THE POEMS OF ANDREW MARVELL

LONGMAN ANNOTATED ENGLISH POETS

General Editors: John Barnard and Paul Hammond
Founding Editor: F. W. Bateson

Titles available in paperback:

BLAKE: THE COMPLETE POEMS
(Revised Second Edition)
Edited by W. H. Stevenson

DRYDEN: SELECTED POEMS
Edited by Paul Hammond and David Hopkins

THE POEMS OF ANDREW MARVELL
(Revised Edition)
Edited by Nigel Smith

MILTON: PARADISE LOST
(Second Edition)
Edited by Alastair Fowler

MILTON: COMPLETE SHORTER POEMS
(Second Edition)
Edited by John Carey

SPENSER: THE FAERIE QUEENE
(Revised Second Edition)
Edited by A. C. Hamilton

TENNYSON: A SELECTED EDITION
(Revised Edition)
Edited by Christopher Ricks

Anon., Andrew Marvell, Portrait, *c.* 1657–62. By courtesy of the National Portrait Gallery, London.

THE POEMS OF ANDREW MARVELL

EDITED BY
NIGEL SMITH

REVISED EDITION

PEARSON
Longman

Harlow, England • London • New York • Boston • San Francisco • Toronto
Sydney • Tokyo • Singapore • Hong Kong • Seoul • Taipei • New Delhi
Cape Town • Madrid • Mexico City • Amsterdam • Munich • Paris • Milan

PEARSON EDUCATION LIMITED

Edinburgh Gate
Harlow CM20 2JE
United Kingdom
Tel: +44 (0)1279 623623
Fax: +44 (0)1279 431059
Website: www.pearsoned.co.uk

First edition published in 2003

Revised (paperback) edition published in Great Britain in 2007

© Pearson Education Limited 2003, 2007

ISBN-13: 978-1-4058-3283-0

British Library Cataloguing in Publication Data
A CIP catalogue record for this book can be obtained from the British Library

Library of Congress Cataloging in Publication Data
Marvell, Andrew, 1621–1678.
  [Poems]
  The poems of Andrew Marvell / edited by Nigel Smith. — Rev. pbk. ed.
    p. cm. — (Longman annotated English poets)
    ISBN-13: 978-1-4058-3283-0 (pbk.)
    ISBN-10: 1-4058-3283-5 (pbk.)
    I. Smith, Nigel. II. Title. III. Series.
PR3546.A1 2006
821'.4—dc22

                                    2005057893

10 9 8 7 6 5 4
14 13 12 11

Set by 35 in 9.5/11.5pt Galliard
Printed in Great Britain by Henry Ling Limited, at the Dorset Press,
Dorchester, DT1 1HD

CONTENTS

NOTE BY THE GENERAL EDITORS

Longman Annotated English Poets was launched in 1965 with the publication of Kenneth Allott's edition of *The Poems of Matthew Arnold*. F.W. Bateson wrote that the 'new series is the first designed to provide university students and teachers, and the general reader with complete and fully annotated editions of the major English poets'. That remains the aim of the series, and Bateson's original vision of its policy remains essentially the same. Its 'concern is primarily with the *meaning* of the extant texts in their various contexts'. The two other main principles of the series were that the text should be modernized and the poems printed 'as far as possible in the order in which they were composed'.

These broad principles still govern the series. Its primary purpose is to provide an annotated text giving the reader any necessary contextual information. However, flexibility in the detailed application has proved necessary in the light of experience and the needs of a particular case (and each poet is by definition, a particular case).

First, proper glossing of a poet's vocabulary has proved essential and not something which can be taken for granted. Second, modernization has presented difficulties, which have been resolved pragmatically, trying to reach a balance between sensitivity to the text in question and attention to the needs of a modern reader. Thus, to modernize Browning's text has a double redundancy: Victorian conventions are very close to modern conventions, and Browning had firm ideas on punctuation. Equally, to impose modern pointing on the ambiguities of Marvell would create a misleading clarity. Third, in the very early days of the series Bateson hoped that editors would be able in many cases to annotate a *textus receptus*. That has not always been possible, and where no accepted text exists or where the text is controversial, editors have been obliged to go back to the originals and create their own text. The series has taken, and will continue to take, the opportunity not only of providing thorough annotations not available elsewhere, but also of making important scholarly textual contributions where necessary. A case in point is the edition of *The Poems of Tennyson* by Christopher Ricks, the Second Edition of which (1987) takes into account a full collation of the Trinity College Manuscripts, not previously available for an edition of this kind. Yet the series' primary purpose remains annotation.

The requirements of a particular author take precedence over principle. It would make little sense to print Herbert's *Temple* in the order of composition even if it could be established. Where Ricks rightly decided that Tennyson's reader needs to be given the circumstances of composition, the attitude to Tennyson and his circle, allusions, and important variants, a necessary consequence was the exclusion of twentieth-century critical responses. Milton, however, is a very different case. John Carey and Alastair Fowler, looking to the needs of their readers, undertook synopses of the main lines of the critical debate over Milton's poetry. Finally, chronological ordering by date of composition will almost always have a greater or lesser degree of speculation or arbitrariness. The evidence is usually partial, and is confused further by the fact that poets do not always write one poem at a time and frequently revise at a later period than that of composition. In the case of Marvell, the 1681 *Miscellaneous Poems* is the principal source for most of the poems, while for the Restoration satires the Longman text is the result of a new collation of the surviving printed texts and manuscripts. This text is accompanied by extensive annotation of the literary, intellectual, and political contexts of Marvell's poetry, providing a unique resource for the student of Marvell's work and its age.

John Barnard
Paul Hammond

INTRODUCTION

This edition includes all of Marvell's poems. Most are in English, but there are also eighteen in Latin and one in Greek. It contains all of the poems considered without doubt to be Marvell's. Cases are also made for the inclusion of other poems as Marvell's, or partly Marvell's: the authorship of these poems has been a matter of debate in the past and will probably remain so in the future. Several poems once thought to be Marvell's, or possibly Marvell's, but now, with reasonable certainty, not, have been either placed in Appendix 1, or excluded and listed in Appendix 4. The headnotes contain full details of dating (where possible), manuscript and print publication and circulation, historical context, literary sources, details of prosody and other matters of style, and considerations of major debates in modern criticism concerning the poems. The annotations contain extensive glossing of vocabulary, and further contextual and literary material, such as echoes, allusions and the manipulation of source texts. Editing a poet whose language is as rich and whose biographical details are as obscure as Marvell's necessarily means reliance upon a substantial body of scholarship in previous editions and in books and scholarly articles. Wherever possible, it has been acknowledged. In this edition is also much new work concerning all aspects of the poetry: new arguments for dating and contextualization, new source material and a larger record of contemporary echoes and allusions than has previously been presented. In this respect, the edition is designed to be used alongside the new Yale University Press edition of Marvell's prose, edited by Annabel Patterson, Martin Dzelzainis, N.H. Keeble, Jeremy Maule† and Nicholas von Maltzahn.

Canon

The idea of a printed canon, sustained over several years, is entirely alien to how Marvell saw his verse. For the most part, our texts of the lyric poems and the Cromwell poems, for which Marvell is best known, and in which area his reputation is secure, are based on one witness, *Miscellaneous Poems* (1681), which was published three years after his death. Ten

poems appeared in print in Marvell's lifetime: the two panegyrics of Charles I (one in Greek, one in Latin); the verse epistle to Lovelace; the Villiers and Hastings elegies (the former unsigned); the two prefatory poems to James Witty's translation of a medical text; *The First Anniversary of the Government of the Lord Protector*, also unsigned; and *On Mr Milton's Paradise Lost*. Four lapidary epigraphs were made and erected (one further epitaph, for James Harrington, remains lost: see Aubrey (1898), i. 288, 293). Comparatively few MS witnesses to these poems have survived, and very few indeed that can be dated with certainty to Marvell's lifetime.

By contrast, the body of Restoration verse satire that has been attributed to, or associated with, Marvell, survives in very great numbers of MSS. The poems in this corpus that have, hitherto, been most confidently ascribed to Marvell's authorship, do not, in fact, occur in many MS copies or, in these copies, with a great many textual variants. However, there are good reasons for associating Marvell with several works that do survive in many variant readings. These variants are sometimes significant factors in discussions of authorship, although much of this textual evidence is often unyielding. Seldom does it tell an editor what he or she would like to know.

Miscellaneous Poems (hereafter *1681*) was printed three years after the poet's death. The note in the volume, by Mary Marvell,[1] claims that they were assembled from the poet's own papers. Naturally enough, this note asserted textual accuracy and implied that the poems were all Marvell's: 'these Poems, as also the other things in this Book contained, are Printed according to the exact Copies of my late dear Husband, under his own Hand-Writing, being found since his Death among his other Papers.' However, few have examined *1681* and not been struck by the indifferent quality of its construction, and worried by its reliability as evidence of a Marvell

---

[1] Once doubted, but now argued to have been the genuine wife of the poet: see Philip Withington, *The Politics of Commonwealth: Citizens and Freemen in Early Modern England* (Cambridge University Press, 2005), 224–7.

canon of verse, and its status as a witness for the text of Marvell's poems. Editorial judgement and a now long tradition of critical discussion have established a set of internal characteristics that have been seen to typify Marvell's verse: tight, terse syntax that often admits ambiguity, a quality that is related to the poet's skill with Latin; highly inventive imagery that expresses the interpenetration of different media, or different perspectives, or states of awareness.

Several poems that appear in *1681* have been excluded from the canon by editors on the grounds of absence of these internal qualities, although other reasons, such as lack of appearance in other witnesses, or unlikely ideological alignment, are also advanced. The poems in question are: *A Dialogue between Thyrsis and Dorinda*, *Tom May's Death* (doubted by Lord, xxxii), *On the Victory obtained by Blake over the Spaniards, in the Bay of Santa Cruz, in the Island of Tenerife, 1657* (doubted by Lord, xxxii, and Duncan-Jones, *EMS*, 5 (1995), 107–26). The Villiers elegy, also doubted by Lord, xxxii, is accepted by all other recent editors. I accept one, *Tom May's Death*, as firmly Marvell's, and leave different degrees of doubt for *A Dialogue between Thyrsis and Dorinda* and *On the Victory obtained by Blake over the Spaniards, in the Bay of Santa Cruz, in the Island of Tenerife, 1657*. Specific arguments for and against Marvell's authorship are set out in the Headnotes to each poem. Significant factors that weigh in favour of Marvell's authorship of these poems are his extraordinary ability to mimic other poetic voices, and indeed to construct poems by imitating and then mutating extant poems by other poets. It is plausible that Marvell took extant circulating lyrics and altered lines, or added his own material, thereby making the poem his own. It is also possible that verse surviving in his papers after his death was poetry by others that was in the process of being transformed, either into new versions of the original poem, or into entirely new verse constructions.

1681 was published as part of a Whig propaganda campaign at the end of the Exclusion Crisis. The significance of the arrangement of the poems, as a document of Whig affiliation, has been a subject of scholarly attention (see Patterson, in Condren and Cousins, eds (1990), 188–212). Soon after its printing, the Cromwell poems were cancelled from most of the copies that have survived. Like several of Marvell's prose works, *1681* exists in several variant states. This is clear evidence of considerable interference and revision during the printing process, to remove mistakes, and for political reasons. The two elegies and one verse epistle to Royalist heroes or poets, from the late 1640s, two of them published under Marvell's name, do not appear in *1681*. This is presumably because of the Whig slant of *1681*.

We may suppose that the lyric poems circulated in MS form on a very limited basis: there are very few copies of Marvell's lyrics in contemporary MSS, and very few unmistakable echoes of the poems in other MS and printed verse of the period. The three poems addressed to Thomas, Lord Fairfax most probably circulated entirely within the very local community at Nun Appleton. 'The Picture of Little T.C. in a Prospect of Flowers' may well have been produced entirely for a family known to Marvell in north Lincolnshire. 'Bermudas' was a household poem written while Marvell was resident with John Oxenbridge in the mid-1650s. Some of the panegyrical verse clearly circulated in the Protectoral court and among the bureaucracy of the regime: the songs celebrating the marriage of Mary Cromwell and Lord Fauconberg, and, in a different way, *An Horatian Ode upon Cromwell's Return to Ireland*. *The Character of Holland* was first of all a presentation poem, designed to help secure Marvell a position in the government; only later, during the Restoration, was its role as a printed satire realized. The Latin poems on Cromwell and Queen Christina of Sweden were meant to be dispatched as diplomatic gifts. The Latin verse letter to Dr Ingelo was another presentation poem for Queen Christina. The *First Anniversary* was published as a propaganda pamphlet, in the context of Cromwell's vexed relationship with his parliaments. All of this is to say that most of Marvell's poetry was intended either for private use, or for presentation, entertainment or advocacy within very restricted communities. As we have seen, Marvell did not regard his verse as a printed canon, or even a manuscript corpus designed for circulation, although, if Mary Marvell is to be believed, he kept his poems in a collection among his papers. A 'Marvell' canon of state poems in print is the creation of those in the years following the revolution of 1688–89 who wanted to offer the world a Whig patriot, assembling texts from a few printed pamphlets, and from the manuscript separates and collections that had circulated in the Restoration, and that would continue to do so. The entire Marvell canon of lyric, panegyric and state poems was then progressively established in collected editions from the earlier eighteenth century onwards, starting with Cooke's edition of 1726 (see below, *Abbreviations*).

Chronology

The composition dates of many Marvell non-lyrical poems are known, either with certainty or reasonable probability. There is also a good deal of information concerning the dates of MS and printed circulation of poems in Marvell's lifetime. But most of the poems did not appear in print until 1681. Since so many of the lyrics remain undatable with any certainty, and since the organization of *1681* is significant, this edition presents the poems as they appeared in *1681*. The early poems that did not appear in *1681* are listed in chronological order of composition and appearance in print. The Restoration satires are also printed in the order of composition and first appearance in MS and print. Full details of circumstances of composition and publication, where known, are given in the headnotes to each poem.

Copy-texts

For most of the pre-Restoration poems there is no choice of copy-text: *1681* provides the only witness. However, the existence of one unusual witness does create complications for the editor. Bodleian Library, MS Eng. poet. d. 49 (*Bod. 1*), an annotated copy of *1681*, has readings which seem so sensible that they have often been accepted by previous editors (especially Donno). The volume is assumed to have belonged to Marvell's nephew William Popple, with whom the poet corresponded, and to whom he appears to have been deeply attached. Did Popple, or whoever was the annotator, have access to manuscript copies of the poems that reflected more faithfully the poet's intentions? The readings of *Bod. 1* have been accepted to some extent in this edition, although by no means in every case. There are many instances where *1681* provides a reading that remains more persuasively consistent with Marvell's characteristic way of writing poetry. The cancelled Cromwell poems and the Restoration verse satires were written in to *Bod. 1*. They are therefore not printed poems with some emended readings but discrete manuscript witnesses drawn from different sources. In *Bod. 1*, most of *An Horatian Ode* is written in stanzas, unlike the continuous verse of *1681*, with a different punctuation scheme and several

distinctive variant readings. It is in effect a different poem, and any editor would be entitled to present both versions.

The Restoration satires, as already noted, exist in a very great number of MSS. Dating of these MS copies is extremely difficult: few are close to the original date of composition. There are very many instances of corruption in the process of copying, as well as additions of lines in the course of time. The texts in this edition are constructed from what appears to be the most plausible reading, and one that is confirmed by a consonance of manuscript readings with late 1660s and early 1670s printed texts. The texts of the Advice to a Painter poems are based on the texts in *Bod. 1*, with a small number of readings taken from a congruence of witnesses in other manuscript and printed copies. In some instances, as with *The Loyal Scot*, a witness other than *1681* or *Bod. 1* has been preferred. In some cases, as with *Janae Oxenbrigiae Epitaphium*, the witness (transcriptions of an epitaph engraved on stone that no longer exists) is closer to the final form in which the poet intended the poem to stand than the version in *1681*.

Where a printed edition of a poem exists before *1681*, it is evident in most cases that some very minor revision took place after the initial composition, presumably by Marvell. In the case of *The First Anniversary*, the poem was complete at the time of its first publication, and it was this edition that provided the copy text for *1681*.

Full details of textual variants of the early sources (as opposed to the choices made by modern editors) are given either in the annotations, or, where the detail is very dense, in Appendix 3. Spelling mistakes most probably caused by compositorial error (for instance in Marvell's Latin poems) have been silently corrected. Variant spellings in different texts of English and Latin words are also not shown.

Spelling and Punctuation

As with most Longman Annotated English Poets editions, this one modernizes spelling but mostly retains original punctuation. Very few points of interpretation in Marvell's verse turn on old spellings: where they do, the original spelling is retained and explained in the annotations. Capitalization, often erratic or inconsistent in *1681* and the other texts, is retained only for proper names and clear instances of personification. The fashion for intense capitalization of the names of ideas, over and above personification, had not yet arrived in Marvell's time: this is further evidence for leaving most nouns with lower-case first letters. Italics in the original texts are also removed. Stresses that occur as a result of metre, or as a result of now unfamiliar seventeenth-century punctuation, are either marked or explained in the annotations. *1681* marks contractions, but not all of them. They are almost always introduced to make the word fit the metrical pattern of its line, and are signalled here with apostrophes in place of the missing syllables. Elisions are left for the reader to make, although it was a seventeenth-century practice to use the apostrophe when two vowels come together (e.g. 'Th' eye' for 'The eye').

The punctuation in *1681* is distinctive. This is especially so in the use of colons and semi-colons at some line-endings, and the parenthesis. Punctuation has only been altered if another contemporary witness appears to offer a better reading, or where an alteration helps the modern reader make sense of old conventions. I do not accept the reasoning of some editors (Donno, and especially Ormerod and Wortham) that, since the text of *1681* is in some or many respects corrupt, a modern editor has licence to change the punctuation in accordance with a modern preference for commas. Seventeenth-century verse punctuation practice, itself indebted to humanist innovations in the previous two centuries, placed a high premium on the relationship between punctuation marks and sense. It is rhetorical as opposed to grammatical. Although the shift from the former to the latter was taking place in the later seventeenth century, *1681* remains a rhetorically punctuated volume. The use of parenthesis, the colon and especially the semi-colon is unfamiliar to the modern eye, and often feels awkward. Nonetheless, the semi-colon played an important role in the division of poetic sentences according to the different parts of a subject (see Parkes (1992), 97–114). This is quite different from the modern use of the colon and semi-colon as aids in organizing the logic of a sentence: in effect an extension of syntax. The use of parenthesis in Marvell's verse has been regarded as particularly significant. In one sense, this usage continues in an intensified way extant habits of the period. But the parenthesis enabled Marvell to bring into conjunction in a thematically significant way the public and the private, and the visual and the aural, the multiple voices of a single, sometimes divided, mind: notable features of his verse. In this respect, he

has been called the last great exploiter of *linulae* ('little moons') until the Romantic period (Lennard (1991), 82). Although we cannot trace Marvell's punctuation habits to a collection of poems in his own hand, since none is known to survive, neither can we readily suppose that the punctuation of *1681* is solely that of the compositor (especially in respect of parentheses), even though the compositor(s) of *1681* did provide a distinctive scheme. Where the punctuation of *1681* has been altered for the sake of clarity and better understanding, the revision has been made in a way that is consistent with the original punctuation structure of the whole volume. The punctuation of the Restoration satires, either in print or in MS, is looser. The chosen copy-text has been followed, but emended where necessary for the sake of clarity and sense.

Line numbers are identified in the notes (i.e. 'l.', 'll.'), but page numbers appear as unitalicized numbers. Unpaginated manuscripts are described by folio number and side (e.g. fol. 3^v, fols. 7–11^r). Titles of printed books are given in italic; discrete works (such as poems) within larger collections in roman type between inverted commas. Reference to modern scholarly works is given parenthetically in the headnotes and footnotes by reference to author, date of publication and page number(s); a full bibliography appears at the end of the volume. Scholarly articles are referred to by author, journal issue and page number, but not by title. Essays in edited collections are referred to by author, editor(s) of the collection, date of publication and page number. Throughout this edition, the place of publication is London unless otherwise stated.

Annotation

The extensive annotation of Marvell's works only began in 1927, with H.M. Margoliouth's first edition of the Oxford English Texts *Poems and Letters*. Since then, much effort has been expended on Marvell's text and the interpretation of his poems. Where earlier annotations have become generally accepted, no acknowledgement appears in the footnotes. More recent contributions are acknowledged. All Marvell scholars are greatly indebted to Marvell's earlier and later editors: in particular those who assembled *1681*, William Popple, or whoever annotated and provided additional poems in *Bod. 1*, Cooke, Thompson, Grosart, Margoliouth, Legouis, Duncan-Jones, Donno and Wilcher.

Headnotes

Again in accordance with Longman Annotated English Poets series conventions, the headnotes provide extensive information of date of composition and publication, and the state of early texts, both form(s) of publication and circumstances of circulation. Where relevant, matters of attribution and authorial authenticity are discussed. This is followed by information concerned with context (especially important for Marvell's public poetry), detailing the historical and cultural circumstances surrounding the poem's composition and publication. Much more context is known for the public poems, commendatory, panegyrical or satirical, than for most of the lyrics. The next headnote sections discuss literary and other sources for the poetry, as well as accounts of the genres to which each poem belongs, or which it incorporates. Further information is concerned with poetic structure and matters of prosody. Several of Marvell's poems have been the subject of major critical debate. Where this is so, an account is given in a 'modern criticism' section. Any significant details of early reception are also given at this point. Some of the lesser of the lyrics have been the subject of smaller yet still significant amounts of critical discussion, and details of these discussions are recorded. However, many poems have no 'modern criticism' section.

Footnotes

In addition to providing details of textual variants (except where, as noted above, the variants are numerous), the annotations at the foot of each page yield several kinds of information. First of all, definitions of unfamiliar words are given, especially seventeenth-century vocabulary, no longer in current usage. *Oxford English Dictionary* (*OED*) references are given, where it has been used, and definitions unrecorded in the dictionary are noted, as are significant pre-datings of *OED* references. Some corrections to *OED* are also recorded. Marvell was a master of the pun, and true to his humanist education in several ancient and modern languages, he made poetic capital of the rich linguistic inheritance at his disposal. His reputation, according to Aubrey, as the greatest English Latin poet of his generation, has frequently been noted, as have the Latinate elements of his vocabulary and syntax. Less well known is his exploitation within the English language of the resources of other languages: Greek, Dutch, French, Italian and Spanish. Non-English words, either from classical or European vernacular languages, are noted, as are English words closely related to, and drawn from, words in other languages, including neologisms. Particular political and religious meanings of words in the seventeenth-century public domain, sometimes for limited periods of time, are indicated, as are a small number of words that have special, personal connotations for Marvell.

Second, the annotations extend, where appropriate, the contextual information given in the headnotes. This is especially important in the Cromwell poems and the verse satires of the Restoration. Here, particular attention is given to use made of contemporary printed material (e.g. pamphlet literature) in the construction of the poems, some of it very pointedly and ironically deployed. Thirdly and finally, Marvell's indebtedness to earlier poetry in ancient, continental and English tradition, and his habit of composition by reorganizing other, often recently published poems by other poets, is reflected by setting out echoes of source poems and allusions to related poems and other materials in the notes. In these instances, the abbreviation 'cp.' ('compare') is used: I follow here the practice adopted by Paul Hammond in the LAEP edition of Dryden. Hammond's intention is to invite 'the reader to consider whether [the instance of an echo or allusion] is a direct borrowing by Dryden of a phrase in another writer, or an example of a shared contemporary rhetoric'. I offer the same comparisons with Marvell's verse and the literature that he knew and with which he worked. Since the canon of Marvell's verse is still in several instances a matter of debate, I have noted echoes of other verse by Marvell in particular Marvell poems, and the echoed words or lines are often quoted. The intention is to enforce the claims made for Marvell's authorship in some parts of the canon considered hitherto insecure, and to give the reader a sense of the nature of the coherence of Marvell's verse: the habitual phrases, images and sound shapes that Marvell used to write poetry. In the Cromwell poems, for example, succeeding poems borrow words and phrases from earlier ones, and redeploy them in thematically significant ways. These reworkings too are noted. Although some poems are necessarily more heavily annotated than others, usually on account of the difference in content and context between epideictic verse on public themes and amorous or devotional lyric, the notes as a whole give, within a coherent design, a far more detailed explanation of Marvell's verse than has been hitherto possible.

In accordance with LAEP conventions, prose translations of the one Greek and several Latin poems are supplied. Previous translations (especially those by McQueen and Rockwell) have been used as a basis while fresh translations have been made. The notes to these poems contain some information concerning Marvell's habits and procedures as a Latin poet, and as a translator, as well as providing some insights into how he understood Latin and English verse to interrelate, especially in the case of Latin and English versions of the same poem.

Manuscript and Printed Sources

A comprehensive list of seventeenth-century MSS and printed books in which Marvell's poetry was first published is given in Appendix 2, together with a key to *sigla*. MS and printed sources for each poem are listed in each headnote. I follow the practice of *IELM* of listing first the major MS collections, followed by an alphabetical list of other MSS.

Conclusion

Marvell was a secretive figure: in politics, he seems to have spared no effort to cover his tracks, even, allegedly, by leaving deliberately confusing trails. In his correspondence, there is almost no discussion of literature, and poetry in particular. His views have to be inferred from the poetry, and the political prose works of the 1670s. For this reason, our knowledge of Marvell will grow as we become more skilled at exploring the contents of archives. This edition cannot therefore claim to be definitive. However, as far as Marvell's poetry goes, it is comprehensive, and reflects the achievement of scholarship on Marvell and seventeenth-century literature up to the beginning of the twenty-first century.

Marvell did not, like Milton, sustain a lifelong ambition to be a major, epic-writing poet, thereby producing a substantial oeuvre that in very many ways and instances drastically altered the direction of English verse (to say nothing of his career as a religious and political polemicist and civil servant). Neither did Marvell, like Dryden, set out not merely to change English verse, but also to establish in a set of critical principles a new foundation for English letters. He did, however, reflect deeply on the nature

of poetry, ancient and modern, classical, Renaissance and contemporary, European and English. He thought about the identity of the poet and his responsibilities to public and private realms. He set, as a matter of contemplation, the power of poetry against the power of great men. His occasional and polemical verse appears to reflect on the very relationship between text and context, as words arrange and rearrange historical personalities and events. His poetry is often one of denial: an abnegation of the poet's ego in order to let the matter of his verse be a reflecting surface, or a think tank, for a number of themes: male, female and androgynous sexuality, the relationship between words and other media like music, painting and architecture, the mutual invasiveness of different media and different planes of reality, the power of poetic cliché and the potential for poetic renewal, the dignity of toleration and the claims of godly virtue, the claims in the world and in verse of different kinds of authority, civic and military, and constitution, from monarchy to republic. In all these respects, Marvell's verse offers a coherent response and a view of the civilized legacy offered by literature that is every bit as intelligent and admirable as the larger bodies of work produced by his contemporaries Milton and Dryden. Indeed, more so than in Milton or Dryden, Marvell's verse confronts more profoundly and consistently two problems facing any poet writing in the seventeenth century: on the one hand, the relationship between amorous or private devotional verse and the different kinds of public verse, and on the other, the challenge to principle and fixed beliefs that the mutable world of public life and politics offered. Since Marvell was, in different ways through his career, both of and in this public world, it is no surprise that terms like 'amphibian' and 'chameleon' occur to describe poet, lover and prince. Such a complex of expressed insights becomes even more rewarding when the poetry is placed beside the prose, especially the polemical works of the 1670s. The preparation of the texts in this edition, and the writing of annotations, has been designed to enable the modern reader to have the linguistic, aesthetic and historical materials necessary to see these achievements at work in a poet whose work cannot hope to match the sum achievements of the greatest poets of his age (Donne, Jonson, Milton and Dryden), but whose skill and acuity mean that many of his poems stand as the very best example of their kind in English, or in any language.

ACKNOWLEDGEMENTS

The preparation of this edition has taken place over nearly fifteen years: a preliminary, exploratory period in the summer of 1988, a further eighteen months spent in the preparation of sample work during 1989 and 1990, a concentrated effort to produce text, headnotes and commentary for the lyrics, panegyrics and pre-Restoration satires from the summer of 1994 to the summer of 1997, extensive work on the Restoration satires from 1998 through to the spring of 2000, and on the Latin poems, and one Greek poem, in the spring and early summer of 2000. The whole was finally assembled in the spring, summer and autumn of 2001.

In that time, I also published two monographs (and researched and wrote one of them), two substantial editions (a long autobiography and a library catalogue), as well as several articles, taught English literature for many hours a week, and latterly chaired two English departments, one in Oxford, the other in Princeton. Even without these distractions, the debts incurred in editing Marvell would have been manifold.

I am deeply grateful to the institutions whose practical support has made this edition possible: Keble College, The Queen's College, and the English Faculty, University of Oxford, and Princeton University offered me periods of leave during which the most burdensome tasks of editing were undertaken. I received generous research grants from the British Academy and from the Council of the Humanities at Princeton University, which have enabled me to travel in Britain, Europe and America in order to examine manuscript copies and printed books containing Marvell's poetry. Production costs have been partially absorbed by a very generous subvention from the Committee on Research in the Humanities and Social Sciences, Princeton University.

Most of the research for this edition was conducted in the Bodleian Library, which remains the best collection anywhere for research on early modern English literature. I salute its librarians for their commitment, and for making a civilized, genial environment while enduring the privations of stretched resources. Further work was undertaken in the Rare Books and Manuscripts Departments of the British Library, the National Library of Scotland, at Cambridge University Library, the University of Birmingham, the Brotherton Library, University of Leeds, the Borthwick Institute, University of York, Nottingham University Library, the Newberry Library, Chicago, and the Firestone Library, Princeton. Specific manuscripts and printed books were consulted at All Souls College, Oxford, Worcester College, Oxford, the Fitzwilliam Museum, Cambridge, King's College, Cambridge, the Society of Antiquaries, London, the National Library of Wales, Cardiff Central Library, Boston Public Library, the Library Company of Philadelphia, the Folger Shakespeare Library, Washington DC, the Houghton Library, Harvard University, the Beinecke Library, Yale University, Wellesley College, the libraries of the University of Illinois, Urbana-Champaign, the University of Chicago, Ohio State University, Columbus, the University of Minnesota, Minneapolis, Rutgers University, New Brunswick, the University of California, Los Angeles, and the William Andrews Clark Memorial Library, Los Angeles, the Huntington Library, San Marino, the University of Texas, Austin, the Österreichische National-bibliothek, Vienna, the Royal Library, Copenhagen, and the Royal Library, The Hague. I am also grateful to the following county and city record offices for allowing me to consult material: Bedford, Bedfordshire; Bradford District Archives; Carlisle, Cumbria; Chelmsford, Essex; Lincolnshire Archives Office; City of London; Taunton, Somerset; Warwick, Warwickshire; Chichester, West Sussex.

Many individuals have also helped me. For skilled, diligent and painstaking assistance in checking collations, I am grateful to Lia Lynch and Jerry Passannante, my graduate students in Princeton, as well as to Naomi Baker, Warren Chernaik, John Watkins and Wayne Rebhorn. Several scholars have sent me information or have responded helpfully to queries. In this respect, I am especially grateful to Lyndy Abraham, Gordon Campbell, Tom Corns, James Loxley, John McWilliams, Jonathan Post, Timothy Raylor, Joshua Scodel, Richard Strier,

Winifred Stevenson, Helen Wilcox, Michael Wilding and Chris Wortham. Peter Davidson and Jane Stevenson have put their considerable collective wit and their remarkable hospitality into the furtherance of the project. To Peter, I am indebted for many hours of deliberation on annotation problems, on Latin, and for thinking through where to look next, especially with regard to the Roman Catholic world, and continental European literature. Mira Seo checked and emended translations from the Latin: I am most thankful for her skill in rendering Marvell's often complex Latin usage more faithfully in English. Jane Griffiths of the *Oxford English Dictionary* has been a most resourceful correspondent with regard to Marvell's word usage and its historical context. Several colleagues have either seen or heard material from this edition: I am deeply grateful to the following for their insightful, stimulating comments, which have in several places saved me from errors: Edward Holberton, John Kerrigan, David Loewenstein, David Norbrook, Steve Pincus, Nicholas von Maltzahn, Suzanne Wofford, Blair Worden, Steven Zwicker. Communities make the writing of learned books possible, even when conversation becomes more complicated after becoming a transatlantic person. In this respect, I must acknowledge the mutually beneficial relationship I have enjoyed with the members of the Yale University Press Marvell's prose works editing team: Annabel Patterson, Martin Dzelzainis, Neil Keeble, Jeremy Maule† and Nicholas von Maltzahn. I have received support and encouragement from Elizabeth Story Donno and Donald Friedman, and practical help from the greatest and most long-lived Marvell scholar, Elsie Duncan-Jones. I am grateful to Katherine Duncan-Jones for enabling me to be in touch with her mother. Several colleagues have lived with my long labour, and the obsessions that have been part of it. I acknowledge the following for the encouragement they have offered in the best spirit of collegiality: Malcolm Parkes, Stephen Wall, Ralph Hanna, Margaret Kean and John Carey in Oxford, Peter Lake, Joanna Picciotto, Michael Wood, Tony Grafton and Leonard Barkan in Princeton. In England and America, at home and at work, and across the world over the years, Kate Flint has been a constant source of advice as well as support. I do not know how she has endured the exactions of this part of our lives, but I am deeply appreciative of her presence in this respect, as in all others. Finally, two colleagues must be mentioned as both mentors and guides of this project. Without their patience, experience, critical intelligence and inspiration, none of the following pages would be possible. Paul Hammond first encouraged me to think about editing Marvell, and, as general editor of the series, John Barnard first invited me to submit sample material and commissioned the edition. Both have read several drafts of each poem and the accompanying material. I have learned a great deal from their sense of judgement. General editors generally receive little credit for their demanding work. Let that not be the case this time.

April 2002   Nigel Smith

In this paperback printing, corrections have been made, along with some revisions and the addition of a substantial body of fresh information that has become known to me since the hardback went to press in 2002. Three new copy texts of Marvell poems have been uncovered, while several important historical and critical analyses have been published. Additionally, I have adopted the new English translations of the Latin poems by Estelle Haan, which first appeared as Appendix I in her monograph *Andrew Marvell's Latin Poetry: From Text to Context* (Bruxelles: Éditions Latomus, 2003). I am most grateful to Professor Haan and to Collection Latomus for permission to present these translations here. Finally, I am deeply indebted to Philip Langeskov of Pearson who has taken this edition through to a paperback version.

September 2005   Nigel Smith

LIST OF ILLUSTRATIONS

Publisher's Acknowledgements

We are grateful to the following for permission to reproduce copyright material:

The National Portrait Gallery, London, for frontispiece and Fig. 9; The British Library for Figs 1, 2 and 3; The Bodleian Library, University of Oxford, for Figs 4, 5, 6 and 7; Borthwick Institute, University of York, for Fig. 8.

In some instances we may have been unable to trace the owners of copyright material, and we would appreciate any information that would enable us to do so.

ABBREVIATIONS

Unless otherwise stated, the place of publication is London.

AGP = Andrew Marvell, *An Account of the Growth of Popery and Arbitrary Government* (1677)

Aitken = *The Poems of Andrew Marvell, Sometime Member of Parliament for Hull*, ed. G.A. Aitken (London and New York, 1892)

CPW = John Milton, *The Complete Prose Works*, gen. ed., Don M. Wolfe (New Haven, CT, 1953–80) 8 vols in 10

CSPC = *Calendar of State Papers Colonial*

CSPD = *Calendar of State Papers Domestic*

Collins = Dan S. Collins, *Andrew Marvell, a reference guide* (Boston, MA, 1981)

Cooke = *The Works of Andrew Marvell, Esq.* ed. Thomas Cooke, 2 vols (1726)

Cummings = Robert Cummings, ed., *Seventeenth-Century Poetry. An Annotated Anthology* (Oxford, 2000)

DNB = *The Dictionary of National Biography founded in 1882 by George Smith. The Concise Dictionary from the Beginnings to 1921* (1930)

Donno = Andrew Marvell, *The Complete English Poems*, ed. Elizabeth Story Donno (Harmondsworth, 1972)

EB = *Encyclopaedia Britannica Online* (http://search/eb/com)

Grosart = *The Complete Works and Prose of Andrew Marvell*, ed. Alexander B. Grosart, 4 vols (London, 1872–75)

Henning = Basil Duke Henning, *The House of Commons 1660–1690*, 3 vols (1983)

IELM = Peter Beal, *Index of English Literary Manuscripts* (London and New York, 1980–97)

JHC = *Journal of the House of Commons*, 1547–1800, 55 vols (1803)

JHL = *Journals of the House of Lords. Journals of the House of Lords, beginning anno primo Henrici octavi*, 79 vols (1771 ff.)

Kermode = *The Selected Poetry of Andrew Marvell*, ed. Frank Kermode (New York, 1967)

Legouis = Andrew Marvell, *Poems and Letters*, 2 vols (Oxford, 1971), ed. H.M. Margoliouth, 3rd edn rev. Pierre Legouis, with the collaboration of E.E. Duncan-Jones

Lewis and Short = *A Latin Dictionary: founded on Andrews' edition of Freund's Latin Dictionary.* Rev. enl., and in great part rewritten by Charlton T. Lewis (Oxford and New York, 1879, 1993 impression)

LIMC = *Lexicon Iconographicum Mythologiae Classicae* (Zürich and München, 1984), 8 vols

Lord = *Andrew Marvell: Complete Poetry*, ed. George DeF. Lord (London and New York, 1968; reprinted with corrections, London and Melbourne, 1984)

McQueen and Rockwell = *The Latin Poetry of Andrew Marvell*, eds William A. McQueen and Kiffin A. Rockwell (Chapel Hill, NC, 1964)

Margoliouth = Andrew Marvell, *Poems and Letters*, 2 vols (Oxford, 1952), ed. H.M. Margoliouth, 2nd edn revised

MED = *Middle English Dictionary*, eds Sherman M. Kuhn and John Reidy (Ann Arbor, MI, 1952–)

MPW = *The Prose Works of Andrew Marvell*, 2 vols, eds Annabel Patterson, Martin Dzelzainis, Nicholas von Maltzahn and N.H. Keeble (New Haven and London, 2003)

OED = *Oxford English Dictionary*, 2nd edn, available online (http://dictionary.oed.com)

ODEP = *The Oxford Dictionary of English Proverbs*, 3rd edn revised by F.P. Wilson with an introduction by Joanna Wilson (Oxford, 1970)

OLD = *Oxford Latin Dictionary*, ed. by P.G.W. Glare (Oxford and New York, 1968, 1982)

Ormerod and Wortham = Andrew Marvell, *Pastoral and Lyric Poems 1681*, eds David Ormerod and Christopher Wortham (Nedlands, Western Australia, 2000)

Pepys, Samuel = *The Diary of Samuel Pepys: a New and Complete Transcription*, ed. Robert Latham and William Matthews, 11 vols (1970–83)

Reeves and Seymour-Smith = *The Poems of Andrew Marvell*, eds James Reeves and Martin Seymour-Smith (1973)

RO = Record Office

RT = Andrew Marvell, *The Rehearsal Transpros'd* (1672)

s.sh. = single sheet

Thompson = *The Works of Andrew Marvell, esq., Poetical, Controversial, Political, containing many Original Letters, Poems, and Tracts, never before printed. With a new life of the author, by Capt. Edward Thompson* (1776)

Tilley = Morris Palmer Tilley, *A Dictionary of the Proverbs in England in the Sixteenth and Seventeenth Centuries* (Ann Arbor, MI, 1950)

Walker = *Andrew Marvell*, eds Frank Kermode and Keith Walker (Oxford, 1990)

Whiting = Bartlett Jere Whiting, *Proverbs, Sentences and Proverbial Phrases from English Writings Mainly before 1500* (Cambridge, MA, and London, 1968)

Wilcher = Andrew Marvell, *Selected Poetry and Prose*, ed. Robert Wilcher (Cambridge and New York, 1986)

Williams = Gordon Williams, *A Dictionary of Sexual Language and Imagery in Shakespearean and Stuart Literature*, 3 vols (London and Atlantic Highlands, NJ, 1994)

Yale POAS = *Poems on Affairs of State: Augustan Satirical Verse, 1660–1714*, vol. 1, ed. George deF. Lord (New Haven, CT and London, 1963)

JOURNAL ABBREVIATIONS

BJRL   Bulletin of the John Rylands Library
BLJ   British Library Journal
BNYPL   Bulletin of the New York Public Library
BUSE   Boston University Studies in English
CL   Comparative Literature
CQ   Critical Quarterly
CS   Critical Survey
DUJ   Durham University Journal
EA   Etudes Anglaises
E in C Essays in Criticism
ELH   A Journal of English Literary History
ELN   English Language Notes
ELR   English Literary Renaissance
EMS   English Manuscript Studies
E&S   Essays and Studies
ES   English Studies
HJ   Historical Journal
HLQ   Huntington Library Quarterly
JDJ   John Donne Journal
JEGP   Journal of English and Germanic Philology
JHI   Journal of the History of Ideas
MLQ   Modern Language Quarterly
MLR   Modern Language Review
MP   Modern Philology
N & Q   Notes and Queries
NLH   New Literary History
NRS   Naval Record Society
PLL   Publications in Language and Literature
PBA   Publications of the British Academy
PBSA   Publications of the Bibliographical Society of America
PH   Publishing History
PMLA   Publications of the Modern Language Association of America
PQ   Philological Quarterly
RES   Review of English Studies
RN   Renaissance News
RQ   Renaissance Quarterly
SC   The Seventeenth Century
SEL   Studies in English Literature
SN   Studia Neophilologica
SP   Studies in Philology
TLS   Times Literary Supplement
TSLL   Texas Studies in Language and Literature
UKCR   University of Kansas City Review
YES   Yearbook of English Studies
YULG   Yale University Library Gazette

CHRONOLOGICAL TABLE OF MARVELL'S LIFE AND CHIEF PUBLICATIONS

1621 (*31 March*) Born at Winestead, Holderness, Yorkshire, the son of Andrew, vicar of Winestead and his wife Anne (née Pease)

1624 (*20 September*) Rev. Andrew Marvell appointed Master of the Grammar School and Charterhouse at Hull, and Lecturer at Holy Trinity Church

1629–33 Probably attends Hull Grammar School

1633 (*14 December*) Becomes subsizar (an undergraduate receiving an allowance from the foundation) at Trinity College, Cambridge

1637 First verse published, in Latin and Greek, in a congratulatory volume on the birth of a child to Charles I and Queen Henrietta Maria

1638 (*13 April*) Elected to a scholarship at Trinity College, Cambridge. (*April*) Mother dies. (*November*) Father remarries

1639 (*Lent Term*) Takes BA. Possible brief conversion to Roman Catholicism

1641 Father drowns in Humber. Leaves Cambridge for London

1642 (*February*) Living in Cowcross, London; witnesses three Savile deeds at Gray's Inn

1642/3–47 Travels in Holland, France, Italy and Spain

1646 Meets Richard Flecknoe in Rome early in the year

1647 (*12 November*) Sells property in Meldreth, Cambridgeshire

1648 (*7 July–August*) *An Elegy Upon the Death of My Lord Francis Villiers* written and published

1649 (c. *May*) 'To his Noble Friend Mr Richard Lovelace, upon his Poems' published (written probably in later 1648). (*Late June–July*) 'Upon the Death of Lord Hastings' written and published. Appears to have been moving in London literary circles

1650 (*June–July*) Writes 'An Horatian Ode upon Cromwell's Return from Ireland' (*Late, after 13 November*) Writes 'Tom May's Death'

1650–52 (*Late 1650–later 1652*) Tutors Mary Fairfax at Nun Appleton, Yorkshire

1651 (*Early*) Writes 'To His Worthy Friend Doctor Witty upon His Translation of the Popular Errors' and '*Dignissimo suo Amico Doctori Wittie.*' (*February–early March*) Writes '*In Legationem Domini Oliveri St John ad Provincias Foederatas.*' (*Late June–late August*) Writes 'Upon Appleton House, To My Lord Fairfax' and associated poems

1653 (*21 February*) Recommended by Milton to Bradshaw for a Latin secretaryship. (*Late February–early March*) Writes *The Character of Holland*. (*July*) Employed at Eton as tutor to Oliver Cromwell's ward William Dutton, in the house of John Oxenbridge

1653–54 (*July 1653–December 1654*) Writes 'Bermudas'

1654 (*Late February*) Writes 'A Letter to Doctor Ingelo'

1654–55 (*Late December 1654–early January 1655*) Writes and publishes *The First Anniversary of the Government under His Highness the Lord Protector*

1656 (c. *January–August*) Travels to Saumur, France with Dutton; described there as a 'notable English Italo-Machavellian'

1657 (*late May–9 July*) 'On the Victory obtained by Blake over the Spaniards, in the Bay of Santa Cruz, in the Island of Tenerife, 1657' is written. (*September*) Appointed Latin Secretary to John Thurloe. (*November*) Writes 'Two Songs at the Marriage of the Lord Fauconberg and the Lady Mary Cromwell'

1658 (*Late April–May*) Writes '*Janae Oxenbrigiae Epitaphium.*' (*September–January 1659*) Writes 'A Poem upon the Death of his Late Highness the Lord Protector'. (*23 November*) Walks in Oliver Cromwell's funeral procession

1659 (*January*) Elected joint MP for Hull. (*May*) Loses seat at the Restoration of the Rump, but retains post as Latin Secretary and granted lodgings in Whitehall

1660 (*April*) Re-elected MP for Hull

1662 (*Before 18 March*) Exchanges blows in the House with Sir Thomas Clifford

1662–63 (*June 1662–April 1663*) Absent in Holland on state affairs, and on behalf of the Earl of Carlisle

1663–65 (*July 1663–January 1665*) Secretary to the Earl of Carlisle during an embassy to Russia, Sweden and Denmark

1665 (*25 October*) Joins committee on embezzlement of prizes during Second Dutch War. Shortened and altered version of *The Character of Holland* published

1666 (*April*) Involved in writing and circulation of *The Second Advice to a Painter*. (*Late 1666–January 1667*) Involved in writing and circulation of *The Third Advice to a Painter*. (*3 December*) Writes to Hull Corporation with regard to legislation enabling inspection of accounts

1667 (*After 25 June, before 25 July*) Writes 'Clarendon's Housewarming'. (*31 August–28 November*) Writes 'The Last Instructions to a Painter'. Four editions of 'The Advice to a Painter' poems, and associated poems, printed. (*October–November*) Takes part in impeachment of Clarendon. (*14 and 29 October*) Speaks in Commons against impeaching Clarendon. (*17 October*) Joins committee appointed to inquire into miscarriages of the Dutch War. (*7/11 November*) Moves that one of charges against Clarendon be clarified. (*16 December*) On committee to arrange Clarendon's banishment

1668 (*15 February*) Speaks strongly against Arlington in debate concerning miscarriages. (*21 February*) Speaks against those responsible for paying seamen with tickets, not money

1669 (*September*) Named in a list of the Duke of York's supporters in the House of Commons

1669–70 Writes first version of 'The Loyal Scot' out of ll. 649–96 of 'The Last Instructions to a Painter'

1670 (*9 May–5 August*) Writes Latin and English versions of 'Epigram: Upon Blood's attempt to steal the Crown'

1671 Acquires use of cottage in Highgate. Possibly writes 'The Second Chorus from Seneca's Tragedy *Thyestes*' at this time

1671–72 Writes '*Inscribenda Luparae*'

1672–73 Controversy with Samuel Parker

1672 (*Autumn*) Writes and publishes *The Rehearsal Transpros'd*

1673 (*Early summer*) Writes and publishes *The Rehearsal Transpros'd. The Second Part*

1674 (*Late April–June*) Writes 'On Mr Milton's *Paradise Lost*'. (*Summer*) Mentioned by government spies as member of a Dutch fifth column

1675 (*April*) Writes 'His Majesty's Most Gracious Speech to both Houses of Parliament'. (*July*) Writes 'The Statue at Charing Cross'

1676 (*June*) Publishes *Mr. Smirke: Or, the Divine in Mode* with *A Short Historical Essay Concerning General Councils, Creeds, and Imposition in Religion*

1677 (*27 March*) Speaks in the House of Commons against the Bill to secure the Protestant succession. (*June*) Takes a house in Great Russell Street in order to conceal two bankrupt relatives. (*Late December*) Publishes anonymously *An Account of the Growth of Popery and Arbitrary Government*

1678 (*April*) *Remarks Upon a Late Disingenuous Discourse Writ by One T.D.* licensed. (*July*) Visits Hull and falls ill on return journey. (*16 August*) Dies in the Great Russell Street house of a tertian ague. (*18 August*) Buried in St Giles-in-the-Fields

1681 (*January*) *Miscellaneous Poems* published by Robert Boulter, with notice 'To the Reader' by Mary Marvell

POEMS

POEMS PUBLISHED IN PRINT BEFORE 1650

1
Ad Regem Carolum Parodia

Date and Publication. Late 1636–early 1637. Along with no. 2, the poem was first printed in Συνῳδία *Sive Musarum Cantabrigiensium Concentus et Congratulatio* (1637; [Sig. K4ʳ-L1ʳ]), a collection of Greek and Latin poems by Cambridge students and academics celebrating the birth, on 17 March 1637, of Charles I's fifth child, Anne.

Context, Genre and Source. The poem is a close imitation, as far as contextual circumstances would allow, of Horace, *Carmina* I.ii. Originally, a *parodia* was a counter-song; a reply using very nearly the same words or phrases as the original (Lewis and Short). That *parodia* involved the comic or the ironic was acknowledged by some ancient commentators, and repeated in the sixteenth century by Julius Caesar Scaliger, *Poetices libri septem* (1561), I.xlii. But M. clearly means 'imitation', an exercise required in grammar schools (see below, *Title* n.). Civil war in Rome, finally ended by the rise of Augustus, is replaced by the plague, which had visited Cambridge in late 1636, causing the University to close. Horace takes his occasion from extreme storms and the flooding of the Tiber; M. from apparent flooding of the Cam and Granta. Συνῳδία printed one hundred and ninety poems of various length, the work of one hundred and thirty-five different poets. Other notable poets in the Cambridge collections, or those who would become notable, include Crashaw, Robert Heath, Joseph Beaumont and Henry More. Some important divines and influential tutors also figure: e.g. John Sherman, Nathanael Culverwel (see below, 154), Richard Watson, Robert Gell. Specially bound copies of these collections of occasional verse were presented to the monarch.

One of the other contributors to the volume was Edward King, of Christ's College, who was soon to drown at sea, and become the subject of a volume of elegies, *Justa Edovardo King naufrago* (1638). In this volume was first published Milton's famous elegy *Lycidas*, in which the imagery of storms looms large. *Lycidas* uses the occasion of King's death to lament obliquely the rise of the Laudian bishops in the national church. The poem represents an important moment in the development of Milton's Puritan poetics. M.'s imagery of storm and civil discord is far more formulaic, and obviously derivative of Horace. But in his poem, no less than was the case for Milton in *Lycidas*, M. was discovering the poetic methods that would later enable him to generate the tight, impacted syntax of *An Horatian Ode*, and the exquisitely concise imagery of *Upon Appleton House*.

Several poems in the volume imitate the same Horace poem: e.g. Edward Leek, 'In natalitia Principis mense Martio natae' ([Sig. A4ʳ]); S[amuel] Collins, 'Reginae sacrum puerperae' ([Sig. A4ᵛ-B1ʳ]); John Potts, 'In faustum Illustrissimae Principis verno tempore Natalem Γενεθλιακόν' ([Sig. D1ʳ]). The volume features several other verse genres in different examples. The sense of a collection of academic exercises is unavoidable, and would apply to M.'s poem (he was fifteen at the time) were its imagery not so arresting. This is M.'s only Latin poem not written in elegiacs or hexameters.

M.'s adaptation works at several different levels. First, there is a simple substitution of words into Horace's Latin. Often, the substituting vocabulary has similar sounds or spelling to the words it replaces. In some instances, it seems as if new vocabulary is suggested by the sound shapes of the original, even though the meaning is very different. A predominant feature of change of meaning is reversal of sense (e.g. ll. 23–4). This method of composition by transposition was used by M. as a way of writing English verse throughout his career: see, e.g., below, *The Second Advice to a Painter, General Headnote, Authorship*. In a very few places, the *parodia* fails to meet the seventeenth-century context, at the places where Horace's Latin is followed most closely, word for word (e.g. ll. 25–6). In M.'s adaptation, Apollo becomes Charles I and Erycina, Henrietta Maria. This means that the glorification of Augustus in Horace is not repeated by a similar martial praise of Charles: the royal infant is instead imagined as a future Caesar. The adaptation of ll. 45–9 involves the

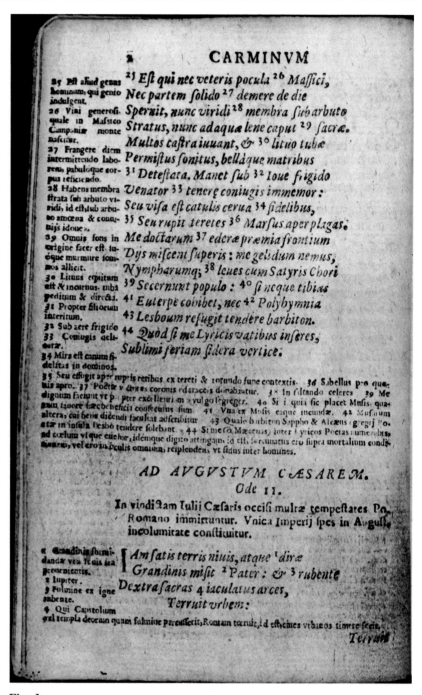

Fig. 1

Quinti Horatii Flacci Poemata. Scholiis siue annotationibus, quae breuis
commentarii vice esse possint à Ioanne Bond illustrata (1630), 2–3.
Permission British Library (1506/29).

LIBER I.

Terruit gentes, graue ne rediret
[1] Sæculum Pyrrhæ, noua monstra [6] questæ,
Omne quum [7] Proteus pecus egit altos
    Visere montes:
Piscium & summâ genus hæsit [8] ulmo,
Nota quæ sedes fuerat [9] columbis:
Et [10] superiecto pauidæ natarunt
    Æquore damæ.
Vidimus [11] flauum Tyberim, retortis
[12] Littore Etrusco violenter undis,
Ire deiectum [13] monumenta regis,
    Templaq; [14] Vestæ:
[15] Iliæ dum se nimium [16] querenti
[17] Iactat ultorem: [18] vagus, & [19] sinistra
Labitur ripa ([20] Ioue non probante) [21] V-
    xorius amnis.
[22] Audiet ciues acuisse ferrum,
Quo graues Persæ melius perirent:
Audiet pugnas, [23] vitio parentum
    Rara iuuentus.
[24] Quem vocet diuûm populus ruentis
Imperi [25] rebus? [26] prece qua fatigent
Virgines sanctæ minus audientem
    [27] Carmina Vestam?
[28] Cui dabit partes scelus expiandi
Iupiter? tandem venias precamur,
Nube candentes humeros [29] amictus
    [30] Augur Apollo.

replacement of just one word: in l. 46, 'Quirini' is
substituted by 'Britanno'. For a full discussion of
Marvell's adaptive ingenuity, see Haan (2003), 35–43.

Ad Regem Carolum Parodia

Jam satis pestis, satis atque diri
Fulminis misit pater, et rubenti
Dextera nostras jaculatus arces
        Terruit urbem.
5   Terruit cives, grave nè rediret
Pristinum seclum nova monstra questum,
Omne cum pestis pecus egit altos
        Visere montes;
Cum scholae latis genus haesit agris,
10 Nota quae sedes fuerat bubulcis;
Cum toga abjecta pavidus reliquit
        Oppida doctus.
Vidimus Chamum fluvium retortis
Littore a dextro violenter undis
15 Ire plorantem monumenta pestis,
        Templáque clausa.
Granta dum semet nimiùm querenti
Miscet uxorem vagus et sinistra
Labitur ripa, Jove comprobante,
20   Tristior amnis.
Audiit coelos acuisse ferrum,
Quo graves Turcae meliùs perirent;
Audiit mortes vitio parentum
        Rara juventus.
25 Quem vocet divam populus ruentis
Imperi rebus? prece qua fatigent
Doctior coetus minus audientes
        Carmina coelos?
Cui dabit partes luis expiandae
30 Jupiter, tandem venias, precamur,
Nube candentes humeros amictus
        Auxiliator.
Sive tu mavis, Erycina nostra,
Quam jocus circumvolat et Cupido,

35 Túque neglectum genus et nepotes
        Auxeris ipsa.
Sola tam longam removere pestem,
Quam juvat luctus faciésque tristis,
Prolis optata reparare mole
40   Sola potésque.
Sive felici Carolum figura
Parvulus Princeps imitetur, almae
Sive Mariae decoret puellam
        Dulcis imago.
45 Serus in coelum redeas, diúque
Laetus intersis populo Britanno,
Néve te nostris vitiis iniquum
        Ocyor aura
Tollat. Hic magnos potiùs triumphos,
50 Hic ames dici pater atque princeps,
Et nova mortes reparato prole
        Te patre, Caesar.

A *Parodia* to King Charles

Enough of plague, and enough of his dreadful thunderbolt has the father already sent, and smiting
our citadels with right hand aglow, he has terrified
the city; terrified the citizens lest should return the
oppressive age of former times, bewailing new prodigies, when plague drove every flock to go to see the
high mountains; when the schoolish stock stuck in
broad fields (till then an abode known to cowherds),
when the scholar cast aside his gown and abandoned
the town in terror. We have seen the river Cam, his
waves violently cast back from his right-hand shore,
proceed in lamentation of the plague's memorials
and the closed churches, while Granta joins his wife
in her excessive complaints, and straying over his left
bank with Jupiter's sanctioning he glides, a sadder
river.

Title. Parodia] the strictest kind of imitation; a school or academic exercise; no sense of ridicule is carried by this term: see
above, *Headnote, Context, Genre and Source*.
2. Fulminis] possibly suggested by the marginal note for
'rubente' (*Carmina*, I.ii, l. 2) in most of the annotated editions
of Horace in the seventeenth century: 'Fulmine ex igne rubente' (see fig. 1).
21. coelos] substitutes for *cives* in Horace; 'the reminiscence of
the original gives the modern reader pause as he reflects that
this was written only five years before open war between King
and Parliament' (McQueen and Rockwell).

22. Turcae] a fleet was in preparation to combat Turkish
pirates; the revenue for this was derived from the contentious
and unpopular Ship Money, the tax levied by Charles I
between 1634 and 1639, during the period of personal rule,
when Parliament was not summoned and parliamentary revenue was hence unavailable.
41–4. Sive . . . imago] the poem was written before the sex of
the royal child was known.
51. reparato] *1637* reparare *Cooke*. Cooke uses the infinitive
form; the corresponding word in Horace is 'equitare'.

Youth made sparse have heard that the heavens have sharpened a sword by which the oppressive Turks should better have perished; they have heard of deaths caused by their parents' vices.

Which of the gods may the people call to the affairs of the tottering empire? By what prayer may a more learned gathering weary the heavens inattentive to their invocations? To whom will Jupiter grant the role of making atonement for the plague? Come at last to our aid, we pray you, your shoulders clad in the whiteness of cloud, or if you prefer, our Erycina, about whom Mirth and Cupid fly, you too aid a neglected people and your descendants.

You alone have the power to take away a plague so long, which is pleased by our grief and sad countenance; you alone have the power to renew through the longed for delivery of your offspring. Whether a little prince imitates Charles in his happy features or whether the sweet image of kindly Mary graces a daughter: return late into the heavens, and may you be happy to remain long among the British people, nor may a swifter breeze steal you away in indignation at our vices. Here rather celebrate mighty triumphs, here may you love to be called father and prince, and make amends for death through new birth and with you, Caesar, as father.

2
Πρὸς Κάρολον τὸν βασιλέα

Date, Publication and Context. See above, *Ad Regem Carolum Parodia, Headnote.*

The poem is the only surviving example of M.'s Greek verse.

῍Ω Δυσαριστοτόκος, Πέντ' ὢ δύσποτμος ἀριθμός! 5 Novemb.
  ῍Ω Πέντε στυγερὸν, Πέντ', ἀίδαο πύλαι! 5 Aug.
᾽Αγγλῶυ ὢ μέγ' ὄνειδος, ὢ οὐρανίοισιν ἀπεχθές!
  ᾽Αλλ' ἀπελύμαινες Κάῤῥολε τοῦτον ἄνα.
5 Πέμπτον τέκνον ἔδωκε μογοστόκος Εἰλείθυια,
  Πέντε δὲ Πένταθλον τέκνα καλοῦσι τεόν.
Εἰ δὲ θέλεις βίβλοις ταῖς ὀψιγόνοισι τίεσθαι,
  Πεντήτευχον ἔχεις παιδία διογενῆ.
῍Η ὅτι θεσπεσίης φιλέες μήστωρας ἀοιδῆς,
10 ᾽Αρμονίην ποιεῖς τὴν Διὰ πέντε Πάτερ.

  ᾽Ανδρέας ὁ Μαρβέλλον, ἐκ τοῦ τῆς Τριάδος

O ill-fated mother of the best of offspring, Five. O, ill-omened number, O hateful five, five, gates of Hades. O great reproach to the English, O hateful to the gods!

But thou, O Charles, didst wipe out this disgrace. Helping Ilithyia has granted a fifth birth, and five children name they pentathalon.

If you wish to be honoured in the books of later generations, you have in these five divinely born children your Pentateuch. Or because you love masters of divinely inspired song, you make here the fifth harmony, Father.

Andrew Marvell, Trinity College

1–2. The sidenotes connect the reference to the number five in these lines to two ominous dates for the royal family, both assassination attempts on James I: the Gowrie Conspiracy 5 August 1600, and the Gunpowder Plot of 5 November 1605.
5. Εἰλείθυια] Ilithyia, the Greek goddess of childbirth (Roman Lucina).

3

An Elegy Upon the Death of My Lord Francis Villiers

Date. July–August 1648. Francis, third son of George Villiers, first Duke of Buckingham (1592–1628), and brother of Fairfax's eventual son-in-law, George, second Duke of Buckingham (1628–87), was born on 2 April 1629, after his father's assassination (see below, ll. 25, 29–30). He was killed fighting for the Royalists in an action near Kingston upon Thames, 7 July 1648. If M. was associated with the Villiers family, or in receipt of their patronage, before and at this time, he would most likely have produced his poem quite soon after Villiers' death, like the poem published by the Villiers' 'servant' (see below, *Sources and Genre*).

Publication. The poem was printed in a quarto pamphlet of one sheet of which only two known copies survive (one at Worcester College, Oxford; the other at the College of Wooster, Wooster, Ohio). The poem was not printed in *1681*: M., his poetic executors, or his publishers, would not have wanted so blatantly a royalist poem in a volume containing panegyrics of Fairfax and Cromwell, both of whom are derided and imagined killed in battle in this elegy (see below, ll. 15, 17). The published poem was unsigned, and M. may well have removed it from his papers long before the 1670s (but see also below, *Structure and Style*).

Attribution. The poem was attributed to M. by George Clarke (in the Worcester College copy), son of William, Secretary to the Army Council (who would have known M.). The younger Clarke's library passed to Worcester College. He was a committed antiquarian, and his many attributions of unsigned works are usually accurate. Clarke's testimony, the fact that M. was intimate with the Villiers family in the 1640s (he had visited Rome with Lord Francis and his elder brother in the mid-1640s; see above, xxiv), and internal evidence, suggest that the poem is M.'s. Ricks, in Patrides, ed. (1978), 110, regards the imagery of reflection and perception in the poem

(especially ll. 51–4) as typical, if not quite unique, of M. Craze (1979), 44–64, accumulates 'many points in favour of Marvell's authorship'. Some still doubt that the poem is M.'s (e.g. Chernaik (1983), 236–7; Donnelly, in Summers and Pebworth (1992), 156–7, n. 6).

Context. After the first Duke of Buckingham's assassination in 1628, the Villiers children were taken into the royal family and educated by the royal tutors, Brian Duppa, Bishop of Chichester, and William Cavendish, Earl of Newcastle. The Villiers brothers were sent to Cambridge, most probably just after M. had left the University in 1641, but they enlisted with Prince Rupert and Lord Gerard in 1642. After the sequestering of their estates in 1643, they were sent on an extensive tour of the continent (Phipps (1985), 4–5).

On their return, Francis joined his elder brother in the Earl of Holland's rising, the purpose of which was to relieve the Royalists besieged in Colchester by Fairfax. It was 'planned to be a major rising, but turned out to be a very damp squib' (Ashton (1994), 408); there is very little printed material concerned with the events in Surrey, most attention being focused on Colchester. Duncan-Jones, *N & Q*, 198 (1953), 102, notes Ludlow's comment that Villiers had a romance with Mary Kirke, daughter of the poet Aurelian Townsend. According to Ludlow's account, it was because Villiers had sent his company before him, having entertained Mary Kirke the night before, that he was exposed to the enemy. He was surprised by Parliamentary soldiers, refused to give himself up, and was killed (Ludlow, 1. 198). Indeed, Villiers was described in detail defending himself valiantly, with his back against a tree, his horse having been shot from under him. The manner of his death was most unchivalric (in keeping with the desperation and bitterness that characterized the Second Civil War), a Parliamentary soldier dashing off his helmet, then running him through from behind:

and (after he was dead) cut off his Nose, and then run him thorow and thorow the neck and cut and mangled his body in a most barbarous and inhumane manner: But that gallant Spirit expired with more honour then ever the proudest of the Rebels, or any of their tainted race will do to the worlds end: He scorned to ask quarter of a Rebel, and fought with 8 or 9 of the stoutest Butchers of the Army. But he is dead.
When they dishonour'd and defam'd shall die,
Valour and Fame shall crown his memory.
(*The Parliament-kite*, 8 (29 June–13 July 1648), 44–5)

To many commentators, the death of the young cavalier was indicative of the senseless waste of war, and the growing acknowledgement of the futility of these late royalist risings. Even the Parliamentarian journalist John Hall lamented: 'the *Lord Francis Villiers*, a fine yo[u]ng Gentleman *expiated* part of the folly of his companions, and dyed by a many wounds, which had been brave enough, had they been received in another cause', *Mercurius Britannicus*, [9] (11 July) 1648, 70.

There has been some debate on the nature of M.'s allegiances in the poem. Guild, *SEL*, 20 (1980), 125–36 (129–32) notes that the poem is apparently the most openly royalist of M.'s works, but qualifies this by stating that the grief expressed is personal (and hence not blatantly political), that the poem is under the sway of the general brutalization of affairs after the outbreak of the Second Civil War, and that Villiers' death is ultimately blamed on fate, not Parliament, as if to suggest (in line with *An Horatian Ode*) that Parliament was destined by fate to victory. Loxley, *SC*, 10 (1995), 47–8, goes even further: he sees the poem as in tension with Royalist elegy, not congruent with its dominant characteristics. The poem is thus concerned not with a loyal subject but a lover; it is 'a poem attempting to mediate between modes of representing its dead'. In this way, the poem has more in common with mourning elegies, and their use of heroic, romance and mythic components, from the pre-war decades (e.g., see below, l. 109 n.). The poem's reflection of court portraiture suggests that M. knew of the close involvement of the Villiers family (even after Buckingham's assassination in 1628) in the artistic and cultural idealism of the Caroline court. Norbrook (1999), 181, argues that Villiers is presented virtually as an art object (see below, ll. 39–50), like the paintings his elder brother had sold to fund the royalist rising. Nonetheless, it is hard to see how the invocation to poets to take up arms (l. 126) could not be read at the very least as an oblique statement of Civil War royalist allegiance, however strained the connection might be between these closing lines and the rest of the poem.

For Hammond, *SC*, 11 (1996), 107–9, the poem is an early example of M.'s concern with valiant, even erotic, male beauty, characterized by Villiers' own self-observing powers: 'There is a narcissistic, self-enclosing movement about the gaze which is directed at himself, and which finds other masculine objects – even the eyes of an enemy soldier – to reflect it back, rather than the eyes of his mistress. Marvell's conceit labours to preserve the all-male circuit of vision.' The inclusion of the Venus and Adonis story not only makes Villiers (through comparison with Adonis) an 'icon of male beauty', but also 'an unattainable object of sexual desire'.

Sources and Genre. The difficulty of precise generic placing for M.'s two earlier elegies (see also below, 25) is due to the relative youth of the genre in English, itself a part of the process by which funeral elegy separated itself from love elegy, to become the genre exclusively named by the word 'elegy' (Draper (1929), 24–92). The closeness of elegy to panegyric in the earlier seventeenth century (Draper, 27–8), and the tendency of elegy to become satirical under the pressure of the Civil War (Smith (1994), 287–94), are further complicating factors. M.'s earlier elegies also display none of the generic discipline associated with his Cromwell elegy, characterized by its overt Puritan and Commonwealth aesthetics, or the verse epitaph on Frances Jones, with its echoes of Donne's *Anniversaries*. The complicated meditative poetry established by Donne in the *Anniversaries* (1611–12) did not find universal favour. Scodel (1991), 86–91, notes the interaction of elegy and epitaph in classical and Renaissance tradition, with epitaphs (normally concerned with the deeds and qualities of the deceased) being incorporated at the ends of elegies (normally concerned with the thoughts and feelings of the mourners). Further comment by M. on the contents of funeral elegies (ll. 41–2) suggests that M. understood that he had in Villiers a subject whose nature was at odds with the conventional components of the genre.

While M. does not obey the latter category in any strict or sustained sense, the poem comments directly upon the tradition of a final epitaph by having Villiers carve his own epitaph (l. 120). Although many printed elegies of the period simply dealt in generalized, even abstract, terms with the subject's virtuous qualities, some did comment on particular roles played in specific events. See, for instance, anon., *An Elegy on the Death of the Right Honourable Spencer, Earl of Northampton* (1643). None, however, go so far as M. does in placing his subject in a heroic romance narrative (associated with the history of the Villiers family), and endowed with a character and a distinctive mode of perception. To this extent, M.'s poem is unique and outstanding in its time. Equally unusual is the near absence of praise of moral virtues (Norbrook (1999), 181). A famous predecessor of sorts is the 'The Movrning Mvse of Thestylis', in Spenser's *Astrophel*, where Sidney's love with 'Stella' is addressed. The imagery of the subject as a plant (l. 39), and the themes of (possibly alchemical) paradisal renewal in marriage (ll. 77–8), and male beauty, are shared with the Hastings elegy (see below, 25). Other features are in keeping with contemporary elegies (e.g. personification (*peripeteia*): ll. 2–16; the topos of tears: ll. 19–24). In common with M.'s other poems written at the end of the 1640s, the poem also contains echoes of late courtly and cavalier non-elegiac verse (e.g., see below, l. 52 n.).

M.'s poem has very little to do with any of the three other printed elegies on Villiers. The *Elegy on the Untimely death of the incomparably Valiant and noble, Francis, Lord Villiers* (dated by Thomason, 11 Aug. 1648) is unrefined and simple: 'Since in him, Courage, Beauty, Blood,/All that is Great, and Sweet, and Good,/All youth's contracted Glories, have-/(Weep, pittying Reader! Weep.) – their Grave.' There are only the very broadest of similarities (based on rhetorical structure rather than verbal echo) with 'Obsequeies on the untimely death, of the never to be too much pitied Francis Lord Villiers', printed in *Vaticinium Votivum* (11 March 1649; spuriously attributed to George Wither: see Norbrook, *N & Q*, 241 (1996), 276–81). *An Elegie and Epitaph, upon the Right Honourable the Lord Francis Villars: Written by an affectionate servant to his Family* (4 August 1648), complete with a woodcut headpiece showing a supine skeleton, rehearses divine right theory and anti-Puritan, anti-Leveller sentiment, although it may have influenced other M. poems. M.'s description of Villiers does, however, develop imagery describing his father, the first Duke of Buckingham, in the largely critical poetry on his assassination. See, e.g., anon., 'Upon the Sodaine Death of the Great D. of B.':

What though, Mars-like, to Pallas thou didst yield?
Yet thou of Venus ever had'st the field.
The nymphes, whose brows bright wreathes of honour
                                                          twine,
Judg'd thee to bee a man neere half divine,
And freely would expose vnto thy pleasure
The curious riches of their hidden treasure.
    (Fairholt (1850), 47; see below ll. 25–6 n., 109–14)

However, M.'s poem shows further affinities with the three MS elegies on Villiers discovered in University College, London, MS Ogden 42, 'C.R.', 'To my worthy friend A: J: invitinge him to write something on the Lord Francis Villers slayne in their uncivill Warrs at Kingston upon Thames' (pp. 3–4); 'A.J.', 'The Answere' (p. 5); 'G.T.', 'On the Death of the Lord Francis Villers' (p. 179). In particular, the four poems share an acknowledgement of Villiers' physical beauty and some classical parallels, as discussed by McWilliams (forthcoming). The opening of G.T.'s poem is indebted to the beginning of M.'s. This suggests that M. was moving in the same circles as the undoubtedly royalist poets collected in this volume. Similarity may also be found between M.'s poem and a Latin elegy 'Illustrissimi Herois Domini FRANCISCI VILLIERS Epicedium' by G.F., published in *Vaticinium Votivum* (1649).

Structure and Style. For all its authentic Marvellian touches, the poem has generally been regarded as technically inferior to most of M.'s poetry. Its absence from *1681* may imply that M. had simply forgotten it, having perhaps written it in a hurry (even in difficult personal circumstances) and having been unable to keep a copy. The unevenness of the poem also suggests hurried composition (e.g. l. 90), followed by hurried publication, and a lack of opportunity to make revisions.

It is, nonetheless, a successful poem, maintaining an appropriate tenor of reserved regret (with occasional emotional heights) within the structure of rhymed heroic couplets, and deftly placed enjambements. Emphatic caesurae (e.g. ll. 1, 6) are more noticeable than in M.'s other elegies, as are reversals of word order (e.g. l. 21). A number of M.'s verse formulations are embryonically introduced: they occur in later poems (largely *An Horatian Ode*) in a more refined way (see below, ll. 14 n., 42 n., 69 n., 119–20 n.), while M.'s conceptual comparisons within single lines are more pronounced (e.g. l. 28). The same is true of a number of images, drawn out into complex conceits (e.g. ll. 39–41). There are a number of images that are quietly placed either for effect, or perhaps, through inexperience, lacking the more confident texturing of the later public poetry (e.g. the personification of revenge (ll. 23–4), the association of Villiers with the life of flowers (ll. 39; 62–3; 81–2; 109–14) [where the presentation of Villiers as a superior Adonis evokes the metamorphosis of that mythical lover into an anenome]). The poem is structurally poised between the cultural forms associated with Villiers' family and early life (romance, courtly portraiture, extravagant buildings) and that which painting cannot represent: war and the pressure it places upon love. Paradoxically, the actual death of Villiers is described not literally, but through a series of romance, epic and mythical images (ll. 93–114). Villiers' last act is a making of his own memorial (the pyramid of slain soldiers): a return to the modes of representation that had marked his life.

An
Elegy Upon the Death of My
Lord Francis Villiers

'Tis true that he is dead: but yet to choose,
Methinks thou Fame should not have brought the news
Thou canst discourse at will and speak at large:
But wast not in the fight nor durst thou charge.
5   While he transported all with valiant rage,
His name eternized, but cut short his age;
On the safe battlements of Richmond's bow'rs
Thou wast espied, and from the guilded tow'rs
Thy silver trumpets sounded a retreat,
10   Far from the dust and battle's sulph'ry heat.
Yet what couldst thou have done? 'Tis always late
To struggle with inevitable fate.
Much rather thou I know expect'st to tell
How heavy Cromwell gnashed the earth and fell,

---

1. 'Tis . . . dead] 'shows an awareness of the many elegies in miscellany manuscripts which ask "Is't true?" or state . . . "I'll not believe it!."' (Hobbs, *EMS*, 1 (1989), 186).
2. Fame . . . news] 'The poem opens with an address to Fame, evoking the world of the rival newbooks which constantly printed rumours of the death of his [Villiers'] enemies', Norbrook (1999), 181.
3. discourse] a) travel (*OED* v. 1) b) discuss (*OED* v. 3). *speak at large*] proclaim a) without restraint b) at length c) in general (as opposed to particular) terms.
4. charge] a) command, order (*OED* v. II 14 a) b) attack, especially on horseback (*OED* v. IV 22 a) c) load and aim a firearm (*OED* v. I 5) d) ready a pike in battle (*OED* v. 21 a).
5. transported all] a) affected all around him (with his gallantry) (*OED* v. 1b, trans.) b) went entirely from this world to the next (*OED* v. 1e, intr.). Both Villiers brothers were known for their impetuosity.
7–8. the safe . . . tow'rs] Craze (1979), 55, suggests an echo in these lines of Virgil, *Aeneid*, IV, ll. 186–7: 'aut summi culmine tecti,/turribus aut altis' (on high roof-tops or high towers).
7. the safe . . . bow'rs] see above, Headnote, Context. *Richmond's bow'rs*] Mary Villiers (1623–85), sister of Francis, became Duchess of Richmond by her second marriage, to James

Stuart, first Duke of Richmond and fourth Duke of Lennox (1612–55). He was Keeper of Richmond Park, which overlooks Kingston, near to where Villiers fell (see above, *Context*).
8. Thou] i.e. Fame.
10. dust] a) dust raised by battle: cp. Virgil, *Aeneid*, XII, ll. 444–5: 'tum caeco pulvere campus/miscetur pulsuque pedem tremit excita tellus' (Then the plain is a turmoil of blinding dust, and the startled earth trembles under the tramp of feet). b) turmoil (*OED* n.¹ 5). c) field of contest (i.e. battlefield): cp. Virgil, *Aeneid*, VII, l. 163: 'domitantquet in pulvere currus' (or break in teams amid the dust). d) toil: cp. Horace, *Epodes*, I, l. 51: 'cui sit condicio dulcis sine pulvere palmae?' (who had the surety of victory's palm without the dust?). *sulph'ry*] a) pertaining to gunpowder (*OED* a. 2 c) b) hell-like ('sulphurous': *OED* a. 3).
11. Yet . . . done] Cp. Milton, *Lycidas*, l. 57: 'Had ye been there . . . for what could that have done?' *late*] a) too late b) indicative of time's advance (*OED* a.¹ 3).
13. expect'st] expected.
14. heavy] a) heavily armed (*OED* a.¹ I 7) b) grave (*OED* a.¹ III 13) c) dull (*OED* a.¹ V 18) d) oppressive (*OED* a¹ VI 22); cp. *An Horatian Ode*, ll. 91–2: 'So when the falcon high/Falls heavy from the sky'.

15 Or how slow Death far from the sight of day
The long-deceivèd Fairfax bore away.
But until then, let us young Francis praise:
And plant upon his hearse the bloody bays,
Which we will water with our welling eyes.
20 Tears spring not still from spongy Cowardice.
The purer fountains from the rocks more steep
Distil and stony Valour best doth weep.
Besides revenge, if often quenched in tears,
Hardens like steel and daily keener wears.
25   Great Buckingham, whose death doth freshly strike
Our memories, because to this so like;
Ere that in the eternal court he shone,
And here a favourite there found a throne;
The fatal night before he hence did bleed,
30 Left to his princess this immortal seed.
And the wise Chinese in the fertile womb
Of earth doth a more precious clay entomb,

Which dying by his will he leaves consigned:
Till by mature delay of time refined
35 The crystal metal fit to be released
Is taken forth to crown each royal feast:
Such was the fate by which this postume breathed,
Who scarcely seems begotten but bequeathed.
    Never was there human plant that grew
40 More fair than this and acceptably new.
'Tis truth that beauty doth most men dispraise:
Prudence and valour their esteem do raise.
But he that hath already these in store,
Cannot be poorer sure for having more.
45 And his unimitable handsomeness
Made him indeed be more than man, not less.
We do but faintly God's resemblance bear
And like rough coins of careless mints appear:
But he of purpose made, did represent
50 In a rich medal ev'ry lineament.

---

16. deceivèd] a) mistaken (*OED* ppl. a.) b) ensnared (*OED* v. 1). *Fairfax*] It is true that Ferdinando, second Baron Fairfax, and a prominent Parliamentary commander, died after an illness on 14 March 1648, just before this poem was written, but M.'s reference is surely to his son, Thomas, the addressee of *Upon Appleton House*, who had been for some time chief commander of the Parliamentary forces, and who frequently featured alongside Cromwell in royalist propaganda and satire.
18. bays] technically a laurel given to a conqueror or poet, but coffins were more usually decorated with rosemary, a symbol of eternity and with a smell that disguised that of putrefaction. (Houlbrooke (1998), 284, 288).
19. welling] overflowing with tears.
20. spongy] a) like a sponge, retaining (as opposed to releasing) moisture (*OED* a. 3a) b) insubstantial (*OED* a. 4).
22. Distil] pour down in drops (*OED* v. 1).
23–4. revenge . . . wears] the image suggests the representation of revenge here as a sword or dagger.
24. keener] a) bolder (*OED* a. 2a) b) more bitter (*OED* a. 5).
25. Great Buckingham] George Villiers, first Duke of Buckingham, father of Francis Villiers, and favourite of both James I and Charles I, was assassinated on 23 August 1628; cp. anon., 'Ad viatorem', printed with *An Elegie and Epitaph, upon the Right Honourable the Lord Francis Villars: Written by an affectionate servant to his Family* (1648), s.sh., ll. 1–4: 'Stay passer by, and pay the yeare/To him who lyes entombed here;/'Tis Villars, Buckinghams brave Sonne, Who hath the Gole of Honour wonne.' *strike*] Buckingham's assassin, John Felton, stabbed him in the chest with a knife. Our memories are struck by Buckingham was struck by Felton's blow, and the deaths of father and son are similar.
25–6. whose death . . . so like] but there were very few elegies on Buckingham, and of those, most were at least to some degree critical; most of the verse on the assassination vindicated Felton or was critical of the Duke's impact on the court and royal policy (see, e.g., Fairholt (1850), especially 36–67; Holstun (2000), ch. 2).
29–30. See above, *Headnote, Context.*

29. fatal] ominous (*OED* a. 4c).
30. his princess] Lady Katherine Manners, Duchess of Buckingham (d. 1629).
31–6. It was believed that Chinese porcelain was hardened by burying its constituent components underground for a hundred years: see Bacon, *Sylva Sylvarum* (1624), 82; *New Atlantis* (1627), 31; Donne, 'Elegie on the Lady Markham' (1609), ll. 21–2; Browne, *Pseudodoxia Epidemica* (1646), II.v.7. Cp. *The First Anniversary*, ll. 19–20: 'Their earthy projects under ground they lay,/More slow and brittle than the China clay.'
33. consigned] given in trust.
37. postume] posthumous child (*OED* B. n. a.); cp. Virgil, *Aeneid*, VI, ll. 763–5: 'Silvius, Albanum nomen, tua postuma proles,/quem tibi longaevo serum Lavinia coniunx/educet silvis' (Silvius of Alban name, thy last-born child, whom late in thy old age thy wife Lavinia shall bring forth in the woodland).
38. bequeathed] to heaven.
40. acceptably] agreeable, satisfying (from the Latin *acceptus*); stressed on first and third syllables.
41. 'Tis . . . dispraise] Cp. Ecclesiasticus 11:2: 'Do not overrate one man for his good looks/or be repelled by another man's appearance.'
42. Prudence . . . valour] Cp. *An Horatian Ode*, l. 33, where Cromwell 'Could by industrious valour climb.' This vocabulary comes from Machiavelli and, more generally, the *discorso* tradition of political theory, which was used increasingly during the 1640s as a means of understanding and assessing the events and the politics of the Civil War (see below, 272; Tuck (1993), especially 39–45, 203–78). M.'s use of these terms in this poem demonstrates his familiarity with political theory at an early stage.
44. more] i.e. 'handsomeness' as well as prudence and valour.
45. unimitable handsomeness] the use of terms that suggest visual representation (see also below, ll. 50, 83) implies that M. may have had the portraiture of the Villiers family in mind. Van Dyck painted Francis Villiers twice (and thus did 'imitate' his beauty), most notably when Villiers was six in 1635, standing alongside his elder brother George.
50. lineament] feature (*OED* 2).

Lovely and admirable as he was,
Yet was his sword or armour all his glass.
Nor in his mistress' eyes that joy he took,
As in an enemy's himself to look.
55   I know how well he did, with what delight
Those serious imitations of fight.
Still in the trials of strong exercise
His was the first, and his the second prize.
     Bright Lady, thou that rulest from above
60   The last and greatest monarchy of love:
Fair Richmond hold thy brother or he goes.
Try if the jasmine of thy hand or rose
Of thy red lip can keep him always here:
For he loves danger and doth never fear.
65   Or may thy tears prevail with him to stay?
     But he resolved breaks carelessly away.
Only one argument could now prolong
His stay and that most fair and so most strong:
The matchless Chlora whose pure fires did warm
70   His soul and only could his passions charm.
     You might with much more reason go reprove
The am'rous magnet which the north doth love.

Or preach divorce and say it is amiss
That with tall elms the twining vines should kiss
75   Than chide two such so fit, so equal fair
That in the world they have no other pair.
Whom it might seem that Heaven did create
To restore man unto his first estate.
Yet she for Honour's tyrannous respect
80   Her own desires did and his neglect.
And like the modest plant at every touch
Shrunk in her leaves and feared it was too much.
     But who can paint the torments and that pain
Which he professed and now she could not feign?
85   He like the sun but overcast and pale:
She like a rainbow, that ere long must fail,
Whose roseal cheek where heaven itself did view
Begins to sep'rate and dissolve to dew.
     At last he leave obtains though sad and slow,
90   First of her and then of himself to go.
How comely and how terrible he sits
At once and war as well as love befits!
Ride where thou wilt and bold adventures find:
But all the ladies are got up behind.

---

51. Cp. Clarendon, *History*, XI.175: 'Lord Francis Villiers, a youth of rare Beauty and comliness of Person.'
52. glass] mirror; contrast Fanshawe, 'Presented to his Highnesse, in the West, Ann. Dom. 1646', ll. 45–8: 'So doe *the People* fix their eyes upon/*The King*, admire, love, honour *Him* alone./In *Him*, as in a glasse, their manners view/And frame, and copie what they see *Him* doe.'
55–8. M. had spent time with the extravagant Villiers brothers in Italy; these lines are based then upon M.'s personal acquaintance of Lord Francis (see above, *Context*). M. refers to his own training in swordsmanship when in Spain: 'To a Friend in Persia', Legouis (1971), II.324.
59–61. Bright Lady . . . Richmond] See above, l. 7 n. The Duchess of Richmond was renowned for her beauty, and was painted several times by Van Dyck, as part of family portraits, on the occasion of her first marriage in 1636 as Venus, and on the occasion of the second in 1637 as St Agnes, patroness of marriage. Given the circumstances of Villiers' liaison with Mrs Kirke, M. may be referring to the former portrait.
62–3. jasmine . . . lip] these details are too conventional to suggest a connection with any particular painting.
69. Chlora] E.E. Duncan-Jones, *N & Q*, 198 (1953), 102, suggests that Chlora was Mary Kirke, daughter of the court poet Aurelian Townshend; the dead Villiers was found wearing a lock of her hair, wrapped in a ribbon. A Chlora also appears in *Mourning*, l. 4, and a Clora in *The Gallery*, l. 1.
74. twining vines] cp. *Upon Appleton House*, ll. 609–10: 'Bind me ye woodbines in your twines,/Curl me about ye gadding vines.'
75. equal fair] i.e. equally beautiful.
76. no other pair] no equals; a wordplay, with 'pair' evoking 'peers'.
78. first estate] i.e. Paradise.
79. Honour's tyrannous respect] Mary Kirke was already married.

81. modest plant] *mimosa pudica*, or sensitive plant; cp. *Upon Appleton House*, ll. 354–7: 'that heaven-nursèd plant,/Which most our earthly gardens want./A prickling leaf it bears, and such/As that which shrinks at every touch'.
83–8. Cp. Francis Quarles, *Argalus and Partheneia* (2nd edn, ?1635), 46: 'His pining thoughts and her projecting feares;/His soliloquies, and her secret teares.'
84. feign] conceal.
86–8. rainbow . . . dew] M.'s simile presents the rainbow as a structure that eventually dissolves into rain, but the cause of rainbows in the refraction of sunlight through falling rain was well known: Bacon and Browne refer to it, and there were continental authorities such as Pererius and Vossius: see Browne, *Pseudodoxia Epidemica*, VII.iv, ed. R. Robbins, 2 vols (Oxford, 1981), II.1089; see also, Browne, *Pseudodoxia*, I.545: 'the Rainebow hath its ground in Nature, as caused by the rayes of the Sunne, falling upon a roride [dewy] and opposite cloud; whereof some reflected, others refracted beget that semicircular variety we generally call the Rainebow.' M. used the same image in his consolatory letter to Sir John Trott (late August 1667): 'The Tears of a family may flow together like those little drops that compact the Rainbow, and if they be plac'd with the same advantage towards Heaven as those are to the sun, they too have their splendour' (Legouis, II.311). *Bod. 1* emends 'compact' to 'compose'.
87–8. roseal . . . dew] the image is twofold a) of the cheek as the petals of a rose-flower separating as happiness turns to an expression of grief b) of Chlora as a rainbow, about to separate back into water-droplets, and fall to earth.
87. roseal] a) rose-coloured (*OED* a. 1) b) by playing on the Latin for dewy, *roscidus*, roseal wittily suggests 'wet' or 'moist'; Chlora is thus aptly portrayed as being tearful.
88. dew] see above l. 87 n. b).
94. got up behind] in the saddle.

95 Guard them, though not thyself: for in thy death
    Th'eleven thousand virgins lose their breath.
        So Hector issuing from the Trojan wall,
    The sad Ilìads to the gods did call
    With hands displayed and with dishevelled hair
100 That they the empire in his life would spare.
    While he secure through all the field doth spy
    Achilles for Achilles only cry.
    Ah ignorant that yet e'er night he must
    Be drawn by him inglorious through the dust.
105   Such fell young Villiers in the cheerful heat
    Of youth: his locks entangled all with sweat
    And those eyes which the Sentinel did keep
    Of Love closed up in an eternal sleep.
    While Venus of Adonis thinks no more,
110 Slain by the harsh tusk of the savage boar.
    Hither she runs and hath him hurried far

    Out of the noise and blood, and killing war:
    Where in her gardens of sweet myrtle laid
    She kisses him in the immortal shade.
115   Yet died he not revengeless: much he did
    Ere he could suffer. A whole pyramid
    Of vulgar bodies he erected high:
    Scorning without a sepulchre to die.
    And with his steel which did whole troops divide
120 He cut his epitaph on either side.
    Till finding nothing to his courage fit
    He rid up last to death and conquered it.
        Such are the obsequies to Francis own:
    He best the pomp of his own death hath shown.
125 And we hereafter to his honour will
    Not write so many, but so many kill.
    Till the whole Army by just vengeance come
    To be at once his trophy and his tomb.

---

96. *eleven thousand virgins*] St Ursula, a British princess, was murdered, along with her eleven thousand female companions when returning from a pilgrimage to Rome.

97–104. *Hector . . . dust*] Cp. anon., *A Mournfull Elegy upon the three Renowned Worthies, Duke Hamilton, the Earle of Holland, and the ever to be honoured Lord Capel* (1649), s.sh.: 'Renowned CAPEL, . . . Whose *actions* manifested him to be/A second *Hector*, or more in degree,/Hated by *Achillis*, 'cause his fame/Did seem to blemish great *Achillis* name.' M.'s simile is a curious conflation of the story: in Homer, Hector's invocations to fight come earlier in the poem (e.g. his general challenge in *Iliad*, VII). It is Achilles who spies out Hector on the battlefield (*Iliad*, XX, ll. 428–9), while Hector is well aware of his disadvantage against the god–man Achilles.

98. *Ilìads*] Trojan women (not in *OED*); see Homer, *Iliad*, VI, ll. 494–502: 'Presently, she [Andromache] came to the well-built palace of man-slaying Hector and found therein her many handmaidens; and among them all she roused lamentation.'

102. *Achilles*] Reference to Achilles was as frequent as that to Hector in Royalist poetry: see, e.g., H.B., 'Heroick Martyr, whose immortall death', in *Verses on the Death of the Right Valiant S' Bevill Grenvill* (1643), 21: 'Achilles like All-Proofe, but in the Heele:/Offring Thy selfe a Resolv'd Sacrifice,/As sure to fall.'

105. *Such*] in this way. *cheerful*] animated, enlivened (*OED* a. 2).

106. *locks . . . sweat*] For another simultaneous association of sweat with amorousness and soldiery, see below *Upon Appleton House*, l. 428 and n.

107–8. *Sentinel . . . Of Love*] i.e. the Sentinel of Love.

109–10. *While Venus . . . boar*] see Ovid, *Metamorphoses*, X, ll. 708–39; one of the most popular classical images of natural love in the Renaissance; frequently represented in emblems; see, e.g., Milton, *A Masque*, ll. 997–1001: 'Beds of hyacinths, and roses,/Where young Adonis oft reposes,/Waxing well of his deep wound/In slumber soft, and on the ground/Sadly sits the Assyrian queen.' Adonis's wound signified the 'wound' of earthly love. Cp. also Patricke Mackgueir, *Tears for the Death of Lodouicke, Duke of Richmond and Lennox* (1624), ll. 47–8: 'But when thy armes were layd aside, she swore,/My sweet

Adonis hath escap'd the Bore.' Van Dyck painted Villiers' parents as Venus and Adonis *c.* 1620. John Hall also called Villiers Adonis: see *Mercurius Britannicus*, 10 (18 July 1648), 75.

111. *him*] i.e. Villiers.

113. *myrtle*] with its fragrant flower, the myrtle plant was considered sacred to Venus, and was an emblem of love.

116. *could*] was able to (*OED* v¹ II 3). *pyramid*] reference to pyramids as funerary monuments was common in Renaissance poetry: e.g. Drummond's pyramid-shaped epitaph 'Of Jet,/Or Propherie' in Walter Quin, ed., *Mausoleum Or, the Choicest Flowers of the Epitaphs, written on the Death of Prince Henrie* (1613), 5; anon., 'Faire Britaine's Prince', in *idem.*, 6, 'Affections flammes huge *Pyramides* doth raise,/All graven with golden letters of his praise'; cp. also P.M., 'Yet boast not Senate: know he could not Dy', in *Verses on the Death of the Right Valiant S' Bevill Grenvill* (1643), 19: 'Neere *Lindsey's*, *Denby's*, or *Northampton's* side/(Who Conquer'd dying) raise his *Pyramide*:/Which may restore him to the World agen,/A Conqueror of Time as well as Men.'

117. *vulgar*] a) ordinary (specifically of common soldiers; *OED* a. II 9 c) b) plebeian, coarse, unrefined (*OED* a. II 13).

119–20. *whole . . . side*] Cp. *An Horatian Ode*, ll. 15–16: 'Did thorough his own side/His fiery way divide'; *The First Anniversary*, ll. 91–2: 'And they, whose nature leads them to divide,/Uphold this one, and that the other side.' *whole troops divide*] a) cut through groups of soldiers b) dismember the bodies of soldiers: see Virgil, *Aeneid*, IX, ll. 750–1: 'mediam ferro gemina inter tempora frontem/dividit impubesque immani volnere malas' (the steel cleaves the brow in twain full between the temples, and with ghastly wound severs the beardless cheeks).

123. *obsequies*] funeral rites. *own*] owed, due.

125–6. *And . . . kill*] Cp. anon., 'To King Charles', Folger MS V.a.219, fol. 16ʳ: 'Strew all the pavement where hee treads/With loyall hearts, or Rebels heads.'; anon., 'Upon yᵉ Death of K Charles yᵉ 1ˢᵗ', Cardiff Central Library, MS 1.482, fol. 47ᵛ: 'I'll sing yʳ Obsequies wᵗʰ Trumpet sounds,/And write thine Epitaphs wᵗʰ Blood & Wounds.'

127. *Army*] the New Model Army.

4

To his Noble Friend Mr Richard Lovelace, upon his Poems

Date. Late 1648. M.'s commendatory poem was included in the first edition of Richard Lovelace's *Lucasta* (1649), sig. a 7^{r-v}. The Stationers' Register entry, 14 May 1649, claims that *Lucasta* was licensed on 7 February 1648. Thomason dated his copy 21 June 1649. It is usually claimed that the references in M.'s poem to harsh censorship (see below, ll. 21–6) imply that M. must have written his poem before *Lucasta* was licensed, even late 1647 (e.g. Margoliouth; Craze (1979), 34; Griffin (1995), 23). But it is more probable that M. wrote his poem between licensing and publication: references in the poem refer to dates in 1648 (see below, ll. 29 n., 31–2 n.), and the preliminaries (in which M.'s poem was placed) were most probably printed after the verse was set, so the licensers would not have seen verse that openly attacks them.

Internal evidence shows that some of the other prefatory poems in the volume were written after the licensing date, and well into 1649 (see, e.g., John Pinchbacke, 'Another, upon the Poems', ll. 26–7). Corns (1992), 225, accordingly prefers a scenario in which composition of the poem did not much precede publication. The absence of regicidal lament from the whole volume (unlike the Hastings elegies, including M.'s, which appeared shortly after *Lucasta*), suggests a date of composition before the trial and execution of the King in the closing months of 1648, and the first weeks of the following year. This is supported by the probable reference to the church government legislation of August 1648 (see below, l. 24 n.). But if the date of composition was late, Norbrook (1999), 172–3, argues that the poem looks back to reflect an immediate post-civil war era.

Although Lovelace's imprisonment, in connection with the sequestration of his estates (between 9 June 1648 and 10 April 1649), is usually cited as the most probable reason for the delay in the printing and publication of the volume, there is also the possibility that *Lucasta* was delayed by political interference. Patterson (1978), 18, argues that M.'s explicit con-nection of the *Lucasta* volume with the sequestration (see below, ll. 27–30) is evidence for the delay between licensing and publication and points to a motive for the poem's composition: Lovelace's name appeared on 5 May 1649 in a list of delinquents whose cases were to be considered for a reduction of their fine; *Lucasta* appeared shortly afterwards.

Publication. 1649, in Richard Lovelace, *Lucasta*, sig. a7^{r-v}. Not in *1681*.

Context. Richard Lovelace (1618–58) came from an old Kentish gentry family. He entered Gloucester Hall, Oxford, in 1634, and quickly gained a reputation for being extremely handsome, virtuous, and courtly ('a most beautiful gentleman . . . and extraordinary handsome man, but prowd' (Aubrey (1898), II.37)). Aubrey also quotes as a correlative Ovid, *Metamorphoses* III, ll. 420–3, where Narcissus' beauty and likeness to the gods, is described; this is a passage elsewhere used by M. (see below, 82). Lovelace was admitted to the degree of MA at Oxford in 1636, and was incorporated at Cambridge the following year, where M. may have first met him. He then joined the court, served in the Scottish campaign of 1639 and continued to write plays and poems. He retired to Kent, and presented to Parliament the pro-royalist petition of Kentish gentry in April 1642. He was consequently imprisoned for some six weeks (during which time he wrote some of the poetry that appeared in *Lucasta*), and on his release continued to fund, and provide soldiers for, the royalist cause. He took up arms again in 1645 and joined the King in Oxford, then served in the French armies after the surrender of Oxford in 1646. On his return to England in 1648, he was again arrested and imprisoned in Petre House, Aldersgate, where he assembled the *Lucasta* volume. He was released on 10 December 1649, but by this time was penniless, and spent the next years in dire poverty, despite the support of friends. He died in London in 1658.

Genre, Sources and Style. The poem is a true poetic epistle, complete with superscription, formal address ('Sir') and signature; it was probably written in this way and sent to Lovelace (for a comparable example, see e.g., Carew, 'To Master W. Montague', l. 1). In that it is concerned with the place of the poet in public life, M.'s poem is faithful to Horatian verse epistles: e.g. *Epistle* I.i, l. 16, 'nunc agilis fio et mersor civilibus undis' (Now I become all action and plunge into the tide of civil life). Yet Horace's poets, both himself and others, do not live in decayed times. They also assume the patronage of the great, including Augustus. This is especially so of the dedicatory epistles (e.g. *Epistle*, I.xiii), and in respect of Horace's interest in the possibility of the poet's personal independence despite patronage (*Epistle* I.xiv, xv), a theme quite contrary to Lovelace's predicament. The poets and dramatists mentioned in the Augustus epistle (*Epistle* II.i) are in part presented, like Lovelace in M.'s poem, as acting characters. The mention of the rabble who fight for crude entertainment on the stage against the aims of the poet-dramatist (*Epistle* II.i, ll. 182–6) is broadly comparable to Lovelace's struggle with the 'rout' of Presbyterian censors.

M.'s use of the verse epistle reflects his awareness of how different a time he lives in, as compared to the verse epistles of the previous generation. Jonson's verse epistles and epigrams are concerned with the unproblematic exercise of the virtue that great Englishmen have inherited directly from ancient Rome; it is people rather than times, who are degenerate. Censure rather than censorship is the convention, and it is exercised by one writer critically on another, rather than arbitrarily imposed by law: such is the case with Jonson, 'To John Donne' (*Epigram* 96) and Carew's 'To Ben Ionson. Vpon occasion of his Ode of defiance annext to his Play of the new Inne.' Their imagery of conflict is explicitly divorced from war: 'That I, hereafter, do not think the Bar/The seat made of a more than civil war' ('An Epigram to the Counsellor that Pleaded and Carried the Cause', ll. 1–2). Similarly, Donne's verse epistles addressed to other poets are concerned with the intimacy of poets in their joint quest for their muses (e.g. 'To Mr T.W.' (sts. I, V, VI), 'To Mr S.B.', 'To Mr B.B.').

The poem's subject matter is typical of much royalist verse written in the 1640–60 period, with its castigation of the 'pamphlet wars', Parliamentary licensing and its plangent, retrospective glance at the high days of the Caroline literary culture in the 1630s (although Lovelace wrote most of his verse during the Civil War decade itself): see Smith (1994), 26–32. The understanding of the predicament of the cavalier poet is startlingly acute, suggesting a profound engagement with the *Lucasta* volume. In keeping with the generic confusion of the time, the poem is a panegyric, but also, by its occasion, an elegy, not for Lovelace, but for the lost halcyon days of pre-war culture. Norbrook (1999), 173, stresses that, with mention neither of king nor court, the lost literary culture is that of Jonson's 'town'.

The poem uses a series of similes to demonstrate the corruption of literary ideals by the Civil War in a way that is harmonious with Lovelace's bearing and M.'s representation of it. Cultural decline is compared to 'complexions' that alter with climate. The result is double standards and paradoxes (ll. 13–14), as opposed to the singularity of a time when values were perspicacious and plain; praise meant praise, and was generously reciprocated (l. 7; see also ll. 36, 49–50). Gradually, lexical repetition, articulating giving and plainness, becomes ironic modulation ('Civil . . . civic', l. 12), followed by paradox (ll. 13–14, 26), and finally, absurd, nonsensical logical propositions (ll. 27–32). Most of the dedicatory poems in the volume praise Lovelace's amorous verse in courtly terms. M.'s poem is singular in catching the sense of the impact of civil conflict on poetry so sharply. It also shares with John Hall's dedicatory poem a sense of the *Lucasta* poems offering a new kind of heroic love poetry for the age of war in which the poet becomes the object of his praise: 'what Ionick sweetnesse thou canst write?/And melt those eager passions that are/Stubborn enough t'enrage the God of war,/Into a noble Love, which may aspire/Into an illustrious Pyramid of Fire' ('To Colonel Richard Lovelace, on the publishing of his ingenious poems', ll. 12–16). Nonetheless, M. places Lovelace firmly in a narrative in which he is seen to act as a character, ultimately a romance hero; Hall opts for direct address alone, as do nearly all of the other dedicatory poems in the volume. Once in romance, Lovelace is described in terms fitting of courtly poetry and poet heroes: the anaphora of ll. 37–8 is typical of Sidney's poetry, especially *Astrophel and Stella*.

The poem goes further than all the other dedicatory verse in the volume by using the literary materials of the new age of civil and military conflict. When M. was writing the poem, anti-Parliamentary journalism flourished in London. M.'s associate

Marchamont Nedham was writing and publishing *Mercurius Pragmaticus*, a newsbook that supported the King, although it was also at times friendly towards the Levellers. Its hatred of Presbyterianism was unqualified. Nedham's (and other journalists') love of hyphenated portmanteau words as part of his repertoire of 'joco-serious' abuse is reflected in M.'s poem at l. 19. M.'s line appears to be a re-ordering of Nedham's terms: 'Paper-pellet . . . Water-rat' (*Mercurius Pragmaticus*, 25 (29 February–7 March 1648), sig. A4ᵛ). Patterson (1978), 18, argues that the poem's sense of deep loss is for 'the age of classical rhetoric when the writer's trade was seen as a positive social and political force'; the poem is indeed lamenting the association of the *ars rhetorica* with the 'innocence' of the court, but rhetoric ought to flourish (as Milton and others reminded readers in the pamphlet exchanges of the 1640s). In M.'s poem, Presbyterian censorship is presented as the threat to civic virtue; any positive picture of public polemical exchange is absent, as we might expect in a poem addressed to a royalist. Satirical attacks on Presbyterianism, from a royalist, Independent or sectarian position, and in verse and prose, were frequent in the second half of the 1640s: see e.g., anon., *The Presbyterians Letany* (1647). The spectacle of the courtly women coming to Lovelace's defence (ll. 33–40) relates not only to romance but also to the women-on-top pamphlets of the period, where the inversion of conventional gender roles functioned as a response to the disorder of the times, and a means of attacking Puritanism by traducing religious rigour as misdirected, superabundant libido (see Wiseman in Holstun, ed. (1992), Turner (2002), ch. 3).

For Norbrook (1999), 172–3, the key public apologist behind the poem is not Nedham but Hall, who was addressing writers like Lovelace and Marvell in order to encourage them to serve in a new public sphere that would revive the nation under a strictly limited monarchy. Thus, M.'s poem may be regarded as in part a response to Hall, and may allude in its first line to the title of his work, *A True Account*

and Character of the Times (1648). See also Cuthbert (1987), 22 ff.

Modern Criticism. The poem has been seen to stand out as one of the most forthright and incisive of M.'s comments on poetry and the nature of the poet's role in society (Chernaik (1983), 16), and has been seen as the 'best and most revealing' of the 'early Royalist poems' (Hodge (1978), 114). In this connection, Friedman, 38–9, notes that the poem is not concerned with a lost *otium*, but the 'vanished correspondence between moral integrity and artistic genius'. There is a critical consensus that the poem is an uncomplicated defence of the view that 'the poet should strive to remain uncompromised by the conditions that prevail in the grubby arena of politics' (Wilcher (1985), 111), but M.'s lexis in the poem suggests that the poet is already tainted by the Civil War, and the politics of its 'paper bullets'. Marcus's view ((1986), 215–18) that M.'s praise of Lovelace as poet first neutralizes then undermines Lovelace as political activist is controverted by Griffin (1995), 24–5, who argues that M. does not directly judge Lovelace's verse, but is more concerned to analyse the nature of the fallen times, and its consequences for poetry. Nonetheless, Lovelace's poetry is implicitly praised in so far as it lives in M.'s lines, but the representation of cavalier ethos is designed to 'lay [that ethos] to rest'. For Norbrook (1999), 172–3, the poem ultimately confesses both the poet's distance from committed civil war allegiances, and M.'s sense of himself as an outsider to the literary and cultural circles the centre of which was Lovelace.

To his Noble Friend Mr Richard Lovelace, upon his Poems

Sir,
Our times are much degenerate from those
Which your sweet Muse with your fair fortune chose,
And as complexions alter with the climes,
Our wits have drawn th'infection of our times.

Title. *Mr*] because Lovelace was an Oxford MA, incorporated at Cambridge, M. addresses him as an equal. Five of the seventeen prefatory poems to *Lucasta* address Lovelace as a Colonel; of the three using 'Mr' or '*Domino*', the two apart from M.'s are by academics (William Rudyerd and John Harmer).

1. *degenerate*] degenerated.
2. *with*] *Donno, Walker*; which *1649*; see R.G. Howarth, *N & Q*, 198 (1953), 330. *fair fortune*] since Lovelace was beautiful (see above, *Headnote, Context*).
4. *drawn*] contracted.

That candid age no other way could tell
To be ingenious, but by speaking well.
Who best could praise, had then the greatest praise,
'Twas more esteemed to give, than wear the bays:
Modest Ambition studied only then,
To honour not herself, but worthy men.
These virtues now are banished out of town,
Our civil wars have lost the civic crown.
He highest builds, who with most art destroys,
And against others' fame his own employs.
I see the envious caterpillar sit

On the fair blossom of each growing wit.
   The air's already tainted with the swarms
Of insects which against you rise in arms:
Word-peckers, paper-rats, book-scorpions,
Of wit corrupted, the unfashioned sons.
The barbèd censurers begin to look
Like the grim consistory on thy book;
And on each line cast a reforming eye,
Severer than the young Presbytery.
Till when in vain they have thee all perused,
You shall for being faultless be accused.

5–10. That . . . men] Cp. Thomas Rawlins, 'To his Honoured and Ingenious Friend Col. Richard Lovelace, on his Lucasta', ll. 6–7: '*When Vertue, Wit, and Learning, wore the bayes,/ Now Vice assumes.*'

5. candid] a) illustrious (*OED* a. 2 a) b) pure (because not tainted with civil conflict (*OED* a. 2 b)); M. recalls the Latin root *candidus* ('white' or 'glistening').

5–6. no other . . . well] i.e. once ingeniousness was only associated with eloquence; now it is associated with craft and deviousness.

6. ingenious] a) clever b) noble. Patterson (1978), 19, suggests a strong echo of the Latin *ingenium*: a) natural talents b) genius. See also above, ll. 5–10 n.

8. An example of ancient magnanimity: noble and selfless behaviour. *bays*] laurel wreath awarded for poetic virtue.

11. town] London, with its theatres and literary circles; not the court; see above, *Headnote, Context*.

12. civic crown] oak wreath awarded for saving the life of a citizen in battle (see *The Garden*, l. 2); cp. Hall, 'To Colonel Richard Lovelace, on the publishing of his ingenious Poems', ll. 7–8: 'on thy happy temples safely set/Both th'Delphick wreath and Civic Coronet.'

15. caterpillar] one who preys upon society; cp. *Mercurius Pragmaticus*, 47 (20–27 March 1649), sig. LI2ᵛ: 'they [the New Model Army commanders] pretend *Democracy*, and like devouring *Caterpillers* eate up even the *buds* of *Loyalty*, though no men can be more ambitiously desirous then they to *rule* like *Kings* without controll'. The author, Marchamont Nedham, is drawing on a Leveller pamphlet at this point. Lovelace wrote a number of poems addressed to (or in one instance, about) animals, using them as an oblique way of commenting on his own and other predicaments. Only one, 'The Grass-hopper' was included in the 1649 collection; seven more were included in *Lucasta. Posthume Poems* (1659).

17. swarms] a standard image of sectarian, radical or mob activity, as in the title of John Taylor's *A Swarme of Sectaries* (1641). German *Schwärm* described the sixteenth-century Anabaptists; a *Schwärmer* is also a zealot or fanatic. Also alludes to the swarms of flies sent by God to plague the Egyptians: see Exodus 8:21–32.

19–20. Word-peckers . . . sons] partisan pamphleteers and journalists, bred from the corruption of wit. Cp. Nedham, *Mercurius Pragmaticus*, 25 (29 February–7 March 1648), sig. A4ᵛ: 'Paper- pellet . . . Water-rat'.

20. wit . . . sons] the image is of journalists as, like insects, bred from corrupted matter, i.e. dung, a common image for pamphlet and newsbook language in the period: see, e.g., ?John Taylor, *A fresh Whip for all scandalous Lyers* (1647), 1–2. *unfashioned*] a) shapeless b) inelegant.

21. barbèd] a) bearded (*OED* ppl. a.¹ 1); comparison between the appearance of Puritan divines and of rabbis was a common feature of anti-Puritan caricature. b) wearing a barb, or sharp hook (as with a warhorse; *OED* ppl. a.¹ 2). c) implying 'barbarous'. *censurers*] a) official censors, those responsible for implementing the terms of the Licensing Acts of 14 June 1643 and 4 October 1647, which renewed the measures of 1643. Milton wrote *Areopagitica* (1644) against the 1643 Ordinance, which empowered the searching of premises, and the seizure of materials, authors and printers, in addition to establishing a licensing system. The licensers were named in 1643, not in 1648 (see below, l. 22 n.). b) moral condemners; cp. Milton, *Colasterion* (1645), *CPW*, II.740: 'Which if ignoble and swainish mindes cannot apprehend, shall such merit therfore to be the censurers of more generous and vertuous Spirits?'

22. consistory] court of presbyters, made up of pastors and lay elders. *Lucasta* would have been examined by the Clerk of the Stationers' Company, but the list of those appointed in 1643 to license books of divinity was impeccably godly, and included several Presbyterians: Thomas Gataker, John Downame, Callibut Downing, Thomas Temple, Joseph Caryll, Edmund Calamy, ?William Carter, Charles Herle, James Cranford, Obadiah Sedgwick, John Batchelour, John Ellis. After the New Model Army's entry into London on 1 December 1648 licensing was put in the hands of military authorities.

24. Severer . . . Presbytery] Cp. Milton, 'On the New Forcers of Conscience under the Long Parliament', l. 20: '*New Presbyter* is but old *Priest* writ large.' *young Presbytery*] The Assembly of Divines had been convened in 1643 to establish a new national church discipline. The Presbyterians had the upper hand at first, and the Assembly's Directory of 1645 put forward a Presbyterian system of church government, although this was never adopted to the extent that it could be called a national church polity. A fuller version of this system, with complicated rules for internal governance and censorship was instituted by an Ordinance of Parliament on 29 August 1648. *Presbytery*] stressed on second syllable.

Some reading your *Lucasta*, will allege
You wronged in her the House's privilege;
Some that you under sequestration are,
30   Because you write when going to the war;
And one the book prohibits, because Kent
Their first petition by the author sent.
        But when the beauteous ladies came to know
That their dear Lovelace was endangerèd so:
35   (Lovelace that thawed the most congealèd breast,
He who loved best and them defended best,
Whose hand so rudely grasps the steely brand,
Whose hand so gently melts the lady's hand.)

They all in mutiny, though yet undressed,
40   Sallied, and would in his defence contest.
And one, the loveliest that was yet e'er seen,
Thinking that I too of the rout had been,
Mine eyes invaded with a female spite,
(She knew what pain 'twould be to lose that sight).
45   'O no, mistake not,' I replied, 'for I
In your defence, or in his cause would die.
But he, secure of glory and of time,
Above their envy, or mine aid doth climb.
Him, valian'st men, and fairest nymphs approve;
50   His book in them finds judgement, with you love.'

---

28. House's privilege] Parliamentary privileges (e.g. freedom of speech, immunity from arrest in civil matters, the power of committing persons to prison) were much and furiously debated in the months before the Civil War broke out. The King was accused of alienating certain Parliamentary privileges (e.g. Bulstrode Whitelocke, *Memorials* (1682), 51, at the point of Charles's arrival at the Commons to seize the five members, December 1641: 'the House was in a great disorder, crying aloud many of them together, *Privilege, Privilege*'). Lovelace also discussed and obliquely abused Parliament in the central poem of the *Lucasta* collection, 'To Lucasta. From Prison', st. vi: 'I would love a *Parliament*/As a maine Prop from Heav'n sent;/But ah! Who's he that would be wedded/To th' fairest body that's beheaded.'

29. sequestration] confiscation of property by legal command: Lovelace's estate was sequestered by order of the House of Commons on 28 November 1648 on account of his taking up arms against the Parliament.

30. going to the war] echoes the title of Lovelace's famous poem, 'To Lucasta, Going to the Wars'.

31–2. Kent ... sent] Lovelace had presented the Kentish Petition to the House of Commons in 1642: a document produced by Sir Edward Dering and other gentry in Kent defending the King's legal rights, and arguing for the use of the Book of Common Prayer. Lovelace was consequently imprisoned in the Gatehouse.

33. beauteous ladies] Cp. John Hall, *Mercurius Britannicus*, 10 (18 July 1648), 75, on the Earl of Holland after his unsuccessful rising in the Second Civil War: 'perhaps be admitted to *London*, to make cringes and shew himself before the Ladies, who may be as glad of the recovery of this Old *Otho*, as they were lately sorrowfull for the death of the young *Adonis* [Lord

Francis Villiers]'. See also above, *An Elegy Upon the Death of My Lord Francis Villiers*, ll. 109–10 n.

36. Echoes l. 13, thereby identifying Lovelace with the old, pre-Civil War standards of virtue.

37. rudely] with great force (*OED* adv. 1). *brand*] blade or sword (*OED* n. II 8 a, b).

39. mutiny] a) discord (*OED* n. 2; often used in romance vocabulary) b) revolt against authority (OED n. 1). *undressed*] a) unarmed and without armour b) not dressed for public appearance.

40. Sallied] issued forth in a sortie from a place of defence (*OED* v.[2] 1 a).

42–6. Thinking ... die] M.'s worried confession of his identification with the world of Parliament and journalists, and also an admission of his admiration for Lovelace. Aubrey (1898), II.37 quoted four lines from Ovid (*Metamorphoses*, III, ll. 420–3), using the description of Narcissus' self-love to describe Lovelace; precisely the passage that features elsewhere in M. (see above and below, 18, 82).

42. rout] disorderly army in retreat (i.e. the censors – see above, ll. 17–32).

44. what pain ... sight] because the censor (as the lady supposes the speaker to be) needs his sight to read books submitted for licensing. *pain*] punishment (*OED* n[1] 1 a).

47. secure ... of time] i.e. his reputation will last.

48. their] i.e. the censurers. *climb*] inviting an association with the same-sounding but different word 'clime' (l. 3), and the sense of that line.

49. valian'st] valiant 1649, Margoliouth; valiant'st *Kermode, Donno, Wilcher, Walker*; bravest *Thompson*.

50. judgement] discernment, wisdom (*OED* 8 a), as opposed to judgement as censure (*OED* 6) or religious profession (*OED* 7 b).

5

Upon the Death of Lord Hastings

Date. Late June–July 1649. Henry, Lord Hastings, son and heir of Ferdinando, Earl of Huntingdon, died, aged nineteen, of smallpox on 24 June 1649, the day before his wedding.

Publication. The poem appeared in the collection of elegies assembled by Richard Brome, entitled *Lachrymae Musarum*, published quite soon after Hastings's death, as the signs of hasty compilation imply (e.g. 74, 77). A second edition was published in January 1650. In both editions, M.'s poem appeared as the first in a 'postscript' of eight further elegies, since the bulk of the volume 'was printed before these following Papers were written or sent in'. The history of the two editions is complex, and there are variants in both. In the first edition, M.'s poem appears on pages 78–80, and in the Huntington Library copy of the first edition (shelf-mark 102355), as well as in the British Library and Huntington Library copies of the second edition (shelfmarks E1247(3) and 102354; 102837 respectively) on unpaginated, inserted leaves, between pages 42 and 43, with the instruction 'Place this after *fol.* 42.' printed at the foot of the first page. By moving the poem forward from the postscript, M. is placed among the company of fellow poets: Herrick, Denham and John Hall (although Nedham and Dryden's elegies remained in the postscript). The poem was not printed in *1681*, and was first added to M.'s canon by Grosart.

Gearin-Tosh (*E & S*, 34 (1981), 105–22 (108–9)) argues that *Lachrymae Musarum* was covertly mourning the regicide, as much as it was commemorating Hastings, who, after all, had achieved little in his young life, despite coming from a famous literary family, and despite the remarkable timing of his death. The leaf after the title-page of *Lachrymae Musarum* contained a decoration of the four crowns of England, Wales, Scotland and France, with insignia, which appeared on other royalist publications at this time. The second edition was received by Thomason on 30 January 1650, the first anniversary of the regicide itself. Some evidence suggests that Hastings was present at the Siege of Colchester (with his uncle, Baron Loughborough, a prominent royalist commander), an event notorious for its Cavalier recklessness during the Second Civil War. McWilliams, *YES*, 33 (2003), 273–89, argues that *Lachrymae Musarum* was meant to be understood not merely as an act of mourning but even one of resistance to the new regime.

Context. The poem incorporates some of the circumstances of the Hastings family, and the marriage of Henry, Lord Hastings (1630–49), son and heir apparent of Ferdinando, seventh Earl of Huntingdon, to Elizabeth, daughter of Sir Theodore Turquet de Mayerne (1573–1655), physician to James I, Charles I, Henrietta Maria and, finally, Oliver Cromwell.

Henry, Lord Hastings' parentage came from two famous literary families. The literary and cultural patronage of the Earls of Huntingdon at their country seat of Ashby de la Zouche in Leicestershire was extensive. Hastings' mother was the daughter of the poet and statesman Sir John Davies. Her mother was the controversial and notorious prophet, Lady Eleanor Davies, whose publications had increased in frequency at the end of the 1640s, but who is, not surprisingly, absent from M.'s poem. She published two versions of a prophecy on the occasion of the death of her grandson in which she found a parallel story in 2 Esdras 9–10. She regarded Henry's death as a symbol of the tragedy that was occurring in the world at large (see Cope in Davies (1995), 146–7). Lucy, Countess of Huntingdon, mentioned by M. at l. 40, wrote a poem on her son's death; this survives in a copy of the second edition of *LM* now owned by the Huntington Library, shelfmark 102354 (see below, ll. 19 n., 37–40 n.).

Mayerne, the other named parent (l. 48), had been excluded from the medical faculty at the University

Fig. 2
Lachrymae musarum; The Tears of the Muses: Exprest in Elegies;
written by divers persons of nobility and worth upon the death of
the most hopefull, Henry Lord Hastings ... collected and set
forth by R[ichard] B[rome] (1649), facing title-page.
Permission British Library (C. 117. b. 32).

of Paris for being a Paracelsan and a Protestant. His presence in England ensured that (al)chemically prepared remedies were incorporated into the English pharmacopoeia. M. refers to Mayerne by name, and builds alchemical and pharmacopoeic imagery into the poem's structure. M. has been seen to represent the union of Hastings and Mayerne as a 'chemical wedding', symbolizing, and even partaking of the alchemical process of purification (see below, ll. 47–54). Hastings' death is thus also the loss of the immortal elixir, or stone (Abraham (1990), 303–4). Mayerne had been involved in the unsuccessful treatment of James I on his deathbed in 1625; Maule, *RES*, n.s., 37 (1986), 399, suggests that this earlier event may be recalled in ll. 57–8, so that 'to lose one member of the royal family might be regarded as misfortune – the death of another [since Hastings claimed royal descent from Edward IV] began to look like carelessness'.

Although the Hastings family was in serious financial straits at the end of the 1640s (and Mayerne was described as a 'person of Great Wealth', Huntington Library, Hastings Papers, Genealogy Box 1 (26)), Hastings's funeral itself was lavish and marked by a public procession in London (his body was finally interred at Ashby de la Zouche in July 1649). Although M.'s poem hints at Hastings' royalism, the other elegies in the volume make much more of this. Both Gearin-Tosh, *ES*, 34 (1981), 112–14, and Loxley, *SC*, 10 (1995), 53, argue that, despite its royalist associations (e.g. ll. 25–6), the poem offers, then withdraws, Royalist implications. Thus, the absence of reference to the Earl of Huntingdon, Hastings' father, who gave the King no assistance, has been seen by Gearin-Tosh as a covert royalist statement, but the reference to the monarchy of heaven (ll. 27–32) paints princes in a tyrannous light.

Genre, Style and Versification. M.'s second funeral elegy is more conventional than his earlier Villiers elegy, although there are some shared elements between the two poems (see above, 11–17). The Hastings elegy does not develop a complex narrative as is the case in the Villiers elegy, but it is notable for the assured unity by which the subject is praised and seen in glory, a unity that is sensitive to and knowledgeable of the circumstances of Hastings' death. Several motifs in the poem have predecessors in earlier elegies on the aristocracy. For instance, the comparison of heaven with the machinery of state (ll. 27–32) is a feature of Patricke Mackgueir, *Tears*

for the Death of Lodouicke, Duke of Richmond and Lennox (1624), ll. 63–9:

> Thou wentst to heare the just decrees of heauen.
> Our g[r]acious King and Councell knew this cleare,
> Thou onely for that purpose left'st vs here:
> Which made with consent together stay
> Their Parliament vntill another day:
> That so the High Assembly of the blist,
> Might first determinate what things they list.

Conventional elegiac motifs lead into a briefer narrative explaining the relationship between Providence, medical endeavour and alchemical hopes. At the same time, there is a sophisticated generic interaction, as the expectations of marriage poetry, and epithalamia, are frustrated by the claims of elegy. Accordingly there are several echoes of epithalamic verse, that rework their components according to the funeral occasion. Ovid, *Heroides*, XXI, ll. 151–68, notes the frustration of Hymen, god of marriage (see below, ll. 43–6) by the untimely death of the bride. In M.'s poem, there are particular echoes of Spenser's *Epithalamion* (see below, ll. 41–6 nn.). The change of appropriate genre was also noted by Lady Eleanor Davies in *Sions Lamentations* (1649): '[Hastings] who Epithalamiums to lamentations exchanged for Epitaphs' (Davies (1995), 274).

The poem is organized in a series of short verse paragraphs, each with a discrete subject and with at least one powerful image: the weeping of tears as a mark of grief (ll. 1–8); Hastings has outrun his time (ll. 9–18); Hastings' perfectibility on earth frustrated by heavenly jealousy and earthly rebellion (ll. 19–26); Hastings is held 'captive' by Heaven (ll. 27–32); Hastings' recreation and joy in Heaven (ll. 33–40); the joy of the gods, except Hymen (ll. 41–6); Mayerne and Aesculapius's sadness at the frustration of Hastings' marriage (ll. 47–54); Mayerne's medical skill nothing against Heaven's will (ll. 55–60). Noting a tradition in funerary verse of equating lines with the years of the deceased, and that nineteen would be a difficult figure for a poet, Maule, *RES*, n.s., 37 (1986), 396, sees a connection between M.'s sixty-line poem and Jonson's 'To Sir William Sidney, On His Birthday' (1616), also written in sixty lines (see below, ll. 17–18 n.). M.'s poem reverses Jonson's imagery: Jonson's conceit is that men burn with the flame of love and with revelry on their birthdays; all flames are extinguished as the wedding is prevented (see below, ll. 45–6).

Imagery of tears or flowing water and the figure of Hymen, god of marriage, recur throughout the poems in *Lachrymae Musarum*. The poem also compresses the passage of a day into forty lines: we begin with morning, but we arrive at a night scene by ll. 44–5. Empson (1930; repr. 1961), 199–201, praised the latter section as a brilliant description of a sunset. The second verse paragraph is a meditation on the pun in Hastings' name. M. is silent on the pun itself, although it is mentioned in Lucy Hastings' poem, and contemporaries would have been well aware of it: 'knowing the infectious Dust/ Might Canker the bright piece with Rust,/Hasted him hence' ('The Bowells of the Earth my bowells slide', ll. 14–16).

It is, of course, unsurprising that a series of poems produced by writers in a relatively closed world, with a shared literary culture, should produce poems of a similar nature when addressing a singular issue. Nonetheless, the interconnectedness of the poems in *Lachrymae Musarum* is striking. Since M.'s poem, along with Nedham's and Dryden's, among others, was submitted at a late stage, it is probable that M. saw some of the earlier compositions and some of those in the postscript, either before or during the writing of his own poem. It is also the case that some of the poems in the collection provided M. with sources for some of his other poems (see below, ll. 18 n., 25 n., 48–52 n.). These interrelationships are discussed further by McWilliams, *YES*, 33 (2003), 273–89.

Upon the Death of Lord Hastings

Go, intercept some fountain in the vein,
Whose virgin-source yet never steeped the plain.
Hastings is dead, and we must find a store
Of tears untouched, and never wept before.
5   Go, stand betwixt the morning and the flowers;
And, ere they fall, arrest the early showers.
Hastings is dead; and we, disconsolate,
With early tears must mourn his early fate.
    Alas, his virtues did his death presage:
10   Needs must he die, that doth out-run his age.
The phlegmatic and slow prolongs his day,
And on Time's wheel sticks like a remora.
What man is he, that hath not heav'n beguiled,
And is not thence mistaken for a child?
15   While those of growth more sudden, and more bold,
Are hurried hence, as if already old.
For, there above, they number not as here,
But weigh to man the geometric year.

1. intercept] cut off. *vein*] underground stream; cp. Thomas Pestel, 'For the Honourable, Lucie, Countess of Huntingdon', in *Lachrymae Musarum* (1649), 16: 'for your pain/Here's water of a Special vein'.
2. virgin-source] the virgin at a wedding ought to have been the bride, not pure water: cp. Jonson, *Epithalamion; or, a Song, celebrating the Nuptials of that Noble Gentleman, Mr Jerome Watson . . . with the Lady Frances Stuart* (1640), l. 41: 'See how she paceth forth in virgin white.'
5. morning] with a pun on 'mourning'.
6. early showers] dew.
8. early tears] wept in the morning, since derived from dew. *early fate*] i.e. a death too soon.
9–10. A classical notion: see Martial, *Epigrams*, X. liii: 'invida quem Lachesis raptum trieteride nona,/dum numerat palmas, credidit esse senem' (Me, snatched away in my ninth three years' span, jealous Lachesis, counting my victories, deemed old in years).
10. out-run] outstrip, leave behind (*OED* v. 2).
11. phlegmatic] having a phlegmatic humour: dull, cold, sluggish; stressed on first syllable.
12. Time's wheel] an emblem of a wheel with a death's head on the top, and entitled 'L'Heure de la Mort Incertaine', occurs in Gilles Corrozet, *Hecatongraphie* (Paris, 1543), sig. Niii[b]. The image is similar to M.'s, the sentiments different. *remora*] *echeneis remora*, or sucking fish, believed to stop the course of ships to which it attached itself. *Remora* is Latin for 'delay' or 'hindrance'.

14. child] a) child b) youth of noble birth, knight (Heninger, in Patrides, ed. (1978), 94).
15–18. Cp. Bathsua Makin, 'In mortem clarissimi Domini, Domini Henrici Hastings' (Huntington Library, Hastings Papers, Literature Box 1 (1), ll. 1, 3–4: 'En duplex aenigma! senex, juvenisque! . . . Non obiit: non bis denos compleverat annos/Heros, qui meritò dicitur esse senex.' (A double riddle! Both old man and young man! He does not die, nor doubly filled up heroic years to merit the name of old man.)
17–19.   number . . . weigh . . . measure] Ormerod and Wortham see an echo of a text associated with numerology, Wisdom 21:11, from the Apocrypha: 'You [God] have ordered everything by measure, number and weight.'
17–18. For . . . year] Cp. Jonson, 'To Sir William Sidney, On His Birthday' (1616), ll. 21–2: 'This day says, then, the number of glad yeeres/Are justly summed, that make you man.' See also above, *Headnote, Genre, Style and Versification*.
18. geometric year] a year calculated with geometry would pass more quickly than a normal year; Heninger, in Patrides, ed. (1978), 95–100, argues that the 'geometric year' is a calculation, in Platonic tradition, that expresses each unit of time as part of a unifying eternity, usually described in the figure of a circle. The emblematic representation of man's life as four quarters of a circle, corresponding to the four seasons of the year is graphically geometrical. M.'s friend, John Hall, used a different sense of the word in his elegy on Hastings: 'To the Earl of Huntingdon, On the death of his Son', in *LM*, ll. 49–50: 'Nothing in him was crooked, lame or flat,/But *Geometrically* proportionate.'

Had he but at this measure still increased,
And on the Tree of Life once made a feast,
As that of Knowledge; what loves had he given
To earth, and then what jealousies to heaven!
But 'tis a maxim of that state, that none,
Lest he become like them, taste more than one.
Therefore the democratic stars did rise,
And all that worth from hence did ostracize.

Yet as some prince, that, for state-jealousy,
Secures his nearest and most loved ally;
His thought with richest triumphs entertains,
And in the choicest pleasures charms his pains:

So he, not banished hence, but there confined,
There better recreates his active mind.
Before the crystal palace where he dwells,
The armèd angels hold their carousels;
And underneath, he views the tournaments
Of all these sublunary elements.
But most he doth th'eternal book behold,
On which the happy names do stand enrolled;
And gladly there can all his kindred claim,
But most rejoices at his mother's name.

The gods themselves cannot their joy conceal,
But draw their veils, and their pure beams reveal:

---

19. Had . . . increased] Cp. Lucy Hastings, Countess of Huntington, 'The Bowells of the Earth my bowells slide', ll. 17–18: 'till the Measure/Accomplish'd bee of the Elect.' *measure*] i.e. rate (not in *OED*).

20–1. Tree of Life . . . Knowledge] See Gen. 2:9: 'And out of the ground made the Lord God to grow every tree that is pleasant to the sight, and good for food; the tree of life also in the midst of the garden, and the tree of knowledge of good and evil.' The Tree of Life was also the source of the knowledge of god in nature, the *prisca theologia*, for Paracelsans. Hastings' learning is also praised by Bathsua Makin, 'In mortem clarissimi Domini, Domini Henrici Hastings' (Huntington Library, Hastings Papers, Literature Box 1 (1), ll. 9–12: 'Quem grave judicium, doctae et faciundia linguae/Ingenii et morum, dexteritate, nitor/Tam benè certarunt ornatum reddere, vix ut/In voto potuit quid superesse cui.' (Grave judgement, and skill in the learned tongue, and splendour and wit, morals and probity, contend so well, with skill, to adorn him, so that hardly in prayer [for an ideal man] could one go beyond him.)

23. maxim] a moral or political principle, expressed in brief, pithy form, fashionable in the early seventeenth century. Popular with some republicans in the 1650s, but more often derided as an instrument of tyranny by others, including Milton and Algernon Sidney: see Dzelzainis, in Armitage, *et al.* (1995), 188–96.

24. one] of the two trees in ll. 20–1.

25–6. In ancient Athens, those who were too wealthy, virtuous, popular or politically able could be banished by a vote in the assembly, in order to prevent a monarchy: see Aristotle, *Politics*, III.viii.1–2.

25. democratic stars] Cp. M[archamont] N[edham], 'On the untimely death of the Lord Hastings', in *Lachrymae Musarum* (1649), 81–5 (ll. 1–2): 'It is decreed, we must be drain'd (I see)/Down to the dregs of a *Democracie*.' *stars*] dominant forces (but not in *OED* until the eighteenth century): see anon., *Englands New Directory* (1647), 4: 'The Privy Councel and Parliament ought fast and pray,/For they are the evil Stars the Scots do say.' *rise*] in rebellion.

26. worth] high personal merit; excellence (*OED* n.[1] 2 b, 3). *ostracize*] banish (*OED* v. 2; M.'s usage here is an example in *OED*).

27–32. Gearin-Tosh, *E & S*, 34 (1981), 113–14, suggests that M. is referring to Henry VII's entertainment of Philip of

Castile (who had been driven ashore in England by a storm) until the Earl of Suffolk, whom Philip was protecting from Henry, was incarcerated in the Tower of London. The story was recounted by Lewis de Mayerne Turquet (the grandfather of Hastings' fiancée) in his *The Generall Historie of Spaine*, trans. Edward Grimeston (1612), 25.4, sig. Ooooiv[v].

27. state-jealousy] see above, l. 23 n.

28. Secures] imprisons (*OED* v. 4).

29. His] i.e. the ally. *triumphs*] official festivity, pageant or spectacle (*OED* n. 4).

30. pains] sufferings, troubles, sorrows (*OED* n.[1] 4).

32. recreates] a) refreshes b) remakes in eternal life, after death. *active*] a) lively, energetic (*OED* a. 5) b) as opposed to contemplative or speculative philosophy; concerned with ethics and the practice of moral action (*OED* a. 1).

33. palace] M.'s elegy has a heavenly building at its centre, whereas in epithalamia it is postponed to the end: 'from the earth, which they may long possesse,/With lasting happinesse,/Vp to your haughty pallaces may mount.' Spenser, *Epithalamion*, ll. 420–2.

34. carousels] chivalric tournaments involving teams of knights in various exercises and entertainments.

36. sublunary elements] earthly life.

37–40. Cp. Lucy Hastings, Countess of Huntingdon, 'The Bowells of the Earth my bowells slide', ll. 16–18: 'Hasted him hence; into his Treasure/Of Blessed Spirits, where till the Measure/Accomplish'd bee of the Elect.'

37. eternal book] the Book of Life (e.g. Phil. 4:3; Rev. 3:5) into which the names of the elect (the 'happy names' of l. 38) are written.

39. claim] legal term : assert as one's own (*OED* v. 2 a).

40. mother's name] Lucy, Countess of Huntingdon, daughter of the poet Sir John Davies.

41–2. An appropriate alternative to Spenser's portrayal of heaven and celestial lights in *Epithalamion*, ll. 410–13: 'And ye high heauens, the temple of the gods,/In which a thousand torches flaming bright/Doe burne, that to vs wretched earthly clods,/In dreadful darknesse lend desired light.' Cp. also Philip Kinder, 'Upon the death of the Lord Hastings' (Bod., MS Ashmole 788, fol. 148[v]), where Hastings is described as an 'off-spring of the gods' and the 'muses morning-star'.

42. veils] clouds (*OED* n.[1] 5 c). *beams*] of light, made by the stars.

Only they drooping Hymeneus note,
Who for sad purple, tears his saffron coat;
45   And trails his torches through the starry hall
Reversèd, at his darling's funeral.
      And Aesculapius, who, ashamed and stern,
Himself at once condemneth, and Mayerne

50   Like some sad chemist, who, prepared to reap
The golden harvest, sees his glasses leap.
For, how immortal must their race have stood,
Had Mayerne once been mixed with Hastings' blood!
How sweet and verdant would these laurels be,
Had they been planted on that balsam tree!

43–6. Hymeneus . . . funeral] Hymeneus (or Hymen), god of marriage, wore a saffron robe and carried a nuptial torch (see Jonson, *Hymenaei* (1606), sig. A4ʳ); Hymeneus was also gloomy at the marriage of Orpheus and Eurydice, where his torch sputtered and smoked: see Ovid, *Metamorphoses*, X, ll. 1–10; purple denoted a person of rank and was the colour used to cover coffins or tombs; Hastings died on the eve of his wedding day; he was to marry a daughter of the King's physician, Sir Theodore Turquet de Mayerne. The passage is a reversal of Spenser, *Epithalamion*, ll. 25–7: 'Hymen is awake,/And long since ready forth his maske to moue,/With his bright Tread that flames with many a flake.' Cp. also Philip Kinder, *Pietati Sacrum . . . Henrici Baronis Hastings* (24 June 1649): 'Pridiè Sponsalium (proh *Hymenae*) Funere luit immaturo' (The day before his wedding (O Hymen!) he suffered his unseasonable burial); Sir Aston Cokaine, 'A Funeral-Elegie upon the death of *Henry* Lord *Hastings*', in *Lachrymae Musarum* (1649), 6: 'Didst thou sleep, *Hymen*? or art lately grown/T'affect the Subterranean, Region? Enamour'd on blear'd *Libentina's* eyes,/Hoarse howling Dirges, and the baleful cries/Of inauspicious voices, and (above/Thy Star-like Torch) with horrid Tombs in love?' Other examples from *Lachrymae Musarum* are discussed by Maule, *RES*, n.s., 37 (1986), 396–8. *saffron*] in addition to the colour of Hymen's coat, saffron was also one of the colours by which the alchemist knew his experiment was moving towards a successful conclusion (Gearin-Tosh, *E & S*, 34 (1981), 120).

44. sad . . . coat] Cp. Lady Eleanor Davies, *Sions Lamentation* (1649), in Davies (1995), 274: 'he born *anno* 1630. about nineteen years of age . . . exchanged . . . The saffron robe for sable mourning.' *purple*] the colour of royal mourning: from Latin *purpura*, the garment of kings and magistrates (Lewis and Short, II.B). *tears*] a) weeps upon (*OED* v.² 2). b) rips (*OED* v.¹ 1). *coat*] translates Latin *palla*, male garment, sometimes meaning the dress of tragic actors (Lewis and Short, II.A), which in turn puns on 'pall': a) robe of a high-ranking person (*OED* n.¹ II 5) b) covering of a coffin at a funeral (*OED* n.¹ I 4).

45. starry hall] night sky (see above, l. 42).

46. Reversèd] carried behind and held downwards.

47–50. Aesculapius . . . leap] the zeugma of the final two words of l. 48 ('and Mayerne'), together with the absence of punctuation, mean that the chemist may be Aesculapius or Mayerne. The image in l. 49 could be seen to ridicule alchemists; M. may have been trying to warn Mayerne of the more tenuous aspects of alchemy. Aesculapius restored the dead Hymeneus to life (see Apollodorus, *The Library*, II.x.3; see also above, ll. 43–6); Maule, *RES*, n.s., 37 (1986), 398–9, argues that M. thus suggests that 'what Aesculapius could do for Hymen, he cannot do for Hastings; and no more can Mayerne'.

47. Aesculapius] god of healing; one of the names of Hermes Trismegistus (one of the Hermetic dialogues is entitled the

Asclepius); Mayerne had been painted by Rubens in 1631 sitting in front of a life-size statue of Aesculapius. Although Aesculapius had the power to cure, and to restore the dead to life, he was also portrayed as suffering in several myths in order to suggest the power of death over man. Gearin-Tosh, *E & S*, 34 (1981), 116–17 suggests that Rubens's portrait transfers this knowledge to a sombre-faced Mayerne, who himself discovered the pigment for purple in painting. The chiaroscuro around Mayerne's face and hands suggests the darker side of a physician's work.

48–52. Mayerne . . . blood] Cp. John Hall, 'To the Earl of Huntingdon, On the death of his Son', in *Lachrymae Musarum* (1649), 46: 'Yet has this *Genius* made sad depart . . . Which the wise-pow'rful MAYERN, (who can give/As much as poor Mortality can receive) . . . Maugre those hopes which did so bravely feign/That a great Race should spring from him again.'

48–9. Mayerne/ . . . chemist] see above, ll. 43–5; Mayerne introduced chemical and alchemical cures (he thought that the philosopher's stone was a panacea), to the fury of traditional herbalists.

49. sad] Cp. Spenser, *The Faerie Queene*, I.v.36, ll. 4–8: 'Where was a Caue ywrought by wondrous art,/Deepe, darke, vneasie, dolefull, comfortlesse,/In which sad *Æsculapius* farre a part/Emprisond was in chaines remedilesse,/For that *Hippolytus* rent corse he did redresse.' Aesculapius was punished by Jove for bringing the dead Hippolytus to life (see also Virgil, *Aeneid*, VII, ll. 765–72), and in Spenser's Christian universe, he is not redeemed. Hamilton, in Spenser (1977), 82, notes that Aesculapius was regarded in some traditions as a false Christ, because he sought to redeem bodies but not souls. *chemist*] alchemist; Mayerne was an alchemist and Paracelsan (see above, *Headnote, Context*).

49–50. who . . . leap] who, hoping to achieve the alchemists' goal of transforming base metal into gold, saw only his glass vessels break.

50. leap] burst, crack (*OED* v. 5 b).

53. laurels] laurel leaves, from the bay tree, woven into a wreath, were worn as a sign of victory, or poetic distinction; appropriate for Hastings' achievements, and the distinction of his lineage.

54. balsam tree] tree yielding balsam resin, used as a soothing balm, but also regarded as a preservative essence in alchemical writing, and thought by Paracelsus to exist in all bodies (see 'balsam': *OED* n. I 4); so, in the image, Mayerne's daughter becomes the essence of Hastings' preservation and perfection. In alchemical theory, the Tree of Life (see above, l. 20) contained the balsam that kept Adam in a state of prelapsarian purity. After the Fall, that balsam could be discovered from within the human body, thereby returning man to the Paradisal state (see Abraham (1990), 272–3).

5   But what could he, good man, although he bruised

         All herbs, and them a thousand ways infused?

         All he had tried, but all in vain, he saw,

         And wept, as we, without redress or law.

         For man (alas) is but the heavens' sport;

60   And art indeed is long, but life is short.

---

55. *bruised*] pounded, crushed (*OED* ppl. a. 3).

56. *herbs*] Aesculapius used herbs to cure Hippolytus: 'Paeoniis revocatum herbis' (recalled by the Healer's herbs), Virgil, *Aeneid*, VII, l. 769; cure by herbs was a godlike action: see Ovid, *Metamorphoses*, I, ll. 521–4; Milton, *Comus*, ll. 628–40. Lady Eleanor Davies implies that Hastings 'by letting blood was cast away', although 'committed to no simple Doctors' (*Sions Lamentation* (1649), in Davies (1995), 272). Maule, *RES*, n.s., 37 (1986), 399, notes that herbal remedies for smallpox were common in the seventeenth century.

57–8. In Paris, Mayerne had been accused of injuring several patients with his treatment, but his reputation for exactitude in diagnosis and prescription remained and grew with the French after he came to live in England. He also wrote long letters of counsel to his patients.

58. *redress or law*] Ormerod and Wortham emend to 'redress of law'; it seems more typical of M., however, to make poetic capital by altering slightly a well-known phrase. *redress*] remedy, assistance (*OED* n. 2). *law*] i.e. recourse to legal redress.

59. *man . . . sport*] Cp. Shakespeare, *King Lear*, IV.i, ll. 36–7: 'As flies to wanton boys, are we to th'Gods;/They kill us for their sport.'

60. *art . . . short*] Hippocrates, *Aphorisms*, 1: 'Ὁ βίος βραχύς, ἡ δὲ τέχνη μακρή, ὁ δὲ καιρὸς ὀξύς, ἡ δὲ πείρα σφυλερή, ἡ δὲ κρίσις χαλεπή'. (Life is short, the Art long, opportunity fleeting, experiment treacherous, judgement difficult.); in an early work of 1603, 'Apologia qua videre est inviolatis Hippocratis . . .', Mayerne had been at pains to show that chemical remedies were in accord with the principles and practices of Hippocrates and Galen. See also Tilley, A332: 'Art is long, life short'. McWilliams, *YES*, 33 (2003), 273–89, argues that the phrase is meant by M. to refer reflexively to the literary art of the elegist.

MISCELLANEOUS POEMS (1681)

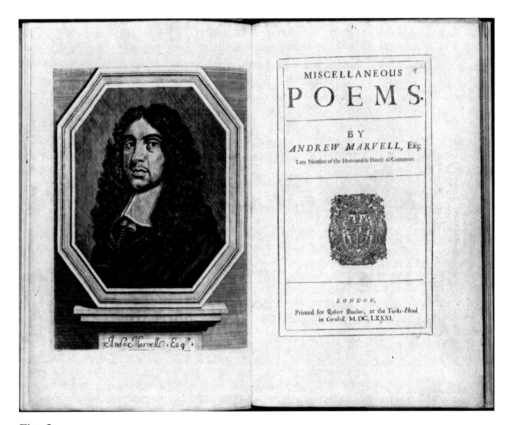

Fig. 3
Andrew Marvell, *Miscellaneous Poems* (1681), title-page and facing engraved portrait.
Permission British Library (C. 59. i. 8).

6
A Dialogue, Between the Resolved Soul, and Created Pleasure

Date. ?After August 1667. Noting that the poem bears echoes of *Paradise Lost*, Leishman ((1966), 31–2, n. 1; see below, ll. 51–4 n.) argues that M. may have written it after the first publication of Milton's epic in 1667.

Manuscript Circulation. The poem appears in Bod., MS Rawl. A 176, fols 80–1 (*Bod. 2*), two conjugate folio leaves copied in the 1670s, and seized from the lodgings of Colonel John Scott in Canning Street, London, on 28 October 1678, by Samuel Pepys.

Printed Publication. 1681. The poem was placed first in this volume. Lewalski in Patrides, ed. ((1978), 251) suggests that this was because of the poem's religious nature.

Sources, Genre and Style. The poem belongs to the tradition of the poetic dialogue (see Bossy, *CL*, 28 (1976), 144–63; Cox (1992)). It mirrors and thematically expands the temptation of Christ in the wilderness (Luke 4:1–13). The theme grows out of the initial ten lines which resemble the verse attached to an emblem (the verse attached to Wither's twenty-fourth *Embleme* (1635) connects, but does not juxtapose, as M.'s poem does, resolve and pleasure). Kermode, *BJRL*, 44 (1961–62), 68–9, argues that the poem includes a full example of the literary banquet of sense: in the first section the soul resists sensual temptation or trial, and in the second, overcomes temptations of women, wealth, worldly glory and improper learning. The senses are treated in ascending order: from taste and touch, dependent upon sense; to smell, positioned between these and the higher senses; to sight and hearing, which operate without contact (although Toliver, *SEL*, 4 (1964), 64, argues that M. deliberately reverses the conventional precedence of sight over sound). By the end, the soul has completed an imitation of Christ. The Soul's position can only be accepted if its premises are granted outright: it thus

requires from the reader an act of faith. For Rees (*N & Q*, 222 (1977), 198–9), the concentration upon the senses and, in the second half of the poem, the sense of sight, the temptations to pleasure, worldly power and knowledge, and the promise of 'one beauty' (l. 53), suggest that M. was also accepting the story of the Judgement of Paris as an informing principle. But if M. knew of this myth (especially as it had been allegorically interpreted by Ficino, *Opera* (Basle, 1576), I. Epistolarum. Lib. 10, 919–20), he reversed Ficino's acceptance that all three choices offered to Paris had to be accepted by rejecting each of them (see Rees (1989), 3). Another mythic parallel reflected in the poem is the Choice of Hercules, which existed in Christianized versions (see Kermode (1971), 86).

The poem is related to one kind of medieval soul–body debate, where a virtuous soul overcomes and chastises a guilty body. Indeed, five of the patristic and medieval Seven Deadly Sins are present in the poem: gluttony (ll. 11–16), sloth (ll. 19–22), pride (ll. 31–4), lust (ll. 51–4), avarice (ll. 57–60). But these generic features are radically transformed by the controlling warfare metaphor. Indeed, the poem has been related to Milton's definition of the 'warfaring Christian' in *Areopagitica*. Rees (1989), 13–22, notes that the poem passes through a series of topics, and their oppositions, well known in devotional tradition: the *vita voluptuosa* (ll. 19–22), *speculum mundi* (ll. 31–4), and the special temptations of music (ll. 41–4). These are all part of a presentation of the trial of pleasure against virtue, exemplified in the stories of ancient mythology and a common theme in seventeenth-century masques. The poem also reflects the traditional tripartite division of pleasurable, active and contemplative lives. The middle category is introduced at l. 24 and then tested in the second half of the poem. The categories used by Pleasure in the first half of the poem occur in Neoplatonic tradition as metaphors for the divine (e.g. the mirror of l. 34; the circle describing the relationship between soul and 'centre'), but

Neoplatonic language is dismissed by the more austere solutions found by the Soul (unlike the use made of Neoplatonic imagery elsewhere in M.'s verse; see below, 154). Stoic (especially Senecan) sources are in fact preferred in the poem (see below, ll. 45–50 n.), a feature that has been attributed to the Senecanism of one of the fellows of Trinity College during M.'s time there (see L.N. Wall, *N & Q*, n.s. 8 (1961), 185–6), but which is consonant with the expressed sentiments of many Puritans (including Milton, see *Paradise Regained*, 1, ll. 155–67, 173–9) after 1660.

If the poem may be seen to bear the traces of Puritan literature, and was indeed written at a later date than was once supposed, it properly belongs with the body of Puritan allegorical writing of which Bunyan's great works are the most famous example (see Keeble (1987), especially ch. 7; Rivers (1991), ch. 3; Philips (1998)). Like *Bermudas*, but unlike *A Dialogue between the Soul and Body*, the poem is a Puritan transformation of a courtly, Neoplatonic form.

Structure, Style and Versification. Leishman ((1966), 203–4) regards the poem not merely as an example of the dialogue, but also a dialogue that may well have been set to music. Friedman (1970), 73, opines that the poem is 'not so much a dialogue as a dramatisation of a temptation and its failure'. The poem is simple, and alternates between the trochaic heptasyllables (and, in the second part, some six-syllable lines) of Pleasure and the Soul's iambic octosyllables, with two choric stanzas, the first of which divides the poem into two halves. The different stanza forms used by Pleasure in the second half contrast with the same stanza forms being used by the Soul: the Soul is faithful to her forms; Pleasure is driven to experiment. The variations in stanza length and rhyme scheme suggest further musical opportunity for a composer. Pleasure addresses the senses successively: taste (ll. 14–16), touch (ll. 19–22), smell (ll. 25–8), sight (ll. 31–4), hearing (ll. 37–40). Friedman (1970), 77, notes the repeated use of soft 'l's at ll. 19–22 in a stanza concerned with touch. In the second part of the poem, Pleasure tempts the soul

with beauty, wealth, glory and knowledge. Where the first part of the poem is concerned with the senses, the second is an attack on the mind.

The participants in the dialogue are distinguished by different prosodies. In the first part of the poem, Created Pleasure speaks in trochaic heptasyllables, while the Resolved Soul responds in iambic tetrameters. In the second part, Pleasure changes to seven-syllable trochaics, alternating with iambic trimeters, but the Soul's metre remains the same. The interdependence of speakers in *A Dialogue of the Soul and Body* is paralleled here by having Pleasure tempt the Soul in terms that apparently answer its own desires. In the second part, the Soul does not merely answer Pleasure, but engages in debate through rhetorical questions, and is more obviously assertive through the use of exclamations.

Modern Criticism. Leishman ((1966), 209) identified eleven instances of syntactical inversion (ll. 14, 22, 26, 31, 38–9, 42, 46, 52, 55, 63, 77) that he considered weakened the poem's grace and strength by their frequency, although Wilcher (1985), 69, sees these, together with the imperative verbs and abrupt sentences, as deliberate attempts to create a sense of earnestness. Similarly, Rees (1989), 20, notes a decline in quality in the second half of the poem, and suggests that this is a deliberate reflection of the poetry that ultimately deals with the contemplative life: contemplation and poetry are incompatible (for a related use of 'bad poetry', see below, *A Poem upon the Death of his Late Highness the Lord Protector, Headnote, Versification and Style*). The same problem is addressed by Toliver, *SEL*, 4 (1964), 59–60: threatening 'pleasurable' imagery is undermined by 'sophisticated and multiple ironies' involving the aesthetic concepts that appear in the first part of the poem. For Hill, in Carey, ed. (1969), 80–1, the Soul is 'militantly Puritan', and the conflicted nature of the poem relates to the 'more obvious conflict of the Civil War', just as for Bateson, in Carey, ed. (1969), 106, the poem reflects the national struggle in that it dramatizes 'the basic human attitudes that have been institutionalized as Anglicanism or Puritanism or whatever it is'.

A Dialogue, Between the Resolved Soul, and Created Pleasure

Charge

Courage my Soul, now learn to wield
The weight of thine immortal shield.
Close on thy head thy helmet bright.
Balance thy sword against the fight.
See where an army, strong as fair,
With silken banners spreads the air.
Now, if thou be'st that thing divine,
In this day's combat let it shine:
And show that Nature wants an art
0   To conquer one resolvèd heart.

Pleasure

Welcome the creation's guest,
Lord of earth, and heaven's heir.

Lay aside that warlike crest,
And of Nature's banquet share:
15   Where the souls of fruits and flowers
Stand prepared to heighten yours.

Soul

I sup above, and cannot stay
To bait so long upon the way.

Pleasure

On these downy pillows lie,
20   Whose soft plumes will thither fly:
On these roses strewed so plain
Lest one leaf thy side should strain.

Soul

My gentler rest is on a thought,
Conscious of doing what I ought.

Title. 1681; A Combat Between the Soule And Sense *Bod. 2.*
Resolved] resolute, determined, settled in purpose (*OED* ppl.
a. 1); see also below, l. 10 n. *Created*] of God's creation (*OED*
ppl. a. a); the threat to the Soul is from Nature (see below,
ll. 9–10) as opposed to the devil; Pleasure is the spokesman for
Nature.
Charge] *Bod. 2*; not in *1681*; a) matter of moral import (*OED*
n. II 9) b) duty, responsibility (*OED* n. II 12) c) attack (*OED*
III 18; see below, l. 49). d) sound signalling an attack (usually
made by a drum or trumpet) (*OED* n. III 19).
2–4. shield . . . sword] see Ephesians 6:16–17: 'Above all, taking
the shield of faith . . . the helmet of salvation, and the sword of
the Spirit, which is the word of God.' Friedman (1970), 74,
argues that the Soul appears as the archangel Michael.
3. Close] in the sense of closing a vizor before battle; also
suggesting the phrase 'closing ranks' (or files), used literally
and figuratively in mid-seventeenth-century English (*OED*
v. III 10 b).
4. Balance] counterpoise (*OED* v. I 3).
5–6. army . . . banners] Rees (1989), 13, suggests a possible
out-of-context echo of a phrase from Cant. 6:4: 'terrible as
an army with banners'. Cp. also Milton's description of the
Satanic army, *Paradise Lost*, I, ll. 545–6: 'Ten thousand banners rise into the air/With orient colours waving.'
8. it] i.e., 'that thing divine' (l. 7), a resolved soul.
9. wants] a) lacks b) needs.
10. one] *1681*; a *Bod. 2. resolvèd*] a) steadfast, determined (see
above, *Title* n.) b) 'dissolved', 'melted', through love for Christ
and an awareness of the need for repentance (*OED* v. II 6 b).
See Griffin (1995), 85–6.
13. crest] helmet (*OED* n.¹ 4).
14. Nature's banquet] referring to the tradition of the banquet
of sense (see above, *Headnote, Sources, Genre and Style*).
banquet] literally, a) a sumptuous feast (*OED* n.¹ 1) b) a light
repast between meals (*OED* n.¹ 2).
15–16. Not in *Bod. 2.* Friedman (1970), 77, argues that
Pleasure makes a theological error: in proposing that the Soul's

state can be enhanced by nature, Pleasure assumes that there
can be extension from soul into body. The Soul effectively
denies this in ll. 17–18.
15. souls] i.e. vegetable souls, the insensible, life-giving faculty
of plants.
16. Stand prepared] a) Pleasure presents the souls of fruit and
flowers as armed soldiers in order to appeal to the Soul's state
b) the fruit and flowers have been lavishly and carefully prepared for a feast ('prepare': *OED* v. 5).
18. bait] break a journey for refreshment (*OED* v.¹ II 7).
19. Cp. Milton, *Paradise Lost*, IV, ll. 333–4: 'sidelong as they
sat recline/On the soft downy bank damasked with flowers.'
downy] i.e. of down, feathery.
21–2. A frequent image in amorous poetry: cp. Spenser,
The Faerie Queene, II.xii.77, l. 1: 'Vpon a bed of Roses she
was layd'; Marlowe, 'The passionate Shepherd to his love'
(1599–1600), l. 9: 'And I will make thee beds of roses'; Carew,
'A Rapture' (1640), l. 35: 'There, a bed/Of Roses . . . shall be
spread' (Rees (1989), 204, n. 8).
21. plain] a) flat (*OED* a. I 1) b) smooth, free from roughness
(*OED* a. I 2).
22. strain] injure (*OED* v.¹ II 13 a).
23–4. M.'s presentation of the conjunction of contemplation
and action appears to echo verbally the temptation to learning
in Milton, *Paradise Regained* (1671), IV, ll. 285–8: 'To whom
our Saviour sagely thus replied./Think not but that I know
these things, or think/I know them not; not therefore am I
short/ Of knowing what I ought.' Cp. also Henry Peacham,
Minerva Britanna (1612), sig. C3ᵛ, where an emblem depicting a woman leaning on a T-shaped cross, and holding a Bible,
is accompanied with these lines: 'My hope is heaven, the crosse
on earth my rest.'
23. gentler] i.e. more comfortable (not in *OED*). *rest*] a) repose
(*OED* n.¹ I 2) b) support (*OED* n.¹ II 13). A 'rest' was the
support on a suit of armour for the butt-end of a lance (*OED*
n.³ 2): the Soul is punning in terms appropriate to his appearance in the poem.

Pleasure

25 If thou be'st with perfumes pleased,
Such as oft the Gods appeased,
Thou in fragrant clouds shalt show
Like another God below.

Soul

A soul that knows not to presume
30 Is Heaven's and its own perfume.

Pleasure

Everything does seem to vie
Which should first attract thine eye:
But since none deserves that grace,
In this crystal view thy face.

Soul

35 When the Creator's skill is prized,
The rest is all but earth disguised.

Pleasure

Hark how music then prepares
For thy stay these charming airs;
Which the posting winds recall,
40 And suspend the river's fall.

Soul

Had I but any time to lose,
On this I would it all dispose.
Cease tempter. None can chain a mind
Whom this sweet chordage cannot bind.

Chorus

45 Earth cannot show so brave a sight
As when a single soul does fence
The batt'ries of alluring sense,
And Heaven views it with delight.
Then persevere: for still new charges sound:
50 And if thou overcom'st thou shalt be crowned.

---

25. *perfumes pleased*] a deliberately cloying alliteration. *perfumes*] i.e. incense.

27. *show*] appear (*OED* v. VI 29), strongly associated in the seventeenth century with public appearances of monarchs and state officials.

29–30. *presume . . . perfume*] rhymed by the Soul to show 'perfume' in its proper immoral light.

31–2. i.e. everything competes to be the first object seen by you.

31. *vie*] contend, oppose (*OED* v. 4).

32. *should*] *1681*; shall *Bod. 2*.

34. *crystal*] it may seem that Pleasure is offering the crystal for the Soul to see its reflection in; however, all relevant *OED* entries refer to the transparent rather than reflective properties of crystals (*OED* A n. 2, 3). 'Crystal' was an abbreviated form of 'crystal-glass' (*OED* A n. 5) or an object made from it (*OED* A n. 6); crystal glass was known for its transparency, but could also reflect. Pleasure also suggests that the Soul is so refined, its proper reflection is the pure transparency of crystals.

35. *prized*] valued (*OED* v.¹ I 1).

36. *all but*] nothing more than.

38. *stay*] a) period of temporary residence; sojourn (*OED* n.³ 6) b) support (*OED* n.² 1 b) c) tether, as in a rope that supports a mast (*OED* n.¹ 1); see below, l. 44 n. *airs*] a) musical airs (*OED* n.¹ A IV 18, 19) b) atmosphere (*OED* n.¹ A I 4).

39. *posting*] hastening (OED vbl. n. 2).

40. *suspend*] a) delay, postpone (*OED* v. I 3) b) hold up, without attachment (*OED* v. II 10 a). *fall*] flow (not in *OED*). Cp. *Upon Appleton House*, ll. 675–8: 'The jellying stream compacts below,/If it might fix her shadow so;/The stupid fishes hang, as plain/As flies in crystal overta'en.'

44. *chordage*] a) music (not in *OED*) b) cordage, i.e. binding ropes (*OED* n.). Cp. Lovelace's less complex figure in 'A forsaken lady to her false Servant that is disdained by his new

Mistris' (1649), ll. 23–7: 'must we/ . . . / . . . Be dragged on still/By the weake Cordage of your untwin'd will,/Round without hope of rest?'

45–50. Cp. Seneca, *De Providentia*, II.viii: 'Nobis interdum voluptati est, si adulescens constantis animi irruentem feram venabulo excepit, si leonis incursum interritus pertulit, tantoque hoc spectaculum est gratius, quanto id honestum fecit.' (We men at times are stirred with pleasure if a youth of steady courage meets with his spear an onrushing wild beast, if unterrified he sustains the charge of a lion.) (Legouis); 2 Tim. 2:3, 5: 'therefore endure hardness, as a good soldier of Jesus Christ . . . And if a man also strive for masteries, yet is he not crowned, except he strive lawfully'; 2 Tim. 4: 7–8: 'I have fought a good fight, I have finished my course, I have kept the faith: Henceforth there is laid up for me a crown of righteousness.'

45. *brave*] a) referring to the Soul's courage b) splendid, inspiring: referring to the quality of the battle as spectacle.

46. *a*] *1681*; the *Bod. 2. fence*] a) fight with a sword (*OED* v. 1) b) ward off (*OED* v. 5).

47. *batt'ries*] a) succession of heavy blows (*OED* n. I 1) b) artillery (image of war) (*OED* n. II 4). *sense*] a) each of the five senses offered by Pleasure; cp. *Upon Appleton House*, ll. 287–8: 'And with five bastions it did fence,/As aiming one for ev'ry sense.' b) *Bod. 2* has an upper-case 'S': 'Sense' is personified as a combatant.

48. *Heaven*] *1681*; heavens *Bod. 2*.

49. *persevere*] Ephesians 6:18: 'watching thereunto with all perseverance and supplication for all saints'. *charges*] sounds signalling an attack (usually made by a drum or trumpet) (*OED* n. III 19).

50. *overcom'st*] Cp. Rev. 2:11: 'He that overcometh shall not be hurt of the second death'; see also 1 John 5.4–5; Rev. 2:7, 17, 26; 3:5, 12, 21; 21:7. *crowned*] Cp. Rev. 2:10: 'Be thou faithful unto death, and I will give thee a crown of life.'

Pleasure
All this fair, and soft, and sweet,
    Which scatt'ringly doth shine,
Shall within one beauty meet,
    And she be only thine.

Soul
55 If things of sight such heavens be,
What heav'ns are those we cannot see!

Pleasure
Wheresoe'er thy foot shall go
    The minted gold shall lie;
Till thou purchase all below,
60   And want new worlds to buy.

Soul
Were't not a price who'd value gold?
And that's worth nought that can be sold.

Pleasure
Wilt thou all the glory have
    That war or peace commend?
65 Half the world shall be thy slave
    The other half thy friend.

Soul
What friends, if to myself untrue?
What slaves, unless I captive you?

Pleasure
Thou shalt know each hidden cause;
70   And see the future time:
Try what depth the centre draws;
    And then to heaven climb.

Soul
None thither mounts by the degree
Of knowledge, but humility.

51–4. Cp. Milton, *Paradise Lost*, IX, ll. 602–9 (Satan to Eve): 'Thenceforth to Speculations high or deep/I turned my thoughts . . . all that fair and good in thy divine/Semblance, and in thy beauty's heavenly ray/United I beheld.' (Leishman (1966), 31–2, n. 1).
51. *this*] *1681*; *thats Bod. 2. fair . . . sweet*] Cp. Cowley, 'The Soul' (1647), ll. 17–19: 'If all things that in *Nature* are/Either soft, or sweet, or fair,/Be not in Thee so'Epitomiz'd'; Anon., 'A Letter to his Mistresse', in Abraham Wright, ed., *Parnassus Biceps* (1656), ll. 10–11: 'What ere is soft is sweet is faire/Are but her shreds.' *soft*] *Bod. 1, Bod. 2*; *cost 1681*.
52. *Which*] *1681*; *That Bod. 2. scatt'ringly doth shine*] Cp. Donne, 'Of Aire and Angels' (1633), l. 22, 'scatt'ring bright'. *scatt'ringly*] dispersed in all directions (*OED* adv.).
53. *one beauty*] Rees, *N & Q*, 222 (1977), 198–9, argues that the single beauty suggests Helen, in the context of broader association with the story of the Judgement of Paris (see above, *Headnote, Sources, Genre and Style*). Cp. below, *The Second Advice to a Painter*, ll. 67–8; see also Lovelace, 'Paris's Second Judgement' (1659–60), l. 16, 'Whilst one, as once three, doth his Soul divide.'
57. *thy*] *1681*; *that Bod. 2*.
58. *minted gold*] coinage.
59–60. Friedman (1970), 91, n. 64, connects Pleasure's offer to the pagan legends of Pluto, Plutus and Mammon. By contrast, the Soul's response at ll. 61–2, 67–8 and ll. 73–4 refers to Christ's sacrifice, His Harrowing of Hell and His establishment of a new kingdom.
60. *new worlds*] Pleasure uses the terminology of colonial exploration in the Americas. Since Pleasure promises in l. 59 that the Soul might own all of the sublunary world, 'new worlds' must literally refer to other, as yet unknown, worlds (cp. Beelzebub on the matter of journeying to Earth in Milton,

Paradise Lost, II, ll. 402–3: 'whom shall we send/In search of this new world . . . ?').
61. *Were't not a price*] i.e. if it were not regarded as valuable.
62. *that*] *1681*; *than Bod. 2*.
64. *That*] *1681*; *Which Bod. 2*.
65. *slave*] *1681*; *slaves Bod. 2*.
66. *friend*] *1681*; *friends Bod. 2*.
68. *captive*] *1681*; *conquer Bod. 2*; capture (*OED* v. a), but with the hint also of 'captivate', i.e. 'enthrall' (*OED* v. b).
69–72. 'The quatrain ranges from Aristotelian metaphysics to contemporary physics, from clairvoyance to universal knowledge; but we must not disregard its clustering reminiscences of Christ, Aeneas, Odysseus and all the heroes of pagan and Christian epic who were attracted to see the future or made perilous descent into hell in the quest of some form of knowledge.' (Friedman (1970), 80.)
69. *each hidden cause*] origins of natural phenomena; 'felix, qui potuit rerum cognoscere causas' (Blessed is he who has been able to win knowledge of the secret causes of things), Virgil, *Georgics*, II, l. 490.
71. *centre*] the centre of the earth, at the heart of the Ptolemaic universe.
73. *degree*] a) literally, the step in an ascent, from Latin *gradus* (*OED* n. 2 fig.) b) increment (*OED* n. 6) c) academic qualification (*OED* n. 7 a).
74. *humility*] i.e. degree of humility. Meekness, humbleness, the opposite of pride (*OED* 1); from ecclesiastical Latin: see e.g., Lactantius, *Divinarum institutionum, liber IV*, cap. XVI [0499A]: 'Propter hanc humilitatem, Deum suum non agnoscentes' (on account of this lowliness, they did not recognize their God [i.e. in Jesus]). Cp. Milton, *Paradise Regained*, I, ll. 158–60: 'I send him forth/To conquer Sin and Death the two grand foes,/By humiliation and strong sufferance.'

Chorus

75   Triumph, triumph, victorious Soul;
     The world has not one pleasure more:

The rest does lie beyond the pole,
And is thine everlasting store.

---

77. pole] sky (*OED* n.² 4).

78. store] sufficient or abundant supply (*OED* n. 4 a); in contrast to the Soul's store, the earthly stores of Nature and Love are passionately consumed in *The Match*; distinctively used in the English Bible: see, e.g., 1 Tim. 6:19: 'Laying up in store for themselves a good foundation against the time to come, that they may lay hold on eternal life.'

7
On a Drop of Dew

Date. Donno assumed that the poem was produced during M.'s stay at Nun Appleton (late 1650–52), but there is no certain evidence for this. The echoed texts in this poem suggest, by comparison with their presence in other M. poems, a more likely composition date to be the late 1640s. Whether it was written before or after its Latin companion poem, *Ros*, is not known.

Publication. 1681.

Sources and Genre. Dewdrops featured in emblem literature and elsewhere: since they were believed to descend from the heavens, they were regarded as a microcosm of eternity. Dew was a symbol of transcience: 'the whole world before thee is as a little grain of the balance, yea as a drop of the morning dew that falleth downe upon the earth' (Wisdom 11:22), but also of the hope of immortality: 'I am a drop of that dew, that dew that lay upon the head of Christ . . . this dew of heaven . . . not dust' (Donne, *Sermons*, X.187). Dew appears in the moral and sacred literature that M. read. Henry Hawkins's *Partheneia Sacra* (1633) contains a long chapter on dew, parts of which appear to be echoed in M.'s poem, although Hawkins regards dew as an analogy of the Incarnation: like dew distilling on plants, Christ and his grace are placed by God in the Virgin Mary. The parallels between Hawkins' text and M.'s poem are detailed by Giles, *The Explicator*, 39 (1981), 14–18. By contrast, M.'s symbolic explanation of the dew is purely and explicitly as an emblem of the soul. The relationship between elements of classical philosophy, platonic and stoical, in this theological literature and M.'s poem are discussed by Wall, *N & Q*, 206 (1961), 185–6, Toliver (1965), 6, 10, 41, 157, and Cook (1986), 148–50.

Revard (in Summers and Pebworth, eds (1992), 39–40) argues that the poem's sources are in fact in third-century Greek epigrammatic verse, notably Synesius of Cyrene's hymn (I [3], ll. 707–19) comparing the soul to a drop of water:

δός με, φυγοῖσαυ
σώματος ἅ ταν,
θοὸν ἅλμα βαλεῖν
ἔπὶ σὰς αὐλάς,
ἔπι σοὺς κόλπους,
ὅθεν α ψυχάς
προρέει παγά.
Λιβὰς οὐρανία
Κέχυμαι κατὰ γᾶς˙
Παρά με δίδου
Ὅθεν ἐζεχύθην
φοιτὰς ἀλήτις
νεύσον προγόνῳ.

    (*Opere*, ed. A. Garzya (Turin, 1989), 756)

(Grant to me to escape the destiny of the body and to spring swiftly even to Thy courts, to Thy bosom, whence floweth forth the fountain of the soul. A heavenly drop, I am shed upon the earth. Do thou restore me to that fountain whence I was poured forth, a wanderer who comes and goes.)

This is in contrast to a patristic usage, in which the blood of martyrs was described as dew drops: see, e.g., Prudentius, *Liber Peristephanos*, ll. 49–50, 740 (and see also Virgil, *Aeneid*, XII, l. 339). M.'s Latin companion to this poem, *Ros*, is more explicitly associated with the erotic elements associated with dew drops and tears in Greek poetry (see below, 43–4). This tradition was inherited by sixteenth-century humanist poets. Ippolito Capilupi ('Ad eandem' [Mariam Virginem], *Carmina* (Antwerp, 1574), 4) Christianizes the erotic elements when using dew to represent divine incarnation:

Cum ros vere rosam penetrat fulgentibus astris,
    Tum rosa, gemma velut, rore referta nitet.
Sic postquam Deus ipse tuam delapsus in aluum est,
    Sole magis, era luce repleta micas.

(When dew from the shining stars in spring penetrates the rose, then like a gem the rose shines, filled with dew; so, after God himself had slipped into your womb, brighter than the sun you beam, filled with true light.)

Here Mary is the rose; in M.'s poem any explicit religious associations beyond the soul's relationship with God are removed.

The association of dewdrops with tears (see below, l. 13) was made in classical literature: see, e.g., Ovid, *Metamorphoses*, IV, l. 263: 'rore mero lacrimisque suis ieiunia pavit' (her hunger fed by naught save pure dew and tears); X, l. 360: 'tepido suffundit lumina rore' (the warm tears fill her eyes). The association is central in late sixteenth and seventeenth-century devotional literature, especially of the Roman Catholic kind: see, e.g., Robert Southwell, *Marie Magdalens Funerall Teares* (1591), 56: 'This dew of devotion never falleth, but the sunne of justice draweth it up, and upon what face soever it droppeth, it maketh it amiable in Gods eie.' See below, ll. 17–18, 39–40, and also *Eyes and Tears, Headnote, Sources and Genre*. See also Hester Pulter, 'A solitary discoars:', ll. 59–64: 'Hee with his Heat exhales above our vew/Which doth Nocturnally descend in Dew/See how the solysequem thrust her Head/Up through the Center from that comon Bed/Into the Liquid Azure Sea above Her/To follow Phoebus her admired Lover.' (University of Leeds, Brotherton MS LT.q.32, pp. 126–7).

Style, Structure and Versification. The poem is self-mirroring in its very structure, just like a real drop of dew, while the second half, on the soul, matches, point for point, the first half, applying the description of the dewdrop to the matter of the soul. The two-part structure may have been suggested by Thomas Stanley's 'The Bud' (1646), which begins with 'See', and uses 'Such' to begin the second section, where the explanation of what the bud represents is made. Wilcher (1985), 64, argues that the first eighteen lines of the poem are governed by the command 'see' (l. 1), and the rest of the poem by the conjunction 'so' (l. 19), in imitation of the structure of an emblem poem. The metre of the first part of the poem (ll. 1–20), concerned with the dewdrop, alternates almost line by line (only two adjacent lines, ll. 4–5, have the same number of syllables). The second half of the poem, concerned with the soul, is marked by groups of lines with similar syllable lengths, notably ll. 27–32 (seven syllables per line), ll. 33–6 (eight syllables) and ll. 37–40 (ten syllables). The rhyme scheme is equally various, with a greater degree of variation in the first twenty lines (abcabcddeffegghhiijj) than the second twenty (klklmmnonoppqrqrsstt). The couplets at the end of each section imply clarity, resolution and stasis, as opposed to the undulating movement implied in the first parts of those sections. The syntax of the first eighteen lines (two nine-line sentences) is extremely difficult. The intention may have been to suggest the integrity of the dewdrop. Just as the spherical drop shape is suggested by variant line length, so the syntax appears to 'run round' the surface of the drop in an endless chain, rather than having a linear logic with a beginning and end point.

However, the nature of description means that the two halves of the poem interpenetrate: the physical description of the dewdrop has symbolic colourings, while the section on the soul continues to use pictorial vocabulary. Each section presents elements of the other in a markedly different kind of poetry. Thus, description and interpretation interpenetrate, just as both dewdrop and tear contain within themselves the greater and higher environment from which they come. In the first half, description of a natural object moves from literal observation through anthropomorphic description to psychological connotations. The manna of l. 37 is made to identify with both dewdrop and soul. The interpenetration of categories may be seen as a meditation upon the complexities of description and interpretation, and the proximity or even interpenetration of subject and object. Yet these senses of fusion are undermined by the consistently impersonal nature of the speaker's viewpoint, which never uses the first person. But then again, impersonality is itself undermined by the refined and fastidious feelings attributed to the dewdrop and the soul.

The forty lines of the poem are related to numerological principle by Muldrow, *ELN*, 23 (1986), 24, who cites Augustine (Letter XV) on the aptness of the number as a 'fit symbol for this life.'

On a Drop of Dew

See how the orient dew,
  Shed from the bosom of the morn
  Into the blowing roses,
Yet careless of its mansion new;
5 For the clear region where 'twas born
  Round in itself incloses:
  And in its little globe's extent,
Frames as it can its native element.
  How it the purple flower does slight,
10   Scarce touching where it lies,
  But gazing back upon the skies,
Shines with a mournful light;
  Like its own tear,

Because so long divided from the sphere.
15   Restless it rolls and unsecure,
  Trembling lest it grow impure:
Till the warm sun pity its pain,
And to the skies exhale it back again.
  So the soul, that drop, that ray
20 Of the clear fountain of eternal day,
Could it within the human flower be seen,
  Rememb'ring still its former height,
  Shuns the swart leaves and blossoms green;
And, recollecting its own light,
25 Does, in its pure and circling thoughts, express
The greater Heaven in an heaven less.
  In how coy a figure wound,
  Every way it turns away:

1–3. Cp. Ippolito Capilupi, 'Ad eandem' (see above, *Headnote, Sources and Genre*); Carew, 'A Pastorall Dialogue' (1640), ll. 1–4: 'See love, the blushes of the morne appeare,/Anow she hangs her pearlie store/(Rob'd from the Easterne shore)/I'th'Couslips bell, and Roses eare.' Dew and roses are also associated by the similarity of their Latin names: respectively, *ros* and *rosa*.
1. See how] Wilcher (1985), 64, notes the similarity of this phrasing with poems in the emblem book and emblematic tradition. See, e.g., Rowland Watkyns, 'The Hen and Chickens', ll. 1–2, in *Flamma Sine Fumo* (1662), 54: 'See how the careful Hen, with daily pain,/Her young and tender Chickens doth maintain.' *orient*] a) brilliant, lustrous, shining (applied to precious stones, especially pearls, from the East; *OED* B a. 2) b) morning (because from the east, and hence associated with daybreak; *OED* B a. 3). Cp. Henry Hawkins, *Partheneia Sacra* (1633), 66: 'it wil looke like an Orient-pearl, and being turnd some other way, becomes glowing Carbuncle, then a Saphir, and after an Emerauld.' Pliny, *Natural History*, 9.107 describes the generation of pearls as the ingestion by the shellfish of 'dew'.
3. blowing] blossoming (*OED* ppl. a. 2).
4. Yet] still. *careless*] disregarding; unaware of (*OED* a. 2).
5–8. Contrast Henry Hawkins, *Partheneia Sacra* (1633), 66: 'if the Sun do but shine upon it . . . it wil looke like an Orient-pearl . . . and al enclosed in a nothing, or a litle glasse of al the greatest beauties of the world.'
6. incloses] *1681+*; encloses *Walker, Ormerod and Wortham*; encloses, perhaps stressing that what is 'in' the dew drop (water) is the same as that which makes its boundary with the outside world. 'inclose' also increases the alliteration in the line. *OED* notes that 'inclose' was the legal and statutory form of enclose with reference to the enclosure of common and waste lands.
7–8. And . . . element] Colie (1966), 282, proposes that the image was suggested by the use of convex mirrors in painting (especially the work of Van Eyck) where a greater environment is reflected in a much smaller space.
8. Frames] a) sets in a frame (*OED* v. 9; but the earliest given usage is 1705) b) shapes (*OED* v. 5) c) conceives of, imagines

(*OED* v. 8 c) d) expresses (*OED* v. 8 b). *as it can*] in so far as it is able. *native element*] a) the sky b) heaven.
9. purple flower] the violet.
13. i.e., as if it was its own tear. *tear*] see above, *Headnote. Sources and Genre*. Cp. *Eyes and Tears*, l. 28.
14. sphere] the sphere of heaven (in the Ptolemaic description of the universe) from which the dewdrop descended.
15. unsecure] a) fearful, apprehensive b) exposed to danger.
17–18. But see Bacon, *Novum Organum* (1620), in *Works*, ed. Spedding *et al.* (1858), I.356: 'Paracelsus autem ait, herbam vocatam *Rorem Solis* meridie et fervente sole rore impleri, cum aliae herbae undique sint siccae.' (And Paracelsus says that a herb called Sun-Dew is filled with dew at midday when the sun is hot and the other grasses around it are dry.) Paracelsus believed that dew was an exudation of the sun and stars. Cp. *Eyes and Tears*, ll. 21–4.
18. exhale] evaporate (*OED* v.¹ 4); cp. Bacon, *Sylva Sylvarum* (1626), 413: 'The November Rose is the sweetest, having been less exhaled by the Sun.'
20. fountain of eternal day] the godhead: see, e.g., Jer. 2:13: 'my people have committed two evils; they have forsaken me the fountain of living waters, and hewed them out cisterns'.
21. human flower] i.e. the human body.
23. swart] Walker; sweat *1681, Margoliouth, Legouis*; sweet *Bod. 1, Thompson, Donno, Wilcher*; dark. John Sparrow, as Legouis reports, conjectured that *1681*'s 'sweat' was a misprint for 'swart' or 'swert' (*OED*; obscure form of 'swart'). By analogy, the blossoms and leaves are either, along with the flower, the human body, or the earth. Very common in the middle ages, 'swart' is still relatively common in poetry even in the seventeenth century, and usually describes foliage and dark skin. Its deployment here is thus entirely appropriate, quite unlike 'sweet'.
24. recollecting] a) gathering again (*OED* v.¹ 2) b) remembering (*OED* v.² 1). 'Recollection' also belongs to the vocabulary of mystical discourse, meaning to concentrate in meditation (*OED* v.² 4).
26. Cp. *Upon Appleton House*, l. 44: 'Things greater are in less contained.'
27. coy] a) shy, modest (*OED* a. 2) b) disdainful (*OED* a. 3).

        So the world excluding round,   35   Moving but on a point below,
30   Yet receiving in the day.   It all about does upwards bend.
        Dark beneath, but bright above: Such did the manna's sacred dew distil;
        Here disdaining, there in love.   White, and entire, though congealèd and chill.
        How loose and easy hence to go: Congealed on earth: but does, dissolving, run
        How girt and ready to ascend.   40   Into the glories of th'Almighty Sun.

29–36. The world or earth according to the Copernican system (Cook (1986), 149).

29. the . . . round] i.e. shutting out the surrounding world.

33. loose] unprepared, 'undressed', as opposed to 'girt' (see below, l. 34). *easy*] not hard pressed (*OED* a. 5). *hence*] i.e. depart from heaven to be on earth.

34. girt] a) prepared (*OED* v.¹ 1 b) b) figuratively: 'armed and ready to fight' ('gird': *OED* v.¹ 3); appropriate since 'girt' and 'gird' refer to wearing a sword-belt, or the encircling defences of a town (*OED* v.¹ 4–6), just as the dewdrop is 'enclosed in itself'.

36. It all about] i.e. its whole spherical surface area.

37–40. manna's . . . Sun] manna was the miraculous food (sent by God to sustain the Israelites in the wilderness) that appeared with the dew in the morning, and melted in the heat of the sun (Exod. 16:11–21). Contrast Henry Hawkins, *Partheneia Sacra* (1633), 66: 'so manie Orient-pearls, so manie drops of *Manna*, wherewith the Heavens seeme to nourish the earth, and to enrich Nature, as being the symbol of the Graces,

wherewith God doth water and fertilize our soules'. Giles, *The Explicator*, 39 (1981), 14–18, associates manna, the 'sacred dew', with Christ.

37. distil] rain down (*OED* v. 1).

38. congealèd] frozen (*OED* ppl. a. 1).

39. dissolving] manna melting into liquid is used as an analogy to describe evaporation.

40. th'Almighty Sun] see Ps. 84:11: 'For the Lord God is a sun and shield'; Jesus was also thought to have been referred to in Mal. 4:2 (thereby involving a pun on Sun/Son of God): 'But unto you that fear my name shall the Sun of Righteousness arise with healing in his wings.' Cp. Mildmay Fane, 'Contemplatio Diurna', in *Otia Sacra* (1648), ll. 1–4, which contrasts with M.'s treatment, since the dew is regarded as an emblem of sin, to be burned off by the Sun of Righteousness: 'When we behold the Morning Dew/Dissolve ith'rising Sun: What should it shew?/But that a Sun to us did rise,/Our Fathers hoary sin to Atomise.'

8
Ros

Date. See above, *On A Drop of Dew, Headnote, Date*. Most editors are not sure which of these two complementary poems came first. Ormerod and Wortham, however, argue that the Latin poem was the first to be composed: the English is more tightly controlled and concisely expressed. The passages from *Ros* apparently omitted in *On a Drop of Dew* were, they suggest, obtrusive, and hence were cut. The poem's terms of endearment and its punning suggest that it may have originated in connection with M.'s tutorship of Mary Fairfax: see Murray (1999), 50; Haan (2003), 57–94.

Publication. 1681.

Genre, Sources and Style. The symbolism of the drop of dew in theological writing was widespread: see, e.g., [Richard Herne], *Ros Coeli. Or, A Miscellany of Ejaculations, Divine, Morall, &c.* (1640), and above, *On a Drop of Dew, Headnote, Sources and Genre*.

Where *The Garden* is concise, allusive and packed with figurative language, and *Hortus* is not, *Ros* and its English counterpart share poetic strategies. 'The object seems to be to present a deliberate emulation of the poet by himself in bi-lingual versions of the same subject' (McQueen and Rockwell, 12). Both attempt to shape words to describe appropriately and wittily the drop of dew, its mediating relationship between heaven and earth, and its status as an analogue for the life of the soul. The consequence is some highly wrought Latin as well as English, where the sense is difficult in places to make out. For most editors and translators, parts of *Ros* have seemed to leave proper (or classical) Latin behind (e.g. ll. 15, 26, 42).

Textual emendations and non-literal translations have been the result. Nonetheless, Empson (1953), 80, contrasted the syntactical obscurity of the first eight lines of *On a Drop of Dew* with the first grammatically clear and complete line of *Ros*. Likewise, Rees (1989), 24, argues that the Latin version is more explicit in its delineation of the soul's journey than is the English. Revard (in Summers and Pebworth, eds (1992), 41), concurs, especially in respect of the soul's fear of earthly taint (ll. 14–15), and the erotic comparison at ll. 17–18. Friedman (1970), 59, 89 n. 33, notes both elements of concision, and of expansiveness when compared with the English version.

Ros

Cernis ut Eoi descendat gemmula roris,
    Inque rosas roseo transfluat orta sinu.
Sollicita flores stant ambitione supini,
    Et certant foliis pellicuisse suis.
5   Illa tamen patriae lustrans fastigia sphaerae,
    Negligit hospitii limina picta novi.
Inque sui nitido conclusa voluminis orbe,
    Exprimit aetherei qua licet orbis aquas.
En ut odoratum spernat generosior ostrum,
10 Vixque premat casto mollia strata pede.
Suspicit at longis distantem obtutibus axem,
    Inde et languenti lumine pendet amans,
Tristis, et in liquidum mutata dolore dolorem,
    Marcet, uti roseis lachryma fusa genis.
15 Ut pavet, et motum tremit irrequieta cubile,
    Et quoties Zephyro fluctuat aura, fugit.

---

1. Cernis] a) see (Lewis and Short, II.A) b) understand (Lewis and Short, II.B).
2. rosas roseo] an example of paronomasia; see also below, ll. 12, 13, 43.
3. ambitione] excessive desire to please (Lewis and Short II.A), but also invoking the Roman republican sense of canvassing for votes (Lewis and Short, I), appropriate for the earthly flowers.
supini] a) literally, lying on the back, i.e. face upwards b) suggested by its use in Latin poetry to describe the hands in prayer: see, e.g., Virgil, *Aeneid*, III, ll. 176–7: 'corripio e stratis corpus tendoque supinas/ad caelum cum voce manus.' (I

snatch myself from my bed, raise my voice and upturned hands to heaven, . . .).
8. aetherei . . . aquas] 'And God made the firmament, and divided the waters which were under the firmament from the waters which were above the firmament: and it was so' (Gen. 1:7).
10. mollia] possibly plays on Mary Fairfax's nickname 'Little Moll.' (Haan (2003), 59).
12. languenti lumine] see above, l. 2 n.
13. dolore dolorem] see above, l. 2 n.
15. irrequieta] 'always in motion' in classical Latin.

Qualis inexpertam subeat formido puellam,
    Sicubi nocte redit incomitata domum.
Sic et in horridulas agitatur gutta procellas,
20   Dum prae virgineo cuncta pudore timet.
Donec oberrantem radio clemente vaporet,
    Inque jubar reducem sol genitale trahat.
Talis, in humano si possit fiore videri,
    Exul ubi longas mens agit usque moras;
25 Haec quoque natalis meditans convivia Coeli,
    Evertit calices, purpureosque toros.
Fontis stilla sacri, lucis scintilla perennis,
    Non capitur Tyria veste, vapore Sabae.
Tota sed in proprii secedens luminis arcem,
30   Colligit in gyros se sinuosa breves.
Magnorumque sequens animo convexa deorum,
    Sydereum parvo fingit in orbe globum.
Quam bene in aversae modulum contracta figurae
    Oppositum mundo claudit ubique latus.
35 Sed bibit in speculum radios ornata rotundum;
    Et circumfuso splendet aperta die.
Qua superos spectat rutilans, obscurior infra;
    Caetera dedignans, ardet amore poli.
Subsilit, hinc agili poscens discedere motu,
40   Undique coelesti cincta soluta viae.
Totaque in aereos extenditur orbita cursus;
    Hinc punctim carpens, mobile stringit iter.
Haud aliter mensis exundans manna beatis
    Deserto jacuit stilla gelata solo:
Stilla gelata solo, sed solibus hausta benignis,
    Ad sua quâ cecidit purior astra redit.

Dew

You see how a little gem of Eastern dew descends and, sprung from a rosy bosom, flows onto roses? The flowers stand opened in their anxious desire, and strive to entice with their own foliage. That gem, however, surveying the heights of its native sphere, disregards the painted thresholds of its new abode, and enclosed within the shining circumference of its globe, it portrays, as far as it can, the waters of the ethereal globe. Look how, of nobler birth, it spurns the fragrant purple and scarcely presses the soft couches with its chaste foot. But it looks up with long gaze at the distant heavens and through love of that region hangs poised with languishing light. Sad and transformed by sorrow into liquid sorrow, it wastes away like a tear pouring down rosy cheeks. How afraid it is as, restless, it trembles on its troubled bed, and as often as the breeze swells with the west wind, it flees. Just as fear overcomes an inexperienced girl if she returns home unaccompanied at night. Thus the drop is stirred up into terrible little storms while it fears everything because of its virginal modesty, until the sun with its warm ray heats its wavering form and draws it back into its engendering radiance. Such is the case, if it could be seen in the human flower, when the exiled soul constantly causes long delays.

    This too contemplating the banquets of its native heaven, shuns the goblets and purple couches. A

17–20. Qualis . . timet] the comparison of the drew drop to a frightened girl has no comparison in *On a Drop of Dew*. McQueen and Rockwell, and Donno, see some comparison with *On a Drop of Dew*, l. 16: 'Trembling lest it grow impure', but this line has more in common with *Ros*, l. 15.

25–6. Haec . . . toros] Through two sets of related metaphor a) the joys of heaven imagined as a feast b) petals and leaves imagined as the cups and couches of a feast, a contrast is made between a heavenly banquet and the earthly banquet of sense, which the dew drop rejects.

26. Evertit] Possibly a mistaken rendering of 'evitat', which is closer to 'shuns' (*On a Drop of Dew*, l. 23) (John Sparrow, recorded by Legouis). *calices, purpureosque toros*] i.e. blossoms and leaves.

28. Tyria veste] Tyre was famous for the substance used to die clothes purple. *vapore Sabae*] Saba was the largest town in Arabia Felix (now the Yemen), famous for its myrrh and frankincense. *vapore*] in classical Latin, steam or warmth.

29. arcem] a) 'arx': fortress, castle, stronghold, citadel (Lewis and Short I.A). b) hinting at 'arcam': the Ark of the Covenant

(Lewis and Short II.b); typologically associated with 'tabernacle', the curtained tent, containing the Ark of the Covenant and other sacred objects, which served as the portable sanctuary of the Israelites during their wandering in the wilderness (*OED* n. 2).

42. Hinc] 1681; *Hic Bod*. 1. *punctim*] McQueen and Rockwell assumed that 'punctim' ('by a point') meant in this instance 'punctatim' ('in an instant'). They were challenged by Legouis, who felt that the normal meaning was intended. This is supportable: 'punctim' is connected to l. 41 and contrasts with l. 35: as it leaves the earth, the whole of the surface of the dew drop is stretched lengthwise, like a shaft; hence, at the end, it is a point, as opposed to the 'speculum . . . rotundum' of l. 35. For a further note supporting this reading, see Ormerod and Wortham. Cp. *On a Drop of Dew*, ll. 35–6: 'Moving but on a point below,/It all about does upwards bend.'

43. mensis . . . manna] see above, l. 2 n.

44–5. Stilla . . . solo] the chiasmus is another poetic device that enhances the sense of circularity: both of the dew drop/soul and the notion of the circular journey from heaven to earth and back again.

drop of the sacred spring, a spark of the eternal light, it is not captivated by Tyrian vestment or the scent of Saba, but utterly withdrawing into the citadel of its own light, it retracts inward, winding itself into brief circles. Following in its mind the vaults of the mighty gods, it moulds a starry globe in a small sphere. How well, contracted into a miniature of the shape opposite, it encloses everywhere its side opposed to the universe! But, adorned, it drinks the rays into its round mirror and is radiant, exposed in the surrounding daylight – glowing where it looks upon the gods above, dimmer below; spurning everything else, it burns with love of the sky. It springs up, demanding that it depart from here in quick movement, and released, is girt on all sides for its heavenly journey. And its entire orbit is stretched into an aerial route; hence plucking its way point by point, it skims a swift journey. Not otherwise did Manna, overflowing with a blessed feast, lie as a frozen drop upon the deserted ground. A frozen drop on the ground but drawn by kindly suns, it returns, purer, to its own stars from which it fell.

9
The Coronet

Date. The indebtedness of the poem to Donne's sequence *La Corona*, and Herbert's 'The Wreath', and the echoes of sixteenth-century verse, suggest an early date of composition, possibly before M.'s tour of the continent began in 1642/43, possibly shortly after his return in 1646 (see below, *Sources and Genre*).

Publication. 1681.

Sources and Genre. Emblem literature provides several vivid predecessors for the images central to the poem: for the coronet and the snake, see M. Claude Paradin, *Devises Héroïques* (Lyons, 1557) (see fig. 4); see also Johannes Camerarius, *Symbolum et emblematum* (Leipzig, 1605), 51. The poem ends with the common Christian image of Christ triumphant over the devil, represented as the serpent.

The poem belongs to a series of divine poems concerned with crowns, of which Donne's sonnet 'La Corona' is the most famous. In this respect, Friedman (1970), 83, regards the poem's proper genre as palinode – a poem of response to a previous poem. Donne's poem makes plain the fact that the crown is a metaphor for the poem itself; M.'s poem treats the crown literally: his speaker is a shepherd. Colie (1970), 79–80, describes this as an 'unmetaphored figure', typical of a poet 'critical of traditions', and in this instance, meant to stand for 'something made out of metaphors, or makes his figure stand for the writing of poetry'. Donne dismisses the crown of bays that might be his reward for writing the 'crown' of words that is the sonnet, in favour of the 'crown of glory' that Christ's crown of thorns won for mankind. M. seeks to replace the crown of thorns with a coronet of flowers, but finds the serpent (representing man's sinfulness) interweaved in it. Hence the coronet can only crown Christ's feet. Gent (*RQ*, 32 (1979), 528) accepts the poem/coronet parallel for M.'s poem and argues that the speaker discovers that the poem he is writing (his coronet) is self-seeking rather than atoning for the crucifixion. Seen in this light, M.'s poem re-arranges Donne's theme.

The poem also contains several echoes of sacred verse by George Herbert: see below, ll. 16 n., 20 n., 21 n. There are more general echoes of 'A Wreath', and of 'Affliction' V, ll. 21–2: 'While blustring windes destroy the wanton bowres,/And ruffle all their curious knots and store.' These are seen by Carpenter (*JEGP*, 69 (1970), 50–1) to reflect M.'s pulling together of several related themes and poems by Herbert. M.'s speaker admits defeat at the end of his poem, whereas Herbert's 'The Wreath' ends with an optimistic offer to substitute a poem of true praise. M.'s poem also intensifies the difference between poet and speaker as compared with Herbert's poem.

Donne's poem belongs to a cycle of seven sonnets, the last ending with the first line of the first, thereby intimating 'an unbroken circle of both prayer and prayer'. Patterson (*ELH*, 44 (1977), 495–6) contends that Donne's structure and Herbert's poem achieve levels of certainty avoided by M.'s poem, which 'remains definitively in the mode of penitential prayer and . . . unresolved'.

The Coronet belongs to a tradition of early seventeenth-century divine poetry concerned to make holy (and hence criticize, reject or 'convert') the literary ingenuity of the late sixteenth-century courtly lyric, exemplified by the verse of Sir Philip Sidney (whose work is also echoed in this poem: see below, l. 22 n.). Accordingly, Everett (in Brett, ed. (1979), 116) notes that the poem changes from narrative to prayer, from meditation to address.

The poem is related to some of the verse produced by M.'s contemporaries and associates in the later 1640s. It could be seen as an expansion of the second stanza of John Hall's 'An Ode' (1646):

> I think I pass
> A meadow gilt with crimson showers
> Of the most rich and beauteous flowers;
>   Yet thou, alas!
> Espi'st what under lowers;
>   Taste them, they're poison; lay
>   Thyself to rest, there stray
> Whole knots of snakes that solely wait for pray.

HEROÏQVES. 191

In ſe contexta recurrit.

Benedices Coronæ anni benignitatis tuæ, *dit* Pſalm. 64.
le Pſalmiſte, faiſant mencion de la grand' grace, que la
bonté, beninité, & prouidence Diuine nous fait : nous
enuoyant annuellement une Reuolucion, coronnee de di-
uerſité de tous biens, s'entreſuiuans & tenans de pres,
ſelon leurs tems, & leurs ſaiſons. Par le Serpent, s'en-
tend l'annee : en enſuiuant l'Egipcienne antiquité.

Fig. 4
Claude Paradin, *Devises Héroïques* (Lyons, 1557). The Bodleian
Library, University of Oxford, Mal. 730.

The question of the poem's religious position has been explored. Both Legouis (1965), 37–8, Carpenter, op. cit., and Patterson, op. cit., assume that the poem is a Protestant, Calvinist, and even Puritan, vehicle. Wilcher (1985), 72, argues that the poem is most successfully achieved, somewhat at odds with its sense of the frailty of all human art, because M. is in fact implicitly criticizing the Puritan castigation of human invention.

Structure and Versification. The first part of the poem is almost a Shakespearean sonnet (the first eight lines make a true octet), of three quatrains and a couplet, but is extended where the final 'turn' of a sonnet would be in l. 14. In fact, the couplet is deferred until the final two lines (ll. 25–6). The second movement of the poem is fourteen lines long: it does not obey a known sonnet form, but ll. 19–24 is an embedded sestet from Petrarchan convention.

The poem uses three metres (iambic pentameters (ll. 1, 4, 6, 8–9, 12, 17–26); iambic tetrameters (ll. 5, 7, 10–11, 13–16), and iambic trimeters (ll. 2–3), and a complicated rhyme scheme (abbacddceffeghghiijkljklmm), both elements of which are at odds with the supposedly simple pastoral speaker. Ormerod and Wortham present the poem as three stanzas of eight, eight and ten lines, on the grounds that it is suggested by the rhyme scheme and 'thought patterning'. The placing of the shorter metres, with the consequence of rapidly changing rhythms, intimates not only the interweaving of flowers in a coronet, but also the confidence of the pastoral speaker. This is replaced by the more prosaic and mentally complicated pentameters of the second part of the poem (like the change between octet and sestet in sonnet tradition). By contrast, the syntax of the first twelve lines is involuted and deliberately 'twisting' (with enjambment at ll. 7–8,

10–12, 13–14), that of the last fourteen lines direct and very clear (although the terms of reference in these lines are highly ambiguous). Colie (1970), 80, regards the first movement as Attic in style, with delayed verbs, and both phrases and clauses thwarting each other, while verbs govern several components (e.g. 'long', l. 1; 'seek', l. 4).

The first rhyme scheme ends at l. 12, where the speaker's confidence ends. The second rhyme scheme, lasting for the next four lines, is interweaved, suggesting the presence of the serpent, and is less certain in its sense of 'wovenness' than the first scheme. The fourth rhyme scheme (ll. 19–24) is the most complicated, and appears at first as unrhymed, suggesting the 'breaking' of the poem by sin, although once understood, a higher order of intelligence, associated with divinity, might be inferred. These lines are framed by two rhyming couplets (ll. 17–18, 25–6), both of which enforce the certainty of divine truth. Pastoral was associated with simplicity, but the poem demonstrates through its stylistic, syntactic and prosodic constitution that sincerity is impossible, and that if eloquence is deceitful, so is plain speech.

The Coronet

When for the thorns with which I long, too long,
　　With many a piercing wound,
　　My Saviour's head have crowned,
I seek with garlands to redress that wrong:
5　　Through every garden, every mead,
I gather flow'rs (my fruits are only flow'rs)
　Dismantling all the fragrant tow'rs
That once adorned my shepherdess's head.
And now when I have summed up all my store,
10　　Thinking (so I myself deceive)
　　So rich a chaplet thence to weave

Title. Coronet] a) garland of flowers for the head (*OED* n. 2 b) b) Christ's crown of thorns (*OED* n. 1 b; see Matt. 27:29, Matt. 15:17, John 19:2).
1. long] a) for a long time (*OED* adv. 1) b) yearn for (*OED* v.¹ 6).
4. garlands] a) wreaths of flowers worn on the head (*OED* n. 1) b) collection of poems (*OED* n. 4). *redress*] a) amend, put right (*OED* v.¹ 7) b) atone for (*OED* v.¹ 13).
5. mead] meadow (*OED*).
6. fruits] cp. Matt. 7:20: 'by their fruits ye shall know them': 'fruits' are usually taken to mean achieved spirituality. Here M.

also recalls Israelite offerings to God: 'And the feast of Harvest, the first fruits of thy labours, which thou has sown in the field' (Exod. 23:16). *flow'rs*] see 1 Peter 1:24: 'The grass withereth, and the flower thereof falleth away.'
7. Dismantling] a) remove, strip off (*OED* v. 2) b) take to pieces (*OED* v. 5). *tow'rs*] high head-dresses worn by women, made of pasteboard, muslin, lace and ribbon; in M.'s pastoral world, they are made of flowers (*OED* n.¹ I 6 b).
9. summed up] gathered together ('sum': *OED* v.¹ 3).
11. chaplet] wreath or garland of flowers for the head; coronet (*OED* n. 1).

As never yet the King of Glory wore:
    Alas I find the serpent old
    That, twining in his speckled breast,
    About the flow'rs disguised does fold,
    With wreaths of fame and interest.
Ah, foolish man, that would'st debase with them,
And mortal glory, Heaven's diadem!

20 But Thou who only could'st the serpent tame,
    Either his slipp'ry knots at once untie,
    And disentangle all his winding snare:
    Or shatter too with him my curious frame:
    And let these wither, so that he may die,
    Though set with skill and chosen out with care.
25 That they, while Thou on both their spoils dost tread,
    May crown thy feet, that could not crown thy head.

12. King of Glory] i.e. Jesus Christ; repeated once in each of the four verses in Ps. 24:7–10.
13. serpent old] see Rev. 12:9: 'that old serpent, called the Devil, and Satan, which deceiveth the whole world'.
14. twining in] a) entwining (*OED* v.[1] I 1d) b) but with a heavy echo of 'twine', to move sinuously and circuitously (*OED* v.[1] I 2), like a serpent. *speckled breast*] Cp. Spenser, *The Faerie Queene* (1590), I.ix.15, ll. 1–2: 'So dreadfully he towards him did pass,/Forelifting up aloft his speckled brest.'
15. fold] coil, wind (*OED* v.[1] 2).
16. wreaths] a) coils (*OED* n. I 1) b) as if the coils of the snake were a coronet (*OED* n. II 11). *fame and interest*] Cp. Herbert, 'The Church-Porch' (Williams MS, l. 228; before 1633), 'A toy shunn'd cleanly is fames interest'. *fame*] a) reputation, renown (*OED* n.[1] 3) b) infamy (*OED* n.[1] 4). *interest*] a) self-advantage (*OED* n. 2, 5) b) worldly business or principles (*OED* n. 4) c) power to influence from personal connections (*OED* n. 6).
17. foolish] a frequent biblical term: see, e.g., Ps. 74:18: 'the enemy hath reproached, O Lord, and that the foolish people have blasphemed thy name'.
18. diadem] crown (*OED* n. 1).
19. Thou . . . tame] see Genesis 3:15: 'And I will put enmity between thee and the serpent, and between thy seed [understood to be Christ] and her seed; it shall bruise thy head, and thou shalt bruise his heel.' See below, ll. 25–6 n. *Thou*] i.e. Christ.
20. knots . . . untie] Cp. Herbert, 'Home' (1633), ll. 60–1: 'O loose this frame, this knot of man untie!/That my free soul may use her wing.'
21. winding snare] a transposed echo of Herbert's 'Is all good structure in a winding stair?', 'Jordan (I)' (1633), l. 3, pointing to the theme of poetic construction and its relationship to worship that becomes prominent at this point in the poem. 'Winding snare' also suggests 'winding sheet', or shroud. *snare*] trap consisting of a running noose on a string (*OED* n. 1).

22. shatter . . . frame] Rees (1989), 35, argues that M. may be referring to eternal damnation as well as physical death. *curious frame*] see Sidney, *Astrophel and Stella*, 28, ll. 1–4: 'You that with allegories curious frame/Of others children changlings use to make,/With me those paines for God-sake doe not take,/I list not dig so deepe for brasen fame.' *curious*] a) skilful, ingenious (*OED* a. II 7) b) delicate, fine (*OED* a II 7b). *frame*] structure, meaning a) the coronet b) the speaker's body: see Ps. 139:15: 'My substance was not hid from thee, when I was made in secret, and curiously wrought in the lowest parts of the earth.' c) the poem itself: a common way of representing the sinfulness of human invention: see, e.g., Ed[ward] May, 'On the deceased Authour', in Thomas Beedome, *Poems Divine, and Humane* (1641), sig. A3[r]: 'I . . . see the flowers of poesie on their stalkes,/Florish in pride of fancy, I beginne,/To thinke Idolatry no sinne.'
23. these] a) the flowers of the coronet b) the body and limbs of the speaker c) the words of the poem. *wither*] see above, l. 6 n.
25–6. while . . . head] See 1 Cor. 15:25: 'For he must reign till he hath put all his enemies under his feet'; see also above, l. 19 n. Colie (1970), 29, regards the ending as apocalyptic; Stocker (1986), 119, as a use of the traditional image of Christ triumphant, standing on the serpent.
25. spoils] a) Christ's 'plunder' as victor, standing on the flowers and the vanquished serpent (OED n. I 1a) b) wasted parts (of the coronet flowers and the serpent) (*OED* n. III 9a) c) pagan art: the 'spoils of Egypt' (Rees (1989), 36).
26. crown . . . crown] Cp. Isa. 28:1, 3: 'Woe to the crown of pride . . . whose glorious beauty is a fading flower . . . The crown of pride shall be trodden under feet.' Lewalski (in Patrides, ed. (1978), 257) notes that the use of 'crown' marks a 'return to the weaving technique of the first eight lines, and this device of closure reinforces the possibility that a new and properly humble poetic crown for Christ may be produced on these new terms.'

10

Eyes and Tears

Date. ?After July 1648. See *Mourning. Headnote, Date.*

Publication. 1681; reprinted in *Poetical Recreations* (1688), Part 2, 26–8, without sts. II, III, V, IX and XI, and the Latin epigram from which st. VIII is drawn. Thompson printed the poem as continuous verse.

Text. A later seventeenth-century MS copy in Bod. MS Tanner 306/2 (*Bod. 7*), f. 388 omits st. IX, and has several minor variants, two of which agree with emendations in *Bod. 1*. Kelliher (1978), 49–50, notes that the volume was compiled by William Sancroft, Cambridge graduate, Master of Emmanuel College and eventually Archbishop of Canterbury. M. and Sancroft could have known each other from their early days and have moved in similar literary circles. Kelliher dates the paper in *Bod. 7* as being possibly produced *c.* 1656. The copy in the Clark Library, Los Angeles (P7455M1 [?1712], Bound, pp. 70–3; *LAC 1*), was made in the eighteenth century from a printed source, with one significant variant.

Sources and Genre. 'Tear' poems were quite common in the Renaissance, and were prominent examples of the achievements of baroque poetry. See, e.g., Erasmo Valvasone, 'Lagrime di Santa Maria Maddalena' (1589), st. 21:

> Aurea carena dal bel collo scende,
> Su'l bel petto le treme aureo monile,
> Et aurea ciata i fianchi annoda, & prende
> Mista di gemme con lauor sottile.

> (Iv'ry-restraining gold that chains her neck,
> Which quivers, ore on snow, above her heart
> Then her more golden sides and flanks entwines
> With panting gems enmeshed with subtle art.)
> (see below, ll. 29–32, 57–60)

Eyes and tears had already been made conjunct by Petrarch: e.g. *Rime Sparse*, 84, ll. 29–35. M.'s poem is usually connected with Crashaw's 'The Weeper' (1646, 1648, 1652 [as 'Sainte Mary Magdalen or the Weeper']), although the reference to the Magdalen in M.'s poem (l. 29) is but one of a series of different illustrations. Wilcher (1985), 17, claims that M. actually cites the precise subject of Crashaw's poem

in st. VII, as if he were performing a commentary upon it. There are also connections with Crashaw's 'The Teare'. Shell (1999), ch. 2, shows how poems of tears and weeping were a very prominent and distinguishing part of English Counter-Reformation poetics (as opposed to being exclusively of the European Counter-Reformation), although they were not invented by it, and were not exclusive to it.

Examples of the fusion of lamentation and seeing or reading (see below, l. *2*) are found in this tradition: see William Alabaster (who veered between Protestant and Catholic throughout his life), Sonnet 21, 'Upon Christ's saying to Mary "Why Weepest Thou?"' (*c.* 1597–98), ll. 7–8: 'When through my tears his love I clearer read,/So now his loss through them doth more augment.' The confusion of eyes and tears themselves is also present in this tradition: see Alabaster, Sonnet 71, ll. 11–13: 'since tears see the best, I ask in tears,/Lord, either thaw mine eyes to tears, or freeze/My tears to eyes'. In this respect the poem reverses the sentiments expressed in verse elegies: see, e.g., Patrick Hannay, *Two Elegies, On the late death of our Soueraigne Queene Anne* (1619), [sig. A4ʳ]: '*She* wastes *her eyes* in *teares*.'

However, M.'s poem begins and remains secular in subject-matter, like other similar examples in the period: see, e.g., Thomas Carew, 'Lips and Eyes' (1640). Only stanza VIII, with the attached Latin version, is religious and certainly may be regarded as part of the English tradition inaugurated by the Elizabethan Jesuit Robert Southwell. It is possible but unlikely that M. did not write the Latin version. We may further speculate that the stanza began life as a separate entity – a Latin epigram – that was later incorporated into the new, longer poem. The poem's appearance in *Poetical Recreations* confirms the transformation from sacred convention to secular lyric (a 'deconversion', so to speak) that the poem's origins and method of composition embody. Similar verse is contained in Bod. MS Rawl. D 204, a Restoration verse miscellany belonging to Sir John Reresby.

Along with the echoes of Shakespeare (see below, *Title* n., l. 55 n.), Wilcher (1985), 13–20, senses the presence of Donne's poems that mention tears (especially 'A Valediction: of Weeping' and 'Twicknam Garden'), but notes a turning away (perhaps critically so) from Donne's dramatic confrontations of tearful lovers. What remains of Donne is an echo of the phrasing of interpenetration: not, as in Donne, of the lovers but of the means of perception and expression: eyes and tears (see below, l. 55n.).

The emblem tradition provides a focus for each successive stanza: see, e.g., Peacham, *Minerva Britanna or a Garden of Heroical Devises* (1612), 142:

Looke how the *Limbecke* gentlie downe distils,
In pearlie drops, his heartes deare quintessence:
So I, poore Eie, while coldest sorrow fills,
My brest by flames, enforce this moisture thence
    In Christall floods, that thus their limits breake,
    Drowning the heart, before the tongue can speake.

Structure, Versification and Style. The poem is written in rhyming couplets of iambic tetrameters, divided into fourteen stanzas of four lines each. The poem is balanced, with six stanzas on each side of the pivotal sts. VII and VIII. Thus, the figure of the Magdalen is at the centre of the poem. Each stanza deals with a different aspect of, or image connected with, the poem's central concern, but some adjacent stanzas are more conceptually relevant than others (e.g. I and II, XII and XIII). Different kinds of cause of tears are dealt with: complaint (st. I), sorrow (st. II), pity (st. VI), grief (st. VII). Different sections of the poem employ repetition in order to create an effect of rising intensity (e.g. the use of 'all' in ll. 7, 12, 15, 19, 21; anaphora in sts. IX and XIII), which sits paradoxically alongside the sense of disruption that weeping brings about. The effect is to focus the reader's attention upon the suspended moment of weeping, as if the entire fifty-six lines were addressing the picture or emblem of a weeper. We are left meditating two objects, suspended, pendant-like, for our attention: eyes, and tears. At the same time, we are made very subtly aware of the different qualities attached to weeping, and to seeing.

Modern Criticism. Leishman (1966), 39, regards the poem as containing neither the peaks nor the troughs of Crashaw's, although Lewalski (in Patrides, ed. 265), takes the poem as a serious investigation of the relationship between nature, grace and penitence. Rees (1989), 41–2, notes the problems created by the poem turning in upon itself in an aesthetic impulse, as opposed to considering God: precisely the conclusion warned against in *The Coronet*. The poem is thus at odds with the achievements of its generic stable-mates: was M. under-inspired by the Magdalen (unlike Crashaw and Vaughan), or was he deliberately parodying the genre (even to the extent of attempting to expose the flaws in Catholic or high Anglican devotional modes)? Against several accusations of disjointedness in the poem, Hartwig (in Summers and Pebworth, eds (1992), 70) argues that the poem discovers a unity of metaphor in a celebration of both the genre of tear poems and the origins of tears themselves. Thus M., like Donne, but in a different way, 'creates an awareness of objects and subjects as the same.' Similarly, Wilcher (1985), 17–18, regards the poem as a kind of interrogation: the grief of sts. VII and VIII evokes a seriousness of emotion that questions the more self-indulgent weeping of the first six stanzas, the aesthetic and ameliorating concerns of sts. IX–XI, and the recklessness of the last three stanzas.

Eyes and Tears

I

How wisely Nature did decree,
With the same eyes to weep and see!
That, having viewed the object vain,
They might be ready to complain.

II

5   And, since the self-deluding sight,
In a false angle takes each height,
These tears which better measure all,
Like wat'ry lines and plummets fall.

Title. Cp. Shakespeare, *Venus and Adonis* (1593), ll. 962–3: 'O how her eyes and tears did lend and borrow/Her eyes seen in the tears, tears in the eyes.'
1. decree] 1681+; *agree Bod. 7*.
3. That . . . vain] Cp. Ecclesiastes 1:14: 'I have seen all the works that are done under the sun; and behold, all is vanity and vexation of spirit.' *object vain*] a) the empty or futile object (with 'vain' as an adjective) b) the object viewed vainly ('vain' as adverb).
4. They] 1681; *We Bod. 1, Bod. 7*.
5–6. since . . . height] the self-deceiving eye inaccurately measures heights because of the effect of perspective. The eye

measures inaccurately, viewing from below, as opposed to the plumb-line of the tear in ll. 7–8, which measures from above as it falls. Cp. *A Poem upon the Death of his Late Highness the Lord Protector*, ll. 269–70: 'The tree erewhile foreshortened to our view,/When fall'n shows taller yet than as it grew.'
5. And] 1681, Bod. 7; *Thus Bod. 1. self-deluding*] see above, l. 3 n.
6. angle] line of observation (see above, ll. 5–6 n.).
8. wat'ry lines] suggesting a vertical line made by drops of falling water; however a 'water-line' was also a rope in seventeenth-century nautical usage (*OED* 1). *plummets*] lead weights tied to the end of a string (M.'s 'lines') to measure a height accurately (*OED* n. 1).

III

Two tears, which Sorrow long did weigh
10   Within the scales of either eye,
        And then paid out in equal poise,
        Are the true price of all my joys.

IV

What in the world most fair appears,
Yea, even laughter, turns to tears:
15   And all the jewels which we prize,
        Melt in these pendants of the eyes.

V

I have through every garden been,
Amongst the red, the white, the green;
And yet, from all the flow'rs I saw,
20   No honey, but these tears could draw.

VI

So the all-seeing sun each day
Distills the world with chemic ray;

But finds the essence only show'rs,
Which straight in pity back he pours.

VII

25   Yet happy they whom grief doth bless,
        That weep the more, and see the less:
        And, to preserve their sight more true,
        Bathe still their eyes in their own dew.

VIII

        *So Magdalen, in tears more wise
30   Dissolved those captivating eyes,
        Whose liquid chains could flowing meet
        To fetter her Redeemer's feet.

IX

Not full sails hasting loaden home,
Nor the chaste lady's pregnant womb,
35   Nor Cynthia teeming shows so fair,
        As two eyes swoll'n with weeping are.

9–12. Cp. Flecknoe, 'Song', in *Miscellania* (1653), ll. 10–12: 'Why Pearls and Diamonds fall and rise:/Their prices iust goe high or low,/As they are worne in Coelia's eyes.'
11. poise] a) weight (*OED* n. I 3) b) balance (*OED* n. II 5).
12. true . . . joys] a penitent sense of redemption through sacrifice, the tears being 'paid' for Christ's atonement, but a clear religious context at this point in the poem is absent.
16. pendants] hanging objects (*OED* n. II 2).
17–18. Cp. *The Nymph Complaining for the Death of her Fawn*, ll. 71–2: 'I have a garden of my own/But so with roses overgrown.'
20. but] a) except b) only.
21–4. The sun is presented as an alchemist, searching for the quintessence of things, but finding it to be water. This stanza is conceptually if broadly related to Cowley's translation of Anacreon, 'Drinking' (1656), ll. 9–12: 'The busie *Sun*/ . . . /Drinks up the *Sea*, and when h'as done,/The *Moon* and *Stars* drink up the *Sun*.'
21. So] 1681; *Lo Poetical Recreations.*
22. distills] extract essence by means of heat (*OED* v. 4, 4 b).
chemic] alchemical (*OED* a. A 1).
23. the] 1681+; *its Bod. 7. essence*] i.e. quintessence (*OED* n. 2 b), refined substance, separate from the other four elements, and present in all objects; its recovery was one of the goals of alchemy.
25–8. Cp. Carew, 'A Pastorall Dialogue' (1640), ll. 17–22: 'Shepherd: If thine eyes guild my pathes, they may forbeare/Their uselesse shine./Nymph: My teares will quite/Extinguish their faint light./Shepherd: Those drops will make their beames more cleare,/Loves flames will shine in every teare.'
25. happy they] an echo of Horace's famous 'Beatus ille' (*Epode* II).

27. sight more true] i.e. spiritual insight or emotional wisdom.
28. dew] tears (*OED* n. 3 b).
29–33. A Latin translation of this stanza is given at the end of the poem in *1681* (see below). Hartwig (in Summers and Pebworth, eds (1992), 72) argues that this stanza may be seen as a kind of origin for the poem, growing as it may have done from the Latin, and offering a 'completeness with which it informs and unites the other stanzas.'
29. Magdalen] Mary Magdalen, the disciple of Christ (see, e.g., Matt. 27:56), a repentant harlot, identified with the sinner woman who washed Christ's feet with tears: Luke 7:37–8.
30–2. captivating . . . feet] an apparent reversal: 'Her thoughts were arrested by euery thread of Christes Sindon [shroud], and she was captive in so manie prisons, as the tombe had memories of her lost maister', Robert Southwell, *Marie Magdalens Funerall Teares* (1594, 3rd edn), sig. K12ᵛ. Cp. Crashaw, 'The Weeper' (1646 edn), ll. 137–8: 'we go to meet/A worthier object, *Our Lord's* feet.'
31. liquid chains] strings of tears, suggesting a string of rosary beads.
32. fetter . . . feet] Cp. *A Dialogue between the Soul and Body*, ll. 1–4: 'O who shall, from this dungeon, raise/A soul inslaved so many ways?/With bolts of bones, that fettered stands/In feet; and manacled in hands.'
34. A compression and revision of st. 21 of Crashaw's 'The Weeper': 'Say watry Brothers/Yee simpering sons of those fair eyes,/Your fertile Mothers./What hath our world that can entice/You to be borne? what is't can borrow/You from her eyes swolne wombes of sorrow.' *the chaste lady's*] the Virgin Mary.
35. Cynthia teeming] the full moon. *teeming*] 1681+; *seeming Bod. 1*; being full, as if ready to give birth (*OED* v.¹ 3).

X

The sparkling glance that shoots desire,
Drenched in these waves, does lose it fire.
Yea, oft the Thund'rer pity takes
0   And here the hissing lightning slakes.

XI

The incense was to heaven dear,
Not as a perfume, but a tear.
And stars show lovely in the night,
But as they seem the tears of light.

XII

5   Ope then mine eyes your double sluice,
And practise so your noblest use.
For others too can see, or sleep;
But only human eyes can weep.

XIII

Now like two clouds dissolving, drop,
50   And at each tear in distance stop:
Now like two fountains trickle down:
Now like two floods o'erturn and drown.

XIIII

Thus let your streams o'erflow your springs,
Till eyes and tears be the same things:
55   And each the other's diff'rence bears;
These weeping eyes, those seeing tears.

---

*Magdala, *lascivos sic quum dimisit Amantes,*
        Fervidaque in castas lumina solvit aquas;
      Haesit in irriguo lachrymarum compede Christus,
60   *Et tenuit sacros uda catena pedes.*

---

37. sparkling glance] Cp. Spenser, *The Faerie Queene* (1596), V.vi.38, ll. 6–8: 'despight/The glauncing sparkles through her beuer glared,/And form her eies did flash out fiery light'; Milton, *Comus*, l. 80: 'Swift as the sparkle of a glancing star.'
37–8. sparkling . . . fire] three Petrarchan commonplaces (Hartwig, in Summers and Pebworth, eds (1992), 81). For the glance, see, e.g., Petrarch, *Rime Sparse*, 183; fire, ibid., 182; waves: 34.
38. does] *1681+*; doth *Bod. 7. it*] *1681, Margoliouth*; its *Thompson+* ('it' is frequently found as a possessive in the seventeenth century: see 'it' *OED* pron. B III 10).
39. Yeu] *1681+*; And *Bod. 7. Thund'rer*] God as Zeus or Jove.
40. the] *1681+*; his *Bod. 7. slakes*] extinguishes (*OED* v.¹ II 11).
41–4. Cp. Crashaw, 'The Weeper' (1st edn, 1646), ll. 105–8: 'Does thy sweet breath'd *Prayer*/Up in clouds of Incense climb?/Still at each sigh, that is each stop:/A bead, that is a teare doth drop.'
41–2. incense . . . tear] the suggestion is that the tears flow upwards, as the incense fumes rise, and as the tears literally do in Crashaw, 'The Weeper' (1646), stanza 4.
43–4. stars . . . light] a reversal of a common conceit, comparing eyes (and tears) to stars; cp. Crashaw, 'The Weeper, l. 15: 'Stars they are indeed too true.'
45. sluice] dam or sluice-gate.

47. others] i.e. the beasts.
49. like . . . dissolving] Cp. *An Elegy upon the Death of My Lord Francis Villiers*, ll. 86–8: 'She like a rainbow, that ere long must fail,/Whose roseal cheek where heaven itself did view/Begins to separate and dissolve to dew.' *drop*] drip (*OED* v. 2).
50. in distance] Daniels, *The Explicator*, 35.3 (1977), 8, suggests this means 'at a distance in time' (*OED* v. 11), so that the tears are imagined slowly dripping, interrupted by pauses.
52. o'erturn] i.e. overflow (not in *OED*); with an undertone of 'overwhelm' or 'ruin' ('overturn': *OED* v. 3 a).
53. streams] *1681+*; Springs *LAC 1.*
55. each the other's] Cp. Donne, 'The Ecstasy' (1633), l. 36: 'And makes both one, each this and that.' *diff'rence bears*] Cp. Shakespeare, *A Lover's Complaint*, ll. 42–3: 'our drops this difference bore'.
56. those] *1681+*; these *Bod. 7.*
57–60. Not in *LAC 1.* Bain, *PQ*, 38 (1959), 442, notes that the Latin version is less economical and allusive than the English: see above, st. 8. Here is a more literal English rendering: 'Thus Magdalen, when she dismissed her lecherous lovers dissolved her blazing eyes in chaste waters; Christ was a prisoner in a watery shackle of tears, and held his sacred feet in a liquid chain.'

11
Bermudas

Date. July 1653–December 1654. In July 1653 M. was employed at Eton as tutor to Oliver Cromwell's de facto ward (and projected future son-in-law), William Dutton. M. stayed with his charge in the house of John Oxenbridge, Fellow of Eton College since 1652, who was also Vicar of New Windsor. Oxenbridge was a firm Independent, who had been twice to the Bermudas (where his cousin was governor) between 1635 and 1641. When M. arrived in Eton, Oxenbridge had recently been made (on 27 June) one of the Commissioners for the government of the Bermudas (CSPC, XII.405), and became governor of the Somers Islands Company in 1655. Members of the Trott family, for whom M. was to write epitaphs in the 1660s, were shareholders in the Somers Islands Company, and M. would later sit on a parliamentary committee of inquiry into the islands, but the Oxenbridge connection provides by far the strongest evidence for a date.

Publication. 1681.

Context. English colonists arrived in the Bermudas nearly a hundred years after their discovery by the Spanish (the islands were named after the Spanish explorer Juan Bermudez). The poem is indebted to published accounts of the settlement of the Bermudas, but M.'s idealizing ignores the disputes among the colonists, the punishment of some of them, conspiracies against the governors, the furore and squabbling caused by the pressure to ship ambergris back to England, instances of sodomy, and the unpopularity of Puritan activities in the 1620s and 1630s. Certainly, the islands were abundant in bird life and citric fruits (as well as mulberries and olives, which are not mentioned by M.). In reality, M.'s second paradise was heavily fortified, and planters were advised to come equipped with all the necessities of life. A work ethic was deliberately encouraged for fear that 'idleness' would run rife. The melons of l. 22 were planted by the first settlers, not found naturally growing on the islands as the

poem implies. Some species, such as tortoises, were protected by law, to prevent their extinction on the islands (John Smith, *A Generall Historie of Virginia, New England and the Summer Isles* (1624), 194), and meat or fish were often eaten raw, out of haste and hunger, quite unlike the fruit that falls into the settlers' mouths (l. 21). M. follows the writings on the Bermudas that were published for propaganda purposes, such as Lewis Hughes' *A Letter sent into England from the Summer Islands* (1615), which claims the islands had a special destiny. Where M. appears to be using the other accounts, the negative in the sources is rendered positive in the poem, whose imagined occasion may be the psalm sung by the first English visitors on their arrival after near shipwreck in a storm.

M.'s poem was most probably a compliment to Oxenbridge and his wife, in conscious imitation of psalm poetry, and possibly also in connection with his role as tutor of Dutton (see below, *Sources and Genre*). M.'s letter to Cromwell (28 July 1653) and epitaph for Jane Oxenbridge (see below, 192–4) provide evidence of his affection for the Oxenbridges and his high esteem for their godly household. In the later 1640s, Oxenbridge had served as chaplain to M.'s acquaintance, the Fifth Monarchist and republican Robert Overton, then deputy commander of the Hull garrison, and was appointed to this post by M.'s employer, Lord Fairfax, then its commander. It is possible that M. had met Oxenbridge in Hull. At Magdalen Hall, Oxenbridge's imposition of a Puritan disciplinary system (in the form of a demanding subscription to be taken by his tutees) had resulted in his dismissal by Archbishop Laud in May 1634, and his flight across the Atlantic. Oxenbridge's involvement in experiments in Independent (i.e. Congregational) church discipline, in England, New England, Surinam and the Bermudas, suggests that the poem be read not wholly literally but typologically, pointing up an ideal of spiritual felicity. The description of natural beneficence can be read literally, or symbolically, or as both. Oxenbridge sent a catechism, entitled 'Baby Milk', to the Bermudas, which caused resentment among the settlers, who were resistant to Puritanism and generally royalist in their politics. His interest in different kinds of devotional literature is reflected in M.'s use of psalm translations and Sylvester's translation of du Bartas in his poem.

Sources and Genre. Bermudas is heavily indebted to Waller's mock-heroic 'The Battle of the Summer Islands' (published 1645), especially Canto I and Canto II, ll. 1–28, where the account of the stranded whales begins (see below, ll. 10–11). M. entirely avoids the barbarous treatment of the whales by the colonists in Waller's poem, and concentrates on the paradise described in Canto I, ll. 5–12:

> That happy island where huge lemons grow,
> And orange trees, which golden fruit do bear,
> The Hesperian garden boasts of none so fair;
> Where shining pearl, coral, and many a pound,
> On the rich shore, of ambergris is found.
> The lofty cedar, which to heaven aspires,
> The prince of trees! is fuel for their fires.

These are expanded to ll. 7–28 in M.'s poem. But where Waller's speaker rejoices in the sensuality of his fecund surroundings, M.'s puritanical oarsmen praise God's Providence in giving them an earthly paradise. It is specifically a refound Eden, and not a classical Golden Age, to which Horace recommends retreat from Roman civil strife in *Epodes* XVI. Patterson, *ELH*, 44 (1977), 488–9, suggests that M. was deliberately revising Waller's Epicurean poem in the name of godliness, a point reinforced by the naming of God in the poem, who is the subject of the main verbs between l. 9 and l. 32. By contrast God is absent from earlier English versions of earthly paradises, such as Spenser's Bower of Bliss and Garden of Adonis, *The Faerie Queene*, II.xii. 42 ff., III.vi. 29 ff. Earlier analogues of 'eternal spring' are in Homer, *Odyssey*, VII, ll. 117–21, and Tasso, *Gerusalemme Liberata*, XVI.9–11. M. also avoids the eroticism of these narratives. The calm elements of Virgilian exile (*Eclogues*, IX, ll. 57–8) are replaced by a lively nature, such as the winds that are, as it were, ears of God for the rower's song (l. 4). The line from Virgil, *Aeneid*, III, l. 7, 'Incerti, quo fata ferant, ubi sistere detur' ('Not knowing where the fates bear us, where it is appointed us to settle'), adopted as a motto by the Somers Islands Company in 1622, is replaced by a strong Providentialism. Echoes of

particular psalms and the *Benedicite* from the Book of Common Prayer have been seen in the poem. C.B. Hardman, *RES*, n.s. 32 (1981), 64–7, argues that M. roots his psalmic references in his poem not to any version of the Bible, but to George Sandys' verse paraphrases of the Psalms (1636, 1638, 1648). Hardman notes echoes of Sandys' paraphrases of Psalms 104 and 107. From the latter M. took the image of the singers in a boat, saved by God from a storm (see below, ll. 1–12):

> When they to God direct their Praires,
> His Mercie comforts their Despairs.
> Forthwith the bitter Storms asswage,
> And faming suppresse their Rage:
> Then, singing, with a prosperous gale
> To their desired Harbour saile.

Also not in the Bible but in Sandys' version of Ps. 107 is the picture of God's people as colonists landing in an earthly paradise, and the image of praise spreading across the world (see below, ll. 35–6). Elsewhere (*E in C*, 27 (1977), 93–9), Hardman discusses attitudes among Church Fathers (notably Chrysostom) that associate psalm singing with daily activities.

Hardman, *RES*, n.s. 32 (1981), 65, also suggests that *Bermudas* 'sounds rather like a metrical Psalm'. In fact, M. builds on the regular iambic metre of metrical psalms by inserting spondees at the end of some lines, and reversed iambs (trochees) sometimes at the beginnings of lines to create a dactylic effect (ll. 1, 5, ?7, 12, 20, 33, 36). Of the Sandys' translations used by M., only Ps. 107 is in tetrameters and this is entirely regular in iambic metre. Others in fours in Sandys' collection, such as Ps. 46 and Ps. 51, do contain trochaic feet at the beginning of lines, but not in as sustained a way as in M.'s poem. Sandys' translations were popular at court, and especially with the King. By 1651 they were widely recognized as part of the Royalist literature of lament of which *Eikon Basilike* was the most well-known. To transfer this kind of verse into an obviously puritanical context was to perform the kind of generic relocation characteristic of M.'s political poems (see below, *An Horatian Ode, Headnote, Modern Criticism*, 270–2). Among the religious reforms debated by Puritans in the 1640s and 1650s was a new (and better) translation of the Psalms (see Smith (1994), 260–77). M.'s highly wrought psalmic poem introduces refined courtly verse into the space of a godly household. The metrical variations and the nautical context suggest additionally the singing of a sea shanty. Hardman, *RES*, n.s. 51 (2001), 80–2, has suggested that the poem might have been sung to the tune of, not a shanty, but a well-known ballad. But, whereas music usually lightens the burden of labour, this relationship is reversed in a poem that makes the praise of God pre-eminent: the work of rowing keeps time to the music, rather than vice versa.

The sense of *koinonia*, of the fellowship of believers, so central to Independent ecclesiology (see Nuttall (1957)), is enhanced by the devices that merge realms of experience, so that the new is always also familiar. The islands are like a boat (l. 1), and the rowers are already in a boat; they are mother ships to the small long boat of the rowers. They initially appear to be landing on the coast for the first time, but they already know what is ashore, as if they are merely about their daily colonial business. God's actions alternate between past and present tenses: His omnipresence makes the sense of return to Eden possible. In this respect, and in the context of 1650s religious politics, some have felt that *Bermudas* carries millennial overtones (see, e.g., Lewalski, in Patrides, ed. (1978), 274). Ormerod and Wortham list further symbolic references: biblical typology, ll. 21, 25–8 nn.; numerology, ll. 1–4 n.; iconography, ll. 17, 19 nn.

Modern Criticism. Until the early nineteenth century, *Bermudas* remained unmentioned, but then appeared in an anthology in 1819 (Campbell, 1819). Hazlitt, *Lectures on the English Poets* (1818), 163, commended the poem, as did Lamb, *Examiner* (16 January 1820), 39, who thought it was a contemplation of possible voluntary exile. Several Victorian commentators thought that the poem was among M.'s most successful achievements, and it has a strong claim to have been the best known of M.'s pre-Restoration poems in the nineteenth century and the early twentieth century. Extensive contextual discussion of the poem has produced the suggestion (Cummings, *MP*, 67 (1969–70), 331–40, Fizdale, *ELH*, 42 (1975), 203–13) that the apparently positive perspective of the poem is ironic and undermining. M. is 'concerned with showing just how unfit man is for paradise in his fallen state' (Fizdale, 207). This view has not gained general acceptance, although the disparity of the two views has left a marked impression. Hence, the 'poem allows us a destination, and its creating (not merely communicating) art makes satisfying things that are from the world but not to be possessed in it' (Brockbank, in Patrides, ed. (1978), 190). The treatment of nature has been seen as less startling and more superficial than it is in *The Garden*. Accordingly, *Bermudas* is 'a fantasy, self-indulgently dispensing with the laws that generate Marvell's real and imagined universes' (Hodge (1978), 89). Rees (1989), 43, sees the poem as signalling a shift in mood in *1681* from the poems that express a mistrust of created pleasure to those openly celebrating it, reconciling nature and grace in a paradisal landscape where man's free will and God's guidance are in harmony, where pleasure, action and contemplation are fused, and where freedom is experienced within the fellowship of a true Christian, even millennial, community.

Bermudas

Where the remote Bermudas ride
In th'ocean's bosom unespied,
From a small boat, that rowed along,
The list'ning winds received this song:
5   'What should we do but sing his praise
That led us through the wat'ry maze,
Unto an isle so long unknown,

---

1. ride] the islands are imagined as ships riding at anchor; cf. George Sandys, paraphrase of Ps. 104:26: 'And high-built ships upon her bosom ride.'
2. unespied] unnoticed; Colie, *RN*, 10 (1957), 75, and Brockbank, in Patrides, ed. (1978), 178, argue that the rowers, as much as the islands, are 'unespied'.
4. list'ning winds] a reversal of a poetic convention, where to speak to the winds is to waste one's breath: see Lucretius, *De Rerum Natura*, IV, l. 931; Ovid, *Amores*, I.vi, l. 42.
5–8. The first English seafarers to reach the Bermudas (a party bound for Virginia, headed by Sir Thomas Gates, Sir George Summers and Captain Newport) survived potential shipwreck in a storm off the dangerously rocky coast of the islands. This was interpreted as an act of Providence: God had kept mariners away from the Bermudas by means of inaccessibility through natural dangers in order to reserve it for Englishmen (Lewis Hughes, *A Letter, sent into England from the Summer Islands* (1615), sigs. A3ᵛ–4ʳ).
6. wat'ry maze] the approaches to the islands were extremely difficult to navigate; see also *The First Anniversary*, l. 1, 'Like the vain curlings of the wat'ry maze'. Mazes were frequent points of reference in seventeenth-century verse. 193 instances are noted by the English Poetry Database, but Marvell's image of a liquid maze is unique.
7. so long unknown] the Bermudas were discovered by Juan Bermudez in 1515.

And yet far kinder than our own?
Where He the huge sea-monsters wracks,
10   That lift the deep upon their backs.
He lands us on a grassy stage;
Safe from the storms, and prelates' rage.
He gave us this eternal spring,
Which here enamels ev'rything;
15   And sends the fowls to us in care,
On daily visits through the air.

He hangs in shades the orange bright,
Like golden lamps in a green night.
And does in the pom'granates close,
20   Jewels more rich than Ormus shows.
He makes the figs our mouths to meet,
And throws the melons at our feet;
But apples plants of such a price,
No trees could ever bear them twice.
25   With cedars, chosen by His hand,

---

8. kinder] a) more benign b) more natural.

9. sea-monsters] whales (see above, *Sources and Genre*); see also Ps. 74:13–14, 'thou breakest the heads of the dragons in the waters. Thou brakest the heads of leviathan in pieces'; the carcasses of dead whales (often used by the colonists and then cast out to sea) created hazards when washed up against the shores in large numbers. *wracks*] casts ashore (as if the whales were wrecked ships; (*OED* v.² 2)).

11. grassy stage] but the shores of the islands were rocky, and there was little grass on the islands themselves; M. probably has in mind the Latin 'herbosus' (see, e.g., Horace, *Carmina*, III.xviii.9) or 'gramineus' (e.g. Virgil, *Aeneid*, VI, l. 642), both of which occur in scenes of recreation and pleasure (in the latter instance, the Blissful Groves). *Aeneid*, V, l. 287, is more relevant, since it is a 'grassy stage', a grassy plain, surrounded by a theatre, where Aeneas presides over a great festive gathering. The oarsmen are also 'landed' on the 'stage', so it is also a 'landing stage', antedating the earliest *OED* reference to the word by 120 years (*OED* n. 4 g).

12. prelates' rage] see above, *Headnote, Context*.

13. eternal spring] 'The seasons of the yeere are two; a hot season, that beginneth about the middle of *Maie*, and continueth til the middest of *August*: all the rest of the yeere is as a continuall spring', Lewis Hughes, *A Letter, sent into England from the Summer Islands* (1615), sig. B2ᵛ. However, John Smith describes the fact that nothing ripens as an unhealthy stasis, *A Generall Historie of Virginia, New England and the Summer Isles* (1624), 170.

14. enamels] embellishes what is already beautiful (*OED* v. 1d).

15–22. 'God did feed them plenteously with Hogges, Fish, Fowles, and other his good creatures', Lewis Hughes, *A Letter, sent into England from the Summer Islands* (1615), sig. A4ʳ.

15–16. sends the fowls . . . air] 'He rained flesh also upon them as dust, and feathered fowls like as the sand of the sea': Ps. 78:27; quails nourish the wandering Israelites (Ex. 16:11–13 [see also Ps. 105:40]); ravens are sent to succour Elijah (1 Kings 17:6); 'the gray and white Plover, some wilde Ducks and Malards, Coots and Red-shankes, Sea-wigions, Gray-bitterns, Cormorants, numbers of small Birds, like Sparrowes and Robins, which have lately beene destroyed by the wilde Cats, Wood-pickars, very many Cahowes, which since this plantation are kild', Smith, *Generall Historie*, 171; accounts of the Bermudas mention birds' eggs in exposed nests as much as the variety of fowl. But the settlers experienced a plague of ravens in 1614 (Smith, *Generall Historie*, 180).

15. fowls] Bod. 1; fowl's 1681. *in care*] a) i.e. as a matter of God's oversight and protection b) in the care of man (*OED* n.¹ 4 a).

17. He hangs . . . orange bright] Cp. Saint-Amant, 'L'Autonne des Canaries', l. 12: 'L'orange en mesme jour y meurit et boutonne.' (In the same day, the orange dies and buds.) *shades*]

a) i.e. in the shade created by the orange tree leaves. b) Ormerod and Wortham suggest a punning reference to the dark parts of a picture, as in chiaroscuro (*OED* n. 3 a), and appropriate in respect of the still-life and landscape effects that follow.

18. green night] Cp. below, *The Garden*, l. 48: 'green shade'.

19–20. pom'granates . . . Jewels] Rees (1989), 51, suggests that the reader is invited to look through the skin of the pomegranate to its shining interior, thereby suggesting contemplation of the 'inward' as well as 'outward' nature of things.

19. pom'granates] 'Thy plants are an orchard of pomegranates, with pleasant fruits' (Cant. 4:13); the pomegranate was a symbol of eternity (see *OED* n. 1 a fig.). *close*] enclose.

20. Ormus] Hormuz, near the entrance to the Persian Gulf, used by the Portuguese as a market in the sixteenth century; see Milton, *Paradise Lost*, II, ll. 1–2: 'High on a throne of royal state, which far/Outshone the wealth of Ormus and of Ind.'

21–4. Cp. Waller, 'The Battle of the Summer Islands', I, ll. 21, 34: 'Figs there unplanted through the fields do grow'; 'On choicest melons, and sweet grapes, they dine.' Figs were the only fruit in M. mentioned by Lewis Hughes, *A Letter, sent into England from the Summer Islands* (1615), sig. B1ᵛ.

21. figs] 'The fig tree putteth forth her green figs': Cant. 2:13.

22. melons] see above, *Headnote, Context*.

23–4. apples . . . twice] Wilding, *ELN*, 6 (1969), 254–7, notes that pineapples (once assumed to be meant by 'apples') do not grow on trees (see illustration in Richard Ligon, *A True and Exact History of the Island of Barbados* (1657), inserted before sig. Z1). Wilding suggests that the apples are the fruit of the Tree of Knowledge of Good and Evil (which could indeed only be picked once – to precipitate the Fall of mankind). They could equally be fruit of the Tree of Life. Such an interpretation would be consistent with a typological understanding of the poem (see above, *Sources and Genre*). The tree in the Garden of the Hesperides would also bear no fruit after Hercules had picked the golden apples (Lucan, *De Bello Civili*, IX, 356 ff.). It is worth noting that Jourdain described prickly pears in the Bermudas growing upon trees (Silvester Jourdain, *A Plain Description of the Barmudas* (2nd edn, 1613), sig. C3ʳ).

23. apples plants] i.e. plants apples.

24. twice] Hence overgoing the 'eternal spring' in Virgil, *Georgics*, II, ll. 149–50 (Wilson, *N & Q*, 49 (2002), 343).

25–6. cedars . . . From Lebanon] Solomon built his temple from the cedars of Lebanon; M. most probably has in mind Ps. 92:12 or Ps. 104:16. Gates and Sommers built boats from cedar trees on the islands in order to escape (W.C., 'The Epistle Dedicatorie', in Silvester Jourdain, *A Plain Description of the Barmudas* (2nd edn, 1613), sig. A4ʳ); later the trees were felled and their wood put to use at an alarming rate, so that legal controls were necessary.

From Lebanon, He stores the land.   Till it arrive at heaven's vault:
And makes the hollow seas that roar   35   Which thence (perhaps) rebounding, may
Proclaim the ambergris on shore.   Echo beyond the Mexique Bay.'
He cast (of which we rather boast)   Thus sung they, in the English boat,
30   The Gospel's pearl upon our coast.   An holy and a cheerful note,
And in these rocks for us did frame   And all the way, to guide their chime,
A temple, where to sound His name.   40   With falling oars they kept the time.
Oh let our voice His praise exalt,

---

26. *stores*] stocks (*OED* v. 1).

27. *hollow seas . . . roar*] 'Let the sea roar, and the fullness thereof': Ps. 98:7. *hollow*] stormy (from the hollows made in a rough sea) (*OED* a. 2c). See also below, *A Poem upon the Death of his Late Highness the Lord Protector*, l. 106, 'As hollow seas with future tempests rage'.

28. *Proclaim*] the roar of the sea announces the ambergris washed up on the shore. *ambergris*] fragrant substance secreted by sperm whales; see *The Gallery*, l. 38. Cp. Anne Bradstreet, 'Of the four Elements'; 'Water', in *Several Poems* (1678), 16: 'Thy gallant rich perfuming Amber-greece/I lightly cast ashore as frothy fleece:/With rowling grains of purest massie gold,/Which *Spains Americans* do gladly hold.' (see also below, ll. 35–6 n.).

29–30. *He cast . . . pearl*] an inversion of Matt. 7:6: 'neither cast ye your pearls before swine, lest they trample them under their feet'; the godly settlers are not swine. Pearls were supposed to be abundant (in fact, they were not) in the waters around the islands, and the Bermudas were well known for their hogs (assumed by some to have been brought by the Spanish) (see Silvester Jourdain, *A Plain Description of the Barmudas* (2nd edn, 1613), sigs. C1ᵛ, C3ᵛ). See also Matt. 13:45, 'The kingdom of heaven is like unto a merchant man, seeking goodly pearls.'

29. *rather*] more readily (*OED* adv. II 4 a). *boast*] Ps. 44:8: 'In God we boast all the day long, and praise thy name forever.'

31. *rocks*] for Smith, however, the rocks were 'dark and cumbersome places' (*Generall Historie*, 169). *frame*] fashion, shape (*OED* v. 5 a).

35–6. *rebounding . . . Bay*] the sound of the reflected godly song will be heard in Spanish America, the lair of paganism and Catholicism. Plans were already afoot during M.'s stay with Oxenbridge for an expedition into the Caribbean (which would eventually become the unfortunate Western Design): see Armitage, *HJ*, 35 (1992), 531–55. For their part the Spanish were leaving their verse in the New World: see, e.g., the poem inscribed on the E1 Morro rock, New Mexico on 5 August 1629.

35. *(perhaps)*] a) Wilcher (1985), 144, challenges the conventional view that this parenthesis is a doubting of the efficacy of the song, arguing that such a sense would be against the strong faith in God shown by the rowers; rather, it is a sign of a reluctance to presume God's intentions. But it is the rowers' song, and not God, that is doubted. Yoshinaka, *SC*, 13 (1998), 22–35, argues that the parenthesis implies on the one hand, M.'s understanding of the rowers' singular faith, and on the other, the fact that the Bermudas and the rest of the New World are not a paradise, but subject to sublunary contingency. b) J.B. Winterton, *N & Q*, 213 (1969), 101–2, suggests that M. may be offering a doubting of cosmological description: a solid heavenly sphere would function as a reflecting surface, but the 'new philosophy' would put this in doubt.

36. *Mexique Bay*] Gulf of Mexico.

38. *note*] tune, song (*OED* n.² I 3).

39. *And . . . chime*] echoes *Upon Appleton House*, l. 541, 'And all the way, to keep it clean'. *chime*] music.

12
Clorinda and Damon

Date. ?Late 1650–52. The poem is heavily indebted to Spenserian pastoral. The only other poem in M.'s canon to have such sources and echoes is *The Picture of Little T.C. in a Prospect of Flowers*, which was probably written during the stay at Nun Appleton (there are also textual connections between the two poems: see below, *The Picture of Little T.C. in a Prospect of Flowers*, l. 37 n.), and one of the speakers shares a name with M.'s mower, the mower poems also being written during this period. There are some speculative grounds then for attributing the date of the poem to this period. On account of its similarity to *A Dialogue between Thyrsis and Dorinda*, which may be one of M.'s earliest poems, Donno suggests that the poem was written much earlier.

Publication. 1681.

Sources and Genre. Lewalski (in Patrides, ed. (1978), 269), notes the poem's reflection of various aspects of Spenser's poetry, and in particular his pastoral works: the May (see below, l. 20 n.), July and September eclogues of *The Shepheardes Calendar*, and the *Epithalamion* (see below, l. 28 n.; although the poem also specifically echoes parts of *The Faerie Queene*: see below, ll. 3–4 n., 8 n.). The poem reverses the normal roles allotted to pastoral characters, in that the female, Clorinda, functions as the sexual temptress, and purveyor of *carpe diem* sentiments, while Damon is the guardian of virtue. Friedman (1970), 8, regards this as a 'minor innova-tion'. Most English pastoral is concerned with *otium*: M.'s poem studiously rejects it, not least of all with the stychomythic exchanges and interruptions that imply earnestness and mental labour. Other conventional pastoral features (e.g. caves and fountains) are forced to behave in symbolic ways, while the conventionally symbolic becomes relocated in a natural scene (e.g. the 'scutcheon' of grass; a scutcheon (see below, l. 3 n.) being associated with the Petrarchan conceit of love as armed combat) that is finally turned, with every other element, towards the worship of God.

Clorinda's world of simple, sensuous pastoral perceptions is superseded by Damon's landscape of Christian symbols. In this context, Rosenberg, *BUSE*, 4 (1960), 152–61, regards the poem as an extreme example of the use of pastoral as a vehicle for Christian concepts, 'posing Puritan repressive plainness against pagan or epicurean unrestraint' (unlike the residue of Petrarchan femininity that remains in Spenser's Christian eclogues). Friedman (1970), 52, associates the offering of a hymn by Damon (but inspired by Pan) at the end of the poem with Herbert's 'Love (II)', where the triumph of heavenly love over earthly is marked by the offering of a hymn. This is all the more remarkable for the fact that pastoral was regarded in Renaissance literary criticism as unfit for spiritual revelation (hence Damon's comments at l. 21). Kaufmann (1978), 72–3, argues that the poem presents an 'open' Paradise rather than the traditional depiction of Paradise as a restricted enclave.

Clorinda and Damon

C. Damon come drive thy flocks this way.
D. No: 'tis too late; they went astray.
C. I have a grassy scutcheon spied,
    Where Flora blazons all her pride.
5   The grass I aim to feast thy sheep:
    The flowers I for thy temples keep.
D. Grass withers; and the flowers too fade.
C. Seize the short joys then, ere they vade.
    See'st thou that unfrequented cave?
10   D. That den? C. Love's shrine. D. But Virtue's grave.
C. In whose cool bosom we may lie
    Safe from the sun. D. Not heaven's eye.
C. Near this, a fountain's liquid bell
    Tinkles within the concave shell.
15   D. Might a soul bathe there and be clean,

    Or slake its drought? C. What is't you mean?
D. These once had been enticing things,
    Clorinda, pastures, caves, and springs.
C. And what late change? D. The other day
20   Pan met me. C. What did great Pan say?
D. Words that transcend poor shepherds' skill,
    But He e'er since my songs does fill:
    And His name swells my slender oat.
C. Sweet must Pan sound in Damon's note.
25   D. Clorinda's voice might make it sweet.
C. Who would not in Pan's praises meet?

Chorus

Of Pan the flow'ry pastures sing,
Caves echo, and the fountains ring.
Sing then while he doth us inspire;
30   For all the world is our Pan's choir.

1–2. come drive . . . astray] Cp. Isa. 53:6: 'we like sheep have gone astray' (Wilcher (1985), 53).
3–4. grassy . . . pride] Cp. Spenser, *The Faerie Queene*, II.xii.50, ll. 3–5: 'whose faire grassy ground/Mantled with greene, and goodly beautifide/With all the ornaments of *Floraes* pride.'
3. scutcheon] escutcheon; shield on which a coat of arms is displayed, used here as a metaphor for a lawn, grove or copse.
4. Flora] Roman goddess of flowers. *blazons*] describes in heraldic language (*OED* v. I 1).
5. aim] intend, design (*OED* v. 8).
6. temples] a) sides of the head (*OED* n.² 1) b) ornaments worn on the side of the forehead (*OED* n.² 2).
7. See Isa. 40:8: 'The grass withereth, the flower fadeth: but the word of our God shall stand for ever.'
8. vade] decay, disappear (*OED* v.¹ 3; variant of 'fade'; associated with Latin *vadere*, 'to go [hastily]').
9. unfrequented] Cp. Horace, *Carmina*, III.xxv, ll. 12–14: 'ut mihi devio/ripas et vacuum nemus/mirari libet' (even as I love to stray and to gaze with awe upon the unfrequented banks and groves).
10. den] a den, unlike a cave, was the lair of a wild beast (*OED* n.¹ 1) or the hiding place of a thief (*OED* n.¹ 3): places of danger and immorality. Cp. Matt. 21:13: 'My house shall be called the house of prayer; but ye have made it a den of thieves.' The passage carries a sexual innuendo: Clorinda's cave is associated with the vagina. Accordingly, an obscure seventeenth-century meaning of 'den' is a cavity in the human body (*OED* n.¹ 6).
13. liquid] pure, clear (*OED* a. II 3).
14. Tinkles] a) rings (*OED* v. II 2) b) flows (*OED* v. II 2 b). *concave*] Damon's fears (see above, l. 10 n.) might be enhanced

by the innuendo buried in 'concave': 'con' occurs in English only as an innuendo: it is vulgar French for vagina (Williams (1994), I.289–90).
16. slake its drought] quench its thirst; cp. John 3:13–14: 'Jesus answered and said unto her, Whosoever drinketh of this water shall thirst again: But whosoever drinketh of the water that I shall give him shall never thirst; but the water that I shall give him shall be in him a well of water springing up into everlasting life.'
20. great Pan] Christ: Spenser, *The Shepheardes Calendar*, E.K.'s gloss to the May eclogue: 'Great Pan is Christ, the very God of all the shepheardes'; Milton, 'On the Morning of Christ's Nativity', l. 89: 'the mighty Pan'. An ancient study recorded that at the time of the crucifixion, a voice cried out that 'great Pan' was dead: Plutarch, *De Defect. Orac.*, 418.
21. transcend] exceed (*OED* v. 3).
23. swells] by mentioning the breath inside his pipe, Damon suggests he is inspired by the Holy Spirit, which was defined as a divine breath (Hebrew *ruâch* or Greek πνεῦμα); see below, l. 29. *oat*] pipe made of oaten straw (*OED* n. 5).
26. meet] in the sense of realizing harmony in singing to praise God, as opposed to the proposed amorous meeting in the cave. Clorinda has rapidly shifted her ground: she now proposes a union with Damon within the greater goal of worshipping 'great Pan'. For Wilcher (1985), 54, this is a possible indication of Clorinda's shallowness, for Craze (1979), 294, evidence of her high intelligence.
28. echo . . . ring] echoing the mutating last line of each stanza in Spenser's *Epithalamion*, but especially l. 128: 'That all the woods shal answer and theyr eccho ring.'
29. inspire] see above, l. 23 n.

13

A Dialogue between the Soul and Body

Date. Not earlier than 1652. The echoes of works published in late 1651 or 1652 (notably James Howell's *The Vision: or a Dialogue between the Soul and the Bodie* (dated by Thomason 14 January 1652; see below, ll. 1–2, 19–20, 29–30, 33–6 nn.)), and of works definitely written by M. in this period (notably *Upon Appleton House* (see below, ll. 43–4 n.)), suggest as the most likely composition date either during the latter part of M.'s stay at Nun Appleton, or just after his departure from there. However, the strong echoes of the poem in the prose works of the 1670s (see below, 43–4 n.) give some support for a late date of composition, or revision. This view would be supported by the alterations made in *Bod. 1* (see below, *Text*).

Publication. 1681. The poem was copied from *1681* into a verse miscellany (BL MS Add. 29921, fols. 80–1 (*BL 1*)) probably in the early eighteenth century, although compilation of material in this book may have begun as early as 1668. A good deal of the poetry in this miscellany (including other soul/body dialogues) is of a godly nature, the first 34 pages being copied from a manuscript in the possession of the influential Baptist Hebrew scholar Hanserd Knollys. This gives some indication of the early readership of M.'s dialogue.

Text. The alterations in *Bod. 1* consist of two diagonal lines crossing out the last four lines of the poem, with the words '*Desunt multa*' (much is missing) written below. Leishman (1966), 216, suggests that the original poem may have contained several more ten-line stanzas, of which the last four lines were a remnant. But the comment may mean no more than that the annotator, noting that the last stanza-speech is four lines longer than the others, thought that the poem had been imperfectly copied, possibly from an incomplete copy. He could conceivably have known this for certain, having seen a longer manuscript copy of the poem.

Genre and Sources. Osmond, *ELR*, 4 (1974), 364–403 (especially 387–9), and (1990), 97, 99–101, gives a history of the tradition of soul–body dialogues, their apparent disappearance between the end of the middle ages and the seventeenth century, and their revival in the early 1600s under the impetus of Puritan concerns with introspective spiritual states, soteriology (the business of soul-saving) and the rise of Platonism. These movements took place within the broader context of the importation of pre-Reformation and Counter-Reformation devotional literary forms into reformed pieties as a means of filling the void created by both Protestantism's abolition of non-scriptural literature in acts of worship, and its emphasis upon religious interiority. M.'s poem represents a 'further development away from the moral toward the philosophical dialogue. . . . In content it is very far removed from the medieval dialogues; there is no mention of sin at all, and certainly no distinction between the internal cause and the external manifestation of an act, between will and action' (Osmond, 387–8). It is concerned with the soul/body relationship rather than the themes of death and judgement. The debt to classical philosophy is also held to be obvious, and more so than in similar examples. It is also notable that the poem has no 'definite frame of reference for the debate', and no attempt is made to resolve the problem voiced by the opposing voices (Osmond, 388). The poem's relationship with classical and Renaissance philosophy is also discussed by Datta, *RQ*, 2 (1969), 245–55. However, Bossy, *CL*, 28 (1976), 160, regards the poem as still part of the medieval tradition, since it contains the soul's complaints regarding the tyranny of the body, and a series of echoes of medieval examples; hence it is the 'subtlest' example in the tradition.

The sophistication of M.'s poem is evident in comparison with 'A.W.'s' 'A Dialogue betweene the Soule and the Body', printed in Francis Davison, ed., *A Poetical Rapsody* (1602), 197, which like M.'s poem portrays the interdependence of body and soul:

... Ay me, poore Soule, whom bound in sinful chains
This wretched body keepes against my will!
Body Aye mee poore Body, whom for all my paines,
    This froward soule causlesse condemneth stil.
Soule Causles? whenas as thou striv'st to sin each day?
    Causles: whenas I strive thee to obay.
Soule Thou art the meanes, by which I fall to sin,
Body Thou art the cause that set'st this means awork
Soule No part of thee that hath not faultie bin:
Body I shew the poyson that in thee doth lurke.
Soule I shall be pure when so I part from thee:
    So were I now, but that thou stainest mee.

Other examples are less poised. 'The Convert: A Dialogue', copied into a Restoration and early eighteenth-century poetry miscellany (BL MS Add. 29921, fols. 25ᵛ–27ᵛ), but from an earlier seventeenth-century source, has a soul that succeeds in persuading the body to give up pleasures on the understanding that the body will go to heaven with the soul. Indeed, the poem contains ideas of angelic and heavenly diet and senses, prominent in Milton's *Paradise Lost*, and which solve the dilemmas exhibited in M.'s poem. Others still, unlike M., imply a companionship between soul and body throughout, an appropriate approach given that the body was supposed to be resurrected with the soul at the Last Judgement: e.g. Henry Vaughan's three dialogues, 'Death', 'Resurrection and Immortality', 'The Evening Watch.'

The imagery of the soul imprisoned within the body (ll. 1–2) is literally depicted in an emblem prefacing chapter 38 of Hermann Hugo, *Pia Desideria* (Antwerp, 1624), between pp. 332 and 333, under which is printed in Latin the sentences from Romans 7 transposed by M. at ll. 11–12. M.'s English is indebted in places very closely to Hugo's accompanying Latin verse, in particular the first eight lines:

Libera quae potui spatioso ludere Coelo,
Cernis, ut angusto carcere clausa premar?
Heu dolor! ut miseras me lux effudit in auras,
Ipsa loco caveae membra fuere meae.
Per compes, manicaeque manus, nervique catanae,
Ossaque cancellis nexa catasta suis.
Quo mihi cognati nativa repagula claustri,
Damner ut hospitii compede vincta mei?

(I who could play freely in the wide heavens – do you perceive how I am now pressed close in a narrow dungeon? Alas, what misery! that the light poured me forth on these unhappy airs! My very limbs are a prison to me. Feet fetters, hands manacles, nerves chains, bones a cage for showing off a slave in a market, bound together with its own lattice-work of bars. To what end am I barred in by the natural barrier of a prison so closely kin to me, so that I am condemned to be bound in fetters in the guest-chamber which is my very own?)

The borrowings are discussed by Datta, *RQ*, 2 (1969), 242–55: in her view Hugo's poem, which outdid any previous English treatment of the topic, directly provoked M. to write his poem. Yet this does not discount echoes from native works (see below, ll. 1–2 n., 7–8 n., 19–20 n., 29–30 n., 37–8 n.). In this respect, M.'s poem is related to Cowley's 'The Despair' (1647), st. 4 (ll. 28–30): 'Ah sottish *Soul*, said I,/When back to its *Cage* again I saw it fly;/Fool to resume her *broken Chain*.' Millus, *YULG*, 47 (1973), 216–23, argues that M. derived his physiological imagery from the new discoveries in anatomy (of which the work of William Harvey is most famous) and the pictures in anatomical publications, such as Andreas Vesalius's *De humani corporis fabrica* (1543; see below, ll. 7–8 nn.). With reference to the poem, these writings and illustrations are examined by Sawday (1995), 21–2, who also explains the relationship between anatomical representation and public execution reflected in M.'s poem (see below, ll. 7–10).

There are distinct echoes of Shakespeare's *The Tempest*, in particular, of Ariel and Caliban's complaints to Prospero of his imprisonment, although M. puts into the mouths of the Soul and Body words that belong in the play to Prospero. As an instance of Marvellian inventiveness, Shakespeare's noun 'pine' becomes a verb in the poem (see below, ll. 21–2).

Structure, Versification and Style. Unlike M.'s other dialogue poems, the speakers here are given quite long stanzas, ten-line lyrics in themselves. Also unusual is that each speaker appears to be talking to a third party rather than to each other, although a dramatic element is sustained by each speaker showing an awareness of the presence of the other. The tone of reproach in each speaker, together with the extravagant conceits (the body described as instruments of torture, the soul as a tyrant; the body as a sorcerer, mental qualities as diseases), irony, punning, hyperbole and paradox, create a sense of humour for the reader: the speakers are a 'comic duo' (see Berek, *MLQ*, 32 (1971), 144–7). The last four lines of the poem, given to the body, remove the balance between soul and body throughout the poem (see above, *Text*). Rather than mere opposed and distinct exchange, the two speakers produce arguments that reveal the interdependence of body and soul: how could the body be aware of sin were it not for the consciousness of the soul? How can the body think so sharply and inventively without the soul?

A Dialogue between the Soul and Body

Soul

O who shall, from this dungeon, raise
A soul inslaved so many ways?
With bolts of bones, that fettered stands
In feet; and manacled in hands.
5   Here blinded with an eye; and there
Deaf with the drumming of an ear.

A soul hung up, as 'twere, in chains
Of nerves, and arteries, and veins.
Tortured, besides each other part,
10   In a vain head, and double heart.

Body

O who shall me deliver whole,
From bonds of this tyrannic soul?
Which, stretched upright, impales me so,
That mine own precipice I go;
15   And warms and moves this needless frame:
(A fever could but do the same).
And, wanting where its spite to try,
Has made me live to let me die.
A body that could never rest,
20   Since this ill spirit it possessed.

1–2. dungeon . . . ways] Cp. James Howell, *The Vision: or A Dialog between the Soul and the Bodie* (1652), 1: 'Soul. . . . What cause have I to repent that ever I was thrown into that dungeon, that corrupt mass of flesh?' *dungeon*] i.e. the body.
3–8. fettered . . . veins] Cp. a Pythagorean account of the soul in Thomas Stanley, *The History of Philosophy*, 3 vols (1655–60), 3.103: 'The fetters of the soul are Veines, Arteries, and Nerves; but when she is strong, and composed within her selfe, her fetters, are Reasons, and Actions.'
3. bolts] irons for fastening legs; a fetter (*OED* n.[1] 6).
3–4. fettered . . . feet] 'fetters' derives from 'feet' (*OED* n.); 'one cannot be fettered in feet – or anything else – unless one already has feet to be bound' (Berek, *MLQ*, 32 (1971), 145); the etymological wordplay suggests the inseparability of body and soul.
4. manacled . . . hands] 'manacle' derives from Latin *manus* (hand).
5–6. Cp. *Upon Appleton House*, ll. 289–92: 'When in the east the morning ray/Hangs out the colours of the day,/The bee through these known allies hums,/Beating the *dian* with its drums.'
6. ear] Referring to the ear-drum (*OED* n[1] III), or tympanum (*OED* 2).
7. hung up] Millus, *YULG*, 47 (1973), 221–2, suggests that M. may have derived this image from the picture of a cadaver (showing an interior view of the muscles) hung up by a rope in Vesalius' *De humani corporis fabrica* (1543).
7–8. chains . . . arteries] Millus, *YULG*, 47 (1973), 221, suggests that M. may have derived this image from the illustrations of the nerve and arterial systems in Vesalius' *De humani corporis fabrica* (1st edn, 1543). *in chains . . . veins*] Cp. John Hall, 'An Epicurean Ode' (1646), ll. 8–9: 'Since that the soul doth only lie/Immers'd in matter, chain'd in sense.' *chains*] another common form of fetter (*OED* n. I 2).
10. vain] a) empty (*OED* a. I 2) b) futile (*OED* a. I 1) c) vainglorious (*OED* a. I 4) d) punning on 'vein.' *double*] a) literally, because of the heart's two ventricles b) duplicitous.
11–12. A transposition of Romans 7:24: 'O wretched man that I am! who shall deliver me from the body of this death?'; cp. also the motto below the woodcut in Hugo's *Pia Desideria* (see above, *Headnote, Genre and Sources*): '*Quis me liberabit de corpore mortis huius?*' (Who will deliver me from the body of this death?).
11. deliver] set free, release (*OED* v.[1] 1).

12. bonds] another word for shackles or fetters (*OED* n.[1] I 1).
13–14. stretched . . . go] the body imagines the soul as a torturing rack, upon which victims were stretched; cp. *RT*, 30: 'after he [Bishop Parker] was stretched to such an height in his own fancy, that he could not look down from top to toe but his Eyes dazled at the Precipice of his Stature'.
13. impales] thrusting a stake through the fundament, to come out of the mouth, usually as a form of torture or capital punishment (*OED* v. 4 a). *OED* v. 4 b quotes this line in the sense of 'to transfix upon, or pierce through with, anything pointed'; fig. to torment or render helpless as if transfixed', but M. is making an image out of the literal meaning of the previous entry.
14. a) the soul has made the body stand upright, so that it always risks falling over (see below, *That mine*). b) the body moves ('I go') as a living precipice. As a creature that prefers to move horizontally across the ground, the body identifies itself as a soulless beast, like the serpent cursed by God (Gen. 3:14: 'upon thy belly thou shalt go'). *That mine*] i.e. 'that over mine'. *precipice*] loftiness; steep height (*OED* n. 3). Cp. *Upon Appleton House*, ll. 374–5: 'And, from the precipices tall/Of the green spires, to us do call.'
15. needless] having no wants (*OED* a. 3); Berek, *MLQ*, 32 (1971), 146, argues that since 'needless' can also mean 'unnecessary[:] the body inadvertently trivialises itself, playing directly into the soul's viewpoint.'
17. its] 1681+; 'tis *LAC 1*.
19–20. body . . . possessed] Cp. James Howell, *The Vision: or A Dialog between the Soul and the Bodie* (1652), 27: 'Add hereunto, that there is a *malus Genius* an ill Spirit that is always busie about me, and are irresistible.'
20. ill] evil (*OED* a. 1), but playing on the sense of the word that the Body would most easily recognized: unwell, disordered (*OED* A a. 8 a). *spirit it possessed*] a) the soul is the body's possession b) the body is 'possessed' by the soul (in the technical sense of a body being occupied by an alien, evil spirit that must be cast out by exorcism). The body has either inaccurately described the soul as a mere spirit, or it has confused 'soul' with 'spirit', a position taken by some radical Puritans at the time (see Smith (1989), 272, 276); to this extent the body takes a theologically unorthodox position. Cp. *RT*, 111–12: 'the Body is in the power of the mind; so that corporal punishments do never reach the offender, but the innocent suffers for the guilty.'

Soul	*Body*

Soul

What magic could me thus confine
Within another's grief to pine?
Where whatsoever it complain,
I feel, that cannot feel, the pain.
25   And all my care itself employs,
That to preserve, which me destroys:
Constrained not only to endure
Diseases, but, what's worse, the cure:
And ready oft the port to gain,
30   Am shipwracked into health again.

Body

But physic yet could never reach
The maladies thou me dost teach;
Whom first the cramp of Hope does tear:
And then the palsy shakes of Fear.
35   The pestilence of Love does heat:
Or Hatred's hidden ulcer eat.
Joy's cheerful madness does perplex:
Or Sorrow's other madness vex.
Which Knowledge forces me to know;
40   And Memory will not forgo.
What but a soul could have the wit
To build me up for sin so fit?
So architects do square and hew
Green trees that in the forest grew.

21–2. magic . . . pine] Cp. Shakespeare, *The Tempest* (1610–11), I.ii, ll. 291–3: 'it was mine Art,/When I arriv'd and heard thee, that made gape/The pine, and let thee out.'
22. pine] a) suffer (*OED* v. 2) b) become enfeebled (*OED* v. 5).
23. it] i.e. the body.
29–30. ready . . . again] Cp. James Howell, *The Vision: or A Dialog between the Soul and the Bodie* (1652), 2: 'Bodie. . . . you are the Pilot that steers this frail Bark'; ibid., l. 23: '*Soul. And at that port arrive, free./Where I may ever rest from shipwrack.*' See also Seneca, *Agamemnon*, ll. 589–92: 'Heu quam dulce malum mortalibus additum/vitae dirus amor, cum pateat malis/effugium et miseros libera mors vocet/portus aeterna placidus quiete.' (Alas, how alluring a bane is appointed unto mortals, even dire love of life, though refuge from their woes opes wide, and death with generous hand invites the wretched, a peaceful part of everlasting rest.) See also Petrarch, *Rime Sparse*, 80. Bossy, *CL*, 28 (1976), 160–1, notes an example of this image in old French poetry.
29. the port] i.e. death for the body, eternal life for the soul. *gain*] arrive at (*OED* v.² 7).
31. physic] medicine (*OED* n. 4).
33. cramp of Hope] suggests an ironic distortion of the figure of the anchor, the emblem of hope (from a reference in Heb. 6:19: 'Which hope we have as an anchor to the soul.'), since a cramp was a grappling iron (*OED* n.² 1), as well as a muscular pain (*OED* n.¹); see also *The Definition of Love*, ll. 7–8 n. *cramp*] Cp. Shakespeare, *The Tempest* (1610), I.ii, ll. 327–8: 'to-night thou shalt have cramps,/Side-stitches that shall pen thy breath up.'; John Hall, 'To his Tutor, Master Pawson, An Ode' (1646), l. 67: 'Nor anger pull with cramps the soul.'

34. palsy] nervous disease, causing impairment (including involuntary motion) or suspension of muscular action and sensation (*OED* n. 1).
35. pestilence] fatal epidemic, especially bubonic plague (*OED* n. 1, 1 b).
37–8. Cp. James Howell, *The Vision: or A Dialog between the Soul and the Bodie* (1652), 46: 'sadness contracts, and mirth too suddenly dilates my spirits, and makes them break out into violent fits of laughter.'
38. other madness] i.e. weeping.
40. forgo] pass over (*OED* v. 2).
43–4. Cp. *Upon Appleton House*, ll. 1–4: 'Within this sober frame expect/Work of no foreign architect;/That unto caves the quarries drew,/And forests did to pastures hew'; *AGP*, in *MPW*, II. 258: 'men, instead of squaring their Governments by the Rule of Christianity; have shaped Christianity by the Measure of their Government . . . and bungling Divine and Humane things together, have been always hacking and hewing one another, to frame an irregular Figure of Political Congruity'. The body speaks from a similar perspective to M.'s mower (see above, *The Mower against Gardens*), taking the side of nature against art. Duncan-Jones, *N & Q*, n.s. 3 (1956), 383–4, notes a further echo of these lines in M.'s defence of John Howe, *Remarks Upon a Late Disingenuous Discourse* (1678) in which the image of architects hewing trees is disavowed; it is suggested that M. was acknowledging and correcting a mistake made in the poem. Cp. also Cowley, *Davideis* (1656), 4, ll. 31–8, 'Souls form and build those mansions where they dwell,/Whoe're but sees his Body must confess/The Architect no doubt, could be no less.'
43. architects] master-builders (*OED* n. 1). *square*] make timber square or rectangular in cross-section (*OED* v. 1 b).

14
The Nymph Complaining for the Death of her Fawn

Date. Very few clues exist for assisting the dating of composition of this poem. The dating of the earliest usage of vocabulary in l. 1 to the early 1640s is one guide; the echoes of works published in 1647 and 1662 (see below, *Sources and Genre*) another. There are also similarities with the pastoral literature associated with the imprisonment, trial and execution of Charles I (see below, 67). In the light of this evidence, it may cautiously be conjectured that the poem was composed in the late 1640s, possibly in the earlier months of 1649, following the regicide.

The close association of ll. 55–72 with a poem by Rowland Watkyns published in 1662, which M. would most probably not have seen in manuscript before then (see below, *Sources and Genre*), points to the possibility that M. may have written his poem in two stages, with a long period of time in between. But the volume of Watkyns' poetry in which the poem appears, *Flamma sine Fumo* (1662), is markedly royalist: it is most unlikely that M. would have been writing verse like this in the early 1660s.

Publication. 1681. Yale University, Osborn MS b 150 (*Υ 14*), a late seventeenth-century verse miscellany, contains a copy of the poem with some missing lines (ll. 17–24), which may be evidence of more than one version of the poem being in circulation. It is significant that the lines missing are those concerned with divine justice and blood guilt: some of the most politically sensitive lines in the poem. This MS is not listed in *IELM*.

Sources and Genre. Kerrigan, ed. (1991), 66, includes the poem as an example of the lover's complaint, a genre defined by its manifest theme, but including a variety of modes and poetic forms. Allen (1960), 94, identifies the poem as an epicedium (funeral song), but for the song to be performed while the subject is still alive (the fawn dies as the poem concludes) is unusual. Sellin (in Summers and Pebworth, eds (1992), 86–100) argues that the strongest generic presence in the poem is the *calyca*, as practised by Stesichorus,

a lament sung by a young girl dying of love for her lover.

Several Greek and Latin poems deal with the death of favourite pets: the *Greek Anthology*, 7.189–90, 192, 195, 198–207; 386, 530, 549; Catullus, 2; Ovid, *Amores*, II.6 on Corinna's parrot (which closes, like M.'s poem, with a monument to the dead animal). The killing of Silvia's stag by Ascanius in Virgil, *Aeneid*, VII, ll. 475–510, has been seen as a source of M.'s narrative, but this is challenged by Friedman (1970), 102–3, and Spinrad (*PMLA*, 97 (1982), 50–9). The killing of Silvia's deer began the war between the Trojans and the men of Latium, just as Agamemnon's killing of Artemis's deer (Sophocles, *Electra*, ll. 565–72; *Aeneid*, II, ll. 116–17) resulted in the sacrifice of his daughter Iphigenia. These myths exist as significant, threatening shadowy presences behind the poem, relating to its own civil war context. By contrast, William Browne's description of Aletheia rising from the corpse of Fida's hind takes up where M.'s poem stops, developing the themes of rebirth and renewal, as opposed to the metamorphosis into stasis of both fawn and nymph (*Britannia's Pastorals* (1613), 1,4, 155–224).

Ovid's *Metamorphoses* provide several important moments in the Nymph's complaint (below, l. 28 n., 99–100, 116 n.). In *Metamorphoses*, XII, ll. 27 ff., Diana's hind is killed by Agamemnon. More significantly, *Metamorphoses*, X, ll. 104–42, contains the story of Cyparissus, lover and murderer of his deer. In the same passage, Sylvanus (the precursor of M.'s Sylvio) is in turn Cyparissus's lover (see also Spenser, *The Faerie Queene*, I.vi.16–17, where Sylvanus is the murderer of the deer). A more minor affinity is detected by Berger, *MLS*, 3 (1967), 297, who argues that the nymph may be read as both Pygmalion and his statue (*Metamorphoses*, X, ll. 243–97).

Scodel (1991), 224, suggests that the epitaph at the end of the poem (ll. 111–22) is indebted to Ovid's *Heroides* II (Phyllis to Demophoon) and VII (Dido to Aeneas), both of which are lovers' complaints ending in epitaphs that will be inscribed on the tombs of the lovers after they have committed suicide.

The poem is strongly influenced by the traditions of pastoral verse and drama in Renaissance Europe and England. Coughlan (1980), 180–1, finds a close parallel to the description of the fawn in Calpurnius Siculus, *Bucolica*, VI, ll. 25–45:

Lycidas
Fingas plura licet: nec enim potes, inprobe, uera
exprobrare mihi, sicut tibi multa Lycotas.
Sed quid opus unan consumere tempora lite?
Ecce uenit Mnasyllus: erit, nisi forte recusas,
arbiter inflatis noncredulis, improbe, uerbis.

Astylus
Malueram, fateor, uel praedamnatus abire
quam tibi certanti partem committere uocis.
Ne tamen hoc impune feras: en aspicis illum
candida qui medius cubat inter lilia, ceruum?
Quamuis hunc Petale mea diligat, accipe uictor.
Scit frenos et ferre iugum sequiturque uocantem
credulus et mensae non improba porrigit ora.
Aspicis ut fruticat late caput utque sub ipsis
cornibus et tereti pendent redimicula collo?
Aspicis ut niueo frons inretita capistro
lucet et, a dorso quae totam circuit aluum,
alternat uitreas lateralis cingula bullas?
Cornua subtiles ramosaque tempora molles
impliceure rosae rutiloque monilia torque
extreme ceruice natant, ubi pendulus apri
dends sedet et niuea distinguit pectora luna.

(Lycidas: 'More lies you may tell; and yet, you rascal, you can't bring true reproaches against me like all that Lycotas brings against you. But what need to waste our time in fruitless wrangling? See, here comes Mnasyllus. He will be (unless mayhap you shirk the challenge) an umpire undeceived, you rascal, by boastful words.'
Astylus: 'I own I had preferred to depart, even though condemned beforehand, rather than match a bit of my voice against your rivalry. Still, that you may not go unpunished for all this – look, do you see yonder stag that reclines in the heart of the white lilies? Though my own Petale is fond of him, take him if you win. He is trained to bear reins and yoke and follows a call with trustfulness; 'tis no glutton mouth he shoots out for his food. Do you see how his head branches wide with antlers, and how the necklet hangs beneath his very horns and shapely neck? Do you see how his forehead gleams, enmeshed with snowy frontlet, and how from his back the side girth, circling his whole belly, has amulets of glass on this side and on that? Roses twine neatly round his horns and softly round his branching temples; and a collaret with red-gold chain dangles from beneath the neck, where a boar's pendent tusk is set, showing up his breast with snow-white crescent.')

Marc'antonio Flaminio's *Carminum* (Florence, 1552), IV is concerned with a nymph (literally a 'goat-girl') goat that dies:

Adeste ò Satyri, bonique Fauni, &
Quicquid capripedum est ubique Diuum,
Mecum numina sancta lacrimate.
Vestra mortua bella caprimulga est,
Illa candida, bella caprimulga . . . (243)

(Pay attention, o satyrs, fauns and all god-like goat-footed creatures everyone, to my copious holy weeping! Your beautiful nymph is dead; this innocent, beautiful nymph . . .).

Parry, *CS*, 5 (1993), 244–51 (244) argues that the poem is indebted to Guarini's *Il Pastor Fido*, and Fanshawe's 1647 translation of the text. Parallels are noted between M.'s pastoral characters and Guarini's characters of Silvio the huntsman and Dorinda the nymph. Silvio prefers hunting to love, and in II.ii loses a favourite hound in pursuit of a deer. Dorinda finds the hound and tries to exchange it for a kiss from Silvio. A debate on love ensues but the lovers part unhappily, leaving a distressed Dorinda. Parry suggests 'some imaginative reshuffling of this scene on Marvell's part seems to lie behind the central section of his poem', and that the poem, like the Fanshawe translation, is closely related to civil war experiences. In the case of several local echoes, M. appears to be reversing, or complicating, Guarini's Italian and Fanshawe's English.

Williamson, *MP*, 51 (1954), 268–71, notes the strong presence of the language of the Song of Solomon in the poem, especially ll. 71–92. Allen (1960), 98–114 places the poem in the tradition of medieval poetry in which the deer and its slaughter are associated with the life and sacrifice of Christ. Antecedent to this tradition is an ancient notion that deer were special creatures, spirit-bearing, sometimes workers of miracles or prophetic. Thus, noting the Renaissance identification of Diana with the Virgin, Allen (1960), 112, suggests that the statue of the weeping nymph with the fawn at her feet bears comparison with representations of the weeping mother of Christ, and the *Pietà*. Red and white were associated with the Virgin in medieval iconography as much as they were with secular love themes. Skelton, *N & Q*, n.s. 203 (1958), 531–2, notes the similarity of this passage to parts of Rowland Watkyns' 'The Holy Maid', in *Flamma sine Fumo* (1662), 104–6, which is based on the imagery of the Song of Solomon, and which involves the death of the 'Beloved', who corresponds to M.'s fawn:

My Beloved's white and ruddy,
My red sins made him all bloody:
His head is like fine gold, most free
From dross, and all impurity:
His gracious eyes are like Doves eyes;
And in his cheeks composed lies
A bed of spices and flowers sweet,
Where all perfumes together meet:
His mouth breathes roses; and no bliss
Can equal his delicious kiss.
But see, where my Beloved lies,
And courts me with his dying eyes:
He spreads his arms me to embrace;
Who would not love so sweet a face? (ll. 27–40)

Matthew Stevenson's 'Phyllis' Funeral', in *Occasion's Off-spring* (1645), 6–8, is spoken by a shepherdess who is dying in front of her sheep. But where, in Stevenson's poem, the symbolism is focused on Phyllis, in M.'s poem, the fawn is the centre of attention.

Many English pastorals were manifestly concerned with religious and political issues. A poem belonging to Fairfax during M.'s stay at Nun Appleton was his uncle Edward Fairfax's 'An Egloge', an allegorical pastoral dialogue between Lycaon (Roman Catholicism) and Hermes (Protestantism). Flora is allowed by Lycaon to keep her goats, but Hermes predicts their apocalyptic end: 'Sitting on Isis flowrie banke I spied/On a white horse a crowned Monarch ride/Vpon his thigh was write his wonderous name/Out of his mouth a Sword two-edged came/Flora hir beast & and all her goats he slew/And in a lake of fire ther bodys threw' (Bod. MS Fairfax 40, 655–6). M.'s poem echoes this kind of allegorically religious pastoral.

That roses and lilies were the emblems of Charles I and Queen Henrietta Maria leads Parry, op. cit. (247), to construe ll. 71–100 as an allegorical reference to royalty and 'the presence of complex images and ideas that relate to the death of Charles I' (through the association of the regicide with the passion of Christ). To this extent, Parry speculates that the poem is M.'s own version of Charles's posthumous apology, *Eikon Basilike*, noting the reference to the fawn's 'image' in l. 121. Two further contextual issues of the 1640s are echoed in the poem: the desecration of the national church by the forces of Puritan zeal (see below, l. 1 n., and Coolidge, *PQ*, 59 (1980), 11–25), and the accusation of Parliament

that Charles had earned blood-guilt on account of his alleged responsibility for the spilling of blood, for which crime he must be executed (see Crawford, *JBS*, 16 (1977), 41–69). In M.'s poem, the blood-guilt belongs to the troopers: M. is possibly presenting a royalist version of blood-guilt.

But if M.'s poem does relate to regicide literature, the connections are more complex than Parry suggests. There was certainly a considerable body of royalist and regicide literature in pastoral: e.g. *Calvers Royal Vision* (12 October 1648), in which the author describes himself as a divinely inspired 'Poore sily shepheard.' A poem in *The Princely Pellican* (2 June 1649) represents the dead king as 'Albion's Niobe' (see Ovid, *Metamorphoses*, VI, ll. 165 ff.), rather than the fawn. However, to read the nymph as the king puts an unbearable strain of interpretation on the poem. Pastoral elegies that do relate directly and obviously to the regicide tend not to have so much in common with M.'s vocabulary, although there are some similar topoi and narrative patterns. *Orpheus his descerpsion* (February 1649), a manuscript poem in the Thomason collection (E 541(8)), articulates a very different pastoral scene to M.'s:

See see wild Satyrs how they runne
All smeard with Blood, what have they done?
The Muses all in a rout do stray
Phaebus hath flung his harpe away,
    And heer's a Crowne
    Comes tumbling downe
The head rould after which it did weare,
Whose Blood and plaints yet sad the aire.

Yet at the end, and like the nymph and the fawn, the narrating swain and his lover petrify as they look at the monument to the disappeared king. See also Silver, *ELH*, 68 (2001), 29–55 and Hester Pulter, 'The invitation into the Countrey to my D D M.P P P 1647 when his sacred Maj:^tie was at unhappy hour', ll. 71–4: 'But oh those time now changed bee/Sad Metamorphosis wee see./For since Amiintas went away/Shepherds and sheepe goe all astray.' (University of Leeds, Brotherton MS LT.q.32, p. 6).

Style and Versification. The poem consists of eleven verse paragraphs, each between twenty-four and four lines in length. Fowler (1970), 198–9, notes the connection in numerology between eleven and mourning (see also Ormerod and Wortham, 283). The first paragraph is the longest. Goldberg (1986), 15, divides the poem into four sections, which correspond to four modes of organizing speech, and four associated genres concerned with speech: antithesis (sonnet), ll. 1–24; repetition (lyric stanza), ll. 25–39; allegory (Spenserian epic), ll. 55–92; epigraph (epigram), ll. 93–122. The first passage is marked by a high degree of antithesis; statements contradict each other throughout the poem (e.g. l. 29, 'I know'; l. 47, 'I do not know'). The poem's rhymed tetrameters are associated with the speech of satyrs and nymphs in pastoral drama, and with simple speakers (cp. Rowland Watkyns, 'The Holy Maid' (1658)), or verse associated with leisure and retreat (e.g. Dudley, Lord North, 'To winne her from resolving upon a Cloyster'd life', in *A Forest of Varieties* (1645), 18–19). The nymph is given her own simple diction and syntax (six lines are entirely monosyllabic; nine others contain six monosyllables; the word 'it' is repeated twenty-six times), and her own trite punning. The syntax is sometimes awkward (e.g. ll. 7–8), the sentences frequently very brief and exclamatory, as the nymph struggles to express her grief. In this way, repeated conjunctions cloud her logic (see, e.g., ll. 9, 12). The nymph seems barely to know that she is speaking verse, as lines are frequently run on, and periods occur at the caesura. Only the section based upon the Song of Solomon (ll. 71–92) escapes from these paradigms to achieve a less interrupted metre. Although it may be the result of compositorial clumsiness and incomprehension, the punctuation of *1681* aids this effect (where it has been emended here, the original effects are nonetheless preserved). At ll. 35–6 and ll. 41–2 dental consonants and frisking rhythms imitate the playfulness of the fawn; from l. 63 to l. 70 the fawn's agility is intimated in disyllabic trochees: 'little silver', 'pretty skipping'. But none of this should be accepted without Colie's important caveat ((1970), 88) that some vocabulary (l. 16), and some punctuation (l. 5) breaks the fiction of innocence. Reconciling both poles are elements such as the rhyming word 'in' (l. 23) which appears to be typical of the nymph's naivety, yet which is also so placed that the author's (but not the nymph's) interest in religious allegory is apparent.

Modern Criticism. Dove regarded the poem as M.'s masterpiece; its sense of removed wonder, reconciling the actual and the fantastic, attracted other nineteenth-century readers, such as Poe (Collins). As an exemplary pastoral, Dennis (1883), 147–52, thought the middle section, ll. 55–92, the strongest part.

The poem has generated more interpretative difficulties in twentieth-century criticism than any of M.'s lyrics. Much interpretation of the poem has been concerned with the question of whether or not the poem is in some sense an allegory. While some have acknowledged literary presences within the poem that were conventionally understood to be allegorical (such as the Song of Songs), they have nonetheless denied that the poem is referring to anything in particular. Convinced that a psychological realism is intimated by the simple prosody of the poem, Foster, *UKCR*, 22 (1955), 72–8, argues that the poem is an exercise in exploring the primitivism and childlike consciousness of the nymph herself. Others have argued for an understanding of the poem as a record of different kinds of personal history (Asp, *PLL*, 14 (1978), 394–405; Baruch, *EA*, 31 (1978), 152–60). Morgan, in Stanivukovic (2001), 71–93, argues that the nymph's sexuality is lesbian. On the other hand, others have argued that the fawn represents the Anglican church (Emerson, *EA*, 8 (1955), 107–10), Christ (Bradbrook and Lloyd-Thomas (1940), 4–50), the Holy Ghost (Hartman, *EIC*, 18 (1968), 113–35), Charles I (Sandstroem, *SEL*, 30 (1990), 92–114), and the nymph's virginity (Reeves and Seymour-Smith (1969)), or her lost child (Jones, *The Explicator*, 26 (1968), item 73). The nymph herself has been seen as a representation of the soul, as allegorized innocence confronting its inevitable doom in experience (Nevo, *SEL*, 5 (1965), 1–21), as the church recalling the life of Christ (King (1977), 47–65), and as the archetypal 'great mother' (Teunissen and Hinz, *ELH*, 45 (1978), 410–28). Allen (1960), 107–10, sees the nymph's garden as a Platonic representation of the human mind. Although he denies allegory, Guild, *MLQ*, 29 (1968), 385–94, argues that in the context of the postfiguring of the episode from *Aeneid* VII, the poem represents the suffering of nonpartisans in times of war. Hartman, ibid., combines allegory and history in a reading that suggests that the poem portrays an impatience to force 'a reconciliation of nature and spirit, parallel to the regicidal revolt of the Puritans'.

The disjunction of voices and genres in the poem has been regarded both as a failure of generic mixture (Colie (1970), 71), and as a questioning of pastoral and the idea of the contemplative life itself (Norford, *ELH*, 41 (1974), 50–73). Extending this concern with the self-referential, Goldberg (1986), 14–37, argues that the poem is wholly and only concerned with the problems of its own articulation: 'The poem defies referentiality. It is only, and entirely, self-referential, "about" itself, about how the text comes to be, how it relates to antecedent texts, what it represents in the world' (14). Through its series of self-denying voices, the poem becomes 'an apotheosis of the diminutive powers of poetry' (15; quoting Hartman), but through these limitations, M. 'allows us to hear the echo of a voice that is his own' (15).

The Nymph Complaining for the Death of her Fawn

The wanton troopers riding by
Have shot my fawn and it will die.
Ungentle men! They cannot thrive
To kill thee. Thou ne'er didst alive
5 Them any harm: alas nor could
Thy death yet do them any good.
I'm sure I never wished them ill;
Nor do I for all this; nor will:
But, if my simple prayers may yet
10 Prevail with heaven to forget

Thy murder, I will join my tears
Rather than fail. But, O my fears!
It cannot die so. Heaven's King
Keeps register of everything:
15 And nothing may we use in vain.
Ev'n beasts must be with justice slain;
Else men are made their deodands.
Though they should wash their guilty hands
In this warm life-blood, which doth part
20 From thine, and wound me to the heart,
Yet could they not be clean: their stain
Is dyed in such a purple grain.
There is not such another in
The world, to offer for their sin.
25   Unconstant Sylvio, when yet
I had not found him counterfeit,
One morning (I remember well)
Tied in this silver chain and bell,
Gave it to me: nay and I know
30 What he said then; I'm sure I do.
Said he, 'Look how your huntsman here
Hath taught a fawn to hunt his dear.'
But Sylvio soon had me beguiled.
This waxèd tame, while he grew wild,

Title. Nymph . . . Fawn] nymphs (*OED* n. 1) and fauns (*OED* n.) were both kinds of deity in classical mythology. But M. primarily means simply a young maiden (*OED* n. 2) and a young fallow deer ('fawn': *OED* n.¹ 2).

1. wanton] a) undisciplined (*OED* a. A1) b) cruel (*OED* a. A 5). *troopers*] horse soldiers (*OED* n. 1); first used of the Scottish Covenanting Army that invaded England in 1640, then applied to Parliamentary cavalry during the 1640s, although both Royalists and Parliamentarians had 'Troops' (sixty mounted men) of horse. Cp. also Phineas Fletcher, *Sicelides* (1631), I.iii, l. 1: 'Saw you the troope which past along here?'

4. To] That; *Υ 14*.

9–11. if . . . murder] a mutation of Luke 23:34, where the New Testament's 'forgive' is changed to 'forget': 'Then said Jesus, Father, forgive them; for they know not what they do.'

9–12. if my . . . fail] should my simple prayers succeed in persuading heaven to forget your murder, I would add my tears rather than see my plea fail.

9. simple] a) unadorned (*OED* a. A I 3) b) honest (*OED* a. A I 1) c) uneducated (*OED* a. A II 9).

13. so] i.e. unavenged by heaven.

14. register] an account.

15. in vain] treat with contempt (*OED* a. and n. II 6).

17–24. Not in Υ 14.

17. deodands] technically, things (such as animals) given to God (i.e., in fact, to the crown, to be put to pious uses) because they had caused the death of human beings (*OED*); the nymph suggests that men should become deodands for the death of animals, as animals are if they cause the death of men. Parry, *CS*, 5 (1993), 244–51 (246) notes that in Guarini's *Il Pastor Fido* (1647), 435–8, mention is made of a nymph being

sacrificed to Diana (see below, l. 104) for betraying her trust, although no animals are involved in this episode.

18–24. wash . . . sin] in hunting rituals, the hunters washed their hands in the blood of the dead animal to purify themselves. However, the nymph says that the extent of the troopers' crime is such that no such expiation is possible. Roberts, *N & Q*, 49 (2002), 338–43, detects Shakespearian allusions here.

21. stain] i.e. guilt.

22. purple] bloody (*OED* a. 2 d). Latin *purpura* can mean red as well as purple; the association of purple with high office and kings was present in classical literature (see e.g., Virgil, *Georgics*, II, l. 495). *grain*] dye; colour (*OED* n.¹ III 11). Figuratively, 'grain' was also used in connection with moral qualities good and bad, and specifically in connection with the regicide: see, e.g., Henry Thurman, sermon preached at St Mary Magdalen's Church, Oxford, 21 October 1660, reported in Anthony à Wood, *Life and Times*, ed. A. Clark (Oxford, 1891), I.370: 'Sins of so deep a graine as of killing a king.' Wood says this was a blasphemy (although the congregation concurred with the preacher), since Thurman was claiming that Christ would offer no forgiveness for this sin: a sentiment that fits precisely with the nymph's mood.

25. Unconstant] unfaithful (*OED* a. 1).

28. silver . . bell] Cp. Ovid, *Metamorphoses*, X, l. 114, where Cyparissus's stag has a silver boss (*bulla argentea*) on its forehead, translated by Sandys as a 'silver bell'. Like M.'s fawn, the much beloved stag is accidentally killed.

32. dear] a common pun, especially in romance tradition: a) loved one b) deer.

34. waxèd] became (*OED* v.¹ II 9 a).

35 And quite regardless of my smart,
    Left me his fawn, but took his heart.
        Thenceforth I set myself to play
    My solitary time away
    With this: and very well content,
40 Could so mine idle life have spent.
    For it was full of sport; and light
    Of foot, and heart; and did invite
    Me to its game: it seemed to bless
    Itself in me. How could I less
45 Than love it? O I cannot be
    Unkind, t'a beast that loveth me.
        Had it lived long, I do not know
    Whether it too might have done so
    As Sylvio did: his gifts might be
50 Perhaps as false or more than he.
    But I am sure, for ought that I
    Could in so short a time espy,
    Thy love was far more better then
    The love of false and cruel men.
55   With sweetest milk, and sugar, first
    I it at mine own fingers nursed.
    And as it grew, so every day
    It waxed more white and sweet than they.
    It had so sweet a breath! And oft
60 I blushed to see its foot more soft,
    And white (shall I say than my hand?
    Nay any lady's of the land).

        It is a wondrous thing, how fleet
    'Twas on those little silver feet.
65 With what a pretty skipping grace,
    It oft would challenge me the race:
    And when 't had left me far away,
    'Twould stay, and run again, and stay.
    For it was nimbler much than hinds;
70 And trod, as on the foúr winds.
        I have a garden of my own,
    But so with roses overgrown,
    And lilies, that you would it guess
    To be a little wilderness.
75 And all the springtime of the year
    It only lovèd to be there.
    Among the beds of lilies, I
    Have sought it oft, where it should lie;
    Yet could not, till itself would rise,
80 Find it, although before mine eyes.
    For, in the flaxen lilies' shade,
    It like a bank of lilies laid.
    Upon the roses it would feed,
    Until its lips ev'n seemed to bleed:
85 And then to me 'twould boldly trip,
    And print those roses on my lip.
    But all its chief delight was still
    On roses thus itself to fill:
    And its pure virgin limbs to fold
90 In whitest sheets of lilies cold.

35. smart] hurt (*OED* n.¹ 2).
36. heart] a) heart b) hart; see above l. 32 n.
40. idle] a) worthless (*OED* a. 2) b) unoccupied (*OED* a. 4).
41. sport] a) pastime, recreation (*OED* n.¹ I 1) b) merriment (*OED* n.¹ I 2 a–b).
43–4. bless/Itself] make or declare itself happy (*OED* v.¹ 8).
53. then] a standard seventeenth-century spelling of 'than.'
54. men] 1681; man Υ 14.
55. sweetest milk] Cp. Cant. 5:1: 'I have drunk my wine with my milk.'
58. waxed] see above, l. 34 n.
58–9. It . . . breath] Cp. Cant. 5:10, 13, 16: 'My beloved is white and ruddy. . . . His cheeks are as a bed of spices, as sweet flowers: his lips like lillies, dropping sweet smelling myrrh. . . . His mouth is most sweet.'
62. lady's] ladies 1681.
63. fleet] swift (*OED* a. 1).
64. silver] white (*OED* a. 12).
65. pretty . . . grace] Cp. Cant. 2:8: 'Behold, he cometh leaping upon the mountains, skipping upon the hills.'
69–70. Cp. Ps. 104:3: 'who walketh upon the wings of the wind.'
69. hinds] a) female deer (*OED* n.¹ 1) b) countrymen (*OED* n.² 3).
70. as] 1681+; as if Υ 14.
71–92. The rose and the lily (Cant. 2:1; 5:13) were identified with the beloved, who was interpreted as Christ, a frequent figuration in seventeenth-century verse. See, for instance, 'The

Lover', anon. *Eliza's Babe's* (1652), ll. 9–12: 'For He's the purest red and white,/In whom my soule takes her delight:/He to the flowrs their beauty gives,/In him the Rose and Lilly lives.' See also above, *Headnote, Sources and Genre*.
74. wilderness] densely planted section in a formal garden, designed to seem uncultivated (*OED* n. 1 c). Cp. Bacon, *Essay* XLVI (1625), 'Of Gardens' (ed. M. Kiernan (Oxford, 1985), 143): 'For the *Heath*, which was the third part of our Plot, I wish it to be framed, as much as may be, to a *naturall wildnesse*. . . . I like also little *Heaps*, in the Nature of *Mole-hils*, . . . to be set. . . . Some with Red-Roses; Some with Lilium Convallium.' The garden at Wilton, drawn by Isaac de Caus in the 1640s, contained a wilderness of regularly planted trees, bracketed together to give the effect of woodland, bracketed by long tunnels of greenery, through which a river flowed unhindered. The wilderness was placed between intricate broderie patterns and shaped shrubs, and the amphitheatre or 'circus'. See Hunt, in Greengrass *et al.* (1994), 328.
81. flaxen] white (*OED* a. A 2 b); see Gervase Markham, *The Country Farme* (1616), 515: 'That kind of Wheat which among the English is called Flaxen-wheat, being as white or whiter than the finest Flax.'
82–3. Cp. Cant. 2:16: 'My beloved is mine, and I am his: he feedeth among the lillies.'
90. As opposed to the hot 'sheets' of flame that engulf that other martyr, Captain Douglas: see below, *The Last Instructions to a Painter*, ll. 677–80.

Had it lived long, it would have been
Lilies without, roses within.
   O help! O help! I see it faint:
And die as calmly as a saint.
95 See how it weeps. The tears do come
Sad, slowly dropping like a gum.
So weeps the wounded balsam: so
The holy frankincense doth flow.
The brotherless Heliades
100 Melt in such amber tears as these.
   I in a golden vial will
Keep these two crystal tears; and fill
It till it do o'erflow with mine;
Then place it in Diana's shrine.
105   Now my sweet fawn is vanished to
Whither the swans and turtles go:

In fair Elysium to endure,
With milk-white lambs, and ermines pure.
   O do not run too fast: for I
110 Will but bespeak thy grave, and die.
   First my unhappy statue shall
Be cut in marble; and withal,
Let it be weeping too: but there
Th'engraver sure his art may spare;
115 For I so truly thee bemoan,
That I shall weep though I be stone:
Until my tears, still dropping, wear
My breast, themselves engraving there.
There at my feet shalt thou be laid,
120 Of purest alabaster made:
For I would have thine image be
White as I can, though not as thee.

97. *balsam*] tree whose sap was held to have healing powers (*OED* n. II 8); see above, *Upon the Death of Lord Hastings*, l. 54 n.; cp. Crashaw, 'The Weeper' (1646), ll. 67–70: 'There is no need at all/That the Balsame-sweating bough/So coyly should let fall,/His med'cinable Teares.'

98. *frankincense*] aromatic gum resin yielded by trees of the *Boswellia* genus (*OED* n. 1); burned as incense in services of worship.

99–100. *brotherless Heliades . . . these*] the Heliades, daughters of Helios, weeping for their dead brother Phaethon, were turned into poplar trees, their tears into amber: Ovid, *Metamorphoses*, II, ll. 340–66; the Heliades are also mentioned in a later passage just preceding the account of the killing of Cyparissus's stag: *Metamorphoses*, X, l. 91 (see above, l. 28 n.).

100. *Melt . . . tears*] Cp. Ovid, *Metamorphoses*, tr. Golding (1575), II, l. 455: 'Now from these trees flow gummy teares that Amber men doe call'; *idem*, tr. Sandys (1632), 53: 'From these cleere dropping trees, teares yearely flow:/They, hardned by the Sunne, to Amber grow', and Crashaw's 'The Weeper' (1646), ll. 43–4: 'Not the soft Gold which/Steales from the Amber-weeping Tree.'

101–2. *I . . . tears*] Cp. Ps. 56:8: 'Put thou my tears into thy bottle: are they not in thy book?'; Crashaw, 'The Weeper' (1646), ll. 34–6: 'Angels with their Bottles come;/And draw from these full Eyes of thine,/Their Masters water, their owne Wine.'

104. *Diana*] goddess of hunting and virginity; Diana's stag was killed by Agamemnon during a hunt: see Ovid, *Metamorphoses*, XII, ll. 27 ff.

106. *turtles*] turtledoves; Cant. 2:12: 'the voice of the turtle is heard in our land'.

107. *Elysium*] in Greek mythology, abode of the blessed after death.

108. *ermines*] stoats, animals of the weasel family, whose fur is wholly white in winter, except for a black tip on the tail (*OED* n. 1).

110. *bespeak*] a) make arrangements for (*OED* v. 5) b) be the evidence of [by becoming a statue] (*OED* v. 7) c) tell of [in ll. 111–20].

112. *marble*] cp. Guarini, *Il Pastor Fido*, trans. Fanshawe (1647), l. 4108: 'Art thou a tender breast, or marble hard?'

113. *there*] *1681*; here Υ 14.

115. *bemoan*] lament (OED v. 1).

116. *weep . . . stone*] recalling Niobe, who was turned into a statue but continued to weep after her excessive pride was punished by Latona, Diana and Apollo with the death of her children: Ovid, *Metamorphoses* VI, ll. 165 ff., especially ll. 286–312. An engraving depicting the young, deceased Lord Hastings surrounded by weeping muses, and with Latin verses by Edward Montagu that make reference to Niobe, was attached to the second edition of *Lachrymae Musarum* (1650), in which M.'s *Upon the Death of the Lord Hastings* appeared (see fig. 2). Cp. also Hester Pulter, 'Upon the Death of my deare and lovely Daughter J.P. Jane Pulter, baptized May 1 1625 and died Oct 8 1646 Aet. 20', ll. 56–8: 'Whilst Shee (ah mee) clos'd up her lovely eyes/Her soule being seated in her place of birth/I turned a Niobe as shee turn'd earth.' (in Stevenson and Davidson, eds (2001), 193).

120. *alabaster*] fine-grained, soft white, opaque or translucent stone, used for statues or vases; by 'purest', the nymph means 'whitest'. Cp. Guarini, *Il Pastor Fido*, trans. Fanshawe (1647), l. 4109: 'I would not idolize fair Alabaster.'

Date. ?Late 1640s–early 1650s. The poem is extremely hard to date. The sources are common with those lyrics that can be more confidently dated to the later 1640s or very early 1650s. The subject matter relates to two poems associated with the early 1650s (*The Picture of Little T.C. in a Prospect of Flowers* and *Upon a Eunuch: a Poet*). The aesthetic experimentation, great refinement of form and sentiments, and political undertones, suggest any point within this general period.

Publication. 1681.

Genre and Sources. The poem is derived from a classical tradition in which an adult amorously solicits the love of a child or youth. Leishman (1966), 167, notes in particular an epigram by Philodemius in the *Greek Anthology* (V.124; see also V.33):

Οὔπω σοι καλύκων γυμνὸν θέρος οὐδὲ μελαίνει
    Βότρυς ὁ παρθενίους πρωτοβόλων χάριτας·
Ἀλλ' ἤδη θοὰ τόξα νέοι θήγουσιν Ἔρωτες,
    Λυσιδίκη, καὶ πῦρ τύφεται ἐγκρύφιον.
φεύωμεν, δυσέρωτες, ἕως, βέλος οὐκ ἐπὶ νευρῇ
    Μάντις ἐγὼ μεγάλης αὐτίκα πυρκαϊῆς.

(Your summer is not yet bare of its sheathes, nor darkening is the grape-cluster now first out-shooting maiden graces; but already young Loves are sharpening swift arrows, Lysidice, and fire is smouldering concealed. Let us fly, we wretched lovers, while as yet the shaft is not upon the string: I prophesy a mighty conflagration soon.)

Horace, *Carmina*, I.xxiii, is an address of an older male to a timid young girl who shuns him, while *Carmina*, II.v, is a description of an as yet immature girl, on the brink of sexual initiation. Horace fused elements of the Greek poets, the anthologists, Anacreon and Theocritus, and this type of poem found its way into Latin and vernacular anthologies of the sixteenth and seventeenth centuries (e.g., ?John Gough, *The Academy of Compliments* (1646)). But, unlike the classical poems, M.'s young love is categorized as a child, and there is a jealous father.

The topos occurs in verse by M.'s contemporaries. Carew's 'The second Rapture' (1640), ll. 7–17, is uncompromisingly erotic, containing none of M.'s delicate discrimination:

Give me wench about thirteen,
Already voted to the queen
Of Lust and lovers; whose soft hair,
Fann'd with the breath of gentle air,
O'erspreads her shoulders like a tent,
And is her veil and ornament;
Whose tender touch will make the blood
Wild in the aged and the good;
Whose kisses, fast'ned to the mouth
Of threescore years and longer slouth,
Renew the age.

Structure, Style and Versification. The poem is written in trochaic heptasyllables, organized in four-line stanzas and rhyming abab. Jonson used the form in his two Catullan seduction poems in *Volpone* (1606) ('Come, my Celia, let us prove' (III.vii, ll. 166–83); 'Kiss me, sweet: the wary lover' (III.vii, ll. 236–9); also published in *The Forest* (1616)). The first line of M.'s poem is exceptional, having an extra syllable: the poem begins with a dactyl. Notable conciseness of syntax (e.g. ll. 24–5) is accompanied by only one prosodic feature within the regular metrical pattern: the exaggerated caesura in l. 17. St. V uses the *carpe diem* motif. The poem is divided into two halves, the first ending in ritual sacrifice, the second in ritual crowning. The argument works by a series of discrete 'clarifications' and redefinitions in each stanza, until the moment of reciprocal crowning in the final stanza, which has been seen in its tonal qualities as combining the gravity of high courtliness with the simplicity and circularity of a nursery rhyme (Bradbrook and Lloyd-Thomas (1940), 50; Rees (1989), 92).

Modern Criticism. There is a general agreement that the tone of the poem is uncertain, and that our capacity to engage with the poem personally is hindered by the adoption of personifications. Uncertainty is enhanced by an unstable shift of direction between one stanza and the next: green innocence (st. III) is replaced by the image of a sacrifice (st. IV), thereby converting love into lust despite an explicit dissociation of the two realms. This effect is enhanced by the close proximity of logical connectives within related but distinct arguments: 'So' (ll. 21, 28, 29), 'Thus' (l. 25). Whatever the claims to pleasure, there is always a threat: time might defeat pleasure; the sacrifice to pleasure is the death of innocence. Yet what has struck most commentators is the exclusion of 'mature passion', and 'womanhood', a quality that has sometimes been seen as a limitation (Martz in Patrides, ed. (1978), 210; Ellrodt in Patrides, ed. (1978), 220). In fact, st. IV celebrates masculine sexuality, while the infant addressed remains ungendered, and is likened to a king rather than a queen in st. VII (see Hammond, *SC*, 11 (1996), 109). The poem seems thus to be latently homoerotic, and is certainly deprived of most of the signals associated with heterosexual desire. Colie (1970), 54, notes that the poem exhibits a predatory love by an elder for a younger person, as opposed to the protective love offered in *The Picture of Little T.C. in a Prospect of Flowers*.

What most commentators have taken as an analogy, Venuti (lecture at Renaissance studies conference, University of Reading, 1989; confirmed by correspondence, June 2001) regards as a serious comment, by means of analogy, on the nature of the state. The mutual coronation in sts. VII–VIII is regarded as a demonstration through a love poem of the mutual responsibilities of monarchs and subjects, even an image of elective monarchy.

Young Love

I

Come little infant, love me now,
    While thine unsuspected years
Clear thine agèd father's brow
    From cold jealousy and fears.

II

5   Pretty, surely, 'twere to see
    By young Love old Time beguiled:
While our sportings are as free
    As the nurse's with the child.

III

Common beauties stay fifteen;
10   Such as yours should swifter move;
Whose fair blossoms are too green
    Yet for Lust, but not for Love.

IV

Love as much the snowy lamb
    Or the wanton kid does prize,
15 As the lusty bull or ram,
    For his morning sacrifice.

---

1. infant] the word derives from Latin *infans*, meaning a young child, one not yet able to speak (*OED* n.[1] 1 a), but in English 'infant' can technically mean one who has not reached his or her majority (*OED* n.[1] 2).

2. unsuspected] innocent (of sexual impropriety, because the young lover is sexually immature). The word is appropriate because Latin *suspicio* means 'to look upwards at' (as a child would to an adult) as well 'to mistrust.'

4. cold jealousy] as opposed to the 'hot jealousy' of a rival lover.

5. Pretty] a) beautiful (*OED* a. II 4) b) clever, ingenious (*OED* a. II 2 b) c) admirable (*OED* a. II 3).

6. young Love old Time] suggesting two well known allegorical figures, prominent in emblem literature: Cupid with his bow and Father Time with his sickle. *beguiled*] a) charmed (*OED* v. 3) b) deceived (*OED* v. 1) c) diverted (*OED* v. 4); in the sense of 'wiling away the time'; see, e.g., Shakespeare, *Twelfth Night* (1601), III.iii, ll. 40–1: 'I will bespeak our diet,/Whiles you beguile the time.'

7. sportings] a) pleasant pastimes ('sport': *OED* n.[1] I 1) b) amorous encounters ('sport': *OED* n.[1] I 1 b). Latin *lascivus*

translates 'sport' as a) playful and b) lewd. The speaker fails to free 'sporting' entirely from its lascivious associations. See below, l. 14 n. *free*] a) innocent (*OED* a. II 7) b) without obligations (*OED* a. II 6).

9. Common] ordinary (*OED* a. II 11). *stay fifteen*] wait until they are fifteen.

10. move] i.e. mature; there are, however, undertones of the young love 'moving' the passions of the speaker ('move': *OED* v. 7).

11. green] i.e. young, immature (*OED* a. A II 8); but green was associated with lechery: see Williams (1994), II.620.

12. Lust . . . Love] cp. Carew, *The Second Rapture* (1640), ll. 7–9 (reprinted above in *Headnote, Genre and Sources*).

13. snowy] white: suggesting innocence, gentleness, meekness, obedience.

14. wanton] obstinate, unmanageable (*OED* a. A 1 b). Also translates as Latin *lascivus* (see above, l. 7 n.).

15. lusty] a) healthy, vigorous (*OED* a. 5a) b) full of sexual desire (*OED* a. 5).

V

Now then love me: Time may take
    Thee before thy time away:
Of this need we'll virtue make,
20   And learn love before we may.

VI

So we win of doubtful Fate;
    And, if good she to us meant,
We that good shall antedate,
    Or, if ill, that ill prevent.

VII

25 Thus as kingdoms, frustrating
    Other titles to their crown,
In the cradle crown their king,
    So all foreign claims to drown,

VIII

So, to make all rivals vain,
30   Now I crown thee with my love:
Crown me with thy love again,
    And we both shall monarchs prove.

17–20. See above, *Headnote, Structure, Style and Versification.*
18. *before thy time*] i.e. early, before the youth's life has run its natural course.
19. *need*] necessity (*OED* n. 3 a).
20. *may*] a) are able (*OED* v. B II 2) b) are permitted (*OED* v. B II 4).
21. *doubtful*] a) uncertain (*OED* a. 1) b) causing apprehension and fear (*OED* a. 3, 4).
23. *antedate*] enjoy before its (supposed) proper time. Cp. *A Dialogue between Thyrsis and Dorinda,* ll. 27–8: 'How I my future state/By silent thinking antedate.'
24. *ill*] i.e. the possibility that the youthful and ancient lovers may never meet, and enjoy each other. *prevent*] forestall (*OED* v. II 5).

27. *cradle . . . king*] Hammond, *SC,* 11 (1996), 109, writes: 'If Marvell had wanted us to see the child as a girl, he could easily have made the comparison refer to a queen. Critical commentary on this poem has assumed that the child is female, but there is no evidence for this, and the logic of Marvell's similes clearly points the other way.'
28. *So . . . to*] i.e. in order . . . to. *drown*] an image derived from the literal fate suffered by possible claimants to thrones: the Duke of Clarence is stabbed and drowned in a butt of malmsey in Shakespeare's *Richard III* (1592), I.iv.
29. *vain*] a) without hope, futile (*OED* a. I 1) b) seem vainglorious (*OED* a. I 4).

16
To His Coy Mistress

Date. Late 1640s–early 1650s. The poem is assumed by many to be early (e.g. Margoliouth, Donno): a courtly lyric associated with M.'s youthful activities, and showing the influence of the great poets of the early part of the century (especially Donne).

The truncated and variant manuscript version in the hand of Sir William Haward and dated to 1672 (Bod. MS Don. b. 8 (*Bod. 12*), pp. 283–4, reproduced in fig. 5; see Kelliher, *N & Q*, 215 (1970), 254–6) may have been copied from memory, or, despite its obvious corruptions, from an earlier manuscript version of the poem. This is no certain evidence that the version in *1681* was a late revision, but it does suggest that there may well have been earlier incomplete versions of the poem in circulation in M.'s lifetime. Hammond (*SC*, 11 (1996), 115; and in Bell *et al.*, eds (2001), 28) suggests that the Haward MS, with its two extra bawdy lines, and other coarsened elements, may have circulated among coffee-house wits, 'being made more salacious in order to suit the fashionable masculine taste of the 1670s'. This would support a case, made by Hammond, in Bell *et al.*, eds (2001), 25–6, for *Bod. 12* being revised from the text that appeared in *1681*.

The reference to the conversion of the Jews, an event supposed to take place just before the Second Coming of Christ (l. 10), has led some to date the poem in the mid-1650s (1656 being a date regarded by many contemporaries as likely for the start of the Millennium), or, in the light of the reference to 'ten years before', to 1646 or thereabouts (see Sharrock, *TLS*, 31 October 1958, 625; challenged by Duncan-Jones, *TLS*, 5 December 1958, 705).

Given the weight of allusion to, and echo of, poetry published and circulating in the late 1640s and early 1650s in the poem, it seems likely that M. may have drafted the poem in this period. The Haward copy could then be a version corrupted in its copying, in common with many examples of amorous and erotic verse in the Restoration (see Hammond, *ES* (1993), 39–62).

Printed Publication. 1681.

Manuscript Circulation. Copied, *c.* 1672 in *Bod. 12* (see above, *Date.*), and, *c.* 1715, with very minor variations in Leeds, Brotherton Library, MS Lt. 61, fols. 24ᵛ–25ᵛ (*L 3*).

Context. Worden, *HJ*, 27 (1984), 525–47, argues that M. was intimate with a number of poets and men of letters in London in the late 1640s and early 1650s, including John Hall and Marchamont Nedham. The echoes of the works of these other men in M.'s elegiac and panegyrical poetry of these years is attested. There is even a case for suggesting that these poets, including M., constituted a 'school'. Proof of influence by M., or upon M., of contemporary poems is difficult, but *To His Coy Mistress* is a poem in which the presence of other poets is at its greatest.

Sources, Genres and Structure. The poem has been seen as broadly in the tradition of Latin love elegy, pre- and post-Ovidian. More precisely, the poem is an example (almost to a self-parodic degree) of the *carpe diem* motif, most famously exemplified in Catullus' famous and much-imitated fifth poem 'Vivamus, mea Lesbia, atque amemus' (Let us live, my Lesbia, and love). Rees (1989), 93, associates the coy mistress with the *castas puellas* ('decent girls') of another Latin elegist, Propertius (*Elegies*, I.i, l. 5). However, Coughlan (1980), 106, argues that the influence of the Latin elegiac tradition is overestimated: this tradition, and in particular Catullus and Propertius, is richer in range than *carpe diem* poetry, which she locates earlier in the *Greek Anthology*. In several instances, classical *topoi* are reversed (see below, l. 39), or rejected: there is no celebration of the flesh by recourse to flower imagery – *carpe florem*. Within this structure come a series of allusions to the Greek and Latin erotic lyric tradition, the epigram, echoes of Lucretius's *De Rerum Natura*, and a more concrete set of local echoes to English poems (and, less frequently, plays) in or near this tradition, many of them circulated or published in the later 1640s and 1650s, in addition to echoes from the service for the burial of the dead in the Book of Common Prayer. Coughlan (1980), 106 ff., notes the similarity of several epigrams from the *Greek Anthology*, in addition to the directly echoed V.85 (see below, ll. 25–32 n.). See, for instance, V.72: 'Τοῦτον βίος, τοῦτ' αὐτό· Τρυφή βίος. Ἔρρετ' ἀνίαι·/ξωῆς ἀνθρώποις ὀλίγος χρόνος. ἄρτι Λυαίος,/ἄρτι χοροί, στέφανοί τε φιλανθέες, ἄρτι γυναῖκες·/σήμερον ἐσθλὰ πάθω· τὸ γὰρ αὔριον οὐδένι δέλον.' (This is life, and nothing else is; life is delight; away, dull care! Brief are the years of man. Today wine is ours, and the dance, and flowery wreaths, and women. Today let me live well; none knows what may be tomorrow.); V.80: 'Μῆλον ἐγώ· Βάλλει μὲ φίλων σέ τις. Ἀλλ' ἐπινεύσον,/Ξανθίππη· Κἀγὼ καὶ σὺ μαραινόμεθα.' (I am an apple; one who loves thee throws me at thee. But consent, Xanthippe; both thou and I decay.) There are several echoes of different but consecutively placed lyrics in Cowley's *The Mistress* (1647), Herrick's *Hesperides* (1648) and Thomas Stanley's *Poems* (1651), some words and phrases frequent in Benlowes's *Theophania* (1652), and some very direct reworkings of images from John Hall's *Poems* (1646) (see below, ll. 41–6 nn.). There are further echoes of two incompetent poems by Matthew Stevenson, 'To my Coy and Captious Mistress' and 'To my Cozen Coy' in *Occasion's Off-spring* (1645), 16, 36–9 (see below, ll. 19–20, 31–2 nn.). Finally, M.'s poem shares a title with one by Sir Robert Ayton (*c*. 1629–32), which is further evidence that M. was responding to a cliché identified by William Paulet, 'To *the Ingenious Author* Mr Alexand. Brome', ll. 23–6, in Alexander Brome, *Songs and other Poems* (London, 1664), B1ʳ: 'Shall I whine/To a coy Mistress, swear, and lye, and pine,/And dye, and live again, and change more shapes/Then Proteus did, or four and forty Apes.'

Brody (*ELH*, 56 (1989), 53–79 (74)) argues that this 'parodic deconstruction of a cluster of inherited literary forms – the lover's complaint, the blazon, the *carpe diem* exercise' transcends the limitations of these forms, and their clichés to produce a 'radically new, outspoken, and vigorous evocation of sexual intimacy'. Colie (1970), 59, describes this collective effect as 'literally, an expansion', pushing time, space and the abilities of praise poetry beyond its customary limits.

Stewart (in Miner (1971), 133–50) relates the poem to the *ars moriendi* tradition, seeing the sensuous depiction of death, the three-part formula encompassing past, present and future, and the speed of the moment of death as components therein. The poem appears to echo (and perhaps parody) *ars moriendi* religious writing:

> Yea, let us gather our selves together before the supreme decree of death passe out against us at unawares, that so we may meet it with as much readinesse of mind, so it is willing with greediness to receive us, who should not be drifters off of repentance, like *Salomon* sluggard; or any more supersede, flatter, or foster ourselves with vaine and deceitful conceits of the immortalitie of this melting mortalitie, or admire this dying carcasse, which the worms must feed upon ere it be long, or be ravished with the astonishing fabrick of our bodies which are but clay tabernacles, and death at our floating will dissolve the pinnes thereof.
>
> (Ninian Campbell, *A Treatise upon Death*
> (Edinburgh, 1635), sig. E2ʳ⁻ᵛ)

The Epicurean philosophy of living for the moment has been detected in the poem (see, e.g., Diogenes Laertius, *Lives of Eminent Philosophers*, X.125–6), but Coughlan (1980), 171, notes that *carpe diem* poetry is customarily anti-philosophical. Yet, as Smith (in Smuts, ed. (1996), 177–209 (183)), argues, the *carpe diem* motif was used by continental epicureans, such as Montaigne, from the late sixteenth century onwards. The poem is, in that view, a very serious parody (from a Puritan point of view) of epicurean beliefs, then prevalent at the exiled court in Paris, and made public through publications by royalists, such as Cowley in *The Mistress* (1647). Epicurean beliefs are also undermined by being placed ironically alongside providentialist references (e.g. ll. 29–30, 45–6). Images from Cowley are combined to rebut epicureanism with exaggeratedly expressed Christian teachings concerning mortality (l. 24): Cowley, it is argued, is under attack. The reference to human desire as animalistic (l. 38) is also epicurean: M.'s representation is seen as ironically self-defeating at the speaker's expense, who is presented as an epicurean with no knowledge of the realm of grace. Several alchemical resonances are discussed by Abraham (1990), 287–319.

Ray, *RES*, 44 (1993), 386–8, notes echoes with Sandys' translation of Ovid's *Metamorphoses* (1632), remarking that the male speaker of M.'s poem is voicing Ovid's echo (hence the word-play at l. 27), and that the mistress corresponds to Narcissus (both are proud 'that neither youth nor Mayden' might them touch). Hammond (*SC*, 11 (1996), 112–13) similarly notes the presence of vocabulary and thematic echoes from the Narcissus episode in Golding's earlier translation of Ovid's *Metamorphoses* (see below, ll. 26 n., 33–6 n.). These similarities are enhanced by further echoes from Ovid's Latin and from Renaissance commentaries on Ovid (see footnotes for details). In accordance with other sources (see below, 234, l. 591 n.), M. may also have been attracted by finding his name in Latin three times in the Latin ('miratur . . . mirabilis . . . mirantia', *Metamorphoses*, III, ll. 424, 503). Hammond argues that 'there are sufficient traces of the Narcissus story in Marvell's text to suggest that when he composed this poem about desire for a woman, Marvell's imagination was dwelling on other forms of desire'. This sense of another preoccupation is offered to the extent that the poem is noticeably less interested in the heterosexual erotic than its sources in Donne and Herrick.

Several commentators have seen the structure of the tripartite logical syllogism in the poem. Leishman (1966), 70, regards the poem as one that out-Donnes Donne in its continuous argument, its rigidly syllogistic structure and its 'essentially dramatic tone'. For Low and Pival, *JEGP*, 68 (1969), 414–21, these correspond to the vegetable, mineral and finally animal states, the purpose of the first two being to persuade the mistress of the attractiveness of the animal state of lust, where pleasure and pain are one (l. 43); this honest and unironic ending being itself a reversal of the lightness usually found in *carpe diem* conclusions. Sokol, *ES*, 71 (1990), 244–52, argues that not the formal syllogism, but another kind of logical argument, the *reductio ad absurdum* (1. a proposition and a chain of reasoning from A to B; 2. the impossibility of 1; 3. therefore, not A), and a travesty of it, is present. The conclusion that lust must be satisfied is a fallacious conclusion, built on top of the opening proposition of 'Had we but world enough' and the following acknowledgement of the foreshortening of time. Thus, the poem succeeds through a 'contrived collision between its emotional impulse and its purported form'. Sokol contends further that the poem parodies an already acknowledged fallacious form of logic, the *modus tollens* (1. if P then Q; 2. not Q; 3. not P). To travesty logic to this extent is for Sokol to parody (but not destructively) the *carpe diem* motif, since the presence of this rigour, however fallacious, undermines the softness

of love elegy. To this extent, logic and emotional mood coalesce, as the statement of hypothesized premises and absurd conclusions are mirrored by tones expressing mockery of the proposition and its justification (see below, ll. 5–20). So, M. 'uses logic and illogic to disturb stereotypes, expose assumptions, and test the use of reason itself'. In this way, the mistress is compelled not to think of her honour but to see that the only response to the claim of death is to seize life in a culminating moment of sexual fulfilment.

Style and Versification. The three parts correspond generically and rhetorically to an erotic blason, notable for its precise but absurd arithmetical exaggeration and its sense of a slowing down of time (ll. 1–20); a briefer, second section echoing an epigram from the Greek anthology, and most densely indebted to emblems (ll. 21–32); and the final section in which the majority of the Ovidian echoes are located, which is abundant in erotic energy (in opposition to the previous section) and verbs of (sometimes violent) action, and which demands the mastery of the present over the passing of time (in opposition to the first section) (ll. 33–46). In the first part there is an emphasis on sight, then sound, and finally, touch.

The focus of interest in the poem is in the conceits which are progressively more difficult to interpret, but the poem is delivered throughout in an effortlessly achieved prosody that matches speech rhythms with an often perfect iambic line. Animation of the speaker's voice is heightened with enjambement, the occasional reversal of an iambic foot (e.g. ll. 6–8, 12), and the irregular placing (ll. 7–8, 14, 38, 46), or the removal, of the caesura. The force of the speaker's claim for the instant consummation of his desire is enforced through a flattening of rhythm in the poem's last line: the final six syllables are all stressed. A further counterpoint to the presence of speech rhythms is the use of several thematically significant rhymes (e.g. 'time/crime' [ll. 1–2], 'grow/slow' [ll. 11–12], 'strife/life' [ll. 43–4]).

The tone of the speaker is crucial to the interpretation of the poem, but the images are deceptive in their apparently changing direction. The speaker reserves the indirectly named lower parts (including the genitalia) for the greatest praise through time, but then devotes better time (the 'last age', the millennium itself) to the mistress's heart. Elsewhere, conceptual opposites are used with pointed effect:

not only is a very long lifetime (ll. 1–20) contrasted with the absence of time because of death, but vast space and distance (ll. 5–7) and absolute open space (l. 24) are contrasted with the confinement of the interment vault (l. 26).

Modern Criticism. From a very early stage, perhaps even before Addison's prose pastiche of it in *The Spectator* (89 (12 June 1713; ed. Donald F. Bond (Oxford, 1965), 378)), the poem has been praised as M.'s finest love lyric. It has been regarded widely as the best love poem in the metaphysical tradition, and even as the best love poem in the language (Millgate, *The Listener*, 63 (1960), 701–2). Very few have passed negative judgements on the poem. Reed (1912), 273–8, thought it 'flawed by inappropriate touches of humour', despite its intensity; others have felt that it was old-fashioned and belonging to the poetics of a previous generation.

Leishman (1966), 71–2, echoing T.S. Eliot, notes the poem's remarkable speed, and regards the mock-serious argument and witty hyperbole as akin to a Donne elegy. Yet Leishman (1966), 77, claims that M.'s revivifying of the *carpe diem* topos marks this poem off strongly from Donne's analytical, introspective rebelliousness. Friedman (1970), 117, regards the poem as typically *carpe diem*, as opposed to the reversal of that *topos* in *Daphnis and Chloe*. Hill (in Carey, ed. (1969), 82–3) notes the poem's placing of physical passion in a subordinate place: the conclusion is Puritan rather than libertine, although Colie (1970), 124, stresses that the poem is concerned with desire rather than love. For Ellrodt (in Carey, ed. (1969), 152), the poem avoids a universal truth: 'it is a dramatic moment that owes all to its uniqueness in time and space'. This achievement, for Rees (1989), 94, is because the poem is a 'magnificent predatory assault on the imagination, disguised as an assault on the reason'. The rhetoric of the poem is enhanced by the impersonal nature of the mistress (Colie (1970), 60). For Belsey (in Machin and Norris, eds (1987), 105–21 (119)), this moment of difficulty (or obscurity) is because the poem sits on a crucial historical watershed, embodying 'a collision between the asceticism it both defies and defers to and the humanism which it cannot yet recognize'.

That the poem might have a 'philosophy' has troubled some critics. If the idealism of Neoplatonism is parodied in the first twenty lines, Epicureanism, the philosophy of pleasure, has been seen as present in the last thirteen. If this is so, most are agreed that it is an Epicureanism qualified because the poem deliberately forgets the idea of a future after death (see above, *Sources, Genres and Structure*). For Rees (1989), 103, the poem in this sense is finally ironic: voluptuousness is a result of restricted vision and is therefore self-limiting.

Goldberg (in Carey, ed. (1969), 1670–1) notes the poem's high civilization, 'and its subject . . . in which those values are necessarily obliterated'. If that is the case, the poem's meaning has been startlingly expanded by Hammond's (*SC*, 11 (1996), 112–15) argument that the poem be regarded as 'homosocial', written 'to impress a male audience'. Moreover, the poem provides evidence, through its Ovidian echoes of the Narcissus story, that M. 'could only write about courting a woman if he imagined himself courting a boy'. M.'s poem also 'echoes', 'not simply in the sense that it reverberates in the vault, but because, like Echo's cries, it can only imitate the fragments of other men's speech'. The raunchier version in *Bod. 12* might then be seen as M. 'trying to demonstrate his heterosexual credentials' at a time when he was being derided in print for his homosexual interests (Hammond, in Bell *et al.*, eds (2001), 30–1).

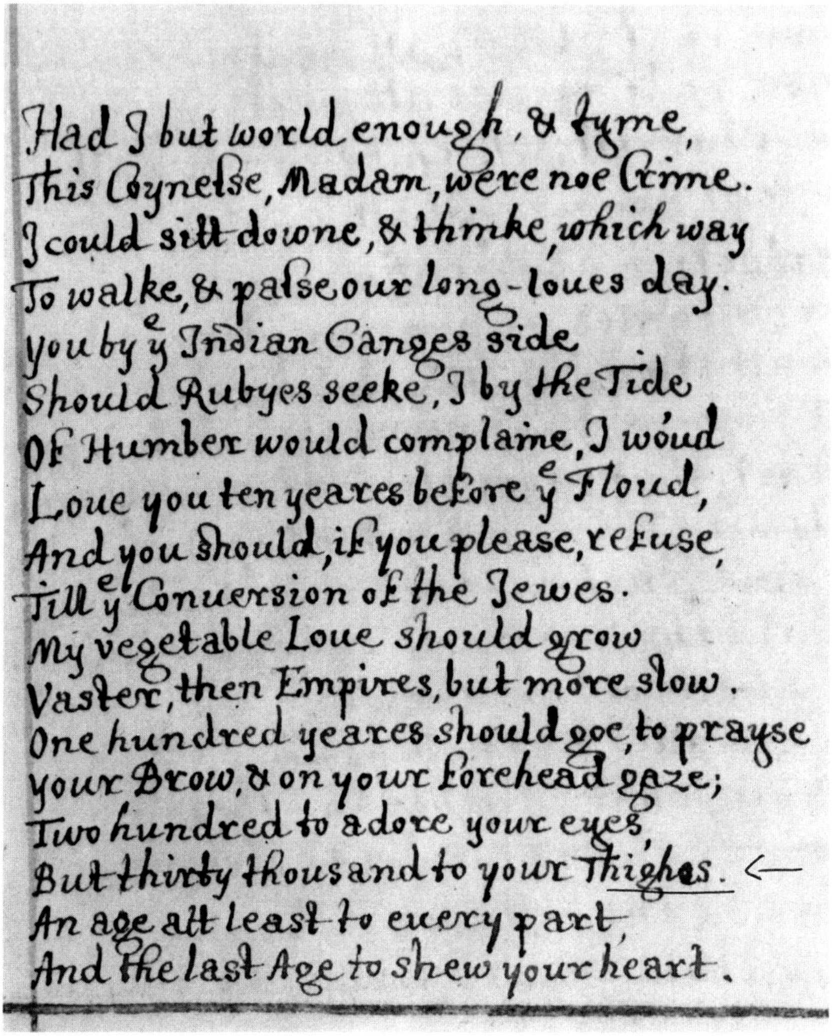

Had I but world enough, & tyme,
This Coynelse, Madam, were noe Crime.
I could sitt downe, & thinke, which way
To walke, & palse our long-loues day.
You by y̆ Indian Ganges side
Should Rubyes seeke, I by the Tide
Of Humber would complaine, I wou'd
Loue you ten yeares before y̆ Floud,
And you should, if you please, refuse,
Till y̆ Conuersion of the Jewes.
My vegetable Loue should grow
Vaster, then Empires, but more slow.
One hundred yeares should goe, to prayse
Your Brow, & on your forehead gaze;
Two hundred to adore your eyes,
But thirty thousand to your Thighes. ←   ramble
An age att least to euery part,
And the last Age to shew your heart.

Fig. 5(a)
The Bodleian Library, University of Oxford, MS Don. b. 8, pp. 283 and 284
(the Haward Manuscript).

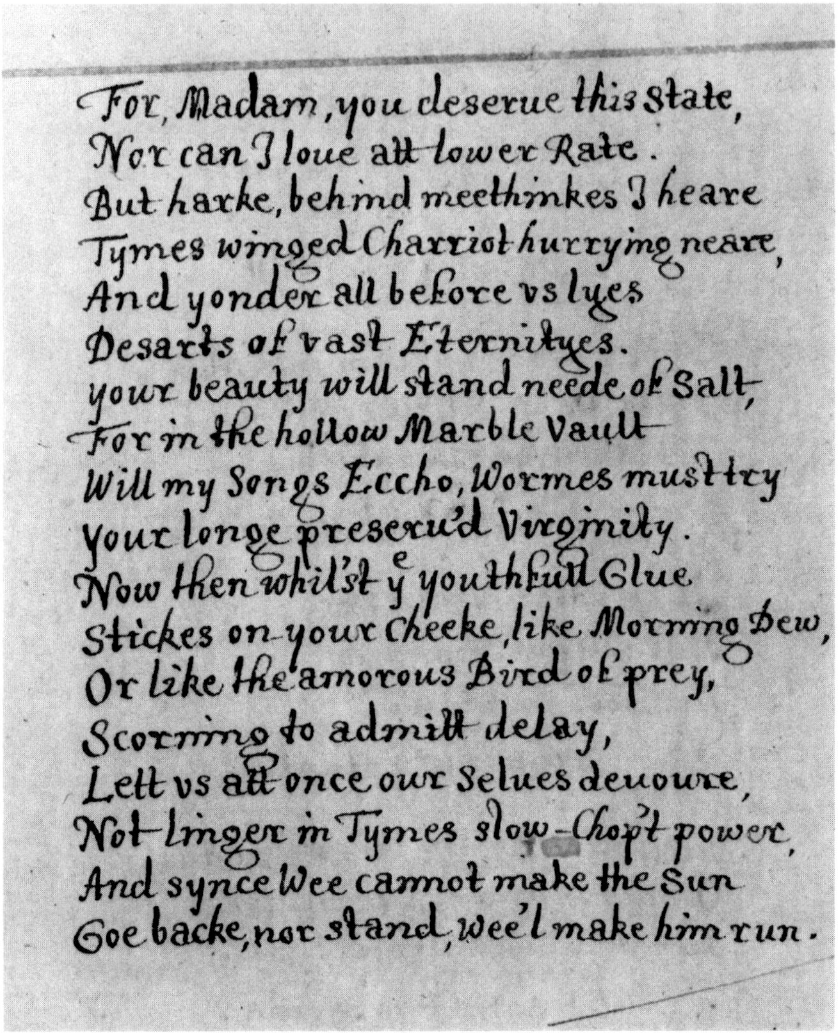

For, Madam, you deserue this state,
Nor can I loue att lower Rate.
But harke, behind meethinkes I heare
Tymes winged Charriot hurrying neare,
And yonder all before vs lyes
Desarts of vast Eternityes.
your beauty will stand neede of Salt,
For in the hollow Marble Vault
Will my Songs Eccho, Wormes must try
Your longe preseru'd Virginity.
Now then whil'st ÿ youthfull Glue.
Stickes on your Cheeke, like Morning Dew,
Or like the amorous Bird of prey,
Scorning to admitt delay,
Lett vs all once our Selues deuoure,
Not linger in Tymes slow-Chop't power,
And synce Wee cannot make the Sun
Goe backe, nor stand, wee'l make him run.

Fig. 5(b)

To His Coy Mistress

Had we but world enough, and time,
This coyness lady were no crime.
We would sit down, and think which way
To walk, and pass our long love's day.
5 Thou by the Indian Ganges' side
Shouldst rubies find: I by the tide
Of Humber would complain. I would

Love you ten years before the flood:
And you should, if you please, refuse
10 Till the conversion of the Jews.
My vegetable love should grow
Vaster than empires, and more slow.
An hundred years should go to praise
Thine eyes, and on thy forehead gaze.
15 Two hundred to adore each breast:
But thirty thousand to the rest.

Title. Coy] a) modest, shy b) disdainful. Rees (1989), 93, argues that the word carried also an 'aura of affectation'; 'coy' derives from the Latin *quietus* ('at rest, still'); cp. Robert Heath, *Clarastella* (1650), 'Dialogue between Sylvio and Mirtillo', l. 29: 'Repent not then thy well plac't love, though she/with the like coyness slight its modestie!/For who asks doubting lest he should obtain,/Instructs his Mistress to a coy disdein'; Randolph, 'A complaint against Cupid that he never made him in Love' (1638), ll. 150–1: 'Give me a Mistresse in whose looks to joy/And such a Mistresse (Love) as will be coy.' The tradition of coyness, both as an exceeding of Protestant teaching on the marital sexual 'mean', the reconciliation of the two extremes in Herrick, and the case for a feminine exception in the verse of Katherine Philips, is explored by Scodel, *Criticism*, 28 (1996), 239–79. M.'s collocation of coyness and time occurs in a republican tract of 1659, with a reference appropriate to the poem (construing delay as a missed Machiavellian *occasione*), from a circle in which M. moved: 'But if with *Miles* the Friers man, we flout and abuse this coy Mistress TIME, and improve not the advantage and opportunity thereof, she will be gone, and then repentence may come too late', *Chaos* (1659, 21 June), 3. Cp. also Charles Aleyn, *The Historie of Henrie the Seventh* (1638), ll. 453–4: 'Death's a *Coy Mistresse*, court her she's not wonne,/Of those which sought her, she was rarely found'; Evelyn, *Sylva* (1670, 2nd edn), 235: 'Here [in ancient gardens] the most beloved and coy Mistress of Apollo rooted.'
1. we] *1681*; I *Bod. 12.*
2. lady] *1681*; Madam *Bod. 12.*
3. We would] *1681*; I could *Bod. 12.*
4. long love's] *1681*; long-loue's *Bod. 12. love's day*] recalls 'loveday': a) day for lovemaking b) day for settling disputes amicably.
5–7. Ganges'... Humber] In Drayton, *Polyolbion* (1613), XXVIII, l. 475, the River Humber compares himself favourably with the Ganges.
5. Thou] *1681*; You *Bod. 12. Ganges' side*] Cp. Robert Chamberlain, 'In Praise of a Country Life' (1638), ll. 23–4, 'For all the precious wealth, or sumptuous pride/That lies by *Tiber, Nile or Ganges* side.' *Ganges*] largest river of the Indian subcontinent, sacred to Hindus; associated in the early modern period with wealth and opulence.
6. rubies] Cp. Proverbs 31:10: 'Who can find a virtuous woman? for her price is far above rubies.' *find*] *1681*; seeke *Bod. 12.*
7–10. I would... Jews] the conjunction of the deluge and the conversion of the Jews (supposed to presage the Millennium) is explained by Zachery Crofton, *Bethshemesh Clouded* (1653),

3–4: 'There is an argument for it, it is analogical. It was in 1656 [BC], the flood came on the old world, and lasted fourty daies. Ergo in that year 1656 fire must come on this world and last fourty years.' Millenarian ideas were popular among mid-seventeenth-century Puritans and negotiations were begun in the 1650s between the Commonwealth government and the Jews of Amsterdam in the hope that the return of the Jews to England would help bring on the Millennium. See Katz (1982).
7. Humber] broad estuarial river making the border between Lincolnshire and Yorkshire, on the eastern side of northern England. M.'s place of childhood residence and education, Hull, lay on the north bank of the Humber, and his place of birth, Winestead, not far from it. M.'s father drowned in the river. *complain*] as in the genre of the 'lover's complaint' (see Kerrigan (1991)), and in contradistinction to l. 13, 'praise'.
8. flood] see Gen. 6:7–8:22.
9. please] *1681*; pleas'd *L 3.*
10. conversion of the Jews] the conversion of the Jews to Christianity was one of the events supposed to precede the Second Coming of Christ.
11. My vegetable love] if 'vegetable' is regarded (in witty terms) as a metaphorical noun, as well as an adjective, the phrase implies a long, slow erection of the penis. Epicureans thought that plants could love in the same way as humans: see Smith (in Smuts, ed. (1996), 205). *vegetable*] plantlike or treelike: characterized by slow, steady growth (in the Aristotelian scheme of vegetative, sensitive and rational souls, the first is characterized only by growth); cp. Herbert of Cherbury, 'You well compacted groves' (?1620), ll. 13–14: 'Pleasure of such a kind, as truly is/A self-renewing vegetable bliss.'
13–18. An hundred... heart] Cp. Catullus, *Carmina*, V, ll. 7–10: 'da mi basia mille, deinde centum,/dein mille altera, dein secunda centum,/deinde usque altera mille, deinde centum,/dein, cum milia multa facerimus. . . .' (Give me a thousand kisses, then a hundred, then another thousand, then a second hundred, then yet another thousand, then a hundred. Then when we have made up many thousands . . .); Cowley, 'My Dyet' (1647), ll. 15–19: 'a sigh of Pity I a year can live,/One Tear will keep me twenty at least,/Fifty a gentle Look will give;/An hundred years of one kind word I'll feast:/A thousand more will added be'.
13. An] *1681*; One *Bod. 12.*
14. Thine eyes] *1681*; Your Brow *Bod. 12. thy*] *1681*; your *Bod. 12.*
15. each breast] *1681*; your eyes *Bod. 12.*
16. the rest] *1681*; your Thighes *Bod. 12.*

An age at least to every part,
And the last age should show your heart.
For Lady you deserve this state;
20   Nor would I love at lower rate.
      But at my back I always hear
Time's wingèd chariot hurrying near:

25   And yonder all before us lie
Deserts of vast eternity.
Thy beauty shall no more be found;
Nor, in thy marble vault, shall sound
My echoing song: then worms shall try
That long preserved virginity:

---

18. *last age*] the Millennium, the thousand-year reign of Christ, immediately preceeding the Last Judgement: see above, *Headnote, Sources, Genre and Structure*, and ll. 7–10 n. *should*] *1681*; to *Bod. 12.*

19–20. *state . . . rate*] Cp. Herrick, 'Upon a delaying Lady' (1648), ll. 7–12: 'I scorne to be/A slave to state:/And since I'm free,/I will not wait,/Henceforth at such a rate,/For needy state' (Friedman); Matthew Stevenson, 'To my Cozen Coy' (1645), ll. 7–12: 'Those things most take men's palates ever,/They purchase with most hard endeavor./And that's the reason that yee maids,/Hold up the rate of maidenheads./Which if you were not coy and nice/Alack a day! would beare no price.'

19. *Lady*] *1681*; Madam *Bod. 12. state*] a) condition (including the Aristotelian tripartite division: see above, l. 11 n.) (*OED* n. I 1, 4) b) high status (*OED* n. II 16).

20. *Nor . . . rate*] Cp. Sir Robert Howard, 'The Opinion' (1668), ll. 23–4: 'That must above the Common rate,/Not reward passions but create.' *would*] *1681*; can *Bod. 12.*

21–4. *But at . . . eternity*] Cp. Thomas Stanley, 'Celia Singing' (1651), ll. 5–8: 'The winged Chariot of the Light,/Or the slow silent wheels of Night;/The shade, which from the swifter Sun,/Doth in a circular motion run.'

21. *at my back I always*] *1681*; harke, behind meethinkes I *Bod. 12.*

22. *Time's . . . near*] Cp. Euripides, *Madness of Hercules*, ll. 506–7: 'ἐλπίδας μὲν ὃ χρόνος οὐκ ἐπίσταται/σώζειν, τό δ' αὑτόν σπουδάσας διέπτατο.' (nothing careth Time to spare our hopes:/Swiftly he works his work, and fleets away); Seneca, *Hercules Furens*, ll. 177–80: 'vivite laeti; properat cursu/vita citato volucrique die/rota praecipitis vertitur anni' (live happily; life speeds on with hurried step, and with winged days the wheel of the headlong year is turned); Quarles, *Emblems* (1635), 3.12: 'The secret wheels of hurrying time do give/So short a warning.' *Time's wingèd chariot*] The representation of time as a clock with wings in emblem books was quite common: e.g. Guillaume de la Perrière, *La Theatre des Bon Engins* (Paris, 1539), no. 71 (see also Henkel and Schone (1967), 1340–1). Cronos (Saturn) was fused with Chronos in emblem books: this single figure representing Time was depicted holding a scythe and driving a chariot (see below, ll. 39–40 n.). See also *Greek Anthology*, VII.225, ll. 1–2: 'ψήχει καὶ πέτρον ὃ πολὺς χρόνος οὐδὲ σιδήρου/φείδεται, ἀλλὰ μιῃπάντ' ὀλέκει δρεπάνῃ' (Time wears stone away and spares not iron, but with one sickle destroys all things that are); Seneca, *Hippolytus*, l. 1141: 'Volat ambiguis mobilis alis' (On doubtful wings flies the inconstant hour).

23. *lie*] *1681*; lyes *Bod. 12.*

24. *Deserts . . eternity*] Cp. Herrick, 'Eternitie' (1647), ll. 7–8: 'th'Sea/Of vast Eternitie; Cowley, 'My Diet' (1647), l. 21:

'And all beyond is vast *Eternitie*'; Cowley, 'Sitting and Drinking in the Chair made out of the Reliques of Sir Francis Drake's Ship' (pub. 1663), ll. 65–8: 'The streits of time too narrow are for thee,/Launch forth into an undiscovered Sea,/And steer the endless course of vast Eternity,/Take for thy Sail this Verse, and for thy Pilot Me'; Cowley, 'The Wish' (1647), ll. 36–7: 'She who is all the world, and can exclude/In desarts Solitude'. This image of the death is notable for its exclusion of any idea of romantic or theological afterlife. The classical source behind all the seventeenth-century English versions may be Lucretius, *De Rerum Natura*, I, l. 1103: 'deffugiant subito magnum per inane soluta' (space without end or limit lies open to us in all directions). *Deserts*] uninhabited places (*OED* n.² 1). *vast*] undermining the fulsome sense of 'vast' at l. 12. *eternity*] *1681*; Eternityes *Bod. 12.*

25–32. *Thy beauty . . . embrace*] an embedded version of an epigram from the *Greek Anthology* (V.85), attributed to Asclepiades: 'Φείδῃ παρθενίης Καὶ τί πλέον; οὐ γὰρ ἐς Ἀδην/ἐλθοῦσ εὑρήεις τὸν φιλέοντα, κόρη./ἐν ζωοῖσι τὰ τερπνὰ τὰ Κύπριδος Ἐν δ' Ἀχέροντι/ὀστέα καὶ σποδιή, παρθένε, κεισόμεθα' (You'll stay a virgin? to what end?/Hades holds no living friend;/Among the living we must know/Cyprian sweetness – there below/In the darkness when we die,/Bones and ash uncoupled lie.) (translation by Stella Revard, in Summers and Pebworth, eds (1992), 33).

25. *Thy beauty shall no more be found*] *1681*; Your beauty will stande need of Salt *Bod. 12.*

26. *Nor, in thy marble vault, shall sound*] *1681*; For in the hollow Marble Vault *Bod. 12. thy*] *1681+*; the *L 3. marble*] Cp. Ovid, *Metamorphoses*, III, l. 419: 'ut e Pario formatum marmore signum' (like a statue carved from Parian marble.)

27–9. *then worms . . . dust*] Cp. Francis Wyrley, 'A Privat discourse with a Mistress', Rosenbach Library, Philadelphia, MS 1083/17, f. 91^r·v: 'The wormes shall in the Caskett sport/Wherein that hidden pearle doth ly/And feed out with rude gluttony.' The poem was identified by Maule, *EMS*, 8 (1996), 150. See also Marotti (1995), 81. Belsey, in Machin and Norris (1987), 105–21 (110–11), associates this image with the medieval Dance of Death, still current in the seventeenth century, where a Death figure danced with the living, specifically reminding them of the limitations of human love.

27. *My echoing song: then*] *1681*; Will my Songs Eccho *Bod. 12.* The phrase is a playful allusion to the Ovidian echoes (at ll. 26 and 33–6), in which the speaker literally speaks the words of Ovid's nymph Echo (in English translation). Just as Echo's own words will not be heard after the 'death' of her joining with Narcissus, so the speaker will not be heard in the vault of the dead mistress. *shall*] *1681*; must *Bod. 12.*

28. *That*] *1681*; Your *Bod. 12.*

dignitary magi

And your quaint honour turn to dust;

30 And into ashes all my lust.

narrow, deprived

The grave's a fine and private place,

But none I think do there embrace.

   Now, therefore, while the youthful glew

Sits on thy skin like morning dew,

35 And while thy willing soul transpires

At every pore with instant fires,

Now let us sport us while we may;

And now, like am'rous birds of prey,

comma the our line

Rather at once our Time devour,

40 Than languish in his slow-chapped power.

possibly of earlier manuscript version

29–32. Not in *Bod. 12*.

29–30. *dust . . . ashes*] Cp. The Order for the Burial of the Dead, *The Book of Common Prayer* (1559), ed. John E. Booty (Charlottesville, VA. 1976), 310: 'we therefore commit his body to the ground, earth to earth, ashes to ashes, dust to dust, in sure and certain hope of resurrection'; [Jeremiah Rich], *An Elegie on the Death of the Right Honourable Iohn Warner, Lord Mayor of London* (1648), s.sh.: 'And if thy Monument shall leave his trust,/And turn to ashes like thy mouldring dust.'

29. *quaint*] a) proud (*OED* a. II 9) b) prim (*OED* a. II 10). There is also a pun on ME 'queynte' (vagina); Williams (1994), 3.1125 notes that 'quaint' was used in this sense until the mid-nineteenth century. *honour*] a) reputation (*OED* n. 1) b) chastity (*OED* n. 3) c) literally: maidenhead (*OED* n. 3b) *dust*] *Cooke*+ durst *1681*.

31–2. A reversal of a convention in love elegies; see e.g., Propertius, *Elegia*, II.xv, l. 36: 'huius ero vivus, mortuus huius ero' (hers will I be in life, hers will I be in death); cp. also Matthew Stevenson, 'To my Coy and Captious Mistress' (1645), ll. 13–14: 'No, though one carelesse smile would save/Thy cast-of carkass from the grave.'

31. *fine and*] *1681*+; fine, a *L 3*.

32. *none . . . embrace*] a reversal (by stressing the idea of a physical meeting between lovers) of a classical sentiment, repeated in the Renaissance, that lovers did meet in the grave (e.g., Propertius, *Elegies*, IV.vii, ll. 93–4; Donne, 'The Relique' (1633), ll. 1–11; see Allen, *MLN*, 74 (1959), 485–6).

33–6. *Now . . . fires*] Cp. Ovid, *Metamorphoses*, trans. Arthur Golding (1564), III, ll. 612–17: 'But fainting straight for paine,/As lith and supple waxe doth melt against the burning flame,/Or morning dew against the Sunne that glareth on the same:/Even so by piecemeal being spent and wasted through desire,/Did he consume and melt away with Cupid's sweet fire/His lively hue of white and red'; *Metamorphoses*, trans. Sandys (1632) 'Narcissus seen, intending thus the chace;/She forth-with glowes, and with a noiselesse pace/His steps pursues; the more she did persew,/More hot . . . she grew:/And might be likened to a sulph'rous match,/Which instantly th'approached flame does catch.' M.'s use of Ovid makes the speaker's voice correspond to Echo's in Ovid, the Mistress to Narcissus (see above, l. 27 n.).

33. *therefore, while*] *1681*; then whilst *Bod.12*, l. 29. *glew*] *Bod. 1*; glue *Bod. 12*, l. 29, *Donno*; hew *1681*, *Margoliouth, Macdonald, Lord, Legouis*, hue *Kermode, Walker*, a) sweat; the sexual connotations of sweat are evident in Milton's *Comus* (1634), l. 916, where the Lady is ensnared with Comus's 'gums of glutinous heat'; not in *OED*. b) glow; Wilcher notes that M. may have known a medieval northern dialect form for 'glow', most apparent in the 'glew' spelling (see 'gle', n. 4, 'glouen'.v. 1, in *MED*). Secondary, conceited senses of '(sexual) ardour' (see 'glow', *OED*, v.¹ 6; Tilley, H 86) and 'perfume' ('glue', *OED* n. 3 b; 'gum', *OED* n.² 2). The original reading was presum-

ably 'glew . . . dew', i.e. the sweat sits on the skin like dew on grass. The editor or compositor of *1681* did not recognize the image and assumed some error of transcription: he thought that the image was comparing the woman's rosy cheeks with the rosy sky at dawn, and so produced the reading 'hew . . . glew' (i.e. 'hue . . . glow' in modern English). Whoever produced *Bod. 12* seems to have thought that 'glew' meant 'glue', and made the image obvious by remembering 'sits' as 'sticks'. The agreement of *Bod. 1* and *Bod. 12* is sufficient evidence that 'glew . . . dew' is the correct reading, since they obviously come from quite separate textual traditions. For a full discussion, see Hammond, in Bell *et al.*, eds (2001), 28–31.

34. *Sits on thy skin*] *1681*; Stickes on your Cheeke *Bod. 12*, l. 30. *dew*] *Bod. 1*, *Bod. 12*, l. 30, *Cooke*+; glew *1681*, *Lord*.

35–6. *And . . . fires*] Cp. Crashaw (1652), 'To the Name above Every Name, the Name of Jesus', ll. 211–14: 'with wider pores/Inlarge thy flaming-brested Louers/More freely to transpire/That impatient Fire.'

35. *transpires*] passes out as vapour through the skin (*OED* v. 3).

36. *instant fires*] Cp. Ovid, *Metamorphoses*, trans. Sandys (1632), 89: 'instantly th'approached flame does catch'.

37. *sport us*] take our pleasure; make love.

38. *And now, like*] *1681*; Or like the *Bod. 12*, l. 31. *am'rous birds of prey*] Brody (*ELH*, 56 (1989), 53–79 (67 n. 31)) suggests that the image of the birds of prey are opposites to the 'love bird' or 'bird of Venus', usually doves, who draw the chariot of the goddess. Smith (in Smuts, ed. (1996), 177–209 (204–7)), argues that the simile is a perversion (in the service of the speaker's epicurean perspective) of the proper order according to the chain of being: after human love comes higher kinds of love, such as that enjoyed by angels, not the lower love of the beasts.

39–40. *Rather . . . power*] it has been suggested that the retaliation of the lovers upon Time is a response to the myth of the pre-Hellenic deity Cronus (Cronos or Kronos; later identified with Saturn), who devoured five of his six children. The story was a topic in pictorial representation (e.g. by Rubens in 1636), while Cronus was the original Father Time figure, being depicted with a sickle or curved sword. Elsewhere, Chronos (i.e. Time, not specifically Cronus) is depicted flying away with time: Otto van Veen, *Amorum Emblemata* (1556), 236–7. Cp. Ovid, *Metamorphoses*, XV, ll. 263–6, trans. Sandys: 'Still-eating Time, and thou ô envious Age,/All ruinate: diminisht by the rage/Of your devouring teeth, all that have breath/Consume, and anguish by a lingring death.'

39. *Rather at once our Time devour*] *1681*; Lett vs att once our Selues devoure *Bod. 12*, l. 33. *our Time devour*] cp. Ovid, *Ex Ponto*, IV.x, l. 7: 'tempus edax igitur praeter nos omnia perdet' (So devouring time will destroy all things but me).

40. *Than languish in his slow-chapped*] *1681*; Not linger in Tymes slow-Chop't *Bod. 12*, l. 34. *slow-chapped*] slowly-devouring (from 'chaps': jaws (*OED* n.² 2 pl.)).

Let us roll all our strength, and all
Our sweetness, up into one ball:
And tear our pleasures with rough strife,

45   Thorough the iron gates of life.
     Thus, though we cannot make our sun
     Stand still, yet we will make him run.

41–6. Cp. John Hall, 'To his Tutor, Master Pawson. An Ode' (1646), ll. 13–16: 'Come, let us run/And give the world a girdle with the sun;/For so we shall/Take a full view of this enamelled ball.'

41–2. roll . . . ball] Cp. Lucan, *De Bello Civili*, IV, ll. 73–4: 'densos/Involvere globos' (rolled into dense round masses).

42. ball] Many different kinds of ball have been suggested (see Carey, ed. (1969), 63); in the context, cannonball, a medicinal bolus, and ball-money (coins thrown through churchyard gates at the bride and groom at some English wedding ceremonies: see Brett, *CQ*, 20 (1978), 5–17) are more likely; the ball was a symbol of perfection, so that alchemists described the elixir or philosopher's stone as a ball (see Abraham (1990), 313); cp. Henry Peacham, 'Protegere Regium', ll. 3–4, in *Minerva Britanna* (1612), 31: 'My dutie is the Citie gate to guard,/And to rebate their Rammes, and fierie balls.'

43. tear our pleasures] Cp. John Hall, 'To his Tutor, Master Pawson. An Ode' (1646), ll. 50–1: 'O, let us tear/A passage through/That floating vault above'; Ovid, *Metamorphoses*, trans. Sandys (1632), 89: '*On me thy pleasure take*, the Nymph replyes.'

44. Thorough] *1681+*; Through *L 3*; spelt with the extra syllable to keep the metre; see also below, *An Horatian Ode*, l. 15 n. *iron gates*] Cp. *In Legationum Domini Oliveri St John ad Provincias Foederatas*, l. 10: 'Clavibus his Jani ferrea Claustra regis' (With these keys thou rulest the iron gates of Janus); Lucan, *De Bello Civili*, I, ll. 61–2: 'pax missa per orbem/Ferrea belligeri conspecat limina Iani' ('Let peace through all the world in this blest state/Once more shut warre like *Ianus* Iron gate' [May]). The sense of the gates as the threshold between this world and the next is enforced by Horace, *Carmina*, III.xxvii, l. 41, when Europa wonders whether she is awake or visited in a dream by a phantom that had flown through the *porta eburna* (ivory gate). *gates of life*] an inversion of the gates of death (Ps. 9:13: 'thou that liftest me up from the gates of death'), which were iron: an image from the Harrowing of Hell; cp. also Ps. 106:16: 'For he hath broken the gates of brass, and cut the bars of iron in sunder'; Lucretius, *De Rerum Natura*, I, l. 415: 'vitai claustra resolvat' (open the gates of life [i.e. 'die']). See also The Collect, Easter Day, *The Book of Common Prayer* (1559), ed. John E. Booty (Charlottesville, VA, 1976): 'Almighty God, which through thy only begotten

Son Jesus Christ hast overcome death, and opened unto us the gate of everlasting life.' Brody (*ELH*, 56 (1989), 71–2), argues that M.'s echo of the Prayer Book is a parody of the Christian doctrine of resurrection: death is overcome not by resurrection in the afterlife but by life. Smith (in Smuts, ed. (1996), 177–209 (207)) argues that this was meant in an ironic way: the speaker thinks that lust will be rewarded with more pleasure in life; the Christian knows that the wages of sin (i.e. lust) are death. *gates*] *1681, Cooke, Margoliouth, Legouis, Wilcher*; grates *Bod. 1, Donno*. Randall, in Summers and Pebworth, eds (1992), 47–69, argues in favour of 'grates' on the grounds of its frequency as an image of a fortified door, and on the revival of English ironwork in the seventeenth century. He also notes contemporary references to the vagina as a portcullis, and that in Renaissance tennis hitting the ball into the grille at one end of the court won the point in play. But Wilcher's sense that the unexpectedness of 'gates of life' (reversing 'gates of death' and the commonness of 'iron grates') 'has the ring of Marvellian wit' is more convincing.

45–6. though . . . still] in Joshua 10:12–14, Joshua commanded the sun and moon to stand still while the Israelites avenged themselves upon the Amorites; in Psalm 19:6 the sun is imagined 'running': 'Which is as a bridegroom coming out of his chamber, and rejoiceth as a strong man to run a race'; also a refinement of Catullus's invocation of the sun (*Carmina*, V, l. 4–6), here rendered by Jonson, 'Song. To Celia' (1616), ll. 6–8: 'Suns that set may rise again;/But if once we lose this light,/'Tis with us perpetual night'; and an 'overgoing' of a couplet from Lovelace in 'Dialogue. Lucasta, Alexis' (1649), ll. 30–1: 'So in each other if the pitying Sun/Thus keep us fix't;/nere may his Course be run!'; see also Herrick, 'Corinna's going a Maying' (1648), ll. 61–2: 'Our life is short; and our dayes run/As fast away as do's the Sunne.' Bearing in mind the reference to Time in l. 39, cp. also Carew, 'A Pastorall Dialogue' (1640), ll. 32–3: 'Then let us pinion *Time*, and chase/The day for ever from this place.'

45. Thus, though we cannot make our] *1681+*; And synce Wee cannot make the *Bod. 12*, l. 35.

46. Stand still, yet we will] *1681+*; Goe backe, nor stand, wee'l *Bod. 12*, l. 36. *yet . . . run*] the opposite view is expressed in *RT*, 135: 'the world will not go the faster for our driving.'

17

The Unfortunate Lover

Date. 1648–49. *The Unfortunate Lover* is closely related to the courtly poetry written at the end of Charles I's life, some of which was connected with his execution. It is likely that M. saw Lovelace's poems in the months before they were published in June 1649, and that, as Margoliouth noted, M. may have been struck by the couplet in Lovelace's 'Dialogue – To Lucasta', ll. 15–16, 'Love near his standard when his host he sets,/Creates alone fresh-bleeding bannerets', so that it influenced l. 57 of *The Unfortunate Lover*. P.R.K.A. Davidson and A.K. Jones, *N & Q*, n.s. 32 (1985), 170–2, note the similarity between M.'s poem and two epigrams designed by Sir Richard Fanshawe to represent the plight of Charles I's second son James, just after the execution of the father on 30 January 1649 (see below *Sources and Allusions*). M. might have seen these in manuscript circulation.

While this is a conjecture (and there are other similar echoes from poems written and published earlier – e.g. Cleveland, 'To Prince Rupert' (?1642, publ. 1647), l. 4, 'Dub'd at adventures Verser Banneret!'), there are also similarities in words and phrases with *Upon Appleton House*, which would support a date between late 1650 and ?July 1652, the duration of Marvell's residence at Nun Appleton. Craze (1979) 106–9, also notes similarities with *An Horatian Ode* (June–July 1650), and the stanza forms of *Upon Appleton House*, *Upon the Hill and Grove at Bilbrough*, *Damon the Mower* and *The Garden*, the first three of which are thought to have been written in the Nun Appleton years.

However, the earlier date seems more likely, as the poem is very resonant with forms of Royalist iconography in the months before and immediately following the execution of Charles I (see below, *Sources and Allusions*). The stanza form was then developed in M.'s verse of the early 1650s.

Publication. 1681.

Sources and Allusions. Palmer, *English Miscellany*, 24 (1973–74), 19–57, sees close parallels between *The Unfortunate Lover* and Giordano Bruno's *De Gli Eroici Furori* (1585). There is no evidence that M. was directly indebted to Bruno, but M. does employ a number of enigmatic conceits, very similar to Bruno's. Where Bruno's characters interpret poems in a dialogue, M. leaves the task to his readers. The external furies, and the internal discord of stanzas III–V, is abstractly and separately represented by Bruno: 'the suffering imposed upon him by the war he wages with the contraries external to him. . . . He shows how he endures the division and discord within himself . . . because he is not in the temperance of indifference, but in the excess of contraries' (trans. Paul E. Memmo, 1964, 101–2). More impressively, Bruno's heroic lover describes himself as an 'unfortunate lover': 'Lasso, que'giorni lieti/Trancommi l'efficacia d'un istante,/Che femmi a lungo *infortunato amante*' (455). See also Lady Hester Pulter's 'The Unfortunate Florinda', Leeds University, Brotherton Library, MS Lt. q. 32, 2ᵛ–36ᵛ, and unbound papers.

Elaborating upon the idea of the poem's Italianate design, a circular structure representing a form of cosmic order has been proposed by Røstvig, in Friedenreich, ed. (1977). An Italian form in nine stanzas, recited by nine men in a circle, *in ordine di ruota*, represented the governing nine spheres of the universe, and the wheels of fortune and of nature. Within this formation, life was described as a circle, subject to alternate rising and falling motions, concepts with which M. would have been familiar from his knowledge of Nicholas of Cusa and Bruno. The poem moves in a circular way as follows: st. 1 – love; st. 2 – wave/rock; st. 3 – breast/day; st. 4 – cormorants; st. 5 – cormorants; st. 6 – day/breast; st. 7 – rock/wave; st. 8 – love. The second half of the poem is an exact mirror image of the first half, with pairs of objects chiastically reversed in the second half.

Bradbrook and Lloyd-Thomas (1940), 29 n., have been influential in viewing the poem as a series of emblematic pictures. They suggest as influences upon

M. the depiction of the lover's torments in Otto van Veen, *Amorum Emblemata* (Antwerp, 1608) and Crispin de Passe, *Thronus Cupidinis* (1618). However, it is hard to see a probable influence upon M. when these works are examined. More convincingly, Leishman (1966), 34–5, suggests Alciati's emblems and illustrated epigrams of 1531, especially numbers 5 and 134. Number 28 shows Prometheus being eaten by birds in punishment for stealing fire from heaven; 'De Morte et Amore' (52) depicts Cupid and Death throwing arms at people (broadly reflecting below, ll. 42–4); number 97, 'In Statum Amoris', has a blindfolded Cupid holding arms and standing in flames (see below, l. 47). The rock (15, 52) has a precedent in Henry Peacham, *Minerva Britanna* (1612), 158, which shows an emblem of a rock surrounded by a stormy sea, under which is printed 'Amid the waves, a mightie Rock doth stand,/ Whose ruggie brow, had bidden many a shower'. Peacham's rock, unlike M.'s is interpreted as 'manlie constancie', against which the ship of 'opinion' threatens to break, steered as it is by 'pride' and 'vain desire', and burning with 'hot passions'. Schwenger, *MLQ*, 35 (1974), 364–75, argues for the use of the armorial device.

Most agree that the poem uses the Petrarchan convention of the lover sailing on a sea of passion, and that the poem generally displays the extreme literalism and contorted mannerism of late Petrarchanism. More recently, the dramatic vocabulary in the poem has led to speculation on the connection with masque: 'masque of quarrelling elements' (l. 26), 'spectacle' (l. 42), 'play' (l. 43). Stocker (1986), 268–72, detects echoes of Inigo Jones and Sir William Davenant's masque, *Salmacida Spolia* (1640), ll. 111–18, 124–31, 360–3 (see below, *Modern Criticism*). Like a masque, the poem mixes comedy with higher modes of apprehension, and avoids mention of specific events, but clearly, unlike the masque, it neither praises nor offers advice.

The motifs in the poem have a common source in romance. Bruno and M. offer condensed versions of patterns given much more extensive treatment in poetic and prose romance, with antecedents in epic poetry. Of particular importance is the salvation of the young from tempests, instanced in the discovery of Pyrocles in a shipwreck and after a sea battle at the beginning of Sidney's *New Arcadia* (1593), 'a young man . . . who sat as on horseback, having nothing upon him but his shirt . . . holding his head up full of unmoved majesty, he held a sword aloft in his fair arm, which often he waved about his crown as though he would threaten the world in that extremity' (ed. M. Evans (1977), 64). Charles I read and enjoyed Sidney's *Arcadia*, which is used in the chief text of post-execution martyrology, *Eikon Basilike* (1649), and attacked by Milton precisely for this association in *Eikonoklastes* (1649). The story of Amphialus's painful desire for Philoclea (*New Arcadia*, III.iii) is also relevant: 'alas, that tyrant love (which now possesseth the hold of all my life and reason) will no way suffer it. It is love, it is love, not I which disobey you' (ed. Evans (1977) 450–1; see below, l. 45). Thirdly, there is the speech of Philanax to Euarchus, lamenting the death of Basilius in figurative terms: 'here is before your eyes the pitiful spectacle of a most dolorously ending tragedy, wherein I do but play the part of all this now miserable province which, being spoiled of her guide, doth lie like a ship without a pilot, tumbling up and down in the uncertaine waves, till it either run itself upon the rock of self-division or be overthrown by the stormy wind of foreign force' (*Old Arcadia* (1590, ed. J. Robertson, Oxford, 1973), 360, see below, ll. 13–16). For another shipwrecked lover, see also Marston, *Antonio and Mellida* (1599), I.i, ll. 1–29. William Cartwright's 'Ariadne *deserted by* Theseus, *as She sits upon a rock in the Island* Naxos, *thus complains*', written before 1648, has the disconsolate speaker ('Drown'd first by my own Tears; then in the deep', l. 80.) call down a vengeance upon Theseus similar to M.'s lover's torment: 'The Ravenous Vulture tear his Breast,/The rowling Stone disturb his rest', ll. 21–2 (see below, ll. 14–15, 27–37).

Behind the romance elements is the presence of Virgil's *Aeneid*, Book I, particularly the storm imagery and the punishment of Ajax by Juno (see below, ll. 9–10, 48). Contemporary translations of *Aeneid*, I, ll. 44–5 bear close comparison with the description of M.'s rock-bound lover: 'Him breathing flame, his breast quite thorow struck,/ With whirlwinds snatch'd, and on a sharp rock stuck' (John Ogilby, 1650); 'With whirlwinds took the guilty lover, stuck/Him, gasping flame, upon a pointed rock!' (James Harrington, 1658). Duncan-Jones in Brower *et al.* (1973), 215–77, also suggests Lucretius, *De rerum natura*, V, ll. 222–5, 'tum poro puer, ut saevis proiectis ab undis/navita nudus humi iacet, infans, indigus omni/vitali auxilio, cum primum in luminis oras/nixibus ex alvo matris natura profundit' (then further the child, like a sailor cast forth by the cruel waves, lies naked upon the ground, speechless, in need of every kind of vital support, as soon as nature has spilt him forth with throes from his mother's womb into the regions of light).

Within this broad tradition, P.R.K.A. Davidson and A.K. Jones, *N & Q*, n.s. 32 (1985), 170–2, detect a similarity between M.'s poem and a 'prophetic epigram' written by Sir Richard Fanshawe on Charles I's son, James, Duke of York:

Effigei inscriptum

Altissimae sicut prosopiae ita et indolis Adolesentuli Jacobi Ducis Eboracensis serenissimi Caroli primi (Magnae Britanniae Regis) Filii secundo-geniti, secundi Fratris nunc unici; aetate eius circiter 13, Ore (ut Moribus) virgineo; sorte Profugi; Mari tumultante peribundo similis; ejecto Nauclero; conclamato nauigio; Infixi scopulo; Innixi Anchorae; Thalassi-Archarum Tridenti, ad quod munus jam tunc designatus, primo quidem ab Inclytissimae Memoriae patre, post autem a fratre Augustissimo.

Epigramma Propheticum
Anno Domini 1648

Uno fratre minor Jacobus in orbe Britanno
    Altera stat vidui gloria spesque Soli.
Uno fratre minor Tabula depingitur ista
    Ferrea Fraternis Iura daturus Aquis.
En! Armata Venus, pelagoque (ut Cypria) pascens,
    Heu, tumido non hoc Marmore digne puer.
Sed subsidente Aquae, ne vestras induat iras,
    Cui tenera virtus aspere fronte latet.

(An epigram inscribed upon a likeness of James, Duke of York, a distinguished youth, son of His Serene Majesty King Charles the First of Great Britain, the second son of a second son, aged about thirteen, virginal in his countenance as in his life, an exile by fate, he is represented as one in peril on a stormy sea, the captain thrown overboard, the ship broken up, thrust upon a rock, but clinging to an anchor, the trident of the ruler of the sea. To this office he was even then marked out first by his father of illustrious memory, and afterwards by his very august brother.)

Prophetic Epigram
AD 1648

Younger than his only brother, James stands out in the British World as a secondary glory and hope of the widowed throne. Younger than his only brother, he is depicted in the tablet as destined to reign with despotic sway over his brother's seas. Lo! a Venus in armour, a child of the sea, like the Cyprian, still a boy, hardly yet worthy of this pompous marble. Yet sink down ye waves, lest he should clothe himself in fury like yours, he in whom rough valour lies hidden under a gentle appearance.)

Despite the 'striking similarity' between the two pieces, and the possibility that M. might have seen the Fanshawe lines or even a finished (but now lost) relief, there is no proof of Fanshawe's influence upon M., or vice versa. Moreover, there is no certainty here as to the identity of the Lover in M.'s poem, be it Charles I, James, or his brother, the future Charles II (sent away to the Scilly Isles during the 1640s; see below, *Modern Criticism*). The affinity does suggest the existence of a distinctive late Caroline iconography, but where Fanshawe's epigram is definitely Royalist in sentiment, the affiliation of M.'s poem is oblique and suspended. Other examples of this iconography also connect with *The Unfortunate Lover*. Mildmay Fane's 'A game at Tables' ('Fugitive Poetry', Harvard UL fMS Eng. 645, fol. 16) is similarly concerned with the two brothers, and describes social advancement in the Interregnum in terms very similar to the emblematic ending of M.'s poem (see below, ll. 63–4): 'Till I thinke Hells broke Loose/And all Conditions sexes & Degrees/Contend for Pedigrees/To Blazon out in urgent field/A Dart Gules yts wth malice steeld'. Likewise, some elegies for Charles I did depict him as a romance figure:

When ghastly Death's astonishing Arrest
    In all her terrors, and grim wardrobe drest,
    From a green Treaty nipt ere fully blown,
    And soft amusements of a vestured throne,
    He meets with cheerfull combat, and arm'd breath,
    A vigorous Resignation, not a Death
        When *His unlimited forgiveness* flies
    High as *His blood's* shrill voice, and towring cryes,
    Not spun in *scanty half denying prayers*,
    But Legacie obliging to His Heirs.
        (*An Elegie on . . . Charles I*, in [John Cleveland],
            Monumentum Regale (1649), 19)

Versification, Style and Rhetoric. The poem consists of eight stanzas, numbered in roman numerals, of eight lines each, in iambic tetrameters. The stanza form is shared with *Upon Appleton House, Upon the Hill and Grove at Bilbrough, Damon the Mower* and *The Garden: The Unfortunate Lover* is probably the earliest use of this form. Craze (1979), 106, suggests that the stanza may derive from Saint-Amant's stanzas of five octosyllabic couplets. Saint-Amant was influential in England in the 1640s, and translated by Fairfax (see also *The Garden, Headnote*). Interaction between sentence and regular line are provided by enjambements (ll. 9–10, 24–5, 31–2, 35–6, 41–6, 55–8) and trisyllables to fit the iambic pattern (l. 16).

The transition from the past to the present tense is clearly signalled in stanza VI, l. 41, when the Lover is presented as a mature man. 'Presents' (l. 25) is a Latinate use of the present in a *dum* (while) clause: it should be read as 'presented'. The same is true of l. 37: 'Thus while they famish him'. The vocabulary is characterized by kinetic words, enhancing the sense of activeness: 'meteors' (l. 6), 'shipwrack' (l. 9), 'waves' (ll. 13, 47). The poem is an exercise in prosopopeia, the Lover being put on the same level as the personified elements with which he interacts. The conceits describing the Lover's feelings in stanzas I–III are hyperbolic.

Modern Criticism. The earliest opinion was not complimentary: 'probably the worst love poem ever written by a man of genius' (H.C. Beeching, *National Review*, 37 (1901), 747–59). For some, the Caesarian birth of l. 16 was distasteful. However, other and later comment, generally finding more merit in the poem, has sought to understand the poem through its bringing together of different forms and genres. Legouis (1965), 32, among others, has seen the lover as a romance hero treated sympathetically: 'a cursed hero after the heart of Byron or Hugo, of a *roseau sentant* who scorns the universe eager for his downfall'.

Several lines of criticism regard the instances of hyperbole in the poem as one consistent, and sometimes also multi-layered, allegory. This seems to be encouraged by the distancing from passion achieved by the condensed figuration. Bertoff in *MLQ*, 27 (1966), 41–50 reads the poem as an allegory of the soul as it emerges from eternity into time-bound finitude, returning in the death of the lover to eternity. King (1977), 77–88, argues for the poem to be regarded as a series of emblems, each of which recalls some stage in the life and death of Christ. Duncan-Jones in Brower *et al.*, eds (1973), 224, finds contemporary references to Christ as 'God's banneret' (see below, l. 57).

Claims for a political allegory have also been made. The Lover's mother ship becomes the ship of state, the nation or, possibly also, the church. R. Syfret is reported by Bradbrook and Lloyd-Thomas (1940), 29–30 n., to read l. 30 as a reference to Charles, Prince of Wales, who had been cast away in the

Scilly Isles after Royalist defeats in the west country in 1646. Newton, *Cambridge Quarterly*, 6 (1972–73), 138, regards the poem as a codified lamentation for Prince Charles' loss of his crown. More recently, Stocker (1986), 267–305, has argued extensively that the poem represents a cryptic account of Charles I's loss of his crown through the events of the civil war. As *Philogenes* (the name of the 'King's Majesty' in Jones and Davenant's *Salmacidia Spolia* (1640)), lover of his people, and the royal son of his mother, England (l. 14), Charles fails by paying too much attention to the self-deluding image presented in the court masque, and through the perfidy of the Bishops (represented by the greedy cormorants of l. 27). The sea becomes a metaphor for political unrest as well as violent passion. But recent historical criticism is cautious: the poem 'seems, however, rather to be using some contemporary political metaphors to catch an allusive amatory state than the other way round' (Norbrook (1999), 168).

The more extensive the allegorical interpretations become, the more they risk offering unconvincing and unprovable interpretations. The absence of courtship in the poem enhances the force of the allegorical claim, but Schwenger's suggestion (*MLQ*, 35 (1974), 371) that the tense avoidance of passion reveals homosexual love is difficult to justify. Stocker's argument (1986), 267–305, depends upon a sophisticated control of a wide variety of contextual material. Local observations are convincing – the Lover, making 'impression upon Time' (l. 8) and fighting Fortune does look like a prince, even a Machiavellian one – but there is no final proof that the stormy sea represents the people, or that the Lover is Charles I. She also allows herself to take political views expressed by Marvell in his later political writings and project them back onto the earlier material. The poem has the ability to ruin the effectiveness of any interpretation, however subtle, which attempts to render it clear. None the less, it is also evident that the poem is related to the poetry of embattled Royalism and eventual lament for the execution of Charles I. It is characteristic of this poetry to be obscure, given the dangerous political context of its production and publication, and equally characteristic of a pre-1650 lyric by M. to be so wilfully unrevealing of its public context.

The Unfortunate Lover

I

Alas, how pleasant are their days
With whom the infant Love yet plays!
Sorted by pairs, they still are seen
By fountains cool, and shadows green.
5 But soon these flames do lose their light,
Like meteors of a summer's night:
Nor can they to that region climb,
To make impression upon Time.

II

'Twas in a shipwrack, when the seas
10 Ruled, and the winds did what they please,
That my poor lover floating lay,
And, ere brought forth, was cast away:
Till at the last the master-wave
Upon the rock his mother drave;
15 And there she split against the stone,
In a Caesarean sectiòn.

III

The sea him lent those bitter tears
Which at his eyes he always wears:
And from the winds the sighs he bore,
20 Which through his surging breast do roar.

---

1. pleasant] a) pleasing, agreeable (*OED* a. 1) b) merry, gay (*OED* a. 3).

2. infant Love] not Cupid, but M.'s child figure bears obvious comparison with the infants (including Cupid) of the emblem book tradition; see also *Musick's Empire*, ll. 1–2: 'First was the world as one great cymbal made,/Where jarring windes to infant Nature played'.

3. still] always (*OED* a. 3).

4. fountains] see Rev. 21: 6: 'I will give unto him that is athirst of the fountain of the water of life freely'; *The Garden*, l. 49: 'the fountain's sliding foot'. In Platonic writing, the fountain is a metaphor for the transcendental force which impels life. *shadows green* Cp. *The Garden*, l. 48: 'a green thought in a green shade'.

7–8. Figuratively, the lovers, glowing like meteors, cannot ascend to the higher realm in the heavens where their incandescence would show for eternity; literally, lovers, being (typically young) people, are subject to change and decay – they are not immortal.

7. region] heaven; see *The First Anniversary of the Government under O.C.*, ll. 47–8: 'Learning a music in the region clear,/To tune this lower to that higher sphere'.

8. impression] a) a mark (*OED* n. 2) b) an assault (*OED* n. 1b). An 'impression' was a name for a meteor (*OED* n. 5): see Samuel Purchas, *A Theatre of Politicall Flying-Insects* (1657), 10, 'hot impressions in the air' (see above, ll. 7–8 n.).

9–10. See Virgil, *Aeneid*, I, ll. 82–5: 'ac venti, velut agmine facto,/qua data porta, ruunt et terras turbine perflant./incubuere mari totumque a sedibus imis/una Eurusque Notusque ruunt creberque procellis/Africus et vastos volvunt ad litora fluctus' (when lo! the winds, as if in armed array, rush forth where passage is given, and blow in storm-blasts across the world. They swoop down upon the sea, and from its lowest depths upheave it all – East and South winds together, and the South-wester, thick with tempests – and shoreward roll vast billows). The description of shipwreck follows in *Aeneid*, I, ll. 102–23.

9. shipwrack] shipwreck. The old spelling is kept here because of its commonness in the seventeenth century and because its sound is more appropriate to the overall effect of the stanza (see also the rhyme at ll. 27–8).

11. lover floating] the description of the lover in the womb has resonances with the birth of Old Testament prophets: see Jer. 1.5, 'Before I formed thee in the belly I knew thee; and before thou camest forth out of the womb I sanctified thee, and ordained thee a prophet unto the nations'. For other connections with Old Testament figures, see below, ll. 23–4 n., 61 n.

14. rock] cp. the use of the rock as a device on the flag of the Parliamentarian Colonel Sir Edward Hartop, with the motto 'Irritus ingenti scopulo fluctus assultat' (To no avail the wave dashes against the mighty rock) (Young (1995), 102). *drave*] archaic, Northern form of 'drove' (*OED* v. A2), mostly fifteenth-century in usage, but present in seventeenth-century poetic vocabulary: see Cowley, 'The Usurpation' (1647), l. 12: 'thou, their *Cov'etous Neighbours*, drav'st out all'.

15. split] a) suffer shipwreck (*OED* v. I 1 b) b) give birth.

16. Caesarean sectiòn] a birth achieved by a surgical incision through the abdomen into the side of the womb, as was the case with the birth of Julius Caesar. The image implies that the Lover will have as uncanny and prodigious a career as Caesar himself, and invites the reader to treat the Lover as a political figure. P.R.K.A. Davidson and A.K. Jones, *N & Q*, n.s. 32 (1985), 170–2 (171) suggest an oblique and paronomasic reference to the execution of Charles I, so that the phrase is taken literally as the 'sectioning' of Caesar, and enforced by *An Horatian Ode*, ll. 23–4, 'And Caesar's head at last/ Did through his laurels blast'.

17. those] Bod. 1; these 1681.

18. wears] Bod. 1; bears 1681.

17–20. A reversal of Bruno: 'da gli occhi, copiose lacrime che fluiscono al mare; manda dal petto la grandezza e moltitudine de suspiri a l'aria capacissimo' (from his eyes, he pours forth copious tears which flow into the sea; from his breast he sends an abundance and multitude of sighs to the immense receptacle of the air), 395, trans. Memmo, 145.

No day he saw but that which breaks
Through frighted clouds in forkèd streaks;
While round the rattling thunder hurled,
As at the fun'ral of the world.

IV

25 While Nature to his birth presents
This masque of quarr'lling elements;
A num'rous fleet of corm'rants black,
That sailed insulting o'er the wrack,
Received into their cruel care
30 Th'unfortunate and abject heir:
Guardians most fit to entertain
The orphan of the hurricane.

V

They fed him up with hopes and air,
Which soon digested to despair;
35 And as one corm'rant fed him, still
Another on his heart did bill.
Thus while they famish him, and feast,

He both consumèd, and increased:
And languishèd with doubtful breath,
40 Th'amphibium of Life and Death.

VI

And now, when angry Heaven would
Behold a spectacle of blood,
Fortune and he are called to play
At sharp before it all the day:
45 And tyrant Love his breast does ply
With all his winged artillery;
Whilst he, betwixt the flames and waves,
Like Ajax, the mad tempest braves.

VII

See how he nak'd and fierce doth stand,
50 Cuffing the thunder with one hand;
While with the other he does lock,
And grapple, with the stubborn rock:
From which he with each wave rebounds,
Torn into flames, and ragg'd with wounds;

22–3. See *An Horatian Ode*, ll. 13–16: 'like the three-forked lightning, first/ Breaking the clouds where it was nursed,/ Did thorough his own side/ His fiery way divide'. Pursuing the link with *An Horatian Ode* further, the purported Lover King, born in a Caesarean section, witnesses only the new 'day' of thunder and lightning (in *An Horatian Ode*, Cromwell's Providential power) which 'Caesar's head at last/ Did through his laurels blast' (ll. 23–4).
23–4. An allusion to the apocalyptic events described in the Book of Revelation during the Last Judgement: 'And I heard a voice from heaven, as the voice of many waters, and as the voice of a great thunder' (Rev. 14: 2).
26. masque] See *Headnote, Sources and Allusions. elements]* the turmoil of earth (the rock), air (winds, sighs), water (seas, tears) and fire (lightning) in stanzas II and III.
27. corm'rants] the name of the large, scavenging bird, cormorant was also used to signify a greedy, rapacious person (*OED* n. 2 fig.). Craze (1979), 109, suggests the black-suited functionaries of the Court of Wards (see also Corvino in Ben Jonson's *Volpone* (1607)). By means of reference to Rev. 19:17–18 ('all the fowls that fly in the midst of heaven . . . eat the flesh of kings'), and contemporary sermons, Stocker (285–8) suggests the English episcopacy, especially the Laudians. Wilcher (2001), 306–7, argues that the Scots and Parliamentarians who imprisoned the King at Newcastle and Holdenby are the more appropriate presences behind this late 1640s poem.
28. insulting] a) scornfully triumphing (*OED* vbl. n. a) b) assaulting (*OED* vbl. n. b).

30. abject] a) cast off, rejected (*OED* ppl. a. A1) b) downcast, degraded (*OED* ppl. a. A2) c) low in spirit (*OED* ppl. a. A3).
31. Guardians] proper legal term for a person entrusted with the custody of a ward, such as the orphaned Lover: see above, l. 27 n.
34. despair] without hope; common in romance: Sidney, *Old Arcadia* (1590, ed. Jean Robertson, Oxford, 1973), Second Eclogues, 141, 'And I am here the same, so mote I thrive and thee,/ Despaired in all this flock to find a knave but thee'.
36. bill] peck (*OED* v.² 1).
37–8. 'Or in questa vita tal pastura e di maniera tale, che piu accende, che possa appagar il desio' (Now in this life the pecularity of such nourishment is that it enflames the desire more than it can satisfy it), Bruno, 368; trans. Memmo, 116.
39. languishèd] became weaker and more feeble (*OED* v. 1). *doubtful]* uncertain.
40. Life and Death] 'Mors et Vita' ('Death and Life'), Bruno, 447.
43–4. play/At sharp] to duel with unblunted swords (*OED* n.¹ 1 b).
45. ply] assail incessantly (*OED* v.² 4 a).
46. winged artillery] Cupid's arrows.
48. Ajax] son of Oileus, destroyed by Minerva with his fleet in a storm because he had attacked Cassandra in the goddess's temple during the fall of Troy. The story is recounted by Virgil, *Aeneid*, I, ll. 39–45. Ajax was regarded as an exemplar of folly.
49. nak'd] a) unclothed (*OED* A a. 1) b) unarmed (*OED* A a. 4).
54. ragg'd] torn to pieces (*OED* v.¹ 1 a).

5   And all he says, a lover dressed
    In his own blood does relish best.

VIII

This is the only banneret
That ever Love created yet:

60 Who though, by the malignant stars,
    Forced to live in storms and wars;
    Yet dying leaves a perfume here,
    And music within every ear:
    And he in story only rules,
    In a field sable a lover gules.

55–6. all he says . . . best] Donno represents says as ''says'', the aphetic form of 'assays' (attempts). Wilcher, on the contrary, maintains that 'less violence is done to the text by taking 'all he says' as the object of 'relish'; the couplet can then be paraphrased: 'A lover covered in his own blood can best appreciate everything that this unfortunate lover says.' Neither commentator is quite correct. Quite simply, the lover will still maintain that despite his suffering, either a) a lover is best appreciated this way (as if he were a dish of food 'dressed' in the sauce of his blood), or b) the lover's senses are at their most sensitive in this state.

56. relish] a) taste (*OED* v.¹ 2) b) enjoy (*OED* v.¹ 3).

57–64. Wilcher (2001), 307, argues that this stanza encapsulates the story of martyrdom in *Eikon Basilike* (1649) and its laudatory reception.

57. banneret] a) kind of knight, equal to a baron, having vassals under his own banner (*OED* 1a) b) one knighted on the field of battle for valour (*OED* 1b). The last banneret to be created in this second sense was Major General John Smith, knighted for his recapture of the royal standard at the Battle of Edgehill, 1642: see Edward Walsingham, *Britannicae Virtutis Imago* (Oxford, 1644), 15. See also headnote, *Date*.

59. malignant] a) of evil influence, specifically an astrological term (*OED* A a. 3) b) applied between 1641 and 1660 by Royalists to supporters of the Parliament and Commonwealth (*OED* A a. 1 b, c); cp. the 'democratic stars' of *Upon the Death of Lord Hastings*, l. 25.

61. perfume] from Ecclesiasticus 49:1: 'The remembrance of Josias is like the composition of the perfume that is made by the art of the apothecary: it is sweet as honey in all mouths, and as musick at a banquet of wine'. Such imagery was part of the iconography of Charles I: e.g. Martin Parker, 'Upon defacing at *White-hall*' (1643–167[?3]), ll. 11–12, 29–30 – 'Nor shew a reason from the stars/ What causeth Peace or Civil Wars. . . ./ With rich perfume in every room,/ Delightful to that Princely Train'. However, the word was not specifically reserved for the king: e.g. Mildmay Fane, 'Upon ye Perfume [Philip, Earl of] Pembroke left when he was sent to bid this World good night', 'Fugitive Poetry', Harvard UL, fMS Eng. 645, 35. Lady Eleanor Davis identified Josias with the subject of another M. poem, Henry, Lord Hastings, in *Sions Lamentation* (1649), 8: see above, 23, l. 29 n.; see also Cope in Davies (1995), 146–7.

63–4. Cp. Cleveland, 'The Mixt Assembly' (1647), 37–40: 'Strange Scarlet Doctors these, they'l passe in Story/ . . . /The fading Sables and the coming Gules'; Joseph Beaumont, *Psyche* (1648), I.xii, ll. 4–6: 'The front display'd a goodly-dreadful sight,/Great Satan's Arms stamp'd on an iron shield,/A Crowned Dragon Gules in sable field.'

63. story] a) narrative of past events, either historically true, or fictional (*OED* n.¹ I 1); b) pictorial representation of a historical subject (*OED* n.¹ II 8). Cp. *An Elegie on . . . Charles the I* in [John Cleveland], *Monumentum Regale* (1649), 17: 'But the afflicted quill whose penance lies/Through all His thorns, must stories martyr rise:/What hardy plume dares register His cares?'

64. gules] heraldic red. 'Gules' is used here as an adjective, but also occurs as a verb ('to stain red with blood') in seventeenth-century epic and romance: see, e.g., Thomas Heywood, *The Iron Age* (1632), Part 2, III, l. 357, 'Till Hecub's reverent lockes be gul'd in slaughter'. Ormerod and Wortham note that M.'s heraldry is technically incorrect: a colour may only be imposed on a metal background: silver or gold, but not black.

Date. ?After July 1650; early 1650s. The mention of the royal paintings in the past tense in l. 48 (they were sold by Act of Parliament in July 1650), and the echoes from several of M.'s poems written in the late 1640s and early 1650s, give some sense of when the poem was composed. Since the verb in l. 48 could be a subjunctive, and hence not a past tense usage, this evidence is not wholly persuasive. As is the case with *Upon Appleton House*, the poem echoes lines from poems by William Cartwright that M. would most likely have read in his *Comedies, Tragi-Comedies, With Other Poems* (1651) (see Wilcher, *N & Q*, n.s. 39 (1992), 462–3, below, *Headnote, Sources and Genre*, and 203, 228–30, 237). Also like *Upon Appleton House* and *Musick's Empire*, the poem appears to be influenced by sections of Davenant's *Gondibert* of 1651. This evidence (together with a close echo of *Upon Appleton House*; see below, l. 35 n.) further strengthens the case for an early 1650s dating.

Publication. 1681.

Sources and Genre. Verse commenting upon accompanying emblems were common in the Renaissance; these, and elements of emblematic iconography have been seen as the generic sources of *The Gallery*. Giambattista Marino's *La Galeria* (Venice, 1620) was an influential collection of poems on mythological subjects, portraits of real people and sculptures: it may have supplied M. with the idea for his title. A French version was Pierre Le Moyne's *Peintures Morales* (1640–43). But M.'s poem is not concerned with a single image. Rather, it fuses different elements from these traditions in a poem that takes as the centre of its conceit the common poetic notion that the lover has the image of his beloved engraved in his heart or soul.

M.'s knowledge of painting in the context of his travels in Europe, the revival of portrait painting in the Renaissance, and English collectors of art, is discussed by Hinnant, *RQ*, 24 (1971), 26–37. Hagstrum (1958), 117, associates the second

and the fourth stanzas with the brooding light of Rembrandt, Rubens and Caravaggio.

The Gallery also documents a transition in artistic taste from the pictorial narratives of arras-hangings popular in Tudor and Jacobean England to the cosmopolitan fashions of Mannerist painting embraced by the Caroline court, and in particular the genre of allegorical or mythical portrait. The poem moves historically from the abandonment of the arras, so to speak, to the dispersion of Charles I's impressive collection of paintings in July 1650, a collection that had been substantially augmented by the acquisition of the Duke of Mantua's paintings in 1629. Pastoral subjects were a major topic in which the change from Mannerist to Baroque style was registered. M.'s speaker appears to return to the image of an innocent lover very early in their acquaintance, but the manner of the painting refers to this further change of painting style. The recounting of different states of passion is thus also an account of an artistic fashion and the dependence of that fashion upon a political regime and its vision of civilization.

Several poems in Richard Lovelace's *Lucasta* (1649) use images from paintings. In particular, M.'s poem inverts in several senses Lovelace's 'Amyntor's Grove'. Lovelace's poem begins with Chloris, a shepherdess, M.'s poem ends with a pastoral vision of the female lover (ll. 1–12). Amyntor's Grove has several rooms, one of which is full of paintings (ll. 29–44), whereas M.'s poem interiorizes a single picture gallery as an image of the soul. Pictures of saints in this gallery are surrounded by gems which have the effect of making them appear connected and like 'one continued Tapistrie' (l. 62); whereas M.'s pictures have displaced the tapestries. Lovelace names his painters ('*Titian, Raphael, Georgone*' (l. 31)), and Amyntor may refer to Endymion Porter, who travelled abroad acquiring pictures for Charles I, whereas M. has only implicit references to particular painters and pictures. If M. did write the poem in the early 1650s, it displays no reference to the iconography of Commonwealth portraiture, that was an exaggeration, and sometimes a subversion, of Caroline court styles (see Peacock, in Lake and Sharpe, eds (1992), 226–8). Lovelace is at pains to show nature's transcendence of art (in the beauty of two young lovers), whereas M. meditates upon the interaction of love and artistic representation.

Wilcher, *N & Q*, n.s. 39 (1992), 462, detects in the second half of the penultimate stanza (ll. 45–8) lexical and conceptual echoes from another poem concerned with painting, William Cartwright's 'To a Painter's handsome Daughter' (1651), ll. 3–6:

> So lively, and so fresh, that we may swear
> Instead of draughts, He hath plac'd Creatures there;
> People, not shadows; which in time will be
> Not a dead Number, but a Colony.

The passage in Davenant's *Gondibert* (1651) from which parts of *Upon Appleton House* and *Musick's Empire* draw (and to which Cartwright's lines are also related) is preceded by stanzas dealing with the power of visual art. Book 2, Canto 6, stanzas 62 to 75 deal with a series of painted representations of Eve, the Flood and the post-Noachian dispensation. The paintings become progressively more gloomy, as do those in *The Gallery*, until the scene is redeemed by Lord Astragon and his assembly dressed in many colours, and likened to pastoral virgins, just like the mistress, as she appears in M.'s final stanza.

Versification and Style. The poem is written in iambic tetrameters, organized in seven stanzas of eight-line rhymed couplets. The central conceit of the speaker's soul as a picture gallery is notable for the clarity of its articulation, with each stanza corresponding to a different picture, alternating between violent, passion-filled people and perfect female deities in sts. II–V. After the introductory stanza, st. II contrasts the female (murderess) with the male (tyrant), st. III is concerned with the representation of Aurora, st. IV with the sorceress and witchcraft, st. V with Venus, and st. VII with the human pastoral. In successive stanzas, indoors is juxtaposed with outdoors. This clarity is enhanced by a use of syntax and punctuation that sharpens the focus of the pictorial details: see, e.g., the two *caesurae* and six stressed syllables of l. 16. Clipped consonants are a feature of sts. II and IV, as opposed to the heavy sibilants of sts. III and V. The extreme variations of tone, from 'parodistic hyperbole' to 'quasi-ritualistic incantation', are discussed by Warnke, *SEL*, 5 (1965), 23–6.

The Gallery

I

Clora come view my soul, and tell
Whether I have contrived it well.
Now all its several lodgings lie
Composed into one gallery;
5 And the great arras-hangings, made
Of various faces, by are laid;
That, for all furniture, you'll find
Only your picture in my mind.

II

Here thou art painted in the dress
10 Of an inhuman murderess;
Examining upon our hearts
Thy fertile shop of cruel arts:

---

2. *contrived*] a) devised (*OED* v.¹ 3) b) understood (*OED* v.¹ 4).
3–6. *several lodgings . . . various faces*] suggesting several previous mistresses.
3. *lodgings*] living rooms and bedrooms (*OED* vbl. n. 3 a).
4. *gallery*] a building specifically devoted to the display of works of art (*OED* n. 6, where the first usage recorded is 1591, in Shakespeare, *1 Henry VI*, II.iii, l. 37).
5. *arras-hangings*] tapestries hung on walls or moveable screens, with colourful figures and scenes woven into them (*OED* 4).
6. *faces*] a) panels (not in *OED*) b) woven representations of human visages (*OED* n. I 1 c) *by are laid*] i.e., discarded.
7. *furniture*] movable articles in a dwelling, whether useful or ornamental, including fittings and drapery (*OED* n. 7).
9–17. *Here . . . the other side*] signifying a double-sided portrait. See also below, l. 33.
11. *Examining*] testing (*OED* v. 10).
12. *shop*] shopful (*OED* n. 2 c), with 'shop' meaning 'workshop': *OED* n. 3 a, c).

Engines more keen than ever yet
Adornèd tyrant's cabinet;
15   Of which the most tormenting are
Black eyes, red lips, and curlèd hair.

III

But, on the other side, th'art drawn
Like to Aurora in the dawn;
When in the east she slumb'ring lies,
20   And stretches out her milky thighs;
While all the morning choir does sing,
And manna falls, and roses spring;
And, at thy feet, the wooing doves
Sit pèrfecting their harmless loves.

IV

25   Like an enchantress here thou show'st,
Vexing thy restless lover's ghost;
And, by a light obscure, dost rave
Over his entrails, in the cave;
Divining thence, with horrid care,
30   How long thou shalt continue fair;
And (when informed) them throw'st away,
To be the greedy vulture's prey.

V

But, against that, thou sit'st afloat
Like Venus in her pearly boat.

13–14. Engines . . . cabinet] Cp. *RT*, 60, in *MPW*, I. 208–9: 'It were a worthy Spectacle . . . to see his Majesty . . . busied in his Cabinet among those Engines whose very names are so hard that it is some torture to name them.'; 'A Short Historical Essay' in *Mr Smirke* (1676), 72–3, *MPW*, II. 170: 'Indeed, whatsoever the Animadverter saith of the Act of Seditious Conventicles here in *England*, as if it were Anvill'd after another of the *Romans* Senate, the Christians of those Ages, had all the finest tooles of Persecution out of *Julian's* shop, and studied him then as curiously as some do now *Machiavel.*'
13. Engines] instruments of murder or torture (*OED* n. 5 b).
14. tyrant's] Kermode, Walker, Wilcher, Ormerod and Wortham+; tyrants *1681, Margoliouth, Lord*; a tyrant's *Thompson, Donno. cabinet*] a) private or secret room (*OED* n. II 7 a). b) a picture gallery (*OED* n. I 4), and a figure for secret or hidden intentions, such as a tyrant might have (*OED* n. I 6).
17–24. th'art . . . loves] Hinnant, *RQ*, 24 (1971), 30–2, argues that this stanza is more indebted to pictures of the sleeping Venus (several of which were in English collections) than to pictures of Aurora, who is usually portrayed with other mythological characters, and in active situations.
18. Aurora] goddess of the dawn: 'Et iam prima novo spargebat lumine terras/Tithoni croceum linquens Aurora cubile' (And now early Dawn, leaving the saffron bed of Tithonus, was sprinkling her fresh rays upon the earth), Virgil, *Aeneid*, IV, l. 585.
20. milky] milk-white (*OED* a. 1).
21. morning choir] usually birdsong; iconographically, the group of angelic, winged figures surrounding the goddess.
22. manna] substance miraculously supplied as food to the Children of Israel in the wilderness (Ex. 16:31).
22–3. roses . . . doves] attributes of the Sleeping Venus (see above, ll. 16–24n.).
23. wooing] the copy owned by the University of Illinois at Urbana-Champaign (no shelfmark) alters 'wooing' in a late-seventeenth or early-eighteenth-century hand to 'cooing'. The

reading of *1681* is consistent with M.'s wit (the doves woo because they are lovers (see l. 24)), but the annotation expresses one of the poet's intentions: he means to make us think of the more expected 'cooing'.
24. harmless] innocent (*OED* a. 3).
25–33. here . . . against that] see above, ll. 9–17 n.: another double-sided portrait.
25–32. Ovid, *Elegia* VIII, features the old enchantress Dipsas giving advice to young women on how to treat their men. This, however, is a young enchantress, a sadistic woman superstitiously sacrificing her lovers in order to find out how long she will remain beautiful. Hinnant, *RQ*, 24 (1971), 32, notes the absence of mythological and metamorphosis themes in this stanza, unlike conventional enchantress portrayals of Circe, Armida and the Witch of Endor.
27. light obscure] the enchantress's candle or torch light, and/or the light of her divining fire; also playing on chiaroscuro, the style of pictorial art where only light and shade, but not colours, are used (*OED* 1). Enthusiasm for the various effects of obscurity was widespread: see, e.g., Contantijn Huygens, *Briefwisseling*, ed. J.A. Worp (The Hague, 1911–18), I.94.
27–8. rave/Over] poke or pry into (*OED* v.³ b).
28. entrails] innards; contents of the abdominal cavity (*OED* n.¹ II 3).
29. Divining] ancient divination involved three steps: a) killing the animal, b) observing the state of the organs, c) burning the entrails and making a prophecy from the way they burnt. See John Potter, *Antiquities* (1818), i. 367. *thence*] i.e. from thence. *horrid*] shocking, detestable (*OED* a. 2). *care*] a) anxiety (*OED* n.¹ 2) b) attentiveness (*OED* n.¹ 3).
30. fair] beautiful.
34. Venus . . . boat] Venus sprang from the foam of the sea, and was depicted in Renaissance paintings (such as Botticelli's *Birth of Venus*) as seated in a conch shell on a calm ocean. As in previous stanzas, M. eliminates other figures from his portrayal of a well-known painting subject (see Hinnant, *RQ*, 24 (1971), 33–5).

35 The halcyons, calming all that's nigh,
    Betwixt the air and water fly.
    Or, if some rolling wave appears,
    A mass of ambergris it bears.
    Nor blows more wind than what may well
40 Convòy the perfume to the smell.

VI

    These pictures and a thousand more,
    Of thee, my gallery dost store;
    In all the forms thou can'st invent
    Either to please me, or torment:
45 For thou alone to people me,

    Art grown a num'rous colony;
    And a collection choicer far
    Than or Whitehall's or Mantua's were.

VII

    But, of these pictures and the rest,
50 That at the entrance likes me best:
    Where the same posture, and the look
    Remains, with which I first was took.
    A tender shepherdess, whose hair
    Hangs loosely playing in the air,
55 Transplanting flow'rs from the green hill,
    To crown her head, and bosom fill.

---

35. halcyons] birds believed to build their nests at sea, so calming the winds and waves: see *Upon Appleton House*, ll. 669–72 and n.: 'The modest halcyon comes in sight,/Flying betwixt the day and night;/And such an horror calm and dumb,/Admiring Nature does benumb.' See also, ibid., ll. 673–5.
38. ambergris] fragrant substance secreted by sperm whales.
40. Convòy] escort (*OED* v. I 1), appropriate to a marine scene; the naval use of the word originates during the English Civil War period (*OED* gives 1641 as the earliest date of this sense); also implies the more expected 'conveys', which is in fact the second general sense of 'convoy' (*OED* v. II 5). *perfume*] the substance (here, ambergris), as opposed to the smell it makes.
42. dost] *1681*; do *Bod. 1. store*] stock.
45–8. For . . . were] See above, *Headnote, Date* and *Sources.*
45. people] populate.
47–8. collection . . . were] Charles I bought some of the paintings of Vincenzo Gonzaga, Duke of Mantua in 1629, and integrated them into the royal collection at Whitehall; the most famous and expensive item, Mantegna's 'Triumphs of Julius Caesar', were hung in the state apartments of the Commonwealth and Protectorate: see Kelsey (1997), 39.

48. or . . . or] either . . . or.
51. posture] position and carriage of the body (in a painting) (*OED* n. 1).
53. tender shepherdess] paintings of aristocratic women as pastoral shepherdesses were a particular feature of the Platonic love cult inspired by Queen Henrietta Maria. Mary Villiers, Duchess of Richmond (the 'fair Richmond' of *An Elegy Upon the Death of My Lord Francis Villiers*, l. 61), was painted in this way by Van Dyke.
55. Transplanting] Cp. Carew, 'On a Damaske rose sticking upon a Ladies Breast' (1640), ll. 3–4: 'Let scent and lookes be sweete and blesse that hand,/That did transplant thee to that sacred land.'
55–6. flow'rs . . . fill] the goddess Flora was usually painted with a floral crown and an armful of flowers, as in Botticelli's *Primavera*. Hinnant, *RQ*, 24 (1971) 36–7, regards ll. 53–6 as a reference to Botticelli's painting, and specifically the last panel, showing the metamorphosis of the shepherdess Chloris into Flora. Botticelli took the myth from Ovid, *Fasti*, V, ll. 183 ff. Wind (1958; rptd. 1980), 114–17, discusses the allegorical meaning of the painting.

19
The Fair Singer

Date. ?1647–48. The evidence for dating is based upon the supposed dates for other poems that are largely imitations of a European or English love poem (see below, *The Match, Mourning, Headnote, Date*).

Publication. 1681.

Sources and Genre. The poem is an exercise in Petrarchan conventions betraying for many commentators not so much feeling as an interest in the capacity to manipulate clichés ('lyricism of the untouched heart': Colie (1970), 44). It appears to be very closely related to two Italian poems by Marino, *Canto Insidioso, Lira* (1622), Pt. II:

> Fuggite, incauti amanti,
> la canora omicida,
> ch'asconde, empia ed infida,
> sotto note soavi amari pianti.
> Quelle corde sonore
> sono i lacci d'Amore;
> quella che sembra cetra
> e d'Amor la faretra;
> quell'arco, arco è d'Amor;
> que'dolci accenti
> son saette pungenti.

(Flee, unwary lovers, the melodic murderess, who, wicked and faithless, hides bitter tears in pleasant notes. Those sonorous chords are the cords of Love; that which seems a lute is the quiver of Love; that bow is the bow of Love; those sweet accents are pungent darts.)

> E con la voce e con la vista intanto
> Gir per due strade a saettare i petti.
> > *Adone*, VII, 39

(And with voice and glance together, in two ways she pierces hearts.)

Their relationship with M.'s poem is discussed by Mirollo (1963), 245–6. Leishman (1966), 49–58, discusses the poem's similarity to a number of contemporary examples (by Milton, Waller and Robert Heath), none of which is a source, although they demonstrate the poetic topos of the address to a singing woman. M.'s poem is superior to the others by virtue of its 'intellectualisation' (ibid., 49).

Carew's second 'Song. Celia singing' (1640) is, however, a possible English source:

> You that thinke Love can convey,
> > No other way,
> But through the eyes, into the heart,
> > His fatall Dart:
> Close up those casements, and but heare
> > This Syren sing;
> > And on the wing
> Of her sweet voyce, it shall appeare
> That Love can enter at the eare.

Lovelace's 'Gratiana dauncing and singing' (1649) presents the woman replicating the movement of the spheres with her arts. Unlike M.'s singer, who captures hearts with her looks and minds with her song, she captures male desire with her dancing: 'Chain'd to her brave feet with such arts' (l. 15).

Structure, Style and Versification. The poem is written in six-line iambic pentameters (the only amatory lyric by M. with this metre), organized in three six-line stanzas, and rhyming ababcc (also unusual in M.). They are like three sestets, each from a Petrarchan sonnet. Each stanza is a sentence. Craze (1979), 51, notes the peculiarly Latinate syntax, with little inversion of word order, and then only to achieve a rhyme. The stanzas move successively from the singer as enemy, to the speaker taken prisoner, then being defeated.

The poem is most remarkable for its effortless achievement. Leishman (1966), 46, regarded the poem as blemished by a first and third stanza that failed to match the achievement of the second. Nonetheless, his praise is elsewhere unqualified: 'In poems of which Marvell's *Fair Singer* is the supreme example, what they have given us, however ingenious and intellectualised, are still essentially descriptions, analytic and defining, precise and comparatively sober, of a sight or sound, which are simultaneously descriptions, often metaphorical, of its effect upon spectators or hearers' (57). Colie (1970), 43–4, notes the fusion of amatory commonplaces 'so intricately intertwined and so trickily played off against one another, that they are difficult to take seriously'. Yet the poem makes the conventional description of the woman seem natural, while the prosodic regularity points to 'composure and sanity'.

The Fair Singer

I

To make a final conquest of all me,
Love did compose so sweet an enemy,
In whom both beauties to my death agree,
Joining themselves in fatal harmony;
5   That while she with her eyes my heart does bind,
She with her voice might captivate my mind.

II

I could have fled from one but singly fair:
My disentangled soul itself might save,
Breaking the curlèd trammels of her hair.
10   But how should I avoid to be her slave,
Whose subtle art invisibly can wreathe
My fetters of the very air I breathe?

III

It had been easy fighting in some plain,
Where victory might hang in equal choice.
15   But all resistance against her is vain,
Who has th'advantage both of eyes and voice,
And all my forces needs must be undone,
She having gainèd both the wind and sun.

---

2. compose] a) made an alliance with (*OED* v. II 10 b) b) fashion (*OED* v. I 1).
4. fatal harmony] a paradox. *harmony*] a) agreement (*OED* 1) b) pleasing combination of musical notes (*OED* 4).
5. bind] a) tie up (*OED* v. 2) b) enchant (*OED* v. 2 b).
6. She . . . mind] Cp. Waller, 'Of my Lady Isabella, Playing the Lute' (1645), ll. 11–12: 'Music so softens and disarms the mind,/That not an arrow does resistance find.' *captivate*] a) enchant (*OED* v. 3) b) keep in subjection (*OED* v. 2).
7. singly] of a single quality (*OED* adv. 1).
8–9. Echoing the notion of the soul freeing itself from the body at death: cp. Virgil, *Aeneid*, XI, ll. 828–9: 'tum frigida toto/paulatim exsolvit se corpore lentaque colla' (Then, growing chill, she slowly freed herself from all the body's bonds).
8. disentangled] free from complications (i.e. clear-sighted) (*OED* v. 1 b).
9. curlèd trammels] Cp. Drayton, 'The second Nimphall', *The Muses Elizium*, l. 236: 'In the curld Tramels of thy hayre.' *trammels*] a) plaits, braids or tresses (*OED* n.¹ IV 6) b) nets (*OED* n.¹ I. 1) c) hobble, to prevent a horse from straying; device that shackles or fetters (*OED* n.¹ II 2–3).

11. wreathe] twist, coil (*OED* v. 1).
12. fetters . . . breathe] based on the ancient and Renaissance depiction of eloquence as a Heracles or Hercules leading men by chains attached to his tongue and their ears: see Lucian, *Heracles*, 1–6; Alciati, *Emblemata*, clxxx.
13–18. Cp. Milton, *Areopagitica*, *CPW*, II.562: 'When a man hath . . . drawn forth his reasons, as it were a battell raung'd . . . calls out his adversary into the plain, offers him the advantage of wind and sun.'
14. hang] Cp. the scales held by Zeus, determining the fight between Hector and Achilles (Homer, *Iliad*, XXII, ll. 209–12; Virgil, *Aeneid*, XII, ll. 725–7). *in equal choice*] i.e. evenly balanced.
16. advantage] another military term used figuratively: a place of vantage on higher ground afforded superiority over the enemy (*OED* n.¹ I 3), as opposed to the flat plain of l. 13.
17. forces] a) army, troops (*OED* n.¹ I 1 pl.) b) physical strength (*OED* n.¹ I 1).
18. gainèd . . . sun] naval and military allusion: gaining the windward and sunward side of an enemy.

20
Mourning

Date. Noting the possible connection of the Chlora of this poem (l. 4) with the Chlora of *An Elegy upon the Death of my Lord Francis Villiers* (l. 69), Donno suggests a *terminus a quo* of July 1648. Like the Chlora in this poem, the Chlora of M.'s elegy also weeps (ll. 86–8).

Publication. 1681.

Sources and Genre. Poems concerned with a (usually female) weeper constitute a distinct subgroup in the period: see, e.g., John Hall, 'Julia Weeping' in *Poems* (1646), ll. 1–4, 15–18: 'Fairest, when thy eyes did pour/A crystall shower,/I was persuaded that some stone/Had liquid grown. . . . Those pearly drops in time shall be/A precious sea;/And thou shall like thy coral prove,/Soft under water, hard above.' See also above, *Eyes and Tears. Headnote. Sources and Genre.* The picture of a possibly insincere female weeper is present in Cowley's 'Weeping' (1647), several echoes of which are present in M.'s poem (see below, ll. 1–4 n.). To this extent, M.'s Chlora is a 'silent woman', of the kind made famous by Jonson in his play *Epicoene* (1609); for echoes of this play in the poem, see below, ll. 35–6 n. Delany, *MLQ*, 33 (1972), 30–6 (30) identifies a source in the proverb 'Marry widow before she leave mourning'.

The poem is a pastoral mock-elegy. Leishman (in Carey, ed. (1969), 120) finds a strong resemblance between the presentation of Chlora's dissimulation and Étienne Pasquier's (Stephanus Paschasius) Latin poem 'De Amoena vidua':

> Certior vt facta est vxor de morte mariti,
> 　　Mirum quàm variis sit cruciata modis.
> Nullus in urbe locus, quo non gemebunda feratur,
> 　　Nec sibi, nec lachrimis parcit ubique dolor.
> Quinetiam Superos atque inuida Numina damnat;
> 　　Conqueriturque suo se super esse viro.
> Vt lachrimis quaestus, sic tristia vora querelis
> 　　Addit, & expertem se sore connubii.
> His tamen in lachrimis nihil est ornatius illi,
> Perpetuusque sub est eius in ore nitor,
> Siccine, defunctum quae deperit orba maritum,
> 　　Semper aget viduo foemina maesta thoro?
> Quae flet culta, suum non luget, Amoena, maritum,
> 　　Quid facit ergo? alium quaerit Amoena virum.
> 　　　　(*Deliciae C[entum] Poetarum Gallorum*, ed.
> Janus Gruterus (Ranutius Gherus) (1609), ii. 875)

As a wife is tested at the time of her husband's death, it is wondrous how many ways she suffers torments. There is no place in the city she may frequent without groaning; everywhere her grief spares neither herself, nor her tears. She even curses the gods and the malignant powers, and laments that she has survived her husband. Just as she increases tears with indignation, so to her complaints she adds mournful prayers that she might always be free of marriage. Yet, amid these tears, nothing could be handsomer than she, and there hides a perpetual brightness in her face. Will she, who, widowed, pines for her dead husband, always thus play the sorrowing wife on her bereaved bed? Amoena, she who weeps elegantly does not mourn her husband. What, then, is she doing? Amoena seeks another husband.

The questioning of the sincerity of tears was a topic in English love poetry too. See, e.g., Sir Robert Howard, 'Song at Amaranta's Command, set to the Tune of Archibella' (1668), ll. 10–12: 'Those streams from springs like ours might flow,/The tears can ne'r united grow,/Of feigned grief and reall woe.' The eighth and penultimate lines of M.'s poem bear a close resemblance to the opening lines from a poem by John Eliot, 'A New-years Gift', not published until 1658, but circulating in manuscript at least by 1642, when publication was first planned ('To the Reader', *Poems* (1658), sig. A2ʳ):

> Could I but dive into the Oceans Breast,
> Or climbe those Rocks, that with the clouds contest,
> If I could sayl unto the Persian shore,
> Or rob the wealthy *Indies* of their Oare.
> Your private walks, and Arbours I would pave
> With orient Pearl, and you should Diamonds have.
> 　　　　　　　　　　　　　　　　　　　　(ll. 1–6)

Hobbs, *EMS*, 1 (1989), 187, also suggests that ll. 29–31 are indebted to Davenant's 'Go, hunt the whiter ermine' (1638), ll. 9–15:

> Goe, dive into the Southerne Sea, and when
> Thou'st found (to trouble the nice sight of men)
> A swelling Pearle, and such whose single worth
> Boasts all the wonders which the Seas bring forth
> Give it Endymions Love: whose every Teare
> Would more enrich the skill full Jeweller.
>
> How I command! How slowly they obey!

In addition to these precise sources and analogues, the poem contains references to what by the 1640s were a series of clichés, some carefully embedded in the narrative that explains Chlora's situation: e.g. the eye as window of the soul (l. 24), tears as coins (ll. 25–8). Wilcher (1985), 22, argues that these relocations and revivifications are a 'cynical' refurbishment of poetic materials, reflecting the dubious nature of Chlora's integrity. The poem is thus in some ways a denial of the high status given to weeping in *Eyes and Tears*, to which poem *Mourning* is intimately linked.

Structure, Versification and Style. The poem is divided into nine stanzas of four iambic tetrameters, each rhyming abab. Only the first line, with its trochaic first foot, is irregular. Such regularity allows the poet to exploit the tonal qualities of his sentences. Thus, the clear, urgent clauses of the first three stanzas, where the weeping is described, are replaced by a wry, insinuating tone in the rest of the poem. Yet the earnest voice of the first three stanzas describes a complicated phenomenon, and it is not clear that the speaker understands entirely what he is seeing; the second four stanzas are in no doubt of their judgement. The relative impersonality of the speaker's voice is modified by the introduction of the first person in the final stanza, where a 'silent judgement' (i.e. no personal comment, complementing Chlora the 'silent woman') is promised, only to be delivered ambiguously in the final line: 'it is to be supposed they grieve'. The final impression, bolstered by the startling imagery of st. VIII, is of a deep intimacy shared with an onlooker deeply engaged in the interpretation of an event. The cultivation of enigma in the poem is matched by the seamless joining of literary components, as the reader moves from the genre of lachrymose poetry in the first third of the poem, via pastoral figures, to a concretely social, even urban, picture of Chlora in her house, and further to the exotic imagistic climax in stanza 8, even though this itself, the speaker implies, may be a hollow world.

Modern Criticism. Comment on the poem is scarce. Wilcher (20–3) regards the speaker's dissociation from the two rumours, while also undermining his own unqualified support for Chlora's integrity, as an example of a refusal to 'simplify the enigma of experience'. M. declines 'to resolve some dispute activated by his poetry', offering instead a 'final neatly balanced assessment'. For Delany, *MLQ*, 33 (1972), 30–6 (33), the fulcrum of this balance is Chlora's auto-eroticism (ll. 19–20) 'in which the psychological congruity of the kindred passions of grief and lust is translated into a literal congruity, as the eyes' moisture flows into . . . the genital moisture of Chlora's loins'. Chlora is thus like Narcissus (or one of M.'s Narcissus figures [see above, 22, 82]), but immune through her toughness to Narcissus's weakness.

Mourning

I

You, that decipher out the fate
Of human offsprings from the skies,
What mean these infants which of late
Spring from the stars of Chlora's eyes?

II

5   Her eyes confused, and doubled o'er,
With tears suspended ere they flow,
Seem bending upwards, to restore
To heaven, whence it came, their woe.

III

When, moulding of the wat'ry spheres,
10   Slow drops untie themselves away;
As if she, with those precious tears,
Would strow the ground where Strephon lay.

IV

Yet some affirm, pretending art,
Her eyes have so her bosom drowned,
15   Only to soften near her heart
A place to fix another wound.

V

And, while vain Pomp does her restrain
Within her solitary bow'r,
She courts herself in am'rous rain;
20   Herself both Danaë and the show'r.

VI

Nay others, bolder, hence esteem
Joy now so much her master grown,
That whatsoever does but seem
Like grief, is from her windows thrown.

1–4. Cp. Cowley, 'Weeping' (1647), ll. 7–10: 'As Stars reflect on waters, so I spy/In every drop (methinks) her Eye./The Baby which lives there, and always plays/In that illustrious Sphere.'
1. An address to astrologers; cp. *To a Gentleman that only upon the sight of the Author's writing, had given a Character of his Person and Judgement of his Fortune*, ll. 25–6: 'Hinc mihi praeteriti rationes atque futuri/Elicit; astrologus certior astronomo' (Hence, interpretations of the past and future/He elicits; an astrologer more certain than an astronomer). Cp. also Cleveland, 'The hecatomb to his Mistresse' (1651), ll. 77–80: 'Say the Astrologer, who spells the Stars,/In that fair Alphabet reads Peace and Wars,/Mistakes his Globe, and in her brighter eye/Interprets Heavens phisiognomy.'
3. infants] tears, although usually 'infants' or 'babies' were the reflections of people in the pupils of another person's eyes (from the pun on Latin *pupilla*); Latin *infans* means 'that which cannot speak', just as tears are silently eloquent.
4. Spring . . . Chlora's] a pun on 'spring' since 'Chlora' derives from Greek *chlora*, 'green'. *stars . . . eyes*] standard language for praising women; see the striking picture of a sonnet woman with suns for eyes in Charles Sorel, *The Extravagant Shepherd*, trans. John Davies (1654), leaf inserted between 22 and 23.
5–8. Her . . . woe] Chlora's eyes are turned upwards towards heaven, whereas in Crashaw's 'The Weeper' (1646), ll. 19–20, it is the tears that flow upwards: 'Upwards thou dost weepe,/Heavens bosome drinks the gentle streame.'
5. confused] a) bewildered (*OED* ppl. a. II 2) because looking upward towards heaven and downwards to Strephon b) mixed together (with the tears; *OED* ppl. a. II 4); from Latin *confusion*: mixture, union (Lewis and Short: I.A.2). *doubled o'er*] the tears form an extra layer over the cornea of the eye; their

presence causes 'double' or blurred vision. Delany, *MLQ*, 33 (1972), 30–6 (32) suggests that 'doubled' infers treachery.
6. tears suspended] as opposed to the tears of *Eyes and Tears*, ll. 7–8, that fall immediately and vertically to make a 'plummet.' *suspended*] a) temporarily stopped (*OED* v. I 2 b) b) hung up (*OED* v. II 10 a).
9. moulding . . . spheres] the tears take their shape from the eyes; cp. Jonson, 'The Mind' (publ. 1640), ll. 55–6: 'So polished, perfect, round, and even,/As it slid moulded off from heaven.'
12. Cp. Milton, *Lycidas* (1637), l. 151: 'To strow the laureate hearse where Lycid lies.' (Hobbs, *EMS*, 1 (1989), 187).
13. pretending] indicating (*OED* v. I 11). *art*] craftiness (*OED* n. III 13).
16. wound] i.e. from one of Cupid's arrows.
17. vain Pomp] echoes The Book of Common Prayer, Catechism (1603 version): 'That I should forsake the deuill and all his workes, the pomps and vanities of the wicked world.'
18. bow'r] inner chamber, bedroom (*OED* n.¹ 2).
19. She . . . rain] Cp. Henry Reynolds, 'So glides along the wanton brook', 'Courting the banks with amorous rain.' (Hobbs, *EMS*, 1 (1989), 186).
20. Danaë and the show'r] Zeus made an amorous assault upon Danaë by pouring onto her in the shape of a golden shower; Perseus was the result of the union (see Ovid, *Metamorphoses*, IV, ll. 610–11); interpreted (e.g. by Horace, *Carmina*, III.16) as a fable concerning the corrupting power of money. The subject was painted by Orazio Gentileschi, *c.* 1621; M. could have seen the picture when in Italy (see Garrard (1989), 242–3).
21. hence] from these premises, therefore (*OED* adv. III 7).
24. is . . . thrown] as if she were throwing favours to new suitors. *windows*] i.e. eyes.

VII

5   Nor that she pays, while she survives,
To her dead love this tribute due,
But casts abroad these donatives,
At the installing of a new.

VIII

How wide they dream! The Indian slaves
0   That dive for pearl through seas profound,
Would find her tears yet deeper waves,
And not of one the bottom sound.

IX

I yet my silent judgement keep,
Disputing not what they believe:
35   But sure as oft as women weep,
It is to be supposed they grieve.

27. donatives] gifts officially made to mark an occasion (here, the 'installation' of a new lover, as if he were being presented to an ecclesiastical benefice (*OED* n. B 1)).

29. wide] a) broad-ranging b) wide of the mark. *dream*] fancy, imagine (*OED* v.² 6).

29–31. The Indian . . . waves] Cp. Herbert, 'Marie Magdalene' (1633), ll. 10–12: 'Though we could dive/In tears like seas,/our sins are piled/Deeper than they.' See also above, *Headnote, Sources and Genre.*

30–1. pearl . . . tears] Cp. Crashaw, 'The Weeper' (1646), l. 54: 'Her richest Pearles, I mean thy Teares'; Thomas Bancroft, 'To the never-dying Memory of the Noble Lord *Hastings*, &c.', in *Lachrymae Musarum* (1649), 56: 'His fame . . . with all the weight of Worth that Youth could have,/Sank to the restful centre of the Grave,/As th'Indian dives for Pearls.' Delany, *MLQ*, 33 (1972), 30–6 (35) writes: 'Marvell's poetic gift often seems to reach its highest pitch when he unites paradox with hyperbole, as he does here: the wit of imagining her tears as bottomless seas is reinforced by the implicit *identity* of tears and pearls.' Diving for pearls was more conventionally regarded as an example of human vanity and lustfulness: 'Alas!

who was it . . . / . . . /That sought out Pearles, and div'd to find/Such pretious perils for mankind!' (Henry Vaughan, 'The First White Age', translation of Boëthius, *De Consolatione Philosophiae*, Lib. 2, Metrum 3 (1651), ll. 34, 35–6.

30. dive] Bod. 1; sink 1681; presumably by using a weight. *profound*] deep (*OED* a. 1).

31–2. Cp. William Alabaster, Sonnet 18, ll. 11–12: 'burning love doth make my tears more deep,/And deeper tears cause love to flame above.'

32. sound] a) strike; touch the bottom (verb: *OED* v.² 4) b) firm (adjective; *OED* a. 4 a); a) implies that Chlora's grief (as expressed by her tears) is unfathomably deep, but b) suggests that her grief is insincere.

33. silent] unwritten or unspoken (*OED* a. 2).

34. they] the 'some' of l. 13 and 'others' of l. 21.

35–6. Cp. Jonson, *Epicoene* (1609), 1.1, ll. 94–6: 'Lady, it is to be presumed,/Though art's hid causes are not found,/All is not sweet, all is not sound'; Donne, 'Twicknam Garden' (1633), ll. 24–5: 'Nor can you more judge a womans thoughts by teares,/Then by her shadow what she weares.'

21
Daphnis and Chloe

Date. ?Late 1640s. Legouis (1971, 1.258) cited L.N. Wall for an apparent echo of the title of a tract of 1647 (see below, l. 107 n.), but this has not been preferred by subsequent editors as a *terminus ad quem*. Griffin (1995), 26, suggests that the reference to beheading in ll. 97–100 associates the poem with the regicide, so that a date of 1649 would be likely. A stronger piece of evidence, however, is the similarity of the treatment of love and death with *To His Coy Mistress* (see below, ll. 6, 68 n., 74–6 n.).

Publication. 1681. An abridged version, containing stanzas I–III, V–VII, X–XV, XXII–XXV, was printed in George Ellis, ed., *Specimens of the Early English Poets* (1st edn, 1790; 2nd edn, 1801), 3.266–9. The consequence of the omitted stanzas is to remove the cynicism from the poem and diminish the overtones of playfulness: the sense of pain at the parting of the lovers is the main focus, and the poem becomes a complaint.

Genre and Sources. Although the poem has been compared to M.'s *Mourning* in respect of the gap between character and the narrator's awareness (Wilcher (1985), 78), the poem is in fact unique in M.'s oeuvre for its comparative length and its cynical treatment of the relationship between two lovers. To this extent, it is like a short epyllion, of which genre Marlowe's *Hero and Leander* (1593–98) is the most famous example in English. The title reflects the third-century Greek romance *Daphnis and Chloe*, by Longus, translated into English by Angel Day from the French of Jacques Amyot in 1587, and could be understood as a revision of Longus' sympathetic treatment of the adolescent pastoral lovers' incomprehension of their love, or how to consummate it. Colie (1970), 48, regards M.'s cynical lovers as a deliberate and ironic undermining of Longus' pair. Hardin (2000), 57, suggests that Longus' sophist narrator, a 'libertine manipulator of innocence and our own experience', is transformed into the specious Daphnis in M.'s poem. Walton (1955), 125, compares M.'s manner and tone in the poem with Chaucer's *Troilus and Criseyde*, specifically Chaucer's attitude to Criseyde, while also noting M.'s familiarity with other poems by Chaucer. Daphnis and Chloe are also names of pastoral figures in earlier elegiac and amorous Latin verse: see John Barclay, *Poematum Libri Duo* (1615), 43–8, 80–1.

The poem combines a coy Ovidian narrative with an extended metaphysical conceit: the moment of parting between the lovers is compared to a person's death, but the conceit playfully exploits the association of death with sexual pleasure and climax (see Dollimore (1998)). Personification is the dominant figure, in addition to the heavy use of paradox. Daphnis initially appears innocent of the connotations of his language but, when his apology is revealed to be a mere persuasion to love, his naivety must be regarded as questionable. Chloe is named in l. 6 as a 'coy mistress': to some extent, the poem analyses 'coyness' through her eyes as well as through her lover's, thereby containing more perspectives than *To His Coy Mistress*. The proximity of Chloe to Nature suggests that the poem is akin to an allegory (where Daphnis should be associated with Art), which associates the poem with the allegory of Nature and Love in *The Match* (see below, ll. 13–16 n., 25).

Style, Structure and Versification. Heptasyllabic lines in quatrains with an abba rhyme are found first in Shakespeare's *The Phoenix and the Turtle*, and then in Carew's 'Separation of Lovers'. M.'s heptasyllables here are trochaic. The heavily accentuated rhythms, relentless and crude as they are, enhance the ironic distance between characters and narrator. Carefully chosen vocabulary that jars with the situation enhances the sense of mockery on the narrator's part (e.g. l. 6, 'dismal'). Elliptical or obscure lines (e.g. ll. 61, 78–9) make Daphnis seem more emotionally intense at first but, by the end of the poem, all the more artfully deceitful. There are five 'scenes' of death: death in bed (ll. 27–8, 37–40); death by execution (ll. 53–6, 66–8, 97–100); death by fasting (ll. 69–70); death by over-eating (ll. 78–80); necrophilia (ll. 73–6).

Modern Criticism. Colie (1970), 46, notes that the reader comes to understand that Daphnis is more interested in the drama he creates than in Chloe: to this extent he is as 'coy' as any mistress, and self-obsessed too. Detecting that the poem is indebted to the equivocation that governs the *ars amatoria*, Rees (1989), 127, argues that the poem presents 'love as possession and freedom as licence'. For Ellrodt (in Patrides, ed. (1978), 224), the poem is an exposure of the 'false appearances of passion', thereby doubting the 'reality of an inner life whose "bottom" one may not "sound"'. The difficulty of coming to terms with the poem is well-expressed by Nevo, *SEL*, 5 (1965), 17: the poem is itself 'an analogue of change', offering an experience rooted in the 'very fabric of erotic nature . . . its milieu in the adulterate and ambiguous motivations of sophisticated society'. Yet Griffin (1995), 31–4, presents the poem as an allegory of Charles I's negotiations with Parliament in the later 1640s, seen by hostile or critical contemporaries as duplicitous.

Daphnis and Chloe

I

Daphnis must from Chloe part:
Now is come the dismal hour
That must all his hopes devour,
All his labour, all his art.

II

5 Nature, her own sex's foe,
Long had taught her to be coy:
But she neither knew t'enjoy,
Nor yet let her lover go.

III

But, with this sad news surprised,
10 Soon she let that niceness fall;
And would gladly yield to all,
So it had his stay comprised.

IV

Nature so herself does use
To lay by her wonted state,
15 Lest the world should separate;
Sudden parting closer glues.

V

He, well-read in all the ways
By which men their siege maintain,
Knew not that the fort to gain
20 Better 'twas the siege to raise.

VI

But he came so full possessed
With the grief of parting thence,
That he had not so much sense
As to see he might be blessed.

---

2. *dismal*] miserable (*OED* a. A 4).
3. *devour*] destroy (*OED* v. II 4).
4. *art*] a) i.e. the art of love b) cunning (*OED* n. III 13).
5. *her*] a) i.e. Chloe b) i.e. Mother Nature, a female, is the enemy of women.
6. *coy*] see above, *Headnote, Genre and Sources.*
10. *niceness*] reserve (*OED* 4).
12. *comprised*] included (*OED* v. 3).
13–16. Cp. *The Match*, ll. 13–16: 'But likeness soon together drew/What she [Nature] did sep'rate lay;/Of which one perfect beauty grew,/And that was Celia.'

13. *use*] act (*OED* v. II 6).
14. *wonted*] customary (*OED* ppl. a. B).
16. *glues*] 'allusive of sexual conjunction', Williams (1994), II.604–5. Cp. *To his Coy Mistress*, l. 33 n.
17–20. Cp. Suckling, ''Tis now since I sate down before', ll. 1–4: ''Tis now since I sate down before/That foolish Fort, a heart,/(Time strangely spent) a Year, and more,/And still I did my part' (Duncan-Jones, *N & Q*, 198 (1953), 430).
19. *fort*] a) the heart; Chloe's affections (see above, ll. 17–20n.) b) 'woman' or 'vagina', Williams (1994), I, 531–3.
20. *raise*] end.

VII

25   Till Love in her language breathed
       Words she never spake before;
       But than legacies no more
       To a dying man bequeathed.

VIII

       For, alas, the time was spent,
30   Now the latest minute's run
       When poor Daphnis is undone,
       Between joy and sorrow rent.

IX

       At that 'Why', that 'Stay my dear',
       His disordered locks he tare;
35   And with rolling eyes did glare,
       And his cruel fate forswear.

X

       As the soul of one scarce dead,
       With the shrieks of friends aghast,
       Looks distracted back in haste,
40   And then straight again is fled.

XI

       So did wretched Daphnis look,
       Frighting her he lovèd most.
       At the last, this lover's ghost
       Thus his leave resolvèd took.

XII

45   'Are my hell and heaven joined
       More to torture him that dies?
       Could departure not suffice,
       But that you must then grow kind?

XIII

       Ah my Chloe how have I
50   Such a wretched minute found,
       When thy favours should me wound
       More than all thy cruelty?

XIV

       So to the condemnèd wight
       The delicious cup we fill;
55   And allow him all he will,
       For his last and short delight.

XV

       But I will not now begin
       Such a debt unto my foe;
       Nor to my departure owe
60   What my presence could not win.

XVI

       Absence is too much alone:
       Better 'tis to go in peace,
       Than my losses to increase
       By a late fruitión.

25–6. her . . . she] Chloe.

25. Love] Hymen, god of love; see also below, l. 96 n.

27. than legacies no more] i.e. they were no more than legacies.

30. latest] last (*OED* a.¹ 1).

32. rent] torn (*OED* v.² 1 c).

34. tare] i.e. tore.

35. rolling eyes] commonly associated with heightened desire or imagination: cp., e.g., Shakespeare, *A Midsummer Night's Dream* (1595–96), V, i, ll. 10–13: 'the lover, all as frantic,/ Sees Helen's beauty in a brow of Egypt:/The poet's eye, in a fine frenzy rolling,/Doth glance from heaven to earth.'

36. forswear] i.e. renounced (*OED* v. 1).

37–40. As . . . fled] Cp. Donne, 'A Valediction: Forbidding Mourning', ll. 1–4: 'As virtuous men pass mildly away,/And

whisper to their souls, to go,/Whilst some of their sad friends do say,/The breath goes now, and some say, no.'

40. straight] immediately.

44. resolvèd] Friedman (1970), 116, suggests that the 'resolved' Daphnis is to be compared ironically with the resolved Soul of *A Dialogue, Between the Resolved Soul, and Created Pleasure.*

48. kind] a) loving, affectionate, intimate (*OED* a. II 6) b) sexually complaisant (Williams (1994), II.760–1).

53. wight] man (*OED* n. 2).

58. foe] i.e. Chloe.

61. alone] i.e. by itself.

64. fruitión] a) enjoyment; pleasurable possession (*OED*) b) punning on 'fruit': 'sex' and sexual parts, Williams (1994), I.560–2.

XVII

55 Why should I enrich my fate?
'Tis a vanity to wear,
For my executioner,
Jewels of so high a rate.

XVIII

Rather I away will pine
70 In a manly stubbornness
Than be fatted up express
For the cannibal to dine.

XIX

Whilst this grief does thee disarm,
All th'enjoyment of our love
75 But the ravishment would prove
Of a body dead while warm.

XX

And I parting should appear
Like the gourmand Hebrew dead,
While he quails and manna fed,
80 And does through the desert err.

XXI

Or the witch that midnight wakes
For the fern, whose magic weed
In one minute casts the seed,
And invisible him makes.

XXII

85 Gentler times for love are meant.
Who for parting pleasure strain
Gather roses in the rain,
Wet themselves and spoil their scent.

65–8. *Why . . . rate*] Since the clothes of the condemned were customarily kept by the executioner: see William Hone, *The Table Book of Daily Recreation and Information* (n.d.), 766. M. appears to enlarge the custom to include jewellery.
68. *so high a rate*] Cp. *To His Coy Mistress*, ll. 19–20: 'For Lady you deserve this state;/Nor would I love at lower rate.'
69. *away will pine*] i.e. will pine away.
71. *express*] specifically (*OED* B adv. 3).
72. *dine*] eat (*OED* v. 2).
73. *grief*] hardship (*OED* n. 1).
74–6. Craze (1979), 42, notes a similarity between these lines and the necrophilia of *To His Coy Mistress*, ll. 27–8: 'worms shall try/That long preserved virginity.'
75. *ravishment*] rape (*OED* n. 2).
76. *dead while warm*] i.e. still warm, very recently dead.
78–80. A conflation of Numbers 11, where the Israelites, living on manna, complained to Moses of lack of flesh to eat. The Lord provided a vast quantity of quails, but then visited a plague on the people 'while the flesh was yet between their teeth' (Numb. 11:33). The sin of 'lusting' had also occurred at this point, and those who had 'lusted' are buried in verse 34: this provides an apt association with the subject of M.'s poem, and in particular the imagery of st. XIX.
78. *gourmand*] greedy (*OED* A a.).
79–80. *he . . . And*] Rees (1989), 125–6, argues against Cooke's emendation, accepted by all editors thereafter (although Legouis was unhappy with it): the 'original does throw up a real and bizarre confusion between feeding and being fed on, which seems central to Marvell's treatment of erotic love'. She also claims that the lines as such are 'obviously garbled'. An intransitive use of the verb 'feed' is listed in *OED* (v. 3), but used with 'of' or 'on', which is missing in M. Further complication is added by the switch from past ('fed') to present ('does err').
79. *he*] 1681; with Cooke +.
80. *And*] 1681; He Cooke +. *desert*] wilderness (*OED* n.[2] 1). *err*] wander (*OED* v.[1] 1).
81–4. It was believed that ferns had invisible seeds; it was believed that possession of them made humans invisible. See Shakespeare, *1 Henry IV*, II, ii, l. 96 (Margoliouth).
83. *casts the seed*] 'ejaculates semen' is the obscene or erotic innuendo: see Williams (1994), I, 215; III, 1214; in other words, the suggestion is that Daphnis will 'come' and die (i.e. 'disappear') immediately.
85–9. Cp. Suckling, *Aglaura*, III.i, ll. 119–22, 'Gather not roses in a wet and frowning hour,/They'll lose their sweets then, trust me they will, sir,/What pleasure can love take to play his game out/When death must keep the stakes.' (Duncan-Jones, *N & Q*, 198 (1953), 430). The heroine is appealing to her husband not to consummate their marriage until his life is no longer in danger.
85. *Gentler times*] Friedman (1970), 117–18, suggests a reference to the pastoral genre as the true setting for innocent love.

XXIII

Farewell therefore all the fruit
90   Which I could from love receive:
     Joy will not with sorrow weave,
     Nor will I this grief pollute.

XXIV

     Fate I come, as dark, as sad,
     As thy malice could desire;
95   Yet bring with me all the fire
     That Love in his torches had.'

XXV

     At these words away he broke;
     As who long has praying ly'n,

To his headsman makes the sign,
100   And receives the parting stroke.

XXVI

      But hence virgins all beware.
      Last night he with Phlogis slept;
      This night for Dorinda kept;
      And but rid to take the air.

XXVII

105   Yet he does himself excuse;
      Nor indeed without a cause.
      For, according to the laws,
      Why did Chloe once refuse?

89. fruit] see above, l. 64 n.
92. pollute] i.e. with one final (and first) act of sexual intercourse (see Williams (1994), II.1071).
93–6. Daphnis imagines himself as not unlike M.'s picture of the disappointed Hymen in *Upon the Death of Lord Hastings*, ll. 43–6.
96. Love] Hymen, god of love, who characteristically wears yellow and carries torches; see also above, ll. 25–6 n.
98. i.e. the prayer vigil sometimes kept by the condemned before execution. *ly'n*] *1681*; the correct form of the verb would be 'lain', but this does not fit the rhyme.
99. headsman] executioner (*OED* 2).
100. parting stroke] playing on execution as a synonym for copulation: Williams (1994), I.451–2.
101–4. Daphnis is now viewed as a philanderer, although he appears as inept earlier in the poem.
102. Phlogis] derived from Greek φλόξ, flame, suggesting that she is implicitly fiery and passionate; also associated with φλόγινος, a precious stone. But Daphnis' true attitude to women is underlined by the direct meaning of Phlogis in Greek: a piece of broiled meat.

103. Dorinda] a common pastoral name: see, e.g., ?Sir John Reresby, 'A dialogue between a shepheard and his Fancy in a pastorall straine', 4 (Bod., MS Rawl. D 204, fol. 88ʳ); see also below, *A Dialogue between Thyrsis and Dorinda. kept*] a) watched for b) reserved.
104. rid] to 'ride' was a synonym for copulation: Williams, III.1154–5.
107. laws] L.N. Wall (cited by Legouis (1971, 1.258)) suggests that M. is echoing the subtitle and concerns of *A Parliament of Ladies: with their Lawes newly enacted* ([16 April] 1647), attributed to Henry Nevile. In this bawdy prose pamphlet, a collection of city wives respond to their husbands' proclamation that a man may have two wives with the equal and opposite law that a woman may have two husbands. But the 'laws' could simply be those of brief and shallow amatory exchange, or, as Friedman (1970), 114, suggests, of the amatory Courts of Love (or a travesty thereof) popular in early seventeenth-century France, and imported into the court of Charles I's Queen, Henrietta Maria (see also Veevers (1989)).

Date. ?1649–51. Since the poem is constructed out of a highly dense set of echoes to late sixteenth and earlier seventeenth-century literature, none of which is particularly predominant as a model or source for the poem (unlike the case with many other poems by M. that appear to be 'improving' or responding to particular poems), there may be some grounds for thinking that *The Definition of Love* was composed first at an early stage in M.'s career, perhaps before the trip to the continent. But the echoes of poems in Cowley's *The Mistresse* (1647), Lovelace's *Lucasta* (1649) and Robert Heath's *Clarastella* (1650), together with the interest in philosophy and education, and the very distinct focus upon particular poetic genres, topoi, and emblems, suggests a date of composition at the turn of the decade. In its complicated forms of self-awareness and self-reflection, the poem belongs with *To His Coy Mistress*: these are good grounds for seeing it as being composed during the same period.

Publication. 1681.

Genre and Sources. The poem comes relatively late in a line of poems that play with the formal philosophical sense of 'definition', but it does not fulfil the usual characteristics of the genre since it is concerned with specific loves: it distinguishes but does not define (see Kermode, *RES*, n.s. 7 (1956), 183–5). Where most discourse on the nature of love is concerned with the fulfilment of love through union, M.'s poem is concerned with the two perfect, but irreconcilable, loves. Similarly, where hope usually precedes despair in descriptions of the progress of love, in M.'s poem the opposite is true. Neither is the subject a 'she' in any definite sense: the lover of the speaker remains unnamed and without gender.

The poem has been seen as the most akin of M.'s to Donne's metaphysical lyric, and specifically 'A Valediction: Forbidding Mourning', 'not as a deliberate and inferior imitation . . . but . . . with the likeness of a peer'. Moreover, for Colie (1970), 76,

M.'s poem 'outdoes' Donne's geometric imagery, and for Wilcher (1985), 47–8, the poem is at least a 'challenge', at most a 'patronising' deflation of Donne's romantic claims for the union of lovers. Donne's poem is suffused with apparent personal engagement, whereas M.'s poem 'is simply performing, with characteristic seventeenth-century intellectuality, ingenuity, hyperbole and antithesis, an elaborate series of variations on the ancient theme of star-crossed lovers' (Leishman (1966), 68–9). Donne's paradox is reduced to antithesis: the poem achieves a lessening of the powers of the tradition to which it belongs, even as it technically excels. Furthermore, where Donne uses his famous compasses conceit to suggest the connectedness of the lovers, M. reaches opposite conclusions (unlike most of Donne's followers: see, e.g., Carew, 'To my Mistresse in absence' (1640), ll. 7–10: 'Then though our bodyes are dis-joyned,/As things that are to place confin'd;/Yet let our boundlesse spirits meet,/And in loves sphaere each other greet'; Lovelace, 'To Lucasta, Going beyond the Seas' (1649), ll. 13–18: 'Though Seas and Land betwixt us both,/Our Faith and Troth,/Like separated soules,/All time and space controules:/Above the highest sphere wee meet/Unseene, unknowne, and greet as Angels greet'). The treatment of Donne has been seen as a deliberate differentiation of M.'s position from that of the earlier poet.

Lexically, the poem contains a more than usually dense set of echoes from a wide variety of mostly English love lyrics. Where there are echoes of whole lines or stanzas, the purpose is almost always to subvert the original. Stanza VIII appears to complicate and finally reverse lines from Cowley's 'Impossibilities' (1647):

As *stars* (not powerful else) when they *conjoyne*,
    Change, as they please, the Worlds estate;
So thy *Heart* in *Conjunction* with mine,
    Shall our own fortunes regulate;
And to our *Stars themselves* prescribe a *Fate*.

There are more distant, yet distinct, echoes of Herbert's 'The Search' (1633), ll. 41–52:

> Thy will such a strange distance is,
>   As that to it
> East and West touch, the poles do kisse,
>   And parallels meet.
>
> Since then my grief must be as large,
>   As is thy space,
> Thy distance from me; see my charge,
>   Lord, see my case.
>
> O take these barres, these lengths away;
>   Turn, and restore me:
> Be not Almightie, let me say,
>   Against, but for me.

Still another source from a poem that *The Definition of Love* reverses, Lovelace's 'To Lucasta, Going beyond the Seas' (1649), st. III, involves a pun on angels/angles at l. 18 (see below, l. 26):

> Though Seas and Lands betwixt us both,
>   Our Faith and Troth,
>   Like separated soules,
>   All time and space controules:
> Above the highest sphere wee meet
> Unseene, unknowne, and greet as Angels greet.

Other echoes suggest that M. exaggerated the conceptual opposites that he found in some previous poems. Robert Heath's 'Hope' and 'Fear' become 'Despair' and 'Impossibility', with 'Hope' explicitly rejected: ''Tis a child of Phansies getting,/Brought up between *Hope* and *Fear*' ('The Quare: What is Love?' (1650), ll. 1–2; see below, ll. 3–8).

The extent to which the poem refers either to geometry or astronomy and astrology, or both (see below, Title, sts. V–VIII) has been debated by Davison, *RES*, n.s. 6 (1955), 141–6, Schmitter and Legouis, *RES*, n.s. 12 (1961), 49–55. The conjunction of astrology and astronomy existed in Herrick's poetry: 'Make me a heaven; and make me there/Many a lesse and greater spheare./Make me the straight, and oblique lines;/The Motions, Lations, and the Signes.' ('The Eye' (1648), ll. 1–4).

Davison (*RES*, n.s. 6 (1955), 146), regards the conjunction of these materials as evidence of M.'s commitment to the Platonic love cult of the early seventeenth century, an allegiance he was to exploit later in *The Rehearsal Transpros'd* (1672). Here, the figure of Necessity (Fate in ll. 11–19) is the iconic means of mocking Bishop Parker's desire for absolute authority:

Neither are you more distinct in the matter of Necessity, wherein, it being the Original from which you first derive all this Absolute and Unlimited Government, it behooved you if ever to have *shown your Heraldry*. For though Necessity be a very honourable Name of good extraction and alliance, yet there are several Families of the Necessities, as in yours of *Bayes*, and though some of 'm are Patrician, yet others are Plebeian. There is first of all a necessity; that some have talk'd of, and which I have mention'd you in my former Book, that was pre-eternal to all things, and exercised dominion not only over all humane things, but over Jupiter himself and the rest of the Deities, and drove the great Iron nail thorough the Axle-tree of Nature. I have some suspicion that you would have men understand it of your self, and that you are that Necessity. (*The Rehearsal Transpros'd: The Second Part* (1673) in *MPW*, II. 321–2.)

Structure. The poem is an exercise in different kinds of explanation, logic, and logic's subversion by paradox and oxymoron. Geometry, through Euclidian rules, is a structure for the poem: 'given: love itself; required: its definition; construction, the images of space and line; proof, the argument from those images that culminates in the QED of the last stanza' (Rees (1989), 128). To this extent, 'Socratic irony lies at the heart of the poem' (Toliver, in Lord, ed. (1968), 75). Several commentators have detected Platonic concepts of ideal love in the poem, although Berthoff's suggestion that the poem contains an allegory of the temporal soul's longing for its higher part (*RES*, 17 (1966), 16–29; see below, ll. 9–10) has not been generally accepted (see Carey, ed. (1969), 68; Bateson, *E in C*, 27 (1977), 109–11). Toliver, in Lord (1968), 74–84, refers to several Platonic thinkers – Plotinus, Ficino and Pico, as well as Plato – to show that M. is echoing a Platonic tradition that the absolute union of loves is not only very difficult but also dangerous. With a closer focus, Sokol, *N & Q*, n.s. 35 (1988), 169–70, argues that the poem is an ironic reversal of the genealogy of Love (the child of Resource and Need) in Plato, *Symposium*; 203b–c, as the child of Despair and Impossibility. To this extent, M. returns to Socrates' earlier formulation in the *Symposium* that Love is but the want of something lacking. But the poem also employs an Aristotelian mode of definition to define love: definition by difference. Thus, magnanimity is confronted by despair (l. 5), hope by fate (ll. 7–11). The sphere imagery of the second half of the poem is reminiscent of Plato's description of love as a sphere (*Symposium*; 189e–193b), but redefined so that the sphere is not an image of sexual union, but of likeness and attraction held in permanent, separated suspension. The poem involves a series of 'definitions', and is thus concerned with the very nature of definition itself, and the fear that definition may after all be a circular process, 'since to say that definitions are by *definition* universally valid has to be self-validating' (Rees (1989), 128). Most poems in the tradition are concerned merely with the subject of definition as opposed to the nature of definition itself.

The poem is written in nine octosyllabic iambic quatrains with alternate rhyming lines. The prosody is briskly paced by suppressing caesuras, and by running together the two lines of each half stanza. This effect is aided by monosyllabic vocabulary that is only seldom, and then markedly, replaced with polysyllabic words (of the 190 words, 145 are monosyllabic). There are only four caesuras in thirty-two lines, and only one pair of lines (ll. 7–8) based upon antiphonal balance (elsewhere a common feature of M.'s verse). The axis of the earth's rotation (l. 18) is suggested by six stressed monosyllables in this line.

Modern Criticism. The absence of emotions in the poem has been very widely noticed. 'It is a contemplative poem which has love for its subject. The extreme discrepancy between the personal subject and the impersonal mode reflects the tension of forces within the poem itself' (Rees (1989), 137–8). Friedman (1970), 180, sees this as an integral part of the poem's meaning: 'that *this* love shares the attributes of the heavenly bodies, not only in being uncircumscribed by the limitations of lovers in the flesh, but also in being capable of abstraction and geometric expression'.

The Definition of Love

I

My love is of a birth as rare
As 'tis for object strange and high:
It was begotten by Despair
Upon Impossibility.

II

5   Magnanimous Despair alone
Could show me so divine a thing,
Where feeble Hope could ne'er have flown
But vainly flapped its tinsel wing.

Title. Definition. a) action of stating what a thing is, or a word means (*OED* n. 3) b) precise statement of the essential nature of a thing (*OED* n. 4) c) limitation, restriction (*OED* n. 1): a play on the Latin *definio*, to limit, or, less commonly, to terminate d) in geometry, the agreed signification of words (not in *OED*; see Hobbes, *Leviathan* (1651), 1.4.12). Hence the title has been seen as a paradox: the meaning and the end of love. Kermode, *RES*, n.s. 7 (1956), 184, suggests that the title was possibly added by mistake after the poem had been written. *1. My love*] the feelings of the speaker, but the collocation suggests (before the reader reaches l. 3) that a Petrarchan mistress is being named. In other words, the poem begins with confusion rather than definition. *birth*] lineage. *rare*] a) seldom seen (*OED* a. 2d) b) distinguished, excellent (*OED* a. 6).
2. object] a) in metaphysics, a thing or being of which one thinks, as opposed to the thinking subject (*OED* n. I 6) b) the end to which effort is directed; the objective (*OED* n. 5a) *strange*] a) unfamiliar, hitherto unknown (*OED* a. 7) b) exceptionally great (*OED* a. 9a) c) exciting wonder (*OED* a. 10a). *high*] a) elevated, exalted (*OED* a. A II 5a) b) extreme (*OED* a. A II 15a).
4. Impossibility] contrary to the belief, present in several English and continental authorities that desire grew only out of the possible (see Rees (1989), 129–30). Cp. Cowley, 'The Vain Love', ll. 41–2: 'Now my desires are worse and fly/At an *Impossibility*'. See also Walter Montagu, *The Shepherds' Paradise* (?1632), II.vi, ll. 78–9: 'he that will have the glory of a love that out of choice affects impossibilities must needs delight in suffering'.
5. Magnanimous Despair] an oxymoron, possibly generated in direct opposition to the more conventional collocation: see, e.g., Spenser, *The Faerie Queene*, IV.viii.51, ll. 7–9: 'And all dismayd through mercilesse despaire,/Him wretched thrall vnto his dongeon brought,/Where he remaines, of all vnsuccour'd and vnsought.' *Magnanimous*] a) valiant (*OED* a. 1) b) nobly selfless and generous (*OED* a. 2).
7–8. feeble Hope . . . wing] M. appears to be giving hope a new emblematic shape: in emblem tradition, hope is represented as an anchor, a staff and a detached tree-branch sprouting leaves; a ball with wings in George Wither's *A Collection of Emblemes* (1635), 101, 109, 139, 174, represents 'fickle fortune'.
7. feeble Hope] Cp. Spenser, *The Faerie Queene* (1596), IV.vi.34, ll. 1–3: 'But *Scudamour* whose hart twixt doubtfull feare,/And feeble hope hung all this while suspense,/Desiring of his *Amoret* to heare.'
8. vainly] a) ineffectually (*OED* adv. 1) b) foolishly (*OED* adv. 2); cp. Cowley, 'The Vain Love' (1647), ll. 45–6: 'What Lover can like me complain,/Who first *lov'd vainly*, next *in vain*.' Cowley's 'vainly' also suggests (unlike M.) 'conceitedly' (*OED* adv. 3). *tinsel*] glittering (*OED* n.³ and a. 6).

III

   And yet I quickly might arrive
10 Where my extended soul is fixed,
   But Fate does iron wedges drive,
   And always crowds itself betwixt.

IV

   For Fate with jealous eye does see
   Two perfect loves, nor lets them close:
15 Their union would her ruin be,
   And her tyrannic power depose.

V

   And therefore her decrees of steel
   Us as the distant poles have placed,
   (Though Love's whole world on us doth wheel)
20 Not by themselves to be embraced:

VI

   Unless the giddy heaven fall,
   And earth some new convulsion tear;
   And, us to join, the world should all
   Be cramped into a planisphere.

---

9. quickly] a) feelingly (despite the elevated, ethereal love) (*OED* adv. 1) b) rapidly (*OED* adv. 2).

10. i.e., where my soul is directed, or has gone, to the object of its desire. *extended*] a) possessing dimensions in time and space (*OED* ppl. a. 4) b) strained (*OED* ppl. a. 2 a). That the soul as well as the body might have extension was a contentious philosophical debate, intensified in the mid-seventeenth century by the spread of Cartesian ideas. Henry More, the most prominent of the Cambridge Platonists, vigorously maintained that the soul did have extension: 'let us first consider [the soul] a while, what she is in her own Essence, without any reference to any *Body* at all, and we shall find her a *Substance extended and indiscerpible* . . . she hath as ample, if not more ample, *Dimensions* of her own, then are visible in the Body she has left' (*The Immortality of the Soul* (1659), 3.2.1). M.'s speaker suggests that, unconfined by his body, his soul reaches out to the object of its desire. *soul*] a) in metaphysics, the vital, sensitive or rational principle in plants, animals or human beings (*OED* n. I 5) b) also carrying an erotic sense of tumescence and orgasm (with 'soul' meaning 'sperm'; Williams (1994), III.1274). *fixed*] a) directed towards (*OED* ppl. a. 3 a) b) firmly attached (*OED* ppl. a. 2).

11–19. Another piece of translated iconography (see above, ll. 7–8 n.). M. derives his figure of Fate from that of Necessity, specifically mentioned by Horace, *Carmina*, I.xxxv, ll. 17–19, the source for the beginning of this passage (see below, ll. 11–12 n.) Although Fate first appears as neuter (l. 8), Necessity was represented in Orphic theology as a female (mother of the Fates, wife of Demiurgus [fashioner of the world], mother of destiny), revolving the world on a spindle held on her lap (Plato, *Republic*, 616C). In M.'s version, Fate follows Horace's Necessity in holding iron wedges, then she separates the two lovers by making them the opposite poles of the world: they become Necessity's spindle. The image occurs elsewhere in Marvell: see above *Headnote, Sources and Genre.*

11–12. Cp. Horace, *Carmina*, I.xxxv, ll. 17–19: 'te semper anteit saeva Necessitas,/clavos trabales et cuneos manu/ gestans aëna' (Before thee ever stalks Necessity, grim goddess, with spikes and wedges in her brazen hand).

11. iron wedges] Cp. Spenser, *The Faerie Queene* (1596), IV.v.35, ll. 6–9: 'His name was *Care*; a blacksmith by his trade,/That neither day nor night, from working spared,/ But to small purpose yron wedges made;/Those be vnquiet thoughts, that carefull minds inuade.'

12. crowds] forces, thrusts (*OED* v.[1] II 6 a).

14. loves] i.e. the love that each lover has for the other, not the lovers themselves. *close*] come together, unite (*OED* v. III 11 intr.).

18. poles] the extremities of the axis of a rotating sphere. Davison, *RES*, n.s., 6 (1955), 143, suggests that the poles are not terrestrial, but celestial: the spirits of lovers ascended to the celestial sphere of love. These lines are still governed by Plato's image of rotating spheres that fit inside each other: they are imagined as eight whorls (the weights that turn a spindle) fitting inside each other (*Republic*, 616D–617C; see above, ll. 11–19 n.).

19. i.e. Love, as a replication of the celestial sphere, or like the revolving earth, rotates around the poles of the two loves.

20. i.e. being at opposite poles, the two loves can never touch each other. *themselves*] i.e. each other.

21–4. M. imagines a violent disturbance in heaven that causes an equally catastrophic effect on earth; the falling heavens cause the earth to be squashed into a flat plane, but the syntax is not entirely clear.

21. giddy heaven] i.e. inducing dizziness on account of its height.

22. earth . . . tear] i.e. the earth, by a new convulsion, becomes torn; alluding to classical view that the world was originally in a state of chaos: see, e.g., Ovid, *Metamorphoses*, I, ll. 5–20. See also *Upon Appleton House*, ll. 762–6 and n. *convulsion*] violent physical disturbance. *OED* gives the first use of the word in this sense as 1703 (n. 4); with the earth personified, M. uses the anatomical sense of 'convulsion' figuratively for an involuntary contraction (*OED* n. 2 a).

23–4. Cp. Chapman, *Bussy D'Ambois* (?1604), V.i, ll. 22–3: 'And may both points of heavens strait axeltree/Conjoyne in one, before thy selfe and me'; Donne, 'Sermon LXVI', in Donne (1953–62), VII.69: 'If you look upon this world in a Map, you find two Hemispheares, two half worlds. If you crush heaven into a Map, you may find two Hemispheares too, two half-heavens.'

23. world] a) the universe (i.e. the celestial sphere; *OED* n. II 9) b) the earth (i.e. the terrestrial sphere; *OED* n. II 7 a).

24. planisphere] map formed by the projection of a sphere, or part of one, on a flat surface. M.'s planisphere appears to be a map both of the heavens (the proper location of perfect loves) and of the earth (with lines of latitude and longitude; the latter meeting at the poles). See above, *Sources.*

VII

25 As lines so loves oblique may well
Themselves in every angle greet:
But ours so truly parallel,
Though infinite, can never meet.

VIII

Therefore the love which us doth bind,
30 But Fate so enviously debars,
Is the conjunction of the mind,
And opposition of the stars.

---

25. lines oblique] lines of longitude, meeting in angles at the poles (Schmitter, *RES*, n.s., 12 (1961), 49). *lines*] circles of the terrestrial or celestial sphere (*OED* n.² 10 a). *oblique*] the axes of the celestial and terrestrial spheres are oblique (i.e. slanting, so that, relative to each other, they meet) when at any part of the earth's surface except for the poles and the equator (*OED* a. 2 b).

26. angle greet] see above, *Headnote, Genre and Sources. angle*] a) Crook, *The Explicator*, 32 (1974), item 73, suggests an echo of Horace, *Carmina*, I.ix, ll. 21–2: 'nunc et latentis proditor intumo/gratus puellae risus ab angulo' (the sweet laugh of the girl who gives herself away as she hides deep in the corner) b) name of the four astrological 'houses', at the cardinal points of the compass (*OED* n.² 7).

27. parallel] the parallel unmeeting lines correspond to lines of latitude – parallel meridians that never meet (Schmitter, *RES*, n.s. 12 (1961), 49).

28. Though . . . meet] Alluding to the notion that a straight line, if extended infinitely, will eventually meet in a circle: the lines of each lover may each make circles (an emblem of perfection), but the two circles will remain parallel; cp. *RT*, in *MPW*, I. 146,

'And, as a streight line continued grows a Circle, he had given them so infinite a Power, that it was extended unto Impotency.'

31–2. conjunction . . . stars] a play on astrological and astronomical ideas (see the technical definitions given below): the love which binds the speaker and his beloved is a mental conjunction (a meeting of minds), but the lovers are permanently separated because the stars which govern them are opposed (as in Shakespeare's 'star-cross'd lovers' (*Romeo and Juliet* (1593–96), Prologue, l. 6)). Cp. Cowley, 'Friendship in Absence' (1656), ll. 11–12, 'Like loving *Stars*, which oft combine,/Yet not themselves their own *Conjunctions* know.'

31. conjunction . . . mind] Cp. Henry King, 'The Boy's answere to the Blackmore', ll. 17–18: 'the Conjunction of our . . . lipps/Not kisses make, but an Ecclypse'. *conjunction*] a) union, combination (*OED* n. 1) b) marriage c) in astrology, the presence of two planets in the same zodiac sign; the conjunction is supposed to have an influence upon earthly events.

32. opposition] in astrology and astronomy, the relative position of two heavenly bodies when exactly opposite to each other as seen from the earth's surface.

23

The Picture of Little T.C. in a Prospect of Flowers

Date. 1652. If the poem was written for Theophila Cornewall (see below, *Context*), the most likely date for the poem's composition would have been during the stay at Nun Appleton. Duncan-Jones, *HLQ*, 20 (1956–57), 183–4, notes echoes in the poem of Edward Benlowes' appropriately titled *Theophila* (1652), 3.22–5, which narrows the probable date even further. Theophila would have been 6–8 years of age at this time, which fits the figure in the poem perfectly. Before this period, M. was either abroad or engaged in London poetry and politics; after this period, he was preoccupied with the search for patronage and in the writing of political verse.

Publication. 1681. A copy of the poem, made from *1681*, in the Waller family papers (*WTC*; see *IELM*, II.2.34, MaA 54) dates, apparently, from not before the late 1690s. It is conjectured that the text was a fair copy in the hand of the poet Edmund Waller's daughter, possibly deriving from another copy in his possession (Warren Chernaik, private communication).

Context. Margoliouth (*MLR*, 17 (1922), 351–61 (359–60); see also Lincolnshire Archives Office, Parish Register of Thornton Curtis, fiche no. 06 32 001 02A) identified T.C. as Theophila (baptized 26 September 1644), daughter of Humphrey Cornewell, of Berington, Herefordshire, whose mother, also called Theophila, was a member of the Skinner family with whom M. was familiar. The Cornewalls were living at Thornton Curtis, Lincolnshire, on the south bank of the Humber, not very far from Nun Appleton and Hull, when Theophila was baptized. She had an elder sister also called Theophila who died in early infancy (baptized 23 August 1643; buried 25 August 1643). This circumstance is usually taken to explain ll. 35–40.

Genre, Structure and Sources. The poem is a fusion of pastoral idyll with the poetic language of Petrarchan desire, but, as Friedman (1970), 175, notes, it is the opposite of a persuasion to love. A qualified *carpe florem* is also included in the final stanza. Colie (1970), 52–4, notes an oblique treatment of the *carpe diem* convention: the speaker acknowledges the inevitability of sexual desire and love in T.C.'s future, but all suggestion of a directly engaged sexuality is absent from both speaker and subject. The poem is in fact an apology for self-control. Cullen, *PMLA*, 84 (1969), 1559–70, discusses the poem's revision of the tradition of golden age, 'messianic' or 'prophetic' pastoral in classical and Renaissance verse, in which the perfection of the natural world is encountered. Virgil's *Eclogue* IV addresses a baby boy (possibly the son of the consul C. Asinius Pollio), whose arrival the poet prophesies, and who will bring on a new fructifying golden age (the poem is supposed to be referring to a golden age under the Emperor Augustus; see also below, *A Letter to Doctor Ingelo*). See also the golden age evoked by the chorus at the end of the first act of Tasso's *Aminta*, translated by Henry Reynolds (1632), sigs D[1]ᵛ–D2ᵛ. Paradoxically, the fulfilment of M.'s poem is not in the golden age itself (which T.C. facilitates in st. IV), but an 'iron age' of tyranny when a grown-up T.C. will 'slay' her lovers. Several epigrams in the Greek Anthology, and some by Anacreon, express praise of infant charms and warnings of future embroilments in love. Leishman (1966), 165–69, discusses several, although most are not very closely related to M.'s poem. Philodemus (Greek Anthology, V.124) is the nearest relative to M.'s poem:

Οὔπω σοὶ καλύκων γυμνὸν θέρος, οὐδὲ μελαίνει
    Βότρυς ὃ παρθενίους πρωτοβόλων χάριτας.
Ἀλλ' ἤδη θοὰ τόξα νέοι θήγουσιν Ἔρωτες,
    Λυσιδίκη, καὶ πῦρ τύφεται ἐγκρύφιον.
Φεύγωμεν, δυσέρωτες, ἕως βέλος οὐκ ἐπὶ νευρῇ·
    μάντις ἐγὼ μεγάλης αὐτίκα πυρκαϊῆς.

(Your summer is not yet bare of its sheaves, nor darkening is the grape cluster now first out-shooting maiden graces; but already young Loves are sharpening swift arrows, Lysidice, and fire is smouldering concealed. Let us fly, we wretched lovers, while as yet the shaft is not upon the string: I prophesy a mighty conflagration soon.)

This tradition was drawn upon by Horace, *Carmina*, II.v, which was imitated by several seventeenth-century poets. While echoes of Horace's poem are absent in M.'s, a poem in that tradition written by Thomas Stanley in 1646 may have been seen by M., although it was never printed (see below, ll. 1–6 n.). Stanley initially treats the bud as a symbol for the young woman: M. treats T.C. quite literally. Fowler (1970), 78, identifies st. III as derived from the iconography of the triumph: T.C. appears as the triumph over, and the triumph of, Love (cp. Spenser, *An Hymne in Honour of Beautie*, ll. 267–80). The same stanza is regarded as mock-heroic by Bradbrook and Lloyd-Thomas (1940), 51, modulating the epic vocabulary and tone of st. II (Wilcher (1985), 74). There are other elements from unexpected places, such as royal panegyric (see below, l. 10 n.). Ekphrastic elements are discussed below, *Title* n. With T.C. imagined in the future as a conqueror of men, the poem contrasts with the pessimistic advice offered by Carew in 'Good counsell to a Young Maid'. Simpler examples of other kinds of poems related to M.'s would include Robert Heath's 'On Carastella walking in her Garden' (1650), where the mistress is the sole life-giving force among the flowers. William Hammond's 'The Walk' (1655) contains a similar passage that is very close to M.'s description of T.C.:

> The violet,
> Bowing its humble head down at her feet,
> Pays homage for the livery of her veins:
> Roses and lilies, an what beautous stains
> Nature adorns the Spring with, are but all
> Faint copies of this Original.
> She is a moving Paradise, doth view
> Your greens, not to refresh herself but you.
>   (ll. 3–10; see below, ll. 4–7, 25–32)

Duncan-Jones, *HLQ*, 20 (1956–57), 183–4, notes the four stanzas from Edward Benlowes' *Theophila* (1652; see above *Date*), 3.22–5 which M.'s text appears to echo (see below, ll. 6, 35, 37; there are further places of comparison throughout this canto):

This all-informing Light i'th'pregnant mind,
    The babe Theophila enshrin'd:
Grace dawns when Nature sets:
    dawn for fair day design'd.

Breathe in thy dainty bud, sweet
    rose; 'tis Time
Makes thee to ripened virtues climb,
When as the Sun of Grace shall
    spread thee to thy prime.

When her life's clock struck twelve
    (Hope's noon) so bright
She beam'd, that queens admir'd her sight,
Viewing, through Beauty's lantern,
    her intrinsic light.

As, when fair tapers burn in crystal frame,
    The case seems fairer by the flame:
So, does Heav'n's brighter love
    brighten this lovely dame.

The poem has been seen as an exploration of a reborn classical golden age, although this view has been challenged because of the poem's careful, deeply emotional tonalities, that have been seen to belie much personal knowledge of the addressee and her family on M.'s part. Summers (in Carey, ed. (1969), 148) notes how the poem's evocation of a golden age in nature inevitably makes plain the nature of the plants, the dissonances and imperfections of the natural world in which we live. For Leishman (1966), 187, the poem creates a moment of a reborn golden poetry too: the 'poem has a kind of extra dimension, and seems to inherit and renew whole centuries of poetic tradition and achievement'.

Style and Versification. Inversions for the sake of rhyme, and the use of the auxiliary 'does', have been regarded as clumsy and a weakness. Yet the poem exploits, ironically and otherwise, the placing of words. Extreme changes of poetic mode, tone and chronological perspective are matched by a transition from the address to the reader in sts. I and II, to the speaker in st. III and to Little T.C. in sts. IV and V, although the addresses are all made in the intimate space between speaker and reader: there is no sense that T.C. hears the warning voice, or is intended to hear it. The result is an oblique effect that has divided readers. Dyson and Lovelock (1976), 37–46, discuss the texture of the poem at length.

The Picture of Little T.C. in a Prospect of Flowers

I

See with what simplicity
This nymph begins her golden days!
In the green grass she loves to lie,
And there with her fair aspect tames
5   The wilder flowers, and gives them names:
But only with the roses plays;
      And them does tell
What colour best becomes them, and what smell.

II

Who can foretell for what high cause
10   This darling of the gods was born!
Yet this is she whose chaster laws
The wanton Love shall one day fear,
And, under her command severe,
See his bow broke and ensigns torn.
15   Happy, who can
Appease this virtuous enemy of man!

III

O then let me in time compound,
And parley with those conq'ring eyes;
Ere they have tried their force to wound,
20   Ere, with their glancing wheels, they drive

Title. 1681; The Picture of my little neece ['Hardey' crossed out] in a Prospect of Flowers. *WTC. Picture*] Colie (1970), 106, suggests that the poem 'is an exact poetic parallel to pictures of children ringed with emblematic flowers indicating the transience both of childhood and beauty'. *T.C.*] see above, *Headnote. Context. Prospect*] visible scene or landscape (*OED* n. I 3); two other meanings are relevant in the context of the poem's contents: a) survey, description (*OED* n. II 6) b) consideration of the future (*OED* n. II 8). Sambras (*Imaginaires*, forthcoming) sees a reflection in the poem of the genre of portrait painting where the subject is surrounded by painted flowers. *1–8.* Cummings sees st. I as indebted to the description of the goddess Flora in Ovid, *Fasti*, V, ll. 207–14.
1. See . . .] Cp. Stanley, 'The Bud' (1646), ll. 1–4: 'See how this infant bud, so lately borne,/Swelld with the Springs warme breath and dew o'th'morne,/Contracted in its folded leaves doth beare/The richest treasure of the teeming yeare.' *simplicity*] a) without deceit or artifice (*OED* n. 3), hence b) innocence.
2. golden] as in the classical golden age: see, e.g., Tasso, *Aminta*, trans. Henry Reynolds (1632), sigs D[1]': 'O Happy Age of Gould; happy houres; . . . Without the toyle or care of Man,/And Serpents were from poyson free.' See also below, l. 37 n.
3. green . . . lie] Carey (in Patrides, ed. (1978), 151), argues that T.C.'s innocence is signalled by her willingness to lie horizontally in grass. Giving a lover a 'green gown' was a synonym for sexual intercourse in the period (see Williams (1994), II.620–1).
4. fair aspect] in Spenser, 'fair aspects' are always a threat: e.g. *The Faerie Queene*, II.xii.53, l. 1: 'Much wondred *Guyon* at the faire aspect/of that sweet place' (on the Bowre of Blisse); V.viii.2, ll. 8–9: 'Such wondrous powre hath wemens faire aspect,/To captiue men.' *aspect*] a) appearance (*OED* n. III 11) b) facial expression (*OED* n. III 10).
4–5. tames . . . names] naming the plants was an Edenic activity, although associated with Adam rather than Eve (see Gen. 2:19). The rhyme 'tame/name' (or vice-versa) was commonly associated with this notion. See, e.g., Robert Aylett, 'The Brides Ornaments' (1654), I.i, ll. 64–5, 67–8: 'Then

first thy free love did to man appear,/Whom after thine own Image thou didst frame, / . . . /Much fruit on Earth: and gav'st him power to tame/Thy handy-works, to which he gave a name.'
6. roses plays] Simmons, *The Explicator*, 22 (1964), item 62, notes that the origins of the name of the prayer rosary come from 'a place where roses grow', and that 'plays' sounds very like 'prays'.
7. tell] a) announce (*OED* v. B 3) b) discern, determine (*OED* v. B 7).
10. darling of the gods] Theophila means 'dear to the gods'. Cp. Spenser, 'An Hymn of Heavenly Beautie', ll. 183–5: 'There in his bosome *Sapience* doth sit,/The soueraine daerling of the *Deity*,/Clad like a Queene in royall robes'; Carew, 'Upon the King's Sickness', l. 37: ''That darling of the gods and men doth wear/A cloud on's brow, and in his eye a tear.'
11. she . . . laws] T.C. is likened to Diana, the goddess of chastity.
12. wanton Love] i.e. Cupid. *wanton*] a) amorous (*OED* A a. 2) b) roguish, unruly (*OED* A a. 2). *one*] *1681*; on *WTC*.
16. Appease] bring to peace, pacify (*OED* v. 1 a). *enemy of man*] a name usually applied to Satan; see e.g. Milton, *Paradise Lost*, IX, l. 494: 'So spake the enemy of mankind.'
17. in time] i.e. timely; before it is too late (*OED* n. IV 42 b). *compound*] pay for committing an offense of injury (*OED* v. II 13); Royalists 'compounded' during the Interregnum by accepting the terms of composition in order to avoid prosecution (*OED* v. II 15 b).
18. parley] negotiate with an enemy (*OED* v. 2 a).
18–22. conq'ring . . . yield] Cp. Stanley, 'The Bud' (1646), ll. 5–6: 'By whose young growing beauties conquerd yield/The full-blowne glories of the painted field.'
18–20. eyes . . . wheels] see Ezek. 10:12: 'And their whole body, and their backs, and their hands, and their wings, and the wheels, were full of eyes round about, even the wheels that they four had.'
20. glancing] a) strike obliquely (*OED* v.¹ 1) b) rapid (*OED* v.¹ 2) c) with a momentary, intense look (*OED* v.¹ 5; see above, l. 18).

In triumph over hearts that strive,
And them that yield but more despise.
   Let me be laid,
Where I may see thy glories from some shade.

    But most procure
That violets may a longer age endure.

IV

25 Meantime, whilst every verdant thing
Itself does at thy beauty charm,
Reform the errors of the spring;
Make that the tulips may have share
Of sweetness, seeing they are fair;
30 And roses of their thorns disarm:

V

But O young beauty of the woods,
Whom Nature courts with fruit and flowers,
35 Gather the flowers, but spare the buds;
Lest Flora angry at thy crime,
To kill her infants in their prime,
Do quickly make th'example yours;
    And, ere we see,
40 Nip in the blossom all our hopes and thee.

---

21. triumph] Fowler (1970), 78, detects a reference to the tradition, in words and pictures, of the allegorical triumph. The nymph is both the *Trionfi della Pudicizia* and the *Trionfi della Morte*. See above, Headnote, *Genre and Sources*. *strive*] fight (*OED* v. 4).

22. Missing from *WTC*. *but*] even.

23–4. The speaker imagines himself viewing the prospect from the grave (in these lines, he regards himself as being buried), the safest place for any man under the gaze of T.C. The case is supported by an echo from pastoral tradition in Tasso, *Aminta*, trans. Henry Reynolds (1628), sig. C[1]ʳ: 'Neere where my bloudlesse carkasse shall be lay'd.'

24. shade] a) place protected from the sun (*OED* n. III 9) b) 'shades' were a name for Hades, the underworld, and abode of the dead (*OED* n. I 2 b).

26. charm] a) bewitch (*OED* v.¹ 1) b) delight (*OED* v.¹ 5) c) soothe (*OED* v.¹ 4).

27. Reform the errors] a phrase deriving from the terms of Protestant Reformation.

28. tulips] King, *N & Q*, n.s. 16 (1969), 100, notes an apparent transposition of iconography. T.C. appears as a simulacrum of the Virgin Mary, who was usually described surrounded by roses, lilies and violets (John Hall associates these three flowers with Christ: 'A Pastoral Hymn' (1646), ll. 15–17). M. may have replaced lilies by tulips precisely because lilies mentioned in the Bible (Matt. 6:28, 29) were thought to be tulips (see John Gerard, *Herball*, ed. Thomas Johnson (1636), 33).

29. sweetness] i.e. sweet-smelling. Tulips are odourless; M. urges that they be made to smell because they are visually beautiful.

31. procure] bring about, cause (*OED* v. II 4 b).

32. violets] violets were well known for their transience; hence what is imagined is a contradiction in terms. See John Gerard, *Herball* (1636), 852: 'The floures [of the violet] for the most part appear in March, and at the farthest in Aprill.'

33–40. A reworking of Vertumnus's *carpe diem* appeal to Pomona in Ovid, *Metamorphoses*, XIV, ll. 761–4: 'quorum memor, o mea, lentos/pone, precor, fastus et amanti iungere, nympha:/sic tibi nec vernum nascentia frigus adurat/poma, nec excutiant rapidi florentia venti!' (Have a thought of these, I pray you, and put away, dear nymph, your stubborn scorn; yield to your lover. So may no late spring frost ever nip your budding fruit, and may no ravaging winds scatter them in their flower.) Further aspects of M.'s use of this text are discussed by Leishman (1966), 182–4.

35. Simmons, *The Explicator*, 22 (1964), item 62, suggests that this line reverses Herrick's 'Gather ye Rose-buds while ye may' ('To the Virgins, to make much of Time' (1648), l. 1). Cp. the contrast with *Upon Appleton House*, ll. 741–2: 'Whence, for some universal good,/The priest shall cut the sacred bud.'

36–40. Flora was the Roman goddess of flowers. In Spenser's *The Faerie Queene*, II.xii.50–1, Flora appears, and the heavens protect the buds and leaves from extremes of hot and cold, but in Ovid, *Fasti*, V, ll. 311–26, Flora neglects to guard the countryside on account of neglect by the Roman senate.

37. prime] youth, beginning, first age (*OED* n.¹ 6). 'Prime' was also the 'golden number' (*OED* n.¹ II 4), used to calculate the lunar calendar and sometimes supposed to be nineteen years. There may be an intended echo of l. 2 above, 'golden days'. Cp. Spenser, *The Faerie Queene*, II.xii.75, ll. 6–7: 'Gather the Rose of loue, whilest yet is prime,/For soone comes age, that will her pride deflowre.'

39. ere] *1681*; are *WTC*.

24

Tom May's Death

Date. Late 1650. Thomas May (1599–1650), historian, poet, playwright, pamphleteer and translator, died on 13 November 1650. May's death is usually taken as the date for the composition of most of the poem, although Reedy, *SEL*, 20 (1980), 137–51, argues that an earlier version may have been composed in response to May's *The History of the Parliament* (1647). A possible reference in ll. 85–7 to the exhumation of May's remains from Westminster Abbey in 1661 has also led to suggestions that there was further revision at this stage (Rees, *MLR*, 71 (1976), 481–8 (485)).

Publication. 1681.

Attribution. The absence of the poem from *Bod. 1* has led some (in particular, Lord) to doubt M.'s authorship. It was also oddly placed in *1681* between 'The Picture of Little T.C.' and 'The Match'. The exclusion is most likely due to the embarrassment the poem caused a Whig editor who was planning a new edition of M.'s works: see Chernaik (1983), 208–9; von Maltzahn, in Chernaik and Dzelzainis (1999), 64–5, 73–4. Aubrey (Bod. MS Wood F39, fol. 414) assumed that the poem was M.'s, although this may be a judgement based solely upon its inclusion in *1681*. But Aubrey was usually very well informed about his contemporaries. Internal evidence confirms M.'s authorship (see below, *Versification and Style*).

Context. May's decision to follow Parliament (he was appointed its official historiographer) was not lightly forgiven by his former friends who decided to follow the King. In the 1620s and 1630s, May had been a successful poet, playwright and translator, enjoying a considerable reputation at court. Aside from several Parliamentary pamphlets, and his *History*, May was granted a licence to publish *The King's Cabinet Opened* (1645), a collection of captured royal correspondence used by Parliament to maximum propaganda effect. In his *Brief Lives*, Aubrey commented that May's 'translation of Lucan's excellent poeme

made him in love with the republic, which tang ['odorem' inserted here] stuck by him'. Elsewhere, Aubrey reported from the witness of others that, as a young man, May was 'debaucht *ad omnia*' (MS Wood F39, fol. 414). May's poverty, mocked in M.'s poem (l. 81), was in fact the result of unfulfilled expectations. He had been in line to inherit considerable property, but was a disappointed heir (see Chester (1932), 11–30). This circumstance ended May's hopes of a career in court politics, and was the main reason for his recourse to a career in letters.

The poem is a travesty of May's views, and of the way his poetry and his prose were engaged in public affairs. Although May was certainly partly responsible for the development of republican thought in mid-seventeenth-century England, he did not discountenance the possibility of a settlement with the King. His association with pro-Protestant foreign policy aristocrats in the 1620s places him in line with a tradition of belligerently anti-Catholic foreign policy stretching back to Elizabeth's reign. It was also in line with the views of prominent Parliamentary nobility in the Civil War, such as the Earl of Essex (who is compared to Brutus in May's *History*, 3.2). Only in the Latin translation of May's *Continuation* of Lucan's *De Bello Civili*, *Supplementum Lucani* (1640), where passages recording imperial clemency were suppressed, is genuine hostility to the monarchy registered.

The charge against May that he has treacherously swapped sides is only secondary. His real failing, in the eyes of the poem's main speaker, the dead Ben Jonson, is that he has alienated the true role of the poet by expressing classical republican views in partisan pamphlets and histories. Some of May's earlier poems adhere closely to Jonsonian themes of the fraught but necessary interaction of learning and noble patronage (see, e.g., BL MS Add. 25303, fols. 186ᵛ–187ʳ). However, *Tom May's Death* understands that May's 'decline' began with the translation of Lucan's *De Bello Civili* or *Pharsalia* (1627), which the poem presents not as the complicatedly ambiguous epic it was for readers in the 1620s and 1630s, but very much as the reading matter of republicans and of commonwealth supporters. It is *The History of the Parliament*, however, that has most offended Jonson's ghost (ll. 71–4).

Yet none of May's published pamphlets contains the parallels between ancient republicans and modern Parliamentarians suggested in the poem. May's *History* does not make the blatant parallels between contemporary figures and Brutus, Cassius and Spartacus; neither does his more clearly republican *Breviary* of 1650. Of the comparisons between classical figures and contemporaries made by May in the *History*, only one is referred to in the poem (the Brutus/Essex parallel is tentatively and indirectly made). Cassius is mentioned in the *History*, but he is compared to no one; Spartacus is not mentioned in the *History*. Unsurprisingly, M.'s poem pays no attention to May's own account of his developing historiography or to his changing use of classical histories within the *History*, from the partisan Lucan and Tacitus to the relatively impartial Dio Cassius (see Smith (1994), 342–4).

Such a misrepresentation may be connected with the fact that May was assumed by contemporaries to have been involved in the writing and production of Parliamentary propaganda and newsbooks during the First Civil War of 1642–45 (in particular *Mercurius Britanicus*, now thought to be the work of others, notably Marchamont Nedham, who was to compose the inscription on May's tombstone): 'he calls not himself Mercury, yet is *Majanatus*, who failing of the laureat wreath, envies the Crowne it selfe, and puts his fictions into grave prose, as if he stood to be a City Chronicler: and sure however poets have got an ill name, I had rather believe in the supplement of *Lucan*, then the relation of the battell of *Newbury*' (*Britanicus Vapulans*, 1 ([4 November] 1643), 2). In his prefatory poem to May's translation of Lucan, Jonson had called May 'Mercury' (l. 24), but now he was assumed to be a Mercury of an undesirable sort. John Taylor, for instance, assumed that May was a joint author of *Mercurius Britanicus* (*Mercurius Aquaticus* (1643), sig. b2ʳ). And yet it could be that May played a larger role in the newsbooks than is usually thought to be the case. The development of Nedham's republican views grew partly from his acquaintance with May, and May either was, or was assumed to be, responsible for the recessed republican parallels between Roman and English Civil War history that appeared in issues of *Mercurius Britanicus* and, just before May died, the early issues of *Mercurius Politicus*. Moreover, the poem gives evidence (ll. 39–46) of the alehouse meetings of republicans in the later 1640s, well witnessed in contemporary printed and manuscript sources. These were notoriously drunken, as Nedham himself admitted (BL MS. Add. 28,002, fol. 59.), and, where May was concerned, they must have appeared to Royalists as a specific perversion of Tribe of Ben tavern culture.

The poem has puzzled critics because it follows on chronologically from *An Horatian Ode*, in which M. expresses his pro-Commonwealth and pro-Cromwell sentiments. Reedy, *SEL*, 20 (1980), 137–51, argues that M. was using Jonson's voice to castigate May as an Essex sympathizer. The publication of May's *History* was a gesture in support of Essex's pro-Scottish attempt at a reconciliation with the King (opposed by Fairfax and Cromwell): M. may, then, have written the poem earlier, in 1647, in support of the emergent Fairfax/Cromwell faction. He therefore cannot have seen the pro-Fairfax and pro-Cromwell *Breviary* which May published in June 1650. This view assumes that M. was back in England by 1647, and that he was already a Cromwell supporter, although he wrote Royalist elegies until the end of the 1640s.

The mentions of Spartacus, Guelphs and Ghibellines are very much classical republican references from the early years of the Commonwealth (as opposed to the later Rota Club mentioned by Rees, *MLR*, 71 (1976), 485), and point back to an as yet unidentified piece of journalism by May, or a mistaken attribution by someone else to May: equally possibly, it is a deliberately fictitious suggestion. The voice of Jonson complains against the 'Roman-cast similitudes' discussed by 'novice Statesmen', the kind of discussion of reason of state, 'interest' theory, and republicanism that prevailed among some journalists like May and Nedham, and gentlemen like Henry Marten, from the later 1640s onwards, and which would lead eventually to the full-blown classical republicanism of the 1650s (see Worden *et al.* (1981), Tuck (1993), 221–53, and Smith (1994), 177–200). The evidence is scanty, but suggests that the hired pens of the Council of State, and some of the gentlemen within it or close to it, discussed and decided to project in print an image of a republic in the months leading up to May's death (Worden, in Amussen and Kishlansky, eds (1995), 325–7). In effect, some of the 'Sons of Ben', Jonson's younger companions and admirers who kept him company in taverns during his declining years in the 1620s and 1630s, had become (in Jonson's ghost's view) anti-monarchist journalists (and desecrators of poetry) in the 1640s.

How M. could have written *Tom May's Death* so shortly after *An Horatian Ode* is a question often raised. Nedham, a possible associate of M.'s in the late 1640s, infamously changed sides and wrote both for and against the same figures and causes at different points in his career. Whether he is viewed sympathetically or not, his dilemmas and views have been seen as very similar to those of M., especially during the difficult early Commonwealth period (see Wallace (1968), 6, 63; Worden, *HJ*, 27 (1984), 533–4). To write from the opposite point of view to that which one is supposed to support, or is paid to support, is entirely possible. There is no reason why M. cannot have written *An Horatian Ode* and then *Tom May's Death*. Chernaik (1983), 177, goes as far as to suggest that the two poems are 'companion pieces', although there is no hard evidence of how the poem circulated or was received in the period following the occasion of its composition. While he is unconvinced that M.'s objection to May is personal or moral (upstanding M. versus turncoat May), Norbrook (1999), 272, 280, argues that *Tom May's Death* is a 'staggering reversal' of the *Ode*. The poems are 'rival experiments', 'exploring the challenges of different poetic modes both for opening alternative worlds of political connection and for their own linguistic challenges'.

The politics of the poem are not, however, extensively developed. There are no complicated contextual relationships between *Tom May's Death* and contingent events as there are in the Cromwell poems, *Upon Appleton House*, and the verse satires of the Restoration years. The real concern of the poem is poetry itself, and the role of the poet as a commentator on public affairs. For this reason, *Tom May's Death* should be considered alongside the poems on Lovelace and Flecknoe, all three constituting mutually reflecting explorations of the role of the poet in different kinds of public sphere.

Sources and Genre. The poem belongs to the group of classical satirical forms put to use in the paper wars of the 1640s, and described by Faber (1992). In their use of the journey to the underworld motif, their use of fantasy, and in their dialogue form, they belong to the Lucianic tradition, given wide circulation by the northern humanists of the early sixteenth century, and in particular, Erasmus, More and Rabelais. In their mixture of prose and verse, and in their combination of dialectic and fantasy, resolving matters of church and state through ridicule, they belong to the Menippean tradition. For instance, the anonymous *The Passage of Thomas Strafford* (1641) describes Strafford's passage across the Styx to Hades, where the residents discuss the state of England and of the English in Hell. Ben Jonson's own addiction to and use of Lucian makes the model particularly apt, since his ghost speaks sixty-one lines of the poem. Jonson's dramatic satire of Marston, *Poetaster* (1601), is in part a Lucianic trial, conducted by the great classical poets. Here, Virgil's instructions that 'some Gallo-Belgic phrase' (V.iii, l. 53) be avoided in poetry is a reference to the early continental newsbook, prefiguring Jonson's critical treatment of news in *The Staple of News* (1626), and in line with the sentiments of M.'s poem and its immediate predecessors. Lucianic satire was also used in masques, and May's connection with masques features in the poem (l. 38). Jonson's love of drink was also used in a Menippean satire designed to mock a wine patent, *The Copie of a Letter sent from the Roaring Boyes* (1641):

> First came the Poets, of each land, and tooke
> Their place in order, learned *Virgill* struck
> In for the first, *Ben Johnson* cast a glout,
> And swore a mighty oath hee'd pluck him out,
> And wallowing towards him, with a cup of Wine,
> He did so rattle him with *Catiline*,
> That had not *Horace* him appeas'd, 'tis said
> He had throwne great *Sejanus* at his head. (sig. A1ᵛ)

In the underworld of M.'s poem, be it Elysium or Hades, the true state of the world is apparent and we see it with clarified vision. However much Jonson had valued May in life, and however he praised the virtue and patriotism of Roman republican heroes in his plays, his ghost revises his opinions.

Another Lucianic motif relevant to M.'s poem, and to his English source poems, was the Olympian trial. A similar source in this tradition was Seneca's *Apocolocyntosis* in which the Emperor Claudius presumes apotheosis but, like M.'s May, is expelled from heaven. Faber (179–80) detects clear resemblances between descriptions of Claudius and May (the stammer and the limp: see below, l. 27 n.). Like May too, Claudius is expelled for lack of principle, and he reveals his literary pretensions by speaking in Homeric verse, as May spoke through Lucan.

One Menippean satire to which M.'s poem directly refers is the anonymous *The Great Assises Holden in Parnassus by Apollo and His Assessors* (1645). It has been attributed to Wither, but his authorship is unlikely. M.'s indebtedness to this poem for his description of Jonson (ll. 10–15) is clear:

> For sterne aspect, with *Mars* he might compare,
> But by his belly, and his double chinne,
> Hee look'd like the old Hoste of a *New Inne*.
> *(The Great Assises, 9)*

The satire puts various newsbook writers and pro-Parliamentarian journalists on trial for their desecration of letters. The judges and officials of the mock court are distinguished English and European literary forebears: Bacon, Budé, Sidney, Pico della Mirandola, Erasmus, Scaliger, Lipsius, Barclay, Selden, Grotius. Newsbooks and the 'lying pamphlets' of the early 1640s are under attack, but so also are some of the poets: *The Great Assises* is an expression of the uneasiness induced in authors by the effect of the pamphlet battles of the Civil War and by press freedom. Thus, May becomes a paragon of unreliability:

> his suit it was,
> That *May* on his arraignment might not passe:
> For though Poet hee must him confesse,
> Because his writings did attest no lesse;
> Yet hee desir'd hee might be set aside,
> Because hee durst not in his truth confide . . .
> *(The Great Assises, 16)*

But there is also a political dimension, which makes *The Great Assises* and *Tom May's Death* quite unlike a slightly earlier Menippean satire such as Sir John Suckling's 'The Wits', a poem that is wholly literary in its concerns, as is a continental example such as that of May's friend Daniel Heinsius in *Hercules tuam fidem* (1609). In *The Great Assises*, Apollo is a 'Great Prince' who has been rebelled against by the press, which suggests that he represents Charles I. M.'s figure of Ben Jonson uses Apollo's words, but with far stronger sentiments (see below, l. 32). Faber (185–7) sees parallels between the Italian poets jostling for Apollo's favour and members of Charles I's court. No doubt there is a parallel between Apollo and Charles I, but the comparison of god with king serves, in true Lucianic fashion, to undermine kingly status, while pointing up the futility of attempts to reach a settlement between King and Parliament. Unlike M.'s poem, *The Great Assises* condemns neither Parliamentarians nor Royalists, neither poets nor

newsbook writers. Rather, all possibility of impartial judgement is seen to be lost in an age where high and unimpeachable moral standards have been lost. More relevant to M.'s poem, although May is condemned for his 'ingratitude' in *The Great Assises*, he is not as harshly dealt with as William Camden, who offended his monarch (James I) as much as May did his. *Tom May's Death* takes the anxious concern with the state of poetry during the civil crisis in *The Great Assises* and uses it as a vehicle for anti-republican sentiments.

There are some links with works by poets close to M. at this time. Lovelace's 'On Sanazar's being honoured with six hundred Duckets by the Clarissimi of Venice', was not in the *Lucasta* (1649) collection that M. read and for which he provided a commendatory poem. It is a mid-1650s poem, and like *Tom May's Death*, is both anti-republican and uses Ben Jonson as a figure of judgement, associating literary quality with monarchy. The poem carries several echoes of *Tom May's Death*, and both M. and Lovelace were well aware of the effect of the national crisis on courtly verse. To this extent, the recourse to Jonson as arbiter by both poets relates closely to M's conclusion in his poem to Lovelace (ll. 12–14). Duncan-Jones, *PBA*, 61 (1975), 77, suggests that the virtuous poet of ll. 65–6 is Davenant, who had recently completed *Gondibert*, and was in prison on the Isle of Wight, in some danger of his life for his royalism. She notes in particular affinities between M.'s poem and Davenant's Postscript published in 1651:

> if my POEM were not so severe a representation of Vertue (undressing Truth even out of those disguises which have been most in fashion throughout the World) it might arrive at fair entertainment, though it makes now for a Harbor in a Storm.
> (Ed. David F. Gladish (Oxford, 1971), 251)

Davenant, preferred by Charles I to May as Laureate, 'laughs' to see the heavy irony of May's death as a confirmation of his self-denying Roman austerity (ll. 87–9). Davenant's own position was as complicated as M.'s: he was a diehard royalist, but *Gondibert* itself is critical of courts, and Davenant accepted the authority of the Commonwealth, even though *Gondibert*'s preface, and Thomas Hobbes' published reply to it, launched a distinctly anti-populist neoclassical and rational aesthetic.

It was unconventional to have Jonson (and not a classical figure) passing judgement in a Menippean satire, and to an extent that Jonson's authority is almost mocked (the parallel figures in the *Apocolocyntosis* are Hercules and Jupiter). At the same time, Jonson's political views are made decidedly monarchical with the help of allusions to Dante (ll. 17–18). Jonson's own earlier portrayal of Brutus and Cassius in *Sejanus* was as protectors of liberty. The allusion to one of Jonson's masques at the end of the poem suggests that M. had Jonson the court poet and entertainer, not Jonson the classicist, in mind, although the poem contains echoes in Jonson's ghost's words of his great classical authority, Horace. M. is furthermore suggesting that Jonson, had he lived through the 1640s, would have substantially modified his views of classical literature and republics. Here M. the satirist wears a specific mask: that of a royalist Menippean.

Jonson's voicing of the role of the true poet (ll. 65–70) is also a reversal of the real Jonson's commendatory poem to May's translation of Lucan:

When, Rome, I read thee in thy mighty pair,
And see both climing up the slippery stair
Of fortunes wheel, by Lucan driven about,
And the world in it, I begin to doubt:
At every line some pin thereof should slack
At least, if not the general engine crack. (ll. 1–6)

It is worth noting, however, that one republican, known to M. and closely associated with May, Marchamont Nedham, misquoted Dante (probably via Machiavelli) in his famous *The Case of the Commonwealth Stated* (May 1650, ed. P.A. Knachel (Charlottesville, 1969), 118). Nedham argues that Dante says that virtue is not transmitted in a hereditary way (*Purgatorio*, VII, ll. 121–3). In fact, Dante says that virtue is *rarely* transmitted in family lines; the speaker is the dubious Sordello, so the framework of interpretation is even more qualified and complex. In this context, M.'s poem offers a corrective to the republican misappropriation and coarsened reading of Dante's poem.

Style and Versification. ll. 21–4 and ll. 39–96 are spoken by Jonson's ghost. Both he and the narrator speak in rhymed iambic pentameters. Where there is a departure from regular metre in Jonson's lines, the effect enhances the sense of drunken outrage in his manner. The poem relies upon a series of parodic echoes, especially of Jonson mocking (sometimes gently, sometimes fiercely) May's poetic, historiographical and polemical procedures. This is an inversion itself, since May was an early admirer of Jonson. Further inversion includes Jonson's travesty of May's imitation and translation of Lucan's epic opening (ll. 21–4). Reversed iambs (trochees) at the starts of lines coincide with reference to alcohol, rebels or disproportion: 'Such did he seem for corpulence and port' (l. 11); 'Brutus and Cassius, the people's cheats' (l. 18); 'Pressed for his place among the learned throng' (l. 28) (see also ll. 39, 41, 96–8). They come between regular iambic lines and work in rhythmic contradistinction to them. When the centre of Jonson's judgement comes, the metre breaks into reversed dactyls, that is, anapaests for the first half of the line: 'When the sword glitters o'er the judge's head' (l. 63). The imagery comes almost entirely from the travestied sources of the poem, and figures of speech are absent: a fitting testimony to Ben Jonson's own predilection for a plain style. In keeping with the decorum of Lucianic verse, the poem lacks the sophisticated tonal irony of Horatian or Juvenalian satire, a further comment on the drabness, in the poem's view, of May's work and activities.

Modern Criticism. The poem has attracted very little critical attention. More energy has been expended on the question of attribution. For many commentators, the poem has been evidence of M.'s desire to distance himself from classical republicanism or even from politics itself. For Hyman, *PMLA*, 73 (1958), 477, the writing of *Tom May's Death* is a denunciation of the stance of *An Horatian Ode* yet still 'a logical outcome' from M.'s own ambivalent responses to the competing forces in the nation. Aubrey felt that the poem 'falls very sever upon' May (Bod. MS Wood F39, fol. 414), but most commentators have chosen to steer clear of it, sometimes using the argument that it was not by M. to do so (Patterson (1978), 119, n. 13). Duncan-Jones, *PBA* (1975), 268–90 (283), thinks that the poem is 'not exactly a savage satire', but mixes merriment and anger, in a Lucianic manner. However, in line with Aubrey, Rees (*MLR*, 71 (1976), 481) regards the fusing of literary judgement, morality and political vision as troubling. The longest commentary on the poem is in Chernaik (1983), 82–4, 174–82, for whom it is a crucial witness of M.'s belief in the function of the poet as a warrior in the cause of virtue: its tight structural parodies are an instance of that virtue. The poem's main attraction is its 'ethical argument', in 'which the poet shows that his opponent, unlike himself, is not worthy of trust or respect' (176).

Tom May's Death

As one put drunk into the packet-boat,
Tom May was hurried hence and did not know't.
But was amazed on the Elysian side,
And with an eye uncertain, gazing wide,
5 Could not determine in what place he was,
(For whence, in Stephen's Alley, trees or grass?)
Nor where *The Pope's Head*, nor *The Mitre* lay,
Signs by which still he found and lost his way.
At last while doubtfully he all compares,
10 He saw near hand, as he imagined, Ayres.
Such did he seem for corpulence and port,
But 'twas a man much of another sort;
'Twas Ben that in the dusky laurel shade
Amongst the chorus of old poets laid,
15 Sounding of ancient heroes, such as were
The subject's safety, and the rebel's fear.
And how a double-headed vulture eats
Brutus and Cassius, the people's cheats.
But seeing May, he varied straight his song,
20 Gently to signify that he was wrong.
'Cups more than civil of Emathian wine,
I sing' (said he) 'and the Pharsalian Sign,
Where the historian of the Commonwealth
In his own bowels sheathed the conquering health.'
25 By this May to himself and them was come,
He found he was translated, and by whom.
Yet then with foot as stumbling as his tongue
Pressed for his place among the learned throng.

---

1. drunk] In his *Brief Lives*, John Aubrey noted that May 'came of his death after drinking with his chin tyed with his cap (being fatt); suffocated.' *packet-boat*] boat making regular voyage between ports and carrying mail (originally state papers between England and Ireland); M.'s association of a boat run by the state with Charon's boat that crossed the River Styx to reach the underworld points up May's purported political ignorance and irresponsibility in a typically Lucianic way: see *Headnote, Sources and Genre*.

3. amazed] a) astonished b) dazed. *Elysian*] in Greek culture, the blessed lived in the Elysian Fields after death.

4. uncertain] a) unsteady, unfocused (because May is either still drunk or hungover) (*OED* a. 5) b) doubting (*OED* a. 6).

6. Stephen's Alley] St Stephen's Alley, or Canon Row, near King Street and Tothill Street, once the property of the dean and canons of St Stephen's Chapel, but the home of various noblemen and gentlemen in the seventeenth century, and notorious for its taverns. May lived there.

7. The Pope's Head ... The Mitre] these seem to be fictitious inn names, with Catholic and prelatical associations, thereby pointing up May's sense of irreverence.

10. Ayres] Rees, *MLR*, 71 (1976), 281–8 (282, n. 6) notes that Henry Ayres was a member of the Vintners' Company in the 1640s.

11. corpulence and port] see below, l. 13.

13. Ben] Ben Jonson (?1572–1637), poet and playwright. Jonson's fatness and his reputation for drinking were as famed as his literary prowess. He advertised it himself: 'My mountain belly, and my rocky face' ('My Picture Left in Scotland' (1619), l. 17). See above l. 11.

14. laid] 1681, Margoliouth, Kermode, Lord, Wilcher; layed Donno, Walker, as if to suggest a pun: to find Jonson 'laid' (in the sense of resting) among the old poets in Elysium is expected, but the reader is then surprised by the sense of laying as 'singing a lay or song'. Yet the fact there is no evidence of 'lay' as a verb strongly suggests that the reading is far-fetched.

15. Sounding] singing (*OED* v.[1] I 2b).

16. subject's ... fear] Jonson's 'ancient heroes' are princes or monarchs who protect their subjects in part by suppressing rebellion. The safety of the people was a common phrase in Civil War political controversy: '*salus populi suprema lex est.*'

17–18. double-headed ... cheats] Brutus and Cassius, who led the conspiracy to assassinate Julius Caesar, were regarded as heroes by republicans, but as villains by monarchists and royalists. M. appears to be modifying a passage from the undoubtedly monarchical Dante's *Inferno*, XXIV, ll. 64–9, where Satan as a three-headed winged monster gnaws Judas, Brutus and Cassius. May praises Brutus and Cassius as humane defenders of popular liberty in *The History of the Parliament*, 3.2.

17. And] Cooke, Donno; But 1681.

19. straight] straightaway; immediately.

20. he] i.e. May.

21–4. A parody of the first three lines of May's influential translation of Lucan's *De Bello Civili*. Self-defeat by drinking replaces civil conflict, and the heroic field of Pharsalia becomes an inn:

> Warres more then civill on Aemathian plaines
> We sing: rage licens'd; where great Rome disdaines
> In her owne bowels her victorious swords.

May's drinking also parodies the Roman republican ritual of drinking sacrificial blood, represented in the engraving on the title-page of May's *A Continuation of Lucan's Historicall Poem* (1650).

21. Emathian] Cooke+; Emilthian 1681. Emathia was the part of Thessaly (or Macedonia) where the Battle of Pharsalia was fought (see Lucan, *De Bello Civili*, VI, l. 332 ff.).

23. historian of the Commonwealth] May was an apologist for Parliament in the 1640s and author of two histories of it. To use 'commonwealth' and not 'Parliament' is further evidence of the post-regicide dating of the poem: see above, *Headnote, Date, Context.*

24. Parodying the Roman way of honourable suicide by falling on one's sword.

26. translated ... whom] transported by Death to Elysium and mockingly parodied by Jonson. 'Translated' carries a double sense of its own function in that it represents both 'transported' and 'parodied'. This is also a reversal of Jonson's commendatory poem to May's translation of Lucan: 'so the work will say:/ The sun translated, or the son of May.' (ll. 23–4)

27. foot ... tongue] May is supposed to have had a stammer, except among close friends, but he is also still drunk at this point. See Clarendon, *Life*, l. 32.

But Ben, who knew not neither foe nor friend,
30   Sworn enemy to all that do pretend,
Rose; more then ever he was seen severe,
Shook his grey locks, and his own bays did tear
At this intrusion. Then with laurel wand –
The awful sign of his supreme command,
35   At whose dread whisk Virgil himself does quake,
And Horace patiently its stroke does take –
As he crowds in, he whipped him o'er the pate
Like Pembroke at the masque, and then did rate:
   'Far from these blessèd shades tread back again
40   Most servile wit, and mercenary pen.
Polydore, Lucan, Alan, Vandal, Goth,
Malignant poet and historian both.
Go seek the novice statesmen, and obtrude

On them some Roman-cast similitude,
45   Tell them of liberty, the stories fine,
Until you all grow consuls in your wine.
Or thou, Dictator of the glass, bestow
On him the Cato, this the Cicero;
Transferring old Rome hither in your talk,
50   As Bethlem's house did to Loreto walk.
Foul architect that hadst not eye to see
How ill the measures of these states agree;
And who by Rome's example England lay,
Those but to Lucan do continue May.
55   But thee nor ignorance nor seeming good
Misled, but malice fixed and understood.
Because some one than thee more worthy wears
The sacred laurel, hence are all these tears?

37–8. whipped . . . masque] At the performance of a masque before the King and Queen by gentlemen of the Inns of Court in February 1634, the Lord Chamberlain, Philip Herbert, Fourth Earl of Pembroke, broke his staff over May's shoulders, not realizing who he was (May was at this time in favour with Charles). Pembroke apologized the next day and paid May fifty pounds in compensation. Pembroke died in 1650, and a satirical commemoration tied this event to May's later affiliations: 'To *Tom May* (whose pate I broke heretofore at a *Masque*) I give Five Shillings; I intended him more, but all that have read his *History of the Parliament* thinke *Five* shillings to muche' (Anon., *The Earle of Pembroke's Last Speech* (1650), 3).
37. rate] utter strong reproofs (*OED* v. 2).
41. A catalogue associating mercenary and malignant writers (in Jonson's view) with barbaric, warlike tribes, who are treacherous and wreak havoc on peaceful states. Polydore Virgil (d.1555) was an Italian historian, whose *Historia Anglica*, compiled for Henry VII, was regarded as both flattering and libellous. Lucan ironically flattered Nero in the *Pharsalia*, while the poem itself is a defence of the lost Roman republic. The Alani were Scythians (mentioned in *Pharsalia*, VIII, l. 223, X, l. 454) who joined with their conquerors the Huns to invade the Roman Empire: they are thus like Vandals and Goths. In *The Great Assises*, 17, May asks to be exiled to 'Scythian snowes' if the charge of his ingratitude can be sustained.
42. Malignant] rebel against God and constituted authority; applied first by Parliamentarians to Royalists from 1641, and then vice versa, from 1642 (*OED* a. A 1b, c); see also below, l. 56, *malice*.
43–9. M. dwells on May's parallels, implicit in his translation, and explicit in his history, between Rome and England. May had initially shown how England was as much unlike as like Rome, but the *Breviary* and especially its Latin translation emphasized the parallel to the extent that May was manufacturing English classical republicanism. See *An Horatian Ode, Headnote, Genre and Allusion*.
43. obtrude] to force upon importunately (*OED* v. 2), as a malignant would.
47. Dictator] originally a magistrate in ancient Rome, elected in times of emergency, with absolute authority.

48. Cato . . . Cicero] Marcus Porcius Cato the Elder (and 'Censor') (234–149 BC), Roman soldier and statesman, was a fierce opponent of corruption and luxury, and commonly regarded as the epitome of Roman virtue. However, M. refers to his great-grandson of the same name (95–46 BC), philosopher, soldier and politician. He defended the free state, and was associated with Pompey and Cicero against Caesar. He was not present at Pharsalia, and famously retreated across the Libyan desert (with disastrous consequences for his men: see Lucan, *De Bello Civili*, IX, ll. 564–937), finally committing suicide at Thapsus. Marcus Tullius Cicero (106–43 BC), orator, philosopher and politician, exemplar of Roman eloquence and republican liberty; Lucan portrays him (fictitiously) as present at Pharsalia, where he makes a reckless, bellicose speech before the battle. In Lucan's view, the eloquence of this speech masks its poor logic (*De Bello Civili*, VII, l. 63 ff.).
50. Bethlem's . . . walk] The town of Loreto, south of Ancona in Italy, had been a major place of pilgrimage since the fifteenth century. According to legend, the House of the Virgin was transported by angels from Nazareth (not Bethlehem as M. has) to Trsat near Rijeka in 1291, and from there to Loreto on 10 December 1294.
51. Foul] ugly, disfigured, unattractive (*OED* a. III.11), but the quality attaches to the 'architecture' of May's writings, rather than the architect himself.
52. measures] dimensions; proportions.
53. who . . . lay] i.e. 'those who place England alongside the example of Rome'.
54. May's comparison of Rome and England supposedly carries on Lucan's work, but the achievement is purely May's. *continue*] May first published his *A Continuation of the Subject of Lucan's Historicall Poem till the Death of Julius Caesar* in 1631. A Latin translation of this work appeared in 1640.
55. thee] Kermode+; the *1681, Margoliouth, Legouis*.
56. malice] In his trial in *The Great Assises, Mercurius Aulicus'* objection that he should not be tried by May because of his malice is sustained by Apollo (16–17).
57–8. some one . . . laurel] Sir William Davenant was made Poet Laureate on Jonson's death in 1637. May's malice purportedly grew from Charles' preference for Davenant over himself. See *Headnote, Context*.

Must therefore all the world be set on flame,
Because a gázette writer missed his aim?
And for a tankard-bearing muse must we
As for the basket, Guelphs and Ghib'llines be?
When the sword glitters o'er the judge's head,
And fear has coward churchmen silencéd,
Then is the poet's time, 'tis then he draws,
And single fights forsaken Virtue's cause.
He, when the wheel of empire whirleth back,
And though the world's disjointed axle crack,
Sings still of ancient rights and better times,
Seeks wretched good, arraigns successful crimes.
But thou, base man, first prostituted hast
Our spotless knowledge and the studies chaste,
Apostatizing from our arts and us,
To turn the chronicler to Spartacus.

75 Yet wast thou taken hence with equal fate,
Before thou couldst great Charles his death relate.
But what will deeper wound thy little mind,
Hast left surviving Dav'nant still behind,
Who laughs to see in this thy death renewed,
80 Right Roman poverty and gratitude.
Poor poet thou, and grateful senate they,
Who thy last reck'ning did so largely pay;
And with the public gravity would come,
When thou hadst drunk thy last to lead thee home;
85 If that can be thy home where Spenser lies,
And rev'rend Chaucer; but their dust does rise
Against thee, and expels thee from their side,
As th'eagle's plumes from other birds divide.
Nor here thy shade must dwell. Return, return,
90 Where sulph'ry Phlegethon does ever burn.

---

60. *gázette writer*] See above, *Headnote, Context*.
62. *basket*] *a*) basket used for distributing alms (*OED* n. 1 b) b) bag or *borsa* used to receive votes in Florentine elections. *Guelphs and Ghib'llines*] parties in medieval Italy, infiltrating political assemblies as well as the sympathies of individual rulers; respectively supporters of the Pope and the Holy Roman Emperor. No English republican referred to these parties extensively in print before 1651, although they are present in one text alluded to in M.'s poem, Dante's *Divine Comedy* (e.g. *Paradiso*, VI, ll. 31–3, 100–10, XVI, l. 154). It is the image of decision-making through the votes of a popular assembly that offends Jonson's ghost here.
63. *sword . . . head*] an image suggesting the dangers that come with power; also an image of usurpation (and decollation): the sword is de facto power, threatening the de jure power of the magistrate; the source is the story of the sword suspended by a single hair over the head of the courtier Damocles, after he had extravagantly praised the happiness of the tyrant Dionysius (see Horace, *Carmina*, III.i, l. 17).
64. *coward churchmen*] the Presbyterians had objected to the trial of the King in 1648–49, but to no effect.
65–6. *poet's time . . . Virtue's cause*] Duncan-Jones, *PBA* (1975), 268–90 (282–3) argues that the poet is Davenant, imprisoned at the time of May's death on a charge of treason and in danger of his life: see above, *Headnote, Sources and Genre*. Davenant's heroic poem *Gondibert* had just been published. A parallel is drawn between the role of the poet in M.'s poem, Davenant's preface, and Cowley's commendatory poem: 'So much more thanks from human kinde does merit/The Poets Fury, then the Zealots Spirit.' But Jonson might equally have found Cowley and Davenant's views (especially their open political engagement) unacceptable, unless M. is assuming that Jonson's views have also been changed by the Civil War; elsewhere M. appears to mock Davenant (*Upon Appleton House*, l. 456).
67. *wheel of empire*] see above, *Headnote, Sources and Genre*.
68. *world's . . . crack*] the axis upon which the earth was presumed to rotate is mentioned in Lucan, *De Bello Civili*, usually as an image of the unchanging. Jonson's ghost picks up on the fact

that this is not what happens in Lucan. In the political world, things fall apart, but in the natural world: 'sed, qui non mergutur undis/Axis inocciduus gemina clarissimus Arcto,/Ille regit puppes' ('but the pole-star, which never sets or sinks between the waves, the brightest star in the two Bears, he it is that guides our course'), *De Bello Civili*, VIII, ll. 174–6 (see also VII, l. 422); see also Horace, *Carmina*, III.iii, l. 7: 'si fractus inlabatur orbis' ('were the vault of heaven to break and fall upon him').
69. *ancient rights*] see *An Horatian Ode*, l. 38.
74. *Spartacus*] (73–71 BC), leader of the slaves' revolt against Rome; again, it is hard to find a specific English figure to whom M. refers other than Oliver Cromwell; Julius Caesar is regarded as a second Spartacus by the republicans in Lucan (*De Bello Civili*, II, ll. 552–4).
75. *equal*] just, equitable (*OED* a. 5).
76. *great Charles . . . relate*] at the end of his *A Breviary of the History of the Parliament*, 215, May wrote: 'But by what means, or what degrees, it came at last so far, as that the King was brought to tryal, condemned, and beheaded; because the full search and enarration of so great a business would make an History by it self, it cannot well be brought into this Breviary, which having passed over so long a time, shall here conclude.'
78. *Dav'nant*] see above, ll. 57–8.
80. A parodic view of the standard Roman virtues of magnanimity and selflessness.
82. The Council of State voted £100 for May's funeral in Westminster Abbey (*CSPD* (1650), 432).
85–7. May was interred in Westminster Abbey; M. reverses here the compliment that Jonson had paid to Shakespeare in his memorial verse: 'I will not lodge thee by /Chaucer, or Spenser', ll. 19–20.
87–8. *expels . . . divide*] a possibly deliberate reworking of *An Horatian Ode*, ll. 15–16.
88. *th'eagles . . . divide*] it was supposed that when eagle feathers were mixed with those of other birds, they would destroy them. *divide*] a) separate (*OED* v. I 1) b) echoes Latin 'divexare', to tear asunder, and hence destroy.
90. *Phlegethon*] fiery river in Hades.

Thee Cerberus with all his jaws shall gnash,
Megaera thee with all her serpents lash.
Thou riveted unto Ixion's wheel
Shalt break, and the perpetual vulture feel.
95   'Tis just, what torments poets e'er did feign,

Thou first historically shouldst sustain.'
     Thus by irrevocable sentence cast,
     May, only Master of these Revels, passed.
     And straight he vanished in a cloud of pitch,
100 Such as unto the Sabbath bears the witch.

---

91. Cerberus] three-headed dog guarding the entrance to Hades. The image associates with the two-headed vulture chewing Brutus and Cassius at ll. 17–18. May becomes the third 'cheat', and thus, by comparison with Dante's original image, is associated with Judas, thereby enhancing the theme of betrayal voiced at l. 73. Being chewed in all three of Cerberus's jaws, May becomes Judas, Brutus and Cassius.

92. Megaera] one of the Furies, often represented with a torch in one hand and snakes in the other.

93. Ixion's wheel] Ixion, King of the Lapithae, tried to rape Juno, for which he was banished to Hades, and bound to a whirling wheel (see Ovid, *Metamorphoses*, VI, l. 461); precisely the punishment that May calls down upon himself in *The Great Assises* (17) if it can be proven that he transgressed in being ungrateful to Charles I. Claudius is threatened with Ixion's wheel towards the end of Seneca's *Apocolocyntosis*, but other punishments are found. Ixion's wheel is represented in George Wither, *A Collection of Emblemes* (1635), 69.

94. Shalt break] referring to the punishment of being broken on a wheel: being bound to a wheel and then having one's limbs broken. *perpetual vulture*] Prometheus was punished for stealing fire from heaven by having his constantly renewing liver continually eaten out by a vulture.

96. historically] because May, in the eyes of Jonson, is a bad historian. *sustain*] undergo (*OED* v. 9).

98. Master of these Revels] see above, l. 38.

99–100. straight . . . witch] see Jonson, *The Masque of Queenes* (1609), ll. 326–8: 'A cloud of pitch, a spur, and a switch,/To hast him away, and a whirlwind play/Before, and after, w'th thunder for laughter.' But the House of Fame in this masque rests upon statues of Homer, Virgil and Lucan (ll. 684–6), the last poet being castigated in M.'s poem. May's descent identifies him with the antimasque, as opposed to the masque heroes, who usually ascend heavenwards on masque machinery. For the significance of this, see above, *Headnote, Sources and Genre*.

25

The Match

Date. ?1647. The affinity to Donne (see below, *Sources, Genre and Structure*) suggests that the poem is early. The series of echoes to poetry by Cowley and Philipott (published in 1647 and 1646 respectively) is some evidence for a composition date not before this time. Donno suggests that the Celia of l. 16 associates the poem with the Celia of *To His Worthy Friend Doctor Witty upon His Translation of the Popular Errors*, ll. 17–27, but the earlier date seems more likely.

Publication. 1681.

Sources, Genre and Structure. The poem consists of a tightly controlled pair of analogies (woman as the creation of Nature; man as the creation of Love) construed as an aetiological myth or allegory that explains physical union. The rigidity of this format has been seen as indicative of an ironic treatment of a set of very well-worn love poetry conventions: M. is sending up the genre (Colie (1970), 124–5, 127). The poem is in several ways indebted to Donne and his own inflection of the Petrarchan inheritance, in addition to lyrics from Abraham Cowley's *The Mistresse* (1647). For instance, 'The given Heart' describes amorous frustration as an explosion:

> Wo to her stubborn *Heart*, if once mine come
> Into the self same room;
> 'Twill tear and blow up all within,
> Like a *Grenado* shot into a *Magazin*. (ll. 9–12)

More precise echoes suggest that M. was reworking parts of Thomas Philipot's *Poems* published in 1646, making even more rigorous conceits on top of Philipot's own wit, and again making consummation replace the frustration of male desire:

> Thou art Natures Magazine,
> Or her casket rather, in
> Whose narrow precincts she hath pent
> The treasure that both Indies sent.
> ('A Pastorall Court-ship', ll. 9–12)

If this small spark which bore so thin a blaze,
Could in each part so much resentment raise . . .
My martyr'd heart must struggle with, which fries
In flames of Love, first kindled by your eyes.
('On a sparke of fire fixing on a Gentlewomans Breast', ll. 1–2, 7–8)

Fire as an image of sexual desire is of course common in this tradition. So are references to sighs and tears, but both are absent in M.'s poem.

The poem has been seen as reversing the argument and sentiments of *The Definition of Love* (Klause (1983), 62; Rees (1989), 136), just as the creations of Nature and Love are not the intended consequences of their actions. Hodge (1978), 91–2, argues that the two personified entities are not expressions of abstract, macrocosmic realities, but representations of active principles in the world, according to Paracelsan theory.

Structure, Versification and Style. The poem consists of ten four-line stanzas, with alternating iambic tetrameter and trimeter lines, rhyming on alternate lines. The metre is highly regular, or, as Leishman (1966), 36, put it, 'rather plodding and mechanical'. Four stanzas are given to Nature and Celia, five to Love and the speaker: this corresponds to the association of even numbers with the female, odd numbers with the male (see Henry Cornelius Agrippa, *Female-Prae-eminence*, trans. H. Care (1670), 9). The logic of the poem works until l. 24, when the literally described explosives become figures for the distractions of sexual desire and passion. Then there is a leap between the penultimate and final stanzas, almost as if some stanzas were missing. The speaker confesses that he is the product of Love's explosive materials, but in the last stanza, beginning with the spurious connective 'So', the consummation seems already to have happened; it is not visible to us. Our awareness that the argument is faulty makes us readjust our understanding of the poem: it is but a persuasion to love.

The Match

I

Nature had long a treasure made
    Of all her choicest store;
Fearing, when she should be decayed,
    To beg in vain for more.

II

5   Her orientest colours there,
    And essences most pure,
With sweetest perfumes hoarded were,
    All as she thought secure.

III

She seldom them unlocked, or used,
10   But with the nicest care;
For, with one grain of them diffused,
    She could the world repair.

IV

But likeness soon together drew
    What she did sep'rate lay;
15   Of which one perfect beauty grew,
    And that was Celia.

V

Love wisely had of long foreseen
    That he must once grow old;
And therefore stored a magazine,
20   To save him from the cold.

VI

He kept the sev'ral cells replete
    With nitre thrice refined;
The naphtha's and the sulphur's heat,
    And all that burns the mind.

Title. a) partnership of lovers (not specifically a marriage: *OED* n.[1] II 10) b) device that ignites explosives (*OED* n.[2] 2). Donno cites several other definitions of the word current in the seventeenth century that colour the reader's awareness: antagonist, counterpart, equal, contest, pairing, alliance.
1. Nature] A version of Dame Nature, so important in the poetry of Spenser and his followers: see, e.g., *The Faerie Queene*, VII.vii.
2. store] treasure reserved for future use (*OED* n. 7 a).
3. decayed] i.e. in advanced age, beyond the bloom of youth and fertility (*OED* v. 4); the notion that nature was in a state of deterioration since the Fall was current in medieval and early modern Europe. Contrast Spenser *The Faerie Queene*, VII.vii.13, ll. 1–2, Dame Nature is a 'great Grandmother . . . euer young yet full of eld'.
5. orientest] most brilliant ('orient': *OED* a. B 2 b). *colours*] a) colours b) outward appearances (*OED* n. III 11).
6. essences] internal sources of being (see above l. 5 n. 'colours') (*OED* n. 7), but there is a play on 'essence' as perfume (*OED* n. 10), especially in the light of l. 7, 'sweetest perfumes'.
10. nicest] most scrupulous (*OED* a. 11 b).
11. grain] smallest possible quantity (*OED* n. II 9). *diffused*] spread abroad (*OED* ppl. a. II 2).
12. world repair] restore to its state of prelapsarian purity ('repair': *OED* v.[2] 2).

13–16. Cp. *A Dialogue, Between the Resolved Soul, and Created Pleasure*, ll. 51–4: 'All this fair, and soft, and sweet,/Which scatt'ringly doth shine,/Shall within one beauty meet,/And she be only thine.'
16. Celia] see *Headnote, Date*.
18. once] one day (*OED* adv. B 1 b).
19. magazine] a) storehouse (*OED* n. 1 a) b) arsenal (*OED* n. 2 b); see above, *Headnote, Sources, Genre and Structure*. Cp. also W.L., 'To the fair, Vertuous, and nobly honoured Lady, Mrs R.G.', in M. de Harst, *A Panegyrick of the most renowned and serene Princess Christina*, trans. W.L. (1656), sig. [F7ʳ]: 'That which we falsly call a Wart, doth prove/To be the very Magazin of Love,/The strongest Tower of warlike Cupid.'
21. cells] store closets (*OED* n.[1]).
22. nitre] potassium nitrate or saltpetre, the essential ingredient of gunpowder (*OED* n. 1 b). *refined*] purified; freed from impurities (*OED* v. 3 b).
23. naphtha] highly volatile liquid issuing naturally from the earth (*OED*). *sulphur's heat*] the non-metallic element sulphur is highly flammable, was used to make gunpowder, and was popularly associated with the fires of hell, and with thunder and lightning (*OED* n. 1); 'sulphur' was also a name for the discharge of gunpowder (*OED* n. 4).
23–4. sulphur's . . . mind] Cp. Cowley, 'The Monopoly' (1647), ll. 1–2: 'What *Mines of Sulphur* in my breast do ly,/That feed th'eternal burnings of my heart?'

VII

25 He fortified the double gate,
    And rarely thither came;
For, with one spark of these, he straight
    All Nature could inflame.

VIII

Till, by vicinity so long,
30   A nearer way they sought;
And, grown magnetically strong,
    Into each other wrought.

IX

Thus all his fuel did unite
    To make one fire high:
35 None ever burn'd so hot, so bright:
    And Celia that am I.

X

So we alone the happy rest,
    Whilst all the world is poor,
And have within ourselves possessed
40   All Love's and Nature's store.

---

25. double gate] an arsenal had a double gate for reasons of security, and to minimize damage to the outside world if it did ignite.
27. these] i.e. nitre, naphtha and sulphur.
29. vicinity] a) nearness (*OED* 1) b) likeness (*OED* 2).
31–2. grown . . . wrought] Cp. Donne, *The First Anniversary* (1611), ll. 220–2: 'She that should all parts to reunion bow,/ She that had all Magnetique force alone,/To draw, and fasten sundred parts in one.'

31. magnetically] a) with powers of attraction like those of a magnet ('magnetic': *OED* A a. 2) b) magically ('magnetic': *OED* A a. 1 c).
32. wrought] fashioned (not in *OED*).
37. the happy] i.e. the happy ones. *rest*] a) relax (*OED* v.¹ I 1) b) remain (*OED* v.² 2).
39. possessed] enjoyed (not in *OED*).

The Mower Poems

The four Mower poems were printed in *1681* in the sequence adopted here (and by most editors). They are usually assumed to have been first composed during M.'s stay at Nun Appleton, but there is no absolute certainty to this supposition. Each Mower poem represents a significant transformation (and in some instances reversal) of prevailing bucolic and country house poetic conventions, and, as with *Upon Appleton House*, some of the Mower poems reflect the literary interests of M.'s employer, Lord Fairfax. It may be that parts of the mower poems were originally envisaged as sections of *Upon Appleton House*. This is especially so of *Damon the Mower*, which has the same stanzaic form as *Upon Appleton House*. All four poems are notable for their extremely regular metres.

There is a degree of interconnection between the sources of the poems that is not immediately apparent in each poem when considered alone. For instance, the grafting of trees discussed in *The Mower against Gardens*, ll. 21–6, is said by Pliny (trans. Philemon Holland (1634), 1.522–3) to take place best just before the hottest season (upon 'the rising of the Dog-starre'), when trees are, as lovers, at their most amorous. Intense summer heat and the dog star are the subjects of *Damon the Mower* (ll. 17–18). The mowing of grass to make hay took place in June and July, before harvest time. The sequence of the poems mirrors the chronology of the mower's brief appearance, moving from very late spring, through the heat of summer to the mower's final nighttime disappointment, and his acknowledgement of mortality. Wilcher (1985), 89, argues that the four poems, printed in the sequence adopted in *1681*, realize their fullest significance by revealing 'the process of disorientation that transforms the confident champion of pastoral values in "The Mower against Gardens" into the alienated dealer of death in "The Mower's Song"'. For Haber (1994), 123, the three later mower poems 'arrive gradually at a logical, self-conscious view of the relation of innocence to experience'. Rees (1989), 147, argues that each poem is

made formally distinct, but 'resembles a musical form such as a sonata, with a prominent leitmotif and contrasts of mood and tempo'. Each poem is rooted in a specific aspect of rural culture and its literature. These are successively: gardens versus meadows; pastoral; the authority of Pliny's natural history; the survey. The idea of a closely knit sequence is challenged by Colie (1970), 30 and Kegel-Brinkgreve (1991), 547. The apparent naivety of the mower's mind, its closeness to nature, and the distinctive character of his self-reflection, are topics of frequent critical debate. Specific discussions are mentioned below in the headnotes to each poem.

Mowers are present in the earliest pastoral poetry: M.'s use of the mower instead of the shepherd is not as unusual as has often been claimed. Theocritus's *Idyll*, X, is a dialogue between two reapers, and Scaliger listed mower poems as a subcategory of pastorals (*Poetices libri septem* (1561), III.xcix). In this respect, M.'s poems are closer to the older generic categorization, as opposed to the relegation of pastoral below georgic, or its reconstruction within georgic terms that began to occur in the 1650s (see Fowler and Chambers in Leslie and Raylor, eds (1992), 81–9, 173–94). Nonetheless, in the history of pastoral, M.'s mower is one of a number of figures and voices that usurped the shepherd, furthering the disintegration of the genre (Laing (1982), 10, 186–91).

'Reaper' was the more proper translation from some languages than 'mower'. Mowers and reapers were signified by the same word in Hebrew (*qôtsêr*, from the root 'to cut down'). In the AV translation, 'mower' is used in Ps. 129:7, where the enemies of Zion are said to wither like grass on rooftops, not gathered by mowers. But in the olive oil culture of the ancient world, reaping was associated with the harvesting of olives and vines. Unlike many treatments of mowers and reapers, especially in classical tradition, M.'s figures do not mention that they, unlike the shepherds, are waged labourers. By the mid-seventeenth century, mowers were firmly present in English verse, although they did not usually speak: 'No unexpected Inundations spoile/The Mowers hopes, nor mocke the Plough-mans toyle' (Denham, *Coopers Hill* (A Text, 1642), ll. 199–200). Similarly, in Milton's 'L'Allegro' (?1631), l. 66, the mower appears alongside the ploughman, the milkmaid and the shepherd. Edward Fairfax's early seventeenth-century allegorical pastoral 'Egloge', which was in the possession of M.'s employer, Thomas, Lord Fairfax, begins with mowers: 'The sweatie Sith-man wth his rasor keene/Shore the perfumed beard from medowes greene' (Bod. MS Fairfax 40, 647). One exception would be Aurelian Townshend's 'A Dialogue betwixt Time and a Pilgrime' (1653), where Time is presented as an old man mowing a field. Alpers (1996), 27, claims that M. was the first poet to make the mower a representative pastoral lover.

The mower had a more widely known symbolic life as an emblem of death (Time, the grim reaper). Like M.'s mower, Spenser's Time is an enemy of gardens: 'in the Garden of Adonis springs,/Is wicked Time, who with his scyth addrest,/Does mow the flowring herbes and goodly things' (*The Faerie Queene*, 3.6.39). The moral associations of reapers varied: Milton represented Cain as a 'sweaty reaper' (and Abel as a shepherd; *Paradise Lost*, 11, ll. 434–7), but Christ was assumed by commentators to be the reaper named in Rev. 14:14 (see Stocker (1986), 349, n. 88).

M.'s mower is, by virtue of the vocabulary given to him, a committed observer of agriculture, and a traditionalist. This is most evident in *The Mower against Gardens*, but throughout the sequence, there is a sustained attack on ornamentation in gardens, and the innovations in horticultural and agricultural technique that were beginning to take hold in mid-seventeenth-century England. The mower represents a rural culture of accumulated experience, where memory, custom and ready reckoning took precedence over learning, experiment and print (see Markham, *The English Husbandman* (1635), 9; Fox *et al.* (1996), 92). Paracelsus and his followers believed that the common people had a knowledge of the healing powers of herbs and plants that was part of the lost *prisca theologia*, and Fairfax's interests were broadly in line with this tradition. Rogers (1996), 62–4, argues that the mower's consciousness betrays 'an organic immersion in a vitalist world of self-moving matter' – akin, in his view, to the monist views of matter that were discussed by a variety of radical and philosophical reformers in the

period. The mower is also a defender of his workplace, the fields and meadows, and is resistant to the landscaping that broke down the traditional barrier between the enclosed garden and land put to agrarian use (see Leslie and Raylor, eds (1992), Part Two). Such a transgression is apparent in the layout of the estate at Nun Appleton, especially in the way that the wooded path extends away through the woods from the house and garden (see fig. 8). The elaborate plans for agricultural development discussed, publicized and proposed by the Hartlib circle (especially by Hartlib himself, John Beale and Cressy Dymock) effectively turned enclosed land into a domain that was as intricately cultivated as the garden, and that had fruit and plant gardens at its centre (Hunt, in Greengrass *et al.*, eds (1994), 321–42). The mower is hostile to horticultural innovation, and displays no awareness of moves for agricultural improvement. Conversely, there is hardly any reference to mowers and mowing in writing on agriculture and agricultural improvement. Reference to mowers was most common in ballads and other forms of popular verse, the form of print with the widest, most popular, circulation in the period: see, e.g., John Taylor, 'The Exale-tation of Ale' (1651), ll. 61–2.

Kegl (in Harvey and Maus, eds (1990), 89–118) argues that the poems reflect the growth of agricultural waged labourers including mowers (who lived on less than subsistence wages) during the seventeenth century, noting also the parallels drawn by contemporaries between the enclosure of common land to make fields and the improvement of gardens. Yet little in fact is given away with regard to the economic conditions of M.'s mower. There is, for instance, no reference made to the enclosure of fields, and the literature it generated, either for or against. Neither is there any explicit awareness of the factor that all commentary on mowers acknowledged: that mowers were needed only in two summer months; it was not possible to live as a mower for the whole of the year. Whether waged or not, it is most likely that the mowers at Nun Appleton came from the local community, some of them living in the cottages depicted in the more detailed 1596 map of the estate (Borthwick Institute of Historical Research, University of York, PR. B/P 15). During the civil disruption of the mid-century, travelling labourers who found work as mowers included decommissioned soldiers and uprooted sectaries (Hessayon (1997), ch. 4).

Marcus (1986), 233–40, argues that the Mower is a construction in deliberate contradistinction to the festive rural figures of Cavalier verse, itself part of a deliberately constructed courtly aesthetic and religious attitude: the 'Mower is a countryman apparently untouched by Laudian teaching as to the proper relationship between country pastimes and religious observance' (234). The mower claims that the fields are paradisal, but the garden enthusiasts also represented their improvements as Edenic, or at least near approaches to that state: see Evelyn, *Kalendarium Hortense* (1666), 2.

The lexical history of the word 'mower' is complex. Baldwin, *The Explicator*, 35.3 (1976), 25–6, notes 'mower' (*OED* n.^{2}) as 'One who makes mouths; a jester, a mocker', a fitting definition of M.'s sceptical, sardonic and disappointed speaker. No instance of the noun is noted after 1530, but 'mow' as grimace (*OED* n.^{2}) and 'to mow', to make mouths or grimaces (*OED* v.^{3}) remained in usage until the mid-eighteenth century.

To 'mow' in the seventeenth century meant to have sexual intercourse: it was a form of bawdry in England and explicitly literal in Scotland (Williams (1994), II.919–20). M. signifies his awareness of these meanings in his Latin poem *Upon an Eunuch: a Poet*, where the sickle is used to describe male virility: 'Falcem virginae nequeas immitere messi' (You cannot thrust a sickle at the virgin harvest). The sickle or scythe accordingly was used to name the penis ('Priapus when hee's but half man'd/Without a prick or sickle in it stand', R. Fletcher, *Ex Otio Negotium* (1656), 99; see also Williams (1994), III.1248).

Mowers were also described in martial terms (see, e.g., Wye Saltonstall, *Picturae Loquentes* (2nd edn, 1635), sig. G10^v–11^r). By a similar token, imagery of mowers and mowing was frequent in Civil War battle descriptions:

the Cavaliers came on to assault *Glocester* and got within Pistoll shot of the City, whereupon Colonell *Massey* made a breach in his works, and drew up six or seven pieces of Ordnance charged with Muskets bullets to the breach, which he fired upon them, and slew a great many of them, cutting them off as Mowers cut grasse, and forced them to retreat. (*Certaine Informations*, 34 (4–11 September 1643), 264.)

Cromwell was even likened to a mower by Payne Fisher:

Not much unlike a Husbandman, who goes
Through all the fields, and with his sickle mowes
The riper Corne and the first Grass for hay, . . .
Where e're he comes making an open way,
Alaies those Plants which did so glorious stand,
Like to dead stubble on the mowed land.
                    (*Veni: Vidi; Vici. The Triumphs of the Most
                    Excellent & Illustrious Oliver Cromwell*,
                    trans. Thomas Manley (1652), 63–4)

Arresting passages of angelic reapers bringing on the millennium will be found in George Foster, *The Sounding of the Last Trumpet* (April and November 1650), 14, 49–50, a work that envisages Fairfax as the deliverer of a just commonwealth. M. makes no explicit reference in these poems to public events, yet Wilcher (1985), 104, notes the classical understanding of Virgil's *Eclogues*, and in particular, symbolic associations between on the one hand shade and genuine retirement from public life, and on the other, heat and exile, slavery and discord. In this context, the amorous torment of the mower is where 'an original sense of well-being in the countryside converts to anarchy and violence' (Marcus (1986), 236) so that he is 'symptomatic of disturbances in the very fabric of seventeenth-century life' (Wilcher, op. cit., loc. cit.).

26

The Mower against Gardens

Date. 1668. Developing an argument made first by Pritchard, *SEL*, 23 (1983) 371–88, Hammond (*N & Q*, 2006, forthcoming), argues that the poem in fact belongs to 1668, along with *The Garden*, despite being part of a group of poems most of which were written in 1650–52. Hammond detects several echoes of Cowley's 'The Garden' and other poems and essays, published in 1668, including shared rhymes (see also below, ll. 29–30 n.), and where M.'s gardener disagrees with the horticulturalist sentiments of Cowley's poem. This dating might explain the one heavy echo of 'The Garden' in the poem (see below, l. 17); Hammond would see both of M.'s poems as different responses to Cowley's 'The Garden', and links the imagery of sexual impropriety with M.'s anti-court verse satires of the later 1660s and M.'s response to Milton's *Paradise Lost*, first published in 1667. Poetic elements suggesting an earlier date remain, but do not detract from the force of this argument.

Publication. 1681.

Context. The poem picks up on contemporary anxieties aroused by garden fanaticism, *furor hortensis*, but builds on a tradition of resistance to artificiality imposed on nature that was well embedded in English poetry by the mid-seventeenth century (see, e.g., Spenser, *The Faerie Queene*, VII.vii.8, ll. 3–7). Moreover, those who sought gardens for mere pleasure and self-indulgence were generally frowned upon: self-improvement and spiritual recreation were prerequisite qualities (see Leslie and Raylor, eds (1992), 7). But the mower appears to despise all kinds of garden as perversions of the order of nature. Any notion that the garden was in some measure an attempt to restore Eden is absent. Plants were to be used for their medicinal qualities: Damon the Mower makes use of common wayside plants when he cuts himself (see below, *Damon the Mower*, l. 83). Botanical gardens could be dangerous places, replicating the associations and imagery of the Civil Wars: 'There is a Plant called *Noli me tangere*, neer which

if you put your hand, the Seed will spurtle forth suddenly, in so much that the unexpectnesse of it made the valiant Lord *Fairfax* to start, as Master *Robert* [corrected to Bobart in Bod. Vet. A3.f.7] at the Physick Garden in *Oxford* can tell you,' William Coles, *The Art of Simpling* (1656), 39. The garden imagery in this poem is so ornate and contrived that M. most probably had in mind an Italian or Italianate garden (see Hunt (1978), 44). As James Howell put it: 'As hee traverseth the Countrey hee must note the trace, forme and site of any famous *Structure*, the Platforms of *Gardens, Aqueducts, Grots, Sculptures*', *Instructions for Forreine Travell*' (1642), 109. M.'s mower is against gardens of any kind, but the intellectually fashionable view by the mid-seventeenth century was that the garden was the final form of man's cultivation of nature after the intermediary stages of agricultural cultivation.

Sources and Genre. The poem is written in the form of a regular Horatian epode, with alternating iambic pentameter and tetrameter lines. It therefore echoes, but presents a complication of, the sentiments expressed in Horace's famous second epode ('Beatus ille qui procul negotiis'). Jonson, who had translated the second epode, also praised country life in 'To Sir Robert Wroth', including mowing:

> The whilst, the several seasons thou hast seen
> > Of flowery fields, of copses green,
> The mowed meadows, with the fleeced sheep,
> > And feasts that either shearers keep. (ll. 37–40)

Maxwell, *N & Q*, n.s., 8 (1961), 309, lists other examples of English epodes with the same metre in the period. Kermode, *N & Q*, 197 (1952), 136–8, saw M.'s poem as a response to Thomas Randolph's somewhat longer poem, 'Upon Love fondly refus'd for Conscience sake' (1647). M. certainly reworks several concepts in Randolph's poem while not relying upon the poem as a verbal source. Randolph's speaker is a young lover, searching for innocence (and an innocent definition of youthful pleasures) in a refound golden world, away from the 'tyrant conscience'. Nature is alluring to the speaker in this sense (and beyond man's control), and grafting is simply an enhancement of this perfection. Fairies, elves and goblins are superstitious fictions, like the claims of conscience. M.'s poem banishes human love in order to exhibit a 'higher wisdom' in the voice of the mower, who introduces a distinction between gardens and nature beyond gardens, and who speaks with a knowledge of fairies and fauns, who, for him, are vitally real. Randolph's positive reference to horticulture is reversed. The attack on cosmetics at ll. 1–2, 5–8, 11–14, 23–30 is shown by Parker, *N & Q*, forthcoming, to be drawn from du Bartas, *Divine Weeks*, trans. Sylvester, II.iv.4. 4.94–220, a passage describing the death of Jezebel at the command of Jehu; e.g., II.iv.4.119–22, 145–6, 158–62: 'Close in her Closet, with her best Complexions,/Shee mends her Faces wrinkle-full defections,/Her Cheek shee cherries, and her Ey shee cheers,/And fains her (fond) a Wench of fifteen years; . . . with vile Drugs adultering her Face,/Closely allures th' Adulterers Imbrace. . . ./The Lillies of her brests, the Rosie red/In either Cheek, and all her other Riches,/Wherewith shee bleareth sight, and sense bewitches;/Is none of hers: it is but borrow'd stuff,/Or stoln, or bought, plain Counterfet in proof: . . .'

Blatt, *N & Q*, forthcoming, suggests that Henry Vaughan's 'Corruption' (1650), provides another source, notably in the stanza form, and in a series of echoes. In Vaughan's poem, fallen man is in the countryside, like M.'s mower, but, unlike the mower, he longs for the garden of Eden (ll. 17–20). The countryside affords glimpses of Paradise to man (ll. 21–8), whereas M.'s mower seems wholly content with fairy-filled meadows. Vaughan notes that the mortality of plants came with the Fall (ll. 11–12), so that decay follows as soon as plants seed; by contrast, M.'s mower is outraged by the total absence of seed through the grafting process. Vaughan's poem is the opposite of Randolph's, since a longing for Eden against the reality of original sin is answered in the promise of it shown in aspects of natural landscape. The last two lines of Vaughan's poem contain the voice of the angel in Rev. 14:15, where reaping is identified with redemption, and the separation of the saved from the damned: '*Arise! Thrust in thy sickle.*' M.'s poem presents horticulture as the Fall, but replaces the apocalyptic endings to Vaughan's poem with a relocation of the mower's 'Eden' in the

agricultural world, so reinstating Randolph's initial sentiments in natural rather than human terms. Although M.'s mower is against grafting, the poem is, in effect, a verbal grafting of two different poems to form a hybrid: it therefore imitates in its form the subject of its complaint.

M.'s mower speaks against a weighty tradition in favour of gardens, stemming back to the portrayal of Paradise as a garden (Gen. 2:15). Seventeenth-century horticulturalists aspired to recreate Eden, just as religious and political radicals believed that their reforms would bring about a recreated Eden. M.'s mower believes that nature, experienced by the mower as the world of basic English agriculture, is 'pure', not the garden (l. 4).

Versification and Style. In addition to the imitation of the Horatian epode (see above, *Sources and Genre*), the poem is notable for the extended conceit, maintained for thirty lines, of man as pander, brothelkeeper or polygamous tyrant, seducing flowers and plants away from nature and into his garden–prison–brothel–seraglio, where, doped with lusciousness, they are made to wear alluring cosmetics and perfumes in an unnatural fashion. In short, they fall from natural beauties to become courtesans. The worst crime is to interfere with the order of nature by grafting trees.

The poem is precisely focused around a shift in l. 19 from the past tense to the subjunctive mood. Badley (1994) notes a significant degree of numerological design in the poem, part of a strategy designed to point up themes. 'Proud' (l. 20) is at the centre of the poem, being the ninetieth word, occurring at the end of the twentieth line.

Modern Criticism. King, *HLQ*, 23.3 (1970), 237–42, sees a parallel between the stance of M.'s mower and the visionary calls for a return to Eden through the cultivation of common land in Digger pamphlets. Gardening is 'an imperialist takeover' (McKeon, *YES*, 13 (1983), 46–65 (60)), a view that fuses gardening with enclosure issues. The mower speaks against gardens because they are 'enclosed' (l. 31), and this has been seen as a reference to protests against enclosure (see also Hill) in Carey (1969), 83–5). These views are placed in the context of M.'s debt to the Cavalier lyric by Malcolmson (in Burt and Archer, eds (1994), 252): M.'s 'use of the imagery of enclosure cannot be understood apart from its relation to gender: in their poems on the libertine garden, the Cavaliers conceitedly and pornographically describe women in terms of the land and its fruits; . . . Marvell reverses this process and describes the land and its fruits in terms of women'.

Haber (1994), 107, notes how apparently removed from contemporary norms of consciousness the mower in this poem is. He does not regard himself as fallen, or even wholly human. His perception of human skills and human corruption is rendered through a single point of view. The reader, but not the speaking mower, appreciates the irony of the humanizing terms (largely sexual) that are used to describe the garden. The mower is caught up in the processes of human corruption that he descries by his very power of words, but he does not realize this. Thus, he experiences a sense of unity with nature (Haber, 108): the 'us' of l. 40 being both mower, meadows, and any other beings in the meadows. The mower's diatribe invokes the greater world of moral censure, but the poem does not refer allegorically (*pace* Spenserian pastoral) to worlds of politics and religion. It only finally refers to its own world. In doing so, Haber, 109, claims that M. is reconciling 'two versions of pastoral that Sidney forced apart': 'He is presenting pastoral both as the diminished reflection of a greater, uncontrollable reality, and as the metaphoric recreation of a simpler, more innocent existence. . . . the second version . . . is necessarily dependent upon the first.'

Alpers (1996), 238–9, singles out the distinctiveness of M.'s speaker. At first a special identity for the speaker's voice is not apparent: only at the end of the poem is the mower's identity apparent (apart from being signalled in the title). 'The poem thus enacts a general truth about Marvell's pastoralism: conventional figures, literary shepherds or their equivalents, are no longer the *sine qua non* of pastoral expression but are special cases, precipitates as it were, of the pastoral speaker.' If this is so, the poem has a special significance as the first in the mower sequence: for Haber (1994), 123, the other mower poems 'unpack what is already there [in] *The Mower against Gardens*'.

The Mower against Gardens

Luxurious man, to bring his vice in use,
  Did after him the world seduce:
And from the fields the flowers and plants allure,
  Where Nature was most plain and pure.
5 He first enclosed within the gardens square
  A dead and standing pool of air:
And a more luscious earth for them did knead,
  Which stupefied them while it fed.
The pink grew then as double as his mind;
10 The nutriment did change the kind.
With strange perfumes he did the roses taint,
  And flowers themselves were taught to paint.

---

1. *Luxurious*] a) lecherous (*OED* a. 1) b) self-indulgent (*OED* a. 3 a). *vice*] depravity, corruption (*OED* n.¹ 1). *bring . . . in use*] a) bring into practice b) fulfil sexually c) make profitable.
2. *seduce*] a) lead astray (*OED* v. 2) b) induce to surrender chastity (*OED* v. 3).
3. *allure*] attract (*OED* v. 1 b), with an overtone of 'charm' (*OED* v. 3).
4. *plain*] a) flat (*OED* A a. I 1) b) simple (*OED* A a. II I 8).
5. *He first enclosed*] Cp. Randolph, 'Upon Love fondly refus'd for Conscience sake', l. 14: 'Inclosures mens inventions be.' *gardens square*] inviting also the sense of 'garden's square' (emphasizing the unnaturalness of geometrical shapes). Cp. Bacon, *Essay* XLVI, 'Of Gardens' (ed. M. Kiernan (Oxford, 1985), 141–2): 'The *Garden* is best to be Square; Incompassed, on all Foure Sides, with a *Stately Arched Hedge*.'
6. *standing pool of air*] Cp. Sir Henry Wotton, *The Elements of Architecture*, in *Reliquiae Wottoniae* (1624, 2nd edn, 1651), 203: 'Not unexperienced, for want of *Wind*: which were to live (as it were) in a *Lake*, or standing *Pool* of *Aire*'; James Howell, *Instructions for Forreine Travell* (1642), 170 (significantly, on the Dutch): 'Yet in conversation, they are but heavy, of a homely outside, and slow in action, which *slownesse* carieth with it a notable *perseverance*, and this may bee imputed to the quality of that *mould* of *earth*, whereon they dwell, which may

be said to *bee a kind of standing poole of Ayre*'. The source of the phrase is in Leon Battista Alberti, *De Re Aedificatoria* (Florence, 1485), I.sig. aiii^v: 'lacunum stagnum . . . aeris'.
7. *luscious*] sickly, cloying (*OED* a. 2).
7–8. *knead/ . . . fed*] *OED* ('knead' v.) provides examples in some dialects of the short pronunciation of the vowel (i.e. 'kned'), which would make the rhyme regular.
8. *stupefied*] made dull and lifeless (*OED* v. 4); usually used in the period to describe the effect of drugs.
9. *pink . . . double*] a) *caryphillus minor silvestris* or small gilliflower, either single, with a flower of five leaves, or double, with more leaves. But the double occurs naturally and none of the many kinds of pink were assumed by seventeenth-century authorities to be the products of cultivation: see, for instance, John Parkinson, *Paradisi in Sole Paradisus Terrestris* (1629), 314–18. b) 'pink' was used figuratively to describe perfection (*OED* n.⁴ 2 fig.). *double*] a) referring to the double pink. b) duplicitous (*OED* A a. 5).
10. *kind*] a) nature of the species (*OED* n. I 9) b) sex (*OED* n. I 7).
11. *strange perfumes . . . taint*] but perfume (especially in England) was customarily derived from roses. *strange*] foreign, alien (*OED* a. 1, 7); 'strange woman' described a harlot (*OED* a. 4). *taint*] corrupt, contaminate (*OED* v. 4).
12. *paint*] apply cosmetics (*OED* v.¹ 4).

    The tulip, white, did for complexion seek;
      And learned to interline its cheek:
15 Its onion root they then so high did hold,
      That one was for a meadow sold.
    Another world was searched, through oceans new,
      To find the *Marvel of Peru*.
    And yet these rarities might be allowed
20   To man, that sov'reign thing and proud;
    Had he not dealt between the bark and tree,
      Forbidden mixtures there to see.
    No plant now knew the stock from which it came;
      He grafts upon the wild the tame:
25 That the uncertain and adult'rate fruit
      Might put the palate in dispute.

    His green *seraglio* has its eunuchs too;
      Lest any tyrant him outdo.
    And in the cherry he does Nature vex,
30   To procreate without a sex.
    'Tis all enforced, the fountain and the grot;
      While the sweet fields do lie forgot:
    Where willing Nature does to all dispense
      A wild and fragrant innocence:
35 And fauns and fairies do the meadows till,
      More by their presence than their skill.
    Their statues polished by some ancient hand,
      May to adorn the gardens stand:
    But howsoe'er the figures do excel,
40   The gods themselves with us do dwell.

---

13. tulip] tulips were associated with artificial gardens, and were regarded as a kind of fallen plant, being valued only for their beauty since they had no medicinal application: see James Shirley, 'The Garden' (1646), ll. 13–14: 'Those Tulips that such wealth display,/To court my eye, shall lose their name' (Rees (1989), 149). *complexion*] cosmetics (*OED* n. 6).

14. interline] mark with lines in various colours (*OED* v.¹ 5).

15–16. onion root . . . sold] alluding to the extremely high prices paid for bulbs during the largely Dutch tulip mania of the 1630s: see Dash (2000).

15. onion root] tulip bulb.

17. Cp. *The Garden*, ll. 43–6: 'The mind, that ocean where each kind/Does straight its own resemblance find,/Yet it creates, transcending these,/Far other worlds, and other seas.'

18. Marvel of Peru] *mirabilis jalapa*, a plant with multi-coloured, funnel-shaped flowers found in the West Indies and central and south America (*OED* n. 6). See also below, l. 27 n.; Robert Boyle, *Experiments and Considerations touching Colours* (1664), 5: 'such a variety [of colours] we have much admired in that lovely plant which is commonly call'd the *Marvayl of Peru*: for of divers sorts of fine Flowers, which in its season that gaudy Plant does almost daily produce, I have scarce taken notice of any two that were dyed perfectly alike.'

21–2. The production of new breeds by budding (inserting the bud of one tree or shrub under the bark of another) is imagined as pandering on the part of man between plant species. While the sense is of unnatural interference, the image is of human sexual copulation: the bud (penis) is inserted into the tree's vagina (the space between the bark and the tree trunk). *dealt*] had (sexual) intercourse with (*OED* v. II 11 b). The commercial connotations of 'deal' (*OED* v. II 13) are raised by the reference to new world exploration in ll. 17–18.

22. Forbidden mixtures] see Lev. 19:19: 'Ye shall keep my statutes. Thou shalt not let thy cattle gender with a diverse kind: thou shalt not sow thy field with mingled seed: neither shall a garment mingled of linen and woollen come upon thee'; Deut. 22:9: 'Thou shalt not sow thy vineyard with divers seeds: lest the fruit of thy seed which thou hast sown, and the fruit of thy vineyard, be defiled.' (Legouis) Pliny, *Natural History*, XV.15, discusses in wholly positive terms the introduction of foreign trees, and the mixing of trees by grafting.

24. the wild the tame] a juxtaposition usually used to describe animals in the period. *wild*] uncultivated, growing in state of nature (*OED* a. A I 2). *tame*] a) cultivated (*OED* a. 2) b) deficient, dull (*OED* a. 5 a).

25. uncertain] of indeterminate identity (*OED* a. 4 c). *adult'rate*] a) the product of 'adulturous' (i.e. unnatural, improper) union. b) adulterated; full of base, corrupt genres.

26. put . . . dispute] confuse the tastebuds.

27. seraglio] a) enclosure (*OED* I 2) b) harem, place of confinement for wives in a Muslim house (*OED* I 1). *1681* prints the word in italic, which stresses the alien nature of the word, just as the garden contains foreign plants, like the *Marvel of Peru* (see above, l. 18).

28. tyrant] oriental rulers, with seraglios of wives and eunuch servants, were commonly regarded by Europeans as despots or tyrants (see, e.g., Milton, *Paradise Lost*, II, ll. 1–2), whose practice of polygamy and concubinage was depraved.

29–30. cherry . . . sex] this must be a stoneless cherry: stone was a term for testicle (*OED* n. 11). In Charles Estienne's *Maison Rustique*, translated by Richard Surflet, translated and expanded by Gervase Markham (1616), 361, the cause of stoneless cherries is attributed to the fruit growing out of a branch with no pith; this could be achieved by a process involving grafting (see also Carey, in Patrides, ed. (1978), 148–9). M.'s sentiments are the opposite of those expressed by Cowley, 'The Garden' (1667), st. 10, ll. 23–8: 'Even *Daphnes* coyness he does mock,/And weds the Cherry to her stock,/Though she refus'd *Apolloes* suit;/Even she, that chast and Virgin tree,/Now wonders at her self, to see/That she's a mother made, and blushes in her fruit.'

29. vex] distress (*OED* v. I 3).

31. enforced] a) compelled (*OED* v. III 13) b) ravished (*OED* v. II 9). *grot*] grotto: artificial structure imitating a rocky cave (*OED* 2).

33. willing] compliant (*OED* ppl. a.); as opposed to 'enforced' (l. 31).

35. fauns and fairies] The invocation of fairies by M. seems to have no clear connection with any cultural, religious or political alignment (Diane Purkiss, private communication).

37. statues] statues were a well-known feature of ornate gardens (see Hunt, in Patrides (1978), 335–45). *polished . . . hand*] implying that the statues are original classical figures, made by an ancient hand, then resituated in an ornate garden. *polished*] make smooth (*OED* v. B 1).

40. gods] the deities themselves, as opposed to their representations in the statues.

27

Damon the Mower

Date. July–August 1652. The hot summer of 1652, one of the means of dating *Upon Appleton House* (see above), chimes with the references to extreme heat in stanza II.

Publication. 1681. A fragment of the first nineteen lines, almost certainly copied from *1681*, survives in University of Chicago, MS 554, p. 11 (*Ch. 1*), an early eighteenth-century commonplace book that belonged to the Fairfax family.

Sources and Genres. The poem echoes some of the earliest pastoral verse: Kalstone, *ELR*, 4 (1974), 175–88, regards Theocritus's *Idyll*, XI, where the ugly Cyclops Polythemus woos Galatea, as a source for M.'s poem and the origin of M.'s mower's comic deflation (also referred to in M.'s *Remarks upon a late Disingenuous Discourse* (1678), 78). The story is retold in Ovid, *Metamorphoses*, XIII, ll. 740–897. Damon is a character in Virgil's eighth *Eclogue* where he complains at the loss of his love Nysa before committing suicide. Kalstone argues however that M.'s poem in fact has more to do with Virgil's second *Eclogue*, which restates Theocritus's *Idyll* XI, through the character of the suffering shepherd Corydon. Both of these, like Damon, give gifts and are ignored. Corydon reconciles himself to his pastoral world by the end of the eclogue, whereas Damon can only face death. Haber (1994), 116, argues that M. deliberately conflates two opposite kinds of character – Polyphemus and Corydon – in one character, for the sake of achieving an enhanced effect of alienation. ll. 49–56 contain a clear instance of the mower voicing his overgoing of classical, Virgilian shepherds, put incongruously in the voice of the mower, rather than the poet. The 'overgoing' is achieved in terms which put M.'s poem close to Theocritus's ironic method. On this theme, and especially the extent to which Damon is aware (or not) of literary conventions and heroic dimensions, see also Alpers, *NLH*, 14.2 (1983), 277–304.

Haber (1994), 116, regards the echoes of Theocritus, *Idyll* I (see below, ll. 13, 30, 41–2, 58 nn.) as the point at which Damon achieves heroic self-consciousness. M. is blending two Theocritan bucolics with entirely different kinds of character: both are used to reveal the different potentials in Damon.

More significantly, Corydon is in love with a boy, Alexis; the woman Thestylis (who also appears in *Upon Appleton House*, l. 71) is a distraction and is the recipient of Corydon's gifts only because Alexis has spurned him. Homosexual desire is not explicitly present in M.'s poem, but remains submerged in the poem's allusions (see Hammond, *SC*, 11 (1996), 111–12).

The extensive presence of Thomas Randolph's influence in the Mower poems has also been suggested. Damon is a name adopted by Randolph himself in 'An Eclogue to Master Jonson', ll. 74–7, and the poem associates mowers with summer heat:

> The reapers, that with whetted sickles stand,
> Gathering the falling ears i'th'other hand,
> Though they endure the scorcing summers heat,
> Have yet some wages to allay their sweat.

M. ignores Randolph's interest in the fact that mowers, as opposed to shepherds, are paid wages. Leishman (1966), 138–9, sees the immediate source of M.'s interest in extremes of heat and cold in Randolph's *A Dialogue. Thirsis. Lalage* (ll. 1–6):

> My *Lalage* when I behold
>   So great a cold,
> And not a sparke of heat in thy desire,
> I wonder what strange power of thine,
>   Kindles in mine
> So bright a flame, and such a burning fire.

A more convincing case for a source is argued by Baruch, *CL*, 26 (1974), 242–59, through the detection of a series of parallels between *Damon the Mower* and Tristan L'Hermite's 'Les Plaintes d'Acante', in *Les Amours* (1637), translated by Thomas Stanley as 'Acanthus Complaint'. M. read both, and took their conceits to 'logical conclusions', while exploiting material in the French that Stanley had not translated. M. certainly uses pastoral hyperbole (evolving the most famous Petrarchan paradox of icy fire) in his description of Juliana (ll. 25–32). But such poetic women do not harm nature; in Damon's eyes, Juliana is too much, and his fields provide neither fulfilment nor refuge.

Marcus (1986), 233–8, argues that the poem is in fact written in contradistinction to the Cavalier celebration of holiday pastimes, even in its more plangent but still resilient Civil War mode, as instanced in Lovelace's 'The Grasse-Hopper' (see below, l. 11 n.). The references to Anglican liturgy reveal texts used in May Day sermons.

Structure, Style and Versification. There is a contrast between the sophisticated literary use of pastoral and pastoral tradition and Damon's simple consciousness. This is signalled initially by the contrast between the sophisticated awareness and tone of the narrator in the first stanza, and Damon's first speech in the second. Damon's speech is characterized by repetition (e.g. ll. 11, 14), and his habit of speaking in balanced parallelisms (e.g. ll. 20–1, 31–2, 40). As with the mower in *The Mower against Gardens* there is no apparent distance between the self-consciousness of the speaker and nature itself. Damon cannot explicitly compare himself to nature, so he appears to humanize nature. Thus, according to Haber (1994), 112–13, Damon 'turns symbols back upon themselves', depriving them of the chance to signify anything more than nature itself. Damon often expresses himself in terms of paired natural objects, but this is set against the doubleness of the poem's form: like the snake with its second skin (ll. 15–16), it regenerates itself from a previous version of itself. It is both different and the same. But

later in the poem, a kind of heroic self-consciousness grows in Damon (st. VII), supplanting the simplicity of the earlier stanzas, and adding a capacity for self-identification and meditation upon an interior emotional life. Damon then becomes the singular focus of the poem, obsessed with his own emotional life, until he wounds himself (ll. 77–8), when inner and outer worlds are fused. Finally, the doubles of animals and remedies are resolved by Damon meeting his own double: Death (ll. 87–8).

Damon the Mower

I

Hark how the mower Damon sung,
With love of Juliana stung!
While everything did seem to paint
The scene more fit for his complaint.
5 Like her fair eyes the day was fair;
But scorching like his am'rous care.
Sharp like his scythe his sorrow was,
And withered like his hopes the grass.

II

'Oh what unusual heats are here,
10 Which thus our sunburned meadows sear!
The grasshopper its pipe gives o'er;
And hamstringed frogs can dance no more.
But in the brook the green frog wades;
And grasshoppers seek out the shades.

---

2. stung] a conventional way of expressing amorous desire, either referring to female attractiveness or male potency (see, e.g., Carew, 'Upon a Mole in Celia's Bosom' (1640), l. 20; Randolph, 'A Pastorall Courtship' (1638), l. 25), but also an ironic reference to 1 Cor. 15:55–6 that puts the mower's grief in the broader context of mortality and redemption: 'O death, where is thy sting? O grave where is thy victory? The sting of death is sin; and the strength of sin is the law.' The reference links with the end of the poem (ll. 87–8) where death is explicitly invoked and identified with the mower (see Hartman, in Lord (1968), 115, n. 26).
3. seem] the narrator speaks in similes, while Damon fuses signifier and signified in a language both literal and metaphorical. *paint*] decorate.
4. scene] theatrical and pictorial: like the painted scenery for a masque. *complaint*] the poem of complaint that begins in st. 2.
6. care] suffering (*OED* n.[1] 1).

8. withered . . . grass] green was the colour traditionally associated with hope: see Chevalier (1996), but 'withered' recalls the admission of human mortality in Isa. 40:6–8.
9. heats] hot season, summer (*OED* n. 3 b pl.).
11. grasshopper . . . o'er] As opposed to the grasshoppers of two other poets: 'The summer music of the grasshopper', Randolph, 'An Eclogue to Master Jonson' (1638), l. 83; Lovelace's grasshopper 'welcomes' the sun and 'Sporst in the guild-plats of his Beames', 'The Grasse-hopper' (1649), ll. 9–10. Earlier literary grasshoppers do not live in such a hot environment: e.g. Anacreon, trans. Thomas Stanley (1651), 'The Grasshopper. XLIII', ll. 1–3: 'Grasshopper thrice-happy! who/Sipping the cool morning dew,/Queen-like chirpest all the day.' *pipe*] song (*OED* n.[1] 2).
12. hamstringed] disabled (by the heat) (*OED* v. 2).
13. brook] *1681*; brooks *Ch. 1. frog*] Cp. Theocritus, *Idylls*, X, ll. 52–3: 'εὐκτὸς ὁ τῶ βάτράχω, παῖδες, βίος· οὐ μελεδαίνει/ τὸν τὸ πιεῖν ἐγχεῦντα·' (O for the life of a frog, boys! No care has he/For one to pour out his drink).

5   Only the snake, that kept within,
     Now glitters in its second skin.

III

    'This heat the sun could never raise,
     Nor Dog Star so inflames the days.
     It from an higher beauty grow'th,
20   Which burns the fields and mower both:
     Which mads the dog, and makes the sun
     Hotter than his own Phaëton.
     Not Jùly causeth these extremes,
     But Juliana's scorching beams.

IV

25   'Tell me where I may pass the fires
     Of the hot day, or hot desires.
     To what cool cave shall I descend,
     Or to what gelid fountain bend?

30   Alas! I look for ease in vain,
     When remedies themselves complain.
     No moisture but my tears do rest,
     Nor cold but in her icy breast.

V

    'How long wilt thou, fair shepherdess,
     Esteem me, and my presents less?
35   To thee the harmless snake I bring,
     Disarmèd of its teeth and sting;
     To thee chameleons changing hue,
     And oak leaves tipped with honey dew.
     Yet thou ungrateful hast not sought
40   Nor what they are, nor who them brought.

VI

    'I am the mower Damon, known
     Through all the meadows I have mown.

15. snake] making the field like Eden, and through allusion to the Genesis story, hinting at the involvement of women. Haber (1994), 122, notes the self-renewing snake as an image of both death and immortality: eternal life in death is what Damon achieves at the end of the poem. *within*] a) the shade b) its first skin.

18. Dog Star] Sirius, in the constellation of the Greater Dog, or Procyon, in the Lesser Dog, both being bright, were supposed to cause excessive heat when rising: 'in England the heat is not so intense and violent in the Dog-dayes, (especially in the Northern parts of England ['Kingston upon Hull' in margin], where I write this, where nevertheless they fear the biting of this Dog as much as in Spaine . . .)', James Primrose, *Popular Errours*, trans. Robert Witty (1651), 256 (M.'s dedicatory poem to Witty was published in this volume). Cp. Joannes Secundus, *Elegiae*, 1.3, ll. 27–8: 'licet in me/Fervidus ingeminet sidera sicca Puer' (even though the sultry Boy double the Dog Star's days for my benefit). *inflames*] Kermode, Wilcher, Ormerod and Wortham; inflame's *1681*, Margoliouth, Lord, Legouis; inflame Ch. 1, Donno, Walker.
21. mads] Bod. 1; made *1681*.
22. Phaëton] a) chariot (but 'phaeton' as a name for a light, open four-wheeled carriage is not recorded in *OED* until 1739); named after b) the son of the sun-god Helios (or Phoebus), he lost control of the chariot of the sun and scorched the earth: see Ovid, *Metamorphoses*, II, ll. 1–328.
23. Jùly] pronounced according to the regular metre, in order to emphasize the connection with Juliana in l. 24.
24. scorching beams] Cp. Johannes Secundus, *Elegiae*, I.iii, l. 13: 'Heu, Heu! quam meam me caeca face Julia torret!' (Alas! how Julia sears me with her invisible torch!).
27. cool cave] Cp. Ovid, *Metamorphoses*, XIII, l. 777: 'aut fessus sub opaca revertitur antra' (or returned weary to his shady cave).

28. gelid] cool, refreshingly cold (*OED* a. 2; from Latin *gelidus*, icy cold).
30. remedies . . . complain] Haber (1994), 10, believes that M.'s phrase relates to Theocritus' use of the word *pharmakon* (*Idylls*, XI, ll. 1, 7), which means both 'remedy' and 'poison'.
31. No . . . rest] i.e. 'no moisture remains except my tears.'
32. Nor . . . breast] a very obvious use of Petrarchan convention.
34–8. presents . . . dew] more extensive catalogues of gifts are listed by Virgil, *Eclogues*, II, ll. 45–55. See also Ovid, *Metamorphoses*, XIII, ll. 831–7. But Damon's gifts are simple and wholesome compared with the artificial gifts of Marlowe ('The Passionate Shepherd to his Love') and Herrick's swains in *Hesperides* (posies, clothes made from plants and flowers, rings).
34. presents] Haber (1994), 114–15, suggests a pun, with 'presents' implying 'presence'.
35–7. snake . . . chameleons] in Fletcher's *The Faithful Shepherdess* (?1610), III.i, ll. 28–40, the Sullen Shepherd makes Amarillis look like Amoret by using a charm that includes snakes and chameleons.
38. oak leaves . . . honey dew] honey dew was believed to distil when the influence of the Dog Star was at its height (see above, l. 18); it was also thought to be most pure when found on oak leaves: see Pliny, *Natural History*, XI.xii–xiii, trans. Philemon Holland, 315–16 (Wilcher, *N & Q*, 213 (1968), 102–3). Cp. Virgil, *Eclogue*, IV, l. 30: 'durae quercus sudabunt roscida mella' (rough-skinned oaks will sweat with honeydew).
40. who . . . brought] Cp. Virgil, *Eclogue*, II, l. 19: 'despectus tibi sum, nec qui sim quaeris' (you scorn me, never asking who I am).
41–8. Rogers (1996), 62, suggests that this stanza is a recitation of the song that Damon used to sing before he met Juliana.
41–2. Cp. Theocritus, *Idyll*, I, l. 120–1: 'Δάφνις ἐγὼν ὅδε τῆνος ὅ τὰς βόας ὧδε νομεύων,/Δάφνις ὅ τὼς ταύρως καὶ πόρτιας ὧδε ποτίσδων' (I am that Daphnis, he who drove the kine to pasture here,/Daphnis who led the bulls and calves to water at these springs).

On me the morn her dew distills
Before her darling daffodils.
45   And, if at noon my toil me heat,
The sun himself licks off my sweat.
While, going home, the ev'ning sweet
In cowslip-water bathes my feet.

VII

'What, though the piping shepherd stock
50   The plains with an unnumbered flock,
This scythe of mine discovers wide
More ground than all his sheep do hide.
With this the golden fleece I shear
Of all these closes every year.
55   And though in wool more poor than they,
Yet am I richer far in hay.

VIII

'Nor am I so deformed to sight,
If in my scythe I lookèd right;
In which I see my picture done,
60   As in a crescent moon the sun.
The deathless fairies take me oft
To lead them in their dances soft;
And, when I tune myself to sing,
About me they contract their ring.

IX

65   'How happy might I still have mowed,
Had not Love here his thistles sowed!
But now I all the day complain,
Joining my labour to my pain;

---

44. daffodils] spring flowers, now faded by some months at the time of Damon's speech.
46. licks off] i.e. evaporates. *sweat*] the sign of labour, the consequence of the Fall, 'In the sweat of thy face shalt thou eat bread, till thou return unto the ground' (Gen. 3:19); particularly associated with the hard work of mowing: see Wye Saltonstall, 'A Mower', in *Picturae Loquentes* (2nd edn, 1635), sig. G11ᵛ, 'the sweat seems to spring in his forehead'. See also Milton, *Paradise Lost*, XI, l. 434, where Cain is described as a 'sweaty reaper', and *Upon Appleton House*, l. 428.
48. cowslip-water] lotion made from cowslips, used for cleansing and moisturizing, as well as for medicinal purposes: John Parkinson, *Paradisi in Sole Paradisus Terrestris* (1629), 247. Cowslips are also spring flowers (see above, l. 44 n.).
49–56. What . . . hay] Cp. Virgil, *Eclogue*, II, ll. 21–4: 'Mille meae Siculis errant in montibus agnae;/lac mihi non aestate novum, non frigore defit./canto quae solitus, si quando armenta vocabat,/Amphion Dircaeus in Actaeo Aracyntho' (A thousand lambs of mine roam Sicily's hills;/Summer or winter, I'm never out of milk./I sing such songs as, when he called his herds, Amphion of Thebes on Attic Aracynthus). See also Ovid, *Metamorphoses*, XIII, ll. 810–37. Haber (1994), 118, argues that these lines show that Damon is aware of the innovation he is making: supplanting the shepherd with the mower in pastoral tradition. Ormerod and Wortham see a juxtaposition between the shepherd, an image of Christ, and the mower, who resembles with his scythe the traditional figure of Death.
51. discovers wide] uncovers a wide area around him. *discovers*] a) lays bare (*OED* v. 1) b) finds for the first time (*OED* v. 8); Kalstone, *ELR*, 4 (1974), 181, argues that 'discovers' identifies Damon as an explorer (see below, l. 53).
53. golden fleece] the mown hay is compared to the golden fleece sought for by Jason and the Argonauts. Damon thus identifies himself as a hero, but Jason had a disastrous marriage, and possibly committed suicide: see below, l. 88.
54. closes] enclosed fields (*OED* n.¹ 2).

55. wool] wool was the staple commodity of pre-industrial England, from which most of its wealth derived.
57–8. Cp. Virgil, *Eclogue*, II, ll. 25–7: 'nec sum adeo informis: nuper me in litore vidi,/cum placidum ventis staret mare; non ego Daphnim/iudice te metuam, si nunquam fallit imago.' (Nor am I so unsightly; on the shore the other day I looked at myself, when, by the grace of the winds, the sea was at peace and still. With you for judge, I should fear not Daphnis, if the mirror never lies). Ovid's Cyclops acknowledges his ugliness when he sees his reflection and praises it as a virtue (Ovid, *Metamorphoses*, XIII, ll. 840–53); Damon appears to find his deformities lessened by his own perception of his reflection.
58. in my . . . right] Corydon looks at his reflection in the sea (Virgil, *Eclogues*, II, l. 25), as does Polyphemus (personated by Damoetas), who claims that the reflected gleam of his teeth match the fairness of his single eye and beard (Theocritus, *Idyll*, VI, ll. 37–9).
59–60. I see . . . sun] Cp. Ovid, *Metamorphoses*, XIII, ll. 851–3, where the Cyclops compares his one eye to the sun.
59. done] produced, made ('do': *OED* ppl. a. 1), possibly implying Damon's simplicity: he thinks he sees a picture rather than a reflection, although 'picture' could mean 'visible image' (*OED* n. 2 f).
61–4. Cullen (1970), 188, detects an allusion to Spenser, *The Faerie Queene*, VI.x.8–17, where Calidore sees the dance of the Graces on Mount Acidale. See also *Upon Appleton House*, ll. 429–32.
61. deathless] immortal.
64. ring] i.e. circular patterns in grass, 'fairy rings', supposed to be caused by dancing fairies, in fact caused by fungi.
66. thistles] see Gen. 3:18: 'Thorns also and thistles shall it [the ground] bring forth to thee; and thou shalt eat the herb of the field.' Ormerod and Wortham prefer an application of the parable of man whose good seed was corrupted by his enemy, who secretly sowed tares (Matt. 13:24–30).
67. complain] see above, l. 4 n.

And with my scythe cut down the grass,
'0   Yet still my grief is where it was:
But, when the iron blunter grows,
Sighing I whet my scythe and woes.'

X

While thus he threw his elbow round,
Depopulating all the ground,
'5   And, with his whistling scythe, does cut
Each stroke between the earth and root,
The edgèd steel by careless chance
Did into his own ankle glance;

And there among the grass fell down,
80   By his own scythe, the mower mown.

XI

'Alas!' said he, 'these hurts are slight
To those that die by Love's despite.
With shepherd's-purse and clown's-all-heal,
The blood I staunch, and wound I seal.
85   Only for him no cure is found,
Whom Juliana's eyes do wound.
'Tis Death alone that this must do:
For Death thou art a mower too.'

71. *iron*] Damon lives in the brutal Age of Iron, after the Ages of Gold and Silver; see also below, ll. 77–8. 'Iron' could also mean 'affliction' or 'suffering', from a mistranslation of Hebrew in the Vulgate Bible: 'the iron entered his soul' instead of 'his person entered into the iron [fetters]' (Ps. 105:18).

72. *whet*] sharpen (*OED* v. 1). *scythe*] a) scythe b) sigh ('sithe': *OED* v.²).

74. *depopulating*] ravaging, laying waste (*OED* v. 1).

77–8. A biblical echo and the literalizing of an emblem: Joseph's feet are hurt by iron fetters, Ps. 105:18; 'Time devours Things; His Sithe our Legs will hit', 'Owen's Epigrams' in Thomas Pecke, ed., *Parnassi Puerperium* (1659), 112. See also the description of 'wicked Time' as mower in Spenser, *The Faerie Queene*, III.vi.39.

78. *glance*] as Damon had glanced his reflection in his scythe (see above, ll. 57–60). Punning on the Latin *acies*, 'sharp edge' and 'sharpness of vision': cp. *An Horatian Ode*, l. 60; *The Picture of Little T.C.*, l. 20.

80. *mown*] Friedenreich, in Friedenreich, ed. (1977), 154, notes the pun on 'moan' here.

82. *despite*] scorn, contempt (*OED* n. 1).

83–4. In some pastoral poetry, healing plants are associated with the Golden Age: see Jacopo Sannazaro, *Arcadia*, sixth eclogue, ll. 88–92: 'La terra . . . Era allor piena d'herbe salufere,/Et de balsamo e 'ncenso lachrimevole,/Di myrte preciose et oroifere.' (The earth . . . was full then of health-bearing herbs, and of balsam, and weeping incense, or precious and odoriferous myrrhs.)

83. *shepherd's-purse and clown's-all-heal*] shepherd's purse, or *capsella bursa-pastoris*, a weed with large pouch-like pods, and

clown's-all-heal, *panax coloni*, or clown's-wound wort; both were supposed to stop bleeding and cure wounds: Nicholas Culpeper, *The English Physitian Enlarged* (1653), 71, 341. Clown's woundwort was commonly found at the edges of fields, and in ditches (especially near London and in Kent), shepherd's purse near highways and among rubbish: distinctly the common possession of mowers; see Culpeper, 71. Shepherd's purse flowered all summer, clown's woundwort in August. John Gerard recounts his own encounter with a mower who had cut his leg to the bone with a scythe, and had cured the bleeding and the wound himself with clown's woundwort: John Gerard, *The Herball or Generall Historie of Plants* (2nd edn, 1633), 1005.

85–8. It is conceivable that the last four lines of the poem are spoken not by Damon but by the narrator, thereby complementing st. I.

87. *Death*] Kermode, Lord, Walker, Ormerod and Wortham; death 1681, Donno, Wilcher. Death's appearance recalls the famous words spoken by death in pastoral convention: 'Et in Arcadia ego'. Both Theocritus' Polyphemus and Virgil's Corydon are promised new loves; Damon meets only Death, which is an image of himself.

88. *Death . . . too*] the clearest indication of the association between the mower and the emblematic depiction of Time as a mower carrying a scythe: see Wye Saltonstall, *Picturae Loquentes* (2nd edn, 1635), sig. G10ᵛ: 'one that barbes the overgrowne fields, and cuts off the greene lockes of the meddowes. Hee walkes like the Embleme of Tyme, with a Sith upon his backe, and when he cuts the grasse, hee shewes the brevity of mans life, which commeth forth like a flower, and is cut downe.'

28

The Mower to the Glow-worms

Date and Context. See above, *The Mower against Gardens*, Headnote, Date.

Publication. 1681.

Sources. Glow-worms occur in pastoral tradition: 'shee sitts reading by the Glow-wormes light', Jonson, *The Sad Shepherd*, II.viii, l. 57; 'Through still silence of the night,/Guided by the glooe-worms light', Fletcher, *The Faithful Shepherdess*, IV.ii, ll. 3–4. In Mantuan's first eclogue, glow-worms are a sign of harvest, and are associated with marriage:

> Now *Ceres* russel'd in her bristling Corn
> With pendant eares; and when it must be shorn
> The Mower thinks; for nightly now the skies
> With Glow-worms shine, and glist'ring Butterflies:
> Loe now my Marriage, now my genial day
> Approach'd, appear'd.
> (*The Bucolicks of Baptist Mantuan in Ten Eclogues*,
> trans. Thomas Harvey (1656), 8)

In Carew's 'To my worthy friend Master Geo. Sands, on his translation of the Psalmes', l. 16, the glow-worms are associated with an amorous as opposed to heavenly muse; in Stanley's 'The Gloworme', the glow-worm comes to be outshone, even extinguished, by the 'light' of the mistress. In Herrick's 'The Night-piece, to Julia', l. 1, 'Her eyes the Glow-worme lend thee', implying a harmony between the mistress and the glow-worms; M.'s poem presents the opposite case.

M. draws strongly on Pliny's *Natural History* for his information and for several verbal sources (see below, ll. 1–4 n.). Pliny explains that the appearance of glow-worms (and 'glo-birds') in summer was a signal to country people of the time for the sowing of panic grass and millet, or any other plant, to make hay directly after the harvesting of barley. The glow-worms are therefore implicitly associated with the mowers. Pliny compounds this with a mythical

explanation of the origins of glow-worms. Nature would:

> needs give the Husbandman other starres beneath upon the earth, as signs to shew him the true seasons and times when and how to go to worke: as if she cried out and spake unto him after this manner: Why shouldest thou looke up to the heavens, thou that art to till the ground? Why keepest thou a seeking among the stars for thy countrey worke? . . . Behold I scatter and spread here upon the ground, other especiall shining stars. . . . Seest thou not these flies or glo-birds aforesaid couer their bright and glittering light, when they keep their wings close together, and carrie fire-light about them euen in the night?
> (Pliny, *Natural History*, trans.
> Philemon Holland (1635), I.593)

Glow-worms also featured as emblems of prudence and Providence (see e.g., Joachim Camerarius, *Symbolum et Emblematum Centuria* (1590), sig. Aa2r), possibly through an association with the 'Light of Nature'. Sir Thomas Browne discussed at length his observation that the light of a glow-worm could not be abstracted from it, and that the light was coterminous with its life (*Pseudodoxia Epidemica* (1646), III.xxvii.12); Scoular (1965), 105–8, lists further examples of glow-worms in Renaissance literature.

In a theological context, the glow-worm was associated with the limitations of human perception: 'Though the *candle* of *Reason* excell in light the Glow-worms of sense; yet it is but a *candle*, not the *Sun* it self' (Peter Sterry, *The Spirits Conviction of Sinne* (1645), 10). Likewise, glow-worms were sometimes seen as symbolic of illusion and disappointment, instanced in Suckling, *Aglaura* (1638), II.iii, ll. 81–2: 'Then all my feares are true, and shee is false;/False as a falling Star, or Glow-wormes fire.' While the mower refers positively to glow-worms, the word 'glow-worm' itself was a term of contempt in seventeenth-century England (*OED* b, c). Is this a sign of his distorted judgement?

Haber (1994), 104–6, suggests that the displaced mower has an original in the exiled Meliboeus in Virgil's first *Eclogue*, and argues that M. deliberately revises the intimacy of Virgil's two shepherds with the lonely interiority of the Mower. In doing so, he inverts Virgil, making what is metaphoric in the *Eclogues* literal in his own verse, and thereby recreating a Theocritan perspective, in particular 'the coincidence of distance and identity', which is nonetheless still an inversion of Theocritus. A nocturnal figure bemoaning an absent or lost love is the subject of Sannazaro's *Arcadia*, seventh eclogue.

Leishman (1966), 144–5, suggests that M. derived the phrasing of his poem from Sir Henry Wotton's 'On his Mistris, the Queen of Bohemia' (1651):

> You meaner *Beauties* of the *Night*,
> That poorly satisfie our *Eies*
> More by your *number*, then your *light*,
> You *Common People* of the *Skies*;
>   What are you when the *Sun* shall rise?
>
> You Curious Chanters of the Wood,
> That warble forth *Dame Natures* layes,
> Thinking your *Voyces* understood
> By your weake *accents*; whats your praise
>   When *Philomell* her voyce shal raise?
>
> You *Violets*, that first appeare,
> By your *pure purpel mantels* knowne,
> Like the proud *Virgins* of the *yeare*,
> As if the *Spring* were all your own;
>   What are you when the *Rose* is *blowne*?
>
> So, when my *Mistris* shal be *seene*
> In *form* and *Beauty* of her *mind*,
> By *Vertue* first, then *Choyce a Queen*,
> Tell me, if *she* were not design'd
>   Th'*Eclypse* and *Glory* of her kind.

Structure, Style and Versification. The poem is delivered in stanzas that become progressively darker, and where the sense of movement increases, from the stationary nightingale through the wandering mowers to the displaced mind of the speaking mower. But the end is simply an end: there is no conclusion beyond an acknowledgement of emotional disquiet. The poem is thus virtually static: the mower merely voices the cause of his disquiet.

Leishman (1966), 144 ff., regards the source of the poem's success as deriving from its single sentence structure, with the main verb not appearing until the first line of the last stanza. The preceding stanzas are made up of apostrophes in the first line of each stanza, followed by 'balanced relative clauses, whose pattern is almost exactly repeated in each stanza'. Alpers (1996), 58, regards each stanza as 'a sort of miniature pastoral' with which the reader is wholly taken before moving on. But in Leishman's view, the inclusion of the expletives 'do', 'doth' and 'did' (usually in order to produce an infinitive form of the verb for the sake of completing a rhyme), prevents the poem achieving perfection (e.g. ll. 2, 4, 12). A contrapuntal effect is achieved by the deployment of sophisticated, allusive vocabulary within the simplicity of the pastoral frame ('meditate', l. 4; 'portend', l. 5; 'presage', l. 8; 'officious', l. 9; 'courteous', l. 13). The effect is consonant with the emotionally disorientated mower. The simplicity is enhanced by instances of alliteration (ll. 1, 5, 12), locally repeated consonants (ll. 1–2, 4, 5–6), a large number of single-syllable words, and an absolutely regular iambic metre. The poem is 'in number' precise: the word placed exactly halfway in the poem is 'fall' (l. 8), with its connotations of the Fall of man as well as the mowing of grass. But the mower's state of mind (indeed, his 'displacement') is registered in ll. 14–16 by logical connectives, 'Since', 'For', 'so . . . that'.

Modern Criticism. An increasingly sophisticated awareness of the apparently simple nature of pastoral has made the poem a subject of extensive consideration. Haber (1994), 99–105, is concerned with the change of focus in the final stanza, where the mower refers to himself in the first person for the first time, establishing his own sense of separation from stability, and loss of innocence, as the poem ends. At the same time, the poem is remarkable for voicing a fall that is essentially harmless. These features constitute a series of binary ambiguities: 'Separation [of consciousness from world] thus becomes both the means of connection, and the point at which connection is made. . . . The condition of not being symbolic is made to rely on that of being symbolic, and "innocence" is presented as a creation of the Fall.' The result is to go beyond Virgil's allegorical pastoral to restate a Theocritan problem: the coincidence of distance (what pastoral talks about) and identity (what pastoral is): 'these conflicting perspectives themselves are necessarily related and reflective of each other. Any attempt to insist on one alone recreates the other.'

Alpers (1996), 53, argues that the poem is distinctive because it does not give a rustic identity to the speaker, who might easily be a courtly figure. Yet the address to nature in the form of the glow-worms is distinctly pastoral. Thus, the poem exposes two views of the world without forcing the reader to make a choice between them: the country world and the world of affairs of state (ll. 5–6). But the reader is ultimately trapped within the mower's perspective: 'unless you know what the glow-worms presage (that it is time to mow), you cannot know what they portend' (Alpers, 55). The poem is further complicated, however, by the alienation of the mower from his pastoral setting, and through this alienated self-awareness, claims Alpers, 59, the reader becomes aware that the mower represents the pastoral poet. The mower's 'mental displacement . . . is itself a reduction . . . of the situation of any poet who looks for ways of representing or speaking of his situation and world. . . . The poem, then, is something of a double pastoral: the glow-worms are pastoral creatures to the mower, but the mower himself is a pastoral creature to us.'

The Mower to the Glow-worms

I

Ye living lamps, by whose dear light
The nightingale does sit so late,
And studying all the summer-night,
Her matchless songs does meditate;

II

5　Ye country comets, that portend
No war, nor prince's funeral,
Shining unto no higher end
Than to presage the grass' fall;

1–3. Ye .. night] See Robert Boyle, *Experiments and Considerations touching Colours* (1664), 147: 'the Light of a Glow-worm, by which I have been sometimes able to Read a Short Word.'
1. lamps] 'the Greeks name them [glow-worms] Lampyrides', Pliny, *Natural History*, trans. Philemon Holland (1635), I. 593.
2. nightingale] Cp. Fletcher, *The Faithful Shepherdess* (1608–10), 5.3, ll. 58–60: 'The Nightingale, among the thicke leaved spring/That sits alone, in sorrow and doth sing,/Whole nights away in mourning'. See also *Upon Appleton House*, ll. 513–18. The association of nightingales with frustrated love was a well-established poetic topos by the mid-seventeenth century: see Alpers (1996), 56, n. 31; see also Sannazaro, *Arcadia*, seventh eclogue, ll. 1–2: 'Come nocturno ucel nemico al sole,/Lasso! Vo yo per di chiaro in su la terra' (Like the nocturnal bird an enemy of the sun/weary I go among places shadowy and black).
2–4. nightingale . . . meditate] Cp. Pliny, *Natural History*, trans. Philemon Holland (1635), I.286: 'Ye shall have the yong Nightingales studie and meditate how to sing'.
4. matchless] a) peerless, without an equal (*OED* a. 1) b) without a spouse, unmarried (*OED* a. 3). *meditate*] practise, rehearse (from Latin *meditor*); cp. Virgil, *Eclogue*, I, ll. 1–2: 'Tityre, tu patulae recubans sub tegmine fagi/silvestram tenui musam meditaris avena' (You, Tityrus, under the spreading, sheltering beech,/Tune woodland musings on a delicate

reed); Milton, *Lycidas*, l. 66: 'And strictly meditate the thankless muse.'
5–7. country . . . end] Cp. Robert Chamberlain, 'In Praise of Country Life' (1638), ll. 18–20, 'Matters of State, not yet domestick jars,/Comets portending death, nor blazing stars/Trouble his thoughts.'
5. comets] The appearances of comets were understood to bear omens (such as the appearance of Halley's Comet before the Battle of Hastings in 1066); the glow-worms are like comets because they are an omen of the harvest (see above, *Headnote, Sources*, and below, l. 8). *portend*] presage as an omen (*OED* v.[1] 1).
6. Such as one might find in a conventional elegy (e.g. the interpretation of the storm before Cromwell's death (see below, *A Poem upon the Death of his Late Highness the Lord Protector*, ll. 101–32)); also a reversal of Thomas Proctor, *A gorgeous Gallery, of gallant Inuentions* (1578), 'A proper Sonet, how time consumeth all earthly things', ll. 1–4: 'I sighe to see, the Sythe a fielde./Downe goeth the Grasse, soon wrought to withered hay:/ . . . /And Princes passe, as Grasse doth fade away.'
7. end] a) purpose b) finish.
8. grass' fall] see Isa. 40:6–7: 'All flesh is grass, and all the goodliness thereof is as the flower of the field: The grass withereth, the flower fadeth: because the spirit of the Lord bloweth upon it: surely the people is grass.' *grass*] any kind of herbage grown to make hay (*OED* n. 2 c).

<table>
<tr><td align="center">III</td><td align="center">IV</td></tr>
</table>

Ye glow-worms, whose officious flame	Your courteous lights in vain you waste,
10 To wand'ring mowers shows the way,	Since Juliana here is come,
That in the night have lost their aim,	15 For she my mind hath so displaced
And after foolish fires do stray;	That I shall never find my home.

---

9. officious] a) attentive, obliging (*OED* a. 1) b) dutiful (*OED* a. 2). A courtly usage (see below, l. 13).

10. wand'ring . . . way] Cp. Job 12:24–5: 'He taketh away the heart of the earth, and causeth them to wander in a wilderness'; Proverbs 21:16: 'The man that wandereth out of the way of understanding shall remain in the congregation of the dead.'

11. aim] course (*OED* n. 2).

12. foolish fires] a) the English translation of Latin *ignis fatuus*, 'will-o'-the-wisp', 'Jack-a-lantern', a phosphorescent light seen above marshy ground (supposedly the spontaneous combustion of flammable gasses) b) figuratively, that which misleads, and hence, 'fires of love'. Cp. Herrick, 'The Night-piece, to Julia', l. 6: 'No *Will-o'-th'-Wisp* mis-light thee.'

13. courteous] In Philisides's beast fable, part of the third eclogues in Sidney's *Old Arcadia*, glow-worms are described as courteous (ll. 5–7): 'Each thing with mantle black the night doth soothe,/Saving the glow-worm, which would courteous be/Of that small light oft watching shepherds see.'

16. home] Cp. Virgil, *Eclogue*, I, ll. 3–5: 'nos patriae finis et dulcia linquimus arva./nos patriam fugimus; tu, Tityre, lentus in umbra/formosam resonare doces Amaryllida silvas' (We flee our country's borders, our sweet fields, abandon home; you, Tityrus, lazing in the shade, make woods resound with lovely Amaryllis). Where Meliboeus (Virgil's speaker) has really lost his home, M.'s mower speaks metaphorically, but that he speaks alone (rather than in a dialogue, as with Meliboeus) intensifies the sense of loss.

29
The Mower's Song

Date. See *Headnote, The Mower Against Gardens, Date.*

Publication. 1681.

Sources and Genre. The poem has been identified as a dirge, specifically on account of its repeated refrain. Nature as a reflection of the mind is a pastoral commonplace: e.g. Spenser, *The Shepheardes Calendar,* January Eclogue, ll. 19–20: 'Thou barrein ground, whome winters wrath hath wasted,/Art made a myrrhour, to behold my plight.' Pyrocles's poem in Sidney's *Arcadia,* Book 2 (ed. Jean Robinson (Oxford, 1973), 118), is concerned with the reciprocal impacts of nature and mind upon each other. M.'s poem shows the dissolution of this union into vengeful alienation. The mower addresses the meadows as if they were his best friend, but their lushness eventually contrasts with his desolation. Thus, the oneness of mower and meadow, figured as a mirror in stanza one, mutates through figures of difference (the meadows in flower, st. 2; May-games, st. 3; revenge, st. 4) towards a final union where the meadows become the green coat of arms on the mower's tomb (st. 5).

The green commemorative heraldry of st. 5 is an intensification of the pastoral topos where nature actively laments a dead shepherd, as exemplified in the fifth eclogue of Sannazaro's *Arcadia*:

> Pianser la sante Dive
> La tua spietata morte:
> I fiumi il sanno e le spelunch' e y faggi;
> Pianser le verdi rive,
> L'herbe pallide et smorte.

(The holy Goddesses wept your pitiless death; the rivers knew it and the caverns and the beeches; the green banks wept, the grasses pale and withered.)

Everett, *CQ,* 4 (1962), 223–4 (see below, l. 20 n.) discusses the significance of the mower's invocation of revenge tragedy. Others have connected the mower's desire for a universal ruin (l. 22) to an intimation of apocalyptic violence (Colie (1970), 30; Stocker (1986), 234–40; Rogers (1996), 65).

Style and Versification. The Mower's Song is the only lyric by M. to have a refrain of two lines: one tetrameter, matching the previous five lines of the stanza, followed by an alexandrine of twelve entirely regular monosyllables. Craze (1979), 152–3, suggests that the first line of the refrain equates with the action of the mower drawing his scythe to his right, and the second line, the action of the scythe cutting its swathe (as if the twelve monosyllables were individual stalks of grass). The first four lines of each stanza are entirely regular iambic tetrameters rhymed in pairs. Of the four mower poems, *The Mower's Song* has the most exaggerated sense of the mower's closeness to the grassy land: the self-obsession of his mood merges with the land in the final stanza, where he imagines the meadows as his tomb. The reductiveness of the mower's perceptions is enhanced by the repetition of vocabulary (especially, 'grass', occurring eight times), and associated vocabulary beginning with 'g' ('greenness', l. 3; 'green', l. 26). The use of the past tense towards the beginning of each stanza is modulated into the present tense in the refrain, emphasizing the focus of past, present and future in the destructive act of mowing.

The Mower's Song

I

My mind was once the true survey
Of all these meadows fresh and gay;
And in the greenness of the grass
Did see its hopes as in a glass;
When Juliana came, and she
What I do to the grass, does to my thoughts and me.

II

But these, while I with sorrow pine,
Grew more luxuriant still and fine;
That not one blade of grass you spied,
10   But had a flow'r on either side;
When Juliana came, and she
What I do to the grass, does to my thoughts and me.

III

Unthankful meadows, could you so
A fellowship so true forgo,

15   And in your gaudy May-games meet,
While I lay trodden under feet?
When Juliana came, and she
What I do to the grass, does to my thoughts and me.

IV

But what you in compassion ought,
20   Shall now by my revenge be wrought:
And flow'rs, and grass, and I and all,
Will in one common ruin fall.
For Juliana comes, and she
What I do to the grass, does to my thoughts and me.

V

25   And thus, ye meadows, which have been
Companions of my thoughts more green,
Shall now the heraldry become
With which I shall adorn my tomb;
For Juliana comes, and she
30   What I do to the grass, does to my thoughts and me.

1. survey] a) view (e.g. of an estate; *OED* n. 1) b) prospect or map (*OED* n. 5). In fact, this is a metaphorical use of 'survey', since it is understood to be a mirror (see l. 4) of nature.
3–4. greenness . . . hopes] green was the colour symbolic of hope (see Chevalier (1996)).
4. glass] mirror. Cp. Rowland Watkyns, *Flamma sine Fumo* (1662), 'Weak man's estate, as in a glass/Is truly seen in fading grass' (Friedman (1970), 147, n. 64).
7. these] these meadows (see above, l. 2). *while . . . pine*] in the past tense: an imitation of a Latin *dum* (while) clause, with present tense in past time. *pine*] allusive word-play: the Cyclops in Ovid, *Metamorphoses*, XIII, l. 782, plays on a pine-trunk when he laments his unrequited love for Galatea (see above, *Damon the Mower, Headnote, Sources*).
8. luxuriant] growing profusely (*OED* a. 2). Also misused for 'luxurious' (lecherous, unchaste): Badley (1994) notes the apparent male genital configuration of the blade of grass with a flower in each side in ll. 9–10.
10. But had] i.e. 'But it had.'
13. Unthankful] a) unworthy of thanks (*OED* a. 1) b) ungrateful (*OED* a. 2).

14. forgo] abstain from (*OED* v. 6).
15. gaudy] gay, showy (*OED* a.² 3). *May-games*] merrymaking and sports associated with the first of May (*OED* n. 1 a); the context of the encouragement of festive culture and its calendar by the Laudian movement is discussed in relation to the poem by Marcus (1986), 233–8.
19. ought] owed (*OED* v. II 4).
20. revenge] Everett, *CQ*, 4 (1962), 223–4, regards the mower's invocation of revenge as an appropriate acknowledgement of heroic status: 'Like many grander characters, [the mower] requires fellowship in Hell, and pulls down his world upon himself; he enacts the good tragic motif of Revenge on the natural forces that will not suffer the destruction of his mind.' Stocker (1986), 238–9, discusses the possibility that the mower is contemplating suicide.
26. more green] a) more amorous b) more youthful, inexperienced c) more integrated with nature. Cp. *The Garden*, ll. 47–8: 'Annihilating all that's made/To a green thought in a green shade.'
27–8. The grass is imagined by the mower as his blazon (a heraldic device on a coat of arms).
28. shall] *1681; will Bod. 1.*

30
Ametas and Thestylis Making Hay-Ropes

Date. The argument that the poem is connected with the Mower poems (see below, *Location*) provides some evidence that it was written in the early 1650s, during M.'s stay at Nun Appleton. But there is no conclusive evidence for this, or any other date.

Publication. 1681.

Genre and Sources. The poem is a simple pastoral eclogue, although, as Leishman (1966), 119–20, noted, it is complicated by comparison with the eclogues of pastoral's Elizabethan heyday. Nonetheless, Wilcher (1985), 51, stresses that the crudity of the lovers is suggested by the glibness with which they accept the analogies, and by the fact that the poem has fewer possibilities for irony than many of its predecessors and contemporaries. Cullen (1970), 198, maintains that the eclogue is also a witty reversal of a seduction poem in that the woman finally tempts the man. In this respect, Friedman (1970), 101, feels that the poem is so *libertin* it is hard to believe that it is M.'s. Ormerod and Wortham (9–11) treat the poem as a serious example of *discordia concors* in the central image of the twisted hay-rope, with each lover taking a different argumentative position: Ametas is *libertin*, Thestylis, romantic and courtly. In this respect, they argue, Ametas's image of the hay stook as 'love' is a profane parody of the haystack as pictorial symbol of the transience of earthly things, common in emblem books, and which in turn takes its inspiration from Psalmic literature (see, e.g., Ps. 102:11).

Craze (1979), 165, suggests that the episode recounted in M.'s poem may have been inspired by Milton, *L'Allegro* (1645), ll. 87–90, a vignette featuring two pastoral figures, Phillis and Thestylis: 'And then in haste her bower she leaves,/With Thestylis to bind the sheaves;/Or if the earlier season lead/To the tanned haycock in the mead.' Thestylis is a woman in Virgil, *Eclogue*, II, ll. 10–11, adapted by M. in *Upon Appleton House*, ll. 401–8. The

entwining of pastoral lovers is the theme of Carew's 'A Pastorall Dialogue. Celia. Cleon' (1640), but the lovers make a wreath of hair to immortalize their love; before they consummate it, they are surprised. The image of twined threads belongs to the classical representation of Fate, and is found in non-amorous pastoral verse: 'Then happy those whom Fate, that is the stronger,/Together twists their threads, and yet draws hers the longer' (Aurelian Townshend, 'A Dialogue betwixt Time and a Pilgrime' (1653), ll. 20–1).

Location. Rees (1989), 164–5, argues that the placing of the poem just after the mower poems in *1681* serves to mock that group of poems by showing, contrary to their conclusions, that love and nature are not incompatible. Yet Colie (1970), 54, finds Ametas' ready acceptance of Thestylis' assertion of love's inconstancy as an excuse to seize the moment unsettling, just as Wilcher (1985), 51, regards these features, and Thestylis' purely tactical coyness, as indicative of shallowness.

Structure and Style. The metre is trochaic heptasyllables, organized in four quatrains (despite ll. 13–14 being labelled 'IV', and ll. 15–16, 'V'). Simplicity is at a premium in the diction: of the ninety-eight words, eighty-five are monosyllables. But the patterns of thought and sound are sophisticated, both the comparisons between the twining of the hay-rope and the nature of love, and the careful matching of sound against sense (e.g. the opposition of 'st' and 'th' sounds in ll. 1–2; the repeated stresses of l. 4). Even so, Ametas' logic is obviously specious, relying upon the acceptance of a figurative argument as literal, and then exposing its untruthfulness to literal fact. The rhyme pattern of abab obviously enacts in sound the interweaving suggested in the poem's major conceit, and this effect is exaggerated by the maintenance of 'ay' at the end of the second and fourth lines in each quatrain.

Ametas and Thestylis Making Hay-Ropes

I

Ametas

Think'st thou that this love can stand,
Whilst thou still dost say me nay?
Love unpaid does soon disband:
Love binds love as hay binds hay.

II

Thestylis

Think'st thou that this rope would twine
If we both should turn one way?
Where both parties so combine,
Neither love will twist nor hay.

III

Ametas

Thus you vain excuses find,
10   Which yourselves and us delay:
And love ties a woman's mind
Looser than with ropes of hay.

IV

Thestylis

What you cannot constant hope
Must be taken as you may.

V

Ametas

15   Then let's both lay by our rope,
And go kiss within the hay.

---

1. love] Ormerod and Wortham, 10, imagine that 'Ametas treats the spectacle of the stock of hay standing between [himself and Thestylis] as a sort of phallic emblem.' *stand*] a) remain b) become or stay erect (i.e. a pun, whereby 'love' is imagined as a penis; see Williams (1994), III.1305–6).

3. unpaid . . . disband] a military conceit: to 'disband' (*OED* v. II 4) was applied to the breaking up of a company of soldiers; like such a company, if left unpaid, Love will dissolve. *unpaid*] i.e. unrequited.

5. rope] rope made of twisted hay, with two strands twined together in the opposite direction to each other: Thestylis' image for the coming together of the two lovers. However, there are bawdy overtones: 'rope' could also mean the penis (see Williams (1994), III.1170–1; a later seventeenth-century usage, although common sexual slang in the eighteenth century). *twine*] a) twist together b) sexual embrace; coition (Williams (1994), III.1447).

8. twist] a) twist b) copulate (Williams (1994), III.1448; cp. Marston, *The Fawne* (1604–6), 4: 'goe thy waies, twist with whom thou wilt, for my part tha'st spun a faire thread').

9. vain] a) self-regarding (*OED* a. I 4) b) hopeless (*OED* a. I 1).

10. yourselves and us] i.e. you women and us men. *yourselves*] *Bod. 1+; your selve 1681, Margoliouth, Legouis; your selves Lord; yourself Kermode. delay*] a) put off in time (*OED* v.¹ 1) b) assuage, dilute (sexual desire; *OED* v.² 2).

13–14. A version of a well-known proverb: 'take things as you find them' (*ODEP*, 799).

15. lay by] lay aside (*OED* v.¹ VIII 50). *rope*] see above, l. 5 n.

16. kiss . . . hay] the 'hay' was also a winding country dance (just as Ametas and Thestylis have wound a rope), ending in a kiss between partners (*OED* n.⁴); see also *Upon Appleton House*, l. 426. *kiss*] a) kiss b) copulate (Williams (1994), II.761–2).

31
Music's Empire

Date. Late 1650–52. Controversy with regard to the date is focused on the possible identity of the 'gentle conqueror' (l. 23). Fairfax and Cromwell are the two obvious candidates. Cromwell's love of music, and the presence of musical performance in the Protector's household, together with the references to colonial expansion and empire (Title, ll. 12, 19), are pieces of evidence for a date of composition during M.'s employment by the Protectorate government in 1657–58 (Griffin (1995), 90). But the echoes of *Upon Appleton House* (l. 17), and *Upon the Hill and Grove at Bilbrough* (l. 23), together with the strong presence of Davenant's *Gondibert* (see below, *Headnote, Sources and Genre*), a poem of great interest to M. during his stay at Nun Appleton, suggest the time of M.'s residence with Fairfax as the more likely date of composition (see below, *Upon Appleton House, Headnote, Date*).

Publication. 1681. Copied with very minor variations of punctuation only into Leeds, Brotherton Library, MS Lt. 61, fols. 18ᵛ–19ʳ (*L3*; an early eighteenth-century verse miscellany).

Sources, Genre and Structure. The poem has been regarded as a significant but unusual example in the *laus musicae* tradition: see, e.g., Robert South, *Musica Incantans* (Oxford, 1655, 1st edn). This view has been challenged by Friedman, in Summers and Pebworth (1990), 17. M. departed from the tradition in two respects: a) the extended analogy between the development of music and the growth of empires (as opposed to the more conventional imagery of music as state building and government in *The First Anniversary of the Government Under His Highness the Lord Protector*, ll. 45–86) b) the dissociation of music and heavenly harmony: 'the normal notion of practical music as the macrocosmic model of the universal music is certainly rearranged, if not actually reversed' (Hollander (1961, 1970), 310). Moreover, the sounds choose their instruments

rather than music being seen as merely a human product: part of music's empire is its capacity to have an autonomous authority. The analogy between the history of civilization and that of music also avoids the consideration of the different uses of music throughout history that typified contemporary authorities (see, e.g., Charles Butler, *The Principles of Musik* (*sic*; 1636), 102–3). Thus, M.'s poem differs from a poem by Lovelace, which in other respects has close affinities with *Music's Empire*:

> Thus do your *Ayres Eccho* o're
>   The *Notes* and *Anthemes* of the *Spheres*,
> And their whole *Consort* back restore,
>   As if *Earth* too would *blest Heavens Ears.*
>   ('To my Noble Kinsman T.S. Esq.;
>   On his Lyrick Poems composed by Mr J.G.'
>   (1656), ll. 19–22)

M.'s poem displays affinities with several prefatory poems, additional to Lovelace's, that were printed in both 1656 and 1659 editions of John Gamble's *Ayres and Dialogues*.

Earlier analogous treatments of music with affinities to M.'s poem include the *Auditus* section from Chapman's *Ovid Banquet of Sence* (1595), ll. 135–279. The speaker's mistress sings as if she could raise a city (l. 176). More importantly, while the speaker seeks to rule the 'monarchy' of his mistress's face, the 'chaos' of his flesh is organized by her singing: the lover becomes the 'empire' (l. 231) not only of the mistress's gaze, but also of her voice (and her look is also music): 'My life then turn'd to that, t'each note, and word/Should I consorte her looke;/which sweeter sings,/Where songs of solid harmony accord.' (ll. 235–7)

M.'s most immediate source is three stanzas from Davenant's *Gondibert* (1651; 2.6.80–2), noted by Craze (1979), 256–7, and Rees (1989), 175–7, evidence that helps date the poem (see above, *Date*). The stanza form used in *Music's Empire* appears nowhere else in M., but it differs from Davenant's stanza in

Gondibert only in the matter of rhyme. Elsewhere in the second canto, Davenant elaborates a history of music while describing his 'House of Praise' that, like M.'s poem, connects sacred and secular (sts. 47, 48, 49). M.'s 'gentle conqueror' is a less distinctly drawn alternative to Davenant's Duke Gondibert, who is soothed by music, while offering silent prayers of victory (see also below, l. 23 n.). Above all in importance, Davenant's sts. 80–2 provide a direct verbal model for M. (see below, ll. 2, 9–10; 16):

> Yet Musick here, shew'd all her Art's high worth;
> Whilst Virgin-Trebles, seem'd, with bashfull grace,
> To call the bolder mary'd Tenor forth;
> Whose Manly voyce challeng'd the Giant Base.
>
> To these the swift soft Instruments reply;
> Whisp'ring for help to those whom winds inspire;
> Whose lowder Notes, to Neighb'ring Forrests flie,
> And summon Nature's Voluntary Quire.
>
> These, *Astragon*, by secret skill had taught,
> To help, as if in artfull Consort bred;
> Who sung, as if by chance on him they thought,
> Whose care their careless merry Fathers Fed.

M.'s depiction of the growth of music's empire follows an Aristotelian pattern, with imperial dominion growing from a state of nature, through simple and uncivilized living, to the growth of cities, and the establishment of colonies, which are the first steps in the establishment of empire. Such a pattern corresponds to the broadly Machiavellian historiography accepted by M.'s associates (e.g. Milton, Nedham and Hall) in the period just before the Nun Appleton sojourn. M. may be responding further to Davenant, who writes in the preface to *Gondibert* that empire is a quality of mind that leads to boundless speculation (ed. Gladish (1971), 31), unless controlled by a set of regulations as strict as the leader of an army. Just as M.'s allegory reverses its coordinates, so Davenant then changes his argument to show how great military leaders (he must silently be referring to Cromwell) have been obliged to poets. M.'s poem offers an alternative version (with a positive account of the Jews) of the meanings of political and poetic empire to Davenant's scarcely hidden contempt for the new regime and the Jews:

> But perhaps the art of praising Armies into great, and instant action, by singing their former deeds (An Art with which the Ancients made *Empire* so large) is too subtle for moderne *Leaders*; who as they cannot reach the heights of Poesy, must be content with the narrow space of Dominion: and narrow Dominion breeds evil, peevish, and vexatious mindes, and a nationall self-opinion, like simple Jewish arrogance; and the Jews were extra-ordinary proud in a very little Country. (ibid., 32)

M.'s poem also reflects a more Miltonic conception of the state as a vibrant aggregation of (dis)harmonious elements (in *Areopagitica* (1644); for M.'s use of these notions, see below, 290, 90 n.), as opposed to Davenant's image of music as a form of distraction that facilitates social control:

> Others may object that Poesy on our Stage, or the Heroick in Musick (for so the latter was anciently us'd) is prejudiciall to a State; as begetting Levity, and giving the People too great a diversion by pleasure and mirth. To these (if they be worthy of Satisfaction) I reply; That whoever in Government endeavors to make the People serious and grave, (which are attributes that may become the Peoples *Representatives*, but not the People) doth practice a new way to enlarge the State, by making every Subject a *Statesman*: and he that means to governe so mournfully (as it were, without any Musick in his Dominion) must lay but light burdens on his Subjects. (ibid., 39–40)

Soon M. would present Cromwell as the consummate master musician of the protectorate state, knitting together the different parts of the political fabric, and using Milton's writings in part to do so (see below, *The First Anniversary of the Government under His Highness the Lord Protector*). The region that is music's empire, the space between earth and heaven, is, in *The First Anniversary*, the domain of Cromwell. The hints of allusiveness in *Musick's Empire*, be the 'gentler conqueror' Fairfax or Cromwell, make the poem in Griffin's view (1995, 91) link the realms of the public and the private.

Goldberg, *TSLL*, 13 (1971), 421–30 (423), suggests that the 'gentler conqueror' is Christ, the poem a recounting of Christian time from creation to judgement. The poem is thus typological: in medieval iconography, Jubal's invention of music prefigures the crucifixion of Christ (Jubal was a descendant of Cain, and was castigated for his *curiositas*). Numerology may also have relevance. The twenty-four lines of the poem correspond to the association of twenty-four with the union of heaven and earth at the Last Judgement in cabbalistic tradition.

The conceptual structure of the poem is an allegory that Leishman (1966), 220, considers flawed and confused: 'there is a carelessness or inattentiveness in its working out which may be regarded as having

some affinity with that carelessness and slovenliness
Marvell so often displays in his use of inversion'. Yet
the poem appears to proceed precisely by the breaking down of the 'correspondence between literal
and metaphorical'. Wilson, *BJRL*, 51 (1969), 472,
regards the poem accordingly as a fantasy rather than
an allegory, a 'politico-musical conceit'. Legouis
(1965), 82, notes the paradox (as with *The Fair
Singer*) of writing in a most unlyrical metre about the
art that is most closely connected with lyric.

Music's Empire

I

First was the world as one great cymbal made,
Where jarring winds to infant Nature played.
All music was a solitary sound,
To hollow rocks and murm'ring fountains bound.

II

5   Jubal first made the wilder notes agree;
And Jubal tuned Music's first Jubilee:
He called the echoes from their sullen cell,
And built the organ's city where they dwell.

III

Each sought a consort in that lovely place;
10   And virgin trebles wed the manly bass.
From whence the progeny of numbers new
Into harmonious colonies withdrew.

IV

Some to the lute, some to the viol went,
And others chose the cornet eloquent.
15   These practising the wind, and those the wire,
To sing men's triumphs, or in heavens choir.

Title. Empire] see above, *Headnote, Sources, Genre and
Structure*.
2. jarring] sounding with harsh, rough vibration; discordant
(*OED* ppl. a. 1).
5. Jubal] Gen. 4:21: 'the father of all such as dwell in tents,
and of all such as handle the harp and organ'. Repeated in
seventeenth-century music manuals: see, e.g., Charles Butler,
The Principles of Musik (1636), sig. ¶¶2ᵛ: 'the people of God
do truly acknowledge a far more ancient Inventer of this
divine Art: [Jubal the son of Lamech the sixth from Adam:] of
whom it is said, that he was the Father of all that handle the
Harp and Organ: i.e. of all Instruments.' [Butler's eccentric
orthography has been standardized.]
6. first] Bod. 1, Cooke, Lord, Donno; not in *1681, Thompson,
Margoliouth, Kermode, Walker*. *Jubilee*] a) a year of emancipa-
tion kept every fifty years (see Lev. 25); hence fiftieth anniversary (*OED* n. 1, 3) b) exultant and noisy public rejoicing (*OED*
n. 5). The word's usage is particularly apt because of the
Hebrew root of jubilee, *yobel*, meaning 'ram's horn'. The two
senses had been associated since early Christian Latin.
7. echoes] Wilson, *BJRL*, 51 (1969), 476, notes an association
with the nymph Echo in Longus, *Daphnis and Chloe*, Book 4,
whose dismembered parts (she was rent asunder by Pan's
shepherds because she spurned the god) and songs resound in
underground places. Ovid's Echo, spurned by Narcissus, hid in
remote places, such as caves, withering away to a mere voice
(see Ovid, *Metamorphoses*, III, ll. 393–401). *sullen*] gloomy
(*OED* A. a. 4).
8. organ's city] see above, l. 5 n.
9–10. See above, *Headnote, Sources, Genre and Structure*.
9. consort] a) spouse (*OED* n. 1 1) b) musical harmony (*OED*
n. 2 II 3). 'Consort' also meant 'associate' or 'colleague' in a
political sense (*OED* n.¹ 3), which fits with the analogy

between music and civil society, but not with the progenerative
theme of the stanza.
10. In direct contrast to Crashaw, 'Musick's Duell' (1646),
ll. 49–50: 'the grumbling Base/In surly groanes disdaines the
Trebles Grace.'
11–12. Cp. William Cartwright's 'To a Painter's handsome
Daughter' (1651), ll. 4–6: 'He hath plac'd Creatures
there;/People, not shadows; which in time will be/Not a dead
Number, but a Colony.'; *The Gallery*, ll. 45–8: 'For thou alone
to people me,/Art grown a num'rous colony.'
11. progeny] offspring, descendants (*OED* n. 1). *numbers*]
musical periods; groups of notes (*OED* n. IV 18 pl. a).
12. colonies] Latin *colonia* meant 'farm' or 'landed estate', as
well as settlements in new lands; if the poem was intended for
Fairfax, the reference would obviously connect with the Lord
General's retirement. *withdrew*] retired; went away to (M. is
using the verb in an unusual way; *OED* records no instances of
'withdrawing into' a place).
14. cornet] originally made of, and resembling, a horn, before
the invention of the modern brass instrument (*OED* n.¹ 1).
15–16. Cp. an 'old distich', quoted by Charles Butler, *The
Principles of Musik* (1636), 118: '*Non vox sed Votum, non
Musica Chordula sed Cor,/Non Clamans sed Amans, cantat in
aure Dei.*' ('Nor Voice but You, Hearts zeal not Musiks
String;/Love not loud cry, in th'ear of God doth sing.')
15. wire] string instruments (not in *OED*; a figure developed
from 'wire' as metallic musical instrument strings: *OED*
n. II 4).
16. heavens] *1681, Margoliouth, Lord*; heaven's *Thompson,
Kermode, Donno, Walker*; Heaven *Ormerod and Wortham*.
choir] *Thompson, Kermode, Donno, Walker*; quire *1681,
Margoliouth, Lord, Ormerod and Wortham*; sing in chorus
(*OED* v.).

V

Then Music, the mosaic of the air,
Did of all these a solemn noise prepare:
With which she gained the empire of the ear,
20   Including all between the earth and sphere.

VI

Victorious sounds! Yet here your homage do
Unto a gentler conqueror than you;
Who though he flies the music of his praise,
Would with you Heaven's hallelujahs raise.

17. The various sounds, when arranged together in harmony, are likened to the arranged patterns of mosaic pictures or decorations. Like the 'light mosaic' of the book of nature in *Upon Appleton House*, l. 582, the 'mosaic of the air' is a divinely inscribed language, parallel (yet inferior) to the 'mosaic' books of the Bible (i.e. the Pentateuch). *OED* B n. 1 a notes the earliest comparison of music with mosaic *c*. 1400 (but with the terms reversed when compared to M.'s version) in *The 'Gest Hystoriale' of the Destruction of Troy*, ll. 1653, 1660–2: 'Within this palis of prise was a proude halle, . . . With a flore at was fret all of fyne stones, Pauyt prudly all with proude colours, Made after musycke, men on to loke.' See also John Bulwer, *Chironomia* (1644), 141: 'Eloquence receives her beauteous colours, her Musive or Mosaique Excellency, whereby she becomes most accomplished' (noted by Wilson, *BJRL*, 51 (1969), 480–1).
18. solemn] a) sacred (*OED* a. 1) b) imposing; awe-inspiring (*OED* a. 4, 7) c) serious (*OED* a. 6). *noise*] a) pleasant sound (*OED* n. 5) b) company of musicians (*OED* n. 5 b), imagined as an army (see l. 19).
19. empire] territory under complete control (*OED* n. II 5); see above, *Headnote, Sources, Genre and Structure*.

20. sphere] the boundary of heaven (*OED* n. I.1); M. thus excludes heavenly music (the 'music of the spheres') from the music of this poem, although it was frequently invoked in the *laus musicae* tradition (see *The First Anniversary*, ll. 47–8, and above, *Headnote, Sources, Genre and Structure*).
22–3. gentler conqueror . . . his praise] see above, *Headnote, Context*.
23. flies . . . praise] Rees (1989), 176–7, suggests that M. is responding directly to Davenant's comments on the dangers of praise in *Gondibert* (2.6.86–7). Here, praise offered to heaven is seen as proper and appropriate, but as courtly flattery it has the power to wreck monarchies. Hence the wisdom of flying from the music of one's own praise. See also above, *Headnote, Sources and Genre*. Cp. Matthew Stevenson, 'To an Impudent Scold . . .', in *Occasion's Off-spring* (1645), 124: 'You . . . with full cry confound his eares, . . . /Thus like *Acteon* with affrights hedg'd round/Hee flyes the furie of his owne fierce hound.'
24. Heaven's hallelujahs] Fairfax, no less than Cromwell, was a pious Protestant: he adhered to Presbyterian church discipline, and kept a manuscript book of sermons: see below, *Upon Appleton House, Headnote, Context*.

32

The Garden

Date. 1668. The poem has been customarily regarded as a product of M.'s period of retirement (between ?late 1650 and ?July 1652) as tutor to General Fairfax's daughter, Mary, on the Fairfax estate at Nun Appleton, Yorkshire. Donno (255) sees thematic similarities with the Yorkshire poems, *Upon Appleton House* and *Upon the Hill and Grove at Bilbrough*, and regards the first stanza as an inversion of *An Horatian Ode*, ll. 1–8.

However, Pritchard, *SEL*, 23 (1983), 371–88, makes a strong case for a Restoration dating of the poem, probably 1668, based on evidence of the influence of poetry by Katherine Philips (*Poems* (1667)), and Abraham Cowley (*Several Discourses by Way of Essays, in Verse and Prose*, in *Works* (1668)). Assuming family and friendship ties, Pritchard notes similarities with Philips' 'Upon Mr Abraham Cowley's Retirement' (*The Garden*, ll. 1–9, 52), 'A Country-life' (*The Garden*, ll. 15–16, 61–4), 'Upon the graving of her Name upon a Tree in Barnelmes Walks' (*The Garden*, ll. 23–4); 'La Solitude de Saint Amant' (*The Garden*, ll. 18, 49), and Cowley, 'The Garden' (*The Garden*, st. V), 'The Muse' (*The Garden*, st. VI), 'Of Solitude' (*The Garden*, st. VII), 'Claudian's Old Man of Verona' (*The Garden*, l. 66). Although Philips and Cowley might both have seen M.'s poem in MS (though no contemporary MSS survive), and so been influenced by M., Pritchard cites as corroborative evidence to his case the relative absence of verbal parallels between *The Garden* and *Upon Appleton House*, the suspicion that M.'s poetry did not circulate widely in manuscript, and M.'s habit of incorporating influences in his poems from recently published printed volumes. The argument is not absolutely convincing. Apart from the possibility of an unidentified common source, Pritchard plays down the significance of the Hermetic presence, especially when the major Hermetic works were published in the 1650s in English translation and were known to Fairfax. The more striking elements of the vocabulary (e.g. l. 47, 'annihilating') are to be found in devotional literature of the 1640s and 1650s,

rather than the 1660s. There is of course the possibility that M. may have revised the poem in the Restoration, having first composed it during the Interregnum. The argument for a later date is none the less preferable until better evidence to the contrary is produced.

Publication. 1681.

Sources and Genre. Leishman (1966), 295–6, argues that *The Garden* has at its centre the opulent world of Theocritus, *Idylls*, VII, ll. 143–6: 'All nature smelt of the opulent summer-time, smelt of the season of fruit. Pears lay at our feet, apples on either side rolling abundantly, and the young branches lay splayed upon the ground because of the weight of their damsons.' Several commentators have seen the prototype of Marvell's garden in the Epicurean garden described by Horace (*Epistles*, II.ii, ll. 76–8) and in the association of poetry with civilized retirement and contemplation which his poetry celebrates (*Carmina*, I.i, ll. 29–36; I.xxxii, ll. 1–3). Despite this preference for Horatian *umbra* (leisure in the sense of rest) over *otia* (leisure in the sense of idleness), J.M. Potter, *SEL*, 11 (1971), 137–51, notes that the Epicureanism is limited. None the less, a convincing source is Virgil's minor poetry, especially *Ciris* (ll. 1–11), where retirement in Epicurus's Attic Garden is juxtaposed with public life as competing claims for poetic inspiration: the garden produces poetry of wisdom or philosophy, not of the praise of public virtue. Marvell adopts Virgil's language of the verdant shade, '*viridi . . . umbra*' (*Eclogues*, IX, l. 20), but introduces a transcendental dimension to Virgil's depiction of the wandering mind: in Marvell's poem the soul, not the mind, will make the greatest journey (see below, ll. 5, 45–6, 52–5).

To this should be added the stoic tradition and its praise of gardens, represented in seventeenth-century England by the Dutch jurist, Justus Lipsius's popular work *A Discourse of Constancy*, translated by R.G. (1654): 'What *plenty* of Herbs and Flowers! that

Nature may seem to have call'd hither into this little place, whatsoever this *Our* World hath excellent, or the *Other*' (75; see below l. 72). Poggioli, *Daedalus*, 88 (1959), 686–99, contends that *The Garden* is an example of the transition in the late Renaissance from pastoral of solitude to pastoral of self. It is difficult to see the poem as a pastoral: David Kalstone, *ELR*, 4 (1974), 174–88, argues, against Poggioli, that the erotic pastoral scenes depicted in sts. III and IV are reinterpreted and 'purified' in the poem's unique elevation of nature.

The Garden has its place in the tradition of seventeenth-century retirement poetry. Mildmay Fane, Second Earl of Westmoreland's 'To Retiredness', in *Otia Sacra* (1648), 172–4, makes no distinction between the garden and other forms of cultivation in the natural world, though like M.'s poem, the ultimate aim of contemplation is sacred: 'Whether on Natures Book I muse,/Or else some other writes on't, use/To spend the time in, every line,/Is not excentrick but Divine' (ll. 71–4). There are similar treatments of fountains (*Otia Sacra*, 137, 156; see below, l. 49), of invention (*Otia Sacra*, 154; see below, ll. 43–8) and of dials (*Otia Sacra*, 154; see below, l. 66), but Fane's poetry combines a use of conceit which makes nature continuous with human culture and with the epideictic conventions of the country house poem popularized by Ben Jonson. However, the imaginative devices of M.'s poem are seen to be caused by the garden itself.

Hunt (1978), 37 notes the poem's position at the transition between the 'gradual development of an expressive vision at the expense of the emblematic, of an empirical or scientific regard at the expense of the discovery of *a priori* ideas in a garden world. . . . *The Garden* celebrates both an actual and a symbolic world'. For this reason, although M. appears to use elements from Cowley's earlier lyric poetry (see below, l. 24), *The Garden* displays as much familiarity with *Several Discourses by way of Essays*, especially *The Garden*, where Epicureanism and Edenic parallels are combined with observation of fruits in stanza 10 (see below, ll. 34–40).

Like Cowley (*The Garden*, st. VIII), M. sees in his poem the potential for the garden to present to man at least a hint of the paradisal garden from which Adam and Eve were expelled after their Fall (ll. 57–64). The image of Eden, and the possibility of its recuperation, was the most powerful idealistic and utopian image in the century. Cowley's poem, addressed to John Evelyn, praises married life, with the wife's beauty compared to a garden, whereas M.'s paradise is one of a solitary male, before the creation of Eve. While *The Garden* does use ideas in Hermetic philosophy, the suggestion, made by Røstvig (1954), 261 and *English Studies*, 40 (1959), 65–76, that M. is presenting not only a solitary Adam, but the androgynous *Adam Kadmon* of cabbalistic tradition, has not gained general acceptance. The speaker's invigorating interaction with the fruit and flowers, ll. 34–40, does bear a broad comparison with cabbalistic writing, but the genuine cabbalistic and Hermetic poetry of Samuel Pordage in *Mundorum Explicatio* (1661) is very removed from M.'s verse. Hodge (1978), 88, notes that the fruit and flowers of ll. 34–40 are both active or animated and passive, especially the 'curious peach': 'the illusion of movement is achieved this time by eliminating the point of reference, as when the station seems to leave a train'.

The other major Biblical presence is the Song of Solomon, and its tradition in Renaissance poetry of the *hortus conclusus*, or enclosed garden (Cant. 4:12). The Song, traditionally interpreted as an allegory of the marriage between Christ (the Bridegroom) and His Church (the Bride), raises the possibility of an allegorical reading of M.'s poem, since in the Song, the bridegroom compares his bride to a garden, 'Thy plants are an orchard of pomegranates, with pleasant fruits; camphire, with spikenard' (Cant. 4:13). There are echoes of contemporary translations and imitations of the Song of Solomon (see below, ll. 17–18). Stewart (1966), 153, argues that M.'s meditation 'suggests the lush garden eroticism of the allegorized Song of Songs'. But to go further and argue that the garden is the soul, and the soul the Bride of Christ, so making the speaker into a Christ figure, is finally unconvincing. The erotic associations of 'green' in the Song (Cant. 1:16; 2:13) disappear in M.'s poem.

The emblem books whose influence may be detected in many of M.'s lyrics are no less present in *The Garden*. The Jesuit Henry Hawkins' *Partheneia Sacra* (1633) takes the garden as a figurative 'amphitheatre' within which each component has a series of moral and sacred significances. The emblematic poem for the garden itself (13) explains that the garden represents the Virgin, inspired by the Holy Spirit to give birth to Christ, the collective emblems of different virtues in the plants. Unlike M.'s poem, the lily represents 'immaculate Chastitie', the rose 'Shamefastnes and bashful Modestie', and 'the quintessence of beautie, sweets, and graces'. Hawkins' garden is a *hortus conclusus*, 'wherein are al things mysteriously and spiritually to be found', and where the landscape provides material for M.'s account of creativity in stanza VI of *The Garden*: Hawkins' garden is surrounded by an ocean, which can be viewed through a telescope, and there are 'certain risings to be seen of Hils in elevations of mind, and Valleys againe in depressions and demissions of the same mind, through annihilation'. Emblematic creation in Hawkins becomes a description of imagination in M.

Since Fairfax (and Katherine Philips) translated the French *libertin* poet, Marc-Antoine de Gérard, Sieur de Saint-Amant, the influence of his *La Solitude* and *La Contemplation* has been proposed and rejected, largely on account of the seriousness with which M. treats ideas of the natural. In this sense, Klonsky, *Sewanee Review*, 58 (1950), 16–35 treats *The Garden* as a repetition of the metaphors used by Plotinus to describe the birth of the World-Soul and its relationship with Intellect. In both the garden is an allegory for the realm of first forms: 'this principle is in Soul and comes from Intellect, flowing into his garden when Aphrodite is said to have been born' (*Enneads*, III.v. 9). While M.'s poem never concedes allegory in the explicit manner suggested by Klonsky, Plotinus' modes of representation do foreshadow M.'s description of the active mind in the garden. In effect, M. transfers the metaphors of Neoplatonism from the cosmic to the human scale, almost parodying Neoplatonic language: 'Should not abide unchanged when it produces: it is moved and so brings forth an image. It looks to its source and is filled, and going forth to another opposed movement generates its own image, which is sensation and the principle growth in plants. . . . The part before this, which is immediately dependent upon Intellect, leaves Intellect alone, abiding in itself' (*Enneads*, III.ii.1; see below, ll. 41–6).

M. would have known the writings of at least some of the Cambridge Platonists, of whom Nathanael Culverwel wrote *An Elegant and Learned Discourse of the Light of Nature* (1654). On the status of poetic inspiration, he writes 'truly his [Empedocles'] Poetical raptures were not so high as to elevate him above a body, for he presently sinks into ὕλη, he falls down into matter, and makes *Nature* nothing else but that which is ingenerable and incorruptible in material beings' (14; see below, l. 40). Culverwel is concerned with God's imprints in nature and the

imprints of nature on the tabula rasa (56; see below, ll. 23–4, 44–6). The mind of the speaker in st. VI creates, in imitation of God's creation of the world, without becoming part of creation, for 'God, though he leaves prints of himself upon all the souls in the world, nay, upon all the beings in the world, yet these impressions are not particles of himself; nor do they make the least mutation in him, only in the creature; for he was as full and perfect before he had printed any one creature, and if the whole impression of creatures were annihilated, yet his Essence were the same, and he could print more when he pleased, and as many as he pleased' (87–8). Again, the broad patterns of thought behind M.'s poem are evident.

Modern Criticism. In the nineteenth century, the poem was commonly known as 'Thoughts in a Garden', and was regarded by the influential Palgrave as the best example of M.'s nature poetry, with an intensity of feeling which anticipated Shelley (F.T. Palgrave, *Landscape in Poetry from Homer to Tennyson* (1897), 155–6). The 'green silence' of Emerson's 'Humble Bee' has been seen as a consequence of Marvell's influence (O.W. Holmes, *Ralph Waldo Emerson* (1885), 338). There was speculation that Palgrave had access to a manuscript when he substituted 'claps' for 'combs' (l. 54).

The rise of detailed textual analysis in the light of psychological and psychoanalytical theories of expression made *The Garden* a tempting subject. In *Scrutiny*, 1 (1932–33), 236–40, and later in *Some Versions of Pastoral* (1935), 113–39, Empson argued that the poem represented an exploration of the relationship between man and creation, including the different orders of creativity or authorship for man and God. Within this framework, the metaphors of st. VI are seen to represent Freud's understanding of the relationship between self-awareness and primal development: 'the mind as knower is a conscious mirror . . . the unconscious is unplumbed and pathless. . . . On the Freudian view of an Ocean, *withdraws* would make this repose in Nature a return to the womb; anyway it may mean either 'withdraws into self-contemplation' or 'withdraws altogether, into its mysterious processes of digestion' (119–20). Sts. IV and V contain 'the sublimation of sexual desire into a taste for Nature', and the reflection of beasts in land and sea (ll. 43–4) represents in the search for resemblance of kinds a 'desire for *creation*' (120). For Bradbrook and Lloyd-Thomas (61), this process placed M. in the central tradition of metamorphosis in English verse: as with Spenser, M.'s *Garden* was seen to achieve a transcending of mutability in the very act of understanding and accepting it.

Most post-war criticism has been concerned with identifying the generic character of *The Garden* by comparison with traditions and similarities in Classical and Renaissance verse (see above, *Genre and Allusion*). In this way, Kermode, *E in C*, 2 (1952), 225–41, took issue with Empson and others who would read the poem as serious philosophy or theology. The poem uses serious ideas, but lightly, in the tradition of the range of poetic genres which the poem acknowledges and sometimes parodies, from the Golden Age pastoral of Tasso, to the Elizabethan Platonic lyric, the *libertin* or Cavalier lyric and the emblem book. The meeting of Epicurean and emblematic gardens in st. II is a 'joke . . . to give Quiet and her sister plant emblems like those of the active life, and to clash the emblematic and the vegetable plants together' (in Carey, ed. (1969) 258). Leishman (1966), 293–4, challenged the validity of Kermode's generic interpretation, claiming that *The Garden* is the first poem to celebrate the 'philosopher's garden'.

Recent criticism still values the poem highly, and still retains as its central concern the creation, annihilation and transcendentalism of sts. VI and VII. For Rajan, in Patrides, ed. (1978), 166–7, the withdrawal of the mind is to the 'Paradise within', 'the ocean of imagination, the interior garden of Adonis. . . . The mind is now not tied to that exterior reality which it has succeeded in originating fully within itself.' In fashioning the 'green thought', the mind achieves a mimesis of reality, but the creative tranquillity of the garden is subverted by the threat of 'annihilation'. *The Garden*, then, manifests inconclusiveness where 'the energies which constitute the fictive world are also instrumental in undermining what they create'. It is comic, yet serious in its anticipation of an afterlife. The syntactic ambiguities of the poem are not resolved: in some of his last writing, Empson (1979), 43–6, defended himself against Legouis' objections to his original arguments, and again asserted the relevance of the occult tradition which M. would have known from Cambridge and from his time with Fairfax.

The Garden

I

How vainly men themselves amaze
To win the palm, the oak, or bays;
And their uncessant labours see
Crowned from some single herb or tree,
5 Whose short and narrow vergèd shade
Does prudently their toils upbraid;
While all flow'rs and all trees do close
To weave the garlands of repose.

II

Fair Quiet, have I found thee here,
10 And Innocence thy sister dear!
Mistaken long, I sought you then
In busy companies of men.

---

1. *vainly*] a) in a futile manner; without profit (*OED* adv. 1) b) foolishly, senselessly, thoughtlessly (*OED* adv. 2) c) with personal vanity (*OED* adv. 3). *amaze*] a) to put out of one's wits (*OED* v. 1); Donno notes the correlative with the Latin *furor*, 'madness'. b) to drive oneself to stupidity, bewilderment, puzzlement (*OED* v. 5).
2. Wreaths signifying the following virtues: military (made from palm leaves), civic (oak leaves), poetic (laurel ('bay') leaves).
3. *uncessant*] common spelling of 'incessant', *c.* 1550–1690.
4. *single*] A.H. King, *English Studies*, 20 (1938), 118–21, suggests 'single' means 'celibate'.
5. *vergèd*] provided with a border, edged (*OED* v. 1 trans.). The 'herb or tree' casts a small, neat shadow around the heads of those who wear garlands of honour. *Vergèd* suggests a stringent control, as opposed to the fulsome shade of the garden in ll. 7–8. *shade*] shadow; see Virgil, *Ciris*, ll. 2–3: 'Cecropius sauis exspirans hortulus auras/florentis viridi sophiae complectitur umbra' ('the Attic garden, breathing forth sweet fragrance, enwraps me in fine-flowering Wisdom's verdant shade').
6. *prudently*] a) with discretion b) with practical, worldly or politic wisdom. *toils*] a) laborious task (*OED* n. 1 2) b) a struggle, physical or verbal (*OED* n. 1 1) c) a trap or snare (*OED* n. 2). In the seventeenth century a net set as a trap was called a toil. *upbraid*] a) to reprove, to censure (*OED* v. 2) b) to plait into a wreath (not in *OED*, but as in 'braid', *OED* v.1 III 11).
7. *close*] unite, combine (*OED* v. III 11); see *The Definition of Love*, ll. 13–14: 'For Fate with jealous eyes does see/Two perfect loves, nor lets them close.'
8. *repose*] temporary rest, cessation from activity and exertion.
11–12. *I . . . men*] a reworking of George Herbert's seeking in *Redemption*, ll. 9–11, 'I straight return'd, and knowing his great birth,/ Sought him accordingly in great resorts;/ In cities, theatres, gardens, parks, and courts.'

Your sacred plants, if here below,
Only among the plants will grow.
15   Society is all but rude,
     To this delicious solitude.

                    III

No white nor red was ever seen
So am'rous as this lovely green.
Fond lovers, cruel as their flame,
20   Cut in these trees their mistress' name.

Little, alas, they know, or heed,
How far these beauties hers exceed!
Fair trees! Wheres'e'er your barks I wound,
No name shall but your own be found.

                    IV

25   When we have run our passions' heat,
     Love hither makes his best retreat.
     The gods, that mortal beauty chase,
     Still in a tree did end their race:

13–14. A Hermetic notion: 'It is true w<i>thout any lying, certaine & most true, that w<hi>ch is inferiour, or below, is as <tha>t w<hi>ch is superiour or above', Hermes Trismegistus, *Tabula Smaragdina*, trans. John Everard (1640), Bodl. MS Ashmole 1440, fol. 196. Cp. Cowley, *The Garden*, ll. 73–4, 'Upon the Flowers of Heaven we gaze;/The Stars of Earth no wonder in us raise'.
14. will] *1681*+; do MS Clark P7455 M1 [?1712], p. 45.
15. all but] very nearly. *rude*] uncultivated, barbarous, wild (*OED* a. 3b).
16. To] i.e. compared to. *delicious*] a) delightful (*OED* a. 1) b) highly pleasing to bodily senses (*OED* a. 2). *solitude*] a) state of being alone (*OED* n. 1) b) lonely, unfrequented place (*OED* n. 3). Solitude was the subject of several commonplace phrases: 'solitude is best society' (Cicero): 'I am never *lesse alone, then when alone*' (Lipsius). See also Cowley, *Of Solitude*, ll. 25–6: 'Oh Solitude, first state of Human-kind!'. Cowley regarded the commonplace as a 'very vulgar saying' in the first sentence of his essay *Of Solitude* (1668).
17–18. A parody of a convention in amorous expression: cp. W.L., 'The Epistle', in M. de Harst, *A Panegyrick of the most renowned and serene Princess Christina* (1656), sig. [A6ʳ], 'Lillies and Roses enjoyed no Whites and Reds, till her cheeks taught them their complexions.' In *Eyes and Tears*, l. 18, red, white and green are the colours in a garden. Here, however, white (the lily) and red (the rose) are associated with passionate love: see Thomas Randolph, 'In Anguem, qui *Lycorin* dormientem amplexus est' (1638), English version, ll. 7–9, 'Lyllies did strow her couch, and proud were grown/ . . . /Roses fell downe soft pillowes to her head'. For other associations, see *Headnote, Sources, Genres and Allusions.*
18. am'rous] Legouis (1965), 90 n. maintains that *am'rous* could only have its passive and obsolete sense of 'lovely' for M. In reply, J.C. Maxwell, *N & Q*, 213 (1968), 377, quoted Nicholas Hookes's *To Amanda, walking in the Garden*, from *Amanda. A Sacrifice* (1653), 43, where the 'am'rous Queen' Amanda is approached by active plants: 'A short dwarfe flower did enlarge its stalk,/And shot an inch to see *Amanda* walk.' *lovely green*] Cp. Maciej Kazimierz Sarbiewski, *Out of Salomon's sacred marriage songs, The Odes of Casimire*, trans. G. Hills (1646), 85, 'While in the sacred Green, a bow're we see/Doth spread it selfe for thee.' *lovely*] a) beautiful (*OED* a. 3 b) b) amorous (*OED* a. 1 b).
19–20. Cp. Virgil, *Eclogue* X, ll. 53–4: 'malle pati tenerisque meos incidere amores/arboribus: crescit illae, crescitis, amores'

(it is better to suffer and carve my love on the young trees. They will grow; thou, too, my love, wilt grow.)
19. Fond] a) over-affectionate (*OED* n. 5a) b) infatuated (*OED* n. 2) c) foolish (*OED* n. 2).
20. mistress'] mistress *1681*, Bod. 1.
23–4. Whereso'e'er . . . found] M. alludes to the notion, commonly found in occult writings and nature mysticism (especially Paracelsus), of *signatura rerum*, the doctrine of signatures. At the creation, God put into each piece of creation a distinct sign, which was the true name of that object, and which most perfectly expressed what it was. God put into Adam's mind a mental impression of each signature so that he would be able to name and hence know every object in creation. This was the basis of the Adamic knowledge so celebrated in the Hermetic tradition, and which Renaissance occultists sought to recover. M.'s *persona* says that if ever he would be led to carve names in the trees, it would be the (true) name of the trees themselves, not the name of a woman. The trees become the true objects of the *persona*'s love, and the subjects of his exercise of the *prisca theologia* of natural knowledge. See Jacob Boehme, *Signatura Rerum*, trans. John Ellistone (1651), ch. 1, and above, *Upon Appleton House*, sts. LXXII, LXXIII. For *Signatura rerum*, see also stanza VI. *wound/ . . . found*] a good rhyme in seventeenth-century pronunciation.
23. Fair trees . . . I wound] For ancient examples of lovers' names carved in trees, see Virgil, *Eclogues*, X, ll. 53–4; Ovid, *Heroides*, V, ll. 21–30. Cp. Cowley, *The Tree* (1647), ll. 3–4: 'I cut my Love into his gentle Bark,/ And in three days, behold 'tis *dead*.'
25. run our . . . heat] exhausted our sexual desire. *heat* is a pun, referring to intense passion, and to the single course in a race (*OED* n. 10) which is used here as the metaphor for the pursuit of ardent sexual passion. *passions'*] *1681*; a) sexual impulses (*OED* n. 9) b) in the plural, also invoking the northern name for the plant Bistort or Dock (*OED*).
26. retreat] withdrawal a) as if from a battle (*OED* n. 3) b) from the public world into privacy and seclusion, with religious (monastic) echoes (*OED* n. 4); see ll. 11–12.
28. race] a) the chase of Daphne by Apollo b) the gods, since Daphne had turned herself from a divine being into a tree. Ovid's tale (see below, *29–30*) ends with Apollo making the laurel the wreath worn by triumphant Roman generals. The deity of Apollo is also forever in the laurels: 'semper habebunt/te coma, te citherae, te nostrae, laure, pharetrae' (My hair, my lyre, my quiver shall always be entwined with thee, O laurel), *Metamorphoses*, I, ll. 558–9.

Apollo hunted Daphne so,
Only that she might laurel grow;
And Pan did after Syrinx speed,
Not as a nymph, but for a reed.

Into my hands themselves do reach;
Stumbling on melons, as I pass,
40   Insnared with flow'rs, I fall on grass.

V

What wondrous life is this I lead!
Ripe apples drop about my head;
5   The luscious clusters of the vine
Upon my mouth do crush their wine;
The nectarene, and curious peach,

VI

Meanwhile the mind, from pleasures less,
Withdraws into its happiness:
The mind, that ocean where each kind
Does straight its own resemblance find;
45   Yet it creates, transcending these,
Far other worlds, and other seas;

29–30. The story of Phoebus Apollo's chase and attempted rape of Daphne occurs in Ovid, *Metamorphoses*, I, ll. 452–567, and of Pan's attempt to catch Syrinx, I, ll. 698–712. It was extremely common in Renaissance art and literature. For example, a grotto at the Villa Aldobrandini, near Rome, which M. may have visited (see below, ll. 65–6) contained paintings of metamorphoses by Domenichino Zampieri. One depicts the pursuit of Daphne by Apollo (see K.J. Höltgen, *N & Q*, 214 (1969), 381–2; see also Hunt (1978), 107). See also the text of an entertainment, 'Praelectio Musica', with orations, performed on 10 July 1669 for Thomas Lawrence, Vice Chancellor of Oxford University, recorded in the common-place book of Thomas Lessey (Cardiff Central Library, MS 1.482, fol. 40ᵛ): 'Those cherries of yʳ Lips are blood-ripe, & cry come eat me, & you tempt us with the Apples of yʳ eyes, worse yⁿ ever Eve was with that of yᵉ Serpent. But I fear I follow the Metaphor too far I shall pursue you as Apollo did Daphne into a tree, but you would still keep yʳ propriety, for you love to bear fruit in all capacities.'

34–40. *Ripe . . . grass*] see *Bermudas*, ll. 21–4.

33. *is this*] Thompson+ in this *1681, Cooke, Margoliouth, Lord, Walker, Wilcher.*

34. See Sarbiewski, 'The Apple ripe drops from its stalke to thee', Ode 21. Lib. 4, 'Out of *Salomon's* sacred marriage song', *The Odes Of Casimire*, trans. G.H. (1646), 87.

35. *luscious*] see Sarbiewski, 'The luscious fruit from the full Figtree shall/Into thy bosome fall', Ode 21. Lib. 4, 'Out of *Salomon's* sacred marriage song', *The Odes of Casimire*, trans. G. Hils (1646), 87.

37. *curious*] a) dainty, delicate (*OED* a. II 7 b) b) beautifully wrought (*OED* a. II 7) c) inquisitive (*OED* a. II 10).

37–8. *peach . . . reach*] see Ben Jonson, 'To Penshurst', ll. 43–4: 'The blushing apricot and woolly peach/Hang on thy walls, that every child may reach.'

40. *Insnared with . . . grass*] see Job 18:10, 'The snare is laid for him in the ground, and a trap for him in the way'; Isa. 40:6, 'All flesh is grass, and all the goodliness thereof is as the flower of the field.' M. uses vocabulary usually associated with man's mortality and fallen condition in an innocent way, likening his garden to Eden (see ll. 57–64). *Insnared*] 'ensnared' (*OED*).

41. *from pleasures less*] from inferior pleasures (of the senses). Empson ((1935), 118–19) detected verbal ambiguity, especially in 'from pleasure[s] less', which he claimed could mean 'from the lessening of pleasure' or 'made less by pleasure'. In reply, Legouis, *RES*, n.s. 8 (1957), 382–7 (383), argued that only one meaning is possible: 'from the lesser pleasures of the body'. Hodge (1978), 65, pointed out that the phrase did not indicate an absolute division between mind and body, because the mind's awareness includes the body; the mind simply chooses to withdraw into its own 'happiness'. *pleasures*] Bod. 1+; pleasure *1681, Thompson, Margoliouth, Kermode, Walker.*

43–4. The mind, likened to an ocean, has in it a resemblance or image of all the objects in the world. M.'s image depends upon the notion that all species on land had their correspondents in the sea (see Pliny, *Natural History*, IX.i.2; Sir Thomas Browne, *Pseudodoxia Epidemica* (1646), III.xxiv). According to the notion of *signatura rerum* (see above, ll. 23–4.), these were originally placed in Adam's mind by God. *straight*] a) immediately b) exactly.

43. *kind*] group of animals or plants (*OED* n. II 10 a).

45. *Yet it creates*] Far from being passive, so that man simply renames creation in imitation of God's original naming, or after the nature of the objects, the mind is capable of imagining its own original worlds of objects. The use of 'creation' gives the mind a godlike status. *transcending*] a) passing beyond, exceeding b) being above, and independent, like God. *these*] the objects in the world and their resemblances in the mind.

46. *Far other worlds*] Virgil, *Ciris*, ll. 5–6, notes the poetic mind's journey while in the garden: 'ut mens curet eo dignum sibi quaerere carmen/longe aliud studium atque alios accincta labores' (so that my mind desires to go in quest of a sufficiently worthy song, prepared though she is for far different tasks and far different toils). Cp. also Cowley's *The Muse* (1656), ll. 33, 35: the muse has a 'thousand worlds too of thine own . . . a New World leaps forth when Thou say'st, Let it be'. In his notes, Cowley annotates these lines: 'The meaning is, that Poetry treats not only of all things that are, or can be, but makes *Creatures* of her own . . . and varies all these into innumerable Systemes, or Worlds of Invention.' The possibility of more than one world is treated by Lucretius, *De Rerum Natura*, II, ll. 1064–6.

Annihilating all that's made
To a green thought in a green shade.

VII

50 Here at the fountain's sliding foot
Or at some fruit-tree's mossy root,
Casting the body's vest aside,
My soul into the boughs does glide:
There like a bird it sits, and sings,
Then whets, and combs its silver wings;
55 And, till prepared for longer flight,
Waves in its plumes the various light.

VIII

Such was that happy garden-state,
While man there walked without a mate:
After a place so pure, and sweet,
60 What other help could yet be meet?
But 'twas beyond a mortal's share
To wander solitary there:
Two Paradises 'twere in one
To live in Paradise alone.

---

47. *Annihilating*] a) to obliterate (*OED* v. 1) b) to treat as non-existent (*OED* v. 3). In the act of mental creation, the mind blots out all images of objects in the world to produce the 'green thought'. Margoliouth and Donno explain *annihilating* as 'reducing', but this meaning is not recorded in the seventeenth century by *OED*. *Annihilating* was frequently used in M.'s time in a religious sense, to express mortification, and even the obliteration of the self or ego, in order to achieve union with the Godhead: 'if any have been so happy as truly to understand Christian annihilation, extasis, exolution, . . . they have already had an handsome anticipation of heaven', Sir Thomas Browne, *Hydriotaphia* (1658), in Browne, *The Major Works*, ed. C.A. Patrides (1977), 314. M.'s use of the word has such overtones, giving the act of creating a green thought associations of the achieving of transcendental perfection and illumination.
48. *green . . . shade*] an original thought about nature and the garden, made under the influence of the garden (that is, contemplative activity while sitting under the shadow of a bush or tree in the garden). Green thoughts are in part amorous reflections in *The Mower's Song*, l. 26, and anon., *The Reign of King Edward III* (1595), 1.2, ll. 63–4: 'Since green our thoughts, green be the conventicle/Where we will ease us by disburdening them' (Frank Romany, private communication). *green shade*] Cp. Virgil, *Eclogues*, IX, ll. 19–20: 'quis humum florentibus herbis/spargeret aut viridi fontis induceret umbra?' (Who would strew the turf with flowery herbage, or curtain the springs with green shade?). Hodge (1978), 67, suggests that 'shade' could also mean 'image', through the common Latin root *umbra*. In this case, the 'green shade' is not only the garden, but the expression of the thought (e.g. a poem): 'the conclusion of the mind's activity is the creation of an all-subsuming idea in an all-subsuming Image'.
49. *fountain's*] Thompson+; fountains 1681, Margoliouth, Lord. Most probably a mechanical device with a water jet, as opposed to a natural feature, and usually placed at the centre of a formal arrangement of beds. *sliding foot*] Cp. Virgil, *Culex*, l. 17:

'liquido pede labitur unda' (wave glides in its watery course [literally, 'foot']). *sliding*] flowing (*OED* ppl. a. 3 a).
51. *vest*] vesture; clothing. M. imagines the soul as clothed by the body, the body as its temporary clothing.
52–3. M.'s source was Spenser, *An Hymne of Heavenly Beautie* (1596), ll. 24–8: 'to mount aloft by order dew,/To contemplation of th'immortal sky,/Of the soare falcon so I learne to fly,/That flags awhile her fluttering wings beneath,/Till she her selfe for stronger flight can breath.' Cp. also Rowland Watkyns, 'Faith', in *Flamma sine Fumo* (1662), 2, 'Yet like a bird my souls shall fly/Safe from the fowlers tyranny.' In a poem concerned with the ability of the souls of friends to transcend the limitations of time and space and thereby find each other, Cowley uses the bird analogy to describe his recourse to verse as the solution to his friend's absence: 'Just as a *Bird* that flies about/And beats it self against the *Cage*,/Finding at last no passage out/It sits and sings, and so o'ercomes its rage.' Fowler, *TLS*, 12 Dec. 2003, adduces the following earlier sources: the neoplatonic winged soul of Boethius, *Philosophiae consolationis*, IV.i; the legless birds of Jeremy Taylor, and contemporary interest in the bird of paradise, used as an impresa by Fairfax's future son-in-law Buckingham, and figured in Herbert, 'Prayer (I)', l. 12.
54. *whets*] preens. Usually, to whet means to sharpen. As a boar might sharpen its tusks, so the soul as bird takes care of its wings in anticipation of the eventual flight to heaven. *silver wings*] see Ps. 68:13: 'yet shall ye be as the wings of a dove covered with silver'.
56. *various*] varied in colour (*OED* a. 4 a).
57. *garden-state*] alluding to the innocent political order of Paradise; see James Shirley, 'To L. for a wreath of Bayes sent' (1646), ll. 13–14: 'My fancy's narrow yet, till I create/For thee another world, and in a state,/As free as innocence, shame all poets' wit.'
60. *help . . . meet*] see Genesis 2:18: 'And the Lord God said, It is not good that the man should be alone; I will make him an help meet for him'.

IX

the a poth

5   How well the skilful gard'ner drew
     Of flow'rs and herbs this dial new;
     Where from above the milder sun

*became thee's no
death?*

Does through a fragrant zodiac run;
And, as it works, th'industrious bee
70   Computes its time as well as we.
     How could such sweet and wholesome hours
     Be reckoned but with herbs and flow'rs!

*passage of two :
unthreatening*

65–6. In a secondary sense the gardener is God the clockmaker: 'God set up the world as a fair and goodly clock', Nathanael Culverwel, *A Discourse of the Light of Nature* (1654), 16. K.J. Höltgen, *N & Q*, 214 (1969), 381–2, notes that the garden contains here, or is likened to, a floral sundial, like those recorded in emblem books (in Jesuit ones as *impresa* for the power of oratory), and which Marvell may well have seen at Frascati, near Rome, in the grounds of the Villa Aldobrandini, *c.* 1647.
66. *flow'rs and herbs*] Cowley, *Poemata Latina* (1668), title page: 'HERBARUM FLORUM SYLVARUM'; 'The Garden', st. V, l. 9, 'herbs and flowers'; see also below, l. 72.
68. *fragrant zodiac*] the flowers represent the zodiac: the belt of the celestial sphere, within which the apparent motions of the sun, moon and principal planets take place, and which is divided into twelve equal parts called 'signs' or 'houses' (*OED* n. 1). *Hortus*, l. 52, has '*fragrantia signa*', a play upon what

Zodiacal signs would normally be: *flagrantia*, burning. See above, *The Unfortunate Lover*, l. 8 n.
69–70. *th'industrious bee . . . as we*] Cp. Horace, *Carmina*, IV.2, ll. 27–9: 'ego apis Matinae/more modoque/grata carpentis thyma per laborem' (I, after the way and manner of the Mantinian bee, that gathers the pleasant thyme laboriously); Cowley, 'The Praise of Pindar' (1656), ll. 46–9: 'And all inferiour beauteous things/Like the laborious Bee,/For little drops of Honey flee,/And there with humble Sweets contents her Industrie.' *time*] as the quotation from Horace suggests, M. makes a pun here on the herb 'thyme'. See also *Hortus*, ll. 55–6.
72. *herbs and flow'rs*] ambiguous, referring to decay as well as life: 'abstracting from those Arts, and Advantages of *Novelty*, I know them to be *but* Herbs, and Flowers; that is, *suddain*, and *Fading* Things', Lipsius, *A Discourse of Constancy* (1654), trans. R.G., 79.

33
Hortus

Date. 1668? See *The Garden, Headnote, Date.* Whether *Hortus* was composed before its companion poem in English, *The Garden*, has been much disputed. The break between l. 48 and l. 49 appears to be a genuine one of sense, and is not merely an editorial imposition, made after M.'s death. In the corresponding place in *The Garden* come the Neoplatonic lines, the content of which is entirely absent from *Hortus*. The greater concision of *The Garden* is the strongest evidence for McQueen's argument (*PQ*, 44 (1965), 176–7) that the Latin poem came first. Yet the evidence that *The Garden* is lexically indebted to many recently published poems by other authors (see above, *The Garden, Headnote, Sources and Genre*) is reason to think again, and regard the English poem as the earlier composition.

Publication. 1681.

Genre and Sources. Without a Latin version of the complicated, poetically exceptional sts. V–VIII of *The Garden, Hortus* is a much less complex poem. It is an Epicurean treatment of the contrast between the turmoil of sexual love and public affairs on the one hand, and the ordered nature of the garden on the other, of *negotium* and *otium*. To this extent, the poem imitates Horatian Epicurean poetry, as demonstrated by Potter, *SEL*, 11 (1971), 137–51. A broad context for M.'s poem is evident in Horace, *Epistulae*, I.iv, ll. 15–16, 2.2, ll. 76–8, and *Carmina*, IV.ii, ll. 25–6; 4.15, ll. 17–20. More precise sources for M.'s poem are in *Carmina*, I.i, ll. 3–8, 19–22, 29–30, 1.32, ll. 1–4. There is also a near echo of the first line of Horace's first *Satire* in the first line. This is appropriate in the light of Horace's exposure of the pervasiveness and futility of greed and self-interest in public life in his poem. In addition to textual echoes, specific elements of the poem that belong to this tradition are the denial of ambition (ll. 1–20), and the identification of the speaker as a poet, looking specifically for leisure to write (ll. 16,

49). The poet is stressed at the end of the poem, as opposed to God in *The Garden*. Unlike the Latin of *Ros*, which also has an English companion poem, and which is intricate and matches in Latin the poetic complexity of the English poem, *Hortus* is linguistically much simpler than its English counterpart. The limitations in *Hortus* extend to tone, where the speaker is less laughable than his counterpart in *The Garden* because he is less pretentious (Klause (1983), 116).

McQueen, *PQ*, 44 (1965), 173–9, also notes that *The Garden* is more succinct than *Hortus*, not merely in terms of line length, but also in terms of a more concise treatment of corresponding subjects (e.g. *The Garden*, ll. 12–15 and *Hortus*, ll. 20–4). All references in *Hortus* are made explicit; in some instances this is achieved with similes. There is a more extended presence of mythical reference. Power and war are present here, in addition to sexual love, which is the dominant human feature in *The Garden*. Greater compression also means greater allusiveness. In McQueen's view, the composition of the English version suggested themes latent in the Latin that were then developed at greater length.

Williamson, *MLN*, 76 (1961), 590–8, notes that M.'s Latin poem is related to the Epicurean retirement literature that Cowley, Evelyn, Mackenzie and Temple had made popular in English. *Hortus* is different in that love is tamed by nature, rather than being a mere threat to nature. Thus, *Hortus* 'is concerned with the opposition of the love of woman and the love of nature, where Cowley had united them. . . . "The Garden" turns this opposition into an active versus contemplative theme.' Sexual love versus love of poetry in *Hortus* is replaced by the rejection of human sexual love for an innocent interaction with the creation in *The Garden*. Potter, *SEL*, 11 (1971), 141, argues that the peace and the *umbra* celebrated by M. is in classical terms that which the ruler struggles for in *An Horatian Ode* and the Latin poems on Cromwell.

Hortus

Quisnam adeo, mortale genus, praecordia versat?
Heu palmae, laurique furor, vel simplicis herbae!
Arbor ut indomitos ornet vix una labores;
Tempora nec foliis praecingat tota malignis.
Dum simul implexi, tranquillae ad serta quietis,
Omnigeni coeunt flores, integraque sylva.

　Alma Quies, teneo te! et te germana quietis
Simplicitas! Vos ergo diu per templa, per urbes,
Quaesivi, regum perque alta palatia frustra.
Sed vos hortorum per opaca silentia longe
Celarant plantae virides, et concolor umbra.

　O! mihi si vestros liceat violasse recessus
Erranti, lasso, et vitae melioris anhelo,
Municipem servate novum, votoque potitum,
Frondosae cives optate in florea regna.

　Me quoque, vos Musae, et, te conscie testor Apollo,
Non armenta juvant hominum, circique boatus,
Mugitusve fori; sed me penetralia veris,
Horroresque trahunt muti, et consortia sola.

　Virgineae quem non suspendit gratia formae?
Quam candore nives vincentem, ostrumque rubore,
Vestra tamen viridis superet (me judice) virtus.
Nec foliis certare comae, nec brachia ramis,
Nec possint tremulos voces aequare susurros.

　Ah quoties saevos vidi (quis credat?) amantes
Sculpentes dominae potiori in cortice nomen?
Nec puduit truncis inscribere vulnera sacris.
Ast ego, si vestras unquam temeravero stirpes,
Nulla Neaera, Chloe, Faustina, Corynna, legetur:

30　In proprio sed quaeque libro signabitur arbos.
O charae platanus, cyparissus, populus, ulmus!

　Hic Amor, exutis crepidatus inambulat alis,
Enerves arcus et stridula tela reponens,
Invertitque faces, nec se cupit usque timeri;
35　Aut exporrectus jacet, indormitque pharetrae;
Non auditurus quanquam Cytherea vocarit;
Nequitias referunt nec somnia vana priores.

　Laetantur superi, defervescente tyranno,
Et licet experti toties nymphasque deasque,
40　Arbore nunc melius potiuntur quisque cupita.
Jupiter annosam, neglecta conjuge, quercum
Deperit; haud alia doluit sic pellice Juno
Lemniacum temerant vestigia nulla cubile,
Nec Veneris Mavors meminit si fraxinus adsit.
45　Formosae pressit Daphnes vestigia Phoebus
Ut fieret Laurus; sed nil quaesiverat ultra.
Capripes et peteret quòd Pan Syringa fugacem,
Hoc erat ut calamum posset reperire sonorum.

Desunt multa

　Nec tu, opifex horti, grato sine carmine abibis:
50　Qui brevibus plantis, et laeto flore, notasti
Crescentes horas, atque intervalla diei.
Sol ibi candidior fragrantia signa pererrat;
Proque truci Tauro, stricto pro forcipe Cancri,
Securis violaeque rosaeque allabitur umbris.
55　Sedula quin et apis, mellito intenta labori,
Horologo sua pensa thymo signare videtur.
Temporis O suaves lapsus! O otia sana!
　O herbis dignae numerari et floribus horae!

---

2. *simplicis herbae*] 'Corona quidem nulla fuit graminea nobilior, in maiestate populi terrarum principis praemiisque gloriae.... graminea numquam nisi in desperatione suprema contigit ... dabatur haec viridi e gramine decerpto inde ubi obsessos servasset aliquis' (No crown indeed has been a higher honour than the crown of grass among the rewards for the glorious deeds given by the sovereign people, lords of the earth. ... the grass crown has never been conferred except upon the leader of a forlorn hope.... This crown used to be made from green grass pulled up from the site where the besieged men had been relieved by some one). (Pliny, *Natural History*, XXII.iii.4).
19. *Horroresque ... muti*] Cp. *Upon Appleton House*, l. 671: 'And such an horror calm and dumb.'
21. *vincentem*] *Cooke+*; vincentum *1681*. *ostrumque* 'ostrum': literally, the blood of the sea snail, from which purple dye was made (Lewis and Short, n. I, II).

30. *libro*] the bark of the tree (*cortex* in Latin) is imagined as a book.
31. *ulmus*] *Bod. 1+*; ulnus *1681*.
34. *invertitque faces*] Cp. above, *Upon the Death of Lord Hastings*, ll. 43–6: 'Hymeneus . . . trails his torches through the starry hall/Reversed, as at his darling's funeral.'
35. *exporrectus*] *Margoliouth+*; experrectus [i.e. 'awaked'] *1681*.
36. *Cytherea*] Venus, who rose from the sea near the island of Cythera. Cp. below, *The Second Advice to a Painter*, l. 64 n.
38. *tyranno*] i.e. Love.
43. *Lemniacum*] alternative name for Vulcan, who, in mythology, lived on the island of Lemnos.
44. *Nec . . . si*] *1681+*; Dum Veneri Myrtus Marti dum *Bod. 1, Donno.*
45. *Phaebus*] *1681*; Phoebus *Bod. 1*.
52. *fragrantia signa*] see above, *The Garden*, l. 68 n.
56. *thymo*] punning on 'time'; thyme-water was regarded as a cure for emotional passion.

The Garden

What madness, alas, for the palm and the laurel or for the simple grass vexes your hearts, o mortal race, to such an extent that a single tree scarcely adorns your unrestrained labours, nor entirely girds your temples with its grudging foliage, while at the same time, entwined in the wreaths of tranquil repose, flowers of all sorts and the untainted forest come together!

Kindly Repose, I hold you, and you, Simplicity, sister of Repose! For it is you that I have long sought in vain through temples, through cities, through the lofty palaces of kings. But the verdant plants and the shadow with like colour had concealed you far off amid the shady silence of gardens.

O if I could have violated your retreats as I wandered, wearied and panting for a better life! Look after your new countryman and, o leafy citizens, elect me, having obtained my wish, into your flowery kingdoms.

I call to witness you Muses and you, all-knowing Apollo, that the herds of men and the bellowings of the Circus or the lowings of the forum do not please me also; but the sanctuaries of the spring, silent veneration and solitary communities draw me.

Whom does the charm of virginal beauty not hold in suspense, which though conquering snow in its whiteness, and purple in its redness, yet your ardent virtue surpasses, in my judgement. Hair is unable to compete with foliage nor arms with branches, nor can voices equal your tremulous whisperings.

Ah how often have I beheld (who would believe it?) cruel lovers engraving the name of their mistress upon bark, which possesses greater strength, nor were they ashamed to inscribe wounds upon sacred trunks; as for me, if ever I have violated your stocks, no Neaera, Chloe, Faustina, Corinna will be read, but each tree shall bear its own seal on its own bark. O dear plane tree, cypress, poplar, elm!

Here Love, divested of his wings, walks about clad in sandals, laying aside his enervated bows and his hissing weapons, and he upturns his torches and does not wish that he be consistently feared; or else he lies stretched out and falls asleep upon his quiver; not inclined to listen even though Cytherea calls, nor do vain dreams relay his previous wickedness.

The gods above rejoice as the tyrant cools off and although they have known both nymphs and goddesses so many times, now each attains a superior desire in a tree. Jupiter, neglecting his wife, is dying about an aged oak. Juno did not grieve thus for another rival. No traces defile the bed of the Lemnian, not does Mars remember the Venus is the ash is present. Phoebus pressed upon the trail of the beautiful Daphne so that she might become a laurel but nothing beyond that had he sought. And as to the reason why the goat-footed Pan pursued the feeling Syrinx, this was so that he would be able to discover the sonorous reed.

Many lines are missing

Nor will you, the garden's craftsman, depart without a pleasing song, you who in brief plants and abundant blossom have marked out the growing hours and the intervals of day. There a brighter sun traverses the fragrant signs; and in the place of the fierce Bull, in the place of the drawn claw of the Crab, it glides towards the carefree shades of the violet and the rose. Moreover the busy bee intent upon its honeyed toil, seems to mark its tasks by means of thyme, its horologe. O sweet lapses of time! O health-giving ease! O hours worthy to be accounted among herbs and flowers.

34

To a Gentleman that only upon the sight of the Author's writing, had given a Character of his Person and Judgement of his Fortune

Illustrissimo Viro
Domino Lanceloto Josepho de Maniban
Grammatomanti

Date. 1676. Cooke, I.6–7, following Ambrose Philips, *Freethinker*, 253 (22 August 1722), 328–35, assumed that M. had met Maniban in Bordeaux, possibly during M.'s travels in Europe during the 1640s. But at l. 14, M. claims that he did not know Maniban. Legouis, *RES*, 2 (1926), 328–35, and 1971, noted that M.'s nephew, William Popple, lived in Bordeaux from 1670 until after M.'s death, and suggested that M.'s mention of a French Abbot in a letter to Popple of 17 July 1676 (Legouis (1971), II.346) may refer to Maniban. Legouis' inference was that Popple gave a letter of M.'s to Maniban.

Publication. 1681.

Context. M. wrote to William Popple on 15 July 1676, with a postscript dated 17 July, one month after the publication of *Mr Smirke*. The letter reveals a man concerned to maintain secrecy: he talks about the author of *Mr Smirke* in the third person, two passages in the letter are in Latin, and a note on the outside instructs the carrier not to read it. The sensitive public context in which M. found himself at this time is reflected in the speaker's unease at having himself 'discovered' by the graphologist.

Sources, Genre and Criticism. The poem is a verse letter: for M.'s exploitation of this genre, see above, 19–20. Legouis's interest aside, the poem has been almost entirely overlooked until very recently. Creaser (in Chernaik and Dzelzainis, eds (1999), 159–60) seeks to raise the reputation of this 'underrated' poem. He regards the poem not merely as an ironic treatment of predictive astrology, but as an ironic and witty treatment of the relationship between consciousness and expression. Maniban 'reads' people from their writing but since 'Marvell is indeed writing, irony lies in the very existence of the poem. If so secretive a man [as M.] took Maniban seriously, the last thing he would do would be to write about it.' Creaser takes seriously the final comments on the consequence of astrology being a disdain for life. M. 'will have nothing to do with views which deprive individuals of their responsibility for themselves.' The poem thus hints at free will theology, over and against extreme views of determinism, providential or astrological.

To a Gentleman that only upon the sight of the Author's writing, had given a Character of his Person and Judgement of his Fortune

Illustrissimo Viro
Domino Lanceloto Josepho de Maniban
Grammatomanti

Quis posthac chartae committat sensa loquaci,
   Si sua crediderit fata subesse stylo?
Conscia si prodat scribentis litera sortem,
   Quicquid et in vita plus latuisse velit?
5 Flexibus in calami tamen omnia sponte leguntur
   Quod non significant verba, figura notat.
Bellerophonteas signat sibi quisque tabellas;
   Ignaramque manum spiritus intus agit.
Nil praeter solitum sapiebat epistola nostra,
10 Exemplumque meae simplicitatis erat.
Fabula jucundos qualis delectat amicos;
   Urbe, lepore, novis, carmine tota scatens.

Hic tamen interpres quo non securior alter,
   (Non res, non voces, non ego notus ei)
15 Rimatur fibras notularum cautus aruspex,
   Scripturaeque inhians consulit exta meae.
Inde statim vitae casus, animique recessus
   Explicat; (haud genio plura liquere putem.)
Distribuit totum nostris eventibus orbem,
20 Et quo me rapiat cardine sphaera docet.
Quae Sol oppositus, quae Mars adversa minetur,
   Jupiter aut ubi me, Luna, Venusque juvent.
Ut trucis intentet mihi vulnera cauda draconis;
   Vipereo levet ut vulnera more caput.
25 Hinc mihi praeteriti rationes atque futuri
   Elicit; astrologus certior astronomo.
Ut conjecturas nequeam discernere vero,
   Historiae superet sed genitura fidem.
Usque adeo caeli respondet pagina nostrae,
30 Astrorum et nexus syllaba scripta refert.
Scilicet et toti subsunt oracula mundo,
   Dummodo tot foliis una Sibylla foret.

Sub-title. Grammatomanti] 'Graphology' came into use as the term for the study of handwriting in the late nineteenth century. The first recorded usage for the sense of inferring a person's character from the peculiarities of his handwriting (*OED* 2) is 1886. M.'s *grammatomanti* literally means 'diviner of writing', being made up from *gramma* (a stroke of the pen; post-classical Latin) and *mantis* (soothsayer or diviner). The Latin cognates are ambiguous, and M. would have been aware of this: *grammaticus* is an expert on literary or linguistic matters, but a *grammatista* is an elementary schoolmaster.
1. chartae] *charta*: originally papyrus (Lewis and Short).
4. latuisse] *lateo*: in one sense, expressing one of M.'s concerns at this time: the retired life (Lewis and Short, II.A). Cp. Ovid, *Tristia*, III.iv, l. 25: 'crede mihi, bene qui latuit bene vixit' (believe me, he who hides well his life, lives well).
7. Bellerophonteas . . . tabellas] Bellerophon was sent, through the instigation of his wife Stheneboea, by King Proeteus of Argos to King Iobates of Lycia with a letter requesting that the bearer be put to death. Used proverbially to mean any one who carries a message unfavourable to himself (Lewis and Short). See Hyginus, *Fabulae*, 57.2. The legend also appears in Homer, *Iliad*, VI, ll. 152–97, where Bellerophon escaped by performing several heroic deeds. The episode is the only evidence in Homer showing knowledge of the art of writing.
tabellas] written composition, letter, contract; transferred in plural from *tabella*: writing tablet.
8. spiritus intus agit] a conflation of Virgil, *Aeneid*, VI, ll. 726–7, where 'agit' humorously replaces 'alit': 'spiritus intus alit, totamque infusa per artus/mens agitat molem' (a spirit within sustains, and mind, pervading its members, sways the whole mass) (McQueen and Rockwell).
9. nostra] translated as 'my' by McQueen and Rockwell, who assume the use of the word as the possessive genitive of the first person (Lewis and Short, I.A). Yet M. could be referring to

himself and William Popple: the letter was sent from Marvell to Popple (see above, *Headnote. Context*).
13. securior] surer in the sense of a) certain, accurate b) free from apprehension (see l. 14, 'non ego notus ei').
14. voces] words: transferred from *voco*, to name (Lewis and Short, B 5), hence 'names'; 'voces' also carries undertones of *vocalis*: prophetic speech (see, e.g., Ovid, *Metamorphoses*, XIII, l. 716), which Maniban must interpret. M. means that Maniban saw a letter in English (Margoliouth).
15–16. Cp. Juvenal, *Satire*, VI, ll. 550–1: 'haruspex;/pectora pullorum rimabitur, exta catelli' (a soothsayer, he will probe the breast of a chicken, or the entrails of a puppy).
15. aruspex] haruspex, an Etruscan diviner who foretold future events by inspecting the entrails of sacrifices.
16. exta] organs from which the *haruspices* made their prognostications (the heart, lungs and liver).
19. i.e. he shows how each part of the zodiac determines my fortunes.
20. cardine] axes of the celestial sphere. *sphaera*] the celestial sphere.
23–4. Ut . . . caput] Draco, a northern constellation of thirty-one stars. In astrology, the head was beneficent, but the tail malignant. See, e.g., John Tanner, 'Common Notes of the Year 1676' in *Angelus Brittannicus. An Ephemeris for the Year of our Redemption* (1676), sig. A1ᵛ: 'The Names and Characters of the Seven Planets', 'Saturn, Jupiter, Mars, Sol, Venus, Mercury, Moon,/Dragons And a Tail.'
27. Ut] *Contra* McQueen and Rockwell, Legouis argues that 'ut' must mean 'so that'.
32. foliis] a) plant leaves (upon which the Sibyll wrote) (Lewis and Short, I) b) leaves of paper (Lewis and Short, III). *Sibylla*] the Cumaean Sibyl (see Virgil, *Aeneid*, III, ll. 441–52), a woman who prophesied by writing symbols on leaves; the wind blew the leaves about, leaving men to guess their contents.

Partum, Fortunae mater Natura, propinquum
    Mille modis monstrat mille per indicia:
5 Ingentemque uterum quâ mole puerpera solvat;
    Vivit at in praesens maxima pars hominum.
Ast tu sorte tuâ gaude celeberrime vatum;
    Scribe, sed haud superest qui tua fata legat.
Nostra tamen si fas praesagia jungere vestris,
10 Quo magis inspexti sydera spernis humum.
Et, nisi stellarum fueris divine propago,
    Naupliada credam te Palamede satum
Qui dedit ex avium scriptoria signa volatu,
    Sydereaque idem nobilis arte fuit.
15 Hinc utriusque tibi cognata scientia crevit,
    Nec minus augurium litera quam dat avis.

To That Renowned Man
Lord Lancelot Joseph
de Maniban, A Graphologist

Who henceforth would entrust his feelings to talkative paper if he believed that his own destiny underlies his pen; if the guilty letter betrays the fortune of the writer and whatever in life he would wish had been more concealed? Nevertheless in the flexings of the pen everything is read of its own accord; what the words do not signify, the shape denotes. Each signs for himself the tablets of Bellerophon and a spirit within activates the ignorant hand. Our letter had a taste of nothing beyond what was customary, and was an example of my simplicity – the sort of gossip that delights charming friends, utterly abounding in the city, wit, news, poetry. Still, this interpreter, than whom no other is more assured (not the subject-matter, not the voice, not I were known to him) a shrewd soothsayer, he pries into the entrails of my little marks, and gaping, he consults the innards of my writing. Then immediately he unfolds the events of my life and the recesses of my mind (I should think that no more is obvious to my guardian spirit). He apportions the entire zodiac to my fortunes, and teaches by what pole the sphere whirls me along; what adversities the sun in opposition, and Mars may threaten, or where Jupiter, the moon, and Venus may assist me; how the tail of the fierce Dragon threatens wounds upon me, how in the manner of a serpent his head may alleviate the wounds. Hence an astrologer, more assured than an astronomer, he elicits for me computations of the past and of the future. Although I may be unable to distinguish conjectures from truth, still the horoscope overcomes the reliability of history. To such an extent does the page of heaven correspond with ours, and the written syllable represent the interworkings of the stars. Undoubtedly oracles underlie the entire universe provided that a single Sibyl exists in so many leaves. Nature, the mother of Fortune, reveals in a thousand ways and through a thousand signs an imminent birth, and by what childbearing labour she may relieve the enormity of her womb; yet the greatest part of men dwells in the present. But you, most famous of seers, rejoice in your lot; write, but no one remains who can read your prophetic utterances. However, if it is right to join our presentiments to yours, the more you have examined the stars, the more you spurn the earth, and unless you are the stars' divine offspring, I would believe that you are sprung from Palamedes, son of Nauplius, who provided written symbols from the flight of birds, and was likewise famous in the art of the stars. Hence the related knowledge of both has increased in you; the letter provides no less augury than the bird.

33–5. An allusion to Virgil, *Eclogue*, IV, ll. 4–10, in which the rebirth of the classical Golden Age is predicted (and was taken to refer to the birth of Christ). McQueen and Rockwell are puzzled by the apparent disconnectedness of the two lines from the rest of the poem. But the allusion was suggested to M. by the mention of the Cumaean Sibyll at l. 32. M. had made extensive use of this eclogue in his Latin poem praising Queen Christina of Sweden, verse that expounds Protestant millennial themes (see below, *A Letter to Doctor Ingelo, then with my Lord Whitelocke, Ambassador from the Protector to the Queen of Sweden,* ll. 15, 22–3, 83 nn.). This poem was written in 1654. Stocker, *SP*, 84 (1987), 163–4, argues that in his later poem, M. is ridiculing Maniban further by juxtaposing dubious graphology with vatic prophecy. But in l. 36, M. also appears to express doubts concerning the usefulness of millenarian predictions, as if he were reversing the confidence of 1650s millennial poetry.

42–3. Naupliada . . . volatu] Palamedes, son of Nauplius, King of Euboea, was supposed to have added the letter 'Y', Latin 'V', (and others) to the alphabet after seeing cranes in flight (see Pliny, VII.lvi.192; Martial, *Epigrams,* XIII.lxxv, l. 2). The reference contains another critical (and this time, threatening) remark: Palamedes was stoned to death in front of Troy because of a forged letter that Ulysses concealed under his bed. For other versions, see Hyginus, *Fabulae,* 105.

35

Flecknoe, an English Priest at Rome

Date. Not earlier than March 1646. Richard Flecknoe, English secular priest, probable Jesuit, poet, musician and exile, arrived in Rome in 1645. M. arrived in Rome towards the end of 1645. He may well have dined with Flecknoe at the English College in Rome in late December 1645 (27th and 30th), but not earlier (see below, *Context*). However, the reference to Lent (l. 46) makes a March date as *terminus ad quem* most likely.

Publication. 1681. However discriminating this satire might have seemed at the supposed time of its composition, it would most probably have seemed virulently anti-Catholic at the time of its publication, in the aftermath of the Popish Plot (1679). Anti-Catholic verse satire was popular at this time: see, e.g., John Oldham, *Satyrs upon the Jesuits* (1681); John Wilmot, Earl of Rochester *et al.*, *Rome Rym'd to Death* (1683).

Context. Richard Flecknoe (*c.* 1605–*c.* 1677) was born in the vicinity of Little Harrowden, Orlingby Hundred, Northamptonshire (not Ireland, as was once supposed; see Mayer, in Flecknoe (1987), xlvi, clii–clv). He was supposed to have been converted to Roman Catholicism by a Jesuit at Liège *c.* 1620 and was imprisoned in Newgate shortly thereafter before he returned to Saint-Omer to study philosophy and theology. However, his connections with English Catholic peers in Northamptonshire, notably Lord Vaux, may mean that his Catholicism was actually rooted in his home background. He was ordained priest (probably by the Jesuits; he was most probably a lay-priest) in 1636, returned to England and offended non-Jesuit priests in London with his staging of a 'lascivious play' (either *Love's Kingdom*, or another work now lost) in early 1638. In 1640, Flecknoe left England, spent some time in the Spanish Netherlands, but left for Italy in 1644 because of continued violence in the north, and was in Rome by January 1645. The young Duke of Buckingham elevated Flecknoe to his 'poeticall Academy' of exiles in Rome, and the poet-musician-priest's associates while in Rome (including the Duchess of Lorraine, Cardinal Caraffa and the Duchess Maidalchini) are at odds with the picture painted by M., although Flecknoe's tiny quarters, as portrayed by M., would not have been inconsistent with his way of life. In the later 1640s, Flecknoe left Rome for Spain, Portugal and America, before eventually returning to England in the 1650s.

Flecknoe thrived upon, and made much of, his patronage by aristocrats, in England and on the continent. He was an accomplished lutenist, and was much sought after as an entertainer in great houses. As a priest, he could offer advice, but he was also a minstrel and a raconteur. Most of his works were written quickly and geared specifically to the sensibilities of his patrons, eschewing aesthetic innovation.

Marvell dined in the English College, but not because he was tutor to a member of the Skinner family, as was once supposed. Chaney (348–50) makes the case that Marvell in fact received patronage from the second Duke of Buckingham and his brother, Lord Francis Villiers, for whom M. was later to write an elegy (see *An Elegy upon the Death of My Lord Francis Villiers*). M. may have met Flecknoe while dining with Buckingham at the College. The young M. would have been useful to Flecknoe as an avenue to Buckingham, whose patronage the (by this time) impoverished exile urgently sought. Norbrook (1999), 168, suggests that M.'s poem offers Buckingham a warning about the 'kinds of company he should avoid keeping'. Full detail of Flecknoe's relationships with his continental patrons is given by Burdon, *N & Q*, n.s. 217 (1972), 16–18.

Sources and Genre. The resonances, in content and in style, of M.'s poem with earlier satires are many and complex. Despite this eclecticism, M.'s satire is highly original, developing an extended conceit in which the function of the emaciated poetaster's manuscript copies as clothing becomes the site for a series of playful, sometimes lurid, but not overtly hostile, observations upon, and engagements with, Roman Catholic habits and worship. Despite this levity, the poem nonetheless profanes Catholic sacramental language, and images that profanity in its own structure (Norbrook (1999), 168).

Flecknoe himself is presented as a priestly version of one of the characters at Trimalchio's dinner in Petronius's *Satyricon*: Seleucus (l. 42), for instance, is a bore, as is Flecknoe with his bad verse, while Ganymedes (l. 44) complains of poverty. Dinner is also the setting for the earlier satires of Horace, especially II.viii. Flecknoe's persistence echoes the tiresome speaker of I.ix, who resorts to verse (ll. 26–34), while poetic hackery for the sake of advancement, hinted at by M. (and certainly a major purpose behind Flecknoe's verse) is identified in II.v, ll. 74–6 as a means of legacy-hunting: 'scribet mala carmina vecors:/laudato' (Will the idiot write poor verses? Praise them). As with Petronius, the satire of bodily excess in Horace seems to be inverted in M.: 'quin corpus onustum/hesternis vitiis animum quoque praegravat una/atque adfigit humo divinae particulam aurae' (Nay more, clogged with yesterday's excess, the body drags down with itself the mind as well, and fastens to earth a fragment of the divine spirit). (II.ii, ll. 77–9; see below, ll. 49–51).

The influential English satires of the late sixteenth and early seventeenth centuries, most notably those of Donne and Joseph Hall, are not models for Marvell (*pace* Legouis; see also Patterson (2000), 73). Both earlier satirists attack character types and manners rather than individuals, or in Hall's case, where individuals are involved, disguised names are used. Nonetheless, clear similarities are evident. The dining location is associated with religious practice by Hall, *Virgidemiarum*, III.iii, ll. 1–4. Donne's *Satire* I exemplifies his use of extended conceit and his interest, like M., in enclosed space:

> Leave mee, and in this standing woodden chest,
> Consorted with these few bookes, let me lye
> In prison, and here be coffin'd, when I dye;
> Here are Gods conduits, grave Divines; and here
> Natures Secretary, the Philosopher;
> And jolly Statesmen, which teach how to tie
> The sinewes of a cities mistique bodie. (2–8)

Just as the speaker's encounter with the bizarre courtier in Donne's *Satire* IV, ll. 17 ff. is a confident adaptation of Roman conventions, so M.'s poem makes its own way with a multitude of classical topoi and conventions.

The theological and literary jokes bear a close relationship with some contemporary satires, and in particular Thomas Jordan's 'A Poet's farewell to his threadbare Cloak': 'He that would Cloak it in the new Translation,/Must have his Taylor cut it Pulpit-Fashion' (Bodl. MS Rawl. poet 84, fol. 75ʳ). This was published in printed form first in Sir John Mennes and James Smith's 1655 collection *Musarum Deliciae*, but some manuscript copies of the poem indicate an earlier (possibly considerably earlier) date for the composition and initial circulation of the poem. Where the cloak of M.'s Flecknoe covers his transparency, Jordan's poet's threadbare cloak is the object of transparency: 'Transparent garment, proof against no weather,/Men wonder by what art thou hang'st together' (Bodl. MS Rawl. poet 84, fol. 74ᵛ).

The funeral imagery in the poem bears close affinities, almost to the point of echo, not with Donne's satires, but with his elegiac poetry, as Donne's conceits are lifted from a panegyrical context and placed in a diametrically opposite framework. In *The Anniversaries*, the dead Elizabeth Drury is imagined as wrapped in the 'rags of paper' of the poet's verse ('A Funeral Elegy', ll. 11–12); in M.'s poem, Flecknoe dresses in the rags of his poetry. Elizabeth Drury was so pure it was as if she was transparent (ibid., ll. 59–60); Flecknoe is transparent because he has eaten so little. Hartwig, *SEL*, 36 (1996), 171–212 (172), argues that there are structural and conceptual affinities between M.'s poem and another Donne poem, 'Infinitati Sacrum, 16 August 1601. Metempsychosis. Poêma Satyricon. The Progresse of the Soule': Flecknoe passes through a series of changing identities and associations that achieve satirical purchase in a parody of the 'progress of the soul' narrative: pelican, lute, frog/toad, chameleon, camel, God, Perillus. Flecknoe in his 'coffin' of a room replaces Donne's soul in its initial 'low room' (l. 70) of Adam's body. Some of Donne's conceited imagery is also a source for M.: 'th'ends did themselves digest/Into ten lesser strings, these fingers were:/And as a slumberer stretching on his bed,/This way he this, and that way scattered/His other legge' (ll. 142–6; see below, ll. 41–4).

Much of M.'s poem appears to be a riposte to Flecknoe's ideals, beliefs, behaviour and poetry. Flecknoe's idealistic poetic, not unlike Milton's, sees music and poetry as a harmonious combination that reflects divine truth: 'which ballads . . . was in manner the sole relict of this divine Science, until *Claudio Montanvendo* [*sic*] (in our Fathers days) principally revived by his admirable Skill (like another *Prometheus*) conjoyning in one body again the scattered limbs of *Orpheus* (Musick and Poetry)', *Ariadne Deserted by Theseus* (1654), sigs. A4ᵛ–A5ʳ (see below, ll. 6–7). While Flecknoe developed his own version of simple bawdy drollery and satire in the later 1650s (see, e.g., *Life of Tomaso the Wanderer* (1667)), he also had an explanation for the simple diction and syntax of his idealizing earlier verse: 'so have I endeavour'd short periods and frequent rithmes, with words smooth and facile, such as most easily might enter into the mind, and be digested by the understanding', *Ariadne Deserted by Theseus* (1654), sig. A7ʳ. If Flecknoe was interested in mock-heroic drollery as early as the time that M. met him, some of the poem's imagery could be seen as an appropriate mock-heroic response (e.g. ll. 41–4), as well as an attack upon Flecknoe's notorious snobbery.

Flecknoe published little before the mid-1650s, but his later collections contain poems from the period when he met M. His poverty and his ceaseless search for patronage is documented in his own poetry:

> I must beg of you, Sir, nay what is more,
> ('Tis a disease so infectious to be poor)
> Must beg you'd beg for me: which whilst I do,
> What is't but even to make you beggar too?
> > 'To Sir K[enelm] D[igby] in Italy, Anno 46
> > Recommending to him a certain Memorial'
> > (see below, ll. 48–9, 53)

What to M. was Flecknoe's 'hideous verse . . . in dismal tone' (l. 20) could be represented by many examples, one of which is these lines from *Love's Kingdom* (?1638, publ. 1664), 17:

> Now Children, in a word to tell,
> what noble love is, (mark me well)
> it is the counterpoise that mindes
> to fair and vertuous things inclines;
> it is the gust we have, and sence,
> of every noble excellence.

Style, Structure and Versification. The poem is notable for highly wrought and sustained conceits and puns. Reilly, *JDJ*, 2 (1983), 51–62, notes the construction of complex metaphors out of puns, usually directed towards the mockery of Catholicism. ll. 9–18 are thus developed around the conceit of Flecknoe's room as a coffin, the theme being death, the decorations presenting Catholicism as 'a religion

of spiritual death'. The space-saving ingenuity with which the room is constructed invokes the priest-holes of English Recusant houses, with its associations of secrecy and (in Protestant eyes) deceit, as well as duress.

Thus, within the governing genre of satire, the poem moves through a series of religious situations. The first is martyrdom, with the humorous presentation of the Protestant speaker being a 'martyr' to the Catholic priest's vile poetry. Foxe's *Acts and Monuments* is a background presence here: the reference to Nero (l. 126) recalls Foxe's account of the primitive church; both Foxe and M. use Suetonius as a source. Duncan-Jones, *PBA*, 61 (1975), 276, suggests that M.'s speaker is identifying with St Lawrence, since he turns first one, then another 'burning ear' to Flecknoe, just as the saint asked his torturers to turn him over on the gridiron. Then comes Flecknoe's fasting for Lent, itself succeeded by the parodic communion of the meal. Flecknoe's body is wittily presented as the host, enabling allusions to the Catholic theology of transubstantiation (ll. 58–62), the doctrine of the Trinity and the authority of the Church's teaching (ll. 75–8), and Protestant–Catholic disputes concerned with the reading of the Latin Bible and the understanding of Scripture, in addition to the ridicule of Flecknoe's poetic practice.

The poem makes a series of obscure and abstruse references in the services of humour, but it does so through the voice tone of a speaker that is supremely confident. The requirement of the rhyming couplet is expertly and unforcedly met yet effortlessly combined with lively speech rhythms and conversational manners, which offer suspension, balance and interruptive variety (with sentence endings often occurring in the first or second, or the penultimate or final, feet) within the regular iambic pattern. As an early poem, M. offers what the reader is meant to take as a thoroughly virtuoso, precocious performance, over and against the awful grotesquery of Flecknoe's songs, and their tuneless performances by the youth.

Modern Criticism. There is very little sustained commentary or criticism on the poem. Hammond, *E in C*, 35 (1985), 315–30 (315), doubts that M.'s poem can have been an influence upon Dryden's *Mac Flecknoe*, since that poem was written before M.'s poem was published. James Granger, *A Biographical History of England* (1769–74), praised *Flecknoe* as the best of Marvell's satires. Chernaik (1983), 165–74, admires the poem as a satire, in particular the 'construction of the sympathetic and credible narrator', whose 'pursuit of uncompromising truth is problematic', although the poet's cruelty in the portrayal of Flecknoe's poverty is acknowledged. Martin, *E in C*, 40 (1990), 54–66, argues against a long line of negative assessments that the poem is remarkably subtle, the poet revealing his own earlier encounter with Catholicism in Cambridge, and showing an awareness of the shortcomings and corruptions of the satirist as well as those of his target of attack. This assessment is upheld by Hartwig, *SEL*, 36 (1996), 171–212, who provides the first extensive theological and iconographic reading of the poem. Her judgement that M. 'devastates Flecknoe for the reader, but we do not emerge from the poem without recognizing that Flecknoe creates a field of energy even as he remains especially unmoved by others' responses' (206) points up M.'s early

concerns with the potentials and limitations of other poets as a means of understanding his own identity and capability.

Flecknoe, an English Priest at Rome

Obliged by frequent visits of this man,
Whom as priest, poet, and musician,
I for some branch of Melchizedek took,
(Though he derives himself from my Lord Brooke)
5   I sought his lodging; which is at the sign
Of the sad Pelican; subject divine
For poetry: there three staircases high,
Which signifies his triple property,
I found at last a chamber, as 'twas said,
10   But seemed a coffin set on the stairs' head.
Not high'r than sev'n, nor larger than three feet;
Only there was nor ceiling, nor a sheet,

1. Obliged] a) morally bound (*OED* ppl. a. 1) b) compelled (*OED* ppl. a. 2). M. chooses a word central to the patronage relationships which Flecknoe sought to exploit: 'I esteem more this occasion to have found a Treasure, as in effect 'tis one to oblige ones Friends. You may give this inclosed to Monsieur d'Avencourt, who will make no difficulty to deliver you the sum therin exprest, neither does know wherefore 'tis, but may imagine I owe it you,' Flecknoe, quoting Mme de Beauvais to himself in a letter to Lord Marquis Cavallo Bajan, Rome, 1645, *A Relation of Ten Years Travel* (1656), 36.
2. poet . . . musician] see below, l. 3 n.
3. branch] descendant (*OED* n. II 5b). *Melchizedek*] a) King of Salem, 'priest of the most high God' and blesser of Abraham (Gen. 14:18) b) seen as a type of Christ because he was a priest but not of the priesthood ('not after the law of a carnal commandment, but after the power of an endless life' (Heb. 7:15–21)), so making the genealogical connection even more deflatingly ironic. Hartwig, *SEL*, 36 (1996), 171–212 (190), suggests that because Melchizedek was regarded also as a theophanic pre-incarnation (the bodily appearance of the Lord upon earth), since he had neither father nor mother (Heb. 7:3), Flecknoe, whose body is 'constituted' out of papers, is a parodic imitation of him.
4. Lord Brooke] M. presents this association as a typical Flecknoe boast, and therefore as an untruth. Poetically, Flecknoe did have great respect for Fulke Greville, Lord Brooke (1554–1628), regarding him as an important poet ('Whose *Master-strokes*, great wits do look upon/With reverence and admiration', '*On the Works of* Fulk Grevil, *Lord* Brook', ll. 3–4, in *Epigrams* (1671), 10), and, along with Sidney, as responsible for the introduction of courtly wit from Italy, of which he regarded himself as the true inheritor (*A Treatise of the Sports of Wit* (1662), sig. A4ᵛ). In the 1640s, the most well known Brooke, was Robert, son of Fulke, Puritan, theological writer and Parliamentarian commander. In fact, Flecknoe was patronized by a staunchly Catholic branch of the Brooke family, Sir Basil Brooke of Madely, Shropshire, and his daughter-in-law, Lady Neville Brooke, to whom Flecknoe's *The Affection of a Pious Soule* (1640) was dedicated.

5–6. sign . . . sad Pelican] an inn name: there was a Pelican Inn in Little Britain, London, mentioned in the will of John Oxenbridge, Boston Public Library, MS Am. 1502, v. 2, no. 15). M. also described the bookshop selling Samuel Parker's *Tentamina* at the same place: 'But where was his Shop? *Ad insigne Pelicani*. A very Emblematical sign where you digged and pick'd your very Heart-blood and Brains out to nourish your young *Tentamina*. Where was this? *in parva Britannia*', *RT*, 260. Hartwig, *SEL*, 36 (1996), 171–212 (172–84), discusses the iconographic and emblematic traditions of pelican representation in the Renaissance. The self-sacrificing pelican (tearing its breast to feed its young) sometimes symbolized Christ; just so, Flecknoe suffers for his religion and his art. However, these associations are reversed at l. 127 where Flecknoe is identified with the other symbolic values attached to the pelican: gluttony and garrulity. The lodging itself might have been one of the considerable properties of the English College, which before the Reformation had been a pilgrim-hospice since 1362.
7–8. three staircases . . . triple property] a joke at the expense of Flecknoe's Catholicism, parodying the triple tiara of the Pope. For Flecknoe's 'properties', see above, l. 2.
10. head] top.
11. M. appears to literalize and invert one of Flecknoe's conceits, although he presumably did not see it when he first wrote the poem: 'while their [cardinals'] Bodies inhabit whole Acres of Palaces, their souls in their straight narrow bosoms are stifled for want of room', *A Relation of Ten Years Travells* (1656), 34. *sev'n . . . three*] two of the most sacred numbers.
12. ceiling] a) screen of tapestry, curtain (*OED* vbl. n. II 3) b) wall panelling (*OED* vbl. n. II 4; see below, l. 14 n.) c) wall hangings; black hangings were employed at funerals (see *The First Anniversary of the Government under his Highness the Lord Protector*, l. 331) d) undercovering of roof or floor (*OED* vbl. n. II 5). *sheet*] a) article of bed-clothing (*OED* n.1 3) b) winding sheet (*OED* n.1 2) M. offers puns on both words, but through the influence of l. 10, suggests that the funerary meanings prevail.

Save that th'ingenious door did, as you come
Turn in, and show to wainscot half the room.
15 Yet of his state no man could have complained;
There being no bed where he entertained:
And though within one cell so narrow pent,
He'd stanzas for a whole *apartement*.
    Straight without further information,
20 In hideous verse, he, and a dismal tone,
Begins to exercise, as if I were
Possessed; and sure the Devil brought me there.
But I, who now imagined my self brought
To my last trial, in a serious thought
25 Calmed the disorders of my youthful breast,
And to my martyrdom prepar\`ed rest.
Only this frail ambition did remain,
The last distemper of the sober brain,
That there had been some present to assure

30 The future ages how I did endure:
And how I, silent, turned my burning ear
Towards the verse; and when that could not hear,
Held him the other; and unchang\`ed yet,
Asked still for more, and prayed him to repeat:
35 Till the tyrant, weary to persecute,
Left off, and tried t'allure me with his lute.
    Now as two instruments, to the same key
Being tun'd by art, if the one touch\`ed be
The other opposite as soon replies,
40 Moved by the air and hidden sympathies;
So while he with his gouty fingers crawls
Over the lute, his murm'ring belly calls,
Whose hungry guts to the same straitness twined
In echo to the trembling strings repined.
45   I, that perceived now what his music meant,
Asked civilly if he had eat this Lent.

---

13. ingenious] cleverly or skilfully constructed (*OED* a. I 3 b).
14. wainscot] wainscot was wooden panelling (usually oak) used to line walls of a dwelling; hence to line with wooden panel-work (*OED* v. 1); the door opens inwards to function as panelling for half the room.
16. There . . . entertained] Reilly, *JDJ*, 2 (1983), 51–62 (55–6) suggests an allusion to the Protestant belief that Catholic priests were guilty of sexual immorality, although customarily nobles received visitors while in bed.
18. stanzas] a) rooms (Italian; *OED* 2) b) groups of lines of verse (*OED* 1). *apartement*] set of rooms (French; *OED* 1); a jibe at Flecknoe's love of the large salon gatherings of his patronesses: '*From thence they went to Supper, and having supp'd, retired into a large* Apartement, *lluminated by the six fair* Christal Branches, *and bordered about with* Silver sconzaes, *in which were inchac'd* Concave Mirrours *of* Oval Form *for better reflection of the* Light' (*A Treatise of the Sports of Wit* (1662), 10).
20. and] *1681*; in a Bod. 1. *dismal*] Cp. Virgil, *Eclogues*, III, ll. 26–7: 'non tu in triviis, solebas/stridenti miserum stipula disperdere carmen?' (Was it not you, Master Dunce, who at the crossroads used to murder a sorry tune on a scrannel straw?).
20–2. he, and a . . . Possessed] Flecknoe later claimed that music (in association with poetry) cast out evil spirits: *Ariadne Deserted by Theseus* (1654), sig. A4ʳ.
21. exercise] a) to perform (in this case, to recite; *OED* v. 5ᵃ) b) to conduct a religious service or expound scripture (*OED* v. 7) c) with the meaning of 'exorcize' – to drive evil spirits from a person possessed with them (*OED* v. 2).
24. last trial] the 'last trial' of Paul by King Agrippa is recounted in Acts 26.
27–8. frail ambition . . . sober brain] see Milton, *Lycidas* (1637), ll. 70–1: 'Fame is the spur that the clear spirit doth raise/ (That last infirmity of noble mind).'
27. frail] morally weak (*OED* a .3).
31–3. ear . . . other] Cp. Matt. 5:39: 'But I say unto you, That ye resist not evil: but whosoever shall smite thee on thy right cheek, turn to him the other also.'

32. could not hear] *1681*; could n *1681* (BL c.59.i.8).
33. unchang\`ed] not dead (see *OED* n. 1 d).
36. allure] charm (*OED* v. 3); Hartwig, *SEL*, 36 (1996), 171–212 (184), argues that M.'s speaker makes a lewd reference to the lute's role as an instrument of seduction, as much as its music was seen to symbolize divine harmony. *lute*] 'travelling into *Italy* I found that Musick I intended to introduce, exceedingly in vogue, and far advanced towards its perfection, which made me study the perfectioning myself therein', Flecknoe, *Ariadne Deserted by Theseus* (1654), sig. A3ᵛ.
40. hidden sympathies] usually expressed as 'secret sympathies': see, e.g., Du Bartas, trans. Sylvester, *Divine Weekes and Workes* (1621), 'The Imposture', l. 203, but see also Francis Kynaston, *Rhodon and Iris* (1631), l. 737. *sympathies*] a) affinity between things, by which they can influence one another (*OED* n. 1 a) b) in the light of ll. 41–3, hinting at *OED* n. 1 b, a relation between bodily organs, where one induces the condition of the other.
41. gouty] swollen (*OED* a. 3).
43–4. hungry guts . . . repined] a witty comparison: instrument strings were made from twined animal guts; Flecknoe's guts are so taut and empty with hunger, they twine themselves into strings inside him and sound in echo to the lute. Hartwig, *SEL*, 36 (1996), 171–212 (189), notes that lute bodies were frequently buckled by the tension of the strings within a year or two of use; similarly, Flecknoe's body is 'sunk' by the 'strings' of his stomach. Cp. Fletcher, *Love's Cure* (1622/23), 2.1, in F. Bowers, ed., *The Dramatic Works in the Beaumont and Fletcher Canon*, 3 (1976), 27: 'they say her guts shrunk all into Lutestrings, and her nether-parts cling'd together like a Serpents Taile, so that though she continued a woman still above the girdle, beneath she was monster'. In the same discussion, the notion that poets live upon nothing in that they live upon their wits is raised.
43. straitness] a) tightness (*OED* n. 1 a) b) privation (*OED* n. 4).
44. repined] murmured with discontent (*OED* v. 1 intr.).
46. civilly] a) politely (*OED* adv. 6) b) 'morally' as opposed to spiritually, as distinct from Flecknoe's religiosity (*OED* adv. 4).

He answered yes; with such, and such an one.
For he has this of gen'rous, that alone
He never feeds; save only when he tries
With gristly tongue to dart the passing flies.
I asked if he eat flesh. And he, that was
So hungry that, though ready to say Mass,
Would break his fast before, said he was sick,
And th'ordinance was only politic.
Nor was I longer to invite him scant:
Happy at once to make him Protestant,
And silent. Nothing now our dinner stayed
But till he had himself a body made.
I mean till he were dressed: for else so thin
He stands, as if he only fed had been
With consecrated wafers: and the Host

Hath sure more flesh and blood than he can boast.
This *basso relievo* of a man,
Who as a camel tall, yet eas'ly can
The needle's eye thread without any stitch,
(His only impossible is to be rich)
Lest his too subtle body, growing rare,
Should leave his soul to wander in the air,
He therefore circumscribes himself in rhymes;
And swaddled in's own papers seven times,
Wears a close jacket of poetic buff,
With which he doth his third dimension stuff.
Thus armèd underneath, he over all
Does make a primitive *sottana* fall;
And above that yet casts an antique cloak,
Torn at the first Council of Antioch;

---

47. yes . . . one] to eat in company implies that Flecknoe persuaded others to pay for his meals.

48. gen'rous] from nobility (*OED* a. 1 absol.); Flecknoe was known for pursuing noble patronage at any expense of producing verse (see above, *Headnote, Context*).

49–50. save . . . flies] Hartwig, *SEL*, 36 (1996), 171–212 (190), notes the association of frogs and toads with the devil. Giovanni Valeriano, *Hyroglyphica* (Basel, 1550), 210–12, associates nine human states with frogs, including 'imperfectus', 'poetae' and 'longo post tempore progrediens' (slow to learn).

51. eat flesh] abstinence from the eating of meat is practised during Lent.

52–3. Mass . . . before] Roman Catholics were and are not supposed to eat before attending mass.

54. ordinance was only politic] M. has Flecknoe claim that he can eat before mass because a) he is ill b) the requirement to fast before mass is an instruction from the Pope; it is mere 'policy'.

55. scant] ungenerous (*OED* A. a. 6).

56. Protestant] since Protestants do not fast before their communion service (see above, l. 51).

57. now our dinner] Bod. 1; now dinner 1681. *silent*] Flecknoe can neither sing nor speak while eating; nor will his stomach rumble.

58. body] a parodic allusion to the Roman Catholic doctrine of transubstantiation, where the bread and wine of the communion service are believed to turn into the actual body and blood of Christ (Reilly, *JDJ*, 2 (1983), 59).

61. consecrated wafers] unleavened bread used in holy communion services, and dedicated sacrally to that purpose. *Host*] the consecrated wafers.

63. basso relievo] Italian: bas-relief – sculpture or carving which does not project from its surface in proportion to its length and breadth.

64–6. camel tall . . . rich] 'It is easier for a camel to go through the eye of a needle, than for a rich man to enter into the kingdom of God' (Matt. 19:24).

65. stitch] a) pain (*OED* n. 1 2) b) of sewing: Flecknoe's meagre clothes are threadbare (*OED* n. 1 II).

66. impossible] impossibility (*OED* B n.).

67. subtle] a) thin (*OED* a. 3) b) delicate, fine (*OED* a. 6). *rare*] thin in substance (*OED* a.¹ 1).

69. circumscribes] to write around with an inscription (as on a coin) (*OED* v. 4).

70. swaddled] a parody of the nativity scene: see Luke 2:7: 'And she brought forth her firstborn son, and wrapped him in swaddling clothes.' *seven*] parodying the frequent number of repetitions in both Old and New Testaments: e.g. Lev. 4:6: 'And the priest shall dip his finger in the blood, and sprinkle of the blood seven times before the LORD'; Luke 17:4: 'And if he trespass against thee seven times in a day, and seven times in a day turn again to thee, saying, I repent; thou shalt forgive him.'

71. close] dense in substance (*OED* a. A II 13), as opposed to 'subtle' and 'rare' at l. 67. *buff*] tough leather, used for military attire (*OED* II 2 b).

72. third dimension] depth; see above, l. 63 n.

74. primitive] a) simple b) old-fashioned, both deriving from 'primitive' in the sense of the early or primitive church (*OED* a. A I 2); see also below, l. 75 n. *sottana*] Italian: cassock, outer garment worn by Roman Catholic priests.

75. antique cloak] extravagant clothes associated with masquers and, satirically, with ecclesiastical vestments: see *Upon Appleton House*, ll. 591–2, 'Under this antic cope I move/Like some great prelate of the grove', and Milton, *An Apology for Smectymnuus* (1642; *CPW*, I.930), 'It had no Rubric to be sung in an antic Cope upon the Stage of a High Altar'. *antique*] a) variant spelling of 'antic': bizarre, fantastic, ludicrous, grotesque (*OED* A a.) b) of ancient times (*OED* A a. 1) c) old-fashioned (*OED* A a. 3). *cloak*] see above, *Headnote, Sources and Genres*.

76. Torn] Bod. 1, Wilcher; Worn 1681, Thompson, Margoliouth, Kermode, Lord, Walker. *first . . . Antioch*] the first of three third-century synods held in Antioch took place in 264; all three were concerned with rebutting the anti-trinitarian theology of Paul of Samosata, who argued that although Jesus was miraculously born of a virgin, and was penetrated by the divine Logos, yet was only a man, and not a God-man (see Hefele (1871), 118–26). The torn cloak is thus both the divided Church at Antioch, and, more importantly, the doctrine of the Trinity. Continuing the analogy between Flecknoe and Christ, M. gives the poet his final embodiment in the doctrine of the Trinity. Anti-trinitarianism had become a controversial (often radical) Protestant heresy by the mid-1640s, but nothing is made of it in this poem.

Which by the Jews long hid, and disesteemed,
He heard of by tradition, and redeemed.
But were he not in this black habit decked,
80 This half-transparent man would soon reflect
Each colour that he passed by; and be seen,
As the chamelion, yellow, blue, or green.

     He dressed, and ready to disfurnish now
His chamber, whose compactness did allow
85 No empty place for complimenting Doubt,
But who came last is forced first to go out;
I meet one on the stairs who made me stand,
Stopping the passage, and did him demand:
I answered, 'He is here Sir; but you see
90 You cannot pass to him but thorough me.'
He thought himself affronted, and replied,
'I whom the palace never has denied
Will make the way here;' I said, 'Sir, you'll do

Me a great favour, for I seek to go.'
95 He gath'ring fury still made sign to draw;
But himself there closed in a scabbard saw
As narrow as his sword's; and I, that was
Delightful, said, 'There can no body pass
Except by penetration hither, where
100 Two make a crowd, nor can three persons here
Consist but in one substance.' Then, to fit
Our peace, the priest said I too had some wit:
To prov't, I said, 'the place doth us invite
By its own narrowness, Sir, to unite.'
105 He asked me pardon; and to make me way
Went down, as I him followed to obey.
But the propitiatory priest had straight
Obliged us, when below, to celebrate
Together our atonement: so increased
110 Betwixt us two the dinner to a feast.

---

78. tradition] the Roman Catholic Church regarded its traditions as authoritative, as opposed to the Protestant preference for the authority of Scripture and scriptural interpretation; being a Catholic, Flecknoe is seen to follow tradition. *redeemed*] a) recovered, as in out of pawn b) another theological pun: Flecknoe recovered the cloak as Christ saves mankind from sin.
80–2. This . . . chamelion] unlike the poet in Marston's *Satyre* I, ll. 1–2: 'I cannot show in strange proportion,/Changing my hew like a Camelion.'
82. chamelion] Hartwig, *SEL*, 36 (1996), 171–212 (192), notes that chameleons were not associated with positive values in emblem literature, but with flattery and changeability. Hartwig, *SEL*, 36 (1996), 196, suggests that M.'s picture of Flecknoe's 'airy' body chimes silently with the other feature attributed to chameleons: that they lived on air. *yellow . . . green*] Cp. Alciati, *Emblemata* (Paris, 1536), trans. Jean Lefèvre, no. 88, 'In Adulatores' ('Flateurs'): 'Cameleon soufflant sans cesse/Vivant dair/n affixes couleurs./Adonc bleu/verd, ou iausne/& laisse/Rouge & blanc/taincts de grands valeure' (The chameleon breathing ceaselessly, living on air, does not have fixed colours. It is now blue, now green, now yellow, but never red or white, hues of great value).
83. disfurnish] divest of furniture; used because Flecknoe and the speaker are the only objects in the impoverished apartment, and thus its only 'furniture'; see *Upon Appleton House*, l. 68, 'new furniture of friends'.
84–5. whose . . . Doubt] constructed as a personification.
85. complimenting Doubt] a) i.e. flattering each other to see who should for the sake of decorum leave the room first b) as in 'complement': that which makes complete.
86. But . . . out] an inversion of Matt. 19:30: 'But many that are first shall be last; and the last shall be first.'
87. stand] a) stop (*OED* v. 4) b) take up a position against an enemy (*OED* v. 10).
88. demand] ask for (*OED* v. 8).
90. You . . . me] Cp. John 14:6: 'I am the way, the truth, and the life: no man cometh unto the Father, but by me.'
92. the palace] probably the Casa Barberini; Cardinal Antonio Barberini, nephew to Pope Urban VIII, was one of the most influential nobles and churchmen in mid-seventeenth-century

Rome. His house was known as the Palace, and he was protector of the English Catholics. See N.N., *The Scarlet Gown, Or the History of all the Present Cardinals of Rome*, trans. Henry Cogan (1653), esp. 71.
98. Delightful] a) charming (*OED* a. 1) b) delighted (*OED* a. 2).
98–9. There can . . . hither] the passage is so narrow that one person can pass another only by passing through the other's body (i.e. by *penetration*), which is an impossibility; see *An Horatian Ode*, ll. 41–2, 'Nature that hateth emptiness,/Allows of penetration less'. The bawdy (and homoerotic) connotations of these lines are apparent when juxtaposed with verse by Wye Saltonstall, *Picturae Loquentes* (1631), sig. A11ʳ: 'For Mayds are vessels, and but weake ones too,/ . . . They know no *vacuum* but must be fild.' In this respect, see also Lucretius, *De Rerum Natura*, IV, ll. 1111–12: 'nec penetrare et abire in corpus corpore toto;/nam facere velle et certare videntur' ('For bodies cannot pierce, nor be in bodies lost:/ As sure they strive to be, when both engage', trans. Dryden, ll. 78–9).
100–1. three persons . . . substance] parody of the doctrine of the Holy Trinity: the godhead exists as a trinity (three identities, father, son and holy ghost united in one substance); cp. also Matt. 18:20: 'For where two or three are gathered together in my name, there am I in the midst of them.' In numerological theory, two symbolized excess and defect, three reconciliation; see Rivers (1978), 179.
104. By] Bod. 1+; But *1681. unite*] ally, associate, as opposed to the hostility which the visitor previously but mistakenly thought the speaker to be offering.
107. propitiatory] a) appeasing, conciliating (*OED* 2 B a.) b) atoning, especially with reference to Christ (*OED* 2); in this sense Flecknoe imitates Christ. 'Propitiatory' was used as a negative term to describe Popish worship by Reformers.
108. Obliged] see above, l. 1 n. *celebrate*] parodying the celebration of a Mass or Holy Communion.
109. atonement] a) reconciliation (*OED* n. 2) b) parodying the theological sense of conciliating God by the expiation of sins (*OED* n. 3, 4b).
110. feast] parodying 'feast' as a meal marking a religious anniversary, most usually applied to the Passover.

Let it suffice that we could eat in peace;
And that both poems did and quarrels cease
During the table; though my new-made friend
Did, as he threatened, ere 'twere long intend
15 To be both witty and valiant: I loath,
Said 'twas too late, he was already both.
    But now, alas, my first tormenter came,
Who satisfied with eating, but not tame,
Turns to recite; though judges most severe
20 After th'Assizes dinner mild appear,
And on full stomach do condemn but few:
Yet he more strict my sentence doth renew;
And draws out of the black box of his breast
Ten quire of paper in which he was dressed.
25 Yet that which was a greater cruelty
Than Nero's poem he calls charity:
And so the pelican at his door hung
Picks out the tender bosom to its young.
    Of all his poems there he stands ungirt
30 Save only two foul copies for his shirt:
Yet these he promises as soon as clean.
But how I loathed to see my neighbour glean
Those papers, which he pillèd from within

Like white flakes rising from a leper's skin!
135 More odious than those rags which the French youth
At ordinaries after dinner show'th
When they compare their *chancres* and *poulaines*.
Yet he first kissed them, and after takes pains
To read; and then, because he understood
140 Not one word, thought and swore that they were good.
But all his praises could not now appease
The pròvoked author, whom it did displease
To hear his verses, by so just a curse
That were ill made condemned to be read worse:
145 And how (impossible) he made yet more
Absurdities in them than were before.
For he his untuned voice did fall or raise
As a deaf man upon a viol plays,
Making the half points and the periods run
150 Confus'der than the atoms in the sun.
Threat the poet swelled, with anger full,
And roared out, like Perillus in's own bull;
'Sir, you read false.' 'That anyone but you
Should know the contrary.' Whereat, I, now
155 Made mediator, in my room, said, 'Why,
To say that you read false Sir is no lie.'

---

111. Let it suffice] Cp. Ezek. 45:9: 'Thus saith the Lord GOD; Let it suffice you. O princes of Israel: remove violence and spoil, and execute judgement and justice, take away your exactions from my people, saith the Lord GOD.'
113. table] eating (*OED* n. I 6 c).
115. loath] reluctant, disinclined (*OED* a. 4) (to witness a display of wit).
120. Assizes] periodically held county courts that administered civil and criminal justice; presided over by itinerant judges.
123. black box] box for official (e.g. legal) papers (not in *OED*); see Congreve, *The Way of the World* (1700), IV.i.633: 'some proof you must let me give you; – I'll go for a black box, which Contains the Writings of my whole Estate.'
124. quire] sheets of writing paper (there were usually twenty-four or twenty-five in a quire).
126. Nero's poem] see Suetonius, *Lives of the Emperors*, VI.xxiii.1–2: among other attempts at competitive excellence in arts and sports, Nero sang verse to an audience; no one was allowed to leave while he was singing.
127–8. pelican . . . young] see above, l. 6 n.
129. ungirt] an inversion of 1 Peter 1:13: 'Wherefore gird up the loins of your mind, be sober, and hope to the end for the grace that is to be brought unto you at the revelation of Jesus Christ.' Cp. also Sir Thomas Browne, *Pseudodoxia Epidemica* (1646), V.XXII.13, 'for by a girdle or cincture are symbolically implied Truth, Resolution, and Readiness unto action.'
130. foul copies] draft versions.
133. pillèd] peeled (*OED* v.¹ II 5).
134. white flakes . . . leper's skin] see Lev. 13:10–11: 'if the rising be white in the skin . . . It is an old leprosy'.
136. ordinaries] prayers, religious service or lecture (*OED* n. II 10; n. III 12).

137. chancres] French; ulcers occuring in venereal disease (*OED*). poulaines] French: long, pointed shoes (*OED*).
138. kissed] parodying a Catholic priest kissing a Bible in a service of worship.
139–40. understood . . . word] Reilly, *JDJ*, 2 (1983), 55, suggests that M. repeats a typical Protestant joke: the reader does not understand Flecknoe's poem, just as many Catholics were supposed not to understand the Latin of their Bible and services.
145. impossible] i.e. 'impossible though it is to believe'.
149. half points and the periods] points (from the Italian *punto*) were a) short phrases of melody (*OED* n.¹ 9 a), or b) an important phrase in a contrapuntal composition (*OED* n.¹ 9 b); periods were complete musical sentences; M. is drawing a distinction between shorter and longer musical units.
152. Perillus in's own bull] Perillus built for the tyrant Phalaris a hollow bull; the bull 'roared' when a person was placed inside it and it was roasted; Phalaris first tested the device on its inventor, but was also eventually burnt in the bull by the people. See Ovid, *Ars Amatoria*, I, l. 653; Ovid, *Ibis*, 439. Hartwig, *SEL*, 36 (1996), 203–4, notes that in Lucian's account of the story (*Dialogues*, I, ll. 17–19) Perillus is unpleasant, while the groanings of the person being roasted in the bull made a sweet music to the listeners outside.
153–4. 'That . . . contrary'] i.e. anyone apart from you will know the truth is contrary to your assertion.
155. mediator] i.e. the narrator parodies the role of Christ. *room*] official function (*OED* n. B III 12); the speaker now takes on Flecknoe's role as he had reconciled the speaker and the youth in his tiny dwelling (see above, ll. 101–2).
156. is no lie] a) is the truth b) is no occasion for a challenge (as in 'to give the lie', i.e. to accuse of lying; *OED* n.¹ 2 b).

Thereat the waxen youth relented straight;
But saw with sad despair that 'twas too late.
For the disdainful poet was retired
160 Home, his most furious satire to have fired
Against the rebel, who, at this struck dead,
Wept bitterly as disinherited.
Who should commend his mistress now? Or who

Praise him? Both difficult indeed to do
165 With truth. I counselled him to go in time,
Ere the fierce poet's anger turned to rhyme.
   He hasted; and I, finding myself free,
As one 'scaped strangely from captivity,
Have made the chance be painted; and go now
170 To hang it in St Peter's for a vow.

---

157. *waxen*] smooth (*OED* a. 2 b) because a) youthful b) pale (with 'sad despair' [l. 158]).
158. *'twas*] *Bod. 1+*; *was 1681, Thompson*.
160. *satire*] probably M. means a 'pasquil', a satire that was posted in a public place, a common Roman practice.
163–6. *Who . . . rhyme*] the speaker implies that the youth wanted to have Flecknoe write sonnets to his mistress for him, and to address panegyrics to the youth himself; the speaker fears that Flecknoe will instead ridicule the youth in satires.
168. *strangely*] astonishingly, surprisingly (*OED* adv. 5).

169–70. *Have . . . vow*] The events the poem describes have been turned into an ex-voto painting. In the light of ll. 167–8, the sense is 'as I have escaped from this captivity, I offer this painting to St Peter as thanks'. The offering is appropriate in the light of St Peter's own miraculous escape from prison with the help of an angel (Acts 12:7–9). There is an element of parody here: Evelyn describes 'vows' of gold in Roman Catholic churches (Evelyn, *Diary*, ed. E.S. de Beer, 6 vols (Oxford, 1955), II.200). Cp. also Horace, *Carmina*, I.v, ll. 13–16.
169. *chance*] the falling out of events (*OED* n. 1).
170. *St Peter's*] St Peter's Basilica. *vow*] votive offering (*OED* n. 6).

36
Dignissimo suo Amico Doctori Wittie
De Translatione Vulgi Errorum D. Primrosii

Date. Later 1650. See below, *To His Worthy Friend Doctor Witty upon His Translation of the Popular Errours, Headnote, Date.*

Publication. 1651, 1681.

Text. There are a very few emendations in *1681*, including corrections of compositorial error, changes in punctuation in order to enhance emphasis, and one change of vocabulary in order to introduce a pun. In *1651*, the poem is signed '*Andrew Marvell. A.F.* [*Andreae filiae*].'

Context. In *Popular Errours*, chs 31–4 (325–40), Primrose attacks several conceptions concerning tobacco: that it is a narcotic, that it is healthy to consume it immoderately, that it is good for consumptive conditions, that its consumption should be accompanied with drinking, that it enters the brain, and that it is a preservative against the plague. He also recommends tobacco for the treatment of fatness, as good for old men and 'cold stomachs', and warns of the withdrawal symptoms if a regular tobacco smoker completely abstains from it. Where M.'s English poem deals with the matter of translation itself, his Latin poem contains echoes of and

allusions to the treatment of plague and tobacco in Primrose's Latin original: see Haan (2003), 105–11.

Dignissimo suo Amico Doctori Wittie

De Translatione Vulgi Errorum D. Primrosii

Nempe sic innumero succrescunt agmine libri,
    Saepia vix toto ut jam natet una mari.
Fortius assidui surgunt a vulnere praeli:
    Quoque magis pressa est, auctior Hydra redit.
5 Heu quibus Anticyris, quibus est sanabilis herbis
    Improba scribendi pestis, avarus amor!
India sola tenet tanti medicamina morbi,
    Dicitur et nostris ingemuisse malis.
Utile Tabacci dedit illa miserta venenum,
10 Acri veratro quod meliora potest.
Jamque vides olidas libris fumare popinas:
    Naribus O doctis quam pretiosus odor!
Hac ego praecipua credo herbam dote placere,
    Hinc tuus has nebulas Doctor in astra vehit.
15 Ah mea quid tandem facies timidissima charta?
    Exequias siticen jam parat usque tuas.
Hunc subeas librum sancti ceu limen asyli,
    Quem neque delebit flamma, nec ira Jovis.

Title. D. Primrosii] Not in *1651*.
2. Saepia] cuttlefish, which secreted a black liquid, from which ink was made.
3. praeli] variant spelling of 'preli' ('prelum'), wine-press, generally used to mean the printing-press in the period. *vulnere*] the wound of the cuttle-fish, made to extract the ink.
4. pressa est] *1681*; premitur *1651*. The revision in *1681* introduces a pun on the printing-press. *Hydra*] water-serpent with seven heads that lived near the Lernean lake, killed by Hercules. When one head was severed, two grew in its place. See, e.g., Lucretius, *De rerum natura*, V, l. 27; Ovid, *Metamorphoses*, IX, l. 192. The invocation of the Hydra is appropriate, because, like the cuttlefish, it is a marine creature.
5. Anticyris] Anticyra was a name shared by three towns, one in Phocis, one on the Sinus Maliacus and one in Locris, each famous for hellebore, believed by the ancients to be a cure for madness and other mental diseases.

7. India] i.e. the West Indies.
10. Acri] *1681*; Acci *1651*. *veratro*] 'veratrum', another name for hellebore. On the relationship between hellebore and tobacco, see Primrose, *Popular Errours*, trans. Witty, 326: 'Tobacco doth purge the body both upwards and downwards in a violent manner like Hellebore, or Antimony. And any man shall as soone prove Hellebore to bee a narcotick, as persuade mee that Tobacco is so.'
11. Jamque . . . popinas] alluding to the practice of making spills from the pages of books, especially to light pipes.
13. praecipua . . . dote] i.e. the special property of causing men to burn books containing 'vulgar errors.' *praecipua*] *1681*; praecipû *1651*.
14. tuus . . . Doctor] i.e. Primrose.
16. siticen] 'siticines' were funeral musicians.

Fig. 6
James Primrose, *Popular Errours. Or The Errours of the people in Physick, first written in Latine by the learned physitian James Primrose Doctor in Physick . . . Translated into English by Robert Wittie Doctor in Physick (1651)*, facing title-page. The Bodleian Library, University of Oxford, Vet. A3 e. 982.

To His Most Worthy Friend Doctor Witty On His Translation of the Vulgar Errors of Dr Primrose

Assuredly do books increase in such a countless troop that scarcely does a single cuttle-fish swim in the whole sea. They arise more strongly from the wound of the incessant press, and the more she has been pressed, the more enlarged does the Hydra return. Alas, by what Anticyras, by what herbs is curable the base plague, the greedy passion for writing! India alone possesses remedies for so great a disease, and is said to have groaned at our misfortunes. In her pity she gave the useful poison of tobacco, which has greater potency than sharp hellebore. Already you behold a stinking bistro giving off smoke from books: O how precious is the odour to learned nostrils! I believe that the herb pleases by virtue of this particular quality; from this source your doctor carries these little clouds up to the stars. Ah, my most fearful page, what in the world will you do? Already the funeral-musician is preparing your obsequies! May you enter this book as though it were the threshold of a hallowed sanctuary, which neither the flame nor the wrath of Jupiter will destroy.

37

To His Worthy Friend Doctor Witty upon His Translation of the Popular Errors

Date. Later 1650. Witty's dedication is dated 30 November 1650, and his preface to the reader is signed 'From my house at Hull, Decemb. 2, 1650'.

Publication. James Primrose (or Primerose), *Popular Errours. Or the Errours of the People in Physick*, trans. Robert Witty (1651), sigs. A8ᵛ–B1ʳ. *1681.*

Context. While M.'s Latin dedicatory poem addresses the contemporary issue of publication, his English poem relates more extensively to the contents of *Popular Errours*, a Galenist defence of (male) physicians against superstition, mountebanks, empiricks, Paracelsan medicine and the practice of popular diagnosis and treatment by women. The last theme is emphasized by a woodcut in which an angel holds back a woman so that a sick man can be treated by a physician (see fig. 6). M. makes reference to this image in ll. 29–30, although the concerns of *Popular Errours* are much broader.

Witty was a Hull physician, who had been an usher in the Grammar School there between 1635 and 1642. George Fox disputed with Witty when imprisoned in Scarborough Castle in 1665, calling him a 'great Presbyterian' (Fox (1998), 355–6). Witty was friendly with members of the Fairfax family in the Restoration (see BL MS Eg. 2146, fol. 6 ff.); it is likely that he was acquainted with them before 1660. This itself provides further evidence of M.'s social circle during his time at Nun Appleton.

Primrose was the son of Gilbert, a Scottish divine, who had been received into the French reformed church, and had taught at Saumur, before he became a minister in the French church at London in the 1620s. Although admitted to the College of Physicians by Harvey, James attacked the theory of the circulation of blood in a published work of 1630. He published *De Vulgi in Medicina Erroribus* in Latin in 1638. Witty had translated Primrose's *The Antimoniall Cup twice cast* (1640), which was added to the end of *Popular Errours*. Primrose was living in Hull when he died in 1659, and was probably resident there at least by 1650, when he added extra material for Witty's translation ('The Translator to the Reader', *Popular Errours*, sig. A6ʳ.) It is highly likely that M. would have known Primrose as well as Witty.

Witty dedicates his translation to Frances Strickland, daughter of Thomas, Earl of Winchelsea, so that one kind of (gentle)woman is praised and educated, while another, the female physician, is rebuked. Editors have usually taken M.'s Celia to be his tutee Mary Fairfax. There is also the possibility that M. is obliquely addressing Frances Strickland.

Genre. As a prefatory poem on a translation, M.'s poem is closely related to contemporary ideas and debates on translation. Although Primrose's text is medical in subject matter, M. treats it as if it were a poem. M.'s paradoxical notion that the less given in English the more the Latin flourishes in translation is in opposition to the description of 'free translation' by Sir John Denham, where the translator must add his own 'spirit' in order to avoid 'evaporation' in the original (Denham (1969), 159).

To His Worthy Friend Doctor Witty upon His Translation of the Popular Errors

Sit further, and make room for thine own fame,
Where just desert enrolls thy honoured name –
The good interpreter. Some in this task
Take off the cypress veil, but leave a mask,
Changing the Latin, but do more obscure
That sense in English which was bright and pure.
So of translators they are authors grown,
For ill translators make the book their own.
Others do strive with words and forcèd phrase
10 To add such lustre, and so many rays,
That but to make the vessel shining, they
Much of the precious metal rub away.
He is translation's thief that addeth more,
As much as he that taketh from the store
15 Of the first author. Here he maketh blots
That mends; and added beauties are but spots.
　　　Celia whose English doth more richly flow
Than Tagus, purer than dissolvèd snow,
And sweet as are her lips that speak it, she
20 Now learns the tongues of France and Italy;
But she is Celia still: no other grace
But her own smiles commend that lovely face;
Her native beauty's not Italianated,
Nor her chaste mind into the French translated:
25 Her thoughts are English, though her sparkling wit
With other language doth them fitly fit.
　　　Translators learn of her: but stay, I slide
Down into error with the vulgar tide;
Women must not teach here: the Doctor doth
30 Stint them to caudles, almond-milk, and broth.
Now I reform, and surely so will all
Whose happy eyes on thy translation fall.
I see the people hast'ning to thy book,
Liking themselves the worse the more they look,
35 And so disliking, that they nothing see
Now worth the liking, but thy book and thee.
And (if I judgement have) I censure right;
For something guides my hand that I must write.
You have Translation's statutes best fulfilled,
40 That handling neither sully nor would gild.

1. Sit further] 'sit further away', as if the speaker were a portrait painter, talking to his subject; M. figuratively asks Witty to make space for the commendatory poem by moving the translation further along in the volume.
3–6. Some . . . pure] M. voices the opposite view to that of Denham in 1655 (1969), 159: 'I conceive it a vulgar error in translating Poets, to affect being *Fidus Interpres*; let that care be with them who deal in matters of Fact, or matter of Faith'.
4. cypress] a light, transparent material (*OED* 3, 1c).
8. ill] bad, poor.
10–12. lustre . . . rub away] in making the metal extremely shiny, polishing entirely obliterates it, just as (Paracelsan) alchemy damages base metal by vainly attempting to turn it into gold. The use of real or fake gold as medicine is attacked in *Popular Errours*, 160, 204.
16. spots] blemishes.
17. Celia] see above, *Headnote, Context*.
18. Tagus] River flowing from its source in Spain above the Serrania de Cuenca, east of Madrid, westwards through Portugal and into the sea at Lisbon. It is celebrated in the Portugese epic of exploration, Luis de Camões' *Os Lusíadas*, of which Sir Richard Fanshawe's translation was published in 1655. As the river flows through two nations (and forms their border in places), so Celia's speech contains the languages of more than one nation. Like Celia, the river must 'translate'.
19–26. Here M. agrees with Denham: a translation into English should not permit the language to be corrupted or diluted by French and Italian elements or fashions (Denham, (1969), 160).

23. Italianated] made sexually enticing, in imitation of Italian fashion (*OED* ppl. a. 2). The comment is consonant with the rejection of foreign (probably Italianate) architecture registered in *Upon Appleton House*, sts. I–III.
24. chaste . . . translated] possibly a reference to the more sexually explicit *libertin* poetry (including some of Saint Amant's verse) being read at Appleton House.
27–30. I slide . . . broth] Taken directly from Primrose's precise delimitation of the medical role of women, Primrose, *Popular Errours*, book I, chapter 5, trans. Witty, 19: 'For it is not a thing of such consequence, not ought any Physician of note, or Surgeon to think worse of Women, which are borne for the care and service of men, if they doe their whole endeavour for the good of Mankinde; for they know how to make a bed well, boyle pottage, cullices, barley broth, make Almond milke, and they know many remedies for sundry diseases.'
27–8. I slide . . . tide] Cp. *Upon Appleton House*, ll. 644–5: 'Stretched as a bank unto the tide,/Or to suspend my sliding foot.'
30. Stint] restrict (*OED* v. II 14). *caudles . . . broth*] 'for they know how to make a bed well, boyle pottage, cullices, barley broth, make Almond milke', Primrose, *Popular Errours*, trans. Witty, 19. *caudles*] warm drinks made of gruel and wine or ale, sweetened and spiced, and given to sick people, especially women in labour (*OED* n. 1): 'That Midwives does ill, who give to women/in Childbed nothing but hot drinks,' Primrose, *Popular Errours*, trans. Witty, 177. *almond-milk*] a medicinal application, made of sweet blanched almonds and water, for softening skin and muscles. See above, *Headnote, Context*.
33. hast'ning] 1681; hasting *1651*.

38
On Mr Milton's Paradise Lost

Date. Late April–June 1674. M.'s commendatory poem was written for and published in the second edition of Milton's *Paradise Lost* (1st edn, 1667), which was registered for publication on 6 July 1674. The reference to Dryden's operatic version of Milton's epic (licensed on 17 April, see below, ll. 18–22) limits the period of probable composition to just over two months.

Publication. John Milton, *Paradise Lost* (2nd edn, 1674; hereafter *1674*), sig. [A3^{r-v}], placed after S[amuel] B[arrow]'s Latin poem, 'In Paradisum Amissam Summi Poetae Johannis Miltoni' (sig. A2^{r-v}), before Milton's note on 'The Verse' (sig. [A4^{r-v}]), and signed 'A.M.'; both poems are additions to the printed text of *Paradise Lost*. The poem did not appear in the fourth (the first folio; 1688) edition of *Paradise Lost*, most probably out of deference to Dryden (the publisher was Dryden's publisher, Tonson), three of whose couplets replaced it. *1681*. A copy in a scribal hand, subscribed 'A. Marvell', is inserted after p. 60 in an exemplum of *1681*, now in the library of Wellesley College, Massachusetts.

Context. M. had known Milton personally since at least 1653, and had probably been familiar with some of his publications, especially the poems published in 1645, and some of the anti-episcopal tracts, before then. A further version of the shorter poems was published in 1673, and poems in this volume are also reflected in M.'s poem. M. had read *Paradise Lost* (in both ten and twelve book versions [see below, l. 3]) carefully: his prefatory poem contains many verbal allusions to various places throughout the text of Milton's epic.

The poem is apparently concerned only with the narrow context of M.'s response to *Paradise Lost*, Dryden's attempt to dramatize it and the debate (addressed most famously by the dispute between Dryden and Sir Robert Howard in the 1660s, and by Milton's preface to his poem) on the status of rhyme in verse (see Zwicker in MacLean (1995), 137–58

for an account of the controversy). However, by arguing that the 'town-Bayes' (l. 47) may not only refer to Dryden (following the Duke of Buckingham's representation of Dryden as Mr Bayes in his play *The Rehearsal* (1672)), but also to any other 'hack poet', Lippincott, *ELN*, 9 (1972), 270, and Wittreich, in Patrides, ed. (1978), 289, suggest that M. is also referring to polemical attacks on Milton in the early 1670s. M. had defended Milton as part of his polemic in *The Rehearsal Transpros'd*, Part I (1672), and had indeed referred to Samuel Parker (in his attack on John Owen) as a rhymer in prose, 'yet . . . if rhiming be the business, and you are also good at *tagging of points in a Garrett*' (*MPW*, I. 128), because he had used so many 'ism' endings in his naming of erroneous ways. These are the same words used by M. in his poem (ll. 49–50), but while this context does broadly inform the poem, the reference to Dryden's version of *Paradise Lost* in ll. 18–22, the fact that the 'Town-Bayes' is referred to in the singular (l. 47), and the particular issue of rhyme (ll. 48–50), still points overwhelmingly to Dryden as the figure mentioned. In later years, and after he had reverted to using blank verse on the stage, Dryden remembered the joke in his translation of Persius's first satire: 'Studious to please the Genius of the Times,/With Periods, Points, and Tropes, he slurs his Crimes . . . /Sweet sound is added now, to make it Terse,/'Tis tagged with Rhyme' (ll. 169–70, 184–5).

Lippincott, 269–70, further suggests that in this poem M. was also continuing his defence of Milton, in answer to *The Transproser Rehears'd* (1673; formerly attributed to Richard Leigh, now to Samuel Butler (see von Maltzahn, *SP*, 92 (1995), 492–4)), where Milton had suffered an unprovoked attack, including the accusation that he hypocritically used internal rhymes having rejected them in his prefatory remarks and his earlier attack on Bishop Joseph Hall (42). Butler associates M. with several republicans, Puritans and commonwealth-men (and republican reading habits), including Milton (repeatedly),

Nedham, Bradshaw, Cromwell and Ireton. M. replied by defending Milton's reputation in the second part of *The Rehearsal Transpros'd* (1673). The specific defence of Milton's prosodic methods associated non-rhyming poetry with anti-monarchical, anti-episcopal stances, despite M.'s own coy admission of guilt in the matter of rhyme (l. 51). Butler declared that 'rhyming' (i.e. jesting) in prose in *The Rehearsal Transpros'd* was little different from writing unrhymed blank verse (41). By writing in rhymed couplets, while acknowledging the superiority of Miltonic unrhymed verse, *On Mr Milton's* Paradise Lost praises Milton and triumphantly preserves M.'s identity as the 'transproser'. M. was also repeating the terms and even phrasing he had used to praise Milton's *Defensio Secunda* (1654) to the poet in the letter of 2 June in that year (see below, l. 53).

This seemingly narrow context had much broader ramifications. The absence of rhymes (and the inclusion of highly unusual and daring internal rhymes) in *Paradise Lost* occasioned sufficient worry on the publisher's part for the inclusion of the note explaining Milton's strategy of versification as early as the fifth issue of the first edition (1668). Milton's aversion to rhyme at this late stage of his career soon became a target for his enemies, in as much as he associated rhyme with bondage, tyranny and custom. Freedman, *HLQ*, 24 (1961–62), 337–44, argues that Milton's note relates closely to the dispute between Sir Robert Howard (a great admirer of Milton and the inventor of the original 'town-Bayes' [see below, l. 47]) and Dryden, on the fittingness of rhymed verse in drama, although M. does not refer in any detail to the matter of this dispute in the poem. The controversy was, however, widely known and mentioned, notably in other examples of commendatory verse at this time: 'In troth, I have no faculty at praise,/My *Bush* is very full of *thorns*, tho it seems *Bays*,' Walter Pope, 'To his Worthy Friend Mr Flatman', in Thomas Flatman, *Poems and Songs* (1674), sig. A5ʳ.

According to Aubrey, Dryden had sought and gained Milton's permission to put *Paradise Lost* on the stage as *The State of Innocence and the Fall of Man: An Opera* (first registered as *The Fall of Angels and Man in Innocence*), and this meant putting the epic into rhyming couplets. M.'s use of 'tagging points' to describe adding rhymes to blank verse in *The Rehearsal Transpros'd*, antedates Milton's use of the phrase in his meeting with Dryden. If Aubrey's account is authentic, Milton may have taken his lead from M.'s original coining. Winn (1987), 266, defends Dryden's 'tagging' as faithful to Milton's own lexis (with hardly any of Dryden's characteristic vocabulary) and based on a deep knowledge of *Paradise Lost*, with rhyming words being transplanted from within a single line, or from related contexts in the poem. Dryden worked very hard for four weeks probably in March–April 1674 to compress more than ten thousand lines of verse into a performance that would not have exceeded two hours. The pressure for a rapidly produced text probably came from the players of the King's Company, who needed a play for their new theatre, to compete with Dryden's version of *The Tempest*, then being acted by the rival company. The machinery and scenic complexity of the play made it prohibitively expensive for the company. It was never acted, but was finally published in 1677. Ll. 25–6 in M.'s poem possibly hint at the frustration of Dryden's aims; ll. 49–50 suggest that M. knew precisely what Milton had said to Dryden, since he uses and extends the same analogy between rhyming words and the tags and points of clothing as reportedly used by Milton: 'Mr Milton received him civilly, and told him he would give him leave to tagge his verses' (Aubrey, II, 72). M. appears not to have seen a copy of Dryden's opera before he wrote his poem.

Shifflett (*RQ*, 49 (1996), 803–23) notes further parallels between M.'s poem and Jonson's prefatory poem to Thomas May's translation of Lucan. M. echoes Jonson in particular at the beginning and the end of his poem, thereby using the allusion to Jonson as a frame through which to view the comments on Milton and *Paradise Lost*. Moreover, 'to praise Milton in a Jonsonian manner is, in this outstanding case, to praise him for having written a Lucanic poem'. Like Jonson, M. uses asyndeton, while both poets explore their subjects as poems of divine inspiration and note the precise adherence to poetic decorum. Shifflett argues that M.'s purpose was to echo Jonson's defence of stoic values and literary procedures in Lucan, in May's translation and in his own poem and so to present Milton as a stoic. Lucan had defiantly composed a republican epic under Nero. M. had also defended Milton in stoic terms in *The Rehearsal Transpros'd*, Part 2; Jonson and M. understood that stoic retirement implied continuing resistance, rather than capitulation (in Milton's case, to the monarchy). For Scodel, in Norton, ed. (1999), 546, these qualities make M.

'the greatest son of Ben', even as he was also adapting Jonson's own master, Horace.

Style and Versification. The poem appears to take its shape, in a series of phrasal echoes, notably in ll. 1–16, from Ben Jonson's 'To my Chosen Friend, The Learned Translator of Lucan, Thomas May, Esq.' (see above, *Headnote, Context*). While the rhetorical procedure of praise through doubt was known in stoical literature, most famously Seneca, and was extensively used by Jonson, Shifflett, *RQ*, 49 (1996), 807–8, argues that M. revised the conventions of commendatory verse by repeatedly 'straining praise through the sieve of doubt'. Herz, *MLQ*, 39 (1978), 239–63 (244) argues that M. adopts the first person of a Miltonic narrator's or speaker-poet's persona in the poem. The 'I' 'speaks out of the experience of *Paradise Lost* as M. makes himself undergo the process of uncertainty, error, correction of vision, and affirmation that is Milton's strategy in the poem'. She further argues that the form of the poem compresses the scope of *Paradise Lost* into an extended kind of Miltonic sonnet, with the first ten lines constituting the octet, the next six the sestet. The reader is also made a spectator to *Samson Agonistes* (ll. 9–10), assimilating its own daringness to that of *Paradise Lost*. Some of M.'s Miltonic echoes in the poem appear critical: e.g. describing Milton through Milton's words for Satan (l. 2), and referring to Milton's age (l. 9).

M.'s couplet does full justice to Milton in its echoes of Miltonic verse and its further imitations of the prosodic ingenuity of *Paradise Lost*, although the Miltonic echoes are less dense between l. 17 and l. 30. These latter features include: suspending the

caesura until late in the line (l. 5); the running over of sense from one line to the next, with one meaning generated at the turn of the (unpunctuated) line (l. 21); epic lists (ll. 3–4); extended, repetitive use of a consonant, significant for the poem's meaning (ll. 32–3). In this way, M. imitates Milton's embedding of prose style effects within blank verse (see Corns (1990), ch. 2), and this is done with a flexibility absent in Dryden's more rigid attempts to tame Miltonic verse for his own rhymed ends (for instance, in *Absalom and Achitophel* (1681)). At the same time, M.'s poem is also very much a part of the new age of controversial, satirical verse (as *Paradise Lost* never was): imagistic invention is severely limited, and the speaker's tone is carefully cultivated in order to generate implied fine discrimination and even irony.

Modern Criticism. The poem was one of the few by which M. had a reputation in the eighteenth century and the Romantic period. Herz, *MLQ*, 39 (1978), 239–63 (246) finds the poem remarkable in its many-faceted engagement in Miltonic forms, while also establishing distinctly Marvellian perceptions and expression. The poem thus demonstrates a central Marvellian truth that reading is re-creation.

On Mr Milton's *Paradise Lost*

When I beheld the poet blind, yet bold,
In slender book his vast design unfold,
Messiah crowned, God's reconciled decree,
Rebelling angels, the forbidden tree,
5 Heaven, hell, earth, chaos, all; the argument

Title. On Mr Milton's Paradise Lost] *1681;* On Paradise Lost *1674.*

1. When I beheld] see Milton, Sonnet XVI: 'When I consider how my light is spent'; M., letter to Milton, 2 June 1654 (on Milton's *Defensio Secunda*; Legouis, II.306): 'When I consider how equally it turnes and rises with so many figures.'

2. slender book] the first edition of *Paradise Lost* (1667) contained ten rather than twelve books; M. may also mean that Milton's poem is slender when compared with its source text, the Bible, or that it was simply a small book, being only an octavo (see 'slender', *OED* a. I 4). *vast*] usually associated with Satan; see, e.g., *Paradise Lost*, VI, l. 109. *design*] always used in a negative sense in *Paradise Lost*: e.g. II, l. 630: 'Satan with thoughts inflamed of highest design.'

3. Messiah crowned, God's reconciled decree] *Paradise Lost* recounts mankind's transgression of God's initial commandment

not to eat the forbidden fruit, and the Son's atonement for mankind's sins. M. refers here to the opening passage of Book XI – clear evidence that he had inspected the additions to the new twelve-book version of the poem: see Milton, *Paradise Lost*, XI, ll. 46–7: ' "All thy request for man, accepted Son,/ Obtain, all thy request was my Decree." ' *reconciled*] see 2 Cor. 5:18–19: 'And all things are of God, who hath reconciled us to himself by Jesus Christ, and hath given to us the ministry of reconciliation. To wit, that God was in Christ, reconciling the world unto himself, not imputing their trespasses unto them; and hath committed unto us the word of reconciliation.'

5. argument] a possible reference to the prose 'Argument' added, at the request of the printer/publisher, along with the paragraph on 'The Verse', for the fifth issue of the first edition. The line provides further evidence of which text of *Paradise Lost* M. may have first read.

Held me a while misdoubting his intent,
That he would ruin (for I saw him strong)
The sacred truths to fable and old song
(So Sampson groped the Temple's post in spite)
0   The world o'erwhelming to revenge his sight.
　　Yet as I read, soon growing less severe,
I liked his project, the success did fear;
Through that wide field how he his way should find
O'er which lame Faith leads Understanding blind;
5   Lest he perplexed the things he would explain,
And what was easy he should render vain.
　　Or if a work so infinite he spanned,
Jealous I was that some less skilful hand
(Such as disquiet always what is well,
0   And by ill imitating would excel)
Might hence presume the whole creation's day
To change in scenes, and show it in a play.
　　Pardon me, mighty poet, nor despise

25   My causeless, yet not impious, surmise.
But I am now convinced, and none will dare
Within thy labours to pretend a share.
Thou hast not missed one thought that could be fit,
And all that was improper dost omit:
30   So that no room is here for writers left,
But to detect their ignorance or theft.
　　That majesty which through thy work doth reign
Draws the devout, deterring the profane.
And things divine thou treats of in such state
As them preserves, and thee, inviolate.
35   At once delight and horror on us seize,
Thou sing'st with so much gravity and ease;
And above human flight dost soar aloft
With plume so strong, so equal, and so soft.
The bird named from that Paradise you sing
40   So never flags, but always keeps on wing.
　　Where couldst thou words of such a compass find?

---

6. *misdoubting*] suspicious of; fearing.
6–10. 'Marvell's admission to initial "misdoubting" (l. 6) fear that Milton had tainted Christianity with classical myth in revenge for his blindness hints at Milton's bitterness over the Restoration, since *Paradise Lost* associates Milton's blindness and political isolation' (Scodel, in Norton, ed. (1999), 546).
7. ruin] reduce (*OED* v. I 1 trans.).
8. fable and old song] in *Paradise Lost*, XI, ll. 10–14, Adam and Eve's prayers of repentance are compared to those 'in fables old' of Deucalion and Pyrrha to Themis to restore mankind after the deluge. In both prose and poetry, Milton usually uses 'fable' pejoratively and 'song' in a positive sense.
9. So Sampson . . . spite] alluding to Milton's *Samson Agonistes* (1671), and the first instance in the tradition of comment associating Samson with Milton himself; the Biblical account is at Judges, 16:29–30. *groped*] suggesting Milton's old age as well as his blindness. Cp. also [Samuel Butler], *The Transposer Rehears'd* (1673), 41: 'the *blind* author of *Paradise Lost* . . . begins his third Book thus, groping for a beam of *Light*'. M. seems here to reflect Butler's own critical view of Milton's abilities, but the rest of the poem defends Milton's reputation.
13. wide field] two very frequent Miltonic words, but never collocated in his poetry.
14. lame. . . . blind] an inversion, since faith is usually associated with strength (especially by Milton), and blindness with error. It is also a reversal: in Andrea Alciato's well-known *Emblemata* (Lyons, 1550), 173, a blind man carries a lame one in an image entitled 'Mutuum auxilium' (mutual help), the source for which is *Greek Anthology*, IX.xii. In *Of Reformation*, the lame and the blind are the victims of greedy prelates: *CPW*, I.611, l. 4. 'lame' may be suggested by the 'lame metre' referred to in Milton's note 'The Verse'. The line also appears to respond to the title page of Sir Roger L'Estrange's attack on Milton, *No Blinde Guides* (1660): 'If the Blinde lead the Blinde, Both shall fall into the Ditch.'
15. perplexed] confused (*OED* v. 1).
16. vain] worthless (*OED* a. I 1).
17. spanned] encompassed.
18–22. Jealous . . . play] See above, *Headnote, Context*.

20. would excel] see *Paradise Lost*, II, ll. 883–4 (of Sin): 'She opened, but to shut/Excelled her power.'
24. impious] see *Paradise Lost*, VI, l. 188: 'He on his impious foes right onward drove.'
25. and] *1674, 1681*; that *Bod. 1.*
30. detect] reveal (*OED* v. 1).
31. majesty] Shifflett, *RQ*, 49 (1996), 818, and (1998), 123–4, suggests an allusion to the stoic concept of majesty as inner self-governance (see Milton, *Paradise Regained*, II, ll. 458–86), which could thus be read as a joke at the expense of Charles II. For Scodel, in Norton, ed. (1999), M. 'wittily implies Milton transcended anger by creating his own godly poetic kingdom.'
33. treats] *1681, Bod. 1*; treatst *1674.*
35. delight and horror] Cp. Lucretius, *De Rerum Natura*, III, ll. 28–30: 'his ibi me rebus quaedam divina voluptas/percipit adque horror, quod sic natura tua vi/tam manifesta patens ex omni parte retecta est' (Thereupon from all these things a sort of divine delight gets hold upon me and a shuddering, because nature thus by thy power has been so manifestly laid open and uncovered in every part). Capel Lofft noticed this echo in his edition of *Paradise Lost*, Books 1 and 2 (Bury St Edmund's, 1793), xlv. Lofft also states that M. would have been more faithful to the nature of Milton's poem had he imitated Lucretius more closely. See also below, l. 53n.
36–7. Thou sing'st . . . aloft] echoes the narrator's claim in *Paradise Lost*, I, ll. 12–16, 'I thence/Invoke thy aid to my adventurous song,/That with no middle flight intends to soar/Above the Aonian mount, while it pursues/Things unattempted yet in prose or rhyme.'
39–40. bird . . . wing] the Bird of Paradise, so called after its bright plumage, and supposed to fly perpetually, and, accordingly, to have neither legs, feet nor wings, although authorities before Milton's time challenged the latter belief. An emblematic figure of poetic perfection and longevity, typical of M., rather than the Miltonic bird figure of divine inspiration at *Paradise Lost*, I, l. 21.
41. compass] See *Paradise Lost*, IX, l. 59: 'From compassing the earth, cautious of day'.

Whence furnish such a vast expense of mind?
Just heaven thee like Tiresias to requite
Rewards with prophecy thy loss of sight.
45   Well mightst thou scorn thy readers to allure
With tinkling rhyme, of thine own sense secure;
While the town-Bayes writes all the while and spells,
And like a pack-horse tires without his bells:

Their fancies like our bushy points appear,
50   The poets tag them, we for fashion wear.
I too transported by the mode offend,
And while I meant to praise thee must commend.
Thy verse created like thy theme sublime,
In number, weight, and measure, needs not rhyme.

42. *Whence furnish . . . expense*] a possible reference to
Milton's straitened financial circumstances after 1660. *Whence*]
1674, 1681; Where *WC. expense*] 'expense' carries echoes of
'expanse': Milton's treatment of the vast spaces of chaos and
heaven has always been centrally connected to the 'sublimity'
of *Paradise Lost*, e.g. II, l. 1014: 'Into the wilde expanse'; IV,
l. 456: 'Pure as th'expanse of heav'n'.
43. *Tiresias*] Jupiter gave Tiresias the power of prophecy
after Juno strainded him: Ovid, *Metamorphoses*, III, ll. 336–8. In
Paradise Lost, III, ll. 26–36, Milton compares himself with two
blind poets, Thamyris and Maeonides (Homer), and two blind
prophets, Tiresias and Phineus. The latter two are added as an
afterthought to the former two. Shifflett, *RQ*, 49 (1996), 814,
and (1998), 117, argues that the choice of Tiresias emphasizes
stoic themes (see above, *Headnote, Context*).
45. *mightst*] *1674, Bod. 1*; might *1681*.
46. *tinkling rhyme*] cf. Milton, 'The Verse': 'the jingling sound
of like endings'. *thine*] *Bod. 1*; thy *1674, 1681*.
47. *town-Bayes*] see above, *Headnote, Context. spells*] out other
words, syllable by syllable in a laborious manner, to search for
rhymes (*OED* v.² 3).
48. *pack-horse*] in Milton's *The Reason of Church-Government*
(1642), the bishops are likened to drudging packhorses in
writing their sluggish defenses of episcopacy (*CPW*, I.822);
synonym for a drudge (*OED* n. b).
49–50. *fancies . . . wear*] poetic inventiveness or 'fancies' are
like the tassells of a hose-fastening ('bushy point'), but they are
constrained by the rhyme of the couplet, just as the fastening is
'tagged'. M. might be suggesting in the 'we' that the unfastened
'bushy points' are the fancies he shares with Milton, but this
most un-Miltonic association of verse with fashions in clothing,
and M.'s implication of himself in the crime of 'tagging' (see
l. 51), infers that Milton's unrhyming poetry is of quite
another order to that of contemporary (poetic) fashion: see
above, l. 35, and *The First Anniversary*, l. 316 n. Aubrey, *Brief
Lives*, ed. A. Clark (Oxford, 1898), I.205 recalls Davenant's
reference to tags and points being superseded by hooks and
eyes, so that they were obviously old-fashioned by the time of
the Restoration: is this another indication of Milton's age?
49. *bushy points*] *1681*; Bushy-points *1674*; tasselled fastenings
for hose; see above, *Headnote, Context*.
50. *tag*] supply rhymes.
51. *I . . . offend*] as a show of humility or even guilt, M. places

himself among the poets who have offended Milton: 'some
famous modern poets, carried away by custom', Milton, 'The
Verse'. Samuel Butler noted M.'s 'happy talent of *Rhyming*, in
Transversing the Treatise of *Schism*, and for the Titles *dear sake*
you might have made all the Verses rung *Ism* in their several
Changes', which would have made *The Rehearsal Transpros'd*
more acceptable than the blank verse *Paradise Lost* (*The
Transproser Rehears'd* (1673), 30). *transported*] carried away
by a fit of enthusiasm (*OED* v. 3); see also below *The Loyal Scot*,
l. 274.
52. *And . . . commend*] Cp. Jonson, 'To Mr Joshua Sylvester'
(1616), ll. 1–2: 'If to admire were to commend, my praise/
Might then both thee, thy work and merit raise.' *commend*] i.e.
because 'praise' does not rhyme with 'offend'. 'Commend' was
also preferred to 'praise' in the King James version (1611) of
2 Cor. 3.1 ('Do we begin again to commend ourselves?').
Tyndale (1535), the Great (1540) and Geneva (1560) Bibles
have 'praise' (e.g. Geneva: 'Do we beginne to praise our selves
againe?'). The King James Bible was closely identified with the
restored Church of England, as opposed to the earlier translations which were often preferred by Puritans. 'Commend' was
also preferred in the Rheims (Roman Catholic; 1582) and
Bishops' (1602) Bibles.
53. *sublime*] M. had previously praised Milton's *Defensio
Secunda* (1654) because it achieved the sublimity of Roman
eloquence (in the terms of the title of his friend John Hall's
translation of Longinus's *On the Sublime*): 'the most compendious Scale, for so much, to the Height of the Roman
eloquence. . . . it seems to me a Trajans columne in whose
winding ascent we see imboss'd the severall Monuments of
your learned victoryes.' Letter to John Milton, 2 June 1654
(Legouis (1971), II. 305–6). See also above, l. 1 n.
54. *In number . . . measure*] see Wisdom 11:20, 'thou hast
ordered all things in measure, number, and weight'. Milton,
'The Verse', says that English tragedy, like classical verse,
'consists only in apt numbers, fit quantity of syllables, and the
sense variously drawn out from one verse into another'.
Cp. also Herbert, 'The Grief' (1633), ll. 16–18: 'some lover's
lute,/Whose grief allows him music and a rhyme;/For mine
excludes both measure, tune, and time'; Jonson, 'To my
Chosen Friend, The Learned Translator of Lucan, Thomas
May, Esq.' (1627), ll. 7–8: 'But when again I view the parts so
peised,/And those in number so, and measures raised.'

39
Inscribenda Luparae

Date and Context. 1671–72. Duncan-Jones (*TLS*, 26 April 1957, 257) provides details of a competition instituted by Colbert for the best inscription to be set up on the pediment of the great colonnade of the Louvre, which had been completed in 1670. The prize was a thousand pistols. The pediment stones were hoisted into position in 1672. M.'s distichs were written in response to the competition, notwithstanding his anti-French and pro-Dutch sentiments at this time. Whether they were presented in the French court is unknown.

Publication. 1681.

Genre and Sources. The first and fourth distichs are concerned with architecture (the fourth evidently reworking an image from the opening section of *Upon Appleton House*: see below, ll. 7–8 n.), the second, third, fifth and sixth with Louis XIV and his status. Many other Latin distichs from the competition survive in English sources: e.g. Bod., MS Sancroft 18, 4; Bod., MS Rawl. poet 69, fol. 57.

The poem was written in the wake of Emanuele Tesauro's popular *Il cannocchiale aristotelico* (1655) which elevated epigraphy to a distinct and demanding rhetorical art. Tesauro also redefined epigraphy to include all 'eulogies, epitaphs, dedications, epigrams, mottoes, and every kind of inscription', be they written or carved in stone. Although lapidary poems had been published in printed books widely before the 1650s, the inclusion of this poem in *1681* does chime with a strong European fashion (see Petrucci (1993), ch. 7).

Inscribenda Luparae

Consurgit Lupurae dum non imitabile culmen,
  Escuriale ingens uritur invidiâ.

Aliter
Regibus haec posuit Ludovicus templa futuris;
  Gratior ast ipsi castra fuere domus.

Aliter
5 Hanc sibi sideream Ludovicus condidit aulam;
  Nec se propterea credidit esse deum.

Aliter
Atria miraris, summotumque aethera tecto;
  Nec tamen in totò est arctior orbe casa.

Aliter
Instituente domum Ludovico, prodiit orbis;
10 Sic tamen angustos incolit ille lares.

Aliter
Sunt geminae Jani portae, sunt tecta Tonantis;
  Nec deerit numen dum Ludovicus adest.

---

2. *Escuriale*] the Escurial, the royal palace in Madrid, burned for a fortnight in June 1671. *uritur*] a) blushes, flushes b) burns.
3. *Ludovicus*] Louis XIV.
7–10. *Atria . . . lares*] Cp. *Upon Appleton House*, ll. 49–56: 'Yet thus the laden house does sweat,/And scarce endures the Master great:/But where he comes the swelling hall/Stirs, and the square grows spherical;/More by his magnitude distressed,/Than he is by its straitness pressed:/And too officiously it slights/That in itself which him delights.'
7. *tecto*] *Bod. 1, Margoliouth, Donno*; fecto *1681*.
8. *Nec . . . casa*] Echoes an inscription on the pediment of the Sancta Sanctorum of the Church of St John Lateran in Rome: 'Non est in toto sanctior Orbe locus' (There is not in the world a more holy house), reported in John Raymond, *An Itinerary Contayning a Voyage, Made through Italy, in the yeare 1646, and 1647* (1648), 81 (noted by Duncan-Jones in Legouis (1971)).
11. *geminae Jani portae . . . Tonantis*] the Gates of Janus were open in times of war and shut in times of peace; the indistinct reference implies that Louis has control of both war and peace. Cp. also *In Legationem Domini Oliveri St John*, ll. 8–10: 'Ast scriptum ancipiti nomine munus erat;/Scilicet hoc Martis, sed pacis nuntius illo;/Clavibus his Jani ferrea claustra regis.' (Your office was written in your double name:/In the last, the messenger of war, but in the first of peace./With these keys you control the iron locks of Janus.) *Tonantis*] name for Jupiter.
12. *adest*] *Bod. 1, Margoliouth, Donno*; adect *1681*.

To be Inscribed on the Louvre

While the inimitable summit of the Louvre rises up,
the huge Escurial burns with envy.

In another manner

Louis built this temple for future kings, but for
himself the camp has been a more pleasing domicile.

In another manner

Louis founded this starry palace for himself, and did
not believe that on account of this he was a god.

In another manner

You are amazed at the halls and the sky driven up by
a roof; however no more confined a house exists in
the whole world.

In another manner

While Louis was setting up a dwelling-place, the
world advanced. Thus however does he inhabit a
narrow household.

In another manner

There are twin gates of Janus, there are roofs of the
thunderer, nor will divine power be lacking while
Louis is present.

40

Upon a Eunuch: a Poet

Date. ?After 1650. Whether Hammond's argument (see below, *Context*) is accepted or not, the poem contains considerable reflection upon the relationship between personal identity and poetry. It therefore probably belongs to the period of reflection on the nature of poetry (see above, *To His Coy Mistress*, *Headnote*, *Context*), and probably to the later part of that time in the early 1650s. It may also have been written later still, during the polemical exchanges of the late 1660s and 1670s.

Publication. 1681.

Context. M. was described as a eunuch (as well as effeminate, a sodomite and a homosexual) in a number of satirical responses to *The Rehearsal Transpros'd* (1672), notably 'A Love-Letter to the Author of the Rehearsall Transpros'd' (1673–74; Royal Society, MS 32, pp. 45–8). That these allegations were part of a polemic attack has led nearly every commentator to dismiss them, and to deny any specific connection with M.'s poem, which itself is usually seen as a meditation upon the nature of poetic creativity. However, Hammond (*SC*, 11 (1996), 96–7, 101) rejects both of these earlier positions. Although there is no certain evidence, it may be conjectured that M. addressed the poem to himself, and, since specific reference to sexual disability and preference is rare in the period, it is possible that the poem and the satirical allegations are connected. The reference to Ovid's version of the Narcissus story (*Metamorphoses*, III; see below, l. 5), in which the poet is cast in the role of Echo, occurs elsewhere in M.'s verse, 'the principal myth – through which sexuality is imagined in Marvell's poetry' (Hammond, 101).

Genre and Sources. The poem is labelled as a fragment, but it exists discretely as an epigram. The tradition of (often bawdy) epigrams in which poetic activity is compared to sexual virility is most famously embodied in Martial's epigrams. See, e.g., I.xxxv:

> Versus scribere me parum severos
> nec quos praelegat in schola magister,
> Corneli, quereris: sed hi libelli,
> tamquam coniugibus suis mariti,
> non possunt sine mentula placere.
> quid si me iubeas thalassionem
> verbis dicere non thalassionis?
> quis Floralia vestit et stolatum
> permittit meretricibus pudorem?
> lex haec carminibus data est iocosis,
> ne possint, nisi pruriant, iuvare.
> quare deposita severitate
> parcas lusibus et iocis rogamus,
> nec castrare velis meos libellos.
> Gallo turpius est nihil Priapo.

(That I write verses little squeamish, and not such as a schoolmaster would dictate, is your complaint, Cornelius; but this volume cannot please, any more than husbands can please their wives, without a prick. What if you bade me indite a marriage song not in the words of a marriage song? Who brings garments into Flora's festival, and permits prostitutes the modesty of the stole? This is the rule assigned to jocular poems, to be unable to please unless they are dirty. Wherefore lay aside your squeamishness, and leave my pleasantries and my jokes be, I beg you, and do not seek to castrate my poems. Nothing is more shameful to Priapus than a eunuch priest of Cyebe.)

M.'s poem has its starting point as the opposite sexual premise to Martial's. Sir John Davies, John Weever, Sir John Harington and Ben Jonson made the epigram popular in the 1590s and the early seventeenth century, although Jonson dissociated himself from Martial's bawdry (see *Epigram* LIX, 'To a Playwright'). One of Donne's epigrams ('Raderus' (1602)) described an expurgated edition of Martial as a castration of the poet. Among those volumes that heavily influenced M., Herrick's *Hesperides* (1648) contained many epigrams, some associating writing poetry with sexuality. See, e.g., '[To his Book] Another':

To read my Booke the Virgin shie
May blush, (while *Brutus* standeth by:)
But when He's gone, read through what's writ,
And never staine a cheek for it.

M.'s epigram is closer to Martial's mode of comparison, and again quite contrary to Herrick's acknowledgement of feminine heterosexual embarrassment.

Upon a Eunuch: a Poet

Fragment

Nec sterilem te crede; licet, mulieribus exul,
Falcem virgineae nequeas immitere messi,
Et nostro peccare modo. Tibi Fama perennè
Praegnabit; rapiesque novem de monte sorores;
5 Et pariet modulos Echo repetita nepotes.

Upon an Eunuch: a Poet
Fragment

And do not believe that you are sterile, albeit, as an
exile from women, you are unable to thrust a sickle
at the virgin harvest or to sin in our manner. By you
will Fame be forever pregnant, and you will lay hold
of the nine sisters from the mountain, while Echo,
repeatedly struck, will give birth to music as your
offspring.

---

1. mulieribus] contains an incorrect quantity for the line (Kelliher, cited in Legouis (1971)).
2. Falcem . . . messi] see above, *The Mower Poems, Headnote.*
4. novem . . . sorores] the poetic Muses. *monte*] monse *1681*; the Muses are variously described as coming from Olympus, Parnassus or Helicon. *rapies*] 'snatch' ('rapio', Lewis and Short, I.A) but with the connotation of 'rape' ('rapio', Lewis and Short, III.B.1).

5. Et . . . nepotes] Recalling the birth of music from the city of notes and echoes in *Musick's Empire*, ll. 7–12. *modulos*] referring to poetic rhythm or metre, as well as music ('modulus', Lewis and Short, I.4). *repetita*] literally, 'strike again' ('repeto', Lewis and Short, I).

41

In the French Translation of Lucan, by Monsieur De Brebeuf are these Verses

Date. 1656–57. See below, *Sources and Context.*

Publication. 1681.

Sources and Context. Georges de Brebeuf's French translation of Lucan's *De Bello Civili* (or *Pharsalia*) was published in 1655. M. supplies a Latin version of *La Pharsale*, III, ll. 395–8. De Brebeuf expanded on two lines in Lucan's original, *De bello civili*, III, ll. 220–1: 'Phoenices primi, famae si creditur, ausi/ Mansuram rudibus vocem signare figuris' (These Pheonicians first made bold, if report speak true, to record speech in rude characters for future ages.) A French prose translation by De Marolles of 1647 (2nd edn, 1654) is literally faithful to Lucan's Latin, whereas De Brebeuf investigates the aesthetic concept of *ut pictura poesis est*, and points this up in his prefatory 'advertissement'. No less a French authority than Corneille was said to have held De Brebeuf's lines in high esteem (Legouis (1965), 24; (1971), I.275).

In *Bod. 1*, an English translation has been added under M.'s Latin, and attributed to Sir Philip Meadows, who was preferred to M. for a Latin secretaryship in 1653:

> He that ingenious Art did first descry
> Of painting Words, & speaking to ye Eye;
> And by ye several Shapes of Figures wrought,
> Gave Colour & a Body to a Thought.

Beyond the details of the translations of Lucan and Brebeuf, there is no contextual evidence associated with this poem. But if Meadows was responsible for the English lines in *Bod. 1*, it may be conjectured that M.'s Latin lines were written in connection with his bid (successful in 1657) to become a Latin secretary. With their notable economy and poise, were they intended to be a further affidavit of M.'s skills with words? Or, if they were written during M.'s stay in France (January–August 1656), were they intended as a compliment, as suggested by (Legouis (1971), I.275)? Or as an example for his pupil William Dutton?

In the French Translation of Lucan, by Monsieur De Brebeuf are these Verses

> C'est de luy que nous vient cet art ingenieux
> De peindre la parole, et de parler aux yeux;
> Et, par les traits divers de figures tracées,
> Donner de la couleur et du corps aux pensées.
>
> 5   Facundis dedit ille notis, interprete plumâ
> Insinuare sonos oculis, & pingere voces,
> Et mentem chartis, oculis impertiit aurem.

With eloquent signs as the quill interpreted he granted the art of implying sounds to the eyes and of painting words, and he bestowed the mind to paper, the ear to the eyes.

Title. Verses] *1681*; Verses. lib: 3 *Bod. 1*.
1. luy] the Phoenician who invented the alphabet.
2. aux] ava *1681*.
5. plumâ] *Bod. 1*; plumas *1681*.

7. Et . . . aurem] *1681*; Conspicuamque levi mentem transmittere chartâ (He looked forward by that which is written on paper to transforming the mind to agility). *Bod. 1*.

42

The Second Chorus from Seneca's Tragedy Thyestes

Date. ?1671. Craze (1979), 307–8, suggests that M. wrote the poem on the occasion of his removal to Highgate in 1671. The poem bears some marks of indebtedness to both Milton's *Paradise Regained* (1671) and Cowley's version of Seneca's lines (1668) (see below, *Source* and l. 2 n.). Further support for a later date is given by Wilcher (1985), 107 (see below, ll. 1–2 n.)

Publication. 1681. The poem appeared later in Henry Playford's *Banquet of Musick* (1691). The translation was copied into BL MS Add. 29921, fol. 81ʳ⁻ᵛ (*BL 1*), as well as Bod., MS Rawl. poet 90, fol. 165ʳ⁻ᵛ (*Bod.* 5, a late seventeenth-century verse miscellany), and Bod., MS Rawl. poet 196, fol. 15ᵛ (*Bod.* 11, an early eighteenth-century songbook, possibly of Scottish provenance; in this copy, the last line of the poem is repeated as a refrain).

Context. If Craze's conjecture for the date is correct (see above, *Date*), the poem would belong with M.'s late interest in the Horatian theme of retreat (see above, *The Garden, Headnote, Sources and Genre*), itself reflected in Cowley's *Essays*. Writing to William Popple towards the end of April 1671, M.'s contempt for Charles II's court is clear: 'I think it will be my Lot to go on an honest fair Employment into *Ireland*. Some have smelt the Court of Rome at that Distance. There I hope I shall be out of the Smell of our' (Legouis (1971) II.323). 1671 also saw the beginnings of the 'country' (as opposed to 'court') faction, which would soon become the Whig party. The poem may be a personal statement; it may also be the political badge of an emergent grouping. In this respect, the apparent echo of an Anglican divine (see below, l. 2 n.) may be seen as the appropriation of a theological voice associated with the restored regime by an author whose own association with that regime's enemies (the Puritans, the Cromwellian Protectorate and republicanism) was well known. However it was constructed, the voice of retreat was for M. very much a stance: 1672 would see the publication of the first part of *The Rehearsal Transpros'd*; its impact

generated the greatest public controversy of M.'s career. See also the discussion in Shifflett (1998), 71–2.

Source. The poem is a direct translation from the end of Seneca, *Thyestes*, ll. 391–403:

> *Stet, quicumque volet, potens*
> *aulae culmine lubrico:*
> *me dulcis saturet quies;*
> *obscuro positus loco,*
> *leni perfruar otio;*
> *nullis nota Quiritibus*
> *aetas per tacitum fluat.*
> *Sic cum transierint mei*
> *nullo cum strepitu dies,*
> *plebeius moriar senex.*
> *Illi mors gravis incubat,*
> *qui, notus nimis omnibus,*
> *ignotus moritur sibi.*

(Let anyone who shall so wish stand in power on the slippery top of a palace: but let sweet repose satisfy me. Planted in some obscure place, let me enjoy calm leisure. Let my age flow smoothly on, a stranger to law suits; and when my days have thus passed without clatter, let me die unaristocratic but old. On that man death lies heavy who, known only too well to the world, dies still unknown to himself.)

The passage was quite commonly translated during the Renaissance: in England by Wyatt (*c.* 1530–42), Jasper Heywood (1560; in his translation of the entire tragedy), Cowley (1668; in *Several Discourses by Way of Essays, in Verse and Prose, 3. Of Obscurity*), Sir Matthew Hale (1676), and after M.'s death, John Norris (1684) and George Granville, Baron Lansdowne (1712). Cowley's version takes twenty-six lines to render Seneca's thirteen strophes, and Hale twenty-two. M.'s fourteen lines are by far the closest to Seneca. Cowley's version is looser than M.'s:

> Upon the slippery tops of human State,
>   The guilded Pinnacles of Fate,
> Let others proudly stand, and for a while
>   The giddy danger to beguile,
> With Joy and with disdain look down on all,

Till their Heads turn, and down they fall.
Me, O ye Gods, on Earth, or else so near
   That I no fall to Earth may fear,
And, O ye Gods, at a good distance seat
   From the long Ruines of the Great,
Here wrapt in th'Arms of Quiet let me lye;
Quiet, Companion of Obscurity.
Here let my life, with as much silence slide,
   As Time that measures it does glide.
Nor let the Breath of Infamy or Fame,
From Town to Town echo about my Name.
Nor let my homely Death embroidered be
   With Scutcheon or with Elogie
   An old *Plebeian* let me die,
Alas, all then are such as well as I.
   To him, alas, to him, I fear,
The face of Death will terrible appear,
Who in his life flattering his senceless pride
By being known to all the world beside,
Does not himself, when he is Dying know
Nor what he is, nor whither he's to go.

Translation and Versification. M.'s translation is in trochaic heptasyllables. These were probably meant to be closer to Seneca's glyconics than the pentameters of Wyatt and Cowley. The poem is divided into two groups of three lines, rhyming aaa, that frame two more groups of four lines, the first in rhyming couplets,

the second rhyming abab. l. 4 and l. 6 contain additions to the original in the shape of two strong images. The presence of death at l. 14 is not in the original. M. follows Wyatt's translation in this respect, as opposed to the twenty-two lines of Hale's translation.

The Second Chorus from Seneca's Tragedy *Thyestes*

Stet quicunque volet potens Aulae culmine lubrico etc.

Translated

    Climb at court for me that will
    Tottering favour's pinnacle;
    All I seek is to lie still.
    Settled in some secret nest
5   In calm leisure let me rest;
    And far off the public stage
    Pass away my silent age.
    Thus when without noise, unknown,
    I have lived out all my span,
10 I shall die, without a groan,
    An old honest countryman.
    Who exposed to others' eyes,
    Into his own heart ne'er pries,
    Death to him's a strange surprise.

Title. Lord, Donno, Walker; Senec. Traged. ex Thyeste Chor. 2 *1681*; The honest Country Man: *Bod. 5*; [No title, but placed under header 'Songs'] *Bod. 11*; A Translation of the Second Chorus from Seneca's *Thyestes Kermode*.
2. Tottering favour's pinnacle] *1681*, *BL 1*; Tott'ring favours Pinnacle, all I see *Bod. 5*; Giddy favour's slipp'ry hill *Bod. 1*. Craze (1979), 307, prefers *1681* because 'pinnacle' is closer to *culmen* ('peak', 'summit') than 'hill'. But this reading relegates *lubrico* ('slippery'). 'Tottering' is meant to refer to *lubrico* and may have been suggested by Jasper Heywood's 1560 translation: 'In tyckle top of court delight to stand'), but 'giddy' adds the extra dimension of the sense of vertigo at being on such a precarious height. Both versions appear to respond to the first four lines of Cowley's translation (see above, *Headnote, Source*). 'Pinnacle' is probably taken from Matt. 4:5: 'Then the devil taketh him up into the holy city, and setteth him on a pinnacle of the temple.' See also Luke 4:9, and Milton, *Paradise Regained*, IV, l. 549. Widespread theological debate over the meaning of the pinnacle episode involved the suggestion that it prefigured the crucifixion of Christ (Carey in Milton, ed. Carey (1997), 507). Duncan-Jones (as reported in Wilcher (1985), 107), detects an echo from Richard Allestree's *The Causes of the Decay of Christian Piety* (1667), 112: 'He who desires to be *great* only *in the Kingdom of Heaven*, laughs at the busie *aspirings to secular greatness*, and wonders at the force of that *enchantment*, which engages men with so extream a toil, to climb a tottering *pinnacle*, where the standing is uneasie, and the fall deadly.' For *culmen*, cp. also Lucan, *De Bello Civili*, V, ll. 249–51: 'Haud magis expertus discrimine Caesar in ullo est,/Quam non e stabili tremulo sed culmine cuncta/

Despiceret staretque super titubantia fultus' (In no peril was Caesar more clearly taught how insecure and even tottering was the eminence from which he looked down upon the world, and how the ground he stood on quaked beneath him.)
3. All I seek is to] *1681+*; Is to *Bod. 5. seek*] *1681+*; wish *Bod. 11*.
4. secret] *1681+*; saccrid [i.e. sacred] *Bod. 11*.
5. leisure] specifically, free unoccupied time (*OED* n. 3). M. closely translates Seneca's *otio* (*otium*: in this context, freedom from business).
7. silent] a) unnoticed, unrecorded (*OED*. A 3 c) b) i.e. making no impact. From Seneca's *tacitum* where silence is a descriptive figure for the smooth flowing of a river (i.e. the figure of the river of life), which was adapted from Virgil, *Aeneid*, IX, ll. 30–1: 'ceu septem surgens sedatis amnibus altus/per tacitum Ganges' (even as Ganges, rising high in silence with his seven peaceful streams). *age*] lifetime.
8. Thus when] *1681+*; When thus *Bod. 11*. Thus] closely following Seneca's *Sic*.
9. I have] *1681+*; I've *Bod. 5*.
10. I shall die] a perfectly correct translation of Seneca's *moriar*.
11. countryman] Tarrant, in Seneca (1985), 148, argues that by *plebeius*, Seneca (along with other moralists) would have meant 'common' or 'ordinary' in a favourable sense.
12–14. Who . . . surprise] the freest part of the translation, reversing the order of Seneca and most of the English translations. Craze (1979), 307, suggests that M. adopts Wyatt's 'daised with dreadful face', but in a manner 'more tenderly . . . more dramatically'. There might also be an echo of Cowley's 'The face of Death will terrible appear' (l. 22).
13. pries] *1681+*; spys *Bod. 11*.

43
Janae Oxenbrigiae Epitaphium

Date. Late April–May 1658. Jane, wife of John Oxenbridge (see above, *Bermudas, Headnote, Context*) died on 23 April 1658. Her burial is recorded in Eton parish register on 28 April. The witness for the date of her death is the text of the epitaph in *1681*. Wood's dating of the death as 22 April 1655 (Bod. MS Wood B.12, 252), and Le Neve's date of 23 April 1653 (he also claims she was aged 77, as do Baker, Huggett and Cole; see below, *Publication*), are now discounted.

Publication. The epitaph was originally engraved on a black marble surface, placed beneath Jane Oxenbridge's monument, erected on the south wall of Eton College Chapel, under an arch over the second ascent to the altar, and near the entrance to Lupton's Chantry. Over the monument were set the arms of Oxenbridge impaling those of Butler: a silver lion rampant against a red background with a green border, with gold shells, against three gold covered cups (see BL, Add. MS 4843, fol. 153ʳ; see also the drawing in Bod. MS Ashmole 1137, fol. 119). Under the epitaph was set a shorter memorial inscription to Oxenbridge's second wife, Frances, daughter of the Puritan divine Hezekiah Woodward. M.'s lines were obscured by whitewash at the Restoration; apparently an erasure of an object with Commonwealth and Puritan associations ('this larg epitaph giving offence to the Royalists at the Kings Restauration, an. 1660, it was daubed out with paint', Bod. MS Wood B.12, 253); the monument itself was removed during alterations made in 1699. A copy of the epitaph was printed in *1681*. Seven MS copies survive. Four are in eighteenth-century antiquarian works, while three were made in the seventeenth century, including two before M.'s death:

BL 13   BL, Lansdowne MS 1233, fol. 99ʳ·ᵛ. Copy in a composite volume of topographical notes and epitaphs; made on 8 May 1661

Bod. 10   Bod., MS Wood B.12, 251–2. Copy in Anthony Wood's hand in his autograph volume of notes on chapels in Windsor and Eton; 1677

Bod. 9   Bod., MS Ashmole 1137, fol. 119. Copy in Elias Ashmole's hand in a folio composite volume of Ashmole's antiquarian collections; late seventeenth century

BL 11   BL, Harley MS 3614, fol. 5ᵛ. Copy in the hand of the antiquary John Le Neve in a folio volume of monumental inscriptions made between 1651 and 1675; early eighteenth century

BL 12   BL, Harley MS 7034, 312–13. Copy in the hand of the antiquary Thomas Baker in a folio volume of his collections; early eighteenth century

BL 9   BL, Add. MS 4843, fol. 153ʳ·ᵛ. Copy in the hand of Rev. Roger Huggett, Librarian of Eton College in his folio volume of materials for a history of Eton College; mid-eighteenth century

BL 10   BL, Add. MS 5831, fols. 62–3. Copy in the hand of the antiquary William Cole in vol. XXX of his miscellaneous collections; eighteenth century

Text. *BL 13, Bod. 9* and *Bod. 10* present the epitaph as strophic verse, line by line, in accordance with the actual inscription, as opposed to the continuous prose of *1681*. Kelliher (1978), 73, and *BLJ*, 4 (1978), 134–9, establishes that several early MS copies (*BL 9–13*) derive from a careless transcript made by the chapel clerk at Eton, 'Taffy' Woodward (see *BL 10*): several faults were introduced at this stage. This transcriber (and whoever made the transcription in *Bod. 10*; possibly Anthony Wood himself) read the words through the paint, and evidently had difficulties reading some words and numbers. The existence of *BL 13* enables the recovery of the text of the original engraved inscription. As with the Trott epitaphs, the text in *1681*, was set from a draft or fair-copy made by M. before final changes were introduced. Kelliher (1978), 72, contains a reconstruction of the original transcription.

Context. Jane Oxenbridge (b. 1620–21) was the daughter of Thomas Butler of Newcastle, merchant, and Elizabeth Clavering, of Callaley. She married John Oxenbridge (1608–74) in 1634, shortly after he was expelled from Magdalen Hall, Oxford. For Oxenbridge's career, and M.'s residence with the Oxenbridges in Eton, during the time that he was tutor to Oliver Cromwell's ward, William Dutton, see above, *Bermudas, Headnote, Context,* 54–5. The arms above the monument, on top of the arch, were sketched in *Bod. 10,* and described in *Bod. 9* as a silver lion rampant, 'a bord v^t charged with escall. Ag. A chev. Betw. 3. cups covered.' A brief epitaph to Oxenbridge's second wife, Francis, daughter of Hezekiah Woodward, stood near it. Wood later called it a 'large canting inscription', in which Oxenbridge made 'a grievous puling' after his wife (Bod. MS Wood B12, 251–2). But Wood confirmed the implication in M.'s lines that Jane Oxenbridge was more than a merely pious wife, since he reports that she used to 'preach among ye women'. In *Athenae Oxonienses,* this statement was preceded by the observation that she preached 'amongst her gossips', a phrase among many objected to in the *Memoirs of Mr Ambrose Barnes* (written *c.* 1709; *Publications of the Surtees Society,* 50 (Durham, 1867), 63), brother-in-law of Jane Oxenbridge. Barnes' *Memoirs,* 64, attest to Jane Oxenbridge's prowess as a scriptural commentator: 'a schollar beyond what is usual in her sex, and of a masculine judgement in the profound points of theologie, [her husband] loved commonly to have her opinion upon a text of scripture before he preacht from it'.

By common reputation, Puritans and funerary monuments do not go hand in hand. Cavalier verse made much of godly contempt for monuments, and derided Puritan habits of commemoration. Extravagant expense was discouraged, and there was objection to the use of images of the departed: it was seen as a kind of idolatry. There are recorded instances of the desecration of monuments by soldiers, and, allegedly, by Puritan separatists. Parliament, however, understood the importance of the monuments as a means of sustaining social hierarchies through a visible and material sign of status and family identity. Jane Oxenbridge's epitaph is very much in keeping with refined Puritan epitaphs, emphasizing her piety and her domestic virtues. A royalist satire of her husband's patron, Oliver Cromwell, bitingly mocked Puritan scruples with monuments: 'no Stone/Shall stand this Epitaph; *That he has None*' ('Cromwell's Panegyrick', *Rump: Or an Exact Collection of the Choycest Poems* (1662), 225). Ironically, M.'s Puritan epitaph of Jane Oxenbridge was itself a victim of Royalist iconoclasm. The history of the early modern epitaph is explored by Scodel (1991): see, especially 22–3, 208–9, and ch. 7.

Janae Oxenbrigiae Epitaphium

Juxta hoc marmor, breve mortalitatis speculum,
  Exuviae jacent Janae Oxenbrigiae.
    Quae nobili, si id dixisse attinet,
Paterno Butleriorum, materno Claveringiorum genere orta,
5 Johanni Oxenbrigio Collegii AEtonensis socio nupsit.
Prosperorum deinceps et adversorum consors fidelissima.
    Quem, religionis causa oberrantem,
    Usque ad incertam Bermudae insulam secuta:
Nec mare vastum, nec tempestates horridas exhorruit:
10   sed, delicato corpore,
Quos non labores exanclavit? quae non, obivit itinera?
    Tantum mariti potuit amor, sed magis Dei.
Tandem cum, (redeunte conscientiarum libertate) in patriam redux,
    Magnam partem Angliae cum marito pervagata;
15 Qui laetus undequaque de novo disseminabat Evangelium.
    Ipsa maximum ministerii sui decus,
      et antiqua modestia
Eandem animarum capturam domi, quam ille foris exercens.
    Hic tandem divino nutu cum illo consedit:
20 Pietatis erga Deum, charitatis erga proximos
    Conjugalis et materni affectus, omnium virtutum
    Christianarum exemplum degebat inimitabile.

6. *Consors fidelissima*] BL 13, BL 12; Consors ei fidelissima *Bod. 9, BL 11, BL 10, BL 11*; ei Consors fidelissima *1681.*
7–9. *Quem . . . exhorruit*] Cp. *Bermudas,* l. 12: 'Safe from the storms, and prelates' rage.' *Quem*] BL 13+; Quam BL 12.
14–15. *Magnam . . . Evangelium*] in contrast to the hope that the gospel will spread beyond the Bermudas: 'Which thence (perhaps) rebounding, may/Echo beyond the Mexique Bay' (*Bermudas,* ll. 35–6).
15. *disseminabat*] BL 13+; disseminasset BL 9, BL 10, BL 11.
16. *sui*] not in BL 12.

17. *et antiqua modestia*] Cp. *An Epitaph upon Frances Jones,* ll. 9–10: 'To say she lived a virgin chaste,/ In this age loose and all unlaced.'
18. *ille*] BL 13+; illo BL 12.
20. *Pietatis*] BL 13+; Ubi pietatis Bod. 9, 1681.
20–1. *charitatis . . . virtutem*] BL 13; conjugalis & materni affectus, erga proximos charitatis, omnium denique Virtutum *1681.*
22. *degebat*] 1681+; decebat *Bod. 9*; [a blank space] *BL 13.*

Donec quinque annorum hydrope laborans,
Per lenta incrementa ultra humani corporis modum intumuit.
25   Anima interim spei plena, fidei ingens,
Stagnanti humorum diluvio tranquillè vehebatur.
Et tandem, post 37 peregrinationis annos, 23 Apr. Aº 1658.
Evolavit ad Coelos, tanquam columba ex arca corporis:
          Cujus semper dulci, semper amarae memoriae,
30   Moerens maritus posuit.
Flentibus juxta quatuor liberis,
Daniele, Bathshua, Elizabetha, Maria.

Epitaph of Jane Oxenbridge

Beside this stone, a brief reflection of her mortal life, lie the remains of Jane Oxenbridge. She was born, if it is proper to mention, of the noble line of the Butlers on her father's side, of the Claverings on her mother's. Thereafter, she married John Oxenbridge, a fellow of Eton College. She was a most faithful wife to him in prosperity and adversity. When he was driven into exile for the sake of his religion, she followed him to the troubled island of Bermuda, fearing neither the great sea nor its rough storms. But frail of body, what toils did she not undergo, from what journeys did she shrink? So much could love of her husband accomplish, but more, her love of God. When, finally, upon the rebirth of liberty of conscience, she returned to his homeland, she travelled with her husband through much of England, wherever it was his joy once again to preach the gospel. She herself was the greatest glory of his ministry; her old-fashioned purity of character enacted in her household the same illumination of souls as did his public preaching. It was here, that by God's will, she ultimately came to settle with him; she performed the works of Christian piety, acts of charity towards her neighbours, maternal and conjugal affection, and offered an inimitable example of all Christian virtues, until, suffering five years with dropsy, by gradual stages she became swollen beyond the limit of the human form. Yet all the while her soul was full of hope, great in faith, until it was peacefully washed away with the accumulation of body fluids. And at length, after thirty-seven years of her earthly pilgrimage, on April 23, 1658, her soul flew to heaven as a dove from the ark of her body; her grieving husband placed [this stone], along with their four weeping children Daniel, Bathsheba, Elizabeth, Mary, to the ever painful memory of one who was always sweet.

---

23. *hydrope*] dropsy: morbid condition characterized by accumulation of watery fluids in the serous cavities, or connective tissues, of the body (OED 1). Cp. Donne, *Holy Sonnet*, III, l. 9 (1633): 'Th'hydroptique drinkard, and night-scouting thiefe.'
25–8. *Anima . . . corporis*] a conceit in which Jane Oxenbridge's death is compared to the biblical deluge (Gen. 6:6–8). The flight of her soul from her body is likened to Noah releasing the dove from the ark to search for dry land (Gen. 8: 8, 10, 12). The conceit appears extravagant, of the kind that pushes comparison to breakdown or parody (see above, *To his Coy Mistress*, ll. 7–16). However, the image is apt as an attempt to describe a grossly swollen body, even though the impression of the soul being swept away by the deluge of retained body fluids defies the idea of the separation of body and soul that is the conceit's subject.
27. 37] *BL 13, 1681; 77 BL 9, BL 10, BL 11, BL 12. 1658*] *BL 9, 1681; 1653 BL 10, BL 11, BL 12; 1655 BL 13.*
28. Evolavit] *1681+; volabat BL 13, Bod. 10, Bod. 11.*
29. dulci] *Bod. 10+; dulcis BL 13.*
32. Bathshua] *BL 13+; Kather Bod. 10.*

44
Johannis Trottii Epitaphium
and
45
Edmundi Trottii Epitaphium

Date. Late August–September 1667. Although funerary verse was almost always written soon after the death of the subject, and was in effect part of the formal grieving process that took place, M. was in Russia when John Trott died on 28 June 1664. Edmund Trott died on 11 August 1667. That the two poems were written at the same time is supported by their similarity. M. also wrote to Trott in August 1667 expressing his condolences for the loss of both sons. See further Von Maltzahn (2005), 97.

Publication. The epitaphs were engraved on monuments in the Church of St Mary the Virgin (now the Old Church), Laverstoke, Hampshire. *1681*.

Text. By consulting the monuments at Laverstoke (see below, *Context*), Margoliouth was able to provide a full text, as opposed to the version with abbreviated lines in *1681*. He was also able to provide a number of minor corrections, some of which had already been identified by earlier editors, including the annotator of *Bod. 1*.

Context. John (1642–64) and Edmund Trott (1643–67) were the sons of Sir John Trott (d. 1672; created Baronet, 12 October 1660) of Laverstoke Manor in Hampshire, nine miles east of Andover, which he had purchased in 1653. He was a local official during the Commonwealth and Protectorate, and was MP for Andover during the Restoration. He served with M. on the committee investigating misconduct after the Second Dutch War. Trott retained his nonconformist sympathies during the Restoration, and voted with the opposition. Duncan-Jones (*N & Q*, n.s. 13 (1966), 26–7) suggests that he was an exemplar of virtue for M.,

as opposed to the corrupt Clarendon. Like Trott, Clarendon had lost his hopes of issue (not his sons, but his infant grandsons, in May and June 1667), but there the comparison ended (see also below, *The Second Advice to a Painter, General Headnote, Manuscript Circulation*).

The poem tells us that John attended school at Winchester. Both sons matriculated at Oriel College, Oxford on 7 December 1660, aged 18 and 17 respectively. John became a student of the Inner Temple in 1661, and Edmund in 1664. Both died of smallpox, John on 28 June 1664, Edmund on 11 August 1667.

Monuments to the family were erected in the Church of St Mary the Virgin, Laverstoke, which became in 1874–75 the mortuary chapel of the Portal family and is known as the 'old church'. Among these were the tablets to John and Edmund Trott. Margoliouth saw these lapidary texts and corrected the versions in *1681* in accordance with them. According to Pevsner (1967), the monuments were moved to Hinton Ampner.

Genre, Structure and Style. The epitaphs are typical of their genre and time in lamenting (albeit young) honest men: see Scodel (1991), 148–50; see also above, *Janae Oxenbrigiae Epitaphium, Headnote, Context*. Such critical comment as there is on the epitaphs is impressed by M.'s Latin syntax. McQueen and Rockwell (78) note the parenthesis in the first epitaph (ll. 7–8): 'an excellent instance of the possibilities of Latin word order which make Latin for some purposes a more satisfactory vehicle than a non-inflected language. . . . The idea of the boy's merits, modestly voiced, being unheard in the clamor of his parents' grief, is a mild but very characteristic conceit.'

Johannis Trottii Epitaphium

    Charissimo Filio Iohanni Trottio
      Iohannes Trottius
  (E Laverstoke In Agro Hantoniensi Baronettus
    Pater Et Elizabetha Mater
5   funebrem tabulam curavimus.
    Age Marmor, & pro solita tua humanitate,
(Ne inter Parentum Dolorem & Modestiam
Supprimantur praeclari Juvenis meritae laudes)
   Effare Johannis Trottii breve Elogium.
10   Erat ille totus Candidus, Politus, Solidus,
    Ultra vel Parii Marmoris metaphoram,
    Et Gemma Scalpi dignus, non Lapide:
  E Schola Wintoniensi ad Academiam Oxonii,
Inde ad Interioris Templi Hospitium gradum fecerat:
15 Summae Spei, Summae Indolis, ubique vestigia reliquit;
     Supra Sexum Venustus,
     Supra AEtatem Doctus,
     Ingeniosus supra Fidem.
  Et jam vicesimum tertium annum inierat,
20 Pulcherrimo undequaque vitae prospectu,
    Quem Mors immatura obstruxit.
Ferales Pustulae Corpus tam affabre factum
Ludibrio habuere, & vivo incrustarunt sepulchro.
   Anima evasit Libera, AEterna, Faelix,
25   Et morti insultans
Mortalem Sortem cum Foenore accipiet.
    Nos interim, meri vespillones,
Parentes Filio extra ordinem Parentantes,
Subtus in gentilitia crypta reliquias composuimus,
30   Ipsi eandem ad Dei nutum subituri.
Natus est XXVII° Sept^is An° MCDXLII obiit XXVIII°
     Junii MDCLXIIII
   Reviviscet Primo Resurrectionis.

Epitaph of John Trott

For our beloved son, John Trott, John Trott (Baronet from Laverstoke in Hampshire) the father, and Elizabeth, the mother, have established this funeral tablet. Act your part, O marble, and with your customary humanity (lest amid the grief of his parents and the modesty of the distinguished youth his merited praises should be kept secret) speak the brief epitaph of John Trott. He was wholly unblemished, refined, genuine, even beyond the metaphor of Parian marble and worthy to be carved on a gem, not stone. From the school at Winchester to Oxford, thence to quarters in the Inner Temple he made his way: everywhere he left signs of the highest promise, of the greatest ability; charming beyond his sex, learned beyond his age, talented beyond belief. And he had just begun his twenty-third year, with the fairest prospect of life on all sides, which untimely Death obstructed. The deadly pox made sport of his well-made body and encrusted him in a living tomb. Yet his soul escaped, free, immortal, happy, and, mocking death, will receive its mortal fate with profit. We, meanwhile, are mere undertakers, parents, contrary to custom, sacrificing for a son. Below in the family crypt we have interred the remains, likewise we ourselves shall be submitted to the will of God. He was born September 27, 1642. He died June 28, 1664. He will rise on the morn of Resurrection.

1–4. *Laverstoke+*; Charissimo Fili o & c./Pater Et Mater & c. *1681.*
10. *Candidus . . . Solidus*] applying both to John in l. 9, and the Parian marble of l. 11.
11. *Parii Marmoris*] white marble from the Aegean island, in the Cyclades group, of Paros, highly valued by the ancients for statuary.
19. As Legouis notes, there is a discrepancy between the claim in this line and the dates given at ll. 31–2 below.
26. *Sortem*] a) fate (Lewis and Short: 'sors', D) b) financial capital (Lewis and Short: 'sors' D 2). The metaphor of economic benefit is strongly embedded in Christian thought and language (see, e.g., Matt. 25:14–30; Smith, *English*, 36 (1987), 197–232), but M.'s deployment of it here may have been

suggested by Sir John Trott's business activities. He was involved in the East India Company from an early stage.
27. *vespillones*] corpse-bearers, but those who carried the bodies of the poor at night (Lewis and Short, 'vespillo'); M. suggests that the parents are impoverished by the loss of their son, and in comparison with his accession to heavenly glory.
28. *Parentes . . . parentantes*] a sound play on two words with different meanings in Latin: 'parento' (Lewis and Short, I) means to offer a solemn sacrifice in honour of deceased parents. The further consequence is a paradox of sense, as the line suggests.
31–3. *Laverstoke*; Natus est & c. reviviscet/Primo Resurrectionis. *1681.*

Edmundi Trottii Epitaphium

Dilectissimo Filio Edmundo Trottio
Posuimus Iidem Iohannes Pater Et Elizabetha Mater
    Frustra superstites.
Legite Parentes, vanissimus hominum ordo,
    Figuli Filiorum, Substructores Nominum,
    Fartores Opum, Longi Speratores,
Et nostro, si fas, sapite infortunio.
        Fuit Edmundus Trottius.
E quatuor masculae stirpis residuus,
Statura justa, Forma virili, specie eximia,
Medio juventutis Robore simul & Flore,
Aspectu, Incessu, sermone juxta amabilis,
Et siquid ultra Cineni pretium addit.
    Honesta Disciplina domi imbutus,
        Peregre profectus
    Generosis Artibus Animum
    Et exercitiis Corpus firmaverat.
    Circaeam Insulam, Scopulos Sirenum
        Praeternavigavit,
Et in hoc naufragio morum & saeculi
Solus perdiderat nihili, auxit plurimum.
        Hinc erga Deum pietate,
    Erga nos Amore & Obsequio,
Comitate erga Omnes, & intra se Modestia
    Insignis, & quantaevis fortunae capax:
    Delitiae AEqualium, Senum Plausus,
    Oculi Parentum (nunc, ah, Lachrymae)
In eo tandem peccavit quòd mortalis.
    Et fatali Pustularum morbo aspersus
        Factus est

(Ut verae Laudis Invidiam ficto Convitio levemus)
    Proditor Amicorum, Parricida Parentum,
        Familiae Spongia:
    Et Naturae invertens ordinem
35   Nostri suique Contemptor,
        Mundi Desertor, defecit ad Deum.
Undecimo Augusti AErae Christianae 1667 suae xxiiii
    Talis quum fiuerit Coelo non invidemus.

Epitaph of Edmund Trott

For our most beloved son, Edmund Trott, we, his father John and his mother Elizabeth, have placed in vain these surviving words. Read, parents, the most futile rank of humans, fabricators of sons, founders of names, stuffers of moneybags, nourishers of distant hopes, and, if it is possible, be wise by our misfortune. Edmund Trott is no more. The last of four sons, proper in stature, with a manly form and distinguished appearance, in the midst of both the strength and the beauty of youth, attractive in aspect, in carriage, in speech equally, and whatever else adds worth to ashes. Imbued with virtuous discipline at home, he left home to strengthen his mind in the noble arts, and his body with exercises. He circumnavigated, and in Circe's island, and of the age he alone lost nothing, he gained much. Hence, with piety toward God, with love and obedience toward us, with kindness toward all, within himself both an exceptional modesty and a fitness for any fortune,

---

1. Dilectissimo] *Laverstoke*; Charissimo *1681.*

2. Iidem . . . Mater] *Laverstoke*; Pater & Mater *1681.*

3. Frustra] because the line has been extinguished with Edmund's death.

5–6. Figulis . . . Substructores . . . Fartores . . . Speratores] the startling comparison of parents to tradesmen as well as merchants exaggerates the sense of earthly mundanity in comparison with mortality and the afterlife.

5. Nominum] *Laverstoke*, *Bod. 1*; Hominum *1681. Speratores*] possibly a financial speculator (see above, *Johannis Trottii Epitaphium*, l. 26 n.).

6. Fartores Opum] see above, *Johannis Trottii Epitaphium*, l. 26 n.

9. Sir John Trott and his wife had five children: one daughter and four sons, two of whom died in infancy, and the two young men who are the subjects of the epitaphs.

18. Circaeam Insulam] Circe was a sea-nymph and sorceress, daughter of the Sun and Perse; after her flight from Colchis, she was reputed to live in the region of the promontory of Circeii in Latium. See, e.g., Virgil, *Eclogues*, X, 70; *Aeneid*, VII, ll. 20, 191; Ovid, *Metamorphoses*, XIV, 247ff. *Scopulos Sirenum*] the Sirens were birds with the faces of virgins who dwelt on the southern coast of Italy, where they lured seafarers

with their sweet voices and then killed them; see Virgil, *Aeneid*, V. l. 864. The *scopuli Sirenum* were three small rocky islands on the south west coast of Campania, between Surrentum and Capreae.

20. hoc . . . saeculi] a reference to the crisis of the Restoration and Clarendon's government (see above, *The Advice to a Painter Poems*, *General Headnote*, *Context*). Margoliouth compares ll. 20–1 with *An Epitaph upon Frances Jones*, ll. 10–12.

27. Oculi] a) darling, jewel ('oculus', Lewis and Short, II A) b) literally, eyes, since he becomes tears at the end of the line ('oculus', Lewis and Short, I).

32. Proditor . . . Parricida Parentum] similar to the wordplay in *Johannis Trottii Epitaphium*, l. 28, augmented this time with alliteration. The language of Roman public life refers the knowing reader back to the context of political corruption surrounding Clarendon's ministry.

33. Spongia] because, being the sole surviving male heir, he will erase the name of his family.

37. Christianae] *Laverstoke*; Christae *1681. Suae xxiiii*] not in *1681.*

38. Not in *Cooke, Thompson* and *Grosart. Coelo*] *Bod. 1, Margoliouth*; Coeeo *Laverstoke*; Calo *1681.*

however great: the delight of his peers, the applause of the old, the darling of his parents' eyes (now, ah, tears), in death he at last has sinned, because mortal. And bespattered with the fatal disease of the pox, he has become (That we may lighten the envy of true praise with a feigned reproof) a betrayer of friends, a parricide, the sponge of his family: and perverting the order of Nature, a despiser of our affairs and his own, a deserter of the world, he has defected to God. On August 11, 1667, of the Christian era, the twenty-fourth year of his own. When such a one goes to heaven, we do not begrudge it.

46
An Epitaph upon Frances Jones

Date. 1672. Although published in *1681*, M.'s poem was carved on a memorial tablet in the crypt of St Martin-in-the-Fields, London, marking the burial of Frances Jones, 1633–72: see Brogan, *RQ*, 32 (1979), 197–9. Prefacing the epitaph are these words: 'Here lyes buried the body of Mistress Frances IONES daughter of ARTHUR Lord vicecount of Ranelagh, by his wife the Lady KATHERINE BOYLE, who was daughter to RICHARD BOYLE Earl of Corke, and Lord high Treasurer of Ireland. She dyed in the prime of her Age, haveing never been marryed, the XXVIII of March in the year MDCLXXII.'

Publication. The precise date of the erection of the monument is unknown; presumably *c*. 1672. *1681*.

Context. Frances Jones was born 23 December 1633. Her mother, somewhat unhappily married, had a notable intellect, and she was sister to the soldier, playwright and politician, Roger Boyle, Lord Broghill, later Earl of Orrery, and Robert Boyle, the celebrated scientist. After her husband's death in 1669, Lady Ranelagh lived in Pall Mall, and, according to Edward Phillips, frequently visited Milton when he was living in Petty France. M. perhaps met Lady Ranelagh and her daughter through Milton.

Genre and Sources. The poem is M.'s only verse epitaph in English. Scodel (1991), 225–30, notes that the poem both exploits and criticizes the contemporary mood of nostalgia in epitaphs: M. 'simultaneously attacks those who idealize the dead out of partisan self-interest and, while purporting not to, idealizes the deceased for his own polemical purposes as a virginal, virtuous Protestant whose exceptional virtues reveal all that is wrong with the Restoration settlement and society'. Unlike other early seventeenth-century epitaphs, M. does not suggest that his poem can influence society: Frances Jones' ideals have no currency in her age, yet it is judged by her. The very deliberate echoes of Donne and of Jonson (ll. 9, 19–20) are for Scodel (232) an instance of M.'s attempt to show poetry's loss of power in a decadent age.

The poem consists of an extended and paradoxical *occupatio*: praise is made by arguing that further praise is unnecessary. This 'self-denying' motif is continued through the poem. Where epitaphs were supposed to sum up the virtues of the deceased, M. claims that the extent of Frances Jones' virtue was the daily summation of her entire life. By such protestation of poetic disempowerment, M.'s speaker imitates the self-denying lifestyle of the godly Puritan. The poem ends in a sharp turn that emphasizes the absence inherent in epitaph representation, so making the 'reader feel the loss of one whose perfection he or she can only know from a distance, through a distorting representation, once it is gone' (Scodel (1991), 230).

Connections have also been made between the treatment of the epitaph genre in the poem with M.'s comments on funerary remarks in *The Rehearsal Transpros'd* (also 1672), where Parker is accused of diminishing the honour of the deceased by excessive praise that is really self-serving (see Scodel (1991), 228–9).

An Epitaph upon Frances Jones

Enough: and leave the rest to Fame.
'Tis to commend her but to name.
Courtship, which living she declined,
When dead to offer were unkind.
5   Where never any could speak ill,
Who would officious praises spill?
Nor can the truest wit or friend,
Without detracting, her commend.
To say she lived a virgin chaste,

10   In this age loose and all unlaced;
Nor was, when vice is so allowed,
Of virtue or ashamed, or proud;
That her soul was on heav'n so bent
No minute but it came and went;
15   That ready her last debt to pay
She summed her life up ev'ry day;
Modest as morn; as midday bright;
Gentle as ev'ning; cool as night;
'Tis true: but all so weakly said;
20   'Twere more significant, 'She's dead.'

Title. An Epitaph upon Frances Jones] An Epitaph upon _____
1681. The identity of Frances Jones remained unknown until
Brogan's discovery (see above, *Headnote, Date*).
1–2. Fame . . . name] the middle term 'commend' becomes the
necessary rhyme word in *On Mr Milton's Paradise Lost*, l. 51–2:
'I too transported by the mode offend,/And while I meant to
praise thee must commend.' See also below, l. 8.
3. Courtship] a) courteous or courtly behaviour (*OED* 1 b)
b) referring to the fact that Frances Jones did not marry.
4. unkind] a) a courtly paradox: it would be discourteous
('unkind': *OED* a. 6) to remember someone in courtly terms
when they had spurned courtliness while alive b) unnatural
(*OED* a. 4).
5. could] i.e. were allowed to (see above, l. 3).
6. officious] a) attentive, courteous (*OED* a. 1) b) dutiful (*OED*
a. 2). *spill*] waste, squander (*OED* v. I 6).
8. commend] see above, ll. 1–2 n.
9. To say] Cp. Jonson, 'To Alphonso Ferrabosco, on his
Booke', l. 11, 'To say, indeed, shee were the soule of heaven.'
10. age . . . unlaced] Scodel (1991), 229–30, suggests that
this comment links closely with M.'s attack on Parker in *The*

Rehearsal Transpros'd (1672) for encouraging moral laxity
while enforcing religious conformity and perpetuating superstition. *loose*] a) ungirt, naked (*OED* a. 1 e) b) wanton; morally
lax (*OED* a. 7). *unlaced*] with the fastenings of clothes undone;
cp. *On Mr Milton's Paradise Lost*, ll. 49–50, where, as opposed
to the immoral ways of Restoration society (alluded to here as
being undressed), the poets are described fastening their
clothes (i.e. rhyming their verse to form couplets).
11. when] where *1672*. *allowed*] a) permitted (*OED* v. III 8 a)
b) approved of (*OED* v. I 2 a).
12. or . . . or] i.e. either . . . or.
14. No minute but it came and went] i.e. no minute passed
without her soul being aware of its heavenly destiny.
17–18. Modest . . . night] these four similes do seem to be
clichés, and hence are 'weakly said' (see below, 19).
19–20. 'Tis true . . . dead] Cp. Jonson, 'To Alphonso
Ferrabosco, on his Booke', ll. 17–18: 'The proofes of all these
bee/Shed in thy Songs;'tis true: but short of thee.'
19. weakly] feebly (*OED* a. 1).
20. She's dead] Cp. Donne, 'The First Anniversarie', l. 183:
'Shee, shee is dead, shee's dead.'

47

Epigramma in Duos Montes Amosclivum et Bilboreum. Farfacio

Date and Context. See below, *Upon the Hill and Grove at Bilbrough, Headnote, Date.* Almscliff Crag overlooks Huby from the north-west, five miles to the south of Harrogate.

Publication. 1681.

Cernis ut ingenti distinguant limite campum
    Montis Amosclivi Bilboreique juga!
Ille stat indomitus turritis undique saxis;
    Cingit huic laetum fraxinus alta caput.
5   Illi patra minax rigidis cervicibus horret:
    Huic quatiunt virides lenia colla jubas.
Fulcit Atlanteo rupes ea vertice caelos:
    Collis at hic humeros subjicit Herculeos.

10 Hic ceu carceribus visum sylvaque coercet:
    Ille oculos alter dum quasi meta trahit.
Ille giganteum surgit ceu Pelion Ossa:
    Hic agit ut Pindi culmine nympha choros.
Erectus, praeceps, salebrosus, et arduus ille:
    Acclivis, placidus, mollis, amoenus hic est.
15 Dissimilis domino coiit Natura sub uno;
    Farfaciaque tremunt sub ditione pares.
Dumque triumphanti terras perlabitur axe,
    Praeteriens aequa stringit utrumque rota.
Asper in adversos, facilis cedentibus idem;
20   Ut credas Montes extimulasse suos.
Hi sunt Alcidae Borealis nempe columnae,
    Quos medio scindit vallis opaca freto.
An potius, longe sic prona cacumina nutant,
    Parnassus cupiant esse Maria tuus.

---

1. *Cernis*] with the sense of 'perceive' as well as 'visually discern'. 'Cerno' is frequently used by Lucretius: see, e.g., *De Rerum Natura*, I, ll. 265–8: 'Nunc age . . . /nequa forte tamen coeptes diffidere dictis,/quod nequeunt oculis rerum primordia cerni' (Now mark me . . . that you may not by any chance begin nevertheless to distrust my words because the first-beginnings of things cannot be distinguished by the eye). *campum*] the plain stretches eastwards between Bilbrough Hill and Almscliff Crag for some sixteen miles; it is the flood plain of the River Wharfe. The major Fairfax residence of Denton is situated a further nine miles upstream to the east. See also *Upon the Hill and Grove at Bilbrough*, l. 24 n.
4. *huic*] disyllabic; see also *A Letter to Doctor Ingelo*, l. 38. *fraxinus*] in Howell's *Dendrologia* (2nd edn, 1644), 115, the ash represents the great warrior-king, Gustavus Adolphus, of Sweden. Cp. also René Rapin, *Hortorum*, trans. John Evelyn the Younger (1672), 'warlike ash' (printed in Evelyn, *Sylva* (1679, 2nd edn), 276.
6. *Huic . . . jubas*] the figurative association of helmet crests (of which some were made from horse manes) with the crests of the hills occurs in *Upon the Hill and Grove at Bilbrough To the Lord Fairfax*, ll. 33–4, just as in Virgil, *Aeneid*, VII, l. 785, *juba* (mane) is used to figure the crest of a helmet. Was M. led to his figure by the similar sound of *collis* (hill) to *collum* (neck), converting *viridis collis* (as in Lucretius, *De rerum natura*, II, l. 322) into M.'s *'virides . . . jubas?*
7–8. *Atlanteo . . . Herculeos*] Atlas was depicted carrying the earth on his head and with his arms, Hercules on his shoulders: see *LIMC*, III.1.4–6.

9–10. *carceribus . . . meta*] terms from chariot-racing in ancient Rome: the *carceres* restrained the horses at the start; the *metae* were pillars at each end of the circus, around which the chariots raced seven times. Both terms are used to form similes in well-known ancient literature: for *carceres*, see Lucretius, *De Rerum Natura*, II, l. 264; Virgil, *Georgics*, I, l. 512; Horace, *Satires*, I.i, l. 114; for *metae*, see, e.g., Horace, *Carmina*, I.i, l. 5.
11. *giganteum . . . Ossa*] two giants, Ephialtes and Otus, the sons of Aloeus, imprisoned Mars and attempted to reach the heavens by piling three mountains, Pelion, Ossa and Olympus, on top of each other. Both were killed by Apollo. See Claudian, *De Bello Gothico*, ll. 67–76.
12. *Hic . . . nympha choros*] the image of Bilbrough Hill as dancing nymphs appears to be suggested by the grove of trees on its summit. Adapted from Virgil, *Georgics*, IV, ll. 532–3: 'Nymphae,/cum quibus illa choros lucis agitabat in altis' (the Nymphs, with whom she was wont to tread the dance in the deep groves) [Legouis]. *Pindi*] Pindus (now Mezzara), a mountain in Thessaly, believed to be the seat of the Muses. See, e.g., Ovid, *Metamorphoses*, VII, ll. 224–6.
18. Cp. Ovid, *Amores*, III.ii.12: 'nunc stringam metas interiore rota'.
21. *Alcidae Borealis*] Fairfax. *columnae*] the pillars of Hercules straddled the straits of Gibraltar: taken now to be the rock of Gibraltar itself, and Mount Acha at Ceuta, North Africa, or Jebel Musa, west of Ceuta.
23–4. *cacumina . . . Parnassus*] Parnassus had two peaks.
24. *cupiant*] 1681+; cupiunt *Aitken, Ormerod and Wortham.* *Maria*] Mary Fairfax.

An Epigram on the two mountains, Almsclif and Bilbrough: To Fairfax

You see how the summits of the mountains Almscliff and Bilbrough mark the plain with a huge boundary! The former stands untamed with towering rocks on every side; the lofty ash surrounds the latter's glad head. On the former a threatening rock stands erect with rigid neck; on the latter smooth necks shake their verdant manes. That cliff supports the heavens with an Atlantean summit; but this hill submits Herculean shoulders. This confines the view with its forest as if by barriers, while that other draws the eyes just as a turning-point. That rises giant-like just as Pelion on Ossa; this, like a Nymph, leads the dancing on the summit of Pindus. That one is erect, sheer, rugged and steep; this is sloping, gentle, soft, lovely. Nature has joined different hills under a single master; and equally do they tremble under the dominion of Fairfax. And while he glides across the lands in his triumphal chariot, as he passes, with his even wheel he draws both together – harsh towards his enemies, likewise accommodating to those who yield, so that you would believe that his own mountains were his motivation. These are indeed the pillars of the Hercules of the North, which a shady valley divides with its middle strait, or rather thus do the peaks bow down from a distance; they wish to be your Parnassus, Mary.

48
Upon the Hill and Grove at Bilbrough
To the Lord Fairfax

Date. Late 1650–52. Hodge, *MP*, 71 (1974), 347–55, argues that the mention of Lady Fairfax in the past tense in l. 43 must mean that the poem should be dated after her death in 1665 (the Fairfaxes were interred in the church at Bilbrough). But the reference to Lady Fairfax is to her courtship by Thomas Fairfax in the context, present in the companion Latin poem, of their daughter Maria Fairfax and her future. We might expect from a post-1665 poem some of the echoes of 1660s' published verse found by Pritchard (*SEL*, 23 (1983), 371–88) in *The Garden*, but there are none. There are, however, several echoes of *The Garden* in the poem, which, if Pritchard's dating of that poem as 1668 is allowed to stand, might be understood as M. using the Bilbrough poem as a source for his later poem. There are fewer echoes of *Upon Appleton House*, but the two works have very similar imagistic and prosodic strategies.

Publication. 1681.

Context. Bilbrough was another Fairfax house and estate, purchased by Sir William Fairfax in 1546; it was the main residence of Fairfax's great grandfather, also called Sir Thomas (d. 1599). The hill lies five miles to the north-west of Nun Appleton, and rises only 145 feet, but does so from flat country. Wilson, *TLS*, 31 March 1972, 367, notes the flattening and disfiguring of the hill through gravel-quarrying, although a farmer had restored something of the hill's soft brow in the early 1970s. The trees in M.'s poem had also disappeared. Wilson points out that hills like Bilbrough, formed by glaciers, are often smooth and symmetrical: M.'s description may not be as fanciful as might at first appear.

Sources and Genre. The poem is indebted to two poetic traditions: the mountain poem and the grove poem (Scoular (1965), 154, 159–62). Retirement to woods for peace and health is a topos in classical verse (see, e.g., Horace, *Epistolae*, I.iv, ll. 4–5; Tacitus,

Dialogus, XII.i). The status of groves as sacred places for ancient people was known in the seventeenth century (see Evelyn, 'An Historical Account of the Sacredness and Use of Standing Groves', in *Sylva* (2nd edn, 1670, Bk. 4)). An ancient naturalist like Pliny understood that superior wood was produced from trees that grew in high, exposed places. The oak and the ash (the two tree species M. mentions as growing on Bilbrough Hill), being the most useful woods, and serving military needs in particular, are appropriate in a poem praising a great soldier: 'the speare or launce of *Achilles* made [of ash]' (Pliny, *Natural History*, trans. Philemon Holland (1601), 1.645). Oak groves were associated with worship in the Old Testament, and the tree was sacred to the Romans (who associated it with Jupiter), as well as the Druids, who were valued as the guardians of an authentic British religion (see, e.g., Cowley, *Plantarum* (1668), Bk 6, 339).

The poem is in the tradition that presents groves as sacred places for worship, meditation and retirement: see, e.g., Ovid, *Amores*, III.i, ll. 1–6; Sarbiewski (see below); Henry Vaughan, 'Upon the Priory Grove, His Usual Retirement' (1645–46). High places were similarly regarded: see, e.g., Mantuan, *Eclogue* VIII, translated by Thomas Harvey (1656), 75: 'the divine and holy Fathers chose/Retired houses, places of repose/Among the mountains'. The deity in the grove in M.'s poem is Fairfax himself. Like M., Sir Thomas Salusbury presented the grove as the site for the union of patron and wife (fusing prothalamion and estate poem, but in Edenic rather than pagan terms) in 'Kensington Grove . . . To the Earl of Carbery and the Fair Lady, that Styled a Paradise on Earth: May 15th: 1637.' Several such poems were written in the mid-seventeenth century: see, e.g., Rowland Watkyns, 'Upon the Golden Grove in the County of Carmarthin, the Habitation of the Right Honourable the Lord Vaughan, Earl of Carbery, Now Lord President of the Marches of Wales' (*c.* 1660), properly a country house poem. Here the grove is idyllic, its owner exemplary in virtue but, unlike the hill in M.'s poem, the grove is not a representation of the owner.

The presence of hills in this tradition of verse, with reference to Sarbiewski and Denham, as well as M., is discussed by Røstvig (1954), 237–42. Sarbiewski's Ode to Paulus Coslovius (35.4) describes temples on hill-tops. In G. Hill's translation ((1646), 103), the poetry is Marvellian in its use of mirror concepts and personification:

> Here, tops of Hills, themselves behold,
> In all their flowry pride unfold.
> The Poplar now that shakes, when th'East winds blow,
> Stood cloth'd in gray, under the ling'ring snow.

M.'s poem contains clear echoes of Hill's translation of Sarbiewski's epode on the estate of the Duke of Bracciano ((1646), 107–8):

> A Bow're growes green, set round with trembling Okes
> Which fanns the Heavens with gentle strokes.
> It clothes the Hills, and spreads it selfe all over
> To th'open Theaters a cover.
> Close joyn'd to the walls, the Nymphs coole Arbour
> Which to the Sunny shore commands.
>
> (see below, ll. 33–4, 43–4)

Sarbiewski and Denham both anticipate M. by implying an ethical stance through the mode of a description of nature. Ethics and morals were taught by the emblem tradition which has been seen as reflected in several lines or stanzas in the poem (see below, ll. 23–4 n.).

The tradition of the grove as a place of retirement, meditation and contemplation is reflected in the titles of theological, political, ethical and practical manuals. The Sir John Vaughan of Golden Grove, who inspired Rowland Watkyns' poem, was the brother of William Vaughan, whose *The Golden-groue, moralized in three books* was published in 1600. Vaughan's book was likened in its prefatory poetry (sigs. A5ʳ, B1ʳ, B2ᵛ) to the Garden of the Hesperides, a 'harbour of delight', quite unlike the gaunt, windy hill in M.'s poem. An influential allegorical satire of the 1640s was James Howell's *Dendrologia* (1640; 1644; French translation 1641). Where M.'s speaking trees offer a panegyric to Fairfax, Howell's express views on contemporary European politics. Prefatory verse (2nd edn, sig. A3ᵛ) claims that groves were the favourite contemplative places of the Druids. By the mid-1650s, groves were associated with the then disestablished Anglicans, latter-day Druids: the grove suggested a place of retirement for a way of worship that was suffering a

kind of internal exile: see, e.g., Jeremy Taylor, *The Golden Grove, Or, A Manuall of Daily Prayers and Letanies* (1655). The association of oaks with monarchy was literally enforced in 1650 when Charles II made his escape after the Battle of Worcester by hiding in an oak tree (see the verse quoted in Evelyn, 'An Historical Account of the Sacredness and Use of Standing Groves', in *Sylva* (2nd edn, 1670), 617). In Cowley's *Plantarum*, Bk 6 (1668), 339, the Druids are seen to cultivate the oak because they foresaw that it would achieve the great triumph enabling Charles's escape. In contrast, Summers (1953; in Carey, ed. (1969), 140) regards the humanized landscape in stanzas I and II of M.'s poem as a representation of the 'Republican gentleman'.

M.'s attitude to trees reflects none of the botanical work associated with the Dutch florists of the previous hundred years, and their English followers, or the proposals for arborial reform made by John Evelyn in *Sylva* (1664), in the context of the depletion of forests in early modern Europe. There is, furthermore, no association of 'arboriculture' with paradisal or millennial themes as expressed by Evelyn and other Hartlibians like John Beale. This material is explored by Parry, Leslie and Chambers in Leslie and Raylor, eds (1992), 130–94 (and for responses to deforestation in the period, see Grove (1995), ch. 1). All of M.'s tree sources could be and probably were in classical literature. It is unlikely that Cowley, Evelyn or Beale read Marvell, since all were prone to extensive citation and quotation, yet none refers to any M. poem.

Structure, Style and Versification. The eight-line stanza of tetrameters organized in rhyming pairs is familiar from *The Unfortunate Lover*, *The Gallery* and *Upon Appleton House*. The first four stanzas are devoted to the hill, then four to the grove, followed by two concluding stanzas: the organization provides the poem with a firm logic, and the poem is notable for its high degree of functional unity. Wilson, *N & Q*, 222 (1977), 126–7, suggests that this organization is symbolic, with significance attaching to the numbers four and ten. There are four pairs of four-beat lines in each stanza; eight eight-syllable lines form the stanza. Four, argues Wilson, connotes solidity and reliability (from the 'four-square' man praised by the ancient Greeks): 'the square [is] likened to the earth, which perchaunce might be the reason that the Prince of Philosophers in his first booke of the *Ethicks*, termeth a constant minded man, euen egal and direct on all sides, and not easily ouerthrowne by euery litle aduersitie, *hominem quadratum*, a square man' (Puttenham, *The Arte of English Poesie* (1589), sig. Niii^r), qualities shown by Fairfax. Multiples of four suggest balance, an attribute of perfection itself. The ten stanzas suggest the Pythagorean *tetractys* or *decad*, the number expressive of perfection, partly because derived by addition of the first four numbers. Pythagorean number theory received extensive treatment in Thomas Stanley's *History of Philosophy* (3 vols, 1655–60), 3.56–7, published with Fairfax's help. The focus of poetic invention is a series of conceits (by which Bilbrough Hill and the trees of the grove are variously personified), but they are never allowed to detract from the literal landscape being described: nature and art are in this respect fused. Leishman (1966), 250, regards the poem as unique in the seventeenth century in this respect: the balance, the equivalence, between the literal and the metaphorical, the factual and the hyperbolical, the pictorial and the conceptual. The description of harmony involves, almost unnoticeably, stasis that moves (l. 5), while disorder is rendered in portmanteau words that are made to seem ugly: a violence in nature that is matched by disfigured words (ll. 11, 13, 28). Roles are reversed: the ground rises up on the hill, or the hill rises on level ground (ll. 23–4; see Carey, in Patrides, ed. (1978), 147). Indeed, so familiar are some conceits (e.g. the 'crest' of the hill implying that it is like either a head or a helmet) that the distance between the figure and the referent

disappears: at this point Fairfax himself appears. In the penultimate stanza, the terms of signifier and signified are reversed (now the battlefield is described as a mountainous landscape with trees) as the outer world of Fairfax's military career is introduced (ll. 67–8). Syntactic control works in a similar way to achieve a sense of reconciliation between distinct objects: art and nature, hills and groves, height and retirement (e.g. ll. 79–80). The conceits and diction are generally far less extravagant and playful than those in *Upon Appleton House*: fitting poetical features for a simpler, more lonely environment. Accordingly, the poem has been regarded as having some merits, but as a lesser achievement than *Upon Appleton House* and related pieces by other poets (e.g. Denham's *Cooper's Hill*: see Bowles (1806) in Carey, ed. (1969), 36). For Leishman (1966), 246, it is but a 'delightful trifle'.

Upon the Hill and Grove at Bilbrough
To the Lord Fairfax

I

See how the archèd earth does here
Rise in a perfect hemisphere!
The stiffest compass could not strike
A line more circular and like;
5 Nor softest pencil draw a brow
So equal as this hill does bow.
It seems as for a model laid,
And that the world by it was made.

---

1. archèd] a) in the shape of an arch b) in the general sense that the earth is round.
2. perfect hemisphere] an oblique compliment to Fairfax in the light of Pythagorean notions of balance and harmony: 'A good wise person . . . / . . . like the world it self, is smooth and round,/In all his polish'd frame no blemish found' (attributed to Ausonius, in Thomas Stanley, *The History of Philosophy* (1660), 3.50).
3. compass] i.e. a pair of compasses.
4. like] even, regular.
5–8. Nor . . . made] Cp. *Upon Appleton House*, ll. 5–8: 'Who of his great design in pain/Did for a model vault his brain,/Whose columns should so high be raised/To arch the brows that on them gazed.'

5. pencil] paintbrush (*OED* n.¹ 1 a). *brow*] a) top edge of a hill (*OED* n.¹ 6) b) eyebrow or forehead (*OED* n.¹ 3, 5), as if the pencil were painting a portrait.
6. equal] symmetrical, evenly proportioned. *bow*] a) curve (*OED* v.¹ 3) b) there is a hint of *OED* v.¹ 6 (to bend the body in a mark of respect): the hill and grove has civility (see below, l. 21), and shows fear and respect for Fairfax (see below, l. 41).
7. model] a) three dimensional representation of a projected structure (*OED* n. I 2) b) exemplar (of sphericality), object adopted for imitation (*OED* n. II 10) c) a painter's model (*OED* n. II 11), continuing the analogy between hill and portrait introduced in l. 5.

II

    Here learn, ye mountains more unjust,
10 Which to abrupter greatness thrust,
    That do with your hook-shouldered height
    The earth deform and heaven fright,
    For whose excrescence ill-designed,
    Nature must a new centre find,
15 Learn here those humble steps to tread,
    Which to securer glory lead.

III

    See what a soft access and wide
    Lies open to its grassy side;
    Nor with the rugged path deters

20 The feet of breathless travellers.
    See then how courteous it ascends,
    And all the way it rises bends;
    Nor for itself the height does gain,
    But only strives to raise the plain.

IV

25 Yet thus it all the field commands,
    And in unenvied greatness stands,
    Discerning further than the cliff
    Of heaven-daring Tenerife.
    How glad the weary seamen haste
30 When they salute it from the mast!
    By night the northern star their way
    Directs, and this no less by day.

9–16. Cp. Sarbiewski, 'To Paulus Iordanus Ursinus, Duke of Braciano. Ode I.Lib. Epod.', trans. G. Hills (1646), 107: 'A gentle Cliffe from a steep Hill doth rise/That even to Heaven, mounts by degrees' (Røstvig (1954), 240). Wilcher (1985), 125, suggests that the thrusting mountains suggest the kind of ambition typified in M.'s view of 'restless Cromwell'.

9. unjust] irregular (*OED* a. 4).

10–16. Cp. Denham, *Cooper's Hill* (1642), ll. 56–60: '*Windsor* her gentle bosome doth present:/Where no stupendous Cliffe, no threatning heights/Accesse deny, no horrid steepe affrights,/But such a Rise, as doth at once invite/A pleasure, and a reverence from the sight.'

10. abrupter] higher, more precipitous ('abrupt': *OED* n. 4).

11. hook-shouldered] i.e. hunch-backed; cp. *The Last Instructions*, l. 163.

13. For] on account of. *excrescence*] abnormal, disfiguring protuberance (*OED* n. 3).

14. A new geometrical centre, since the mountains have distorted the perfect sphere of the earth. Cp. *Upon Appleton House*, ll. 25–6: 'But all things are composèd here/Like Nature, orderly and near.'

15–16. An invocation of Christian humility, like Fairfax's (see *Upon Appleton House*, ll. 31–2, 41–4), expressed through the New Testament metaphor of walking for living: see, e.g., Ephesians 4:1–2: 'I therefore, the prisoner of the Lord, beseech you that ye walk worthy of the vocation wherewith ye are called./With all lowliness and meekness, with longsuffering, forbearing one another in love.'

15. humble . . . tread] Cp. Herbert, 'Marie Magdalene', ll. 4–6: 'Shewing his steps should be the street,/Wherein she thenceforth evermore/With pensive humbleness would live and tread.'

17. access] approach (*OED* n. I 1).

21. courteous] see above, l. 6 n.

22. all . . . bends] a more extended description of how the hill 'bows' (see above, l. 6 n. *bow*] b)).

23–4. Colie (1970), 23, n. 14, suggests consonance with an emblem of a hill and fields, representing the relationship between humility and greatness (Jacobus Camerarius, *Symbolum et Emblematum ex re Herbaria . . .* (Frankfurt, 1654), sig. T3ʳ).

24. raise] a) lift to a higher position (*OED* v.¹ III 17) b) promote or advance (continuing the courtly metaphor (*OED* v.¹ III 18) c) as opposed to the plain in *Upon Appleton House*, l. 452, *rased* lower by the cattle chewing its grass. *plain*] is this the same eastward-looking plain as described in the Latin companion poem (see *Epigramma in Duos Montes Amosclivum et Bilboreum*, l. 1 n.)? The plain extending northwards from Bilbrough Hill, through which flows the River Ouse above York, contains the site of one of Fairfax's (and Parliament's) greatest victories, the Battle of Marston Moor (2 July 1644), which ended Royalist power in the north.

25. field] a) land below the hill b) battlefield (*OED* n. I 6). *commands*] a) looks down upon (*OED* v. III 6 b) b) dominates or controls by strategic superiority (*OED* v. III 6); a military reference: the hill reflects Fairfax's qualities and career.

26. unenvied] not regarded enviously (*OED* ppl. a. 2).

27. Discerning] distinguishing objects at a distance with the eye (*OED* v. 5); another military term: see, e.g., Milton's figurative usage, *Paradise Lost*, I, ll. 326–7: 'His swift pursuers from heaven gates discern/The advantage.'

28. Tenerife] the volcanic peak on the Canary Island of the same name; it rises to 12,192 feet, whereas Bilbrough Hill is but 145 feet high.

29–30. Wilson, *TLS*, 31 March 1972, 367, considers that the reference is to boats sailing up the River Ouse to York, which was still a considerable port in the seventeenth century.

29. haste] pronounced 'harst' in the seventeenth century.

31. northern star] i.e., the Pole-Star.

V

Upon its crest this mountain grave
A plump of agèd trees does wave.
5　No hostile hand durst e'er invade
With impious steel the sacred shade.
For something always did appear
Of the great Master's terror there:
And men could hear his armour still
40　Rattling through all the grove and hill.

VI

Fear of the Master, and respect
Of the great nymph did it protect,
Vera the nymph that him inspired,
To whom he often here retired,
45　And on these oaks engraved her name;
Such wounds alone these woods became:
But ere he well the barks could part
'Twas writ already in their heart.

---

33. crest] a) summit (*OED* n.¹ 5 b) b) likening the top of the hill to a soldier's helmet (*OED* n.¹ 4). *grave*] weighty, authoritative, respected (continuing the association with Fairfax; *OED* a. A 1).

34. plump] *Margoliouth, Legouis, Donno*; plum *1681*; plume *Cooke, Wilcher, Walker*; clump (*OED* n.¹ c); a military usage: a 'plump of spears' described a body of armed men; an archaism, but used in the early seventeenth century (*OED* n.¹ a). 'Cromwell's Plump', a small tree-covered hillock, was the Parliamentary command point during the Battle of Marston Moor (2 July 1644), a few miles to the north of Bilbrough Hill. 'Plume' fits with the figurative likening of the hill to a helmet (*OED* n.¹ 2): cp. Pliny, *Natural History*, tran. Philemon Holland (1601), 1.465: 'A tall tree this is [the ash], and groweth round, bearing leaves set in manner of feathers or wings.' A plumed helmet is likened to a hill with almond trees on the top in Spenser, *The Faerie Queene*, I.vii.32, and was copied by Marlowe, *Tamburlaine the Great*, II, IV.iii, ll. 119–24.

35–6. No hostile hand] in Ovid, *Metamorphoses*, VIII, ll. 741–76, Erysichthon felled the oaks in the sacred grove of Ceres. See Wilson, *BJRL*, 51 (1969), 453–70. Cp. also the destruction of the sacred grove outside Massilia by Caesar and his army in Lucan, *De Bello Civili*, III, ll. 429–31: 'Sed fortes tremuere manus, motique verenda/Maiestate loci, si rebora sacra ferirent,/In sua credebant reditoras membra secures' ('the Souldiers valiant hands/Trembld to strike, mov'd with the Majestie,/And think the *Ax* from off the Sacred Tree/Rebounding back, would their own bodies wound' (May); the translation in the 1776 edition of *Sylva*, published in York, bears a closer affinity to M.'s English: 'None dares with impious steel the bark to rend,/Lest on himself the destin'd stroke descend').

36. impious] irreverent. *sacred shade*] clumps of trees were thought by the ancients as sacred, and were treated as sites of worship (see above, *Headnote, Sources and Genre*). See also below, ll. 69–72 n.

37–40. Cp. the description of the wood of Argiletum, Virgil, *Aeneid*, VIII, ll. 347–58, especially ll. 351–4: ' "hoc nemus, hunc", inquit, "frondoso vertice collem,/quis deus incertum est, habitat deus; Arcades ipsum/credunt se vidisse Iovem, cum saepe nigrantum/aegida concuteret dextra nimbosque cieret" ' ("This grove", he cries, "this hill with its leafy crown, though we know not what god it is – is yet a god's home: my Arcadians believe they have looked on Jove himself, while oft his right hand shook the darkening aegis and summoned the storm-clouds").

38. great Master] Fairfax. *great Master's terror*] Cp. Sarbiewski, 'To Paulus Iordanus Ursinus, Duke of Braciano. Ode I. Lib. Epod.', trans., G. Hills (1646), 107: 'we may descry/A displayd Banner from on hye,/Which to th'Imperiall force a terrour was,/A terrour to great *Borgias*.'

42–3. great nymph . . . Vera the nymph] Ann, Lady Fairfax, daughter of Sir Horace Vere (d. 1665); see below, *Upon Appleton House*, l. 36 n. A 'great nymph', Lauretta, protectress of rural life, is the subject of the second part of Mantuan, *Eclogue*, VIII: Pollux met her on a mountain, although 'she was no Godddess of the Mounts or Trees,/Nor of the Muses' (trans. Thomas Harvey (1656), 77).

43–4. The courtship of the Fairfaxes took place at Denton, not Bilbrough, but M. is imagining Lady Fairfax as the deity of a sacred grove, Fairfax as her devotee.

44. retired] signalling the genre of the retirement poem.

45–8. See *The Garden*, ll. 23–4: 'Fair trees! Wheres'e'er your barks I wound,/No name shall but your own be found.' Cunnar (in Summers and Pebworth, eds (1992), 129–30) notes that these lines represent a correction of the ancient and Petrarchan tradition where lovers violate nature by writing their lovers' names in trees: see, e.g., Theocritus, *Idyll*, XVIII, ll. 47–8; Virgil, *Eclogue*, X, ll. 52–4; Propertius, *Elegy* I.xviii, ll. 21–2. For later versions, see, e.g., Jonson, 'To Penshurst', ll. 15–16. M. is fusing amorous convention with the notion of *signatura rerum*, that God wrote a name in or on all the objects in creation, and placed the names in Adam's mind so that he could perfectly name nature. Cp. Evelyn, *Sylva* (3rd edn, 1679), 265, where trees (and other flora) are themselves 'the most natural and instructive *Hieroglyphicks* of our expected *Resurrection* and Immortality'. According to Howell, the Druids cut their learning into trees (*Dendrologia* (2nd edn, 1644), sig. A3ᵛ).

46. became] a) suited (*OED* v. III 7) b) graced (*OED* v. III 9).

47. barks could part] i.e. separate by cutting into (*OED* v. I 4 b).

48. writ . . . heart] a version of the hermetic notion that all the objects in creation had their true name, the *signatura rerum*, imprinted in or on them by God: the 'true name' of these trees is Vera. See below, *The Garden*, ll. 23–4 n.

VII

For they ('tis credible) have sense,
50   As we, of love and reverence,
And underneath the coarser rind
The Genius of the house do bind.
Hence they successes seem to know,
And in their Lord's advancement grow;
55   But in no memory were seen,
As under this, so straight and green.

VIII

Yet now no further strive to shoot,
Contented if they fix their root.
Nor to the wind's uncertain gust,

60   Their prudent heads too far intrust.
Only sometimes a flutt'ring breeze
Discourses with the breathing trees;
Which in their modest whispers name
Those acts that swelled the cheek of Fame.

IX

65   'Much other groves', say they, 'than these
And other hills him once did please.
Through groves of pikes he thundered then,
And mountains raised of dying men.
For all the civic garlands due
70   To him, our branches are but few.
Nor are our trunks enow to bear
The trophies of one fertile year.'

49–56. M. uses the trees as a conceit for family trees. Cp. *Upon Appleton House*, ll. 489–92.
49. sense] consciousness or recognition of (*OED* n. II 17 a).
51. rind] bark of a tree (*OED* n.¹ 1).
52. Genius of the house] guardian spirit or deity of the place; *genius loci*. Referring to the classical notion that nymphs or tutelary genii lived within trees: see Evelyn, *Sylva* (3rd edn, 1679), 267.
56. this] i.e. this Lord. *straight*] a) vertical (*OED* a. A 7) b) tall (not in *OED*) c) figuratively: honest, proper, right (*OED* a. A 6); does M. mean the ash (see *Epigramma in Duos Montes Amosclivum et Bilboreum*, l. 4) rather than the oak (see above, l. 45) trees? Oaks were known to grow sideways quickly but upwards very slowly (see, e.g., Evelyn, *Sylva* (1664), 9).
57. shoot] a) grow (*OED* v. I 6) b) figuratively: fire (*OED* v. III 21; the trees now reflect Fairfax's restrained military ambitions in retirement).
58–9. fix . . . gust] '*Seneca* observes *Woods* most expos'd to the *Winds* to be the most *strong* and *solid*', Evelyn, *Sylva* (1664), 12.
58. fix their root] contrast *The Garden*, l. 49: 'Here at the fountain's sliding foot.'
59–60. Cp., Evelyn, *Sylva* (3rd edn, 1679), 258, where such imagery is taken allegorically: 'our late *Enthusiasts* amongst us; who, when their *Quaking* fits possess them, resemble the giddy motion of *trees*, whose heads are agitated with *every wind of Doctrine*'.
63–4. Cp. Sir Thomas Salusbury, 'Kensington Grove . . . To the Earl of Carbery and the Fair Lady, that Styled a Paradise on Earth: May 15th: 1637', ll. 43–5: 'The very trees do prophesy success/To your chaste loves, and promise happiness/Eternal as your souls.' Salusbury looks forward, M. backwards, in time. Cp. also T.P., 'On the Vocall Forest', in Howell, *Dendrologia* (2nd edn, 1644), sig. A4ᵛ: 'the wagging leafes first mutter,/At th' change, and streight *State-Language* they doe utter./The pleasant *Arbour* gently whispers This.' Howell then claims that once trees spoke and moved like men (ibid., 1). Fruit trees were supposed to talk (and always tell the truth), either directly

to the conscience without words, or to speak all languages: see Ralph Austen, *A Dialogue, Or Familiar Discourse, and conference between the Husbandman, and Fruit-Trees* (Oxford, 1676), 1–2.
64. swelled the cheek] as Fame drew in air to blow her trumpet (Fowler (1994)).
65. other groves] Cp. Milton, *Lycidas* (1637), ll. 172–4: 'So Lycidas sunk low, but mounted high. . . . Where other groves, and other streams along'; *The Garden*, ll. 43–6: 'The mind, that ocean where each kind/Does straight its own resemblance find;/Yet it creates, transcending these,/Far other worlds, and other seas.'
67. groves of pikes] Cp. Waller, 'The Battle of the Summer Islands' (1645), 3, ll. 53–4: 'Their fixed javelins in her side she wears,/And on her back a grove of pikes appears.' Waller describes the hunting of a whale, and compares it to an island rising out of the sea at l. 56, just as M.'s hill rises from the plain. *thundered*] Fairfax is imagined as Jove.
69–72. Cp. *A Poem upon the Death of his Late Highness the Lord Protector*, ll. 261–4: 'Not much unlike the sacred oak which shoots/To heaven its branches and through earth its roots:/Whose spacious boughs are hung with trophies round,/And honoured wreaths have oft the victor crowned.'
69. civic garlands] of oak, given to him who saves a city from slaughter and ruin by an enemy (see *The Garden*, l. 2); Augustus was given such a crown of oak *in perpetuum* for his protection of the lives of the citizens (Ovid, *Fasti*, I, l. 614).
71. enow] enough (*OED* a. 2 b).
72. trophies] 'It was upon the trunk of a knotty and sturdy Oak the ancient heroes were wont to hang the arms and weapons taken from the enemy, as trophies', Evelyn, *Sylva* (2nd edn, 1670). For Parry (in Leslie and Raylor, eds (1992), 143), Evelyn's comment shows an understanding of how the active life paid tribute to the contemplative. *one fertile year*] Cp. *An Horatian Ode*, ll. 73–4: 'And now the Irish are ashamed/To see themselves in one year tamed.'

X

'Tis true, ye trees, nor ever spoke
More certain oracles in oak.
75   But peace (if you his favour prize):

That courage its own praises flies.
Therefore to your obscurer seats
From his own brightness he retreats:
Nor he the hills without the groves,
80   Nor height but with retirement loves.

---

73. *ye*] *Bod. 1*; the *1681*.
74. Alluding to the sacred (and oldest) Greek oracle at Dodona: see above, *Headnote, Genre and Sources*. See Claudian, 'Panegyric on the Third Consulship of the Emperor Honorius', ll. 116–18: 'te pulcher Enipeus/celasque Dodone stupuit rurusque locutae/in te Chaoniae moverunt carmina quercus' (Fair Enipeus and lofty Dodona look upon thee in amaze, and the oaks of Chaonia, finding tongues once more, utter oracles in thine honour). *certain*] dependable (*OED* a. I 3).

75. *peace*] a) i.e. 'silence!' b) a reminder that Fairfax, once a general and a man of war, has become a man of peace.
76. See *Musick's Empire*, ll. 21–3: 'here your homage do/Unto a gentler conqueror than you;/ . . . though he flies the music of his praise.'
77. *obscurer*] more remote, secret, retired (*OED* a. 5).
79–80. *Nor . . . Nor*] imitating a Latin '*nec . . . nec*' construction.

49

Upon Appleton House, To My Lord Fairfax

Date. Late June–late August 1651. M. stayed at Nun Appleton, one of the Yorkshire residences of Thomas, third Baron Fairfax of Cameron, between late 1650 and later 1652, as tutor to Fairfax's daughter, Maria. Several allusions to recently published works provide the *terminus a quo*, in particular Robert Waring's dedicatory poem to William Cartwright's *Poems, Plays and Miscellanies*, dated by the bookseller Thomason 23 June (see below, ll. 449–53, 629–33). Hirst and Zwicker, *HJ*, 36 (1993), 247–69, argue that a series of references to agricultural activity, Fairfax's movements, and public affairs (especially a series of threats to the fledgling 'free state'), associate the poem with the summer months of July and August.

Publication. 1681.

Context. Having been chief commander of the Parliamentary forces by the end of the First Civil War, and during the Second Civil War, Fairfax withdrew from public life in June 1650 (not without expressions of betrayal on the part of some Parliamentarians). He resigned his command when he refused to lead an army into Scotland, which he regarded as the invasion of a foreign country without provocation (see above, *An Horatian Ode, Context*). He had taken no part in the trial of Charles I and expressed his revulsion at the regicide in an unpublished poem. In his Yorkshire retirement, he devoted himself to his manuscripts and books, to writing, to the building of new houses at Nun Appleton and in York (see BL, MS Add. 71448), and to the future of his family in the shape of his daughter's marriage. Nun Appleton was settled on Fairfax and his heirs by his grandfather, Thomas, the first Lord Fairfax (d. 1640), on the occasion of his marriage to Anne Vere in 1640.

Although the substantial house built at Nun Appleton by Fairfax, and designed by John Webb (sketched by Daniel King *c.* 1656; Bod. Gough Maps 1, fol. 1, see fig. 7) was once generally regarded as

the house in M.'s poem, Erikson, *ELR*, 9 (1979), 158–68 (163–5), argues that M. was in fact referring to the much smaller dwelling built out of the nunnery and standing next to the ruined church. This makes sense of the references in the poem itself (ll. 71–4, 87–8). Fairfax did not build the larger house, or expand the smaller house to make it larger (see Powell, *N & Q*, n.s. 43 (1996), 281–4), until the mid-1650s (as opposed to the earlier dating of 1637–50), and he did so in order to enhance his daughter's dowry. But the reference to the grand intentions of the 'foreign architect' in sts. 1–3 suggests that Fairfax was planning the new house at this time, and that M. knew of this. While the subject of the poem is the house at Nun Appleton, details of other Fairfax residences and estates, especially Denton, find their way into the poem (see below, l. 466). A full discussion of the relationship between the estate as it was in M.'s time, as it is today, and the poem, may be found in Post, *Ben Jonson Journal*, 11 (2004), 163–205.

The poem is, in the fullest sense, the product of a patronage relationship, and is quite unlike the published panegyrics that still praised Fairfax's martial heroism even after his retirement: (see, e.g., Samuel Colvile, 'Ad Illustrissimum Heroem Dominum Thomam Fairfaxium Baronem de Cameron' (1650), Anon., 'Ad Fairfaxum Imperio post attritas regis copias usum' (1651)). M. deals in depth with many aspects of Fairfax's antiquarian and literary interests, and the place of the Fairfax family in history. There are several allusions to, and uses of, texts that were in Lord Fairfax's library, from the poetic to the contemplative and occult. M.'s poem is also related to the verse that was produced by other members of the Fairfax family in this period.

Several commentators have argued that the poem addresses Fairfax's role as a military leader and a prominent Parliamentarian. Hirst and Zwicker, op. cit., regard the poem as advice to Fairfax not to indulge excessively in meditative, and possibly enthusiastic, interests that would go against the

Fig. 7
Daniel King, Appleton House. The Bodleian Library, University of Oxford, MS
Gough Maps 1, fol. 1.

public standards of the Commonwealth (but Wilding (1987), 143, doubts whether a hired tutor would be in any position to give advice or criticism). Although Fairfax was no supporter of extreme radicalism, he had succeeded in having appointed many hard-line Puritans as officers at the formation of the New Model Army in 1645, and his treatment of the Diggers in 1649 was moderate. Despite the easy retirement that the poem appears to offer, the north of England in 1651 experienced a most uneasy peace, with the enduring threat of a royalist rising, and further Leveller insurgency against enclosure just to the east of the Fairfax estates. With the threatened invasion of a Scottish army at this time, the Council of State turned to Fairfax for his active participation, since the situation was now the one in which Fairfax had said he was ready to take up arms before he resigned. Fairfax's dilemma was whether he should take up arms for an uncertain cause, before the survival of the Commonwealth was guaranteed by its victory at Worcester on 3 September 1651. The choices facing Fairfax in the summer of 1651 are mapped onto the experiences and expressions of the various characters in the poem, but M. is respectful of Fairfax's judgement by placing no final judgements in the voice of the poem's narrator.

There is nonetheless no explicit reference to public events involving Fairfax in the period immediately preceding the poem's composition (and no reason for them to be included). M. makes no reference to the fracas in which one of Fairfax's cousins was involved, in early April 1651, while representing the republic in Holland. These facts should have been known to M. through the extensive newsbook and pamphlet collection being assembled by Fairfax.

Just as the Fairfaxes were very interested in their family history, so that history is registered in the poem. Griffin, *SEL*, 28 (1988), 61–76 (62–7), suggests that the apparent invention of William Fairfax's rescue of Isabel Thwaites, with legal right on his side, may have functioned as an explanation designed to deter the fear that those who occupied former monasteries committed sacrilege. Some country house poems explicitly praised those who avoided the re-use of monastic fabric (e.g. Herrick, 'A Panegyrick to Sir Lewis Pemberton' (1648), l. 127). Fairfax employed the important antiquarian Roger Dodsworth to copy and preserve manuscripts in York both before and after the siege there in 1644. Fairfax's own interest in medieval learning (he possessed manuscripts that may have belonged to Isabel Thwaites) is reflected in the early part of M.'s poem. Elsewhere, M. appears

to take elements of local medievalism, and shows (as he does in other poems) how they have been positively transformed in the post-Reformation age.

The impeccably Protestant heritage presented in this history of the Fairfax family, and the anti-episcopal reference at l. 366, chimed with Fairfax's Presbyterianism and, more so, that of his wife. Noting the absence of Lady Fairfax by name, and elsewhere present only three times, in the poem, Hirst and Zwicker, op cit., 260–2, contend that Prioress Langton in the poem is a representation of the strong-willed wife of the Lord General. She interrupted from the public gallery during the trial of the King, was in contact with Presbyterian Royalists, and seems to have successfully pressured her husband to resign his command in June 1650. A Catholic allegory for intramarital Protestant politics was an appropriate way for M. to distance Fairfax from his wife's dangerous activities, while not drawing disapproval from Lady Fairfax herself. June 1651 saw the trial and execution of Christopher Love, a Presbyterian minister, found guilty of conspiring with the royalists. Further allusions in the poem to Catholic elements within the Fairfax family are discussed by Cotterill, *ELH*, 69 (2002), 103–32.

Sources and Genre. Poems on country houses and estates stem back to classical verse: on the one hand the praise of humble retreats in Horace and Martial, and on the other, the grand architecture acknowledged by Statius and Sidonius Apollinaris. The vogue, however, caught on in a serious way in the seventeenth century, as shown by Fowler (1994). M.'s poem is unusual and innovative in a number of ways: the indistinctness of the description of both house and estate, the presence of an observing persona, and sheer length. M.'s demonstration of his mastery of the genre's repertoire is signalled by the exhaustive range of possibilities, from park poem, to retirement and digressive observation.

M.'s debt to his greatest English predecessor in this mode, Ben Jonson's 'To Penshurst' (1612), is apparent in several ways. Although M. eschews the festiveness invoked by Jonson (and Herrick), his poem follows 'To Penshurst''s modesty topos, its attentiveness to the trees and animals on the estate, and its floods. But where Jonson's natural world is the object of sumptuous production, M.'s is the opportunity for contemplation. Jonson's poem returns to the household itself, whereas M.'s stays in natural contemplation while still praising the Fairfax line. M. is also far less obviously indebted to classical poetry than is Jonson, and the poem avoids Jonsonian gravity.

The conjunction of praise of family members, of an estate, with reference to painting, is made in Richard Lovelace's 'Amyntor's Grove' (*c.* 1641), addressed to Endymion Porter, who had an estate at Woodhall in Hertfordshire. M.'s poem extends and clarifies the conceits and mode of representation in Lovelace's poem, which he would have known well. The poem contains echoes of estate poems by Fairfax's kinsman, Mildmay Fane, second Earl of Westmoreland, and, more intriguingly, the Dutch poet Constantijn Huygens. The presence of the military world in Renaissance gardens, either in the real sense of fortified gardens, and the incorporation of military structures in garden designs, or in a symbolic way in didactic literature, is discussed by Turner, *E in C*, 38 (1978), 288–301; *idem*, (1979), 55, 70. For further discussion of the garden context, see Whitaker, *HLQ*, 62 (2000–1), 297–311.

Upon Appleton House is also a 'prospective' poem, another new and fashionable genre, popularized by Sir John Denham's *Coopers Hill* (1641/42), and influenced by developments in landscape painting. Prospective poetry exploited the illusions presented to the viewer by landscapes, and derived social and political commentary from views. Although M.'s poem deals with a history of the Fairfax family, as Denham's uses landscape as an opportunity to meditate upon English royal family history, M. is more exclusively concerned with illusion and the eye's survey of the Appleton estate (e.g. sts. XI, LVIII). For Fitter (1995), 289, these concerns make the poem not a true example of the 'landskip' genre. There are some echoes of Denham's poem in M.'s (see below, l. 640); the pre-Reformation history in *Upon Appleton House* is effectively pitched against the worries concerning the Reformation and regret for the destruction of the monasteries in Denham's poem. Likewise, the River Thames in *Coopers Hill* threatens to ruin the work of the mowers, whereas the Wharfe's flood for M. is a condition of regeneration; Windsor Forest and the flood strive against each other in Denham, but in M. the former is a comforting refuge from the latter. Turner (1979), 61, deems the poem 'the longest and most complicated topographical poem in English.' Colie (1970), 210 ff. discusses the relationship between the elements of verbal distortion in the poem, and paintings exploiting optical illusion and distortion.

M. would have been one of the first to stay at Nun Appleton since Fairfax's retirement. We may never know the nature and extent of their interaction, and whether Fairfax's verse influenced M.'s, or vice versa, or both. What is clear is that *Upon Appleton House* is full of echoes and reworking of some Fairfax poems, and in particular his translation of Saint Amant's 'La Solitude' (1625; see below, l. 495 n.). Fairfax's translation replicates Saint Amant's vivid interest in ruins and the quarries from which the rocks came, and their representation of an absolute retirement. For M., ruins (ll. 87–9) are not the objects of contemplation but the occasion of the narrative of William Fairfax's rescue of Isabella Thwaites from the nuns – a small gothic fiction. Other Fairfax poems contain interests in creation and perspective similar to *Upon Appleton House*: e.g. 'Wisdomes Antiquity' (Leeds, Brotherton Library, Fairfax MS Acc. No. 24719), fols. 295–6: 'Whilst yet the earth unframed was,/ . . . I was, and when I wisely set/ The Hanging clouds I (th'Architect)/Gave to the sea itt circled shore' (cp. below, sts. I, LXXXXVI). Finally, there are also poems by other members of the Fairfax family (whom M. would have known) that bear significant resemblances to sections of M.'s poem (see below, ll. 13, 65–6).

Upon Appleton House also carries significant echoes of a variety of retirement poems, either in their original languages, or in English translation:

> after noone he takes a kind of pride
>   To th'Hills to walke, or River side,
> And midst the pleasant Okes, a shade doth find,
>   T'avoyd the blasts o'th'Southern wind;
> To th'darksome shore, by the deeper poole he goes,
>   And through, with nimble Boat he rowes;
> Sometimes the sporting fish, his baite thrown in,
>   Hee pluckes up with his trembling line.
> 'A Palinode to the Second Ode of the booke of
> (Epodes of Q.H. Flaccus', *Odes* (1646), Sarbiewski,
> (trans. G. Hills, 133))

Sarbiewski's verse was among the contents of the extensive library of Henry Fairfax, uncle of Thomas and Rector of Bolton Percy, in which parish Nun Appleton was situated.

The poem contains within itself, and is a meditation upon, epic poetry. Evander's garden and house, with its cattle, humble house and strewn leaves is the digression in the *Aeneid* that provides a model for M.'s much-expanded praise of the retired general Fairfax (*Aeneid*, VIII, ll. 362–73). The entire praise of Fairfax is a series of digressions, although the general himself is unmistakably a military figure. To this extent, Wallace (1968), 240 ff. argues that M. is replying to Davenant's recently published heroic poem *Gondibert* (1651), with its pretentious claims of producing epic literature on subjects distanced from the present time, its grand claims for poetry as high architecture, its preference for books (as opposed to the book of nature), and the influence in its preface of Hobbes' psychological and political theories (see below, ll. 3, 20, 355–6). To all of these themes, *Upon Appleton House* replies in the negative, most notably through its concern with a living hero who, unlike Davenant's heroes, confronts military action before retreating. *Gondibert* describes a Baconian natural utopia, whereas M.'s poem enacts one; *Gondibert* reveals a suspicion of courts, described at first by Davenant as gardens, whereas M. makes the garden the centre of Fairfax's noble life. Rhodalind's beauty is compared in *Gondibert* to alchemical processes, but the poet doubts that 'Verse has Chymick pow're' (1.4.4, l. 1); Maria Fairfax effects an alchemical transformation, communicated through the verse.

There are some elements of medieval and pre-Reformation vocabulary and literature in the poem (e.g. see below, l. 675 n.). Although *The Pricke of Conscience* is not among the surviving Fairfax MSS (unlike poetry by Chaucer, Gower and the *Cursor Mundi*), it was a popular text in Yorkshire monasteries and nunneries. The successive comparison of the world as sea, wilderness, forest, battlefield, in the second book of *The Pricke* (1212–56) is comparable to M.'s similes and metaphors in the poem; where *The Pricke* points to mortification, M. is concerned to demonstrate the potential for man's regeneration through contact with the natural world (see also below, ll. 355, 568).

The text most fundamentally behind the poem, and the source of many individual episodes and phrases, is the Bible. The narrative is founded upon a series of carefully deployed allusions to and echoes of biblical language, from a variety of books, albeit largely Genesis and, secondarily, Revelation. Again, this was a compliment: Fairfax's own reverence for Scripture is attested by Brian Fairfax: 'He red diviner things then Druids knew,/Such mistery's were then reveald to few,/For his Chiefe study was Gods sacred Law,/And all his Life did Comments on it draw'. (BL, MS Eg. 2146, fol. 2ᵛ).

Several sections of the poem draw on the narrative of the plight of the Israelites in Egypt supplied by Josuah Sylvester's popular translation of Du Bartas' *Divine Weeks* (1607). Indeed the passage in the middle of M.'s poem, concerned with the mowers in the meadows, is effectively a truncated version of sections of Sylvester (see below, ll. 322–3, 369–70, 484–6, 629–33). The translation was commonly used as an educational text: M.'s recourse to it at this time may be connected with his role as tutor in the Fairfax household. Sylvester praises the Hebrew and Roman patriarchs because they were countrymen (and not courtiers) turned soldiers and statesmen: 'And ord'red there with as good Discipline,/The Fields of Corne, as Fields of Combat first;/And Ranks of Trees, as Ranks of Souldiers yerst' (I.iii, ll. 1057–8). River valleys are at the heart of the description of England: 'Th'inammell'd Valleys, where the liquid glasse/Of silver Brookes in curled streames doth passe,/Serve us for Gardens; and their flowerie Fleece/Affords us Syth-worke' (II.ii.3, ll. 699–702).

Finally, the poem is indebted to the tradition of the masque. Thomas Randolph's pastoral drama *Amyntas* (1638) contains references to the language of the birds (see below, l. 570) and masque entertainment (see below, ll. 585–6), in addition to a character called Thestylis.

Structure and Versification. The poem is a meditation upon the meaning of the 'sober frame', by which is meant the house, the grounds, and the various perspectives offered by the associations that grow up within the 'picture' of the poem, in the following sequence:

Sts. I–X. The initial 'frame': the humble architecture of the house (suggesting Fairfax's humility).

Sts. XI–XXXV. The history of the Reformation at Nun Appleton, and its relationship with the union of Fairfax and Thwaites.

Sts. XXXVI–XLVI. The description the flora of the Nun Appleton gardens, with military details supplied literally by Fairfax, as well as through the military lens suggested to the poet by Fairfax's martial career.

Sts. XLVII–LX. The passage concerned with the meadows, displaying the most exaggerated distortions of size and space in the poem.

Sts. LXI–LXXXI The wood is the subject of a further eighteen stanzas, punctuated by three stanzas concerned with the river.

Sts. LXXXII–LXXXXVII. The river remains the scene for the final sixteen-stanza section of the poem, which begins with the arrival of evening and Mary Fairfax, and culminates in the praise of the Fairfax line, set now to reside on the site of a reborn Eden at Nun Appleton.

O'Loughlin, in Lord, ed. (1968), 123–4, argues that this sequence is a dialectical progression from contemplation to action, then to contemplation again, in which each section manages to engage with, or is undermined by, its opposite.

Grossman (in Summers and Pebworth, eds (1988), 193–5) describes the structure of the poem as the conjunction of a historical and iconic allegory with an irony (working through word-play and allusions) that undermines allegory's speculative bent. The point of conjunction is defined here as the rebus: 'not only . . . a pictorial pun on the sound of a word, but also . . . [using] . . . words to evoke a picture, which, at the moment of perception, refers itself to a second verbal text'. There are other forms of conjunction and doubleness in the poem. The action fits within one day, from dawn (l. 289) until dusk (l. 775), but the middle of the poem, between stanzas XLVII and LIX, recounts at least several days' work of harvesting hay and grazing the stubble, followed by the flooding of the meadows (albeit presented as a courtly entertainment (ll. 385–6)).

The poem is written in eight-line stanzas of octosyllabic iambic couplets. Puttenham called it the 'square or quadrangle equaliter', and associated it with the earth and the constant-minded-man on account of its regularity and solidity. This was a form used by Saint Amant; M. had already used it with success in *The Gallery* and *The Unfortunate Lover*, and he would do so again in *The Garden*. The couplets have been noted for being 'at once riddling and conversational . . . [with] elliptically contorted or pleonastic syntax, . . . conspicuous enjambment, and yet . . . even Spenserian pace, their casual inclusiveness' (O'Loughlin, in Lord, ed. (1968), 122).

Numerological patterns have been adduced by Røstvig, in Friedenreich, ed. (1977), 245–67, and Brooks-Davies, *N & Q*, 225 (1980), 336–9. The former suggests a pattern of 10 + 75 (i.e. 3×25) + 12. Within this structure, a series of structural 'circles' is described arranging the stanzas so that their subject-matter 'balanced': specifically sts. XI and XXXV, XXII and XXIV, XXI and XXV, XIII and XXXI–XXXIII. The latter notes a thematic division in the poem's central stanza (XXXXIX), a shift from active to contemplative subject matter. The halfway points in each of the two halves (sts. XXIV and LXXIV) mirror each other, with the nuns being set off against the sibyls. The opening passage, describing the house, is ten stanzas long: a perfect number. William and Mary Fairfax occupy other subsidiary

centres, while symbolism and significant coincidences of fives are used to highlight the superiority of Fairfax's choices over Catholic superstition. The poem also divides into unequal halves of 46 and 51 stanzas, the former group representing the forty-six years taken to rebuild the Temple of Jerusalem, and associated with the regeneration of the human body (see John 2:19–221). More tentatively, Brooks-Davies suggests that 51, divided by 3 into 17, implies the fifty years of Jubilee and the one eternal year of 'true rest'.

Modern Criticism. Despite its length and its centrality in M.'s canon, *Upon Appleton House* has not occasioned the critical debate that surrounds M.'s most famous lyrics. Early nineteenth-century commentators saw in the poem's rural observations evidence that M. 'had the eye and feeling of a true poet . . . a real lover of nature, and a witness of her beauties in her most solitary retirement', as opposed to the mannered structures of Pope (Whittier, in Carey, ed. (1969), 36). In short, the poem confirmed to the Victorian view that M. was a proto-Romantic. Yet while *Upon Appleton House* was admired by the Victorians, it was also frowned upon for the extravagance of its conceits, and thought inferior to the shorter pastoral and garden poems. These views were repeated by T.S. Eliot in his influential essay on M., where parts of the poem deploy 'undesirable images . . over-developed or distracting . . . misshapen' (T.S. Eliot in Carey, ed. (1969), 51). This tradition continues in the view of the poem as 'thin and artificial', and incapable of resolving its contradictions (Goldberg in Carey, ed. (1969), 161, 167), or as 'insignificant as poetry, though it is impregnated with Marvell's brilliant and lively sense of comedy' (Grove, in Carey, ed. (1969), 294).

Christopher Hill takes *Upon Appleton House* as a prime example of M.'s ability to show the tensions and interactions between the forces of good and evil, and of M.'s capacity to create landscapes that reflected the crisis of his times, while reminding the reader of the central dream of the time: the return to a state of Edenic innocence. For Hill, unlike many others, M. was no escapist, as history's presence in the poem, and the poetic persona's own restlessness, testify (Hill, in Carey, ed. (1969), 92). Influenced by Hill, Chambers (in Summers and Pebworth, eds (1992), 139–53), argues that the poem acknowledges its historical moment by rejecting (in the satire of the nuns) the culture of medieval antiquarian gothicism, upon which claims to Stuart ancestral privilege had been made (but see above, 214, and below, ll. 551–2,

739–42 nn.). Later twentieth-century critics have been more impressed by the poem's structural and tonal sophistication, ambition and generic complexity. This range includes for Ellrodt the capacity to discuss cold (and congealing) as well as hot objects (Ellrodt in Carey, ed. (1969), 154): 'his sensibility craves freshness and humidity, but his mind demands the definite contours of the solid universe'. This was regarded as a 'surreal' effect by Broadbent (Broadbent in Carey, ed. (1969), 158), and as a 'vertiginous succession of surfaces [becoming] a mirror of unity' (Gray, *ELR*, 9 (1979), 169–82). For Healy (in Healy and Sawday, eds (1990), 172), the subversions of vision in the poem undermine the reassurance offered to Fairfax in his retirement.

The most extended acounts of the poem have been concerned to develop the initial contextual dimension offered by Hill either in terms of the themes of redemption from corruption in the union of contemplative man and contemplated creation (so that the flood represents a baptism: Røstvig in Carey, ed. (1969), 291), other kinds of Christian symbolism and sacramentalism (Warnke in Patrides, ed. (1978), 234–50), a document of class occlusion (Wilding (1985), 138–74), or even as a grandly coded explanation of the efficacy of alchemy (Abraham (1990), 39–64). Wallace (1968), 232–57, regards the aesthetic playfulness of the poem as a confirmation of the poet's most deeply meditated insights into the interrelationship between private retirement and public loyalty or action. The rhetorical work of

the poem has been judged to achieve its own version of the historical process, fusing an awareness of human history with natural process in a movement towards a 'gentle' apocalypse (Rogers, in Summers and Pebworth, eds (1992), 209). Or its expansive conjunctions of meaning reflect and embody the paradox of a new self-awareness emergent in the mid-seventeenth century, where persons understand themselves as 'known to be destined but . . . experienced as radically indeterminate' (Grossman in Summers and Pebworth, eds (1988), 201) and where a 'world more nearly modern and seculer can be glimpsed' (Brand, *ELR*, (2002), 477–510). Some attempts to connect the events recorded in the poem with the events of the English Revolution often involve manipulations as far-fetched as some of the poem's conceitedness.

Upon Appleton House, To My Lord Fairfax

I

Within this sober frame expect
Work of no foreign architect;
That unto caves the quarries drew,
And forests did to pastures hew;
5   Who of his great design in pain
Did for a model vault his brain,
Whose columns should so high be raised
To arch the brows that on them gazed.

1–8. Cp. Jonson, 'To Penshurst' (1616), ll. 1–5, 'Thou art not, Penshurst, built to envious show,/Of touch, or marble; nor canst boast a row/Of polished pillars, or a roof of gold: . . . but standst an ancient pile.'

1. sober] unextravagant (*OED* a. 10). *frame*] building (*OED* n. 8 b).

2–4. foreign architect . . . hew] extravagant proportions, with high columns and arches specifically for the houses of high-ranking people, were associated with the anthropomorphic architectural theorist and practitioner Filarete (Antonio Averlino), fl. 1451–65. See Onians (1988), 158–70. David Papillon, a Huguenot, may have submitted a proposal for the house; John Webb was the architect finally chosen by Fairfax: see Bold (1989).

3–4. caves . . . hew] Cp. Jonson, 'Another Lady's Exception, Present at the Hearing' (1640), ll. 11–12: 'To make the mountain quarries move,/And call the walking woods.'

3. unto . . . drew] mined the quarries for stone until they became caves; in direct contrast to the palace in *Gondibert* (1651), 2.2.6: 'To that Proud Palace which once low did lie/In *Parian* Quarries, now on Columnes stands:/*Ionique* Props that bear their Arches high.' *drew*] a) moved b) extracted, so that the quarries become caves (*OED* v. III 49) c) as in the architect 'drawing' his design (*OED* v. V 60).

4. hew] cut with blows so as to shape (*OED* v. II 3), but with overtones of 'cut down' (*OED* v. II 4).

5–6. In the mental exertion of inventing an architectural design, the architect extended his imagination, and used this 'stretched brain' as a model for the building. The notion that buildings reflected their designers was commonplace: 'A house being a mere artificial and no natural thing hath its first subsistence in the idea of man's brain, according to whose model, good or ill, the house proves good or ill.' (Henry Hawkins, *Partheneia Sacra* (1633), 166).

5. in pain] 'pain' means the trouble taken to achieve something (*OED* n. 5), but the use of the preposition 'in' also implies that such effort is physically painful, hinting at the analogy between artistic creation and childbirth.

6–8. model . . . brows] In Constantijn Huygens, *Hofwyck* (1651), ll. 980 ff., the house is imagined as the head, the gardens as the body of a person. Vitruvius stipulates that temple architecture should take its proportions from a fine example of the human body: *De Architectura*, I.c.i.

6. vault] a) raise and cover in the manner of a vault (*OED* v.[1] 3) b) leap over (*OED* v.[2] 2).

7–8. Whose column . . . gazed] the columns are so high that beholders raise their eyebrows in surprise or disapproval.

II

Why should of all things man unruled
0   Such unproportioned dwellings build?
The beasts are by their dens expressed:
And birds contrive an equal nest;
The low-roofed tortoises do dwell
In cases fit of tortoise-shell:
5   No creature loves an empty space;
Their bodies measure out their place.

III

But he, superfluously spread,
Demands more room alive than dead.
And in his hollow palace goes
0   Where winds as he themselves may lose.
What need of all this marble crust
T'impark the wanton mote of dust,
That thinks by breadth the world t'unite
Though the first builders failed in height?

IV

25   But all things are composèd here
Like Nature, orderly and near:
In which we the dimensions find
Of that more sober age and mind,
When larger-sizèd men did stoop
30   To enter at a narrow loop;
As practising, in doors so strait,
To strain themselves through heaven's gate.

V

And surely when the after age
Shall hither come in pilgrimage,
35   These sacred places to adore,
By Vere and Fairfax trod before,
Men will dispute how their extent
Within such dwarfish confines went:
And some will smile at this, as well
40   As Romulus his bee-like cell.

---

9. *unruled*] ungoverned, disorderly (*OED* ppl. a. 1), but hinting at its geometrical or architectural sense, 'irregular' (*OED* ppl. a. 3).
10. *unproportioned*] lacking in proportion or balance; see above ll. 6–8 n.
11. *expressed*] described (*OED* v. 9 c).
12. *equal*] a) adequately fitting or appropriate (to the birds' shape and size; *OED* a. 3) b) uniform in dimensions and proportions (*OED* a. 7).
13–14. *low-roofed . . . tortoise-shell*] Cp. Wither, *A Collection of Emblemes* (1635), 222: 'The *Tortois*, doubtlesse, doth no house-roome lack,/Although his *House* will cover but his back.' The tortoise, living in its shell, was, among other things, an emblem of the self-contained man, the man of policy, of silence, and one who keeps to his home – all qualities applicable to Fairfax. Cp. below, ll. 772–3.
13. *low-roofed*] close to the ground; 'Our roofs are too low for so lofty a head', Charles Fairfax, Leeds, Brotherton MS Fairfax, Acc. No. 24722, unnumbered leaves.
15. *No creature . . . space*] an animal version of the dictum that nature abhors a vacuum: cp. *An Horatian Ode*, l. 41: 'Nature that hateth emptiness,/Allows of penetration less.'
17. *superfluously*] a) beyond what is necessary (*OED* adv. 1) b) extravagantly (*OED* adv. 3).
20. *Where . . . lose*] Cp. Davenant, *Gondibert* (1651), 2.2.7: 'So vast of heighth, to which such space did fit/As if it were o're-cyz'd for Modern Men;/The ancient Giants might inhabit it;/And there walk free as winds that pass unseen.'
21. *marble crust*] marble surfaces of floors, steps, walls and roofs.
22. *impark*] to confine in a park, as with beasts of the chase (*OED* v. 1). *mote*] Bod. 1; *mose* 1681; speck. Grosart argued for 'mote' as a misprint of 'mole', which he took to mean 'an unformed mass'; Cummings, *ELN*, 24.1 (1986), 22–5, suggests 'mese' (house, dwelling (*OED* n.²)), so that 'mese of dust' refers to the body of the houseowner.
23–4. Man attempts to join up the world by building a structure as wide as the earth, to embrace all languages and

tongues, even though the earlier idealistic builders of the Tower of Babel (Gen. 11:1–9) failed in their aim to make it reach to heaven. The Tower of Babel was built by Nimrod, prime biblical representative of monarchical tyranny in the period.
25. *composèd*] a) well put together (*OED* ppl. a. 2) b) tranquil (*OED* ppl. a. 4).
26. *near*] a) close at hand, proximate (*OED* adv.² 1) b) thrifty (*OED* adv.² 10).
29–30. *When . . . loop*] Cp. Aeneas's visit to Evander's house, *Aeneid*, VIII, ll. 359–68, especially ll. 362–3, 366–7: ' "haec", inquit, "limina victor/Alcides subiit . . ." '/ . . . et angusti subter fastigia tecti/ingentem Aenean' ('These portals', he cried, 'victorious Alcides stooped to enter . . .', . . . and beneath the roof of his lowly dwelling led great Aeneas).
29. *larger-sizèd men*] the giants; see above, l. 20 n.
30. *loop*] circular or oval shape of primitive door opening (in M.'s time a 'loop' was an opening in a wall, to afford vision, or to launch missiles (*OED* n.² 1).
31–2. *in doors . . . gate*] see Matt. 7:14: 'strait is the gate, and narrow is the way, that leadeth to destruction, and many there be which go to heaven'.
31. *strait*] narrow.
33. *after age*] future generations.
36. *Vere*] Anne, Lady Fairfax (d. 1665), daughter of Sir Horace Vere, under whose command Fairfax served in the Low Countries, 1629–32. She married Sir Thomas in 1637. See below, *Upon the Hill and Grove at Bilbrough*, ll. 43–4.
37. *extent*] dimensions (*OED* n. II 4).
39–40. *And some . . . cell*] i.e. some will, with amusement, disbelieve that the Fairfaxes could have lived in such a small space, as much as they disregard the claim that Romulus, founder of Rome, lived in a thatched hut on the Palatine Hill: see Ovid, *Fasti*, II, ll. 183–4; Virgil, *Aeneid*, VIII, l. 654; Vitruvius, *De Architectura*, II.i. The hut is compared to the single, tiny compartments of a honeycomb made by bees.
40. *cell*] humble dwelling of one room (*OED* n.1 I 2c).

VI

Humility alone designs
Those short but admirable lines,
By which, ungirt and unconstrained,
Things greater are in less contained.
45 Let others vainly strive t'immure
The circle in the quadrature!
These holy mathematics can
In ev'ry figure equal man.

VII

Yet thus the laden house does sweat,
50 And scarce endures the Master great:
But where he comes the swelling hall
Stirs, and the square grows spherical;
More by his magnitude distressed,
Than he is by its straitness pressed:
55 And too officiously it slights
That in itself which him delights.

VIII

So Honour better lowness bears,
Than that unwonted Greatness wears.
Height with a certain grace does bend,
60 But low things clownishly ascend.
And yet what needs there here excuse,
Where ev'ry thing does answer use?
Where neatness nothing can condemn,
Nor pride invent what to contemn?

IX

65 A stately frontispiece of poor
Adorns without the open door:
Nor less the rooms within commends
Daily new furniture of friends.
The house was built upon the place
70 Only as for a mark of grace;
And for an inn to entertain
Its Lord a while, but not remain.

---

42. *admirable*] wonderful, surprising (*OED* a. 1).
43. *ungirt*] left loose (*OED* ppl. a. 2 b).
45. *immure*] enclose, imprison (*OED* v. 2).
46. *circle . . . quadrature*] the ancient problem of squaring the circle. *quadrature*] the Italian *quadratura*, the basic structure and balance of any building, expressed on paper by drawing an elevation of a building within proportioned squares: see Onians (1988), 209, 232–3.
47–8. *These holy . . . equal man*] as in the circle encompassing the human figure with outstretched arms and legs (in fact, a circle set within a square), as drawn by both Leonardo da Vinci and Albrecht Dürer (see Heninger (1977), 144–58); Constantijn Huygens built a house and estate with all its proportions designed to reflect the human form: see above, ll. 6–8 n.
49–52. *Yet . . . distressed*] Cp. *Inscribenda Luparae*, ll. 9–10.
52. *square grows spherical*] Markham (1870), 366, thought this a reference to the cupola built above the hall in the new building at Nun Appleton. However, the image seems much more involved with the geometrical concerns of ll. 46–8: here, indeed, the square is made into a circle, thereby inverting the ancient problem.
53. *distressed*] a) put under strain (*OED* v. 1 b fig.) b) defeated; a witty allusion to Fairfax's military prowess (*OED* v. 2 a).
55. *officiously*] a) obligingly (*OED* adv. 1) b) unduly obstrusive (*OED* adv. 3) *slights*] disrespects; in so 'expanding', the house disrespects the humility that Fairfax admired, thereby doing the opposite of the other meaning of 'to slight' – to make level.
56. *That*] humility (see above, l. 43).

60. *clownishly*] clumsily, awkwardly (as of peasants or rustics) (*OED* a. 2).
64. *invent*] make up (*OED* v. 2 c) (pace *Grosart, Legouis, Donno, Wilcher, Walker, Ormerod* and *Wortham*: 'find out') *contemn*] scorn.
65–6. *A stately . . . door*] poor people awaiting alms function as an adornment for the entrance to the house; cp. Huygens, *Hofwyck* (1651), ll. 1064–5: 'Twee Poorten seggen meer: onthael ick vriend of gast,/'T en is niet door een' deur, 't is door twee open' deuren' (Two gates there are also there to welcome friend or guest. It's not through a door, but through two open doors); Charles Fairfax, 'Come, come my good Shepherds' (*c*. 1650), ll. 15–16: 'Content and sweet chearfulness open our door/They smile with the simple, & feed the poor', Leeds, Brotherton MS Fairfax, Acc. No. 24722, unnumbered leaves.
65. *frontispiece*] front of a building, especially a decorated entrance; Grummitt, *The Coat of Arms*, 11 (1996), 22–36 (228) suggests the 'frontispiece' would normally include a coat of arms; in M.'s poem it is replaced by the poor. *poor*] poor people.
67. *commends*] a) entrusts (*OED* v. 1) b) adorns (*OED* v. 4).
71. *inn*] Cp. Fairfax, 'Upon the New-built House att Apleton', Bodl. MS Fairfax 40, p. 593, ll. 1–4: 'Think not, O man that dwells herein/This house's a stay, but as an inn,/Which for convenience fitly stands,/In way to one not made with hands'; this poem is called 'Upon Appleton-House' in the Fairfax poetry collection acquired in 1994 by the Brotherton Library, Leeds University (Acc. No. B24719); see also *Headnote, Context*.

X

Him Bishop's-Hill, or Denton may,
Or Bilbrough, better hold than they:
But Nature here hath been so free
As if she said, 'Leave this to me'.
Art would more neatly have defaced
What she had laid so sweetly waste;
In fragrant gardens, shady woods,
Deep meadows, and transparent floods.

XI

While with slow eyes we these survey,
And on each pleasant footstep stay,
We opportunely may relate
That progress of this house's fate.
A nunnery first gave it birth
(For virgin buildings oft brought forth),
And all that neighbour-ruin shows
The quarries whence this dwelling rose.

XII

Near to this gloomy cloister's gates
There dwelt the blooming virgin Thwaites;

Fair beyond measure, and an heir
Which might deformity make fair.
And oft she spent the summer suns
Discoursing with the subtle nuns.

95 Whence in these words one to her weaved,
(As 'twere by chance) thoughts long conceived.

XIII

'Within this holy leisure we
Live innocently as you see.
These walls restrain the world without,

100 But hedge our liberty about.
These bars inclose that wider den
Of those wild creatures, callèd men.
The cloister outward shuts its gates,
And, from us, locks on them the grates.

XIV

105 'Here we, in shining armour white,
Like virgin Amazons do fight.
And our chaste lamps we hourly trim,
Lest the great Bridegroom find them dim.
Our orient breaths perfumèd are

110 With incense of incessant prayer.

---

73. Bishop's-Hill, or Denton] other Fairfax properties acquired through the estate of Isabel Thwaites. Bishop's-Hill was in the city of York (and was plundered in 1642 (BL MS Eg. 2146, fol. 24ʳ)), Denton in Wharfdale, thirty miles from Nun Appleton. Denton was the senior residence of this branch of the Fairfax family. See below, l. 466 n.
74. Bilbrough] another Fairfax residence, purchased by Sir William in 1546, its grounds being the subject of another M. poem; see above, *Upon the Hill and Grove at Bilbrough*. Thomas and Lady Fairfax were buried at Bilbrough.
77. neatly] a) tidily (*OED* adv. 1–2) b) cleverly (*OED* adv. 4) c) elegantly (*OED* a. II 7 a).
78. laid . . . waste] a) left uncultivated (*OED* a. 1 a) b) alluding to the military sense of 'devastated' (*OED* a. 3 b).
81. slow] slowly-scanning.
83. opportunely] appropriately (as parts of the estate give occasion).
87. neighbour-ruin] the remains of the nunnery next to the house.
90. the blooming virgin Thwaites] Isabel Thwaites, who was married to William Fairfax in 1518. The story of the complications of this match is expounded below until l. 280. See *Headnote*, *Context*.
94. subtle] a) discriminating (*OED* a. 9) b) cunning, crafty (*OED* a. 10).
100. hedge] a) defend (*OED* v. 1) b) confine (*OED* v. 5 b).

101. bars] the Fairfax coat of arms consisted of a black lion rampant on six bars, that 'may signify the liberty of the subject. who was long opprest by Danes Normans and during the Civill Warrs but now strongly asserted by yᵉ two Judges father and son' (Bod. MS Fairfax d. 1, p. xxii). *inclose*] 'the very walls themselves within which they are inclosed do guard them from all such dangerous and spirituall incursions', [Lawrence Anderton], *The English Nunne* (Saint Omer, 1642), 36.
103–4. gates . . . grates] Cp. Lovelace, 'To Althea, From Prison', ll. 1–4: 'When Love with unconfined wings/Hovers within my Gates;/And my divine *Althea* brings/To whisper at the Grates.'
105. shining armour] the nuns' habits. *white*] Cistercian habits are white.
106. virgin Amazons] recalling the Amazon warriors led by Radigund in Book V of Spenser's *The Faerie Queene*; Brian Fairfax later described the nuns as 'Vestal Virgins' in 'Upon cutting down the Woods at Nun Appleton, 1679', l. 6 (BL MS Eg. 2146, fol. 2ʳ).
107–8. lamps . . . dim] an allusion to the parable of the wise and foolish virgins (Matt. 25:1–12).
108. great Bridegroom] Jesus Christ; the conventional interpretation of the Bridegroom in the Song of Solomon; all nuns are described as 'brides of Christ'.
109. orient] a) precious (*OED* a. 4) b) fresh (*OED* a. 1).

And holy-water of our tears
Most strangely our complexion clears.

XV

    'Not tears of grief; but such as those
    With which calm pleasure overflows;
115 Or pity, when we look on you
    That live without this happy vow.
    How should we grieve that must be seen
    Each one a spouse, and each a queen;
    And can in heaven hence behold
120 Our brighter robes and crowns of gold?

XVI

    'When we have prayèd all our beads,
    Someone the holy legend reads;
    While all the rest with needles paint
    The face and graces of the saint.
125 But what the linen can't receive
    They in their lives do interweave.
    This work the saints best represents;
    That serves for altar's ornaments.

XVII

    'But much it to our work would add
130 If here your hand, your face we had:

By it we would Our Lady touch; *blasphemous?*
Yet thus She you resembles much.
Some of your features, as we sewed,
Through every shrine should be bestowed.
135 And in one beauty we would take
    Enough a thousand saints to make.

XVIII

    'And (for I dare not quench the fire
    That me does for your good inspire)
    'Twere sacrilege a man t'admit
140 To holy things, for heaven fit.
    I see the angels in a crown
    On you the lilies show'ring down:
    And round about you glory breaks,
    That something more than human speaks.

XIX

145 'All beauty, when at such a height,
    Is so already consecrate.
    Fairfax I know; and long ere this
    Have marked the youth, and what he is.
    But can he such a rival seem
150 For whom you heav'n should disesteem?
    Ah, no! and 'twould more honour prove
    He your *devoto* were, than love.

---

112. strangely] wonderfully (*OED* adv. 5).
114. pleasure] used as a term in Catholic devotional and allegorical literature. E.g., Henry Hawkins, *Partheneia Sacra* (1633), 2: 'see a goodlie HOUSE of pleasure, standing therein before you.'
116. vow] of devotion to the Cistercian Order; more specifically, of chastity.
118. spouse] see above, l. 108. *queen*] in imitation of Mary, the Virgin Queen.
120. brighter robes] see 2 Sam. 13:18: 'And she had a garment of divers colours upon her: for with such robes were the king's daughters apparelled.' *crowns of gold*] see Esther 8:15: 'And Mordecai went out from the presence of the king in royal apparel of blue and white, and with a great crown of gold.' Cp. Bunyan, *The Pilgrim's Progress* (1678), ed. R. Sharrock (1965), 201: 'In that place you must wear crowns of gold.'
121. prayèd . . . beads] prayers counted off on rosary beads.
122. legend] saints' lives, e.g. Jacobus de Voragine's *Golden Legend* (c. 1255–66).

123. paint] i.e. embroider.
131. Our Lady] the Virgin Mary.
132. Yet thus] even as you are.
133. sewed] punning of 'sowing', as in sowing seed: Hirst and Zwicker, *ELH*, 66 (1999), 632, argue that the abbess offers embroidery as an alternative form of reproduction to progeneration; contemporary aesthetic theory would have defined such images as iconic, which would be appropriate for a Roman Catholic form of worship, offensive to Protestants.
134. Through . . . bestowed] the embroidered images of Isabel Thwaites as the Virgin will be used to decorate shrines.
139–40. sacrilege] profanation of the sacred (*OED* n.¹ 1 b).
141–2. angels . . . lilies] Cp. Chaucer, *The Second Nun's Tale*, ll. 220–1, 'This angel hadde of roses and of lilie/Corones two, the which he bar in honde.'
141. crown] ring (*OED* n. 13 b).
142. lilies] lilies signified virginity (*OED* A n. 3 a).
146. consecrate] dedicated to heaven.
152. devoto] Italian or Spanish: religious devotee.

XX

'Here live belovèd, and obeyed:
Each one your sister, each your maid.
55 And, if our rule seem strictly penned,
The rule itself to you shall bend.
Our abbess too, now far in age,
Doth your succession near presage.
How soft the yoke on us would lie,
60 Might such fair hands as yours it tie!

XXI

'Your voice, the sweetest of the choir,
Shall draw heav'n nearer, raise us higher.
And your example, if our head,
Will soon us to perfection lead.
65 Those virtues to us all so dear,
Will straight grow sanctity when here:
And that, once sprung, increase so fast
Till miracles it work at last.

XXII

'Nor is our order yet so nice,
70 Delight to banish as a vice.

Here pleasure piety doth meet;
One perfecting the other sweet.
So through the mortal fruit we boil
The sugar's uncorrupting oil:
175 And that which perished while we pull,
Is thus preservèd clear and full.

XXIII

'For such indeed are all our arts;
Still handling Nature's finest parts.
Flowers dress the altars; for the clothes,
180 The sea-born amber we compose;
Balms for the grieved we draw; and pastes
We mould, as baits for curious tastes.
What need is here of man, unless
These as sweet sins we should confess?

XXIV

185 'Each night among us to your side
Appoint a fresh and virgin bride;
Whom if Our Lord at midnight find,
Yet neither should be left behind.
Where you may lie as chaste in bed,
190 As pearls together billeted.

---

156. rule . . . bend] M. apparently effects a pun: the rule is in the first instance the discipline governing the convent, but a rule that bends is a 'Lesbian rule' (i.e. made of lead and designed to fit the curves of a moulding, but also figuratively used to describe accommodating judgements, especially in the seventeenth century – OED a). The reference might be said to allude wittily to the implied Lesbian sexual practices in the convent (see below, l. 191 n., l. 200 n.), but the word 'Lesbian' as a description of female homosexuality was not used until the 1890s according to *OED*. M.'s usage is most probably an unusual coincidence rather than a remarkable case of lexical foresightedness.
157. Our abbess . . . age] Lady Anna Langton, Prioress of Nun Appleton, who nonetheless ruled for twenty-four more years after 1518. She had only just been succeeded when the nunnery was surrendered in 1539, and still qualified for a pension.
158. succession] to be abbess.
164. perfection] moral perfection, highest achievement of holiness in this life (*OED* n. 4); an important term in medieval theology: see, e.g., Hampole, *Psalter* (1340), xiv.5: 'this perfeccioun is that the deuel & the warld haf na pousle in vs.' See also below, l. 172.
166. straight grow sanctity] immediately grow as sanctity; there is also a pun on 'straight' in the context of the plant metaphor – the plant of virtues will grow 'upright' as sanctity. *sanctity*] saintliness, holiness of life.
169. nice] strict (*OED* a. 7 b, c).

171. pleasure] see above l. 114 n.
172. perfecting] see above l. 164 n.; Pecock, *The Represessor of Over Much Blaming of the Clergy* (1449), V.xiii: 'for this cause of the more perfiting lordis and ladies it is allowable . . . hem to have mansiouns covenable for hem within the monasteries'.
173–6. So through . . . full] spiritual purification (and hence immortalization) is likened to the process of preserving fruit by boiling it in sugar: 'We shall be so candied, by being swallow'd up of Life. . . . That we shall be, as if we were all of Spirit, when in truth, it is but this Body that is swallowed up of Life', John Bunyan, *The Resurrection of the Dead* (?1665), *Miscellaneous Works* vol. III, ed. J. Sears McGee (Oxford, 1987), 224.
174. uncorrupting oil] i.e. preserving syrup.
175. pull] pluck (the fruit from the tree).
179. clothes] altar-cloths.
180. sea-born amber] ambergris, a wax-like secretion of the sperm-whale, found floating in tropical seas, and used as a perfume; see *Bermudas*, l. 28 n. *compose*] arrange.
181. grieved] afflicted with injury or disease (*OED* ppl. a. 2). *draw*] infuse or distil (*OED* v. III 41).
182. baits] a) refreshments b) enticements. *curious*] fastidious (*OED* a. 2).
183–4. What need . . . confess] a man is only necessary if the preparation of perfumes, balms and foods are to be confessed to a priest as sins.
187–8. Whom if . . . behind] see above, ll. 107–8.

All night embracing arm in arm,
Like crystal pure with cotton warm.

XXV

Lesbian

'But what is this to all the store
Of joys you see, and may make more!
195 Try but a while, if you be wise:
The trial neither costs, nor ties.'
Now Fairfax seek her promised faith:
Religion that dispensèd hath,
Which she hence forward does begin;
200 The nun's smooth tongue has sucked her in.

XXVI

Oft, though he knew it was in vain,
Yet would he valiantly complain.
'Is this that sanctity so great,
An art by which you finelier cheat?
205 Hypocrite witches, hence avaunt,
Who though in prison yet enchant!
Death only can such thieves make fast,
As rob though in the dungeon cast.

XXVII

'Were there but, when this house was made,
210 One stone that a just hand had laid,
It must have fall'n upon her head
Who first thee from thy faith misled.
And yet, how well soever meant,
With them 'twould soon grow fraudulent:
215 For like themselves they alter all,
And vice infects the very wall.

XXVIII

'But sure those buildings last not long,
Founded by folly, kept by wrong.
I know what fruit their gardens yield,
220 When they it think by night concealed.
Fly from their vices. 'Tis thy 'state,
Not thee, that they would consecrate.
Fly from their ruin. How I fear
Though guiltless, lest thou perish there.'

XIX

225 What should he do? He would respect
Religion, but not right neglect:
For first Religion taught him right,
And dazzled not but cleared his sight.
Sometimes resolved his sword he draws,
230 But reverenceth then the laws:
For Justice still that Courage led;
First from a judge, then soldier bred.

XXX

Small honour would be in the storm.
The court him grants the lawful form;
235 Which licenses either peace or force,
To hinder the unjust divorce.
Yet still the nuns his right debarred,
Standing upon their holy guard.
Ill-counselled women, do you know
240 Whom you resist, or what you do?

---

191. *All night . . . arm*] here and at l. 200, M. appears to imply that the nuns engage in Lesbian sexual practices, the context of which is discussed in Holstun, *ELH*, 54 (1987), 835–57. The records show impropriety of an entirely heterosexual kind. Of the nineteen nuns in the Priory when it was surrendered in December 1539, three are noted as having borne children (presumably while under vows), including a Fairfax, Jane, daughter of Robert, who committed incest with Guy Fairfax of 'Laysthorpe besides Gilling' and lived with him after the dissolution (Cross and Vickers (1995), 580–2). See also above, l. 156 n.
197–200. *seek . . . her in*] seek her promise of marriage, which has been annulled by the religious life she is beginning, since she has been persuaded by the nun.

197. *promised faith*] betrothal.
198. *Religion*] i.e. monastic life. *that*] the promise.
200. see above, l. 191 n.
204. *finelier*] more cunningly.
219–20. 'It was a commonplace of scurrilous anti-Catholic propaganda that nuns buried their illegitimate babies at midnight in the nunnery's grounds' (Ormerod and Wortham).
221. *'state*] estate, i.e. inheritance, property.
222. *consecrate*] see above, l. 146.
229. *resolved*] determined.
232. *judge . . . soldier*] Sir William Fairfax's father (also Sir William) was Judge of Common Pleas, his mother the daughter of George Manners, twelfth Earl Roos, a distinguished soldier.

XXXI

Is not this he whose offspring fierce
Shall fight through all the universe;
And with successive valour try
France, Poland, either Germany;
45 Till one, as long since prophesied,
His horse through conquered Britain ride?
Yet, against fate, his spouse they kept;
And the great race would intercept.

XXXII

Some to the breach against their foes
50 Their wooden saints in vain oppose.
Another bolder stands at push
With their old holy-water brush.
While the disjointed abbess threads
The jingling chain-shot of her beads.
255 But their loud'st cannon were their lungs;
And sharpest weapons were their tongues.

XXXIII

But, waving these aside like flies,   *Faerie Queene*
Young Fairfax through the wall does rise.
Then th'unfrequented vault appeared,
260 And superstitions vainly feared.
The relics false were set to view;
Only the jewels there were true.

But truly bright and holy Thwaites
That weeping at the altar waits.

XXXIV

265 But the glad youth away her bears,
And to the nuns bequeaths her tears:
Who guiltily their prize bemoan,
Like gypsies that a child had stol'n.
Thenceforth (as when th'enchantment ends,
270 The castle vanishes or rends)
The wasting cloister with the rest
Was in one instant dispossessed.

XXXV

At the demolishing, this seat
To Fairfax fell as by escheat.
275 And what both nuns and founders willed
'Tis likely better thus fulfilled.
For if the virgin proved not their's,
The cloister yet remainèd her's.
Though many a nun there made her vow,
280 'Twas no religious house till now.

XXXVI

From that blest bed the hero came,
Whom France and Poland yet does fame:

---

241. offspring fierce] Sir Thomas Fairfax, son of the Fairfax/Thwaites marriage, fought in Italy and Germany; his son, Thomas, first Lord Fairfax, was knighted for gallantry at Rouen; four of his sons fell fighting abroad; the Lord Fairfax of M.'s poem fought in the Low Countries: see above, l. 36 n. The various volumes of Fairfax family genealogy, heraldry, history and poetry (*Analecta Fairfaxiana*) contain detailed accounts of these martial exploits, together with copies of the epitaphs of those who fell abroad.
244. either] a) 'or' (abbreviating 'either . . . or') b) i.e. Holland, and what were then the German-speaking principalities.
245. one] Fairfax himself.
248. intercept] interrupt, and hence bring to an end.
251. at push] on the attack.
252. holy-water brush] also known as holy-water sprinkle, or aspergillum.
253. disjointed] distracted (*OED* v. 1 b).
257–8. waving . . . flies] Cp Spenser, *The Faerie Queene*, I.i.23, where the Red Cross Knight is described fighting the monsters and serpents as a shepherd brushing aside gnats. For earlier versions of the simile, see Homer, *Iliad*, II, ll. 469–71; Ariosto, *Orlando Furioso*, XIV, 109. Flies were associated with devils

and spirits: see Spenser (1977), 39.
259. unfrequented] a) unvisited b) not honoured with religious observance ('frequent': *OED* v. 3 b). *vault*] chamber underneath church floor, crypt.
260. vainly] a) pointlessly (*OED* adv. 1) b) foolishly (*OED* adv. 2).
268. had] Bod. 1; hath 1681.
269–70. th'enchantment . . . rends] M. chooses a strong romance motif to end this passage (cp. the disappearance of Busirane's house after the rescue of Amoret, Spenser, *The Faerie Queene*, II.xii.24). Fairfax wrote a prose romance entitled 'Berlam and Josaphat K. of Judea', which until recently was owned by the Fairfax family. It was sold at Sotheby's in December 1993.
270. rends] bursts apart (*OED* v.[1] 6).
271. wasting] decaying (*OED* ppl. a. 2 a).
272. dispossessed] the nunnery was finally surrendered in 1539.
273. demolishing] dissolution of the monasteries.
274. escheat] a) a term in feudal law for the reversion of property from the tenant to the lord of the manor in the absence of an heir (*OED* n. I 1) b) plunder (*OED* n. II 6).
281. the hero] probably Sir Thomas Fairfax, son of William Fairfax and Isabel Thwaites.

Who, when retirèd here to peace,
His warlike studies could not cease;
285 But laid these gardens out in sport
In the just figure of a fort;
And with five bastions it did fence,
As aiming one for ev'ry sense.

XXXVII

When in the east the morning ray
290 Hangs out the colours of the day,
The bee through these known allies hums,
Beating the *dian* with its drums.
Then flowers their drowsy eyelids raise,
Their silken ensigns each displays,
295 And dries its pan yet dank with dew,
And fills its flask with odours new.

XXXVIII

These, as their Governor goes by,
In fragrant volleys they let fly;
And to salute their Governess
300 Again as great a charge they press:
None for the virgin Nymph; for she
Seems with the flowers a flower to be.
And think so still! though not compare
With breath so sweet, or cheek so fair.

XXXIX

305 Well shot, ye firemen! Oh how sweet,
And round your equal fires do meet;
Whose shrill report no ear can tell,
But echoes to the eye and smell.

283–4. See *An Horatian Ode*, ll. 9–10.
285–8. But . . . sense] Cp. Benlowes, 'Pneumato-Sarco-Machia', *Theophila* (1652), ll. 23–4: 'Then be sure/That all thy outworks stand secure.' See also below, ll. 349–50 n.
286–7. just . . . fence] Turner (1979), 70–1, notes the similarity between Fairfax's military garden and the picture of the garden as bastion in Diego Saavedra de Fajaro's *Idea Principis Christiano-Politici* (Brussels, 1649), 31. A miniature fort 'in perfect proportion, with his ramparts, bulwarks, counterscarps, and all other appurtenances', in the place of a flowerbed in the garden at Ware Park, Hertfordshire, home of Sir Henry Fanshawe, was reported by John Chamberlain as newly completed in October 1606. But it was replaced by a pond and fountain in 1613 (*The Chamberlain Letters*, ed. Elizabeth McClure Thomson (1965), 61, 99). Duncan-Jones, *RES*, n.s., 52 (2001), 192–3, assumes that Sir Thomas Fairfax did have a garden fort constructed, and that it was still extant during the period of M.'s residence.
287. bastions] projecting parts of a fortification, in the shape of an irregular rectangle; bastions were incorporated within landscaped gardens; in Sidney's *Arcadia* (1593), 60, Basilius's garden is described as being star-shaped, and surrounding a lodge also mostly in the shape of a star. *fence*] defend (*OED* v 4).
288. ev'ry sense] the five senses of touch, taste, sight, smell and hearing; in *A Dialogue, Between the Resolved Soul, and Created Pleasure*, Pleasure attacks each of the five senses in turn. Duncan-Jones, *RES*, n.s., 52 (2001), 193, suggests an allusion, most probably on the part of the poet, to the five bulwarks or bastions of the Castle of Alma in Spenser's *The Faerie Queene*, II.xi.7–14. The Sir Thomas Fairfax who built the fort could have read Spenser; his descendant, M.'s employer, liked *The Faerie Queene* and had a horse called Brigadore, named after the steed stolen by Braggadochio from Guyon (V.ii.29).
289–320. Cp. Shirley, *The Imposture* (1640), 1.2., ll. 41–9, where nuns in a besieged Mantua commemorate battles with their horticulture: 'Where flowers shall seem to fight, and every

plant/Cut into the forms of green artillery,/And instruments of war, shall keep alive/The memory of this day' (Elsie Duncan-Jones, private communication). M. is unlikely to have seen a printed version of the play, since this did not appear until early 1653.
291–2. The bee . . . drums] see Cleveland, 'Fuscara; or the Bee Errant', ll. 51–2, 'Tuning his draughts with drowsy hums,/As Danes carowse by Kettle-drums.' In pastoral verse, the opposition of the martial and the natural was stressed, as opposed to M.'s incorporation of the former in the latter. See, e.g., Henry Vaughan, 'The First White Age', translation of Boëthius, *De Consolatione Philosophiae*, Lib. 2, Metrum 3 (1651), l. 21: 'No stirring Drum had scarr'd that age.'
291. allies] a) allies b) alleys.
292. dian] trumpet-call, or drumroll, at early morning; reveille (Fr. *diane*).
293–6. Then . . . new] Cp. Phineas Fletcher, *The Purple Island* (1633), vi.68, ll. 3–4: 'Yet in the Spring in troups new mustered/Peep out again from their unfrozen tomb.'
294. ensigns] standards; flags.
295. pan] part of the lock on a musket (or pistol) containing the priming powder.
296. flask] in which the gunpowder was kept.
299. Governess] Lady Fairfax.
300. charge] a) amount of gunpowder (*OED* n. I 3 a) b) attack (*OED* n. III 18 a).
301. virgin Nymph] Maria Fairfax; see above, *Headnote, Context*.
303. not compare] Miller, *ELN*, 25.3 (1988), 26–8, suggests 'not' was a misprint for 'nought'. Equally, 'none' could be substituted. But this would lose the connection of sense with the first part of the line. *compare*] comparable.
305. firemen] gunners (*OED* n. 1).
305–6. sweet . . . meet] referring to the equally proportioned length and curving shape of the plant petals.
306. fires] petals (as if they 'shot' from the barrel (i.e. the stem) of the plants).

See how the flowers, as at parade,
10 Under their colours stand displayed:
Each regiment in order grows,
That of the tulip, pink, and rose.

XL

But when the vigilant patrol
Of stars walks round about the Pole,
15 Their leaves, that to the stalks are curled,
Seem to their staves the ensigns furled.
Then in some flow'r's belovèd hut
Each bee as sentinel is shut;
And sleeps so too: but, if once stirred,
20 She runs you through, nor asks the word.

XLI

Oh thou, that dear and happy isle   *England*
The garden of the world ere while,   *fashioning it as*
Thou Paradise of fóur seas,   *paradise*
Which heaven planted us to please,
25 But, to exclude the world, did guard

With wat'ry if not flaming sword;
What luckless apple did we taste,
To make us mortal, and thee waste?   *despairing 'greto at irrecoverable past*

XLII

Unhappy! Shall we never more
330 That sweet militia restore,
When gardens only had their towers,
And all the garrisons were flowers,
When roses only arms might bear,
And men did rosy garlands wear,
335 Tulips, in several colours barred,   *— Charles I: connoisseur of Tulips!*
Were then the Switzers of our guard.

XLIII

The gard'ner had the soldier's place,
And his more gentle forts did trace.
The nursery of all things green
340 Was then the only magazine.
The winter quarters were the stoves,
Where he the tender plants removes.

309–16. See ... furled] Grummitt, *The Coat of Arms*, 11 (1996), 222–36 (226–7), notes that the flowers embody the Fairfax arms (as incorporated with the Vere arms). The three red-flowered plants of l. 312 represent the three blazoned gules (red) bars of the Fairfax family. The stars of l. 314 correspond to the 'mullet of five points argent' of the first quarter of the Vere arms.
310. colours] regimental standards.
312. pink] form of *Dianthus*, a popular garden plant. *rose*] Fowler, *TLS*, 12 Dec. 2003, suggests that the rose is a 'muscat-rose' (*OED* 5, from French *rose muscate*) thereby enhancing the military presence in the garden with the pun on 'musket.'
313–14. vigilant ... Pole] stars in the Lesser Bear and Great Bear constellations are known as the 'guards of the Pole' (Cummings).
316. staves] flagpoles.
320. She] In Cleveland's poem 'Fuscara; or the Bee Errant' (1651), the bee is male, whereas M.'s is female. *nor*] Cooke, *Thompson, Donno, Ormerod and Wortham*; or *1681, Kermode, Wilcher, Walker*. Kermode suggests that 'or' means 'ere'. *word*] password.
321. dear and happy isle] England.
322–3. garden ... seas] M. appears to be using phrases from Shakespeare's *Richard II*: 'This other Eden, demi-paradise' (II, ii, l. 42); 'When our sea-walled garden, the whole land,/Is full of weeds, her fairest flowers chok'd up' (III, iv, ll. 43–4). M.'s speaker appropriates the lamenting voices of John of Gaunt and one of the gardener's assistants.
322–3. garden of the world ... Paradise] Cp. du Bartas, *Divine Weekes*, trans. Josuah Sylvester, (1607), 'All-hail (dear Albion) Europ's Pearl of price,/The Worlds rich Garden, Earth's rare

Paradise'; Giles Fletcher, 'Upon the most lamented departure of the right hopefull, and blessed Prince Henrie Prince of Wales', ll. 20–1: 'The Garden of the World, whear nothing wanted,/Another Paradise'; Fane, 'Anglia Hortus', ll. 1–2: 'The Garden of the world, wherein the Rose/In chief Commanded, did this doubt propose/To be resolv'd in;/Whether sense to prise/For umpire to Create it Paradise.'
326. flaming sword] see Gen. 3:24: 'So he drove out the man; and he placed at the east of the garden of Eden Cherubims, and a flaming sword which turned every way, to keep the way of the tree of life.'
331. towers] trees.
335. barred] striped.
336. Switzers] a tulip 'with a fair red and pale white or straw colour' called a 'Swisse' (John Parkinson, *Paradisi in Sole Paradisus Terrestris* (2nd edn, 1656), 60); M. makes an association with the Swiss guards ('Switzers') of the Vatican, who wore red, yellow and black striped uniforms. But Simons, *N & Q*, n.s. 36 (1989), 434, notes that a 'Switser' in Holland was a relatively cheap, single colour variety. Either way, M. is forcing the comparison, and in doing so, he is also a) enhancing the military overtones (the Dutch often named tulips after military heroes), b) raising the profile of enemies to Fairfax's cause in the poem (Charles I was a connoisseur of tulips; the real 'Switzers' guarded the head of the Roman Catholic church).
338. forts] punning on 'fortes' (strengths), which was spelt as 'forts' in the seventeenth century (Cummings).
340. magazine] building for storing arms and ammunition (*OED* n. 2 a).
341. stoves] hothouses for plants (*OED* n.¹ 3).
342. removes] technical term for lifting a siege (*OED* v. 3 c).

But war all this doth overgrow:
We ordnance plant and powder sow.

XLIV

345   And yet there walks one on the sod
Who, had it pleased him and God,
Might once have made our gardens spring
Fresh as his own and flourishing.
But he preferred to the Cinque Ports
350   These five imaginary forts:
And, in those half-dry trenches, spanned
Power which the ocean might command.

XLV

For he did, with his utmost skill,
Ambition weed, but conscience till.

355   Conscience, that heaven-nursèd plant,
Which most our earthly gardens want.
A prickling leaf it bears, and such
As that which shrinks at every touch;
But flowers eternal, and divine,
360   That in the crowns of saints do shine.

XLVI

The sight does from these bastions ply,
Th'invisible artillery;
And at proud Cawood Castle seems
To point the batt'ry of its beams.
365   As if it quarrelled in the seat
Th'ambition of its prelate great.
But o'er the meads below it plays,
Or innocently seems to graze.

---

344. ordnance] artillery.
349. Cinque Ports] originally five, but later more, ports on the east Sussex and Kent coast which functioned as an incorporation under a Lord Warden, and which were originally charged with providing the Royal Navy. In 1650, the Lord Warden's responsibility reverted to the Council of State, of which Fairfax was a member, for the first half of 1650: hence M.'s reference. Used as a metaphor for the five senses: see Benlowes, *Theophila* (1652), 'Pneumato-Sarco-Machia', ll. 26–9: in 'Design/With constant care a watch o'er every part;/Ev'n at thy Cinque-ports, and thy heart/Set sentinels'. See above, ll. 285–8.
351. spanned] harnessed (*OED* v.[2] 1).
352. Power . . . command] The authority of the Lord High Admiral was also taken by the Council of State in 1650.
354. Ambition] Fairfax's grandfather, however, described him as dangerously proud and spendthrift, to the extent that he would imprudently ruin the family estate; when Thomas Fairfax altered the entailment so that a female as opposed to a male could inherit his property, some members of the family thought that his grandfather's fears would be realized: see *Fairfax Correspondence*, ed. G.W. Johnson, 2 vols (1848), I.314–16.
355–7. Conscience . . . prickling leaf] as in the fourteenth-century poem *The Pricke of Conscience* of which other echoes may be found in the poem (see above, *Headnote, Context*; l. 568 n.). A stained-glass window (*c.* 1410–20) in the church of All Saints, North Street, York, is based on the poem.
356. earthly] *1681*; earthy *Bod. 1. want*] a) lack b) need.
358. that which . . . touch] the sensitive plant, *herba mimosa*, at least one kind of which is prickly. See above, *An Elegy Upon the Death of My Lord Francis Villiers*, l. 81.

361. sight] vision, but also punning on *OED* n.[1] 14 b: gunsight. *ply*] employ (*OED* v.[2] I 1).
363. Cawood Castle] a residence of the Archbishop of York, two miles south-east of Nun Appleton. It had been empty since October 1642.
365. quarrelled] objected to, reproved (*OED* v 4–5). *seat*] place.
366. Th'ambition . . . great] John Williams (1582–1650) was the last Archbishop of York before the interruptions of the Civil War and Interregnum. He was high-minded, and offended people of all parties (including Fairfax) in his aim of avoiding extreme policies. He had considerable influence at court, and although he counselled accommodation with the leading Parliamentarian aristocrats, he earned the ire of the House of Commons in his defence of episcopacy. He avoided imprisonment, was enthroned in York in June 1642, and fortified Cawood Castle, which then became a royalist garrison (Fairfax, *Short Memorials* (1699), 52–5). He fled in October to his native Conway, where he led the royalist community. *prelate*] high-ranking clergyman – in this case, the Archbishop.
367. plays] a) moves lightly (*OED* v. 3) b) discharges, fires (*OED* v. 6 c; the sight is imagined as artillery).
368. graze] *Bod. 1*; gaze *1681*; a) touch by a beam of light: cp., e.g., R. Montagu, *Acts and Monuments* (1642), 78: 'Then be the tops of the mountains graised on by the beames appearing.' (*OED* v.[2] 2 b). b) ricochet: see, e.g., Thomas Fuller, 'The Holy and Profane State' (1642), V.i.358: 'Those bullets which graze on the ground do most mischief to an army.' (*OED*, v.[2] 2).

XLVII

And now to the abyss I pass

70 Of that unfathomable grass,
Where men like grasshoppers appear, *a la Gullieir's Travels*
But grasshoppers are giants there:
They, in their squeaking laugh, contemn
Us as we walk more low than them:

75 And, from the precipices tall
Of the green spires, to us do call.

XLVIII

To see men through this meadow dive,
We wonder how they rise alive.
As, under water, none does know

80 Whether he fall through it or go.
But, as the mariners that sound,
And show their lead the ground,
They bring up flowers so to be seen,
And prove they've at the bottom been.

XLIX

85 No scene that turns with engines strange
Does oft'ner than these meadows change.

For when the sun the grass hath vexed,
The tawny mowers enter next;
Who seem like Israelites to be,

390 Walking on foot through a green sea.
To them the grassy deeps divide,
And crowd a lane on either side.

L

With whistling scythe, and elbow strong,
These massacre the grass along:

395 While one, unknowing, carves the rail,
Whose yet unfeathered quills her fail.
The edge all bloody from its breast
He draws, and does his stroke detest;
Fearing the flesh untimely mowed

400 To him a fate as black forbode.

LI

But bloody Thestylis, that waits
To bring the mowing camp their cates,
Greedy as kites, has trussed it up,
And forthwith means on it to sup:

405 When on another quick she lights, *self-referential.*
And cries, 'He called us Israelites;

369–70. *abyss . . . unfathomable*] the meadows are imagined as an ocean; cp. du Bartas, *Divine Weeks*, trans. Sylvester (1598), 'Eden', ll. 14: 'This Ocean hath no bottome, nor no shoare'; Marino, trans. Crashaw, 'Sospetto d'Herode' (1646), V, ll. 1–2, 'Below the Botome of the great Abysse,/There where one Center reconciles all things.'

369. *abyss*] with a pun on 'abbess'; cp. [Lawrence Anderton], *The English Nunne* (Saint Omer, 1642), 134: 'an *abysse* of delights'. As with ll. 355–7 above, M. points to the replacement of the world of unnatural Roman Catholicism with a godly appreciation of nature.

370. *unfathomable*] immeasurably deep (*OED* a. 2 a).

371–2. *grasshoppers . . . there*] See Numbers 13:32–3: 'And they brought up an evil report of the land which they had searched unto the children of Israel, saying, The land, through which we have gone to search it, is a land that eateth up the inhabitants thereof; and all the people that we saw in it are of a great stature. And there we saw the giants, the sons of Anak, which come of the giants: and we were in our own sight as grasshoppers, and so we were in their sight.' Wilding (1985), 160, notes the Leveller use of this text to describe their sense of persecution by the republic in the third Agreement of the People (rptd D.M. Wolfe, ed., *Leveller Manifestoes of the English Revolution* (New York, 1944), 401).

373. *contemn*] treat with scorn or contempt (*OED* v. 1).

380. *go*] go forwards.

381. *sound*] take soundings of water depth.

382. *show*] display (the mark or residue of the seabed). *ground*] seabed.

385. *scene . . . strange*] scene change in a court masque effected by complicated machinery.

389. *Israelites*] a common description of the English nation as God's chosen people since the mid-sixteenth century. By contrast, the Scots, the immediate threat during summer 1651, were compared to the Israelites' captors, the Egyptians: 'they are like the Egyptians fail them that trust them, they are given to flattery and lying', anon., *A new and true declaration* (1651, 23 June), 8. There were also specific uses of the name in agricultural discourse: 'And which doth he think were heardsmen and shepheards, which were plowmen and tillers of land, the *Israelites* in the land of *Goshen*, or the *Aegyptians* in the land of *Aegypt*', [Joseph Lee], *Considerations concerning Common Fields* (1653), 31.

390. *Walking . . . sea*] just as the Israelites crossed the Red Sea (Exod. 14: 21–2).

394. *along*] flat, along the ground (*OED* a.² 6).

395. *rail*] the landrail, or corncrake.

401. *Thestylis*] Thestylis prepares food for the reapers in Virgil, *Eclogues*, II, ll. 11–12, although it is savoury garlic and thyme, rather than rails. See also above, *Headnote. Sources and Genre*, and *Ametas and Thestylis Making Hay-Ropes*.

402. *cates*] provisions (*OED* n.¹ 1).

405. *quick*] a) quickly b) alive.

406. *Israelites*] see above, ll. 388–9.

But now, to make his saying true,
Rails rain for quails, for manna, dew.'

The women that with forks it fling,
Do represent the pillaging.

LII

Unhappy birds! What does it boot
410 To build below the grass' root;
When lowness is unsafe as height,
And chance o'ertakes, what 'scapeth spite?
And now your orphan parents call
Sounds your untimely funeral.
415 Death-trumpets creak in such a note,
And 'tis the sourdine in their throat.

LIV

425 And now the careless victors play,
Dancing the triumphs of the hay;
Where every mower's wholesome heat
Smells like an Alexander's sweat.
Their females fragrant as the mead
430 Which they in fairy circles tread:
When at their dance's end they kiss,
Their new-made hay not sweeter is.

LIII

Or sooner hatch or higher build:
The mower now commands the field;
In whose new traverse seemeth wrought
420 A camp of battle newly fought:
Where, as the meads with hay, the plain
Lies quilted o'er with bodies slain:

LV

When after this 'tis piled in cocks,
Like a calm sea it shows the rocks:
435 We wond'ring in the river near
How boats among them safely steer.
Or, like the desert Memphis sand,
Short pyramids of hay do stand.

407–8. But now . . . dew] See Exod. 16:13–15, where the Lord provides quails and manna for the Israelites to eat. But in Numb. 11:31–4, God punished the Israelites with plague for gathering too many of the quails left for them (Ormerod and Wortham).
409. What does it boot] what good does it do (see 'boot', *OED*, v.¹ 3).
413–14. And now . . . funeral] Cp. Virgil, *Georgics*, IV, ll. 511–15, 'qualis populea maerens philomela sub umbra/amissos queritur fetus, quos durus arator/observans nido implumis detraxit; at illa flet noctem, ramque sedens miserabile carmen/integrat, et maestis late loca questibus implet' (even as the nightingale, mourning beneath the poplar's shade, bewails the loss of her brood, that a churlish ploughman hath espied and torn unfledged from the nest: but she weeps all night long, and, perched on a spray, renews her piteous strain, filling the region round with sad laments).
413. orphan] echoing the Latin *orbus*, meaning 'bereaved'. Latin *orbitas*, 'bereavement', refers to the loss of children or parents.
414. untimely] premature.
415. Death-trumpets] i.e. announcements of death.
416. sourdine] French: trumpet mute.
419. traverse] a) way, path (*OED* n. III 11a) b) view (*OED* n. IV 13b) c) masque scenery (*OED* n. IV 13a).
420. camp] plain, field (*OED* n.² IV 11), appropriate because of its more familiar military usages.
425. careless] carefree (*OED* a. 1).

426. hay] a) grass b) winding country dance (*OED* n.⁴) c) military file (*OED* n.² 3).
428. Alexander's sweat] 'his body had so sweete a smell of it selfe, that all apparell he wore next unto his body took thereof a passing delightful savour, as it had been perfumed. And the cause hereof peradventure might be, the very temperature and constitucion of his body, which was hot and burning like fire', Plutarch, *Life of Alexander*, trans. Sir Thomas North, IV.2.
430. fairy circles] fairy rings: circle of grass of a different shade from the grass around it, supposed to have been made by dancing fairies; the women are thus compared to the fairies.
433. cocks] haycocks; heaps of hay (*OED* n.²).
435–6. We wond'ring . . . steer] the eye, 'wondering' its gaze across the meadows to the river, is deceived, and appears to see boats travelling among the hay heaps.
437. Memphis] city in ancient Egypt; hence a synecdoche for Egypt.
438. Short] a) low b) of a brief duration. *pyramids*] ornamental and monumental trapezoid columns called 'pyramids' were a feature of country house grounds: Constantijn Huygens built one, and wrote a brief poem on it. It was depicted in the engravings accompanying *Hofwyck* (1651) with a Latin inscription beneath it from Martial, *De Spectaculis*, 1: 'Saxea Pyramidum sileat miracula Memphis:/Inuidia Coeli lignea digna fuit' (The stones of the Pyramid do not disclose the miracle of Memphis. The jealousy of Heaven made wood worthy) (see below, l. 439 n.).

And such the Roman camps do rise
40   In hills for soldiers' obsequies.

Or rather such is the *toril*
Ere the bulls enter at Madril.

LVI

This scene again withdrawing brings
A new and empty face of things;
A levelled space, as smooth and plain,
As cloths for Lely stretched to stain.
45 The world when first created sure
Was such a table rase and pure.

LVII

For to this naked equal flat,
450 Which Levellers take pattern at,
The villagers in common chase
Their cattle, which it closer rase;
And what below the scythe increased
Is pinched yet nearer by the beast.

---

439. Roman camps] tumuli (including burial mounds) thought in M.'s time to be Roman, but in fact Ancient British. Sir Thomas Browne attributed burial mounds to the Romans, the Saxons and the Danes ('Of Artificial Hills, Mounts or Burrows', in *Works*, ed. Geoffrey Keynes (1928), III.88). *rise*] a) ascend b) wittily playing on 'rise', *OED* v. B I 5 b, to take up arms, and *OED* v. B I 6, to break up camp.

440. obsequies] funeral rites or commemorations.

441. scene] as in the intricate machinery of a court masque; see also descriptions of Fairfax's prowess: 'Fairfax the Greate what glorious things have bene/Acted by him upon our English Sceane/Which wee all knowe Hee only will not owne/Bidds us Singe Paeans to the Lambe and Throne', John Favour, 'To the Honorable S[r] Thomas Widdrington Kn[t] one the Commissioners for the Great Seale of England. Vpon the death of the Right Honourable Ferdinando Lord Fairfax.', ll. 17–20, Leeds, Brotherton Library, Fairfax MS, Acc. No B24720, fol. 351[r].

444. cloths] canvasses. *Lely*] Sir Peter Lely (1618–80). Lely was born in Holland but came to England with William, Prince of Orange, in 1641 on his marriage to Princess Mary. Although best known for his portraits (of Charles I, Cromwell, Charles II, and many courtly women (see below, *Last Instructions*, l. 61), and M. himself (see Vertue, II.22; Hunt (1978), 15–16)) he also painted landscapes. M.'s reference may be related to Lely's proposal, along with Gerbier and Geldorp, to produce a series of paintings for Whitehall celebrating Parliament's victories since the beginning of the Civil War. These would have included scenes of battles and sieges as well as portraits.

446. table rase] i.e. *tabula rasa*, a blank writing tablet; one on which the writing has been erased; already in use as a metaphor for explaining cognition; see also below, l. 452.

447. toril] M. means the bullring, but the *toril* is the pen where the bulls are kept before they enter the ring.

448. Madril] Madrid; common English name for Madrid in the seventeenth century.

449–52. For . . . rase] Cp. Robert Waring, 'To the Memory of his deceased Friend. Mr William Cartwright', in Cartwright, *Comedies, Tragi-Comedies, with other Poems* (1651), sig. *7[r]: 'But there's a Toleration now; the Hill/Levell'd to a Plain, all bellowing cattle fill.'

449. naked] bare, devoid of trees and bushes. *equal*] entirely level. *flat*] river plain (*OED* n.[3] 5).

450. Levellers] the Levellers were an association of radical Puritans and fellow travellers, largely among the 'middling sort', in London and the New Model Army, who campaigned for an extension of religious toleration and political liberties, notably an increased franchise. They had emerged as an organization by 1646–47. Although their threat to the Commonwealth was ended by the crushing of Leveller mutinies in 1649 (in which Fairfax played a significant role), some Levellers remained active in the next decade, even close to Nun Appleton (see *Headnote, Context*). If not democrats in the modern sense of the word, they were widely perceived to be so by contemporaries. The concerns of the Levellers were largely urban, but, as Cummings notes, there are calls for an abandonment of enclosure, and for the reversion of formerly common land to 'free and common use, and benefit of the poor' (Richard Overton, 'Certaine Articles for the good of the Common wealth' in *An Appeale from the Degenerate Representative Body* (1647), 68). However, M. may mean the True Levellers, or Diggers, who cultivated land in common, regarding the earth as a common treasury. They were radical Puritan, agrarian communists. The most important commune was at St George's Hill, near Cobham, Surrey, on 1 April 1649, and was led by Gerrard Winstanley, by far the most important Digger thinker and writer. Since he was responsible for the security of Surrey, Fairfax was called on by local landowners: he interviewed Winstanley and William Everard in 20 April, and visited the commune in late May. *take pattern at*] use as a model.

451. in common] a) together b) on the common land. *chase*] drive (*OED* v.[1] 10).

452. cattle . . . rase] Cp. Nemesianus, *Eclogue* I, ll. 6–7: 'dum salices haedi, dum gramina vaccae/Detondent' (while the kids nibble at the willow twigs, the cows crop the grass). *cattle*] The Surrey Diggers (see above, l. 450 n.) were found guilty of trespass, and, because they could not afford the fines, cattle in the keeping of Winstanley was taken from him, although not his property. The cattle took on a special significance to Winstanley: see, e.g., *A Letter to the Lord Fairfax* (9 June 1649), 2–3; *A Watchword to the City of London* (August 1649), in C. Hill, ed. (1973), 139–44. *rase*] shave (*OED* v[1] 4c); see also above, l. 446.

453. increased] grew.

454. beast] Bod. 1; breast *1681*; Hill (1974), 81–204, discusses the widespread description in the seventeenth century of the people as a many-headed beast.

455 Such, in the painted world, appeared
    Dav'nant with th'universal herd.

LVIII

    They seem within the polished grass
    A landskip drawn in looking-glass.
    And shrunk in the huge pasture show
460 As spots, so shaped, on faces do.
    Such fleas, ere they approach the eye,
    In multiplying glasses lie.
    They feed so wide, so slowly move,
    As constellations do above.

LIX

465 Then, to conclude these pleasant acts,
    Denton sets ope its cataracts;
    And makes the meadow truly be
    (What it but seemed before) a sea.
    For, jealous of its Lord's long stay,

470 It tries t'invite him thus away.
    The river in itself is drowned,
    And isles th'astonished cattle round.

LX

    Let others tell the paradox,
    How eels now bellow in the ox;
475 How horses at their tails do kick,
    Turned as they hang to leeches quick;
    How boats can over bridges sail;
    And fishes do the stables scale.
    How salmons trespassing are found;
480 And pikes are taken in the pound.

LXI

    But I, retiring from the flood,
    Take sanctuary in the wood;
    And, while it lasts, myself embark
    In this yet green, yet growing ark;

455–6. Such . . . herd] In Sir William Davenant's *Gondibert* (1651) (2.6), Astragon's palace contains a series of pictures, including some of the Creation. M. alludes specifically to 2.6.60: 'Then strait an universal herd appears;/ First gazing on each other in the shade;/ Wondring with levell'd Eies, and lifted Ears,/Then play, whilst yet their Tyrant is away.' The scene presented to the poet by the Nun Appleton estate, being natural, is the opposite of the artificial palace in Davenant. To put Davenant with his herd suggests that M. is mocking him, given the elitist sentiments expressed in the Preface to *Gondibert*. But M. seems primarily to stress the manner in which habits of perception and representation determine how we view and describe what we see. See above *Headnote, Context*.

457. polished grass] i.e. nearly 'polished glass'.

458. Pictures painted on glass with a mirror background were fashionable in the mid-seventeenth century. *landskip*] slightly earlier spelling of 'landscape', derived from Dutch *landschap*; technical term for picture representing natural scenery (*OED* n. 1 a); the first usage recorded in *OED* is 1603.

460. spots] beauty-patches.

461. Such] i.e. so.

462. multiplying glasses] E.W. and N.S. Hetherington, *ELN*, 13 (1975), 123–4, note that M. is probably referring not to the microscope, but to the short tubes in which fleas were trapped between a plate of plain glass and a small, thick glass lens; by looking through the lens, the flea would look very large. A 'multiplying-glass' was also the name for a lens with many flat facets ground onto its convex, thereby giving many reflections of the object viewed (*OED* 2). *lie*] a) are placed b) deceive.

465. pleasant acts] see above, l. 385.

466. cataracts] in the plural, flood- or sluicegates, as well as waterfalls (*OED* n. 1; from the Vulgate translation of Gen.

7:11: 'cataractae caeli apertae sunt' ('the windows of heaven were opened')). Barnard, *RES*, n.s. 31 (1980), 310–15, argues that M. is referring to the sluicegates controlling the flow of water from the fishpond on the Denton estate into the River Wharfe. This would have caused flooding at the Nun Appleton estate thirty miles downriver, and M. is eliding the periodic sluicing of Denton's ponds with the annual spring flooding of the Wharfe. The more threatening broader context was some disastrous flooding in Holland and Yarmouth in March 1651.

472. isles . . . round] surrounds with water. *astonished*] Bod. 1; astonish 1681; bewildered.

474. eels . . . ox] i.e. because the eels are swallowed by the drinking oxen; their bellowing now sounds like the eels trying to escape; resembles the story of Perillus' bull (see above, *Flecknoe an English Priest at Rome*, l. 152 n.).

475–6. horses . . . quick] it was popularly believed that horse-hairs turned into leeches under water.

477–80. See Ovid, *Metamorphoses*. I, ll. 295–6: 'ille supra segetes aut mersae culmina villae/navigat, hic summa piscem deprendit in ulmo' (one sails over his fields of grain or the roof of his buried farmhouse, and one takes fish caught in the elm-trees' top.).

478. fishes . . . scale] i.e. the fishes cover the stables in scales as well as 'climb' them.

480. taken . . . pound] a) trapped in a pen for animals, and hence b) taken into custody. *pound*] a) animal enclosure (*OED* n.² I.1 a) b) prison (*OED* n.² 2); 'pound' recalls 'pond', the usual place to confine a pike.

483. embark] a) go aboard b) enclose in bark.

484–6. Cp. du Bartas, *Divine Weeks*, trans. Sylvester (II.iii.1, ll. 101–2): 'from the All-drowning *Flood*/He sav'd the worlds seed in an Arke of wood.'

85 Where the first carpenter might best
Fit timber for his keel have pressed.
And where all creatures might have shares,
Although in armies, not in pairs.

LXII

90 The double wood of ancient stocks
Linked in so thick, an union locks,
It like two pedigrees appears,
On one hand Fairfax, th'other Vere's:
Of whom though many fell in war,
Yet more to heaven shooting are:
95 And, as they Nature's cradle decked,
Will in green age her hearse expect.

LXIII

When first the eye this forest sees
It seems indeed as wood not trees:

As if their neighbourhood so old
500 To one great trunk them all did mould.
There the huge bulk takes place, as meant
To thrust up a fifth element;
And stretches still so closely wedged
As if the night within were hedged.

LXIV

505 Dark all without it knits; within
It opens passable and thin;
And in as loose an order grows,
As the Corinthean porticoes.
The arching boughs unite between
510 The columns of the temple green;
And underneath the wingèd choirs
Echo about their tunèd fires.

---

485. *first carpenter*] Noah (see Gen. 6:14–22 for the building of the ark).
486. *pressed*] a) commandeered (*OED* v.² 2 c) b) with the trees imagined as men being pressed into military service (*OED* v.² 2 a).
487. *shares*] allotted portions.
488. *armies*] see above, l. 486 n. b). *pairs*] see Gen. 6:19.
489. *stocks*] tree trunks (*OED* n.¹ 2 a), but with an echo of the figurative sense (*OED* n.¹ 3 a) of stock as a line of familial descent developed in the following lines.
491. *pedigrees*] family trees.
493. *many . . . war*] a) many trees were felled to make weapons and ships b) many Fairfaxes and Veres fell in battle.
494. *shooting*] the image of Fairfax and Vere souls as shooting stars ascending to heaven recalls the star in the Vere coat of arms, and (so it was thought) the Anglo-Saxon origin of the Fairfax name: 'Fairfax or as in some old deeds . . . Fairvex, so calld by yᵉ English-Saxons á pulchro capillitio feré their fair locks or hair, for Fax and Vere are yᵉ same', Henry Fairfax, in Bod., MS Fairfax, d.1, p. 19. Daniel King, who stayed with the Fairfax family in the later 1650s, prepared a genealogy of the Veres for presentation to Lady Fairfax: 'A Short Discourse of yᵉ Descent of the Right honorable, prudent, & pious Lady, Anne Vere', BL, Add. MS 71449, fols. 37ʳ–51ᵛ.
495. *And . . . decked*] Saint Amant, 'La Solitude', trans. Fairfax, ll. 6–10: 'Oaks that such spreading branches bear,/Which, from old time's nativity/And the'envy of so many years,/Are still green, beautiful and fair/As at the world's first day they were.'
498. *wood not trees*] an inversion of the proverb 'not to see the wood for the trees': Whiting (1968), W561.
499. *neighbourhood*] proximity (*OED* 3 a).

501. *takes place*] a) comes into being (*OED* n. 27 a) b) occupies space c) takes precedence (*OED* n. 27 c).
502. *fifth element*] the fifth essence, or quintessence: heavenly substance, latent in all earthly bodies, and extracted by the alchemical process.
505. *Dark all without*] i.e. it seems from the outside as if it were dark inside. *knits*] closes up.
506. *thin*] sparsely wooded.
507–8. *And in . . . porticoes*] grows in the light and airy manner of the Corinthian colonnade. Corinthian design was supposed to have originated in imitation of growing plants. Webb's designs for the new house at Nun Appleton contained Corinthian capitals for the north entrance. These capitals had plants in relief, in addition to the conventional Corinthian pattern, and the Fairfax lion. See Bold (1989), 163–5.
507. *order*] a) arrangement b) architectural order. The Corinthian order is described in the next five lines.
509–12. *The arching . . . fires*] Cp. Constantijn Huygens, *Hofwyck* (1651), ll. 341–5: 'De Bercken staen om mij als Toorsten, die in Kercken/Niet hald soo dienstigh staen en druippen opde Sercken,/Blanckstammigh is de Boom, gelijck 't was vande Bije/Sijn maker werdt onthaelt; noch is 't veel dat ick 't sie,/ Soo duyster is 't in 't groen, soo groen is 't in den duyster' (My birches abound as white as church tapers,/Which drip their wax in graves, stand not so strong,/White-barked this tree, white as the virgin wax/New gathered form the hive; I see things but dimly,/So shadowy the greenness, and so green the shade).
509–10. Columns were supposed to have originated in tree trunks.
512. *fires*] a metaphor for birdsong (not in *OED*) meaning: birdsong as a) gunfire b) passions, enthusiasms. The 'choir' in a church (see above, l. 511) was also where 'church-buckets' were kept in case of fire (*OED*).

LXV

The nightingale does here make choice
To sing the trials of her voice.
515 Low shrubs she sits in, and adorns
With music high the squatted thorns.
But highest oaks stoop down to hear,
And list'ning elders prick the ear.
The thorn, lest it should hurt her, draws
520 Within the skin its shrunken claws.

LXVI

But I have for my music found
A sadder, yet more pleasing sound:
The stock-doves, whose fair necks are graced
With nuptial rings their ensigns chaste;
525 Yet always, for some cause unknown,
Sad pair unto the elms they moan.
O why should such a couple mourn,
That in so equal flames do burn!

LXVII

Then as I careless on the bed
530 Of gelid strawberries do tread,
And through the hazels thick espy
The hatching throstle's shining eye,
The heron from the ash's top,
The eldest of its young lets drop,
535 As if it stork-like did pretend
That tribute to its Lord to send.

LXVIII

But most the hewel's wonders are,
Who here has the holt-felster's care.
He walks still upright from the root,
540 Meas'ring the timber with his foot;
And all the way, to keep it clean,
Doth from the bark the woodmoths glean.
He, with his beak, examines well
Which fit to stand and which to fell.

513. nightingale] nightingales were conventionally associated with wooded groves: see, e.g., Henry Vaughan, 'Upon the Priory Grove, His Usual Retirement' (1645–46), ll. 5–10. In medieval iconography, the nightingale was associated with Christ, its song with Christ's lament for his death but, as with the stock doves below (l. 523), M. frees the bird from overt religious associations. Cp. Fairfax, 'The Solitude', ll. 23–4: 'Sad Philomela's mournful song/Doth sweetly entertain my grief'; Huygens, *Hofwyck* (1651), ll. 403–6: ''K spreeck van geen' Nachtegael; die heeft'er oock sijn nest,/En maeckt'er meer meer geschals dan all'de vlugge rest:/'K spreek van gevogelte met kotelicker veeren,/Veel aerdiger gebackt en in veel langer kleeren' (I speak not now of nightingales, although they nest/Within my grove, outsinging the other darling birds/I speak of one more eminent).
516. squatted] pressed down.
518. elders . . . ear] Reid, *N & Q*, n.s. 42 (1995), 447–8, shows that M. refers to 'jew's ear' (*auricula auricula*) a fungus that was commonly supposed to grow only on the elder (in fact it grows on other trees too). Through the pun on 'elder', M. imagines the trees as the elders of a congregation, reflecting Presbyterian church government, the preference of the Fairfaxes.
519–20. Yet proverbial wisdom has the nightingale pressing itself against the thorn, which makes it sing: see Marston, *The Dutch Courtesan* (1603–5), I, ii, ll. 117–18: 'I love to sleep 'gainst prickle,/So doth the nightingale.'
523. stock-doves] wild pigeons; presented for sacrifice at the Temple (Luke 2:24) and hence prefigurations of Christ's sacrifice, but see above l. 513 n.

526. Sad . . . moan] Virgil, *Eclogues*, I, l. 58: 'nec gemere aërea cessabit turtur ab ulmo' (and the turtledoves shall not cease their moaning from the skyey elm).
528. flames do burn] flames of passion: cp. Cowley, 'Written in Juice of Lemmon' (1647), ll. 22–4: 'require/A more gentle *Ordeal Fire*,/ And bid her by *Loves-Flames* read it again'.
530. gelid] cold.
532. hatching] incubating (*OED* v.¹ 1). *throstle*] thrush.
535–6. As if . . . send] storks were supposed to leave one of their young behind as a tribute to the owner of the house where they nested. M. may well have heard this in a sermon at Trinity College, Cambridge, given by one of the fellows: 'The Stork is said to leave one of her young ones where she hatcheth, as it were out of some instinct of gratitude', John Sherman, *A Greek to the Temple* (1641), sig. ¶2ᵛ. Datta, *JWCI*, 31 (1968), 437–8, adduces further sources in Konrad Gesner, *De avium natura* (Zürich, 1555), 254; Arnold Freitag, *Mythologia Ethica* (Antwerp, 1579), 250; Bartholomaeus Anglicus, trans. Stephen Bateman, *Batman upon Bartholome* (1582), xii, 8; Drayton, *Noahs Floud* (1630), ll. 406–7.
537. hewel] green woodpecker (see *OED*: 'hickwall').
538. holt-felster] forester; keeper of the woods. Duncan-Jones and Wilcox (*N & Q*, n.s. 48 (2001), 395–7) suggest that 'holt-felster' is not a variant of 'holt-feller' (*OED* 'holt' 1, 5), meaning 'woodcutter', as suggested by Margoliouth, but is derived from Dutch 'hout-vester', 'overseer' or 'keeper of the woods'. Dutch 'v' is pronounced as an 'f'. 'Hout-vester' appeared as 'hout-vorster' in Henry Hexham's *Copious English and Netherduytch Dictionarie* (1648); Hexham had served in the Low Countries under Fairfax.

LXIX

45 The good he numbers up, and hacks;
    As if he marked them with the axe.
    But where he, tinkling with his beak,
    Does find the hollow oak to speak,
    That for his building he designs,
50 And through the tainted side he mines.
    Who could have thought the tallest oak
    Should fall by such a feeble stroke!

LXX

    Nor would it, had the tree not fed
    A traitor-worm, within it bred.
55 (As first our flesh corrupt within
    Tempts ignorant and bashful Sin.)
    And yet that worm triumphs not long,
    But serves to feed the hewel's young.
    While the oak seems to fall content,
60 Viewing the treason's punishment.

LXXI

    Thus I, easy philosopher,
    Among the birds and trees confer:
    And little now to make me, wants
    Or of the fowls, or of the plants.
565 Give me but wings as they, and I
    Straight floating on the air shall fly:
    Or turn me but, and you shall see
    I was but an inverted tree.

LXXII

    Already I begin to call
570 In their most learned original:
    And where I language want, my signs
    The bird upon the bough divines;
    And more attentive there doth sit
    Than if she were with lime-twigs knit.
575 No leaf does tremble in the wind
    Which I returning cannot find.

---

550. *tainted*] diseased.
551–2. *Who could . . . stroke*] 'Was't not enough the *Hatchet* did hew down/Those well-grown Oaks, and Pillars of the Crown', Marchamont Nedham, 'On the untimely death of the Lord Hastings', *Lachrymae Musarum* (1649), 81–3 (ll. 5–6). Larson, *DUJ*, 80 (1987), 27–35, notes the association of tree symbolism with the royalist cause. Not only was the oak associated with monarchy, but several authors, including Howell, Herrick, Cowley, Lovelace and Evelyn, linked trees with the royalist cause and the court, probably in the light of the destruction of woodland by Puritans. M.'s reference to the destruction of the oak is an oblique reference to regicide and the passing of a kind of civilization, as well as a comment on the limitations of such fables (see Smith (1994), 8).
554. *traitor-worm*] compound forms for 'traitor' existed, although usually with a verb (e.g. 'traitor-led').
556. *bashful*] a) dismayed (*OED* a. 1) b) shameful (*OED* a. 4).
558. *hewel's*] see above l. 537 n.
561. *I, easy philosopher*] the speaker's definition of himself bears comparison with a later description of Fairfax during his retirement: 'He red diviner things then Druids knew./Such mistery's were revealed to few,/For his chiefe study was Gods sacred law,/And all his Life did comments on it draw/ . . . Like some Religious Hermit now he seemed', Brian Fairfax, 'Upon cutting down the Woods at Nun Appleton, 1679', ll. 35–8, 41 (BL MS Eg. 2146, fol. 2ᵛ).
563. *wants*] is lacking.
568. *inverted tree*] a commonplace, with sources in Plato and Aristotle, explored by Chambers, *SR*, 8 (1961), 261–9; see also *The Pricke of Conscience*, I, ll. 672–87; Evelyn, *Sylva* (1664), 11: '*Homo* is but *Arbor inversa*.'
570. *learned original*] sounds made by birds and beasts were assumed in the occult tradition to be part of the 'language of nature', the signs which God originally placed in nature and gave as names to Adam. Hence, before the Fall, the 'language of nature' was equivalent to the 'original language' spoken by Adam and Eve. The aim of the magus was to return, through illumination, to the Adamic state and, in doing so, M.'s speaker comprehends the 'natural' and 'original' language of the birds. See John Webster, *Academiarum Examen* (1654), 31–2. Cp. Virgil's Helenus in *Aeneid*, III, l. 361: 'et volucrum linguas et praepetis omina pinnae' ([who knows] the tongues of birds and omens of the flying wing); Tasso, *Aminta*, trans. Henry Reynolds (1632), sig. C3ᵛ: 'Mopso that knows the hid language of birds.' See also above, *The Garden*, l. 24. Srigley, *N & Q*, n.s., 43 (1996), 284–7, notes that the original language was succeeded by the confusion of tongues, after the Tower of Babel was built, when, according to cabbalistic tradition, seventy-two languages were spoken (also the number of the languages of God): the number of the stanza in which this line comes. See also above, *Headnote. Genre and Sources*.
571. *want*] lack.
572. *divines*] interprets by intuition or supernatural insight.
574. *lime-twigs*] twigs coated with a viscous sticky substance prepared from the bark of the holly in order to catch small birds (*OED* n.¹ 1 a).

LXXIII

Out of these scattered sibyl's leaves
Strange prophecies my fancy weaves:
And in one history consumes,
580 Like Mexique paintings, all the plumes.
What Rome, Greece, Palestine, ere said
I in this light mosaic read.
Thrice happy he who, not mistook,
Hath read in Nature's mystic book.

LXXIV

585 And see how Chance's better wit
Could with a masque my studies hit!
The oak leaves me embroider all,
Between which caterpillars crawl:
And ivy, with familiar trails,
590 Me licks, and clasps, and curls, and hales.
Under this antic cope I move
Like some great prelate of the grove.

577–82. Out of . . . read] Cp. Fairfax, 'The Solitude' (*c.* 1650–71), ll. 81–2: 'The marble stones here strewed about/Of characters leave yet some sign.'

577. sibyl's leaves] originally a single prophetess, but, from the fourth century BC, the Sibyls were ten women reputed to have prophetic powers; the Erythraean Sibyl inscribed her prophecies on leaves, arranged as an acrostick so that the initial letters of the leaves always formed a word. The later Sibylline Oracles (AD 150–80) either confirmed Jewish or Christian doctrine or predicted future events, and were regarded by some early theologians as having equal prophetic status with the Old Testament.

579. consumes] uses up (*OED* v.¹ 3), but usually used in a destructive sense.

580. Like Mexique . . . plumes] pre-Conquest Mexican paintings were composed of feathers; see also below, *Last Instructions*, l. 14. Thomas Gage, who had been a Dominican priest in Mexico, but had converted to become a Puritan minister in Kent, dedicated his *The English-American his Travail by Sea and Land* (1648) to Fairfax. A copy may therefore have been available at Nun Appleton. There are several references to featherwork, including an encounter with a 'gallant and amorous' prior (ed. Thompson (1958; 1981), 39), who feasts on poultry, and whose chamber contained a few books that had been neglected in favour of a guitar. It was richly decorated with silk tablecloths, china and paintings made of cotton wool and feathers. The picture, another version of the Roman Catholic 'other' (see above, 219–22), contrasts with M.'s speaker, the 'prelate of the grove', who speaks with the birds as part of his knowledge of the book of nature.

581. Rome, Greece, Palestine] the wisdom of ancient Greece and Rome, and the sacred truths of Scripture.

582–4. I in this . . . book] a reference to the nature mysticism of Hermes Trismegistus, the supposed Egyptian high priest with a knowledge of divinity and the world *thrice* as great as that given to Moses (his *Corpus Hermeticum* is really a collection of sixth-century Alexandrian writings). It was assumed that hermetic knowledge was a wisdom given to Adam, and kept untainted by Trismegistus and Pythagoras. Knowledge of the hermetic secrets conferred on the magus a spiritual purity equal to Adam's before the Fall, in addition to control over the natural world. *mosaic*] M. means the 'book of nature', the 'second scripture' in which the truth of the first scripture could be discerned (see above, l. 581); 'mosaic' is thus a pun, playing on a) the pattern of the leaves, which is like a mosaic, b) the 'book of nature' is like the Mosaic books in the Old Testament, the Pentateuch. Cp. *Music's Empire*, l. 21, where music is the 'mosaic of the air'.

583. Thrice] a) three times as much (OED adv. 2) b) very, extremely (i.e. an intensifier; *OED* adv. 3b); from the Latin

'ter', e.g. Horace, *Carmina*, I.xiii, ll. 17–18: 'felices ter et amplius,/quos inrupta tenet copula' (Thrice happy and more are they whom an unbroken bond unites).

585–6. Chance's . . . masque] Hunt, *PQ*, 59 (1980), 374–7, notes that M. may have seen the highly elaborate fusions of theatre and garden in the Spanish estates referred to later in the poem (see below, ll. 755–6); these included very frequent scene changes and *trompe-l'oeil* as well as the use of gardens as scenery along with painted boards. See also above, *Headnote. Genre and Sources.*

586. masque] a) masque: courtly entertainment with a mixture of drama, music and extravagant set design and machinery. b) disguise.

587–90. Colie (1966), 287–8, proposes that the fusion of the human figure with nature was possibly suggested by anamorphic and grotesque paintings where human figures were painted in terms of natural features, fruit and vegetables.

587. embroider] splendidly decorate (*OED* v. 2a).

589–90. ivy . . . hales] Cp. Thomas Beedome, 'To his Mistresse, when shee was going into the Country' (1641): 'when you see/The trusty Ivy claspe it's much loved tree,/And with its amorous intwinings cover/The welcome waste of it's imbraced lover:/Thinke it our Embleme then.' Ormerod and Wortham note that ivy was an emblem of immortality in Renaissance art, symbolizing the triumph of faith over death.

589. familiar] a) adapted to relations with (*OED* a. 2. e; the earliest date given is 1721) b) intimate (*OED* a. 5) c) in the pattern of armorial bearings (*OED* a. 1 b).

590. hales] pulls, tugs (*OED* v.¹ 3).

591. antic] a) fantastic, bizarre (*OED* a. A 2 c) b) ancient, belonging to former times ('antique': *OED* a. A 1 and 3 a). *antic cope*] see Milton, *An Apology against a Pamphlet* (1642), *CPW*, 1.930: 'it consisted most of Scripture language: it had no *Rubrick* to be sung in an antick Coape upon the Stage of a high Altar'. The next sentence in Milton points up M.'s amused attraction to this passage, and the extent of M.'s own self-portrayal at this point in *Upon Appleton House*: '*It was big-mouth'd* he says; no marvell.' In the light of M.'s reference to Cawood Castle and John Williams, Archbishop of York (see above, ll. 363–6), see also anon., *A Vindication of the late Archbishop of York* (19 May 1647), 4, where Williams is presented as the champion of a traditional English church against Laudian and Arminian innovations, 'When *Altars, Copes,* and such adult'rate ware,/Were by Faction brought into the chair.'

592. prelate of the grove] Larson, *DUJ*, 80 (1987), 27–35 notes that the speaker casts himself here as a kind of druid, one of the guises of royalist poets (as retainers of the 'royal oak', i.e. the monarchy); in his royalist tree allegory, James Howell described himself as 'Druyd like' (*Dodona's Grove* (1640), sig. A2ᵛ). But M.'s figure is free from such overt associations.

LXXV

Then, languishing with ease, I toss
On pallets swoll'n of velvet moss;
95 While the wind, cooling through the boughs,
Flatters with air my panting brows.
Thanks for my rest ye mossy banks,
And unto you cool zephyrs thanks,
Who, as my hair, my thoughts too shed,
00 And winnow from the chaff my head.

LXXVI

How safe, methinks, and strong, behind
These trees have I encamped my mind;
Where Beauty, aiming at the heart,
Bends in some trees its useless dart;
05 And where the world no certain shot
Can make, or me it toucheth not.
But I on it securely play,
And gall its horseman all the day.

LXXVII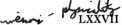

Bind me ye woodbines in your twines,
610 Curl me about ye gadding vines,
And oh so close your circles lace,
That I may never leave this place:
But, lest your fetters prove too weak,
Ere I your silken bondage break,
615 Do you, O brambles, chain me too,
And courteous briars nail me through.

LXXVIII

Here in the morning tie my chain,
Where the two woods have made a lane;
While, like a guard on either side,
620 The trees before their Lord divide;
This, like a long and equal thread,
Betwixt two labyrinths does lead.
But, where the floods did lately drown,
There at the evening stake me down.

593–4. *Then . . . moss*] Cp. Statius, *Silvae*, I.iii, ll. 70–2: 'illic ipse antris Anien et fonte relicto/nocte sub arcana glaucos exutus amictus/huc illuc fragili proternit pectora musco' (There Anio himself, leaving his grotto and his spring, in night's mysterious hour puts off his grey-green raiment and leans his breast against the soft moss hereabouts) (Cummings).
593. *languishing*] growing weak (*OED* v. 1).
594. *pallets*] simple beds.
596. *panting*] perspiring.
598. *zephyrs*] soft, gentle breezes; see Fairfax, 'The Solitude', l. 12: 'Where Zephyrus doth wanton play'.
599. *shed*] separate.
600. *And winnow . . . my head*] 'And winnow from my head the chaff (of my thoughts).' See Matt. 3:12; Luke 3:17. Cp. Milton, *An Apology against a Pamphlet* (1642), *CPW*, 1.945: 'Do but winnow their chaff from their wheat, ye shall see their great heape shrink and wax thin past belief.'
601–8. *How . . . day*] Cummings suggests that the stanza is indebted to the story of Hippolytus (Virgil, *Aeneid*, VII, ll. 761–82) who was hidden in Egeria's grove, safe from the strife of men, the jealousy of the gods, and the violence of horses.
601. *strong*] strongly fortified.
604. *Bends in*] aims at.
605. *certain*] accurate, reliable.
607. *play*] fire, shoot (*OED* v. 7 a).
608. *gall*] harass (military) (*OED* v.¹ 5).
609–11. *Bind . . . lace*] Cp. Randolph, 'A Pastorall Courtship' (1638), ll. 103–6: 'Come let those thighes, those legs, those feet/With mine in thousand windings meet,/And woven in more subtle twines/Then woodbine, Ivy, or the vines.';

William Hammond, 'The Walk' (1655), ll. 20–1: 'By twining woodbines what sweet joys are caught/In such embraces.'
609. *woodbines*] a) general name for climbing plants, including convolvulus and ivy (*OED* 1) b) honeysuckle (*OED* 2).
610. *gadding vines*] Cp. Milton, *Lycidas* (1637), ll. 39–41: 'Thee Shepherd, thee the Woods, and desert Caves,/With wilde Tyme and the gadding Vine o'regrown,/And all their echoes mourn.' *gadding*] of a plant: spreading hither and thither (*OED* v.² 4).
615. Larson, *DUJ*, 80 (1987), 27–35, argues that this line, and l. 624, refer to Druidic practices of sacrifice; but if this is so, M.'s treatment seems entirely innocent of any sinister implications.
616. *nail me through*] clearly meant to evoke Christ's crucifixion.
619–20. *like a guard . . . divide*] see Fane, 'Fullbeck' (1659), ll. 17–18, 'like a lifeguard to the palace stand,/To guide the passenger on either hand'.
621. *This*] the lane.
621–2. *like . . . labyrinths*] the path through the forest is likened to the thread by which Theseus found his way out of the Labyrinth on Crete (see Ovid, *Metamorphoses*, VIII, ll. 152–82).
621. *equal*] Dividing the wood into two equal halves. A 1596 map of the parish of Bolton Percy (University of York, Borthwick Institute of Historical Research, PR. B/P 15) shows a path through the wood in front of the house dividing it somewhat unequally, while a map of 1712 shows a lane dividing the south part of the wood into two equal segments: see Raylor, *N & Q*, n.s., 44 (1997), 186–7, and fig. 8.

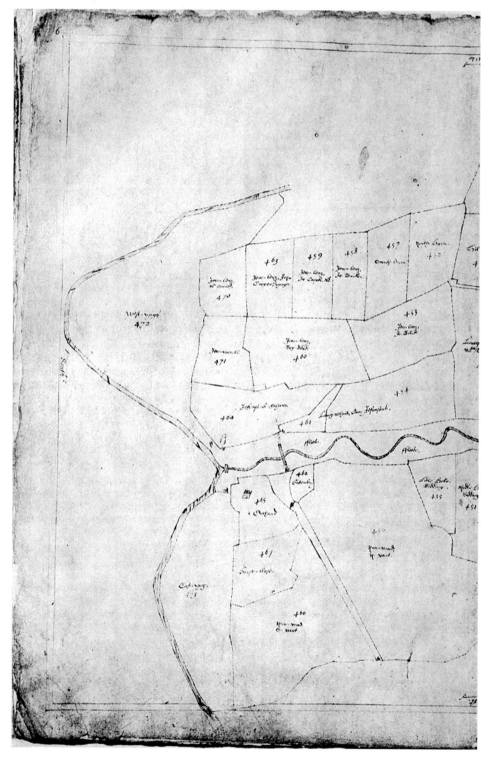

Fig. 8
Survey of Parish of Bolton Percy, including Nun Appleton estate, *c.* 1596. Reproduced
from an original in the Borthwick Institute, University of York, PR B/P 15.

LXXIX

25 For now the waves are fall'n and dried,
And now the meadow's fresher dyed;
Whose grass, with moister colour dashed,
Seems as green silks but newly washed.
No serpent new nor crocodile
30 Remains behind our little Nile;
Unless itself you will mistake,
Among these meads the only snake.

LXXX

Plot

See in what wanton harmless folds
It ev'rywhere the meadow holds;
35 And its yet muddy back doth lick,
Till as a crystal mirror slick;
Where all things gaze themselves, and doubt
If they be in it or without.

— Paradise Lost . L.460

And for his shade which therein shines,
640 Narcissus-like, the sun too pines.

LXXXI

Oh what a pleasure 'tis to hedge
My temples here with heavy sedge;
Abandoning my lazy side,
Stretched as a bank unto the tide;
645 Or to suspend my sliding foot
On th'osier's underminèd root,
And in its branches tough to hang,
While at my lines the fishes twang!

who poetic-control?

LXXXII

But now away my hooks, my quills,
650 And angles, idle utensils.

629–32. Cp. du Bartas, *Divine Weekes*, trans. Sylvester, II.ii.3, ll. 777–80, 'About thy borders (O Heav'n-blessed ILE)/There never crawles the noysome Crocodile;/Nor Bane-breath'd Serpent, basking in thy sand,/Measures an Acre of thy flowerie Land.' See also Robert Waring, 'To the Memory of his deceased Friend. Mr William Cartwright', in Cartwright, *Comedies, Tragi-Comedies, with other Poems* (1651), sig. *7ʳ: 'The Crocodile, which like Nile's streames, still growes/Bigger as't runns, and with fresh vigour flowes.'
629–30. *No serpent . . . Nile*] like the River Nile, the River Wharfe becomes fertile through flooding; unlike the Nile (as was popularly believed), the Wharfe does not breed crocodiles from its slime.
631. *itself*] that is, the River Wharfe.
632. *snake*] see Fairfax, 'The Solitude' (*c*. 1650–71), ll. 31–2, 36, 'the murmuring streams,/In shady valleys running down,/ . . . As winding serpents in the grass'; Jonson, 'To Sir Robert Wroth' (1640), ll. 17–18: 'Alongst the curlèd woods, and painted meads,/Through which a serpent river leads.'
633. *wanton*] unrestrained; cp. Milton, *Paradise Lost*, IV, ll. 626–9: 'Yon flow'ry arbors, yonder alleys green,/Our walks at noon, with branches overgrown,/That mock our scant manuring, and require/More hands than ours to lop their wanton growth.'
636–40. *Till . . . pines*] Cp. Fairfax, 'The Solitude' (*c*. 1650–71), ll. 131–4: 'Sometimes soe cleare & so serene/Itt seemes ast were a looking glass/And to our vewes preventing seemes/As heaven beneath the water was.'
636. *slick*] smooth, shiny (*OED* a. 1).
637. *gaze*] see.
639–40. *And for . . . pines*] Cp. Fairfax, 'The Solitude' (*c*. 1650–71), ll. 135–40: 'The sun in it's so clearly seen/That, contemplating this bright sight,/As, 'twas a doubt whether it had been/Himself or image gave the light,/At first appearing to our eyes/As if he had fallen from the skies.'
639. *shade*] image (i.e. reflection) (*OED* n. II 5 b).
640. *Narcissus-like . . . pines*] Narcissus pined away for love of his reflection until he turned into a flower; cp. Denham,

Coopers Hill, Draft A, ll. 219–22: 'The Stream is so transparent pure & Cleare/That had the selfe enamoured youth gaz'd here,/So fatally deceav'd, he had not beene,/While the bottome, not his face had seene'; Girolamo Preti, 'Salmacis', trans. Sir Edward Sherburne (1651), 8, 'The Flowers which on its fertile Borders grow,/As if on Love with their own Beauties shew:/Bending their fragrant Tops, and slender Stems/*Narcissus*-like, to gaze on the clear Streams.'
641–4. *Oh . . . tide*] M.'s speaker appears as a river god.
641–2. See Milton, *Lycidas* (1637), ll. 104–5, 'Next Camus, reverend sire, went footing slow,/His mantle hairy, and his bonnet sedge.' M's speaker is crowned, as Camus (usually identified as Milton's tutor Joseph Mede) is in *Lycidas*.
642. *sedge*] coarse, grassy, rush-like, green-brown plant that grows in wet places.
645. *sliding foot*] see Virgil, *Culex*, l. 17, 'liquido pede labitur unda' (waves glide in their watery course); *The Garden*, l. 49.
646. *osier*] kind of willow, associated with public weakness: '*I have always observed him . . . a plain-hearted man, an English Oake, and not an* Osier *that wil warp and winde with every wind*', Daniel Friend on Sir Arthur Hesilrige in [Friend], *Musgrave Muzl'd* (1651), sig. A2ʳ. This description of Hesilrige makes an apt comparison with the retiring Fairfax. Similar associations attached to willows in royalist iconography: 'But He unmov'd in faith their *Lillies* fled,/And to th'unstable Willows wandered', Rachel Jevons, *Exultationis Carmen* (1660), ll. 81–2. In the *Aeneid*, VI, ll. 136–9, the osier is the key to the underworld. *undermined root*] the river has exposed the root by washing away the earth around it.
648. *twang*] pluck (*OED* v. 9).
649. *quills*] fishing floats (*OED* n.¹ 3 e); see Sir Henry Wotton, in Izaak Walton, *The Compleat Angler*, ed., J. Bevan (Oxford, 1983), 77: '*Let me live harmlessly, and near the brink/Of* Trent *or* Avon *have a dwelling place,/Where I may see my* quil *or cork down sink,/With eager bit of* Pearch, *or Bleak, or Dace.*'
650. *angles*] fishing rods (originally the fishing hook: *OED* n.¹ 1). *idle utensils*] a paradox: instruments of idleness.

The young Maria walks tonight:
Hide trifling youth thy pleasures slight.
'Twere shame that such judicious eyes
Should with such toys a man surprise;
655 She that already is the law
Of all her sex, her age's awe.

And on the river as it flows
With ebon shuts begin to close;
The modest halcyon comes in sight,
670 Flying betwixt the day and night;
And such an horror calm and dumb,
Admiring Nature does benumb.

LXXXIII

See how loose Nature, in respect
To her, itself doth recollect;
And everything so whisht and fine,
660 Starts forthwith to its *bonne mine*.
The sun himself, of her aware,
Seems to descend with greater care;
And lest she see him go to bed,
In blushing clouds conceals his head.

LXXXV

The viscous air, wheres'e'er she fly,
Follows and sucks her azure dye;
675 The jellying stream compacts below,
If it might fix her shadow so;
The stupid fishes hang, as plain
As flies in crystal overta'en;
And men with silent scene assist,
680 Charmed with the sapphire-wingèd mist.

LXXXIV

665 So when the shadows laid asleep
From underneath these banks do creep,

LXXXVI

Maria such, and so doth hush
The world, and through the ev'ning rush.

---

651. Maria] Mary Fairfax (1638–1704), redeemed, like the house and the gardens, from the dangers of civil war: 'my *Daughter*, not above five Years old, being carried before her Maid, endured all this retreat a Horseback; but Nature not being able to hold out any longer, she fell into frequent Swoonings, and in appearance was ready to expire her last', Thomas Fairfax, *Short Memorials* (1699), 56.
653. judicious] serious, discriminating.
654. toys] trifling things. *surprise*] come upon unexpectedly (*OED* v. 3), with an echo of 'to capture' (*OED* v. 2 b).
657. loose] primarily a) untidy, but also alluding to b) unchaste, as if Maria redeems Nature's 'looseness' (see Williams (1994), II.826).
659. whisht] silent.
660. bonne mine] shown to good advantage: another military term; *bonne* is disyllabic, as in French.
668. ebon] black, dark (*OED* a. B 3). *shuts*] shutters (*OED* n. 1 b).
669–72. The modest ... benumb] the halcyon (i.e. kingfisher) was reputed to build floating nests, having pacified the wind and waves; Pliny notes that, when inland, kingfishers 'haunt rivers, & sing among the flags and reeds', *Natural History*, trans. Philemon Holland (2ⁿᵈ edn, 1634), 287. Cp. above, *The Gallery*, ll. 35–6, in a stanza describing a painting of Venus: 'The Halcyons, calming all that's nigh,/Betwixt the air and water fly.' Royalist poets looked back from the turmoil of civil war and defeat to the 'halcyon days' of the 1630s. Emblematically, the halcyon represented the good king who brings peace and prosperity. M. relocates the

halcyon's association with Fairfax, and more importantly, Mary Fairfax.
671. horror] a) rippling of the water surface (*OED* n. 2 a) b) roughness (i.e. on account of the dark: *OED* n. 1 a; cp. Virgil, *Aeneid*, trans. Dryden (1697), VII. 41: 'Which thick with Shades, and a brown Horror, stood.').
673. viscous] glutinous, sticky (*OED* a. 1 a). *she*] the halcyon.
674. azure dye] the kingfisher is 'for the most part of her pennage, blew, intermingled yet among with white and purple feathers', Pliny, *Natural History*, trans. Philemon Holland (2ⁿᵈ edn, 1634), 287.
675. jellying stream compacts] in alchemical theory, the halcyon was believed to calm seas by making them solid with a substance called *halcyonium*, 'spuma maris concreta' (solidified sea foam), William Johnson, *Lexicon Chymicum* (1652), 120. Also cp. Fairfax, verse translation of *The Song of Solomon*, 'Thy nostrils wᵗʰ a blast hath laid/The liquid seas on solid heaps/The floating waves therwᵗʰ was staid/As Ice congeld in the depths', BL, MS Add. 11,744, fol. 13ᵛ. *jellying*] congealing. *compacts*] solidifies (*OED* v.¹ 1 b); see also M.'s letter to Sir John Trott: 'The Tears of a family may flow together like those little drops that compact the Rainbow' (Legouis, II.311), and *An Elegy Upon the Death of My Lord Francis Villiers*, ll. 86–8 n.
677. stupid] a) senseless (*OED* a. A 3 c) b) astonished (*OED* a. A 1) c) paralysed (*OED* a. A 1 c).
678. crystal] this must in fact mean amber: see below, 386, l. 682.
679. men ... assist] Maria's attendants are imagined as carrying masque scenery, but not speaking parts. *assist*] attend.
680. sapphire-wingèd] see above, l. 673 n.

No new-born comet such a train
Draws through the sky, nor star new-slain.
85 For straight those giddy rockets fail,
Which from the putrid earth exhale,
But by her flames, in heaven tried,
Nature is wholly vitrified.

LXXXVII

'Tis she that to these gardens gave
90 That wondrous beauty which they have;
She straightness on the woods bestows;
To her the meadow sweetness owes;
Nothing could make the river be
So crystal-pure but only she;
95 She yet more pure, sweet, straight, and fair,
Than gardens, woods, meads, rivers are.

LXXXVIII

Therefore what first she on them spent,
They gratefully again present:
00 The meadow carpets where to tread;
The garden flowers to crown her head;
And for a glass the limpid brook,

Where she may all her beauties look;
But, since she would not have them seen,
The wood about her draws a screen.

LXXXIX

705 For she, to higher beauties raised,
Disdains to be for lesser praised.
She counts her beauty to converse
In all the languages as hers;
Nor yet in those herself employs
710 But for that wisdom, not the noise;
Nor yet that wisdom would affect,
But as 'tis heaven's dialect.

LXXXX

Blest Nymph! that couldst so soon prevent
Those trains by youth against thee meant;
715 Tears (wat'ry shot that pierce the mind);
And sighs (Love's cannon charged with wind);
True praise (that breaks through all defence);
And feigned complying innocence;
But knowing where this ambush lay,
720 She 'scaped the safe, but roughest way.

684–6. star new-slain . . . exhale] meteors, which were thought to shoot out from the earth.
686. putrid] a) decomposing (*OED* a. 1) b) crumbling (*OED* a. 4).
687. flames] Cp. Fairfax, 'An Epitaph on A.V. dieng Young': 'Least the earth should be burnd/By the scorching beames of that bright star,' BL, MS Add. 11,744, fol. 45ᵛ.
688. vitrified] turned to glass; two of St John's visions in Revelation involve the vitrification of the sea: e.g., Rev. 15:2: 'And I saw as it were a sea of glass mingled with fire: and them that had gotten the victory over the beast, and over his image, and over his mark, and over the number of his name, stand on the sea of glass, having the harps of God.' For the view that all nature would be turned to glass on the last day, see *Operum mineralium M. Ioannis Isaaci Hollandi, sive de lapide philosophiae*, in L. Zetzner, ed., *Theatrum Chemicum* (1602–22), 3.513: 'vitrum omnium extremum est, ac post iudicium quicquid sub firmamento comprehensum est, omne in vitrum diuina ordinatione conuerte tur' (Glass is the end of everything, since after the judgement everything under heaven will be seized, and by divine command, all will be turned into glass). See also Rev. 4:6. Scoular (1965), 178, notes several

analogues, including Drayton, *Idea* (1593), 53, l. 4, 'Thy Cristall streame refined by her Eyes.'
691. straightness] honesty; a quality approved by Puritans, applied here metaphorically to the trees (see 'straight', *OED* a. 6. a; John Preston, *New Covenant* (1634), 233: 'a right and straight man').
695–6. The adjectives in l. 695 correspond in reverse order to the nouns in l. 696; an example of *versus rapportati*. The lines are also a reworking of Donne's 'Sappho to Philaenis', ll. 27–8, in which the negative comparison of Philaenis to objects of natural beauty is transposed into a demonstration of Mary Fairfax's excelling of the landscape of the Nun Appleton grounds: 'Thou art not soft, and cleare, and strait, and Faire,/As down, as Stars, Cedars, and Lilles are.'
701. glass . . . brook] Cp. Fairfax, 'The Solitude', l. 38: 'Upon the watry plains of glass.' *glass*] mirror. *limpid*] clear.
707–8. She . . . hers] see above, ll. 569–84; Mary Fairfax excelled at languages: see *To his Worthy Friend Doctor Witty*, ll. 17–26.
712. heaven's dialect] connected by Srigley, *N & Q*, n.s., 43 (1996), 287, with the 'original' language of st. LXXII, l. 570, a coincidence of similar numbers 'by accident or design'.
713. prevent] anticipate (OED v I 2).
714. trains] of artillery (*OED* n.¹ III 9 b).

LXXXXI

This 'tis to have been from the first
In a domestic heaven nursed,
Under the discipline severe
Of Fairfax, and the starry Vere;
725 Where not one object can come nigh
But pure, and spotless as the eye;
And goodness doth itself entail
On females, if there want a male.

LXXXXII

Go now fond sex that on your face
730 Do all your useless study place,
Nor once at vice your brows dare knit
Lest the smooth forehead wrinkled sit:
Yet your own face shall at you grin,
Thorough the black-bag of your skin;
735 When knowledge only could have filled
And virtue all those furrows tilled.

LXXXXIII

Hence she with graces more divine
Supplies beyond her sex the line;
And, like a sprig of mistletoe,
740 On the Fairfacian oak does grow;
Whence, for some universal good,
The priest shall cut the sacred bud;
While her glad parents most rejoice,
And make their destiny their choice.

LXXXXIV

745 Meantime, ye fields, springs, bushes, flowers,
Where yet she leads her studious hours,
(Till Fate her worthily translates,
And find a Fairfax for our Thwaites)
Employ the means you have by her,
750 And in your kind yourselves prefer;
That, as all virgins she precedes,
So you all woods, streams, gardens, meads.

---

723. discipline severe] a reference to the household discipline associated with the Presbyterianism of the Fairfaxes, especially Lady Fairfax. BL, MS Add. 4929 contains notes on sermons by several (mostly) Presbyterian divines by Sir Thomas and Lady Fairfax. Hers are the more exacting of the two. A rigorous *Order for the House at Denton* and *Remembrance for Servants* in the Fairfax family also survives (but this may well have originated with earlier Fairfaxes): see J. Croft, ed., *Excerpta Antiqua* (York, 1797), 30–1.
724. see above, l. 494 n.
726. But pure] 'but must be pure'. *spotless*] untainted, immaculate.
727. entail] a) attach (*OED* v.² 3) b) settle an inheritance (*OED* v.² 1); Fairfax had ensured that Mary, his only child, would inherit the Nun Appleton estate (see above, *Headnote, Context*).
729. fond] foolish.
730. useless study] i.e. gazing at oneself in a mirror.
734. black-bag] mask; a 'full mask disguising the ravages of dissolute living [and/or disease], drawn against the face by a bead held between the teeth: hence the grin' (Cummings); cp. Benlowes, *Theophila: The Prelibation* (1652), I.XLVIII: 'Time, strip the writhell'd witch; pluck the black bags/From off Sin's grizzly scalp; the hag's/Plagu-sores show then more loathsome than her leprous rags.'; anon., 'Newcastle Cole mines', Bod., MS Locke e. 17, p. 91: 'The Northerne Lad his bony Lasse throws downe/And gives her a Black bag, for a Greene

gowne.' This poem occurs in a collection of Commonwealth and Restoration verse, and is placed with the earlier poetry, which may date its composition to the 1650s.
738. line] lineage.
739–42. like . . . bud] Maria is imagined as mistletoe growing on the oak-tree of her father, but the image of the Druidic priest cutting the mistletoe as part of a fertility ritual (see Selden's notes to Drayton *Poly-Olbion* (1613), Song IX), pulls the attention of the poet back to her eventual marriage, and the continuation of the Fairfax line (see above, *Headnote, Context*). Larson, *DUJ*, 80 (1987), 27–35, notes that Druids were associated with royal culture, although M.'s reference here is exclusively concerned with the Fairfaxes. Cp. Brian Fairfax, 'Upon cutting down the Woods at Nun Appleton, 1679', ll. 9–20, where the nuns are referred to as the opposites of the druids, so that virginity and the absence of marriage preserves both mistletoe and oaks (BL, MS Eg. 2146, fol. 2ʳ).
741. for . . . good] At the Druidic new year ceremony (Alban Arthuan, at the winter Solstice), the priests distributed mistletoe among the people as a sign of the happiness and success that the future would bring (Carr-Gomm (1991), 114); see also Ralph Knevett, 'The Newyeares Gift', ll. 2–7.
748. And find . . . Thwaites] Mary Fairfax was married to George Villiers, second Duke of Buckingham, in 1657: see above *Headnote, Context*.

LXXXXV

For you Thessalian Tempé's seat
Shall now be scorned as obsolete;
55 Aranjuèz, as less, disdained;
The Bel-Retiro as constrained;
But name not the Idalian grove,
For 'twas the seat of wanton Love;
Much less the dead's Elysian fields,
60 Yet nor to them your beauty yields.

LXXXXVI

'Tis not, what once it was, the world;
But a rude heap together hurled;
All negligently overthrown,

outward judgment

post-lapsarian

Gulfs, deserts, precipices, stone.
765 Your lesser world contains the same,
But in more decent order tame;
You, heaven's centre, Nature's lap.
And Paradise's only map.

LXXXXVII ?

But now the salmon-fishers moist
770 Their leathern boats begin to hoist;
And, like Antipodes in shoes,
Have shod their heads in their canoes.
How tortoise-like, but not so slow,
These rational amphibii go!
775 Let's in: for the dark hemisphere
Does now like one of them appear.

---

753. Thessalian Tempé] valley in Thessaly, northern Greece, renowned for its beauty (see Virgil, *Georgics*, II, l. 469; Horace, *Carmina*, I.vii, l. 4, xxi, l. 9); cp. Fane, 'To Sir John Wentworth, upon His Curiosities and Courteous Entertainment at Summerly in Lovingland' (written before 1648), 27–30: ' "Wouldst thou be sheltered under Daphne's groves,/Or choose to live in Tempe, or make loves/To any place where shepherds wont to lie/Upon the hills." ' Fairfax visited Summerly in September 1648 and was much impressed: Rushworth, IV.ii.1263. Aurelian Townshend's masque *Tempe Restored* was published in 1631.
755–6. Aranjuez . . . Bel-Retiro] royal residences near Madrid in Spain with impressive gardens, hermitages, and frequent masque performances. 'Bel-retiro' is properly *Buen Retiro*, so M. makes a Protestant and anti-Catholic joke ('Bel' is from 'Bell and the Dragon' in the Apocrypha).
756. constrained] cramped.
757. Idalian grove] Idalum was a town in Cyprus, where Aphrodite/Venus was worshipped.
759. Elysian fields] according to Greek mythology, home of the blessed after death.
761–8. 'Tis not . . . map] Wilcher, *N & Q*, n.s. 39 (1992), 463, notes a series of echoes from William Cartwright's 'On the Marriage of the Lady *Mary* to the Prince of *Aurange* his Son. *1641*', ll. 11–14, which M. would have read in Cartwright's 1651 collection (see above, *Headnote, Date*): 'Love from that Masse did leap;/And what was but an Heap/Rude and Ungathered, swift as thought, was hurld/Into the beauty of an Ordered World.' Cartwright's poem is of course appropriate to M.'s concern at this point: the future marriage of Mary Fairfax, mentioned at ll. 737–44.
761. 'Tis not . . . world] i.e. after the Fall; possibly also a reference to contemporary theories that the earth was gradually decaying through the passage of time.
762–6. rude heap . . . tame] see Vitruvius, *De Re Architectura*, 2.8: 'Ita enim non acervatim, sed ordine structum opus poterit esse sine vitio sempiternum' (For thus the work is not built all of a heap but in order, and can last). See also Ovid, *Metamorphoses*, I, ll. 5–7 (but offering a different natural history): 'Ante mare et terras . . . chaos: rudis indigestaque

moles' (Before the sea and lands . . . chaos: a rough, unordered mass of things); cp. John Joynes, 'On the incomparable Lord Hastings', in *Lachrymae Musarum* (1649), 29: 'this carcase, World,/Is into her first, rude, dark Chaos, hurl'd'.
762. rude] rough, uncultivated, wild (*OED* A a. 10).
763. overthrown] a) upset b) thrown too strongly.
765. lesser world] the Nun Appleton estate.
769–72. But now . . . canoes] a transposition from Cleveland, 'Square-Cap' (1647), ll. 17–20: 'Then Calot-*Leather-cap* strongly pleads,/And faine would derive the pedigree of fashion:/The *Antipodes* weare their shoes on their heads,/And why may not he in their imitation?'
770. leathern boats] coracles. Cummings suggests a possible pun on 'boots.'
771–4. See above, ll. 13–14.
771. Antipodes] men from the opposite side of the globe, who, being supposed to live upside-down, were assumed to walk on their heads. Cp. Richard Brome, *The Antipodes* (1640), II.ii.12–14: 'The comedy being the world turn'd upside down,/That the presenter wear the capital beaver/Upon his feet, and on his head shoe leather.' McGaw, *ELN*, 13 (1976), 177–80, notes the popularity of this perception, quoting Brome's *Antipodes* (1640), I.vi, ll. 86–95.
772–3. shod . . . tortoise-like] Zacharias Heyns, *Emblemata* (Rotterdam, 1625), 7, depicts a giant tortoise shell in use as a boat (as well as sun-shade, i.e. a house: see above, ll. 13–14).
772. Cp. Martial, *Epigrams*, XII.xlv: 'Haedina tibi pelle contegenti/nudae tempora verticemque calvae/festive tibi, Phoebe, dixit ille/qui dixit caput esse calceatum' (As you cover with a kid's skin your temples and the crown of your bald pate, he made a happy remark to you, Phoebus, who told you your head was well shod).
773. tortoise-like] carrying their coracles upon their heads, the salmon-fishers look like tortoises, and, like Roman soldiers in *testudo* formation, with their shields on their heads.
774. rational amphibii] amphibious creatures, like the tortoise, that live on land, or in the water, but being men, have reason, unlike the tortoise.

50
A Dialogue between Thyrsis and Dorinda

Date. c. 1646–54: see below *Authorship.*

Manuscript Publication. No other lyric poem by M., or attributed to him, exists in so many MS copies: it evidently circulated quite widely, and was set to music at least twice. Before it was printed, the poem was a popular success in both of its two major forms, and in all the minor variations of these versions.

The manuscripts are arranged in chronological order as follows:

Bod. 6   Bod. MS Rawl. poet. 199, 52–3 (signed H: R:amsay; the volume is an Oxford verse miscellany of the 1630s)

BL 4   BL MS Add. 31432, fols. 12ᵛ–14 (a musical setting by William Lawes, in an autograph songbook by Lawes, *c.* 1638–45)

UCO   University College, London, Special Collections, Ogden MS 42, pp. 6–7 (a folio miscellany of royalist poems and songs; 1650s).

Lo. 1   Single folded sheet unbound in Parcel 5 of the Whitelocke Papers at Longleat House. Unknown italic hand; 'pastorall' written on outside of sheet in Whitelocke's hand. Microfilmed as Reel 16 in Film no 96795 (Wakefield: EP Microfilm, 1972).

CUL 1   CUL, Add. MS 79, fol. 19ᵛ (headed Mʳ Symonds A Pembro. Canta. M.A. 1653), in a Cambridge verse miscellany, *c.* 1653–1660s; probably printed from this MS in *1663*)

BL 2   BL, Add. MS 29396, fol. 78ᵛ (ll. 1–11 in a songbook compiled by Edward Lowe, *c.* mid-seventeenth century–1670s)

AT   University of Texas at Austin, MS (Killigrew, T)/Misc./B., fols. 22ᵛ–3. (in a folio verse miscellany, partly compiled by Thomas Killigrew)

CK   King's College, Cambridge, Hayward Collection, H.11.13, fols. [14ᵛ–15] (in a verse miscellany *c.* 1674)

P 1   Princeton University Library, Robert H. Taylor Collection, Restoration MS 3, 264–6 (in a miscellany of poems on affairs of state, *c.* 1680s–1690s)

BL 3   BL, Add. MS 29397, fols. 18ᵛ–21ᵛ (in the musical setting by Matthew Locke, *c.* 1682–90)

Bod. 5   Bod., MS Rawl. poet 90, fols. 168ᵛ–9ᵛ (in a late seventeenth-century verse miscellany)

Bod. 4   Bod., MS Rawl. poet. 81, fols. 27ᵛ–8 (a verse miscellany *c.* 1700)

F 1   Folger, MS W.b.515, 11–15 (Locke's setting in a music book, *c.* 1700)

Bod. 3   Bod., MS Mus. Sch. C. 96, fols. 6ᵛ–7 (Locke's setting in an early eighteenth-century songbook)

BL 1a,
BL 1b   BL, Add. MS 29921, fols. 108, 123ʳ⁻ᵛ (ll. 44–8 and the entire poem in a late-seventeenth–early eighteenth-century verse miscellany; early eighteenth-century)

MCh. 1   Chetham's Library, Manchester, Halliwell-Phillipps MS 2220 (a leaf from an early eighteenth-century verse miscellany)

L 1   University of Leeds, Brotherton Collection, MS Lt. 67, fol. 7ʳ⁻ᵛ (in an early eighteenth-century verse collection)

Y 1   Yale University, Osborn Collection, MS fb 142, 44–5 (in an early eighteenth-century verse miscellany)

CF   Fitzwilliam Museum, Cambridge, MU.MS 120, 1–4 (Locke's setting in a music book, *c.* 1728)

Printed Publication. The poem was published in the following:

John Gamble, *Ayres and Dialogues,* 'The Second Book' (1659), 66–9 (with music)

Samuel Rowlands, *A Crew of Kind London Gossips* (1663; 2nd edn) 'Ingenious Poems', 92–4

Robert Veel, *New Court Songs and Poems* (1672), 132–3

John Playford, *Choice Ayres* (1675), 80–4 (with music by Matthew Locke; the pagination and layout in this volume is irregular) *1681*

Text. The version in *Bod. 6*, attributed to 'H. Ramsay', and *UCO*, contains the following briefer concluding lines, from l. 21 to the end:

> They know not what it is to feare,
> Free from the wolfe and horrid beare:
> There the lambs are allwayes full
> Of grasse softer then our wooll.
> A fixt spring, a constant sun,
> A day that ever is begun.
> Oaten pipes of gold that play
> A never ceasing roundelay.
> There continuall rivers flow,
> Flowers live and garlands grow.
> Shepheards there beare aequall sway,
> Every nymph is queene of May.
>
> D: Oh! T: Dorinda why dost cry?
> D: I am sicke and faine would dye.

UCO contains the following variants: *27–8.* Speares instead of Pipes that play/An Everlastinge Roundelay. *31. aequall*] Kingly. *32. Every*] And every.

CUL 1 and *1663* contains the following inserted lines, between l. 22 and l. 23:

> No Wars, unless our Rames well fed,
> Butt at each others curled head:
> No work, unless, perhaps you find
> Bees dig in Kin-cupes Golden Mine:
> No fold to keep one Lamb from harmes,
> Only *Dorinda* thee mine armes.

'*Music*' appears in the right hand margin at ll. 12, 18 and 26. *P 1* replaces ll. 45–8 with a couplet:

> Dor: Then thou and Ile pluck poppeys which weele steep
> In wine, and drink and die away in sleep.

Bod. 4 attributes ll. 45–8 to a chorus. *Y 1* omits all dialogue signals. Other variants are shown in Appendix 3.

Authorship. The absence of the poem from *Bod. 1*, elements of corruption in the text of *1681*, its unusual location in *1681* (at 109–10, between *On the Victory obtained by Blake over the Spaniards, in the Bay of Santa Cruz, in the Island of Tenerife, 1657* and *The Character of Holland*), the comparatively early date for its composition (the version set to music by William Lawes must have been before September 1645, when Lawes was killed; by this time M. was

24), attribution to other authors, and the purported unfamiliarity of the poem's main themes within M.'s oeuvre, have led some, notably Lord, Kelliher (1978), 48–9 and Chernaik (1983), 207–8, to reject the poem from the canon. Kelliher notes that most of Lawes' work was completed between 1634 and 1639, and that most of the poems in one of the dialogue's MS versions are associated with Oxford, and were written *c.* 1634–35. M. was 13–14 then and went to Cambridge. Chernaik accordingly attributes the poem to Henry Ramsay (to whom the poem is assigned in *Bod. 6*) of Christ Church, a minor poet.

However, Klause (1983), 170, n. 25, 185, n. 28, entertains the possibility that the poem, if not originally by M., was rewritten by him. In addition to numerous minor changes, the poet, in his view, entirely rewrote and extended the latter part of the poem, thereby adding Dorinda's discussion of suicide. *BL 4* and *Bod. 6* thus represent earlier versions of the poem before M. came into contact with it. Against Lord, Klause finds the themes of the poem consonant with M.'s concerns elsewhere (for instance, Thyrsis and Dorinda present a related version (arguably a development) of the discussion between Clorinda and Damon; see also below, *Genre and Sources*). He conjectures further that the concern with suicide may have been suggested to M. by the first printed publication of Donne's *Biathanatos* (1644): William Popple's copy of Donne's treatise survives; M. is known to have suggested readings from it to his nephew. Rees (1989), 59–63, builds upon this hypothesis, showing how the revised version of the poem is more sophisticated in the nature of exchange between the speakers: philosophical and transcendental elements (absent in the shorter version) now enter the poem. Of the elements added in the longer version, some vocabulary (e.g. l. 28, 'antedate') and some topoi (e.g. l. 26, the music of the spheres) seem distinctly Marvellian.

Among the complete editions, Margoliouth, Legouis and Donno accept the poem as M.'s, but Lord and Walker do not. That M. was responsible for the earliest dateable version of the poem is unlikely. The possibility that the version in *1681* involved M.'s hand remains neither proven nor disproven with certainty, but the hints of M.'s presence are sufficient to keep the poem within the canon. The echoes of other verse, and the one case of the revised version's influence (see below, *Genre and Sources*), suggest a composition date of *c.* 1646–54, and possibly the narrower period of 1648–52 within this time. *CUL*

1, the earliest surviving text of the longer and later version, is dated at the earliest to 1653. Its existence therefore provides some further support to this dating argument.

Genre and Sources. Leishman (1966), 105, notes that the poem is typical of lyrics in seventeenth-century song collections where Elizabethan pastoral survived long after its heyday. Another Restoration example is ?Sir John Reresby, 'A dialogue between a shepheard and his Fancy in a pastorall straine', 4 (Bod., MS Rawl. D 204, fol. 88 ff.). Other examples of pastoral dialogues concerning lovers who follow each other into death include Herrick's 'Charon and Phylomel, a Dialogue Song' (1648).

Thomas Washbourne's 'A Pastoral Dialogue Concerning the Joyes of Heaven, And the Paines of Hell', in *Divine Poems* (1654), 84–6, is clearly derived from the longer version of the poem, that is, the version associated with M., rather than by Lawes (as claimed by Wall (see Legouis, I.248)). The contemplation of suicide is replaced by a longer section describing hell, so that the poem balances eternal rewards with a pastoral vision of punishment for the sinful.

The poem's qualities as a specifically Marvellian pastoral have been variously celebrated, in addition to being used as a way of justifying M.'s authorship (see above, *Headnote, Authorship*). Ellrodt (in Patrides, ed. (1978), 219) claims that, of all seventeenth-century poets, only M. 'wrote about death and heaven in terms meant to be spiritual and yet definitely not Christian'. For Lewalski (in Patrides, ed. (1978), 251), the dialogue's vision of a heaven that seems identical to classical Elysium is a product of authorial irony: the 'naive' shepherds have 'somewhat comic misconceptions of religious truth'. But for Colie (1970), 128–9, the dialogue exploits pastoral's capacity for psychological complexity. Unlike *Clorinda and Damon*, heaven is presented by Thyrsis in terms that Dorinda would understand. To this extent, Colie imagines him as a 'Jesuit proselytizing', as opposed, presumably, to the 'Protestant' rigour of Damon's questioning of the pleaures of the pastoral world. But the easiness and simplicity with which

Dorinda produces her death-wish is designed by the poet to point us back to the problems of genuine holy living and holy dying: the mere mention of suicide would have raised this perspective abruptly in the reader. Further to her argument that M. was complicating an earlier poem by adding elements that enhance a transcendental perspective (see above, *Headnote, Authorship*), Rees (1989), 62–3, proposes that Thyrsis's attempt to describe heaven to Dorinda is an example of the dangers that conversation (even when well meant) present to those who abandon Dorinda's 'silent thinking'. Whereas Thyrsis began as teacher, Dorinda becomes the dominant presence, and his accession to her death-wish is thus delivered with unheroic deflation.

Versification and Style. The poem does not offer different metres for the respective speakers but a generally lengthening line-length as the poem progresses. The first speech contains a tetrameter, a trimeter and two heptasyllabic lines, and heptasyllabic lines predominate until l. 22, nearly halfway through the poem. Tetrameters then predominate to l. 44, and the last four lines of the poem are pentameters. There are tetrameters at ll. 12–14, and pentameters at l. 27 and l. 29. The longer lines correspond to an awareness of heaven: most of the tetrameters in the second half of the poem are the vehicle for Thyrsis' vision of the heavenly pastoral. The final resolve of the lovers' suicide pact is made in pentameters, as is Dorinda's first expressed understanding of her future state. The second part of Thyrsis' vision, ll. 31–9, is a typical Marvellian eight-line tetrameter stanza, of the kind used in, for instance, *Upon Appleton House* and *The Garden*. Taken by itself, it bears a close resemblance to the pastoral sections of *Upon Appleton House* (especially ll. 425–32).

A Dialogue between Thyrsis and Dorinda

> *Dorinda.* When Death shall part us from these kids,
>   And shut up our divided lids,
>   Tell me Thyrsis, prithee do,
>   Whither thou and I must go.

Dorinda] a pastoral name not quite as common as Thyrsis: see, e.g. ?Sir John Reresby, 'A dialogue between a shepheard and his Fancy in a pastorall straine', l. 4 (Bod., MS Rawl. D 204, fol. 88ʳ).
2. divided lids] eyelids.

3. Tell . . . do] Cp. the similar form of address in Théophile de Viau, Ode 48, l. 1: 'Dis moy Thyrsis sans vanité'; cp. also Bartholomew Yonge, *The Sheepheard* Carillo *his Song*' (1598), ll. 1–2: 'I pre-thee keepe my Kine for me / *Carillo*, wilt thou?' See also below, l. 45 n.

Thyrsis. To the Elysium: *Dorinda.* Oh, where is't?

Thyrsis. A chaste soul can never miss't.

Dorinda. I know no way but to our home;
 Is our cell Elysium?

Thyrsis. Turn thine eye to yonder sky,
 There the milky way doth lie;
 'Tis a sure but rugged way,
 That leads to everlasting day.

Dorinda. There birds may nest, but how can I
 That have no wings and cannot fly?

5 *Thyrsis.* Do not sigh (fair nymph) for fire
 Hath no wings, yet doth aspire
 Till it hit, against the pole:
 Heaven's the centre of the soul.

Dorinda. But in Elysium how do they
 Pass eternity away?

Thyrsis. Oh, there's neither hope nor fear,
 There's no wolf, no fox, no bear.
 No need of dog to fetch our stray,
 Our Lightfoot we may give away;
 No oat-pipes needful; there thine ears
 May sleep with music of the spheres.

Dorinda. Oh sweet! Oh sweet! How I my future state
 By silent thinking antedate:
 I prithee let us spend our time to come
30 In talking of Elysium.

Thyrsis. Then I'll go on: There, sheep are full
 Of sweetest grass, and softest wool;
 There, birds sing consorts, garlands grow,
 Cool winds do whisper, springs do flow.
35 There, always is, a rising sun,
 And day is ever, but begun.
 Shepherds there, bear equal sway,
 And every nymph's a Queen of May.

Dorinda. Ah me, ah me! *Thyrsis.* Dorinda, why dost cry?

40 *Dorinda.* I'm sick, I'm sick, and fain would die:
 Convince me now, that this is true;
 By bidding, with me, all adieu.

Thyrsis. I cannot live, without thee, I
 Will for thee, much more with thee die.

45 *Dorinda.* Then let us give Carillo charge o'th sheep,
 And thou and I'll pick poppies and them steep
 In wine, and drink on't even till we weep,
 So shall we smoothly pass away in sleep.

---

5. *Elysium*] place for the blessed after death in Greek mythology; hence heaven.
13–14. *birds . . . fly*] playing on the image of the soul as a bird
(see below, *The Garden*, ll. 52–6).
16. *aspire*] a) rise up (*OED* v. III 5) b) hopes for, ardently
desires (*OED* v. II 4).
17. *pole*] sky (*OED* n.² 4).
18. *centre of the soul*] point to which the soul is attracted (*OED*
n. 6 b).
21–48. See above, *Headnote Text*.
22. *wolf . . . fox*] Cp. Herrick, 'The Country Life, to the
honoured M. End. Porter' (1648), 41: 'safe from the Wolfe
and Fox'.
26. *music of the spheres*] the 'music' made by the seven heavenly
spheres rotating in harmony: see above, *Musick's Empire*, l. 20
n., *The First Anniversary*, ll. 47–8.
28. *silent thinking*] i.e. meditating to herself, without speaking.
antedate] anticipate (*OED* v. 6). Cp. *Young Love*, ll. 21–4: 'So

we win of doubtful Fate;/And, if good she to us meant,/We
that good shall antedate,/Or, if ill, that ill prevent.'
31–2. *sheep . . . wool*] Cp. Herrick, 'The Country Life, to the
honoured M. End. Porter' (1648), ll. 10–13: 'view thy
flocks/Of sheep . . . /And find'st their bellies there as full/Of
short sweet grasse, as backs with wool.'
33. *consorts*] harmonies of several voices (*OED* n. II 3).
38. *Queen of May*] young woman chosen to preside over the
festivities of May-day.
44. *die*] with the familiar pun on 'die' as sexual climax. Rees
(1989), 63, notes that the pun is remarkable since it enables
the poet to turn an exploration of 'an extreme and literal
choice of eternity' into a 'parody of the *vita voluptuosa*'.
45. Leishman (1966), 106, notes a source for the name in one
of the songs (*The Sheepheard* Carillo *his Song*') in Bartholomew
Yonge's translation of Montemayor's *Diana* (1598), reprinted
in *England's Helicon* (1600). See also above, l. 3 n.

51

The Character of Holland

Date. Late February–early March 1653. The poem celebrates English success in the First Dutch War (1652–54) which came during the winter of 1653, after eight months of indecision and occasional Dutch supremacy. On 26 November 1652, Robert Blake, George Monck and Richard Deane were appointed to command a reformed English fleet after complaints of inefficiency and cowardice. The Three Days' Battle of 18–20 February 1653 was a notable success for the Commonwealth and M.'s poem most probably marks this event.

M. had travelled in Holland during the 1640s, but while some of the details in the poem no doubt have their roots in personal observation derived from this tour, others were derived from publications concerned with the Dutch. Legouis (1965), 92–3, suggests that M. may have written the poem as part of his unsuccessful attempt to gain employment from the government in this year, an idea supported by the panegyrical elements in the poem (see below, *Sources and Genre*; see also Kenyon, in Brett (1979), 22). Milton's (unsuccessful) letter to Bradshaw, recommending that M. be appointed his assistant, is dated 21 February 1653, just after the Battle: it assumes that Bradshaw will interview M. on the following day. The poem was most probably produced in these days immediately following the victory, to solicit the republic's patronage.

Publication. The poem first appeared whole in *1681*. During the Second Dutch War (1665–67), the first hundred lines of the poem were published anonymously in *1665* under the same title but with an eight-line ending more relevant to the current situation:

> Vainly did this *Slap-Dragon* fury hope,
> With sober *English* valour ere to cope:
> Not though they Primed their barb'rous mornings-draught
> With Powder, and with Pipes of Brandy fraught:
> Yet *Rupert, Sandwich*, and of all, the *Duke*.
> The *Duke* has made their Sea-sick courage puke.
> Like the three Comets, sent from heaven down
> With Fiery Flailes to swinge th'ingratefull Clown.

Robert Horn entered the poem in the Stationers' Register in London on 13 June 1665, ten days after the English victory at Solebay. Three extant copies survive in Lincoln Cathedral, Texas and the Huntington Library (no. 78432) (siglum *1665*). John Barnard, *PBSA*, 81 (1987), 459–464, notes another 1665 edition, printed at York by Stephen Bulkeley (*1665Υ*). During the Third Dutch War in 1672, Horn republished the text of the 1665 London edition (*1672*). The shorter and later version was also reprinted in the *Harleian Miscellany* (1744–46), again taken from the 1665 London edition. A MS copy derived from *1672* exists at the University of Minnesota, MS 690235f, pp. 53–6 (*Mn.*), a verse and prose miscellany from the 1690s. The variants in these lines are slight: *3. primed*] *1665*; prime *1672, Mn. mornings*] *1665, 1672*; morning *Mn. 5. Rupert, Sandwich*] *1665*; Sandwich, Rupert *1672, Mn. 6. their*] *1665, 1672*; yᵉ *Mn.*

Context. Rivalry between the British and the Dutch, largely of an economic nature, was no new matter in the 1650s. In 1608 James I challenged the right of the Dutch to fish freely for herring in what he claimed were English waters. The King wanted a share in the Dutch trade, which was worth £1 million, approximately half of the total export value of British goods at this time. Against such claims, the Dutch were able to use the work of the great humanist, Hugo Grotius, who wrote *Mare Liberum* (1609; see below, l. 26) against Portugese territorial claims: 'Can the vast, the boundless sea be the appanage of one country alone, and it not the greatest? Can any one nation have the right to prevent other nations which so desire . . . from bartering with one another?' (trans. R. van Dernan Magoffin (New York, 1916), 4). The only jurisdiction here, said Grotius, belonged to God. Against Grotius, English lawyers, John Selden the foremost among them, argued that a statute from King Edgar's reign (AD 964), in which the king was named *Rex Marium Britanniae*, proved British territorial sovereignty in the seas (Selden, *Mare Clausum* (1632), II.xii). To this the Dutch were implacably opposed (see Schama (1987), 230–2).

Despite the genuine similarities and mutual sympathy between Dutch religion and politics and the practices of those who were gaining the upper hand in England in the 1640s (see Dunthorne, in Oresko *et al.* (1997), 125–48, and Pincus (1996), ch. 3), godly zeal also enhanced aggressive mercantilism in England. Many merchants had Puritan leanings, and the 1640s saw a campaign in press and Parliament from a broad spectrum of interests to find a means of breaking Dutch trading pre-eminence, by force of arms if necessary. In 1651, the new Republic, Cromwell in particular, sought security in a proposed 'alliance and union' with the Dutch, which would also help in silencing Royalist refugees in exile. The Dutch, bewildered at first, were not prepared to compromise their own independence, in politics and trade, and the negotiations failed. The two British ambassadors sent to The Hague, St John and Strickland, were reputedly abused, especially by English Royalists and their Dutch supporters. They returned, insulted and angry, while the mercantile polemics in England grew.

The legal consequence of the failure of the alliance plan was the 1651 Navigation Act, which prohibited the import of goods to England in any other vessel than that of the country of origin of the goods, or of England. The valuable trade in carrying was denied to the Dutch. In addition, the Act insisted that the Dutch offer a deferential salute to English vessels when encountering them in waters where British sovereignty was claimed (Gardiner (1897), ii.80–7, 107–14).

Economic motives should not, however, be overstressed. Pincus (1996), Pt. 1, shows that ideological rather than economic motives were paramount in turning the minds of English leaders towards war. The Dutch were divided between the pro-Stuart Orange party, strong in the northern provinces, and the Statist or Republican party, which was broadly pro-Commonwealth. English hopes for an alliance were raised by the death of the Stadholder, Willem II, and the States General's decision not to name a successor. Thought to be fellow travellers in the cause of Reformation and in trade, the Dutch were revealed as false brethren when they eventually refused the alliance. Some Dutch statesmen regarded English enmity as caused by the very existence of their Republic, and its prosperity. Lacking in ingenuity, the English, they thought, were forced to resort to

legal intimidation and naval thuggery in order to plunder the fruits of Dutch success.

Attitudes hardened, especially among naval commanders. Hostilities began when, on 12 May 1652, English and Dutch ships met in the English Channel. In a complicated series of manoeuvres, in which some Dutch ships did at first strike sail, Admiral Maarten Harperszoon van Tromp, with a fleet of forty-two ships, did not strike sail to fifteen English ships led by Blake. Some evidence suggests that Van Tromp may have wished to negotiate first. Whatever the truth, a battle ensued until the arrival of English reinforcements forced the Dutch to retreat to the French coast.

The Dutch, aware of the large volume of trade they had to protect with a comparatively small fleet, sent extra ambassadors to London. Certainly some members of the Council of State, equally well aware of English naval superiority, pressed for very high demands of the Dutch, and won the upper hand with their peers. The negotiations in London failed, and the war began in earnest. By June 1653, the English were ready to negotiate but a settlement was not reached until the Treaty of Westminster was signed in the spring of 1654.

In addition to the Three Days' Battle (see above, *Date*), several events in the war are also alluded to towards the end of the poem: Dutch successes in November 1652 (l. 124); the reinforcement of the English fleet in late 1652 and early 1653 (l. 127); the inquiry and dismissals of some officers after the November 1652 defeat (ll. 133–4).

Sources and Genre. The poem is not so much an imitation of a particular classical model or tradition – Horatian, Juvenalian or Varronian – as the product of two major influences: the impact of Dutch culture upon the English, and the new satirical writing, in verse and prose, of the Civil War, most of it published in brief pamphlet or newsbook form. Nearly every line in the poem has a source or an echo in anti-Dutch writing from the previous twelve years.

Cleveland's 'To Prince Rupert' (written December 1642; published 1647) is the source of a number of images: ''Twas the Mount *Athos* carv'd in shape of man' (l. 109; see below, ll. 108–9); 'At least the Countesse will, *Lust's Amsterdam*,/That lets in all religious of the game' (ll. 133–4; see below, ll. 71–6). M. is also following Cleveland in using the possibilities of the character writing genre to satirize public events (cp. Cleveland's *The Character of a London-Diurnall* (1644 and 1647)). Owen Felltham's *A Brief Character of the Low-Countries* (written *c.* 1629–30; published in pirated and incomplete form, 1648, and 1652; first complete and authorized edn, 1652), may have provided M. with the idea for the end of the poem, and for the imagery at ll. 17–18: 'they are so low, that they have a shorter cut to Hell than the rest of their neighbours. And for this cause, perhaps all strange Religions throng thither, as naturally inclining towards their Center. Besides, their Riches shewes them to be *Pluto's* Region' (3). But if M. had read Felltham before he wrote his poem, he nonetheless did not follow all of Felltham's stereotypes.

The Character of Holland is also deeply indebted to a whole host of popular satires and anatomies of the Dutch from the 1640s and early 1650s. M.'s is a refined version of popular satirical verse: 'Though *Van Trumpe* fight,/And *Grotius* write/That the Trade of fishing is free:/Yet if *Selden* or *Blague*/ Should saile to the *Hague,*/The *Hoghens* must beg on their knee', anon., *Amsterdam, And Her Other Hollander Sisters put out to Sea* (1652), sig. A1ʳ. The role of the presses on both sides of the North Sea was considerable in generating hostile popular feelings, and limiting the efforts of statesmen in favour of peace. English newsbooks carried accounts of Dutch satires of the English, which only served to fuel English ire. Pincus (75) goes so far as to claim that war broke out 'not because of their irreconcileable differences, but because popular images had been created on each side of the North Sea which made it impossible to negotiate a peaceful settlement'.

Occasional verse concerned with Anglo-Dutch similarity or opposition is present in the manuscript collections of M.'s circles of friends and acquaintances. Mildmay Fane's collection, 'Fugitive Poetry' (Harvard UL, fMS Eng. 645, fol. 4), contains an epigram in Latin and English by Hugo Grotius himself, '*De Mirandis Bataviae ad J. Dousam*'. Classical nautical deities, the watery landscape and wealth are celebrated here in terms that pre-empt M.'s vilification of them: 'Our Sellars full wth vessells stand/ Yet heer no Vines for th'Pruners hand/ . . . Our Dwellings to ye waters ioygn/Yet Dowse our Thirsts we quench wᵗʰ wine'.

In the English verse written to celebrate victories against the Dutch, there were no fixed conventions but rather a mixing of genres, among which M.'s poem appears as one more example of experimentation. *Concordia rara sonorum, Or A Poem Upon the late Fight at Sea* (1653), commemorating the same action as *The Character of Holland*, locates anti-Dutch satire within epic (especially Lucanic) representations of sea battles. These representations themselves are given a realistic edge by virtue of the journalistic style of the newsbooks: 'Men now, with men contend, and Ships with Ships,/ One body 'gainst another; here one skips/ Into his enemies Deck; but beaten back,/ He leaps to's owne' (10). This body of poetry is concerned largely with the naval war. It could be that the first hundred lines of M.'s poem, which deals with the general state of the Dutch, was written before the war (or at least the Three Days' Battle) and reflects the intensification of anti-Dutch sentiment in 1651–52. The last fifty-two lines of the poem are concerned more directly with the events of the war itself, and are a panegyric for the navy and the Republic. If M. intended the poem to gain him employment with the government (see above, *Date*), ll. 101–52 show M. offering praise poetry in a similar mould to that which republican propagandists printed, dwelling upon similar themes and displaying similar images. *Anglia Victrix/Ad Praelium Navale, in quo Classis Britannica de Batavá & Belgicá victoriam reportavit, diebus 18, 19, 20. Februarij 1652* [i.e. 1653] is an *epinicion* or song of victory, supposedly written abroad, but published by Marchamont Nedham in *Mercurius Politicus*, 144 (10–17 March 1653), 2296, and translated from Latin into English, through which process it becomes a republican poem. As with M., the '*Belgick Lyoness*' is turned into a bear (see below, ll. 19–20), baited by the '*English Mastiff*', while both poems acknowledge the claim made for sovereignty of the sea by Selden. Where M. uses the sea as a source of figures to represent the Dutch, this poem and *Concordia rara sonorum* dwell on the heroism and horror of sea battles in a manner that is Homeric, Virgilian and Lucanic. Nevertheless, *Anglia Victrix* combines conceited form with ridicule in a similar way to *The Character of Holland*: after the battle 'The Fish seem'd pickled in their native Brine', which nearly achieves the effect of M.'s transposition of fish and burghers (see below, ll. 29–30). The poem is also, like M.'s, in two parts, the last twelve lines being a praise of the English Republic, and where the translator's influence is most apparent, notably in the reference to the three generals as '*Triumvirs*'. If M. was looking for a model and a sentiment to follow in praising the new regime, this literature, circulating in educated circles close to the

Commonwealth government, as well as in printed propaganda, would have presented a ready source and example, although there is the equal possibility that M.'s poem itself may have influenced other Republican panegyrics.

For Todd, in Summers and Pebworth, eds (1992), 169–91, M.'s conceptual indebtedness to Felltham's *A Brief Character* is crucial because Felltham's book is in two parts, the first hostile, the second sympathetic in its nature. This enabled Felltham to present the Dutch as in an equilibrium, caught between the warring elements in a state of 'suspenseful wonder'. Felltham's imaginative and insightful formula allowed M. to make more of the anti-Dutch rhetoric of the pamphleteers, and to a) place the Dutch in a historical context in which, unlike the English, they are committed to a perpetual struggle with the elements, and b) to develop an interplay of English and Dutch language that reflects back questioningly upon English national identity as much as it does upon the Dutch (see below, *Modern Criticism*).

Anti-Dutch sentiment in verse was expressed even by Royalist sympathizers. However, M.'s poem would have served a further purpose of opposing the English verse that supported the Dutch and defamed the Commonwealth: Matthew Stevenson's 'The Fleets' (in *Occasion's offspring* (2nd edn, 1654), 92) is a poem in two columns: when read down the columns, the sentiment is anti-Dutch and pro-commonwealth; when read across the columns, the sentiment is pro-Dutch, anti-commonwealth and royalist.

Versification and Style. In the 1665 and 1672 editions, the verse paragraphs of the poem are set separately as stanzas of varying length. Unlike the sustained ambiguity, achieved by the concision, ellipses and balance of the lyrics, *The Character of Holland* relies largely upon the appeal of visually based conceits, supported by puns and word play (paranomasia) which are obvious rather than confusing in their meanings. Needless to say, this is characteristic of a strategy designed to ridicule. There are two major types of word play, both of which are part of a design: to transform, or metamorphose, the Dutch into a 'true' picture of their silly vulgarity. The first is the use of Dutch words, which are quoted and then found to have a hitherto unrealized meaning by virtue of their similarity with another (usually English) word (e.g. 'herring'/'Heeren', l. 34). The

second involves transferred meanings within linked terms, some of which enhance the festive vocabulary used to ridicule the Dutch, others of which provide ironic and negative revelations. There is here the use of traductio (e.g. 'blind'/'blinkard', l. 41; 'drowned'/'draines', l. 42), parallelism (e.g. 'rising sun'/'rising lands', ll. 43–4), and anaphora (e.g. 'Among the hungry'/'Among the blind', ll. 40–1). The strategy is taken to an intricate degree of achievement: we witness an antimetabole of letters rather than of words (e.g. 'case-butter'/'bullet-cheese', l. 120). 'Athos' (l. 98) and 'amity' (l. 101) are both undercut by 'arms' (l. 100), the similar sounds yoking the words together. Elsewhere, repetition is used to leave no doubt in the reader's mind (e.g. 'vainly', ll. 139, 152).

In a similar but distinct way, ellipsis, asyndeton and polysyndeton are used to intimate the dividedness of the Dutch (e.g. 'Turk-Christian-Pagan-Jew', l. 71 for asyndeton). While the iambic metre and couplet rhymes are fairly consistent, there is relatively little use of tonal variation to achieve an ironic effect. Metrical regularity is interrupted for the sake of introducing a demonstrative effect (e.g. ll. 55–8), a voice of common sense and authority, simulating a truthful or historical account. This is necessary since so much of the poem consists of denigrating descriptive catalogues, connected by conjunctions and prepositions, which do not always have a demonstrative effect (e.g. ll. 1–6). 'Therefore' (l. 37) is an exception to this observation, 'Sure' (l. 66) is not. Long sentences characterize the opening of the poem, but this changes after l. 38, when the degree of ellipsis and parallelism increases. Towards the end of the poem, from l. 123 onwards, the more balanced syntax and diction of panegyric is employed, some of which clearly echoes M.'s Horatian poetry (e.g. l. 133, 'besides'; see *An Horatian Ode*, l. 117).

Modern Criticism. The Character of Holland has been used more as an example of a satirical English view of the seventeenth-century Dutch by historians than it has been the subject of critical attention. This phenomenon continues to the present: see Schama (1987), 262–3, 265–7. Comment on the poem is rare, and is usually critical of its morality, rather than its art. In 1833 Hartley Coleridge complained that the poem had 'contributed to influence the national prejudices of the vulgar against the Dutch, and what is still worse, he makes the natural disadvantages which it was the glory of that industrious race to have surmounted, a topic of ridicule and insult' (in Carey, ed. (1969), 37). In 1880, Goldwin Smith professed indifference: 'in Marvell's satires there is no amber: they are mere heaps of dead flies. . . . The curious may look at *The Character of Holland*, the jokes in which are as good or as bad as ever, though the cannon of Monk and De Ruyter have ceased to roar' (ibid., 42).

More recent criticism has valued the way in which the poem artfully or wittily represents Dutch landscape and culture. Hunt (1978), 34–5, stresses M.'s response to the apparent Dutch intermixture of land and sea, the profusion of sects and religion, and the Dutch taste for paintings. Norbrook (1999), 296–7, argues that despite the dominant patriotic pro-war sentiment of the poem, some images (e.g. ll. 17–22) elicit sympathy and admiration for Dutch ingenuity and industry. The strongest defence of the poem comes from Todd in Summers and Pebworth (1992), 191, who argues that M.'s poem amounts to a commentary on English anti-Dutch stereotypes. To make the Dutch state appear as in a perpetual limbo, its resources pulled one way by the land, the other by water, is to make satire do the work of serious geo-political analysis. But 'to portray one's neighbours in this way, similar to oneself but at the

same time "*Half-anders*", is thus to realize what it is to be oneself'.

The Character of Holland

Holland, that scarce deserves the name of land,
As but th'off-scouring of the British sand;
And so much earth as was contributed
By English pilots when they heaved the lead;
5 Or what by th'oceans slow alluvion fell,
Of shipwracked cockle and the mussel-shell;
This indigested vomit of the sea
Fell to the Dutch by just propriety.
   Glad then, as miners that have found the ore,
10 They with mad labour fished the land to shore;
And dived as desperately for each piece
Of earth, as if't had been of ambergris;
Collecting anxiously small loads of clay,
Less than what building swallows bear away;
15 Or than those pills which sordid beetles roll,
Transfusing into them their dunghill soul.
   How did they rivet, with gigantic piles,
Thorough the centre their new-catched miles;
And to the stake a struggling country bound,
20 Where barking waves still bait the forced ground;
Building their wat'ry Babel far more high
To reach the sea, than those to scale the sky.

Title. Character] description of an object's qualities (*OED* n. II 14 b). Huntington Library MS HM198, an early seventeenth-century commonplace book, contains a brief 'Character' (fols. 110ᵛ–111ʳ): 'That there are dutchmen I thinke no man doubts, but whether for the most part of time they be men or no, I thinke the state of the question.'

2. off-scouring] to 'offscour' is to cleanse from defilement. *Off-scouring* then is that which is removed during cleansing: filth; rubbish.

4. lead] sounding-lead (*OED* n.1 6), a lump of lead on the end of a length of string, lowered from a ship to ascertain the depth of the water.

5. alluvion] wash or flow of the sea against the shore (*OED* 1); inundation or flood, especially when the water contains much matter in suspension (*OED* 2, obs.).

6. Of] *Bod. 1+*; *The Mn.*

7. indigested vomit] contemporary satirical illustrations of the Dutch showed the effects of excessive drinking: vomiting and urinating into the sea (Schama (1987), 263–5). *indigested*] cp. Ovid, *Metamorphoses*, I.7: 'rudis indigestaque moles' (a rough, unordered mass of things).

8. just propriety] an allusion to the dispute between the English and the Dutch concerning the ownership of, and right to navigate upon, the sea bordering a nation's coastline – see *Headnote, Context*, and below, l. 26.

10. mad] frantically; with excessive enthusiasm – hinting at Dutch religious fervour.

12. ambergris] odoriferous wax-like substance found in intestines of sperm whale, and floating in tropical seas; used in

perfumes and in cooking. See *The Gallery*, l. 38; *Bermudas*, l. 28.

15–16. those pills . . . dunghill soul] according to one representation, the Dutch were first bred from horse excrement (see below, l. 94). *Transfusing*] *1665, 1665Y, 1672, Bod. 1*; *Tranfusing 1681*; transfer or permeate from one body into another body (*OED* v. 2). Among modern editors, Margoliouth and Legouis are alone in adopting the apparent misprint in the *Miscellaneous Poems*: 'Tranfusing' does not appear in *OED*.

17–18. How . . . miles] Cp. du Bartas, *Divine Weeks*, trans. Sylvester, II.iv.4: 'If you haue been, where, you haue seen som-whiles,/How with the Ram they driue-in mighty Piles/In *Dover* Peer, to bridle with a Bay/The Sand-cast Current of the raging Sea.' (Parker, *N & Q*, forthcoming).

18. the] *1681*; *their Mn.*

19–20. to the stake . . . forced ground] See *Headnote, Sources and Genre*. An image of bearbaiting; Dutch maps portrayed the Netherlands as a lion rather than a bear (Schama (1987), 55). *barking waves*] 'Scylla wept,/And chid her barking waves into attention', Milton, *Comus* (1633), ll. 256–7. *forced*] a) produced with effort or violence (*OED* ppl. a. 3, 1) b) distorted (*OED* ppl. a. 3b) c) artificial (*OED* ppl. a. 4). The sea was an image of rebellion in Civil War epics: see Abraham Cowley, *The Civil War* (1642–43), i.187–8, 'mutinous waves above their shore did swell,/And the first storme of this dire *Winter* fell.'

21. wat'ry Babel] alluding to the Tower of Babel of Gen. 11:1–9, in order to stress a) the arrogance of the Dutch b) their confusion of religions – see below ll. 71–2. See also *Upon Appleton House*, l. 24; *The Loyal Scot*, l. 252.

Yet still his claim the injured ocean laid,
And oft at leap-frog o'er their steeples played:
As if on purpose it on Land had come
To show them what's their *Mare Liberum*.
A daily deluge over them does boil;
The Earth and Water play at level-coil;
The fish oft-times the burgher dispossessed,
And sat not as a meat but as a guest;
And oft the Tritons and the Sea-Nymphs saw
Whole shoals of Dutch served up for *cabillau*;
Or as they over the new level ranged
For pickled herring, pickled *Heeren* changed.

35   Nature, it seemed, ashamed of her mistake,
Would throw their land away at duck and drake.
    Therefore Necessity, that first made kings,
Something like government among them brings.
For as with pygmies who best kills the crane,
40 Among the hungry he that treasures grain,
Among the blind the one-eyed blinkard reigns,
So rules among the drowned he that drains.
Not who first sees the rising sun commands,
But who could first discern the rising lands.
45 Who best could know to pump an earth so leak,
Him they their Lord and country's Father speak.

---

24. leap-frog] the Dutch were known as 'frogs' by the English in the seventeenth century (OED 3). This image of inundation was a theme in seventeenth-century Dutch painting, e.g. Willem Schellinks, 'The Collapse of the St Antonisdyk', Historical Museum, Amsterdam. There are also republican connotations here: in satirical iconography, the Venetian Republic was represented as a frog: engraving entitled 'De Caesare et Venetis', in Ulrich von Hutten, *Ad Divum Maximilianum Bello in Venetos Euntem Exhortatio* ([Vienna, 1517?]). In the Commonwealth newsbooks, frogs also became an image of religious extremism: the Orangists in Holland were compared with the English Ranter sect who 'bring in the Turfe boores of the fens in their blew bookes [present lower-class, immoral sectarian fenlanders in their publications], like the froggs of ditches croaking against you', *Mercurius Politicus*, 112 (22–9 July 1652), 1767 (see also below, ll. 67–76).

26. Mare Liberum] The Dutch jurist Hugo Grotius published his *Mare Liberum* in 1609, arguing that the sea belonged to no one, against the Portuguese claim of private possession of eastern waters. Grotius's book played an important role in the later disputes concerning navigation rights and customs between the English and the Dutch, a major cause of the First Dutch War. See also *Headnote, Context*.

28. level-coil] a noisy, boisterous game, played at Christmas, in which each player is in turn driven from his seat and supplanted by another; from the French 'lever le cul'. As in l. 24, M. draws on the festive culture condoned by James I's *Book of Sports* (1618; 1633), and celebrated in Caroline lyric poetry: '*Buggins* is Drunke all night, all day he sleepes;/This is the Levell-coyle that *Buggins* keeps', Robert Herrick, '*Upon* Buggins', *Hesperides* (1648). In the late 1640s, level-coil became a token of resistance and disaffection for defeated Royalists: 'wee play Rebells all att Level coyle', Mildmay Fane, 'All game at Tables', *Fugitive Poetry*, Harvard UL, fMS Eng. 645, fol. 16.

29. burgher] inhabitant of a borough or corporation, a citizen. In early modern Dutch and German a 'burger' was a citizen of a 'burg' or fortified town.

31. Tritons] classical name of a sea god (e.g. Virgil, *Aeneid*, I, l. 144), later applied in the plural to semi-human inferior sea-deities or sea goblins; characteristically portrayed as bearded men, with the hindquarters of a fish, and holding a trident or shell-trumpet.

32. cabillau] a) codfish, salted and hung for a few days, but not thoroughly dried b) a dish of mashed cod, specifically associated with the Dutch.

33. level] flat tract of land reclaimed from the sea (*OED* n. 6).

The feature was as much a feature of the (eastern) English landscape, as it was of the Dutch: cp. N.N., *A Narrative of all the Proceedings in the Draining of the Great Level of the Fens, Extending into the Counties of Northampton, Lincoln, Norfolk, Suffolk, Cambridge and Huntingdon, and the Isle of Ely* (1661). Contemporary commentators saw similarities between the shared climate, geography and cultures of East Anglia and Holland (see also above, l. 24 n.).

34. pickled herring] the staple of the Dutch diet, and one of the sources of Dutch wealth: 'His soule is Composed of English beere . . . and his bodye is of pickled Herringe', J.S., 'Observations of the Lowe-Countries', Bod. MS Rawl. D 1361, fol. 5^r. *Heeren*] polite form of address in Dutch: 'Gentlemen'.

35. her] 1681; their *Mn*.

36. duck and drake] the game of making flat stones bounce across a water surface. See above, l. 28.

37. Therefore Necessity, that first made kings] 1665, 1672, 1681, Bod. 1; Therefore that *Need*, which some say first made Kings 1665*Y*. A version of a political commonplace, cp. Sallust, *Bellum Catilinae*, II.i, 'Igitur initio reges – nam in terris nomen imperi id primum fuit' (Accordingly in the beginning kings (for that was the first title of sovereignty among men)). Margoliouth suggested an allusion to Hobbes's *Leviathan* (1651), but this is unlikely: necessity is not discussed substantially in *Leviathan*, and not linked to the origins of kingship in Hobbes's other works (e.g. *De Cive* (1640), II.iii). *Necessity*] constraint having its basis in the natural constitution of things (*OED* n. 2 a).

38. like . . . them] 1681; among y^m like government *Mn*.

39. pygmies . . . crane] 'the Trojans came on with clamour and with a cry like birds, even as the clamour of cranes ariseth before the face of heaven, when they flee from wintry storms and measureless rain, and with clamour fly toward the streams of Ocean, bearing slaughter and death to Pygmy men', Homer, *Iliad*, III, ll. 2–8. Sir Thomas Browne, *Pseudodoxia Epidemica* (1646), IV.xi, calls this a 'pleasant figment in the fountain', in addition to doubting the existence of the pygmy.

43. sees] 1665, 1665*Y*, 1672, Bod. 1; see 1681.

45. pump] the use of windmills as pumps to drain land gave the Dutch landscape its most famous feature; even this feature was made the stuff of hostile scatology: 'They banne Tariffes, and drayne their groundes wth windmylls, As yf the Chollicke, were a remedye ffor the stone', Prefatory letter, Huntington Library, MS HM1181, fols. 6–7. *leak*] leaky.

46. Him they . . . Father speak] They regard him as the Lord and father of their country.

To make a bank was a great plot of state;
Invent a shovel and be magistrate.
Hence some small dyke-grave unperceived invades
50	The power, and grows as 'twere a King of Spades.
But for less envy some joint States endures,
Who look like a Commission of the Sewers.
For these *Half-anders*, half wet, and half dry,
Nor bear strict service, nor pure liberty.
55	'Tis probable religion after this
Came next in order; which they could not miss.
How could the Dutch but be converted, when

Th'Apostles were so many fishermen?
Besides the waters of themselves did rise,
60	And, as their land, so them did re-baptize,
Though herring for their God few voices missed,
And Poor-John to have been th'Evangelist.
Faith, that could never twins conceive before,
Never so fertile, spawned upon this shore:
65	More pregnant than their Marg'ret, that laid down
For *Hans-in-Kelder* of a whole Hans-Town.
	Sure when religion did itself embark,
And from the east would westward steer its ark,

---

47. *bank*] hinting at Dutch financial prowess as well as water defences (Todd, in Summers and Pebworth, eds (1992), 189).
48. *be magistrate*] *1665, 1665Y, 1672, Bod. 1*; be a Magistrate *1681*. *Bod. 1* has a mark above the 'el' of shovel to indicate a disyllable. This would seem to stress metrical regularity, and so strengthens the case for the omission of 'a'.
49–50. Alluding to the revolt of Dutch against the Spanish in 1572, and the foundation of the modern Dutch state (C.D. van Strien, as reported in Todd, in Summers and Pebworth, eds (1992), 189, n. 34).
49. *dyke-grave*] official in charge of upkeep of dikes and sea-walls. The term was used in England, as well as in Holland, especially in Lincolnshire.
50. *The power*] i.e. the institutions of government. *King of Spades*] as in a pack of playing cards. The pun is twofold: the spades refer to the shovels, but also to the colour black, and hence the dirtiness which comes from working with drains and ditches.
51–4. *But for less . . . pure liberty*] 'they shew the foggy, boggy, dirty constitution of the land', *Mercurius Politicus*, 111 (15–22 July 1652), 1749.
51. *less envy . . . States endures*] an allusion to the republican government of the United Provinces, and the mixture of authority, between communal assemblies in the cities and the States General, and the protective role of the Stadholder, whose support was mainly in the provinces.
52. *Commission of the Sewers*] the English body centrally in charge of drainage throughout the provinces. The reference to sewers continues the suggestions of uncleanness in l. 50.
53. Half-anders] Hollanders; an example of paronomasia, using Dutch *anders* ('other[wise]', 'different'). '*Halfanders*' is not a Dutch word, but M.'s word reverses Dutch *anderhalf*, 'one and half', listed in Henry Hexham's *Copious English and Netherduytch Dictionarie* (1648). For interpretation, see Todd, in Summers and Pebworth, eds (1992), 190–1.
54. *Nor bear . . . liberty*] 'Tell them of Monarchy but in jest, and they will cut your throat in earnest; the very name they think beares tyranny in its forehead; and they hate it more than a *Jew* doeth images', anon., *The Dutch Drawn to the Life* (1664), 39.
60. *re-baptize*] referring to adult baptism, the mark of con-version and acceptance into a baptist church. Before 1640, Holland was a place of refuge for many English Baptists, and the English General Baptists (who rejected the doctrine of predestination to damnation) had their origins in the Dutch

Waterlander church, whose name is of course significant for Marvell's imagery throughout the poem.
61–2. *Though herring . . . Evangelist*] 'There is nothing like a Bastinado to bring these poor *Johns* and pickled herrings to their senses again', *Mercurius Bellonicus*, 2 (9–16 February 1652), 7.
61. *for their*] *1665Y, 1681*; to be *1665, 1672, Mn.* herring] see l. 34 n.
62. *Poor-John*] usually hake, salted and dried for food. *Evangelist*] St John the Evangelist.
65–6. *More pregnant . . . Hans-Town*] When staying at The Hague, on 1 September 1641, Evelyn wrote 'I [now] rod out of Towne to see the Monument of the Woman, reported to have borne as many Children as are dayes in the Yeare: The Basins wherein they were baptis'd, together with a large Inscription of the mat<t>er of fact is affixed to the Tomb, & inchased in a Compartiment of Carved Worke, in the Church of Lysdune, a desolate plase', *The Diary of John Evelyn*, ed. E.S. de Beer (1959), 32. *Hans-in-Kelder*] a child in the womb: see Lovelace, 'Being Treated. To Ellinda' (1649), ll. 22–4, 'pregnant sister in prime beauty,/Whom well I deem, ere few months elder,/Will take out Hans from pretty kelder'. 'Hans' was a general name for a Dutchman: 'it being in his [the dyke-grave's] power to turn the whole country into a salt-lough when he list, and so to put Hans to swim for his life', James Howell, 'To my Brother', 1 April 1619, *Epistolae Ho-Elianae* (1640). *Hans-Town*] Hansa town – a port in the Hanseatic League. This prodigy of multiple births, and the Dutch idiom in l. 66, had been used by *Mercurius Britanicus*, 70 (10–17 February 1645), 550–1, in an attack on Cleveland's Royalist satire on Parliamentary newsbooks, *The Character of a London Diurnall*: 'it might (perhaps) have been happier for this *Nation*, if she had died a *Hans-en-Kelder*. The Comtesse of *Zealand* was brought to bed of an *Almanacke*: as many children as dayes in the yeare, and it is likely that his Majesties *hermaphrodite* privy-counsell, is of the same lineage.' M. has transferred imagery in English political journalism back to its country of origin.
67–8. *when religion . . . its ark*] see Herbert, 'The Church Militant', ll. 16–17, referring to the ark's voyage: 'The Course was westward, that the sunne might light/As well our under-standing as our sight'. The sentiment is however much closer to Donne, *Satire III*, where religion aids the 'mutinous Dutch' (l. 17). Shipwrecks and tempests were commonly associated with Dutch waters.

It struck, and splitting on this unknown ground,
Each one thence pillaged the first piece he found:
Hence Amsterdam, Turk-Christian-Pagan-Jew,
Staple of sects and mint of schism grew;
That bank of conscience, where not one so strange
Opinion but finds credit, and exchange.
In vain for Catholics ourselves we bear;
The universal Church is only there.
   Nor can civility there want for tillage,
Where wisely for their court they chose a village.
How fit a title clothes their governors,
Themselves the hogs as all their subjects boars!

Let it suffice to give their country Fame
That it had one Civilis called by name,
Some fifteen hundred and more years ago;
But surely never any that was so.
85   See but their mermaids with their tails of fish,
Reeking at church over the chafing-dish.
A vestal turf enshrined in earthen ware
Fumes through the loop-holes of a wooden square.
Each to the temple with these altars tend,
90   But still does place it at her western end:
While the fat steam of female sacrifice
Fills the priest's nostrils and puts out his eyes.

69–72. It . . . grew] Parker, *N & Q*, forthcoming, argues for the influence of Sylvester's translation of du Bartas, *Divine Weeks*, II.iv.4.252–6: 'Their Country-gods with the true God they ming:/They mix his Service, plow with Ass and Ox;/Disguise his Church in suits of Flax and Flocks,/Cast (in one wedge) Iron and Gold together:/*Iew-Gentiles*, both at-once: but, both is neither.'

71–2. Amsterdam . . . schism grew] Amsterdam was famous for its religious toleration of various Protestant churches. The public worship of Catholics was not tolerated. There was a large, intellectually and economically active Jewish community in the city, but 'Turk' (a geographical exaggeration) and 'Pagan' (an anachronism) are included for the sake of satirical effect. *Staple*] a) town given exclusive right of export (*OED* n. 2 1) b) storehouse (*OED* n. 2 2). *mint of schism*] associates Amsterdam's economic proliferation with its religious diversity: 'They countenance only Calvinisme, but for Trades sake they *Tolerate* all others, except the Papists, which is the reason why the treasure and stock of most nations is transported thither', anon., *The Dutch Drawn to the Life* (1664), 48–9. Religious sectarianism prospered in mercantile circles.

75. ourselves] *1681*; yᵉ Character *Mn*.

76. universal Church] money and commerce is the universal activity in Amsterdam, binding all together in a 'church', despite religious differences. The claim of the Roman Catholic religion literally to be the universal church is ousted by the universal activity of trade.

77. tillage] cultivation; nurture (*OED* v. 1 I 6 fig.).

78. village] The Hague (Den Haag), where the *Dutch* court of Provinces sat, and where the Stadholder usually resided, was itself denied the status of a town or city, and therefore a voice in the national assembly of the States.

80. hogs] a play on 'Hoog-mogenden' (high and mighty), used in the official title of the States-General, and a frequent butt for English satire: 'A true description of those so called *Hoghens Mogens*; set out to the life; with the manners of their Quagmire Bog', anon., *Amsterdam, And Her Other Hollander Sisters put out to Sea* (1652), title page. *boars*] a pun, with the secondary meaning of 'boers' – small farmers, peasants: 'you may as well get a Wild Boar into a Dublet, as to make one of those Borish Dutchmen to button his Dublet', 'Holland Anatomised' in, anon., *Amsterdam, And Her Other Hollander Sisters put out to Sea* (1652), 11.

82. Civilis] Claudius Civilis was an ancient Batavian leader (but not, according to Grotius, a king) who led a revolt against the occupying Romans in AD 69. He was celebrated in contemporary histories of the Dutch people as a strong but considerate warrior (keeping women and children in the rear of his armies when in battle). M.'s point is that the meaning of his surname is inconsistent with the Dutch character, thereby providing a conclusion to the question raised in l. 77.

84. that] *1681*; since *Mn*.

85–6. mermaids . . . chafing-dish] Dutch women are described as mermaids who cook their fishy tails as they sit in church on their chafing-dishes – portable grates which held a burning fuel such as charcoal, or, in this case, peat. A woodcut in Francesco Guicciardini's *Description de Touts Les Pays-Bas* (Arnhem, 1613), 358, depicts a mermaid sitting in her house. Legouis (1965), 11, suggests that this is a literary version of the distorted human figures painted by the Van Ostade brothers.

85. of] *1681*; & *Mn*.

87–8. vestal turf . . . wooden square] scatological, comparing the piece of peat (with 'turf' sounding like 'turd') in the chafing-dish to incense burning in a censer; see Owen Felltham, *A Brief Character of the Low Countries* (1652), 10, ''Tis the Port-Esquiline of the world, where the full earth doth vent her crude black gore, which the Inhabitants scrape away for fuel, as men with spoones do excrements from *Civet-Cats*'. The fumes of the peat, unpleasantly imagined as decomposing human excrement, replace in worship the scent of the incense. *vestal*] a) fiery or smoking b) virgin; fresh. Both meanings derive from M.'s ironic comparison in 'vestal' of the Dutch women with the chaste priestesses in the temple of Vesta at Rome, whose task it was to guard the sacred fire.

88. of a wooden square] *1665, 1665Y, 1672*; of wooden square *1681, Bod. 1*. The addition of the indefinite article makes the metre regular.

90. western end] posterior; see Sir Thomas Browne, *Pseudodoxia Epidemica* (1646), II.iii, 'Paracelsus . . . according to the cardinall points of the world divideth the body of man, and therefore working upon human ordure, and by long preparation rendring it odoriferous, he termes it *Zibeta Occidentalis*, Westerne Civet; making the face the East, but the posteriors the America or Westerne part of his microcosme.' Browne's source is Paracelsus, *Archidoxis* (1570), ch. 7. Altars are of course placed at the east end of churches, but the Dutch women invert this custom.

91–2. fat steam . . . puts out his eyes] literally, blinded temporarily, by making the eyes water.

Or what a spectacle the skipper gross,
A water-Hercules butter-coloss,
95 Tunned up with all their sev'ral towns of beer;
When stagg'ring upon some land, snick and sneer,
They try, like statuaries, if they can
Cut out each other's Athos to a man;
And carve in their large bodies, where they please,
100 The arms of the United Provinces.
      But when such amity at home is showed;
What then are their confed'racies abroad?
Let this one court'sy witness all the rest;

105 When their whole navy they together pressed,
Not Christian captives to redeem from bands:
Or intercept the western golden sands:
No, but all ancient rights and leagues must vail,
Rather than to the English strike their sail;
To whom their weather-beaten province owes
110 Itself, when as some greater vessel tows
A cock-boat tossed with the same wind and fate:
We buoyed so often up their sinking state.
      Was this *Jus Belli et Pacis*? Could this be
Cause why their burgomaster of the sea

---

93. skipper] Dutch *schipper*: sea captain. *gross*] Dutch *groot*: huge, large.

94. butter-coloss] 'coloss' was a more frequent term in the seventeenth century for colossus, a huge statue, much more than life-size: see Henry King, 'On the Earl of Essex' (1646), ll. 25–9: 'no Monstrous Birth, with Pow'r endu'd/By that more Monstrous Beast the Multitude;/No State-*Coloss* . . . / Can hold that ill-proportion'd Greatness still'; hence the Dutch skipper is a vast man made of butter, which the Dutch were supposed to eat in vast quantities: e.g. Jonson, *Volpone*, I, i, l. 41–3: 'You shall have some will swallow/A melting heir as glibly as your Dutch/Will pills of butter.' A 'butter-box' was a contemptuous name for a Dutchman (*OED* 2) and was frequent in verbal and visual representations of the Dutch. A broadsheet entitled *The Dutch-mens Pedigree* (1653) contains a scatological woodcut with an accompanying explanation of how the Dutch were first bred from the excrement of a monstrous horse which had been smeared around the inside of a butter-box.

95. Tunned up . . . with beer] full of beer, and hence drunk (*OED* v. 1 b): 'to tun' is to fill a tun or cask (*OED* v. 1). *towns of beer*] some Dutch towns have names with a 'Bier' prefix. Drunkenness was another frequently attributed Dutch characteristic: 'when Rotterdam's or Breda's Beer, or new *Meghen's Mull*, or *Brandt* Wine puffs them up, for then they fear not hanging, strappadoing, or damming', anon., *Amsterdam, And Her Other Hollander Sisters put out to Sea* (1652), 5.

96. snick and sneer] snick and snee – thrust and cut (Dutch *steken* and *snijen*): 'I see/Thy *Brandy-wine*, will make them *Snick* and *Snee*', J.W., *Brandy-Wine, In the Hollanders Ingratitude* ([30 July] 1652), 6. The violence of the Dutch was deeply embedded in English memories of the murder by the Dutch in 1623 of some East India Company employees at Amboyna. See also l. 115.

97. statuaries] sculptors of statues (*OED* n. 1).

98. Cut out . . . to a man] The Macedonian sculptor Deinocrates (or Cheirocrates) proposed to Alexander the Great to fashion Mount Athos into his likeness, 'representing him as pouring a libation from a kind of ewer into a bowl', Strabo, *Geography*,

XIV.i.23. The Dutch sailors, in a drunken sword fight, cut each other as if they were sculpting each other. See Cleveland, 'To P. Rupert' (Dec. 1642), ll. 109–10, ''Twas the Mount *Athos* carv'd in shape of man/(As't was destin'd by th'Macedonian)'.

99. where] *1681*; if *Mn*.

104. pressed] a) assembled b) impressed (i.e. formed a navy by the compulsory acquisition of ships and men).

107. ancient rights] The English claimed that their ownership of the land below the sea was an ancient right (see above, *Headnote, Context*). *vail*] to lower (a flag or sails) as a sign of respect, as the Dutch were expected to do in English waters. See, e.g., Davenant, *Gondibert* (1651), 1.1.68, l. 1: 'They vayl'd their Ensignes as it by did move.' The ancient rights and leagues must be lowered (i.e. ignored), rather than the English claim be honoured. On 19 May 1652, a Dutch fleet, led by Admiral Martin van Tromp, appeared off Dover, and refused to salute when requested to do so by Blake. This incendiary act helped to start the First Anglo-Dutch war.

108. strike their sail] to lower sails as a salute, or, more rarely, as a sign of surrender (*OED* v. IV 17). Clearly, the former meaning only is meant here.

111. cock-boat] small ship's boat, often towed behind coasting vessel.

112. buoyed . . . up] to keep from sinking; to sustain (*OED* v. 2): England keeps the declining Dutch state from sinking. Dutch hostility to English trading claims and moves for union was seen as ungratefulness after English military support in the late sixteenth century for the Dutch against the Spanish.

113. Jus Belli et Pacis] Hugo Grotius published his *De Iure Belli ac Pacis* in June 1625. It was to become his most influential work, clarifying his previous thoughts, but also representing a novel break with Aristotelian ideas of justice. For Grotius, the law of nature was rooted in man's sociability. However, the content of the law was not to be the observation of principles of justice, as with Aristotle, but the imperative of respecting another's rights. M.'s sarcasm arises in the light of a discrepancy between Dutch political theory and actual behaviour.

114. burgomaster] chief magistrate of a Dutch town; *burgomaster of the sea*] Admiral Martin van Tromp.

15 Rammed with gunpowder, flaming with brand wine,
    Should raging hold his linstock to the mine?
    While, with feigned treaties, they invade by stealth
    Our sore new circumcisèd Commonwealth.
        Yet of his vain attempt no more he sees
20 Than of case-butter shot and bullet-cheese,
    And the torn navy staggered with him home,
    While the sea laughed itself into a foam.
        'Tis true since that (as Fortune kindly sports),
    A wholesome danger drove us to our ports,
25 While half their banished keels the tempest tossed,
    Half bound at home in prison to the frost:
    That ours meantime at leisure might careen,

    In a calm winter, under skies serene;
    As the obsequious air and waters rest,
130 Till the dear halcyon hatch out all its nest.
    The Common wealth doth by its losses grow;
    And, like its own seas, only ebbs to flow.
    Besides that very agitation laves,
    And purges out the corruptible waves.
135 And now again our armèd *Bucentore*
    Doth yearly their sea-nuptials restore.
    And now their Hydra of sev'n provinces
    Is strangled by our infant Hercules.
    Their tortoise wants its vainly stretchèd neck;
140 Their navy all our conquest or our wreck:

115. Rammed with gunpowder] Grosart claimed that sailors reputedly fortified spirits with gunpowder. The image also makes Van Tromp into a cannon, which links with the scatological images of the Dutch urinating, excreting and farting as human artillery in contemporary satirical illustrations. *brand wine*] brandy (from the Dutch *brandewijn* – burnt wine). 'Brandy' was used as early as 1657, but the fuller form was retained in official (i.e. customs) use. The Dutch fondness of brandy was frequently noted: 'Oh *brand* Wine! takes away the fear of death', anon., *Amsterdam, And Her Other Hollander Sisters put out to Sea* (1652), 5. *Mercurius Politicus*, 107 (17–24 June 1652), 1683, describes Van Tromp (and another admiral, De Witt) as 'booze and barkish, and are for war'. See also l. 96.
116. linstock] staff of approximately one yard long, with a pointed foot to wedge in a deck or the ground, and a forked head to hold a lighted match, which would set off a cannon. *mine*] charge of gunpowder, usually ignited in an excavated mine, underneath the enemy. M. perhaps makes a visual conceit of the drunken Dutch Admiral igniting his own magazine, instead of firing broadsides. Another possibility would be to read mine as a metaphor for war: Van Tromp's incendiary action started a war (see *Headnote, Context*).
117. feigned treaties] a considerable body of opinion in the Dutch States, mostly within the republican party, did not favour a war with England. Rather, they favoured a mutually beneficial alliance, such as that originally sought by Strickland and St John. Dutch ambassadors were in London to this end right up to the outbreak of naval hostilities. M. refers both to the seemingly contradictory Dutch diplomatic signals, and to the endlessly deferred alliance of the republics (see *Headnote, Context*).
118. circumcisèd] Gen. 17.11: 'And ye shall circumcise the flesh of your foreskin; and it shall be a token of the covenant betwixt me and you.' Metaphorically, and in Christianity, circumcision meant a spiritual purifying, and was a type of baptism. M. refers to the newly born and purified republic. See also below, ll. 141–2 n.
120. case-butter shot] Case-shot were collections of small projectiles placed inside a cannister and fired from a cannon. M. imagines the Dutch making their cannisters from butter. *bullet-cheese*] Bullets made from cheese: 'His body is built of pickled *Herring*. And they render him testy: these with a little Butter, Onyons & *Holland* Cheese are the ingredients of an ordinary *Dutchman*', Owen Felltham, *A Brief Character of the Low-Countries* (1652), 28.

123. kindly] according to its (here, fortune's) nature (*OED* adv. I.1a). Also, there is the secondary sense of fortune sporting in a good-natured way, or at least without evil intent (*OED* adv. II.2), a meaning hinted by the image of the sea laughing in the previous line.
127. careen] an intransitive use of a verb usually transitive in M.'s time: a) to turn a ship over on one side for cleaning, caulking or repairing (*OED* v. 1) b) to cause a ship to heel over under sail (*OED* v. 3).
129. obsequious] dutiful.
130. halcyon] In ancient belief, a bird which was supposed to charm the wind and sea to produce calm seas during the winter solstice (halcyon days), when it bred on a floating nest. Usually identified with the kingfisher, for which halcyon is a poetic name. The halcyon was a subject in emblems: see Alciati, *Emblemata* (1531), 16, 'His comptae Alcyones tranquilli in marmoris unda/Nidificant pullos involucresque' (The caring halcyon builds a nest, a shelter for its young, on calm, marble waves).
131. Common wealth] the spelling of commonwealth as two words is retained from *1681*, emphasizing the mercantile prosperity of the English Republic.
133. laves] washes, bathes, clean. Associated with rebirth: see Milton, *Lycidas* (1637), l. 175, 'With nectar pure his oozy locks he laves.'
135–6. Bucentore . . . *restore*] Bucentaur (*bucintoro*), Venetian state barge, used in the yearly ritual of the marriage of Venice and the Adriatic Sea, when the Doge dropped a ring from the barge into the water. Another example of M. supplying the English Republic with the trappings of the greatest maritime republic, Venice.
137–8. Hydra . . . *Hercules*] the Hydra was the many-headed snake of the marshes of Lerna, killed by the infant Hercules as his second labour. Holland is likened to the Hydra because it has many provinces within it. Milton cited in translation lines from Seneca's *Hercules Furens* (ll. 922–4) in defence of the execution of Charles I in *The Tenure of Kings and Magistrates* (1649). Following Milton, M. gives the English Republic heroic and mythic status. An English ship called the 'Hercules' was captured by Van Tromp in November 1652.
137. now] *Bod. 1*; how *1681*. *their*] *1681* (Huntington Library Copy), *Bod. 1*; the *1681*.
139. tortoise] not merely an image, but a reference to a siege engine (*OED* 2a); see Norbrook (1999), 298. *wants*] lacks. *vainly*] a) futilely b) arrogantly; see also *The Garden*, l. 1.

Or, what is left, their Carthage overcome
Would render fain unto our better Rome.
Unless our Senate, lest their youth disuse
The war, (but who would) peace if begged refuse.
145   For now of nothing may our State despair,
Darling of Heaven, and of men the care;

Provided that they be what they have been,
Watchful abroad, and honest still within.
For while our Neptune doth a trident shake,
150 Steeled with those piercing heads, Deane, Monck and ▋
And while Jove governs in the highest sphere,
Vainly in Hell let Pluto domineer.

141–2. their Carthage. . . . better Rome] the likening of England and Holland to Rome and Carthage during the First Punic War was made by *Mercurius Politicus*, 130 (25 November– 2 December 1652), 2053: 'The *Romans* were the younger State, but better limb'd, and those limbs knit together with the stronger ligaments both of Power and Policy: the *Carthaginians* elder, and of large dimensions, but so ill joynted as if they had been upon the Rack, the members of that body having no coherence.' *fain*] content in the circumstances (of naval defeat; *OED* a. A 2).

143–4. lest their youth . . . refuse] the difficulty of the first phrase is compounded by the ambiguity created by the paren- thesis, which functions as a zeugma, governing both preceding and succeeding phrases (although the comma associates it with the latter). The Senate (Parliament) fear that a negotiated peace will make the young men feeble through lack of practice in war. The parenthesis implies on the contrary that it is foolish to refuse peace if begged (presumably by the enemy), and also casts doubt on the view that the young men would become so weak.

151–2. A direct reversal of Dutch images of the English: 'one of the Pamphleteers is a Rimer, who after he hath made this country a *Star* and *Heaven*, and the men Angels, vouch- safes *England* no other name then Hell, and the men Devils', *Mercurius Politicus*, 111 (15–22 July 1652), 1749.

52

In Legationem Domini Oliveri St John
ad Provincias Foederatas

Date. February–early March 1651. Oliver St John and Walter Strickland were chosen by Parliament on 14 February 1651 to negotiate an alliance with the Dutch. St John set sail on 8 March: see *Joyful Newes from Holland* (7 April 1651). The poem was thus written in the early months of M.'s stay at Nun Appleton (late 1650-later 1652).

Publication. 1681.

Context The desired alliance was regarded by the English government as the prelude to the union of the English and Dutch republics, the two exemplary non-monarchical, godly, seafaring nations. The English delegation arrived in The Hague on 17 March, but three months of negotiation ended in failure. Dutch support for the alliance was only partial and hindered by the power of pro-Royalist Orange influence, despite the recent death of Willem II. In late April, St John arranged for the ambassadors to be recalled. By the summer of the following year, the two nations would be at war. M.'s comment at l. 6 is thus remarkably prescient and quite at odds with available public information in early 1651. We may reasonably infer that M. was party to information limited to the circles of government; more than that, M. has a 'strong awareness of the ideological stakes' of the mission (Norbrook (1999), 283). But it is also the case that the perceived threat of war was simply generated by the suggestiveness and centrality of the Janus image in the poem. St John and Strickland's mission is considered in detail in Pincus (1996), ch. 2.; see also Kelsey (1997), 65–7, 138.

Oliver St John (?1598–1673) was Hampden's counsel during the Ship Money question, and from 1648 Chief Justice of Common Pleas. By his first and second marriages, he was connected with Cromwell, and by his third with John Oxenbridge (see above, 54–5, 192–4). Of the two ambassadors, St John was regarded as the senior partner, and was chosen not for his linguistic ability (his command of European vernaculars was not strong), but because he was skilled in reconciling differences, especially for the sake of Protestant unity. St John's own reluctance to accept the mission (he feared assassination; an earlier ambassador for the republic, Isaac Dorislaus, had been killed in 1649), and his own worries with regard to the legitimacy of the republic, are of course absent from the poem. Like St John in his ambassadorial role, the poem is a committed extension of the English republic's polity.

The poem may have been written in order to win employment with the new government. Its sentiments are undoubtedly republican and apocalyptic, reflecting M.'s connections just before he left London for Yorkshire. Norbrook (1999), 287, suggests that the poem also expresses (in the several instances of images of peace and war) the poet's anxieties concerning his commitment to the new regime, and the dangers it might hold for him.

Genre and Sources. The poem is a *propemptikon* (a poem on a ruler or great person going away on a mission). It 'adapts the conventions of epideictic poetry to new political conditions' (Norbrook (1999), 281). For an ancient example, see Horace, *Carmina*, I.iii, and for a contemporary example in English (by a royalist), see Sir Richard Fanshawe, 'Presented to his Highnesse the Prince of Wales, At his going into the West, *Anno* M.DC.XLV.' It is thus the generic opposite of the *prosphonetikon*, which is exemplified in *An Horatian Ode*.

In Legationem Domini Oliveri St John ad Provincias Foederatas

Ingeniosa viris contingunt nomina magnis,
    Ut dubites casu vel ratione data.
Nam sors, caeca licet, tamen est praesaga futuri;
    Et sub fatidico nomine vera premit.
5   Et tu, cui soli voluit respublica credi,
    Foedera seu Belgis seu nova bella feras;
Haud frustra cecidit tibi compellatio fallax,
    Ast scriptum ancipiti nomine munus erat;
Scilicet hoc Martis, sed pacis nuntius illo:
10   Clavibus his Jani ferrea claustra regis.
Non opus arcanos chartis committere sensus,
    Et varia licitos condere fraude dolos.
Tu quoque si taceas tamen est legatio nomen
    Et velut in scytale publica verba refert.
15   Vultis Oliverum, Batavi, Sanctumve Johannem?
    Antiochus gyro non breviore stetit.

On the Embassy of Lord Oliver St John to the United Provinces

Apt names befall mighty men with the result that you would doubt whether they have been given by chance or by reason. For Fortune, although blind, nevertheless is a predictor of the future, and conceals the truth beneath a prophetic name. As for you, to whom alone the Republic wanted to be entrusted, whether you bring to the Dutch treaties or new wars, it was not in vain that this elusive encounter has befallen you; rather the duty was inscribed in your twofold name: in the latter, to be sure, messenger of war, but in the former, that of peace; by means of these keys do you rule over the iron bolts of Janus. There is no need to entrust hidden meanings to paper and to bury permitted deceptiveness in various forms of guile. Even if you too are silent, yet your name is an embassy, and it relays official words just as in a code. Is it Oliver or the sainted John that you want, Dutchmen? No shorter was the circle in which Antiochus stood.

---

1. Ingeniosa] the source of a complex word-play: *ingeniosus* means 'apt' in this context, but compliments St John with its other meaning, 'gifted', or 'intellectually superior'. The further suggestion in *ingeniosa* of *ingens* ('great', 'remarkable') echoes 'viris . . . magnis'.
8. ancipiti] double; literally 'two-headed' (associating St John with *ancipiti* Janus (see e.g., Ovid, *Metamorphoses*, XIV, l. 334; see also below, l. 10)). M. exploits a word rich with apt associations for a diplomatic context: in post-Augustan Latin, *anceps* meant 'dangerous' (Lewis and Short, B.3).
9. hoc] St John; not St John of Patmos, the prophet of the Book of Revelation, but St John the Apostle, called (with James) Boanerges or sons of thunder (Mark 3:17). In Luke 9:54, James and John ask Jesus to make heavenly fire consume the Samaritans. Nonetheless, contemporaries certainly did connect St John and his mission with the author of the Book of Revelation and its apocalyptic contents: see, e.g., *A Perfect Diurnall*, 60 (27 January–3 February 1651), 804. *Martis*] Mars, the god of war, but used in a transferred sense for war itself (Lewis and Short, II. A). *illo*] a pun on 'Oliver': the olive branch was a symbol of peace (cp. *The First Anniversary*, l. 258).
10. Clavibus . . . regis] In ancient Rome, the doors of the covered passage dedicated to Janus were open in time of war, and closed in time of peace; cp. *Inscribenda Luparae*, l. 11; see also above, l. 8 n.

11. Non . . . sensus] Secret policy, recorded in private letters, was closely associated in the Parliamentarian mind with Royalism, and enforced famously after the capture of royal letters at the Battle of Naseby, which were subsequently published as *The King's Cabinet Opened* (1645). To some extent, the Parliamentarians could claim a degree of government by openly expressed intention: see Potter (1989), 2, 59–64.
14. scytale] code used by the Lacedaemonians; formed by writing on a strip of paper wrapped spirally around a staff; the message could only be read when the parchment was wrapped again around a similar-sized staff. Norbrook (1999), 282, also suggests a pun: a *scytale* was also a small, cylindrical (i.e. non-tapering) poisonous snake (see, e.g. Lucan, *De Bello Civili*, IX, l. 717), hence underlining the dual potential for peace and war.
16. Antiochus . . . stetit] The Roman consul Popilius drew a circle in the sand around King Antiochus and told him he could not step out until he had made a commitment not to attack the Romans' allies in Alexandria: see Livy, *History*, 45.10; Polybius, *Histories*, 29.27. For Norbrook (1999), 282, both historians, writing of the young Roman republic, emphasize that Popilius was condemned for his temper, and proposes that in using the story, M. is pointing up the military strength felt by the English 'free state', with its republican aspirations.

53

A Letter to Doctor Ingelo, then with my Lord Whitelocke, Ambassador from the Protector to the Queen of Sweden

Date. Late February 1654. Longleat House, MS 124a (*Lo. 2*) is dated 'Etonse 7 Kal. March 1653', i.e., 23 February, 1654 (see below, *Headnote, Publication.*). Nathaniel Ingelo was chaplain to Bulstrode Whitelocke when the latter was Ambassador Extraordinary to Queen Christina of Sweden in 1653–54. The poem appears to have been written after the mission departed in November. Successful negotiations were concluded in April; Whitelocke left Sweden in June and returned to London by the beginning of July. Christina saw the poem on 30 March (see below, *Publication*), one week after the poem arrived in Sweden (see Kelliher, *RES*, n.s. 20 (1969), 55).

Publication. The poem was originally written, in all probability, for personal presentation to Christina (although it is concerned with matters solely relevant to Ingelo, as well as praising Christina), along with the two brief poems on Cromwell's image that accompanied his portrait (see below, 313). During an audience with the Christina on 30 March, Whitelocke showed her copies of poems by M. and Sir Charles Wolseley, having previously showed her verse by Daniel Whistler: 'je lui ai donné beaucoup de contentement par la lecture de certains vers Latins, envoyés d'Angleterre (a Monsieur Ingelo) qui estoyent excellemment composes, et ausi d'une Ode qu'on m'a envoyé d'Angleterre, et que sont ici devant escrits. Les quels la Reyne m'a desire lui donner' (*Lo. 2*, f.186ʳ). The closest copy to that which was presented to Christina has been discovered by Holberton (*EMS*, 12 (2005), 233–53) in Longleat House, MS 124a (*Lo.*), the earliest surviving version of Whitelocke's journal, apparently composed during the mission. It is entitled 'Angelo suo Marvellius', playing on Ingelo's name, and is signed 'Tuus Marvelliuss'. This copy of M.'s poem is not in Whitelocke's hand, but may well have been transcribed directly from M.'s original letter to Ingelo. Whitelocke was as impressed by the poem as the Queen: 'excellemment composes.' That Whitelocke

removed the poem from later versions of his journal suggests that he regarded M. as an obscure figure. A copy of M.'s poem (either from the original, or another intermediary copy) made by Jean Scheffer, a protégé of the Queen, was eventually published in Arckenholtz (1751–60), II.68–70, also under the title 'Angelo suo Maruellius'. The poem was printed in *1681*.

Text. The text in Arckenholtz is considerably different from *1681*, containing only half of the complete poem (ll. 1–70). However, this version was closer to the copy that Christina saw than *1681*, which is almost certainly a revised version. The absence of the second half is most likely to have occurred from a missing leaf in Scheffer's MS. It is most likely that this copy was tipped into Arckenholtz's MS (now Royal Library, Stockholm, MS Engstr.Saml.B.1.2.21–22), and part of it became detached or lost in Amsterdam, or on the way there (confirmed with the help of Peter Davidson). In *Lo. 2* and Arckenholtz, the following distich is added between l. 66 and l. 67: 'Ipsa sed & prono connivent sydera coelo/Et flores lassis procubuere stylis' (And when these stars close their eyes in the declining sky and the flowers sink down on weary stems). Kelliher, *RES*, n.s. 20 (1969), 53–5, suggests that these lines may have been passed over by the compositor of *1681*. He also discusses the revisions M. introduced to the text after the first version was sent to Sweden, and suggests that the rather rough state of the Arckenholtz text may have been the result of rapid composition after an urgent commission from Cromwell. Holberton, op. cit., discusses the relationship between the texts of *Lo.*, Arckenholtz and *1681*, arguing that after 1654 M. revised his poem with publication very much in mind, introducing some readings that are more classically correct, and less pointedly connected to the original diplomatic context. *Lo. 2*'s distinct punctuation suggests that its transcriber read the abdication context into the poem.

Context. Bulstrode Whitelocke (1605–75) was appointed ambassador to Sweden in September 1653. He was preferred to Viscount L'Isle, who had been intended for an earlier mission to Sweden. Whitelocke was a remarkably intelligent lawyer and a very shrewd choice as ambassador. He had sat in the Parliament of 1626, became a key figure in the Long Parliament, and rose to be Keeper of the Great Seal, Acting Speaker and President of the Council during the Commonwealth. The pinnacle of his career was as ambassador to Sweden.

Nathaniel Ingelo (?1621–83), Independent divine and Fellow of Eton College, had formerly resolved to travel with L'Isle, and was invited by Whitelocke on 21 September to accompany him as one of his chaplains; he was employed in a number of sensitive matters during the mission. M. knew Ingelo from his sojourn at Eton (he had been there since July 1653): M.'s remarks towards the end of the poem suggest a brief friendship that had produced a serious discussion of poetry and letters. Ingelo was similar to M. in many ways. In addition to being of the same age, and deeply scholarly, both were by the 1650s rather unlikely Puritans since they both maintained a strong interest in music as well as poetry. Both were adept at political and religious survival: Ingelo remained at Eton after the Restoration. The final section of the poem (ll. 128–34) thus continues M.'s exploration of the nature of poetry by considering another poet. In its way, M. does from home in verse what Ingelo was required to do in person in Sweden: to perform diplomacy, the first act of which was praise.

Christina (1626–86), daughter of the great monarch and warrior, Gustavus Adolphus, was by any account a remarkable figure. After her father's death at the Battle of Lützen in 1632, she came to the throne at the age of six. Sweden was ruled by a regency while she remained a minor. M.'s poem attests to her extensive and rigorous education: she kept scholarly habits for the rest of her life. Once ruling in her own right, she soon found herself in disagreement with the nobility who had ruled in her place. Although she played a significant role in the ending of the Thirty Years' War, her works of educational reform, improvement and philanthropy came at a great expense. She was particularly repelled by advice concerning a prudent marriage. As early as 1651, she began to consider abdicating in favour of her younger cousin, the future Charles X. Whitelocke was in fact privy to her final deliberations

before she relinquished the throne (at one point, Christina even suggested that England underwrite the financial terms of her abdication agreement, should the Swedish government in future renege on it) and witnessed the remarkable abdication scene on 10 May 1654 (see Garstein (1992), 716–21). Åkerman (1991) considers Christina's intellectual life in the context of European thought and the politics of her abdication. Given the purpose of the poem, it is notable that during her long residence in Rome after her abdication, Christina was a member of the 'Arcadian Academy', which was dedicated to the 'purification' of poetry.

The poem is exceptional for the fact that M. reconciles two apparently contrary facts: that Christina was a queen and that Cromwell was a regicide. M. does not reveal the matter of Christina's abdication (probably he knew nothing of it); in the Latin poem by Daniel Whistler, and in Whitelocke's English translation of it, the abdication is the central subject, figured at one point as a regicide (Whitelocke (1772), I.508–10, II.474–5; see also Milton, *Defensio Secunda* (*CPW*, IV.i.606)). But if M.'s poem was read by Christina, she may have seen in it imagery sympathetic with her emergent Catholic sympathies (see below, ll. 89–92 n.). Christina's role as a Protestant prince was still celebrated in English publications after her conversion to Catholicism (see, e.g., M. de Harst, trans. W.L., *A Panegyrick of the most renowned and serene Princess Christina* (1656)).

The poem's adherence to courtly protocol reflects the practice of the English administration. The Commonwealth and Protectorate governments, although not monarchies, maintained courtly practice in matters of foreign policy (see Hirst, in Wallace, ed. (1985), 17–53; Kelsey (1997), 58–68). The poems that accompanied Whitelocke and Ingelo had to demonstrate courtly felicity; Whitelocke's skill as a dancer won him the favour of the Queen.

M.'s reference to portraiture in the poem was apt. During the latter stages of the mission, Christina gave gold chains attached to medals on which were struck her image to several members of the English mission, including Ingelo (Whitelocke (1772), 2.140–1). When, after her abdication, Christina made her way to Rome, she took the portrait of Cromwell with her.

Sources and Genre. The poem is a verse epistle in elegiac distichs: Whitelocke also used a verse epistle (probably from his friend Sir Charles Wolseley) as a means of impressing Christina (Whitelocke (1772), II.10–11; (1990), 346). Its imagery is eclectic, and gathered from a wide range of well-known Latin literature. Although Christina is not likened to the goddess Astraea by name (by M. or any other panegyrist of the Queen), Stocker, *SP*, 84 (1987), 159–79, argues that the poem contains a version of Astraean return, which was linked in the Renaissance with the most famous invocation of a returning golden age, Virgil's fourth Eclogue (see also *To a Gentleman*, ll. 33–5 n.). Just as Elizabeth was likened to Astraea, so is Christina responsible for a new golden age (and understood since the Reformation to have millenarian connotations); where Elizabeth was coupled with Henri IV of France (imagined as an idealized marriage), Christina is coupled with Cromwell, not of course as potential marriage partners, but as the two spearheads of a militant Protestant European alliance (see below, ll. 23–6, 101–12). The final seven lines invoke another kind of pastoral topos: the lament for an absent shepherd-poet.

Haan (2003), 133–41, regards the poem as related to Ovid's exile writings, notably the *Tristia*, with Ingelo as the second Ovid, but where 'the inhospitable and barbarous' conditions of Tomis are in fact transformed into an encomium of Sweden's cultural and political climate. Further allusions to Virgil's poetry are discussed on 141–9.

M.'s poem was but one among many panegyrics addressed to Queen Christina, most of them Latin. M.'s contribution is discussed alongside an extensive collection of ninety Latin panegyrics in Kajanto (1993). Although M. refers to Christina's learning, his poem makes no attempt to locate her in a line of female scholars and teachers stemming back to ancient Greece (see M. de Harst, trans. W.L., *A Panegyrick of the most renowned and serene Princess Christina* (1656), 61–3). Some of the imagery is common to panegyrics on Scandinavian monarchs: see, e.g., John Barclay, 'Ad Serenissimum Daniae

Regem; Christianum IV', in *Poematum Libri Duo* (1615), 23–7.

M. read Milton's *Defensio Secunda* (30 May 1654). Although it is impossible to tell with certainty which work came first, the similarity of materials (see below, ll. 59–74 nn.) suggests that there was some exchange of views on the subject-matter of Christina between the two poets in this period. That Milton refers to the abdication (*CPW*, IV.i.606), unlike M., is evidence that at least Milton finished his tract after M.'s poem, and it suggests that Milton was more likely to have been responding to M. rather than vice versa. Rees, *N & Q*, 222 (1977), 200, suggests that if Milton did know M.'s poem when he wrote his tract, 'there may be a hint of friendly irony in the association of such conceits [both poets refer to the Judgement of Paris story; see below, ll. 57–60n.] with youthful poets (Marvell in his thirties would still qualify as an *adulescens* in Ciceronian usage).'

A Letter to Doctor Ingelo, then with my Lord Whitelocke, Ambassador from the Protector to the Queen of Sweden

Quid facis arctoi charissime transfuga caeli,
    Ingele, proh serò cognite, rapte citò?
Num satis hybernum defendis pellibus astrum,
    Qui modo tam mollis nec bene firmus eras?
5   Quae gentes hominum, quae sit natura locorum,
    Sint homines, potius dic ibi sintne loca?
Num gravis horrisono polus obruit omnia lapsu,
    Jungitur et praeceps mundus utraque nive?
An melius canis horrescit campus aristis,
10 Annuus agricolis et redit orbe labor?
Incolit, ut fertur, saevam gens mitior oram,
    Pace vigil, bello strenua, juste foro.
Quin ibi sunt urbes, atque alta palatia regum,
    Musarumque domus, et sua templa Deo.

---

1. arctoi] commonly used in panegyric of Christina: see, e.g., Philippus Columna, in Giuseppe Francesco Mostarda, *Festosi Applaus . . . alla Serenissima Christina* (Rome, 1656), sig. [A2ᵛ]: 'Sophiae Coelo ad Arctoo'; Dominus Eques Columna, in Mostarda, op. cit., sig. [A3ʳ]: 'Arctoum sidus salue terrorque Trionum.'
9–10. An . . . labor] An allusion to the Hyperboreans, a fortunate people who lived in a fertile land of perpetual sunshine beyond the north wind (McQueen and Rockwell).

9. canis . . . aristis] makes a pun in Latin upon the ambassador's name, Whitelocke. The stalks of corn are compared to hair. The collocation is common enough in its literal sense in Latin literature (see, e.g., Ovid, *Metamorphoses*, I, l. 110: 'gravidus canebat aristis'); Legouis follows Lewis and Short in finding a source for the figurative sense in Persius, *Satire* III, l. 115 ('cum excussit membris timor albus aristas' (when pale fear sets a harvest of your bristles up on your body)).

15   Nam regit imperio populum Christina ferocem,
          Et dare jura potest regia virgo viris.
      Utque trahit rigidum magnes aquilone metallum,
          Gaudet eam soboles ferrea sponte sequi.
      Dic quantum liceat fallaci credere famae,
20   Invida num taceat plura, sonetve loquax.
      At, si vera fides, mundi melioris ab ortu,
          Saecula Christinae nulla tulere parem.
      Ipsa licet redeat (nostri decus orbis) Eliza,
          Qualis nostra tamen quantaque Eliza fuit.
25   Vidimus effigiem, mistasque coloribus umbras:
          Sic quoque sceptripotens, sic quoque visa dea.
      Augustam decorant (raro concordia) frontem
          Majestas et Amor, Forma Pudorque simul.
      Ingens virgineo spirat Gustavus in ore:
30   Agnoscas animos, fulmineumque patrem.
      Nulla suo nituit tam lucida stella sub axe;
          Non ea quae meruit crimine nympha polum.
      Ah quoties pavidum demisit conscia lumen,
          Utque suae timuit Parrhasis ora deae!
35   Et, simulet falsa ni pictor imagine vultus,

          Delia tam similis nec fuit ipsa sibi.
      Ni quod inornati Triviae sint forte capilli,
          Sollicita sed huic distribuantur acu.
      Scilicet ut nemo est illa reverentior aequi;
40   Haud ipsas igitur fert sine lege comas.
      Gloria sylvarum pariter communis utrique
          Est, et perpetuae virginitatis honos.
      Sic quoque nympharum supereminet agmina collo,
          Fertque choros Cynthi per juga, perque nives.
45   Haud aliter pariles ciliorum contrahit arcus
          Acribus ast oculis tela subesse putes.
      Luminibus dubites an straverit illa sagittis
          Quae fovet exuviis ardua colla feram.
      Alcides humeros coopertus pelle Nemaea
50   Haud ita labentis sustulit orbis onus.
      Heu quae cervices subnectunt pectora tales,
          Frigidiora gelu, candidiora nive.
      Caetera non licuit, sed vix ea tota, videre;
          Nam clausi rigido stant adamante sinus.
55   Seu chlamys artifici nimium succurrerit auso,
          Sicque imperfectum fugerit impar opus:

---

15. Nam regit] Cp. Virgil, *Eclogue*, IV, l. 6: 'Iam redit.' *Nam*] Kelliher, *RES*, n.s. 20 (1969), 54, argues that the Arckenholtz text's reading of 'Num' for 'Nam' means that the first eighteen lines of the poem read as an unbroken series of questions.

16. regia virgo] points forward to the comparison of Christina and Elizabeth I by echoing a memorial to the English Queen in which she was portrayed as Astraea: 'Quae fuit in terris Dea, Virgo, Regia virgo/Nunc est in coelis Regia, Virgo, Dea' (*Threno-thriambeuticon* (Cambridge, 1603), sig. D1ʳ; see also Yates (1975), 79). Cp. also anon., 'Ad Christinam Suecorum Reginam', in Giuseppe Francesco Mostarda, *Festosi Applaus ... alla Serenissima Christina* (Rome, 1656), sig. [A3ᵛ]: 'Mustasti Regni exuuisas cum Virgine Virgo,/Altera & alterius Regia serta tulit.'

19. licat ... famae] Cp. *In Legationem Domini Oliveri St John. ad Provincias Foederatas*, l. 7: 'Haud frustra cecidit tibi compellatio fallax.'

21. mundi ... ortu] since the birth of Christ (McQueen and Rockwell).

22. Saecula Christinae] Cp. Virgil, *Eclogue*, IV, l. 5: 'saeclorum ... orde'.

23. redeat ... Eliza] Cp. Virgil, *Eclogue*, IV, l. 6: 'redeunt Saturnia regna.' *Eliza*] Elizabeth I of England. The comparison with Elizabeth was made in Whitelocke's first ambassadorial address to Christina on 30 December 1653 (see Whitelocke (1772), I.271), and in other verse elegies on the queen: see Kajanto (1993), 58, 63, 67, 75.

25. effigiem] portraits of Christina and Cromwell were exchanged as a diplomatic courtesy (see above, *In eandem Reginae Sueciae transmissam*). Although merely working as Dutton's tutor in Oxenbridge's household at this time, M. appears to have been allowed into Cromwell's inner circles.

27–8. raro ... Amor] cp. Ovid, *Metamorphoses*, II., ll. 846–7: 'non bene conveniunt nec in una sede morantur/maiestas et amor' (Majesty and love do not go well together, nor tarry long in the same dwelling-place) (Duncan-Jones in Legouis).

27. Augustam] the parallel between Christina and Augustus suggests a further one between M. and Virgil: see Stocker, *SP*, 84 (1987), 166–7.

29. Gustavus] King Gustavus Adolphus (Gustavus II) of Sweden (1594–1632) (see above, *Headnote, Context*).

32. nympha] Callisto, one of Diana's nymphs, raped by Jupiter, changed in revenge by Juno into a bear, and finally turned by Jupiter into the constellation of the Great Bear: see Ovid, *Metamorphoses*, II, ll. 409–507.

34. Parrhasis] another name for Callisto, originally a town in Arcadia, and hence meaning here 'from Arcadia': see Ovid, *Metamorphoses*, II, l. 460.

36. Delia] Diana (from the name of her birthplace in Delos [which means 'clear, visible']).

37. Triviae] Trivia, another name for Diana (from an epithet for deities whose temples were erected at places where three roads met). See Virgil, *Aeneid*, VI, l. 511: 'tria virginis ora Dianae'; Horace, *Carmina*, III.xxii, ll. 3–4: 'ter vocata ... diva triformis'; Wind (1958; 1980), 249, 251.

43–4. Sic ... nives] Cp. Virgil, *Aeneid*, I, ll. 98–101: 'Qualis in Eurotae ripis aut per juga Cynthi/exercet Diana choros, quam mille secutae/hinc atque hinc gloroerantur Oreades; illa pharetram/fert umero, gradiensque deas supereminet omnes' (Even as on Eurotas' banks or along the heights of Cynthus Diana guides her dancing bands, in whose train thousand Oreads troop right to left); Ovid, *Metamorphoses*, III, l. 182: 'ipsa dea est colloque tenus sepereminet omnis' (but the goddess stood head and shoulders above all the rest).

44. Cynthi] Cynthus, a mountain of Delos, celebrated as the birthplace of Diana and Apollo.

49–50. Alcides ... onus] In his first labour, Hercules (Alcides) slew the Nemean lion and wore its skin afterwards; during his eleventh labour, the theft of the golden apples in the Garden of Hesperides, he held up the world for a while.

55. chlamys] broad, woollen upper garment worn in Greece; also a military or state cloak.

Sive tribus spernat victrix certare deabus,
  Et pretium formae nec spoliata ferat.
Junonis properans et clara trophaea Minervae;
  Mollia nam Veneris praemia nosse piget.
Hinc neque consuluit fugitivae prodiga formae,
  Nec timuit seris invigilasse libris.
Insomnem quoties nymphae monuere sequaces
  Decedet roseis heu color ille genis.
Jamque vigil leni cessit Philomela sopori,
  Omnibus et sylvis conticuere ferae.
Acrior illa tamen pergit, curasque fatigat:
  Tanti est doctorum volvere scripta virum.
Et liciti quae sint moderamina discere regni,
  Quid fuerit, quid sit, noscere quicquid erit.

Sic quod in ingenuas Gothus peccaverit artes
  Vindicat, et studiis expiat una suis.
Exemplum dociles imitantur nobile gentes,
  Et geminis infans imbuit ora sonis.
75 Transpositos Suecis credas migrasse Latinos,
  Carmine Romuleo sic strepit omne nemus.
Upsala nec priscis impar memoratur Athenis,
  Aegidaque et currus hic sua Pallas habet.
Illinc O quales liceat sperasse liquores,
80 Quum dea praesideat fontibus ipsa sacris!
Illic lacte ruant illic et flumina melle,
  Fulvaque inauratam tingat arena Salam.
Upsalides Musae nunc et majora canemus,
  Quaeque mihi Famae non levis aura tulit.

57–60. *tribus spernat . . . piget*] an allusion to the judgement of Paris, who has to choose the fairest from Juno, Minerva and Venus, awarding the winner the golden apple. As bribes, Juno offered a kingdom, Minerva intellectual and military renown, and Venus love; Paris chose Venus. M. suggests that Christina possesses the qualities of Juno and Minerva but shuns those of Venus. The moralizing of the story in literary tradition and in this example is discussed by Rees, *N & Q*, 222 (1977), 197–200. In his *Defensio Secunda*, Milton presented himself as Venus being grateful for the queen's judgement (*CPW*, 4.i.656): this is evidence of an interconnection between M.'s poem and Milton's tract (see above, *Headnote, Sources and Genre*, and below, l. 82 n.).

59–74. *Junonis . . . sonis*] Cp. Milton, *Defensio Secunda* (1654, in *Works* (1933), VIII.106): 'Jam tu quidem haud temerè, tot conquisita undique volumina, tot literarum monumenta congessisti, non quasi te illa quicquam docere, sed ut ex illis tui civies de discere, taequae virtutis ac sapientiae praestantiam contemplari possint; cujus ipsa Divae species, nisi tuo animo penitùs insedisset, & quasi oculis conspiciendam se tibi praebuisset, haud ullâ profectò librorum lectione, tam incredibiles amores excitâsset in te sui' (It was not for nothing that you collected from every source so many costly books, so many works of literature, not as if they could teach you anything, but so that from them your fellow-citizens could learn to know you and contemplate the excellence of your virtue and wisdom. If the very image of the goddess of wisdom herself had not been present to you within your own mind, if she had not offered herself to you for your eyes to behold, she could not by any mere reading of books have aroused in you such unbelievable love of herself (translation from *CPW*, IV.i.605)).

61–74. *Hinc . . . sonis*] Christina was particularly interested in the movement for the renovation of learning (especially library reform) in England that focused on the circle of Samuel Hartlib: see Åkerman (1991), 134–6.

61–2. *Hinc . . . libris*] See above, *Headnote, Context*.

63–4. *Insomnem . . . genis*] Cp. Anthonius Sfortia, in Giuseppe Francesco Mostarda, *Festosi Applaus . . . alla Serenissima Christina* (Rome, 1656), sig. [A2ᵛ]: 'Haec Gymnas teneram format Regina Iuventam: Eridit & primis flectere verba modis' (This wrestling fashioned the queen in her tender youth: she learned and above all considered the nature of words).

66. Arckenholtz has two inserted lines here: see above, *Headnote, Text*.

71. *Sic . . . artes*] M. refers to the pillaging of Rome by the Goths. One of Christina's Swedish panegyrists, Olaus Verelius, wrote and edited works on the Goths: see, e.g., Goethrek, King of the West Goths, ed. Verelius, *Gothrici & Rolfi regum historia* (Uppsala, 1664).

72. *una*] Stocker, *SP*, 84 (1987), 172, suggests an allusion to Spenser's Una, the virgin of the Reformation in *The Faerie Queene*, Book I, and hence a further comparison with Elizabeth.

74. *geminis . . . sonis*] Swedish and Latin. A similar figure to the 'double name' of *In Legationem Domini Oliveri St John ad Provincias Foederatas*, l. 8.

75. *Transpositos*] imitates the transposition of the Virgilian eclogue conducted in the poem (Stocker, *SP*, 84 (1987), 173).

78. *Aegidaque . . . habet*] The aegis (shield; armour) and the chariot were attributes of Pallas Athena (Minerva to the Romans), goddess of war and wisdom. She is associated with Uppsala because of its university, founded in 1477. M. de Harst, trans. W.L., *A Panegyrick of the most renowned and serene Princess Christina* (1656), 42, compares the real Christina to the Minerva that once so many 'Poeticall inventions faigned'. Cp. also, Anthonius Sfortia, in Giuseppe Francesco Mostarda, *Festosi Applaus . . . alla Serenissima Christina* (1656), sig. [A2ᵛ]: 'Erudit ad messem Palladis arte labor. . . . Foemina Palladios vincere docta viros' (She learned from the example of Athena the art of hard work . . . through Pallas woman surpasses the teachings of men).

81. *lacte . . . melle*] Cp. Exod. 3:7–8: 'And the Lord said . . . I am come down to deliver them out of the hand of the Egyptians, and to bring them up out of that land unto a good land and a large, unto a land flowing with milk and honey.'

82. *Salam*] Sala, a town in central Sweden, forty miles from Uppsala, famous for its silver mines (rather than gold, as M. implies). *inauratam* implicitly compares the river Fyris (which M. confuses with Sala, the town through which it flowed) with the Tagus, known for its golden sands. Cp. Milton, *Defensio Secunda* (1654; in *Works* (New York, 1933), VIII.106): 'quin & ipsa terra illa, tot metallis faecunda, si aliis noverca, tibi certè alma parens, te summis enixa viribus totam auream produxisse videtur' (In fact, that very land, so rich in metals, if to others a stepmother, to you certainly seems to have been a kind parent, who strove with all her might to bring you forth all gold (translation from *CPW*, IV.i.605)).

83. *Upsalides . . . canemus*] Echoes Virgil, *Eclogue* IV, l. 1: 'Sicelides Musae, paulo maiora canamus' (Sicilian Muses, let us sing a somewhat loftier strain). See also above, *Headnote, Sources and Genre*.

85   Creditur haud ulli Christus signasse suorum
      Occultam gemma de meliore notam.
  Quemque tenet charo descriptum nomine semper,
      Non minus exculptum pectore fida refert.
  Sola haec virgineas depascit flamma medullas,
90   Et licito pergit solvere corda foco.
  Tu quoque Sanctorum fastos Christina sacrabis,
      Unica nec virgo Volsiniensis erit.
  Discite nunc reges (majestas proxima caelo)
      Discite proh magnos hinc coluisse deos.
95   Ah pudeat tantos puerilia fingere coepta,
      Nugas nescio quas, et male quaerere opes.
  Acer equo cunctos dum praeterit ille Britanno,
      Et pecoris spolium nescit inerme sequi.
  Ast aquilam poscit Germano pellere nido,
100   Deque Palatino monte fugare lupam.
  Vos etiam latos in praedam jungite campos,
      Impiaque arctatis cingite lustra plagis.
  Victor Oliverus nudum caput exerit armis,
      Ducere sive sequi nobile laetus iter.

105   Qualis jam senior Solymae Godfredus ad arces,
      Spina cui canis floruit alba comis.
  Et Lappos Christina potest et solvere Finnos,
      Ultima quos Boreae carcere claustra premunt.
  Aeoliis quales venti fremuere sub antris,
110   Et tentant montis corripuisse moras.
  Hanc dea si summa demiserit arce procellam
      Quam gravis Austriacis Hesperiisque cadat!
  Omnia sed rediens olim narraveris ipse;
      Nec reditus spero tempora longa petit.
115   Non ibi lenta pigro stringuntur frigore verba,
      Solibus, et tandem vere liquanda novo.
  Sed radiis hyemem regina potentior urit;
      Haeque magis solvit, quam ligat illa polum.
  Dicitur et nostros moerens audisse labores,
120   Fortis et ingenuam gentis amasse fidem.
  Oblatae Batavam nec paci commodat aurem;
      Nec versat Danos insidiosa dolos.
  Sed pia festinat mutatis foedera rebus,
      Et libertatem quae dominatur amat.

85–6. Creditur . . . notam] Christina is presented as the white stone (signalled by *gemma*) of Rev. 2:17; in it was written the mark or seal (*nota*) by which the chosen would know themselves.

87–8. Quemque . . . refert] Legouis compares these lines to Exod. 28:29, which describes the names carved on Aaron's breastplate, but Christina has the names *in* her heart, as well as 'inscribed' externally in her name.

87. Quemque] Referring to Christ.

89. Sola . . . medullas] the depiction of Christina as a divinely-inspired virgin is redolent of Catholic iconography. If Christina did read the poem, she would have been especially attracted to these lines while contemplating her conversion to Catholicism: see above, *Headnote, Context*; below, l. 92 n.

92. virgo Volsiniensis] St Christina drowned in Lake Bolsena in AD 278. 'The legend of St Christine venerated at Lake Bolsena in Tuscany is simply that of St Christine of Tyre imported from the East and adapted to local conditions' (Attwater (1965), 84–5). Both saints share the same day, 24 July.

97. ille] Cooke+; illa *1681*; Cromwell.

99. aquilam] the eagle was the emblem of the Holy Roman Empire.

100. lupam] a) the Roman Catholic church; see John 10:12: 'the wolf catcheth them, and scattereth the sheep.' b) a she-wolf was the emblem of the Palatine. c) the whore of Rev. 17:1; 19:2.

102. cingite . . . plagis] Cp. *An Horatian Ode upon Cromwell's Return from Ireland*, l. 50: 'He wove a net of such a scope.'

105. Godfredus] Godfrey of Bulloigne, the hero of Tasso's *Gerusalemme Liberata* (1581), trans. Edward Fairfax (1600).

106. Spina . . . comis] Godfrey wore a crown of thorns, and not a crown of gold and precious stones, when entering the Church of the Holy Sepulchre after the capture of Jerusalem. Like Godfrey, Cromwell had and would refuse a crown (see below, 283). *canis . . . coms*] suggests a pun on the name of the ambassador, Whitelocke (Margoliouth): see above, l. 9 n.

108. Boreae] the north.

109–10. Aeoliis . . . moras] Cp. Virgil, *Aeneid*, I, ll. 52–6: 'hic vasto rex Aeolus antro/luctantis ventos tempestatesque sonoras/imperio premit ac vinclis et carcere frenat./illi indignantes magno cum murmure montis/circum claustra fremunt' (Here in his vast cavern, Aeolus, their king, keeps under his sway and with prison bonds curbs the struggling winds and the roaring gales. They, to the mountain's mighty moans, chafe blustering around the barriers). Christina is obliquely compared to Juno, who in this passage of the *Aeneid* (I, ll. 34–123) seeks the aid of Aeolus in confounding the voyaging Trojans with tempests.

111. dea] see above, l. 110 n.

112. Hesperiisque] the west (Hesperus: Lewis and Short, 2), poetic name for Italy or Rome; cp. Horace, *Carmina*, I.xxxvi, l. 4: 'qui nunc Hesperia sospes ab ultima' (who now returned from the farthest west).

113–14. rediens . . . reditus] suggesting that M. may have had Horace's ode on joyful return in his mind: see above, l. 112 n.

120. ingenuam] Stocker, *N & Q*, 231 (1986), 31–2, argues that M. means 'uncorrupted' (as in true, reformed religion) and not the 'free-born' of McQueen and Rockwell.

25   Digna cui Salomon meritos retulisset honores,
      Et Saba concretum thure cremasset iter.
      Hanc tua, sed melius, celebraverit, Ingele, musa;
        Et labor est vestrae debitus ille lyrae.
      Nos sine te frustra Thamisis saliceta subimus,
30   Sparsaque per steriles turba vagamur agros.
      Et male tentanti querulum respondet avena:
        Quin et Rogerio dissiluere fides.
      Haec tamen absenti memores dictamus amico,
        Grataque speramus qualiacumque fore.

A Letter to Doctor Ingelo, then with my Lord Whitlocke, Ambassador from the Protector to the Queen of Sweden

What are you doing, dearest Ingelo, deserter to the Northern zone, o lately known, swiftly abducted? Do you adequately ward off the wintry star by means of hides, you who lately were so delicate and infirm? Say, what are the races of men, what is the nature of the regions, are there men there or rather regions? Does the heavy Pole overthrow everything with its dreadfully sounding rotation while the precipitous world is joined together by one layer of snow on top of the next? Or does the plain grow bristly all the better with white blades of corn, and the annual toil return in its cycle to the farmers. A gentler race, so it is said, inhabits the cruel shore, vigilant in peace, vigorous in war, just in trade. Indeed there exist there cities and the lofty palaces of kings, the dwelling of the Muses and God's own temples. For Christina rules by her authority a fierce people; a royal virgin, she has the power to give laws to men. As a magnet draws inflexible metal to the north, so the iron offspring rejoices in following her of its own accord. Say to what extent can deceptive Rumour be believed, and whether in her envy she keeps many things silent or whether she proclaims them in her loquacity. But if belief is true, no ages since the beginning of a better universe have borne Christina's equal, even if Elizabeth herself, the glory of our world, were to return, though our Elizabeth was such as she and as great. We have seen her picture and the shades mingled with colours: thus did she appear both powerful in her sceptre, and both a goddess. Majesty and love, beauty and modesty (a rare concord) at the same time adorn her august brow. The mighty Gustavus breathes in her virginal countenance: you could recognize the spirit and the lightning of her father. No star beneath its own pole has shone so brightly, not that Nymph who earned the sky for her crime. Ah how often, aware of her guilt, did Parrhasis cast down her timorous glance and how she feared the face of her goddess! And unless the artist is dissembling her countenance with a false image, Delia herself was not so similar to her except for the fact that Trivia's hair is by chance unadorned, but hers is punctiliously divided with a pin – indeed since no one has a greater respect for justice than she, not even her very hair does she carry without a law. She constitutes equally the glory of the forests and of the state, and the adornment of perpetual virginity. Thus too does she tower by a head over the troops of Nymphs and she leads the dancing over the peaks of Cynthus and over the snow. No differently does she contract the equal bows of her eyelids without you thinking that weapons lay beneath her fierce eyes. You would doubt whether she has slain by means of her eyes or her arrows the wild beast which warms her lofty neck with its skin. Hercules, covering his shoulders with a Nemean skin, did not in this manner endure the burden of the tottering world. Alas, such a neck which joins a breast colder than ice, whiter than snow. But it was not permitted to behold the rest, and scarcely all

125–6. *Salomon . . . Saba*] the opulence of Solomon and the Queen of Sheba is documented in 1 Kings 10:1–10. Milton also compares Christina to the Queen of Sheba (*Defensio Secunda* (CPW, IV.i.605–6)). Whitelocke was compared to Solomon and Christina to the Queen of Sheba in a letter sent from Jonathan Pickes, received on 16 March 1653 (see Whitelocke (1772), I.506); see also M. de Harst, trans. W.L., *A Panegyrick of the most renowned and serene Princess Christina* (1656), 41, and W.L., 'To the Fair, Vertuous, and nobly honoured Lady Mrs R.G.', in de Harst, op. cit., 5.

129. *Thamisis*] M. wrote from Eton, which lies on the River Thames.
132. *Rogerio*] Benjamin Rogers of Windsor (1614–98), an accomplished musician, who gained the BMus. at Cambridge through Ingelo's intervention in 1658. Ingelo took with him to Sweden some of Rogers's compositions which were performed for Christina to her pleasure.

those features, for her bosom is enclosed in stiffened steel. Whether the chlamys came to the assistance of this overly daring artist and thus, unequal to the task, he fled the unfinished work, or whether in her victory she shuns competition with three goddesses and, without being despoiled, carries off the prize for beauty in her haste – the famous trophies of Juno and Minerva – for it is shameful to have known the gentle rewards of Venus. Hence in her lavishness she has had no thought for fleeting beauty nor has she been afraid to stay awake late over books. How many times have her attendant Nymphs warned her, sleepless, that alas that colour would depart from her rosy cheeks. And already wakeful Philomela has yielded to gentle sleep and the wild beasts in all the woods have fallen silent. Still the more keenly does she proceed, wearying her cares; of such value it is to peruse the writings of learned men and to learn the nature of the government of a lawful reign, to know what has been, what is, and whatever will be.

Thus whatever wrong the Goth has committed against the liberal arts, she alone vindicates and atones for it by means of her studies. People ready to be taught imitate her noble example, and the infant imbues his lips with twofold sounds. You would believe that the Latins had been transposed and had passed over into Sweden; thus does the whole grove resound to the song of Romulus. Uppsala is said to be not unequal to Athens of old, and here does Pallas possess both her aegis and chariot. O what waters one can hope for from that source since the goddess herself presides over the sacred springs; rivers flow with milk on this side, honey on that, and golden sand dyes the gilded Sala. Upsalian Muses, now we will sing of even greater things, things which the not slight breeze of Fame has borne to me. Christ is believed to have marked for none of his own the secret sign from a better jewel. And in her faithfulness she bears equally inscribed in her heart one whom she holds forever described by her dear name. This is the only flame that consumes her virgin marrow, and she proceeds to unfold her heart at this lawful hearth. You too, Christina, will make hallowed the feast days of the Saints, and the virgin of Bolsena will not be unique. Learn now, kings (majesty closest to heaven), learn, o, to worship from this source the

mighty gods. Ah, may it be shameful for so many to form childish undertakings, some trifles or other, and to seek wealth improperly, while he keen-spiritedly overtakes all on his British horse and does not know how to pursue the unarmed prize of the flock. But he demands to drive the eagle from its German nest and to put the she wolf to flight from the Palatine hill. You too, join the broad plains for the sake of booty, and surround the dens of impiety with tightly-fitting nets. The victorious Oliver takes his bare head out of its armour, happy to lead or to follow a noble route. Just as Godfrey the Elder went to the citadel of Jerusalem, on whose white locks flowered the white thorn. Christina has the power to loosen both the Lapps and the Finns, whom the remotest barriers of the north wind suppress in imprisonment, just as the winds roared beneath the caves of Aeolus and attempt to snatch away the hindering mountains. If the goddess should send this squall from the top of her citadel, how heavy would it fall on the Austrians and the Spanish! But returning, you yourself will one day narrate everything; and I hope that your return does not take a long time. Slow words are not bound there in sluggish cold, to be melted at last by the sun and a new spring; but the Queen, more powerful, burns winter with her rays, dissolving the Pole more than winter binds it.

She is said to have listened in lamentation even to our troubles and to have loved the free-born faith of a brave race. Neither is she obliging to the Dutch ear in the offer of peace nor does she treacherously contemplate Danish trickery, but she hastens pious treaties in changing circumstances, and she who has dominion, loves freedom. She is deserving that Solomon should have reported her merited honours and Sheba's Queen would have burned the congealed route by means of incense. But, Ingelo, your Muse might celebrate her better, and that task is owing to your lyre. Without you in vain do we traverse the willows of the Thames and wander, a scattered throng, through barren fields. And the reed-pipe makes a poor response to whosoever attempts to make lament; indeed even Roger' strings have burst asunder. Nevertheless mindful we declare these things to an absent friend and hope that they will be pleasing, such as they are.

54

An Horatian Ode upon Cromwell's Return from Ireland

Date. June–July 1650. At the time of the execution of Charles I in January 1649, Oliver Cromwell was second-in-command of the New Model Army, and politically influential in the purged House of Commons, the Rump Parliament. In the summer of 1649, he led a military expedition to Ireland where he achieved a series of victories against the Royalist and Catholic alliance at the battle of Drogheda and Wexford, and the siege of Clonmel. Shortly after the latter, in late May 1650, he returned to England, landing at Bristol on the 28th, and reaching Windsor on the 31st. The Irish threat to the new republic of England had been contained, but the Scottish threat remained. On 12 June, Sir Thomas Fairfax was appointed commander-in-chief of the army for a Scottish campaign, with Cromwell still as second-in-command. However, Fairfax refused to enter Scotland without provocation, by which he meant a Scottish invasion of England. On 26 June, sitting high in public esteem after the Irish success, Cromwell replaced Fairfax as commander-in-chief. On 22 July, the Parliamentary forces invaded Scotland. The poem looks back upon the regicide, the birth of the republic, and the Irish campaign, and forward to the Scottish venture. It must have been composed in this brief interlude between Cromwell's two celtic forays. Worden, *HJ*, 27 (1984), 531–2 notes the rise of patriotic feeling at this time, whatever feelings concerning the regicide might be. Accordingly, contemporary newspapers reflect M.'s call (ll. 1–8) for the 'forward youth' to leave behind the activities of peacetime: 'a regiment is raised in these parts for his Excellency the Lord General, and many young men of quality are seeking that employment, desiring to do something worthy of their births . . . for where there is discourse of war, it is a shame for a gentleman to say that he hath read it only, [not] that he saw it', *Perfect Passages*, 5 July 1650.

Manuscript Circulation. The poem evidently circulated in small, elite circles: there are apparent echoes in Manley's translation of Fisher (1652) (see Norbrook (1999), 251), and in Dryden's Restoration verse (see Hammond, *N & Q*, 35 (1988), 173–4), which suggests that M. continued to show the poem to poets whom he encountered. A further inference is that he wrote the poem in pursuit of patronage from the new regime. The *Ode* exists in manuscript in *Bod. 1*, but in a significantly different version to *1681*. Manuscript circulation evidently resulted in more than one copy. Thompson may well have used *Bod. 1*. It is also possible that Thomas Gent, Yorkshire antiquarian, saw a copy of the poem in some form before 1735: the King who 'meekly laid down his Neck' (*Annales regioduni Hullini* (1735), 167), is like M.'s depiction, where Charles 'bowed his comely head,/ Down as upon a bed'.

Printed Publication. The poem was included in *1681*, but was cancelled from most copies. Two known uncancelled copies are British Library C.59.1.8 and Huntington Library 79660. Thompson was the first to reprint the poem, with some errors, in his quarto edition of 1776.

Genre and Allusion. One of the two poems that represent M.'s earliest published work, *Ad Regem Carolum Parodia* (1637), is a close imitation of the second ode in the first book of Horace's odes, or *Carmina* (see above, 5–9). Horace, who fought for the republicans at Philippi, eventually accepted the rule of Augustus Caesar, and celebrated in verse the peace that prevailed under his rule. Such Horatian poetry (as opposed to the later vogue for Horatian satire) became a model for royalist panegyrics: a famous example is Sir Richard Fanshawe's *An Ode Upon occasion of His Majesties Proclamation 1630. Commanding the Gentry to reside upon their Estates in the Country.* Fanshawe's *Selected Parts of Horace* (1652), contains translations of Horace's odes using the same metre as that of M.'s *Ode*. Since Fanshawe was translating these as early as 1648, it has been assumed that M. might have seen and been influenced by them. The compilation and translation of Horatian odes was in part a reaction to the experience of Civil War: Mildmay Fane, Second Earl of Westmoreland's 'Fugitive Poetry' (Harvard UL, fMS Eng. 645) contains nineteen of Horace's odes in Latin and English, and two epodes, all decidedly royalist.

William Simeone, *N & Q*, 197 (1952), 317–18 notes the similarity between the metre of Fanshawe's Horatian Ode (BL MS Add. 15,228, reprinted in Fanshawe, *Poems and Translations*, ed. Peter Davidson, 2 vols (Oxford, 1997–99), I.36–7) and M.'s poem. Fanshawe's poem acknowledges the dangerous enchantments of poetry, which can detract from careers and livelihoods. M. obliquely refers to the same concerns in the *Ode* (ll. 1–5). Fanshawe's published translations have close parallels with M.'s expression of Cromwell's divine protection and diligent effort: 'What is't but *Neros* can effect,/ Whom Heav'ns with prosperous Stars protect,/ And their own prudent care/ Clews through the Maze of War' (*Selected Parts of Horace* (1652), II.4; see below, ll. 11–12, 25–6, 113–14, 119–20). See also Leishman (1965), 284. Norbrook (1999), 252–5, argues that M. deliberately overturns Fane's royalist Horatianism with a republican poetics favouring action. He notes similar direct revisions of Horace's praise of retirement in the verse of the republican Henry Marten.

Several candidates among Horace's odes suggest themselves as models for M. in his Horatian ode on Cromwell: I.ii, xxxv, xxxvii; IV.iv, v, xiv, xv. IV.iv is a *prosphonetikon*, the celebration of a hero's return, like M.'s poem. Hannibal is defeated by Drusus Nero (see also IV.iv), and he speaks a lament in the poem (ll. 50–72), just as Marvell's Irish acknowledge their conqueror (ll. 77–80). When Horace was writing, the name Nero did not have the unfortunate associations it was later to have. Drusus Nero, full of youthful strength (l. 5, 'olim iuventas et patrius vigor'), swoops as a hunter or raider (see below, ll. 109–10) on the sheep-folds (ll. 9–10, 'mox in ovilia/ demisit hostem vividus impetus').

Carmina, I.xxxv is addressed to the goddess Fortuna, who stands between grim Necessity and Hope and Fidelity. The ode looks forwards to Caesar's invasion of Britain, which is about to happen. With regret at Roman losses, Horace finally looks forward, as does M., to a future of martial glory. I.xxxvii records the fall of Cleopatra, whom the future Augustus is seen to chase as a hawk and

a hunter. Erskine-Hill (1983), 196, sees a broad comparison between Cleopatra and Charles I, noting that three years after Cleopatra's defeat at Actium, Octavian 'restored' the republic when he named himself the first Emperor, Augustus (see below, ll. 81–2). IV.v and IV.xv praise the Augustan peace; M. praises the victor in a war. Likewise, *Carmina*, III.i, while admitting the strain placed upon rulers, and their subjection to higher powers, praises the simple life of retreat (ll. 47–8, 'cur valle permutem Sabina/ divitias operosiores?' Why should I change my Sabine dale for the greater burden of wealth). If no identical treatments of subject-matter are apparent, and reversals or inversions are the most common relationship between Horace and M., it is rather in the condensed diction and cryptic syntax of the *Ode* (see below, *Versification and Style*), the sense of detachment and poise, and the simultaneous rendering of past, present and future, that similarities lie.

The mock *propemptikon* (formal ode of farewell; the opposite of *prosphonetikon*) was a feature of 1640s satire, and there is at least one example treating Cromwell's departure for Ireland: *The Loyal Subjects Jubilee, or Cromwels Farewell to England, being a Poem on his advancing to Ireland, July the 11, 1649*. This poem uses theatrical imagery as it predicts Cromwell's downfall at the hands of the Irish: 'His *Exits* come, *Ireland* the stage must be,/ Where he must act his latest Tragedie' (ll. 29–30). M.'s poem answers back in kind (ll. 53–6).

Similarities between the *Ode* (ll. 1–24, 113–14) and passages in Lucan's *De Bello Civili* or *Pharsalia*, I, ll. 144–57, 225–32, 239–43, also exist. Fane's perception of Lucan as a poet appropriate for a society at war is telling: 'If Lucan were againe to write/The Art & Stratagem of fight/Now wth a swifter stile t'enforce/The onsett by th'Courageous horse' (Harvard UL, fMS Eng. 645, 49). It is also evident that M. knew Tom May's translation of Lucan (1st edn, 1626–27):

>   sed nescia virtus
> Stare loco, solusque pudor non vincere bello;   145
> Acer et indomitus, quo spes quoque ira vocasset,
> Ferre manum et nunquam temerando parcere ferro,
> Successus urguere suos, instare favori
> Numinis, inpellens, quidquid sibi summa petenti
> Obstaret, gaudensque viam fecisse ruina.   150
> Qualiter expressum ventis per nubila fulmen
> Aetheris inpulsi sonitu mundique fragore
> Emicuit rupitque diem populosque paventes
> Terruit obliqua praestringens lumina flamma;

In sua templa furit, nullaque exire vetante 155
Materia magnamque cadens magnamque revertens
Dat stragem late sparsosque recolligit ignes.
           Lucan, *Pharsalia*, I, ll. 144–57
But restlesse valour, and in warre a shame
Not to be Conqueror; fierce, not curb'd at all,
Ready to fight, where hope, or anger call,
His forward Sword; confident of successe,
And bold the favour of the gods to presse:
Orethrowing all that his ambition stay,
And loves that ruine should enforce his way;
As lightning by the wind forc'd from a cloude
Breaks through the wounded aire with thunder loud,
Disturbs the Day, the people terrifies,
And by a light oblique dazels our eyes,
Not *Ioves* own Temple spares it; when no force,
No barre can hinder his prevailing course,
Great waste, as foorth it sallyes and retires,
It makes and gathers his dispersed fires.
        Thomas May, translation of *Pharsalia*
             (2nd edn, 1631, sig. A3^v)
'Hic', ait, 'hic pacem temeratque iura relinquo; 225
Te, fortuna, sequor. Procul hinc iam foedera sunto;
Credidimus satis his, utendum est iudice bello.'
Sic fatus noctis tenebris rapit agmina ductor
Inpiger, et torto Balearis verbere fundae
Ocior et missa Parthi post terga sagitta, 230
Vicinumque minax invadit Ariminum, et ignes
Solis lucifero fugiebant astra relicto.

. . .

Rupta quies populi, stratisque excita iuventus
Deripuit sacris adfixa penatibus arma, 240
Quae pax longa dabat: nuda iam crate fluentes
Invadunt clipeos curvataque cuspide pila
Et scabros nigrae morsu rubiginis enses.
      Lucan, *Pharsalia*, I, ll. 225–32, 239–43
Here Peace, and broken Lawes I leave, quoth he,
Farewell all Leagues: Fortune Ile follow thee
No more weele trust: Warre shall determine all:
This said, by Night the actiue Generall
Swifter then Parthian back-shot shaft, or stone
From Balearicke Slinger, marches on
T'invade Ariminum; when every star
Fled from th'approaching Sunne but Lucifer,

. . .

With this sad noise the Peoples rest was broke,
The young men rose, and from the temples tooke
Their Armes, now such as a long peace had marr'de.
And their old bucklers now of leather's bar'de:
Their blunted Piles not of a long time us'd,
And Swords with th'eatings of blacke rust abus'd.
       Tom May, translation of *Pharsalia*
         (2nd edn, 1631, sigs. A4^v–A5^r)

There is also a parallel between the description of Pompey (IX, ll. 192–200) and Cromwell (ll. 81–90)

as worthy servants of the republic. More dubious is the parallel between the death of Pompey (VIII, ll. 613–17) and the death of Charles I (ll. 56–64), suggested by Sir Edward Ridley, *TLS*, 5 February, 1920, 86. In between come a series of less obvious, but none the less present echoes in M. of Lucan and May: 'great *Pompey* feares/That his piraticke Laurell should giue place/To conquerede France' (sig. A3^r; cf. *Ode*, ll. 23–4), 'Nor now can *Caesar* a superior brooke,/Nor *Pompey* brooke a peere' (sig. A3^r; see *Ode*, ll. 17–20); 'his Theaters loud shout/Was his delight; new strength he sought not out,/Relying on his ancient fortunes fame,/And stood the shadow of a glorious name' (sig. A3^r; see *Ode*, ll. 3, 53–64, 118), 'Vnheard-of Starres by night adorne the skies:/Heaven seemes to flame, and through the Welkin fire/Obliquely flyes: state-changing comets dire/Display to us their blood portending haire' (sig. B1^r; see *Ode*, ll. 13–16, 26), '*Titan* hides,/(When mounted in the midd'st of heaven he rides)/In cloudes his burning Chariot, to enfold' (sig. B1^r; see *Ode*, l. 21), 'Ghosts from out their quiet vrnes did grone' (sig. B1^v; see *Ode*, l. 118).

It is clear from these examples that M. is not simply echoing Lucan and May. It is possible to see a pattern of transformations in M.'s borrowings, by which the ironic structure of the *Ode* is partly achieved. The treatment is seen by Coolidge, *MP*, 63 (1965), 111–20, as a reversal of May's attitude to the uses of Roman history. Unlike M.'s claim in *Tom May's Death*, May made comparisons between Rome and England in his *History of Parliament* (1647) to show how the histories of the two nations did not agree: 'May's historical similitudes invite extrapolation; M.'s deliberately frustrate it' (113).

In M.'s poem, recollections of Horace and Lucan serve to evoke Roman responses to the ambiguities of power and right, centring on the name of Caesar. Lucan, Nero's reluctant Laureate, sees Julius Caesar as a power over, against and above, law. Pompey, in Lucan's eyes, is as ambitious as his opponent, even if he is the servant of the Senate. Lucan's real hero is Cato, the representative of republican virtue, who supported the losing side in the Roman civil wars. Charles I is called Caesar in the *Ode* (l. 23), but the context can only be his downfall (in May's *History of the Parliament*, Charles is presented as Caesar the usurper). By l. 101, Cromwell has become the Julius Caesar who triumphantly overruns France, the point at which the *Pharsalia* begins. From this position, following the parallel with Caesar, M. could be seen to hint at Cromwell's ambition for the crown of England, an accusation made by Royalist and radical pamphleteers, and a possibility that Cromwell actively rejected in the mid-1650s (see below, 283). Syfret, *RES*, n.s. 12 (1961), 160–72 (167–8) also makes the case for Cromwell as a Pompey figure, seeing parallels between *Pharsalia*, IX, ll. 192–200 and *Ode*, ll. 29–30, 81–96. From this observation, M. would seem to be reversing the outcome of Lucan's poem, though Lucan was writing when Pompey was dead; M. catches Cromwell in mid-career.

In terms of poetic models, a point of wit is made by situating Lucanic enormity inside Horatian restraint. This would also chime with M.'s interest in a poetry of the sublime, signalled by his echoes of John Hall's translation of Longinus (see below, ll. 21–2 n.). Longinus thought that Pindar's odes were the best sublime poems. It has been suggested that M.'s 'elliptical account of Cromwell's career, with its sublime imagery and its long digression about Charles', may be seen as an attempt to place a Pindaric ode inside a Horatian Ode (Norbrook (1999), 269–70), just as Milton had been trying to locate Pindaric form inside the sonnet. Both Milton and M. may be seen to be replying to Cowley's 1647 announcement of an intention to write a royalist sublime ('To the Reader', *The Mistresse* (1647), 115). A recently noticed source (see Hopkins, *N & Q*, n.s. 48 (2001), 19–20) related to this group of texts is Charles Aleyn's *The Historie of that wise and Fortunate Prince, Henrie of that Name the Seventh* (1638): see below, ll. 13–14 n., 53–8 n., 119–20 n.

M. was acquainted with Richard Lovelace, and the falcon simile in the *Ode* (ll. 91–6) may owe something to Lovelace's *The Falcon*. Though the heron kills the falcon as he is killed by the bird of prey, there is a connection between the battle of heron and falcon and the wars fought between Charles I and Parliament. The heron is a 'public martyr of the sky' (l. 76), and piercing bills strike 'Swift as the thunderbolt' (l. 81; see below ll. 13, 63–4). The falcon in Lovelace's poem is female, as was the case with hunting falcons, a fact that is not acknowledged in M.'s poem.

Versification and Style. Early comments, like Goldwin Smith (380–3) and Trench (394, 398–9), enthusiastically acknowledge the *Ode* as one of the best, if not the best, English Horatian Ode, being faithful in measure, diction and spirit. In his translations of Horace, begun in 1648 though not published

until 1652, Sir Richard Fanshawe had begun to use the metre which Everett, in Brett, ed. (1979), calls a 'remarkable thinking metre', 'an unusual pattern of pairs of rhymed four-beat and then three-beat lines, the delicate monosyllables of the second pair, the short lines, in effect undercutting the first pair' (74). The alternate couplet lengths have been seen as antiphonal in character, as if two distinct voices were speaking. The diction is notable for the high incidence of words with a wide semantic range, always significantly deployed by M., while the syntax features Latinate inversions, the two effects combining to engender the famous reserved and ironic tone of the poem. The confusion or ambiguity is enhanced by grammatical openness: *blast* (l. 24) may be transitive or intransitive, Caesar's head subject or object; does Victory crown Cromwell or sit on his helmet (l. 98)? See also *burning* (l. 21), *hold or break* (l. 39). Many verbs take a conditional construction, and nouns and verbs could have either a passive or an active application. There are ellipses: ll. 31–2, 92, 101–2. Adjectives can also be nouns or adverbs (e.g. *restless*, l. 9). Adverbs are frequently truncated (*true* (l. 27), *reserved, austere* (l. 30)). *Nor* (ll. 3, 61, 81, 111) is a Latinism for 'And not' (see Horace, 'quaerere distuli,/nec scire fas est omnia', *Carmina*, IV. 4, ll. 21–2); 'what he may' (l. 87) a direct rendering of 'qua licet'. *So* (ll. 9, 63) is deployed for a similar effect.

In *1681* the poem is printed in continuous verse, but from the second page onwards of the copy in *Bod. 1*, the poem is written in four-line stanzas. Horace's odes were written and printed both ways in the seventeenth century: there seems to be no particular cause determining these two modes, and neither appears to grow in popularity over any period of time. Did the annotator of *Bod. 1* simply follow his own habit when copying into the volume, or was the copy he had in stanzas which he failed to register initially? The poem is represented here in stanzaic form.

Modern Criticism. An Horatian Ode has generally been admired for its style (Arnold found it '*belle et fort*' (beautiful and vigorous), Letter to Saint-Beuve, 31 December 1863, quoted in Collins, 52–3) and regarded as confusing for its political ambivalence. Nineteenth-century commentators, whose political culture was closer to that of the seventeenth century than is ours, knew M. as a patriot and Parliamentarian, the constitutional monarchist of the Restoration, rather than the Interregnum republican. Indeed, one anonymous reviewer (*American Review*, 77 (May 1851)) omitted the lines sympathetic to Charles I in order to portray M. as the dignified republican, Waller as the shifty time-server. The experience of revolution in France led some, for instance Saint-Beuve (*Noveaux Lundis* (1879), VIII.100–2), to admire M.'s portrayal of the powerful man of the moment, Cromwell.

Towards the end of the century, when M.'s reputation as a lyricist began to grow, the ode came to be regarded as a lyric masterpiece, which was able to rise above politics. But if the prosodic majesty and metrical balance or poise of the poem has sustained universal acclaim since then, the political meaning of the poem has continued to puzzle critics. Disagreements have always been concerned with how sympathetic is M. to Charles I, and how critical of Cromwell he is in a poem ostensibly of praise. The difficulty of the ode in this respect has made it a major example in critical debates concerned with the relative merits of internal and 'aesthetic' interpretation, and contextual or 'historical' interpretation.

Legouis' attempt (1965), 14–15, to pinpoint the fulcrum of the poem as the acceptance of de facto government by an erstwhile monarchist, switching allegiances to one who, with the power of Providence, and despite the barbaric execution of the king, holds the best prospects for peace, has been the most resilient and far-sighted judgement in the last sixty years. It has not however been unchallenged. The twelve lines recounting the regicide, Legouis reminds us, were frequently memorized in the nineteenth century as a eulogy to the martyr-king. One critical trend, starting with Hazlitt (who spoke on hearsay from Lamb in *Lectures on the English Comic Writers* (1818–19), not having read the *Ode* himself) took the poem as openly or covertly royalist (*Collected Works*, ed. A.R. Waller and Arnold Glover (1903), VIII.54). Brooks (*English Institute Essays* (1947), rptd in Carey, ed. (1969), 179–98), attempting to demonstrate the reductive simplicity of historically contextual readings, and the superiority of close textual observation, finds the poem covertly royalist: sympathy with Charles I is compounded with lack of sympathy for Cromwell in the host of ambiguous qualifiers (e.g. 'restless', l. 9). The doubleness of the poem is stressed, 'we do not have to choose between readings . . . they support each other', though this does not exclude apparent over-reading, as the erect sword (l. 116) is seen to indicate that 'those who

take up the sword shall perish by the sword' (194). Brooks was controverted by Douglas Bush (*Sewanee Review*, 60 (1952), reptd in Carey, ed. (1969), 199–210) and accused of constructing a Cromwell out of his own preoccupations, since lacking a historical context. A 'Puritan Stalin' was the result, to which one could add a Cromwell based on Clarendon's model, and an implicit belief that those who commit murders should be punished (204–8). While acknowledging that Brooks did go to context when it suited him, Bush used close reading to argue against Brooks's interpretations (e.g. ll. 25–6).

The Lucanic parallels explored by R.H. Syfret (*RES*, n.s. 12 (1961), 160–72), especially the parallels between Julius Caesar and Cromwell, and the human regret for Charles make for a conclusion: 'in so far as there is a moral or emotional judgement made in the poem, it goes against Cromwell' (172). Taking the Lucanic and Horatian presences together, Coolidge (*MP*, 63 (1965), 111–20, reptd in Lord, ed. (1968), 85–100) sees a much more balanced poem, taking into account Lucan's own hostility to Nero: 'Recollections of Horace and Lucan serve to evoke Roman responses to the ambiguities of power and right' (115). The poem's classicism is confirmed in the detection of numerous instances of Latinate syntax, puns and paronomasia by A.J.N. Wilson, *CQ*, 11 (1969), 325–41, and he developed this interpretation to present the poem as an embodiment of a victory of Fate over Christian morality.

That Horace, *Odes*, I.12, presented Augustus as second only to Jove, was both praise and admonition for the Emperor. That M.'s *Ode* should be read as a panegyric, and so subject to rhetorical conventions, tended to limit the more extreme speculations of earlier readings. For Wallace (1968), 100–4, the poem was a deliberative oration, a moderate delivery on a difficult subject, looking for possible advantages in the future. Thus, the poem divides into a *narratio* (ll. 9–24), *divisio* (ll. 25–56), *confirmatio* (ll. 57–80), *refutatio* (ll. 81–96) and *peroratio* (ll. 96–120). A simpler partition is offered by Craze (1979), 120, of prologue (ll. 1–8), time past (ll. 9–72), time present (ll. 73–96), and the future (ll. 97–112), though the divisions are very unequal, and not consistent with rhetorical prescriptions. Wilson, *CQ*, 11 (1969), 327, and Patterson (1978), 59–68, prefer a demonstrative form of *encomium* which shows or indicates rather than evaluates or weighs. Considering the architectonic structure of Renaissance verse generally,

Fowler (1970), 76–84, notes the unexpected presence exactly half way through a panegyric on Cromwell of the execution of Charles I. Then again, such a placing serves equally to point up the regicide as Cromwell's greatest achievement. Recent studies, made in the light of work on seventeenth-century occasional verse, have sought to locate the *Ode* among the sub-genre of poems celebrating the return of a ruler or hero, the *prosphonetikon* or *epibaterion*, developed by Menander (Anselment, *JDJ*, 3 (1984), 181–201; Norbrook (in Healy and Sawday, eds (1990), 147–69)). Here, what for Fowler is an unexpected structural inversion, becomes for Norbrook a digression, in imitation of Horace, necessarily diminishing in its treatment of Charles. Brooks (193) felt that the praise from the Irish (ll. 73–9) had to be heavily ironic, given their suffering. But government propaganda played up the willingness with which some of the Irish greeted Cromwell. In this context, Norbrook (159–60) suggests that the Irish speak a conventional form of panegyric within the greater frame of an entirely new kind of praise poem.

To some extent, the *Ode* has been aligned with M.'s other poetry for the characteristic of genre revision. Toliver (1965) sees the poem playing out the concerns of M.'s lyrics, 'like the microcosm of the individual soul, the state is under continual siege' (3). Somewhat more convincingly, Friedman (1970), 6, notes the dependence of the opening lines upon pastoral modes of analogy and emblem.

Wallace's (9–105) detailed presentation of the Engagement Controversy as the immediate context within which to situate and interpret the *Ode* remains the most unchallenged of the historical studies. His idea of a rapid switch of loyalties in the aftermath of the regicide, when justice was overcome by power, has been challenged by Nicholas Guild, *SEL*, 20 (1980), 125–36, doubting the degree of M.'s royalism in the 1640s, and the importance of 'sides' in the writing of poetry. Worden, *HJ*, 27 (1984), 525–47, finds as much evidence of rapid change as Guild finds to the contrary.

J.A. Mazzeo, *JHI*, 21 (1960), 1–17, raised the possibility of M. portraying Cromwell in the *Ode* as both the Machiavellian 'novus princeps' of *The Prince*, and the man of *virtù* who seizes power to found a republic in *Discourses*, 1.10. He was immediately refuted on the grounds of insufficient evidence and unfamiliarity with Machiavelli's writings themselves by Hans Baron, *JHI*, 21 (1960), 450–1. However, after recent scholarship on English Machiavellianism, the idea of the *Ode* as a Machiavellian poem has been revived by Worden, and in greater detail by Norbrook, in the context of republican apology of the early 1650s. Scholars are agreed now that this was the period when Machiavelli's influence was at its greatest. Norbrook (in Healy and Sawday (1990), 147–69, and (1999), 243–71) argues that the poem describes a 'revolution' in the old sense of a return to original liberty through the exercise of Machiavellian *virtù*, and that the apocalyptic description of Cromwell accords with this tradition in Italian political discourse. Also wishing to dispel the conception of the *Ode* as a poem of balance and equipoise, Michael Wilding (1987), 114–37, stresses the silences in M.'s poem, that the Irish campaign was not popular with many soldiers in the New Model Army, and that there had been Leveller mutinies before the troops departed for Dublin. He also notes that, while Cromwell is seen by M. as being servant to the Parliament, the Army itself had already purged Parliament once in December 1648. Colie (1970), 65 and Wilding (133) note how in the execution scene itself, blood-guilt is displaced from Cromwell and given to the 'armed bands' (l. 55).

An Horatian Ode upon Cromwell's Return from Ireland

The forward youth that would appear
Must now forsake his Muses dear,
    Nor in the shadows sing
    His numbers languishing:

5 'Tis time to leave the books in dust,
   And oil th'unusèd armour's rust;
     Removing from the wall
     The corslet of the hall.

   So restless Cromwell could not cease
10 In the inglorious arts of peace,
     But through advent'rous war
     Urgèd his active star:

---

1. *forward*] a) prompt, ready (*OED* a. 6) b) inclined to a cause or person (*OED* a. 6b) c) eager, spirited, zealous (*OED* a. 6c); see Tourneur, *The Atheist's Tragedy*, II. i, l. 100, 'His forward spirit press'd into the front' d) precocious (*OED* a. 7). In the mid-seventeenth century, *forward* was associated with military usages (e.g. 'at an advanced point': '*to secure the landing of Irish or* Welsh *supplies so much the forwarder towards the East*', Joshua Sprigge, *Anglia Rediviva* (1647), 189). *appear*] a) to come into view (*OED* v. 1) b) to present oneself, as if before a commanding officer for military service; to volunteer (*OED* v. 4) c) to play a role in the public or active world; see Shakespeare, *Coriolanus*, IV, iii, l. 35, 'Your noble Tullius Aufidius will appear well in these wars.'
2. *now*] suggests the urgency of the recruiting drive for the Scottish campaign; ironically echoes and inverts Horace, *Carmina*, I.xxxvii ('*nunc est bibendum*'); the first instance of Machiavellian vocabulary in the poem, with the injunction of *occasione*, seizing the moment: a portrait of Henry Marten, the republican, by Lely, with the word 'now' inscribed on it hangs in the National Portrait Gallery (see Norbrook (1999), 257). *Muses*] a) the nine goddesses inspiring poetry and music (*OED* n.[1] 1) b) liberal arts (*OED* n.[1] 2 b). Duncan-Jones, in Legouis, claims that *muses* was used as a collective noun for Oxford and/or Cambridge, though no such usage is given in OED.
3-4. *shadows . . . languishing*] the withdrawn youth is supposed to be writing love lyrics, like those composed by Marvell, or Richard Lovelace. *Sing/ . . . languishing*] Norbrook (1999), 266-7, suggests that the weak rhyme here signals courtly avoidance of harsh realities in the public realm. *shadows*] the Roman *vita umbratilis*, not favoured by moralists. *languishing*] a) said of a sickness (*OED* a. 1b); see *The Unfortunate Lover*, l. 39, 'And languished with doubtful breath.' b) pining with love or grief (*OED* a. 2a). c) suffering from, or exhibiting, weariness, ennui, lethargy (*OED* a. 3). Cicero commonly rejects languishing for the claims of republican virtue. For instance: 'nam cum otio languaeremus at is esset rei publicae status ut eam unius consilio atque cura gubernari necesse esset', *De Natura Deorum*, I.iv.7 (Thus, we can languish with leisure, but public matters necessitate that we use singular standards, and besides, necessity requires that we offer advice on government carefully). Similar sentiments to Cicero's became frequent in public poetry during the 1650s: for instance, *Panegyrici Cromwello Scripti* (London, 1654), 18.
5-8. Cp. *RT*, 120, where forgotten controversial divinity (in book form) is likened to 'the rusty obsolete Armour of our Ancestors', hung up 'for derision rather than service'.
5. *time*] not only the sense of readiness, but also of a particular moment in history; see *Tom May's Death*, ll. 65-6: 'the poet's time, 'tis then he draws,/And single fights forsaken virtue's cause.'
6-8. Cp. Cowley, 'An Ode upon the return of his Majestie', in *Irenodia Cantabrigiensis* (1641), sig. F1[v], on the anticipated avoidance of war: 'Their Armour now may be hung up to sight,/And onely in their Halls the children fight.' See also anon., *The City* (Oxford, 1643), ll. 83-6: 'They never us'd to fright the King, nor draw/Tumults together to affront the Law,/No nor good houses, their Corslets slept and all/The armes hung up in each mans hall.' (McWilliams, *N & Q*, 52 (2005), 315-17, who discusses other echoes on this Royalist poem in M.'s ode, and suggests that seeing it would have meant a later departure date for M.'s continental tour than is usually supposed.)
8. *corslet*] piece of armour covering the body.
9. *restless Cromwell*] Cromwell was 'as restless in his own Sphere', according to Marchamont Nedham, *Mercurius Politicus*, 7 (18-25 July 1650), 109. *restless*] a) constantly stirring or acting (*OED* a. 2) b) of an uneasy spirit (*OED* a. 1). The sense of impatience is also implied, but *OED* records no such usage before 1719. *cease*] shares the sense of the Latin 'cessare', to rest.
11-12. *through advent'rous . . . star*] The syntax is ambiguous: either Cromwell 'urged his active star' through the dangers of war, or used adventurous war to urge his 'active star'.
11. *advent'rous*] a) risky, hazardous, perilous (*OED* a. 2) b) enterprising, daring (*OED* a. 4).
12. *Urgèd*] a) brought forward, presented, pressed (*OED* v. I 1) b) advised earnestly, pressed with importunity (*OED* v. I 2) c) caused to move (*OED* v. I 6 b). *active star*] astrological; the star, or celestial power, guiding and protecting Cromwell. The line is finely balanced: the star should rule Cromwell, but he acts on the star itself, making more of the lot which the higher powers allocate to him. The sense is consonant with the Machiavellian image of the man of *virtù* having the capacity to overcome the obstacles which *fortuna* leaves in his path.

And like the three-forked lightning, first
Breaking the clouds where it was nursed,
15   Did thorough his own side
    His fiery way divide.

(For 'tis all one to courage high,
The emulous or enemy;
    And with such to inclose
20   Is more than to oppose.)

Then burning through the air he went,
And palaces and temples rent;

And Caesar's head at last
Did through his laurels blast.
25   'Tis madness to resist or blame
The force of angry heaven's flame;
    And, if we would speak true,
    Much to the man is due:

Who, from his private gardens, where
30   He lived reservèd and austere,
    As if his highest plot
    To plant the bergamot,

13–14. See above, *Headnote, Genre and Allusion.*

13. lightning] Cromwell's rise in M.'s poem is described in the same terms adopted by some Royalist elegies to describe the death of Charles I: see, e.g., anon., 'An Elegie Upon King Charles the First', in [John Cleveland], ed., *Monumentum Regale* (1649), 42, ll. 70–1, 'His *Soul*, of this her triumph proud,/Broke, like a flash of lightning, through the cloud/Of flesh and blood.'

15. thorough] Bod. 1, Th.; through *1681*. The longer spelling of the preposition fits the poem's metre. David Crane, *N & Q*, n.s. 33 (1986), 464, suggests that Milton was influenced by M.'s poem when he wrote *To the Lord General Cromwell* in May 1652. If this was the case, then in addition to common classical sources (Virgil, *Aeneid*, X, l. 809; Horace, *Carmina*, IV.5, l. 14) Milton took the clouds of the *Ode* (l. 14) and saw in the preposition 'thorough' the verb 'to thorough' or make furrows: 'Guided by faith and matchless fortitude/To peace and truth thy glorious way hath ploughed' (ll. 3–4). *side*] Cromwell emerges as a leader of the Parliamentarian (and more specifically, the Independent) party or side, just as lightning breaks through the side of the cloud which produces it.

16. divide] raises the hint of Cromwell dividing his own way as well as his own side; hence Ricks' picture of Cromwell as 'self-divided' (in Patrides, ed. (1978), 130), but in an unexpected way, since self-division is usually ruinous (see Sir Philip Sidney, *Old Arcadia* (1590, ed. Jean Robertson, 1973), 360).

18. emulous] used as a noun here, but usually an adjective in English: Lat. 'aemulus' can be an adjective or a noun; a) those desirous of rivalling, imitating (*OED* a. 1a); (see Letter to Cromwell, 28 July 1653 (Legouis, II.304), 'Emulation which is the Spurr to Virtue'). b) those greedy of praise or power; the envious (*OED* a. 3). Such a degree of courage in Cromwell makes no distinction between those on his own side who aspire to his example, and his enemies: it is therefore in his nature to rise forcefully above the ranks on his own side.

19–20. Cp. Julius Caesar's speech in Lucan, *De Bello Civili*, III, l. 368, after the inhabitants of Marseilles ask him to lay down his arms and enter the city: 'Iam non excludere tantum,/ Inclusisse volunt' (now they want not to exclude me but to have inclosed me).

19. inclose] variation of 'enclose', associated with the legal and statutory permission for the enclosure of common or waste-land, a process which had begun in the seventeenth century (*OED*). To enclose Cromwell among lesser talents on the same side will provoke more reaction from him (since highly restricting) than to pit him against enemies.

21–2. The Republicans were held by Royalists to threaten 'that they will invade France, and after that run through Germany, Italy, and all Europe, throwing down kings and monarchs', *Several Proceedings*, 11–18 July 1650, 616. See also Payne Fisher, *Veni; Vidi; Vici*, trans. T. Manley (1652), 3, 'you do seek *Charybdis* to fly,/And would putt off the Rule of

Monarchy'. *burning*] used by John Hall, man of letters, republican apologist and friend of Marvell, to translate Longinus on the activities of sublime poets, who '*burn* up all before them', their poetry 'wheresoever it *seasonably* breaks forth, bears down all before it like a whirlwind', περὶ ὕψους, *Or Dionysius Longinus of the Height of Eloquence* (1652), sigs. C2ʳ, F7ᵇ. This sense would be consistent with the portrayal throughout the *Ode* of Cromwell as a supreme artist.

24. laurels blast] Cromwell's divine agency, working over and against nature, is enhanced, since lightning was supposed not to strike laurel trees: see Pliny, *Natural History*, XV.xl.

25. madness] 'it must needs be as much madness to strive against the stream for the upholding of a power cast down by the Almighty as it was for the old sons of earth to heap up mountains against Heaven', Marchamont Nedham, *The Case of the Commonwealth, Stated* (1650), ed. P.A. Knachel, Virginia (1969), 13.

26. heaven's] see Nedham, *Mercurius Politicus*, 7 (18–25 July 1650), 109: 'it is a Privilege of this *General*, consigned to him from Heaven, to conquer wheresoever he comes'.

29–32. Cromwell might have lived in rural withdrawal, but his ambition in this retirement was to aspire to the height of horticultural art, in anticipation of the military excellence to come. See *The First Anniversary of the Government under His Highness the Lord Protector*, ll. 229–32.

30. reservèd] a) averse to showing familiarity (*OED* ppl. a. 3) b) retired (*OED* ppl. a. 3c); used in this sense in the royalist Isaak Walton's *The Compleat Angler* (1653, xi.205) c) restrained, restricted (*OED* ppl. a. 4). *austere*] a) severe in self-discipline (*OED* a. 4) b) rigorous, stern (*OED* a. 3) c) grave, sober (*OED* a. 5) d) unadorned, simple (*OED* a. 6).

31. plot] a) patch of ground in a garden marked off for specific use (*OED* I n. 2) b) design, relating to the theatrical language of state (*OED* n. II 5); see below, ll. 53–4 n. W.R. Orwen, *N & Q*, n.s., 2 (1955), 340–1, argues that 'plot' suggests 'plotting', so that ll. 31–2 obliquely hints that Cromwell was from the very beginning plotting to become king.

32. bergamot] the bergamot pear was considered to be the pear of kings: 'Regium pyrum, quod *soppede groenken* a colore viridi & succo copioso dicunt, vel *bergamotten* a Bergamo, Italiae oppido. Colore est herbido, minimo omnium pediculo, & compressae rotunditatis; adeo ut sessile videatur, serotinum est, sapore praestantissimo succi pleno. Merito ergo ab antiquis regium nomen accepit' (The pear of kings, the 'juicy green one', said to be green in colour, and very juicy, or 'bergamot' precisely from Bergamo in Italy. It is grass-coloured, with a small stalk, a compact roundness; it is seen to grow low, and late, with an excellent taste and full of juice. Thus it has been called since antiquity the fruit of kings) (Theophrastus, *Historia Planetarum*, annotated by Johannes Bodaeus (Amsterdam, 1644), 396).

Could by industrious valour climb
To ruin the great work of time,
   And cast the kingdoms old
   Into another mould.

Though Justice against Fate complain,
And plead the ancient rights in vain;
   But those do hold or break,
   As men are strong or weak.

Nature that hateth emptiness,
Allows of penetration less:
   And therefore must make room
   Where greater spirits come.

45 What field of all the civil wars
Where his were not the deepest scars?
   And Hampton shows what part
   He had of wiser art:

---

33. *industrious*] a) showing skilful, purposeful work (*OED* a. 1, 3) b) showing enterprise and diligence (*OED* a. 4). *valour*] retains its chivalric associations (i.e. courage, bravery), but the two words were used in Edward Dacre's translation of Machiavelli's *The Prince* (1640), 16, 23, to render *industria* (applied skill) and *virtù* respectively. Sir Thomas Elyot, *The Boke named the Governor* (1531), I.xxiii defines industry, which 'hath not been so long time used in the English tongue', as the ability, through wit and experience, to exploit circumstances by invention and counsel. Elyot's example of the ruler who best combines industry with the power of providence is Julius Caesar. *climb*] Cromwell was portrayed in Royalist and radical literature as a social climber. Although the line as a whole praises Cromwell's skills, *climb* is not free of the associations it had for M. when he translated the lines from Seneca's *Thyestes*: 'Climb at court for me that will/ Giddy favour's slippery hill.' 35. *kingdoms*] Bod. 1; kingdom 1681. The plural rendering implies that Cromwell will recast the kingdom of Scotland as well as those of England and Ireland. Still, he had not yet invaded Scotland, and the Scots had proclaimed Charles II king. 36. *mould*] a) a pattern or style by which something is shaped (*OED* n. 3 I 1) b) distinctive nature or form of something, indicative of its origins (*OED* n. 3 II 9). The word is cognate with common political metaphors in the period – the body of the kingdom, with the king as the head, and the ship of state: 'For discomposition of the present frame, may not, I pray this be a Topicke for any Government, though never so ill grounded, never so irregular, or never so Tyrannical? Should we sit still, and expect that those in whose hands it is, should quietly resigne it, or new-mould it themselves, or some fine chance should do it to our hands?', John Hall, *The Advancement of Learning* (1649), 20. Classical republican echoes would have been apparent to a contemporary readership: see Jonson, *Catiline* (1611), I, ll. 502–6, 'My self, then, standing/Now to be consul . . . I've power to melt,/And cast in any mould.' Cp. also James Howell, 'To the Earl of Bristol', 23 April 1630, in *Epistolae Ho-Elianae* (1645), 'If this new conqueror [Gustavus Adolphus] goes on with this violence, I believe it will cast the policy of all Christendom into another mould.' 38. *ancient rights*] a concept used by nearly every political group during the Civil War: e.g. 'our antient rights, the Rights of our inheritance', *Sir Iohn Holland His Speech in Parliament* (1641), 4, against royal prerogative. *Ancient rights* refers not to the theory of the divine right of monarchs, but to the place of the monarch in an ancient constitution; see also *Tom May's Death*, ll. 69–70, 'Sings still of ancient rights and better times,/Seeks wretched good, arraigns successful crimes.' 39–40. A general statement of conquest theory: right is with those who have might, so that allegiance should be given to whoever is the successful conqueror. The argument was widely used in the Engagement Controversy by the apologists for the new government. Hodge (1978), 123, among others, has claimed that M. is thinking along the same lines as Thomas Hobbes in his *Leviathan* (1651). This is not the case: M.'s

statements in this poem do not accord with Hobbes's metaphysical framework (e.g. ll. 41–4, where M. appeals to natural and fundamental laws). *hold or break*] Craze (1979), 123, suggests that the 'rights' are likened to cables or ropes on a ship. 41–4. Nature abhors a vacuum, and dislikes even more the simultaneous occupation of the same space by two separate objects ('penetration'). Therefore, when a greater ruler arises than the one already in power, that extant ruler, by nature, must be removed. Cp. Charles Aleyn, *The Historie of that wise and Fortunate Prince, Henrie of that Name the Seventh* (1638), ll. 1325–6: 'To have no *meane* a *vacuum* doth imply/Abhor'd in states, as in Philosophy.' M.'s *therefore* completes a specious syllogism. The effect of the lines is really achieved through simultaneous apprehension by the reader of: a) a power vacuum, sucking matter (Cromwell) in to fill the gap (left by Charles). b) no two physical objects can occupy the same space in time. c) the implication in the syntax (*And therefore must*) that rational demonstration is being offered. *And therefore must* is elliptical: between *therefore* and *must* might come either 'Charles I' or, as the sentence itself would suggest, 'Nature'. By this second choice, Nature is seen to outdo itself, and Cromwell to outdo the forces of nature, even though ll. 41–2 make Cromwell's rise an effect of nature. This inconsistency nicely contains the ambiguity present in Parliamentarian apology when an appeal to natural law was made: the king had violated the laws of nature, which Parliament represented and sought to protect. Nevertheless, even natural law (as opposed to the theory of divine right kingship) could be superceded by a higher power: 'We confess indeed the land of *Palestine* was the favourite of Heaven, and much indebted to the divine influence above other Lands; yea, things went there sometimes contrary to the Law of Nature', Peter Cunaeus, *Of the Common-wealth of the Hebrews* (1653), 43. 46. *scars*] the wounds Marvell imagines the valorous Cromwell receiving in battle, thereby dignifying his bravery (see Shakespeare, *Antony and Cleopatra*, IV, vii, ll. 4–10), but the line could also mean that the scars are the wounds which Cromwell has inflicted on his enemies. Cromwell himself went unscathed in battle (see *A Poem upon the Death of O.C.*, ll. 195–6). 47–52. Hampton Court Palace, on the south bank of the Thames, where Charles I stayed until he fled to Carisbrooke Castle on the Isle of Wight on 11 November 1647. He remained in Carisbrooke until 1 December 1648. The contemporary suspicion that Cromwell, in a supreme act of Machiavellian statecraft, had arranged for Charles, first in 1647, to flee to the Isle of Wight, where he was betrayed to the Governor, and second, to attempt an escape, so that the King could more easily be brought to trial, is now thought to be groundless (Norbrook (1999), 262). Charles had left Hampton Court fearing a Leveller plot to murder him. M.'s image echoes Horace, *Carmina*, I.xxxvii, ll. 17–21, where Octavius's pursuit of Cleopatra is likened to the hawk pursuing a dove, and the hunter chasing a hare. See below, l. 91 n.

Where, twining subtle fears with hope,
50   He wove a net of such a scope
       That Charles himself might chase
       To Caresbrook's narrow case:

That thence the royal actor born
The tragic scaffold might adorn,
55   While round the armèd bands
       Did clap their bloody hands.

He nothing common did, or mean,
Upon that memorable scene;

But with his keener eye
60   The axe's edge did try.

Nor called the Gods with vulgar spite
To vindicate his helpless right;
       But bowed his comely head
       Down, as upon a bed.

65   This was that memorable hour,
     Which first assured the forcèd pow'r.
       So when they did design
       The Capitol's first line,

---

49. twining subtle fears] Cromwell is imagined as a spider spinning a web to catch the King. Cp. a similar image in the Leveller newsbook, *The Moderate*, 28 (16–23 January 1649), 261: 'our Laws were formerly like Spiders Webs, to catch the small flies, and let the great ones go'. *subtle*] a) of a fine or delicate texture (*OED* a. 2; the fears and hopes are the threads Cromwell weaves into a net) b) intricate (*OED* a. 8).

50. net] Sandra Billington, *N & Q*, 223 (1978), 512–13, notes that the net was the devil's property in the Morality drama, and was used to ensnare victims; see ll. 53–64 n. Cp. Fisher, trans. Manley, *Veni, Vidi, Vici*, 32, where Cromwell's Scottish foes are: 'beset by barking Hounds, intangled in a net'. *scope*] M. means 'degree' or 'extent' (the net is so 'large' that however Charles moves he inevitably travels to Carisbrooke), but the word has further resonances: a) plan, method of treatment b) ingenuity.

51. Margoliouth proposed the reading of the net chasing Charles to Carisbrooke. But taken as an adverbial clause, so that Charles chases himself, the line is more consistent with M.'s understanding of events, and what is now accepted as historical reality. *chase*] a) i) pursue (*OED* v.¹ 2 a). ii) hunt (*OED* v.¹ 1 a) b) hurry, rush, run with speed (*OED* v.¹ 6).

52. Caresbrook's] the seventeenth-century spelling fits the metre. *case*] a) box, prison (*OED* n.² 1). b) casement window (*OED* n.² 5) in Caresbrook, from which Charles tried to escape in March 1648. The Levellers called Caresbrook the mousetrap into which Cromwell had lured Charles.

53–64. scene (l. 58), like *actor* (l. 53) and *tragic* (l. 54), is a theatrical word. M. employs the contemporaneous theatrical imagery of the journalists, especially Royalist ones, some of whom had been playwrights. The practice dates from 1647, when some actors attempted to perform plays, despite prohibitions, and petitioned Parliament for freedom to act. The Royalist journal *Mercurius Vapulans* (27 November 1647), 7, likens Parliamentary proceedings to a performance of Shakespeare's *The Comedy of Errors*, and the movement against the King a revised version of Beaumont and Fletcher's *A King and No King*. Marchamont Nedham described the execution of the Marquis of Hamilton as if it were a theatrical performance: '*Be it knowne too, that when the three Lords were murther'd upon that stage of Tyranny*, Cromwell, Bosvile, *and divers others of the savage crew stood in a room belonging to the Star-*

Chamber, *scoffing, and triumphing in the ruine of the* Nobility; *and made use of perspective-glasses, that they might feed their eyes with those bloody Spectacles*', *Digitus Dei* (1649), 22. An older drama was seen in the regicide by a royalist sympathizer: 'This scene was like yᵉ Passion tragedie,/His sensuous Person none could act, but he.' (Anon., fragment of elegy on Charles I, Cardiff Central Library, MS 1.182, fol 33ʳ). See also Smith (1994), 70–92.

53–8. Cp. Charles Aleyn, *The Historie of that wise and Fortunate Prince, Henrie of that Name the Seventh* (1638), ll. 1987–90: 'Thus *he* was brought to act his fatall houre/ Upon a scaffold: to let *greatnesse* know/The twofold danger of too great a Pow'r,/To him that *hath* it, and the *giver* too.'

55–6. While . . . hands] Cp., *UCO*, 182–3: 'Him they diverted to the hands/Of those accursed bloody bands.'

57. common . . . mean] Charles became immediately famous for his dignified behaviour on the scaffold.

58. memorable] on the scaffold, Charles I is purported to have said to Bishop Juxon 'Remember', possibly to give his St George cross to Prince Charles: *King Charls His Speech Made upon the Scaffold* (1648), 13.

59–60. keener . . . edge] Cp. Herbert, 'The Search' (1633), ll. 53–6: 'When thou dost turn, and wilt be neare,/What edge so keen,/What point so piercing can appeare/To come between?'

59. keener eye] see l. 60 n.

60. axe's] a pun on Latin 'acies', which means both 'keen eyesight' and 'blade'. In addition to 'eyesight', 'acies' could mean intellectual keenness or debate. Friedman (1970), 265, notes 'in neo-Platonic psychology, *acies* denotes not only the gaze of the eye, but the interaction of the mind upon the image presented to it by the imagination', so that 'Charles is shown at the last moment to be aware of the personal, the political, and even the symbolic meanings of the fate he is about to meet'. Hence the *keener eye* of l. 59. *try*] test.

61. Charles does not rail against the gods on account of his unfortunate plight, as if he were a character in a conventional stage tragedy.

66. assured] a) legal; made sure of possession or reversion (*OED* v. 3) b) ensured, made secure (*OED* v. 1). *forcèd*] obtained by force, echoing the Latin phrase frequent in contemporary political writing: *vi et armis*, by force of arms.

A bleeding head where they begun,
Did fright the architects to run:
   And yet in that the State
   Foresaw its happy fate.

And now the Irish are ashamed
To see themselves in one year tamed.
   So much one man can do,
   That does both act and know.

They can affirm his praises best,
And have, though overcome, confessed
   How good he is, how just,
   And fit for highest trust:

Nor yet grown stiffer with command,
But still in the Republic's hand:
   How fit he is to sway
   That can so well obey.

85   He to the Commons' feet presents
A kingdom, for his first year's rents.
   And, what he may, forbears
   His fame, to make it theirs.

And has his sword and spoils ungirt
90   To lay them at the public's skirt.
   So when the falcon high
   Falls heavy from the sky;

67–72. Several Roman historians recount the discovery, during the construction of the temple of Jupiter Capitolium, of 'a man's head, face and all, whole and sound: which sight . . . plainly foretold that [Rome] should be the chief castle of the empire and capital place of the whole world', Livy, *Annals*, I.lv.6, trans. Philemon Holland (1600), sig. E1ʳ. The story is also related by Pliny, *Natural History*, XXVIII.iv and, earliest of all, Varro, *De Lingua Latina*, V.xli, but in all three, the head is not bleeding. Tarquin the Proud (the tyrant king who was expelled, resulting in the foundation of the republic) found a bleeding head, according to Livy a good omen for the greatness of empire (*Ab Urbe Condita*, trans. Holland, I.38). But at a feast later on, a serpent appeared before Tarquin and his guests, who were frightened, leaving Tarquin to ponder the meaning of the event. Hodge (126) suggests that M. may be conflating the head tale with the Tarquin story in order to communicate an ambiguous omen: the prospects for the republic are good, but the future may be bloody, the return of tyranny a possibility.

70. fright the architects] The execution of Charles I horrified many Parliamentarians and many supporters of the Parliament during the 1640s refused to condone the trial (notably Fairfax).

71. State] meant specifically as a republic (*OED*, n. IV.28 b); cp. Hobbes, *Leviathan* (1651), IV, ch. 45: 'when Augustus Caesar changed the State into a monarchy'.

73–80. Headnote, Modern Criticism.

73. Irish . . . ashamed] One treatise speaking on behalf of the defeated Catholic forces, its author being a member of the 'old Irish', did in fact shamefully acknowledge Cromwell's superiority to the royalist leader Ormond: anon., *Aphorismical Discovery* (after 1652), in Gilbert (1879–80), II.48, 53. The treatise invokes Lucan's description of Caesar's advance on Rome as a way of describing Cromwell, as does M. (see above, 268–71), although from a different source. See also Norbrook (1999), 247; Rankin (1999).

74. one year] Cromwell arrived in Ireland on 15 August 1649.

76. act and know] qualities attributed to Julius Caesar by Sallust, *Bellum Catilinae*, VIII.v.

81. Nor yet] not yet in time, implying negatively that Cromwell might go beyond his role of servant of the Republic in the future. *stiffer*] stubbornly contesting, hard (*OED* a. 8d); grown stronger in his unyielding nature. Craze (1979), 127, suggests the metaphor is from wax.

82. still] always, consistently.

83–4. A well known *sententia*: Plato, *Laws*, VI.762E, 'No one will ever make a commendable master without having been a servant first.'

85. Commons'] Bod. 1, Thompson; Common 1681. The annotated copy's reading makes Cromwell responsible to the House of Commons, the Rump Parliament, the major representative chamber of the republic. This reading is more consistent with the politics of the republic (the extreme radicals had been defeated), and with the Roman parallel of Pompey's relationship with the Senate (see *Headnote, Genre and Allusion*).

87. what he may] in so far as he can.

90. public's skirt] a version of the body politic image, which M. has largely avoided in the *Ode*, despite its prevalence in Roman and contemporary political consciousness. In an act of humble respect for the republic, Cromwell kneels before the feet of the national body politic, giving it his weapons and what he has won with those weapons.

91. falcon] 'Oliver is a Bird of Prey, you may know by his Bloody Beak', Clement Walker, *The History of Independency* (1660), II, 104. See also John Cleveland, *The Character of a London Diurnall* (1647), 5. Beyond such echoes in contemporary pamphlet literature, there is also a direct predecessor of this image in Dante's description of the flight of Geryon down to the eighth circle, *Inferno*, XVII, ll. 127–32:

> Come il falchon ch'e stato assai sull'ali,
>   che senza veder logoro o uccello,
>   fa dire al falconiere: 'Oime tu cali!' –
>
> discende lasso, onde si mosse snello,
>   per cento rote, e da lungi si pone
>   dal suo maestro, disdegnoso e fello.

(As the falcon, that has been long upon his wings – that, without seeing bird or lure, makes the falconer cry, 'Ah, ah! thou stoopest' – descends weary; then swiftly moves himself away with many a circle, and far from his master sets himself disdainful and sullen.)

Despite the purported rarity of Dante allusion in English Renaissance verse, Margoliouth notes the clear presence of *Inferno*, XXXIV, ll. 55–67, in *Tom May's Death*, ll. 17–18.

She, having killed, no more does search,
But on the next green bough to perch;
95   Where, when he first does lure,
         The falc'ner has her sure.

What may not then our isle presume,
While Victory his crest does plume?
         What may not others fear,
100   If thus he crowns each year?

A Caesar he ere long to Gaul,
To Italy an Hannibal,
         And to all states not free
         Shall climacteric be.

105   The Pict no shelter now shall find
         Within his parti-coloured mind;
         But from this valour sad
         Shrink underneath the plaid:

---

96. sure] Falconry and hawking manuals were at pains to give falconers ways of making sure that birds of prey did return to their lures: see, e.g., Edmund Bert, *An Approved Treatise of Hawkes and Hawking* (1619), II.iv, vii. If in the practice of falconry, the bird often does not return to the falconer, *sure* may read in a double sense, one of certainty, and one ironically sharing with the reader what falconers know through frustrating experience. The allusion to Dante (l. 91) would support this reading.

100. he crowns] Bod. 1, Thompson; *he crown 1681. he* is Cromwell, expected to crown England or Britain ('our isle', l. 97) with the honour of a conquered nation in each successive year. *crowns* suggests kingship and monarchy, though the *plume* (l. 98) is one of victory, not monarchical right. De facto power is thus enhanced.

102. Hannibal] Carthaginian general who invaded Italy in 218 BC, and left Italian soil undefeated in 203 BC, before being beaten in north Africa by Scipio Africanus at the Battle of Zama, 202 BC. Without ironic intent Cromwellian panegyrics compared their subject to Hannibal: Payne Fisher, *Irenodia Gratulatoria* (1652), trans. Thomas Manley as *Veni, Vidi, Vici* (1652), 10, 26–7, 71–2; *The Moderate Intelligencer*, 244 (28 June–5 July 1649), 1. It is the specific occasion, the threat of an invasion, which matters.

103. all states not free] Parliamentarian and Royalist journalists, though for different reasons, spoke of Cromwell eventually invading Europe to battle against the forces of the Counter-Reformation and, in prophetic and millennial rhetoric, Anti-Christ. France and Rome were the two places most frequently named. *free* 'the excellency of a Free State above a Kingly Government', Marchamont Nedham, *The Case of the Commonwealth, Stated* (1650), title page. 'Free state' was derided as the jargon of deceitful usurpers by Royalist writers, e.g., anon., *Traytors Deciphered* (1650), *passim*.

104. climacteric] pertaining to, or constituting, a critical period ('climacter') in the life of a person, institution or object. Associated with changes in health and fortune. Cp. Robert Gomershall, 'Upon the death of his worthy friend Mr Iohn Deane of New-Colledge', in *Poems* (1633), 8: 'Happy Deane then, who mayst call/Thirty, Climactericall,/And in spite of Envies sport/Prove thy good life by thy short'; Thomas Pestell, 'On the untimely death of *Henry* Lord *Hastings*', in *Lachrymae Musarum* (1649), 19: 'Up, Beldame *Muse!* thy Climacterick's past.'

105. Pict] The Scots. *Pict* (late Latin) could come from the *Pictavi* and *Pictores* in Gaul, but the Latin 'picti' means, 'painted' or 'tattooed'. Also associates with 'pictus' – 'empty', 'vain', 'deceptive': 'Hence then you proud Imposters, get you gone,/You Picts in Gentry and Devotion', John Cleveland, *The Rebel Scot* (1644), ll. 111–12.

106. parti-coloured] *1681* and *Bod. 1* have 'party-coloured', though this was the less common spelling at the time. Partly of one colour, partly of another; varied, diversified, chequered; takes from the significance of *Pict* (l. 105), and was part of the anti-Scottish vocabulary of the period, which was often of a non-specific nature. Here, however, the word is associated with republican criticism of the Scots, and their associates, the English Presbyterians, who had objected to the regicide, and some of whom refused the Oath of Allegiance: 'I wish this *parti-coloured* Doctor[,] that doth thus interlace excellent professions with so little adequateness of performance (to speak no worse) would consider how erratick his pen is from truth, (through the blindness of his passion) in his said vindication', [Anthony Ascham], *An Answer to the Vindication of Doctor Hamond* (1650), 1–2. See also *Mercurius Pragmaticus*, 27 (14–21 March 1648), sig. C3ᵛ: 'a *party-colour'd* coat of *Presbyterie*.'

107. sad] a) steadfast, firmly established in purpose (*OED* a. I 2) b) grave, serious (*OED* a. I 4) c) strong, valiant (*OED* a. I 3; M. deliberately uses a word with obsolete, chivalric associations) d) dark-coloured (*OED* a. II 8b; in opposition to the 'parti-coloured' picts). There is also an association with e) in martial terms, of blows delivered with vigour (*OED* a. II 10; like c), the meaning is already antiquated by the seventeenth century).

Happy if in the tufted brake,
10   The English hunter him mistake,
     Nor lay his hounds in near
     The Caledonian deer.   *allusion to Nimrod*

     But thou the War's and Fortune's son
     March indefatigably on;

115   And for the last effect
      Still keep thy sword erect:

      Besides the force it has to fright
      The spirits of the shady night;
      The same arts that did gain
120   A pow'r must it maintain.

---

109. tufted brake] clump of (fern or bracken) bushes. A 'brake' also meant a cage of wooden or iron bars and a trap or snare (*OED* n.⁶ 1).

110. hunter] an allusion to Cromwell as Nimrod (Gen. 10.8–10), the first emperor, who ended a patriarchal republic, but who acted by God's appointment. Nimrod became a tyrant and led his minions to build the Tower of Babel, cursed by God with the confusion of tongues. The Royalist press called Cromwell 'proud Nimrod in Ireland', *The Man in the Moon* (26 December–2 January 1650), 258. Writers defending the engagement used Nimrod, along with Julius Caesar, as examples of usurping tyrants to whom obedience was due by right of conquest. Milton explores Nimrod's later deeds in *Eikonoklastes* (1649), *CPW*, III.466, 598 and *Paradise Lost*, XII, ll. 24–63. M.'s reference seems only to underline the invincible power of Cromwell. *mistake*] a) pass by without noticing (because the plaid acts as camouflage) b) mistake for an animal (given the associations of 'brake', l. 109).

111. lay his hounds in near] put the hunting hounds on the scent of the Scottish deer.

112. Caledonian] Caledonia was the Roman name for northern Britain. In the seventeenth century it was a common literary term for Scotland.

113. War's] Bod. *1*; Wars *1681*; Wars' Donno. *Fortune's son*] 'Fortunae filius', Horace, *Sermones*, II.vi, l. 49.

114. indefatigably] unwearied; with unremitting perseverance.

115. last] lasting. *effect*] from the Latin, *efficere*, to accomplish; a) achievement (of Cromwell's art of state; *OED* n .7) b) impression rendered on the beholder (*OED* n. 6; Cromwell is seen again as an artist – see above, l. 21 n.).

116. sword erect] There has been considerable debate over whether Cromwell is carrying his sword upside down, to make the sign of the cross, warding off the 'spirits of the shady night', or simply drawn ready for battle. Generals on battlefields were usually portrayed carrying not a sword but the baton of their office. Duncan-Jones (*EA*, 15 (1962), 172–4) argues that M. is alluding to the pagan belief that cold iron terrified the spirits of the underworld (Homer, *Odyssey*, XI, l. 48; Virgil, *Aeneid*, VI, l. 260). The 'spirits of the shady' night would then become those defeated and killed by Cromwell, the ghosts of Charles I and the royalists. Given the rise of public sympathy for the executed king, instanced in the widespread circulation of the

Eikon Basilike (1649), the Puritan and republican identification of royalism and episcopacy with superstition and idolatry (connoted by 'shady'), and the reference to what Cromwell must do to remain in power in the future (ll. 119–20), M. is obliquely referring to the continued threat of royalist revival and counter-invasion. In *The Tenure of Kings and Magistrates* (1649), Milton used allusions to Shakespeare's *Macbeth*, in order to associate the Scots and the Presbyterians with superstition and perfidy. In a related way Marvell evokes the supernatural in order to warn of the power of revenge. Cromwell appears as guardian of state and religion, with an erect sword of magistracy, in William Faithorne's engraving *The Embleme of England's Distractions* (1658; see fig. 9).

118. spirits of the shady night] in Virgil, *Aeneid*, VI, ll. 290–4, Aeneas strikes with his sword at the bodiless monstrous forms: 'et frustra ferro diverberet umbras' (and vainly cleft shadows with the steel).

119–20. A sententia which goes back to Sallust, *Bellum Catilinae*, II.iv: 'Nam imperium facile eis artibus retinetur quibus initio partum est'. Womersley, *N & Q*, n.s. 34 (1987), 327, notes a similar pair of lines in Shakespeare, *King John*, III, iii, ll. 135–6, 'A sceptre snatched with an unruly hand/Must be as boisterously maintained as gained.' Cp. also Charles Aleyn, *The Historie of that wise and Fortunate Prince, Henrie of that Name the Seventh* (1638), ll. 1480–2: 'In Policie/'Tis a rul'd Case, *That as a State is gain'd,*/By the same Arts that state must be maintained.' M. is using the language of usurpation associated with the stage but in the context of the birth of the English republic. Cp. also anon., 'A Sonnet' (BL MS Harley 6918, fols. 22ᵛ–23ʳ), ll. 6–9: 'and by fierce warres obtaine a bloudy crowne/must by their sword maintaine their good renowne./And by continued force make their progression;/the self same Art that gets must still preserue' (James Loxley, private communication). Injunctions to maintain that which had been won by the sword were common during the summer of 1650 (see Norbrook (1999), 260–1), although M.'s lines also carry an echo of the ominous warning in Lucan, *De Bello Civili*, I, ll. 510–11: 'O faciles dare summa deos eademque tueri/Difficiles!' ('You gods that easily giue prosperity,/But not maintain it' (May, sigs. A8ᵛ–B1ʳ).

119. arts] the arts of war in the first instance, though also those of supreme statecraft generally. In Machiavellian terms, there is no difference between the arts of war and of peace.

Fig. 9
William Faithorne, *The Emblem of England's Distractions* (1658). By courtesy of the National Portrait Gallery, London.

The First Anniversary of the Government under His Highness the Lord Protector

Date. Late December 1654–early January 1655. The poem was probably written not for the anniversary, but after it, to be circulated in print as a propaganda poem. Topical references to events just after the anniversary (see below, l. 305 n.) support this dating. Harvard, MS Eng 1035, fols. 2–8 (*H 1*) appears to be dated 1655, then corrected erroneously to 1650.

Publication. A quarto edition of the poem appeared, unsigned, in the first month of 1655: Thomason dated his copy 17 January, and the pamphlet was advertised in *Mercurius Politicus*, 240 (1–18 January 1655) as 'newly printed and published'. *The First Anniversary* was entered in the Stationers' Register by its printer Thomas Newcomb (also the government's printer) only on 29 May, along with Waller's panegyric. There is no apparent explanation for this delay, although the entry confirms M. as the author. The poem was printed in *1681*, but cancelled from most copies.

Text. The text of the poem in *1681* was clearly derived from *1655*, as is the MS copy in Bod., Eng. poet d. 49 (*Bod. 1*), which was copied from *1655* (see below, *Title* n.). *1655* was prepared with particular care (*pace* Donno), its punctuation replicated in *1681*, and substantially followed, according to the same general pattern, in *Bod. 1*. These three texts carry more authority than the texts (related to each other) in Harvard, MS Eng 1035 (*H 1*), fols. 2–8 (a mid-to-late seventeenth-century verse collection, 'written for Gregory Boteler'), in BL MS Burney 390 (*BL 5*), fols. 19^v–22^r, and Bod. MS Eng. poet e. 4 (*Bod. 8*) (both late seventeenth-century verse collections in which *The First Anniversary* copies probably derive from earlier texts in circulation), despite the preferences shown by some editors, notably Donno, for *Bod. 8*. Indeed, the copies of the poem in all three MSS are erroneously attributed to Waller and have several lines missing (ll. 33–6, 65–6, 145–8). Both have entirely different punctuation schemes to the text deriving from *1655*, and are in some instances

insensitive to the nuances of the poem, in addition to other readings that are inconsistent with the poem's grammar (e.g. l. 24). I have accordingly preferred *1655* in nearly every instance.

Context. The Protectorate of Oliver Cromwell was established on 16 December 1653. The Rump Parliament, the centre of the republican government since its inception in 1649, was ejected in April 1653. Two months of great indecision followed until the establishment in July of Barebone's Parliament, notable for its radical membership. The internal incoherence of this assembly resulted in its removal by a coup on 12 December, and the acceptance by the army of the Protectorate constitution, Cromwell having refused the offer of the crown from some army officers.

The poem presents as Cromwell's success his rule by the Instrument of Government (l. 68), a written constitution drawn up by Colonel John Lambert and his associates. The Instrument represented a rejection of absolute parliamentary sovereignty, and of republican government, and a return to the tradition of a mixed constitution that was deeply rooted in national tradition. By the Instrument, power was in the hands of the Protector and a Council of State. The latter was meant to exercise a check over the executive. There was also to be an elected Parliament (which met first in September 1654), and successive election to the Council of State achieved by a complicated voting system involving Protector, Parliament and Council.

The Protectorate was a godly government, and its first nine months (before the Parliament met) could boast impressive, zealous reformation, together with the settling of the war with Holland, and treaties with France and Denmark. M.'s poem addresses the particular context of the first Protectorate Parliament of September 1654, which attempted to revise the Instrument, taking back some authority for Parliament from the Protector. M. is sensitive to the millenarian expectations generated by its meeting.

Despite the debate and hostility it aroused, the Instrument remained substantially unaltered, and was still the subject of debate when Cromwell dissolved the Parliament five days after *The First Anniversary* appeared. Then began a process of further constitutional experiment which resulted in the 'rule' of the Major-Generals, later in 1655. Of these matters the poem is entirely unaware.

The first year of the Protectorate was notable for a number of crises, many of which were indicative of the continuing instability of the state. On the domestic scene, republican hostility to the Protectorate was vigorous in the presses, and there were attempts by royalists and some disaffected republicans on Cromwell's life. The Quakers began to emerge as a significant force in the religious life of the nation: their message and their behaviour often frightened and produced hostility, especially in provincial places. Many Puritans, among the backbone of support for the Commonwealth, were disappointed by the government's failure to remove tithes. There were further complaints of legal abuses, and fears that a Protectoral court would lead to tyranny. Symbolic gestures against the Protector were frequent. Particularly relevant, in the light of M.'s praise of the navy (ll. 351–74) and his depiction of Cromwell with a faulchion (l. 384), is an example reported in *The Weekly Post*, 209 (9–16 January 1655), 1865: 'There being a stately ship in the Dock a[t] Wollage, with the statue and portraiture of his Highness the Lord Protector, erected above the stern, with a sword in the one hand, and a pistol in the other, trampling the Scots under his feet, was in the night exceedingly defaced, by having the Nose of this rich and glorious picture cut off.'

Yet none of these issues and movements feature explicitly in the poem. The sole public force of opposition to the Protectorate that M. mentions is the Fifth Monarchist movement (the 'Chammish crew' (l. 293)), an association of radical Puritans, mostly Independents and Baptists, who expected the imminent Second Coming of Christ to rule over his saints for a thousand years before the Last Judgement. Fifth Monarchists applied the prophecies in the Books of Daniel and Revelation to their own time, and they believed that it was necessary (even by force of arms) to reform society in order to help bring on the Millennium. They regarded the Protectorate as illegal, and protested against it from its inception.

Many Fifth Monarchists had previously looked to Cromwell as the hope of their godly vision:

John Spittlehouse, for instance, quoted Cromwell's speeches to Barebone's Parliament in his vindication of the Fifth Monarchists (*An Answer to . . . the Lord Protector's Speech* (1654)). Cromwell himself shared a degree of millenarian sentiment, but he was bold in his opposition to the Fifth Monarchists because he thought they disturbed property relations, and because they were spiritually fractious:

> But, I say, there are others more refined, many honest people, whose hearts are sincere, many of them belonging to God, and that is the mistaken notion of the Fifth Monarchy. . . . A notion I hope we all honour, wait, and hope for, that Jesus Christ will have a time to set up his reign in our hearts, by subduing those corruptions and lusts and evils that are there, which reign now more in the world than, I hope, in due time they shall do. And when more fullness of Spirit is poured forth to subdue iniquity and bring in everlasting righteousness, then will the approach of that glory be. (Cromwell (1988), 437.)

M. echoes the Protector's use of millenarian language in his speeches (e.g., see below, ll. 133–4), and like Cromwell, he presents this as the true form of waiting upon the Lord, as opposed to more militant forms of millenarianism.

Perhaps the most publicly extravagant Fifth Monarchist demonstration was the prophesying of Anna Trapnel in Whitehall during the early months of 1654, in response to the interrogation of the Fifth Monarchist minister Vavasor Powell by the Council of State (see Smith (1989), 44–53). Like M., Trapnel compared Cromwell to Gideon (see below, l. 249). There were many pamphleteers among the Fifth Monarchists, but it is notable that M. singles out Christopher Feake, the most important of the London Fifth Monarchists, and John Simpson, to whose congregation Trapnel belonged. Both men broke silence in mid-December 1654 to speak out against the Protector, both having previously prophesied against Cromwell at the very beginning of the Protectorate, on 19 December 1653: M.'s reference to them helps to date the poem (see below, l. 305 n.).

However, M. discusses none of the Fifth Monarchist speculation as to the kind of state which would immediately precede and prevail during the Millennium. He refers to their 'new king', but this betokens disrespect on M.'s part towards the Fifth Monarchists, since the king was supposed to be King Jesus. The Fifth Monarchists are instead reviled for their outlandish prophetic behaviour. They are deliberately confused with Quakers and Ranters (ll. 298, 305–7) (which reflects the actual fluidity of sect membership), while their particular interpretation of Scripture is presented by M. as a gross defacement of truth (ll. 315–16). No reference is made to the moderate political approach of many Fifth Monarchists (see Capp (1972), 136–51): M. celebrates Cromwell's victory (actually achieved through a series of arrests, extended imprisonments and trials) over what he presents as an unruly and dangerous crew, with heresies more numerous than armed rebels. All matter of constitutional speculation (Fifth Monarchists assumed that there would be rule by the elect in revived Hebraic assemblies or sanhedrins) is ignored for the sake of a discussion of Cromwell's role as a biblical magistrate, interestingly enough, in millennial terms. The discussion of magistracy begins early in the poem, considerably before the Fifth Monarchists are mentioned.

M.'s poem deftly responds to Fifth Monarchist key images and uses of the Bible: the poem avoids the passages from Daniel and Revelation popular with the Fifth Monarchists, and constructs an alternative image of the millennial state. Where the Fifth Monarchists saw destruction as a probable consequence of the Protectorate ('The Lord Jesus is making great hast, to break in pieces all these Kingdoms both new and old', Christopher Feake, *The New Nonconformist* (1654), sig. G2ʳ), M.'s Cromwell builds. To this extent, this portrait of Cromwell has been seen as that of the millenarian, Machiavellian state-builder, akin to the character of Olphaus Megalator (a thinly-disguised and idealized Cromwell) in James Harrington's *Oceana* (1656) (ed. Pocock (1977), 37; see also Norbrook (1999), 343–4).

The poem has been seen as an urging of Cromwell to be King (Wallace (1968), 106–44). There were continued attempts to offer the crown to Cromwell, and settle the succession on his heirs, in order to provide stability in the state. This was in opposition to the argument for an elective Protectorate, based upon the notion of an advantageous constitutional balance: 'If war be, here is the Unitive virtue (but nothing else) of *Monarchy* to encounter it; and here is the admirable Counsel of *Aristocracie* to manage it: if Peace be, here is the industry and courage of *Democracie* to improve it' ([Marchamont Nedham], *A True Case of the State of the Commonwealth*, 51).

Hirst (in Wallace, ed. (1985), 17–53), however, argues that the poem is a celebration of the Protector pure and simple: it closely mirrors the Protectorate understanding of statehood (Cromwell is a prince to the world, but a citizen at home). This was common Commonwealth propaganda (Hirst, 23), as was the picture of Cromwell as Providential ruler. The attachment of prophetic language to the figure of the Protector relates to Cromwell's own religious interests and behaviour (see Worden in Beales and Best, eds (1985), 55–99). Finally, the theme of anti-monarchical and yet imperial sobriety (see below, ll. 387–90) was much echoed as a way of appreciating the godly government of the Protector: 'to salute their Rulers and victorious Commanders with the names of *Caesares* and *Imperatores*; and after Triumphs, to erect for them their *Arcus Triumphale*: But if I mistake not, this day, is not any such outward Pomp or Glory, but that those who have been delivered together, might rejoice together', 'Mr Recorders Speech to the Lord Protector', *Mercurius Politicus*, 92 (9–16 February 1654), 3263–78 (3267). Thus, the detection of the various ways in which the poem presents Cromwell as an Old Testament judge (see Zwicker, *Criticism*, 1 (1974), 1–12), or the ways in which different models and ideals of governance are applied to the Protector (see Patterson (1978), 59–94), are best seen as argumentative devices in putting the Protector's case.

Yet if the poem offers apparent support to the Protector, the opinions of its author may not be so readily identified with this stance. Six months before composing *The First Anniversary* M. had expressed republican sentiments in a letter to Milton. Although M. does not so obviously qualify his praise of the Protector as Milton did in his *Second Defence* (May 1654), it may be that, like Nedham and Milton, M. voiced outward support for the Protectorate, while remaining privately worried by its threat to liberty. There are, significantly, no explicit references to the republican opposition to the Protectorate, while the imagery of Parliament as a building (ll. 87–98) constitutes an implicit modification of republican imagery from the early years of the Commonwealth (the *Second Defense* is also echoed: see below ll. 221–32). M. was friendly with the republican army officer, Robert Overton, who was placed under arrest in late December.

Sources. Even more so than *An Horatian Ode*, *The First Anniversary* is dense with allusion not only to contemporary politics, but also to the forms of expression by which that politics was constructed. At one level, the poem plays with the interest in the meaning and passage of time in the period. Some anti-Protectorate propaganda used astrology (sometimes in verse) to predict, from the early months of 1654, a coming calamity (e.g. 'Raphael Desmus', *Merlinus Anonymus* (1654)). Royalist astrology attacked William Lilly's pro-Protectorate astrology. M.'s poem looks back over the year, ridiculing these predictions (alongside his ridicule of Fifth Monarchist prophecy), by providing a reverse scenario – the history of the Protector's first year (which was by then in contrast a historical truth) in millenarian terms. The poem amplifies the 'official' astrology of the government-sponsored newsbooks: 'From Natural causes we predict that the influence of the superior Bodies in this month do rather intend high and admirable consultation . . . that the whole Western, and Northwest parts of Europe seemingly aim at peace' (*Certain Passages*, 74 (20 December–5 January 1654), 151).

Astrology aside, the poem is also a reply to hostile anti-Protectorate propaganda, a large part of which was written in verse. For instance, the resurrected royalist newsbook *Mercurius Aulicus* (possibly edited in this version by the republican John Streater) printed a series of poems that mock Cromwell by praising him: '*Indeed, my Lord, you'r mightier then a King,/He brings in glittering Trains, but you the Spring.*' 1 (13–20 March 1654), 6. M.'s poem responds in kind (see below, ll. 226, 255, 387–9), and is more generally related to a large number of anti-Protector poems. The Fifth Monarchists also published poetry as well as prose in their campaign. Some poetry was prophetic; some fused prophecy and scriptural interpretation with satire in order to attack the Protector: 'Nor shall from henceforth our *Protector* choose/Not to binde *Dragons*, but to set them loose' ('A Reply to the Libellers Satyrical Rythmes', in Edward Allen *et al.*, *Vavasoris Examen, & Purgamen* (30 March 1654), 45). Several versions of 'The Character of a Protector' poem circulated from at least June onwards; one was found in the possession of the republican Robert Overton (Thurloe, iii.75–6). For further echoes of these poems in *The First Anniversary*, see below, ll. 49–56, 200–3.

Large sections of the poem are indebted to the Bible: comparisons are made between Cromwell and a number of Old Testament figures. Hirst (in Wallace, ed. (1985), 24–6, 31) notes the appropriateness of presenting Cromwell as a prophet and magistrate rather than a king. These passages bear a direct relationship with Cromwell's parliamentary speeches.

Noah was regarded as a regal figure, but M. was at pains to show how Cromwell was neither vulnerable, nor kingly, like Noah. The Gideon parallel is entirely apt: like Gideon, Cromwell did refuse the crown. But the surprising omission is comparison with Moses, the leader and magistrate frequently invoked in Puritan literature both orthodox and radical. The Fifth Monarchists frequently expressed their demands in terms of the reintroduction of a Mosaic code. Instead, Cromwell as an agent of Christ is invoked by M., going beyond Mosaic comparison to outmanoeuvre the Fifth Monarchists in the description of an imminent millenarian future.

The debt of *The First Anniversary* to Waller's 'Upon his Majesty's Repairing of Paul's' (?1635) has been frequently noted (first by Nevo (1963), 26, n. 7, 111). In particular, M. compares Cromwell to Amphion as Waller does with Charles I:

> He, like Amphion, makes those quarries leap
> Into fair figures from a confused heap;
> For in his art of regiment is found
> A power like that of harmony in sound.
>   (11–15; see ll. 49–74 below)

Thus, M. takes an image hitherto associated with royalty and attaches it to the princely Protector. The allusion, which would have been immediately apparent to contemporary literati, is designed to enhance the sense of Cromwell as the leader who outstrips all monarchs. Charles' renovation of St Paul's Cathedral was a project begun by his father, while Cromwell, who renovates not merely one church but an entire state, starts from the beginning. (The poem's use of Waller may catch a further irony, since St Paul's was threatened with demolition throughout the 1650s, and during 1654 the south wall partially collapsed.) In Waller's poem, Charles is the recipient of heavenly benevolence, whereas Cromwell, as prophet and magistrate, is associated with divine agency (Charles is given good weather for his building, but he cannot bring rain (ll. 47–50), Cromwell brings the storm that purges the land (ll. 233–8); Charles is shone on by the sun (ll. 51–3), Cromwell *is* the sun (ll. 342–4); Charles breeds admiration in foreign princes (ll. 61–4), Cromwell breeds fear in them (ll. 377–8)). Amphion was a more appropriate political musician than King David, who remained a strong component in Royalist iconography (see Potter (1989), 161). Wilcher, *N & Q*, n.s. 41 (1994), 79–81, notes a similar set of ironic inversions, borrowing from and responding to lines from Francis Quarles's *Divine Fancies* (1632), IV.69, 'To King CHARLES' (see below, ll. 53–4, 67–74, 101–2, 348 nn.).

One of the sources for the Amphion story was Seneca's well-known *Hercules Furens*, ll. 262–3. Milton had quoted from this play against monarchical tyranny, while Royalist men of letters continued to publish translations of classical tragedies as veiled accounts of the tyranny of Parliament. Ancient tragedy remains a presence in M.'s poem until ll. 209–11, where the tragic chorus is invoked to explain the sense of impending grief at Cromwell's death in the coaching accident. Like Hercules in Seneca's play, Cromwell survives catastrophe and avoids a tragic end.

Revard, in Summers and Pebworth, eds (1988) detects an earlier debt to Pindar (especially his *Pythian Ode* 1, which begins with a reference to the pacifying powers of the lyre) and the tradition of Pindaric imitation in the Renaissance (see also below *Structure and Versification*). Other Cromwellian panegyrists also invoked Pindar, such as John Harmer's allusion to the *Olympian Ode* 10 (in his *Oratio serenissimi protectoris elogium complectans* (1654). Like Pindar, M. was interested in praising the achievements of a period of rule, while also recognizing the difficulties faced by the ruler and his government. Although most of Pindar's rulers were autocratic military rulers, they were sympathetic to democracies and hostile to tyrannies. These complexities chime well with Cromwell's own predicament and preferences. Like Pindar, M. sees his ruler as an agent of God, and does so with musical metaphors. Pindaric lyres were symbols of the cosmos since the lyre was also a constellation in the Greek sky, thus associating with M.'s uses of stellar imagery (ll. 101, 343). Although M.'s poem uses primarily biblical imagery, it shares with Pindar the presentation of enemies as serpents (with rulers as angels), and the presentation of the idealized ruler as an accomplished charioteer. The coaching accident, like Pindar's comparison of Hieron and Philoktetes (*Pythian Ode*, II, ll. 50–5), reminds Cromwell that he is mortal as well as an agent of heaven.

M. also took notice of the poetry published in the newsbooks. Raymond, *HLQ*, 62 (2001), 313–50, shows that M. used sections of George Wither's poem 'A Rapture occasioned by the late miraculous Deliverance of his Highness the Lord Protector from a Desperate Danger', and in particular the likening of

the riding accident to a mishap in an ancient chariot race. Wither's poem was published in *The Faithful Scout*, 201 (13–20 October 1654), 1610, and was an early version of the longer *Vaticinium Casuale*, published after M.'s poem, in 1655.

A number of individually and collectively published panegyrics on the Lord Protector were published in the first year of his rule. Many of these were in Latin. The academic collections, published in June in the aftermath of the peace treaty with Holland compared Cromwell with Augustus (e.g. John Owen, 'Ad Protectorem', in *Musarum Oxoniensium* (Oxford, 1654), 1). Most of these poems dwell on England's maritime power, and are concerned to document the Dutch war. To this extent, they hark back to the poetry of the previous year, with which M.'s *The Character of Holland* distinctly belongs. A few instances of Cromwell as pacifier of the cosmos are used: 'Ex tanto Melibaee Chao *Cromwellius* orbem/Restituit, formam rebus nobisque; quitem/ Praebuit', Rowland Guynne, 'Aecloga congratulatoria', *Musarum Oxoniensium*, [30]. This chimes with *The First Anniversary* in some respects (see, e.g., ll. 99–102). However, M.'s poem is more finely tuned to the constitutional and millenarian themes that dominated public life in the last three months of 1654. Some of these poems make reference to attempts on the Protector's life, an element absent from M.'s poem (e.g. *Musarum Oxoniensium*, 52, 55–6). Of these poems *The First Anniversary* borrows mostly from verse panegyric published in the newsbooks, and *Mercurius Politicus* in particular.

Genre, Structure, and Versification. Unlike *An Horatian Ode*, *The First Anniversary* does not adhere strictly to the pattern of an extant poetic genre. The poem consists of sixteen verse paragraphs of varying length. Wallace (1968), 114, divides the poem into seven sections: the comparison of Cromwell with the monarchs (ll. 1–48); the building of the harmonious state (ll. 49–116); the advent and postponement of the Millennium (ll. 117–58); the coaching accident (ll. 159–220); proof that Cromwell has not used arbitrary power (ll. 221–92); the attack on the Fifth Monarchists (ll. 293–324); the tribute of foreign monarchs to Cromwell's success (ll. 325–402). These sections are seen, principally by Wallace, to correspond to the parts of a classical oration: *exordium, divisio, confirmatio, refutatio, digressio, peroratio*. Each part is designed as an integral part of the poem's thesis, although M. departs from the classical insistence upon correct chronology by placing the consideration of achievements before birth and parentage, while a hypothetical lament for Cromwell's death precedes the account of education and choice of destiny. For Wallace (1968), ch. 3, the poem is an example of demonstrative rhetoric, seeking to present a case, while for Patterson (1978), 68 ff., the poem is deliberative rhetoric, an act of interpretation.

Patterson (1978), 79–80, regards the accident passage as an example of *soteria*, that part of rhetoric dealing with preservation from danger. The poem is exceptional here in that it evaluates near loss by actually imagining Cromwell dead. In this respect, the poem appropriates for the Protector the themes of triumphant escape, naval prowess and the excelling of other monarchs, voiced in Edmund Waller's *soteria*, 'Of the danger his Majesty [being Prince] escaped in the Road at Saint Andrews' (1623, publ. 1645). Norbrook (1999), 340, suggests that M. may in any case have been responding to Waller's *Panegyrick* on Cromwell, or Waller may have been responding to M., since the poems were so close to each other. He further speculates that M. would have been irked by the later attribution of his poem to Waller (see above, *Headnote, Text*).

Much of the poem's metaphorical, prosodic and syntactic inventiveness is dedicated towards support of the demonstrative structure. Thus, while there are instances of verbal ambiguity, these are harnessed to the purpose of demonstrating the viability of the Protectorate, rather than left in the more suggestive manner of *An Horatian Ode*. For the most part, one section or paragraph will end by triggering thematically the contents of the next one (e.g. ll. 43–4). Most of the poem is notable for its clarity, and this quality is at its greatest in the passages that are related to the printed propaganda of the Commonwealth (e.g. l. 22 ff.). The assured tone of the syntax (unlike that of the Cromwell elegy: see below, *A Poem upon the Death of his Late Highness the Lord Protector, Headnote, Style*), with sentence and clause breaks working confidently in and around the rhyming couplets, helps to generate the poem's persuasiveness. Syntactic inversion, where it occurs, not only affects rhymes, but may also mimic the care necessary for the proper ordering of the commonwealth (e.g. l. 96), or produce an arresting effect in the reader's mind, so as to draw attention to a particular point of reason or image (e.g. ll. 115–16, 201–2, 355).

The demonstrative rhetoric is framed by a series of powerful images that give the figure of Cromwell a dominant presence in the poem. The poem begins with the image of the sinking weight creating a maze of ripples in smooth waters: likewise, the brief tumult of a human life raises 'ripples' that are soon lost in the smooth flow of time. Cromwell transcends this limitation in order to confront the tempests of state: he 'raises' his head above malice and praise (l. 399) as opposed to mere men who raise ripples when they sink in time. The poem ends with the picture of Cromwell, as the angel of the commonwealth, troubling these stormy waters in order to calm them. The opening imagery of building and of stars returns in carefully deployed places later on (e.g. ll. 245–8; 343). There are similar double images on a local level (e.g. l. 186 where tears of grief turn to those of joy; see also l. 341). In another kind of juxtaposition, the demands upon the reader made by the musical and architectural images of construction are set against local instances of very clear images, examples of the *rebus*: e.g. the burying of china-clay to bake it (ll. 19–20). The most cryptic aspects of the poem are the usages of Old Testament prophecy. They are worked into the poem's language so deeply (and quite unlike their extravagant appearance in Fifth Monarchist tracts) that they appear to be part of the historical certainty that the poem offers. This certainty is only verbally disrupted to point up that which works (in vain) against it: thus there are some words that appear at first to be nouns or adjectives, but are actually verbs (e.g. l. 27).

Criticism. The poem attracted hardly any attention until the twentieth century. The exception is Samuel Parker's hostile remarks written *c.* 1687 (Parker (1727), 332–49), where the poem (the first 130 lines are summarized) is described as a panegyric on the Protector by virtue of its satire on 'all rightful Kings'. Parker is incensed by M.'s association of monarchs with Saturn, and he may have been inspired by M. to begin his history with a description of the Interregnum as an age of Saturn. The opening image of the poem was also apparently alluded to in another panegyric of 1656, in such a way as to suggest that M. had acknowledged in his poem the frailty of the commonwealth: 'And though some curlings of the waves appeare/The storm is past and in the calme we are' (anon., 'A Panegryric To his Highness My Lord Protector', in anon, *The Unparalleld Monarch* ([22 September] 1656), sig.

[13^r]). Legouis (1928), 208, asserted that the poem was inferior to Waller's *Panegyrick* on Cromwell because it lacked classical sobriety and clarity. Most twentieth-century comment has been concerned with understanding the context and formal structure of the poem, as opposed to offering any critical evaluation. Fowler (1970), 76–84, for instance, notices the effect of surprise by placing Cromwell's coaching accident at the centre of the poem. Hensley, *Ariel*, 3 (1970), 7, argues that M.'s poem is superior to Wither's on the same subject, but also contends that the richness of the imagery undermines the poem's success by being overwrought, even though M. displays 'a sophistication and sureness of control that Wither can hardly hope to match'. Nevo (1963), 113–14, notes the poem's presentation of Cromwell's singularity as leader and servant of Providence, showing 'judgement, guidance, and control', while the 'true inward nature of the heroic role is presented in a final brilliant metaphor of intelligent mission'. Zwicker (1993), 75–89, acknowledges these qualities, yet also admires the poem's evocation of a *gravitas* appropriate for the Protectorate, but regards its embattled brilliance as 'finally incoherent . . . both as form and as an act of social imagination. The poem is set within time and within society, but its energies are devoted to escaping those structures.'

Norbrook (1999), 340, regards these contrary movements as reason for admiration. The poem is 'wild and tormented . . . Marvell was trying to create a different kind of readership, one that was wary of Augustan cliché and open to religious enthusiasm and to Milton's calls for a radical sublime'.

The First Anniversary of the Government under His Highness the Lord Protector

Like the vain curlings of the wat'ry maze,
Which in smooth streams a sinking weight does raise;
So man, declining always, disappears
In the weak circles of increasing years;
5   And his short tumults of themselves compose,
While flowing Time above his head does close.
    Cromwell alone with greater vigour runs,
(Sun-like) the stages of succeeding suns:
And still the day which he doth next restore,
10   Is the just wonder of the day before.
Cromwell alone doth with new lustre spring,
And shines the jewel of the yearly ring.
'Tis he the force of scattered Time contracts,
And in one year the work of ages acts:
15   While heavy monarchs make a wide return,
Longer, and more malignant than Saturn:

---

1. *curlings*] ripples on the surface of the water ('curl', *OED* n. 3 c). *wat'ry maze*] i.e. the pattern of ripples in the water caused by the sinking weight.
2. *sinking weight*] in the nominative case: i.e. the weight makes the ripples in the water.
5. *compose*] settle (*OED* v. 9 a).
7–10. *Cromwell . . . before*] Cp. Jo. Ailmer, in *Musarum Oxoniensium* (1654), 96: 'our *Great Oliver* from a budding *Star*/Full blown a *Sun*, and fixt in's golden *Sphear*,/Beauty and warmth displaies, and with a *ray*/Of his *own light* creates us a *new Day*'.
7. *vigour*] Cp. Horace, *Carmina*, IV.iv, ll. 5–6: 'olim iuventas et patrius vigor /nido laborem propulit inscium' (at first youth and native strength drive him forth, ignorant of toils from out his nest). See also below, l. 11, and *A Poem upon the Death of his Late Highness the Lord Protector*, ll. 34, 252.
8. *stages*] periods of time, i.e. days, the periods of the sun's 'journey' around the earth.
9. *restore*] a) free from sin (*OED* v.^{1} 4 a) b) for Norbrook (1999), 339, 97, carrying a sense of Machiavelli's *ridurre ai principii* (reduction or return to first principles or lost perceptions). See Machiavelli, *Discorsi*, III.i.
10. *just*] deserved (*OED* a. 3a).
11. *lustre*] a) brilliance (*OED* n.^{1} 4 fig.) b) magnificence (*OED* n.^{1} 4c).
12. *jewel . . . ring*] the sun at the centre of the zodiacal ring; Cromwell's coat of arms contained a 'demi-lion rampant holding

in its dexter paw a gem ring or'. The sun was the tutelar planet of the lion: heraldry and astrology are merged (Margoliouth).
14. *in one . . . acts*] cp. *An Horatian Ode*, ll. 34–6: 'To ruin the great work of time,/And cast the kingdoms old/Into another mould.'
15–16. *heavy . . . Saturn*] Saturn, the planet understood (before the discovery of Uranus, Neptune and Pluto) to have the greatest distance from the sun, the longest orbit, and hence the longest year, was associated with lead, the heaviest metal. Under certain circumstances, Saturn could also effect a backwards motion. Saturn was appropriated as the 'muse' of royalist astrologers: 'Saturn's my servitor', 'Raphael Desmus', *Merlinus Anonymus* (1654), sig. A3^r. The Commonwealth's astrologer William Lilly associated Saturn with monarchy in a more critical sense: 'when *Saturn* is got into *Leo*, he gets into a Regall Sign, wherin he hath no right of Dominion, he stirs up in the minds of many men in those Regions . . . a desire to rule like a company of Kings or Tyrants', *Merlini Anglici* (1653), sig. B1^v.
15. *wide return*] very broad orbit, figuratively implying a deviation from the aims of government.
16. *malignant*] astrological term: having an evil influence (*OED* a. 3); 'malignant' was also used by Parliamentarians and Royalists as a term for each other as mutual opponents during the Civil War and Interregnum (*OED* a. 1 b, c).

And though they all Platonic years should reign,
In the same posture would be found again.
Their earthy projects under ground they lay,
20   More slow and brittle than the China clay:
Well may they strive to leave them to their son,
For one thing never was by one king done.
Yet some more active for a frontier town,
Took in by proxy, begs a false renown;
25   Another triumphs at the public cost,
And will have won, if he no more have lost;
They fight by others, but in person wrong,
And only are against their subjects strong;
Their other wars seem but a feigned contest,
30   This common enemy is still oppressed;
If conquerors, on them they turn their might;

If conquerèd, on them they wreak their spite:
They neither build the temple in their days,
Nor matter for succeeding founders raise;
35   Nor sacred prophecies consult within,
Much less themselves to pérfect them begin;
No other care they bear of things above,
But with astrologers divine, and Jove,
To know how long their planet yet reprieves
40   From the deservèd fate their guilty lives:
Thus (image-like) an useless time they tell,
And with vain sceptre strike the hourly bell;
Nor more contribute to the state of things,
Than wooden heads unto the viol's strings.
45   While indefatigable Cromwell hies,
And cuts his way still nearer to the skies,

---

17. *Platonic years*] calculated at between 26,000 and 36,000 solar years, and held by some to be the period in which a complete cycle of human history would take place, which would then be repeated in the following Platonic year. See Plato, *Timaeus*, 39d: 'The complete number of Time fulfils a complete Year when all the eight circuits, with their relative speeds, finish together and come to a head, when measured by the revolution of the Same and Similarly-moving' (Margoliouth). Cp. 'In Augustalia Serenissimi Domini & Principis, OLIVARII D. Protectoris', ll. 27–30, in *Mercurius Politicus*, 92 (9–16 February 1654), 3270: 'Protinus ad primum remeabunt omnia punctum,/Sanctus eritque *Plato* magnus Apollo mihi;/Aurea Saturni referetque *Platonicis Annis*/Secula; cum aeternis solibus *Annus* eat!' (From the first, everything turns back to its point of origin, claim holy Plato and my great Apollo; and golden Saturn concerns the period of Platonic years; with the eternal sun, the year flourishes!) Hirst in Wallace, ed. (1985), 39, attributes this poem to Marchamont Nedham.
19. *earthy projects*] worldly schemes.
20. *More . . . clay*] See above, *An Elegy Upon the Death of My Lord Francis Villiers*, ll. 31–6 n.
21–32. A critique of monarchy typical of the republic (whereas defenders of the Protectorate began to use the language of kingship): 'Monarchy having stood in *England* for many hundred years, accompanied with Troubles and Charges to the People sufficient; for whether Peace or War, the Supream was still in a height of Expence; in War, usually to feede his distempered thirst after conquest or revenge; in Peace to keepe up vaine (and often sinfull) pleasures', *Mercurius Republicans*, 1 (22–29 May 1649), 1.
23–4. *some . . . renown*] in September 1654, Turenne captured Arras for Louis XIV from the Spanish, who had held it since 1640.
23. *some*] a singular usage.
24. *proxy*] the action of a deputy (*OED* n. I 1).
25. *Another*] probably Philip IV of Spain.
27. *wrong*] a) harm b) perpetrate injustice c) dispossess.
30. *common enemy*] a relocation of a common Latin phrase, *communis hostis*, the enemy of the country (see Cicero, *Verrine Oration*, II.ii.6); for monarchs, the enemy of the state is the people who live in it; 'common enemy' had become a keyword among Parliamentarians: 'A New Representative must [b]e

had, but sit it cannot till the dissolution of this; if all chuse, then the chosen will be *royal* . . . Away therefore with that term the *Common Enemy*', *A Modest Narrative of Intelligence*, 6 (5–12 March 1649), 41.
33–4. *They neither . . . raise*] David instructs Solomon on the building of the temple in 1 Chron. 28.
36. *pérfect*] a) complete (*OED* v. 1 a) b) improve (*OED* v. 3).
37. *bear*] have.
38. *astrologers*] but M. was not ignorant of the advice offered to Cromwell's enemies by pro-Commonwealth astrologers: 'the *conjunction* of *Saturn* and *Jupiter* upon their last *Mutation* of *Triplicity* into another, such Nativities, I say, thus, or so concurring, was in the 8. deg. of *Sagitarius*, and the 19 deg. of *Aries*, the Cusp of the 4. House. If his *Highness* Enemies knew the force of what is delivered in the last Aphorism, and how it might be seriously applyed, none would conspire against him', William Lilly, *Ephemeris* (1655), sig. B1ᵛ. Cp. William Godolphin, in *Musarum Oxoniensium* (1654), 98: 'Tell me, Astrologers, th'Event; and make/From this conjunction a new *Almanacke*.' *Jove*] The classical god was sometimes used in the newsbooks as a name for the Pope. See, e.g., 'In Augustalia Serenissimi Domini & Principis, OLIVARII D. Protectoris', l. 10: 'Dein tremit *Italici* trina corona *Jovis*' (So trembles the triple crown of the Italian Jupiter), *Mercurius Politicus*, 92 (9–16 February 1654), 3270. See above, l. 17 n.
41–2. Like the lifeless, mechanical figures that strike the hour on clock-faces; 'image-like' also suggests an association with the frequent republican and Puritan charge that kings were icons and hence idols.
44. *wooden heads*] ornamental, carved head of the viol, into which the tuning pegs fit.
45. *indefatigable*] inexhaustible. Cp. *An Horatian Ode*, l. 114; *RT*, 24; James Fraser, Diary, Aberdeen University Library, MS 2538 (3 vols), I, fol. 33: 'as to his witt he [Cromwell] was a great headpeece, a most cautious, circumspect and prudent person always vigilant, indefatigable both in body and mind'. *hies*] speeds (*OED* v. 2).
46. *cuts . . . skies*] Cp. Tasso, *Gerusalemme Liberata*, trans. Edward Fairfax (1600), I.xiv, ll. 5–6: 'Thus clad he cut the spheares and circles faire/And the pure skies with sacred feathers clift.'

Learning a music in the region clear,
To tune this lower to that higher sphere.
   So when Amphion did the lute command,
Which the god gave him; with his gentle hand,
The rougher stones, unto his measures hewed,
Danced up in order from the quarries rude;
This took a lower, that an higher place,
As he the treble altered, or the bass:
No note he struck, but a new story layed,
And the great work ascended while he played.
   The list'ning structures he with wonder eyed,
And still new stops to various time applied:
Now through the strings a martial rage he throws,
And joining straight the Theban tow'r arose;
Then as he strokes them with a touch more sweet,
The flocking marbles in a palace meet;
But, for he most the graver notes did try,
Therefore the temples reared their columns high:

65 Thus, ere he ceased, his sacred lute creates
Th'harmonious city of the seven gates.
   Such was that wondrous order and consent,
When Cromwell tuned the ruling Instrument;
While tedious statesmen many years did hack,
70 Framing a liberty that still went back;
Whose num'rous gorge could swallow in an hour
That island, which the sea cannot devour:
Then our Amphion issues out and sings,
And once he struck, and twice, the pow'rful strings.
75   The commonwealth then first together came,
And each one entered in the willing frame;
All other matter yields, and may be ruled;
But who the minds of stubborn men can build?
No quarry bears a stone so hardly wrought,
80 Nor with such labour from its centre brought;
None to be sunk in the foundation bends,
Each in the house the highest place contends,

47–8. Learning . . . sphere] the music of the spheres was made by the planets rotating in their proper order; Cromwell is learning this celestial example in order to reorder the sublunary world according to such a perfect pattern: see Plato, *Timaeus*, 47c: 'through learning and sharing in calculations which are correct by their nature, by imitation of the absolutely unvarying revolutions of the God we might stabilize the variable revolutions within ourselves'; see also Plato, *Republic*, vii.530d.
49–56. Amphion . . . played] Amphion was the legendary founder of the city of Thebes; he built the walls of the city with the magical music of this lyre, as M. recounts: see Ovid, *Metamorphoses*, VI, ll. 176 ff.; Horace, *Ars Poetica*, ll. 394–6; Seneca, *Hercules Furens*, ll. 262–3. M.'s invocation is a positive counter to the Royalist use of Amphion: cp., anon., *Stipendariae Lachrymae* (14 July 1654), 8, 'sweet *Amphions* lyribliring tones./For whereas he could move but woods or Stones/I shall move men, and turn them into such,/If they already be not duller much.' A mock encomium on Cromwell invokes another mythical lyre-player, Orpheus, *Mercurius Aulicus*, 1 (13–20 March 1654), 3. See above, *Headnote, Sources*. Cp. also Lovelace's 'To my Noble Kinsman T.S. Esq.; On his Lyric Poems composed by Mr J.G.', ll. 13–16: 'As when *Amphion* first did call/Each listning stone from's Den;/And with the Lute did form his wall./But with his words the men.'
51. measures] a) tunes b) measurements, proportions c) appropriate action (legal).
52. Possibly echoed in anon., *The Burning of London* (York, 1667), ll. 99–100: 'Then shall it's Harmony our *Thebes* advance,/And make *rude Stones* into a *City* Dance.' *order*] a) in proper ranks b) legislative instruction. *rude*] rough, rugged (*OED* a. 10).
53–4. Cp. Francis Quarles, '69. *To King* CHARLES', *Divine Fancies* (1632), ll. 2–4: 'The divers sorts of people represent/The *strings*, all differing in *degrees*, in *places*,/Some *trebles*, and some *Meanes*, and some are *Bases*.'
55. story] a) stage or portion of a building (*OED* n.² 1) b) narrative, tale (*OED* n.¹ 5). *layed*] a) laid b) sang (see *Tom May's Death*, l. 14: 'Amongst the chorus of old poets layed').

58. And . . . applied] Cp. Milton, *Lycidas* (1637), l. 188: 'He touched the tender stops of various quills' (John Creaser, private communication). *stops*] action of pressing finger on the string of a lute to make a note (*OED* n.² 15b). *various time*] different time signatures.
59–63. Now . . . try] Hollander in Lord (1968), 34, argues that the 'martial rage' corresponds to the Phrygian musical mode, the 'touch more sweet' to the Hypolydian, and the 'graver notes' to the Dorian mode.
60. Theban tow'r] see above, l. 49.
63. graver] a) more serious and solemn (*OED* a.¹ 3b); *grave* is the technical term in music for a slow, solemn movement b) deeper in pitch (*OED* a.¹ 6).
66. There were six 'notes' of music, and one more to complete the octave; in the mid-seventeenth century, London had seven gates, including the postern at the Tower, or (more probably) London Bridge.
67–74. Cp. Frances Quarles, '69. *To King* CHARLES', *Divine Fancies* (1632), ll. 1, 5, 7: 'The Common-wealth is like an Instrument;/ . . . /The potent Rulers the *Musitians* are;/ . . . /The Lawes are like the *Ruled Bookes* that lye.'
67. consent] a pun: a) 'consent': compliance, voluntary acquiescence (*OED* n. 1) b) 'concent': harmony (*OED* n. 1) and hence 'agreement' (*OED* n. 2; 'consent' (*OED* n. 2)).
68. Instrument] a pun: the Instrument of Government was the constitutional proclamation of 16 December 1653 (more monarchical than republican in character) by which Cromwell ruled as Protector. See above *Headnote, Context*.
69. hack] a) break a note (*OED* v.¹ 6) b) chop (*OED* v.¹ I 1).
70. The attempts (mostly Parliamentarian, but also including the efforts of the constitutional royalists) to reform government in accordance with what was understood to be the ancient constitution.
71. num'rous] extensive (*OED* a. 1c).
72. island] Britain.
76. willing] a) accommodating b) compelling.
79. hardly] a) vigorously (*OED* adv. 1) b) with such difficulty.

And each the hand that lays him will direct,
And some fall back upon the architect;
85   Yet all composed by his attractive song,
Into the animated city throng.
     The common-wealth does through their centres all
Draw the circumf'rence of the public wall;
The crossest spirits here do take their part,
90   Fast'ning the contignation which they thwart;
And they, whose nature leads them to divide,
Uphold, this one, and that the other side;
But the most equal still sustain the height,
And they as pillars keep the work upright;
95   While the resistance of oppos**è**d minds,
The fabric as with arches stronger binds,

Which on the basis of a senate free,
Knit by the roof's protecting weight agree.
     When for his foot he thus a place had found,
100 He hurls e'er since the world about him round;
And in his sev'ral aspects, like a star,
Here shines in peace, and thither shoots in war.
While by his beams observing princes steer,
And wisely court the influence they fear;
105 O would they rather by his pattern won
Kiss the approaching, nor yet angry Son;
And in their numbered footsteps humbly tread
The path where holy oracles do lead;
How might they under such a captain raise
110 The great designs kept for the latter days!

---

85. *composed*] a) constituted (*OED* ppl. A. 3) b) made calm (*OED* ppl. a. 4) c) constructed (*OED* ppl. A. 2). *attractive*] a) pleasing b) that which attracts; compelling.

87–98. Cp. the parodic description of the commonwealth as carpentry in Thomas Randolph, *The Muses' Looking-Glass* (1638), III.ii, ll. 60–6: 'lest the disproportion break the frame,/He [the statesman] with the pegs of amity and concord/As with the glue-pot of good government,/Joints 'em together: makes an absolute edifice/Of the republic. State-skill'd Machiavel/Was certainly a carpenter.'

87–8. *The common-wealth . . . wall*] see *The Character of Holland*, ll. 17–18: 'How did they rivet, with gigantic piles,/Thorough the centre their new-catched miles.'

89–90. Those most contentious and antagonistic to order nonetheless help to secure it by their very transverse position.

89. *crossest*] a) lying most transverse (in the structure) (*OED* a. 1) b) most contrary, oppositional and quarrelsome (*OED* a. 5).

90. *contignation*] a) structure formed by joining beams together (*OED* 2) b) boarded floor or stage (*OED* 3), and hence suggesting the public sphere. Cp. Milton, *Areopagitica* (1644), *CPW*, II, 555: 'And when every stone is laid artfully together, it cannot be united into a continuity, it can but be contiguous in this world; neither can every peece of the building be of one form.'

92. *this one . . . the other*] the walls (of the state).

93. *most equal*] an oxymoron expressing the tensions within the political institution of the Protectorate; M. seeks to present them as productive forces.

94. *as*] like.

97. *senate free*] the first Protectorate Parliament of September 1654; but ninety of its members had been excluded for refusing to sign an engagement to the Protector as well as the Commonwealth; in any case, Cromwell had forced the disbanding of the more democratically elected Barebone's Parliament in the autumn of 1653. 'I said you were a free Parliament. And so you are whilst you own the Government, and Authority that call'd you hither.' *His Highnesse the Lord Protector's Speech to the Parliament . . . 12th of September, 1654* (1654), 2.

98. *roof's . . . weight*] the roof represents Cromwell, signalled by 'protecting', and implying his distinct influence on the decisions of his Parliament. Cromwell was 'sorry to understand, That any of them should go about to overthrow what was so settled, contrary to their Trusts received from the People, which could not but bring on very great Inconveniences. To prevent which . . . he was neccesitated to appoint a Test or Recognition of the Government', *A Declaration of the Proceedings of*

His Highness (1654 [14 Sept.]), 6. Yet Cromwell's own version of the building image gives the protecting role to Parliament: 'If the Lord's blessing and His presence go along with the management of affairs at this Meeting, you will be enabled to put the topstone to the work, and make the nation happy', Speech of 4 September, in Cromwell (1846), ed. Carlyle, 34–5. *99–102.* Norbrook (1999), 346, argues that the image introduces the dominant place of foreign policy in M.'s representation of Cromwell.

101–2. like . . . war] Cp. Frances Quarles, '69. *To King CHARLES', Divine Fancies* (1632), l. 6: 'The musicke, sometimes *peace*; and sometimes *warre*.'

101–3. like. . . . steer] 'Governours are like the heavenly bodies, much in veneration, but never in rest; and how can it otherwise be expected, when they are not made for themselves, or their owne glory. . . . We see the Sun by its Beams, serving the eye of the meanest Flye, as well as of the greatest Potentate', 'Mr Recorders Speech to the Lord Protector', *Mercurius Politicus*, 92 (9–16 February 1654), 3263–78 (3265). But see also the critical 'To his Highness the Lord Protector', ll. 3–6, *Mercurius Aulicus*, 2 (20–27 March 1654), 13: 'well I may/Have mine eyes dazled by the illustrious Ray/of so much luster, whose effecting Steel/Made Princes fall.'

101. aspects] a) gazes (*OED* n. I 1a) b) astrological influence (*OED* n. II 4). *like a star*] Cp. Pindar, *Olympian Ode* I, ll. 1–8, where Hieron of Syracuse is compared to a bright day star.

103. observing] a) watchful (*OED* ppl. A. 1) b) compliant, obsequious (*OED* ppl. A. 2).

105. pattern won] model of government established.

106. Kiss . . . Son] Ps. 2:12: 'Kiss the Son, lest he be angry, and ye perish from the way, when his wrath is kindled but a little. Blessed are all they that put their trust in him.' This Psalm is addressed to the kings of the earth. *Son*] Jesus Christ; the context is the widespread anticipation of Christ's Second Coming, which some Fifth Monarchists in particular (such as Vavasor Powell) thought would be in 1656.

107. numbered] another millenarian word from the prophecy of the end of Belshazzar's reign in Dan. 5:26: 'This is the interpretation of the thing: MENE; God hath numbered thy kingdom, and finished it.'

108. holy oracles] See also Dan. 7:18: 'But the saints of the most High shall take the kingdom, and possess the kingdom for ever, even for ever and ever'; Dan. 10:14: 'Now I am come to make thee understand what shall befall thy people in the latter days: for yet the vision is for many days.'

But mad with reason, so miscalled, of state,
They know them not, and what they know not, hate.
Hence still they sing hosanna to the whore,
And her whom they should massacre adore:
15 But Indians whom they should convert, subdue;
Not teach, but traffic with, or burn the Jew.
　　Unhappy princes, ignorantly bred,
By malice some, by error more misled;
If gracious heaven to my life give length,
20 Leisure to time, and to my weakness strength,
Then shall I once with graver accents shake
Your regal sloth, and your long slumbers wake:
Like the shrill huntsman that prevents the east,
Winding his horn to kings that chase the beast.
25 　　Till then my muse shall hollow far behind
Angelic Cromwell who outwings the wind;
And in dark nights, and in cold days alone
Pursues the monster thorough every throne:
Which shrinking to her Roman den impure,
30 Gnashes her gory teeth; nor there secure.
　　Hence oft I think, if in some happy hour
High grace should meet in one with highest power,
And then a seasonable people still

Should bend to his, as he to heaven's will,
135 What we might hope, what wonderful effect
From such a wished conjuncture might reflect.
Sure, the mysterious work, where none withstand,
Would forthwith finish under such a hand:
Foreshortened Time its useless course would stay,
140 And soon precipitate the latest day.
But a thick cloud about that morning lies,
And intercepts the beams of mortal eyes,
That 'tis the most which we determine can,
If these the times, then this must be the man.
145 And well he therefore does, and well has guessed,
Who in his age has always forward pressed:
And knowing not where heaven's choice may light,
Girds yet his sword, and ready stands to fight;
But men alas, as if they nothing cared,
150 Look on, all unconcerned, or unprepared;
And stars still fall, and still the dragon's tail
Swinges the volumes of its horrid flail.
For the great justice that did first suspend
The world by sin, does by the same extend.
155 Hence that blest day still counterpoisèd wastes,
The ill delaying, what th'elected hastes;

---

111. reason ... of state] the body of secular theories and practices of governance popular with Renaissance European princes and their advisers, and commonly seen by contemporaries as acting, if necessary, against law and Christian teaching: see Peter Burke in Burns, ed. (1991), 479–84.
113. whore] the Whore of Babylon (see Rev. 17:1).
115. Indians] a reference to the Spanish as opposed to English treatment of native Americans: see Evans (1996).
116. traffic] trade.
117. Unhappy] a) causing misfortune (*OED* a. 1) b) unfortunate (*OED* a. 2) c) unsuccessful (*OED* a. 2 c).
121. graver] a) more sombre b) more injurious.
123. shrill] shrill-toned. *huntsman*] Cromwell was frequently figured, positively and negatively, as Nimrod the hunter (Gen. 10:8–9), who was supposed to have overcome the heathen kings: see, e.g., Christopher Feake, *The Oppressed Close Prisoner* (1654), 3; see also above, *An Horatian Ode*, l. 110 n. *prevents the east*] appears before dawn.
124. Winding] blowing (OED v.² 3 b); cp. William Price, quoted in Christopher Wase, 'Certaine Illustrations of the *Cynegeticall* Poem of *Gratius*' (1654), 70: '*Come Lads and Wind your Horns, and Summon up/Your well-tun'd hounds unto yon mountains top.*' The kings in this line are imagined as the huntsman's dogs.
125. hollow] call (to the hounds in hunting) (*OED* v. 1 b).
128–9. monster ... her] the beast, Antichrist, commonly identified with the Church of Rome (see Rev. 11:7) or the Whore of Babylon. See also Rev. 17:3–18.
130. Gnashes] frequently used in the English Bible: see, e.g., Job 16:9, Ps. 37:12. *gory teeth*] see Rev. 17:6: 'And I saw the woman drunken with the blood of the saints, and with the blood of the martyrs of Jesus.'
132. High grace] being of God's elect.

133. seasonable] occurring at the right time (*OED* a. 1 a).
136. wished] desired. *conjuncture*] forecast (*OED* n. 1).
137. withstand] resist, oppose.
139. Foreshortened] a nonce use of a term describing an effect of visual perspective: apparently shortened in the directions not lying in the plane perpendicular to the line of sight. *OED* cites this as the earliest example (v. 2).
140. precipitate] bring on suddenly (*OED* v. II 3 b). *latest day*] Day of Judgement.
141–4. As opposed to the Fifth Monarchist sense that the moment of the Millennium had practically arrived: 'Let not him say as they said of old, who put the day far from them, that the Vision was for many days, for a time yet far off; But let them accept of the day and time that thou hast put into their hand: The Lord is building his Temple', Anna Trapnel, *The Cry of a Stone* (1654), 29.
148. 'The General . . . being girt with both Swords of War and Civil Justice', Marchamont Nedham, *A True Case of the State of the Commonwealth* (1654), 22. *Girds yet*] keeps on.
151–2. A compression of Rev. 12:3–4.
152. Swinges] lashes (*OED* v.¹ 4); see also Milton, 'On the Morning of Christ's Nativity' (1629), ll. 168–72: 'The old dragon under ground . . ./Swinges the scaly horror of his folded tail' (Margoliouth). *volumes*] coils of a serpent (*OED* n. III 11). *flail*] the tail is imagined as the hand-held weapon with spikes at the striking end (*OED* n. 2).
153. suspend] in water, at the Flood (Gen. 6:17).
154. the same extend] i.e. sin delays the last things; Dan. 9:26 predicts a final flood: 'and the end thereof shall be with a flood.'
155. counterpoisèd] kept in balance. *wastes*] decays, dwindles (*OED* v. II 12 a).
156. The ill] the reprobate.

Hence landing Nature to new seas is tossed,
And good designs still with their authors lost.
    And thou, great Cromwell, for whose happy birth
160 A mould was chosen out of better earth;
Whose saint-like mother we did lately see
Live out an age, long as a pedigree;
That she might seem, could we the Fall dispute,
T'have smelt the blossom, and not eat the fruit;
165 Though none does of more lasting parents grow,
Yet never any did them honour so;
Though thou thine heart from evil still unstained,
And always hast thy tongue from fraud refrained;
Thou, who so oft through storms of thund'ring lead
170 Hast born securely thine undaunted head,
Thy breast through poniarding conspiracies,
Drawn from the sheath of lying prophecies;
Thee proof beyond all other force or skill,
Our sins endanger, and shall one day kill.
175   How near they failed, and in thy sudden fall
At once assayed to overturn us all.
Our brutish fury struggling to be free,
Hurried thy horses while they hurried thee.
When thou hadst almost quit thy mortal cares,

180 And soiled in dust thy crown of silver hairs.
    Let this one sorrow interweave among
The other glories of our yearly song.
Like skilful looms which through the costly thread
Of purling ore, a shining wave do shed:
185 So shall the tears we on past grief employ,
Still as they trickle, glitter in our joy.
So with more modesty we may be true,
And speak as of the dead the praises due:
While impious men deceived with pleasure short,
190 On their own hopes shall find the fall retort.
    But the poor beasts wanting their noble guide,
(What could they more?) shrunk guiltily aside.
First wingèd Fear transports them far away,
And leaden Sorrow then their flight did stay.
195 See how they each his tow'ring crest abate,
And the green grass, and their known mangers hate,
Nor through wide nostrils snuff the wanton air,
Nor their round hoofs, or curlèd manes compare;
With wand'ring eyes, and restless ears they stood,
200 And with shrill neighings asked him of the wood.
    Thou Cromwell falling, not a stupid tree,
Or rock so savage, but it mourned for thee:

157–8. Cp. [Nedham], *A True Case of the State of the Commonwealth*, 34: 'it was high time, some Power should pass a Decree upon the wavering humors of the People, and say to this Nation, as the Almighty himself said once to the unruly Sea; *Here shall be thy Bounds, hitherto shalt thou come, and no further.*'
157. landing] coming into land from the sea.
160. mould] see *An Horatian Ode*, ll. 35–6, 'And cast the Kingdom old/ Into another mould'.
161–2. Whose . . . pedigree] Elizabeth Cromwell (née Steward), Oliver's mother, died on 16 November 1654, at the age of 93.
161. saint-like] 'Madam . . . Your life it was most full of Love/ To creatures in distress', J. L[onge], *An Epitaph On the late deceased, that truely-Noble and Renowned Lady ELIZABETH CROMWELL* ([25 November] 1654), broadsheet.
162. pedigree] line of ancestors (*OED* n. 2 a).
166. Yet . . . so] 'Thou for us hast born and bred/One truely such another/ In Wisdom, Valour, and Goodness,/That freed us from the chains/Of Tyrants great', J. L[ONGE], *An Epitaph On the late deceased, that truely-Noble and Renowned Lady ELIZABETH CROMWELL* ([NOV., 25], 1654), broadsheet. 'Contrary to her expressed wishes, [Elizabeth Cromwell's] funeral was solemnized with great pomp and she was buried in Westminster Abbey on the following Sunday evening' Abbott, III.506.
170. undaunted] undismayed (*OED* ppl. a. 3).
171–2. Cromwell faced several conspiracies and assassination attempts, in addition to the activities of the Fifth Monarchists, during his first year as Protector: see above *Headnote, Context.*
171. poniarding] lethal: literally, 'stabbing with a poniard', a poniard being a short dagger, designed for assassination.
175. How near] i.e. 'by what a narrow margin'.

176. assayed] a) tried b) made a test of.
177–80. Our brutish . . . hairs] Cromwell's coach overturned while he was driving its six horses in Hyde Park on 29 September 1654.
177. brutish] a) wild, of the animals (but they were gifts from the Count of Oldenburgh) (*OED* a. 2) b) British (*OED* obscure).
178. Hurried] agitated (*OED* v. 3). *hurried*] went with speed (*OED* v. 1).
182. yearly] i.e. anniversary.
184. purling ore] gold or silver thread used in embroidery.
186. Still] a) yet b) frozen, since fixed in a piece of embroidery.
189. impious] irreligious, wicked.
190. retort] turn back against them (*OED* v.[1] II 5).
191–200. Echoes the lament of the horses for Automedon, slain by Hector: Homer, *Iliad*, XVII, ll. 426–40.
191. poor beasts] i.e. the coach horses.
195. abate] lower.
197. wide . . . air] Cp. Virgil, *Georgics*, I, ll. 375–6: 'aut bucula caelum/suspiciens patulis captavit naribus auras' (or the heifer looks up to heaven, and with open nostrils snuffs the breeze). *wanton*] healthy (*OED* A a. 7 b).
200–3. him . . . groan] M.'s depiction of Pan's response to Cromwell's accident is a reply to contemporary uses of Pan as a figure of retirement from public life during the Commonwealth period: 'As times come right so I become a Man/Of a right minde And list ye who Tis *Pan*/ Take Horne and Feather who wil But if none please/To give themselves a little Pannick ease/Ile keep them somewhere', anon., *The Paynim's Songs* (1654, 8 July), 5.
201. stupid] senseless (*OED* a. 2).
202. savage] wild.

And all about was heard a panic groan,
As if that Nature's self were overthrown.
5　It seemed the earth did from the centre tear;
　　It seemed the sun was fall'n out of the sphere:
　　Justice obstructed lay, and Reason fooled;
　　Courage disheartened, and Religion cooled.
　　A dismal silence through the palace went,
0　And then loud shrieks the vaulted marbles rent.
　　Such as the dying chorus sings by turns,
　　And to deaf seas, and ruthless tempests mourns,
　　When now they sink, and now the plund'ring streams
　　Break up each deck, and rip the oaken seams.
5　　But thee triumphant hence the fiery car,
　　And fiery steeds had borne out of the war,
　　From the low world, and thankless men above,
　　Unto the kingdom blest of peace and love:
　　We only mourned ourselves, in thine ascent,

220　Whom thou hadst left beneath with mantle rent.
　　　For all delight of life thou then didst lose,
　　When to command, thou didst thyself depose;
　　Resigning up thy privacy so dear,
　　To turn the headstrong people's charioteer;
225　For to be Cromwell was a greater thing,
　　Than ought below, or yet above a king:
　　Therefore thou rather didst thyself depress,
　　Yielding to rule, because it made thee less.
　　　For, neither didst thou from the first apply
230　Thy sober spirit unto things too high,
　　But in thine own fields exercised'st long,
　　An healthful mind within a body strong;
　　Till at the seventh time thou in the skies,
　　As a small cloud, like a man's hand didst rise;
235　Then did thick mists and winds the air deform,
　　And down at last thou poured'st the fertile storm;

---

203. panic] a) of the god of nature, Pan (*OED* a. 1 a) b) of excessive fear (*OED* a. 1 b); cp. anon., 'Obsequies. To the Memory of the truly Noble, Right Valiant, and Right Honourable, Spencer, Earl of Northampton' (1643) in Cleveland, *Poems* (1669), 128: 'Wast not a Pannick dread surpriz'd thy soul/Of being made servile to his high controul?' c) universal (*OED* a. 3).

205–6. In the Ptolemaic system of astronomy, the earth is at the centre of the universe, the sun in the fourth of the concentric spheres around it; both are knocked out of their place by Cromwell's accident. Norbrook (1999), 347, suggests that these hyperboles might have been found in an elegy for Charles I.

208. disheartened] see above, l. 70 n. *cooled*] lost its zeal.

209–11. See above, *Headnote, Sources and Genre.*

209. dismal] a) sinister (*OED* B a. 2) b) gloomy, depressing (*OED* B a. 4).

213–14. The opposite of Cromwell's stated intentions: 'that this ship of the Commonwealth may be brought into a safe harbour, which I assure you it will not well be without your counsel and advice', Speech to the Parliament, 4 September 1654, Cromwell (1988), 442.

214. seams] rivets fastening overlapping edges of a clinker-built boat (*OED* n.⁴).

215–20. See 2 Kings 2: 11–13: Cromwell is figured here as Elijah, who was taken up to heaven in a whirlwind after the appearance of a fiery chariot and horses, leaving his mantle behind. M. may be turning around Christopher Feake's comparison of Cromwell with Ahab, exposed by Elijah at 1 King 21:20 (Feake, *The Oppressed Prisoner* (1654, 19 December), 82–3). In *A Jolt on Michaelmas Day* (1654), Cromwell is compared to Phaeton (being saved only for the hangman's cart), and in Wither's *Vaticinium Causuale* (1654), to Hippolytus, the lucky escape being the work of Providence. Cromwell's accident represents a reversal of the image of tyranny described by Plato, *Republic*, viii.566, which is itself indebted to Homer's description of the death of the charioteer Cebriones (*Iliad*, XVI, l. 776): 'then obviously that protector does not lies prostrate, "mighty with far-flung limbs", in Homeric overthrow, but overthrowing many others' towers in the car of

state transformed from a protector into a perfect and finished tyrant.'

218. See Milton, *Lycidas* (1637), l. 177: 'In the blest kingdoms meek of joy and love' (Margoliouth).

219–20. We . . . mantle rent] Elijah's mantle falls from him, to be recovered by Elisha, who had just 'rent' his own clothes in two: 2 Kings 2:12–13. Unlike Elisha, the 'we' left below do not take up the mantle and assume Elijah's (Cromwell's) authority.

221–32. Cp. *An Horatian Ode*, ll. 27–32, and Milton, *Second Defence* (1654), 150–1: 'non evehi te quidem, sed tot gradibus ex sublimi descendere, & velut in ordinem cogi, publico commodo, . . . regium nomen majestate longè majore aspernatus' (*CPW*, IV.i.672: 'You suffered and allowed yourself, not indeed to be borne aloft, but to come down many degrees from the heights and be forced into a definite rank, so to speak, for the public good. . . . The name of king you spurned from your great eminence, and rightly so. For if when you became so great a figure, you were captivated by the title which as a private citizen you were able to send under the yoke and reduce to nothing.')

222. depose] dethrone (from his state of privacy).

224. turn] become.

226. ought] anything.

227. depress] a) lower in station and dignity (*OED* v. 3, 4) b) lower in vigour (*OED* v. 5).

233–8. Till at . . . king] see 1 Kings 18:43–45: M. compares Cromwell to the cloud that appeared 'like a man's hand' out of the sea, seen on the seventh time of looking by Elijah's servant; a great storm followed (see below, l. 238).

236. thou poured'st . . . storm] there had been an official fast for rain in March 1654; Cromwell was held to have the power to bring rain by his prayers: Abbott (1945), III, 228. Waller noted that Charles I had been unable to invoke rain: 'Upon His Majesty's Repairing of Paul's' (?1635), ll. 48–50. See also Jo. Forde, 'Awake thou stupid World', ll. 28, 30–2, in *Musarum Oxoniensium* (1654), 100: 'Heav'ns to us have signes of favour borne./ . . . When they spake through the Clouds what we would have; To wit, when our late Fast they did prevent;/And store of Raine before we sought it, sent.'

Which to the thirsty land did plenty bring,
But though forewarned, o'ertook and wet the king.
    What since he did, an higher force him pushed
240 Still from behind, and it before him rushed,
Though undiscerned among the tumult blind,
Who think those high decrees by man designed.
'Twas heaven would not that his pow'r should cease,
But walk still middle betwixt war and peace;
245 Choosing each stone, and poising every weight,
Trying the measures of the breadth and height;
Here pulling down, and there erecting new,
Founding a firm state by proportions true.
    When Gideon so did from the war retreat,
250 Yet by the conquest of two kings grown great,
He on the peace extends a warlike power,
And Israel silent saw him raze the tower;
And how he Succoth's Elders durst suppress,
With thorns and briars of the wilderness.
255 No king might ever such a force have done;

Yet would not he be Lord, nor yet his son.
    Thou with the same strength, and an heart as plai
Didst (like thine olive) still refuse to reign;
Though why should others all thy labour spoil,
260 And brambles be anointed with thine oil,
Whose climbing flame, without a timely stop,
Had quickly levelled every cedar's top.
Therefore first growing to thyself a law,
Th'ambitious shrubs thou in just time didst awe.
265   So have I seen at sea, when whirling winds,
Hurry the bark, but more the seamen's minds,
Who with mistaken course salute the sand,
And threat'ning rocks misapprehend for land;
While baleful Tritons to the shipwreck guide,
270 And corposants along the tacklings slide.
The passengers all wearied out before,
Giddy, and wishing for the fatal shore;
Some lusty mate, who with more careful eye
Counted the hours, and every star did spy,

---

238. though forewarned] Ahab was warned by Elijah to prepare for rain when he rode to Jezreel in his chariot: 1 Kings 18:44. Here Ahab obliquely represents Charles I.
239. since] i.e. since 1649. *higher force*] Providence (see l. 243).
241. tumult] disorderly crowd (*OED* n. 1).
243–4. Cp. *An Horatian Ode*, ll. 25–6: 'So restless Cromwell could not cease/In the inglorious arts of peace.'
244. One of the Cromwell family mottoes was *pax quaeritur bello* (Margoliouth). Cicero (*Phillipics*, VIII.i.4) declared that this was impossible: 'cum inter bellum et pacem medium nihil sit' (between war and peace is no middle ground) (Duncan-Jones).
249–56. See Judges 8:1–23. After his defeat of Zeba and Zalmunna, Gideon refused the crown of Israel for himself and his heirs, because he claimed the Lord was the true ruler. Cromwell was compared to Gideon, and ironically so by Fifth Monarchists during the Protectorate: see Anna Trapnel, *The Cry of a Stone* (1654), 29. The biblical episode corresponds with Cromwell's expulsion of the Rump and Barebone's Parliaments, before he refused the crown. See Loewenstein (2001), 167–9.
250. two kings] Cromwell had also conquered two kings: Charles I and Charles II.
252. raze the tower] of Penuel (Judges 8:17).
253–4. Succoth's Elders ... wilderness] Judges 8:16: 'And he took the elders of the city [of Succoth], and thorns of the wilderness and briers, and with them he taught the men of Succoth.' Gideon's action is exactly comparable with Cromwell's in dissolving parliaments: the men of Succoth had refused to provide supplies for the army, just as the Rump and Barebone's had shown a similar reluctance.
257–62. This passage is drawn from Judges 9:7–15, Jotham's fable of the trees' attempt to elect a king from among themselves; they are eventually forced to turn to the bramble, who represents Abimelech, a bastard son of Gideon, with whom the trees (the men of Shechem) are happy. But in M.'s version, the brambles obliquely represent the Levellers, republicans and millenarians whose progress the Protectorate was designed to

stop (see l. 262), while the olive is Cromwell himself. See also *RT*, 24.
258. still refuse to reign] Cromwell had refused an offer of the crown just before the adoption of the Instrument of Government on 12 December 1653; a proposal to offer the crown was made in the Council of State on 23 December but withdrawn. Similar proposals were again discussed in June 1655; Cromwell was formally offered the crown in May 1657.
260–2. See Judges 9:15: 'And the bramble said unto the trees, If in truth ye anoint me king over you, then come and put your trust in my shadow: and if not, let fire come out of the bramble, and devour the cedars of Lebanon.' Anointing oil was used of magistrates as well as kings.
264. ambitious shrubs] One of Anna Trapnel's visions was of the saints as 'little shrubs', who are saved from 'great Oaks' (monarchs and Cromwell) by the 'lovely tree' of Christ: Trapnel, *The Cry of a Stone* (1654), 12–13. *ambitious*] Latin *ambitiosus* means 'embracing' or 'twining round'. The literal image is of the shrubs clinging to Cromwell, threatening to bring him down. *in just time*] a) exactly as calculated (*OED* a. 9) b) just in time. *awe*] a) restrain with fear (*OED* v. 1) b) inspire with wonder (*OED* v. 3).
265–78. Cp. Cromwell, Speech to the First Parliament, 4 September 1654: 'It's one of the great ends of Calling this Parliament, that the Ship of the Commonwealth may be brought into a safe harbour' (Carlyle, 35); 'to save a sinking Nation out of the gulf of mistery and confusion, caused by the changeable Counsels and corrupt Interests of other men', [Nedham], *A True Case*, 28.
266. Hurry] a) propel with excessive speed (with regard to the first clause of the sentence) (*OED* v. 1) b) worry, agitate (with regard to the second clause) (*OED* v. 3).
267. salute] incline towards (*OED* v. 5).
268. misapprehend] mistake for.
269. baleful] malign. *Tritons*] sea deities or sea monsters.
270. corposants] balls of light sometimes seen about the masts or yard-arms of ships during storms (from *corpus sanctum*, 'holy body'); also known as St Elmo's fire. *tacklings*] ship's rigging (*OED* vbl. n. 1 b).

75 The helm does from the artless steersman strain,
    And doubles back unto the safer main.
    What though a while they grumble discontent,
    Saving himself he does their loss prevent.
      'Tis not a freedom, that where all command;
80 Nor tyranny, where one does them withstand:
    But who of both the bounders knows to lay
    Him as their father must the state obey.
      Thou, and thine house, like Noah's eight did rest,
    Left by the wars' flood on the mountain's crest:
85 And the large vale lay subject to thy will,
    Which thou but as an husbandman wouldst till:
    And only didst for others plant the vine
    Of liberty, not drunken with its wine.
      That sober liberty which men may have,
90 That they enjoy, but more they vainly crave:
    And such as to their parent's tents do press,

    May show their own, not see his nakedness.
      Yet such a Chammish issue still does rage,
    The shame and plague both of the land and age,
295 Who watched thy halting, and thy fall deride,
    Rejoicing when thy foot had slipped aside;
    That their new king might the fifth sceptre shake,
    And make the world, by his example, quake:
    Whose frantic army should they want for men
300 Might muster heresies, so one were ten.
    What thy misfortune, they the Spirit call,
    And their religion only is to fall.
    Oh Mahomet! now couldst thou rise again,
    Thy falling-sickness should have made thee reign,
305 While Feake and Simpson would in many a tome,
    Have writ the comments of thy sacred foam:
    For soon thou mightst have passed among their rant
    Were't but for thine unmovèd tulipant;

---

275. artless] unskilful. *strain*] grip tightly (*OED* v.[1] I 3 b).
276. main] open sea (*OED* n.[1] 5).
281. bounders] limits (*OED* n. II 4).
283–4. Cromwell, his wife and six surviving children are compared to Noah and his family. The ark resting on Mount Ararat is represented in the top left hand corner of William Faithorne's engraving of Cromwell between the pillars (1658; see fig. 9).
286–94. See Gen. 9:20–25, where Noah becomes a husbandman, plants a vineyard, and lies drunken and naked in his tent. Ham saw him and told his brothers Shem and Japheth, for which impiety he and his descendants were cursed. Cromwell, unlike Noah, remains sober, but the 'sons of Ham' (the religious and political radicals: see below, l. 293 n.) in seeking to enter Cromwell's tent and see his 'nakedness' only reveal their own.
286. husbandman] 'That he knows how and when to answer the expectation of the Husbandman, and when to hear, even the mourning of the brute Beast, who will yet much more hear the desires of them that fear him, and that in the fittest season,' *By the Lord Protector. A Declaration of his Highness, Setting apart* Tuesday *the 23. of this present* May *for a publique day of thanksgiving* (9 May 1654), in Cromwell (1988), 290–1.
293. Chammish] like or of Ham ('Cham' is the Vulgate spelling), second son of Noah, and progenitor of the tyrant Nimrod.
297. new king] the Fifth Monarchists expected the literal return of Jesus as King; M. might be referring to the Fifth Monarchists' most likely military leader, Thomas Harrison, who had been confined to his father's house in Staffordshire in February 1654, but who was not imprisoned until 15 February 1655. *fifth sceptre*] an allusion to the Fifth Monarchists: see above *Headnote, Context . .*
298. quake] an allusion to the Quakers.
299–300. for men . . . ten] One heresy is equal to ten men; an army made of heresies would thus be very large indeed; cp. Cowley, *The Civil War*, III, ll. 187–8: 'Theise are the loathsome Haeresies that sent/An Army forth for theire deare Parlament.'
301. the Spirit] all religious radicals claimed the direct inspiration of the Holy Spirit: see Nuttall (1946).
302–4. And their . . . reign] the sects are compared to Mahomet, who prophesied during epileptic fits.

302. fall] into a fit.
304. falling-sickness] epilepsy.
305. Feake and Simpson] Christopher Feake (1612–*c.* 1683) and John Simpson (d. 1662), leaders of the Fifth Monarchist movement. Both had been imprisoned together in Windsor Castle since January 1654, but Simpson was released in July on the condition that he came no closer to London than ten miles. Simpson flouted this requirement and preached in his old pulpit, Allhallows, on the two days following the anniversary of the Protectorate, while Feake's denunciation of Cromwell, *The Oppressed Close Prisoner in Windsor Castle* was issued on 19 December. Simpson preached at Allhallows on Christmas Day; Feake remained imprisoned (*Certain Passages*, 74 (20 December 1654–5 January 1655), 157). Marchamont Nedham, who was connected with the production and publication of M.'s poem, attended and informed on Fifth Monarchist meetings in December 1653, leading to the imprisonment of Feake, and in February 1654, after which he stressed the preaching powers of both Feake and Simpson. The famous Fifth Monarchist prophet Anna Trapnel, who prophesied in trances, was a member of Simpson's Baptist congregation. Feake and Simpson were important to M. because they had prophesied against the Protectorate at its start and on its first anniversary: his poem is a reply in kind. Cromwell had interviewed them both in December 1654, an instance of the closeness of his relationship with his antagonists (because former friends), which leads Hirst (1985), 43, to suggest that M. was warning Cromwell away from the Fifth Monarchists.
306. foam] saliva produced during an epileptic fit.
307. rant] a general term for sectarian preaching, but with an allusion to the Ranters, the most libertarian of the sects (if still active in 1654–55, they had ceased to be very visible since their persecution by the Rump in 1650–51).
308. tulipant] turban; Muslims, like Diggers and Quakers, refused to uncover their heads; like Diggers and Quakers, Mahomet would not be accepted among the Fifth Monarchists (most of whom were less extreme Independents and Baptists, but in some of Feake's meetings, hats were kept on (J.N., *Proh Tempora! Proh Mores!* (1654)) because he would not remove his turban.

As thou must needs have owned them of thy band
310 For prophecies fit to be Alcoran'd.
    Accursèd locusts, whom your king does spit
Out of the centre of th'unbottomed pit:
Wand'rers, adult'rers, liars, Münzer's rest,
Sorc'rers, atheists, Jesuits, possessed;
315 You who the scriptures and the laws deface
With the same liberty as points and lace;
Oh race most hypocritically strict!
Bent to reduce us to the ancient pict;
Well may you act the Adam and the Eve;
320 Aye, and the serpent too that did deceive.
    But the great captain, now the danger's o'er
Makes you for his sake tremble one fit more;
And, to your spite, returning yet alive
Does with himself all that is good revive.
325   So when first man did through the morning new
See the bright sun his shining race pursue,
All day he follow'd with unwearied sight,
Pleas'd with that other world of moving light;
But thought him when he missed his setting beams,

330 Sunk in the hills, or plunged below the streams.
While dismal blacks hung round the universe,
And stars (like tapers) burned upon his hearse:
And owls and ravens with their screeching noise
Did make the fun'rals sadder by their joys.
335 His weeping eyes the doleful vigils keep,
Not knowing yet the night was made for sleep:
Still to the west, where he him lost, he turned,
And with such accents, as despairing, mourned:
'Why did mine eyes once see so bright a ray;
340 Or why day last no longer than a day?'
When straight the sun behind him he descried,
Smiling serenely from the further side.
    So while our star that gives us light and heat,
Seemed now a long and gloomy night to threat,
345 Up from the other world his flame he darts,
And princes, shining through their windows, starts;
Who their suspected Counsellors refuse,
And credulous Ambassadors accuse.
'Is this', saith one, 'the nation that we read
350 Spent with both wars, under a captain dead?

---

310. Alcoran'd] Turned into a holy book, like the Koran, which had been translated into English for the first time in 1649, and was regarded by the orthodox as a further encouragement of heresy.
311–12. Abaddon or Apollyon was angel king of the bottomless pit in Rev. 9:1–11, out of which come monstrous locusts who torment men not sealed by God for five months; the image was common in anti-sect literature: see, e.g., John Tickell, *The Bottomles Pit Smoaking in Familisme* (Oxford, 1651).
311. locusts] A common pejorative term for sectaries in antipuritan and heresiographical writing: e.g. John Taylor, *The Anatomy of the Separatists* (1642), 2, 'they are like the Egyptian Locusts, covering the whole land'.
313–14. See *The Character of Holland*, l. 71: 'Hence Amsterdam, Turk-Christian-Pagan-Jew'.
313. Münzer's rest] the remnant of the Anabaptist rising at Münster in 1534, led by Thomas Münzer (Müntzer or Monczer), that abolished the institutions of marriage and private property.
316. points] intricate thread lace made wholly with the needle (*OED* n.[1] VI 31).
317. strict] in church discipline and manners; radical Puritans were frequently accused of taking discipline to an absurd extreme.
318–19. Both the ancient picts and Adam and Eve were examples of naked people; the Adamites were a fictitious sect who supposedly went naked; the Ranters were accused of being Adamites; early Quakers sometimes 'went naked as a sign' of their innocence and the world's sinfulness. For Adamites, see Cressy (2000), ch. 15.

325–42. See Statius, *Thebaid*, IV, ll. 282–4: 'hi lucis stupuisse vices noctisque feruntur/nubila et occiduum longe Titana secuti/desperasse diem' ('tis said that, struck with terror at the change from light to murky darkness, they followed far the setting Titan, despairing of the day); Manilius, *Astronomica*, I, ll. 66–70: 'Nam rudis ante illos nullo discrimine vita/in speciem conversa operum ratione carebat/et stupefacta novo pendebat lumine mundi,/tum velant amisso maerens, tum laeta renato' (Before their time man lived in ignorance: he looked without comprehension at the outward appearance and saw not the design of nature's works; he gazed in bewilderment at the strange new light of heaven, now sorrowing at its loss, now joyful at its rebirth). Lucretius, *De Rerum Natura*, V, ll. 973–6, treats the story as untruthful.
331. blacks] funeral hangings (*OED* n. 5 a).
335. vigils] nighttime watches (*OED* n.[1] 3 a, 4).
341–2. When ... side] Cp. Nicholas Brookes, in *Musarum Oxoniensium* (1654), 60: 'So breakes the Morning forth with Golded smiles/Fringing the East with glories, so unveiles/The Cheerefull Heavens, when their Azure light/Begins t'appeare after a Gloomy night.'
341. descried] caught sight of (*OED* v.[1] III 6).
347. suspected] of collaboration with foreign powers. *refuse*] reject.
348. credulous] believing too readily (*OED* a. 1c), but the ambassadors are nonetheless convinced: cp. Frances Quarles, '69. To King CHARLES', *Divine Fancies* (1632), ll. 13–14: 'whosoever to thy Land repayres,/ May thence returne amaz'd, and tell the Story.'
350. both wars] the Civil Wars and the First Dutch War of 1652–54.

Yet rig a navy while we dress us late;
And ere we dine, raze and rebuild our state.
What oaken forests, and what golden mines!
What mints of men, what union of designs!
55 Unless their ships, do, as their fowl proceed
Of shedding leaves, that with their ocean breed.
Their's are not ships, but rather arks of war,
And beakèd promontories sailed from far;
Of floating islands a new-hatched nest;
60 A fleet of worlds, of other worlds in quest;
An hideous shoal of wood-Leviathans,
Armed with three tire of brazen hurricanes;
That through the centre shoot their thund'ring side
And sink the earth that does at anchor ride.
65 What refuge to escape them can be found,
Whose wat'ry leaguers all the world surround?
Needs must we all their tributaries be,
Whose navies hold the sluices of the sea.
The ocean is the fountain of command,
70 But that once took, we captives are on land.
And those that have the waters for their share

Can quickly leave us neither earth nor air.
Yet if through these our fears could find a pass;
Through double oak, and lined with treble brass;
375 That one man still, although but named, alarms
More than all men, all navies, and all arms.
Him, all the day, him, in late night I dread,
And still his sword seems hanging o'er my head.
The nation had been ours, but his one soul
380 Moves the great bulk, and animates the whole.
He secrecy with number hath enchased,
Courage with age, maturity with haste:
The valiant's terror, riddle of the wise;
And still his falchion all our knots unties.
385 Where did he learn those arts that cost us dear?
Where below earth, or where above the sphere?
He seems a king by long succession born,
And yet the same to be a king does scorn.
Abroad a king he seems, and something more,
390 At home a subject on the equal floor.
O could I once him with our title see,
So should I hope yet he might die as we.

351. rig a navy] during the autumn of 1654, the navy, after the Dutch war, was refurbished and a fleet sent out in what became known as the Western Design: the taking of Spanish possessions in the Caribbean by aggression in the name of religion and trade (see Capp (1989), 87–91, 136–9; Armitage, *HJ*, 35 (1992), 531–55). The policy had been discussed within the Council of State since the Treaty with the Dutch had been signed in April. Intelligence accounts of the fleet's movements were frequently published; the instructions to the fleet were published on 4 December.
352. The monarch (who uses the royal 'we'), speaks in fear of his own possessions and in the sense that England would have been his (see below, l. 279). This presumably makes him the King of Spain. Earlier in 1654, both France and Spain offered to pay England subsidies in order to avoid war.
354. union of designs] a) unified purpose b) the unified nations of England, Scotland and Ireland.
355–6. fowl . . . breed] it was believed that Solan geese were bred from leaves falling into water: see Cleveland, *The Rebel Scot* (1644), ll. 125–6: 'A *Scot*, when from the Gallows-Tree got loose,/Drops into Stix, and turns a Soland Goose.'
358. beakèd promontories] see Milton, *Lycidas* (1637), l. 94: 'That blows from off each beaked promontory.'
359–66. Cp. *Mercurius Aulicus*, 1 (13–20 March 1654), 4: 'The flying Castles the River Ocean range/And render London now the World's Exchange;/When Peace arrives, our all-commanding King/Will hatch a plenty with his spreading Wing.'
361. hideous] a) terrible (*OED* a. 1) b) immense (*OED* a. 1 b).
362. tire] rows of cannon (*OED* n.³). *brazen hurricanes*] bronze cannon.
363–4. the centre . . . ride] see above, l. 205 n.
363. side] broadside.

366. wat'ry leaguers] a leaguer is a camp of ensiegement, or a siege force itself; hence the battleships are the watery leaguers.
368. sluices] water gates (*OED* n. 1 c)
371–2. waters . . . air] as with the division of the earth, air and water between the sons of Chronos (Margoliouth).
374. double oak . . . brass] the fabric of the warships; taken from Horace, *Carmina*, I.iii, ll. 9–12: 'illi robur et aes triplex/circa pectus erat, qui fragilem truci/commisit pelago ratem/primus' (Oak and triple bronze must have girt the breast of him who first committed his frail bark to the angry seas).
378. sword . . . head] a reference to the sword of Damocles; placed over the head of the flatterer Damocles by the tyrant of Syracuse, Dionysius (see Horace, *Carmina*, II.i, l. 17).
381. enchased] inlaid.
384. falchion] broad curved sword, with sharpened edge on the inside curve; see above, *Headnote, Context*. *knots unties*] the man who cut the Gordian knot was to be master of the world: in 330 BC Alexander the Great reached the city of Gordium in Phrygia. In this city a knot tied the yoke of a chariot to its pole. Whoever untied the knot would conquer Asia. Some sources report that Alexander cut through part of the knot to loosen it; others that he removed a pin, thus enabling him to untie the knot easily (see Plutarch, *Lives*, XVIII.2).
389–92. See above, *Headnote, Context*. M.'s foreign monarch accurately describes Cromwell's intention and appearance. He did appear as a prince, if not a monarch, to foreign ambassadors, but scrupulously avoided regal trappings at home, and stressed the legislative power of the Protectorate Parliament. Despite this, it did seem to some that a Cromwellian 'court' emerged, and 'O.P.' was one decidedly regal form adopted in documents and letters.

But let them write his praise that love him best,
It grieves me sore to have thus much confessed.'
395　　Pardon, great prince, if thus their fear or spite
More than our love and duty do thee right.
I yield, nor further will the prize contend;

So that we both alike may miss our end:
While thou thy venerable head dost raise
400　　As far above their malice as my praise.
And as the angel of our commonweal,
Troubling the waters, yearly mak'st them heal.

401–2. From John 5:4: 'For an angel went down at a certain season into the pool, and troubled the water: whosoever then first after the troubling of the water stepped in was made whole of whatsoever disease he had.' Cp. Herrick, 'To the King, To cure the Evill' (1648), ll. 3–4: 'To finde *Bethesda*, and an Angel there,/Stirring the waters, I am come.' The angel of the covenant was associated with Christ by one of Cromwell's chaplains: see Hirst in Wallace, ed. (1985), 41; Cromwell prefigures, then, as well as helps to make possible, the return of Christ. For contrast, see an apocalyptic image of watery destruction from 1655 of the kind M. argued against in this poem (see below, 312, l. 324 n.): 'And for the *Covetous persons*, and all you who in sight of all Warnings will go on skill, and like a Whirlpool, *suck, suck, suck* all into your *Gulfs*, those *insatiable Hells*, know that *Tophet* is fitted for all to *suck* all such insatiable spirits into it' [William] [Finch], *A third great and terrible Fire, Fire, Fire* (1 June 1655), 5.

401. angel of our commonweal] see William Lilly, 'Observations for the moneth of February', in *Certain Passages of Every dayes Intelligence*, 81 (26 January–2 February 1655), 164–5: 'the *Tutelary Angel of England* seems to direct the Noble *Protector*, who by wisdom prevents all mistakes.'
402. yearly] annually. *them*] i.e. the waters (signifying the state), rather than the people. M. thus introduces an extra metaphor in his adaptation of John 5:4. *heal*] a) become calm b) effect healing. Alludes to Cromwell's central concern of 'healing and settling' the state: see, e.g., *His Highnesse the Lord Protector's speech to the Parliament . . . the 4ᵗʰ of September, 1654* (Abbott (1945), III.436); George Smith, *God's Unchangeableness* ([15 January] 1655), sig. A2ᵛ: 'The Lord Protector, whom Providence hath exalted . . . to be a *nursing father* . . . and a skilfill *Esculapius*, to heal the distempers of three sick and wounded nations.'

56

A Poem upon the Death of his Late Highness the Lord Protector

Date. September 1658–January 1659. Oliver Cromwell died on 3 September 1658. In the Stationers' Register for 20 January 1659, Henry Herringman registered a volume entitled *Three poems to the happy memory of the most renowned Oliver, late Lord Protector of this Commonwealth, by Mr Marvell, Mr Driden, Mr Sprat.* A version of the poem had therefore been written in these four months and three weeks since Cromwell's death. Allusion to newsbook and pamphlet publications from these months (especially September 1658; see below *Context*) within the poem confirms this deduction.

Publication. 1681. M.'s poem was withdrawn from *Three Poems* (see above, *Date*), and replaced with Edmund Waller's, 'Upon the Storme and Death of his Late Highnesse Ensuing the same'. By the time *Three Poems* actually appeared in the spring, printed by William Wilson, Richard Cromwell's hold on power was uncertain, if not over. In these circumstances, M.'s praise of Richard as a conciliatory ruler was singularly inappropriate. Given his association and apparent strong sympathy (see Legouis, II.307–8) at this point with the supporters of the Protectorate, as opposed to the republicans, who had gained ground in the Protectorate Parliament, M. himself may have wished to withdraw the poem for reasons of political prudence (see Norbrook (1999), 393). The poem was cancelled from most copies of *1681*, and survives in only one known copy (BL C 59.i.8), where the poem is printed from the beginning up to l. 184. Another version with significant variants was copied into *Bod. 1*; it was this version, or a version very close to it, that Thompson used.

Context. As one of the Latin Secretaries to the Council of State, M. walked in Cromwell's funeral procession on 23 November, and had his mourning clothes paid for by the state. Several commentators have felt that the poem reveals an unusual intimacy with the Cromwell family. Larson, *Mosaic*, 19.2 (1986), 59–60, argues that M.'s description of Cromwell's corpse at ll. 247–53 suggests that M. was one of the few people to see it, as opposed to the vast majority who saw only a wax effigy. Certainly, public information surrounding the Protector's death was tightly controlled by the government: both official newsbooks published identical accounts of Oliver's death and the proclamation of Richard Cromwell as Protector (*The Publick Intelligencer*, 141 (30 August–6 September 1658), 794–[800]; *Mercurius Politicus*, 432 (2–9 September 1658), 802–8). Cromwell's affection for his family was, however, acknowledged in published literature: 'all these his Children, married and honourably disposed of in his lifetime; so that we may truly say, that he lived, to be an Eye-witness of God's great Mercy & Blessings, powred on himself and whole Family . . . a most Tender and Indulgent Father', Thomas L'Wright, *A More Exact Character of . . . Oliver Cromwell* (1659), 5–6. Cromwell's affection for his second daughter, Elizabeth Claypole, his distress at her death from cancer on 6 August 1658, and its connection with his own deterioration, was also public knowledge: see Henry Walker, *A Collection of Severall Passages Concerning His Highnesse* (1659), 1, 10. After Elizabeth's death, Cromwell effectively ceased public activity: another factor in the aptness of M.'s choice of subject. But the poem reflects nothing of Cromwell's elaborate and extravagant funeral ceremony, upon which £60,000 was spent despite the poor state of public finances. Neither is there any trace of Elizabeth's funeral, which took place at midnight on Tuesday, 10 August in Henry VII's Chapel, and which Cromwell did not attend on account of his gout.

M. idealizes Cromwell's relationship with Elizabeth, supposed to be his favourite daughter, but whose haughtiness as an adult (she is frequently noted for assuming the status of a princess) gave Cromwell concern as to her spiritual well-being. She interceded with her father on behalf of several political offenders, including Harrington: she was able to assure the return of the confiscated manuscript of

Oceana. She was also supposed to have reproached her father for his bloodshed on her deathbed. Naturally, none of these details enter the poem.

Whatever the extent of M.'s closeness to the Cromwell family, the presentation of the Lord Protector is in line with that of the private man, who excels in public life all monarchs and princes, of *The First Anniversary,* and the victorious agent of Providence of *An Horatian Ode.* The care for his daughter is consistent with the elaborate state funeral accorded to his mother, Elizabeth, who died in November 1654, aged 93, an event celebrated in *The First Anniversary,* ll. 161–2.

M. wrote his poem soon after Cromwell's death, and inevitably with the necessity of paying respect to Oliver's son and successor as Protector, Richard. Larson, *Mosaic,* 19.2 (1986), 60–6, argues that M.'s poem is in fact a praise of Richard, appropriate to his powers of political reconciliation, and sympathetic to the infant deaths among Richard's own children. Many of the poems in the academic volume *Musarum Cantabrigiensium Luctus & Gratulatio: Ille In Funere Oliveri . . . Haec de Ricardi Successione Felicissima* (1658) praise Richard as well as lament Oliver (and some are concerned wholly with Richard), although not in such problematic terms as does M.. By the time the poem was ready to appear in print, Richard had manifestly failed, and the poem had lost a large part of its moment. It was more appropriate and prudent to reprint a well-known and conventionally martial praise of Oliver Cromwell in Waller's poem. For further details, see also above, *Headnote, Publication.*

Structure. The poem is structured as a series of verse paragraphs in which the attention of the reader is repeatedly returned to Cromwell's private virtues. The first three, ll. 1–20, begin as we might expect of the soldier and statesman with Providence and the public scene, but the next five paragraphs (ll. 20–70) are concerned with Cromwell's relationship with his daughter Elizabeth and the effect of her death on him. This passage comes from the tradition of courtly panegyric and elegy, as opposed to the martial verse more usually applied to Cromwell. The next paragraph (ll. 101–40) describes Nature's own elegy for Cromwell in the storm that accompanied his death, the topos of Waller's poem. The following five paragraphs (ll. 141–200) detail in a much more conventional way Cromwell's military prowess, his place in English history and the godliness of his

valour. Then from l. 201 until l. 216, Cromwell's private virtue of friendship is praised, and after a further paragraph on the public virtue of prudence (ll. 217–26), both private and public virtues are merged in a paragraph (ll. 227–46) that emphasizes Cromwell's excellence in his ability to outdo all of these qualities in others. Through their unique combination in him, he is a paradoxical paragon.

The poem turns abruptly at this point to focus on the actual sight of Cromwell's corpse (ll. 247–86), the occasion for some more meditation on the Protector's future martial fame, before a paragraph providing a vision of Cromwell in glory (ll. 287–98), and a further six lines concerned with the burden of Cromwell's loss in this world. The final three paragraphs (ll. 305–18) are concerned with Richard Cromwell's succession to his father as Lord Protector.

Genre. M.'s poem is quite unlike any of the other elegies for Cromwell in that it focuses upon Cromwell as an exemplary father and private, godly man, as well as a martial hero, prince and agent of Providence. Thus, although for Patterson (1978), 90, the poem is a well-defined example of the classical *epicedion,* or funerary poem, describing deeds and lineage, its range of subjects is much broader than any other example. Other elegies, especially the famous ones by Dryden, Waller and Sprat are wholly concerned with Cromwell's military and imperial identity. Thomas Sprat's 'To the Happie Memory of the most Renowned Prince, Oliver, Lord Protector, &c. Pindarick Ode', sts. 5–6, acknowledges the rise of the private man, but this is as nothing to the careful and extensive attention given in M.'s poem. 'On Oliver Ld Protector Occasion^d by ye many coppies of verses made after his death' (Bodl. MS Locke e.17, pp. 82–6), an Oxford poem most probably written in the late 1650s, is concerned with Cromwell's respect for learning as well as his martial prowess and his greatness exceeding all other men. It also uses classical allusions, analogies (such as with trees) and natural imagery that are akin to elements of M.'s poem; still, the topic of domestic life is excluded. Samuel Slater's *A Rhetoricall Rapture As Composed into a Funeral Oration At the Mournfull Moving of His Highness Stately Effigies from Somerset-House* (1658), a broadsheet elegy, with verse epitaph, contains brief mentions of Cromwell's mother and daughter, but is largely concerned with the martial Cromwell and his glorification in these heroic terms.

There are some passages of distant affinity between this poem and M.'s, but Slater, living at Bury St Edmunds, reveals himself in his other compositions on Cromwell's death to be under the influence of earlier Cromwellian panegyric, including M.'s: see Slater, *The Protector's Protections* (1659), sig. A3ʳ, 47.

Neither does the elegy easily fit with the general pattern of elegies in the period. The execution of Charles I, and the spate of royalist elegies that followed, made royalist elegy in the late 1640s and 1650s highly fashionable, and a highly distinct branch of the genre. Parliamentarian, republican and Commonwealth elegy tended to be as much panegyric as lament, and yet M.'s poem manages to create its own genuine and original terms of loss (see Smith (1994), 287–94). Moreover, M.'s poem defies the genre of funerary elegy in that it is called a 'poem' rather than an 'elegy'. The other singular Cromwell elegy is George Wither's *Salt upon Salt: Made out of certain Ingenious Verses upon the Late Storm And the Death of His Highness Ensuing* (1659), which, unlike M.'s poem, is critical as well as affirmative of the Protector, and extensively meditative upon the sins of the nation and God's punishment of them, as well as (characteristically) Wither's own state of mind.

One common feature of the elegies for Cromwell was an exaggeration of the topos concerned with the excellence of the subject. Cromwell defies the powers of all poets to commemorate him adequately, because he is such an outstanding leader and hero: e.g. 'G.G.', in *Musarum Cantabrigiensium* (1658), sig. G4ʳ, 'Mars *envi'd thee, nor can we blame him for't;* . . . Saturn *in brazen walls thou didst confine,/* Joves *thunder was not so much feard as thine'*. J.H.'s *An Elegie Upon the much lamented Death of his Highnesse Oliver The late Lord Protector* (?1658/59) clumsily strains conceits and heroic comparisons to achieve this effect: 'He Illeads in Nutshells small/Or Points must put for Letters Capitall,/And then look through a Magnifying glass/That would in part, for thy describer pass.' It has been argued that some of the shortcomings of M.'s poem are deliberate gestures in the direction of this kind of effect (see below, *Style and Versification*). And despite the distinctiveness of M.'s poem, it does share local verbal effects with many of the published elegies on Cromwell.

M.'s poem more closely resembles, and in some cases, depends upon, the prose publications lamenting Cromwell's death and celebrating his achievements, where some space at least is given to Cromwell's private virtues and his domestic life: see, for instance, anon., *The Portraiture of his Royal Highness, Oliver Late Lord Protector* (1659), 7–8, 57–8. M.'s poem still exceeds these in its concern with Cromwell's private life.

The poem bears several echoes of both Virgil's *Aeneid* and Lucan's *De Bello Civili* (see below, ll. 156, 243–4, 254 nn.), the latter being one of the key texts behind *An Horatian Ode*. M. engages in the contemporary awareness of the relationship between the two epic poems, where the *Aeneid* was associated with royalism and lament for Charles I, and *De Bello Civili*, republicanism and praise for the Protector (see Smith (1994), 203–33). The Virgil allusions provide M. with a register of lament (and are another instance of M. transferring language associated in the period with kingship to Cromwell), Lucan with images of heroism. As with the *Ode*, the language of Thomas May's translations of Lucan (as well as of Virgil's *Georgics*) are present in the poem. Patterson (1978), 91–2, sees an intricate relationship between a passage at the beginning of *De Bello Civili* (trans. May (1627), sig. A3ʳ⁻ᵛ) and M.'s poem, ll. 257–68:

> one in yeares was growne,
> And long accustomde to a peacefull gowne
> Had now forgot the Souldier: . . .
>   . . . new strength he sought not out,
> Relying on his ancient fortunes fame,
> And stood the shadow of a glorious name.
> As an old lofty Oake, that heeretofore
> Great Conquerors spoiles, and sacred Trophies bore,
> Stands firme by his owne weight, his roote now dead,
> And through the ayre his naked boughes does spread,
> And with his trunke, not leaves, a shadow makes:
> Hee though each blast of Easterne winde him shakes,
> And round about well rooted Trees doe grow,
> Is onely honour'd.

In Lucan, the oak represents Pompey about to be blasted by the lightning of Julius Caesar, whereas M.'s oak is a simile for Cromwell struck down by the inevitability of age, understood as God's ordering of all creation. The further echo of Lucan (in May's translation), 'Not *Ioves* own Temple spares it', in l. 266, compounds the irony communicated by the web of allusion between *An Horatian Ode* and *A Poem*. Once Cromwell was Caesar blasting Pompey/Charles I through his laurels; now he is Pompey blasted by the certainty of mortality. By contrast, the fallen trees in Waller's 'Upon the Late Storm, and of the Death of his Highness Ensuing the

Same', ll. 1–14, are merely the consequences of the storm, despite the web of heroic associations they are then made to invoke.

The echoes of Milton's 'Lycidas' (see below, ll. 22, 303) suggest that M. may have been attempting to generate a distinct kind of Puritan elegy, in addition to revealing the growing influence of Milton on his own verse, despite Milton's own disillusion with the Protectorate. Milton and M. had worked together in the government for some time when Cromwell died. There is evidence in *A Poem* of textual connections with *Paradise Lost* as well as Milton's earlier poetry (see below, ll. 289–90), although this raises questions for the dating of Milton's poetry that cannot be discussed here.

The poem is notable for its reworking in significant ways of M.'s previous elegies and Cromwell poems (direct echoes are recorded in the footnotes). None of this happens in a negative way. M. avoids, for instance, references to the architectural imagery he had used so prominently in *The First Anniversary*, unlike George Wither, who used the building metaphor to question the stability of the Protectorate in the wake of Cromwell's death: see Wither, *Salt upon Salt: Made out of certain Ingenious Verses upon the Late Storm And the Death of His Highness Ensuing* (1659), 3. For Low (1985), 291, this absence is an indication of M.'s disappointment in the Protectorate record of reform; that is, of delayed or imperfect state building. Architecture is replaced by imagery derived from Georgic tradition. Earlier panegyrics of Cromwell stressed in Georgic terms Cromwell's ability to calm damaging storms: Payne Fisher, trans., Thomas Manley, 'A Gratulatory Ode of Peace', in Fisher, *Veni; vidi; vici* (1652), 22: 'The beeches fall, the husbandman doth finde,/His broken corn lodg'd by this furious winde,/And nipt his blooming hopes even in their bud.' In Virgil's *Georgics*, II, l. 523, the husbandman is presented as a happy father among his children, and the storm preceding the assassination of Julius Caesar is described at 1, ll. 464–97 (whereas Cromwell survived several assassination attempts to die a natural death). There are some particular echoes of Virgil's *Georgics* but M. is substantially concerned with a development of vine imagery (ll. 89–100), where Cromwell and his daughter become the vine in danger of being pruned in *Georgics* II, ll. 397–419, as opposed to the state vine cultivated by Cromwell in *The First Anniversary* (ll. 287–8). This is apt because imagery of Cromwell as 'that Plant of Renown,

under whose shadow the tired and drooping spirits of his people have been refreshed and quickned' ('*The Humble Remonstrance and Representation of the Major and Burgesses of the Borough of St Ives*', *Mercurius Politicus*, 549 (6–13 January 1659), 147) was a component of public discourse in the Protectorate.

The first twenty lines rework aspects of *An Horatian Ode*, moving in reverse from the public world of the political stage to the private world of domestic concerns. The stage and its audience, more theatrical as a simile, as opposed to the theatre of execution in the *Ode*, are disappointed by Cromwell's unheroic death (a heroic death would be in battle, as predicted in M.'s elegy on Villiers, l. 14). It is the people as spectators, and not Charles I, who are now disappointed. In the next passage, Cromwell lamenting Elizabeth takes the place of Hymeneus grieving for Hastings in that earlier elegy (ll. 43–6). Elizabeth's virtue shines through in this poem (l. 40), echoing Cromwell's preeminence in *An Ode* (l. 15).

The apocalyptic and millenarian elements in the earlier two Cromwell poems are almost wholly absent here (the one exception is l. 272). In *The First Anniversary*, l. 139, 'foreshortened time' describes an imagined apocalypse brought on by Cromwell's excellent rule. In *A Poem*, there is a reversal in the very unapocalyptic image of Cromwell as a 'foreshortened' tree to human sight, whose immense height can only be appreciated when it is fallen and dead (ll. 269–70).

There are several further references to *The First Anniversary*. Cromwell outruns time in the earlier poem (ll. 9–10) and is commemorated by every day in the later one (ll. 141–2). The horses involved in the overturning of Cromwell's carriage (*First Anniversary*, ll. 175–200) now become the willing sacrifices to Cromwell's honour in death (ll. 123–6), and a storm is the consequence of both events. Oliver's storm (*First Anniversary*, ll. 233–8) that unfortunately destroyed Charles I, returns at the end of the funerary poem as a means of illustrating the degree of clemency expected of Richard Cromwell (ll. 321–4), who will only bring a 'shower'. Where Cromwell had tended the vine of liberty in *The First Anniversary*, ll. 286–8, he is the vine in *A Poem*, wasting away through his daughter's, an offshoot's, death. Where superstitious man in *The First Anniversary*, ll. 329–30, thought that the sun at night was 'plunged below the streams', apotheosized

Cromwell 'plunges' in the swimming baths of heaven (l. 290). In *The First Anniversary*, Cromwell is likened to the huntsman who leads sleepy monarchs in the royal sport (ll. 120–4), and who will hunt the beast of the Roman Church (ll. 125–30), thereby giving more substance to the frequent contemporary description of Cromwell as the Old Testament hunter Nimrod (see above, 278, l. 110 n.). In *A Poem*, hunting for 'wild deer' (l. 245) is quite simply (and less threateningly) one of the Protector's heroic qualities. Hunting was a royal sport, but Charles I had been portrayed as a stag in Sir John Denham's *Coopers Hill* (1641–42, 1655), Sir William Davenant had presented hunting as tyranny in *Gondibert* (1651), 1.2.24–41, and Edmund Waller's commendatory poem to Christopher Wase's translation of the hunting poem by Gratius, *Cynegeticon* (1654), had called for a poem on the modern hunting of 'beasts'. *The First Anniversary* answers that call, while *A Poem* carefully avoids an image of hunting that presents Cromwell in his persecuting role, without sacrificing the association of Cromwell with hunting.

One less obvious link is in the Nisus and Scylla story (Ovid, *Metamorphoses*, VIII) alluded to in ll. 67–8. In George Sandys' commentary on Ovid, attached to his translation (1632), there is a description of the founding of the tower in Megaera, Nisus's city (286): Apollo laid his harp on a stone, and this, striking with a pebble, caused the tower to rise as harmonious, perpetual music. The story echoes the Amphion tale at the beginning of *The First Anniversary*, but this time building has negative associations: it was from the top of the tower that Scylla first saw Minos, her love for him being the cause of the betrayal of the lock (see below, ll. 67–8 n.).

Versification and Style. The poem is written in a series of continuous verse paragraphs, of varying size, between six and twenty-four lines of rhyming pentameter couplets. Most of these have a concluding couplet, the sense of which turns round, or shifts the reader's perspective on the paragraph itself. Within this structure, the major theme of mutuality and reflexiveness is located, and usually expressed in very clear syntax. Thus, Providence, described as a mirror, looks into *itself* to discover Cromwell's fate. Nature and Cromwell are identical: Nature appears to fight Nature for Cromwell's death (l. 133). The infant Eliza replaced the milk in her mother's breasts with love (l. 36). Cromwell and his daughter are likewise mutual reflections of each other's love, to the extent that they become the same entity: as the disease 'melts' his daughter, so Cromwell also inwardly wastes away (here they are not mirrors – Eliza is a wax model of her father within him). This is compounded by vocabulary of 'doubling' (ll. 57, 66), and by paradoxes that enhance the sense of a closeness that is poignantly harmful to both father and daughter. Eliza's dying breath tarnishes the 'polished mirror' of her father's breastplate, and this is enough to set him in his decline (and later on Richard Cromwell, the glittering image of his father, has his 'beams' 'obscured' by grief for his father's death; see also below, l. 78 n.). The image of life on the mirror of Cromwell's dead face (ll. 257–60) suggests that he will return to life.

A further mirroring effect is achieved by the recurrence of vocabulary with somewhat different uses and meanings later in the poem. Love and Grief are consigned to despatch Cromwell gently (l. 21), and later he prefers neither to love nor grieve for his dead daughter (l. 85), as if the personified deities and their allotted roles had come alive in Cromwell's actions. The sea is instructed to retreat beneath its 'abyss' (i.e. seabed) (l. 168), but Cromwell is later seen happily bathing in the 'abyss' of heaven. At l. 18 what he 'least affected was most admired', but with such strong 'affections', he 'affected most what best deserved' (ll. 207–8). Such lexical mirroring occurs within one line: e.g. at l. 182, the soldiers have nothing to fear because they fear God.

By contrast, there are a number of deliberately obscure passages. Among the purported weaknesses detected by critics in the poem are the nebulous and difficult sentences, usually an effect of syntactical inversion, or *hysteron proteron* (e.g. ll. 13–18, 223–6, 273–6), and less commonly, ellipsis (e.g. ll. 128, 189–90, 216, 276). Ambiguity is not cleverly poised, as in the previous two Cromwell poems (and especially *An Horatian Ode*), but is an effect of blurred and indistinct syntax. Would M. have let such a poem be entered for a collection that would eventually be published, or are the apparent blemishes genuine examples of poetic failure, perhaps induced by haste in the circumstances of the Protector's death? One solution is that the poem is marked by deliberate failures of poetic sentence: Cromwell's death brings about the end of good poetry. Ellipsis is a kind of 'choking' in the voice of grief – an effect by no means unknown in mannered seventeenth-century elegies. Moreover, what begins as characteristic inversion (ll. 15–18) ends as deliberate distortion. The effect is the opposite of the distorted impression of height we had of Cromwell when he was alive (see ll. 269–70), and is an obscuring opposite to the bright mirrors and images of Providence, Cromwell and his two offspring who feature in this poem. Syntactic obscurity is also an effect of our dim, sublunary perceptions, in which 'we ourselves betray' (l. 298), while, more often than not, obscure lines are unravelled by the bright day of concluding couplets. To confirm this, lines concerned with the will of heaven are also syntactically difficult (e.g. ll. 107–8). Some sentences 'fool' the reader, appearing to be pointing to one meaning for the first half, and then effecting a reversal and clarification in the second half: 'Pity it seemed to hurt him' – 'more that felt/Each wound himself which he to others dealt' (ll. 197–8). Cromwell, these features tell us, though dead, is always ready to bounce back.

Modern Criticism. M.'s elegy on Cromwell has attracted almost no extensive comment, despite Thompson's generous annotation: 'The English language does not boast a more elegant elegiack poem, than this to the memory of the magnanimous and noble Cromwell' (III.513). Legouis (1965), 111, confessed that the poem was M.'s finest 'official' verse, but that, despite its public function, it was 'so touching, so heart-felt, and so free from the political preoccupation', as if it were 'a friend mourning for a friend'. Friedman (1970), 284, 288–9, regards the poem as a 'mixture of [M.'s] best metaphysical techniques, confused sequences of images and subjects, and hackneyed terms of elegiac praise', and therefore considers it inferior to the elegies of Dryden and Waller. He is impressed by M.'s 'undiminished ability to . . . express correspondences between individual events and their abstract meanings', and by the 'sincerity and depth of [M.'s] sense of

catastrophe', but regards ll. 255–6 in particular as particularly bad, and guilty of 'Shelleyan inanities'. Despite her defence of the poem's formal design, Patterson (1978), 94, finds that it 'competes effectively neither with the strenuous mental activity of the earlier Cromwell poems nor with the voluptuous emotional activity of an elegy'. Donnelly, in Summers and Pebworth, eds (1992), 167–8, argues that the poem's failure is a consequence of the resources in elegiac tradition being unable to match the man who excelled all men.

If Thompson's sentiments are an exaggeration, Legouis's judgement is preferable: the poem is, by a considerable distance, the best of all surviving elegies on Cromwell, and has been unjustly neglected.

A Poem upon the Death of his Late Highness the Lord Protector

> That Providence which had so long the care
> Of Cromwell's head, and numbered ev'ry hair,
> Now in itself (the glass where all appears)
> Had seen the period of his golden years:
> 5   And thenceforth only did attend to trace
> What death might least so fair a life deface.
>
>   The people, which what most they fear esteem,
> Death when more horrid, so more noble deem;
> And blame the last act, like spectators vain,
> 10   Unless the prince whom they applaud be slain.
> Nor Fate indeed can well refuse that right
> To those that lived in war, to die in fight.
>
>   But long his valour none had left that could
> Indanger him, or clemency that would.
> 15   And he whom Nature all for peace had made,
> But angry heaven unto war had swayed,
> And so less useful where he most desired,
> For what he least affected was admired,

Title. Bod. 1; A Poem upon the Death of O.C. *1681.*
2. *numbered ev'ry hair*] see Matt. 10:30, 'But the very hairs of your head are all numbered.'
3. *glass*] mirror (*OED* n.[1] 8); see also 2 Cor. 3:18: 'But we all, with open face beholding as in a glass the glory of the Lord, are changed into the same image from glory to glory.' The image is applied by Charles Darby to Richard Cromwell: *'which of His mind/So clear a Mirrour shows, who sees, would say't/His Fathers Ashes were Vitriolate', Musarum Cantabrigiensium* (Cambridge, 1658), sig. H1ʳ.
4. *seen*] foreseen. *period*] ending, completion (*OED* II 5 a).
7–10. *The people . . . be slain*] the scene described is the performance of a tragedy at a public theatre; the last act is

regarded as flawed unless the hero prince is slain. There is also an allusion to the execution of Charles I, frequently described in theatrical terms, by M. in *An Horatian Ode*, among many others: see above, *Headnote, Genre.*
13–14. *But long . . . would*] his valour had long since overcome all that could have threatened him, and his statesmanship had reconciled others who would have opposed him.
16. *angry heaven*] see *An Horatian Ode*, l. 26: 'The force of angry heaven's flame.'
18. *what . . . affected*] i.e. being a soldier *affected*] a) regarded with fondness, cherished (*OED* ppl. a. 2) b) displayed artificially (*OED* ppl. a. 4).

Deservèd yet an end whose ev'ry part
Should speak the wondrous softness of his heart.
  To Love and Grief the fatal writ was signed;
(Those nobler weaknesses of human kind,
From which those powers that issued the decree,
Although immortal, found they were not free),
That they, to whom his breast still open lies,
In gentle passions should his death disguise:
And leave succeeding ages cause to mourn,
As long as Grief shall weep, or Love shall burn.
  Straight does a slow and languishing disease
Eliza, Nature's and his darling, seize.
Her when an infant, taken with her charms,
He oft would flourish in his mighty arms;
And, lest their force the tender burden wrong,
Slacken the vigour of his muscles strong;
Then to the mother's breast her softly move,
Which while she drained of milk, she filled with love.
But as with riper years her virtue grew,
And ev'ry minute adds a lustre new;
When with meridian height her beauty shined,
And thorough that sparkled her fairer mind;
When she with smiles serene and words discreet
His hidden soul at every turn could meet;
Then might y'ha'daily his affection spied,
Doubling that knot which destiny had tied.
While they by sense, not knowing, comprehend

How on each other both their fates depend.
With her each day the pleasing hours he shares,
And at her aspect calms his growing cares;
Or with a grandsire's joy her children sees
Hanging about her neck or at his knees.
Hold fast, dear infants, hold them both or none!
This will not stay when once the other's gone.
      A silent fire now wastes those limbs of wax,
And him within his tortured image racks.
So the flow'r with'ring which the garden crowned,
The sad root pines in secret under ground.
Each groan he doubled and each sigh he sighed,
Repeated over to the restless night.
No trembling string composed to numbers new,
Answers the touch in notes more sad, more true.
She, lest he grieve, hides what she can her pains,
And he to lessen her's his sorrow feigns:
Yet both perceived, yet both concealed their skills,
And so diminishing increased their ills:
That whether by each other's grief they fell,
Or on their own redoubled, none can tell.
  And now Eliza's purple locks were shorn,
Where she so long her father's fate had worn:
And frequent lightning to her soul that flies,
Divides the air, and opens all the skies:
And now his life, suspended by her breath,
Ran out impetuously to hasting death.

---

21. To . . . signed] Love and Grief are imagined being given Cromwell's death warrant by Providence: they are his executioners. *fatal writ*] death warrant. *signed*] assigned.

22. *kind*] Bod. 1; mind 1681.

26. *gentle*] a) noble (*OED* a. A 1b) b) of family (*OED* a. A 2) c) mild (and not warlike) (*OED* a. A 7). *passions*] a) loving emotions (*OED* n. III 8), but with the secondary senses of b) physical affliction or illness (*OED* n. I 4) and c) martyrdom (*OED* n. I 2).

30. *Eliza*] Cromwell's second daughter, Elizabeth (b.1629), wife of John Claypole, died on 6 August 1658, just one month before her father's death.

31. *taken with*] delighted by.

39. *meridian*] period of greatest splendour (like the sun's power at mid-day (*OED* a. 2b). Elizabeth Claypole died when she was twenty-nine years old.

41–2. *When she . . . meet*] See *Headnote, Context.* 41. *and*] 1681; in Bod. 1.

45. *sense*] a) instinct (*OED* n. I 2) b) feeling (*OED* n. I 8). *not knowing*] not by reason.

48. *aspect*] a) gaze (*OED* I 1) b) appearance (*OED* III 10) *his*] Bod. 1; her 1681.

52. *This*] this one.

53–4. *A silent . . . racks*] Cromwell suffers to see Elizabeth, an image of himself, waste away. The image refers to the practice in witchcraft of melting the wax effigy of an intended victim.

53. *silent fire*] it was understood by many close to the Protector that the physicians could not diagnose Elizabeth's illness; it is now thought that she died of cancer. Cancer was regarded as consuming, and therefore a 'burning' condition; 'silent' is therefore possibly meant in the sense of invisible, of a 'fire' (i.e. fever) of which one cannot see 'burning' symptoms.

62. *feigns*] disguises (in contrast to its meaning at l. 259: imagine).

63. *skills*] knowledge (*OED* n.I 7).

64. *diminishing*] a) decreasing in physical strength b) disregarding, playing down the importance of (their own illnesses) (*OED* v. 3).

66. *redoubled*] repeated.

67. *purple locks were shorn*] Ovid, *Metamorphoses*, VIII, ll. 6–151, contains the story of Scylla, daughter of Nisus, King of Megara, whose city was besieged by King Minos of Crete. Scylla fell in love with Minos, and, intending to win him, cut from her father's head the purple lock of hair upon which depended the safety of his throne and his life. In M.'s transformation of the story, Eliza occupies the position of Nisus, and Cromwell the city of Megara, or, emphasizing the unity of Cromwell and his daughter, Eliza's fateful locks are Cromwell's too. The feminine naivety, deceit and disloyalty in Ovid's tale are entirely removed. More broadly, Elizabeth is the reversal of Scylla, Cromwell the reversal of Nisus.

69–70. *And frequent . . . skies*] see *An Horatian Ode*, ll. 13–16.

Like polished mirrors, so his steely breast
Had every figure of her woes expressed;
75   And with the damp of her last gasps obscured,
Had drawn such stains as were not to be cured.
Fate could not either reach with single stroke,
But the dear image fled, the mirror broke.
     Who now shall tell us more of mournful swans,
80   Of halcyons kind, or bleeding pelicans?
No downy breast did ere so gently beat,
Or fan with airy plumes so soft an heat.
For he no duty by his height excused,
Nor though a prince, to be a man refused:
85   But rather than in his Eliza's pain
Not love, not grieve, would neither live nor reign:
And in himself so oft immortal tried,
Yet in compassion of another died.
     So have I seen a vine, whose lasting age
90   Of many a winter hath survived the rage.
Under whose shady tent men every year
At its rich blood's expense their sorrow cheer,
If some dear branch where it extends its life

Chance to be pruned by an untimely knife,
95   The parent-tree unto the grief succeeds,
And through the wound its vital humour bleeds;
Trickling in wat'ry drops, whose flowing shape
Weeps that it falls ere fixed into a grape.
So the dry stock, no more that spreading vine,
100 Frustrates the autumn and the hopes of wine.
     A secret cause does sure those signs ordain
Foreboding princes' falls, and seldom vain.
Whether some kinder powers, that wish us well,
What they above cannot prevent, foretell;
105 Or the great world do by consent presage,
As hollow seas with future tempests rage;
Or rather heav'n, which us so long foresees,
There fun'rals celebrates while it decrees.
But never yet was any human fate
110 By Nature solemnized with so much state.
He unconcerned the dreadful passage crossed;
But oh what pangs that death did Nature cost!
     First the great thunder was shot off, and sent
The signal from the starry battlement:

---

73. polished mirrors] several contemporary paintings, engravings and woodcuts showed Cromwell wearing a breastplate: see, e.g., the full length portrait by Robert Walker (Cromwell Museum, Huntingdon) and William Faithorne's engraving *The Embleme of England's Distractions* (1658; see fig. 9).

74. figure] image, appearance; see below, l. 78 n.

75. damp] noxious exhalation (*OED* n.1 1 a).

77. either] either of the two (Elizabeth and her father). Fate cannot take away the one (Elizabeth, here the image), without also taking the other (Cromwell, the mirror).

78. image] cp. Gilbert Burnet's comments on Cromwell's chaplain, Peter Sterry's alleged words to Richard Cromwell in Burnet, *Bishop Burnet's History of Hs Own Time* (1724), I.82–3: 'Sterry, praying for *Richard*, used those indecent words, next to blasphemy, *make him the brightness of the father's glory, and the express image of his person.*'

79–80. mournful . . . pelicans] swans were believed to sing only once, before they died, halcyons to calm stormy, winter seas, pelicans to feed their young with their own flesh.

84. prince] Cromwell is presented not as a monarch, but as a prince (from the Latin, *princeps*, the chief authority of a state), a key concept in Machiavellian theory, and in contemporary understanding of Cromwell in Machiavellian terms: 'There is nothing (saith *Machiavel*) gaines a *Prince* such repute as great exploits and rare trials of himself in heroick Actions. . . . He [Cromwell] is a *new Prince*, but hath the beauties and features of all the old-spirited Gallants', Anon., *The Unparalleld Monarch* (1656), 3, 11. See also *The First Anniversary*, l. 395.

87. And in . . . immortal tried] when tested for his own qualities (in war and politics), he proved immortal.

92. rich blood] wine.

96. vital humour] sap.

97–8. whose flowing . . . grape] the sap trickling from the vine are like tears wept because they will not become fulsome grapes.

99–100. So . . . wine] cp. Samuel Slater, *A Rhetoricall Rapture As Composed into a Funeral Oration At the Mournfull Moving of His Highness Stately Effigies from Somerset-House* (1658), ll. 28–30: 'Thy *Daughter* (know)/Toll'd thy Great Bell; the *Prim-rose* fading young,/The old *Stock-Gilly-flower* could not last long.'

99. dry stock] dead stump of a vine.

101–40. A secret . . . past] the description of the storm corresponds to dispersed passages in Wither's *Salt upon Salt* (1659), 11–12, 21–23.

101. secret] supernatural, divine.

106. hollow seas] noise of sea echoes ('hollow': faintly-voiced (*OED* a. A 4)); cp. *Bermudas*, ll. 26–7: 'he . . . makes the hollow seas, that roar,/Proclaim the ambergris on shore.'

108. i.e. celebrates the funerals of those who will die while at the same time determining the demise of the elect in the world below. *There*] Their *1681+. celebrates*] Bod. 1; celebrate *1681*.

111. dreadful passage] crossing to the underworld, in the manner of a classical death description.

112. pangs that death] deathpangs; the opposite of birthpangs; see also Wither, *Salt upon Salt* (1659), 11, 'Nature, at his Death was passionate'; Samuel Fuller, in *Musarum Cantabrigiensium* (1658), sig. H3ʳ, ''twas Nature sigh'd when she did fear/That she should lose thrice famous *Oliver*'.

113. great thunder was shot off] the storm which raged on 2 September, the day before Cromwell's death (and which was rumoured to have carried him off), is imagined as an artillery salute from heaven. There is a contrast here with Wither, *Salt upon Salt* (1659), 12, 'Yet, these vain Blasts for Fame, oft, sound as loud/As *Cannons*, or as *Thunder* from a Cloud.' See also Thomas Fuller, 'An Elegie upon *Oliver* late Lord Protector', in *Musarum Cantabrigiensium* (1658), sig. G3ᵛ: '*Suppose a cloud with tempests bid to rend/In Angry Thunders, and our Fate portend.*'

5   The winds receive it, and its force outdo,
    As practising how they could thunder too:
    Out of the binder's hand the sheaves they tore,
    And thrashed the harvest in the airy floor;
    Or of huge trees, whose growth with his did rise,
0   The deep foundations opened to the skies.
    Then heavy show'rs the wingèd tempests led,
    And pour the deluge o'er the chaos' head.
    The race of warlike horses at his tomb
    Offer themselves in many a hecatomb;
5   With pensive head towards the ground they fall,
    And helpless languish at the tainted stall.
    Numbers of men decrease with pains unknown,
    And hasten, not to see his death, their own.
    Such tortures all the elements unfixed,
0   Troubled to part where so exactly mixed:
    And as through air his wasting spirits flowed,
    The universe laboured beneath their load.
        Nature it seemed with him would Nature vie;
    He with Eliza, it with him would die.

135   He without noise still travelled to his end,
        As silent suns to meet the night descend.
        The stars that for him fought had only power
        Left to determine now his fatal hour;
        Which, since they might not hinder, yet they cast
140   To choose it worthy of his glories past.
            No part of time but bare his mark away
        Of honour; all the year was Cromwell's day:
        But this, of all the most auspicious found,
        Twice had in open field him victor crowned:
145   When up the armèd mountains of Dunbar
        He marched, and through deep Severn ending war.
        What day should him eternize but the same
        That had before immortalized his name?
        That so who ere would at his death have joyed,
150   In their own griefs might find themselves employed;
        But those that sadly his departure grieved,
        Yet joyed rememb'ring what he once achieved.
        And the last minute his victorious ghost
        Gave chase to Ligny on the Belgic coast.

115–18. The winds . . . floor] cp. Wither, *Salt upon Salt* (1659), 20, 'The *Air*, by *Storms* and *Blastings*, *Frosts* and *Snows*,/ Destroy'd our *last Crops*, in their fairest shows.'

121. led] lead Grosart, Margoliouth+; dead *1681*, Bod. *1*.

123–6. The race . . . stall] A reversal of the creation in Virgil, *Georgics*, I, ll. 12–14: 'great *Neptune*, thou,/Whose trident strokes did first from earth produce/A warlike horse.' (trans. T. May (1628), 2); cf. Wither, *Salt upon Salt* (1659), 23, 'Our ablest *Horses*, (ev'n those perhaps, wherein/More *trust* reposed was, then should have bin) Die suddenly, and Ditches are bestrow'd/With those *Bones*, whereupon our *Gallants* rode.'

123. horses] Cromwell's interest in horses extended as far as an intention to establish the Arabian breed in England. They were a sign of the 'courtliness' of the Protectorate, and some of the Protector's horses were the gifts of foreign princes. The Protectorate household establishment for horses was extensive: see Sherwood (1977), 57–8.

124. a] Bod. *1*; an *1681*. *hecatomb*] a public sacrifice of many animals (properly oxen): cp. G.G. in *Musarum Canta-brigiensium* (1658), sig. G4ʳ, 'We . . . offer too,/Whole *Hecatombs of Captive Souls*.'

125. pensive] a) anxious (*OED* a. 2 b) b) mournfully serious, gloomy (*OED* a. 3).

127–8. Numbers . . . own] low fever struck in May 1658; cf. Wither, *Salt upon Salt* (1659), 23, 'Much, of our pretious *Life-Blood* up is drunk.'

128. not . . . own] in order not to see his death, but their own.

129. elements] the four elements of earth, air, fire and water. *unfixed*] unsettled, unstable (*OED* ppl. a. 2).

130. so exactly mixed] in Cromwell, the perfect man.

132. universe] *1681*, Bod. *1*; world with throes *Thompson*.

133. Nature . . . vie] cf. Shakespeare, *Antony and Cleopatra*, V, ii, ll. 97–100: 'nature wants stuff/To vie strange forms with fancy, yet to imagine/An Antony were nature's piece, 'gainst fancy,/Condemning shadows quite.'

136. silent suns] not shining, but usually applied to the moon (*OED* a. 5 a); cf. *Samson Agonistes* (1671), ll. 86–7: 'The sun to me is dark/And silent as the moon'.

137. stars . . . fought] see *An Horatian Ode*, l. 12, 'urged his active star' and Judges 5:20.

139. cast] reckon, calculate (in an astrological sense) (*OED* v. VI 37, 39).

141–2. No part . . . honour] no individual part of time was involved in Cromwell's glory and his death: all of time was occupied.

141. mark] sign, indication (*OED* n.1 III 10).

142. all . . . day] cp. J.H., *An Elegie Upon the much lamented Death of his Highnesse Oliver The late Lord Protector* (?1658/59), single sheet: 'Each single act doth speak so much, that they/Do witnesse the good works of every day.'

143–6. The day of Cromwell's death, 3 September, was the anniversary of two previous victories: at Dunbar in 1650 and Worcester in 1651.

143. auspicious] of good omen, betokening success (*OED* a. 1).

146. through deep Severn] At the Battle of Worcester, Cromwell built a bridge of boats across the River Severn in order to launch an attack on the flank of the Scottish army. 'Through' echoes the description of Cromwell's rise in *An Horatian Ode*, ll. 15–16.

151. sadly] with regret and lament, but also invoking the 'valour sad' (steadfast, serious, valiant) of *An Horatian Ode*, l. 107.

153–4. his victorious . . . coast] On 3 September 1658 a Spanish force under the Prince de Ligne was defeated in Flanders by a French army with an English contingent; see also Waller, 'Upon the Late Storm', ll. 14–15: 'Our dying hero from the continent/Ravished whole towns; and forts from Spaniards reft.' Cf. Abraham Cowley, *The Civil War* (1643), 1, ll. 497–8, on the reunion of Charles I and his queen at the site of the recent Battle of Edgehill (and on the same day, 13 July, as the Royalist victory at Roundway Down): 'Through the glad vale ten thousand *Cupids* fled,/And chac'ed the wandring *Spirits* of *Rebells* dead.'

155 Here ended all his mortal toils: he laid
    And slept in peace under the laurel shade.
        O Cromwell, Heaven's favourite! To none
    Have such high honours from above been shown:
    For whom the elements we mourners see,
160 And heav'n itself would the great herald be;
    Which with more care set forth his obsequies
    Than those of Moses hid from human eyes:
    As jealous only here lest all be less,
    That we could to his memory express.
165   Then let us to our course of mourning keep:
    Where heaven leads, 'tis piety to weep.
    Stand back ye seas, and shrunk beneath the veil
    Of your abyss, with covered head bewail
    Your monarch: we demand not your supplies
170 To compass in our isle; our tears suffice;
    Since him away the dismal tempest rent,

    Who once more joined us to the continent;
    Who planted England on the Flandric shore,
    And stretched our frontier to the Indian ore;
175 Whose greater truths obscure the fables old,
    Whether of British saints or worthies told;
    And in a valour less'ning Arthur's deeds,
    For holiness the Confessor exceeds.
        He first put arms into Religion's hand,
180 And tim'rous Conscience unto Courage manned:
    The soldier taught that inward mail to wear,
    And fearing God how they should nothing fear.
    'Those strokes', he said, 'will pierce through all belo
    Where those that strike from heav'n fetch their blow
185 Astonished armies did their flight prepare,
    And cities strong were stormèd by his prayer;
    Of that forever Preston's field shall tell
    The story, and impregnable Clonmell;

---

156. laurel shade] The palm, not the laurel, was the usual sign of military eminence. The suggestion here is that Cromwell's military achievement is like a poetic excellence (see above, *An Horatian Ode*, l. 21 n.). But see also Virgil, *Aeneid*, VI, ll. 656–9: 'conspicit ecce alios dextra laevaque per herbam/vescentis laetumque choro paena canentis/inter odoratum lauri nemus, unde superne/plurimus Eridani per silvam volvitur amnis' (Lo! others he sees, to right and left, feasting on the sward, and chanting in chorus a joyous paean within a fragrant laurel grove, whence, in the world above, the full flood of the Eridanus rolls amid the forest).

161. obsequies] funeral rites.

162. Moses . . . eyes] See Deut. 34:6: Moses died in land of Moab and was buried there by God 'but no man knoweth of his sepulchre unto this day'.

163–4. Heaven puts on a memorial show for Cromwell to forestall any greater demonstration by men on earth.

166–70. Cp. Samuel Slater, *A Rhetoricall Rapture As Composed into a Funeral Oration At the Mournfull Moving of His Highness Stately Effigies from Somerset-House* (1658), ll. 57–63: 'To congratulate thy Sereness, rise,/Flying quick into thy Followers eyes: Where such an Inundation of Tears,/That out-vied *Thamesis*, shrinking with Fears,/Glides ghastly to the Main-guard for recruit:/The mobled Ocean . . . flowes to th'Funerall/Of his Great *Master*, and outweeps 'um all.'

169–70. we . . . suffice] Cp. Cowley, *The Civil War*, III, ll. 615–16: 'Soe wide a Charity in each Teare was found,/Each like a Sea compasst our Island round.'

169. monarch] as much as Cromwell was described as a prince (see above l. 84), so also the language of kingship was frequently applied to him by supporters and opponents: see, e.g., anon., 'King Cromwell' (Thomason Tracts, 19 May 1653); anon., *The Unparalleld Monarch* (1656), 3, 8, 43; Cromwell was offered (and refused) the crown in May 1657. *supplies*] of salt water.

170. compass] encircle (*OED* v.[1] III 7).

171. dismal] depressing, gloomy (*OED* B a. 4).

172–4. An Anglo-French force captured Dunkirk from the Spanish in 1658; Jamaica was taken in 1655; see Waller, 'Upon the Late Storm', ll. 21–2: 'Under the tropic is our language spoke,/And part of Flanders hath received our yoke.'

173. planted] established (as if to settle or found a colony) (*OED* v. I 3 a).

176. British saints] see below, l. 212. *worthies*] a) heroes of antiquity b) eminent men in church and state. Thomas Davyes described Cromwell as the 'tenth worthy' in a single sheet collection of elegiac verse published after the Protector's death, alluding to the nine worthies of England (or London), celebrated in several popular histories (see, e.g., Robert Fletcher, *The Nine English Worthies* (1606)).

177. valour] Cp. *An Horatian Ode*, l. 107. *Arthur's deeds*] Arthur was one of the Nine Worthies. Cf. B. Turner, in *Musarum Cantabrigiensium* (1658), sig. H1[v], where Cromwell is '*Arthur's* Metempsuchsis'.

178. holiness . . . exceeds] King Edward the Confessor (d.1066), known for his piety.

180. manned] a) in a military sense, furnished with soldiers (*OED* v. 2b) b) made courageous: Cromwell turns conscience into courage (by bringing to manhood).

181. inward mail] the armour of faith – see Ephesians 6:11; a reference to the intense religious discipline and debate in the New Model Army. *inward*] a keyword in Puritan devotional language; 'inward sense and feeling . . . a Copy written by the Spirit of God upon the hearts of believers', Vavasor Powell, Epistle, in Henry Walker, ed., *Spirituall Experiences, Of Sundry Believers* (1653), sigs. A2[v]–3[r].

185. Astonished] a) stunned by blows (*OED* ppl. a. 1) b) dismayed (*OED* ppl. a. 3).

187. Preston's field] Cromwell defeated the Scots under the Marquis of Hamilton at Preston in August 1648.

188. impregnable Clonmell] Clonmell was extremely well defended, but evetually surrendered on 18 May 1650 after an open artillery assault on the walls and a fierce battle: 'The Lord General used more then ordinary industry in reducing this Town . . . *We found in Clonmell . . . the stoutest enemy that ever was found by our Army in* Ireland', [Henry Fletcher], *The Perfect Politician* (1660), 81–3.

And where the shady mountain Fenwick scaled,
'0 The sea between, yet hence his prayer prevailed.
What man was ever so in heav'n obeyed
Since the commanded sun o'er Gibeon stayed?
In all his wars needs must he triumph when
He conquered God, still ere he fought with men.
'5   Hence, though in battle none so brave or fierce,
Yet him the adverse steel could never pierce.
Pity it seemed to hurt him more that felt
Each wound himself which he to others dealt;
Danger itself refusing to offend
'0 So loose an enemy, so fast a friend.
   Friendship, that sacred virtue, long does claim
The first foundation of his house and name:
But within one its narrow limits fall;
His tenderness extended unto all.
'5 And that deep soul through every channel flows,
Where kindly Nature loves itself to lose.
More strong affections never reason served,
Yet still affected most what best deserved.
If he Eliza loved to that degree,
'0 (Though who more worthy to be loved than she?)
If so indulgent to his own, how dear

To him the children of the highest were?
For her he once did Nature's tribute pay:
For these his life adventured ev'ry day.
215 And 'twould be found, could we his thoughts have cast,
Their griefs struck deepest, if Eliza's last.
   What prudence more than human did he need
To keep so dear, so diff'ring minds agreed?
The worser sort, as conscious of their ill,
220 Lie weak and easy to the ruler's will;
But to the good (too many or too few)
All law is useless, all reward is due.
Oh! ill-advised, if not for love, for shame,
Spare yet your own, if you neglect his fame;
225 Lest others dare to think your zeal a mask,
And you to govern only heaven's task.
   Valour, Religion, Friendship, Prudence died
At once with him, and all that's good beside;
And we Death's refuse, Nature's dregs, confined
230 To loathsome life, alas! are left behind.
Where we (so once we used) shall now no more,
To fetch day, press about his chamber door;
From which he issued with that awful state,
It seemed Mars broke through Janus' double gate:

189–90. where . . . prevailed] The Battle of the Dunes (4/14 June 1658) preceded the capture of Dunkirk. English regiments successfully attacked sand dunes defended by Spanish troops. Lieutenant-Colonel Roger Fenwick was mortally wounded in the action.
190. The sea between] although the English Channel separated Fenwick and the English soldiers from Cromwell. *his prayer prevailed*] Cromwell and the Council of State called a day of public prayer and fasting to coincide with the battle.
191–2. Joshua commanded the sun to stay at its noon position until the Israelites had defeated the Amorites: Joshua 10:12–14.
194. He conquered God] like Joshua, Cromwell won God's favour; an allusion to Jacob's wrestling with God disguised as a man, Gen. 32:24–9 *still*] always (*OED* adv. 3).
197–8. Cromwell was more hurt by the pity he felt for his enemies as he defeated them than he was by the blows of their weapons.
200. loose] unrestrained, at liberty (*OED* a. 1 a–b).
201–2. Friendship . . . name] Cromwell's great grandfather was Richard Williams, nephew to Thomas Cromwell, later Earl of Essex, the great statesman of Henry VIII's reign. Thomas Cromwell effectively adopted his nephew, who took his name and received a knighthood.
203–4. Friendship is usually extended to individuals, but Cromwell extended his love to all people.
208. affected] cherished (*OED* v.¹ 2); see also above, l. 18.
212. children of the highest] the elect, the saints, the army: 'In his Army he reckoned the choicest Saints, his chiefest Worthies', '*The humble Address of the Officers in your Highness Armies*', *Mercurius Politicus*, 434 (16–23 September 1658), 845. See above, l. 176.
213. Nature's tribute] death.
214. adventured] risked.

215. cast] guessed (*OED* v. VI 38); see above l. 139.
217. prudence] a) wisdom b) foresight.
218. dear . . . diff'ring] the various Puritans and groups upon which support for the republic and Protectorate was based; they are 'dear' (that is, beloved) to Cromwell and to God.
219. as] Bod. 1; so *Thompson*.
220. A reference to the republican (and largely secular) opposition to the Protector: it was, for the most part, easily contained by the Protectorate intelligence system. See Smith, in Armitage *et al.* (1995), 137–55; Norbrook (1999), 310–25; Holstun (2000), ch. 8.
221–2. A reference to the spiritual pride or perfectionism of some Puritans (since they believed that grace put them above laws). In theological terminology, this is Antinomianism, traces of which were to be found among the Independents and Baptists, as well as the more extreme groups of the period.
225–6. A reference to the view, held by Royalists and republicans alike, that Puritan zeal was a deceit for aggressive egotism. From this viewpoint, rule by the saints was a gross travesty of a political order that should properly follow a divine pattern (and for hard Royalists, this was monarchy by divine right).
227. Valour] see above, ll. 151, 177, and *An Horatian Ode*, l. 107 n.
229. refuse] Bod . . 1; refuge *Thompson*.
233. awful] a) terrible b) causing profound respect.
234. Mars . . . gate] Janus' gates were closed in time of peace, and open in time of war. Cromwell as Mars, god of war, cannot help but signify war although peace was his intention: an apt description of the compounding of peace with force under Cromwell's rule. Cf. James Howell, *Dendrologia Dodonas Grove* (1640, 1644), 102: '*turn'd the match, to powder; Mars thrust Hymen out of dores, and Janus gates flew wide open*' (of James I's threats of war to Spain in the 1620s).

235 Yet always tempered with an air so mild,
    No April suns that e'er so gently smiled;
    No more shall hear that powerful language charm,
    Whose force oft spared the labour of his arm;
    No more shall follow where he spent the days
240 In war, in counsel, or in prayer, and praise;
    Whose meanest acts he would himself advance,
    As ungirt David to the ark did dance.
    All, all is gone of ours or his delight
    In horses fierce, wild deer, or armour bright.
245 Francisca fair can nothing now but weep,
    Nor with soft notes shall sing his cares asleep.
        I saw him dead. A leaden slumber lies
    And mortal sleep over those wakeful eyes:
    Those gentle rays under the lids were fled,
250 Which through his looks that piercing sweetness shed;
    That port which so majestic was and strong,
    Loose and deprived of vigour, stretched along:

    All withered, all discoloured, pale and wan,
    How much another thing, no more that man?
255 Oh human glory vain, Oh death, Oh wings,
    Oh worthless world, Oh transitory things!
        Yet dwelt that greatness in his shape decayed,
    That still, though dead, greater than death he laid;
    And in his altered face you something feign
260 That threatens death, he yet will live again.
        Not much unlike the sacred oak which shoots
    To heaven its branches and through earth its roots:
    Whose spacious boughs are hung with trophies roun
    And honoured wreaths have oft the victor crowned.
265 When angry Jove darts lightning through the air,
    At mortals' sins, nor his own plant will spare;
    (It groans, and bruises all below, that stood
    So many years the shelter of the wood.)
    The tree erewhile foreshortened to our view,
270 When fall'n shows taller yet than as it grew.

---

236. April suns] mild, spring sunshine.
237. powerful language charm] 'his speech alwaies mixt with humility and zeal, and so piercing, that it could not but leave some impression upon those that heard him', Henry Walker, *A Collection of Severall Passages* (1659), 4.
241. meanest] a) most undignified (*OED* a.[1] II 3 c) b) most inferior, most debased (*OED* a.[1] II d).
242. ungirt David . . . dance] David honoured God by dancing before the Ark: 2 Sam. 6:13–15; cp. also Carew, 'To my worthy friend Master Geo. Sands, on his translation of the Psalmes' (1638), l. 14: 'Her Lyrick feet may dance before the Arke.' *ungirt*] must mean without kingly trappings and arms, since David wore a linen ephod or priestly garment.
243–4. his delight . . . bright] see Virgil, *Aeneid*, VI, ll. 653–5: 'quae gratia currum/armorumque fuit vivis, quae cura nitentis/pascere equos, eadem sequitur tellure repostos' (The selfsame pride in chariot and arms that was theirs in life, the selfsame care in keeping sleek steeds, attends them when hidden beneath the earth).
244. horses fierce] see above *Headnote, Context*, and above, l. 123.
245. Francisca] Cromwell's youngest daughter, Frances, who married Robert Rich in 1657.
246. soft notes] gentle singing.
247–50. These lines bear a close resemblance to John Hall's 'To the Earl of Huntingdon, On the death of his Son', in *Lachrymae Musarum* (1649), 43–8 (ll. 24–9): 'I saw a paleness sit/Upon his lips, and lurid darkness break/And chase the Orient Purple of his cheek./I saw his Eyes seal'd to eternal *Night*,/And all those Spices which Corruption fright/Strew'd on his Waxen Limbs.'
248. mortal] deadly. *wakeful*] a) continually active (*OED* a. 2 c) b) vigilant (*OED* a. 2).
249. rays] eyebeams. *lids*] eyelids.
251. port] manner, deportment (*OED* n.[4] I 1).
252. stretched along] the corpse is, of course, horizontally laid out.
254. How much . . . man?] see Virgil, *Aeneid*, II, ll. 274–6: 'quantum mutatus ab illo/Hectore, qui redit exuvias indutus

Achili/vel Danaum Phrygios iaculatus puppibus ignis!' (how changed from that Hector who returns after donning the spoils of Achilles or hurling on Danaan ships the Phrygian fires!).
259. feign] imagine (*OED* v. II 4).
261–8. This passage echoes a simile near the beginning of Lucan's *De Bello Civili* (see above, *Headnote, Genre*). The oak was associated with royalty: James Howell's *Dendrologia Dodonas Grove* (1640, 1644), a political allegory using trees as a vehicle (and which M. appears to echo in this poem, see above l. 234), repeatedly associates the oak with the English monarch, and specifically with James I and his children (35, 65, 101–2). Blatantly royal imagery is thus applied to this description of Cromwell. See also *Upon Appleton House*, ll. 545–60). In Payne Fisher's 'A Gratulatory Ode of Peace', the stout oak is used as a simile for the Scottish forces routed by Cromwell at the Battle of Worcester: 'Like to a happy Oake, whose Trunke so great/Is both to birds and beasts a safe retreat, which hath endur'd the shocks of wind and weather/Untouch'd and free for a long time together;/Laid at, at last, with Axes doth begin/His lofty head towards the earth to leane,' *Veni; vidi; vici*, 64. The reverse of Cromwell's death medal showed a healthy oak tree next to the stump of another, with the words 'Non defitient Oliva Sep. 3, 1658' (the olives (or Olivers) will not fail); this should correctly read 'Non deficient olivae'. Knoppers (2000), 153, suggests that the oaks represent respectively Richard and Oliver. See also *Headnote, Genre*.
264. honoured wreaths] oak wreaths honoured civic achievement (see *To his Noble Friend Mr Richard Lovelace*, l. 12; *The Garden*, l. 2).
266. nor his . . . spare] See *Headnote, Genre*.
267–70. Cp. J.H., 'Epitaph upon K. Charles', *Eikon Basilike* (1649; Wing E306), 2nd pagination sequence, 8, 'So falls that stately Cedar, while it stood/That was the only glory of the wood.'
269–70. The tree looks shorter than it really is when it is standing and we look up at it from below; when it is fallen, we see it at its true height.

So shall his praise to after times increase,
When truth shall be allowed, and faction cease,
And his own shadows with him fall. The eye
Detracts from objects than itself more high:
75 But when death takes them from that envied seat,
Seeing how little we confess, how great.

Thee, many ages hence, in martial verse
Shall th'English soldier, ere he charge, rehearse:
Singing of thee, inflame themselves to fight,
80 And with the name of *Cromwell* armies fright.
As long as rivers to the seas shall run,
As long as Cynthia shall relieve the sun,
While stags shall fly unto the forests thick,
While sheep delight the grassy downs to pick,
85 As long as future time succeeds the past,
Always thy honour, praise, and name, shall last.
Thou in a pitch how far beyond the sphere
Of human glory tower'st, and reigning there
Despoiled of mortal robes, in seas of bliss,

290 Plunging dost bathe, and tread the bright abyss:
There thy great soul at once a world does see,
Spacious enough, and pure enough for thee.
How soon thou Moses hast, and Joshua found,
And David, for the sword and harp renowned;
295 How straight canst to each happy mansion go?
(Far better known above than here below)
And in those joys dost spend the endless day,
Which in expressing, we ourselves betray.

For we, since thou art gone, with heavy doom
300 Wander like ghosts about thy lovèd tomb;
And lost in tears, have neither sight nor mind
To guide us upward through this region blind.
Since thou art gone, who best that way couldst teach,
Only our sighs, perhaps, may thither reach.

305 And Richard yet, where his great parent led,
Beats on the rugged track: he, virtue dead,
Revives, and by his milder beams assures;
And yet how much of them his grief obscures.

---

272. truth . . . cease] the one apocalyptic line in the poem, as opposed to the profuse apocalyptic reference in the earlier Cromwell poems, but no text from the Book of Revelation is invoked here.
273. shadows . . . fall] an extension from the oak image: when the tree falls, the shadows disappear. *shadows*] lesser imitators, whether supporters, opponents or simply comparable men; see also *An Horatian Ode*, l. 3.
273–4. The eye/Detracts] unlike Cromwell, who was 'the Master of Political Opticks', Anon., *The Unparalleld Monarch* (1656), 6.
274. Detracts] subtracts (*OED* v. 1).
275–6. Being envious of the great, we only praise them according to their worth when they are dead.
275. seat] throne, and hence height.
278. rehearse] recite (*OED* v. 1).
282. Cynthia] the moon goddess.
287–90. Thou in a pitch . . . abyss] cf. 'R.H.', '*Mount O Seraphick soul, advance a Throne Above the shade of earth's dark gloomy cave . . .*', *Musarum Cantabrigiensium* (1658), sig. H1ʳ.
287. pitch] highest point (*OED* n.² IV 19); Donno notes that the word is part of the language of falconry (*OED* n.² IV 18), which would therefore echo *An Horatian Ode*, ll. 91–6.
289. Despoiled] stripped (without the sense of spoliation (*OED* v. 3 b)).
290. Plunging] the image of Cromwell bathing in the seas of heaven bears a general resemblance to Lycidas washing his hair in heaven (Milton, *Lycidas* (1637), l. 175; see above *Headnote, Genre and Context*). However, there are several closer parallels with Milton's *Paradise Lost*, all of them concerned with Satan, the rebel angels and Adam's experience of the Fall: 2, l. 172, 'And plunge us in the flames?'; II, l. 441, 'plung'd in that abortive gulf'; 10, l. 476, 'Th'Untractable Abysse, plung'd in the womb'; X, l. 844, 'I find no way, from deeper to deeper plung'd!' The Miltonic position of a reversal in the character of Satan of words attaching to the praise of Parliamentarians and republicans before 1660 is apparent here. It is usually supposed

that Milton had not completed book ten of *Paradise Lost* by late 1658–early 1659, so the possibility that M. was echoing Milton is slight. It is a possibility that Milton is echoing M., and doing so significantly. *abyss*] the span of heaven.
291. at] Margoliouth; yet Bod. 1.
293. Moses . . . Joshua] See '*The humble Address of the Officers of your Hiness Armies*', in *Mercurius Politicus*, 434 (16–23 September 1658), 845, 'alas this our *Moses* (your dear and blessed Father) the Servant of the Lord is dead:'; H[enry] D[awbeny], *Historie and Policie Re-Viewed, In The Heroick Transactions of his Most Serene Highnesse, Oliver, Late Lord Protector* (1659), Sig. A4ʳ, addressing Richard, 'how all we your people, look upon you, as our second *Joshua*, in the place of our second *Moses*'.
294. David . . . renowned] unlike Moses and Joshua, the figure of David was much more readily associated with the monarchy, and with royalist apology: see the engraved frontispiece to Virgilio Malvezzi, *Il Davide Perseguitato* (1647), featuring King David with the face of Charles I.
298. i.e., in saying these things, we reveal our own earthliness and our sense of loss.
301. lost in tears] 'from our eyes/Drop at his shrine a melting sacrifice', Thomas Fuller, 'An Elegie . . .'; Charles Darby, 'Exact a summe of tears from every Poll', *Musarum Cantabrigiensium*, sigs. G3ᵛ, G4ᵛ.
302. region blind] the earth. *blind*] dark, obscure (*OED* a. III 6).
303. Since . . . gone] cp. *Lycidas* (1637), ll. 37–8, 'now thou art gone,/Now thou art gone, and never must return!'
305–6. Richard . . . track] cp. Thomas Resbury, '*Ad Illustrissimum Celsissimumque Dominum* Ricardum . . .', in *Musarum Cantabrigiensium* (1658), sig. E4ʳ, 'te nunquam *Phaetontaeus* stimulaverat ardor/Ante diem Patrii tentare pericula currûs'.
305. Richard] Richard Cromwell (1626–1712) was declared Lord Protector on the day of his father's death.
307. milder beams] it was hoped that Richard Cromwell, without his father's forceful personality and history, would be able to achieve a greater degree of reconciliation between different groups and interests in the nation.

He, as his father, long was kept from sight
310 In private, to be viewed by better light:
But opened once, what splendour does he throw?
A Cromwell in an hour a prince will grow.
How he becomes that seat, how strongly strains,
How gently winds at once the ruling reins?
315 Heav'n to this choice prepared a diadem,
Richer than any eastern silk or gem:

A pearly rainbow, where the sun enchased
His brows, like an imperial jewel graced.
We find already what those omens mean,
320 Earth ne'er more glad, nor heaven more serene:
Cease now our griefs, calm peace succeeds a war,
Rainbows to storms, Richard to Oliver.
Tempt not his clemency to try his power,
He threats no deluge, yet foretells a shower.

---

311. *opened once*] Richard Cromwell as being kept inside a cabinet – associated with secret, courtly government, and another instance of a courtly image being applied to Protectorate government.
313. *seat*] see above, l. 275.
314. *gently winds . . . reins*] a conflation of two different senses. Richard Cromwell, as the husbandman of state, is imagined turning horses with gentle but firm experience (*wind, OED* v.[1] I 9), but there are also senses of the reins being coiled around the people, as an image of control (*wind, OED* v.[1] I 16), and

of the reins being used to control by subtle and insinuating means (*OED* v.[1] I 11).
317. *enchased*] set with gems (*OED* v.[2] 2).
324. *He threats . . . shower*] cp. Samuel Fuller, in *Musarum Cantabrigiensium* (1658), sig. H4[v], 'Thus we have sun-shine mixed with our rain.' There are millenarian connotations here: the Hebrew in the title of a work by the Fifth Monarchist John Rogers, *Sagrir: Or a Doomsday drawing Nigh* (1654), translates as 'torrential rain'. Richard's milder shower promises a less anxiously expectant time.

57
In Effigiem Oliveri Cromwell

Publication. 1681.

Date and Context. See above, *A Letter from Doctor Ingelo, Headnote, Context.* Norbrook (1999), 339, notes that the poem 'enacts a tension between Augustan [i.e. peaceful] and Puritan [warlike] emphases' of Cromwell's Protectoral rule.

A copy of the painting to which this poem was an accompaniment, one of two made most probably by Robert Walker, survives in the collection of the Duke of Grafton and is reproduced in Maurice Ashley, *The Greatness of Oliver Cromwell* (1957). (Edward Holberton, private communication; see also below, *In eandem Reginae Sueciae transmissam, Headnote, Context*).

In Effigiem Oliveri Cromwell

Haec est quae toties inimicos umbra fugavit,
  At sub qua cives otia lenta terunt.

On a Portrait of Oliver Cromwell

This is a representation which has routed the enemy so many times, but beneath which citizens pass sluggish leisure.

---

1. umbra] image (Lewis and Short, II.A); but mostly used in a negative sense on political topics: see, e.g., Cicero, *De Officiis*, III.xvii.69: 'veri juris germanaeque justitiae solidam et expressam effigiem nullam tenemus, umbra et imaginibus utimur' (we possess no substantial, life-like image of true love and genuine Justice; a mere outline of a sketch is all that we enjoy).

2. qua] standing for *umbra*; now used in other figurative senses: protection (Lewis and Short, II.B). The Emperor Augustus provided an *umbra* for his poets.

58
In eandem Reginae Sueciae transmissam

Date. See above, *A Letter from Doctor Ingelo*, *Headnote*, *Context*.

Publication. 1681.

Text. Manuscript copies exist at BL MS Add. 34362, fol. 41ʳ (*BL 6*), a verse miscellany, *c.* 1680s, belonging to the Danvers family; BL MS Add. 32906, fol. 184 (*BL 7*), in a single octavo leaf, made in the early eighteenth century, and owned by the Malet family, baronets of Wilbury, Wilts.; BL MS Add. 36270 (*BL 8*), fol. 97 (with a translation on fol. 98ʳ), mid-eighteenth-century papers of the Yorke family, Earls of Hardwicke; University of Leeds, Brotherton Collection, MS Lt. q. 52, fol. 20ᵛ (*L2*), entitled 'In Picturam Oliveri Protectoris Christianae Sweciae Reginae Dedicatam', and endorsed 'A.M. on Oliver's Picture, sent to Q. Christina', on the verso of a single folio leaf of verse in an unbound bundle of verse assembled by Jonathan Gibson (1630–1711) of Welburn, near Kirkby Moorside, North Yorkshire, late seventeenth century; Worcester College, Oxford, MSS 6.13, p. 112 (*OW 1*), in a verse miscellany compiled in part by George Clarke (1661–1736), late seventeenth–early eighteenth century.

Attribution. Toland (1699), 1.38, and Visiak, *N & Q*, 176 (January–June 1939), 200–1, suggested that the lines were possibly by Milton and M., but the closeness of the lines to the previous two poems has convinced most scholars that M. was the author (see, e.g., MacKellar (1930), 363–4).

Context. The poem seems to have been intended to accompany Cromwell's portrait, which was dispatched to Sweden at the conclusion of the Treaty of April 1654. Toland (1698), 1.38, correctly understood the poem to be spoken by Cromwell: M.'s poem gives the portrait of Cromwell a voice.

In 1727 Isaac Le Heup claimed that 'Oliver in return for the chain, and its ornaments [from Christina], sent his own picture, represented with it as about his neck, and eight elegant lines at the bottom of it, composed by Milton, and which are given in that poet's works, beginning, Bellipotens Virgo. The picture which the protector sent is now remaining at Sweden.' The picture at Gripsholm Castle shows no chains and may have arrived earlier in Sweden than 1653–54; its description is consistent with one owned by the Duke of Grafton. 'In most portraits Cromwell wears a cuirass of polished armour with a simple collar of white cloth protruding. His person is usually unornamented, although in some Walker portraits a page ties a sash around his waist, as though Cromwell were preparing for battle. The Grafton portrait is altogether different: the pose, armour and head are very similar to several other portraits of Cromwell by Walker, but Walker wraps Cromwell's armour in a sumptuous, bright fabric which frames the gleaming Swedish chain and pendant. . . . the Grafton portrait shows him dressed up to make a fit appearance in Christina's gallery.' (Edward Holberton, private communication).

In eandem Reginae Sueciae transmissam

Bellipotens virgo, septem regina trionum.
   Christina, arctoi lucida stella poli;
Cernis quas merui dura sub casside rugas;
   Sicque senex armis impiger ora fero;
5   Invia Fatorum dum per vestigia nitor,
   Exequor et populi fortia jussa manu.
At tibi submittit frontem reverentior umbra,
   Nec sunt hi vultus regibus usque truces.

On the Same Sent Across to the Queen of Sweden

Virgin, powerful in war, Queen of the Seven Oxen, Christina, gleaming star of the North Pole, you see what wrinkles I have earned beneath a cruel helmet; thus an old man I actively confront warfare; while I press forward through the pathless tracts of the fates and with my troops follow through the sturdy orders of the people. But this representation submits its brow more reverently to you, nor is this countenance forever savage towards kings.

Title. 1681; by And. Marvell. Writt under Cromwells picture presented to yᵉ Queene of Sweden. *BL 7;* Andrew Marvell's Verses inscrib'd on Cromwell's picture presented to Christina Queen of Sweden. *BL 8.*
1. septem regina trionum] deriving from Septentriones, the seven stars of the constellation of the Great Bear (also the Wain, and Little Bear); hence a name for the northern regions of the heavens or the earth.
3. Cernis . . . rugas] Cp. *An Horatian Ode,* ll. 45–6: 'What field of all the civil wars/Where his were not the deepest scars?' *Cernis*] *1681+*: Aspice *BL 8.*
4. Sicque] *1681+*; Utque *BL 6, BL 7. fero*] *1681+*; gero *BL 7.*
7. umbra] see above, *In Effigiem Oliveri Cromwell,* l. 1 n.

59

Two Songs at the Marriage of the Lord Fauconberg and the Lady Mary Cromwell

Date. November 1657. Mary Cromwell (1637–1712), third daughter of Oliver Cromwell, was married to Thomas Belasyse, second Viscount Fauconberg (or Falconbridge; 1627–1700), on Thursday, 19 November 1657, at Hampton Court. M. wrote his *Two Songs* for this occasion. The internal evidence of both songs suggests that they would have been performed shortly after the wedding ceremony, but there is no absolute certainty since the celebrations are reported to have continued during the following week.

Publication. 1681.

Context. The two songs were probably part of a musical entertainment devised for the wedding. Davenant wrote an epithalamium for the marriage, which was entered in the Stationers' Register on 7 December, but the poem does not survive in printed or manuscript form. Fauconberg was related matrilineally to Fairfax, and was a Yorkshireman: it is therefore possible that he was well known to M. Despite the closure of the theatres, and the public hostility of the Parliamentarian and Commonwealth regimes to plays, entertainments continued to be performed in private houses throughout the 1640s and 1650s; pastoral themes and characters were popular (see Smith (1994), 70–92; Randall (1995), ch. 10). Many Commonwealth grandees were in favour of drama, and various kinds of officially tolerated theatre began to be performed again during the 1650s. Cromwell himself was fond of music, and maintained a considerable musical establishment, using it to entertain guests (see Sherwood (1977), 137–8). M.'s use of Platonic elements points up the revival of Caroline masque themes inside Protectoral circles; with the Restoration, this kind of masque was to disappear (Maguire (1992), 83–101).

In comparison with the wedding of another Cromwell daughter, Frances, at Whitehall the previous week, this wedding was modest and a private affair: Fauconberg requested that the cost of the wedding be allocated to the dowry. However, such modesty is not attributable to Puritanism. The women in Cromwell's family had Anglican preferences, and the Belasyses were known Royalist sympathizers (the groom had also, at one point, been suspected of Catholicism by the government). The marriage ceremony was conducted by Dr John Hewitt, reputedly using the Book of Common Prayer (just seven months later he would be tried and executed for his alleged part in a Royalist conspiracy). However Puritan M.'s songs appear, they were written for, and performed (if indeed they were) within a courtly and Anglican context. To this extent, they contributed to an atmosphere that must have felt somewhat like a reversion to the 1630s. The marriage itself represented a consolidation of the Cromwell family's rise to the ranks of the nobility. The marriage settlement was worth £15,000, while Fauconberg's estate was worth £35,000 p.a.

Genre and Sources. The songs are pastoral in nature, and are hence thoroughly in keeping with epithalamic tradition. In the first eclogue, Endymion represents the bridegroom, Cynthia the bride and Jove, Cromwell himself. In the second, the bride and groom are alluded to under the names of Damon and Marina; Menalca is Cromwell. Whether the newly-weds and the Lord Protector actually performed in the songs, another customary feature of entertainments, is not known.

The debt to Miltonic pastoral is strong: at the moment of the wedding, during the peace of the Protectorate, the Catholic threat, represented by the 'grim wolf' in *Lycidas* is kept well as bay (l. 2). Further Miltonic echoes occur at the end of the first song (l. 57). The First Song involves no resolution in the union of a human and a deity: Endymion explains why the two spheres must be kept apart, and in doing so he demonstrates the honesty and courage that win Cynthia's favour. In effect, this is a nuptial version of the Platonic and Christian masque in which a human demonstration of faith wins grace.

The poem also explicitly reworks earlier M. poems. In the first instance, there are echoes from other pastoral dialogues (e.g. *Clorinda and Damon*; see also below, l. 24 n.). More significantly, M. refers to his previous panegyrics of Cromwell (see below, Second Song, 11. 15–16).

Friedman (in Summers and Pebworth, eds (1992), 21–8) suggests that Henry Lawes may have been the composer of the music for M.'s songs, although other candidates would have been John Hingston, master of music to the Lord Protector, or perhaps one of the other seven ex-court protectorate musicians. These men, together with the 'two lads brought up to music' would have presumably performed the music at the wedding (see Sherwood (1977), 135–8, 170). Lawes played a prominent role in musical innovation, furthering the humanist goal of balancing text and melodic line. By the mid-seventeenth century English song had abandoned polyphony and conventional formulae for monody which subjected musical line to the poetic text. The dramatized persona of the singing voice and argumentative structure were emphasized, preferences that would have suited the fanciful, ironic and self-conscious nature of M.'s poems.

Versification. The metre of the first song is M.'s favoured iambic tetrameter, with trochaic inversions. Most of the individual speeches are in quatrains, although others vary from half-lines to six lines. The second song features mostly heptasyllabic lines, with the choruses speaking in prosodic forms that vary from one or two iambic feet to full pentameters. Friedman (in Summers and Pebworth, eds (1992), 24) notes that most comparable entertainment verse is regular: M. produces a verse that is expressive rather than formulaic, 'highlighting and emphasizing rhymes, line-ends, and particular points of argument rather than strophic, repeated, or ornamental elements'. Although no music for the songs survives, it may well have been that the tension between regularity of poetic metre and discontinuous cadences (in the style of the music outlined above) would also enhance the playfulness of M.'s sophisticated prosody.

Two Songs at the Marriage of the Lord Fauconberg and the Lady Mary Cromwell

First

Chorus. Endymion. Luna.

Chorus

Th'astrologers' own eyes are set,
And even wolves the sheep forget;
Only this shepherd, late and soon,
Upon this hill outwakes the moon.
5   Hark how he sings, with sad delight,
Thorough the clear and silent night.

Endymion

Cynthia, O Cynthia, turn thine ear,
Nor scorn Endymion's plaints to hear.
As we our flocks, so you command
10   The fleecy clouds with silver wand.

Cynthia

If thou a mortal, rather sleep;
Or if a shepherd, watch thy sheep.

Endymion

The shepherd, since he saw thine eyes,
And sheep are both thy sacrifice.
15   Nor merits he a mortal's name,
That burns with an immortal flame.

Cynthia

I have enough for me to do,
Ruling the waves that ebb and flow.

Endymion

Since thou disdain'st not then to share
20   On sublunary things thy care;

Personae. Endymion] represents Lord Fauconberg (see above, *Headnote. Context*).

1. set] i.e. as the sun sets.

3. late and soon] so late that it is very early.

6. clear] free from cloud and mist (*OED* a. I 1 c).

7. Cynthia] the moon, but plainly identified as Mary Cromwell at l. 33, below. In Elizabethan iconography, Cynthia was Queen Elizabeth herself: Mary Cromwell takes her place as heroic Protestant female.

Rather restrain these double seas,
Mine eyes' uncessant deluges.

Cynthia
My wakeful lamp all night must move,
Securing their repose above.

Endymion
25 If therefore thy resplendent ray
Can make a night more bright than day;
Shine thorough this obscurer breast,
With shades of deep despair oppressed.

Chorus
Courage, Endymion, boldly woo,
30 Anchises was a shepherd too;
Yet is her younger sister laid
Sporting with him in Ida's shade:
    And Cynthia, though the strongest,
Seeks but the honour to have held out longest.

Endymion
35 Here unto Latmus' top I climb:
How far below thine orb sublime?
O why, as well as eyes to see,
Have I not arms that reach to thee?

Cynthia
'Tis needless then that I refuse,
40 Would you but your own reason use.

Endymion
Though I so high may not pretend,
It is the same so you descend.

Cynthia
These stars would say I do them wrong,
Rivals each one for thee too strong.

Endymion
45 The stars are fixed unto their sphere,
And cannot, though they would, come near.
Less loves set off each other's praise,
While stars eclipse by mixing rays.

Cynthia
That cave is dark.

Endymion
    Then none can spy:
50 Or shine thou there and 'tis the sky.

Chorus
    Joy to Endymion,
For he has Cynthia's favour won.
    And Jove himself approves
With his serenest influence their loves.
55   For he did never love to pair
    His progeny above the air;
    But to be honest, valiant, wise,
Makes mortals matches fit for deities.

21–2. double . . . deluges] Cp. *Eyes and Tears*, ll. 38, 45; *Mourning*, ll. 17, 30–2.
21. double seas] the streams of tears from each eye.
22. uncessant] incessant, unceasing.
24. their repose above] their [the 'deluges': the sea and the tears] peacefulness from heaven.
30–2. Anchises represents here Robert Rich, grandson and heir to the Earl of Warwick, who married Frances Cromwell on 11 November 1657. Anchises consorted with Venus on Mount Ida on Crete, so that Frances Cromwell is compared to the goddess of love. Since Anchises was the father of Aeneas, the implication is that the union between Rich and Cromwell families will produce a new hero for the English nation.
33. Cynthia] Mary Cromwell.
35. Latmus] mountain in Caria where Cynthia (as Selene) wooed Endymion. See Pliny, *Natural History*, V.xxxi.113.
40. reason] Cynthia lives in the realm of pure reason, and

expects Endymion to exercise his reason to reach her. M. thus uses a Platonic conception: see below, l. 49 n.
42. so] i.e. by the same measure.
45. sphere] place of fixed orbit in the Ptolemaic system.
47. Less] i.e. lesser. *set off*] enhance, complement (*OED* v[1] 142 e(a)).
49. cave] a reference to Plato's allegory of the cave (*Republic*, VII.514 ff.): man's perception of the world of real ideas is likened to a person in a darkened cave who only sees shadows of objects moving past in the outside world on the wall of the cave. See also above, l. 40.
53–4. Friedman, in Summers and Pebworth, eds (1992), 25, argues that this is an allusion to the marriage of Mary Fairfax and George Villiers, second Duke of Buckingham in September 1657, in which Cromwell played a role. Fraser (1973; 1989), 641–2, suggests that the lines refer to an earlier rumour of marriage with Charles II.

Second Song

Hobbinol. Phillis. Tomalin.

Hobbinol

Phillis, Tomalin, away:
Never such a merry day.
For the northern shepherd's son
Has Menalcas' daughter won.

Phillis

Stay till I some flow'rs ha'tied
In a garland for the bride.

Tomalin

If thou would'st a garland bring,
Phillis you may wait the spring:
They ha'chosen such an hour
10 When she is the only flow'r.

Phillis

Let's not then at least be seen
Without each a sprig of green.

Hobbinol

Fear not; at Menalcas' hall
There is bays enough for all.
15 He when young as we did graze,
But when old he planted bays.

Tomalin

Here she comes; but with a look
Far more catching than my hook.
'Twas those eyes, I now dare swear,
20 Led our lambs we knew not where.

Hobbinol

Nor our lambs own fleeces are
Curled so lovely as her hair:
Nor our sheep new washed can be
Half so white or sweet as she.

Phillis

25 He so looks as fit to keep
Somewhat else than silly sheep.

Hobbinol

Come, let's in some carol new
Pay to Love and them their due.

All

   Joy to that happy pair,
30 Whose hopes united banish our despair.
      What shepherd could for love pretend,
   Whilst all the nymphs on Damon's choice attend?
      What shepherdess could hope to wed
      Before Marina's turn were sped?
35   Now lesser beauties may take place,
      And meaner virtues come in play;
         While they,
         Looking from high,
         Shall grace
40 Our flocks and us with a propitious eye.
         But what is most, the gentle swain
         No more shall need of love complain;
         But virtue shall be beauty's hire,
      And those be equal that have equal fire.
45   Marina yields. Who dares be coy?
      Or who despair, now Damon does enjoy?
         Joy to that happy pair,
      Whose hopes united banish our despair.

---

2. *Never*] i.e. 'never was there'.
3. *northern shepherd's son*] Fauconberg, like his kinsman, Fairfax, was a Yorkshireman; the northern shepherd was Henry Belasyse, first Viscount Fauconberg (d. 1652).
4. *Menalcas'*] Oliver Cromwell. Reference to both Charles I and Charles II was often made in pastoral terms, but the reverse side of Cromwell's death medal depicted a shepherd minding sheep, together with an olive tree (see Randall (1995), 207).
8–10. *wait . . . flow'r*] a reference to the fact that the wedding takes place in the winter.
12. *green*] the colour of love and of hope: see above, 145, ll. 3–4 n.
14. *bays enough*] a reference to Cromwell's achievements: he has won all the bays. Cromwell was portrayed on medals wearing a wreath.
15–16. Friedman, in Summers and Pebworth, eds (1992), 26, argues that M. is echoing his former praise of Cromwell in *An Horatian Ode*, ll. 29–36.
17. *she*] Marina.
24. *Half . . . she*] Cp. *The Nymph complaining for the death*

of her Fawn, l. 58: 'It waxed more white and sweet than they.'
25. *He*] Damon.
26. *silly*] defenceless; conventional epithet for sheep (*OED* a. A 1 c); see, e.g., Francis Quarles, *Judgement and Mercy* (1646), 73: 'The silly *Sheep* reposed in their warm fleeces.'
27. *carol*] song, often accompanied by a dance (*OED* n. I 2).
30. A reference to the supposed political implications of the marriage: not merely a favourable alliance for both the Cromwells and the Belasyses, but also a further healing of national division by the reconciliation of a former royalist family with the Protectorate. In the light of the manner in which the wedding was conducted, and the conspiracy about to occur, the sentiments of the poem were, to say the least, hopeful.
31. *pretend*] try to win in marriage (*OED* v. II 13 b).
40. *propitious*] favouring (*OED* a. 1).
43. *virtue shall be beauty's hire*] i.e. virtue will be the reward of beauty. *hire*] reward (*OED* n. 3).
45. *coy*] see above, *To His Coy Mistress*, Title n.
48. See above, l. 30 n.

THE
ADVICE-TO-A-PAINTER
AND ASSOCIATED POEMS

The Advice-to-a-Painter Poems

Edmund Waller celebrated the English naval victory over the Dutch at Lowestoft in June 1665 with *Instructions to a Painter*, published first in short form as a broadsheet in 1665 (ll. 1–50, 55–64), then in 1666 as a thin folio volume (entered in the Stationers' Register on 1 March). In response, the Advice-to-a-Painter poems appeared, most probably first in manuscript, then shortly afterwards in print. The poems were part of a series of verse satires on the Second Dutch War, which developed from a concern with naval maladministration and court corruption into an attack on the bishops of the Church of England. They constituted a major means by which discontent with Clarendon's government was registered, and opposition focused, before the divisions of the Exclusion Crisis led to the clear identification of Whig and Tory factions.

After the Revolution of 1688–89 in particular, the poems were variously attributed to M. in the *Poems on Affairs of State*, as were some in manuscript form. In this way, the poems were part of the larger freight of Restoration verse satire attributed to M., where a 'Marvell' poem signified resistance to Stuart iniquities (see below, 330).

Authorship. Of all the Advice-to-a-Painter poems, no doubt has been cast on M.'s authorship of the *Last Instructions to a Painter*, which contains plenty of internal evidence of Marvellian poetic language. The *Fourth* and *Fifth Advices*, recounting events between the Parliamentary session beginning in September 1666 and the flight of Clarendon on 29 November 1667, have generally been assumed not to be M.'s work: they are shorter, different in design, and considered generally inferior to the three poems associated with M. The earlier events they cover are the same as those recalled in the *Last Instructions*.

In 1776 Thompson (I, xxxix) reported that after he had completed his edition and life of M., he received the manuscript 'written by Mr Popple' (now considered to be *Bod. 1*) in which were several poems by M. hitherto unprinted. In particular, by 'this manuscript I also find, that those two excellent satires, entitled, A Direction to a Painter concerning the Dutch War in 1667, and published in the State Poems, Vol. I, p. 24, as Sir John Denham's, are both of them compositions of Mr Marvell.' These were the *Second* and *Third Advices*. Inclusion in the manuscript, and perhaps other unstated reasons, inclined Thompson to attribute them to M. In other MSS, presumably unknown to Thompson, there are also attributions of the poems to M.: e.g. the copy of *The Second Advice* in an Oxford anthology of orations and poems (Cardiff Central Library, MS 1.482 (*Ca.*)).

Lord, *BNYPL*, 62 (1958), 551–70, argued on grounds of thematic and some aesthetic continuity that M. was responsible for the *Second* and *Third Advices*. He was confuted by Fogel, *BNYPL*, 63 (1959), 223–36, 292–308 on the grounds of the weakness of this evidence in the context of the total body of available evidence, and by Wallace (1968), 152–5, on the grounds of the strategic implausibility of the positions adopted in these two poems, quite unlike the carefully positioned *Last Instructions*. Fogel believed that each poem was written by a different author. (Lord replied to Fogel in *BNYPL*, 63 (1959), 355–66; the dispute was reprinted in Erdman and Fogel, eds (1966), 25–44, 69–114.) O Hehir (1968, 210–29) attempted to reattach the authorship of the poems to Sir John Denham, who was named as the author of the poems in many of the early MS copies, and in all the early printed editions.

Legouis (1965), 164, n. 1, reaffirmed Margoliouth's earlier exclusion of the poems from the canon. Donno agreed on grounds of poetic quality. But Lord was supported by Farley-Hills (1974), 74, on the grounds of a poetic quality that was recognized by contemporaries such as the Royalist poet Christopher Wase (see his *Divination* (1666), ll. 69–90). Patterson (*PBSA*, 71 (1977), 473–86, and (1978), 111–17, revised (2000), 76–8), reaffirmed the case for M.'s authorship, this time on the basis of a more closely argued appreciation of the application of aesthetic theory, as well as underlining the importance of the inclusion of the poems in *Bod. 1*, as is the case with both *The Second* and *Third Advices*. While this argument did not win complete assent (Chernaik (1983), 211, ignored it, stood by Fogel, the rarity of contemporary attributions to M., and his own sceptical view of the authority of *Bod. 1*), more recent detailed attention to diction, prosody and rhyming, by Patterson *SEL*, 40 (2000), 395–411, and in the following notes, provide strong evidence that *The Second* and *Third Advices* contain the work of M.: in them he can be seen reworking familiar parts of his earlier lyric and public poetry (see below, 333, 371, 344–6, 353–4; see also Patterson (2000), 85). At the very least, sections of the two poems may be said to be M.'s. There is the possibility of joint or collaborative authorship, but also the possibility, or in Patterson's view, probability, that M. was responsible for all of the poems.

The problem of quality remains: *The Last Instructions* is undoubtedly a superior poem to the two *Advices*, both in terms of its design and its prosodic qualities. For instance, it is hard to believe that the inept ll. 175–6, or the obscure and unmetrical l. 286 of *The Second Advice* could be M.'s work. Such an observation strengthens the claim for collaborative authorship in the earlier poems. But a longer gestation time for *The Last Instructions*, and a poetry aimed at a very different readership, with a very different purpose, are still plausible causes of this difference. The findings of John Burrow (*MLR*, 100 (2005), 281–97) using computer stylistics analysis confirm M.'s authorship of the Advice-to-a-Painter poems, but not 'Clarendon's Housewarming.'

If we admit the *Second* and *Third Advices* to the canon of M.'s works, one final question remains. Despite their superiority to other poems in the Advice-to-a-Painter group associated with the Second Dutch War, there is no doubt that these poems are aesthetically and intellectually inferior both to *The Last Instructions* and to *The Loyal Scot*, which uses a passage from the earlier poem. The absence of sustained and intentional ambiguity in the *Second* and *Third Advices* cannot be ignored. *The Last Instructions* seems to have circulated little in manuscript: it is three times as long as *The Second Advice* and more than twice as long as *The Third Advice*. Its length would have made it difficult to function as a single piece of printed propaganda: it may be that M. reserved its readership to a more restricted audience. On the other hand, *The Second* and *The Third Advice* were both possibly written

quite quickly for a broad distribution, and with the clear political intention of embarrassing the war administration. It has taken a long time to find a reliable means of discerning M.'s hand in these poems: he may well have had an interest in keeping his identity quiet, and this might explain the use of Denham's name as author not merely as a literary joke, but also as a false trail. The latter possibility is enhanced by neither poem containing Denham as a fictional speaker, nor imitating his poetry. When *The Loyal Scot* emerged in its longer form in the 1670s, M.'s ventriloquizing of the voice of Cleveland was far more successful (as well as being part of the poem's point). And by the 1670s, M.'s role in public affairs was no longer a secret. As the punishments meted out to the publishers of one of the Advice volumes make clear, it was in M.'s interests to keep his involvement in the project quiet (see below, 323).

Text. A total of 193 individual MS copies of Painter poems that have been associated with M. are known to have survived. Of those accepted in this edition as M.'s, or involving M.'s hand, there are forty-seven examples of *The Second Advice*, twenty-eight of *The Third Advice*, and six of *The Last Instructions*. Very few of these can be dated to the late 1660s, and specifically to the brief period before the printed texts of 1667 appeared. Most belong to the later years of the seventeenth century, and some to the early eighteenth century. Since there are clear connections between some manuscript versions and the early printed editions, it is likely that at least as many MSS copies were made from the printed texts as from other manuscripts. Further details are given in the headnotes to each poem in the series.

Printed Publication. The Second Advice was published as a single octavo item in *1667*. *The Second* and *Third Advices* were then published as a single octavo volume in the same year (*1667²*). *Directions to a Painter*, containing the Second, Third, Fourth and Fifth Advices, and *Clarendon's Housewarming*, was also published in this year (*1667³*), although Wood (1691–92), II. 348 claimed that it was 'printed by stealth' in October 1666. The government and the Stationers' Company investigated the production and distribution of *1667²*: the nonconformist and radical publisher Francis Smith was alleged on 26 July 1667 to be organizing the printing of *1667²* (*CSPD* 1666–67, 430). More remarkably, Elizabeth Calvert, widow of the publisher of radical books, Giles, was interrogated on 5 December 1670 for publishing and selling *1667³* (Corporation of London Record Office, Sessions File 205; Ariel Hessayon, private communication; see also Maureen Bell, *PH*, 35 (1994), 29–30). The document refers back to the offence of publishing *1667³* committed on 20 May 1668. It may be that the book was printed on Calvert's secret press in Southwark. On 10 March 1671, Elizabeth Calvert was fined twenty marks for publishing a seditious book, and another bookseller, Thomas Palmer, was fined forty marks and pilloried for dispensing libels. *1667³* was the text in question for Calvert, and one of the texts for Palmer.

Dzelzainis (forthcoming) has now established that *1667³b*, actually published in 1671 or after, was a pirated edition of *1667³* – the latter prepared by George Larkin, at once a printer with nonconformist associations and an informer for the government. In *1667³b*, in respect of the *Fourth Advice*, 'all lines specifically criticizing the king are absent.' Elizabeth Poole's residence in Southwark had been searched in April 1668; Larkin most probably printed *1667³* in a room rented from Elizabeth Poole; Calvert was the publisher, Joshua Waterhouse the compositor and Thomas Willes the disperser.

This information is significant in two ways. The poem clearly had an import in printed publication (as well as in MSS circulation) beyond the immediate context of the Second Dutch War. Calvert's involvement is evidence of links between Parliamentary circles and the wider body of extra-Parliamentary disaffected persons and groups, many of them with former Commonwealth or radical connections. Indeed, M. probably made available to Calvert a brief record of an interrogation he had jointly conducted in connection with investigations of the cause of the Great Fire. It appeared in *London's Flames* (1667), 7, a rabidly anti-catholic account of the origins of the Fire. Could it be that M. felt that the findings of the Parliamentary committee needed to reach a larger readership, and also that the committee itself would be frustrated if its findings remained within the walls of Parliament? That Calvert had appealed in 1664 to the man whom M. was then serving as secretary, the Earl of Carlisle, for protection, is also suggestive. For a fuller discussion, see Smith and Bell, *TLS*, 5104 (26 January, 2001), 14–15. We can begin to glimpse the formation of a country, Puritan and Whig or neo-Whig alliance, a set of associations that would eventually blossom in the opposition politics of the Exclusion Crisis (1679–81), and which was to a significant degree continuous with the anti-monarchical, anti-episcopal groupings of the 1650s.

Manuscript Circulation. Most of the surviving MS witnesses are poetry anthologies made later in the century, often in professional scribal hands: the Advice-to-a-Painter poems contained in these books were presumably transcribed from single copies ('separates') of the poem made for circulation in 1666–67, or from other anthologies. Other surviving MSS were clearly copied from the early printed editions. There are very few surviving separates, although those that do survive can be connected with the 1660s (see below, *The Second Advice To a Painter*, *Headnote*, *Manuscript Circulation*). We might expect successive copying of the poem to result in disturbances such as alterations of line order, omissions and revisions. While this is the case with some of the later MSS, these features are also found in MSS that appear to be relatively early (e.g. *BL 29*, bound as a book in 1667; *Ca.*, dated 1670, and referring to the poem as 'lately happened'). There are more than twice as many surviving MS copies of *The Second Advice* as *The Third Advice*. Even so, the number of variants and disturbances in copies of the former poem is remarkable, given the relative stability in the state of the latter. By early 1668, the printed satires were being sent directly to MPs in an attempt to influence the shape of debates in Parliament (see Patterson (1978), 33, n. 25).

Bod., MS Gough London 14 (*Bod. 21*), an annotated copy of *1667³*, is corrected in accordance with the texts in *Bod. 1*, including the epigraph from Persius. This would appear to be a late emendation, made at the end of the century. Yale, MS Osborn b. 136 (*Υ 6*) contains the Second and Third Advices (apparently copied from *1667*) and several other painter poems, as well as (after a Latin epitaph on the death of Mazarin, with prose preface) M.'s Latin epitaphs for John and Edmund Trott, the letter to Sir John Trott, and the following prose epitaph, presumably copied (but not perfectly or in identical order) from *1681*. The MS cites Denham as the author of the *Advices* but the inclusion of the Trott material may signify a sense of connection between the two groups of writing, and at the very least the political innuendo detected by Duncan-Jones (*N & Q*, n.s. 13 (1966), 26–7), juxtaposing the virtuous Trott with Clarendon.

Political Context. The Second Anglo-Dutch War (1664–67) was caused both by economic competition, and by continuing ideological tensions between the two nations; specifically Stuart interest in restoring the power of the Prince of Orange, against the interest of the dominant Dutch republican presence (see Pincus (1996), Pt. III). Initial victory against the Dutch was undermined by an inability to exploit naval advantages, and by a failure of the war administration. The navy was hampered by a dual authority structure in which one half was often at odds with the other. Money became increasingly scarce. Supply to the fleet and preparations for coastal defence were inadequate. English trade was paralysed, even to the extent that English colliers were kept out of London in the winter of 1666–67. Coal could not be had for heating (this seems to be mentioned in one version of *The Second Advice to a Painter*; see below, l. 60 n.), and a psychological victory had been won by the Dutch, who, by contrast, had men, munitions and money. The English victory off Lowestoft in June 1665 was succeeded by the embarrassing failure of the navy to punish the Dutch fleet at Bergen, and the debacle of the Four Days' Battle (June 1666), when defeat was only narrowly avoided. At home, further disruption and demoralization came with the Great Plague, which raged throughout 1665–66, and the Great Fire of London, of 2–6 September 1666. Finally, in June 1667, came the humiliation of the Dutch raid on the Medway. After this, England sued for a settlement with the Dutch. In domestic political life, the consequence was the breakdown of Clarendon's control of Parliament and the King's confidence in him: he was removed from office in the autumn of 1667, and went into exile late in the year. 1667 saw the issue of religious toleration re-emerge: the tide began to turn in favour of the supporters of the Nonconformists and away from the Tory and Anglican alliance that had controlled the Cavalier Parliament. The religious issues that would dominate the following decade had their first sounding in these years. In the court and in Parliament, several emerged who championed calls for a more efficient government, and more religious toleration: foremost among them was M.'s old acquaintance, and husband of Mary Fairfax, George Villiers, second Duke of Buckingham, and Arthur Annesley, Earl of Anglesey. The former would be invited to be the King's chief minister, and would quickly fail; the latter was a gifted administrator and trained lawyer, with whom M. would have much to do in the 1670s.

While the press had been subject to a severe censorship since the Restoration, it is now accepted that public opinion played an important role in the politics of the war and of toleration (Pincus, chs 18–19). Although the crisis of the late 1660s was not a party dispute, the minds of contemporaries were conscious of a survival of issues from the 1640s and 1650s. The government, through its information officer and censor, Roger L'Estrange, certainly identified a republican fifth column: *The Intelligencer* reported that a republican faction had encouraged the Dutch to war on the grounds that the English government would misuse the supply it had been voted. Wase suspected the author of *The Second Advice* of Commonwealth sympathies (*Divination*, l. 160). Opinion invented phantom identities that would feed the fears of various participants, and which, though unfounded, were very real in that they could determine the decisions of key actors. In this context, the Painter poems played an important role.

While the Painter poems were concerned with the domestic response to a war against a foreign enemy, the politics of Anglo-Dutch relations themselves also enter the poems. Although mercantile competition was an important factor in the tensions that would lead to war, ideology also mattered, as it had done in the First Dutch War of 1652–54. Stuart support in the Netherlands during the Interregnum had been rooted in the Orangists; Charles II and his new government disapproved of the sway held by the republican faction over the young Prince of Orange, who was the King's nephew (see below, *The Second Advice to a Painter*, ll. 329–34). Likewise, the Dutch government (with the republican faction at the height of its powers) had no liking for the continuance of the English monarchy. They feared English influence on behalf of the Orangist cause, and used the printing presses to circulate hostile pictures of Charles II and the English. M. would have learned of this when he visited Holland as part of Sir George Downing's mission in 1662.

Between 1662 and January 1665, M. was absent from England for a total of two years and four months, including the whole of the crucial year of 1664. In that time, and in part in reaction to the activities of Dissenters and republicans in 1662–63, the hold of the government and the Anglican Royalist presence in Parliament had greatly increased. When M. returned to English politics in 1665, he found the Triennial Act, which guaranteed the calling of Parliament every three years, repealed, and the Conventicle Act, which imposed severe penalties on Dissenters, in place. The trade restrictions imposed against the Dutch in 1664 are now seen as part and parcel of the Anglican reaction: the Dutch had to be opposed because they supported nonconformity, and the idea of an English Commonwealth.

Throughout the cycle of Painter poems, M.'s knowledge of events and personalities is not tied to any particular source (e.g. particular newsbooks); rather, it appears to be based upon a conglomeration of opinions and specific information on events. Although M. often differs in his estimation of people from as well informed an observer as Pepys, his intelligence is often as apparently discerning and accurate. Indeed, the account of the Battle of Lowestoft in *The Second Advice* bears a very close resemblance to a letter of intelligence from William Coventry to Albemarle, that Pepys read (Pepys, 6.122–3). That all three Painter poems presented here were written some months after the events they describe suggests the use of accumulated information, unlike the partially informed nature of publications closer to the events. None of this is surprising, given that M. was appointed to the Parliamentary Committee investigating the misappropriation of prizes on 25 October 1665 (*JHC*, 8.621). In this context, the Painter poems may be seen as a more intimate kind of poetic as well as political exchange: another member of the same committee was Waller himself. The questioning of the justness of the war in *The Second Advice*, ll. 313–30, is particularly apt in this context, and reads almost as a list of a committee's findings. In *1667³* and several MSS these lines are placed at the end of the poem.

The advantageousness of the anonymous authorship of controversial material by an MP is well-expressed by Patterson (1978), 33: 'Inside knowledge could, in effect, create an outspoken but anonymous lobby for positions which could only be held discreetly in the House.' Perhaps in order to cover himself, M. spoke against Clarendon's impeachment several times, but after Clarendon had fled, in December 1667, he joined the committee that arranged Clarendon's banishment. Earlier in 1667, he was involved in illegal nonconformist pamphlet activity. The three Painter poem pamphlets published in 1667 were printed and distributed by surviving members of the radical press of the Commonwealth years (see above, 322–3).

The most curious omission is the absence of mention of the plague that was raging in London in 1665. This may be to do with the fact that, as an MP, M. had followed the court and parliament when it moved to Oxford.

The chronology of events is as follows:

1665
3 June   Battle of Lowestoft

25 October   M. and Waller join Committee on embezzlement of prizes

1666
1 March   Longer version of Waller's *Instructions* licensed
April   *Bod. 1* dates *Second Advice* to this month
1–4 June   Four Days' Battle; Monck's defeat only avoided by arrival of Rupert
October   Wood suggests this is the date for the *Directions* volume
3 December   M. writes to Hull Corporation with regard to legislation enabling inspection of accounts
14 December   Pepys sees copy of *The Second Advice*

1667
20 January   Pepys sees *The Third Advice*
21 January   Commons sets aside £380,000 for new supply of seamen's wages
8 February   King prorogues Parliament
10–12 June   Dutch raid on the Medway
19 June   Pett interrogated by Privy Council on a charge of negligence
1 July   Pepys and friends read several Advice-to-a-Painter poems: most probably *1667²*
25 July   Parliament reconvened
26 July   Francis Smith reported to have attempted to have *Second* and *Third Advice* printed (probably to coincide with the parliamentary session).
24 August   Treaty of Breda
4 September   *Bod. 1* and *BL 28* date for *Last Instructions*
16 September   Pepys sees *Fourth Advice*
10 October   Parliament reconvened
14 October   M. speaks in Commons against impeaching Clarendon
17 October   M. joins committee appointed to inquire into miscarriages of the Dutch War
26 October   Impeachment proceedings against Clarendon begin
29 October   M. speaks again against impeaching Clarendon
31 October   M. defends Pett in House of Commons
7/11 November   M. moves that one of charges against Clarendon be clarified
14 November   Pett investigated by M.'s committee
29 November   Flight of Clarendon
16 December   M. on committee to arrange Clarendon's banishment
19 December   Parliament adjourned

1668

6 February   Parliament reconvened

12 February   MPs receive printed verse satires

15 February   First debate against miscarriages; M.
   speaks strongly against Arlington

21 February   M. speaks against those responsible
   for paying seamen with tickets, not money

Sources, Genre and Aesthetics. The *Second* and *Third
Advices* were ascribed to Denham, but there is no
imitation of any of the poetic modes in which
Denham wrote. This is quite unlike the imitation and
reformation of Cleveland's poetry in *The Loyal Scot,*
and the other examples of M.'s engagement with the
work of other poets. Rather, Denham's name functions as a disguise (or a decoy) and a joke, although
his activities in Parliament at this time were significant and have been overlooked (see above and
below, 321, 369, ll. 65–8). The answering of Waller's
panegyric in its own terms is the starting point of the
cycle, but in *The Third Advice* and *Last Instructions*
it is merely the starting point. Imitation of a Waller
panegyric as a form of critical rebuttal (from both
royalist and republican viewpoints) had been common in the 1650s, when Waller published his
panegyric and elegy on Cromwell: see Norbrook,
SC, 11 (1996), 61–86. Waller was himself imitating Giovanni Francesco Busenello's panegyric of
Venetian naval prowess *Prospettiva del nauale
ripotato dall Republica Serenissima contra il Turco*
(Venice, 1656), translated by Thomas Higgons as *A
Prospective of the Naval Triumph of the Venetians over
the Turk* (1658), for which Waller provided a prefatory poem (sig. B2).

The three poems attributed to M. are united by
their concern with the poetic interpretation of paintings. They therefore relate to the central Renaissance
topos of *ut pictura poesis est,* even to the extent of
literalizing in the *Third Advice* (through the figure
of the Duchess of Albemarle) the idea of the
speaking picture. The tradition, as it was picked up
from classical sources in the continental renaissance,
and transmitted as a concern to seventeenth-century
English culture, is discussed by Patterson (1978),
117–39, revised (2000), 79–85. M.'s grotesque portrayals of courtiers employ a licence that is faithful to
Horace's original *dicta* in his *Ars Poetica,* as opposed
to the strictures concerning decorum among the
Italian theorists. M.'s satires may be seen as a disturbance and reversal of the entire tradition of Stuart

art and letters. The Painter device permits the poet
a critical stance that stands in opposition to the
heroic narrative beloved of Waller, Dryden and other
apologists for the government (see, e.g., Samuel
Wiseman, *A Short and Serious Narrative of Londons
Fatal Fire* (1667)). The fusion of heroic narrative
and painting was a feature of influential Italian art
theory, e.g. in the works of Gianpaolo Lomazzo
(?1538–1600). In addition to the imitation of Waller,
and like him, the poems adopt in some respects the
manner of contemporary painting manuals (see
below, Title n.).

By considering the comments on the relationship
between poetry and painting throughout the three
poems, Farley-Hills (1974), 75, argues that M. was
a serious and reflective comic satirist. The thematic
elevation of paintings may also be seen as a reflection, and a means of signalling, the difficulty of publishing printed attacks on the government in these
years. It was particularly appropriate in light of
the widespread fashion of heroic portrait and naval
painting. Such works are frequently noted in contemporary descriptions of public and private rooms.
In this context, the Painter poems may be seen as
a central part of a critical counter-culture of official
portrayals of national life. In this official culture, the
King was presented as sensitive to the importance
of the advancement of trade through naval prowess
and colonial endeavour. The relationship between
empire, politics, trade and naval poetry is explored
by Armitage, *HJ,* 35 (1992), 531–55, O'Brien (in
Black, ed. (1997), 146–52), Hoxby (2002).

The painter motif was not confined to govern-
mental, courtly or naval affairs, but in the mid-1660s
became widespread: see, e.g., William Austin,
Ἐπιλοίμια ἔπη. *Or, the Anatomy of the Pestilence*
(1666), 74, 'Paint it, that with *Alecto* it may
stand/*Sister* to *Pest,* with *Furies whip* in hand.' The
same poem gives evidence that the subject matter of
sea could equally be applied to domestic and urban
themes. Austin treats a ship in a violent storm at
sea as an analogy for life, specifically the ravages of
the plague (Austin, 4–7). If it is harder to read
heroic or mock heroic accounts of naval battles as
allegories of public matters or inward states of mind,
it is easier through this evidence to see that the
Painter poems could have a broad appeal, and to see
how it was unremarkable for M. to proceed from the
mode of the *Second* and *Third Advices* to the *Last
Instructions.*

Date. 1666. *Bod. 1* gives the date of April 1666; this follows the entry in the Stationers' Register of the complete version of Waller's *Instructions* by one month. Pepys received a copy of *The Second Advice* on 14 December.

Manuscript Circulation and Print Publication. Manuscript copies of the text began to circulate at least by late 1666, if not earlier. It was also printed in *1667*, *1667²*, *1667³* and *1667³b*. Forty-six MS copies survive, although it is impossible to tell with certainty whether any date from the late 1660s. Most are copies made in the late seventeenth century and early eighteenth century. They are as follows:

Bod. 1. Bod., MS Eng. poet d. 49

Bod. 12 Bod., MS Don. b. 8, pp. 237–46

BL 20 BL, Add. MS 23722, fols. 37ᵛ–41ᵛ

BL 14 BL, Harley MS 7315, fols. 1–8ᵛ

P 4 Princeton University Library, Robert H. Taylor Collection, MS 1, pp. 1–13

AC Alnwick Castle, Vol. XIX, fols. 88ʳ–93ʳ; copy owned by Duke of Northumberland

AH 2 Arbury Hall, MS A 414, fols. 50ʳ–55ʳ; copy owned by Viscount Daventry. Microfilm held in Warwickshire Record Office: Mi 351/3

Be. Bedfordshire Record Office, L 31/340, No. 25

Bi. University of Birmingham Library, Special Collections, MS 13/i/22 fol. [12]

BL 29 BL, Add. MS 69823, pp. 38–49

BL 30 Add. MS 72899, fols. 140ʳ–147ᵛ; formerly Bowood House, Petty Papers, Vol. 2, No. 64

Bod. 18 Bod., MS Don. e. 23, fols. 9–15ᵛ

Bod. 24 Bod., MS Eng. misc. e. 536, pp. 1–12

Bod. 8 Bod., MS Eng. poet. e. 4, pp. 213–22

Bod. 21 Bod., MS Gough London 14, fols. 44–50

Bod. 25 Bod., MS Locke e. 17, pp. 160–74

Br. Bradford District Archives, Hopkinson MSS, Vol. XVII, fols. [211–15]

Ca. Cardiff Central Library, MS 1.482, fols. 26ᵛ–31ᵛ

Cm. Cumbria Record Office, Carlisle, D/Lons/L 2/Box 142, recorded in *IELM* as D/Lons/L Miscellaneous 11/6/33, fols. [1–5]

Co. Royal Library Copenhagen, Denmark, Gl. Kgl. Saml. 3579, 8vo, pp. 183–8

CUL 2 Cambridge University Library, Add. MS 42, fols. 4–7ʳ

Es. Essex Record Office, D/DW Z3 (iii), pp. 1–17, 53

F 4 Folger Shakespeare Library, MS V.a.103, Part II, fols. 79ᵛ–87ᵛ [i.e MS 1.28]

F 5 Folger Shakespeare Library, MS V.a.220, Part II, pp. 7–17

G Georgetown University [no ref. or page numbers]

H 2 Harvard University, MS Eng. 624, pp. [1–12]

L 5 University of Leeds, Brotherton Collection, MS Lt. 38, fols. 36–8ᵛ, 30ᵛ–1

L 6 University of Leeds, Brotherton Collection, MS Lt. 54, pp. 390–405

LAC 2 Clark Library, Los Angeles, M3915M3 S445 [16—] Bound, fols. 2–6ᵛ

LAUC University of California, Los Angeles, 170/68, pp. 90–3

N 7 University of Nottingham, Portland MS Pw2, V 5 (i)

N 8 University of Nottingham, Portland MS Pw2, V 5 (ii)

N 9 University of Nottingham, Portland MS Pw2, V 5 (iii)

N 10 University of Nottingham, Portland MS Pw2, V 5 (iv)

NLW 2 National Library of Wales, MS Chirk F, 12633, pp. 10–20

OA 1 All Souls College, Oxford, MS 174, fols. 21–7

OW Worcester College, Oxford, MSS TC. 20. 11, fols. 12–15ᵛ.

Copy owned by Robert S. Pirie (*IELM*, MaA 349; not seen)

SA   Society of Antiquaries, MS 330,
            fols. 16–19[v]
T   Somerset Record Office, DD/TB,
            Box 11, F.L. 14, [no item number]
Wa.   Warwickshire Record Office,
            CR 341/277, pp. 1–10
Y 5   Yale University, Beinecke Library,
            MS Vault, Section 15, Drawer 3
Y 6   Yale University, Beinecke Library, Osborn
            Collection, b 136, pp. 2–16
Y 11   Yale University, Beinecke Library, Osborn
            Collection, c 160, fols. 1–8
Y 10   Yale University, Beinecke Library, Osborn
            Collection, fb 140, pp. 53–64
Y 12   Yale University, Beinecke Library, Osborn
            Collection, fc 161, pp. 1–8

IELM lists Princeton University Library, Robert H.
Taylor Collection, MS 3, pp. 284–9 (*P 1*), which
is called 'The Second Advice to a Painter', 'By y[e]
author of y[e] S[at] A.M.' However, the poem itself is
entirely different to 'The Second Advice.' The MS is
dated 1684 on the inside front fly-leaf.

Text. Bod. 1 (and some of the texts from the 1690s
associated with it) was an attempt to establish an
accurate, 'correct' text. It is used as the basis for the
text here. Lord took *Bod. 1* as his text in *Yale POAS*,
but removed the few lines unique to *Bod. 1*, or rare
in other witnesses, in his complete edition of M.'s
verse (1968), while keeping in this volume most of
Bod. 1's vocabulary preferences. Its readings may
derive from earlier MSS that are closer to the date of
composition. In some cases, its readings differ from
other plausible readings (some of which are in MS,
some in the printed editions of 1667). These are
either shown in the annotations, or preferred in the
text. In a few instances, it seems as if the *Bod. 1* reading has been refined, in a way that is out of character
with the texts that can be associated with the late
1660s. The widespread copying of the poem in
many MSS, sometimes in contexts and locations
in time and place far removed from Westminster
in 1665–67, has lead to a great many variants and
evident corrupt readings or simple mistranscriptions.
Minor variants that have at best only a very small
impact on sense, or that make no sense, are not
recorded. Other variant readings are shown, in order
to give the reader a sense of the many ways in which
the poem was experienced by seventeenth-century
readers.

Some significant features of the surviving MSS
are as follows. *Bod. 18* appears to be copied from
the printed text of 1667 (*1667[2]*). Es. was probably
copied from *1667[3]*. *N 8* is written on three half-
sheets folded lengthwise and placed inside each
other, to form long, narrow pages, the whole being
then folded twice into a small rectangle, as if it were
for carrying in a pocket. This was probably an early
copy (*pace* Beal in *IELM*, who dates it late seventeenth century), made for surreptitious distribution.
Although most of the copies with many lines missing
are from the late seventeenth or early eighteenth
centuries, two Oxford anthologies, both *c.* 1670, fall,
into this category, *Ca.* and *L 5*. The same is true
of *BL 29*, a verse miscellany datable to the late 1660s.
L 5, BL 29, Ca., and the one other early MS (*F 5*,
dated in *IELM* to *c.* 1667) all display a number of
significantly variant local readings. The later MSS are
characterized more by mistakes of transcription and
of sense, the latter being perhaps induced by a lack of
understanding of context on the part of the copier.
It is apparent that many of the later MSS were copied
from one or other of the printed editions, or other
MSS based on printed editions (e.g. *Es.*). The copier
of *Bi.* gave up quite quickly, perhaps realizing the
unsuitable nature and preferences of a poem for a
commonplace book in which the dominant theme is
the defence of episcopacy.

Whereas most of the MSS that are not single
copies form part of a miscellaneous collection of state
poems and satires, *Co.* is written at the end of a MS
copy of Milton's *Pro Populo Anglicano Defensio*
(1651), probably owned at one point by the 'H.
Dixon' who signed the endpaper, and purchased by
the Danish man of letters, Christoph Friedrich
Temler in London on 24 August 1750. In two
places, it is claimed, erroneously, that the Milton
tract is in the author's own hand.

Authorship. For a general discussion of authorship in
the Advice-to-a-Painter poems, see above, 321–2.
In *Divination* (1666), ll. 47–68, his poetic response
to *The Second Advice*, Christopher Wase was certain
that the poem bore the characteristics of neither
Denham nor Waller, and he was a friend of both
poets. In *Bod. 1*, Thompson in 1776 wrote of *The
Second Advice*: 'This hath been unjustly attributed to
Sir John Denham. and are [*sic*] given as such, in the
first Vol. of State poems p. 24.' (p. 157). *F 4* has at
the end of the poem 'J. Smith Esq. fecit.', but this is
presumably a reference to the scribal copier.

Patterson, *SEL*, 40 (2000), 407–8 notes an indebtedness in ll. 53–72 (the description of the Duke and Duchess of York) to passages from M.'s earlier lyrics, and in particular *The Gallery*, ll. 33–8 and *Upon Appleton House*, ll. 629–32. Thematic and topical inversions of passages in earlier poems include the speech of the sailor (ll. 135–40) which reverses lines from *The First Anniversary* (ll. 283–8) and a couplet from *Upon Appleton House* (ll. 485–6). At the very least, M. seems to have made a contribution to the poem, although he may not have been the sole author. Wase hinted obliquely that the author was Buckingham (*Divination*, ll. 103–14). For this to be true, Buckingham would have had to have studied much of M.'s unpublished poetry before he wrote the entire poem. Collaboration seems much more likely.

Context. The poem is a critical response to Waller's panegyric, *Instructions to a Painter* (1665). The chief event in both poems is the Battle of Lowestoft, the first set-piece battle of the Second Dutch War, which took place on 3 June 1665, in which the English won a clear victory, and which was celebrated as such throughout the country. But what should have been a crushing victory was marred when a courtier (Henry Brouncker) pretending to have the authority of the Lord High Admiral, the Duke of York, called off the pursuit of the Dutch fleet. M.'s poem presents this debacle as but one example of a series of manifestations of courtly behaviour that were doing great damage to the nation. Towards the end of the poem, two further naval failures are described. In July de Ruyter, returning with a weakened East India convoy, managed to evade Sandwich's fleet off the Dogger Bank (ll. 245–52, 259–70). At the same time, a foolish attempt to subvert the alliance between the Danish and the Dutch resulted in an English squadron under Sir Thomas Teddeman suffering severe loss and damage from combined Dutch and Danish fire as he tried to attack a Dutch fleet in Bergen harbour (ll. 253–8, 271–86). Finally, although Sandwich did capture part of the Dutch East Indies fleet, he allowed the cargo to be looted, even taking some of the goods himself. This lead to further criticism at home, while at sea, once again, the naval advantage was not pressed home. Charles saved Sandwich by appointing him ambassador to Spain (ll. 287–316). The naval scenario ends with the division of command between Rupert and Monck in early 1666.

The Battle of Lowestoft was not viewed by contemporaries merely within the context of the Dutch war. Looking back in 1667 on defeat, plague and possibly also the Great Fire, the Quaker George Bishop reminded the King of a prophetic warning that came to him from God just after the Battle, in which Bishop was told that plague would come on England because of the persecution of Dissenters (see George Bishop, *The Warnings of the Lord* (1667), 19).

M.'s Commonwealth and Protectorate sympathies are not far from the surface of the poem. The heroes are, by and large, men who had prospered in the Commonwealth navy: of these, Sandwich was the most eminent. The villains are former Royalists, many of whom were in exile during the 1650s, and who returned to reap honours and profits in the 1660s. M.'s estimations of men thus often differ from those in other sources. Pepys greatly valued Sir William Coventry as mentor and colleague, but M. presents him as the minister of death. M. was effectively constructing the 'patriot' tradition, so valued by those supporters of the Revolution of 1688–89 who encountered *The Second Advice* as part of the *Poems on Affairs of State* in the editions of 1689, 1694, 1697 and thereafter (see *Yale POAS*, xxv–lvi, Legouis, II.225–34; von Maltzahn, in Chernaik and Dzelzainis (1999), 50–74). M.'s poem is notable for its equivocation: the Dutch are less reviled than the representatives of English corruption. This is in contradistinction to Jasper Mayne's *To His Royall Highnesse The Duke of Yorke* (Oxford, 1665), a verse panegyric on the Battle of Lowestoft that points up Dutch greed, murderousness, religious toleration and republicanism.

Genre, Sources and Style. The poem is one of the earliest English Painter poems (see above, *The Advice-to-a-Painter Poems, Headnote*, 326), and the first in the long series inspired by Waller's panegyric. As such, it is closely related to Waller's poem (which it exceeds by only thirty-two lines in length), often closely if not patiently inverting Waller's original, and reusing much of Waller's vocabulary. Later poems in the series are less governed by Waller. However the question of authorship is resolved, the poem is less carefully constructed than the prosodically and imagistically intricate *Last Instructions*. This points to probable hasty composition, in order to meet the needs of a defamation campaign. The major political objections to Waller's poem are twofold: first, that the patriotic, self-sacrificial courage celebrated in *Instructions to a Painter* is more likely to be an angry rebuke to an irresponsible home government; second, the war may not have been just, but was rather a design to aggrandize the Duchess of York and the other courtiers.

Not everyone was impressed by the poem:

No happy Picture whose rich features show
Vandike thy labour or thine Angelo . . .
Who after Waller sings yᵉ Holland fight
Tells but how ill 'tis pissble to write.
Who fain would throughly show his want of skill
From Lely drawers my Cleveland ill.
                  'To my Lord of Dorsett', Yale, MS fb 108, p. 15

Yet the poem is a clever travesty, and it was influential on contemporary Dutch war verse (see below, 343). The painter is on the verge of 'shaking' (l. 3), presumably with rage, or pitiful laughter. The painter, as much as his painting, is now a spectacle. The poem introduces mock-heroic spectacles (e.g. ll. 8, 87–8, 93–4), but the action described is plainly unheroic: a poetics of cowardice is the result. Where Waller's poem expounds its propaganda function openly in the instructions to paint, *The Second Advice* inserts the domestic and courtly causes of neglect

as a framing device before the description of the naval engagements. The other remarkable feature is the inclusion of a disaffected speaker (ll. 135–54), akin to similar voices in ancient satire (making more sense of the epigraph from Persius as an informing presence).

The Second Advice To a Painter
for drawing the History of our Naval Business

In Imitation of Mr Waller

navem si poscat sibi peronatus arator
Luciferi rudis, exclamet Melicerta perisse
          frontem de rebus.
          — Persius, *Satire* 5, ll. 102-
                    London, April 16

Nay, Painter, if thou dar'st design that fight
Which Waller only courage had to write;
If thy bold hand can without shaking draw
What ev'n the actors trembled when they saw;
5 Enough to make thy colours change like theirs,
And all thy pencils bristle like their hairs;
    First in fit distance of the prospect vain,

Title. Cp. anon., *A Book of Drawing, Limning, Washing* (1666), 2: 'Directions in drawing of a Face'; 'Further Directions about a Face.' *Advice*] counsel (*OED* n. 5).
Epigraph. 'If a hobnailed countryman, who knows nothing of the morning star, were to ask for the command of a ship, Melicerta would declare that modesty had perished from off the earth.' Several texts have additional quotations: 'Clutorius Priscus', 'Studia illi, ut plena uecordiae, ita inania et fluxa sunt; nec quicuam graue ac serium ex eo metuas qui suorum ipse flagitorum proditor non uirorum animis sed muliercularum adrepit. Cedat tamen urbe et bonis amissis aqua et igni arceatur; quod perinde censeo ac si lege maiestatis teneretur' (His occupations are as futile and erratic as they are charged with folly; nor can any grave and considerable danger be expected from a person who by betraying his own infamy insinuates himself into the favour not of men but of silly women. Expel him, however, from Rome, confiscate his property, ban him from fire and water: this is my proposal and I make it precisely as though he were guilty under the law of treason), [Tacitus, *Annales*, III.50] *AC, F 5, Bod. 21*; 'Pictoribus atque Poetis,/Quidlibet Audendi semper fuit [aequa] potestas. . . . Humano Capiti cervicem pictor equinam,/Iungere si velit' (Painter and poets you say have always had an [equal] right in hazarding anything . . . If a painter chose to join a human head to the neck of a horse) Horat. de Arte Poet [ll. 9–10, 1–2]

1667² [on title page], *Wa*; First half of Horace quotation, with Juvenal, *Satire 1*, epigraph: 'Difficile est satyram non scribere', on facing page, *Bi*.
1. dar'st] picks up from the quotation of Horace, *De Arte Poetica*, ll. 9–10, that appears as an epigraph in some copies; the echo is enforced by the English translation published by Alexander Brome in 1666: 'But equal power, to Painter, and to Poet,/Of daring all, hath still been given.' *design*] sketch, draw (*OED* v. III 14a).
2–3. Waller . . . can] Cp. Waller, *Instructions to a Painter* (1665), l. 15: 'Let thy bold pencil hope and courage spread.'
2. courage . . . write] There is a reference here to the question of Waller's honesty: if he had drawn or painted rather than written verse, he would have had to tell the truth. Waller argues that painters are limited to portraits; only poets can illuminate the confusions of battle: *Instructions to a Painter*, ll. 287–98.
4. actors] the participants in the war. *trembled*] trembled (in fear and dread) at (*OED* v. 3). In *Bod. 1, Bod. 21, G, Yale, 1667³b*, 'at' is interpolated after 'trembled', which ruins the metre (the interpolator must have assumed 'th'Actors'; two rather than three syllables).
6. pencils] paint brushes. *bristle*] ironically recalling epic literature: e.g. Virgil, *Aeneid*, X, l. 178: 'mille rapit densos acie atque horrentibus hastis' (A thousand men he hurries to war in serried array and bristling with spears).

Paint Allin tilting at the coast of Spain:
Heroic act, and never heard till now
Stemming of Herc'les' Pillars with his prow.
And how two ships he left the hills to waft
And with new sea-marks Dover and Calais graft.
    Next let the flaming *London* come in view
Like Nero's Rome, burnt to rebuild it new.
What lesser sacrifice than this was meet
To offer for the safety of the fleet?
Blow one ship up, another thence does grow:
See what free cities and wise courts can do!
So some old merchant, to insure his name
Marries afresh, and courtiers share the dame.
So whatsoe'er is broke, the servants pay't;

And glasses are more durable than plate.
No mayor till now so rich a pageant feigned
Nor one barge all the companies contained.
25   Then, Painter, draw cerulean Coventry,
Keeper, or rather chanc'llor of the sea:
Of whom the captain buys his leave to die,
And barters or for wounds or infamy;
And more exactly to express his hue,
30   Use nothing but ultramarinish blue.
To pay his fees one's silver trumpet spends:
The boatswain's whistle on his place depends.
Pilots in vain repeat the compass o'er
Until of him they learn that one point more:
35   The constant magnet to the pole does hold,

---

8. Allin . . . Spain] Sir Thomas Allin, first Baronet (1612–85) led a disastrous, unprovoked attack on the Dutch Smyrna fleet on 2 December 1664; this triggered the Second Dutch War. Cp. Waller, *Instructions to a Painter* (1665), ll. 55–64 (a tactfully patriotic account); Dryden, *Annus Mirabilis* (1667), ll. 685–6. *Bod. 1* has a marginal comment: 'Commander of a squadron in the Straits'. The imagery of jousting is mock-heroic in tone: cp. Don Quixote's tilting at windmills, which he mistook for giants (Miguel de Cervantes Saveedra, *El ingenioso hidalgo don Quixote de la Mancha* (1605), 1.8). Allin is off the coast of Spain, so the connotation might be that he is to be taken as a Quixote figure.
10. Stemming] a) ramming (*OED* v.³ 2) b) damming up (*OED* v.² 2), the former rendering the line as a bawdy innuendo. *Herc'les' Pillars*] the Straits of Gibraltar.
11. two ships] *Nonsuch* and *Phoenix* ran aground on the eastern side of Gibraltar and were abandoned. *Bod. 1* annotates: 'He run 2 of his Ships on ground.' Allin sailed into trouble in the dark, not wishing to risk missing the Dutch by waiting until day: Allin, *Journals*, 2 vols, ed. R.C. Anderson, NRS (1939–40), 1.184. *waft*] *Bod. 1*+; pass *1667³b*; convey safely by water, convoy (*OED* v.¹ 1, 2).
11–12. how . . . graft] The two grounded ships are imagined convoying the African and European sides of the Straits of Gibraltar up the coasts of Spain, Portugal and France, to become new markers for the English Channel, along with Dover and Calais.
12. sea-marks] conspicuous objects discernible at sea, used as guides or warnings for navigation (*OED* n. 2); cp. *RT*, 135: 'after all the fatal consequences of that Rebellion, which can only serve as Sea-marks unto all wise Princes to avoid the Causes.' *graft*] fix upon (*OED* v.¹ 1 b).
13–14. Next . . . new] *London* blew up off the Nore on 7 March 1665: three hundred people drowned, twenty-five survived (Pepys, 6.52–3). The City of London quickly offered to fund a replacement, *Loyal London*, which was launched on 10 June 1666 only to be burned in the Dutch raid on Chatham the following year (see below, 387). The rebuilt ship was celebrated in a poem indebted to Waller's *Instructions*: William Smith, *A Poem on the ship called the Loyal London* (1666).
15–16. What . . . fleet] Cp. *The Garden*, ll. 59–60: 'After a place so pure, and sweet,/What other help could yet be meet!'

18. free] a) self-governing, with 'freemen' elected to the corporation (*OED* A a. 2 a) b) generous (*OED* A a. 4 a).
22. And . . . plate] Cp. *The Last Instructions*, l. 60: 'To make her glassen d—s once malleable!' *glasses . . . plate*] i.e. plate, being metal (unlike glass), would be appropriated to support City fund-raising.
23. pageant] For the role of pageants in processions and entertainments for the Lord Mayor of London, see Bergeron (1971), part 2; Wiseman (1998), 171–88; an ironic parody of the famous pageants that made up Venetian civic ritual (see above, *The Character of Holland*, ll. 135–6).
24. companies] trade guilds originating in the middle ages, known as the London 'City Companies' (*OED* n. 6).
25. cerulean] deep blue (*OED* a). M. takes from Latin *caeruleus* two sets of association: a) sea-green b) dark, gloomy, associated with death and the underworld. Coventry is presented as Pluto: see, e.g., Ovid, *Fasti*, IV, ll. 445–6: 'hanc videt et visam patruus velociter aufert/regnaque caeruleis in sua portat equis' ([Pluto] saw her, and no sooner did he see her than he swiftly carried her off and bore her on his dusky steeds into his own realms). Cp. Busenello, *A Prospective* (1658), trans. Higgons, sig. B5ᵛ: 'Let it not Azure, nor Cerulean be,/But imitate and mock the foam o'th sea.' See also Virgil, *Aeneid*, III, l. 64. *Coventry*] Sir William Coventry (1628–86), secretary to the Duke of York, and one of the four Navy Commissioners (DNB). Opinion was divided on Coventry's ability and probity. Pepys, who was under Coventry's patronage, admired him. Like Clarendon, he had originally been against a war with the Dutch (Pincus (1996), 247, 252–3). In a broader political context, Coventry was held to have instigated an early attack on Clarendon through the bill against the embezzlement of prize goods of 18 October 1665.
26. Keeper] a) custodian (see above, l. 25 n.); a keeper is the name of several offices of state (*OED* n. I 1 c) b) pimp: suggesting that the sea is Coventry's whore, from which he makes a profit.
30. ultramarinish] ultramarine was the name of a blue pigment (for painting), originally derived from lapis lazuli (*OED* B n. 1); Thomas Jenner, *A Book of Drawing, Limning, Washing* (1ˢᵗ edn, 1652, 1666), 12: 'Ultramarine . . . is too good to wash withal, and therefore I leave it out here.'
32. boatswain] naval officer in charge of sails and rigging; summons sailors to duty with a whistle (*OED* n. 1).

Steel to the magnet, Coventry to gold.
Muscovy sells us hemp and pitch and tar,
Iron and copper Sweden, Münster war,
Ashley prize, Warwick, customs; Cart'ret pay;
40 But Coventry sells the whole fleet away.
    Now let our navy stretch its canvas wings
Swoll'n like his purse, with tackling like its strings,
By slow degrees of the increasing gale,
First under sale, and after under sail.
45 Then, in kind visit unto Opdam's gout,
Hedge the Dutch in only to let them out.
(So huntsmen fair unto the hares give law,
First find them, and then civilly withdraw)
That the blind Archer, when they take the seas,

50 The Hamburg convoy may betray at ease.
(So that the fish may more securely bite
The fisher baits the river overnight.)
    But, painter, now prepare, t' enrich thy piece,
Pencil of ermines, oil of ambergris.
55 See where the Duchess, with triumphant tail
Of num'rous coaches, Harwich does assail.
So the land-crabs at Nature's kindly call,
Down to engender at the sea do crawl.
See then the Admiral, with navy whole
60 To Harwich through the ocean caracole.
So swallows buried in the sea at spring
Return to land with summer on their wing.
    One thrifty ferry-boat of mother-pearl

37–8. Iron and copper were imported from Sweden (see Pepys, 4.412; 8.426).
38. *Iron . . . Sweden*] see above, *A Letter to Doctor Ingelo*, l. 82 n., *RT*, 204. *Münster*] Christoph Bernhard von Galen, Bishop of Münster, 1650–78, signed an offensive alliance with England on 3 June 1665: he would invade Holland in return for Dutch territory to which he laid claim. The alliance certainly undermined Dutch security on land, and divided their war effort. But the Bishop's initial success (see Bod., MS Carte 64, 215–16) was short-lived (see Ogg (1934), I.289). A brief verse panegyric, *A Letter to the Bishop of Munster*, appeared in 1666.
39–40. *Ashley*] Anthony Ashley Cooper, first Baron Ashley, later first Earl of Shaftesbury (1621–83), appointed Chancellor of the Exchequer, 1661; Treasurer of Prizes during Second Dutch War. *Warwick*] Sir Philip Warwick (1609–83), assistant to the Earl of Southampton, Lord High Treasurer. *Cart'ret*] Sir George Carteret, first Baronet (*c.* 1610–80), Treasurer of the Navy, one of the most powerful figures in Clarendon's court entourage.
41. *Now . . . wings*] Cp. Virgil, *Aeneid*, I, ll. 34–5: 'in altum/ vela dabant laeti' (were they spreading their sails seaward); Waller, 'To the King on his Navy' (1635), l. 1: 'Where ere thy Navy spreads her canvas wings.'
42. *tackling*] rigging (*OED* vbl. n. 1 b); cp. *The First Anniversary*, l. 270: 'And corposants along the tacklings slide.'
45. *Opdam*] Jacob van Wassenaer (1610–65), Baron van Opdam, Admiral of the Dutch Navy. Opdam (or 'Obdam') was a fierce supporter of the republican interest against the Orangists within the United Provinces. He had been responsible for the republican reconfiguration of the Dutch navy in later 1653, and its prudent behaviour thereafter (Pincus (1996), 153–5). *Opdam's gout*] Cp. anon., *Defiance to the Dutch* (1674), s.sh., 'I hope we shall to prepare the next Bout/ Cure um, as we did *Opdam*, of the gout.'
49–50. *blind Archer . . . ease*] Captain Archer was commanding a convoy that protected the English Hamburg fleet in May 1665. He apparently mistook Van Tromp's fleet for an English fleet, sailed up to it, and allowed the English ships to be taken: *The Intelligencer* [*The Newes*], 46 (15 June 1665), 454.
53 . . . 74] A parody of Waller, *Instructions to a Painter*, ll. 77–90; cp. also below, *The Last Instructions to a Painter*,

ll. 49–78; see also above, *Headnote, Authorship*; Zwicker (in Condren and Cousins (1990)), 92–3.
54. *Pencil of ermines*] brushes made from ermine fur. *ambergris*] fragrant substance secreted by sperm whales; see above *Bermudas*, l. 28 and n., *The Gallery*, l. 38.
55–82. *See . . . she*] Contrast Dryden's 'Verses to her Highness the Duchess', published as a preliminary to *Annus Mirabilis* (written 1666, printed 1667). Although Dryden was living in retirement in Wiltshire when he wrote his poem, he may still have seen circulated MS poems.
55–6. *tail . . . coaches*] relates to visual depictions (usually in engravings) of royal progresses.
55. *Duchess*] Anne Hyde, Duchess of York (1637–71) arrived in Harwich to visit the fleet on 16 May 1665. *tail*] a sexual pun on both 'arse' and vulva: Williams (1994), III.1355. The reading is sustained by the brief moment of suspension for the reader before the next line runs on.
57–8. *So . . . crawl*] Cp. Wild, *Iter Boreale* (1660), ll. 366–9: 'Poor crabs and lobsters have gone down to creep,/And search for pearls and jewels in the deep;/And when they have the booty, crawl before,/And leave them for his welcome to the shore.'
57. *land-crabs*] 'crabs, especially of the tropical family, adapted to a partly terrestrial life' (*Collins English Dictionary*, 3rd edn, (Glasgow, 1991)). *kindly*] natural (*OED* a. I 1).
58. *engender*] copulate (*OED* v. 4).
60. *caracole*] move in a zig-zag course (*OED* v. 1); a term from horsemanship used here to describe a sailing ship tacking. The mention of the coal trade in some MSS is possibly a reference to its successful disruption by the Dutch: see below, 437.
61–2. *So . . . wing*] Sir Thomas Browne, *Pseudodoxia Epidemica* (1646; 2 vols, Oxford, 1981), I.435, records the custom of honouring swallows because their arrival announced the spring rather than the summer. His source is Aelian, *De Natura Animalium*, i.52.
63–4. *One . . . girl*] a description of the iconography of the birth of Venus, of which the most famous painted example is by Botticelli; see above, *The Gallery*, l. 34 n. In Botticelli's painting, Venus rises from a sea shell, here jokingly referred to as a tiny boat.
63. *thrifty*] frugal (*OED* a. 4).

Suffic'd of old the Cytherean girl.
Yet navies are but properties when here,
A small sea-masque, and built to court you, dear,
Three goddesses in one; Pallas for art,
Venus for sport, and Juno in your heart.

    O Duchess if thy nuptial pomp were mean,
'Tis paid with int'rest in this naval scene.
Never did Roman Mark, within the Nile
So feast the fair Egyptian Crocodile:
Nor the Venetian Duke, with such a state,
The Adriatic marry at that rate.

    Now Painter spare thy weaker art, forbear
To draw her parting passions and each tear;
For love alas has but a short delight:
The winds, the Dutch, the King, all call to fight.

80   She therefore the Duke's person recommends
To Brouncker, Penn, and Coventry, as friends:
(Penn much, more Brouncker, most to Coventry)
For they, she knew, were all more 'fraid than she.
    Of flying fishes one had sav'd the fin,
And hoped with these he through the air might spin;
85   The other thought he might avoid his knell
In the invention of the diving bell.
The third, had tried it and, affirmed a cable
Coiled round about men was impenetrable.
But these the Duke rejected, only chose
90   To keep far off, and others interpose.
    Rupert that knew not fear, but health did want,
Kept state suspended in a chaise-volante.
All, save his head, shut in that wooden case,

---

64. *Cytherean*] pertaining to Venus (*OED* a. 1; see, e.g, Virgil, *Aeneid*, I, l. 227); William Killigrew's *Ormasdes* (1665) features Cleandra, Queen of Citherea; Cleandra sounds like Clarinda, M.'s name for the Duchess of York (see below, l. 154); for an alleged connection with one of the Killigrews, see below, l. 133 n.
65. *properties*] accessories in a play or masque (*OED* n. 3).
67–8. *Three . . . heart*] Venus, goddess of love, and Juno, queen of the gods, were respectively the patroness and the enemy of the Trojans in Virgil's *Aeneid*. Pallas Minerva was the goddess of war. In a French medieval illumination, the three goddesses are depicted with Nature, and represent respectively the Amorous, Contemplative and Active lives; the textual source is an allegory in Fulgentius, *Mythologiae*, II.i. The three were often worshipped in an interconnected way; from which Renaissance Neoplatonists derived the view that colliding differences were reconciled in one dominant consonance. For the place of these deities in iconographic and philosophical tradition, see Seznec (1953), 108; Wind (1958), 71, 85, 162–3.
68. *Juno . . . heart*] i.e. the Duchess is already dreaming of becoming queen.
69–70. *O . . . scene*] Cp. *An Horatian Ode*, ll. 57–8: 'He nothing common did, or mean,/Upon that memorable scene.'
69. *mean*] The Duke of York and Anne Hyde were married in secret on 3 September 1660, after her pregnancy had forced James to admit that he had promised to marry her.
71–2. *Never . . . Egyptian*] Cp. Cleveland, 'A Song of Mark Anthony' (1647), ll. 9–11 (refrain): 'Never Mark Anthony/Dallied more wantonly/With the faire Egyptian Queen.'
73–4. *Nor . . . marry*] alluding to the annual ceremony on Ascension Day when the Doge of Venice married the sea by casting a ring into it: see above, *The Character of Holland*, ll. 135–6. *state . . . rate*] Cp. *To his Coy Mistress*, ll. 19–20: 'For Lady you deserve this state;/Nor would I love at lower rate.'
75–6. Written vertically up the page in *F 5*, and clearly marked for insertion. *spare . . . tear*] alluding to the view that painting was weak in respect of representing the emotions (Patterson (2000), 85).

81. *Brounker*] William, second Lord Brouncker (1620?–84), first President of the Royal Society and an extra Commissioner of the Navy, 1664–66. *Penn*] Sir William Penn, Kt. 1660 (1621–70), Commissioner of the Navy; second in command during the Second Dutch War, and Admiral of the Duke of York's flagship. *Coventry*] see above, l. 25 n.
83. *flying . . . fin*] Cp. anon., *Hogan-Moganides: Or, the Dutch-Hudibras* (1674), ll. 1402–4: 'Then sheathing up each fork,/And small fin,/Mounted like Simon on the Dolphin;/One while the Monster he wou'd stride,/Then light again to see himself ride.'
85. *knell*] i.e. death-knell, hence death (*OED* n. b).
86. *diving bell*] Introduced from Sweden in 1661; M. had seen one in operation in Stockholm harbour on 8 September 1664 (Guy Miège, *A Relation of Three Embassies* (1669), 350).
87–8. *third . . . impenetrable*] Penn was not popular with former Commonwealthmen because he had corresponded with royalists in the later 1650s; the allegation of cowardice was regarded as a test of Penn's faith as well as his courage: 'there was a cruel Articling against Pen after one fight, for cowardice in putting himself within a Coyle of Cables, of which he had much ado to quit himself; and by great friends did it, not without remains of guilt, but that his Brethren had a mind to pass it by and Sir H[enry] Vane did advise him to search his heart and see whether a fault or a greater sin was not the occasion of this so great tryall' (Pepys, 4.375 (9 November 1663)).
91. *Rupert*] Prince Rupert (1619–82), Count Palatine of the Rhine and Duke of Bavaria; accomplished soldier in Europe and during the English Civil War on behalf of the King, for which he was rewarded at the Restoration with an annuity of £4,000 and membership of the Privy Council. *health did want*] Rupert was suffering from the aggravation of an old war wound (he underwent three operations in 1664–67; implied by M. to be syphilis (see below, ll. 99–100); Pepys agreed: 'my Lord Fitzharding came thither and fell to discourse of Prince Rupert, and made nothing to say that his disease was the pox and that he must be Fluxed, telling the horrible degree of the disease upon him, with its breaking out on his head' (15 January 1665; 6.12).
92. *chaise-volante*] French: light, easily moved chair.

He show'd but like a broken weather-glass:
95   But arm'd in a whole lion cap-à-chin,
Did represent the Hercules within.
Dear shall the Dutch his twinging anguish know,
And feel what valour, whet with pain, can do.
Curst in the meantime be the trait'ress Jael
100 That through his princely temples drove the nail!
     Rupert resolved to fight it like a lion.
But Sandwich hoped to fight it like Arion:
He, to prolong his life in the dispute,
And charm the Holland pirates, tuned his lute:
105 Till some judicious dolphin might approach,
And land him safe, and sound as any roach.
Hence by the gazetteer he was mistook,
As unconcerned as if at Hinchingbrooke.
     Now Painter reassume thy pencil's care;
110 It hath but skirmished yet, now fight prepare,
And draw the battle terribler to show
Than the Last Judgement was of Angelo.

First, let our navy scour through silver froth,
The ocean's burden and the kingdom's both:
115 Whose very bulk may represent its birth
From Hyde, and Paston, burdens of the earth.
Hyde, whose transcendent paunch so swells of late,
That he the rupture seems of law, and state.
Paston, whose belly bears more millions
120 Than Indian carracks, and contains more tuns.
     Let shoals of porpoises on ev'ry side
Wonder in swimming by our oaks outvied:
And the sea fowl, at gaze, behold a thing
So vast, more strong, and swift than they of wing,
125 But with presaging gorge yet keep in sight
And follow for the relics of a fight.
     Then let the Dutch with well-dissembled fear
Or bold despair, more than we wish draw near.
At which our gallants, to the sea but tender,
130 More to the fight, their queasy stomachs render:
With breasts so panting that at ev'ry stroke

---

94. broken weather-glass] a weather-glass was an early kind of thermometer and barometer, consisting of an upright tube filled with water, and terminating in a bulb at the top, which contained rarefied air. The water sank or rose as the air in the bulb expanded or contracted: 'broken' refers to Rupert's disease (see above, l. 91 n.), the comparison of his head to a bulb of air a comment on the mental properties of the cavalier hero.

95–6. lion . . . Hercules] the skin of the Nemean lion was Hercules's armour; this is apt for Rupert because the heraldic symbol of the Palatinate was a golden lion (Hesse (1986), 25, 70, 117).

95. cap-à-chin] head to backbone ('chine').

99–100. Jael . . . nail] Jael killed Sisera, the captain of Jabin, King of Canaan, and enemy of the Israelites (Judges 4:17–21).

102. Sandwich] Edward Montagu, Earl of Sandwich (1625–72); Admiral of the Blue or Rear Squadron at the Battle of Lowestoft; for his extensive career, see Ollard (1994).

Arion] celebrated cithara player of Methymna, Lesbos, rescued from drowning by a dolphin: see, e.g., Ovid, *Fasti*, II, ll. 79–118.

104. lute] Sandwich was a keen singer and player of several stringed instruments, including the lute (Pepys, 1.218) and the guitar, which he was commending in November 1665 (Pepys, 6.301).

105. judicious] sensible, wise (*OED* a. 1).

106. Cited as an example by Tilley (R 143) but without an explanation.

107–8. gazetteer . . . Hinchingbrooke] *The Intelligencer* made no mention of Sandwich until 15 June, when it described his battle manner as if he were 'as unconcerned as if he had been in his own parlor'; Sandwich was not amused (Pepys, 6.134–5).

108. Hinchingbrooke] Sandwich's country seat, near Huntingdon.

111–12. terribler . . . Angelo] Cp. a correspondent writing from The Hague in *The Intelligencer*, 55 (17 July 1665): 'the

English Fleet . . . has put their Lordships, and indeed this whole Country into such a fit of distraction, that I cannot do better then referre you to *michael Angelo's Day of Judgement* for a Prospect of our *Confusion*.' *terribler*] referring to the Italian critical term *terribilità* (awesomeness of conception and execution), first used in respect of Michelangelo and his school. Patterson (2000), 85–6, considers the Italian art debate in which the term arose in terms of accusations of stylistic impropriety and irreverence, and in the light of Leonardo da Vinci's claim that paintings could not represent battles.

112. of Angelo] Bod. 1+; of Ameslow *G*; of Anneslow *Υ* 5; Ameslow *NLW 1* (i.e. Arthur Annesley, first Earl of Anglesey (see above, 324)).

113. scour] move rapidly in quest of an enemy (*OED* v.¹ 2). *silver froth*] the money raised in Parliament to finance the war (see below, l. 116 n.).

116. Hyde] Edward Hyde, Earl of Clarendon (1609–74), Lord Chancellor; see above *The Advice to a Painter Poems*, Headnote. *Paston*] Sir Robert Paston (1631–83), later Earl of Yarmouth, MP for Castle Rising, Norfolk, gentleman of the privy chamber, 1667–83, who proposed, at Clarendon's connivance, and in the hope of his own reward (many followed from the King), the massive sum of £2.5 million to finance the Dutch War, which was carried in the Commons on 25 November 1664.

118. That . . . seems] 'Tympany' is preferred to 'rupture' in several MSS (see below, 426). 'Tympany': a) swelling, tumour (*OED* n. 1) b) swelling, as of pride and arrogance (*OED* n. 2 fig.).

120. Indian carracks] large merchant ships, built for trade with the east (*OED*). *tuns*] a) large barrels (*OED* n. 1) b) measure of liquid volume (equivalent to four hogsheads) (*OED* n. 2).

125. gorge] throat (*OED* n.¹ 1); in particlar, the 'crop' (*OED* n. I 1), or pouch-like enlargement of the gullet in which food undergoes partial preparation for digestion ('gorge', *OED* n.¹ 3).

131. stroke] discharge of canons (*OED* n.¹ 1 f).

You might have felt their hearts beat through the oak,
While one, concerned most, in the interval
Of straining choler, thus did cast his gall:
5   'Noah be damn'd and all his race accurst,
That in sea-brine did pickle timber first.
What though he planted vines! He pines cut down.
He taught us how to drink, and how to drown.
He first built ships, and in that wooden wall
140 Saving but eight, e'er since endangers all.
And thou Dutch necromantic friar, be damned
And in thine own first mortar-piece be rammed,
Who first invented cannon in thy cell,
Nitre from earth, and brimstone fetch'd from hell.
145 But damn'd and treble damn'd be Clarendine,
Our seventh Edward, and his house and line!
Who, to divert the danger of the war

With Bristol, hounds us on the Hollander.
Fool-coated gownman, sells (to fight with Hans)
150 Dunkirk; dismantling Scotland, quarrels France,
And hopes he now hath business shaped and power
T'outlast his life or ours, and 'scape the Tower:
And that he yet may see, ere he go down,
His dear Clarinda circled in a crown.'
155   By this time both the fleets in wrath dispute,
And each the other mortally salute.
Draw pensive Neptune, biting of his thumbs,
To think himself a slave whos'e'er o'ercomes;
The frighted nymphs retreating to the rocks,
160 Beating their blue breasts, tearing their green locks.
Paint Echo slain, only th' alternate sound
From the repeating cannon does rebound.
Opdam sails in, placed in his naval throne,

---

133. 'Killigrew' written against this line in the left-hand margin of *N 9*, 'A Courtier' in *Br.*; there are some connections between the poem and William Killigrew's *Ormasdes* (1665; entitled *Love and Friendship* in 1666), but none that relate to the sailor's speech (see above, l. 64 n.). Henry Killigrew (d. 1712), son of Henry Killigrew DD (1613–1700), and not related to the dramatists William and Thomas, fought as a lieutenant in the battle. Henry Killigrew, son of the playwright Thomas, and Groom to the Bedchamber of the Duke of York, may also have been present.
135–40. Noah . . . all] see above, *Headnote, Genre and Sources*.
137–8. What . . . drown] See above *The First Anniversary*, ll. 286–94 nn. Noah's drunkenness recalls Clarendon and his fondness for wine. Clarendon was hampered by one consequence of his drinking: severe gout.
140. eight] the number of people who survived the deluge in the ark: Noah, his three sons and their respective wives (see Gen. 7:13).
141. Dutch . . . friar] Berthold Der Schwarze, a fourteenth-century German monk and alchemist who, among others, developed gunpowder (*c.* 1313). He resided at Konstanz and Paris during his lifetime, but the evidence of his discoveries comes from archives in Ghent (*EB*). Epic verse usually, although not exclusively, ascribed the invention of gunpowder and firearms to demonic agency: See Ariosto, *Orlando Furioso*, IX.xxviii ff., xci; Spenser, *The Faerie Queene*, I.vii.13; Milton, *Paradise Lost*, VI, ll. 472–91; Murrin (1994), 80–92, 123–59).
necromantic] magical (*OED* a. 2 b). Necromancers foretold the future by communicating with the dead: the friar takes his brimstone from hell (see below, l. 144).
145. Clarendine] Clarendon.
146. seventh Edward] supposes Clarendon has aggrandized himself to the point of being king (Edward VII); he was in fact grandfather to two queens by virtue of his daughter's marriage: Mary and Anne.
147–8. war . . . Bristol] George Digby, second Earl of Bristol (1612–77), brought a charge of High Treason against Clarendon in the House of Lords on 10 July 1663.
148. hounds] a hunting term: set a hound loose on a quarry (*OED* v. 3).
149. Fool-coated] like the motley coat of a fool. *gownman*] translates Latin *togatus* (an adult Roman); a) civilian, as

opposed to soldier (*OED* 2); member of a municipal corporation (*OED* 3 d) b) lawyer (*OED* 3 a); Clarendon had a legal training. Cp. Lucan, *De Bello Civili*, trans. Thomas May, ll. 155–6: 'to play the gowne man now/He had forgot', when Caesar angrily addresses the senate.
149–50. sells . . . Dunkirk] Dunkirk was sold to France in October 1662 for 5 million livres. It was an unpopular move, and Clarendon knew it to be so (Pincus (1996), 219).
150. dismantling Scotland] Clarendon ordered Lauderdale to sell the four castles built by Cromwell in Scotland. *quarrels France*] Clarendon rebuffed France's offer to mediate between England and Holland.
154. Clarinda] the Duchess of York (see above, l. 55 n.); a heroine's name in John Fletcher's *The Sea Voyage* (1622). *circled . . . crown*] but Clarendon said he did not approve of his daughter's match, and was greatly angered by it.
157–8. Neptune . . . o'ercomes] Neptune is often depicted as actively influencing human affairs, for instance, as a friend of the Trojans, and the builder of Troy, and as the bringer of floods in punishment for human perfidy: see, e.g., Virgil, *Aeneid*, I, ll. 124–43; VII, l. 23; IX, l. 145; Ovid, *Metamorphoses*, XII, ll. 207–10. See also Waller, *Instructions to a Painter*, ll. 83–90.
157. pensive Neptune] Cp. *The Last Instructions*, l. 925: 'The wondrous night the pensive King revolves.' In Busenello, *A Prospective*, trans. Higgons (1658), sig. C 8ᵛ, the sea nymphs and tritons chase the Turkish admiral, who is the 'foul coward'. *pensive*] melancholy, sad (*OED* a. 3).
159. The . . . rocks] Cp. R[ichard] H[ead], *The Red-Sea* (1666), 4: 'The tender *Nymphs* . . . With hair all torn creep into th'hollow Rocks.'
161. Echo slain] mountain nymph, or oread: in Ovid, *Metamorphoses*, III, Echo offended the goddess Hera by keeping her in conversation, thus preventing her from spying on one of Zeus's amours. To punish Echo, Hera deprived her of speech, except for the ability to repeat the last words of another. Also names the technique in Renaissance verse where the repetition of part of the final line of a stanza changes the sense of that line. *alternate*] i.e. reciprocal exchange of cannon fire.
163. Opdam] see Waller, *Instructions to a Painter*, ll. 137 ff.; see also above, l. 45 n.

Assuming courage greater than his own:
165 Makes to the Duke, and threatens him from far
To nail himself to's board like a petar:
But in the vain attempt takes fire too soon,
And flies up in his ship to catch the moon.
Monsieurs like rockets mount aloft, and crack
170 In thousand sparks, then dancingly fall back.
Yet ere this happened Destiny allow'd
Him his revenge to make his death more proud.
A fatal bullet from his side did range,
And battered Lawson. O too dear exchange!
175 He led our fleet that day, too short a space,
But lost his knee (died since) in Glory's race.
Lawson, whose valour beyond fate did go
And still fights Opdam through the lakes below.
     The Duke himself, though Penn did not forget,
180 Yet was not out of Danger's random set.

Falmouth was there, I know not what to act:
Some say 'twas to grow Duke, too, by contact.
An untaught bullet in its wanton scope
Quashes him all to pieces and his hope.
185 Such as his rise such was his fall, unpraised;
A chance-shot sooner took than chance him rais'd:
His shattered head the fearless Duke distains,
And gave the last-first proof that he had brains.
     Berkeley had heard it soon, and thought not good
190 To venture more of royal Harding's blood.
To be immortal he was not of age:
(And did e'en now the Indian prize presage)
But judged it safe and decent, cost what cost,
To lose the day, since his dear brother's lost.
195 With his whole squadron straight away he bore,
And, like good boy, promised to fight no more.
     The Dutch *Urania* fairly on us sailed,

---

166. board] a) deck (not in *OED*) b) ship (not in *OED*). *petar*] i.e. 'petard', a small bell- or box-shaped piece of artillery used to breach a wall or blow in a gate (*OED* n. 1).
167–8. But . . . moon] Opdam had in fact been killed by cannon-fire some time before his ship, *Eendracht*, exploded: *The Intelligencer*, 46 (15 June 1665), 446; Letter from Admiral Tjerck Hiddes de Vries, 13 June 1665 in *Historisch Genootschap Kronijk*, 14, 217. The explosion was the subject of a contemporary engraving: see Nispen (1991), 28. For Dutch verse recording this event and Opdam's demise, see Nispen (1991), 26–31.
169. Monsieurs] applied to European foreigners other than Frenchmen (*OED*).
173. bullet] cannon-ball (*OED* n.¹ 2). *side*] i.e. broadside: full array of artillery discharged from one side of a ship. *range*] travel; specifically of projectiles (*OED* v.¹ 7 d).
174. Lawson] Sir John Lawson (d. 1665), Vice-Admiral of the Red Squadron; dismissed as a republican and Anabaptist in 1656, but helped Monck to re-establish civil government by bringing ships into the Thames and declaring for the Rump. He was wounded in the knee by a musket-shot towards the end of the battle, and died of gangrene poisoning at Greenwich on 29 June.
175–6. He . . . race] see above, *Headnote, Authorship*.
178. lakes] waters of the River Styx in the classical underworld; usually referred to in the singular: the 'Stygian lake'.
180. Danger's random set] danger is first personified, then presented as an image of ordnance set up to fire. *random*] a) violence (*OED* A n. I 1) b) range of a piece of artillery (from the degree of elevation of the muzzle) (*OED* A n. II 5).
181–8. Falmouth . . . brains] a riposte to Waller's heroic description of the Duke of York on deck in battle: *Instructions to a Painter*, ll. 123–36. For Waller, these deaths were happy and glorious: *Instructions*, ll. 149–50.
181. Falmouth] Charles Berkeley, Lord Fitzharding (1663) and Earl of Falmouth (1664) (d. 1665); a favourite of Charles II, who was much troubled by his death; Pepys was worried by his poor reputation as a man of pleasure, but acknowledged that he was also a 'man of great Honour' (Pepys, 6.123–4). See also below, 349, n. 251.

183. untaught bullet] Cp. R[ichard] H[ead], *The Red-Sea* (1666), 5: 'And being about to say, be brave, be bold,/An untought ill-bred Bullet bids him hold.' *untaught*] uninstructed, ignorant; hence, figuratively 'stray' (*OED* ppl. A. 1); the personified bullet suggests the overthrow of courtly refinement in Falmouth by ignorant, brutal violence. *wanton*] undisciplined, hence beyond control (*OED* A a. 1).
184. Quashes] The reading of 'contract' in l. 182 in several witnesses gives 'quash' the sense not merely of 'destroys' (*OED* v. I 2), but 'annuls' (Falmouth's hopes of becoming Duke by contract) (*OED* v. I 1), although this sense is obscure.
186. chance-shot] sounds like 'chain-shot', cannon-balls linked together by chains.
187–8. His . . . brains] Falmouth's brains are smeared across the Duke of York's face, providing the only evidence that Falmouth had any brains at all, so stupid had he seemed in his life. The same shot also killed Lord Muskerry and Richard Boyle: see Colenbrander (1919), 1.189; Pepys, 6.122. Cp. Waller, *Instructions to a Painter*, ll. 145–49.
187. distains] a) discolours, stains (*OED* v. 1) b) defiles (*OED* v. 2).
189–90. Berkeley . . . blood] William Berkeley (1639–66), second Viscount Fitzharding (in the Irish peerage), was younger brother to the Earl of Falmouth. Previously popular as a courtier, he was reviled for apparent cowardice at Lowestoft (Pepys, 6.129), although other accounts report that he gave chase to part of the Dutch fleet. 'Fitz' means 'son of', hence both Falmouth and Berkeley are sons of the Harding line.
192–3. Indian . . . cost] Berkeley was one of the officers involved in the embezzlement of prizes (see below, ll. 305–7; Pepys, 6.263). *Indian*] i.e. because the Dutch East Indies fleet had been attacked.
195. whole . . . bore] see above, ll. 189–90 n.
197. Urania] *Oranje* or *Orange Tree* according to Sandwich, commanded by Bastiaan Centen: *Journal*, ed., R.C. Anderson, NRS (1929), 226. Centen had sworn to board the Duke (Pepys, 6.122).

And promises to do what Opdam failed.
Smith to the Duke does intercept her way
0 And cleaves t'her closer than the remora.
The captain wondered, and withal disdained
So strongly by a thing so small detained,
And in a raging brav'ry to him runs.
They stab their ships with one another's guns;
5 They fight so near it seems to be on ground,
And ev'n the bullets meeting, bullets wound.
The noise, the smoke, the sweat, the fire, the blood,
Are not to be expressed nor understood.
Each captain from the quarter-deck commands,
0 They wave their bright swords glitt'ring in their hands.
All luxury of war, all man can do
In a sea-fight, did pass betwixt them two.
But one must conquer whosoever fight:
Smith took the giant, and is since made knight.
15 Marlb'rough, that knew and dared too more than all,
Falls undistinguished by an iron ball.
Dear Lord, but born under a star ingrate!
No soul so clear, and no more gloomy fate.
Who would set up war's trade that meant to thrive?

220 Death picks the valiant out, the cow'rds survive.
What the brave merit th'impudent do vaunt,
And none's rewarded but the sycophant.
Hence, all his life he against Fortune fenced;
Or not well known, or not well recompensed.
225 But envy not this praise to's memory:
None more prepared was, or less fit to die.
   Rupert did others and himself excel:
Holmes, Tyddiman, Myngs; bravely Sansum fell.
What others did let none omitted blame:
230 I shall record whos'e'er brings in his name.
But unless after stories disagree
Nine only came to fight, the rest to see.
   Now all conspires unto the Dutchman's loss:
The wind, the fire, we, they themselves do cross.
235 When a sweet sleep the Duke began to drown,
And with soft diadem his temples crown.
But first he orders all beside to watch;
That they the foe whilst he a nap might catch.
   But Brouncker, by a secreter instinct
240 Slept not: nor needs it; he all day had winked.
The Duke in bed, he then first draws his steel,

199. Smith] Captain Jeremy Smith (d. 1675). Pepys (6.121–3) read and copied an account of the Battle by Coventry, which included this description of Smith's action: 'Captain Jer. Smith of the *Mary* was second to the Duke, and stepped in between him and Captain Seaton [sic] of the *Urania* (76 guns and 400 men). . . . Killed him, 200 men, and took the ship. Himself losing 99 men, and never an officer but himself and Lieutenant.'
200. remora] sucking-fish, believed to have the power of stopping any ship to which it attached itself.
203. brav'ry] defiance (*OED* n. 1).
204. They . . . guns] Waller repeatedly regards swords as superior to guns (*Instructions to a Painter*, ll. 143, 199–200).
207. The . . . blood] Cp. Busenello *A Prospective* (1658), trans. Higgons, sig. B 8ᵛ: 'Stones, bullets, arrowes, slaughters still increase;/Toils, flights, cries, shocking not a moment cease.'
208. expressed] a) painted (*OED* v. II 5) b) written down (*OED* v. II 8).
211. luxury] from Latin *luxuria*: 'wild, unrestrained behaviour' (*OLD* 2); not in *OED*.
214. took] captured (*OED* v. II 2). *knight*] Smith was knighted for his bravery later in June 1665.
215. Marlb'rough] James Ley, third Earl of Marlborough (1618–65).
216. undistinguished] a) not regarded as distinct, and hence left alone (*OED* ppl. A 1) b) in death, not elevated above other men (as an aristocrat like Marlborough was when alive) c) unremembered; cp. anon., *The Misfortunes of St Paul's Cathedral* ([1666]), 5: 'But most with common things confused lye,/Unless distinguished by an Elegy.'
217. ingrate] unfriendly (*OED* a. 2).
218. clear] pure, untainted, innocent (*OED* a. IV 14).
221. vaunt] boast (*OED* v. 1).

223. he . . . fenced] Marlborough appears to be an 'unfortunate lover': see above, *The Unfortunate Lover*, ll. 43–4: 'Fortune and he are called to play/At sharp before it all the day.'
224. Or . . . or] i.e. either . . . or.
225–6. memory . . . die] the rhyme suggests a contemporary pronunciation of 'memory' with the 'y' as a long 'i'.
228. Holmes] Robert Holmes (1622–92), Kt. 1666, captain of *Revenge*, in Prince Rupert's squadron at Lowestoft. *Tyddiman*] Sir Thomas Tyddiman (Teddeman; d. 1668?), Rear-Admiral of the Blue Squadron, commanded by Sandwich. *Myngs*] Sir Christopher Myngs (1625–66), Vice-Admiral of the White Squadron, under Prince Rupert's command: see below, *The Third Advice*, l. 115 n. *Sansum*] Robert Sansum (fl. 1649–65), Rear Admiral of the White Squadron.
231. after stories] Cp. Busenello *A Prospective* (1658), trans. Higgons, sig. C5ᵛ: 'But destiny relents, and after-times,/O Fates, will count his end among your crimes.'
232. Nine] ironically parodying the Nine Worthies of ancient, medieval and legendary fame (Joshua, David, Judas Maccabeus, Alexander, Hector, Julius Caesar, Arthur, Charlemagne, Godfrey of Bouillon).
234. fire] a) cannon-fire b) fire caused by fireships or magazine explosions.
237. watch] i.e. be on duty, on deck (as in the nautical turn of duty (*OED* n. III 17).
239–44. But . . . Parliament] Cp. Waller's fanciful description of the terror wrought on the Dutch by the Duke at the very thought of their defeat (*Instructions to a Painter*, ll. 259–86).
239. Brouncker] Henry Brouncker (1627?–88), Groom of the Bedchamber to the Duke of York, 1656–67, MP for New Romney, 1665–68; an infamous instance of cowardice by a courtier with a low moral reputation: Brouncker was exposed in Parliament on 19 and 21 October 1666.
240. winked] slept; to have the eyes closed in sleep (*OED* v.¹ 3).

Whose virtue makes the misled compass wheel:
So ere he waked both fleets were innocent.
And Brouncker Member is of Parliament.
245   And now dear painter, after pains like those
'T were time that thou and I too should repose.
But all our navy 'scaped so sound of limb
That a small space served to refresh its trim;
And a tame fleet of theirs does convoy want,
250   Laden with both the Indies and Levant.
Paint but this one scene more. The world's our own;
The halcyon Sandwich does command alone.
       To Bergen now with better maw we haste,
And the sweet spoils in hope already taste.
255   Though Clifford in the character appears
Of supercargo to our fleet and theirs:
Wearing a signet ready to clap on,
And seize all for his master Arlington.

Ruyter whose little squadron skimmed the seas
260   And wasted our remotest colonies,
With ships all foul returned upon our way.
Sandwich would not disperse, nor yet delay,
And therefore, like commander grave and wise,
To 'scape his sight and fight, shut both his eyes;
265   And, for more state and sureness, Cuttance true
The left eye closes, the right Montagu.
And even Clifford proffered, in his zeal
To make all safe, t'apply to both his seal.
Ulysses so, till he the Sirens passed,
270   Would by his mates be pinioned to the mast.
Now may our navy view the wishèd port
But there too (see the fortune) was a fort.
Sandwich would not be beaten, nor yet beat.
Fools only fight, the prudent use to treat.
275   His cousin Montagu, by court disaster

---

242. virtue] power, influence (*OED* n. II 9). *wheel*] turn, deviate (*OED* v. I 5).
243. innocent] doing no harm (*OED* a. 5) to each other; i.e. disengaged.
244. Brouncker . . . Parliament] and so is immune from prosecution through MPs' privilege; but Brouncker was impeached in 1668: see above, 329.
247–8. But . . . trim] The English fleet was repaired and provisioned four weeks after Lowestoft.
248. trim] state of readiness (*OED* n. I 1).
249. tame] weak (*OED* a. 5).
250. Indies . . . Levant] a Dutch fleet returning from the East Indies.
252. The . . . alone] Fearing a threat to the Stuart succession were he killed in battle, the Duke of York was persuaded to relinquish his active service, leaving Sandwich as supreme naval commander. *halcyon*] calm, peaceful (*OED* B a. 2), and hence unwarlike. Lord, in Erdman and Fogel (1959), 108, suggests that 'halcyon' may be read as 'cowardly'; see above, *The Advice-to-a-Painter Poems, Headnote, Authorship.*
253. maw] stomach, i.e., appetite (*OED* n.¹ 1 b, 4).
255. Clifford] Sir Thomas Clifford (1630–73), later Lord Clifford of Chudleigh. M. quarrelled with Clifford in the House of Commons in March 1662 (*JHC*, 8.391). The Speaker decided that M. was responsible for the initial provocation; M. refused to apologize until a threat of expulsion forced a capitulation. Patterson (1978), 32 connects this incident with M.'s decision, two months later, to travel abroad. Along with Arlington and William Coventry, Clifford was deeply pro-war. *character*] official rank (*OED* n. II 15).
256. supercargo] superintendent of a ship's cargo (*OED* n.).
257. signet] seal of authority (*OED* n. 2).
258. Arlington] Clifford was almost certainly Arlington's agent in the fleet; accordingly, Clifford is the agent ('supercargo') for the merchant Arlington (see above, l. 256, and below, 371, l. 129 n.).
259–70. Sandwich heard rumours of De Ruyter's proximity, but he doubted the truth of them. He was also concerned not to over-extend a fleet in which disease had broken out among the men: *Journal*, ed., R.C. Anderson, *NRS* (1929), 255, 258–9.

259–60. Ruyter . . . colonies] De Ruyter took English prizes off the coast of America in June 1665 (*The Intelligencer*, 52 (6 July 1665), 538), after harrying the English off the coast of Guinea during the previous year.
259–70. Ruyter . . . mast] Admiral Michael de Ruyter (1607–76) had been sent in September 1664 to harry English activity on the Guinea coast, and to regain settlements lost to the English. He was successful, and managed to evade Sandwich, who attempted to intercept him between the Dogger Bank and the Naze of Norway.
259. little squadron] De Ruyter had twelve ships.
260. wasted] ravaged (*OED* v. I 1).
261. foul] 'running foul'; sailing in a compromised way (as opposed to 'running clear') (*OED* a. III 18). *The Intelligencer*, 52 (6 July 1665), 539: 'They are in a very unhealthy condition, and but ill mann'd; their Ships very foul, and sail heavily.'
265. state] greatness of rank (*OED* n. II 16). *sureness*] safety (*OED* n. 1), that, it is implied, lacks courage. *Cuttance*] Roger Cuttance (Cutten or Cuttings; fl. 1650–69) was Sandwich's captain. Knighted according to Charnock (1794), I.12, in 1664, but Evelyn says he witnessed the knighting (in recognition of bravery at Lowestoft) on board *Prince* on 30 June 1665.
266. Montagu] Edward (Ned) Montagu (1635–65), nephew of the Earl of Sandwich, MP for Sandwich from 1661.
268. seal] made by pressing his signet ring (see above, l. 257) into molten wax.
269–70. Ulysses . . . mast] Sandwich heard of the De Ruyter's successful evasion only some time later. The Sirens episode occurs in Homer, *Odyssey*, XII.
271. port] Bergen.
272. fort] Danish fort overlooking Bergen harbour.
274. Fools . . . fight] Sir Gilbert Talbot, English envoy at Copenhagen, was attempting to persuade the Danish king to make a defensive alliance with England in order to attack the Dutch. Sandwich delayed any attack while he waited for news of the diplomatic strategy. *use to*] i.e. are accustomed to.
275. Montagu] see above, l. 266 n. *court disaster*] See the margin of *Bod. 1*: 'Montagu was the Master of the Horse to the Queen. One day, as he led her, he tickled her palm. She asked the King what that meant. The King by this means getting knowledge of it, turned Montague out of his place.'

Dwindled into the wooden horse's master;
To speak of peace seemed among all most proper.
Had Talbot then treated of nought but copper?
For what are forts when void of ammunition?
0 With friend or foe what would we more condition?
Yet we three days till the Dutch furnish'd all
Men, powder, cannon, money treat with Wall.
Then Teddy, finding that the Dane would not,
Sends in six captains bravely to be shot.
5 And Montagu, though dress'd like any bride,
Though aboard him too, yet was reached and died.
    Sad was this chance, and yet a deeper care
Wrinkles our membranes under forehead fair.
The Dutch armada yet had th'impudence
0 To put to sea, to waft their merchants hence.
For, as if all their ships of walnut were,
The more we beat them, still the more they bear.
But a good pilot and a fav'ring wind

Bring Sandwich back, and once again did blind.
295   Now gentle Painter, ere we leap on shore
With thy last strokes ruffle a tempest o'er:
As if in our reproach, the winds and seas
Would undertake the Dutch while we take ease.
The seas their spoils within our hatches throw,
300 The winds both fleets into our mouths do blow;
Strew all their ships along the coast by ours,
As easy to be gathered up as flow'rs.
But Sandwich fears for merchants to mistake
A man of war, and among flow'rs a snake.
305 Two Indian ships, pregnant with eastern pearl
And diamonds, sate the officers and Earl.
Then warning of our fleet, he it divides
Into the ports, and he to Oxford rides,
While the Dutch reuniting, to our shames,
310 Ride all insulting o'er the Downs and Thames.
Now treating Sandwich seems the fittest choice

276–82. Dwindled . . . Wall] Montagu would have been the perfect leader of a wooden horse (the raid on Bergen is imagined as the Greek invasion of Troy) had the alliance with the Danes been completed (in which, at the least, they would have allowed the English ships to attack the Dutch in their own port). But Sir Gilbert Talbot, envoy to the Danish court, negotiated for more than a guarantee to purchase an annual quota of copper. The consequent delay allowed the Dutch to supply and man the fort, which finally proved fatal to the English attack.

280. condition] bargain, treat for conditions (*OED* v. 1).

282. Wall] personifies Danish intransigence.

283. Teddy] Sir Thomas Tyddiman: see above, l. 228 n. *would not*] i.e. make a treaty of alliance; Pepys (6.196) also reports a period of protracted negotiation between Tyddiman and the governor of the castle.

284. Sends . . . shot] the total English losses came to 118 men.

285. dressed . . . bride] appearing as a foppish courtier; Montagu was regarded as vain.

286. Metrically at odds with the iambic pentameter of the poem; scans as two anapaests, each followed by an iamb. *reached*] wounded (*OED* v.¹ 3 a).

288. membranes] the skin (as a figure from 'membrane' meaning 'parchment'); the line is complicatedly expressing a frown of concern or dismay.

290. waft] convoy: see above, l. 11 n.

291–2. walnut . . . bear] Comparing raids on Dutch merchantmen with beating walnut trees to gain the nuts; 'A woman, ass, and walnut tree, the more you beat the better be' (Tilley, W 644). Cp. *Defiance to the Dutch* (1674), s.sh., 'The *Dutch* are stubborn, and wil yield no FRUIT,/Till, like the *Wallnut-Tree*, ye Beat 'um to't.'

296. With . . . tempest] There was a storm, taken to be an act of Providence by *The Intelligencer*, 76 (18 September 1665), 891. *ruffle*] the painter is invited to disturb the canvas by painting a storm; 'ruffle' was in fact used to describe the action of turbulent winds (*OED* v.² 3).

298. undertake] entrap (*OED* v. I 1 a).

303–10. The Intelligencer, 76 (18 September 1665), 891, stressed the taking of Dutch prizes.

300–4. In fact, Sandwich feared that an engagement near to the shore would have endangered the larger ships, while fighting at night risked the dispersal of the fleet, and fighting at all risked losing the prizes already taken (see below, l. 305 n.; Ollard (1994), 137).

305. Two Indian ships] taken on 3 September 1665, south of the Dogger Bank.

306. sate . . . Earl] The contents of the holds of prize ships were supposed to be handed over to Prize Commissioners, who would then arrange for their sale, the proceeds of which would be distributed as prize money. However, on 21 September, Sandwich authorized an immediate partial share-out among the flag officers, including himself. An attempt to hide the impropriety by having the admirals not sell their prize goods failed, and scandal soon broke loose (Ollard (1994), 140). *sate*] glut, satisfy to the full (*OED* v. 1 b).

307. warning] notice of termination of employment: Sandwich is imagined as a master laying off a servant (*OED* vbl. n.¹ 6). *fleet . . . divides*] Sandwich sent the frigates to anchor in Hollesley Bay, Suffolk, while the prizes and the first and second rates, sailed into the mouth of the Thames, anchoring at the Nore on 13 September.

308. Oxford] where the King and court were preparing for the assembly of Parliament.

309–10. Dutch . . . Thames] Sandwich had left for Oxford in early October, certain that the fleet required laying up for refurbishment until the following year; but a Dutch fleet appeared at the mouth of the Thames in the middle of the month (Coventry to Ormond, 29 October 1665, Bod., MS Carte 47, fol. 428ʳ).

310. insulting] attacking (*OED* vbl. n. b).

311–12. treating] negotiating (*OED* v. 1 a). *Sandwich . . . Spain*] Sandwich was appointed ambassador to Spain in November: the intention was to finalize a treaty of alliance (against the growing power of France, and her alliance with Holland), and to remove Sandwich from the embarrassing context at home.

For Spain, there to condole and to rejoice.
He meets the French, but, to avoid all harms,
Slips to the Groin (embassies bear not arms!)
315 There let him languish a long quarantine,
And ne'er to England come till he be clean.
    Thus having fought we know not why, as yet
We've done we know not what, nor what we get.
If to espouse the ocean all the pains,
320 Princes unite, and will forbid the bains.
If to discharge fanatics, this makes more;
For all fanatic turn when sick or poor.
Or if the House of Commons to repay:
Their prize commissions are transferred away.
325 But for triumphant checkstones, if, and shell
For Duchess' closet: 't has succeeded well.
If to make Parliaments all odious: pass.
If to reserve a standing force: alas.

Or if as just, Orange to reinstate:
330 Instead of that he is regenerate.
And with four millions vainly giv'n, as spent;
And with five millions more of detriment;
Our sum amounts yet only to have won
A bastard Orange, for pimp Arlington.
335   Now may historians argue con and pro.
Denham saith thus; though Waller always so.
But he, good man, in his long sheet and staff
This penance did for Cromwell's epitaph.
And his next theme must be o' th' Duke's mistress:
340 Advice to draw Madam l'Edificatresse.
Henceforth, O Gemini! two Dukes command:
Castor and Pollux, Aumarle, Cumberland.
Since in one ship, it had been fit they went
In Petty's double-keel'd *Experiment*.

---

312. condole] over the death of Philip IV on 7 September.
rejoice] at the succession of Charles II, Philip's infant son.
314. Groin] sailor's name [i.e. an etymological perversion] for
Corunna, on the north-west coast of Spain.
314–15. embassies . . . quarantine] while in quarantine off
Corunna, Sandwich's ship seized a Dutch merchantman, an act
of war inappropriate to his diplomatic mission.
319. espouse . . . pains] a further reference to the Venetian sea
marriage ceremony: see above, ll. 73–4 n.; the suggestion is
that the war has been fought as a ritual to marry the English to
the sea.
320. Princes unite] with the exception of the Bishop of
Münster, England was diplomatically isolated during the
Second Dutch War. France entered a military alliance with
the United Provinces against England in 1666. *bains*] banns:
public proclamation of an intended marriage (*OED* n. 1).
321. discharge fanatics] purge republicans or separatists, as had
occurred in the navy in the 1650s: see above, 324, 329.
325. checkstones] small, smooth round pebbles, used to play a
children's game (*OED* n).
326. Duchess] the Duchess of York.
328. reserve] maintain (*OED* v. 8). *standing force*] standing
army.
329–34. Orange . . . Arlington] Pincus (1996), 322, notes the
court interest in restoring William, Prince of Orange (his
authority was withheld until he was made Stadholder in 1672).
These lines do not openly imply sympathy with the republican
element in the United Provinces, but they do reveal a complicated attitude towards Dutch politics; the Dutch are not
merely a national enemy. Waller, *Instructions to a Painter*,
l. 188, regarded William as unjustly debarred from active
service even though he was only 14 in 1665. See also above,
Headnote, General Context.
330. regenerate] degenerate (*OED* ppl. a. 3).
331–2. four . . . millions] an estimated cost of the war: £4 million
voted by Parliament, £5 million more of incurred debt.
334. bastard . . . Arlington] in April 1666, Henry Bennet, Earl
of Arlington, was married to Isabel von Beverweert, daughter

of Louis of Nassau, a natural son of Prince Maurice. *pimp
Arlington*] Arlington was one of the managers of the royal
mistresses: see Burnet (1833), 1.183.
336. Denham] Sir John Denham (1615–69), poet. *Waller*]
Edmund Waller: see above, *Headnote, Context*.
337. sheet] covering worn while penance (originally for fornica-
tion) is made (*OED* n.[1] 1 b). See below, l. 338. *staff*] pole for
help with walking.
338. Cromwell's epitaph] Waller wrote an elegy for Oliver
Cromwell: *Upon the Late Storm and the Death of his Highness
Ensuing the Same* (1659).
339–40. Duke's . . . l'Edificatresse] a crude pun: Denham was
appointed Surveyor-General of the Works in 1660; Lady
Denham became the Duke of York's mistress in 1666; Pepys
(7.158–9) records the affair as having recently begun in
10 June, although the poem is dated April. He also names the
Duke's pimps in arranging the liaison as the notorious Henry
Brouncker (see above, 327, 337–8) and the Countess of
Castlemaine (see below, 369–70, 393). *l'Edificatresse*] feminine form of French 'edificateur', builder, erector, and hence,
bawdily, 'builder of erections.'
341–2. Gemini . . . Cumberland] After Sandwich's removal,
command of the Navy was entrusted jointly to Prince Rupert
(Duke of Cumberland) and George Monck, Duke of
Albemarle (i.e. Aumarle). *342. Castor and Pollux*] Cp. anon., *Castor and Pollux: Or,
an Heroique Poeme upon his Majesties Victorious, and Princely
Generals, The Dukes of* [bracketed together] *Cumberland and
Albemarle*, ll. 5–6: 'The most admird Example how one
Mind/May rule two *Bodies*, and their *Judgements* bind.'
344. Petty's . . . Experiment] Sir William Petty (1623–87)
designed four double-keeled ships, with very narrow drafts (as
little as one foot). *Experiment* was the third of three built
in 1662–64, and was launched on 22 December 1664; it was
sailing still in March 1665, but sank shortly afterwards in a
storm in the Irish Sea (Pepys, 6.63, n. 1). *Bod. 18*, fol. 15[r] has
the marginal annotation 'a ship wth two Keeles w[ch] was cast
away'.

To the King

345   Imperial Prince, King of the seas and isles,
    Dear object of our joys and Heaven's smiles,
    What boots it that thy light does gild our days
    And we lie basking in thy milder rays?
    While swarms of insects, from thy warmth begun,
350   Our land devour, and intercept our sun.
        Thou, like Jove's Minos, rul'st a greater Crete
    (And for its hundred cities count'st thy fleet.)
    Why wilt thou that state-Daedalus allow,
    Who builds thee but a lab'rinth and a cow?
355   If thou art Minos, be a judge severe:

    And in's own maze confine the engineer.
    Or if our sun, since he so near presumes,
    Melt the soft wax with which he imps his plumes
    And let him falling leave his hated name,
360   Unto those seas his war hath set on flame.
    From that enchanter having cleared thine eyes,
    Thy native sight will pierce within the skies:
    And view those kingdoms calm of joy and light,
    Where's universal triumph but no fight.
365   Since both from Heav'n thy race and pow'r descend,
    Rule by its pattern, there to reascend.
    Let Justice only draw: and battle cease.
    Kings are in war but cards: they're gods in peace.

347–50. What . . . sun] the sun was a traditional and popular symbol for monarchy: see, e.g., anon., *To the Queen, On her Birthday* (1663), s.sh.: 'So though the Sun Victorious be,/And from a dark Eclipse set free.'

347. boots it] of what value is it (*OED* v.¹ 3 a).

351. Minos] Waller, *Instructions to a Painter*, ll. 315–36, compares Charles to Alcides, Phoebus and, most importantly, Jove, who visits Crete to instruct the Cyclops how to make his thunder. By contrast, Minos, King of Crete is hardly a flattering parallel: an upright ruler, but one who was cuckolded by a bull, was weak in person and power when old, was denied immortality by Jupiter, and, with ass's ears, was no judge of poetry. For M.'s earlier use of another part of the Minos story, see above, *A Poem upon the Death of his Late Highness the Lord Protector*, ll. 67–8.

352. hundred cities] repeats Ovid, *Metamorphoses*, VII, l. 481.

353. state-Daedalus] Clarendon. *allow*] approve (*OED* v. 2).

354. Who . . . cow] Daedalus built the cow that enabled Minos's wife Pasiphae to have her adulterous union with the bull, and the labyrinth within which the monstrous issue of the union, the Minotaur, was imprisoned (Ovid, *Metamorphoses,*

VIII, ll. 131–7, 155–68). Daedalus' underground maze is as deceitful as Clarendon's statecraft: 'turbatque notas et lumina flexum/ducit in errorem variarum ambage viarum' (He confused the usual passages and deceived the eye by a conflicting maze of diverse winding paths) (*Metamorphoses*, VIII, ll. 160–1).

358. Melt . . . plumes] Daedalus made wings from feathers, by which means he and his son Icarus escaped from Crete. But Icarus flew too near the sun, which melted the wax that held his wings, so he plunged to his death in the Aegean (Ovid, *Metamorphoses*, VIII, ll. 183–235). *imps*] engrafts; hence, figuratively, to enhance (one's power).

359–60. leave . . . seas] Cp. Ovid, *Metamorphoses*, VIII, ll. 229–30: 'oraque caerulea patrium clamantia nomen/excipiuntur aqua, quae nomen traxit ab illo' (His lips, calling to the last upon his father's name, were drowned in the dark blue sea, which took its name from him).

362. native] natural, what one is born with (*OED* a. I 1).

367. draw] a) paint (*OED* v. V 60) b) draw a card (*OED* v. III 32).

368. cards] playing-cards, i.e. kings are the instruments of other forces – fortune, or powerful courtiers.

Date. Late 1666–January 1667. Bod., MS Eng. poet d. 49 (*Bod. 1*) is dated 1 October 1666; Pepys saw a copy of the poem on 20 January 1667 (8.21).

Authorship. According to Patterson's argument (*SEL*, 40 (2000), 95–411), M. may have been responsible only for the following lines: ll. 11–20, 65–70, 81–94, 413–22, 451–6.

Manuscript Circulation and Printed Publication. The poem circulated in manuscript from at least early 1667, and was printed in *1667²*, *1667³*, *1667³b*. As with *The Second Advice*, very few MS copies can be dated to the late 1660s. Copies often exist with copies of *The Second Advice*, but evidently fewer copies of *The Third Advice* were made. Twenty-eight MS copies survive:

Bod. 1   Bod. MS Eng. poet d. 49
BL 20   BL, Add. MS 23722, fols. 42–8ᵛ, 55ᵛ–6
BL 16   BL, MS Harley 7315, fols. 8ᵛ–19ᵛ
P 4   Princeton University Library, Robert H. Taylor Collection, MS 1, pp. 13–28
BL 29   BL, Add. MS 69823, pp. 138–58
Bod. 18   Bod., MS Don. e. 23, fols. 15v–22
Bod. 24   Bod., MS Eng. misc. e. 536, pp. 13–16
Bod. 8   Bod., MS Eng. poet. e. 4, pp. 229–41
Bod. 21   Bod., MS Gough London 14, fols. 50ᵛ–8
Bod. 26   Bod., MS Rawl. poet. 123, p. 105
Bod. 27   Bod., MS Rawl. poet. 172, fols. 175–6ᵛ
Cm.   Cumbria Record Office, Carlisle, D/Lons/ L Miscellaneous 11/6/33, fols. [5–10]
Es.   Essex Record Office, D/DW Z3 (iii), pp. 17–35
F 5   Folger Shakespeare Library, MS V.a.220, Part II, pp. 30–45
G   Georgetown University [no ref. or page numbers]
H 2   Harvard University, MS Eng. 624, pp. [12–25]
L 6   University of Leeds, Brotherton Collection, MS Lt. 54, pp. 406–25

LAC 2   Clark Library, Los Angeles, M3915M3 S445 [16—] Bound, fols. 8–14
N 10   University of Nottingham, Portland MS Pw2V 5 (iv)
N 11   University of Nottingham, Portland MS Pw2V 6
OA 1   All Souls College, Oxford, MS 174, fols. 27ᵛ–35
Copy owned by Robert S. Pirie (*IELM*, MaA 382; not seen)
SA   Society of Antiquaries, MS 330, fols. 22ᵛ–6
Wa.   Warwickshire Record Office, CR 341/277, pp. 11–22
Y 5   Yale University, Beinecke Library, MS Vault, Section 15, Drawer 3, pp. [14–32]
Y 6   Yale University, Beinecke Library, Osborn Collection, b 136, pp. 17–33
Y 11   Yale University, Beinecke Library, Osborn Collection, c 160, fols. 8–9ᵛ, 16
Y 10   Yale University, Beinecke Library, Osborn Collection, fb 140, pp. 65–79

See also above, *The Advice-to-a-Painter Poems, Headnote, Publication and Circulation.*

Text. See above, *The Advice-to-a-Painter Poems, Headnote, Text.* The text is based on *Bod. 1*. There are very few textual variants, and most are of very little significance. The single exception is *BL 29*, the only early witness, dated to 1667. As with the early copies of *The Second Advice*, this copy of *The Third Advice* has a number of unique and significant readings, as well as some unique omissions. Of the printed editions, it is most closely related to *1667³*.

Context. The poem is concerned with the Four Days' Battle (1–4 June 1666), in which Monck encountered considerable losses against De Ruyter's fleet. Pepys had himself thought of writing a lampoon on the subject of 'the late fight at seas and the miscarriages there' (15 July 1666; 7.207). The English fleet was weakened since Prince Rupert commanded a squadron of twenty ships which had left late in May to encounter a French fleet under the duc de Beaufort in the Bay of Biscay. Only Rupert's last-minute arrival saved the English from total defeat. Through the voice of Monck's wife, Ann, Duchess of Albemarle, the poem blames the reverse on corruption and bad administration. Although Monck and Rupert would later allege that Arlington's intelligence had falsely reported Beaufort at Belle-Ile (in an attempt to lay the blame on Arlington and Coventry, rather than Clarendon), they were fully responsible for their action. Arlington claimed he had acted on what he thought was genuine intelligence. As the poem acknowledges (ll. 32–4), Monck engaged De Ruyter's superior fleet thinking he could win. Later on, it became clear that Albemarle's letter, requesting Rupert's immediate support, had been delayed by Coventry and Arlington.

In a reversal of the Battle of Lowestoft, the Four Days' Battle took a very heavy toll in lives and ships. The English lost twenty ships, either destroyed or taken, two admirals (one captured) and eight thousand killed, wounded, or taken prisoner, as against Dutch losses of two admirals, four to seven ships and two thousand killed and wounded. Lack of those willing to serve in the navy was now alarming. Impressment was common: many of the dead men floating in the water after the Battle were still wearing their dark Sunday suits, having been impressed directly from church. It was not an absolute defeat but enabled the Dutch to boast their advantage, which in turn occasioned publications designed to maximize the English navy's side of the story, such as *A True Narrative of the Engagement between His Majesties Fleet, and that of Holland* (1666). See further, Fox (1996).

Patterson (1978), 142–4, revised (2000), 89–92, argues that the poem is also responding to two poems that defended the regime and the war policy. Christopher Wase's *Divination* (1666) was an attack on the political critique of *The Second Advice*, although admiring of its poetic achievement. *The Third Advice* appears to pick up on Wase's accusations (see below, l. 3 n.). Dryden's *Annus Mirabilis* (composed summer–autumn 1666, published January 1667) offered a heroic, indeed Virgilian, account of three failures (the division of the fleet, the Four Days' Battle and the Great Fire of London), but if M. is answering Dryden, he must have seen a MS copy of Dryden's poem and its preface before it appeared in print. This seems extremely unlikely.

The poem offers different kinds of travesty. Official accounts of the Four Days' Battle stressed English prowess and suggested that victory was with them. One such work was *A True Narrative of the Engagement between his Majesties Fleet, and that of Holland* (1666) in which a first person plural voice is associated with Monck, as if the Admiral himself were speaking. In *The Third Advice*, the 'truth' is provided by the female voice of his wife. The joke here is complicated and works at the expense of Clarendon and the Presbyterians, of whom the Duchess was one. She was famous for giving outspoken advice to her husband in favour of a Restoration in the late 1650s, and was hence popular with Clarendon. Only after the Restoration did she become an irritant to Clarendon (and almost everyone else). Her reputation for peculation as well as meanness was considerable, so her calls for integrity in the administration and the navy would have seemed not merely hypocritical, but also incredible. Dzelzainis (in Richards and Thorne, eds, forthcoming) argues that M. deliberately chose this improbable prophet to point up the dire national situation. The humorous, near mock-heroic portrait of Monck contrasts with the commissioned heroic paintings of De Ruyter by Ferdinand Bol (on the circulation of printed pictures in the period, see Globe (1985)). After the Four Days' Battle, printed verse was certainly more willing to confess the horror of a naval battle than was Waller, as the lurid vision of R[ichard] H[ead]'s *The Red-Sea* (12 June 1666) made clear. But criticism of the government was still absent from these poems.

Structure, Style and Versification. As with its predecessor, the poem is written within the framework of imagining a painter painting a picture, this time by Richard Gibson, the dwarf miniaturist. But the poem divides abruptly at l. 169 where the Duchess of Albemarle is introduced. In addition to seeing sources for the 'outrageous polysyllabic rhymes' in Butler's *Hudibras* (1662–3), Dzelzainis (in Richards and Thorne, eds., forthcoming) argues that the Duchess' speech is an example of *parrhesia*, free speech by someone not in power urgently addressing a crisis. The Duchess is likened to a series of classical prophets, the Cumaean Sibyl, the Pythia of Delphi, Cassandra, Philomela, and where she is characterized as an 'engastrimyth' rather than a true divinely-inspired prophetess. The comparison of her to various animals gives her a further truth-telling perspective since in this sense she is precisely not a human and not subject to human folly. Thus, she is 'M.'s response to the problematization of truth telling in a rhetorical culture.' In the case of the Duchess, her credentials as one who speaks the truth and nothing but the truth can only be established by severely negative and deflationary means. The Duchess's speech contains many locutions appropriate to her original lowly status. To this extent her speech should be compared with that of the nymph complaining (see above, 65–71), although her complaint also adopts the 'popular' diction of the Presbyterian poet Robert Wild, whose celebration of Monck's role in bringing about the Restoration, *Iter Boreale*, is echoed in her voice. For Wild's complaint mode, see *A Poem upon the Imprisonment of Mr Calamy in Newgate* (1663). M. would have been attracted by Wild's obsession with other poets and his own reputation: see, e.g., 'Dr Wild to the Ingenious Mr Wanley', in *Iter Boreale* (1668), 110–13. The mock heroic nature of the Duchess's speech becomes more pointed in the context of the distribution of printed versions of the poem by Elizabeth Calvert. In the 1640s and 1650s, the Calverts had been responsible for publishing the radical Puritan works that most offended the Presbyterians. Elizabeth Calvert's clientele of former radicals would have found *The Third Advice* more in the vein of the anti-Presbyterian satires of the Leveller Richard Overton.

The voice of the Duchess also embodies other modes of Monckian panegyric: the heroic: see, e.g., T.B., *The Muses congratulatory Address to his Excellency the Lord General Monck* (1660), s.sh., 'In th'chair of presidents must be/Great *George* bigbelly'd with thy history'; the popular, balladic verse that had been used to celebrate Monck's achievements since 1659: see, e.g., anon., *The Noble English Worthies* (1659), s.sh.: 'He made the *Dutch* then vale their Topps;,/And humble be as their

Sack-slops;/ . . . *Oh! This is our brave George!*' The painting context is appropriate: Pepys (8.147) records dining on disgusting food at Albemarle's Whitehall lodgings in the presence of a considerable collection of paintings. The political and religious implications of this depiction are discussed by Patterson (1978), 152–55 (revised 2000), 94–7; see also below, 348–9. Gibson, not unlike M. himself, was a great survivor, having been a page in the court of Charles I, then Cromwell's portraitist, before becoming official miniaturist to the court of Charles II. Ann, Duchess of Albemarle, was a Presbyterian, and aligns herself with the nonconformists who, though expelled from the national church in 1662, remained loyal to the crown. She stands for those religious nonconformists whom M. would defend in his prose works of the 1670s.

The Third Advice to a Painter
London, October 1st, 1666

Sandwich in Spain now, and the Duke in love,
Let's with new gen'rals a new painter prove.
Lely's a Dutchman, danger in his art:
His pencils may intelligence impart.
5   Thou Gibson, that among thy navy small
Of marshalled shells commandest admiral;
Thyself so slender that thou show'st no more
Than barnacle new hatched of them before:
Come, mix thy water colours, and express,
10   Drawing in little, how we do yet less.
    First paint me George and Rupert, rattling far
Within one box, like the two dice of war:
And let the terror of their linkèd name
Fly through the air like chainshot, tearing Fame.
15   Jove in one cloud did scarcely ever wrap
Lightning so fierce, but never such a clap.

Title. *Advice*] see above, *The Second Advice*, Title n.
2. *prove*] put to the test (*OED* v. B 1 a).
3. Sir Peter Lely (1617–80), the pre-eminent England-based portrait painter of the age; see above *Upon Appleton House*, l. 443. The 'danger' is in the excessive realism of Lely's Dutch style and training, which will be embarrassingly revealing in representing the war. In 1666, Lely was commissioned to paint portraits of the English commanders at the Battle of Lowestoft. M. had his portrait painted by Lely (Vertue (1930–55), 2.22).
4. *pencils*] paintbrushes (*OED* n. I 1 a). *intelligence*] part of the 'danger' of Lely's paintings is that they will reveal politically sensitive information.
5. *Gibson*] Richard Gibson (1615–90), a dwarf who painted miniatures, and who copied Lely's work. He taught Queen Anne to draw.

6. *marshalled*] Bod. 1+; muscle- *Es.*, Bod. 8, *Υ* 5, *Υ* 11, 1667. Mussel shells were also used as receptacles for mixing paints: Thomas Jenner, *A Book of Drawing, Limning, Washing* (1st edn, 1652; 1666), 11. Gibson's painting shells are imagined as a miniature navy, with 'shells' a pun: a) mussel shells b) hulls of ships (*OED* n. IV 26 b).
11–12. *First . . . war*] Cp. *The First Anniversary*, ll. 357–8: 'Their's are not ships, but rather arks of war,/And beakèd promontories sailed from far.'
12. *two dice of war*] signifying that war is a gamble; the Greek Palamedes was held to have invented dice during the siege of Troy (Pausanias, *Attica*, II.xx.3).
16. *clap*] a) thunder-clap (*OED* n.[1] I 2) b) gonorrhoea (*OED* n.[2]).

United gen'rals! sure the only spell
Wherewith United Provinces to quell.
Alas, ev'n they, though shelled in treble oak
Will prove an addle egg with double yolk.
And therefore next uncouple either hound,
And loo them at two hares ere one be found.
Rupert to Beaufort hollow: 'Ay there, Rupert!'
Like the fantastic hunting of St Hubert,
When he with airy hounds, and horn of air,
Pursues by Fountainbleu the witchy hare.
Deep providence of state, that could so soon
Fight Beaufort here ere he had quit Toulon!
So have I seen, ere human quarrels rise,
Foreboding meteors combat with the skies.
　　But let the Prince to fight with Rumour go:
The Gen'ral meets a more substantial foe.
Ruyter he spies, and, full of youthful heat,
Though half their number, thinks his odds too great.
The fowler so watches the wat'ry spot
And, more the fowl, hopes for the better shot.
Though such a limb were from his navy torn,
He found no weakness yet, like Samson shorn,
But swoll'n with sense of former glory won,
Thought Monck must be by Albemarle outdone.
Little he knew, with the same arm and sword,
How far the gentleman outcuts the lord.
　　Ruyter, inferior unto none for heart,
Superior now in number and in art,
Asked if he thought (as once our rebel nation)
To conquer theirs too by a declaration.

And threatens, though he now so proudly sail,
He shall tread back his Iter Boreale.
This said, he the short period, ere it ends,
50　With iron words from brazen mouths extends.
　　Monck yet prevents him ere the navies meet,
And charges in, himself alone a fleet;
And with so quick and frequent motion wound
His murd'ring sides about, the ship seemed round,
55　And the exchanges of his circling tire
Like whirling hoops showed of triumphal fire.
Single he does at their whole navy aim,
And shoots them through, a porcupine of flame.
He plays with danger, and his bullets trolls,
60　As 'twere at trou-madam, through all their holls.
In noise so regular his cannon met,
You'd think that thunder were to music set.
Ah, had the rest but kept a time as true,
What age could such a martial consort show?
65　　The list'ning air, unto the distant shore,
Through secret pipes conveys the tunèd roar:
Till, as the echoes vanishing abate,
Men feel a deaf sound, like the pulse of Fate.
If Fate expire, let Monck her place supply:
70　His guns determine who shall live or die.
　　But Victory does always hate a rant:
Valour her brave, but Skill is her gallant.
Ruyter no less with virtuous envy burns,
And prodigies for miracles returns.
75　Yet she observed how still his iron balls
Bricoled in vain against our oaken walls,

19–20. Cp. *The First Anniversary*, ll. 374–6: 'Through double oak, and lined with treble brass;/That one man still, although but named, alarms/More than all men, all navies, and all arms.'
20. *addle egg*] rotten egg that produces no chicken (*OED* a. B 1).
22. *loo*] incite by shouting 'halloo' (*OED* v.²).
23–4. There is an extra syllable in each of these two lines.
23. *Beaufort*] François de Vendôme, duc de Beaufort (1616–69), French naval commander.
24–6. St Hubert (*c.* 657–727) was responsible for many conversions in the Ardennes region of Belgium. He became Bishop of Tongeren, Maastrict in 705/6, and was venerated as the first Bishop of Liège. The story, originally told of St Eustace, was that, while hunting, he saw a stag with a crucifix between its antlers. There was a medieval cult of St Hubert; two churches in England were dedicated to him. He was also a frequent topic in painting: several English examples show him holding a book on which (or at his feet) is a miniature stag.
26. *Fountainbleu*] forest forty miles south-east of Paris, in which by M.'s time stood the famous royal château, originally a thirteenth-century royal hunting lodge. *witchy*] resembling or characteristic of a witch (*OED*: this line is an example in the *OED* entry, the only example before 1903).
28. *Toulon*] principal headquarters and arsenal of the French navy; founded during the reign of Henri IV (1589–1610).
29–30. *So . . . skies*] See *The Last Instructions to a Painter*, l. 551.

42. *outcuts*] outdoes, supplants ('cut': *OED* v. 57 f).
48. *Iter Boreale*] literally, 'the march from the north', made by Monck in 1659, which effectively secured the Restoration of the monarchy; also the title of Robert Wild's poem that celebrated the march (1660).
51. *prevents*] acts more more quickly than, and in anticipation of (*OED* v. I 2).
55. *tire*] broadside or volley; simultaneous discharge of ordnance (*OED* n.³).
59. *trolls*] rolls (as in a game of bowls) (*OED* v. 2).
60. *trou-madam*] troll-madam; ladies' game, resembling bagatelle, in which metal balls were rolled down a table towards eleven holes at the end (*OED*). *holls*] a) obscure form of 'hull' (*OED*) b) ship's hold (*OED* n. 2).
61. *noise . . . met*] Cp. *Musick's Empire*, ll. 17–18: 'Then music . . . /Did of all these a solemn noise prepare.' *noise*] melodious sound (*OED* n. 5).
64. *martial consort*] Cp. *Musick's Empire*, l. 9: 'Each sought a consort in that lovely place.'
65. *list'ning air*] Cp. *Bermudas*, ll. 3–4: 'From a small boat, that rowed along,/The list'ning winds received this song.'
66. *secret pipes*] a) the pipes of a musical instrument. b) pipes for conveying a substance.
72. *brave*] warrior (*OED* n. B 1). *gallant*] lover (*OED* n. B 3).
76. *Bricoled*] rebounded (*OED* v.).

And the hard pellets fell away, as dead,
Which our enchanted timber fillipèd.
'Leave then,' said she, 'th' invulnerable keel:
80 We'll find their foible, like Achilles' heel.'
    He, quickly taught, pours in continual crowds
Of chained dilemmas through our sinewy shrouds.
Forests of masts fall with their rude embrace:
Our stiff sails mashed are netted into lace,
85 Till our whole navy lay their wanton mark,
Nor any ship could sail but as the ark.
Shot in the wing, so, at the powder's call
The disappointed bird does flutt'ring fall.
Yet Monck, disabled, still such courage shows
90 That none into his mortal gripe durst close.
So an old bustard, maimed, yet loath to yield,
Duels the fowler in Newmarket field.
But soon he found 'twas now in vain to fight
And imps his plumes the best he may for flight.
95 This, painter, were a noble task, to tell
What indignation his great breast did swell.
Not virtuous men unworthily abused,

Not constant lovers without cause refused,
Not honest merchant broke, not skillful play'r
100 Hissed off the stage, not sinner in despair,
Not losing rooks, not favourites disgraced,
Not Rump by Oliver or Monck displaced,
Not kings deposed, not prelates ere they die,
Feel half the rage of gen'rals when they fly.
105   Ah, rather than transmit our scorn to Fame,
Draw curtains, gentle artist, o'er this shame.
Cashier the mem'ry of Du Tell, raised up
To taste instead of Death's, his Highness' cup.
And, if the thing were true, yet paint it not:
110 How Berkeley, as he long deserved, was shot,
Though others, that surveyed the corpse so clear,
Say he was only petrified with fear,
And the hard statue, mummied without gum,
Might the Dutch balm have spared and English tomb
115 Yet, if thou wilt, paint Myngs turned all to soul;
And the great Harman charked almost to coal;
And Jordan old, thy pencil's worthy pain,
Who all the way held up the ducal train.

---

78. fillipèd] struck smartly (*OED* v. 3).
80. foible] weak point (*OED* B n.)
81–9. See *London Gazette*, 58 (31 May–4 June 1666), sig. Mmm᷎, report from Harwich, 2 June: 'the *Dutch* being on the Leewards, their Guns mounted so high, that they only shot our Rigging, but did little execution on the Men or Hulls.'
82. dilemmas] literally, a choice between two equally unfavourable alternatives (*OED* n. 2), figuratively representing chain-shot, where two spherical or hemispherical projectiles were linked by a chain and used specifically to destroy masts, rigging and sails. *sinewy*] pronounced as two syllables. *shrouds*] a) sets of ropes attached from the heads of ship masts, designed to relieve lateral stress (*OED* n.² 1). b) tree branches (with the masts imagined as a forest: see below, l. 83) (*OED* n.³).
83. rude] violent (*OED* a. 5 b).
84. mashed] beaten (by ordnance) into a soft mash (*OED* v¹ 1).
85. lay] i.e. helpless, at the mercy of the Dutch. *wanton*] bobbing up and down (*OED* a. 3 c). *mark*] target (*OED* n. 7 a).
86. sail . . . ark] i.e. drift.
88. disappointed] undone, destroyed (*OED* v. 4 b).
90. gripe] grip, grasp (*OED* n.¹ 1 a).
93–4. Cp. *The Garden*, ll. 54–6: 'Then whets, and combs its silver wings;/And, till prepared for longer flight,/Waves in its plumes the various light.'
94. imps] engrafts, in order to repair (*OED* v. 4); cp. *The Second Advice*, ll. 357–8: 'since he so near presumes,/Melt the soft wax with which he imps his plumes.'
101. rooks] gulls; victims of cheats or swindlers (*OED* n.¹ 2 c).
105. scorn] object of mockery or contempt (*OED* n. 3 b).
107. Cashier] discard, put aside (*OED* v. 3). *Du Tell*] Jean Baptiste du Tell (Teil or Tiel; d. *ante* 1688), naval captain of French birth, made the Duke of York's cup-bearer having been dismissed from his commission in June 1666 for doing more damage to his own side than the enemy at the Four Days' Battle. Eventually knighted.

109–10. paint . . . Berkeley] William Berkeley (1639–66; Kt. 1664), younger brother to Charles, Earl of Falmouth (see above, *The Second Advice*, l. 181), one of the Duke of York's favourites. Lely's portrait of Berkeley shows a calm, staid figure, protected by a breastplate.
111–14. Though . . . tomb] Berkeley's corpse was displayed by the Dutch at The Hague in a sugar chest; it was later enbalmed by Ruysch, lay in the Grote Kerk in The Hague and was brought home for interment in Westminster Abbey in August. The poem presents Berkeley as a coward (as in *The Second Advice*, ll. 193–6, but unlike Dryden, *Annus Mirabilis*, ll. 267–8). It was believed by some that Berkeley behaved desperately in the Four Days' Battle, having endured aspersions of cowardice the previous year; it was also the case that his ship was cut off and surrounded.
113. mummied] embalmed.
115. Myngs] Sir Christopher Myngs (1625–66) led the van in *Victory*. He was fatally wounded on the fourth day of the battle and died later on 10 June (Pepys (7.160)); see also above, *The Second Advice*, l. 228 n.
116. Harman] Sir John Harman (d. 1673), Rear Admiral of the White Squadron. *charked*] a) burned to charcoal, coked (*OED* v.²); in the Four Days' Battle, Harman's ship, *Henry* was fired, many of the crew fled, and Harman was lamed by a falling mast, but he managed to extinguish the fire and save the ship. b) playing upon, and being the opposite of 'to chalk', to mark with chalk, and hence, to make white (*OED* v. 2, 2 b): Lely's portrait of Harman is very dark, as if charcoal had been used.
117. Jordan] Vice-Admiral Sir Joseph Jordan (1603–85), Kt. 1 July 1665 for his bravery at Lowestoft, fought no less bravely at the Four Days' Battle in *Royal Oak* (see above, *The Second Advice*, ll. 173–8 and n.); 'It is my part to praise God that hath delivered me and this ship, wonderfully, after so many days battle; the greatest passes, I think, that ever was fought at sea', Jordan to Sir William Penn, 5 June 1666.

But in a dark cloud cover Ascue, when
He quit the Prince t'imbark in Lowestein,
And wounded ships, which we immortal boast,
Now first led captive to an hostile coast.
　　But most, with story of his hand or thumb,
Conceal, as honour would, his Grace's bum.
When the rude bullet a large collop tore
Out of that buttock, never turned before.
Fortune it seemed would give him, by that lash,
Gentle correction for his fight so rash.
But should the Rump perceive 't, they'd say that Mars
Had now revenged them upon Aumarle's arse.
　　The long disaster better o'er to veil,
Paint only Jonas three days in the whale,
Then draw the youthful Perseus, all in haste,
From a sea-beast to free the virgin chaste:
But neither riding Pegasus for speed,
Nor with the Gorgon shielded at his need.
For no less time did conqu'ring Ruyter chaw
Our flying gen'ral in his spongy jaw.
So Rupert the sea-dragon did invade,
But to save George himself, and not the maid,
And so, arriving late, he quickly missed
Ev'n sails to fly, unable to resist.

　　Not Greenland seamen, that survive the fright
Of the cold chaos, and half-eternal night,
145　So gladly the returning sun adore,
Or run to spy their next year's fleet from shore,
Hoping, yet once, within the oily side
Of the fat whale again their spears to hide,
As our glad fleet, with universal shout,
150　Salute the Prince, and wish the second bout.
Nor winds, long pris'ners in Earth's hollow vault,
The fallow seas so eagerly assault,
As fiery Rupert, with revengeful joy,
Does on the Dutch his hungry courage cloy.
155　But, soon unrigged, lay like an useless board,
As wounded in the wrist men drop the sword;
When a propitious cloud betwixt us stepped
And in our aid did Ruyter intercept.
Old Homer yet did never introduce,
160　To save his heroes, mist of better use.
Worship the sun, who dwell where he does rise:
This mist does more deserve our sacrifice.
　　Now joyful fires, and the exalted bell,
And court-gazettes our empty triumph tell.
165　Alas: the time draws near when, overturned
The lying bells shall through the tongue be burned;

119–20. Ascue . . . Lowestein] Sir George Ascue (Ayscue, Ayscough) (*c.* 1615–72), Admiral of the White Squadron under Albemarle. In the Four Days' Battle, Ascue ran aground on the Galloper Sand in *Royal Prince*, and along with his company was taken prisoner by the Dutch, while the ship was burned. A manoeuvre to rescue the crew, and burn the ship before the Dutch arrived, failed. Ascue was held in the Castle of Lowestein and was 'carried up and down The Hague for people to see' (Pepys, 7.169).
120. Prince] 'yᶜ best Ship in England taken by yᶜ Dutch.' *Bod. 18* (margin).
123–6. See *The London Gazette*, 59 (4–7 June 1666), sig. Nnnʳ, report from Whitehall 4 June: 'they left the General well, having only received a slight bruise on the Hand by a Splinter, and his Breeches shot through by another shot'; Sir Joseph Jordan to Sir William Penn, 5 June 1666: 'Sir Wm. Clarke was shot Friday the first engagement and is since dead and the same shot struck my Lord General's thigh and bruised it a little and tore his breeches and coat in many places.'
125. collop] piece of flesh (*OED* n. 3).
129–30. Rump . . . revenged] Monck had given military backing to the restoration of the monarchy with his march from Scotland, thereby ending the republican government of the recalled Rump Parliament (1659–60).
132. Jonas] The prophet Jonah remained in the belly of the fish that swallowed him for three days and three nights (Jonah 1:17).
133. Perseus] Rupert is likened to the Greek mythological hero Perseus, slayer of the Gorgon and rescuer of Andromeda from a sea monster.
135. Pegasus] Perseus's winged horse.
137. chaw] chew roughly, champ (*OED* v. 1).

144–5. A compression of Milton, *Paradise Lost*, III, ll. 14–22; l. 144 echoes *Paradise Lost*, III, l. 18: 'I sung of Chaos and Eternal Night.'
152. fallow] uncultivated (*OED* a.² d), i.e. calm: a stormy sea, with undulating waves, resembles a ploughed field.
155. board] simple piece of thinly sawn wood (*OED* n. I 1), or formed from layers of compressed paper (*OED* n. I 3). The word is not used in its nautical senses (see above, *The Second Advice*, l. 166).
157. propitious cloud] As reported in accounts of the battle: see Colenbrander (1919), I, 337.
159–62. See Homer, *Iliad*, III, ll. 380–4, where Aphrodite saves Paris from Menelaus in battle by covering him in a cloud of mist and transporting him to his chamber.
163. Recalling the celebrations that greeted the restoration of the monarchy in 1660: see Knoppers (1994), 68–76; Jenner, *Past and Present*, 177 (2002), 84–120.
164. court-gazettes] the biweekly journal or newsbook, *The London Gazette*, called *The Oxford Gazette* for the first twenty-three issues, starting in November 1665, when the court was in Oxford in order to avoid the plague in London.
165–8. i.e. the Great Fire will be a punishment for the lies of state propaganda.
165. overturned] a) literally destroyed or damaged in the Great Fire b) invoking the biblical language of divine punishment: see, e.g., Job. 34:25: 'he knoweth their works, and he overturneth them in the night, so that they are destroyed'.
166. lying . . . burned] blasphemy was punished by the offender's tongue being pierced with a hot iron; lies issued by the government are hence regarded here as a kind of sin. *tongue*] a) literally, the clapper of the bell (*OED* n. III 13 d) b) metaphorically, as if the bells had human powers of speech.

Paper shall want to print that lie of state,
And our false fires true fires shall expiate.
   Stay, Painter, here awhile, and I will stay:
170 Nor vex the future times with nice survèy.
See'st not the monkey Duchess, all undressed?
Paint thou but her, and she will paint the rest.
   The sad tale found her in her outer room
Nailing up hangings, not of Persian loom,
175 Like chaste Penelope, that ne'er did roam,
But made all fine against her George came home;
Upon a ladder, in her coat most shorter,
She stood, with groom and porter for supporter.
And careless what they saw, or what they thought,
180 With Hony pensy honestly she wrought.
For in She-gen'ral's britch, none could (she knows)
Carry away the piece with eyes or nose.
One tenter drove, to lose no time nor place,
At once the ladder they remove and Grace.
185 While thus they her translate from north to east,
In posture just of a four-footed beast,
She heard the news: but altered yet no more
Than that what was behind she turned before;
Nor would come down; but with an hankercher,

190 Which pocket foul did to her neck prefer,
She dried no tears, for she was too viraginous:
But only snuffing her trunk cartilaginous,
From scaling ladder she began a story,
Worthy to be had in me(mento)mori,
195 Arraigning past, and present, and futuri;
With a prophetic (if not spirit) fury.
Her hair began to creep, her belly sound,
Her eyes to startle, and her udder bound.
Half witch, half prophet, thus she-Albermarle,
200 Like Presbyterian sibyl, out did snarl.
   'Traitors both to my Lord and to the King,
Nay now it grows beyond all suffering:
One valiant man on land, and he must be
Commanded out to stop their leaks at sea!
205 Yet send him Rupert, as an helper meet:
First the command dividing, ere the fleet.
One may, if they be beat, or both be hit,
Or if they overcome, yet honour's split;
But reck'ning George already knocked o' th' head,
210 They cut him out like beef, ere he be dead.
   Each for a quarter hopes: the first does skip,
But shall snap short though, at the gen'ralship:

---

167. i.e. there will not be sufficient paper to print the official publications putting this false point of view. There were but five newsbooks in 1666–67; none of them took a position critical of the government: only two were concerned with matters of state.

168. expiate] cleanse or purify from guilt (*OED* v. 2); i.e. the coming Great Fire will purge the taint of these 'false fires' celebrating a victory that was effectively a defeat.

170. nice] precise, exact (*OED* a. 8).

171. monkey Duchess] Ann, Duchess of Albemarle (1619–70), née Clarges, the daughter of Monck's regimental farrier, and, according to Aubrey (ii.73), formerly Monck's seamstress. 'Monkey' because a) like a monkey, she is climbing and (almost) naked (see below, l. 177) b) the poet puns on her married name, 'Monck'.

175–6. Penelope was the wife of Odysseus. In Homer's *Odyssey*, during her husband's absence, Penelope avoided the advances of many suitors by insisting that they wait until she has finished weaving a shroud for Odysseus's father.

176. fine] virtuous (*OED* a. 4 b).

177–8. There is an extra syllable in each of these lines.

178. supporter] heraldic term for figure holding up or standing beside a shield in a coat of arms (*OED* n. 4); the Duchess working with the hangings on a ladder is thus imagined as a coat of arms.

180. Hony pensy . . . she] The motto on the English royal coat of arms was also the title of one of the *Two Royal Acrostichs* (1666), which were anti-Dutch satires. Also the motto of the Order of the Garter, of which Monck was a member.

181–2. i.e. she knew that none could bear to look at or smell Albemarle's buttocks: she thus disguises them in the embroidery.

182. piece] embroidered picture on the wall hangings.

183. tenter] tenter-hook, a hook or bent nail used to stretch cloth on a tenter, or frame, after it has been milled (*OED* n.¹ 2).

185. north to east] the Duchess was, as with a compass, at 'north' on the top of the ladder, by falling off, she is relocated on the floor, at the position of 'east'.

187. news] i.e. of the outcome of the battle, and of Monck's wounds in particular.

191. viraginous] like a virago (*OED* a.).

192. trunk cartilaginous] nose. *cartilaginous*] consisting of cartilage (gristle) (*OED* a. 1).

193. scaling-ladder] ladder used in a siege (see 'scaling': *OED* vbl. n.³).

194. in me(mento)mori] From the Latin *memento mori*, 'remember that you have to die'. *Mento*, made to stand out by the parenthesis, refers to the Duchess's ugliness, since it means 'one who has a long chin.'

195. futuri] made into a Latin word in order to complete the rhyme, and following from the use of Latin in l. 194. There may also be a lewd innuendo here, since *futuo* means 'to have intercourse with a woman'.

196. not spirit] i.e. not by the inspiration of the Holy Spirit, which Puritans often claimed as their prophetic resource.

197. hair . . . creep] i.e. the skin on her head began to creep with horror and her hair stood on end (see 'creep', *OED* v. B 6).

200. sibyl] woman in antiquity with powers of prophecy or divination (*OED* n. 1).

204. leaks] i.e. failures.

205. helper meet] Cp. Gen. 2:18: 'And the Lord God said, It is not good that the man should be alone; I will make him an help meet for him.'

206. First . . . fleet] see above *Headnote, Context*.

209. knocked o'th' head] i.e. defeated; literally 'stunned' (*OED* v. 3 b).

210. cut . . . out] divide (*OED* v. VII 56 h).

211. first] possibly Thomas Clifford (see above, 338, l. 255 n.). *skip*] leap (*OED* v.¹ 2).

212. snap short] fail to obtain (*OED* v. I 3 c).

Next they for Master of the Horse agree:
A third the Cockpit begs; not any me.
5 But they shall know, ay, marry shall they do,
That who the Cockpit has shall have me too.
    'I told George first, as Calamy did me,
If the King these brought over, how 'twould be:
Men, that there picked his pocket to his face,
0 To sell intelligence or buy a place,
That their religion pawned for clothes; nor care
('T has run so long) now to redeem't, nor dare.
O what egregious loyalty to cheat!
O what fidelity it was to eat!
5 While Langdales, Hoptons, Glenhams starved abroad,
And here true Roy'lists sunk beneath the load.
Men that did there affront, defame, betray
The King, and do so here, now who but they?
What, say I men? nay rather monsters: men
0 Only in bed, nor (to my knowledge) then.
    'See how they home return, in revel-rout,
With the same measures that they first went out.

Nor better grown, nor wiser all this while,
Renew the causes of their first exìle,
235 As if (to show you fools what 'tis I mean)
I chose a foul smock, when I might have clean.
    'First, they for fear disband the army tame,
And leave good George a gen'ral's empty name;
Then bishops must revive, and all unfix
240 With discontent to content twenty-six.
The Lords' House drains the houses of the Lord,
For bishops' voices silencing the Word.
O Barthol'mew, saint of their calendar!
What's worse? thy 'jection or thy massacre?
245 Then Culp'per, Gloucester, ere the Princess, died:
Nothing can live that interrupts an Hyde.
O more than human Glouc'ster! Fate did show
Thee but to earth, and back again withdrew.
Then the fat scriv'ner durst begin to think
250 'Twas time to mix the royal blood with ink.
Berkeley, that swore, as oft as she had toes,
Does kneeling now her chastity depose,

---

213. Master of the Horse] Albemarle was made Master of the King's Horse on 26 May 1660.
214. Cockpit] Albemarle's lodgings in Whitehall. *any me*] i.e. any person; also a very crude pun on 'enemy'.
215. marry] i.e. 'to be sure' (*OED* int. a), but also hinting in its sense as a verb in the matrimonial context.
216. Cockpit] the Albemarles' residence (see above, l. 214 n.), but also an allusion to the vagina of the Duchess (but 'cockpit' is not in Williams (1994)).
217. Calamy] Edmund Calamy (1600–66), Nonconformist divine, briefly chaplain to Charles II.
218. these] i.e. courtiers who had been exiles in France during the Civil War and Interregnum.
221. religion . . . clothes] i.e. royalist exiles who became Roman Catholics in Europe in order to prosper; now returned home, they remain alienated from their national Protestant religion.
223. egregious] flagrant, outrageously bad (*OED* a. 3 a).
225. Langdales, Hoptons, Glenhams] Marmaduke, first Baron Langdale (1598?–1661); Ralph, Lord Hopton (1598–52); Sir Thomas Glenham (d. 1659?). All three were strong Royalists; Langdale and Glenham lived in poverty in Germany during the Interregnum.
226. Roy'lists] Those supporters of the King who remained in England, and endured penalties, lived in retirement, and risked raising support for Charles II during the Interregnum.
230. The Duchess accuses the courtiers of impotence.
231. revel-rout] boisterous merriment (*OED* n. 1).
232. measures] a) dances (*OED* n. II 20) b) standards (*OED* n. I 7 b) c) policies (*OED* n. IV 21).
236. foul smock] Cp. Aubrey (ii.73) on the Duchess: 'She was not at all handsome, nor cleanly'; and Pepys (6.57): [Lady Carteret] 'exclaims against . . . the Duchess, for a filthy woman, as endeed she is'; *idem*, ' "Our Dirty Besse" (meaning [the] Duchess)'; idem (8.147): 'I find the Duke of Albemarle at dinner with sorry company . . . dirty dishes and a nasty wife at table.'

237. disband the army] the New Model Army was disbanded shortly after the Restoration.
239–40. Then . . . twenty-six] A bill to lessen the severity of legislation against the nonconformists was defeated by 26 votes on 28 November 1660 (*JHC*, VIII, 194).
239. bishops must revive] seven new bishops were consecrated at Westminster on 2 December 1660.
242. the Word] i.e. the preaching of Scripture (by Nonconformists).
243–4. The 1662 Act of Uniformity deprived all clergy without episcopal ordination of their livings. It took effect on 24 August, St Bartholomew's Day, and hence on the anniversary of the massacre of Protestants in Paris in 1572.
243. saint . . . calendar] Once again, the Duchess reveals her Puritan credentials, regarding the Anglicans as if they were superstitious Roman Catholics.
244. 'jection] i.e. ejection.
245. John, first Lord Colepeper (date of birth unknown), Henry, Duke of Gloucester (b. 1639), and Princess Mary (b. 1631) (the latter being brother and sister to Charles II), all died in 1660.
246. an Hyde] i.e. Ann Hyde, Duchess of York, and daughter of Clarendon, who, in this and the previous line, is insinuated as advancing the claims of her husband to the throne by removing obstacles in his way.
249. fat scriv'ner] Clarendon had received a legal education, entering the Middle Temple in 1625; 'scrivener' here means 'notary' (*OED* 2).
250. time . . . ink] i.e. by marriage fuses the royal line with that of the chancellor.
251. Berkeley] Sir Charles Berkeley, later Lord Fitzharding and Earl of Falmouth: see above, *The Second Advice to a Painter*, l. 181 n. M. refers to an intrigue in which Berkeley persuaded several courtiers to provide the Duke of York with evidence of his future wife's sexual misconduct with them.
252. depose] a) deprive, dispossess (OED v. 4 b) b) affirms, bears witness to (OED v. 5).

Just as the first French Card'nal could restore
Maidenhead to his widow, niece and whore.
255 For portion, if she should prove light when weighed,
Four millions shall within three years be paid.
To raise it, we must have a naval war:
As if 'twere nothing but taratantar.
Abroad all princes disobliging first,
260 At home, all parties but the very worst.
    'To tell of Ireland, Scotland, Dunkirk's sad,
Or the King's marriage; but he thinks I'm mad.
And sweeter creature never saw the sun,
If we the King wished Monck, or Queen a nun.
265 But a Dutch war shall all these rumours still,
Bleed out these humours, and our purses spill.
Yet, after one day's trembling fight, they saw
'Twas too much danger for a son-in-law.
Hire him to leave with six score thousand pound;
270 As with the King's drums men for sleep compound.
Then modest Sandwich thought it might agree
With the state-prudence, to do less than he,

And, to excuse their tim'rousness and sloth,
They've found how George might now do less than bo[
275 'First, Smith must for Leghorn, with force enoug[
To venture back again, but not go through.
Beaufort is there, and, to their dazzling eyes,
The distance more the object magnifies.
Yet this they gain, that Smith his time shall lose
280 And for my Duke, too, cannot interpose.
    'But fearing that our Navy, George to break,
Might yet not be sufficiently weak,
The Secretary that had never yet
Intelligence but from his own *Gazette*,
285 Discovers a great secret, fit to sell,
And pays himself for't ere he would it tell:
Beaufort is in the channel. Hixy, here:
Doxy, Toulon: Beaufort is ev'rywhere!
Herewith assembles the supreme divan,
290 Where enters none but Devil, Ned, and Nan:
And, upon this pretence, they straight designed
The fleet to sep'rate, and the world to blind.

253–4. Cardinal Mazarin (1602–61), the chief minister during the early part of Louis XIV's reign, was famous for promoting elevated matches for his nieces, and was alleged (for instance in the *Mazarinades*, satires published during the Fronde) to have an elicit relationship with Louis' mother, Anne of Austria.
255. portion] dowry (*OED* n. I 3). *light*] a) i.e. of insufficient dowry b) delivered of a child (*OED* a.¹ 3).
256. It was originally moved that Parliament should give the King £2.5 million. This sum was later increased by half.
258. taratantar] sound of the trumpet or bugle (*OED* n. 1).
259. disobliging] offending (*OED* v. 3).
260. i.e. offending all factions but the most pernicious (i.e. Clarendon, his supporters and his minions).
261. Ireland . . . sad] See above, *The Second Advice*, ll. 149–50 n.
262. he] i.e. Charles II.
262–4. King's . . . nun] An insinuation that Clarendon's support for Charles II's marriage to Catherine of Branganza was based on a suspicion that she was barren, and hence would help the chances of a Hyde child inheriting the throne.
262. but . . . mad] The poet apparently forgets that the Duchess is speaking at this point, as opposed to Denham, who was periodically mad (*Yale POAS*). But is the joke more refined still, so that part of Denham's madness is that he forgets that he is writing as the Duchess?
266. humours] In ancient and medieval belief, the four bodily fluids determining a person's disposition: blood, phlegm, choler and melancholy or black choler (*OED* n. I 2 b); hence the sadness (melancholy) of l. 261 and the madness (choler) of l. 262.
268. danger . . . son-in-law] The Duke of York (Clarendon's son-in-law) was praised and rewarded for his bravery at the Battle of Lowestoft, but the King agreed to Parliament's address that the heir to the throne no longer be exposed to such danger.
269. six score thousand pound] voted by Parliament in June 1665.
270. i.e. bribe the press gangs to leave them alone (*Yale POAS*). *compound*] agree to pay (*OED* v. II 8 b).

271–2. modest . . . he] see above, *The Second Advice*, ll. 102, 311–12 n.
275–6. When war was declared on France in February 1666, a fleet under the command of Sir Jeremy Smith was sent to the Mediterranean to protect the Levant trade.
275. Smith] Jeremy Smith (d. 1675), Kt. 1665; see above, *The Second Advice*, l. 199 n. *Leghorn*] Livorno, Italian port, situated on the north-west coast of the Italian 'leg'.
276. not go through] i.e. back through the Straits of Gibraltar.
277–8. Beaufort . . . magnifies] Smith's position strategically divided two French fleets (one at Toulon, the other in the Atlantic), but M. implies that the English did not only not realize this, but were actually scared away by Beaufort.
277. dazzling] dazzled (*OED* ppl. a. 1).
280. for] i.e. because. *cannot interpose*] as Smith had been able to do at the Battle of Lowestoft: see above, *The Second Advice*, ll. 199–200.
283. Secretary] Arlington; see above, 338, 343.
283–6. Secretary . . . for't] Patterson (1978), 155, associates this attack upon Arlington with M.'s speech against him in the House of Commons on 15 February 1668, seen by contemporaries as a key point in the debates on administrative incompetence and corruption. For Arlington, see below 371, l. 129 n.
284. Intelligence . . . Gazette] An inversion of actuality that points up government control of the press: the only licensed newsbook, *The London Gazette* took its information from the intelligence service operated by Arlington as Secretary of State.
286. an allegation of further corruption on Arlington's part.
287. Beaufort . . . channel] a rumour; his fleet was actually in the Tagus.
287–8. Hixy . . . Doxy] false Latin used by jugglers or tricksters in their feats (*OED*: 'Hiccius doccius').
289. divan] council (originally oriental; the privy council presided over by the Turkish Sultan) (*OED* n. 1).
290. Ned] Clarendon. *Nan*] the Duchess of York.
291. straight] immediately.

Monck to the Dutch, and Rupert (here the wench
Could not but smile) is destined to the French.
295 To write the order Bristol's clerk they chose;
(One slit in's pen, another in his nose)
For he first brought the news, and 'tis his place:
He'll see the fleet divided like his face,
And through that cranny in his gristly part,
300 To the Dutch chink intelligence may start.
    'The plot succeeds: the Dutch in haste prepare,
And poor pilgarlic George's arse they share.
And now, presuming of his certain wrack,
To help him, late, they write for Rupert back.
305 Officious Will seemed fittest, as afraid
Lest George should look too far into his trade.
On the first draught they pause with statesmen's care,
Then write it foul, then copy 't out as fair,
Then they compare them; when at last 'tis signed,
310 Will soon his purse-strings but no seal could find.
At night he sends it by the common post
To save the King of an express the cost.
Lord what ado to pack one letter hence!
Some patents pass with less circumference.
315 Well, George, in spite of them thou safe dost ride,
Lessened, I hope, in nought but thy backside.

For as to reputation, this retreat
Of thine exceeds their victories so great.
Nor shalt thou stir from thence, by my consent,
320 Till thou hast made the Dutch and them repent.
'Tis true I want so long the nuptial gift,
But, as I oft have done, I'll make a shift.
Nor with vain pomp will I accost the shore
To try thy valour at the Buoy-i'th'-Nore.
325 Fall to thy work there, George, as I do here:
Cherish the valiant up, the cow'rd cashier.
See that the men have pay and beef and beer;
Find out the cheats of the four-millioneer.
Out of the very beer they steal the malt,
330 Powder out of powder, from powdered beef the salt.
Put thy hand to the tub: instead of ox,
They victual with French pork that has the pox.
Never such cotqueans by small arts to wring:
Ne'er such ill housewives in the managing.
335 Pursers at sea know fewer cheats than they:
Mar'ners on shore less madly spend their pay.
See that thou hast new sails thyself, and spoil
All their sea-market and their cable-coil.
Tell the King all, how him they countermine;
340 Trust not, till done, him with thy own design.

293–4. here . . . smile] The Duchess is amused because Rupert, suffering from the 'French disease' (i.e. syphilis), is to fight the French.
295. Bristol's clerk] Arlington.
296. Arlington's nose was marked by a scar from a sabre wound sustained in the Civil War, which he covered and thereby accentuated, with a piece of black plaster.
300. chink] vagina (Williams (1994), II.239–40); Arlington was married to a Dutch noblewoman, through which link it was assumed that the Dutch high command had intelligence of English naval preparations (see Colenbrander (1919), 1.339); hence Arlington is seen in the act of cunnilingus. The point of the satirist is to juxtapose two wounds: Arlington's 'cranny' and his wife's vagina. The representation of the giving of intelligence as sexual intercourse is a feature of Civil War literature. Cp. [Henry Neville], *Newes from the New Exchange* (1650), 3: the Countess of Carlisle 'was put in intelligence in the *Tower*, where she now pines away for want of *fresh-Cod*; and knoweth not which way to lead her *Nags* to water, since the *State* hath cut off all her *Pipes of Intelligence*'. See also Wiseman, in Holstun, ed. (1992). *start*] hastily impart (*OED* v. 4 a).
302. pilgarlic] bald (likened to a peeled head of garlic); associated in the seventeenth century with the consequences of venereal disease (*OED* a.; Williams (1994), II.1029); 'pilgarlic' was also a name for the penis (Williams (1994), II.1029). *share*] cut off (*OED* v.[1]).
303. wrack] ruin (*OED* n.[1] 3).
304. late] i.e. too late.
305. Officious] in the sense of interested in offices (see below, l. 306 n.).
306. George] i.e. Albemarle. *trade*] of selling offices.

308. foul] 'foul copy': draft or first copy, defaced by corrections (*OED* A. a. II 3 a).
310. seal] device impressed on a piece of molten wax and attached by string to an official document as a sign of authentication and attestation (*OED* n.[2] 1).
314. circumference] roundabout way (*OED* n. 5 b, quoting this example).
321. want] lack.
322. make a shift] a) put up with (Albemarle's continued absence) (*OED* n. II 6 d) b) make underclothing or a dress (*OED* n. IV 10); the Duchess had been a dressmaker, and there is a further hint at the Duchess's lack of gentility, since a 'shift' could also mean a set of sails (*OED* n. IV 8 b).
323. accost] approach (*OED* v. 6).
324. Buoy-i'th'-Nore] an important seamark at the mouth of the Thames, just north of the Isle of Sheppey and the entrance to the Medway; used for rendezvous and reconnaissance.
325–38. Albemarle was evidently busy re-supplying the fleet soon after the Four Days' Battle: see Albemarle to Coventry, 16 June 1666 (in Colenbrander (1919), 1.368–70).
328. cheats of the four-millioneer] embezzlers of the supply of £4 million (see above, l. 256 n.).
330. powdered beef] i.e. salt beef.
331. tub] barrel in which salt beef is kept, but playing upon a) sweating-tub used in the treatment of venereal disease (*OED* n. 1 b) b) nonconformist's pulpit (*OED* n. 4).
333. cotqueans] men who act like housewives, out of their sphere (*OED* n. 2). *wring*] extort money (*OED* v. I 7).
338. cable-coil] see above, *The Second Advice*, l. 338.
339. countermine] defeat by a counter-plot (*OED* v. 2).

Look that good chaplains on each ship do wait,
Nor the sea-diocese be impropriate.
Look to the pris'ners, sick, and wounded; all
Is prize: they rob even the hospital.
345 Recover back the prizes too: in vain
We fight if all be taken that is ta'en.
    'Now by our coast the Dutchmen, like a flight
Of feeding ducks, morning and ev'ning light.
How our land hectors tremble, void of sense!
350 As if they came straight to transport them hence.
Some sheep are stole, the kingdom's all arrayed:
And ev'n Presbit'ry's now called out for aid.
They wish ev'n George divided: to command
One half of him the sea, and one the land.
355   'What's that I see? Ha! 'Tis my George again:
It seems they in sev'n weeks have rigged him then.
The curious heav'n with lightning him surrounds
To view him, and his name in thunder sounds,
But with the same shaft gores their navy near,
360 As ere we hunt, the keeper shoots the deer.
Stay heav'n a while, and thou shalt see him sail,
And how George too can lighten, thunder, hail.
Happy the time that I thee wedded, George,
The sword of England, and of Holland scourge.
365 Avaunt Rotterdam-dog, Ruyter, avaunt!
Thou water-rat, thou shark, thou cormorant:
I'll teach thee to shoot scissors! I'll repair
Each rope thou losest, George, out of this hair.

Ere thou shalt lack a sail and lie adrift
370 ('Tis strong and coarse enough) I'll cut this shift.
Bring home the old ones, I again will sew,
And darn them up to be as good as new.
What, twice disabled? Never such a thing!
Now, Sovereign, help him that brought in the King;
375 Guard thy posterior left, lest all be gone:
Though jury-masts, th' hast jury-buttocks none.
Courage! How bravely, whet with this disgrace,
He turns, and bullets spits in Ruyter's face!
They fly, they fly! Their fleet does now divide:
380 But they discard their Trump; our Trump is Hyde.
    'Where are you now, De Ruyter, with your bears?
See how your merchants burn about your ears.
Fire out the wasps, George, from their hollow trees,
Crammed with the honey of our English bees.
385 Ay, now they're paid for Guinea: ere they steer
To the Gold Coast, they find it hotter here.
Turn their ships all to stoves, ere they set forth
To warm their traffic in the frozen north.
Ah Sandwich! had thy conduct been the same,
390 Bergen had seen a less, but richer flame,
Nor Ruyter lived new battle to repeat,
And oft'ner beaten be than we can beat.
    'Scarce has George leisure, after all this pain,
To tie his breeches: Ruyter's out again.
395 Thrice in one year! Why sure the man is wood:
Beat him like stockfish, or he'll ne'er be good.

---

342. impropriate] i.e. do not allow the funds for paying naval chaplains to be taken by corrupt courtiers or administrators. 'Impropriate' (*OED* ppl. a. 2) refers specifically to the taking of an ecclesiastical benefice or its revenue by a lay body.
348. light] land (*OED* v.¹ II 9).
349. hectors] swaggering fellows; braggarts (*OED* n. 2).
351. arrayed] afflicted, put into a considerable plight (*OED* v. 10 b).
356. rigged him] i.e. refitted his fleet.
359. gores] deeply wounds, i.e. considerably damages (*OED* v.¹ 1 b).
365. Avaunt] 'go away!', 'be off!' (*OED* B int.).
366. water-rat] pirate (*OED* n. 2). *shark*] cheat, swindler (*OED* n.²). *cormorant*] greedy, rapacious person (*OED* n. 2).
367. scissors] chain-shot (not in *OED*); like a pair of scissors, chain-shot cut down rigging. The Duchess draws on the vocabulary of her skill: she is a dressmaker.
376. jury-masts] temporary mast replacing one that has been damaged or carried away (*OED*).
377. whet] incited, urged on (*OED* v. 2).
379–80. fleet . . . Trump] The ships commanded by Smith and Tromp became separated from the rest of the battle.
380. Trump] Admiral Cornelius van Tromp with his name altered so that he appears as a playing card. *Our . . . Hyde*] M.

suggests that as the Dutch fleet apparently discards Tromp, so the English should discard Clarendon.
381. bears] punning on Dutch 'boers': farmers, peasants.
382. In early August 1666, an English fleet commanded by Robert Holmes entered the Vlie and destroyed over one hundred and fifty laden Dutch merchantmen, encountering little resistance from Dutch warships.
385–6. Guinea . . . Gold Coast] parts of the west coast of Africa, extending from present-day Sierra Leone to Benin: see above, *The Second Advice*, ll. 259–60 n.
385. paid for Guinea] De Ruyter had harried English ships off Guinea from the autumn of 1664 until the following summer.
387–90. ere . . . flame] see above, *The Second Advice*, ll. 253–8, 271–94 and n.
387. stoves] From the Dutch for foot-stoves, associated with Dutch habits: *stoven*.
395. wood] a) reckless (*OED* a. 2) b) ferocious (*OED* a. 3) c) insane (*OED* a. 1), and hence the need for him to be beaten (a supposed cure for the insane in the period), as recommended in l. 396.
396. stockfish] dried cod, or similar fish, which had to be beaten before cooking (*OED*), and derived from the Dutch *stokvisch*.

I see them both prepared again to try:
They first shoot through each other with the eye;
Then – but that ruling Providence that must
0 With human projects play as winds with dust,
Raises a storm (so constables a fray
Knock down) and sends them both well cuffed away.
Plant now Virginian firs in English oak,
Build your ship-ribs proof to the cannon's stroke,
5 To get a fleet to sea, exhaust the land,
Let longing princes pine for the command:
Strong marchpanes! Wafers light! So thin a puff
Of angry air can ruin all that huff!
So champions having shared the lists and sun,
0 The judge throws down his warder and they've done.
For shame come home, George: 'tis, for thee, too much
To fight at once with Heaven and the Dutch.
    'Woe's me, what see I next? Alas the fate
I see of England, and its utmost date.
5 Those flames of theirs, at which we fondly smile,
Kindled, like torches, our sepulchral pile.
War, fire, and plague against us all conspire:
We the war, God the plague, who raised the fire?
See how men all, like ghosts, while London burns,
0 Wander and each over his ashes mourns!
Dear George, sad fate, vain mind that me didst please
To meet thine with far other flames than these!

'Curst be the man that first begot this war,
In an ill house, under a blazing star.
425 For others' sport, two nations fight a prize:
Between them both religion wounded dies.
So of first Troy, the angry gods unpaid,
Razed the foundations which themselves had laid.
    'Welcome, though late, dear George: here hadst thou been,
430 We'd 'scaped (let Rupert bring the navy in!)
Thou still must help them out when in the mire:
Gen'ral at land, at sea, at plague, at fire.
Now thou art gone, see, Beaufort dares approach:
And our whole fleet, angling, has catched a roach.'
435   Gibson, farewell, till next we put to sea:
Faith thou hast drawn her in effigy!

To the King

Great Prince, and so much greater as more wise,
Sweet as our life, and dearer than our eyes:
What servants will conceal, and couns'llors spare
440 To tell, the painter and the poet dare;
And the assistance of an heav'nly muse
And pencil represents the crimes abstruse.
Here needs no sword, no fleet, no foreign foe;
Only let vice be damned, and justice flow.

---

398. i.e. they view each other through telescopes; the conceit acknowledges the similar shape of the telescope and the gun, both being tubes.
399–402. On 28 August, Monck and Rupert set out again in search of the Dutch. The English fleet, in pursuit of De Ruyter, ran aground on the Galloper shoal. Monck was then recalled to London to help deal with the catastrophe of the Fire of London.
401. fray] disturbance, brawl (*OED* n.¹).
403. i.e. to make masts from the fir trees, while the hulls are made from oak.
404. proof] resistant (*OED* a. 1).
405. exhaust the land] i.e. of trees and men.
407. marchpanes] marzipan (*OED*), made into ornamental structures.
408. huff] bluster, arrogance (*OED* n. 3).
409. lists] space enclosed for jousting (*OED* n.³ II 9).
410. warder] staff or baton carried as symbol of office (*OED* n²).
414. utmost date] end ('utmost': *OED* a. 6).
415. fondly] foolishly (*OED* adv. 1).
416. sepulchral pile] an image of burning London as a funeral pyre (with 'pile' perhaps suggesting 'pyre' as well as a mass of building (*OED* n.³ 4): *OED* records the first use of 'pyre' in 1658 (Sir Thomas Browne, *Hydriotaphia*)).
417. fire . . . plague] the Great Fire of London ended the plague visitation.
418. who raised the fire] the question of who raised the Fire was an important political question; the cause was assumed by

many to be the consequence of a Popish plot (see Smith and Bell, *TLS*, 1504 (26 January 2001), 14–15).
420. ashes] i.e. the ashes of their houses.
422. far other flames] Cp. *The Garden*, ll. 45–6: 'Yet it creates, transcending these,/Far other worlds, and other seas'; *Upon the Hill and Grove at Bilbrough*, ll. 65–6: 'Much other groves', say they, 'than these/And other hills him once did please.' *flames*] i.e. the flames of love.
423. man] i.e. Clarendon.
424. ill . . . star] Pepys records the sighting of a comet on 6 April 1665; see also Waller, *Instructions to a Painter*, l. 7, Dryden, *Annus Mirabilis*, ll. 64–72; cp. Bussenello, *A Prospective*, trans. Higgons (1658), sig. C 7ʳ. *house*] astrological house.
426. religion . . . dies] i.e. the Protestant cause, embraced by both Holland and England.
427–8. Apollo and Poseidon built the walls of Troy for Laomedon, who cheated them of their pay: their act of vengeance was the fall of Troy: see Homer, *Iliad*, 21, ll. 434–67.
427. Troy] London was regarded as the second Troy.
429–32. After his return to London, Albemarle was instrumental in directing fire-fighters, and then in organizing the relief of the devastated capital.
433. Beaufort dares approach] In early September, Beaufort's fleet was reported to be divided: part of it off La Rochelle, the rest off the coast of Ireland (Coventry to Ormond, 22 September 1666, Bod. MS Carte 47, fol. 464ᵛ).
442. abtruse] hidden, concealed (*OED* a. 1).

445 Shake but like Jove thy locks divine, and frown;
Thy sceptre will suffice to guard thy crown.
Hark to Cassandra's song, ere Fate destroy,
By thy own navy's wooden horse, thy Troy.
Us our Apollo, from the tumult's wave,
450 And gentle gales, though but in oars, will save.

So Philomel her sad embroid'ry strung,
And vocal silks tuned with her needle's tongue.
(The picture dumb, in colours loud, revealed
The tragedies of court, so long concealed.)
455 But, when restored to voice, increased with wings,
To woods and groves, what once she painted, sings.

---

447. *Cassandra*] daughter of Priam and Hecuba; beloved of Apollo and gifted by him with prophecy; in Virgil's account (*Aeneid*, II, l. 246; III, ll. 183–7), she prophesied the destruction of Troy, but no one believed her.

449. *Apollo*] the patron deity of Troy. Who is Apollo: Albemarle, Charles or God? Charles is likened to Jove at l. 445, so the likelihood is that the poet means Albemarle.

450. *oars*] rowing boat (*OED* n. 3 a); if by Apollo is meant Albemarle, the image of the chief naval commander rushing to save the burning London or the nation in a rowing boat (the syntax allows either Apollo or 'Us', the English people, to be in the rowing boat) is decidedly mock-heroic.

451–6. *Philomel . . . sings*] having raped Philomela, sister of his wife Procne, Tereus cut out her tongue to stifle her complaints. Imprisoned by Tereus, Philomela wove her story into a tapestry, which she was able to convey to her sister, who rescued her and helped her take revenge. Pursued by Tereus, Philomela was transformed into a nightingale: see Ovid, *Metamorphoses*, VI, ll. 451–674. See also above, *Upon Appleton House*, ll. 513–14.

456. *To . . . groves*] Cp. Ovid, *Metamorphoses*, VI, l. 668: 'quarum petit altera silvas' (one flies to the woods).

62
Clarendon's Housewarming

Date. After 25 June, before 25 July 1667. The last line of the poem refers to the calling of Parliament on 25 July (St James' Fair) as a forthcoming event: it had been officially summoned on 25 June.

Publication. The poem circulated widely in manuscript, often appearing with the Advice-to-a-Painter poems: fifteen manuscript copies are known to survive:

Bod. 1 Bod., MS Eng. poet d. 49, pp. 187–92
Bod. 13 Bod., MS Douce 357, fols. 155ᵛ–7
BL 20 BL, Add. MS 23722, fols. 60–2
BL 14 BL, Harley 7315, fols. 23ᵛ–7
P 4 Princeton, Robert H. Taylor Collection, MS 1, pp. 33–7
Bod. 18 Bod., MS Don. e. 23, fols. 27–9
Bod. 21 Bod., MS Gough London 14, fols. 64–6ᵛ
LAC 2 Clark Library, Los Angeles, M3915M3 S445 [16—] Bound, fols. 22–4
Es. Essex RO, D/DW Z3 (iii), 48–52
H 2 Harvard, MS Eng. 624, pp. [53–9]
V Vienna, Österreichische Nationalbibliothek, Cod. 14090, fols. 7–9ᵛ
SA Society of Antiquaries, MS 330, fols. 29–30ᵛ
VA 2 Victoria and Albert Museum, Dyce Collection, Cat. No. 43 (Pressmark D.25.F.37), pp. 1–6
Y 5 Yale, MS Vault, Section 15, Drawer 3, pp. 46–50
Y 6 Yale, Osborn Collection, b 136, pp. 43–7

It was also printed in 1667 in the Advice to a Painter poems collection entitled *Directions to a Painter*, which appeared under the name of Sir John Denham, and again in the *State Poems* of 1697.

Text. 1667³ has been used as a copy text, a decision originally made by Margoliouth and followed by Legouis. *Bod. 21* is a corrected copy of 1667³: most of its emendations have been adopted here, as have some in *Bod. 1*. Variants between MSS are numerous but mostly minor.

Attribution. There was no direct attribution to M. until Cooke, although the poem appears in *Bod. 1*. Like the Advice-to-a-Painter poems with which it is connected, the poem belongs with the circles of opposition authorship in which M. participated (see above, 322–3). Although the metrical awkwardness of some parts of the poem make it hard to believe that M. was the author (see Burrows, *MLR*, 100 (2005), 281–97), and although the use of Marvellian topoi could be seen as another poet's reworking of M., a series of phrases and individual words (see below, ll. 7–8, 17–20, 43–4, 56, 87–8, 94–6) suggest finally that M. was the author at least in part. Empson, in Brett, ed. (1979), 53–5, argues that the poem was the joint production of several people, all of them probably MPs. He imagines M. as a ringleader, and proposes that the verses that do scan (ll. 41–52, 93–100) are M.'s. The first two stanzas are also given to M., who is imagined beginning a round of composition for four or five other participants. The first line of the poem does not scan. It is highly prosaic, and was perhaps given to the poet as a starting point.

Context. When he returned from exile in 1660 to become Charles II's chief minister, Edward Hyde, Earl of Clarendon, lived in rented accommodation. After much debate, and with the encouragement of the King, who made a grant of open land, a residence was planned and building was begun in 1664. Clarendon House was completed in late 1666 or early 1667. Many reported its grandeur and its architectural success: it was the first great classical house in England, and was to be much imitated in the following decades. The interior was notable for its large and distinguished picture collection and its library. It stood on the north side of present-day Piccadilly, from between Tyburn Ditch and Sackville Street, straddling Albemarle Street. It looked down upon and dwarfed St James' Palace, a significant symbol of Clarendon's power. Building costs exceeded estimated expenditure by one third, to Clarendon's great embarrassment and financial ruin. Burnet reported that the Earl had naively entrusted the management of the building to others (*History of His Own Time*, I. 248). In the context of war, plague and the Great Fire, Clarendon found himself deeply unpopular, his house the object of violent popular demonstrations: 'at my Lord Chancellor's, they have cut down the trees before his house, and broke his windows; and a gibbet either set up before or painted upon his gate, and these three words write: "Three sights to be seen: Dunkirke, Tangier, and a barren Queene"' (Pepys, *Diary*, 14 June 1667 (8.269)). After his fall from power, Clarendon fled the country and his house, which was then leased to James Butler, Duke of Ormond. Christopher Monck, second Duke of Albemarle, acquired the property in 1675 for a little above half its original cost; Sir Thomas Bond purchased the house and demolished it to build tenements (forming Old Bond Street, Albemarle Street and Dover Street) in 1683. The fullest account of the house is in Wheatley (1891), 408–11.

Sources, Genre and Style. The poem is a parody of a country house poem (see Fowler (1994), 310–13), and the genre of poems celebrating civic buildings. 'To describe the metre of *Clarendon's Housewarming* as anapaestic may create a false impression of regularity', wrote Legouis ((1965), 187). In fact, only twelve lines are properly anapaestic, these being arranged as one iamb followed by three anapaests. None the less, anapaestic feet recur throughout the poem, and create its dominant rhythm, although there are extravagant, indeed, completely unmetrical, departures from it. In a true 'droll', M. (and probably others) use accentual verse, a form associated with popular or archaic poetry, one that went against the preference for heroic couplets. It may be that a 'popular' verse form was used in order to evoke the popular discontent that Clarendon was suffering. At the same time, the form would have facilitated easy and rapid composition. There are frequent feminine rhymes (see below, ll. 53–61). While noting M.'s powers of analysis, isolation and judgement in his satirical couplets, Legouis (1965), 189, defends the prosody of this poem for its robust heartiness, and its fluid capacity to carry insults and obscenities.

Clarendon's Housewarming

When Clarendon had discerned beforehand,
  (As the cause can eas'ly foretell the effect)
At once three deluges threatening our land;
  'Twas the season he thought to turn architect.

5 Us Mars, and Apollo, and Vulcan consume;
  While he, the betrayer of England and Flander,
Like the kingfisher chooseth to build in the brume,
  And nestle in flames like the salamander.

But observing that mortals run often behind,
10 (So unreasonable are the rates that they buy at)
His omnipotence therefore much rather designed
  How he might create a house with a fiat.

Title. 'Housewarming' suggests the context of the Great Fire; literally 'the action of celebrating the entrance into the occupation of a new house or home with a feast or Entertainment' (*OED* 2).
1. discerned] recognized (*OED* v. 4).
2. foretell] predict, prophesy (OED v. 1).
3. three deluges] war (the Second Dutch War), plague (the Great Plague of 1665), and fire (the Great Fire of London, 1666), sent respectively by Mars, god of war, Apollo, god of healing and disease, and Vulcan, god of fire (see below, l. 5).
4. architect] master-builder (*OED* n. 1); see above, *Headnote, Context.* Cp. *A Dialogue between the Soul and Body*, ll. 43–4: 'So architects do square and hew/Green trees that in the forest grew.'
6. betrayer . . . Flander] Clarendon was regarded as responsible for a peace with Catholic France, that would have left the low countries vulnerable to the ambitions of Louis XIV (See Pincus, ch. 16).
7. kingfisher . . . brume] kingfishers (halcyons) were believed to build their nests in winter, when the water was calm: see Browne, *Pseudodoxia Epidemica*, III.x, ed. Robin Robbins,

2 vols (Oxford, 1981), I.197: 'these birds . . . bringing forth their young . . . which happeneth about the brumall Solstice, it hath beene observed even unto a proverbe, that the Sea is calme, and the winds do cease.' Cp. *RT*, 229: 'if this course were once effectually taken, the whole year would consist of Halcyon Holy-dayes, and the whole world free from Storms and Tempests would be lull'd and dandled into a Brumall Quiet.' Cp. also *The Character of Holland*, ll. 128–30: 'In a calm winter . . . / . . . /Till the dear halcyon hath out its nest.' Other sources claimed that the halcyon (Browne thought that English kingfishers were not true halcyons) had the power to calm the water: see *The Gallery*, l. 40 n.; *Upon Appleton House*, ll. 669–72 n. *brume*] winter (from the Latin *bruma*, 'winter' [literally, 'the shortest day']).
8. salamander] lizard-like animal supposed to live in fire: see Sir Thomas Browne, *Pseudodoxia Epidemica* (1646), III.xiv.
9. mortals . . . behind] cp. *The First Anniversary*, ll. 125–6: 'Till then my muse shall hollow far behind/Angelic Cromwell.'
10. unreasonable] unfair, inequitable (*OED* a. 2 b).
12. fiat] Latin: 'let it be done'; a command, parodying God's command of creation in Gen. 1:3: 'Let there be light' (*Fiat lux*).

He had read of Rhodopis, a lady of Thrace,
   Who was digged up so often ere she did marry;
And wished that his daughter had had as much grace
   To erect him a pyramid out of her quarry.

But then recollecting how harper Amphion
   Made Thebes dance aloft while he fiddled and sung,
He thought (as an instrument he was most free on)
   To build with the Jew's-trump of his own tongue.

Yet a precedent fitter in Virgil he found,
   Of African Poultney and Tyrian Dide;
That he begged for a palace so much of his ground
   As might carry the measure and name of an Hyde.

Thus daily his gouty inventions he pained,
   And all for to save the expenses of brickbat;
That engine so fatal, which Denham had brained,
   And too much resembled his wife's chocolate.

But while these devices he all doth compare,
   None solid enough seemed for his thong-caster;

He himself would not dwell in a castle of air,
   Though he had built full many a one for his master.

Already he had got all our money and cattle,
   To buy us for slaves, and purchase our lands;
35   What Joseph by famine, he wrought by sea battle;
   Nay, scarce the priests' portion could scape from his hands.

And henceforth like Pharaoh, that Israel pressed
   To make mortar and brick, yet allowed them no straw,
He cared not though Egypt's ten plagues us distressed,
40   So he could to build but make that policy law.

The Scotch forts and Dunkirk, but that they were sold,
   He would have demolished to raise up his walls;
Nay e'en from Tangier have sent back for the mould,
   But that he had nearer the stones of St Paul's.

45   His wood would come in at the easier rate,
   So long as the yards had a deal or a spar:
His friends in the navy would not be ingrate,
   To grudge him some timber who framed them the war.

---

13. *Rhodopis*] 'Rosy-cheeked.' A Thracian courtesan brought to Egypt by Xanthes of Samos. She was supposed to have built the pyramid for King Mycerinus (the smallest of the great pyramids) out of her earnings: see Herodotus, *The History*, II.134–5, who was sure that the story was untrue; Diodorus Siculus, *The Library of History*, I.lxiv.14, who claimed that the governors of the Egyptian provinces were her lovers, and who built the pyramid of Inaros for her; Strabo, *Geography*, XVII.i.33, claimed that Rhodopis was a courtesan who actually married an Egyptian king, and had a pyramid built in her honour; see also Pliny, *Natural History*, XXXVI.lxxxii.

14. *digged up*] had sexual intercourse: Williams (1994), I.386–7.

15. *his daughter*] Anne Hyde, Duchess of York (1637–71); see above, 332–3, and below, 368–9.

16. *pyramid*] see above, l. 13 n. *quarry*] a) stone quarry b) victim of a hunt (*OED* n.[1] 3 c), i.e. the Duke of York, the future James II, married to Anne Hyde in 1660 (and hence a source of wealth) c) innuendo for vagina, but not in Williams.

17–19. Cp. Waller, 'Upon his Majesty's Repairing of Paul's', ll. 11–15: 'He, like Amphion, makes those quarries leap/Into fair figures from a confused heap;/For in his art of regiment is found/A power like that of harmony in sound'; *The First Anniversary*, ll. 49–74.

20. *Jew's-trump*] Jew's-harp (*OED*).

21–2. Virgil, *Aeneid*, I, ll. 335–69, relates the story of the founding of Carthage: Dido of Tyre, fleeing her brother, King Pygmalion, who had killed her husband Sychaeus, negotiated from the Lybians such land as would fit inside the compass of a bull's hide. She cunningly cut the hide into strips thus greatly increasing the area it covered.

22. *African Poultney*] Sir William Poultney (1624–91), one of the original proprietors of the land granted to Clarendon on 13 June 1664. Here, he is figured as the Libyan king, Iarbus (see above, ll. 21–2 n.; Virgil, *Aeneid*, IV, ll. 36, 196).

24. *Hyde*] punning on the bull's hide (see above, ll. 21–2 n.), and the Old English name for a measure of land that would support one family and its dependents (*OED* n.[2] 1).

25. *pained*] suffered; endured (*OED* v. II 3).

26. *brickbat*] pieces of brick (*OED*).

27. *engine ... brained*] Sir John Denham, the poet, became mad for a time in 1666. The poem construes this as the

consequence of a falling brick (Denham had been made Surveyor-General of the Works).

28. *wife's chocolate*] see below, *Last Instructions*, ll. 65–8.

30. *thong*] strip of hide (*OED* n. 1; see above, ll. 21–4). *caster*] a) thrower (*OED* v. I 1) b) knotter (*OED* v. XII 58).

32. *master*] Charles II.

35–6. *What ... hands*] In Genesis 47:13–26, Joseph bought all the land of Egypt for Pharaoh, except the land of the priests, with the corn he had stored during the seven years of good harvests. Clarendon has acquired all the property of the English through the exactions neessary to fight the war against the Dutch.

37–8. *Pharaoh ... straw*] See Exodus 5:6–19.

39. *Egypt's ten plagues*] sent by God because Pharaoh would not release the Israelites: see Exodus 8–12.

40. *he ... law*] i.e. he was prepared to make his rapacious policies law in order to find the means to build his house.

41–8. *Scotch ... war*] Fowler (1994), 312, writes: 'cheap materials parody the spontaneously available natural resources of a serious estate poem'.

41–3. *Scotch ... mould*] Clarendon House was disparagingly referred to as 'Dunkirk House', 'Tangier Hall' and 'Holland House' (Wheatley (1891), 408).

41. *Scotch forts*] Cromwell built four forts in Scotland, at Ayr, Leith, Perth and Inverness. The materials and grounds were given to Scottish nobility or municipalities who put them to a variety of purposes, including commerce. *Dunkirk*] sold to France in 1662 for 150,000 pistoles.

43. *Tangier*] part of Katherine of Braganza's dowry. *mould*] mole (*OED* n.[3] 2), so spelt in *Bod. 13, V*; massive stone breakwater, contructed by the English soon after the acquisition of Tangier.

44. *stones of St Paul's*] the old St Paul's Cathedral was destroyed in the Great Fire, by which time Clarendon House was nearly complete. Clarendon purchased the stone intended to repair the old cathedral to complete his building.

45. *easier rate*] cheaper.

46. *yards*] wooden spars used to extend sails from masts (*OED* n.[2] 5). *deal*] slice, plank or board of fir or pine wood (*OED* n.[3] 1). *spar*] general term for masts, yards, booms (*OED* n.[1] 4).

47. *ingrate*] ungrateful (*OED* a. 3).

48. *framed*] contrived (*OED* v. 8), punning on 'frame' (*OED* v. 4), to prepare timber for use in a building.

To proceed in the model he called in his Allens,
50   The two Allens when jovial, who ply him with gallons,
The two Allens who served his blind justice for balance,
     The two Allens who served his injustice for talons.

They approve it thus far, and said it was fine;
     Yet his lordship to finish it would be unable;
55   Unless all abroad he divulged the design,
     For his house then would grow like a vegetable.

His rent would no more in arrear run to Worcester;
     He should dwell more noble, and cheaper too at home;
While into a fabric the presents would muster;
60   As by hook and by crook the world clustered of atom.

He liked the advice, and then soon it assayed;
     And presents crowd headlong to give good example:

So the bribes overlaid her that Rome once betrayed:
     The tribes ne'er contributed so to the temple.

65   Straight judges, priests, bishops, true sons of the Seal,
     Sumners, governors, farmers, bankers, patentees,
Bring in the whole milk of a year at a meal,
     As all Cheddar dairies club to the incorporate cheese.

Bulteel's, Beaken's, Morley's, Wren's fingers with telling
70   Were shrivelled, and Clutterbuck's, Eager's, and Kipp's;
Since the Act of Oblivion was never such selling,
     As at this benevolence out of the snips.

'Twas then that the chimney contractors he smoked,
     Nor would take his beloved canary in kind:
75   But he swore that the patent should ne'er be revoked;
     No, would the whole parliament kiss him behind.

---

49. model] plan, design (*OED* n. II 7).
49–52. Allens . . . talons] Sir Allen Appsley and Sir Allen Broderick (see below, *The Last Instruction to a Painter*, l. 212 n.) Both were reportedly fond of each other's company and of drink, and both had been rewarded for their loyalty.
51. balance] a) justice (*OED* n. II 8) b) money (i.e. the sum left when debit is subtracted from credit; *OED* n. VI 19). OED records the first instance of the term 'balance of trade' in 1668, the year following the poem's composition.
52. talons] 'talons' as grasping hands (*OED* n. 2 c) is used for 'talents', i.e. wealth (*OED* n. I 1 d).
55–6. The lines seem to refer to Clarendon's advertising of his vast works, so as to appear (he hoped) as a public benefactor, through providing employment. The satire suggests (fictiously) that the advertisement will draw in even more funds in the form of presents (i.e. bribes; see below, ll. 59, 63) so that the house would grow hugely, like a vegetable (cp. *To His Coy Mistress*, ll. 11–12: 'My vegetable love should grow/Vaster than empires.').
57. rent . . . Worcester] Clarendon had rented Worcester House in the Strand from the Marquis of Worcester for £500 per annum.
59. fabric] building (*OED* n. I 1). *muster*] assemble (*OED* v.¹ 2).
60. hook . . . atom] ancient, Epicurean science thought that atoms stuck together by means of hooks: see, e.g., Lucretius, *De Rerum Natura*, II, l. 394: 'aut magis hamatis inter se perque plaicatis' (or because they are more hooked and entangled more closely).
61. assayed] tried out, tested (*OED* v. I 1).
63. The daughter of Spurius Tarpeius, commander of a Roman citadel during the early wars, offered to betray it to the Sabines in exchange for what the soldiers wore on their left arms. In one of three versions given in the source, it is explained that she meant their gold bracelets, but they crushed her to death under their shields: see Livy, *Ab Urbe Condita*, I.xi.5–9.
64. tribes . . . temple] the tribes of Israel contributed to the building of the Temple of Solomon: see Zech. 8:9: 'Let your hands be strong, ye that hear in these days these words by the mouth of the prophets, which were in the day that the foundation of the house of the Lord of hosts was laid, that the temple might be built.'
65–8. Fowler (1994), 313, writes: 'the bribes parody the presents brought by tenants in [Jonson's] "To Penshurst"'.
65. Straight] immediately. *bishops . . . Seal*] Clarendon was Lord Keeper of the Great Seal; he had played a leading role in the re-establishment of episcopacy.

66. Sumners] summoning officers in ecclesiastical courts (*OED*). *governors*] local officials (*OED* 3). *farmers*] tax-farmers: responsible, by royal decree, for gathering of taxes for the crown, for which duty they were paid a considerable sum. *patentees*] those to whom royal letters patent had been granted, giving them sole profit-making rights in specific areas of commerce.
67. Bring . . . meal] i.e. produce at one time the sum that Clarendon would normally have accrued in the space of a year.
68. Cheddar . . . cheese] milk from a number of dairies was pooled to make Cheddar cheese (Lord). *incorporate*] combined in one mass (*OED* pa. ppl. I 1).
69–70. Bulteel's . . . Kipp's] all servants of Clarendon: John Bulteel, d. 1669, MP for Lostwithiel, secretary to Clarendon; Beaken – unidentified; George Morley, Bishop of Winchester, friend and supporter of Clarendon; Matthew Wren, another secretary to Clarendon; Clutterbuck, authorized to pay Clarendon's debts; Agar, mentioned in connection with Kipps and Wren; Kipps was Clarendon's seal-bearer.
69. See collation: an instance of the transience of topical satire, several transcribers clearly did not know who was being attacked.
71. Act of Oblivion] The Act of Indemnity and Oblivion of 1661, which allowed those who had gained property (mostly belonging to royalists) under the Commonwealth to keep it. Legouis rightly detects the sense of bribery: just as Clarendon had received money from perquisites, so those who had received property during the Commonwealth bribed their way to retaining it. But there is also the sense of 'selling' as enforced (see below, l. 72 n., b)); Clarendon, so the poem supposes, compels 'benevolences' just as the Act of Indemnity confirmed unwilling partings with property.
72. benevolence] a) voluntary contribution (*OED* 3) b) forced loan (*OED* 4). *snips*] casual emoluments of an office, apart from salary (not in *OED*).
73. chimney contractors] collectors of the much resented Chimney Money or Hearth Tax. *smoked*] exposed to smoke, so as to make uncomfortable (*OED* v. II 5 b).
74. i.e. he insisted on receiving money rather than wine from the investors in the Canary patent.
75. patent . . . revoked] in October 1666, a Parliamentary Committee had declared the charter for trade with the Canaries an illegal monopoly.
76. parliament . . . behind] during the scatological festivities celebrating the abolition of the Rump Parliament in 1660, apprentices were reported to have cried 'Kiss my Parliament' (Jenner, *Past and Present*, forthcoming). *kiss him behind*] in the sense of 'I'll not give up my patent, even if the whole of Parliament queues up to kiss my arse.'

Like Jove under Etna o'erwhelming the giant,
  For foundation he Bristol sunk in the earth's bowel;
And St John must now for the leads be compliant,
  Or his right hand shall be cut off with the trowel.

For surveying the building, Pratt did the feat;
  But for the expense he relied upon Wolstenholme,
Who sat heretofore at the king's receipt;
  But received now and paid the Chancellor's custom.

By subsidies thus both cleric and laic,
  And with matter profane, cemented with holy,
He finished at last his palace mosaic,
  By a model more excellent than Leslie's folly.

And upon the terrace, to consummate all,
  A lantern like Fawkes' surveys the burnt town,
And shows on the top by the regal gilt ball,
  Where you are to expect the sceptre and crown.

Fond city, its rubbish and ruins that builds,
  Like vain chemists, a flower from its ashes returning,

95 Your metropolis-house is in St James's fields,
  And till there you remove, you shall never leave burning.

This temple of war and of peace is the shrine;
  Where this idol of state sits adorned and accursed:
And to handsel his altar and nostrils divine,
100 Great Buckingham's sacrifice must be the first.

Now some (as all buildings must censure abide)
  Throw dust in its front, and blame situation:
And others as much reprehend his backside,
  As too narrow by far for his expatiation;

105 But do not consider how in process of times,
  That for namesake he may with Hyde Park it enlarge,
And with that convenience he soon for his crimes,
  At Tyburn may land, and spare the Tower barge.

Or rather how wisely his stall was built near,
110 Lest with driving too far his tallow impair;
When like the good ox, for public good cheer,
  He comes to be roasted next St James' fair.

---

77. Jove . . . giant] In ancient mythology, Jove or Jupiter fought Vulcan beneath the volcano of Mount Etna, and imprisoned him there.

78. foundation . . . bowel] George Digby, second Earl of Bristol, had unsuccessfully attempted to impeach Clarendon in 1663, with the result that he had been forced into hiding for two years. He was to begin impeachment proceedings again on 29 July 1667. See also *The Last Instructions to a Painter*, l. 933.

79. St John] Charles Paulet, Lord St John of Basing, member of a group contracted for customs farming. *leads*] to cover the roof of the house. In respect of St John and lead, see M.'s letter to Sir Henry Thompson, 1 December 1674. *compliant*] ready to yield to the desires of others (*OED* a. A 1).

80. trowel] as used by builders.

81. Pratt] Sir Roger Pratt (1620–84), architect, who underestimated the cost of the building by one third.

82. Wolstenholme] Sir John Wolstenholme, another customs farmer.

83–4. Who . . . custom] i.e. Wolstenholme once collected taxes on the King's behalf; now they are for Clarendon alone.

85. laic] pertaining to the laity (OED a. A).

87. mosaic] a) the house is like a Roman mosaic because it has been financed by a great many different contributions b) very grand (i.e. of Moses, lawgiver to the Israelites). Cp. *Musick's Empire*, l. 17; *Upon Appleton House*, l. 382.

88. model] see above, l. 49 n. *Leslie's folly*] Dr John Leslie, Bishop of Orkney, built a palace so strongly fortified, it resisted Cromwell's arms. *folly*] costly, extravagant structure (*OED* n.¹ 5).

89. consummate] complete (*OED* v. 1).

90. lantern . . . Fawkes'] Clarendon House had a domed lantern located centrally on the roof, above the pediment. Guy Fawkes was discovered in the cellars of Parliament about to initiate the Gunpowder Plot with a dark-lantern, capable of concealing its light.

94. vain chemists] Cp. *Upon the Death of Lord Hastings*, l. 49: 'Like some sad chemist.' *chemists*] alchemists.

95. metropolis-house] centre of government ('metropolis': *OED* n. 2 b).

99. handsel] inaugurate with a ceremony (*OED* v. 2).

100. Buckingham's sacrifice] Buckingham is imagined as a sacrificial bull. He supported the Irish Cattle Bill of 1666–67, which Clarendon had opposed, and, for alleged treason, was forced into hiding in February 1667.

102. Throw dust] possibly a reference to the demonstrations against Clarendon (see above, *Headnote, Context*).

103. backside] back premises, including back yard, outhouses and privy (*OED* 2).

104. expatiation] a) walking abroad (*OED* 1) b) expansion (referring to Clarendon's corpulence) (*OED* 2); cp. *The Last Instructions to a Painter*, l. 63.

105. process of times] i.e. in the course of time; the plural is used to rhyme with crimes.

106. Hyde Park] Clarendon House was near the south-east corner of Hyde Park.

108. Tyburn . . . Tower] Tyburn is at the north-east corner of Hyde Park; public executions took place here; hence Clarendon is made out to be a common criminal, not an aristocratic prisoner of state, who would be conveyed in a barge on the Thames to the Tower of London for imprisonment and execution.

109–10. stall . . . tallow] Clarendon is compared to a domestic animal valuable for rendering into fat. Droving could often be a very long process, which would damage the animals' fat-rendering value.

110. tallow] animal fat, eventually used to make suet, candles, soap and leather dressing (*OED* n. 1, 2).

111–12. When . . . fair] Parliament was summoned to meet on St James's Day (25 July 1667). As in l. 76, these lines call to mind the fall of the Rump Parliament, to which Clarendon's imminent demise (so the poem hopes) is likened. The fall of the Rump was celebrated with the roasting of many animals, in a symbolic gesture of punishment: the 'rump' was now cooked.

112. roasted] figuratively speaking, ridiculed (*OED* v. 4 b). *OED* records the first instance of this term in 1726.

63

The Last Instructions to a Painter

Date. Composed between 31 August and 28 November 1667. Clarendon resigned the seals of office on 30 August, and fled to France (not mentioned in M.'s poem) on 29 November. Several MS copies, and a printed edition, carry the date 4 September 1667. On this day, the King granted a long interview to the Duke of Buckingham (Hutton (1989), 252), which marked the beginning of Buckingham's brief period as a chief adviser to Charles. Given M.'s longstanding connections with Buckingham, it may be that the poem was written either for presentation to Buckingham, or for limited circulation among like-minded peers or MPs, as a new, hopefully uncorrupt and efficient, era of government dawned.

Publication. The poem was printed in *The Third Part of the Collection of Poems on Affairs of State* (1689), and in *Poems on Affairs of State* (1697). One copy of a printed edition of the poem (but without a title page) survives in a tract collection originally purchased by Benjamin Franklin and now owned by the Library Company of Philadelphia (*LCP*). Wing dates this edition 1667 from the title, but since the poem was printed with *The Loyal Scot*, the publication date cannot have been before 1672–73, and is on the grounds of appearance most probably a product of the 1690s (von Maltzahn, in Chernaik and Dzelzainis, eds (1999), 61).

The poem circulated in manuscript, but in a more limited way than the previous two Advice-to-a-Painter poems in the series: five MSS of *The Last Instructions* are known to survive (and also one extract):

Bod. 1 Bod. MS Eng. poet d. 49, pp. 193–234
BL 22 British Library, Add. MS 18220, [ll. 29–48]
BL 27 British Library, Add. MS 73540, fols. 1–26ʳ
LAUC University of California, Los Angeles, 170/86, pp. 67–89
N 12 University of Nottingham, Portland MS Pw V 299
Y 13 Yale University, Osborn Collection, PB VII/15

There are, however, forty-six and twenty-eight surviving MSS respectively of the *Second* and *Third Advice to a Painter*. It may be that a very limited circulation, or even none at all, was intended: the *Second and Third Advices* are purely directed against Clarendon, and they may be associated with the opposition factions of Buckingham, Howard, Temple and so on. But *The Last Instructions* mentions Howard and Temple in a mock-heroic way, and in the case of Howard, the picture is certainly offensive (see below, 375, ll. 261–6). The poem was probably part of the campaign led by Buckingham to bring down Clarendon's ministry (see above, 321–5, and below, ll. 983–90 n.). Although the King is addressed directly in the final section, it is doubtful (unlike the previous two painter poems) that Charles was intended as the poem's first reader since he too is shown in a critical light (see below, 391–3).

Although the fragment (ll. 29–48 in *BL 22*) appears to date from 1668 (see below, *Headnote, Text*), and although three of the complete MSS have been dated to the late 1670s or 1680s, no confident claim can be made for a complete version in MS that predates the printed version of 1689.

Text. The fragment in *BL 22* is concluded with a note that it was communicated from Henry North (identified by Kelliher (1978), 99, as the son of Sir Henry, MP for Suffolk) on 10 July 1668, to John Watson, Vicar of Mildenhall, Suffolk, who copied it into a verse commonplace book. The twelve lines in the fragment, the initial satire of St Albans, contain readings that are more directly salacious, and in places readings that are closer to M.'s Commonwealth poems (see below, 449). However, whether this means that there was a complete early version of the poem that was cruder in its wit than the version that survives in most of the MSS and printed editions, or whether this fragment was changed in its copying, remains a matter for conjecture. What is clear is that fragments of the poem circulated at an early stage.

All of the complete MSS are closely related to each other, with the exception of *LAUC*, whose readings are generally inferior. *Y 13* contains a smaller but still significant number of minor variant readings, which, again, are inferior. A pencilled note on the contents page of *BL 27* attributes the copying of the MS to 'Mr Brown' which is evidence of 1680s work (Nicholas von Maltzahn, private communication); all of the poems in the volume are datable to the 1670s, the latest poem being written in 1679 (Warren Chernaik, private communication). *N 12*, a quarto volume comprising only the poem, in a neat hand, and restored from a poor condition, appears to be copy text marked with instructions for, and notes by, the printer (e.g. fol. 1ʳ, '46 pica lines'; 21ʳ, 'allow 4 lines' after 'To the King'). This text is very close to that in *Bod. 1*, but it is not clear that either were used as copy text for either *1689* or *1697*. The readings of *Bod. 1* have usually been preferred by previous editors, but in the vast number of cases the witnesses of the different MSS largely converge. Most of the names of public figures in *1689* are printed only with the first and last letters: e.g. '*A——n*' for 'Alban', '*C——r*' for 'Crowther'.

Authorship. The poem has sufficient internal characteristics of M.'s other poetry for most editors to feel confident of its authorship. *1689* and *1697* attribute the poem to M. For the question of M.'s authorship in the other Advice-to-a-Painter poems of the period, especially the *Second* and *Third Advices*, see above, 321–2.

Context. The poem is remarkable in its detailed and chronologically accurate description of the events of the first three-quarters of 1667. By the mid-1660s, the confidence that accompanied the early days of the Restoration, and in particular the government of Charles II's chancellor, Clarendon, had dissipated. There were accusations that Clarendon had designs on the throne for his descendants, and had married his daughter to the Duke of York, the King's brother and heir, in order to achieve this. A series of incompetences led to naval embarrassment at the hands of the Dutch – quite contrary to the successes of the Commonwealth navy in the previous decade.

However disunited and inferior in naval terms the United Provinces appeared to be, they had able commanders and a system of public credit far superior to England's. The Dutch had the lead in a war of attrition; the English government underestimated them.

The Dutch were determined to secure a treaty that enhanced not merely their honour but also their national profit. For this reason, they were disinclined to compromise in the negotiations at Breda, which began on 4 May 1667. Instead, they decided on a daring military policy that would force major trading concessions from the English. Sixty-four warships left Holland on 27 May. Admiral de Ruyter arrived off Kent on 5 June and on the 10th bombarded Sheerness Fort. On the 12th, his fleet broke the chain across the Medway, burned three of the biggest English ships moored near Chatham, and captured *Royal Charles*, the pride of the Royal Navy. After an attack on the dockyard at Chatham was foiled, the Dutch retreated to the mouth of the Thames, where they set up an indefinite blockade, having broken English naval power. (Fox (1996), 346–8; see also van Waning and van de Moer (1981)).

The management of the Second Dutch War was, like its causes, fraught with court and government factionalism, in particular opposition to Clarendon's ministry (see Davies (1991), 133–58). Those in the party of the Duke of York, the Lord High Admiral, other Cavalier officers and veterans of the First Dutch War, believed that a final victory could be secured over the Dutch; this would mean a rise in employment during the course of the war, and a chance for the making of fortunes and substantial profits for the nation. Careful preparations were marred by disputes over personnel, and the inability of the Navy to man its ships adequately, despite impressment (which in turn generated considerable distrust among the ranks). Supplies were poor, seamen were unpaid and underfed, and the Navy administration was powerless to improve matters. There were mutinies in June 1665; desertion followed. Incompetence in action fuelled factional infighting within the Navy's command structure, and this transferred itself to the court. The considerable victory at the Battle of Lowestoft on 3 June 1665 (the subject of Waller's *Instructions to a Painter*) declined to a series of fiascos involving inaccurate intelligence, strategic errors, bad timing and the inadequate replacement of poor officers. So many senior English commanders were present during the Thames and Medway attack that confusion was abundant. There were Englishmen serving in Dutch ships during the attack on the Medway. M.'s poem follows the energetic response of the government, and the initial investigations into the embarrassments of June 1667, but gives no account of the further recriminations consequent upon the recall of Parliament in October 1667.

Literary attacks on court corruption had intensified. In April, the King watched a performance of and then suppressed *The Change of Crowns*, a play by Edward Howard (brother of the opposition MP Sir Robert (see below, ll. 265–6 n.)) in which preferment by bribery was exposed. In the aftermath of the Dutch raid, popular discontent, and disquiet within the government and the court, were rife, and registered for contemporaries by the circulation of satirical verse:

> Libels are daily sent . . . and brought to yᵉ King by my Lᵈ Anglesey who sayd he found it in yᵉ outward Coͬᵗ at Whitehall another in Harry yᵉ 8ᵗʰˢ Chayre in yᵉ Gallery a 3ʳᵈ at yᵉ K: bedchamber door, strangely insolent. All wᶜʰ I suppose will bee printed since yᵉ Inclosed written long since, & passing from hand to hand in Manuscript now appears publique, wᶜʰ I therefore send yᵗ yʳ Grace may see to wᵗ height of extravagance yᵉ humours of yᵉ people rise: Of this Sr Fr: Hollys yᵉ young angry sea-Captayne is supposed yᵉ Author: I did on Saturday forbear yᵉ folly of yᵉ D. of Buckingham, and am angry I have nothing July, 1667. (Bod., MS Carte 35, fol. 568ʳ)

In addition to the poems that would eventually be published in the poems on affairs of state collections (see *Yale POAS*, 34–158), several other works critical of Clarendon and the court circulated in manuscript. Of these, 'The Century book printed at Oxford' (Bod. MS Eng. hist. *c.* 57), a satirical list of fictitious publications, is particularly close in some thematic and prosopographic respects to *The Last Instructions*. Another poem on Clarendon's fall, albeit a far shorter one of twelve lines, 'The Downefall of the Chancellor' (Vienna, Österreichische Nationalsbibliothek, Cod. 14090, fol. 9ᵛ) repeats some of the charges in M.'s poem.

Zwicker (1993), 98–9, argues that the criticisms of the court offered in the Advice-to-a-Painter and other satirical poems were answered in poetic apologies for the court, such as Dryden's *Annus Mirabilis* (1667). Dryden himself was aligned with some of M.'s targets, notably the Duchess of York, and opposed to the Duke of Buckingham. Dryden sought 'to recall the more hopeful days when royal paternity might tangle together sexual vigor and national abundance', an association played on by M. in his opening salacious picture of Henry Jermyn, Earl of St Albans, a survivor from Charles I's court (ll. 29–48), and more generally in his linking of 'enormity, appetite and luxury' with 'sterility and death' (Zwicker (1993), 109). If the association of

whoring and misgovernment was a common perception in anti-court satire, M.'s poem took the mode to new extremes of pointed refinement, exploiting the symbolic association of distended courtly bodies and a deformed body politic. It should be no surprise that other anti-court satires, including the outrageously frank verse of Rochester, accompanied M.'s poem in some of the printed texts and the MSS, notably *BL 27*. In *1689*, the poem was published alongside 'Rochester's Farewell', a verse satire now thought to be the work of Savile. For a further exploration of this material, see Hammond (in Smith, ed. (1993), 39–62).

M.'s attack on the court also involves a construction of patriotism in terms of elements dissociated from publicly known Stuart preferences. The heroes and virtuous of the poem are those furthest from the court and its ways: Douglas the Scot and probable Catholic (see below, l. 649 n.), who is never seen on English soil; De Ruyter the Dutch admiral. Treasonous republicans like Thomas Dolman are mildly chastised (l. 431), the English pilot who led the Dutch ships into the Medway treated with mock-horror, and given a just motive in being poorly treated by his masters (ll. 583–4).

In the autumn Parliament began to investigate the conduct of the war, and the role of Clarendon. It is notable how poets played a major role in the transactions of the House of Commons:

> After the article of the charge had been debated Mr Marvell pressed that the words that were said to be spoken against the King should not be passed over in silence but be declared; the words as it [is] said are these:
> 'The Chancellor should say that the King was an unactive person and indisposed for government.' Sir Robert Howard pointed at Mr Seymour, who indeed gave the first hint of them. Mr Seymour produced Sir John Denham and Sir John Denham he affirmed that he had it from another who would justify that the Chancellor said so, and made a most excellent and rational speech. (Milward (1938), 116)

Genre and Sources. The poem is far more thematically and aesthetically unified, and ambitious, either than the *Second* or *Third Advices*, but (in part because it is so long), it falls into several discrete sections, each with differing sources. The most discrete is the elegiac section on Douglas (ll. 649–96), which was redeployed with minor alterations in *The Loyal Scot* (see below, 425–6). It may well be that these lines were composed as an entirely separate poem (see below,

l. 649 n.). In general, the purpose of reference to painting in poetry was to enhance the epic scope of the latter. M.'s frustration with the analogy in his poem points up the unsuitability of his subject matter for dignified treatment.

M.'s poem is a response to, and part of, a series of poems on affairs of state initiated by Waller's *Instructions to a Painter* (1665; see above, 321–6).

The sections of the poem concerned with courtly women are parodies of the Advice-to-a-Painter poems that were part of the lyric tradition (see, e.g., Jonson, 'Eupheme', Part III (?after 1633, publ. 1640); Shirley, 'To the Painter preparing to draw M. M.H.' (?1630s; publ. 1646)). For the Italian origins of this genre, see Rowland (1998), 105–8. At the same time, M.'s poem has affinities with some of the verse published on the Great Fire of London (see above, 353, ll. 413–20, and Aubin (1943)). Poetic descriptions of the Fire helped M. describe urban and naval conflagration, and his poem shares the pictorial motif and aesthetic assumptions of some of the Fire poetry: see, e.g. 'The Author to the Graver Upon occasion of a Draught expressing London in Flames', in Simon Ford, *The Conflagration of London* (1667), ll. 349–494.

M.'s reversals of Waller's confidence work on the level of representation as well as theme. Where Waller's painter works with a 'bold pencil' (l. 15), M.'s painter has a 'desperate' (l. 23) and 'lab'ring' (l. 120) pencil, that risks his curse (l. 19), and that is outpaced by the poet's pen (l. 864). The concern with pictorial art extends beyond the Advice-to-a-Painter poems. Gearin-Tosh, *E in C*, 22 (1972), 48–57, argues that explicit and implicit references to court painting point up the failings of the English court. Rubens is named in the poem (l. 119) but his own painting of Lady State is not mentioned: Lady State, and the other genres of state painting, are of course travestied. M. understood that painting, like poetry, relied upon decorum: the mode of representation should fit the moral state of the subject. The poem accordingly invents a fitting series of written images for the court, while calling on the lower forms of painting in ll. 9–12 for help, culminating in the inverse parody of a Lady State picture (ll. 885–908), where Charles is shown attempting to seduce 'England or the peace'. The topos of sea triumph (specifically not a picture of a naval victory, since the Dutch did not have to fight) is reserved for De Ruyter's journey up the Thames (ll. 522–30). But in addition, as the portrayals of the failing or frustrated painter suggest, painting is outdone by a series of verbal devices.

Another important frame of reference is provided by the optical discoveries of the natural philosophers. The poem makes use of the invention of the microscope and the miniscule world that it revealed. In particular, there are specific references to Robert Hooke's work, published in his seminal *Micrographia* (1665) (see below, 367, ll. 16–17). The microscope's extraordinary powers of perception, so the poem argues, reveal truths about courtiers and politicians that are hidden from normal view. Further aspects of natural philosophy in the poem are discussed by Picciotto (forthcoming, ch. 3). In her view, painting is presented as an inferior art to empirical investigation. It may be efficient as a means of delivering appropriate praise or blame, but it cannot objectively and dispassionately describe, as the microscope and the telescope do. There is always the danger that truth will be lost in the painter's attempt to flatter. The painter must therefore aspire to the perceptive powers of the empiricists. By contrast, St Albans and the Duchess of York appear as false empiricists, lost in corrupt pursuits for sensual pleasure and personal advancement, both perversions of disinterested inquiry (see below, ll. 15–68).

Just as the obscene limnings of ll. 9–11 subvert courtly portraiture, so M.'s poem, a sexually grotesque satire circulated in manuscript, subverts the official panegyric of Waller (see above), Dryden's *Annus Mirabilis*, published in print (1667), and other works of courtly panegyric. A further example would be a verse panegyric addressed to the Duchess of York (see below, ll. 49–78) in St John's College, Oxford:

> Mars wee'd assigne your Guard, but that we are
> Assur'd your Duke's a greater God of war.
> The Graces to attend you wee'd call forth,
> But that their All's compris'd in your own worth.
> And Venus with her Cupid too should come,
> But that you have a sweeter Prince at home.
> (Bod., MS Tanner 314, fol. 102, ll. 5–10)

Sexual satire had been used as a way of criticizing the behaviour of courts, monarchs, parliaments, republic, Puritans and Protector throughout the seventeenth century, though with particular vigour from the mid-1640s onwards (see Wiseman, in Holstun (1992), 134–57). Zwicker (in Condren and Cousins, eds (1990)), 86, argues that the particular treatment of sexual corruption in this poem is, along with other poems by M., an acknowledgement of the 'force of sexuality in imaginative exploit, in the argument of heroic venture, in the calculation of human potential, and in the luxuries of retreat'. The reign of Charles II was publicly celebrated at the Restoration as a renewal of fertility; M. responds by attacking the body politic on the level of sexual morality. The language of sexual innuendo is present in the poem to the extent that it has the capacity to render entirely different readings of passages from the ostensible ones (see below, ll. 29–104). Turner (in Chernaik and Dzelzainis, eds (1999), 217–48) locates the forms of sexual representation in the poem in the context of both learned or elite and scurrilous pornography, especially in pictures, from the tradition stemming from Aretino's *Postures*, or in an appropriation of that popular ritual for the punishment of sexual transgressors, the Skimmington ride (Turner (2002), 72–3, 158, 186–7). For Messina (in Friedenreich, ed. (1977), 298–9), the sexual satire is an example of 'low burlesque'. The initial portraits are grotesques, 'gargoyles stuck in the face of the edifice', but the passage dealing with the excise debates is mock-heroic. Thus, even those in Parliament sharing M.'s views are implicated in the 'mindless chaos that England faces'. Appropriately, the description of De Ruyter (ll. 523–34) begins heroically and in a pastoral idyll, but degenerates until the Dutch Admiral succumbs to a sexual appetite not far removed from the English courtiers: another opportunity for a contrast with Douglas.

The one exception to the satirical and parodic modes of the poem is the passage dealing with the heroic death of Archibald Douglas. Hunt (1978), 159–60, suggests that the passage may have pictorial sources in paintings of Ovidian scenes. A more immediate predecessor to M.'s monosexual Douglas (who dies embracing his 'love' the flames) is Waller's description of the death in a sea battle of the Spanish Marquis and his wife:

Spices and gums about them melting fry,
And, phoenix-like, in that rich nest they die;
Alive, in flames of equal love they burned,
And now together are to ashes turned.
('Of a War with Spain, and a Fight at Sea', ll. 83–6;
see also ll. 75–82, 87–100)

Gearin-Tosh, *E in C*, 22 (1972), 52, argues that the passage contains a fusion of Christian and pagan allusions, characteristic of Rubens, and a baroque, fantastic mode in the style of Bernini. The aesthetics of Roman Catholic Europe are suggested. Friedman (in Chernaik and Dzelzainis, eds (1999), 139) argues that the visual point of Douglas's death is the distinction between his 'shape', and the fire enfolding him: 'the identification between what is without and within is complete, because the act of immolation simultaneously registers and enacts his heroism.' In this way, the poem offers a poetic version of martyrological iconography – the truth in painting, in contrast to the allegorical victory painting of Cornelis de Witt, deputy Admiral to the Fleet, presiding over the raid. The English could now plainly not deploy such images.

The Douglas passage contains allusions to Virgil's *Aeneid* (see below, l. 660 n., ll. 693–6 n.). The passage is one of the more obvious examples of the way in which M. was in fact writing his own version of epic language as a form of critique of the jingoistic epic language that was publicly praising the regime (see Smith, *PBA*, 101 (1999), 185–6). Dryden's dense allusions to and echoes of Virgil in *Annus Mirabilis*, his reflections on heroic verse in his letter to Howard prefacing the poem, and the identification in the fire poetry of London as a burning Troy, were among the immediate triggers. After the Medway raid, the Troy of London is threatened by the Greece of Holland and France. The use of epic in the politics of allegiance or opposition was a major feature of literary life during the Civil War, Interregnum and Restoration periods (see Smith (1994), ch. 7, Erskine-Hill (1996), ch. 6, Norbrook (1999), ch. 10). Translations of ancient epics were used to describe public events, while various kinds of mock epic were produced by royalists, originally as a part of cavalier drinking culture, later as a more engaged form of criticism (see Raylor (1994), 113–53). The 1660s saw the publication of Samuel Butler's *Hudibras* (pt. 1, 1663; pt. 2, 1664) and Charles Cotton's translation of Scarron's travesty of the *Aeneid*, *Scarronides* (1664). M. does not take any of these mock epics as his models (although he sometimes uses the false accents, bad rhymes, absurd analogies and clumsy allusion to technique of *Hudibras*) but instead develops his own distinctive epic poetry. For Nevo (1963), 173–8 (175), the poem 'resolves itself not into a consistent caricature of unheroic heroes, but into what is in effect an epic in reverse – an epic of defeat and demoralization, not of triumph and victory. . . . the epic value of the joys of conquest is presented, with a tragic irony, through the eyes of the enemy.' The appearance of the first edition of *Paradise Lost* in the autumn of 1667, with its strong public resonances, which M. was especially well-qualified to notice, provides another important context. Sections of it appear to be echoed in M.'s satire (see below, 369, 371, 393–4).

The Last Instructions is 995 lines long: the length of a longer book in the epic tradition. John Boys's translation of Book VI, *Aeneas His Descent into Hell* (1661) represented Charles II as Aeneas returning from the underworld of the Interregnum, and with prefatory material dedicated to heroes of the Restoration. There are the characteristic disavowals of the epic narrator (ll. 5–8), but these are turned, ironically, to the advantage of the poem's expressive powers. Epic and mock-epic are juxtaposed to suit the mood of national prowess tragically compromised by farcical incompetence (see, e.g. below, ll. 623–48, where the epic simile describing Monck's witnessing of the capture of *Royal Charles* is followed by the comic portrayal of Sir Thomas Daniel). The Duchess of York is presented as a witch, like Alecto (see below, ll. 69–72 n.). Epic narrative enters the poem properly with the description of the monster Excise (ll. 132–46), and is explicitly signalled in the narrator's comments at ll. 146–9. Then follows a mock-heroic representation of a Parliamentary debate as a battle. At l. 337 Buckingham is depicted as a Satan, struck down by a tyrannous Jove. The epic parody is accompanied by a series of echoes of Ovidian verse, in particular the *Metamorphoses*.

The Medway raid was celebrated in Holland by a large and various body of publications, including printed maps and charts, detailed scenic engravings, letters from naval commanders in ships anchored in the Thames and Medway, and verse. M.'s later confession that Dutch satirical iconography of the English rendered a more truthful picture of the English than any native assessment (see *AGP*, 31, 36) presupposes a knowledge of Dutch anti-English literature. It is highly likely that M. saw some of this material, and used it, or at least was helped by its perceptions, to fashion his critique of the government's mismanagement of the war (see below, 381–2).

Structure. The poem is very much a firm response to the first two advice poems: it is 'instructions' rather than 'advice', thereby asserting itself as the equal of Waller's original poem. Several phrases or conceits from the first two advices are developed in the poem.

The poem consists of three central narrative sections: the sitting of Parliament in 1666 (ll. 105–396);

the attempt of the court to secure peace (ll. 397–522); the Dutch invasion of the Thames and the Medway (ll. 523–884). These are preceded by pictures of courtly corruption and debauchery, and succeeded by the depiction of Charles II attempting to force erotic favours of his vision, the naked 'England or the peace', which is followed by the forty-one line address to the king, where the Advice-to-a-Painter motif is not used. These sections are informed by three elements: first, often fragmentary narration and description of the actual world; second, the 'instructions' through which artistic coherence is given, but which, in the debate between poetry and painter (and momentarily between poetry and music), is shown to be impossible; third, a new 'tectonic' structure which abandons the known artistic forms in order to restore faith in an ideal order (Farley-Hills (1974), 77–8, and analysed in detail, 78–96). Throughout the poem, media and different parts of experience are confused, in order to suggest the difficulty of describing the subject.

Miner (*MP*, 63 (1966), 289–90) notes that the longer passages not explicitly concerned with the painting analogy sustain the painting motif by imitating the painting genre of large-scale events, such as sea battles, and satirical engravings. In some cases, these are executed with considerable accuracy. In Patterson's view ((1978), 164), each picture embodies a crisis of representation, where either pictures or words, or both, fail to capture the subject matter (see below, ll. 909–10, 863–5, 633–8). In this context, the appeal to the king (ll. 943–8) is an appeal for the restoration of the *ut pictura poesis* tradition.

Farley-Hills (1974), 78, regards M.'s merely cursory treatment of aesthetic debate in the poem as entirely intended because 'any conventional method will be inappropriate to this chaotic, unconventional situation'. The poem displays considerable flexibility in its use of the rhymed decasyllabic couplet, ranging from the measuring of chaotic subject matter with highly controlled and dignified verse (i.e. the mock-heroic), to grotesque couplets that reflect grotesque subject matter (e.g. ll. 449–56). Equally remarkable is the tight syntax. This is responsible for a degree of obscurity, but it also makes possible the mapping of political events in a remarkably precise way. This feature itself is further evidence that the poem's intended first readers were extremely familiar with the public events of 1666–67.

Modern Criticism. Early comment is extremely rare, although the quotation of ll. 131–46 (the allegory of the monster Excise) as a preface for *The Craftsman's* attack on a proposal for a general excise tax (No. 217; 29 August 1730) is evidence of an acknowledgement of M.'s poetic art as well as his public convictions. Earlier twentieth-century comment is often dismissive (e.g. Bradbrook and Lloyd-Thomas (1940), 23), regarding the poem as lacking in structure (Sutherland, *PQ*, 45 (1966), 46), or fatally compromised by partisanship: cliquish and esoteric exclusiveness win out over political imagination (Piper (1969), 309–10). Farley-Hills (1974), 76, however, goes as far as to suggest that *The Last Instructions* is M.'s finest poetic achievement, that it displays a vitality and 'maturity of outlook' absent from the earlier poetry, and furthermore that it is 'the first of the great Augustan poems' (97–8). Farley-Hills (1974), 97–8, and Korshin (1973), 97, see M.'s satire as corrective or curative rather than damning and abusive.

Chernaik (1983), 83, regards the poem as establishing 'an aesthetic of realism in opposition to the idealising tendencies characteristic of . . . heroic panegyric'. *The Last Instructions* and the other Restoration satires present 'heterogeneous materials . . . yoked by violence together', as opposed to the standards of judgement and aptness recommended by neoclassical critics like Dryden (152). In this way, M. 'seeks to persuade by explicit argument and by recurrent patterns of imagery, Dryden by his controlling myth, embodied in a plot' (200). Against an older view that the poem is 'derisive, tendentious, cynical, and ugly', unlike the graceful lyrics (Lord, *PQ*, 46 (1967), 209), and an insufficiently rich poetry for the purpose of integrating local politics and universal truths (Toliver (1965), 193), Fisher, *ELH*, 38 (1971), 223–38, argues for *The Last Instructions'* 'aesthetic unity, continuity with the lyrics, and experimental virtues, so that it is 'the first public formal satire in English that truly attempts to create poetic experience from the interaction of these . . . sources'. Messina (in Friedenreich, ed. (1977), 297–310) develops this view, arguing that the

poem's sprawl and disjointedness is functional: the many negative pictures of courtly and administrative corruption contrast with the simple, self-denying heroism of Douglas; anarchic, bustling satire, in which artistic control is nearly denied is set against a heroic death that is presented as an act of high art.

Riebling, *EL*, 35 (1995), 137–57, discusses the poem's 'rhetoric of sexual insult', which links 'abuses of sexual power with abuses of political power and a collapse of gender norms with a collapse of political norms'. M., it is argued, presents Clarendon's fall in terms of the infection of an old roué with venereal disease faced with the unpalatability of castration as a cure. England is a virgin facing rape at the hands of the Dutch, inadequately protected by emasculated guardians. The Douglas sacrifice turns a catalogue of shameful, unmanning failure into a moment of honour, presented as an androgynous death. On the level of poetic genre, Douglas restores the pastoral myth to a fallen world, offering 'a moment of clarity in an otherwise discouraging history' (Toliver (1965), 207). For Friedman, (in Chernaik and Dzelzainis, eds (1999), 139), the scene presents a 'kind of integrity of soul [i.e. noble aspects of character] that is sometimes discovered by moments of historical change', like Charles I's execution in *An Horatian Ode* (see also Toliver (1965), 207–8). A similar comparison with Charles is noted by Messina (in Friedenreich, ed. (1977), 301, 309), where Douglas is regarded as a burnt offering. Creaser (in Chernaik and Dzelzainis, eds (1999), 154–6) notes that this moment is accompanied by a displacement of 'pervasive, but unrealized sexuality' by a self-sacrificing consummation. This is also a transfiguration, from virginal locks and soft body to angelic flaming hair and a glowing, statue-like body. But the 'peculiar, Marvellian timbre of the episode comes from interweaving the glory of transfiguration with the poignant but comic displacement of Douglas' unrealized manhood'. Turner (in Chernaik and Dzelzainis, eds (1999), 240–1) also notes the quality of attentive responsiveness paid by the narrator to Douglas, similar to that paid earlier by the Countess of Castlemaine to her footman (see also Smith, *PBA*, 101 (1999), 186).

The Last Instructions to a Painter

London, 4 September 1667

After two sittings, now our Lady State,
To end her picture, does the third time wait.
But ere thou fall'st to work, first painter see
It ben't too slight grown, or too hard for thee.
Canst thou paint without colours? Then 'tis right:
For so we too without a fleet can fight.
Or canst thou daub a signpost, and that ill?
'Twill suit our great debauch and little skill.
Or hast thou marked how antique masters limn
The alley-roof with snuff of candle dim,
Sketching in shady smoke prodigious tools?

    'Twill serve this race of drunkards, pimps, and fools.
But if to match our crimes thy skill presumes,
As the Indians, draw our luxury in plumes.
15   Or if to score out our compendious fame,
With Hooke then, through the microscope, take aim:
Where, like the new Comptroller, all men laugh
To see a tall louse brandish the white staff.
Else shalt thou oft thy guiltless pencil curse,
20   Stamp on thy palette, nor perhaps the worse.
The painter so, long having vexed his cloth –
Of his hound's mouth to feign the raging froth –
His desperate pencil at the work did dart:
His anger reached that rage which passed his art;
25   Chance finished that which Art could but begin,
And he sat smiling how his dog did grin.

Title. Instructions] as in Waller's *Instructions to a Painter*, a parody of 'instruction' as the formal term for a naval order: see *The Intelligencer*, 43 (5 June 1665), 403.

1–2. two sittings . . . third time] portrait painters required their subjects to sit on three occasions: 'The *third sitting* will be only spent in giving the strong *touches* necessary for rounding the *face*, which now will appear better for observation. . . . In this *sitting* therefore observe, what ever may conduce to the *likeness* and *resemblance*, which above all is the principal aime: viz. *skin-molds, smiling*, or *glanceing* of the *eye*', Sir William Sanderson, *Graphice. Or The use of the Pen and Pensil* (1658), 67. The first two 'sittings' are probably the *Second* and *Third Advice to a Painter*. *Lady State*] possibly Britannia is meant (see below, ll. 761–2). Rubens painted the English Lady State as Minerva.

4. It] a) the painting b) the state (if the painting is allegorical: see Gearin-Tosh, *E in C*, 22 (1972), 50–1). *slight*] a) smooth, glossy (*OED* a. A 1) b) of poor texture (*OED* a. A 3) c) unimportant (*OED* a. A 5 b). *hard*] a) i.e. the oil paint has solidified too much for further work b) difficult.

5–8. A parody of the disavowals in heroic poetry: cp. J[ohn] R[avenshaw], Folger MS V.a.148, fol. 35ᵛ: 'Wee nor could manage speare nor Pike advance/But wee can trayle a fancy shall enhance/Thy highborne spirit who art grown to bee/Protector to the muses pedigree.' *colours*] a) paints (*OED* n. II 8) b) rhetorical figures (*OED* n. III 13).

5. Canst . . . colours] i.e. an impossible task; cp. Giovanni Paolo Lomazzo, *A Tracte Containing the Artes of curious Paintinge* (1598), 3.2: 'Of the Necessity of Colouring.'

6. without a fleet] the fleet was laid up, and hence inoperative, in May 1667.

7. signpost] of an inn.

8. debauch] orgy of sensual pleasures (*OED* n. 1).

9–11. antique] a) ancient (*OED* a. A 1) b) grotesque (see 'antic': *OED* a. A 1). Gearin-Tosh, *E in C*, 22 (1972), 48–57 (51) suggests that this refers to *grottesco* art: disproportioned, distorted, deliberately ugly representations of the human form (see Raylor (1994), ch. 6). 'Antique' and 'antic' may have been synonymous terms (Riebling, *SEL*, 35 (1995), 139); for continuity of spelling, see, e.g. Donne, *Elegy IX, The Autumnall* (1631), l. 43: 'Name not these living death-heds unto me/For these not ancient but antique be.'

9. limn] paint (*OED* v. 3).

10. snuff] burnt end of a candle (*OED* n.¹ I 1).

11. tools] penises (*OED* a. 2b). But the 'tools' are also the courtiers who are the instruments of the French ('tool': *OED* n. 3).

14. Indians . . . plumes] see *Upon Appleton House*, l. 580.

15. score out] cancel. *compendious*] a) concise, succinct (*OED* a. 1); hence b) tiny, of no importance.

16–18. With . . . staff] Cp. Simon Ford, *The Conflagration of London* (1667), ll. 395–406: 'Poetry . . . 'Tis the *Minds Microscope*, that helps the Eye/To the *least insect-thought's Anatomy*.'

16. Hooke] Robert Hooke (1635–1703), experimental scientist, Fellow of the Royal Society and author of *Micrographia* (1665). *microscope*] The impact of the microscope on literature is discussed by Picciotto (forthcoming, ch. 3).

17–18. Comptroller . . . staff] In Hooke's *Micrographia* (1665), second inserted sheet, between 210 and 211, one of the detailed engravings of tiny creatures seen under a microscope was a louse, clutching a hair. Cp. also Hooke's prose (*Micrographia*, 211): 'This is a Creature so officious, that 'twill be known to every one at one time or another, so busie, and so impudent, that it will be intryding it self in every ones company, and so proud and aspiring withall, that it fears not to trample on the best, and affects nothing so much as a Crown.' Lord Clifford of Chudleigh, Comptroller of the Household, took office in November 1666. See above, *The Second Advice*, l. 255 n.; see also 'A new letany' (MS Bod. Rawl. poet 172, fol. 80ʳ): 'From empty-headed Phops by Land and by Sea/From rotten Tom Clifford and his brother Bab May.' In March 1662, M. argued with Clifford in the House of Commons. The cause is unknown. M. refused to apologize, and was compelled to do so by the Committee of Privileges.

19. pencil] paintbrush (*OED* n. I 1 a).

21–6. The painter . . . grin] The painter Protogenes, frustrated by his inability to paint the froth at the mouth of his panting dog, threw his sponge at the painting, which accidentally made the picture perfect, 'fortune also met together in the painting thereof': Pliny, *Natural History*, trans. Philemon Holland (1634), vol. 2, XXXV.x.l. 542. Patterson (1978), 160, notes that Pliny's original parable was intended to demonstrate the painter's self-control: M.'s version suggests the opposite. Defending Samuel Parker against M., [Samuel Butler], *The Transposer Rehearsed* (Oxford, 1673; formerly attributed to Richard Leigh), also referred to this episode.

So mayst thou perfect by a lucky blow
What all thy softest touches cannot do.
    Paint then St Albans, full of soup and gold,
30 The new court's pattern, stallion of the old.
Him neither wit nor courage did exalt,
But Fortune chose him for her pleasure salt.
Paint him with drayman's shoulders, butcher's mien,
Membered like mules, with elephantine chine.
35 Well he the title of St Albans bore,
For Bacon never studied nature more.
But age, allaying now that youthful heat,
Fits him in France to play at cards and treat.
Draw no commission lest the court should lie,
40 That, disavowing treaty, asks supply.
He needs no seal but to St James' lease,
Whose breeches were the instrument of peace;

Who, if the French dispute his power, from thence
Can straight produce them a plenipotence.
45 Nor fears he The Most Christian should trepan
Two saints at once, St Germain, St Alban,
But thought the Golden Age was now restored,
When men and women took each other's word.
    Paint then again her Highness to the life;
50 Philosopher beyond Newcastle's wife.
She, nak'd, can Archimedes' self put down,
For an experiment upon the crown.
She perfected that engine, oft assayed,
How after childbirth to renew a maid,
55 And found how royal heirs might be matured
In fewer months than mothers once endured.
Hence Crowther made the rare inventress free
Of's Highness' Royal Society–

---

27. perfect] stressed on first syllable.

29–48. Paint . . . word] The version of these lines in *BL 22*, fol. 23ʳ, is written under the title 'A Libell/Taken out of the Painter, upon H./Jermyn E of Sᵗ Albans.'

29. St Albans] Henry Jermyn, Earl of St Albans (1604?–84), ambassador at the French court for Charles II; sent to France in January 1667 to negotiate a treaty with Louis XIV. As a young man, Jermyn had enjoyed fame for his sexual prowess; later he was suspected of having a long-term affair with Charles I's Queen, Henrietta Maria.

30. stallion] a woman's hired lover (*OED* n. 2 b); Jermyn had the reputation of a rake as a young man.

31. wit] intelligence.

32. salt] lecherous (*OED* a.² b).

33. mien] bearing, carriage or manner (*OED* n.).

34. Membered] a) with limbs b) with a penis. *mules*] mules have impressively large genitals, but are sterile. *chine*] back (*OED* n.² 2). See also *The Loyal Scot*, l. 224.

35–6. Bacon] Francis Bacon (1561–1626), was first Baron Verulam and Viscount St Albans: hence the sarcastic comparison with his namesake. There are also two puns: ('bore' for 'boar', 'Bacon' for 'pig'). Jermyn is even more of a pig than Bacon, and in being so bestial he has studied nature more than his predecessor, the philosopher of nature.

37–8. age . . . treat] in old age, Jermyn liked to gamble at the card table (see, e.g., Pepys, 8.190).

37. allaying] diminishing (*OED* v.¹ 16).

38. treat] a) entertain (*OED* v. 9 b) b) negotiate (*OED* v. 1).

39–40. Draw . . . supply] St Albans acted at first unofficially and informally. M. construes this as an attempt by the court to maximize the funds voted by Parliament. A substantial sum had in fact been voted (see below, ll. 330–3), but the fear of wasted expenditure was a sustained theme in Parliamentary debates.

41. St James' lease] Jermyn acquired a large plot of land in Pall Mall, and planned St James' Square.

42–4. breeches . . . plenipotence] the source of Jermyn's sway in the French court was his relationship with Henrietta Maria (it was rumoured that he had married her). It was through her influence on Louis XIV that negotiations for peace with Holland and Britain were begun.

44. plenipotence] a) full authority b) penis (Williams (1994), II, 1075).

45. The Most Christian] Louis XIV; the traditional style of the French monarchy. *trepan*] cheat (*OED* v.² c).

46. St Germain] the district of Paris where Jermyn resided.

47–8. Golden . . . word] The Golden Age was the first and best age of the world, when mankind lived in prosperity, without fear or laws and with trust (see, e.g. Ovid, *Metamorphoses*, I, ll. 89–112).

49–78. A portrait in opposition to the mythical description of the Duchess of York in Waller, *Instructions to a Painter*, ll. 81–90. The Duchess is mocked in *The Second Advice*, ll. 53–90, defended by Wase, *Divination* (1666), ll. 35–8, and made the subject of a panegyric by Dryden ('Verses to her Highness the Duchess'), which circulated in MS, but was eventually published as a prefatory poem to *Annus Mirabilis* in January 1667.

49. her Highness] Anne Hyde, Duchess of York, privately married to the Duke of York on 3 September 1660. Her status was regarded as quite unsuitable as a match for the heir to the throne.

50. Philosopher . . . wife] Margaret Cavendish, Duchess of Newcastle (1624?–74), philosopher and author.

51. Archimedes] (*c.* 290–280–212/211 BC) philosopher of Syracuse, famous for his discoveries in applied mathematics and mechanics. He discovered the principle of displacement while bathing, and leapt out naked crying 'Eureka!' (I have found it!). *put down*] surpass (*OED* v.¹ V 41 f).

52. experiment . . . crown] i.e. an attempt to secure the succession of the monarchy (for the Clarendon family), since Charles II was without a legitimate child. As Archimedes displaced water when naked, so the Duchess, naked with the Duke, displaces the Stuarts.

53. engine] device (*OED* n. 3). *assayed*] sought after (*OED* v. I 10 b).

54–6. How . . . endured] the Duchess of York gave birth to Charles, Duke of Cambridge, just two months after her marriage.

57. Crowther] Dr Joseph Crowther (d. 1689), chaplain to the Duke of York, married him to Anne Hyde on 3 September, 1660.

57–8. free . . . Royal Society] M. suggests that the marriage is like admitting an eminent scientist to the recently founded Royal Society, of which the Duke of York was a charter member.

Happiest of women, if she were but able
To make her glassen dukes once malleáble!
Paint her with oyster lip, and breath of fame,
Wide mouth, that 'sparagus may well proclaim;
With Chancellor's belly, and so large a rump,
There (not behind the coach) her pages jump.
Express her studying now if China clay
Can, without breaking, venomed juice convey,
Or how a mortal poison she may draw
Out of the cordial meal of the cacao.
Witness, ye stars of night, and thou the pale

70 Moon, that o'ercome with the sick steam didst fail;
Ye neighbouring elms, that your green leaves did shed,
And fawns that from the womb abortive fled;
Not unprovoked, she tries forbidden arts,
But in her soft breast love's hid cancer smarts,
75 While she revolves, at once, Sidney's disgrace
And her self scorned for emulous Denham's face;
And nightly hears the hated guards away
Galloping with the Duke to other prey.
    Paint Castlemaine in colours that will hold
80 (Her, not her picture, for she now grows old):

---

60. To . . . malleáble] M. uses the image of brittle glass to refer to the brief lifespan of her children. *glassen*] like glass, hard, brittle, fragile. *dukes*] referring to the short-lived children of this marriage, Charles, Duke of Cambridge (1663–67), Charles, Duke of Kendal (1666–67); the suppression of the word after its initial letter in *1689* suggests the obscene 'dildoes'; this adds an extra foot to the line, so that to retain the metre 'malleable' would have to be pronounced 'mall'able', which appropriately puns as 'non-functioning' or 'capable of evil'. In this reading, the Duchess is experimenting to produce an unbreakable and indeed more supple dildo (Picciotto, forthcoming, Ch. 3). *malleable*] capable of being beaten into another shape without shattering (*OED* a. 1).
61. oyster lip] a) Lely's portrait of Anne Hyde (now at Hampton Court) shows a wide mouth with compressed lips, possibly suggesting an oyster shell. b) 'whore's vagina': 'oyster' was i) a veneral symbol ii) the vulva iii) a whore (Williams (1994), II. 982–3); 'lip' meant vaginal labia (Williams (1994), II. 819). Pepys, *Diary*, 8.64 (16 February 1667) makes clear the erotic connotations of oysters: 'I went to Mrs Martin's to thank her for her oysters and there yo did hazer tout ce que je would con her, and she grown la plus bold moher of the the orbis – so that I was almost defessus of the pleasure que ego was used para tener with ella.' *breath of fame*] a) rumour (*OED* n.¹ 1) b) infamy (*OED* n¹ 4).
62. Wide . . . proclaim] as a street-vendor of asparagus would call out.
63. With . . . rump] others had a different view of the Duchess: writing of her in 1665, Sir John Reresby recorded that she 'was a very handsome woeman, had a great deale of witt' (*Memoirs*, ed. A. Browning (1936, 1991), 55).
64. jump] a) as in 'jump on to ride' b) copulate with (Williams (1994), II. 752–3).
65–8. The Duchess of York was supposed to have poisoned Margaret, Lady Denham, the Duke of York's mistress, on 6 January 1667 by a poisoned cup of chocolate; a post-mortem proved the charge groundless. Suspicions of poisoning were also raised when Lady Denham fell ill in November 1666 (Pepys, 7.365). The post-mortem also seemed to Pepys (8.8) to cast doubt on the Duke ever having had sex with her.
65–6. As claimed by Julius Caesar Scaliger, *Exotericae Exercitationes* (1557), fol. 136ʳ, and doubted by Browne, *Pseudodoxia Epidemica* (1646), 2.5.7. The Duchess appears here, again, as an experimental scientist.

65. Express] paint (*OED* v. II 5); see below, l. 907.
68. cordial] restorative (*OED* A a. 2). *cacao*] seed of the tropical American tree from which cocoa and chocolate are made; pronounced 'cacaw'.
69–72. Riebling, *SEL*, 35 (1995), 140, suggests that the Duchess is presented as a witch harming the nation with her poisonous brew: the moon (l. 70) representing chastity, the 'green leaves' (l. 71), virginity, and causing abortions among the creatures (l. 72).
70. Cp. Milton, *Paradise Lost*, II, ll. 662–6: 'the Night-hag . . . / . . . comes/ . . . to dance/With Lapland witches, while the labouring moon/Eclipses at their charmes.' *sick steam*] i.e. steam rising from a cauldron. *sick*] corrupt (*OED* A a. III 7 a). *fail*] grow dim (*OED* v. 3 a).
72. fawns . . . fled] i.e. aborted embryos. *fawns*] young animals (*OED* n.¹ 1).
73. forbidden arts] necromancy is hinted at; the Duchess appears now as a witch rather than a 'new philosopher.' Cp. Lucan's witch Errichtho, who brings dead soldiers back to life: *De Bello Civili*, VI, l. 508 ff.
74. love's hid cancer] the Duchess died of breast cancer in 1671, but whether there was any evidence of the illness in 1667 is uncertain.
75. Sidney's disgrace] Henry Sidney (1636–1708), groom of the bedchamber, was dismissed as a result of the Duke's jealousy. For confirmation of his affair with the Duchess, see Pepys, 7.323.
76. emulous Denham's face] see above, ll. 65–8 n. Lady Denham was Sir John's second wife, and eighteen when she married him in 1665. *emulous*] driven by spirit of rivalry (*OED* a. 2).
79. Castlemaine] Barbara Palmer, Countess of Castlemaine (1641–1709), a mistress of Charles II, and in 1667, in love with Jermyn. Her lascivious reputation is attested by a printed mock petition dated 25 March 1668, *The Poor-Whores Petition to the most Splendid, Illustrious, Serene and Eminent Lady of Pleasure the Countess of Castlemayne*, from the 'Undone Company of poore distressed Whores, Bawds, Pimps, and Panders' to their natural protectress, the Countess of Castlemaine, which was connected with the Bawdy House riots of 1668, popular godly resistance to court extravagance and immorality: see Turner (2002), 168–73.

She through her lackey's drawers, as he ran,
Discerned love's cause and a new flame began.
Her wonted joys thenceforth, and court, she shuns,
And still within her mind the footman runs:
85 His brazen calves, his brawny thighs (the face
She slights) his feet shaped for a smoother race.
Poring within her glass she readjusts
Her looks, and oft-tried beauty now distrusts;
Fears lest he scorn a women once assayed,
90 And now first wished she e'er had been a maid.
Great Love, how dost thou triumph and how reign,
That to a groom couldst humble her disdain!
Stripped to her skin, see how she stooping stands,
Nor scorns to rub him down with those fair hands,
95 And washing (lest the scent her crime disclose)
His sweaty hooves, tickles him 'twixt the toes.
But envious Fame, too soon, began to note
More gold in's fob, more lace upon his coat;
And he, unwary, and of tongue too fleet,

100 No longer could conceal his fortune sweet.
Justly the rogue was whipped in porter's den,
And Jermyn straight has leave to come again.
Ah, painter, now could Alexander live,
And this Campaspe thee, Apelles, give!
105   Draw next a pair of tables op'ning, then
The House of Commons clatt'ring like the men.
Describe the court and country, both set right
On opp'site points, the black against the white.
Those having lost the nation at tric-trac,
110 These now advent'ring how to win it back.
The dice betwixt them must the fate divide
(As Chance doth still in multitudes decide).
But here the court does its advantage know,
For the cheat Turnour for them both must throw.
115 As some from boxes, he so from the chair
Can strike the die and still with them goes share.
    Here, painter, rest a little, and survey
With what small arts the public game they play.

81–102. She . . . again] the only record of this purported affair. An 'inversion of the traditional relationship between age and gender', and between pursuer and pursued, where an aging nymph chases a young satyr or centaur (Riebling, *SEL*, 35 (1995), 141).
81. drawers] tightly fitting breeches or hose; a word of low origins (*OED*), appropriate for the servant.
82. Discerned] recognized; distinguish by the intellect (*OED* v. 4); Lady Castlemaine, like the Duchess of York, is presented, ironically, as a philosopher.
83. wonted] usual (*OED* B ppl. a).
85. brazen] strong (*OED* a. 2); also connoting 'shameless' (*OED* a. 3).
86. smoother race] a) i.e. an animal, possibly a horse (see below, l. 96). 'Smooth' is associated in the seventeenth century with descriptions of animals: see *OED* a 'smooth-skinned'. b) copulation (see 'smooth', *OED* a. 7 a: 'pleasing').
87. glass] mirror.
89. assayed] deflowered.
91–6. A parody of Luke 7:37–8: 'And, behold, a woman in the city, which was a sinner, when she knew that Jesus sat at meat in the Pharisee's house, brought an alabaster box of ointment, And stood at his feet behind him weeping, and began to wash his feet with tears, and did wipe them with the hairs of her head, and kissed his feet, and anointed them with the ointment.'
98. fob] small pocket in the waistband of breeches (*OED* n.²). Farley-Hills (1974), 94, notes that the pocket bulging with money replaces the bulge in the servant's breeches (see above, ll. 81–2) that had first attracted the Duchess. The association of money with virility is made by Iago in Shakespeare's *Othello*, I, iii, ll. 340 ff., when he puns on 'purse' as 'scrotum': 'Put money in thy purse.'
99. fleet] quick.
101. porter's den] gatehouse ('porter': gatekeeper (*OED* n.¹ 1 a)).
102. Jermyn] see above, l. 29 n.
103–4. Alexander . . . Apelles] Apelles was court painter to Alexander of Macedon, Campaspe his Theban captive whom Apelles was asked to paint. Apelles and Campaspe fell in love,

and Apelles spoiled his portrait so that Campaspe would have to sit for him again. Alexander eventually surrendered Campaspe to Apelles. See Pliny, *Natural History*, XXXV.x. The story was a topos for painting, instanced in Frans Francken II's picture of the early seventeenth century, one version of which is in the Duke of Devonshire's collection at Chatsworth. In suggesting that the painter should enjoy sexual relations with Lady Castlemaine, M. points up the fallibility of painting: like the obscene graffiti artist (see above, 367), the court painter falls in with the sins he describes, aiding and abetting the crimes of the court.
105–372. Draw . . . fires] Cp. the triumphant, harmonious image of King in Parliament, with Charles as the new 'young Augustus', in Waller, *Instructions to a Painter*, ll. 299–310.
105. pair of tables] folding board for backgammon (*OED* n.¹ 4), called by its older name of 'tric-trac' at l. 109.
106. clatt'ring] a) rattling noise of counters striking each other (*OED* v. 1) b) chatter, prattle (*OED* v. 3). *the men*] backgammon counters (or in its earlier version, pegs that were fixed in holes at the back of the board).
107. court . . . country] not yet organized political factions, let alone parties; nonetheless, there were clearly those loyal to the court, and those opposed to what they regarded as court abuses. For 1660s political behaviour, see Seaward (1989), ch. 4. *right*] a) straight (*OED* a. I 1 a) b) righteous (*OED* a. II 5).
109. lost the nation] i.e. in the war with the Dutch. *tric-trac*] see above, l. 105 n.
111. divide] a) distribute (*OED* v. I 8 e) b) decide (*OED* v. I 1 d).
114. Turnour] Sir Edward Turnour (1617–76), Speaker of the House of Commons, 1661–73; appointed Attorney-General to the Duke of York in 1660, and received gifts from the Treasury of £2,000 in December 1663 and £5,000 in July 1664. These, together with a further gift of 50 gold pieces from the East India Company, seriously damaged his reputation in Parliament (Henning).
115. boxes] dice-boxes (*OED* n.² I 3 d).
116. strike the die] throw the die in a fraudulent manner, so as to cheat (*OED* v. 74). *goes share*] takes his share of the profit.
118. public game] a) backgammon b) statesmanship.

For so too Rubens, with affairs of state,
His lab'ring pencil oft would recreate.
   The close Cabal marked how the navy eats,
And thought all lost that goes not to the cheats;
So therefore secretly for peace decrees,
Yet as for war the Parliament should squeeze;
5 And fix to the revenue such a sum
Should Goodrick silence and strike Paston dumb,
Should pay land armies, should dissolve the vain
Commons, and ever such a court maintain;
Hyde's avarice, Bennet's luxury should suffice,
0 And what can they defray but the Excise?
Excise a monster worse than e'er before
Frighted the midwife and the mother tore.
A thousand hands she has, and thousand eyes,
Breaks into shops and into cellars pries,

135 With hundred rows of teeth the shark exceeds,
And on all trade like cassowar she feeds:
Chops off the piece wheres'e'er she close the jaw,
Else swallows all down her indented maw.
She stalks all day in streets concealed from sight,
140 And flies like bats with leathern wings by night;
She wastes the country and on cities preys.
Her, of a female harpy, in dog days,
Black Birch, of all the earth-born race most hot
And most rapacious, like himself, begot,
145 And, of his brat enamoured, as't increased,
Buggered in incest with the mongrel beast.
   Say, Muse, for nothing can escape thy sight
(And, painter, wanting other, draw this fight),
Who, in an English senate, fierce debate
150 Could raise so long for this new whore of state.

119–20. Rubens . . . recreate] Sir Peter Paul Rubens (1577–1640), court painter of the Spanish Netherlands, was sent by the Infanta to negotiate with England and Holland; he negotiated with the first Duke of Buckingham while supposedly discussing paintings, and was knighted by Charles I in 1630 for his diplomatic services.
120. pencil] see above, l. 19 n. *recreate*] refresh.
121. close] secret (*OED* a. A I 4). *Cabal*] applied in the reign of Charles II to a small committee of the Privy Council, known as the 'Committee for Foreign Affairs', which had the chief management of the course of government; a precursor of the modern Cabinet (*OED* n.¹ 6).
123. secretly for peace] In January and February 1667, the King promised Parliament that he was not engaged in negotiations for peace, but Clarendon, Ormonde, Burlington and Orrery were secretly urging him to do so (Hutton (1989), 240). Clarendon wanted a peace with France, Bennet with the United Provinces. In January, St Albans was instructed to approach Louis XIV; in October, a treaty of peace was offered to the States-General.
124. squeeze] pressure to extort funds (*OED* v. 3 a).
125. fix to the revenue] see below, l. 332 n. *revenue*] stressed on second syllable.
126. Goodrick] Sir John Goodrick, MP for the county of York, sometimes teller for the Court party in the 1664–65 session of Parliament. *Paston*] Sir Robert Paston (1631–83), knighted at the Restoration; created Viscount Yarmouth, 1673, and first Earl of Yarmouth, 1679; MP for Castle Rising; in January 1667 he became a gentleman of the privy chamber. A friend of the King, he benefitted financially from crown patronage. In the 1664–65 session of Parliament, he proposed the enormous appropriation of £2.5 million for the war.
127. vain] a) worthless (*OED* a. I 1) b) powerless (*OED* a. I 1) c) foolish (*OED* a. I 3) d) self-regarding (*OED* a. I 4).
129. Hyde's] Edward Hyde, Earl of Clarendon. *Bennet's*] Henry Bennet, Earl Arlington (1618–85), Keeper of the Privy Purse, 1661–62, Secretary of State, 1662–74, Commissioner of Prizes, 1664–67. Regarded as pompous and over-ambitious, he exploited the favour of royal mistresses for his own aggrandizement. An arch-courtier and crypto-Catholic, he spent lavishly on his properties in London (Goring House, on the site of the present Buckingham Palace) and in Norfolk (Euston

Hall). M. spoke strongly against him in Parliament on 14 or 15 February 1668. Bennet had been made Baron Arlington on 14 March 1665. M. uses this name at l. 934 below; here 'Bennet' fits the metre.
130. defray] spend (*OED* v.¹ 1). *Excise*] tax on home goods imposed during process of manufacture, or before sale to consumers; first imposed in 1643; stressed on second syllable.
132. tore] i.e. Excise tears her mother's womb as she is born; cp. the description of the birth of Death from Sin in Milton, *Paradise Lost*, II, ll. 777–85; see also below, l. 146 n.
136. cassowar] the cassowary, a long-legged running bird related to the ostrich and the emu, and noted for devouring whatever it was offered.
138. indented] a) serrated (*OED* a. I 1), filled with teeth b) authorized or bound by a legal agreement (*OED* ppl. a. 4). *maw*] jaws (*OED* n.¹ 3).
142. harpy] rapacious monster, with female face and body, and bird's wings and claws (*OED* 1). *dog days*] the hottest time of the year, at the time of the rising of the Dog-star; associated here with the 'hot' time of the Civil Wars and Interregnum (see below, l. 143 n.). For dog days, see above, *Damon the Mower*, l. 18 n.; for the appearance of comets in times of war, see above, 343, l. 424.
143. Black Birch] John Birch (1616–91), Protectorate excise official; Auditor for the Excise during the Restoration; a defender of the Navy Board against its critics in 1668, but in the 1670s was distrustful of the court, and became a Whig. *hot*] lustful (*OED* a. 6 c).
144. rapacious] greedy (*OED* a. 2).
146. Buggered . . . beast] shadows the allegory of the rape of Sin, and the birth of Death in *Paradise Lost*, II. Birch is implicitly compared to Satan.
147. Say . . . sight] A clear signal of epic, and particularly Miltonic, epic narration: see, e.g., Milton, *Paradise Lost*, I, l. 27: 'Say first, for heaven hides nothing from thy view.'
149–50. Who . . . state] an apparent conflation, within the terms of the epic imagination, of the Parliament in Hell and the allegory of Sin and Death, in Milton's *Paradise Lost*, Bk II.
149. senate] Parliament.

Of early wittols first the troop marched in,
For diligence renowned and discipline:
In loyal haste they left young wives in bed,
And Denham these by one consent did head.

155 Of the old courtiers, next a squadron came,
That sold their master, led by Ashburnham.
To them succeeds a despicable rout,
But know the word and well could face about;
Expectants pale, with hopes of spoil allured,

160 Though yet but pioneers, and led by Stew'rd.
Then damning cowards ranged the vocal plain,
Wood these commands, Knight of the Horn and Cane.
Still his hook-shoulder seems the blow to dread,
And under's armpit he defends his head.

165 The posture strange men laughed at of his poll,

Hid with his elbow like the spice he stole.
Headless St Denis so his head does bear,
And both of them alike French martyrs were.
Court officers, as used, the next place took,

170 And followed Fox, but with disdainful look.
His birth, his youth, his brokage all dispraise
In vain, for always he commands that pays.
Then the procurers under Progers filed–
Gentlest of men – and his lieutenant mild,

175 Brouncker – Love's squire – through all the field arrayed
No troop was better clad, nor so well paid.
Then marched the troop of Clarendon, all full
Haters of fowl, to teal preferring bull:
Gross bodies, grosser minds, and grossest cheats;

180 And bloated Wren conducts them to their seats.

151–306. A representation of the debate on the excise that took place in a Grand Committee of the House of Commons between 12 October 1666 (when the debate was between a proposed land tax and a general excise) and 8 November, when the government withdrew its proposals (see Milward, ed. (1938), 21–2, 24–5, 35).
151. *wittols*] contented cuckolds (*OED* n. 1).
154. *Denham*] Sir John Denham, poet, soldier and MP; see above, ll. 65–8 n.; see also above, *The Advice-to-a-Painter Poems*, Headnote, 321, 326.
156. *Ashburnham*] John Ashburnham (*c.* 1603–71), who helped to arrange Charles I's flight to the Isle of Wight. He was (unjustly) suspected of having betrayed the King to the Governor of the island. Expelled from the House in November 1667 for taking a bribe from French merchants.
158. i.e., understand how to alter their opinion or vote in order to please their masters.
159. *Expectants*] one who expects an office (*OED* B n. 2 b).
160. *pioneers*] advance soldiers (*OED* n. 1). *Stew'rd*] Margoliouth proposed Robert Steward (1617–72), MP for Castle Rising, Chairman of the Ways and Means Committee, 1666–68, and a prominent member of the Cavalier Parliament. This view is supported by Henning (1983). But Gearin-Tosh, *N & Q*, n.s. 17 (1970), 257, proposes Sir Nicholas Steward (1618–1710), MP for Lymington, a committed royalist, but an unremarkable man (and hence more fitting for one of the 'rout') and one of the two Chamberlains of the Exchequer, a post in the lower exchequer, where revenue was received.
162. *Wood*] Sir Henry Wood (1597–1671), Clerk of the Spicery to Charles II, MP for Hythe and a Clerk Comptroller of the Board of Green Cloth; a courtier since 1623, Treasurer to Henrietta-Maria in 1644; member of Catharine of Braganza's Council from 1662. *Horn . . . Cane*] Wood was responsible for order in the royal household, and for maintaining its accounts (hence he controls its 'horn of plenty'), but his attempts to curb consumption were well-known (Ormonde to Charles, May 1662) (hence he is responsible for punishment, with the 'cane' or 'wand' of office).
163–4. *hook-shoulder . . . head*] Both Evelyn (17 November 1651) and Pepys (4.348–9, 7.290) attest to Sir Henry Wood's eccentric behaviour. Suffering blows points to Wood's unpopularity.

163. *hook-shoulder*] i.e. hunchback; cp. *Upon the Hill and Grove at Bilbrough*, ll. 9–12: Here learn, ye mountains more unjust,/ . . . /That do with your hook-shouldered height/The earth deform and heaven fright.'
165. *posture*] see above, *Headnote, Sources and Genre. poll*] head (*OED* n.[1] I 1).
167. *St Denis*] patron saint of France, beheaded in 272. He is supposed to have carried his head in his hands for six miles to the site where his cathedral would stand.
168. *French martyrs*] i.e. Wood is also a French martyr, because, it is implied, he is a victim of a venereal infection ('the French disease').
169. *as used*] as usual; as customary.
170. *Fox*] Sir Stephen Fox (1627–1716), MP for Salisbury and Paymaster-General of the army. Highly successful, uncorrupt, and yet reputed to be the richest commoner in England.
171. *brokage*] trade; business (*OED* 1 a).
173. *procurers*] a) officials; commissioners (*OED* n. I 1) b) pimps, panders (*OED* n. II 4; Williams (1994), II.1103–4). *Progers*] Edward Progers (1621–1713), MP for Brecon, Groom of the Bedchamber and a procurer (in the eyes of some, a 'pimp of the bedchamber') for the King.
175. *Brouncker*] Henry Brounker (1627?–88), Gentleman of the Bedchamber to the Duke of York and MP for New Romney, 1665–68; responsible for the unauthorized order at the Battle of Lowestoft (see above, *The Second Advice*, ll. 239–44), subsequently impeached, dismissed from the court in August 1667, and from Parliament in April 1668. *Love's squire*] implying that Brouncker, like Progers, is a pimp for Charles. *arrayed*] prepared for battle (*OED* v. I 1).
178. *Haters of fowl*] being gluttons, they preferred to eat red meat. *teal . . . bull*] a play on the name of John Bulteel (d. 1669), MP for Lostwithiel and secretary to the Earl of Clarendon from *c.* 1658. *teal*] small duck (*OED* n. 1).
180. *Wren*] Matthew Wren (1629–72), Fellow of the Royal Society, MP for Mitchell, 1661–72, secretary to Clarendon, 1660–67 (during which time he was accused of corruption (see Pepys, 7.342 n.)), and to the Duke of York as Admiral, 1667–72.

Charlton advances next, whose coif does awe
The Mitre troop, and with his looks gives law.
He marched with beaver cocked of bishop's brim,
And hid much fraud under an aspect grim.
5 Next the lawyers' mercenary band appear:
Finch in the front, and Thurland in the rear.
The troop of privilege, a rabble bare
Of debtors deep, fell to Trelawny's care.
Their fortune's error they supplied in rage,
*0 Nor any further would than these engage.
Then marched the troop, whose valiant acts before
(Their public acts) obliged them still to more.
For chimney's sake they all Sir Pole obeyed,
Or in his absence him that first it laid.
*5 Then comes the thrifty troop of privateers,

Whose horses each with other interferes.
Before them Higgons rides with brow compact,
Mourning his Countess, anxious for his Act.
Sir Frederick and Sir Solomon draw lots
200 For the command of politics or sots;
Thence fell to words, but quarrel to adjourn;
Their friends agreed they should command by turn.
Cart'ret the rich did the accountants guide
And in ill English all the world defied.
205 The Papists but of these the House had none,
Else Talbot offered to have them led on.
Bold Duncombe next, of the projectors chief,
And old Fitzharding of the Eaters Beef.
Late and disordered out the drinkers drew,
210 Scarce them their leaders, they their leaders knew.

---

181. Charlton] Sir Job Charlton (1614–97), MP for Ludlow and Chief Justice of Chester; moved that M. be sent to the Tower when he allegedly struck Sir Philip Harcourt in the House of Commons, 29 March 1677 (Grey (1769), 4.329); described by North as an 'old cavalier' *coif*] judge's white cap (*OED* n. 3).
182. Mitre troop] a) members of the Mitre Court, an Inn of Court b) frequenters of the Mitre tavern (see above *Tom May's Death*, l. 7).
183. beaver] lower part of face-guard of a helmet (*OED* n.² 1). *bishop's brim*] i.e. mitre; not in *OED*.
186. Finch] Sir Heneage Finch (1621–82), later Baron Finch and Earl of Nottingham, Solicitor-General and MP for Oxford University. *Pace* M.'s depiction, Finch was more often admired for his ability and probity. *Thurland*] Sir Edward Thurland (1624–85), MP for Reigate and Solicitor-General to the Duke of York.
187. privilege] Parliamentary privilege involved immunity from punishment for debt. *bare*] a) unarmed (*OED* a. A I 6 b) b) without property (*OED* a. A II 9).
188. Trelawny] Sir Jonathan Trelawny (*c.* 1623–81), MP for Cornwall; gentleman of the privy chamber; Comptroller to the Duke of York, 1668–74; ruined by the sequestration of his property by Parliament in the 1640s; acted six times as teller for supply during the Second Dutch War, including a vote to extend royal favour to all merchants injured by the prohibition of trade with France.
189. i.e. what they had lost at the hands of fortune, they vigorously recovered through the Supply.
190. engage] a) enter into combat (*OED* v. IV 18 c) b) make security for a payment on the liability of incurring debt (*OED* v. II 3).
193. Sir Courtenay Pole (1619–95), MP for Honiton, proposed the Hearth Tax (or 'Chimney-Money'; 2s. per hearth) in 1662.
194. him that first] possibly Sir John Bramston, Chairman of the Hearth Tax committee.
195. privateers] a) volunteer soldiers (*OED* n. 3) b) MPs who served their own interests by presenting private bills.

197–8. Higgons . . . Act] Thomas Higgons (*c.* 1624–91), MP for New Windsor, and court party member, introduced a bill in 1666–67 for the recovery of £4,500 owed to his first wife. It was defeated on 11 January 1667. He had married the widow of the Earl of Essex, publishing an oration delivered at her funeral in 1656, as well as the translation of Busenello's state panegyric from which Waller developed *Instructions to a Painter* (see above, *Headnote, Genre and Sources*).
197. compact] frowning (literally, to push together).
199. Sir Frederick] Sir Frederick Hyde (1614–77), MP for Haverfordwest and court party member. *Sir Solomon*] Sir Solomon Swale (1610–78), MP for Aldborough and court party member.
200. politics] politicians (*OED* B n. 1). *or sots*] a) fools (*OED* A n. 1) b) drunkards (*OED* A n. 2).
203. Cart'ret] Sir George Carteret: see above, *The Second Advice To a Painter*, ll. 39–40 n.
204. ill English] Carteret was poorly educated: Pepys (4.217) attests to his ignorance.
205. Roman Catholics were excluded from the House of Commons.
206. Talbot] probably John Talbot (1630–1714), MP for Knaresborough. A leading court supporter, but consistently against Popery. M.'s view probably derives from the fact that the Talbots were a Catholic family, including at this time, its head, the Earl of Shrewsbury. For the Catholics, see below, 385, l. 649, 379, ll. 407–8 n.
207. Duncombe] Sir John Duncombe, Kt. 1646? (1622–87), MP for Bury St Edmunds, a Privy Councillor, sometime Commissioner of the Ordnance, and of the Treasury (see below, ll. 605, 793, 806); considered a successful administrator but haughty by contemporaries; ridiculed as Sir Gravity Empty in Buckingham and Howard's *The Country Gentleman* (1669). *projectors*] speculators (*OED* n. 1 b).
208. Fitzharding] Sir Charles Berkeley (1599–1668), second Viscount Fitzharding in the Irish peerage, Comptroller of the Household, and hence in charge of the Yeoman of the Guard. *Eaters Beef*] Beefeaters; popular name for the Yeomen of the Guard, part of the royal household, instituted at the accession of Henry VII, 1485. *OED* lists the first usage as 1671.

Before them entered, equal in command,
Apsley and Broderick marching hand in hand.
Last then but one, Powell that could not ride,
Led the French standard, weltering in his stride.
215 He, to excuse his slowness, truth confessed
That 'twas so long before he could be dressed.
The Lord's sons, last, all these did reinforce:
Cornbury before them managed hobby-horse.
     Never, before nor since, a host so steeled
220 Trooped on to muster in the Tothill Field:
Not the first cock-horse that with cork were shod
To rescue Albemarle from the sea-cod,
Nor the late feather-men, whom Tomkins fierce
Shall with one breath, like thistledown disperse.
225 All the two Coventrys their generals chose,
For one had much, the other nought to lose;

Nor better choice all accidents could hit,
While hector Harry steers by Will the wit.
They both accept the charge with merry glee,
230 To fight a battle, from all gunshot free.
Pleased with their numbers, yet in valour wise,
They feign a parley better to surprise;
They that ere long shall the rude Dutch upbraid,
Who in a time of treaty durst invade.
235   Thick was the morning, and the House was thin,
The Speaker early, when they all fell in.
Propitious heavens, had not you them crossed,
Excise had got the day, and all been lost.
For th'other side all in loose quarters lay,
240 Without intelligence, command, or pay:
A scattered body, which the foe ne'er tried,
But oft'ner did among themselves divide;

---

212. Apsley ... Broderick] Sir Allen Apsley (1616–83), MP for Thetford, Treasurer of the Duke of York's household; Sir Allen Broderick (1623–80), MP for Orford and Callington, Cornwall, Surveyor-General, protégé of Clarendon and a former member of the royalist underground during the 1650s. Pepys (7.416; 19 December 1666) heard 'that Sir Allen Brodericke and Sir Allen Apsley did come drunk the other day into the House, and did both speak for half an hour together, and could not be either laughed or pulled or bid to sit down and hold their peace'. Further testimony to their disorderly conduct was given by Sir Richard Ford: see Henning (1.723).
213. Powell] Sir Richard Powell (or Powle) (1628–78), MP for Berkshire, Master of the Horse to the Duchess of York.
214. French standard] venereal disease. *weltering*] reeling (*OED* vbl. n. 6 b).
216. 'twas .. dressed] an obsession with dress made Powell a frequent late-comer for debates.
217. The Lord's] i.e. Clarendon's.
218. Cornbury] Henry Hyde, styled Viscount Cornbury, later second Earl of Clarendon (1638–1709), MP for Wiltshire; eldest son of Clarendon; loyal to his father during his impeachment, Anglican, loyalist and an opponent of the Buckingham and Arlington factions; Chamberlain to the Queen. *hobby-horse*] figure of a horse, or a part thereof, used in a morris-dance, or by children; possibly an allusion to Cornbury's involvement in the Oxfordshire militia.
219. steeled] armed (*OED* ppl. a. 2).
220. muster] assemble; appear in armed array (*OED* v.¹ 2). *Tothill Field*] in Westminster, used for military drilling (spelled 'Tuttle' in the seventeenth century); in every county the militia was mustered annually for four days.
221–2. Alludes to Prince Rupert's rescue of Albemarle at the Four Days' Battle (1–4 June 1666): a 'corked' horse means a ship (whose hull had been 'caulked'); 'cock' may refer to George Cocke, the naval contractor; the couplet is also a sexual innuendo, juxtaposing the supposed prowess of Rupert and De Ruyter, and recalling Albemarle's embarrassment that had been dealt with in *The Third Advice*, ll. 375–6.
221. cock-horse] toy horse (*OED* A n. 1). *cork were shod*] a reference to fashionable footwear during the Restoration, worn by gallants.
222. Albemarle] see above, 348–50. *sea-cod*] the Dutch generally; De Ruyter specifically.

223. feather-men] gallants in the army wearing feathers in their hats. *Tomkins*] Sir Thomas Tomkins (1608?–74), MP for Weobley; a discontented cavalier, who made an infamous speech against a standing army in July 1667 (see Pepys, 8.352–3 and n. 2); see also below, ll. 841–4 n.
224. thistledown] down or pappus crowning the seed-head of the thistle, by which means the seeds are carried along in the wind.
225–6. two Coventrys ... lose] Henry Coventry (c. 1619–86), MP for Droitwich, diplomatist, and known for his empty pocket; Sir William Coventry (1628?–86), Commissioner of the Treasury and of the Navy, younger brother of Sir Henry, accused of accepting bribes and selling offices: see also above, *The Second Advice to a Painter*, l. 25 n.; Henry Coventry's embassy to Sweden was over, and he had as yet no other posting.
227. i.e. no design could better this chance coincidence.
228. hector] braggart (*OED* n. 2). Henry Coventry was considered, like his brother, as quick-witted, but as someone who had compromised his talents with drink (Pepys, 8.70).
230. To fight ... free] alluding to Henry Coventry's alleged cowardice at the Battle of Lowestoft.
232. parley] discussion of terms with enemy (*OED* v. 2).
233–4. They ... invade] Holles and Henry Coventry had set out on their diplomatic mission to Breda in late April 1667. M. mocks the government and the ambassadors for merely complaining when the Dutch have made an attack while peace negotiations were taking place.
233. rude] a) violent (*OED* A a. I 5 b) b) uncivilized (in breaking the truce) (*OED* A a. I 3 b).
235. Thick] foggy, hazy (*OED* a. II 7) *thin*] poorly attended.
236. fell in] took their place in the ranks (*OED* v. X 62 'fall into').
237. Propitious] favourable (*OED* a. 1).
238. Excise ... lost] On 12 October 1666, the court party had unsuccessfully moved for a general excise of all things (Milward (1938), 21); the previous day £1,600,000 had been voted in supply before the whole House had been assembled.
239–44. M. suggests through the military analogy that there is no effective, unified opposition to the court party.
239. loose quarters] scattered billets.
240. intelligence] information concerning the movements of the enemy.
242. But ... divide] Cp. *The First Anniversary*, l. 91: 'And they, whose nature leads them to divide.'

And some ran o'er each night, while others sleep,
And undescried returned ere morning peep.
5 But Strangways, that all night still walked the round
(For vigilance and courage both renowned)
First spied the enemy and gave th'alarm,
Fighting it single till the rest might arm.
Such Roman Cocles strode before the foe,
0 The falling bridge behind, the stream below.
    Each ran, as chance him guides to several post,
And all to pattern his example boast.
Their former trophies they recall to mind
And to new edge their angry courage grind.
5 First entered forward Temple, conqueror
Of Irish cattle and Solicitor;

Then daring Seymour that with spear and shield,
Had stretched the monster Patent on the field.
Keen Whorwood next, in aid of damsel frail,
260 That pierced the giant Mordaunt through his mail;
And surly Williams, the accountants' bane;
And Lovelace young, of chimney-men the cane.
Old Waller, trumpet-general, swore he'd write
This combat truer than the naval fight.
265 Of birth, state, wit, strength, courage, Howard presumes
And in his breast wears many Montezumes.
These and some more with single valour stay
The adverse troops, and hold them all at bay.
Each thinks his person represents the whole,
270 And with that thought does multiply his soul:

---

244. undescried] unnoticed.
245. Strangways] Colonel Giles Strangways (1615–75), MP for Dorset; former Royalist, anti-Dissenter; teller against the Government in several divisions on finance. He made a filibustering speech in the House of Commons that frustrated the government's attempt to rush through the excise. When Strangways died, M. expressed disapproval at his anti-toleration attitude (Legouis, II.342–3).
249–50. Roman Cocles . . . below] Cocles fought Porsena's army single-handedly at the head of a bridge until his companions could demolish it behind him (see Livy, *Ab Urbe Condita*, II.x.2; Virgil, *Aeneid*, VIII, l. 650).
249. Such] in this way.
251. several] different (*OED* a. A 2).
252. Emphasizing the comparison of Parliamentary business to epic action. *pattern*] copy, imitate (*OED* v. I 4).
253. former trophies] victories against Clarendon and the court won in the House of Commons.
255. Temple] Sir Richard Temple, 3rd Bt. (1634–97), MP for Buckingham, 1661–95, a member of Buckingham's faction, and leader of the critics of Clarendon and Coventry in 1667–68; supported the act against the importation of Irish cattle, which passed in January 1667.
256. Solicitor] Sir Heneage Finch: see above, l. 186 n.; Temple had obliged Finch to withdraw an objection to the wording of the Irish Cattle bill, thereby allowing it to pass.
257–8. Seymour . . . Patent] Edward Seymour, 4th Bt. 1685 (1633–1708), MP for Hindon, Wiltshire, a Sub-Commissioner for Prizes for London until March 1666; later Speaker of the House of Commons (1673–78); he attacked the Canary Patent, a monopoly granted by Clarendon, in the Commons on 29 October 1666. Regarded as conceited, ambitious and proud: see Pepys (6.288). In a Commons debate on 7 November 1667, M. exposed Seymour as the bearer of a rumour (ultimately attributable to Clarendon) that the King was not fit to govern (Milward (1938), 116).
259–60. Whorwood . . . Mordaunt] M. implies that Brome Whorwood (1615–84), MP for the City of Oxford, a disillusioned follower of the court, played a leading role in the impeachment of John, first Viscount Mordaunt (1627–75), former Royalist underground leader, and Constable of Windsor Castle. Mordaunt was accused of abusing the daughter of his Paymaster, William Tayleur, in 1664, as well as evicting Tayleur from his residence and imprisoning him. The

impeachment proceedings ran throughout 1667; Mordaunt finally resigned from his position in September 1668. But Henning notes that Whorwood's only verifiable role in the proceedings was to try to stop Finch becoming a member of the impeachment committee. The case was a cause of great resentment in the House of Commons, and a source of friction with the King. See also below, l. 349.
261. Williams . . . bane] Colonel Henry Williams (1625–73), MP for Huntingdonshire, changed his name from Cromwell at the Restoration; member of committees inquiring into the embezzlement of military stores and the hearth-tax returns. Such a committee was established on 21 September 1666.
262. Lovelace . . . cane] John Lovelace (*c.* 1642–93), MP for Berkshire, opponent of the Hearth Tax; investigated by the Privy Council for beating a hearth-tax collector; later a staunch Whig.
263–4. Edmund Waller, the poet: see above, *Headnote, Genre and Sources*. In 1667, he supported the attack on Clarendon.
263. trumpet-general] a reference to Waller's fame for writing panegyrics, especially in connection with wars (as with *Instructions to a Painter* (1665)), and to Waller's prominence in the Commons as an opponent of standing armies and religious persecution.
265–6. Howard . . . Montezumes] Sir Robert Howard (1626–98), MP for Stockbridge, playwright and collaborator with Dryden on *The Indian Queen* (1665), whose hero is Montezuma. Others also used the mock-heroic to ridicule Howard (this time using Cervantes rather than Ariosto (see below, ll. 275–6 n.)): see 'The Session of the Poets' (1668; formerly attributed to Rochester), ll. 63–4: 'the sad Knight, to his grief, did discover/How Dryden had lately robb'd him of his muse.' Howard was an effective critic of Clarendon's ministry. *Montezumes*] presumably Howard is imagined mock-heroically in extravagant warrior dress, since Aztec warriors dressed in dense, feathered costume.
267. single] a) individual (*OED* a. I 1) b) outstanding (*OED* a. I 7) c) as in 'single [man to man] combat' (*OED* a. II 15).
269–70. Cp. Hobbes, *Leviathan* (1651), ed. C.B. Macpherson (1968), 89: 'when a man compoundeth the image of his own person, with the image of the actions of an other man; as when a man imagins himself a *Hercules*, or an *Alexander*, (which happeneth often to them that are much taken with reading of Romants) it is a compound imagination, and properly but a Fiction of the mind'.

Believes himself an army, theirs, one man
As easily conquered, and believing can:
With heart of bees so full, and head of mites,
That each, though duelling, a battle fights.

275 Such once Orlando, famous in romance,
Broached whole brigades like larks upon his lance.
  But strength at last still under number bows,
And the faint sweat trickled down Temple's brows.
E'en iron Strangways, chafing, yet gave back,
280 Spent with fatigue, to breathe a while toback.
When marching in, a seasonable recruit
Of citizens and merchants held dispute;
And, charging all their pikes, a sullen band
Of Presbyterian Switzers made a stand.

285   Nor could all these the field have long maintained
But for the unknown reserve that still remained:
A gross of English gentry, nobly born,
Of clear estates, and to no faction sworn;
Dear lovers of their king, and death to meet
290 For country's cause, that glorious think and sweet;

To speak not forward, but in action brave,
In giving generous, but in counsel grave;
Candidly credulous for once, nay twice,
But sure the devil cannot cheat them thrice.

295 The van and battle, though retiring, falls
Without disorder in their intervals:
Then, closing all in equal front, fall on,
Led by great Garway and great Littleton.
Lee, equal to obey or to command,
300 Adjutant-general, was still at hand.
The martial standard, Sandys displaying, shows
St Dunstan in it, tweaking Satan's nose.
See sudden chance of war! To paint or write
Is longer work and harder than to fight.

305 At the first charge the enemy give out,
And the Excise receives a total rout.
  Broken in courage, yet the men the same
Resolve henceforth upon their other game:
Where force had failed, with stratagem to play,
310 And what haste lost, recover by delay.

271–2. Cp. Virgil, *Aeneid*, V, l. 231: 'possunt, quia posse videntur' (strong are they, for strong they deem themselves) (Legouis).

275–6. Orlando . . . lance] Orlando Furioso's prowess in battle is likened to the spitting of frogs, rather than larks, on a branch (Ariosto, *Orlando Furioso*, trans. Sir John Harington (1591), IX.lxii–lxiii). St. lxvii refers to the capture of birds alive in a net, but Orlando rejects this kind of strategy.

276. Broached] pierced, as if placing on a spit to roast (*OED* v.[1] 1, 3).

278. Temple] see above, l. 255 n.

279. Strangways] see above, l. 235 n. *chafing*] raging (*OED* v. II 10).

280. toback] i.e. tobacco. Strangways was usually encountered by his contemporaries smoking a pipe or drinking; his 'accounts for sack and sherry . . . Falstaffian' (Henning).

281. seasonable] temporary (*OED* a. 1 c). *recruit*] reinforcement (*OED* n. I 1).

283. charging] placing in position for action (*OED* v. IV 21).

284. Switzers] Swiss guards (*OED* n. 2); Geneva was the home of Calvinism, whose views on predestination most Presbyterians followed; but this is also a paradox, since Swiss troops traditionally formed the bodyguard of the Pope.

287. gross of English gentry] known as the 'country gentlemen' as opposed to the courtiers; distinguished at this point by their desire for a land tax rather than a general excise since it was a more limited measure (see Pepys, 5 November 1666 (7.356); Millward (1938), 25, 309).

288. clear] free from liability, such as mortgages (*OED* a. V 16).

289–90. death . . . sweet] Cp. Horace, *Carmina*, III.ii.13: 'Dulce et decorum est pro patria mori' ('Tis sweet and glorious to die for fatherland).

291. forward] zealous (*OED* a. A 6).

292. generous] liberal (*OED* a. 3) because high-born (*OED* a. 1).

293–4. once . . . twice,/ . . . thrice] a common Biblical number: see, e.g., 2 Kings 13:18–19; Matt. 26:34.

293. Candidly] a) honestly, openly b) innocently, i.e. naively.

295. van] vanguard; foremost division of an army (*OED* n.[2]). *battle*] main body of troops (*OED* n. II 9).

296. intervals] periods of time between sessions of Parliament (*OED* n. 1).

297. equal front] equally spaced in a line of battle (see 'front': *OED* n. II. 56).

298. Garway] William Garraway (Garway or Garroway; 1617–1701), MP for Chichester, had been a supporter of the government, but by 1663–64 a leading critic of the court, especially on matters of finance, including the navy; acted with Buckingham, but remained independent; on 7 December 1666, proposed a public accounts commission which was eventually lost at the prorogation. Later satirized in verse for supporting Danby: see 'Upon Mr Garraway', *BL 7*, fol. 35. *Littleton*] Sir Thomas Littleton (*c*. 1621–81), second Bt., MP for Much Wenlock; one of Arlington's faction; critical of government finances and of attempts made to examine finances in the Commission of Accounts of May–June 1667; made Treasurer of the Navy, 1668.

299. Lee] Sir Thomas Lee (1635–91), MP for Aylesbury; nominated to the abortive public accounts commission (Henning). M. visited him in January 1672 (Legouis, II.327).

300. Adjutant-general] officer who assists a general (*OED* 1).

301. Sandys] Colonel Samuel Sandys (1615–85), MP for Worcestershire, a country Cavalier (Henning suggests that M.'s portrayal of him as a standard-bearer reflects his disappointed expectations of the command of a regiment in the new-raised forces in the second Dutch War); nominated to the abortive public accounts commission (Henning).

302. Dunstan (924–88), Bishop of Worcester, was supposedly tempted by Satan in the form of a beautiful women while at work at his forge. He attacked the woman with his pincers, putting Satan to flight. *tweaking*] pulling sharply (with the pincers) (*OED* v. 1).

306. Measures for raising a general excise were frustrated in the House of Commons on 8 November 1666.

309. stratagem] military trick designed to outwit the enemy (*OED* n. 1).

St Albans straight is sent to, to forbear,
Lest the sure peace, forsooth, too soon appear.
The seamen's clamour to three ends they use:
To cheat their pay, feign want, the House accuse.
Each day they bring the tale, and that too true,
How strong the Dutch their equipage renew.
Meantime through all the yards their orders run
To lay the ships up, cease the keels begun.
The timber rots, and useless axe does rust,
Th'unpractised saw lies buried in its dust;
The busy hammer sleeps, the ropes untwine;
The stores and wages all are mine and thine.
Along the coast and harbours they take care
That money lack, nor forts be in repair.
Long thus they could against the House conspire,
Load them with envy, and with sitting tire:
And the loved king, and never yet denied,
Is brought to beg in public and to chide.
But when this failed, and months enow were spent,
They with the first day's proffer seem content,
And to land tax from the excise turn round,

Bought off with eighteen-hundred-thousand pound.
Thus like fair thieves, the Commons' purse they share,
But all the Members' lives, consulting, spare.
335　　Blither than hare that hath escaped the hounds,
The House prorogued, the Chancellor rebounds.
Not so decrepit Aeson, hashed and stewed,
With magic herbs, rose from the pot renewed,
And with fresh age felt his glad limbs unite;
340　His gout (yet still he cursed) had left him quite.
What frosts to fruit, what arsenic to the rat,
What to fair Denham, mortal chocolate,
What an account to Carteret; that, and more,
A Parliament is to the Chancellor.
345　So the sad-tree shrinks from the morning's eye,
But blooms all night and shoots its branches high.
So, at the sun's recess, again returns
The comet dread, and earth and heaven burns.
　　　Now Mordaunt may, within his castle tower,
350　Imprison parents, and the child deflower.
The Irish herd is now let loose and comes
By millions over, not by hecatombs;

---

311. St Albans] see above, 368, ll. 29–48 nn.; but at this juncture, St Albans was not in France. *straight*] immediately. *forbear*] refrain from pressing (*OED* v. 9).
313. The seamen's clamour] Pepys reported riots of seamen on 19 December 1666 (7.413–14), and 14–15 February 1667 (8.60 62–3), caused by lack of pay, or the government failing to redeem vouchers issued in lieu of pay. M. suggests the government exploited the seamen's grievances to their own advantage.
316. equipage] equipment for war (*OED* n. II 3).
317. yards] naval yards.
318. lay . . . up] put away in a dock (*OED* v.¹ VIII 60 g).
320. unpractised] unemployed (*OED* ppl. a 2).
322. stores] Waller, *Instructions to a Painter*, l. 97, had presented the poor supplying of the English fleet as an act of heroic self-denial. *mine and thine*] Proverbial: 'What is mine is yours and what is yours is mine' (Tilley, M980); see also John 17.10: 'And all mine are thine, and thine are mine; and I am glorified in them.'
324. lack] is missing; the intransitive use of the verb (*OED* v.¹ 1).
327–8. loved king . . . chide] On 18 January 1667, the King addressed the Commons in the House of Lords, urging that the need for supply be met (*JHL*, XII.81); but the land grant had been authorized fourteen months previously.
329. enow] enough (*OED* A 2).
330. proffer] provisional payment of a due (*OED* n. 3).
331–2. land . . . pound] the land tax, preferred by the country opposition, passed on 8 November 1666, for raising part of the total sum of the supply: £1,800,000.
331. turn round] suggests a military manoeuvre, turning a line of troops to face in the opposite direction.
333. fair thieves] a) i.e. thieves at a fair b) they share out stolen money fairly.
334. consulting] i.e. having consulted.
335. Blither] more cheerful (*OED* a. 3).

336. prorogued] adjourned (*OED* v. 3 b), on 8 February 1667, by the King.
337–9. In Ovid, *Metamorphoses*, VII, ll. 160–293, Medea renews the life of her father-in-law Aeson by replacing his blood with a special brew. M.'s negative also invites comparison with the following story in Ovid (*Metamorphoses*, VII, ll. 297–350), where, misled by Medea, the daughters of Pelias vainly attempted to renew the life of their father by dismembering him and boiling him in a pot. Hobbes used the latter in *De Cive* (1647), XII.xiii, as an illustration of the dangers of faction.
342. fair . . . chocolate] see above, ll. 259–60 n.
343. Carteret] see above, ll. 202–3 n., and see above, *The Second Advice To a Painter*, ll. 39–40 n.
344. Parliament . . . Chancellor] Viscount Conway reported early in 1667 that Clarendon 'hath a great mind to dissolve this Parliament' (Conway to Ormonde, 2 February 1667, Bod., MS Carte 35, fol. 290ᵛ; see also Pincus (1996), 395).
345. sad-tree] *Nyctanthes Arbor-tristis*, the Night-Jasmine of India or Melancholy tree, which loses its brightness during the day. *OED* records one usage in 1866, but see also the 'arbor triste' reported in Thomas Sprat, *History of the Royal Society*, August 1667 (Duncan-Jones, reported by Legouis). *morning's eye*] i.e. the sun.
348. comet dread] Clarendon is now likened to a comet. See also below, ll. 370–1 n. Comets were associated in the 1660s with dire warnings to monarchies. References to the obscuring of the sun in *Paradise Lost* were allegedly thought by the licenser to be an attack upon the English monarchy (see von Maltzahn, *RES*, 47 (1996), 479–99). *earth . . . burns*] in the Book of Revelation, the earth is consumed with fire (Rev. 8:5–9); the Great Fire of London was regarded as, or associated with, apocalypse, especially by the radicals who had published the earlier Painter poems (see above, *The Advice to a Painter Poems, Headnote, Printed Publication*).
349. Mordaunt] see above, l. 259 n.
351. Irish herd] see above, l. 255 n.
352. hecatombs] a hundred animals (properly oxen) presented as a sacrifice (*OED* n. 1).

And now, now the Canary Patent may
Be broached again for the great holiday.
355   See how he reigns in his new palace culminant,
And sits in state divine like Jove the fulminant!
First Buckingham, that durst to him rebel,
Blasted with lightning, struck with thunder, fell.
Next the twelve Commons are condemned to groan
360   And roll in vain at Sisyphus' stone.
But still he cared, while in revenge he braved,
That peace secured and money might be saved.
Gain and Revenge, Revenge and Gain are sweet
United most, else when by turns they meet.
365   France had St Albans promised (so they sing),
St Albans promised him, and he the King:
The Count forthwith is ordered all to close,
To play for Flanders and the stake to lose,
While, chained together, two ambassadors
370   Like slaves shall beg for peace at Holland's doors.
This done, among his Cyclops he retires
To forge new thunder and inspect their fires.
    The court as once of war, now fond of peace,
All to new sports their wanton fears release.
375   From Greenwich (where intelligence they hold)

Comes news of pastime martial and old,
A punishment invented first to awe
Masculine wives transgressing Nature's law,
Where, when the brawny female disobeys,
380   And beats the husband till for peace he prays,
No concerned jury for him damage finds,
Nor partial justice her behaviour binds,
But the just street does the next house invade,
Mounting the neighbour couple on lean jade.
385   The distaff knocks, the grains from kettle fly,
And boys and girls in troops run hooting by:
Prudent Antiquity, that knew by shame,
Better than law, domestic crimes to tame,
And taught youth by spectacle innocent!
390   So thou and I, dear painter, represent
In quick effigy, others' faults, and feign
By making them ridiculous, to restrain.
With homely sight they chose thus to relax
The joys of state, for the new peace and tax.
395   So Holland with us had the mastery tried,
And our next neighbours, France and Flanders, ride.
    But a fresh news the great designment nips,
Of, at the Isle of Candy, Dutch and ships!

---

353. *Canary Patent*] see above, l. 257 n.
354. *great holiday*] i.e. the Parliamentary recess.
355. *new palace*] see above, *Clarendon's Housewarming, Headnote, Context. culminant*] an astrological word, applied to heavenly bodies: of the greatest height (*OED* a. 1).
356. *the fulminant*] the thunderer (*OED* ppl. a. A 1).
357–8. *Buckingham . . . fell*] Buckingham had been chief supporter of the Irish Cattle Bill, which Clarendon opposed: see above ll. 351–2. On 25 February, Buckingham's arrest for alleged treasonable practices was ordered (one of which was that he had obtained a cast of the King's horoscope: see above, l. 355 n.).
359. *twelve Commons*] the twelve members of the House of Commons forming part of the eighteen Commissioners for the Public Accounts.
360. *Sisyphus' stone*] Sisyphus was punished in Hades for his robberies by the endless task of rolling a stone up a hill which always rolled back again (see Ovid, *Metamorphoses*, IV, l. 460).
361. *braved*] boasted (*OED* v. 6).
363–4. 'Revenge and Gain are sweetest when joined, or [secondarily] when they alternate.'
367. *Count*] St Albans; see above, ll. 29 n., 35–6 n., 39–40 n.; invokes its French version, 'Comte', which in turn puns on French 'Compte', 'count' [money].
368. France wanted peace with England in order to be free to launch designs on Flanders. The 'stake' would be possession of the Spanish Netherlands.
369. *two ambassadors*] see above, ll. 233–4 n.
370. *Holland's doors*] Breda, which was not in any of the seven United Provinces, but in territory conquered from the Spanish: the Dutch had refused to receive the ambassadors at The Hague: hence they are literally at 'Holland's doors'.
371–2. *Cyclops*] one-eyed giants who forged thunderbolts for Jove (see, e.g., Ovid, *Metamorphoses*, I, ll. 253–61, where Jove also fears burning land, sea and heavens: see above, l. 348).

374. *wanton*] a) uncontrollable (*OED*, A a. 1 a) b) profuse in growth (*OED* A. a. 7 a).
375–89. M. describes a Skimmington ride, a custom in which browbeaten husbands and their overbearing wives were ridden on horseback through their community in mockery (see Underdown (1985), 100, 102–3). See also Samuel Butler, *Hudibras*, The Second Part (1664), ll. 592–664.
375. *Greenwich*] Pepys witnessed the event when he called in at Greenwich on 10 June 1667 (8.257).
381. Unlike some of the MPs mentioned earlier in the poem: e.g. Whorwood (see above, ll. 259–60).
382. *partial*] biased (*OED* a. I 1).
384. *jade*] worn-out horse (*OED* n.¹ 1).
385. *distaff*] stick on which wool or flax was spun; hence a symbol of female authority (*OED* n. 1, 3). *grains . . . fly*] presumably used to make rough music.
387. *Antiquity*] recalling Latin *antiquum*: old customs, habits (Lewis and Short, E).
391. *quick*] lifelike (*OED* A a. II 6). *effigy*] likeness, portrait, image (*OED* n. 1). For the four-syllable pronunciation of this word (spelt 'effigie'), see *The Third Advice to a Painter*, l. 436. *feign*] a) contrive (*OED* v. II 2 d) b) pretend (*OED* v. II 5).
396. *ride*] as in a Skimmington Ride, where Holland is the masterful wife, England the beaten husband, France and Flanders the neighbours.
397. *fresh news*] but the news of the Dutch arriving in the Medway actually preceded the Skimmington Ride (Pepys, *Diary*, 10 June 1667; 8.257). *designment*] representation (i.e. the Skimmington Ride as a representation of international relations; *OED* n. 4). *nips*] cuts off; a nautical word (*OED* v.¹ I 1 d).
398. *Of*] *Donno*; *Off 1697+*; 'nips/*Off*' makes sense as the figure derived from the horticultural phrase, but no sense in terms of grammar. *Isle of Candy*] Canvey Island, in the Thames estuary, but see below, l. 402 n.

Bab May and Arlington did wisely scoff
And thought all safe, if they were so far off.
Modern geographers, 'twas there, they thought,
Where Venice twenty years the Turk had fought,
While the first year our navy is but shown,
The next divided, and the third we've none.
They, by the name, mistook it for that isle
Where pilgrim Palmer travelled in exile
With the bull's horn to measure his own head,
And on Pasiphae's tomb to drop a bead.
But Morice learn'd demónstrates, by the post,
This Isle of Candy was on Essex coast.
    Fresh messengers still the sad news assure;
More timorous now we are than first secure.
False terrors our believing fears devise,
And the French army one from Calais spies.

415 Bennet and May, and those of shorter reach,
    Change all for guineas, and a crown for each,
    But wiser men and well foreseen in chance
    In Holland theirs had lodged before, and France.
    Whitehall's unsafe; the court all meditates
420 To fly to Windsor and mure up the gates.
    Each does the other blame, all all distrust;
    But Mordaunt, new obliged, would sure be just.
    Not such a fatal stupefaction reigned
    At London's flame, nor so the court complained.
425 The Bludworth-Chancellor gives, then does recall
    Orders; amazed, at last gives none at all.
      St Albans' writ to, that he may bewail
    To Master Louis, and tell coward tale
    How yet the Hollanders do make a noise,
430 Threaten to beat us, and are naughty boys.

---

399. Bab May] Baptist (Bab) May (1628–84), Registrar of Chancery, Keeper of the Privy Purse; one of Lady Castlemaine's circle. See also above, ll. 17–18 n. *Arlington*] see above, l. 129 n.
401. Modern] new-fashioned, as opposed to ancient (*OED* a. 3 a).
402. May and Arlington mistake Canvey Island for Candia (Crete), which the Venetians had been defending against the Turks since 1645. Dzelzainis (in Chernaik and Dzelzainis, eds (1999), 292–3) suggests that the origins of the confusion lie in Castlemaine's (see below, ll. 407–8 n.) *An Account of the Present War between the Venetians and Turks; with the State of Candie* (1666), in which Charles II was encouraged to think of himself as the state of Venice, the Dutch as the Turks.
403–4. The English navy had failed to follow up its advantage over the Dutch in 1665; the fleet had been divided during the following year between Albemarle and Rupert; in 1667, most of the fleet was out of commission.
406–7. pilgrim Palmer . . . head] a reference to the cuckolding of Roger Palmer, Earl of Castlemaine (1634–1705), whose wife left him to be Charles II's mistress. He then travelled to the Levant in 1664 with the Venetian ambassador Andrea Cornaro, and served in a Venetian squadron.
406. exile] stressed on second syllable.
407–8. bull's horn . . . Pasiphae's tomb] Pasiphae, wife of King Minos of Crete, fell in love with a bull; the Minotaur was the product of their union. Minos had Daedalus build a labyrinth to imprison the beast. In M.'s depiction, the bull's horn reminds Castlemaine that he is a cuckold, Pasiphae's tomb of his estranged wife: see also Ovid, *Metamorphoses*, VIII, ll. 131–7; Virgil, *Aeneid*, VI, ll. 24–6. Comparisons between England and Crete begin earlier in the poetic sequence: see Waller, *Instructions to a Painter*, ll. 329–36, where Charles II is Zeus gathering his thunder (i.e. his navy) from the Cyclops. Castlemaine's status as leading spokesman for the English Catholics is left unbroached, although his tearful posture and 'pilgrim' status may suggest Catholic religiosity, and links with the portrayal of the other (probable) Roman Catholic in the poem, Archibald Douglas. *bead*] a) tear (not in *OED*) b) the Roman Catholic context suggests *OED* n. I 1: 'prayer'.
409. Morice . . . post] Sir William Morice (1602–76), Secretary of State with Arlington, responsible for the Northern Department, MP for Plymouth. Like Arlington, Morice received letters of intelligence concerning the whereabouts of

the Dutch fleet: see Pepys, 8.502. *the post*] official system for transmission of letters (*OED* n.² I 4); *OED* gives 1667 as the first such usage (citing Pepys on 14 March).
410. Isle of Candy] i.e. Canvey Island. 'Candy' was the name for Crete; much of Castlemaine's *An Account of the Present War between the Venetians and the Turk* (1666) was concerned with Crete, as well as the heroic service of Britons for the Venetians, another embarrassing parallel for the English navy.
411. assure] confirm (*OED* v. 10).
413–14. Cp. John Cooke to Charles Beale, 13 June 1667 (Bod., MS Rawl. Letters 113, fol. 66ʳ): 'you are not ignorant how the deceitful optick-glasses, where rumour is at one end & fear at the other, do commonly misrepresent all things . . . the Countrey . . . swarmes with relations of horror & stupefaction, that . . . a numerous Army of French are to be poured in vpon vs.'
413. devise] imagine (*OED* v. 10).
415. Bennet and May] Pepys, 8.274, heard Arlington named as one among many who had withdrawn money from bankers during the invasion scare. For May, see above, l. 399 n. *shorter reach*] a) lesser means b) poorer understanding (since not at the centre of government) (*OED* n.¹ II 7).
418. theirs] i.e. their money.
419–20. the court . . . gates] Pepys, 17 July 1667 (8.275): 'The King and Court are all troubled, and the gates of the Court were shut upon the first coming of the Dutch.'
420. Windsor] Windsor Castle. *mure up*] wall up (*OED* v. 1 b).
422. Mordaunt, new obliged] 'new obliged' to the court, because the charges against him were dropped in the face of the Dutch threat; see above, l. 260 n. *just*] as opposed to Mordaunt's earlier behaviour: see above, l. 260 n.
423. stupefaction] numbness (*OED* n. 1).
424. London's flame] the Great Fire of September 1666.
425. Bludworth-Chancellor] Sir Thomas Bludworth (Bluddell; 1620–82) was Lord Mayor of London during the Great Fire; his conduct during the fire was defended, but M.'s view coincides with that of Pepys (7.269): 'met my Lord Mayor in Canning Streete, like a man spent, with a handkercher about his neck. To the King's message, he cried like a fainting woman, "Lord, what can I do? I am spent! People will not obey me."'
428. Master Louis] Louis XIV.

Now Dolman's disobedient, and they still
Uncivil; his unkindness would us kill.
Tell him our ships unrigged, our forts unmanned,
Our money spent; else 'twere at his command.
435 Summon him therefore of his word and prove
To move him out of pity, if not love;
Pray him to make De Witt and Ruyter cease,
And whip the Dutch unless they'll hold their peace.
But Louis was of memory but dull
440 And to St Albans too undutiful,
Nor word nor near relation did revere,
But asked him bluntly for his character.
The gravelled count did with the answer faint
(His character was that which thou didst paint.)
445 And so enforced, like enemy or spy,
Trusses his baggage and the camp does fly.
Yet Louis writes and, lest our heart should break,
Consoles us morally out of Seneque.

Two letters next unto Breda are sent:
450 In cipher one to Harry excellent.
The first instructs our (verse the name abhors)
Plenipotentiary ambassadors
To prove by Scripture treaty does imply
Cessation, as the look adultery,
455 And that, by law of arms, in martial strife,
Who yields his sword has title to his life.
Presbyter Holles the first point should clear,
The second Coventry the Cavalier;
But, would they not be argued back from sea,
460 Then to return home straight, *infectâ re*.
But Harry's ordered, if they won't recall
Their fleet, to threaten we will grant them all.
    The Dutch are then in proclamation shent
For sin against th'eleventh commandment.
465 Hyde's flippant style there pleasantly curvets,
Still his sharp wit on states and princes whets;

---

430. Cp. *The Second Advice*, l. 196, where William Berkeley 'like good boy, promis'd to fight no more'.
431. Dolman's disobedient] Colonel Thomas Dolman, an English officer, commanded the Dutch troops in the invading fleet. An act for his attainder on a charge of high treason was passed on 30 October 1665. Dzelzainis (in Chernaik and Dzelzainis, eds (1999), 297), notes that M. plays down Dolman's treachery in order to emphasize the charge of corrupt government. *they*] i.e. the Dutch.
434. his] i.e. Louis's.
435. Summon] 'call up (to his memory)', i.e. remind (*OED* v. 7). *prove*] try (*OED* v. B I 4).
436. To . . . love] a technical description of being moved by a rhetorical appeal to *pathos*.
437. De Witt and Ruyter] the Dutch admirals: see above, 361.
440–1. undutiful . . . near relation] M. supposes that St Albans was married to Henrietta Maria: hence he is Louis' uncle. The supposition circulated widely in the 1660s, but was untrue (see Pepys, 2.263; Reresby (1991), 29).
441. Nor . . . nor] neither . . . nor. *word*] i.e. promise.
442. character] official status; credentials (*OED* n. II 15).
443. gravelled] perplexed (*OED* v. 4). *faint*] lose heart (*OED* v. 1).
444. character] a) credentials b) picture (*OED* n. I 6); see above, ll. 29–48.
445–6. 'a letter come last night . . . from my Lord St Albans out of France, wherein he says that the King of France did lately fall out with him, giving him ill names; saying that he had promised to assist our King and to forward the peace; saying that indeed he had offered to forward the peace at such a time, but it was not accepted of, and so he thinks himself not obliged . . . and so made him go out of his sight in great displeasure.' (Pepys, 26 June 1667 (8.294)).
445. enforced] constrained (*OED* ppl. a 2).
446. Trusses] packs (*OED* v. 1).
448. Seneque] French name of Seneca, the Roman moral philosopher: alleging, presumably, that Louis XIV is both extremely politique and bland in his use of rhetoric.

450. cipher] secret mode of writing; code (*OED* n. 5). *Harry excellent*] Henry Coventry: see above, l. 225 n. *excellent*] from 'Excellency', the title of honour for an ambassador.
451. verse the name abhors] i.e. supposedly because 'plenipotentiary ambassadors' is unpoetic although a perfect iambic metre.
452. Plenipotentiary ambassadors] Henry Coventry and Denzil Holles, first Baron Holles (1599–1680), MP for Dorchester and privy councillor. *Plenipotentiary*] invested with full powers, as deputy of a sovereign ruler.
453–4. To . . . Cessation] i.e. negotiation for peace is tantamount to a peace settlement, as (according to the Bible) a lustful glance at a woman is as good as the adulterous act itself.
454. look adultery] Cp. Matt. 5:27–8: 'Whosoever looketh on a woman to lust after her hath committed adultery with her already in his heart.'
456. Who . . . life] i.e. according to the laws of war, a soldier who surrenders should not be killed by his captors.
457. Presbyter Holles] see above, l. 452 n. *Presbyter*] Holles had been a leading opponent of Charles I, but had favoured a peaceful settlement of the kingdom from an early stage. Along with the Earl of Anglesey, he led the Presbyterian interest in the Cavalier Parliament.
458. Coventry the Cavalier] see above, l. 225 n., l. 228 n.
460. infectâ re] Latin: 'with the business unfinished.'
462–3. With widespread fury at the Dutch raid, and a financial crisis, all of the Dutch demands were conceded in a draft treaty signed at Breda on 1 July concluded there three weeks later and ratified in London at the end of the month.
462–3. Not in *Bod. 1*.
463. shent] reproached (*OED* v.[1] 2).
464. eleventh commandment] see above, ll. 453–4.
465–6. Clarendon's initial attitude towards the Dutch was unyielding and contemptuous.
465. curvets] mannered leap of a horse, in which the hind legs leave the ground before the forelegs (*OED* v. 1).
466. whets] sharpens (*OED* v. 3).

(So Spain could not escape his laughter's spleen:
None but himself must choose the King a Queen),
But when he came the odious clause to pen
0 That summons up the Parliament again,
His writing-master many a time he banned
And wished himself the gout to seize his hand.
Never old lecher more repugnance felt,
Consenting, for his rupture, to be gelt.
5 But still in hope he solaced, ere they come,
To work the peace and so to send them home,
Or in their hasty call to find a flaw,
Their acts to vitiate, and them overawe;
But most relied upon this Dutch pretence
0 To raise a two-edged army for's defence.
      First then he marched our whole militia's force
(As if, alas, we ships or Dutch had horse);
Then from the usual commonplace, he blames
These, and in standing army's praise declaims;
5 And the wise court that always loved it dear,

Now thinks all but too little for their fear.
Hyde stamps, and straight upon the ground the swarms
Of current Myrmidons appear in arms,
And for their pay he writes, as from the King–
490 With that cursed quill plucked from a vulture's wing–
Of the whole nation now to ask a loan
(The eighteen-hundred-thousand pound was gone).
      This done, he pens a proclamation stout,
In rescue of the *banquiers banquerout*:
495 His minion imps that, in his secret part,
Lie nuzzling at the sacramental wart,
Horse-leeches circling at the haem'rrhoid vein:
He sucks the King, they him, he them again.
The kingdom's farm he lets to them bid least
500 (Greater the bribe, and that's at interest).
Here men, induced by safety, gain, and ease,
Their money lodge; confiscate when he please.
These can at need, at instant, with a scrip
(This liked him best) his cash beyond sea whip.

467–8. Spain ... Queen] Clarendon had originally been opposed to the proposal by the Portuguese ambassador in the summer of 1660 of marriage between the King and Catharine of Braganza. When it became known that the Queen was barren, Clarendon was accused of planning the marriage in order to secure the crown for his daughter's children (DNB; see above, *The Second Advice to a Painter*, l. 154).

469–70. Clarendon advised the King that he could raise money without having to recall Parliament: Pepys, 25 June 1667 (8.293).

471. writing-master] properly an instructor in penmanship or calligraphy (*OED* n. 1); here a scribe. *banned*] cursed (*OED* v. II 2).

474. rupture] abdominal hernia (*OED* n. 2). *gelt*] castrated (*OED* v.[1] 1 a).

475. solaced] took comfort (*OED* v. 3).

477. hasty ... flaw] i.e. legal impropriety incurred through the rapid calling of Parliament.

478. vitiate] spoil, render invalid (*OED* v. 1).

479–80. In the aftermath of the naval disgrace, twelve regiments were raised. See Ogg (1934), I.313. *two-edged army*] i.e. the militia and a standing army (see below, ll. 481–4).

483. usual commonplace] i.e. that militias were ill-disciplined.

484. These] i.e. the militia. *standing ... declaims*] it was Charles II and not Clarendon who actually addressed the New Militia (Pepys, 13 June 1667; 8.264).

485. it] i.e. the standing army.

488. Myrmidons] a) Ovid, *Metamorphoses*, VII, ll. 615–60, recounts the creation of the Myrmidons from ants by Jove in answer to a prayer from Aeacus b) hired ruffians (*OED* n. 3).

490. vulture's wing] Duncan-Jones (reported by Legouis) suggests a parody of Henry Constable's 'To the K. of Scots, whome as yet he had not seene' (1584), ll. 13–14: 'The pen wherewith thou dost so heavenly singe/Made of a quill pluckt form an angell's winge.' The vulture was almost always mentioned as an emblem of greed in English Renaissance verse, and frequently in connection with the Prometheus myth.

492. The ... gone] see above, ll. 331–2 n.

493. proclamation] See Pepys, 23 June 1667 (8.285): 'the Banquiers cannot till peace returns, ever hope to have credit again; so that they can pay no more money ... an order of Council passed the 17th instant, directing all the Treasurers of any part of the King's revenue to make no payments but such as will be approved by the present Lords Commissioners; which will, I think, spoil the credit of all his Majesty's service. ... But the King's Declaration in behalf of the Banquiers, to make good their assignments for money, is very good.'

494. banquiers banquerout] bankrupt bankers (who have lent money to the King; French). In correcting a mistranscription by Lord, Gearin-Tosh, *SN*, 42 (1970), 310–11, avers that 'banquerout' is an English word, but there is no example in *OED*. Cp. Donne, *Elegie XIV*, ll. 28–9: 'Of store of Bankerouts, and poor Merchants losses/I urged him to speake.' In keeping with the heroic register, '*banquerout*' suggests that the bankers have been 'routed'. Pepys uses 'banquiers' (2.263; 8.285).

495–8. His ... again] In *RT*, 204, M. refers to a court barber, Olivier Le Daim, who sucked Louis XI's piles.

495. secret part] the anus, although usually applied to the genitals (*OED* a. A 1 j).

496–8. Cp. Cleveland, *The Rebell Scot*, ll. 83–6: 'Sure England hath the Hemerods, and these/On the North Posterne of the patient sieze,/Like Leeches: thus they physically thirst/After our blood, but in the cure shall burst.' (Lord).

496. sacramental] i.e. a profane parody of the dispensing of part of the sacrament, where communion wine is regarded as either becoming or representing the blood of Christ. *wart*] the piles.

497. haem'rrhoid vein] tumorous veins about the anus; i.e. piles.

499. farm] tax farm: a yearly amount of public revenue let out to individual gatherers (the tax farmers; in this case, the bankers) (*OED* n.[2] 2).

502. confiscate] used as an adjective.

503. scrip] a) small bag (*OED* n.[1]) b) scrap of paper (*OED* n.[3]). *OED* gives the earliest dating for 'scrip' as a receipt for a loan (n.[4]) as 1762.

505 When Dutch invade, when Parliament prepare,
     How can he engines so convenient spare?
     Let no man touch them or demand his own,
     Pain of displeasure of great Clarendon.
        The state affairs thus marshalled, for the rest
510 Monck in his shirt against the Dutch is pressed.
     Often, dear painter, have I sat and mused
     Why he should still be'n all adventures used,
     If they for nothing ill, like ashen wood,
     Or think him, like Herb John, for nothing good;
515 Whether his valour they so much admire,
     Or that for cowardice they all retire.
     As heav'n in storms, they call, in gusts of state,
     On Monck and Parliament, yet both do hate.
     All causes sure concur, but most they think
520 Under Herculean labours he may sink.
     Soon then the independent troops would close,
     And Hyde's last project would his place dispose.
        Ruyter the while, that had our ocean curbed,
     Sailed now among our rivers undisturbed,

525 Surveyed their crystal streams and banks so green
     And beauties ere this never naked seen.
     Through the vain sedge, the bashful nymphs he eyed:
     Bosoms, and all which from themselves they hide.
     The sun much brighter, and the skies more clear,
530 He finds the air and all things sweeter here.
     The sudden change, and such a tempting sight
     Swells his old veins with fresh blood, fresh delight.
     Like am'rous victors he begins to shave,
     And his new face looks in the English wave.
535 His sporting navy all about him swim
     And witness their complacence in their trim.
     Their streaming silks play through the weather fair
     And with inveigling colours court the air,
     While the red flags breathe on their topmasts high
540 Terror and war, but want an enemy.
     Among the shrouds the seamen sit and sing,
     And wanton boys on every rope do cling.
     Old Neptune springs the tides and water lent
     (The gods themselves do help the provident).

---

506. engines] device (*OED* n. 3).
509. marshalled] arranged in methodical order (*OED* v. II 5); M. intends a heavy irony, since he intends us to see that Clarendon's scheming is hardly methodical.
510. Monck in his shirt] i.e. not fully dressed; unprepared. *Monck*] see above, 345–7. *pressed*] i.e. as if he had been forced to serve by impressment ('press', *OED* v.² 2), as opposed to being joint chief commander of the navy. For the use of impressed men in the navy, see above, 343.
512. Why . . . used] See above, *The Third Advice*, l. 432. *be'n*] i.e. 'be on'.
513. nothing . . . wood] the wood of the ash can be put to many uses; cp. Spenser, *The Faerie Queene*, I.i.9, l. 7: 'the Ash for nothing ill'.
514. Herb John] St John's wort, but also a name for a tasteless herb of neutral qualities, and hence, proverbially, anything inert or indifferent (*OED* 2).
520. Herculean labours] Juno made Eurystheus set Hercules twelve Labours, recounted in Ovid, *Metamorphoses*, IX, ll. 182 ff.
521–2. Soon . . . dispose] Albemarle's demise would consolidate Clarendon's power, both in terms of his authority over the army, and in terms of opposition to the establishment of a standing army itself.
521. independent troops] i.e. the projected standing army. *close*] engage in combat (*OED* v. III 13).
522. last project] Cp. *An Horatian Ode*, ll. 115–16: 'And for the last effect/Still keep thy sword erect.' *dispose*] settle, order (*OED* v. III 8 a).
523. Ruyter] Farley-Hills (1974), 97, points out that De Ruyter remained at the Thames mouth; it was the younger Van Ghent who led the Medway raid. Cp. the representation of the Dutch and De Ruyter as rapists in newsbook accounts of the Newfoundland attacks (see T. Mundy, 'Some Occurences' (1664), Bod. Rawl. A 315, fol. 244ʳ). *curbed*] controlled (*OED* v.² I 2).

524. Sailed . . . rivers] the Dutch knew well that Kent had many rivers: see Rutgerus Hermannides, *Historische Landbeschryinge van Groot Brittanjen* (Middelburgh, 1666), 278–81.
527. vain] useless (for concealing the nymphs) (*OED* a. I 1 b).
532. old] De Ruyter was sixty.
534. his . . . wave] recalling the less optimistic Marvellian lover Damon who catches his own reflection, in part an imitation of Ovid's Cyclops: see above, *Damon the Mower*, ll. 57–60; Ovid, *Metamorphoses*, XIII, ll. 840–53.
535. sporting] a) playful (*OED* ppl. a. 1 b) b) sexually active.
536. witness] manifest, make evident (*OED* v.1 d). *complacence*] desire to please (*OED* v. 3).
537. streaming silks] i.e. streamers, the long, narrow and tapering flags flown from ship masts, as opposed to the colours that signified rank and intention (see below, l. 539 n.).
538. inveigling] a) deceiving (*OED* v. 1) b) seducing (*OED* v. 2).
539. red flags] some Dutch ships flew red flags in battle, although a variety of striped flags and pennants, based on the tricolour of the United Provinces, were also used: see Wilson (1986), 56–60.
540. Terror . . . enemy] cp. Waller, *Instructions to a Painter*, l. 214: 'Terror and death on his [the Duke of York's] loud cannon wait.'
541. shrouds] ropes leading from the top of a mast (*OED* n.² 1).
542. wanton] playful (*OED* A a. 3).
543–50. Old . . . Isle] *Ode sur la dernière Victoire De Mᴿ Ruiter*, 14 June 1666, mocked an English boast that the King was a British Neptune: 'Et vous nous apprestez à rire,/Puisqu'il enchaine vos Tritons.'
543. Old Neptune] Dutch poetry on the Chatham raid satirized the Duke of York as a mock 'sea-god': 'd'Opgeworpe zeegodt Jork/Eigent zich Neptunus vork' (the heated sea-god York, himself Neptune's trident), Joost van den Vondel, *Zeegevier der Vrye Nederlanden* (1667), 11–12. *springs*] sets in motion (*OED* v.¹ IV 21 a), with a play on the spring-tide that aided the Dutch ('spring', *OED* n.¹ IV 13).
544. i.e. 'God helps those who help themselves.' See *Tilley*, F603, G236.

5 And where the deep keel on the shallow cleaves,
With trident's lever, and great shoulder heaves.
Aeolus their sails inspires with eastern wind,
Puffs them along, and breathes upon them kind.
With pearly shell the Tritons all the while
0 Sound the sea-march, and guide to Sheppey Isle.
    So have I seen in April's bud arise
A fleet of clouds, sailing along the skies;
The liquid region with their squadrons filled,
Their airy sterns the sun behind does gild;
5 And gentle gales them steer, and heaven drives,
When, all on sudden, their calm bosom rives
With thunder and lightning from each armèd cloud;
Shepherds themselves in vain in bushes shroud.
Such up the stream the Belgic navy glides,
0 And at Sheerness unloads its stormy sides.
    Spragge there, though practised in the sea command,
With panting heart lay like a fish on land,
And quickly judged the fort was not tenable –
Which, if a house, yet were not tenantable –

565 No man can sit there safe: the cannon pours
Thorough the walls untight, and bullet show'rs;
The neighb'rhood ill, and an unwholesome seat.
So at the first salute resolves retreat,
And swore that he would never more dwell there
570 Until the city put it in repair.
So he in front, his garrison in rear,
March straight to Chatham to increase the fear.
    There our sick ships unrigged in summer lay
Like moulting fowl, a weak and easy prey;
575 For whose strong bulk earth scarce could timber find,
The ocean water, or the heavens wind.
Those oaken giants of the ancient race,
That ruled all seas and did our Channel grace.
The conscious stag so, once the forest's dread,
580 Flies to the wood and hides his armless head.
Ruyter forthwith a squadron does untack;
They sail securely through the river's track.
An English pilot too (O shame, O sin!)
Cheated of pay, was he that showed them in.

---

545. cleaves] sticks fast to (*OED* v.² 1).

547–55. In the English panegyrics, the elements do not side with the Dutch: see, e.g. Dryden, 'Verses to her Highness the Duchess' (1666), ll. 24–5: 'The wind and tide/You bribed to combat on the English side.'

547. Aeolus] god of the winds. *inspires*] blows upon (*OED* v. I 1).

549. Tritons] male sea-deities, half-fish, half-man, usually portrayed holding a trident and blowing a shell-trumpet. Cp. anonymous engraving celebrating De Ruyter's victory see *Yale POAS*, 124–5; cp. also Busenello, *A Prospective*, trans. Higgons (1658), sig. C8ᵛ.

550–60. Sheppey . . . Sheerness] the Dutch ships bombarded Sheerness from the Isle of Sheppey on the evening of 10 June.

551. So . . . arise] Cp. *The First Anniversary*, ll. 265–6: 'So have I seen at sea, when whirling winds,/Hurry the bark'; *A Poem upon the Death of his Late Highness the Lord Protector*, ll. 89–90: 'So have I seen a vine, whose lasting age/Of many a winter hath survived the rage.' This epic simile may be regarded as an ironic continuation of those in the Cromwell poems, since the Dutch are described triumphally entering the Thames (unlike the foreclosed epic simile in *The Third Advice* (ll. 29–30)). *April's bud*] i.e. early April; spring.

553. liquid] clear, transparent (*OED* a. A II 2).

554. The sterns of ships were gilded.

556. rives] splits (*OED* v.¹ B III 10).

559. Such] in this way. *Belgic*] i.e. Dutch.

560. unloads] a) fires (*OED* v. 5 a) b) a pun: Sheerness was a port.

561–8. Spragge . . . retreat] the Dutch bombardment caused the garrison under Spragge to evacuate.

561. Spragge] Sir Edward Spragge (d. 1673), Vice-Admiral of the Blue Squadron, then commanding at Sheerness; a favourite of the Duke of York; widely criticized for his conduct during the Medway Raid; other instances of his naval tactics and strategy were flawed (DNB). Dryden describes him as 'bountiful as brave' (*Annus Mirabilis* (1667), ll. 693–4), and he had been knighted for gallantry after the Battle of Lowestoft.

562. panting heart] a 'breathless' heart is short of blood, i.e. courage.

563. tenable] capable of being held against attack (*OED* a. 2).

564. tenantable] fit for occupation (*OED* a. 1).

565. sit] a) reside as a tenant (*OED* v. B 8) b) reside in an official capacity (*OED* v. B 4).

566. untight] leaky (*OED* a. 2). *bullet*] cannon-ball (*OED* n¹ 2).

567. unwholesome] unhealthy (*OED* a. A 2 b). *seat*] place of residence (*OED* n. III 12).

568. salute] exchange of cannon-fire (*OED* n.¹ 3).

575. bulk] hulls (*OED* n.¹ II 3).

578. Channel] i.e. the English Channel.

579–80. The . . . head] a gesture of retreat, comparable to those made by the poet figure in *Upon Appleton House*: see above, 225; Marvell's seal depicted a stag, although one with antlers.

579. conscious] aware of his weakness (*OED* a. 4b).

580. armless] without antlers.

581. Ruyter . . . untack] Ruyter had in fact already sent a reconnaissance party upriver on 11 June (Hutton (1989), 268). *untack*] detach (*OED* v. 1 b).

582. securely] safely; unthreatened.

583. English pilot] possibly Captain Philip Holland (*CSPD*, 28 April 1672); for the nonpayment of sailors, see above, *Headnote, Context.*

585 Our wretchèd ships within their fate attend,
     And all our hopes now on frail chain depend:
     (Engine so slight to guard us from the sea,
     It fitter seemed to captivate a flea,
     A skipper rude shocks it without respect;
590 Filling his sails more force to recollect.
     Th' English from shore the iron deaf invoke
     For its last aid: 'Hold chain, or we are broke.'
     But with her sailing weight, the Holland keel,
     Snapping the brittle links, does thorough reel;
595 And to the rest the opened passage show;
     Monck from the bank the dismal sight does view.
     Our feathered gallants, which came down that day
     To be spectators safe of the new play,
     Leave him alone when first they hear the gun
600 (Cornbury the fleetest) and to London run.
     Our seamen, whom no danger's shape could fright,
     Unpaid, refuse to mount our ships for spite,
     Or to their fellows swim on board the Dutch,
     Which show the tempting metal in their clutch.
605 Oft had he sent of Duncombe and of Legge

     Cannon and powder, but in vain, to beg;
     And Upnor Castle's ill-deserted wall,
     Now needful, does for ammunition call.
     He finds, wheresoe'er he succour might expect,
610 Confusion, folly, treach'ry, fear, neglect.
     But when the *Royal Charles* (what rage, what grief)
     He saw seized, and could give her no relief!
     That sacred keel which had, as he, restored
     His exiled sovereign on its happy board,
615 And thence the British admiral became,
     Crowned, for that merit, with their master's name;
     That pleasure-boat of war, in whose dear side
     Secure so oft he had this foe defied,
     Now a cheap spoil, and the mean victor's slave,
620 Taught the Dutch colours from its top to wave;
     Of former glories the reproachful thought,
     With present shame compared, his mind distraught.
     Such from Euphrates' bank, a tigress fell
     After the robbers for her whelps doth yell;
625 But sees enraged the river flow between,
     Frustrate revenge and love, by loss more keen,

---

585. within] i.e. in Chatham, behind the defensive chain (see below, l. 586).
586–95. The chain across the Medway was 8 feet 10 inches deep, and held in place by pulleys. Cp. Joost van den Vondel, 'De Zeeleeu op den Teems' (The Sealion on the Thames) (1667), ll. 32–6: 'daer Brittenlant/Trots zijn yzre keten spant:/Maar wat kan een keten baeten/Als de Leeu van Hollant brult,/En de zee met dootschrik vult?' (There the British proudly draw across their chain. But what avail is a chain when the Lion of Holland roars, and fills the sea with mortal fear?).
587. Engine] a) device (*OED* n. 4) b) instrument of war (*OED* n. 5).
588. captivate] capture (*OED* v. 1 b).
589. skipper] sea captain: from the Dutch *schipper* (*OED* n.² 1). *rude*] uncivilized (*OED* a. A I 3 b).
590. recollect] gather (*OED* v.¹ I 1).
591. invoke] call on earnestly (*OED* v. 4).
593–4. The Dutch ships were helped by an unusually high tide (Hutton (1989), 269).
593. keel] ship (*OED* n.¹ 2); appropriate since a) the keel is also the name of the lowest part of the hull (*OED* n.¹ 1), which would have made contact with the chain b) M. may have supposed that keel was related to Dutch *kiel*, a flat-bottomed vessel.
594. reel] rush violently (*OED* v.¹ 3).
596. dismal] boding, causing disaster (*OED* B a. 2).
600. Cornbury] see above, l. 218 n.
604. tempting metal] i.e. coins. English seamen were thought to have been bribed to fight for the Dutch: see Pepys, 8.267; *CSPD* 1667, 323; *Naval Minutes*, 251.
605. Duncombe] see above, l. 207 n. *Legge*] Colonel William Legge (1608?–70), MP for Southampton, Master of the Armouries and Treasurer of the Ordnance.
607. Upnor Castle] two miles from Chatham; inadequately supplied by the ordnance office to repel the Dutch attack. *ill-deserted*] unfortunately neglected (by the government) and

hence undermanned the garrison was ordered to disband on 24 November 1666 (*CSPD*, 1666–7, 287) as well as under-supplied, so the military desertion is by the government rather than the soldiers.
611. Royal Charles] formerly *Naseby* (complete with a Cromwellian figurehead), it carried Charles II to Dover in 1660.
613. keel] see above, l. 593 n.
615. admiral] flagship (*OED* n. 5).
617. pleasure-boat of war] Charles II was fond of recreational sailing, and *OED* dates the first usage of 'pleasure-boat' as 1661.
618. he . . . defied] Monck had sailed for the Commonwealth in *Royal Charles* under its former name, *Naseby* (see above, l. 611 n.).
619. mean] of low degree; undistinguished (*OED* a.¹ I 1).
620. Taught] i.e. by the Dutch.
623–8. Such . . . harm] Parker, *N & Q*, 52 (2003), 318–24, argues that this passage is indebted thematically and textually to two interacting stories, that of Tereus, Procne and Philomela in Ovid, *Metamorphoses*, VI, ll. 426–674 (especially ll. 636–46) and du Bartas, *Divine Weeks*, trans. Sylvester, II.iv.4.245–8; 329, 332–6, 340–2, 345–6, 799–1208: 'The passages from the King James *Bible* and *Du Bartas* II.iv.4. reinforce some of the elements of Ovid's story of Tereus, Procne, and Philomela: the tigress; the dragging away and/or death of the children; and the tearing at the breast. They also supply the missing elements of Marvell's epic simile: the adjective 'fell' applied to the Tygress; the river Euphrates; the Tygress's impotent rage, as conveyed by M.'s *frustrate* revenge' and *useless* claws'; and the 'Robbers', in the person of the Chaldean troops who lead Zedekiah, his wives and his daughters ('whelps') into captivity in Babylon.'
623. Euphrates] possibly induced by the similarity of 'Tigris' to 'tigress', the former being the other major river in the river system of what is now central Turkey and northern Syria. *fell*] fierce (*OED* a. A 1).
626. Frustrate . . . love] i.e. 'love and revenge frustrated'.

At her own breast her useless claws does arm:
She tears herself, since him she cannot harm.
      The guards, placed for the chain's and fleet's defence,
Long since were fled on many a feigned pretence.
Daniel had there adventured, man of might;
Sweet painter, draw his picture while I write.
Paint him of person tall, and big of bone,
Large limbs like ox, not to be killed but shown.
Scarce can burnt iv'ry feign a hair so black,
Or face so red, thine ochre and thy lac.
Mix a vain terror in his martial look,
And all those lines by which men are mistook;
But when, by shame constrained to go on board,
He heard how the wild cannon nearer roared;
And saw himself confined like sheep in pen,
Daniel then thought he was in lion's den.
And when the frightful fireships he saw,

645 Pregnant with sulphur, to him nearer draw,
Captain, lieutenant, ensign, all make haste
Ere in the fiery furnace they be cast.
Three children tall, unsinged, away they row,
Like Shadrach, Meschach, and Abednego.
      Not so brave Douglas, on whose lovely chin
650 The early down but newly did begin;
And modest Beauty yet his sex did veil,
While envious virgins hope he is a male.
His yellow locks curl back themselves to seek,
Nor other courtship knew but to his cheek.
655 Oft, as he in chill Esk or Seine by night
Hardened and cooled his limbs, so soft, so white,
Among the reeds, to be espied by him,
The nymphs would rustle; he would forward swim.
They sighed and said, 'Fond boy, why so untame,
660 That fliest love's fires, reserved for other flame?'

---

629. guards] desertion was reported at Sheerness, and at least one of the ships guarding the chain withdrew from it too soon (Pepys, 8.308–10).

631. Daniel] probably Sir Thomas Daniel, who commanded a company of footguards, who were supposed to defend *Loyal London* or *Royal James*.

634. shown] displayed.

635. burnt iv'ry] fine soft black pigment, created by calcining ivory in a closed vessel (*OED*).

636. ochre] class of earths used as pigments, from yellow to deep brown in colour (*OED* n. 1 a). *lac*] crimson pigment (*OED* n¹ 2; 'lake': *OED* n.⁶ 1).

637. vain] a) useless (*OED* a. I 1) b) conceited (*OED* a. I 4). *terror*] i.e. terrifying look.

638. lines] lines employed in drawing a picture; distinctive features of a composition (*OED* n.² II 7 d); cp. Jonson, 'Epistle. To Katherine, Lady Aubigny', l. 20: 'feare to draw true lines, 'cause others paint.'

642. Daniel . . . lion's den] alluding to the story of Daniel being thrown into the lion's den by King Darius (Dan. 6:10–23).

643. fireships] ships loaded with explosives, and set on fire, then cast adrift among enemy ships. The Bodleian Library copy of a treatise by Richard Allestree, *The Causes of the Decay of Christian Piety* (1667; shelfmark Vet. A3.e.517), has a wood-cut of a ship on fire pasted onto the title page, thereby linking the calamity of the firing of the ships in the Medway, as well as the explicit references to the Great Fire of London, with general themes of moral decay.

647. tall] a) handsome (*OED* a. 2 b) b) brave (*OED* a. 3). *unsinged*] untouched by fire (*OED* ppl. a.).

648. Shadrach . . . Abednego] three companions of Daniel who survived the fiery furnace (see Dan. 3:13–30).

649–96. Not in *1697*; the passage appears, in slightly modified form, at the beginning of *The Loyal Scot*.

649. Douglas] Archibald Douglas, commander of a company of Scottish troops, died in defending *Royal Oak*, which was fired by the Dutch. It was Cowley and not M. whom some expected to honour Douglas in verse: see Sir William Temple to Lord Lisle, August 1667, in Temple, *Works* (1720), 2. 40: 'I would have been glad to have seen Mr Cowley, before he had died, celebrate Captain Douglas, who stood and burnt in one of our ships at Chatham, when his soldiers left him, because it should never be said, a Douglas quitted his post without order.'

Dzelzainis (in Chernaik and Dzelzainis, eds (1999), 290–312) argues that Douglas was in all probability, and was known to be, a Roman Catholic. The significance of Douglas' religion is more important for his appearance in *Loyal Scot*. Nonetheless, M. appears covertly to pick up on the theme of the loyalty of the English Catholics, a fact that was much proclaimed by their apologists. The extraordinary description of Douglas is aesthetically Counter-Reformation, placing the hero as the truest, beatified martyr (for comparisons with M.'s Protestant martyr figures, see Duncan-Jones, *PBA*, 61 (1975), 275–6, 278).

650. early down] the beginnings of a beard. Cp. Virgil, *Aeneid*, IX, ll. 179–81: 'Euryalus / . . . / ora puer prima signans intonsa iuventa' (Euryalus . . . a boy who showed on his unshaven cheek the first bloom of youth). See also below, ll. 693–6 n.

651. modest] a) retiring, not forward (*OED* a. 2) b) chaste; usually applied to women (*OED* a. 3).

655. Esk] The River Esk flows in a north-easterly direction, south of Edinburgh, into the Firth of Forth at Musselburgh. *Seine*] referring to the fact that Douglas' regiment had served in France.

657–8. Among . . . swim] Turner (in Chernaik and Dzelzainis, eds (1999), 239–40), relates M.'s description to painting that combined the heroic and the erotic (e.g. Rubens's painting 'Landing at Marseilles') where the naked nymphs remain in the foreground of the picture.

660. for other flame] Cp. *The Third Advice*, ll. 421–2: 'Dear George, sad fate, vain mind that me didst please/ To meet thine with far other flames than these!' *flame*] Cp. Virgil's use of *ardor* (a) flame, fire (b) eagerness, ardor: 'dine hinc ardorem mentibus addunt,/ Euryale, an sua cuique deus fit dira cupido?' (Do the Gods, Euryalus, put this fire in our hearts, or does his own wild longing become to each man a god?) (*Aeneid*, IX, ll. 184–5; see also below, ll. 693–6 n.). Fire took on a broad dimension of cultural symbolism at this time, beyond the immediate context of war and the Great Fire of London. It was associated with national triumph (through the victory bonfire), and hence with the precariousness of celebrating victory, which could easily turn to disaster. An account of competing English and Dutch bonfires in Brussels in June and July 1666, arranged by the resident of each country, resulted in the near collapse of the very tall Dutch bonfire, and violence among the spectators and guards (Bod., MS Carte 35, fol. 4ʳ).

Fixed on his ship, he faced that horrid day
And wondered much at those that run away:
Nor other fear himself could comprehend
Then, lest heaven fall ere thither he ascend,
665 But entertains the while his time too short
With birding at the Dutch as if in sport:
Or waves his sword, and could he them conjure
Within its circle, knows himself secure.
The fatal bark him boards with grappling fire,
670 And safely through its port the Dutch retire.
That precious life he yet disdains to save,
Or with known art to try the gentle wave.
Much him the honours of his ancient race
Inspire, nor would he his own deeds deface;
675 And secret joy in his calm soul does rise,
That Monck looks on to see how Douglas dies.

Like a glad lover, the fierce flames he meets,
And tries his first embraces in their sheets.
His shape exact, which the bright flames enfold,
680 Like the sun's statue stands of burnished gold.
Round the transparent fire about him glows,
As the clear amber on the bee does close,
And, as on angels' heads their glories shine,
His burning locks adorn his face divine.
685 But when in his immortal mind he felt
His altering form and soldered limbs to melt,
Down on the deck he laid himself and died,
With his dear sword reposing by his side,
And on the flaming plank, so rests his head
690 As one that's warmed himself and gone to bed.
His ship burns down, and with his relics sinks,
And the sad stream beneath his ashes drinks.

---

666. birding] shooting with a musket (*OED* v. 2).

667–8. conjure . . . circle] an image drawn from magic: the conjuror summons supernatural powers within his magic circle, around which were inscribed powerful symbols (see, e.g. the woodcut of Faustus conjuring the devil from within his circle: Christopher Marlowe, *The Tragicall History of the Life and Death of Doctor Faustus* (1624), title page); had he the Dutch within the circle described by his sword (corresponding to a magic wand), Douglas would be able to silence them.

667. conjure] stressed on second syllable.

669. fatal bark] Cp. Milton, *Lycidas* (1637), ll. 100–2: 'It was that fatal and perfidious bark/Built in the eclipse, and rigged with curses dark,/That sunk so low that sacred head of thine.' *grappling fire*] the fireship transmits fire as opposed to men, who would have boarded by means of grappling irons.

670. port] opening in the side of a ship (*OED* n.³ 2 a).

672. known art] i.e. of swimming.

673–4. In *The Humble Apologie* (1666), 34, Castlemaine pointed to 'my Lord *Douglas* [Lord George Douglas] and his brave *Scots* . . . who scorned to receave wages of those that have declared Warr against *England*.' (See also above, 351–2.) In 1674, he published the third version of this work in which the loyalty of Douglas' Scottish Catholics is contrasted with the treachery of Dissenters and republicans during the Medway raid (see Dzelzainis, in Chernaik and Dzelzainis, eds (1999), 295–6).

674. deface] defame, discredit.

676. Monck] see above, 336–8; here Monck plays the role of Neptune in the tradition of epillya (brief epics, usually of an amorous nature); see, e.g. Marlowe, *Hero and Leander* (1598), ll. 649–76 (or Sest. II, ll. 165–92).

677–92. Duncan-Jones, *PBA*, 61 (1975), 276, 278, compares Douglas's martyrdom with the 'martyrdom' of the speaker in *Flecknoe, an English Priest at Rome*, ll. 31–5, alluding, she argues, to the martyrdom of St Lawrence (see above, 163–70). Dzelzainis (in Chernaik and Dzelzainis, eds (1999), 299), argues that, if Douglas was a Catholic, he would have a greater claim than the speaker of *Flecknoe* to be a latterday St Lawrence. His martyrdom thus hints at beatification, although 'the circumstances of Douglas's death both qualify him for and disenable him from being venerated as a saint in the usual way'. Thus, M. institutes 'a cult based purely on images', and one

derived most obviously from the woodcuts accompanying Foxe's *Acts and Monuments* (1583); for critical discussion, see John R. Knott (1993).

677–90. Like . . . bed] Turner (in Chernaik and Dzelzainis, eds (1999), 240–1) regards the portrayal of Douglas's fiery death as 'a posture in the Renaissance sense, a display of copulation transmuted into art', representing a heroic death as an erotic encounter in an 'intimate domestic interior'. Some of the martyrs immortalized by Foxe are described as going to sleep in suffering fiery martyrdom (e.g. Anne Askew: 'being compassed in with flames of fire, as a blessed sacrifice unto God, she slept in the Lord AD 1546'); John Foxe, *The Acts and Monuments*, ed. Josiah Pratt (1877), V.550.

678. sheets] a) of flames b) as if Douglas were embracing the flames as his lover under the sheets on a bed.

679. exact] perfect (*OED* a. I 1).

680. sun's statue] A bronze statue in Rome, massive but beautiful and lifelike, thought to be the image of the sun or of Rome, and to have been brought from Rhodes. The bronze was gilded; it shone in the dark and rotated in a motion equal to that of the sun, which it always faced. Pope Gregory I (or in some sources Sylvester I) ordered it melted with a huge fire. Only the head and one hand, holding a sphere, survived. These were placed on marble pillars in front of the papal palace. (Magister Gregorius, *The Marvels of Rome* (*c.* 13th century), trans. and ed. J. Osborne (Toronto, 1987), 22–3).

681–2. The flames do not penetrate Douglas but preserve him in death as a refuge from dishonour.

682. clear . . . close] Cp. Martial, *Epigrams*, IV.xxxii.1–2: 'Et latet et lucet Phaethonide condita gutta,/ut videatur apis nectare clusa suo' (In an amber-drop the bee lies hid and lightens, so that it seems to be shut in its native sweets) (Duncan-Jones).

683. glories] haloes (*OED* n. 9).

686. soldered] closely united (*OED* ppl. a. 2).

690. As . . . bed] Cp. *The Loyal Scot*, l. 56: 'As one that hugs himself in a warm bed.' The later poem's version occurs also in *BL 27*.

691. His] 'The' in *The Loyal Scot*, l. 57. *relics*] a) remains of a person (*OED* 2) b) bearing the sense of the remaining parts of saints and martyrs, venerated in Roman Catholic devotion; see above, 168–9.

Fortunate boy, if either pencil's fame,
Or if my verse can propagate thy name,
When Oeta and Alcides are forgot,
Our English youth shall sing the valiant Scot.
    Each doleful day still with fresh loss returns:
The *Loyal London* now a third time burns,
And the true *Royal Oak* and *Royal James*,
Allied in fate, increase, with theirs, her flames.
Of all our navy none should now survive,
But that the ships themselves were taught to dive,
And the kind river in its creek them hides,
Fraughting their piercèd keels with oozy tides.
    Up to the bridge contagious terror struck:
The Tower itself with the near danger shook,
And were not Ruyter's maw with ravage cloyed,
Ev'n London's ashes had been then destroyed.
Officious Fear, however, to prevent
Our loss does so much more our loss augment:

The Dutch had robbed those jewels of the crown:
Our merchantmen, lest they be burned, we drown.
So when the fire did not enough devour,
The houses were demolished near the Tower.
715 Those ships that yearly from their teeming howl
Unloaded here the birth of either pole –
Furs from the north and silver from the west,
Wines from the south, and spices from the east;
From Gambo gold, and from the Ganges gems –
720 Take a short voyage underneath the Thames:
Once a deep river, now with timber floored,
And shrunk, lest navigable, to a ford.
    Now (nothing more at Chatham left to burn),
The Holland squadron leisurely return,
725 And spite of Ruperts and of Albemarles,
To Ruyter's triumph lead the captive *Charles*.
The pleasing sight he often does prolong:
Her masts erect, tough cordage, timbers strong,

693–6. Echoes Virgil's memorializing of Nisus and Euryalus, slain by the Rutulians while on a night raid: 'Fortunati ambo! si quid mea carmina possunt,/nulla dies umquam memori vos eximet aevo,/dum domus Aeneae Capitoli immobile saxum/accolet imperiumque pater Romanus habebit' (Happy pair! If aught my verse avail, no day shall ever blot you from the memory of time, so long as the house of Aeneas shall dwell on the Capitol's unshaken rock, and the Father of Rome hold sovereign sway!) (*Aeneid*, IX, ll. 446–9) (Margoliouth; Russell Lynch, private communication). As M.'s narrator appears moved by Douglas's youth and beauty, so Nisus and Euryalus are closely bonded, so that Nisus sacrifices himself to avenge Euryalus's death. Euryalus 'sinks' in, compared to wilting or severed plants (*Aeneid*, IX, ll. 433–7), just as Douglas melts. M.'s homoerotic narrative is thus suggested in part by Virgil's homosocial tragedy.
693. pencil's] paintbrush's: see above, l. 19 n.
694. propagate] a) disseminate (*OED* v. 3) b) reproduce (*OED* v. 1); hinting at the tragic waste of the virgin soldier's death, who has lost the chance to propagate himself and his family's name (Creaser, in Chernaik and Dzelzainis, eds (1999), 156).
695. Oeta and Alcides] Alcides (Hercules) was burned alive on Mount Oeta, on a pyre of his own making (see Ovid, *Metamorphoses*, IX, l. 229 ff.).
698. London . . . burns] *London* was blown up in March 1665 (see above, *The Second Advice To a Painter*, ll. 13–17); the city of London burned in the Great Fire of 1666; now *Loyal London* follows its namesakes. The line shares phrasing with the entry in Evelyn's diary (28 June 1667): 'Here in the River of Chatham, just before the Towne lay the Carkasse of the *Lond.* (now the 3d time burnt).' Cp. also Dryden, *Annus Mirabilis*, ll. 601–16.
699. Royal Oak and Royal James] English ships destroyed by the Dutch.
700. Allied] playing on the sense of a formal military alliance (*OED* ppl. a. 1 b).
702. ships . . . dive] after the Dutch raid, other high-rating ships moored near Chatham were sunk as a measure of protection: it was hoped to raise them later (*CSPD*, 15 June 1667).
704. Fraughting] loading (*OED* v. 1). *oozy*] muddy (*OED* a II 2).

705. bridge] i.e. London Bridge. *contagious terror*] an image derived from plague and Great Fire experience and literature.
707–8. And . . . destroyed] Panic was enhanced during the Great Fire by the fear the foreign invasion was imminent. London was like the first, not the second, Troy: see Simon Ford, *The Conflagration of London* (1667), ll. 89–96.
707. ravage] destruction (*OED* n. 2).
709. Officious] unduly interfering (*OED* a. 3).
711. jewels of the crown] i.e. the ships burned in the Chatham raid. Many of the royal jewels were lost in the London fire of 1541: see John Stow, *A Survey of London* (1598, rev. 1603), ed. Henry Morley (1912; republished 1994), 293. See also above, 706.
712. merchantmen . . . drown] some merchantmen and new fireships were sunk below Woolwich in an attempt to frustrate a Dutch advance up the Thames to London; Pepys, 14 June 1667 (8.270–1), reported that several of the merchantmen were richly laden with goods, that some of the fireships had been newly fitted, and that one of the sunken ships was foreign and had been promised security.
713–14. the fire . . . Tower] part of the supposed mismanagement of the containment of the Great Fire: see Porter (1996), 35–44.
715. teeming] pregnant (*OED* ppl. a. 1). *howl 1689+* hole *1697* 'howle' corrected to 'hole' in *BL 27*; a) ship's hold (variant spelling of 'holl', *OED* n. 2) b) as if it were a verb, the imagined cries of the 'pregnant' ships in labour, giving birth to their cargoes. Margoliouth suggested 'howl' as a north country form of 'hollow' ('holl', *OED* n. 1).
719. Gambo] Gambia. *Ganges*] Cp. *To his Coy Mistress*, ll. 5–6: 'Thou by the Indian Ganges' side/Shouldst rubies find.'
722. shrunk] Cp. *A Poem upon the Death of his Late Highness the Lord Protector*, ll. 167–9: 'Stand back ye seas, and shrunk beneath the veil/Of your abyss, with covered head bewail/Your monarch.'
725. Ruperts . . . Albemarles] who had organized the coastal defences.
726. lead . . . Charles] but the ship ran aground, and was consequently burnt by its captors (Coventry to Ormonde, 15 June 1667, Bod., MS Carte 47, fol. 486ʳ).
728. cordage] rigging of a ship (*OED*).

Her moving shapes, all these he does survey,
730 And all admires, but most his easy prey.
The seaman search her all within, without:
Viewing her strength, they yet their conquest doubt;
Then with rude shouts, secure, the air they vex,
With gamesome joy insulting on her decks.
735 Such the feared Hebrew, captive, blinded, shorn,
Was led about in sport, the public scorn.
     Black day accursed! On thee let no man hale
Out of the port, or dare to hoist a sail,
Or row a boat in thy unlucky hour.
740 Thee, the year's monster, let thy dam devour,
And constant Time, to keep his course yet right,
Fill up thy space with a redoubled night.
When agèd Thames was bound with fetters base,
And Medway chaste ravished before his face,
745 And their dear offspring murdered in their sight,
Thou and thy fellows held'st the odious light.
Sad change since first that happy pair was wed,
When all the rivers graced their nuptial bed.
And Father Neptune promised to resign
750 His empire old to their immortal line!

Now with vain grief their vainer hopes they rue,
Themselves dishonoured, and the gods untrue,
And to each other, helpless couple, moan,
As the sad tortoise for the sea does groan.
755 But most they for their darling *Charles* complain,
And were it burnt, yet less would be their pain.
To see that fatal pledge of sea command,
Now in the ravisher De Ruyter's hand,
The Thames roared, swooning Medway turned her tid
760 And were they mortal, both for grief had died.
     The court in farthing yet itself does please,
(And female Stuart there rules the four seas),
But Fate does still accumulate our woes,
And Richmond her commands, as Ruyter those.
765   After this loss, to relish discontent,
Someone must be accused by punishment.
All our miscarriages on Pett must fall:
His name alone seems fit to answer all.
Whose counsel first did this mad war beget?
770 Who all commands sold through the navy? Pett.
Who would not follow when the Dutch were beat?
Who treated out the time at Bergen? Pett.

---

729. shapes] structures (*OED* n.[1] 3).
733. shouts . . . vex] When the Dutch had succeeded in the difficult task of navigating *Royal Charles* down the Chatham River, they celebrated by firing their cannon (Pepys, 8.343).
734. gamesome] merry, playful. *insulting*] a) triumphing, boasting (*OED* v. 1) b) leaping (*OED* v. 5).
735–6. feared Hebrew . . . scorn] Samson was paraded in sport before the Philistines, before being set between the pillars: see Judges 16:25.
736. scorn] i.e. the object of scorn.
737. hale] sail before the wind (*OED* v.[1] 4).
740. Thee . . . devour] whereas in *Paradise Lost*, II, ll. 785–809, Death rapes his mother Sin, and 'me his parent would full soon devour/For want of other prey'. *dam*] mother (*OED* n.[2] 3).
742. redoubled] made twice as long (*OED* v.[1] 1).
743–5. agèd Thames . . . sight] In Spenser, *The Faerie Queene* (1596), IV.xi.42–3, the Giant Blomius rapes the Nymph Rheusa to produce the three Irish rivers: the Shure, the Newre and the Barow. See below, ll. 747–50 n.
747–50. The marriage of Thames and Medway was recounted in Spenser, *The Faerie Queene*, IV.xi, esp. sts. 45–53. IV.xi. ll. 1–3 contains the apt prophecy that the River Welland 'Shall drowne all Holland with his excrement'.
749. Father Neptune] common form of address in epic: see, e.g. Virgil, *Aeneid*, V, ll. 14, 863.
754. sad tortoise] Gearin-Tosh, *N & Q*, n.s., 215 (1970), 256, notes the belief that the sea tortoise made terrible grievous noises when captured.
757. fatal] a) deadly (*OED* a. 6) b) doomed (*OED* a. 2). *pledge*] a) promise (*OED* n. 3) b) hostage (*OED* n. 1 b).
761–4. The court . . . those] Frances Teresa Stuart (1647–1702), desired by Charles II as his mistress; married Charles Stuart, third Duke of Richmond (1639–72), in March 1667; she was the model for Britannia stamped on the medal celebrating naval victories in 1667. Both it and the farthing of

Charles II carried the motto *Quattuor maria vindico* (I rule the four seas). Cp. *A Dialogue between the Two Horses*, l. 62.
761. farthing] a) i.e. coinage. b) figuratively, very small matters (*OED* n. 2).
762. female Stuart] Riebling, *SEL*, 35 (1995), 151, suggests that there could also be an undertone of reference to an emasculated Charles.
765. relish] make pleasant to the taste (*OED* v.[1] 1a).
766. Whereas punishment should properly follow conviction.
767. miscarriages] instances of maladministration, blunders (*OED* n. 2). *Pett*] Peter Pett (1610–*c.* 1672) Navy Commissioner at Chatham, 1648–67; Master-Shipwright at Chatham, 1664–67; MP for Rochester, FRS (1662); generally blamed for the Medway disaster: dismissed, arrested, threatened with impeachment, but finally allowed to retire into private life. His administration of the navy was criticized by many, and the charges of peculation probably hold truth; however, M.'s sense that he was being made a scapegoat for the shortcomings of others is consonant with other testimony to his administrative and shipbuilding skills. Pepys was present at his interrogation by a Privy Council committee and was sure that he was being framed by Arlington and Coventry, who were 'upon their own purgation' (8.278–9). Lely painted him in a maritime scene featuring 'The Sovereign of the Seas', part of the naval iconography that M.'s satire subverts. M. spoke in Pett's defence in the House of Commons on 31 October 1667. Interestingly, Milward called Pett's defenders, presumably including M., 'sectaries' (Milward (1938), 127).
771. Who . . . beat] It was the Duke of York who would not follow the Dutch fleet, on 3 June 1665: see above, *The Second Advice*, ll. 233–42.
772. Who . . . Bergen] It was the Earl of Sandwich who, having located the Dutch fleet in the harbour at Bergen, negotiated with the Danes (to whom Bergen belonged), thereby allowing the Dutch to have time to defend themselves in Bergen: see above, *The Second Advice To a Painter*, ll. 253–8, 271–86. *treated*] negotiated (*OED* v. 1 b).

Who the Dutch fleet with storms disabled met?
And rifling prizes, them neglected? Pett.
5 Who with false news prevented the Gazette,
The fleet divided, writ for Rupert? Pett.
Who all our seamen cheated of their debt,
And all our prizes who did swallow? Pett.
Who did advise no navy out to set?
0 And who the forts left unrepairèd? Pett.
Who to supply with powder did forget
Landguard, Sheerness, Gravesend and Upnor? Pett.
Who all our ships exposed in Chatham's net?
Who should it be but the fanatic Pett?
5 Pett, the sea-architect, in making ships
Was the first cause of all these naval slips:
Had he not built, none of these faults had been:
If no creation, there had been no sin.
But his great crime, one boat away he sent,
0 That lost our fleet and did our flight prevent.
Then (that Reward might in its turn take place,

And march with Punishment in equal pace),
Southampton dead, much of the treasure's care
And place in Council fell to Duncombe's share.
795 All men admired he to that pitch could fly:
Powder ne'er blew man up so soon so high.
But sure his late good husbandry in petre
Showed him to manage the Exchequer meeter;
And who the forts would not vouchsafe a corn,
800 To lavish the King's money more would scorn.
Who hath no chimneys, to give all is best,
And ablest speaker, who of law has least;
Who less estate, for Treasurer most fit,
And for a counsellor, he that has least wit.
805 But the true cause was that, in's brother May,
The Exchequer might the Privy Purse obey.
       But now draws near the Parliament's return;
Hyde and the court again begin to mourn:
Frequent in council, earnest in debate,
810 All arts they try how to prolong its date.

773–4. *Who . . . neglected*] again, the fault of Sandwich: see above, *The Second Advice To a Painter*, ll. 293–308.
774. *rifling*] plundering (*OED* vbl. n.).
775–6. *Who . . . Rupert*] the fleet was divided in 1666 between the commands of Albemarle and Rupert. In 1666, Rupert sailed westwards to meet a French fleet (on the evidence of a rumour discovered later to be false). In the meantime, Albemarle engaged the Dutch in battle in the Downs; the message to recall Rupert was delayed, so that he arrived only in time for the last day of the Four Days' Battle. See above, *The Third Advice to a Painter*, ll. 283–94, where the blame for the division of the fleet is cast largely on Arlington. *prevented*] anticipated (*OED* v. III 12). *Gazette*] *The London Gazette* which printed news derived from Arlington's intelligence reports.
777–8. *Who . . . swallow*] see above, ll. 314 n., 583 n.
779. *Who . . . set*] According to Evelyn, the culprit was Sir William Coventry (*Diary*, 29 July 1667).
781–2. *Who . . . Upnor*] Sir John Duncombe's duty (see below, ll. 794–8 n.).
782. *Landguard, Sheerness, Gravesend*] Landguard was a fort at Felixstowe attacked by the Dutch in 1667.
783. *Who . . . net*] Pett was specifically blamed for not mooring the higher ratings further up the Thames.
784. *fanatic*] religious nonconformist (*OED* n. B 2); Pett had served as a Navy Commissioner under the Commonwealth, and is thus identified with Puritan zealots.
785. *sea-architect*] i.e. shipbuilder; Pett was originally a master shipwright.
786. *first cause*] taken from the theological definition for the original cause, the Creator of the universe (*OED* n. I 5). Lord detects an ironic parallel between Pett and the first shipbuilder, Noah. *slips*] a) blunders (*OED* n.³ III 10 c) b) stone landing places beside navigable water (*OED* n.³ I 1). *OED* records the first usage of 'slip' as an inclined plane for shipbuilding or repairing in 1769.
787–8. *Had . . . sin*] i.e. the logic by which Pett is blamed would make God himself responsible for the Fall.
789. *one boat . . . sent*] Pepys (19, 30 June 1667, 8.278, 309) reported that Pett was accused of using boats to carry his own goods away from Chatham.

792. *pace*] step (*OED* n.¹ I 1).
793–4. *Southampton . . . share*] Thomas Wriothesley, fourth earl of Southampton (1607–67), Lord High Treasurer (1660–67), had died in the spring; a friend of Clarendon; uncorrupt but ineffective. Sir John Duncombe was made a Treasury Commissioner in May 1667; see also above, l. 207 n.
794. *Council*] i.e. the Privy Council.
795. *admired*] wondered (*OED* v. 2) *pitch . . . fly*] Duncombe is imagined as a bird of prey climbing to the height from which it swoops down on its prey: see 'pitch' (*OED* n.² III 18). Cp. Pepys, 31 May 1667 (8.244): 'Here I saw Duncomb look so big, and takes as much state on him, as if he had been born a Lord.'
797. *petre*] i.e. saltpetre, potassium nitrate, chief constituent of gunpowder; Duncombe had previously been made an Ordnance Commissioner in November 1664, and had made a great success of his office.
798. *meeter*] more fittingly (*OED* B adv.).
799. *corn*] grain of gunpowder (*OED* n.¹ 1 b); but M. plays on his analogy between the Ordnance Commission and agriculture (see above, l. 797, 'husbandry').
801–4. A sarcastic attack on Duncombe's lack of wealth (he has little property, no chimneys, and hence is not subject to chimney tax), knowledge (he knows no law) and talent (he has no wit). The sense appears to be 'it might be thought virtuous to have a man without means in charge of the exchequer', but the real reason for his appointment was so that his brother-in-law could keep control of him, and thus the exchequer would have to obey the demands of the royal household (see above, l. 399 n.).
804. *counsellor*] see above, l. 794 n. *wit*] intelligence.
805. *brother May*] see above, l. 399 n. Duncombe was Baptist May's brother-in-law; for May, see above, 399 n..
806. *Privy Purse*] short for Keeper of the Privy Purse (May), an officer of the royal household charged with the payment of the private expenses of the sovereign ('privy', *OED* a. 9 a.).
807. *Parliament's return*] on 25 July: see below, l. 826 n.
810. *prolong*] postpone (*OED* v. 3).

Grave primate Sheldon (much in preaching there)
Blames the last session and this more does fear:
With Boynton or with Myddleton 'twere sweet,
But with a Parliament abhors to meet,
815 And thinks 'twill ne'er be well within this nation,
Till it be governed by a convocation.
But in the Thames' mouth still De Ruyter laid;
The peace not sure, new army must be paid.
Hyde said he hourly waits for a dispatch;
820 Harry came post just as he showed his watch,
All to agree the articles were clear–
The Holland fleet and Parliament so near–
Yet Harry must job back, and all mature,
Binding, ere th' Houses meet, the treaty sure.
825 And 'twixt necessity and spite, till then,
Let them come up so to go down again.
   Up ambles country justice on his pad,
And vest bespeaks to be more seemly clad.
Plain gentlemen are in stagecoach o'erthrown,
830 And deputy-lieutenants in their own.

The portly burgess, through the weather hot,
Does for his corporation sweat and trot.
And all with sun and choler come adust
And threaten Hyde to raise a greater dust.
835 But fresh as from the mint, the courtiers fine
Salute them, smiling at their vain design,
And Turnour gay up to his perch does march
With face new bleached, smoothened and stiff with star
Tells them he at Whitehall had took a turn
840 And for three days thence moves them to adjourn.
'Not so!' quoth Tomkins, and straight drew his tongue
Trusty as steel, that always ready hung;
And so, proceeding in his motion warm,
Th'army soon raised, he doth as soon disarm.
845 True Trojan! While this town can girls afford,
And long as cider lasts in Hereford,
The girls shall always kiss thee, though grown old,
And in eternal healths thy name be trolled.
   Meanwhile the certain news of peace arrives
850 At court, and so reprieves their guilty lives.

---

811. Sheldon] Gilbert Sheldon (1598–1677), Archbishop of Canterbury; reputedly a womanizer, although this is not borne out by most biographical sources. Pepys heard rumours that Sheldon 'doth keep a wench, and that he is as very a wencher as can be' on 29 July 1667 (8.364) – plausibly information circulated by critics of the government like Buckingham, or the Archbishop's enemies at court, such as Lady Castlemaine. Sheldon had been a friend and admirer of Clarendon's since the 1630s; he was regarded by his opponents as the epitome of a politic divine, using religion as an instrument of government, and at the expense of spirituality, of which he was felt to have very little (DNB). See also below, *The Loyal Scot*, l. 160 n.
813. Boynton . . . Myddleton] Katherine Boynton (d. 1678), Maid of Honour to the Queen from 1660, and Jane Myddleton (d. 1692), wife of Charles, were both court beauties. Cp. Bod. MS Eng. hist *c*. 57, fol. 2ʳ: 'It is a wise child that knowes her owne mother, written by Mʳˢ Warmstry and dedicated to Mʳˢ Boynton with severall presedents, proveing that it is not a Miracle at Court to have our [*sic*] child before marriage.'
815–16. Both lines have, exceptionally, eleven syllables.
816. convocation] provincial assembly of the Church of England.
818. peace not sure] i.e. the peace treaty had not been signed.
819. dispatch] message (from Breda) (*OED* n. II 8).
820. Harry] Henry Coventry, just arrived from Breda; see above, l. 225 n. *post*] with speed (*OED* adv. b).
823. job] i.e. 'rush back', derived from 'job', hurting a horse's mouth with the bit (in order to go faster; *OED* v.¹). *mature*] bring to completion (*OED* v. 2).
826. Parliament met on 25 July and was dismissed four days later.
827. pad] road horse (*OED* n.² 4).
828. vest] long sleeveless garment worn underneath the coat; introduced by Charles II on 8 October 1666, in order to make English fashion distinct from French influence. *bespeaks*] indicates (*OED* v. II 7) *seemly*] a) appropriately (*OED* adv. 2) b) moderately (*OED* adv. 3).

830. own] i.e. their own coaches.
831. burgess] MP for a borough or corporate town (*OED* n. 1 b).
833. choler . . . adust] choler adust (or black choler, black bile) was a supposed thick black, acrid fluid secreted by the renal glands, believed to be the cause of melancholy (*OED*.¹ 4). *choler*] a) bile (*OED* n.¹ 1) b) anger (*OED* n.¹ 2). *adust*] scorched, dried up (*OED* ppl. a. 1).
837. Turnour . . . march] the Speaker; see above, l. 114 n.
838. face] appearance (*OED* n. II 8 a).
839. Whitehall] Whitehall Palace, royal residence and hence the home of the court.
840. adjourn] until 29 July.
841. Tomkins] Sir Thomas Tomkins: see above, l. 223 n.
841–4. Tomkins made a speech against standing armies in the House of Commons on 25 July: it was made amid considerable excitement and became famous (see Pepys, 8.352–3 and n. 2). See also above, l. 223 n.
843. motion] proposal (*OED* n. 8 a).
844. disarm] Cp. Waller, *Instructions to a Painter*, l. 44, 'Disarm'd of that from which their courage grows.'
845–9. Tomkins was an old cavalier: M. suggests that his cavalier ways in the town undermine the issue of security, and the urgent need to raise an army against the Dutch threat.
845. Trojan] a) like the Trojans, when the Greeks had planted their wooden horse, Turnour enjoys himself when he should be attending to business b) name for a merry, roystering, dissolute fellow (*OED* n. B 2 a).
846. cider . . . Hereford] see above, l. 841 n. Tomkin's constituency was Weobley, in Herefordshire. Although Worcester was the 'queen' of cider, Hereford was also a centre of cider production.
848. healths] Cp. Waller, *Instructions to a Painter*, ll. 45–6: 'While the glad English . . . /In healths to their great leader drink the spoil.' *trolled*] merrily sung (*OED* v. IV 10).

Hyde orders Turnour that he should come late,
Lest some new Tomkins spring a fresh debate.
The King that day raised early from his rest,
Expects (as at a play) till Turnor's dressed.
5 At last together Ayton come and he:
No dial more could with the sun agree.
The Speaker, summoned, to the Lords repairs,
Nor gave the Commons leave to say their prayers:
But like his prisoners to the bar them led,
0 Where mute they stand to hear their sentence read.
Trembling with joy and fear, Hyde them prorogues,
And had almost mistook and called them rogues.
    Dear painter, draw this Speaker to the foot;
Where pencil cannot, there my pen shall do't:
5 That may his body, this his mind explain.
Paint him in golden gown, with mace's brain,
Bright hair, fair face, obscure and dull of head,
Like knife with ivory haft and edge of lead.
At prayers his eyes turn up the pious white,

870 But all the while his private bill's in sight.
In chair, he smoking sits like master cook,
And a poll bill does like his apron look.
Well was he skilled to season any question,
And made a sauce fit for Whitehall's digestion,
875 Whence every day, the palate more to tickle,
Court-mushrumps ready are, sent in in pickle.
When grievance urged, he swells like squatted toad,
Frisks like a frog, to croak a tax's load;
His patient piss he could hold longer than
880 A urinal, and sit like any hen;
At table jolly as a country host
And soaks his sack with Norfolk, like a toast.
At night, than Chanticleer more brisk and hot,
And Serjeant's wife serves him for Pertelotte.
885   Paint last the King, and a dead shade of night
Only dispersed by a weak taper's light,
And those bright gleams that dart along and glare
From his clear eyes, yet these too dark with care.

851–2. Hyde . . . debate] see Pepys, 29 July 1669 (8.361): 'Thus, they are dismissed again, to their general great distaste, I believe the greatest that ever Parliament was, to see themselves so fooled and the nation in certain condition of ruin, while the King, they see, is only governed by his lust and women and rogues about him. The Speaker, they found, was kept from coming in the morning to the House on purpose, till after the King was come to the House of Lords, for fear they should be doing anything in the House of Commons to the further dissatisfaction of the King and his courtiers.'
854. Expects . . . dressed] as the King would not visit an actress after a performance until she was properly dressed. *Expects*] waits (*OED* v. I 2).
855. Ayton] Sir John Ayton (or Eaton), Usher of the Black Rod.
857. summoned] by Black Rod.
858. Nor . . . prayers] *JHC* and Milward (1938) 29 July 1667, confirm that the customary morning prayers were not said on this day.
859. the bar] the bar of the House of Lords; the Members of the House of Commons are summoned to the House of Lords to hear the King's proclamation; they have to wait at the bar of the House of Lords while Clarendon (who presides over the Lords as Lord Chancellor) reads the King's message.
861. prorogues] official term for adjourning Parliament (*OED* v. 3).
864. pencil] paintbrush (*OED* n. I 1 a).
866. mace's brain] alluding to the mace, the symbol of authority in the House of Commons, placed in front of the Speaker.
870. private bill] the Speaker received considerable fees from the passage of private members' bills (Henning).
871–6. In . . . pickle] a poetic version of a pictorial grotesque or burlesque: for discussions of the grotesque and burlesque, see Selden (1978), 89–105, Raylor (1994), Pt. 3.
871. smoking] sweating (*OED* ppl. a. 2).
872. poll bill] part of the £1.8 million voted in the session of 1666–67 (see above, ll. 238 n.) was raised by a poll bill.
874. sauce] Turnour's speeches were known for their courtly elegance.
876. mushrumps] a) mushrooms b) upstarts (*OED* n. 2 a).
pickle] a) salt or acid liquor used as a preservative; hence the

'mushrump' courtiers are kept in reserve for Turnour's attention (*OED* n.[1] 1) b) sorry predicament (*OED* n.[1] 4 a).
877. squatted] i.e. squatting.
878. Frisks] dances or gambols briskly (*OED* v. 1).
879. patient] i.e. held back for a long time.
880. urinal] chamber-pot (*OED* n. 3). *sit like any hen*] i.e. hatching eggs.
882. soaks] a) drinks to excess (*OED* v. III 9 c) b) wets with urine. *sack*] a) white wine imported from Spain and the Canary Islands (*OED* n.[3] 1) b) Turnour is imagined sitting on a wool-sack (strictly speaking, for the Lord Chancellor and judges in the House of Lords; Turnour had a legal training). *Norfolk*] James Norfolk, Serjeant-at-Arms of the House of Commons. *toast*] a) piece of bread browned by a fire, used for dipping in wine or water (*OED* n.[1] 1) b) drinking companion; one who drinks to excess (*OED* n.[1] 3).
883–4. At night . . . Pertelotte] an allusion to Chaucer's tale of the cock and the hen, the *Nun's Priest's Tale*.
884. Serjeant's wife] as yet unidentified.
885–942. Paint . . . Pett] Picciotto (forthcoming, Ch. 3), notes that M.'s ironically deferential or belittling treatment of the painter is now replaced by a complete mastery of him, and of the perceptions of the King.
885–906. Zwicker (1993), 117–18, argues that this passage is a redaction of Charles II's pursuit of Frances Theresa Stuart (see above, ll. 761–4, and below, l. 906 n.). Her marriage to the Duke of Richmond, so evading the King's attentions, was rumoured to have been assisted by Clarendon, a further reason for Charles's ire toward the Chancellor (see Pepys, 8.342–3). Richmond's first wife was the sister of Lord Francis Villiers (d. 1648), and the 'Bright Lady . . . Fair Richmond' of M.'s elegy on him: see above, *An Elegy Upon the Death of My Lord Francis Villiers*, ll. 59–61.
885. dead] for a painter, a paradox: without colour (i.e. dark), yet created with colours (*OED* a. A II 13 b); cp. Daniel King, 'Miniatura or the Art of Limming', BL, Add. MS 12461, fol. 18[r]: 'The apparel in dead colours.'
886. dispersed] dissipated (*OED* v. 1 b).

There, as in the calm horror all alone
890   He wakes, and muses of th' uneasy throne;
      Raise up a sudden shape with virgin's face,
      (Though ill agree her posture, hour, or place),
      Naked as born, and her round arms behind
      With her own tresses, interwove and twined;
895   Her mouth locked up, a blind before her eyes,
      Yet from beneath the veil her blushes rise,
      And silent tears her secret anguish speak;
      Her heart throbs, and with very shame would break.
      The object strange in him no terror moved:
900   He wondered first, then pitied, then he loved,
      And with kind hand does the coy vision press
      (Whose beauty greater seemed by her distress):
      But soon shrunk back, chilled with her touch so cold,
      And th' airy picture vanished from his hold.
905   In his deep thoughts the wonder did increase,
      And he divined 'twas England or the Peace.
          Express him startling next with listening ear,

      As one that some unusual noise does hear:
      With cannon, trumpets, drums, his door surround –
910   But let some other painter draw the sound.
      Thrice did he rise, thrice the vain tumult fled,
      But again thunders, when he lies in bed.
      His mind secure does the known stroke repeat
      And finds the drums Louis' march did beat.
915   Shake then the room, and all his curtains tear,
      And with blue streaks infect the taper clear,
      While the pale ghosts his eye does fixed admire
      Of grandsire Harry and of Charles his sire.
      Harry sits down, and in his open side
920   The grisly wound reveals of which he died,
      And ghastly Charles, turning his collar low,
      The purple thread about his neck does show,
      Then whispering to his son in words unheard,
      Through the locked door both of them disappeared.
925   The wondrous night the pensive King revolves,
      And rising, straight on Hyde's disgrace resolves.

---

889. calm horror] Cp. *Upon Appleton House*, ll. 671–2: 'And such an horror calm and dumb,/Admiring Nature does benumb'; a paradox. *horror*] grim and dreadful atmosphere; taken literally from Latin *horror*; cp. Virgil, *Aeneid*, VII, l. 41: 'dicam horrida bella' (I will tell of grim wars).

893. round] well-shaped (*OED* a. I 3 b).

895. blind . . . eyes] Frances Stuart (see above, ll. 885–906 n.) was fond of the game of blindman's buff: see Hartmann (1924), 142.

896. veil] i.e. the blindfold.

897. silent tears] tears make no noise, and she is gagged.

899–906. Messina (in Friedenreich, ed. (1977), 308) argues that the passage constitutes a literary play on the pictorial emblem: the static picture of the woman and Charles symbolizes a land in distress, but when Charles moves, he transforms the emblem, to represent in sexual terms his political irresponsibility. Yet he also learns, for his actions also reveal that the vision is not at all sexual in nature.

900–1. loved . . . press] an accurate description of Charles II's sexual behaviour: see Pepys, *Diary*, 6.267: 'The King doth spend most of his time in feeling and kissing them naked all over their bodies in bed – and contents himself, without doing the other thing but as he finds himself inclined.' Cp. Waller's suppression of Charles's behaviour: *Instructions to a Painter*, ll. 321–2: 'You for these ends whole days in council sit/And the diversions of your youth forget.'

901. kind] affectionate, loving, intimate (*OED* a. 6). *coy*] modest, shy; cp. *To His Coy Mistress*, Title n.

906. England . . . Peace] i.e. embodied in the allegorical form of a naked woman. *England*] see above, ll. 761–4 n.

907. Express] paint (*OED* v. II 5); see above, l. 65. *startling*] starting with sudden surprise or alarm (*OED* vbl. n. 2).

908. unusual] Cp. Waller, *Instructions to a Painter*, l. 7, 'Make Heav'n concern'd and an unusual star/Declare th'importance of th'approaching war.'

911. vain] empty, in the sense of unreal and illusory (*OED* a. I 2), suggesting that the alarmed king is now inventing spectres of his own fear.

912. thunders] is it the sound of cannon and drums or Charles that 'thunders'? The latter possibility is rude: the King farts. A parody of heroic imagery: see, e.g. Waller, *Instructions to a Painter*, l. 336: 'in Great Britain thought the Thunderer born'.

913. secure] overconfident (*OED* a. A I 1); in the sense of overconfident hitherto.

914. Louis'] trisyllabic: pronounced 'Lewis'; Louis XIV: the implication is that Clarendon is Louis's instrument.

916. infect] change the colour of (*OED* v. 1 a). *taper*] candle (*OED* n.¹ 1).

917–24. While . . . disappeared] Gearin-Tosh, *E in C*, 22 (1972), 48–57 (56) argues that the ghosts satirically parody the deities of Peace and Plenty who appear in Rubens' painting *The Triumph of James I*.

917. fixed] i.e. a fixed stare. *admire*] wonder at (*OED* v. 2).

918. grandsire Harry] Henri IV of France, assassinated in 1610, father of Henrietta Maria. *Charles*] Charles I. The executed monarch appears in a dream vision poem ('A Dreame') in John Quarles, *Regale Lectum Miseriae* (1649), 1–4.

921. ghastly] a) horrible, frightful (*OED* a. 1 a) b) deathlike, pale, wan (*OED* a. 2 a).

922. purple] a) bloody (*OED* a. A 1 d) b) signifying royalty (*OED* a. A 1 a). *thread*] used figuratively to suggest a line, but also suggesting a liquid line made of beads of blood ('thread': *OED* n. 4 b).

923. words unheard] which presumably, given the sense of ll. 929–30, acknowledged that Charles was guilty of the charge frequently made by the Parliamentarians, that he was receiving evil counsel from those close to him.

924. Since Henri IV and Charles I are ghosts, they can pass through solid objects like locked doors.

925. revolves] turns over in the mind, considers (*OED* v. 4). *pensive*] anxious (*OED* a. (n.) 2).

926. straight] immediately.

At his first step, he Castlemaine does find,
Bennet, and Coventry, as't were designed;
And they, not knowing, the same thing propose
Which his hid mind did in its depths enclose.
Through their feigned speech their secret hearts he knew:
To her own husband, Castlemaine untrue;
False to his master Bristol, Arlington;
And Coventry, falser than anyone,
Who to the brother, brother would betray,
Nor therefore trusts himself to such as they.
His father's ghost, too, whispered him one note,
That who does cut his purse will cut his throat,
But in wise anger he their crimes forbears,
As thieves reprieved for executioners;
While Hyde provoked, his foaming tusk does whet,
To prove them traitors, and himself the Pett.
    Painter, adieu! How well our arts agree!
Poetic picture, painted poetry!
But this great work is for our monarch fit:
And henceforth Charles only to Charles shall sit.
His master-hand the ancients shall outdo,
Himself the poet and the painter too.

To the King

So his bold tube man to the sun applied,
950 And spots unknown to the bright star descried;
Showed they obscure him, while too near they please,
And seem his courtiers, are but his disease.
Through optic trunk the planet seemed to hear,
And hurls them off e'er since in his career.
955 And you, great sir, that with him empire share,
Sun of our world, as he the Charles is there,
Blame not the Muse that brought those spots to sight,
Which in your splendour hid, corrode your light:
(Kings in the country oft have gone astray,
960 Nor of a peasant scorned to learn the way).
Would she the unattended throne reduce,
Banishing love, trust, ornament, and use;
Better it were to live in cloister's lock,
Or in fair fields to rule the easy flock.
965 She blames them only who the court restrain,
And where all England serves, themselves would reign.

927–8. Castlemaine . . . Coventry] see above, 323. Coventry led the attack on Clarendon, and told Pepys that he had first proposed the Chancellor's removal (Pepys, 8.414–15). Lady Castlemaine was certainly against Clarendon, but Coventry denied any alliance between the two. Arlington had been aligned against Clarendon in 1663; he was associated with Lady Castlemaine on the matter of Clarendon's position in August 1667. Arlington and Coventry were at odds again the following year.
932. See above, ll. 406–7 n.
933. Bristol] George Digby, second Earl of Bristol (1612–77), and the most prominent courtier during the early 1660s; conducted a vendetta against Clarendon during the 1660s: see above, *The Second Advice to a Painter*, ll. 147–8. Clarendon had blocked Bennet's advancement to several posts, and this had forced him into Bristol's camp.
935. i.e. William Coventry would betray his brother Henry.
938. purse . . . throat] Parliament objected to the King's financial demands in the late 1620s, and in the early 1640s; it was the purged House of Commons that committed Charles I to trial, and his execution on 30 January 1649 after his conviction.
940. thieves . . . executioners] Thieves were given their lives on condition that they became executioners.
941. foaming] raging (*OED* v. 5). *whet*] sharpen (*OED* v. 1 b).
942. the Pett] i.e. the scapegoat (see above, l. 767 n.).
944. Poetic . . . poetry] cp. Horace, *De Arte Poetica*, l. 361: 'ut pictura poesis' (A poem is like a picture).
946. And . . . sit] a figure of reflection: see above, *Headnote, Sources and Genre*. Cp. Busenello, *A Prospective*, trans. Higgons (1658), sig. D8ᵛ: 'Then draw thyself in heat of Battell, wrought,/With the same air and looks, as they that fought,/That thy own Figure done by thy own hand,/May over Death it self triumphing stand.'
949–55. J.E. Weiss and N.O. Weiss, *N & Q*, 225 (1980), 339–41, note that M.'s image is derived from the fact that

no sunspots were observed between 1661 and 1671. In M.'s poem, someone looks through a telescope to see a close-up view of the King, as if they were observing the sun. In William Browne, *Britannia's Pastorals* (1616), II, ll. 863–70, a monarch looks through a telescope in order to see the corruption of his subjects by those of high estate. See also the treatment of the telescope in Samuel Butler's satire of scientific virtuosi *The Elephant in the Moon* (1662), ll. 246–60.
949. tube] telescope (*OED* n. I 3).
950–2. spots . . . disease] Riebling, *SEL*, 35 (1995), 152, suggests that the spots connote venereal disease, as well as moral blemishes.
953. optic trunk] telescope (*pace* Wilcher; Walker, who define 'trunk' as 'nerve', and hence 'optic trunk' is the eye); a man looks through the telescope and sees the sunspots, the sun 'hears' this revelation through the telescope (as if it were now an ear trumpet), and casts off the spots. *planet*] i.e. the sun, imagined as a planet, revolving around the earth in its 'career'.
954. career] pathway or course in the heavens (*OED* n. 3).
959–60. Kings . . . way] an allusion to Charles II's escape from the Battle of Worcester, September 1651, when he was guided by peasants. The political uses of this story by different factions during the Restoration are discussed by Weiser, *SC*, 14 (1999), 43–62. For the paintings recording the episode, see David H. Solkin, *JCWI*, 62 (1999), 199–240.
961. she] i.e. the Muse.
963–4. Better . . . flock] referring to a) the monastical or conventual life criticized in *Upon Appleton House*, ll. 89–272, b) the life of simplicity celebrated in pastoral literature.
964. fair fields] cp. Milton, *Paradise Lost*, IV, ll. 268–9: 'that fair field of Enna'.
965. restrain] a) deprive of its proper function (*OED* v¹ 1). b) imprison (*OED* v¹ 1 c). Buckingham had been in hiding, and then imprisoned in early July, 1667.

Bold and accursed are they that all this while
Have strove to isle our monarch from his isle,
And to improve themselves, on false pretence,
970 About the Common-Prince have raised a fence;
The kingdom from the crown distinct would see,
And peel the bark to burn at last the tree.
(But Ceres corn, and Flora is the spring,
Bacchus is wine, the country is the King.)
975   Not so does rust insinuating wear,
Nor powder so the vaulted bastion tear,
Nor earthquake so a hollow isle o'erwhelm,
As scratching courtiers undermine a realm,

And through the palace's foundations bore,
980 Burrowing themselves to hoard their guilty store.
The smallest vermin make the greatest waste,
And a poor warren once a city razed.
     But they, whom born to virtue and to wealth,
Nor guilt to flatt'ry binds, nor want to stealth;
985 Whose gen'rous conscience and whose courage high
Does with clear counsels their large souls supply;
That serve the King with their estates and care,
And, as in love, on Parliaments can stare,
(Where few the number, choice is there less hard):
990 Give us this court, and rule without a guard.

967–72. Bold . . . tree] structurally similar to the argument of *The Mower against Gardens*: just as gardens are an unnatural and perverse separation of one part of nature from another through enclosure, so the King is separated from the kingdom. In the garden, there is a luscious but unnatural mutation of plant species, while the fields are neglected; in the court, sexual impropriety is rife, and the kingdom is threatened with ruin. Arguments identifying the King with his people were common in literature published in response to the Great Fire: see, e.g. Nathaniel Hardy, *Lamentation, Mourning and Woe* (1666), sig. A4ʳ, 25.
968. isle . . . isle] Cp. *Upon Appleton House*, ll. 471–2: 'The river in itself is drowned,/And isles th'astonished cattle round.'
970. Common-Prince] a fusion of 'prince' and 'commonwealth' or 'commonweal', in order to suggest the common identity of the two.
972. And . . . tree] Cp. *The Mower against Gardens*, l. 21: 'Had he not dealt between the bark and tree.'
973–4. Ceres . . . wine] the three deities, goddesses and god of their respective objects, are designed to instil a sense of natural association (to support the idea that 'the country is the king'). But the story of Ceres, whose daughter Persephone was abducted by Pluto and taken to the underworld (see Ovid, *Fasti*, IV, ll. 420 ff.), points back to court corruption. This sense is supported by the apparent echo of Milton in l. 964; the corresponding passage in *Paradise Lost* (II, ll. 268–72) alludes to the Ceres and Persephone story. See also below, *The Loyal Scot*, ll. 241–3.
975. insinuating] entering between the particles of a substance (*OED* ppl. a. 1) *wear*] corrode, waste away (*OED* v.¹ II 9 a).
976. powder] gunpowder.

978. scratching] a) struggling to make money (*OED* v. 5 a). b) rapaciously grasping (*OED* v. 6 a).
980. Burrowing themselves] digging underground in order to hide themselves (*OED* v.¹ 2 a).
981–2. smallest . . . razed] see Pliny, *Natural History*, trans. Philemon Holland (1634), VIII.xxix, 212: 'Nothing is more certain and notorious than this, that much hurt and dammage hath been known to come from small contemptible creatures, which otherwise are of no reckoning and account. *M. Varro* writes, That there was a towne in Spaine vndermined by Connies [rabbits]: and another likewise in Thessalie, by the Moldwarpes [moles].' See also *The Second Advice*, ll. 349–50.
982. razed] Bod. 1; rac't [pierce, penetrate (*OED* v.³ 2 a; but only fifteenth-century usages recorded)] *1697*.
983–90. But . . . guard] the poem strikingly turns in the final verse paragraph in an address to the King to an appreciation of the virtuous landed nobility and gentry, who, not needing court advancement, are beyond corruption and hence are the best advisers to the King. They are the natural friends of the Parliament and would make the court virtuous. The lines appeal generally to country sentiment, but the ideas cohere with Buckingham's vision, and Buckingham was orchestrating most of the opposition to Clarendon in the autumn of 1667.
985. gen'rous] noble, high-minded (*OED* a. 2 a). *courage high*] Cp. *An Horatian Ode*, ll. 17–18: ''tis all one to courage high,/The emulous or enemy.'
987. estates] a) high status (*OED* n. 3 a) b) constituted as a part of the body politic in Parliament (*OED* n. 6 a) c) wealth (*OED* n. 12 a).
989. Where . . . hard] i.e. 'when there are so few virtuous nobles, the King will not find it hard to choose the right advisors'.

VERSE SATIRES
FROM THE 1670S

Date. 1667–73. The lines on Douglas (ll. 15–62) were first composed as part of *The Last Instructions* in the autumn of 1667. The frame in which they sit, concerning the unity of England and Scotland (ll. 1–14, 63–86, 234–85) may well have been composed in 1669–70 when a Parliamentary union between England and Scotland was discussed. Lauderdale, who appears at l. 100 as a moderate, was only so between 1667 and October 1669. The long anti-episcopal section (ll. 87–233) includes the lines on Blood's attempt to steal the Crown jewels, which took place in 1671. Sheldon (see below, 399) did not die until 1677, so this section of the poem may be as late as the mid-1670s: Patterson (1978), 168, suggests the early 1670s, when M. was researching church history for *The Rehearsal Transpros'd*; Chernaik (1983), 210, suggests 1674, between the writing of the two parts of *The Rehearsal Transpros'd* (1672–73) and *Mr Smirke* and *A Short Historical Essay* (1676), although the absence of any mention of Burnet's restoration as Archbishop of Glasgow in September 1674 (see below, l. 100 n.) makes 1672–73 a more likely choice.

Manuscript Circulation. Nine manuscript copies of the poem have survived (although one of these is now lost). Of these, *BL 27* may belong to the 1670s, while *Bod. 13* and *NLS* probably belong to the 1680s, before the poem was printed. Of the other five, *BL 26* seems related to the printed versions, and may derive from them (see below, *Headnote, Text and Authorship*).

Bod. 1   Bod., MS Eng. poet d. 49, pp. 237^b–47
Bod. 13 Bod. MS Douce 357, fols. 49^v–53
NLS   NLS, Adv. MS 19.1.12, fols. 160^v–4
BL 25   BL, Add. MS 72479 [loose papers from the Trumbull family of Easthampstead Park]
BL 26   BL, MS Sloane 655, fols. 18–21^v
BL 27   BL, Add. MS 73540, fols. 26^v–32^v
RS   Royal Society, MS 32, 1–9. Quarto miscellany compiled by Sir George Ent MD (1604–89)

Υ 7   Yale, Osborn Collection, MS fb 106, No. 17
Mg   Margoliouth owned a verse miscellany of at least 196 pages containing *The Loyal Scot* (which he collated in his edition) as well as poems by Oldham; it was 'writt wth a woman's hand'; now lost; recorded in *IELM*, dated late seventeenth century

Printed Publication. The poem was included in the undated printed edition, with missing title page, in the Library Company of Philadelphia (*LCP*), now believed to be a 1690s production (see above, 350), in *1694* and *1697*.

Text and Authorship. Margoliouth doubted that the anti-episcopal passage was by M. (except for the lines on Blood (see below, 411–12)) on the grounds of inferiority and lack of distinctly Marvellian qualities. Legouis agreed to some extent (printing this section in smaller type), as did Lord (omitting the section altogether, and arguing that his case was supported by marks on the text of *Bod. 1*; in fact, these marks indicate the absence of the lines from *1697* (see Chernaik (1983), 208–9)). But Legouis admitted that the section was still imitating Cleveland (if in terms not entirely consistent with the rest of the poem), and that no MS existed of the poem which did not include these lines: both grounds against rejecting the section. The short versions of the poem in *1694* and *1697* attribute it to M.

He also notes that these lines match (in some places to the extent of textual echo, as well as theme), the ecclesiastical concerns of M.'s 1670s prose tracts. Donno tends to favour these lines as part of an integral whole, confirmed in the longest version, *Bod. 1*. Patterson (1978), 168, regards the later parts of the poem as M.'s on the grounds of the 'tone of classical and Christian humanism' that increases towards the end of the poem. Chernaik (210–11) regards both shorter (i.e. without the anti-episcopal passage) and longer versions as authentic, arguing that the anticlerical satire is common to both, that the passage is an expansion of that which precedes it, and 'that transitional passages link the anticlerical passages in both versions with the beginning and end of the poem'. Margoliouth and Legouis, taking *Bod. 13* as their copy-text, do not include ll. 81–7 which occur in *Bod. 1*, *BL 27*, *1694*, *1697*. They are followed by Walker. Lord adopts the shorter text printed in *1694*, but *Yale POAS* does not include the poem. Donno includes all these sections, but omits the lines on Blood since they are absent from *Bod. 1*, her copy-text.

All MS and printed versions of the poem are relatively close to each other. There are numerous cases of mistakes introduced by transcription. There are, however, many various kinds of omission. The 1690s printed texts (which include lines absent from earlier MS texts) may of course derive from copies now lost that predate the 1680s MSS. For this reason, the text presented here is composite. On the whole, as with Margoliouth and Legouis, the readings of *Bod. 13* are preferred, although not always. Even though parts of the anti-episcopal section may be judged inferior, or alien to M.'s distinctive qualities, the connections with M.'s 1670s concern with the bishops are too strong to dismiss the lines entirely.

Significant characteristics and features of the MSS are as follows. *Bod. 13* is a collection of Civil War and Restoration verse with the date '1642' embossed on both sides of the leather binding. M.'s poem is placed between Cowley's *Civil War* (*c.* 1643) and *Oceana and Britannia*, the latter now thought not to be by M.. 'Marvell' is written after the last line in *NLS*; here the poem is placed among other poems dated in the mid-1680s, although it is also placed outside the main sequence of M. poems in the volume. 'Finis. per Andrew Marvell' is written after the last line in *BL 27*, which is probably a late 1670s or early 1680s collection.

Context. The poem begins by repeating the lines on Captain Douglas from *The Last Instructions* in order to address two public issues prominent in the years following the Second Dutch War. These were the discussion in Parliament of the possible union of England and Scotland, and the character and policies of the bishops in Scotland and in England. The two issues were connected in respect of the persecution of Scottish Covenanters by the re-establishment of bishops in Scotland, policies encouraged by opponents of M., who were ministers of Charles II.

The poem is remarkable for its claim that national distinctions are human inventions, and should at least in some circumstances be removed. Patterson (1978), 167–70, notes that the complete reversal of sentiments from *The Character of Holland* (1653) involves a recantation on M.'s part, as much as Cleveland is also made to recant for his earlier anti-Scottish sentiments. She also suggests that M.'s explanation of national division is humanistic, showing the source of nation-naming to be the linguistic confusion caused by the Fall.

M.'s treatment of nationhood may be seen as a response to, and a reflection upon, the tensions between the two nations, despite the monarch they shared. These relationships were further complicated by the different powers of the monarch in each country. However Charles II used his ministers in the 1660s, he had to contend with a Parliament, whereas in Scotland, he was more powerful in church and state, operating through a very few aristocrats. In England, a restored episcopal church gradually if grudgingly accepted toleration of Dissent, in a context of considerable denominational diversity. In Scotland, a reimposed episcopacy attempted to impose conformity on a laity that was, in large parts of the country, strongly Presbyterian. If English Dissenters were imprisoned and subjected to abuse, and some violence, the Scottish Presbyterians (or Covenanters) claimed massive violent persecution in a vivid literature that was republished down to the nineteenth century. Although he had been in favour of reconciliation between 1667 and 1669 (which explains his appearance in a positive light when compared with Burnet (see below, l. 100 n.)), the King's High Commissioner in Scotland from 1669, John Maitland, Earl, then Duke, of Lauderdale, sanctioned extreme measures against the Covenanters. In 1669, Lauderdale had bluntly announced the suppression of conventicles; the following year, preaching in conventicles was made a capital offence. Matters were exacerbated by periods of relative toleration, when the King hoped to win over more Presbyterian clergy to the episcopal church. The beginning and end periods for the composition of this poem (1669 and 1674) correspond to two periods of intense persecution. Such were the obstacles to political union that Charles II and Lauderdale had abandoned all hopes of a negotiated settlement. They allowed the talks to continue in order to provide a ruse for the government to negotiate secretly with Louis XIV in pursuit of an anti-Dutch alliance, a highly contentious matter since French money and military support were offered in exchange for the advancement of the Catholic cause in England.

To M., the Covenanters looked like English Puritans, even though they had not supported the regicide, and though M. had written in support of the republic's invasion of Scotland in 1650. The Solemn League and Covenant of 1643, the document that bound the Parliamentarians together, was essentially a result of Scottish pre-eminence at that early stage of the Civil War: it was publicly burned during the early days of the Restoration. M. had sympathy with the Covenanters (and not with Lauderdale, whom he regarded as a violent persecutor and a danger to Parliamentary freedoms – see M. to William Popple, 24 July 1675; Legouis, II.343), who would have appeared as fellow-travelling Puritans, under even fiercer persecution than their English brethren. The poem is aimed at combating the widespread view that, in the light of the events of the 1640s, the Scots were unreliable. M.'s attitude may have been coloured by his northern associations: the Fairfaxes were Presbyterians, and collaborative, pro-Scottish attitudes existed more commonly in the north and far north, literally through the experience of proximate coexistence (see Barber, *Northern History*, 35 (1999), 93–118).

But M. was also, as ever, writing strategically. The attack on Lauderdale was aimed at minimizing Clarendon's influence, and that of those who replaced him. The later date suggested for part of the poem, 1674, coincides with the proto-Whiggish Earl of Shaftesbury's association with Hamilton's attack on Lauderdale, and with Clarendon's petition to return from exile. Was M. associated with this group through personal principle, or was he cleverly bought off?

The poem's treatment of the bishops (ll. 95–249) has a close relationship with M.'s prose writings of the 1670s, in particular *The Rehearsal Transpros'd*, parts 1 and 2 (1672–73), *Mr Smirke* (1676), and its appended 'Essay on Councils'. Even if M. was not the author of these lines, the nature of the attack, and the named clergymen, point to M.'s interests and personal connections. This is particularly true of Gilbert Sheldon, Archbishop of Canterbury, who had controverted Milton's *Readie and Easy Way* (1660) in *The Dignity of Kingship Asserted* (1660); see also below 407–8. M. was to reflect seriously upon religious liberty and civil authority in his prose writings, using a wide range of materials that included scripture, patristic writing and European literature

as well as the controversial arguments of his contemporaries. The poetry of *The Loyal Scot* does not afford such reflections and insights, but it is none the less aligned with the prose writings in its concern with the abuse of episcopal authority, and the consequent alienation of the religious vision of the Commonwealth divines. M. identified the bishops as part of an alliance with Lauderdale and the 'whole old Cavalier Party' in July 1675, and admired the way Buckingham attacked them ('never the like, nor so infinitely pleasant'), even though they were 'grown so odiously ridiculous' (M. to William Popple, 24 July 1675; Legouis, II.343).

The discovery that Archibald Douglas was probably a Roman Catholic (see below, *Subtitle* n.) raises the broader issue of the relationship between Protestants and Catholics in Restoration England and Scotland. Both Dissenters and Catholics were aligned in the cause of religious toleration from 15 March 1672 when Charles II issued the Declaration of Indulgence, until he withdrew it during the following spring. Parts of the poem may have been produced during this period when the Cabal had the ascendancy in government, itself half-Puritanical, half-Catholic in character.

The poem is spoken by the persona of the ghost of the royalist poet and satirist, John Cleveland (1613–58), who wrote *The Rebel Scot* at the time of the Scottish army's entry into England in January 1644 in order to fight Charles I. In M.'s poem, Cleveland's ghost reverses his earlier hostility to the Scots. Like all of M.'s poems about other poets, *The Loyal Scot* is a means for M. to measure himself against the achievements, reputation and opinions of an influential poet. Cleveland's presence in M.'s earlier verse is strong (see above, 247–8 and below, *Sources and Genre*). Both poets were in Cambridge at the same time: Cleveland was admitted to Christ's College in 1627, and moved to St John's in 1631, becoming a fellow in 1634. He would have known M.'s associate John Hall: some of Hall's poems were ascribed to Cleveland. Unlike Hall's tutor, John Pawson (see above, *To His Coy Mistress*, ll. 41–6 n.), Cleveland, a fervent royalist, was ejected from his fellowship in 1645. He then served Charles I as a journalist and judge, and survived during the Interregnum as a private tutor, but not without interference and imprisonment at the hands of Protectorate officials. Where M. eventually benefited from employment by the Protectorate, Cleveland was forced to petition Cromwell for his release from prison. He managed nonetheless to publish his poetry and prose works (in which his royalism was easily discernible), and allegedly to run a poetic club with Samuel Butler in London.

Collections of his poems (eighteen surviving editions of *Poems* (1st edn, 1651); four of *J. Cleveland Revived* (first edn, 1659)), especially those published posthumously, successively added poems he had not written to his 'canon', until an attempt was made by two former students to establish a true canon in an edition of 1677, *Clievelandi vindiciae, or, Clieveland's genuine poems, orations, epistles, &c.* Like M., 'Cleveland' was the name under which a variety of poems were published, but in his case, all of them were royalist, and most of them approximated to the highly extravagant, conceited verse for which Cleveland was famous. By the time he wrote *The Loyal Scot*, M. was beginning to acquire a similar reputation as the voice of opposition poetry through his involvement in the Advice-to-a-Painter poems, and their accompanying materials. Although M.'s voicing of Cleveland cannot be regarded as an attempt to frustrate the establishment of an authentic canon for Cleveland (which occurred after *The Loyal Scot* was written), the imitation and then reclamation of Cleveland's voice for a kind of early Whiggery, was an exploitation of the instability of Cleveland's canon. The fourth edition of *J. Cleaveland Revived*, appeared in 1668 (containing many unauthenticated poems, and very few poems now considered to be Cleveland's), and a further edition of *Poems* (with unauthenticated poems, but with a greater number of authentic works) in 1669. Dryden had drawn attention to Cleveland's poetic manner in *An Essay of Dramatick Poesie* (1668), in *Works*, Vol. 17 (1971), 10, 29–30, creating the label 'Clevelandism' to name the poet's habit of catachresis, 'wresting and torturing a word into another meaning', and making unfavourable comparisons between Donne and Cleveland, yet reserving for the younger poet the distinction of being the only English poet quoted in the essay (and *The Rebel Scot* is one of the two poems quoted). Cleveland's achievement and reputation was a very real presence in literary affairs when M. came to write his satire. To put the elegy on Douglas (lines that are markedly Marvellian) into the mouth of Cleveland's ghost is to replace Cleveland's voice with M.'s.

Sources, Genre and Structure. The Loyal Scot is a revision of Cleveland's poem 'The Rebell Scot' (1644),

written on the occasion of the Scottish army's entry into England (in support of Parliament). Cleveland's ghost atones for his former views expressed while alive; anti-Scottish sentiment is converted to praise of heroic Scots, and a demonstration of the unity of the two nations. M. had used echoes from Cleveland to construct his satire of the Dutch in *The Character of Holland*, a work that uses national stereotypes for xenophobic purposes. Now M. puts Cleveland to work in the opposite direction, although his later satire is still hostile to the Dutch. While the ghost speaks a poetry purged of the extravagant conceitedness for which Cleveland was famous, there are several echoes of his verse, especially 'The Rebell Scot' (see below, ll. 12–13, 63, 75–80, 120, 262, 301 nn.), in addition to imitations of Cleveland's manner. The informed reader still recognizes the poem as Cleveland's, allowing M. to conceal his imitative method of composition in the guise of a Menippean satire, a satirical poem spoken by a dead person from the underworld, or about to enter it (see above, *Tom May's Death, Headnote, Genre and Sources*, 118–19, and Smet (1996)). The description of Douglas's fiery death, borrowed from *The Last Instructions* becomes a heroic reversal of the satiric description of Scots in 'The Rebell Scot' as red-haired people, inflamed with disease (ll. 14–15), and the rage of the satirist, described as a fire (l. 5). It also chimes with several works that described ecclesiastical strife in Scotland as a kind of national fire: see, e.g., James Stewart, *Naphtali, or, The wrestlings of the Church of Scotland for the kingdom of Christ* (1667). The homoerotic description of Douglas (see above, 366, 385–7) now appears in contrast with Cleveland's own quizzical treatment of hermaphrodites (see, e.g., Cleveland, 'The Authour to his Hermophrodite'). The satire of the bishops is the ghost's recantation for Cleveland's satires against the Puritans, including the Scottish Presbyterians in 'Smectymnuus, or the Club-Divines', 'The Mixt Assembly' and *The Hue and Cry after Sir John Presbyter*. The same is true of *The Scots Apostasie* (1647), which modern editors consider probably, but not certainly, to be by Cleveland (Morris and Withington, eds (1967), xxxv–vi). Which poems M. (or Dryden) regarded as Cleveland's, and which not, is not known. It is likely, however, that M. would have understood the Cleveland canon to be wider than the narrow group of poems accepted today, including a body of verse with its origins in 1630s and Civil War cavalier scatology, most famously anthologized in *Rump Songs* (1662). Thus, M.'s satire of the bishops is related generically to the apocryphal Cleveland poem 'On J.W. A.B. of York', printed in *Poems* (1669).

Benet, in Summers and Pebworth, eds (1992), 198–9, notes that the treatment of the bishops as deceitful actors, rooted in a long tradition of Protestant anti-clerical suspicion, is opposed to the heroic acting of Douglas, although both are, in this life, shown to be subject to forces of fragmentation and instability (Benet, 201–2). Moreover, the lines (ll. 65–74) that follow the Douglas passage in *The Loyal Scot* continue the pattern of metamorphosis, making Douglas's melting the source of the political fusion of the two nations. On the generic level, this Ovidian addition is seen explicitly to replace the ballad of Chevy Chase, the divisive tale concerned with Anglo-Scottish border hostilities (ll. 69–70). In fact, the poem may be said to develop two forms of metamorphosis: heroic and desirable in the case of Douglas, and of the fixed forms of sin and punishment in the case of the bishops. This process is reflected structurally and generically in the mirroring of Cleveland's poem: *The Loyal Scot* is a poetic metamorphosis itself. None the less, the poem has been noted for its 'piecemeal composition and its digressiveness', making it the most 'miscellaneous and formless' of M.'s verse satires (Chernaik (1983), 196).

The Loyal Scot

Upon the Occasion of the Death of Captain Douglas
   burnt in one of his Majesty's Ships at Chatham
By Cleveland's Ghost

    Of the old heroes when the warlike shades
    Saw Douglas marching on the Elysian glades,
    They straight consulting, gathered in a ring,
    Which of their poets should his welcome sing,
5   And, as a favourable penance, chose
    Cleveland, on whom they would the task impose.
    He understood, and willingly addressed
    His ready Muse to court the warlike guest.
    Much had he cured the tumour of his vein,
10 He judged more clearly now, and saw more plain;
    For those soft airs had tempered every thought,
    And of wise Lethe he had took a draught.
    Abruptly he began, disguising art,
    As of his satire this had been a part.
15   'Not so brave Douglas, on whose lovely chin
    The early down but newly did begin;
    And modest beauty yet his sex did veil,
    While envious virgins hope he is a male.
    His shady locks curl back themselves to seek:
20 Nor other courtship knew but to his cheek.
    Oft as he in chill Eske or Seine by night
    Hardened and cooled those limbs so soft, so white,

Sub-title. Douglas] See above, *The Last Instructions*, l. 649 n.; 'It would certainly complete the reversals inflicted on Cleveland if he were made to go from satirizing rebellious Scottish Presbyterians to praising a loyal Scottish Catholic, and sharpen the ironies in which the poem abounds.' (Dzelzainis (in Chernaik and Dzelzainis, eds (1999), 300). Moreover, as a Catholic, Douglas is remote from the differences between Presbyterians and Anglicans, the context of the poem. He is merely loyal, and all the more so for being apparently without faction.

1. shades] ghosts (*OED* n. II 6).
2. Elysian] as in Elysium: home of the blessed after death in Greek mythology. *glades*] open spaces, or passages, in woods or forests (*OED* n.² 1).
3. straight] straightaway, immediately.
5. penance] because, when living, Cleveland as a poet had given offence to his co-poets in the underworld.
8. ready] a) prepared and prompt (*OED* a. A I 5) b) willing (*OED* a. A I 2 b).
9. tumour] bombast, emptiness (*OED* n. 4 b). Cp. Longinus, Περὶ ὕψους, *Or Dionysius Longinus of the Height of Eloquence* (1652), trans. John Hall, 5: 'one of the *nicest* Cautions in all Speech to beware of *Tumour*; for all men naturally aim at *high* things, and ambitiously avoid the imputation of *drought* or *weaknesse*, and therefore suffer themselves to be carried (I know not how) beyond their *due* bounds.' *vein*] characteristic style of expression (*OED* n. III 12). There is also a medical

resonance: in 'The Rebell Scot', ll. 83–6, England is described as diseased from civil war, with the Scots causing the worst part of the affliction.
11. soft airs] of Elysium.
12–13. And . . . art] M. parallels the last two lines from Cleveland's 'The Rebel Scot': 'A *Scot* when from the Gallow-tree got loose/Drops into *Styx*, and turns a *Soland* Goose.'
12. wise Lethe] those who drank from the River Lethe forgot their pasts.
13. Abruptly] without preliminaries ('abrupt', *OED* a. 2 b); cp. Jonson, *Timber: or, Discoveries* (1640), in C.H. Herford, Percy and Evelyn Simpson, eds, *Ben Jonson* (Oxford, 1947), 8.623: 'The abrupt style, which hath many breaches, and doth not seem to end, but fall.' *disguising art*] Apparently a compliment to Cleveland's wit, but the joke is on Cleveland: the 'disguised art' is really M.'s voice which, in this poem, stands for a reformed Cleveland, who now speaks in favour of, rather than against, the Scots.
15–62. This is the section repeated from *The Last Instructions to a Painter*, ll. 649–96; q.v. for annotations; see also above, *Headnote, Sources, Genre and Structure*. *LCP* omits this passage, and by means of a small pointing hand printed next to a marginal '*Vide*.' refers the reader back to the passage in *The Last Instructions* which is marked at the start with a similar pointing hand.
19–62. Not in *BL 27*: the reader is referred to the passage in *The Last Instructions* which precedes it in this MS.

Among the reeds, to be espied by him,
The nymphs would rustle; he would forward swim.
25   They sighed and said, 'Fond boy, why so untame
That fliest Love's fires, reserved for other flame?'
Fixed on his ship he faced the horrid day,
And wondered much at those that run away:
Nor other fear himself could comprehend
30   Than, lest heaven fall ere thither he ascend.
With birding at the Dutch, as though in sport,
He entertains the while his life too short
Or waves his sword, and could he them conjure
Within its circle, knows himself secure.
35   The fatal bark him boards with grappling fire,
And safely through its ports the Dutch retire.
That precious life he yet disdains to save,
Or with known art to try the gentle wave.
Much him the glories of his ancient race
40   Inspire, nor could he his own deeds deface:
And secret joy in his calm soul does rise,
That Monck looks on to see how Douglas dies,
Like a glad lover the fierce flames he meets,
And tries his first embraces in their sheets.
45   His shape exact, which the bright flames enfold,
Like the sun's statue stands of burnished gold.
Round the transparent fire about him glows,
As the clear amber on the bee doth close.
And as on angels' head their glories shine,
50   His burning locks adorn his face divine.
But when in his immortal mind he felt
His altering form and soldered limbs to melt,

Down on the deck he laid him down and died,
With his dear sword reposing by his side:
55   And on the flaming planks so rests his head
As one that hugs himself in a warm bed.
The ship burns down and with his relics sinks,
And the sad stream beneath his ashes drinks.
        Fortunate boy, if e'er my verse may claim
60   That matchless grace to propagate thy fame,
When Oeta and Alcides are forgot
Our English youth shall sing the valiant Scot.
        Skip-saddles Pegasus, thou needst not brag,
Sometimes the Gall'way proves the better nag.
65   Shall not a death so gen'rous now when told
Unite the distance, fill the breaches old?
Such in the Roman Forum, Curtius brave
Galloping down closed up the gaping cave.
No more discourse of Scotch or English race,
70   Nor chant the fab'lous hunt of Chevy Chase.
Mixed in Corinthian metal, at thy flame
Our nations melting, thy colossus frame,
Shall fix a foot on either neighbouring shore,
And join those lands that seemed to part before.
75   Prick down the point (whoever has the art),
Where Nature Scotland does from England part.
Anatomists may sooner fix the cells
Where life resides, or understanding dwells:
But this we know, though that exceed their skill,
80   That whosoever sep'rates them doth kill.
Will you the Tweed the certain bounder call
Of soil, of wit, of manners, and of all?

---

56. As . . . bed] Cp. *The Last Instructions*, l. 690: 'As one that's warmed himself and gone to bed', which is the text in *1697*. For critical comment, see Creaser, in Chernaik and Dzelzainis, eds (1999), 156.
59–60. if . . . fame] the lines are altered from the earlier version since the Advice-to-a-Painter framework is no longer present: see above, *The Last Instructions to a Painter*, ll. 693–4. *1697* adopts the same readings as the text in *The Last Instructions*, ll. 693–4.
63. Skip-saddles] slippery-saddled (see *The Scottish National Dictionary*, 'skip' v.[1] 1); an imitation of Cleveland's fondness for portmanteau neologisms: see, e.g., 'The Rebell Scot': 'Pigwiggin' (l. 12); 'mouth-Granadoes' (l. 24), 'Estrich-Stomacks' (l. 78). *Pegasus*] winged horse that sprang from the blood of Medusa after she had been slain by Perseus, and who opened the Fountain of Hippocrene with his hoof. Associated with poets, whom he supposedly carried to the heights of their genius.
64. Gall'way] Galloway horses were small but strong. The Galloway nag outstrips Pegasus as Douglas outdoes Hercules (see above, ll. 61–2).
65. gen'rous] noble (*OED* a. 1 a).
67–8. Livy, *Ab Urbe Condita*, VII.vi.1–6 tells of a young soldier, Marcus Curtius, who closed a gaping chasm in Rome by riding into it, and thereby offering himself as a sacrifice to the gods.

69. No more discourse] Cp. Milton, *Paradise Lost*, IX, ll. 1–2: 'No more of talk where God or angel guest/With man. . . .'
70. Chevy Chase] the ballad of Chevy Chase, well-known in M.'s day, told of a skirmish in the Scottish borders (*OED* n. 4 a).
71. Corinthian metal] bronze, first made by chance at the burning of Corinth (see Pliny, *Natural History*, XXXIV.iii.5–8). *thy*] Douglas'.
71–4. at . . . before] Douglas's sacrifice makes him (figuratively) into a Colossus, with one foot in Scotland, the other in England, binding the two nations together.
75–80. Prick . . . kill] an inversion of Cleveland, 'The Rebell Scot', ll. 67–70: 'Hence 'tis, they live at Rovers; and defie/This or that Place, Rags of Geographie./They're Citizens o'th World; they're all in all,/Scotland's a Nation Epidemicall.'
77. fix] assign the precise position of (*OED* v. II 11). See also below, l. 222.
77–8. Anatomists . . . dwells] unlike Parker, who, following Descartes, 'will have the Conscience to be seated in the *Glandula Pinealis*' (*RT*, 267). Contemporary investigation of these concerns included William Harvey's *Anatomical exercitations, concerning the generation of living creatures* published in Latin in 1651 and English in 1653.
81. bounder] a) boundary (*OED* n. II 4) b) a personification: one who marks out the boundary (*OED* n. I 1).

Why draw we not as well the thrifty line
From Thames, Trent, Humber, or at least the Tyne?
So may we the state corpulence redress,
And little England when we please make less.
What ethic river is this wondrous Tweed,
Whose one bank virtue, th' other vice does breed?
Or what new perpendicular does rise
Up from her stream, continued to the skies,
That between us the common air should bar
And split the influence of every star?
But who considers right will find indeed
'Tis Holy Island parts us, not the Tweed.
    Nothing but clergy could us two seclude,

No Scotch was ever like a bishop's feud.
All litanies in this have wanted faith.
There's no 'Deliver us from the bishops' wrath.'
Never shall Calvin pardoned be for Sales,
100 Never for Burnet's sake the Lauderdales,
For Becket's sake Kent always shall have tails.
    Who sermons e'er can pacify, and prayers?
Or to the joint-stools reconcile the chairs?
The kingdoms join, yet church will kirk oppose:
105 The mitre still divides, the crown does close.
As in Rogation Week they whisper round
To keep in mind the Scotch and English bound,
What th' ocean binds is by the bishops rent,

---

87. *ethic*] moral (*OED* a. A 1); M. suggests that the bishops treat the river as a moral division between England (virtue) and Scotland (bad). *Tweed*] river that flows 97 miles from Tweed's Wells through southern Scotland to its mouth at Berwick-upon-Tweed in England. 17 miles of its course form the border with England; only the last two miles flow through England alone. Berwick itself was frequently fought over after the Tweed became the border in the twelfth century. It changed hands thirteen times, and was finally surrendered to the English in 1482.
89. *perpendicular*] i.e. a wall or steep cliff, rising at right angles to the horizontal (*OED* C n. 2).
92. *influence . . . star*] a reference to the commonly held belief that the stars had a determining influence upon the sublunary world, and on human events in particular.
94. *Holy Island*] the small island of Lindisfarne, two miles off the Northumberland coast, linked to the mainland by a causeway at low tide; a religious centre since 635 when St Aidan, the first bishop, founded a church and monastery there. The monks fled to Durham in 875 in the face of Danish raids, but the monastery was refounded from Durham in 1082, and it was garrisoned at the end of the sixteenth century. There were sixteen bishops, but the see was finally transferred to Chester-le-Street in 875, and to Durham in 995.
95. *seclude*] separate, keep apart (*OED* v. 6, which uses this instance as an example).
97. *litanies*] appointed forms of public prayer (especially in the Book of Common Prayer) in which the clergy and the people respond in successive supplications (*OED* n. 1).
98. *Deliver . . . wrath*] In the Book of Common Prayer, the fifth supplication for deliverance in the Litany is concerned with 'sedition and privy conspiracy'. In the 1549 prayerbook, this included 'the tyranny of the Bishop of Rome and all his detestable enormities'.
99. *Calvin . . . Sales*] i.e. the bishops will always prefer the Roman Catholic spiritual writer St François de Sales, whose devotional works were popular with English high church divines, to Jean Calvin, after Luther, the most important figurehead of the Reformation in Europe. Sales was a bishop of Geneva, the city with which Calvin was most closely associated.
100. *Burnet's*] Alexander Burnet (1614–84), Bishop of Aberdeen (1663–64), and Archbishop of Glasgow (1664–69, 1674–79), an uncompromising high episcopalian and persecutor of the Presbyterians. He was the chief obstacle to the policy of reconciliation, and was encouraged to be so by Sheldon (see below, 406–7). He protested against Lauderdale's policy under the terms of the Act of Supremacy of 1669,

which was consequently used to extract his resignation on 24 December. *Lauderdales*] John Maitland, second Earl and first Duke of Lauderdale (1616–82); High Commissioner in Scotland from 1669; an enemy of Burnet's, and at times in favour of toleration and conciliation (e.g. 1667–69); see above *Headnote, Context*. Cp. 'To the parliam'' (*c.* 1670s–1680s), ll. 9–11, Essex RO, MS D/DW/Z4 (xiii): 'Would you unravell Popish Plotts./Lord Lauderdale amongst the Scots/And rid the Court of Irish Sotts.' This quotation appears to present Lauderdale as a Roman Catholic.
101. *Becket's . . . tails*] Legouis reports, without citing a source, that Thomas à Becket was said to have cursed the men of Strood for cutting off his horse's tail; their children were thenceforth to be born with tails. The story remains unsubstantiated. In *RT*, 92, 112, Becket appears as the archetypal greedy and persecuting prelate.
103. *joint-stools*] stools made of parts of wood fitted together (*OED* 1); used in the Scottish church, as opposed to the pews in English churches. When the prayerbook was imposed in Edinburgh in 1637, the congregation threw their stools at the Dean. *chairs*] bishops' seats, and hence the symbol of their authority (*OED* n. 4).
104. *church . . . kirk*] 'kirk' (northern English and Scottish form of 'church') was used officially to distinguish the Church of Scotland from the Church of England until the Westminster Assembly of 1645–48. The struggle between episcopacy and Presbyterianism (see above, *Headnote, Context*) in the Restoration was the last phase of a contest that was as old as the Reformation. In 1690, the Church of Scotland finally and lastingly became Presbyterian, and 'kirk' was used to distinguish it from the Church of England and the episcopal church of Scotland.
106. *Rogation Week*] week in which Ascension Day falls (*OED* n. 1 b); associated with donations for alms (see *OED* n. 1 d); the chanting of saints' litanies during processions in Rogation Week was seen by Puritans as Popish.
107. *bound*] border, boundary (*OED* n.¹ 2); also recalls another Anglican custom, 'beating the bounds', tracing the boundaries of a parish, striking certain points along the way with a rod (*OED* v.¹ III 41); this took place in Rogation Week (see above, l. 106n.). Cp. *RT*, 228, 'You that do, as if it were in Rogation week, perambulate the Bounds of government, and leave them *so easie to be understood, and also unnecessary to be transgressed,* why would you here have conceal'd them, or was it in that manner you drew a Line betwixt the Prince and the Subject to serve ever after for their Boundary.'

Their seas make islands in our continent.
110 Nature in vain us in one land compiles
If the cathedral still will have its isles.
Nothing, not bogs, not sands, not seas, not alps,
Separate the world, so as the bishops' scalps.
Stretch for your line their surcingle alone,
115 'Twill make a more inhabitable zone.
The friendly loadstone hath not more combined,
Than bishops cramped the commerce of mankind.
A bishop will like Mahomet tear the moon,
And slip one half into his sleeve as soon.
120 The juggling prelate on his hocus calls,
Shows you first one, then makes that one two balls.
Instead of all the plagues, had bishops come,
Pharaoh at first would have sent Israel home.

From church they need not censure men away,
125 A bishop's self is an anathema:
Where foxes dung, their earths the badgers yield,
At bishops' musk, ev'n foxes quit the field.
Their rank ambition all this heat has stirred:
A bishop's rennet makes the strongest curd.
130   What rev'rend things (Lord) are lawn sleeves and ea
How a clean laundress and no sermons please!
They wanted zeal and learning, so forsook
Bible and grammar for the service book.
Religion has too long the world depraved,
135 A shorter way's to be by clergy saved.
Believe, but only as the church believes,
And learn to pin your faith upon their sleeves,
(Ah, like Lot's wife they still look back and halt,

---

109. islands . . . continent] contrast with official language, which stressed pacification in one island; see, e.g., 'The Answer of the Parliament of Scotland to His Majesties Gracious Letter', in *His Majesties Letter to his Parliament in Scotland* (1669), 10: 'in Your Desires to render this *Island* more happy then ever it was in former Times.'
111. isles] i.e. a pun on 'aisles'.
112. not . . . alps] Cp. Lucan, *De bello civili*, I.686–90: 'Dubiam super aequora Syrtium/Arentemque feror Libyen, quo tristis Enyo/Transtulit Emathias acies. Nunc desuper Alpis/Nubiferae colles atque aeriam Pyrenen/Abripimur.' (The grim goddess of war has shifted the ranks of Pharsalia across the sea to treacherous Syrtis and parched Libya: thither also am I carried. Next am I spirited away over the cloud-capped Alps and soaring Pyrenees.) (Parker, *N & Q*, n.s. 51 (2004), 39).
113. scalps] a) tops or crowns of heads (*OED* n.[1] 1 a), suggesting an association between bishops, and Roman Catholic monks, with their shaven tonsures b) bank in coastal waters providing a bed for shellfish; a Scottish word (*OED* n.[2]).
114. surcingle] belt or girdle tightened around a cassock (*OED* n. 2). Cp. *RT*, 32, 'This Gentleman, in the Dog-dayes, stragling by Temple-Bar, in a massy Cassock and Surcingle, and taking the opportunity at once to piss and admire the Title-page of his Book.'
115. inhabitable] Margoliouth glossed this as 'uninhabitable' (*OED* a.[1]), but Parker, *N & Q*, n.s. 51 (2004), 35–6, suggests 'inhabitable', the physical corpulence of the bishops being in contrast to their mental activity. *zone*] a) region with definite limits; originally each of the five 'belts' encircling the globe and defined by climate (*OED* n. 1) b) belt (*OED* n. 3). 'Zone' derives from Greek ζώνη, meaning 'girdle'.
116. friendly] in the sense of mutually attractive. *loadstone*] magnet (*OED* 1).
118–19. Mahomet . . . sleeve] an elaboration of the Qur'an, Sura 54.1: 'The hour drew night and the moon did rend asunder', one of the stories relating to Mohammed's miraculous demonstration of his mission.
120. hocus] jugglery, trickery, deception (*OED* n. 2). A reapplication of terms used by Cleveland in *The Rebell Scot*, ll. 25–6, and thus an example of his 'recantation': 'Before a Scot can properly be curst,/I must (like Hocus) swallow daggers first.'
122–3. See Exod. 9:13–14.
124–7. From . . . feld] Cp. du Bartas, *Divine Weeks*, trans. Sylvester, II.iv.4. 929, 931–4: 'As the selfe-swelling Badgerd,

at the bay/With boldest Hounds (inured to that Fray)/First at the entry of his Burrow fights,/Then in his Earth; and either other bites.' (Parker, *N & Q*, forthcoming), where the undermining of Jerusalem's walls by Chaldean troops is countermined by the Jewish troops under Ebedmelech.
125. anathema] the curse against sinners (*OED* I 2); bishops do not need to pronounce a formal 'anathema' because they are themselves a deterrent and a curse.
126. dung] drop excrement (*OED* v. 2 a). *musk*] strong-smelling substances secreted from a gland by certain animals, used as a basis for perfumes (*OED* n. 1); associated with whores: Williams (1994), II.925.
128. rank] a) haughty (*OED* a. A I 1) b) excessive (*OED* A II 6 b) c) corrupt (*OED* III 14 b) d) stinking, rancid (*OED* A III 12). *heat*] turbulence in church and state.
129. rennet] mass of curdled milk found in the stomach of an unweaned calf, or any other substance, used to curdle milk in order to make cheese. *curd*] coagulated milk, eaten as food or made into cheese (*OED* n. 1); scatological: sounds like 'turd'.
130. lawn sleeves] sleeves made of lawn (a kind of fine linen), forming part of a bishop's wear, and associated with the dignity of episcopal office. Cp. *RT*, in *MPW*, 109: 'some Clergymen have been so opiniastre that they have rather exposed the State to ruine then they would part with a Pin, I will not say out of their Church, but out of their Sleeve'. See also below, l. 137 n.
132. wanted] lacked. *zeal*] intense and ardent eagerness; associated with Puritan and Nonconformist religious enthusiasm (*OED* n. 4 a).
133. service book] The Book of Common Prayer (reintroduced in 1662).
134. depraved] corrupted, perverted (*OED* v. 2).
136. Believe . . . believes] episcopal religion is made to look like Roman Catholicism: requiring communicants to follow the authority of church tradition.
137. pin . . . sleeves] a version of a common literary proverb (Tilley F32): e.g. William Secker, *The Nonsuch Professor* (1660), 274: 'That was a good saying of Sir Thomas More: I will not pin my faith upon any man's sleeve, because I know not wither he will carry it.' See also above, l. 130 n.
138. Lot's wife . . . halt] In Gen. 19:26 Lot's wife is turned into a pillar of salt when she looks back upon God's destruction of Sodom and Gomorrah. In their surplices the bishops look like pillars of salt; in being backward with regard to faith, they are like Lot's wife, looking back upon old and sinful ways.

And, surpliced, show like pillars too of salt.)
0 Who that is wise would pulpit-toil endure?
A bishopric is a great sine-cure:
Enough for them, God knows, to count their wealth,
To excommunicate, and study health.
A higher work is to their call annexed;
5 The nation they divide, their curates, text.
No bishop? Rather than it should be so,
No church, no trade, no king, no people, no.
All mischief's moulded by these state divines;
Aaron cast calves, but Moses them calcines.
0 The legion-devil did but one man possess;
One bishop's fiend spirits a whole diocese.

That power alone can loose this spell that ties:
For only kings can bishops exorcise.
Will you be treated princes? here fall to:
155 Fish and flesh bishops are your ambigu.
Howe'er insipid, yet the sauce will mend 'em,
Bishops are very good when *in commendam*.
If wealth or vice can tempt your appetites,
These Templar Lords exceed the Templar Knights.
160 And in the baron-bishop you have both
Leviathan served up and Behemoth.
How can you bear such miscreants should live,
And holy ordure holy orders give?
None knows what god our flamen now adores.

141. sine-cure] a) ecclesiastical position without cure of souls (*OED* n. 1); and hence b) a paid office which involves no work (*OED* n. 2). The first usage of a) recorded in *OED* is 1661 and of b), 1676. All of the listed seventeenth-century examples use the two word form, most of them hyphenated.

143. excommunicate] exclude from participation in church services (*OED* v. 1). *health*] a) spiritual well-being (*OED* n. 4) b) personal welfare (*OED* n. 5).

145. divide . . . text] to divide a text was to analyse a section of scripture during a sermon; hence the curates preach while the bishops divide the nation.

146. No bishop] Usually attributed to James I (see, e.g., Fuller, recording the Hampton Court conference, 1604), *The Church History of Britain* (1655), X.1.12: 'it is my *Aphorisme*, No *bishop*, no *king*', but 'No bishop, No King' was in proverbial usage at the time (Tilley, B408).

148. moulded] shaping by acts of statecraft; an instance of terms associated with secular 'reason of state' thinking, and therefore hardly appropriate for clergymen; see above, *An Horatian Ode*, l. 36 n., and *The Last Instructions*, ll. 815–16.

149. When Moses was receiving the tablets from God on Mount Sinai, Aaron made an idol in the shape of a calf from molten gold. When Moses returned to the Israelites, he burned the calf (see Exod. 32). The bishops are equated with Aaron the high priest. *calcines*] burns (*OED* v. 2).

150–3. For the context of these lines in respect of the power of the king to break the Anglican hegemony, see Dzelzainis (in Chernaik and Dzelzainis, eds (1999)), 303.

150. The legion . . . possess] Jesus called on the spirit possessing the man in the country of the Gadarenes by asking its name; the unclean spirit in the man answered 'Legion: because many devils were entered into him.' (Luke 8:30. See also Mark 5:1–20).

151. fiend] evil spirit (*OED* n. 3). *spirits*] a) possesses (not in *OED*) b) stirs up (*OED* v. I 2 d).

153. exorcise] a) drive away an evil spirit (*OED* v. 1) b) a pun on 'exercise': to discipline (*OED* v. 3). Cp. *Flecknoe, an English Priest at Rome*, ll. 20–2: 'In hideous verse, he, in a dismal tone,/Begins to exercise, as if I were/Possessed; and sure the Devil brought me there.'

154. treated] entertained as (*OED* v. 8 b). *fall to*] fall to eating (*OED* v. X 66 e). With 'to' read as 'too', there is a pun that invokes the tradition of 'fall of princes' (*de casibus*) literature.

155. Fish and flesh] the image presents a dish of bishops made of both fish and flesh as fitting for those who want food fit for a prince. 'Flesh' suggests worldliness, and also lust; fish

was the non-lustful food (especially for the clergy), but it was also a sexual emblem (Williams (1994), I.491). For the hearty appetites of bishops, see *RT*, 92. *ambigu*] entertainment at which meat and dessert were served together (*OED*).

157. commendam] a) ecclesiastical benefice; benefice held by a bishop (or other dignitary) alongside his own preferment (*OED* n. 1) b) commandery; landed estate belonging to an order of knights (*OED* 2); hence the reference to Knights Templar in l. 159. Samuel Parker, M.'s butt in *The Rehearsal Transpos'd*, held the archdeaconry of Canterbury *in commendam* with his bishopric. (*DNB*)

159. Templar Lords] bishops (lords of the temple [i.e. cathedrals]). *Templar Knights*] order of knights founded in 1119–20 for the protection of the Holy Sepulchre and pilgrims visiting the Holy Land. They were extremely powerful and wealthy, and were dissolved in 1312.

160. baron-bishop] i.e. lord bishop. *baron*] a) lowest order of the nobility (*OED* n. 2) b) joint of beef consisting of two sirloins left uncut at the backbone (*OED* n. 8).

161. Leviathan] huge sea monster (see Job 41:1; associated with the devil in Isa. 27:1). *Behemoth*] a huge land beast (see Job 40:15–24). Elsewhere, M. writes that Bishop Parker had written a monstrous work (*A Reproof to the Rehearsal Transposed* (1673)) against Hobbes' alleged atheism in *Leviathan*: see *RT*, 214, and by the way upholding the authority of the bishops: 'I do not see but your [Parker's] *Behemoth* exceeds his [Hobbes'] *Leviathan* some foot long, in whatsoever he saith of the Power of the Magistrate in matters of Religion and Civils; save that you have levyed the Invisible Powers to your assistance.' Hobbes published his own *Behemoth*, his history of the Civil War, in 1679; it had been completed earlier but was withheld from publication at the insistence of the King. It is thus unlikely that M. can have seen it. He may well have read and been amused by Hobbes's rebuttal of John Bramhall, Archbishop of Armagh: ' "he . . . will demonstrate that my principles are pernicious both to piety and policy, and destructive to all relations", &c.: my answer is, that I desire not that he or they should so misspend their time; but if they will needs do it, I can give them a fit title for their book, Behemoth against Leviathan' (Thomas Hobbes, *The Questions concerning Liberty, Necessity, and Chance* (1656), 26).

163. ordure] a) filth, dirt (*OED* n. 1) b) excrement (*OED* n. 2). *orders*] ordination (of priests).

164. flamen] priest in Roman antiquity; later used of ancient British priests (*OED* 1, 3).

165 One mitre fits the heads of foùr Moors.
     No wonder if the orthodox do bleed,
     While Arius stands at th'Athanasian Creed.
     What so obdúrate pagan-heretic
     But will transform for an archbishopric?
170 In faith erroneous, and in life profane,
     These hypocrites their faith and linen stain.
     Seth's pillars are no antique brick or stone,

     But of the choicest modern flesh and bone.
     Who views but Gilbert's toils will reason find
175 Neither before to trust him nor behind.
     How oft hath age his hall'wing hands misled,
     Confirming breasts and armpits for the head!
     Abbot one buck, but he shot many a doe:
     Nor is our Sheldon whiter than his Snow.
180 Their company's the worst that ever played,

---

165. mitre] a) bishop's hat and symbol of his office (*OED* n.[1] 2c) b) turban; oriental headdress (OED n.[1] 1 c). *foùr Moors*] the four archbishops of England and Scotland (Gilbert Sheldon of Canterbury, Richard Sterne of York, Alexander Burnet of Glasgow, James Sharp of St Andrews) imagined as oriental, and hence, in Christian terms, heretical, as well as tyrannical, figures.

167. Arius . . . Creed] Arius denied the doctrine of the Trinity; Athanasius led the Council of Nicea in 325, where the co-eternity and co-equality of the Father and the Son were defined and reaffirmed. The Athanasian Creed encompassed the doctrine of the Trinity and the Incarnation and upheld the truth of the gospel accounts of the life of Christ. While M. was critical of man-made creeds, he is voicing criticism of the Restoration bishops whose sympathy for rational theology led them to be cast as anti-Trinitarians by their opponents. Sheldon (see below, l. 174 n.) had encountered Socinian (after the anti-Trinitarian Faustus Socinus (1539–1604)) books at Great Tew in the 1630s, and was probably responsible for the aquisition of some of them by All Souls College, of which he was Warden (1626–48, 1659–60; McLachlan (1952), 65, 124). Although the Book of Common Prayer (1662) required that the Athanasian Creed should be said or sung, standing, by the minister and congregation, Tillotson was in favour of its abolition (McLachlan (1952), 335). If 'Arius' stands for a politic or Latitudinarian bishop, his hypocrisy is being pointed up. John Owen wrote against Socinianism in 1669 and 1672, and M. defended him by accusing Parker of theological laxness, while also observing 'there is a very great neglect somewhere, wheresoever the Inspection of Books is lodged, that at least the *Socinian* Books are tolerated and sell as openly as the Bible' (*RT*, 78).

168. obdúrate] hardened in wickedness (*OED* a. 1 a).

169. transform] undergo a change of form or nature (*OED* v. 2).

171–3. 'Gilbert Sheldon ar. b: of Canterb obiit Nov. 9.1677' written in margin against these lines in *NLS*.

171. linen stain] metonymically suggesting that the bishops abuse their office, since the lawn-sleeves worn by bishops were made of fine linen. In the light of the sexual overtones of l. 175, 'stain' also carries connotations of sexual or fecal as well as moral pollution.

172. Seth's] a) two pillars, one of brick and one of stone, proof respectively against fire and water, erected by the children of Seth who had been told of the deluge to come, and on which were inscribed all discoveries and inventions; it was believed that they survived in Syria: see Flavius Josephus, *Antiquities*, I.3, in *Works*, trans. Roger L'Estrange (1702), 6. b) Seth Ward (1617–89), Bishop of Salisbury, and a persecutor of Dissenters. *pillars*] an obscene reference to the penis (Williams, II.1030).

174. Gilbert] Gilbert Sheldon (1598–1677), Archbishop of Canterbury from August 1663: see above, l. 153 n., and *The Last Instructions*, ll. 811–16. Sheldon played an important role in imposing episcopacy in Scotland in the Restoration, so his

place in the poem is appropriate. However, sources for his life do not support the picture of sexual impropriety given here, despite the rumours that circulated (see above, *The Last Instructions*, l. 811 n.). He had been a critic of the conduct of the court since the Interregnum, and reproved Charles II for his adultery, even to the extent of refusing him Holy Communion. Sheldon was in favour of compelling uniformity in the church, and had a major part in the passing of the Corporation Act of 1670, but he is known to have protected and even promoted individual nonconformist divines. *toils*] a) verbal disputes (*OED* n.[1] 1) b) traps (*OED* n.[2] 3).

175. before . . . behind] 'alluding to vaginal and sodomitical intercourse', Williams (1994), I.93.

176–7. How . . . head] In *RT*, 8, Samuel Parker's prurient misrepresentation of John Owen is regarded as the consequence of his desire for 'a female'. Parker was one of Sheldon's chaplains (*c*. October 1667–7).

176. hall'wing] sanctifying (*OED* ppl. a). *misled*] moved in the wrong direction (*OED* v. 2).

177. Confirming . . . head] the poet imagines, in a confirmation service, the Archbishop salaciously touching the breasts and armpits of those being confirmed instead of their heads. Cp. The Book of Common Prayer, 1662, 'The Order of Confirmation': 'Then all of them in order, kneeling before the Bishop, he shall lay his hand upon the head of every one severally.' *Confirming*] a) ascertaining (*OED* v. 7) b) administering of rite in the Church of England by a bishop to baptized persons who have reached 'years of discretion', which admits them to the full privileges of the church (*OED* v. 5; 'confirmation': *OED* n. 5). *for the*] i.e. instead of.

178. Abbot . . . buck] 'Geo: Abbot arch: B: of Canterbury shooting at a deer kild the Lord Zouch's keeper in Brashall parish [i.e. Bramshill Park, Hampshire] 1621' written in margin of *NLS*. While hunting with his friend Lord Zouch on 24 July 1621, and armed with a crossbow, George Abbot, Archbishop of Canterbury (1562–1633) mistakenly killed Peter Hawkins, a gamekeeper. Since the gamekeeper had already been warned to keep clear of the hunters, Abbot was cleared of any crime, but his authority to consecrate was consequently challenged (see *DNB*).

179. Anthony à Wood records an audience with Sheldon at Lambeth Place on 9 February 1672 in which Ralph Snow was present as an attendant. Afterwards, a group, including Sheldon's chaplains (Samuel Parker among them) and Snow, retired to drink and to smoke: Wood, 'The Life of Anthony à Wood', *Athenae Oxonienses*, 4th edn, I (1813), lxxi. Parker reports that Sheldon disliked those obsessed with religious observances, and liked to say 'Do well, and be merry', a sentence that would obviously give offence to Puritans: Parker, *Bishop Parker's History of his Own Time*, trans. T. Newlin (1728), 42. *Sheldon*] see above, ll. 153 n., 160 n.

180. company . . . played] the bishops are compared to a bad company of actors.

And their religion all but masquerade.
The conscious prelate therefore did not err,
When for a church he built a theatre.
A congr'ous dress they to themselves adapt,
5 Like smutty stories in clean linen wrapped.
Do but their piebald lordships once uncase
Of rochets, tippets, copes, and where's their grace?
A hungry chaplain and a starvèd rat,
Eating their brethren, bishop turn and cat.
0 But an apocryphal Archbishop Bel
Like snake, by swallowing toads, doth dragons swell.
When daring Blood to have his rents regained
Upon the English diadem distrained,
He chose the cassock, surcingle and gown,
5 The fittest mask for one that robs a crown.
But his lay pity underneath prevailed,

And while he spared the keeper's life, he failed.
With the priest's vestments had he but put on
A bishop's cruelty, the crown had gone.
200 Strange was the sight, that Scotch twin-headed man
With single body, like the two-necked swan;
And wild disputes betwixt those heads must grow
Where but two hands to act, two feet to go.
Nature in living emblem there expressed
205 What Britain was between two kings distressed.
But now when one head does both realms control,
The bishop's noddle perks up cheek by jowl.
They, though no poets, on Parnassus dream,
And in their causes think themselves supreme.
210 King's-head saith this, but bishop's-head that do;
Does Charles the Second reign, or Charles the Two?
Well that Scotch monster and our bishops sort,

---

181. masquerade] assembly of people wearing extravagant masks and other disguises, with dancing and other entertainments; a masked ball (*OED* 1). The targets of satire are the ceremonies prescribed by the 1662 Book of Common Prayer.
182. conscious] knowledgeable of his wrong-doing (*OED* a. 4 b).
183. for] i.e. instead of. *theatre*] Sheldon succeeded Clarendon as Chancellor of Oxford University in December 1667. The Sheldonian theatre was built entirely at his expense in Oxford for the performance of the 'Act, or Encaenia', the annual ceremony for the commemoration of founders and benefactors. It was opened on 9 July 1669; Sheldon, who had never been installed as Chancellor, resigned on 31 July. The reference has overtones of popery: Protestant controversialists often referred to the Roman Catholic Mass as a piece of theatre.
184. congr'ous] i.e. corresponding with their natures (referring to the black and white robes of a bishop: the white episcopal rochet, with lawn sleeves, worn over a black cassock).
185. smutty] indecent, obscene (*OED* a 5). *stories*] paintings or sculptures of historical subjects (*OED* n.¹ II 8).
186. piebald] of mixed colours or qualities (*OED* a.). *uncase*] undress (*OED* v. 1 c).
187. rochets] linen surplices, worn by bishops and abbots (*OED* n.¹ 2). Cp. *RT*, 112, ll. 9–13: 'the late War . . . 'Tis four and twenty years ago, and after an *Act of Oblivion*; and for ought I can see, it had been as seasonable to have shown *Caesars* bloody Coat, or *Thomas a Beckets* bloody Rochet.' *tippets*] bands of silk worn round the neck, with the ends hanging in front (*OED* n. 1 c). *copes*] ecclesiastical cloaks (*OED* n.¹ 2).
190–1. apocryphal . . . swell] a complicated allusion to the story of Bel and the Dragon in the Apocrypha, that fuses the two distinct parts. The prophet Daniel reveals to King Cyrus that the Babylonian idol Bel does not eat food, and kills the dragon that the Babylonians also worshipped by making it eat lumps of pitch, fat and hair, which made it burst. Here, the archbishop is an idol, and an apocryphal scripture, without true authority. His worldly lusts make him swell like the dragon.
192–9. See below, *Bludius et Corona, Headnote.*
193. distrained] grasped tightly (*OED* I 1).
194. surcingle] see above, l. 114 n.
196. lay] of the people, as opposed to the clergy. *pity*] 'pity' as compassion and sympathy (*OED* n. 2) was semantically continuous with 'piety' (i.e. devout, *OED* n. II 2), since the

former was a development in late Latin from the latter. *OED* records the last usage of 'pity' as 'piety' in 1687, and of 'piety' as 'pity' in 1606. Hence Blood shows true 'lay piety', as opposed to the doubtful faith of the clergy.
200. Scotch . . . man] the Scottish histories report the birth of a two-headed 'monster' (i.e. what appears to be Siamese twins) at the time of the marriage in 1498 of King James IV to Margaret, daughter of Henry VII of England. The two parts of the creature, which survived for twenty-eight years, were often in disagreement, but felt pain in common and could sometimes make agreements. In William Drummond, *The History of Scotland* (1655), 134, the phenomenon is meant to illustrate symbolically the nature of Anglo-Scottish relations: the peace between the two nations achieved by the marriage treaty broke down soon afterwards. M.'s point, concluded in l. 191, is that now that England and Scotland have one king, there is no need for conflict between the two nations, but which had occurred on account of the bishops' (and others') desire to impose episcopal church government on the Scots. Other accounts exist in George Buchanan, *Rerum Scoticarum Historia* (1668), 444, translated as *The History of Scotland* (1690), pt. 13, 4, where the creature is described as a hermaphrodite, and Robert Lindsay of Pittscottie, *The History of Scotland* (1728), 103. Both note that one part died some time before the other, leaving the survivor to carry the putrified flesh in great misery.
201. two-necked swan] The Swan of Two Necks (or Nicks) was an inn in Ladd Lane, London belonging to the Vintners' Company. From it coaches left London for the north, including, presumably, Scotland (Winifred Stevenson, private communication).
207. noddle] head (colloquial, indicating jest or contempt, dullness or emptiness; *OED* n.¹ 3).
208. Parnassus] because Parnassus, the hill associated with poetry, had two peaks. Cleveland was often associated with Parnassus by his admirers, so that the reference is doubly ironic: Cleveland 'Whose Laureat-Genius rapt with Sacred skill/Prov'd his Extraction from *Parnassus* Hill', Philip Cleveland, *Upon the most Ingenious and Incomparable Musophilist of his time, Mʳ John Cleaveland* (1658), s.sh.
212. sort] correspond to (*OED* v.¹ I 8).

(It was musician too, and dwelt at court).
    Hark, though at such a distance, what a noise
215 Shatt'ring the silent air disturbs our joys:
The mitred hubbub against Pluto moot,
The cloven head must govern cloven foot.
Strange boldness! Bishops even there rebel,
And plead their *Jus Divinum* though in Hell.
220 Those whom you hear more clam'rous yet and loud,
Of ceremonies wrangle in the crowd,
And would, like chemists fixing mercury,
Transfuse indiff'rence with necessity.
To sit is necessary in Parl'ment,
225 To preach in diocese, indifferent;
New oaths tis necessary to invent,

To give new taxes is indifferent;
To conform's necessary or be shent,
But to reform is all indifferent.
230 'Tis necessary bishops have their rent,
To cheat the plague-money, indifferent.
'Tis necessary to rebabel Paul's,
Indifferent to rob churches of their coals.
'Tis necessary Lambeth never wed,
235 Indifferent to have a wench in bed;
Such bishops are, with all their complement,
Not necessary, nor indifferent.
    Incorrigible among all their pains,
Some sue for tithe of the Elysian plains.
240 Others attempt (to cool their fervent chine)

---

213. musician . . . court] James IV had the two-headed creature educated in languages and music; bishops patronized music (especially with cathedral organs, which were offensive to Puritans), and some, like Sheldon, frequented courts.

214–19. The description, for satirical purposes, of the inhabitants of the underworld, or those on their way to it, was popular from the example of Lucian's dialogues. Seventeenth-century versions that placed religious enemies in Hell include Donne's *Ignatius his Conclave* (1611), Cowley's *The Civil War* (1643), II, ll. 365–617, and, in its way, the Parliament in Hell in Milton's *Paradise Lost*, II.

215. silent] quiet, noiseless (*OED* a. A 4).

216. moot] complain, murmur (OED v.^{1} 1, Scottish, 16–17th century).

217. cloven] split into two (*OED* ppl. a. b). The bishops are imagined as governing (with their cloven hats – mitres) the devils (with cloven feet, the goat's feet of traditional devil iconography).

219. Jus Divinum] the argument that episcopacy was instituted by God; hence bishops had 'divine right'.

221. wrangle] argue noisily (*OED* v. 1).

222. chemists fixing mercury] alchemical process whereby mercury, the spirit of life and mother of all metals, is captured and tamed so that the production of the philosopher's stone can take place (Abraham (1998), 78, 124–5). Cp. John Collop, 'To Eugenia' (1656), ll. 39–40: 'Chymists say, who fix *Mercury* can make gold,/Fix me *Eugenia* thou art rich if't hold.' *fixing*] making solid (*OED* v. I 4 a); alchemical 'coagulation' or 'congelation', converting spirit into body (Abraham (1998), 78).

223. i.e. 'turn points on which Christians might legitimately differ into points on which believers are required to obey bishops.' *Transfuse*] permeate, instil (*OED* v. 2). *indifference*] theological principle that, within limits, differences of religious belief or practice, are of no importance; also known as adiaphorism ('indifferency', *OED* n. II 8 b); see, e.g., Hooker, *Laws of Ecclesiastical Policy* (1594), II.iv.4: 'The choice is left to our own discretion, except a principal bond of some higher dutie remove the indifferencie that some things have in themselves.' *necessity*] M. refers ironically to how a seventeenth-century theologian would use 'necessity', a) constraint in the natural or divine order of things (*OED* n. 2; 'necessary' *OED* a. II 5), but he implies that the bishops mean b) compelled by

circumstances (*OED* n. 3), part of the language of reason of state attributed to them; see also above, l. 148 n.

224. Bishops had seats in the House of Lords.

226. oaths] oaths were the means by which the restored Church of England imposed its authority: the Act of Uniformity, 1662, requiring obedience from protestant clergymen, the Corporation Act, with oaths requiring that members of urban corporations receive the Anglican sacrament, and, most important, the Test Act of March 1673, which imposed the oaths of supremacy and allegiance, and the requirement of annual communion in the Church of England on office-holders.

227. new taxes] see *RT*, 138: 'It has been observed, that whensoever his Majesty hath had the most urgent occasions for Supply, other of them [the Lords Spiritual] have made it their business to trinkle with the *Members of Parliament*, for obstructing it.'

228. shent] disgraced (*OED* ppl. a.).

231. plague-money] the charge is that the bishops have purloined money raised in churches for the relief of the families of plague victims.

232. rebabel] Instead of 'rebuild'; build as high as the Tower of Babel (not in *OED*). *Paul's*] St Paul's Cathedral, in the process of reconstruction after the Great Fire of London.

233. coals] possibly punning on 'cole' (*OED* n.^{3}): money; the first recorded usage is 1673.

234. Lambeth] the Archbishop of Canterbury; Lambeth Palace is his London residence. None of the seventeenth-century Archbishops – Abbot, Laud, Juxon and Sheldon – had been married. In *RT*, 154–5, M. claimed that marriage would prevent Parker from becoming Archbishop of Canterbury.

236. complement] a) ceremoniousness (*OED* n. II 8 b) b) accomplishments (i.e. wicked deeds) (*OED* n. I 1 c) c) all the people, administration and materials that come with a bishop (*OED* n. I 4 b).

238. Incorrigible] depraved beyond reform (*OED* a. 1).

239. tithe] tenth part of annual agricultural produce exacted for the support of the clergy (*OED* n.^{1} B 1). *Elysian plains*] home of the dead in Greek mythology.

240. chine] back (*OED* n.^{2} 2); hence a metonym for the penis: Williams (1994), I.238–9, notes that a strong back was regarded in the seventeenth century as a requisite for a sexual athlete. See also *The Last Instructions to a Painter*, l. 34.

A second time to ravish Proserpine.
E'en Father Dis, though so with age defaced,
With much ado preserves his postern chaste.
The innocentest minds there thirst alone,
5 And, unenforced, quaff healths in Phlegeton.
Luxury, malice, superstition, pride,
Oppression, avarice, ambition, id-
leness, and all the vice that did abound
While they lived here, still haunts them underground.
0 Had it not been for such a bias strong,
Two nations ne'er had missed the mark so long.
The world in all does but two nations bear,
The good, the bad, and those mixed everywhere:
Under each pole place either of the two,
5 The good will bravely, bad will basely do;
And few indeed can parallel our climes
For worth heroic, or heroic crimes.
The trial would, however, be too nice,
Which stronger were, a Scotch or English vice,
50 Or whether the same virtue would reflect

From Scotch or English heart the same effect.
    Nation is all but name as shibboleth,
Where a mistaken accent causes death.
In paradise names only Nature showed,
265 At Babel names from pride and discord flowed;
And ever since men with a female spite
First call each other names, and then they fight.
Scotland and England! Cause of just uproar,
Does 'man' and 'wife' signify 'rogue' and 'whore'?
270 Say but 'a Scot', and straight we fall to sides,
That syllable like a Pict's wall divides.
Rational men's words, pledges all of peace,
Perverted, serve dissensions to increase.
For shame, extirpate from each loyal breast,
275 That senseless rancour against interest.
    One king, one faith, one language, and one isle:
English and Scotch, 'tis all but cross and pile.
    Charles, our great soul, this only understands,
He our affection both and will commands.
280 And where twin sympathies cannot atone,

---

241. Proserpine] daughter of Ceres and Jupiter, raped and carried off by Pluto to be queen of the lower world (see Ovid, *Metamorphoses*, V, ll. 391–6; see also Milton, *Paradise Lost*, IX, ll. 268–72).
242. Dis] Pluto, king of the classical underworld.
243. postern] a) a back gate (*OED* n. 1) b) hind part (*OED* n. 3), i.e. anus (as an innuendo usually signifies 'vagina' (Williams (1994), II.1076)). The image is of Dis protecting himself from the advances of bishops intent on sodomizing him.
245. unenforced] subject to no constraints. *Phlegeton*] river of fire, one of the five rivers in Hades, the classical hell.
246–9. Luxury . . . underground] Cp. du Bartas, *Divine Weeks*, trans. Sylvester, II.iv.4.298–32: 'Their wilfull Dumbness, forcing others dumb/(To Sion's grievous Loss, and gain of Rome)/ Their Courting, Sporting, and Non-residence,/Their Avarice, their Sloth and Negligence.' (Parker, *N & Q*, 51 (2005), 318–24).
250. bias] a) oblique trajectory of ball in game of bowls (*OED* B 2 b) b) tendency, prejudice (*OED* B 3).
251. mark] target in game of bowls (see above, l. 250 n. a); *OED* n.¹ 7 f).
258. nice] of very slight difference (*OED* a. 9 b).
262. shibboleth] a) word used to detect foreigners by their pronunciation: see Judges 12:6: 'Then said they unto him, Say now Shibboleth: and he said Sibboleth: for he could not frame to pronounce it right. Then they took him, and slew him at the passages of Jordan: and there fell at that time of the Ephraimites forty and two thousand.' (*OED* 1, 2). Cleveland used the word in *The Rustick Rampant* (1658), 36: 'They had a *Shibboleth* to discover them, he who pronounced *Brot* and *Cawse* for *Bread* and *Cheese* had his head lopt off.'

264. paradise . . . showed] according to a widely accepted theory of the origins of names (especially prominent in occult and hermetic writings), God placed a signature in every object of creation, and enabled Adam to recognize those signatures, and thus to be able innately to name nature. Words could only name one object; puns were a consequence of the Fall. See above, *Upon Appleton House*, ll. 581–2; *The Garden*, ll. 23–4.
265. The episode of the Tower of Babel (Gen. 11:4–9) was regarded as the second linguistic fall: men had built a tower in order to reach heaven, and to have a reputation, but God punished them for their pride by producing many languages in men which were mutually incomprehensible.
266. female spite] cp. *To his Noble Friend Mr Richard Lovelace, upon his Poems*, ll. 39–43: 'They all in mutiny . . . /Sallied . . . /And one, the loveliest that was yet e'er seen,/Thinking that I too of the rout had been,/Mine eyes invaded with a female spite.'
268. uproar] stressed on second syllable.
270. straight] immediately.
271. Pict's wall] The Romans built two defensive walls in northern Britain to keep invading tribes (i.e. the Picts) at bay: Hadrian's Wall (built *c.* AD 122–8; completed AD 136), running for 73 miles from Wallsend to Bowness, and the Antonine Wall (built *c.* AD 142), running for 36.5 miles between the River Clyde and the Firth of Forth. The latter was abandoned in favour of the former in AD 196.
275. interest] right to spiritual privileges, i.e. religious independence (*OED* n. 1 b).
277. cross and pile] a) heads and tails of a coin (*OED* a), hence b) two sides of the same thing (*OED* b).
278. i.e. 'only Charles understands this'.
280. atone] unite (*OED* v. I 2).

Knows the last secret how to make them one.
Just so the prudent husbandman who sees
The idle tumult of his factious bees,
The morning dews, and flowers neglected grown,
285 The hive a comb-case, every bee a drone,
Powders them o'er, till none discern their foes,
And all themselves in meal and friendship close;
The insect kingdom straight begins to thrive,
And each works honey for the common hive.
290   Pardon, young hero, this so long transport,

(Thy death more noble did the same exhort).
My former satire for this verse forget,
The hare's head against the goose giblets set.
I single did against a nation write,
295 Against a nation thou didst singly fight.
My diff'ring crime does more thy virtue raise;
And such my rashness best thy valour praise.'
     Here Douglas, smiling, said he did intend
After such frankness shown, to be his friend;
300 Forewarned him therefore, lest in time he were
Metempsychosed to some Scotch presbyter.

282–9. Just so . . . hive] an adaptation of Virgil, *Georgics*, IV, ll. 67–87. Virgil describes a war between two bee kingdoms; M. describes the faction within one kingdom. ll. 270–1 are closely related to *Georgics*, IV, ll. 86–7: 'hi motus animorum atque haec certamina tanta/pulveris exigui iactu compressa quiescunt' (These storms of passion, these conflicts so fierce, by the tossing of a little dust are quelled and laid to rest). Otherwise, M. replaces Virgil's terminology of epic conflict with vocabulary of nature and of civil conflict (e.g. l. 283, 'factious'). Patterson (1978), 169, notes the similarity of this Augustan imagery with M.'s earlier treatment of Cromwell: see above, *The First Anniversary*, l. 286. M.'s reference back to Virgil provides a further irony: bees were supposed by Commonwealth idealists and scientific reformers to constitute an exemplary, self-governing society: see Samuel Hartlib, *The Reformed Common-Wealth of Bees* (1655); Johns (1998), 267–71, 280–2.
282. husbandman] recalling not only Virgil's virtuous farmer, but also M.'s previous portrayal of Cromwell: see *The First Anniversary*, ll. 285–6: 'the large vale lay subject to thy will,/Which thou but as an husbandman wouldst till'.
283. idle] without significance, or foundation (*OED* A a. 2–3).
285. comb-case] hive with empty combs in it (*OED* n.¹ 9).
286. Powders] the syntax firmly suggests a) *OED* v.¹ I 1: to sprinkle with powder, in order to pacify the bees, but contemporaries would have been aware of 'to powder' as b) to charge with gunpowder (*OED* v.¹ IV 8), and hence, to agitate.
290. Pardon . . . hero] Cp. *On Mr Milton's Paradise Lost*, ll. 23–4: 'Pardon me, mighty poet, nor despise/My causeless, yet not impious, surmise'; *The First Anniversary of the*

Government under His Highness the Lord Protector, l. 395: 'Pardon, great prince, if thus their fear or spite.' *transport*] stressed on second syllable; fit of poetic rage (*OED* n. 3); see also *On Mr Milton's Paradise Lost*, l. 51.
292–3. 'Rebell Scot by Cleavland' written in margin against these lines in *NLS*.
292. My former satire] Cleveland's 'The Rebel Scot.' Asterisked with reference to 'Cleaveland's Rebel Scot' written vertically in left-hand margin in *BL 27*.
293. hare's . . . set] proverbial: 'tit for tat' (Tilley, H161).
295. Against . . . fight] Douglas's heroism against the Dutch.
296. diff'ring] quarrelling, creating differences (*OED* ppl. a. 2).
297. such my rashness] i.e. 'rashness like this.'
301. Metempsychosed] flight of the soul from one body to another (*OED* v.). *Scotch presbyter*] Douglas' ghost fears that Cleveland, freed from his Anglicanism and Royalism might go too far in the opposite direction, to become a staunch Scottish Presbyterian minister, who would, for instance, place the church's authority above that of the monarch (see, e.g., Gilbert Sheldon, *The Dignity of Kingship Asserted* (1660), 137: 'some kinde of *Rigid Scotch Presbytery*, [might] entertain Tenents, which tend to eclipse the *honour* and *respect* due (by *divine right*) to the *Supreme Sovereignty*'; Sheldon is attacking Milton in this passage); cp. another Cleveland satire, 'The Hue and Cry after Sir John Presbyter' (?1646–47), which includes further vilification of the Scots (ll. 39–42): 'Then what Imperious in the Bishop sounds,/The same the *Scotch* Executor rebounds;/This stating *Prelacy*, the *Classick* Rout,/That spake it often, ere it spake it out.'

65

Bludius et Corona

and

66

Epigram: Upon Blood's attempt to steal the Crown

Date. 9 May–5 August 1671. Colonel Thomas Blood attempted to steal the crown jewels on 9 May 1671; the copy in *BL 22* is dated 5 August.

Text. The Latin version was first printed by Thompson apparently from *Bod. 1*, although there are some slight differences between the two versions. Cooke printed only the English version, Thompson printed the Latin in his preface (I.xxxix), and the English version on III.337. Exceptionally, the Latin version comes second in *Bod. 1*. Thirteen MSS copies of the Latin version survive:

Bod. 1 MS Eng. poet d. 49, p. 246
Bod. 13 Bodleian, MS Douce 357, fol. 81
L 5 University of Leeds, Brotherton Collection, MS Lt. 55, p. 18
AH 1 Arbury Hall, MS 185, fol. [2ʳ]
Bod. 15 Bodleian, MS Broxbourne 85.18 (formerly R 359), fol. [30ᵛ]
Bod. 16 Bodleian, MS Rawl. poet. 171, fol. 10ᵛ
BL 17 British Library, MS Harley 6947, fol. 74
BL 18 British Library, MS Sloane 1941, fol. 18
BL 19 British Library, MS Sloane 3413, fol. 29ᵛ
P 3 Princeton, Gen. MSS. Misc. No. AM 14401, pp. 361–2
Υ 4 Yale, MS Vault, Section 10, Drawer 3, Commonplace book, fol. [35]
Υ 4² Yale, MS Vault, Section 10, Drawer 3, Commonplace book, fol. [35ᵛ]
Υ 2 Yale, Osborn Collection, b52/2, p. 159

There are twenty-seven copies of the English version, recorded here in abbreviated form only: *Bod. 1, Bod. 13, BL 17, L 4, NLS, P 4, AH 1, Bod. 15, Bod. 17, BL 22, BL 28, BL 17, BL 18, BL 19, Ch. 2, F 3, V, P 3, VA 2, Υ 4* (two copies), *Υ 2, Υ 3, Υ 10. IELM* reports two copies, attributed to M. and in

the same hand (MaA 279–80), made on 64 and 115 of an exemplum of *1681*, for sale at Sotheby's, New York, 1 May 1990, and a copy, now unlocated, in an octavo miscellany compiled by Richard Duke (1652–1733) of Otterton, Devon (MaA 278).

Authorship. The poem is ascribed to M. in several MSS (*Bod. 13, BL 19*; in *AH 1* (where M. is described as a 'Dʳ'), *NLS, Bod. 15, F 3* to the English version only), although the strongest evidence for his authorship is the inclusion of the English version of the lines within *The Loyal Scot*, ll. 192–9, which are supplied below. But two of the more important MS witnesses to this poem (*Bod. 1, NLS*) do not include the lines on Blood. Although, as with all of M.'s Latin and English parallel poems, it is difficult to tell which version came first, the transcriber of *Bod. 13* wrote 'Marvel' against the English version.

Context. Thomas Blood (or Blud; ?1618–80) was a discontented and deprived landowner: he had lost at the Restoration considerable lands in Ireland that were given to him in payment for his service as a JP during the Commonwealth. He was a Parliament-arian, and Cromwellian, who was subsequently involved in several anti-monarchist revolts during the Restoration: the attempt to seize Ormond in Dublin, 1663; the Fifth Monarchists in England in the mid-1660s; the Covenanters' revolt in Scotland, defeated at Pentland Hills on 27 November 1666; attempts to rescue friends and to hang Ormond in 1670 (allegedly at the instigation of his mentor Buckingham). Blood periodically visited Holland as a refuge from England, and was presented to De Ruyter. Possibly in revenge for his lost estates, he determined to steal the crown, sceptre and orb from the Tower of London. Disguised as a clergyman,

he befriended the keeper three weeks beforehand.
However, the attempt was frustrated by the arrival of
the keeper's son. Had Blood and his three accom-
plices killed the keeper, rather than wounding him
and binding him, they might have been successful.
The King examined Blood, pardoned him, and returned his lands to him. He died of natural causes in
1680. *CSPD*, 1671, 496, contains an informer's letter of 21 September 1671, to Sir Joseph Williamson
suggesting that Blood and M. were connected
because they were both agents of the Duke of
Buckingham. John Woodfall Ebsworth's *DNB* article
summarizes his talents:

> He assumed various disguises and continually changed
> his places of refuge, sometimes assuming to be a Quaker,
> sometimes an anabaptist, an independent, and even a
> Roman Catholic priest. Rapidly flitting about among all
> sorts of people, entering sympathetically into their
> grievances and family affairs, instead of shrouding him-
> self in mystery and thus exciting suspicion, he succeeded
> in baffling pursuers, and became acquainted with many
> desperate characters.

In a letter of 9 August to a friend in Persia, M.
recounts Blood's career, describing him as a 'most
bold, and yet sober, Fellow.' (Legouis, II.326). *Bod.
13* (fol. 81[r-v]) contains two hostile Latin responses to
M.'s lines, both with English translations. 'An
answer to it' attributed to 'D[r] Fuller' follows the two
poems in *AH 1*:

> Blood underneath y[e] holy coat/this was
> A perfect rebus of y[e] good-old-Cause
> To steal a Crown thus drest! By this is shewn
> What you wth cheat of sanctity have done.
> The name, [y[e] crossed out] garb & design do all expresse
> You acting of y[r] hallowed wickednesse.
> But why Blasphemers must y[t] was be blam'd
> Because in y[e] disguise 'twas falsly shamed? . . .
> . . . You murder'd bravely him y[t] wore y[e] crown,
> He pited y[t] poor wretch by whome 'twas shewn . . .
> . . . Did we not learn from your own lawes of fate
> Such is the fortune of y[e] reprobate. . . .

. . . And were o[r] malice like yours to pray
Your Prince might gracious be to y[e] last day.
But more like Xtians to speed your future bliss
In y[e] next world, we wish you hangd in this.

Bludius et Corona

Bludius, ut ruris damnum repararet aviti,
    Addicit fisco dum diadema suo:
Egregium sacro facinus velavit amictu:
    (Larva solet reges fallere nulla magis).
5 Excidit ast ausis tactus pietate prophana,
    Custodem ut servet, maluit ipse capi.
Si modo saevitiam texisset pontificalem,
    Veste sacerdotis, rapta corona foret.

Blood and the Crown

Blood, in order to recover the loss of his ancestral
estate, while he assigned the diadem to his own
treasury, concealed his illustrious deed in a sacred
vestment (no mask is more accustomed to deceiving
kings). But touched by his profane piety he failed in
his daring attempt, preferring to be captured himself,
so that he might save his guard. If only he had
covered a pontiff's cruelty with a priest's vestment,
the crown would have been seized.

Epigram: Upon Blood's attempt to steal the Crown

When daring Blood his rent to have regained
Upon the English diadem distrained,
He chose the cassock, surcingle and gown,
The fittest mask for one that robs a crown.
5 But his lay pity underneath prevailed,
And while he spared the keeper's life he failed.
With the priest's vestments had he but put on
A bishop's cruelty, the crown had gone.

67

The Statue in Stocks-Market

Date. Late May 1672–late October 1674. See below, *Context.*

Publication. The poem was first printed in *1689*, in *1697* and subsequent reprintings. The version in Thompson was printed from a MS book. The poem circulated in the following twenty-two MSS: *Bod. 1*, *Bod. 12*, *BL 20*, *BL 14*, *L 4*, *NLS*, *P 4*, *Bod. 14*, *BL 26*, *LAC 3*, *Li.*, *N 5*, *N 6*, *V*, *P 1*, *P 4*, *VA 1*, *Υ 9*, *Υ10*, a privately owned MS in England (*IELM*, MaA 251), a MS formerly owned by Margoliouth, now un-located (*IELM*, MaA 252).

Text. *Bod. 12* and *Bod. 14* are written without stanza breaks. The many variants are recorded in Appendix 2.

Authorship. Attributed to M. in only one MS, *N 6*, and then only very indirectly ('By the Author of the second Advice to a painter'). There is a copy, how-ever, in the MS poems added to *Bod. 1*. No printed text carried an attribution until Thompson, I.viii–x. There is a possibility that M. may have been imitat-ing this poem, itself written by another author, when he wrote *The Statue at Charing Cross*, the grounds for attribution to M. in that poem being stronger.

Context. Sir Robert Viner (1631–88), alderman of Langborn in the City of London (later Lord Mayor), and Charles II's principal banker, unveiled an eques-trian statue of the King on 29 October 1672. It was thought that the statue was in fact made on the con-tinent and depicted the Polish general John Sobieski (elected king in 1674) in victory over the Turk. The alterations made to the statue (Sobieski to Charles II, the Turk to Oliver Cromwell) left the Turk's turban in place: it was embarrassing evidence of the conver-sion. Viner may have had the statue for some time: a similar gift from Viner had been declined by the Royal Exchange in 1669. The statue was removed in 1736 to make way for the construction of the Mansion House, re-erected in an inn yard in 1779, and presented to a descendant of Viner. It is now at Newby Hall, Ripon, North Yorkshire. James Ralph commented that the statue was 'a thing in itself so exceedingly ridiculous and absurd, that 'tis not in one's power to look upon it without reflecting upon the tastes of those who set it up', *A Critical Review of the Public Buildings, Statues, and Ornaments in and about London and Westminster* (1736), 9. How-ever, Ralph's evidence has been shown to be unreli-able in several ways. Furthermore, a witness from 1737 makes it clear that while Viner had brought the horse in Rome, the figure of Charles II and the pedestal on which the horse rested, were exe-cuted separately, possibly by Jasper Latham (Martin Dzelzainis, private communication).

The poem uses the occasion of the statue's unveil-ing to highlight a number of court and government failings: financial chaos, and the associated charge of decadent overspending; the motives of the government in starting the Third Dutch War. But the treatment of Viner is at least as critical: his court connections and his authoritarian attitude towards the governance of the City of London made him the enemy of many within the city corporation (see De Krey, in Harris *et al.*, eds (1990), 135–6). It is with some of these men that M. had connections.

The Statue in Stocks-Market

As cities that to the fierce conquerors yield
Do at their own charge their citadels build,
So Sir Robert advanced the King's statue, in token
Of bankers defeated and Lombard Street broken.

5   Some thought it a knightly and generous deed,
Obliging the city with a king and a steed,
When with honour he might from his word have gone back;
He that vows for a calm is absolved by a wreck.

But now it appears from the first to the last
10 To be all a revenge and a malice forecast,
Upon the King's birthday to set up a thing
That shows him a monster more like than a king.

When each one that passes finds fault with the horse,
Yet all do affirm that the king is much worse,
15 And some by the likeness Sir Robert suspect
That he did for the King his own statue erect.

To see him so disfigured the herb-women chide,
Who upon their panniers more decently ride,
And so loose in his seat that all men agree
20 Even Sir William Peake sits much firmer than he.

But a market, they say, does suit the king well,
Who the Parliament buys and revenues does sell,
And others to make the similitude hold
Say his Majesty himself is bought too and sold.

25 This statue is surely more scandalous far
Than all the Dutch pictures that caused the war,
And what the Exchequer for that took on trust
May be henceforth confiscate for reasons more just.

But Sir Robert to take all the scandal away
30 Does the fault upon the artificer lay,
And alleges the workmanship was not his own
For he counterfeits only in gold, not in stone.

But, Sir Knight of the Vine, how came't in your thought
That when to the scaffold your liege you had brought
35 With canvas and deals you e'er since do him cloud,
As if you had meant it his coffin and shroud?

Hath Blood him away (as his crown once) conveyed?
Or is he to Clayton's gone in masquerade?
Or is he in cabal in his cabinet set?
40 Or have you to the Compter removed him for debt?

Methinks by the equipage of this vile scene
That to change him into a Jack-pudding you mean,
Or else thus expose him to popular flouts,
As if we'd as good have a king made of clouts.

45 Or do you his beams out of modesty veil
With three shattered planks and the rags of a sail
To express how his navy was shattered and torn
The day that he was both restored and born?

Title. Stocks-Market] also known as Woolchurch Market, and situated where the Mansion House now stands.

3. advanced] erected (*OED* v. III 9), but with an undertone of 'advanced' as 'raised in price' (*OED* v. III 14) appropriate for the subject matter of ll. 3–4.

4. bankers defeated] the government closed the Exchequer in 1672, thereby causing the ruin of many bankers. Viner, who had leant money heavily to the King, was very badly affected. *Lombard Street*] financial centre of the City of London; in particular, Viner's house of business was here, next to the church of St Mary Woolnoth.

17. herb-women] women who sell herbs on the streets (*OED*).

20. Sir William Peake] alderman of London, knighted at Whitehall, 1 October 1663, Sherriff 1660, Lord Mayor 1667.

22. Parliament . . . sell] i.e. bribery of Parliament and sale of tax farms.

24. Say . . . sold] Louis XIV had passed funds to Charles under the terms of the secret Treaty of Dover.

26. Dutch . . . war] see *AGP*, 31, 36; Patterson (1978), 124–5.

32. gold] Viner was a goldsmith as well as a banker.

34. scaffold] the statue stood on an eighteen-feet-high plinth. *liege*] superior to whom is owed feudal allegiance and service (*OED* B n. 1); hence the King.

35. canvas] sailcloth. *deals*] planks of pine or fir-wood (*OED* n.³ 1).

37. Blood] see above, 401–2.

38. Clayton] Sir Robert Clayton (1629–1707), a poor boy who became one of the richest men in London, elected sherriff in 1671; famous for his extravagant banquets and entertainments. *masquerade*] masked entertainments at court or in private houses, involving the king and queen, were frequent. Clayton entertained the King twice in 1672: on 12 and 17 April, the second occasion undoubtedly involving a masquerade (see Wall, in Legouis).

39. cabal] secret meeting of a faction (*OED* n.¹ 4); more specifically in Charles II's reign, a small committee of the Privy Council, with chief management of the course of government (*OED* n.¹ 6 b).

40. Compter] old spelling of 'Counter', and the common name of city prisons for debt (*OED*). The King owed Viner £416,724 13s 1½d. at the point of the Exchequer's closure.

41. equipage] accoutrements, trappings (*OED* n. 4, 4 b).

42. Jack-pudding] mountebank's buffoon.

47–8. To . . . born] the Battle of Southwold Bay was fought on 28 May 1672, during which *Royal James* blew up, with the Earl of Sandwich, the chief commander, on board. The next day, 29 May, was the King's birthday, the anniversary of his restoration, and the day of the unveiling of the statue.

Sure the king will ne'er think of repaying his bankers,
Whose loyalty now all expires with his spankers.
If the Indies and Smyrna do not him enrich,
They will scarce afford him a rag to his breech.

But Sir Robert affirms we do him much wrong;
For the graver's at work to reform him thus long.

55 But alas! he will never arrive at his end,
For 'tis such a king as no chisel can mend.

But with all his faults restore us our King,
As ever you hope in December for Spring,
For though the whole world cannot show such another,
60 Yet we'd better by far have him than his brother.

---

50. spankers] gold coins (*OED* n. 1).
51. If . . . enrich] In March 1672, before the declaration of war, Sir Robert Holmes made an unsuccessful attack on the Dutch Smyrna fleet off the Isle of Wight. His sole aim was to win treasure. In *AGP* (*MPW*, 256) M. suggests that the attack failed because of the competing greed of the English commanders.
54. graver] sculptor (*OED* n. 2 a).

68

The Statue at Charing Cross

Date. July 1675. M. wrote to William Popple on 24 July: 'for more Pageantry, the old King's Statue on Horseback, or Brass, as bought, and to be set up at *Charing-Cross*', which hath been doing longer than Viner's, but does not yet see the Light'. (Legouis, II.341).

Publication. First printed in *Poems on Affairs of State* (1698). MS copies exist in *Bod. 1, Bod. 12, Bod. 13, BL 6, BL 15, NLS, P 4, Bod. 28, Bod. 17, LAC 3, EUL, F 2, NLW 1, N 5, V, P 1, VA 2, Y 7.*

Authorship. Attributed to M. in no MS, but attributed to M. in the 1698 volume, in the contents list alone, and in Thompson; also included in *Bod. 1.* The subject of the poem connects directly with information in M.'s correspondence (see above, *Date.*).

Text. Bod. 17 stops after 'pensions' in l. 22: the last item in the volume. *Bod. 12* is dated 1675; *Bod. 29,* 1676.

Context. The bronze equestrian statue of Charles I was cast by Le Sueur in 1633, but it remained to be erected when the Civil War broke out. Parliament sold the statue to Rivet the brazier, who sold bronze-handled cutlery to Royalists after the regicide because they believed the cutlery to have been cast from the bronze in the statue. Rivet had in fact kept the statue. Danby acquired it after the Restoration and erected it at his own expense in order to appeal to popular sentiment in 1675.

The Statue at Charing Cross

What can be the mystery why Charing Cross
This five months continues still blinded with board?
Dear Wheler impart, for we're all at a loss
Unless Punchinello be to be restored.

5 'Twere to Scaramuchio too great disrespect
To limit his troop to this theatre small,
Besides the injustice it were to eject
The mimic so legally seized of Whitehall.

For a dial the place is too unsecure
10 Since the privy garden could not it defend,
And so near to the court they will never endure
Any monument how their time they mispend.

Were these deals kept in store for sheathing our fleet
When the King in armado to Portsmouth should sail.

---

2. *board*] planks of wood.
3. *Wheler*] Sir Charles Wheler (*c.* 1620–83), 2nd Bt., of Birdingbury, Warwickshire; MP for Cambridge University, and an intimate of Lord and Lady Danby.
4. *Punchinello*] principal character in an Italian puppet-play; the forerunner of 'Punch' (*OED* 1). Margoliouth notes that an Italian puppet-player called Puncihinello performed at Charing Cross in March 1666; see also Pepys, *Diary*, entries for 8 October 1662.
5. *Scaramuchio*] cowardly and foolish boaster in Italian farce (i.e. *commedia dell'arte*), or a puppet version thereof. M. to William Popple, 24 July 1675 (Legouis, II.342): '*Scarramuccio* acting dayly in the Hall of *Whitehall*, and all Sorts of People flocking thither, and paying their Mony as at a Common Playhouse.'
8. *mimic*] comic actor who imitates the manners of others (*OED* B n. 1).

9–10. In a barbaric frolic, Rochester, it was reported, had vandalized the dial on 25 June 1675: see Goldsworthy (2001), 188: 'thought to be the most remarkable clock in all Europe. It was a type of sundial . . . and bore little resemblance to the ordinary appliance with gnomon and dial. It was an elaborate set of chronometers. It was perfectly accurate and phallic in shape. . . . Rochester was the ringleader – shouting . . . 'What, dost thou stand here to fuck time?'
9. *dial*] sundial (*OED* n.¹ 1).
13–14. Charles II sailed from Gravesend to Portsmouth and back in early July; see M. to Sir Henry Thompson, [6 July 1675] (Legouis, II.340): 'I can not requite it but with the good news of the Kings safe arrival from sea this night. For from Sat: til Satuday we were at a losse. He had a most terrible storme.'
13. *deals*] planks of pine or fir-wood (*OED* n.³ 1). *sheathing*] i.e. covering in order to store.
14. *armado*] fleet of warships (*OED* n. 1).

Or the Bishops and Treasurer did they agree't
To repair with such riff-raff our church's old pale?
No, to comfort the hearts of the poor cavalier
The late King on horseback is here to be shown:
What a do with the Kings and the statues is here:
Have we not had enough already of one?

Does the Treasurer think men so loyally tame
When their pensions are stopped to be fooled with a sight?
And 'tis forty to one if he play the old game
He'll shortly reduce us to forty and eight.

The Trojan horse, though not of brass but of wood,
Had within it an army that burnt up the town:
However 'tis ominous if understood,
For the old King on horseback is but an half-crown.

But his brother-in-law's horse had gained such repute
That the Treasurer thought prudent to try it again,
And instead of that market of herbs and of fruit
He will here keep a market of Parliament men.

But why is the work then so long at a stand?
Such things you should never or suddenly do.
As the Parliament twice was prorogued by your hand,
Will you venture so far to prorogue the King too?

Let's have a King then, be he new be he old;
Not Viner delayed us so, though he was broken
Though the King be of copper and Danby of gold,
40 Shall a treasurer of guineas a prince grudge of token?

The houswifely Treasuress sure is grown nice
That so liberally treated the Members at supper.
She thinks not convenient to go to the price,
And we've lost both our King, our horse and our crupper.

45 Where for so many barties there are to provide,
To buy a king is not so wise as to sell,
And however, she said, it could not be denied
That a monarch of gingerbread would do as well.

But the Treasurer told her he thought she was mad
50 And his Parliament-list withal did produce,
Where he showed her that so many voters he had
As would the next tax reimburse them with use.

So the statue will up after all this delay,
But to turn the face to Whitehall you must shun;
55 Though of brass, yet with grief it would melt him away,
To behold every day such a court, such a son.

15–16. *Or ... pale*] an allusion to the bishops' support for Danby's non-resistance test in the spring and summer of 1675. In the same session (on 17 April), legislation was also brought to the House of Commons for the repair of churches damaged during the Commonwealth.
16. *riff-raff*] rubbish, odds and ends (*OED* n. 2). *pale*] fence (*OED* n.¹ 2).
20. *one*] i.e. the statue of Charles II erected by Sir Robert Viner (see above, 413–14).
22. *pensions are stopped*] the consequence of the closing of the Exchequer, and subsequent stoppages.
23. *old game*] i.e. the raising of serious discontent in the King's subjects.
24. *forty and eight*] the year of the Second Civil War, and, in the old calendar, the English Revolution: the trial and execution of the King, the abolition of the House of Lords and the proclamation of a republic.
25–6. *Trojan ... town*] Lord suggests an allusion to the belief (strongly backed in the House of Commons (see Smith and Bell, *TLS*, 5104 (26 January 2001), 14–15)) that the Great Fire was the result of a Catholic conspiracy. But the parallel of the Trojan horse merely suggests the risk of further discord: the Great Fire had of course already taken place.
28. *half-crown*] a) the half-crown of Charles I, picturing the King on horseback, was the only coin from his reign still in circulation b) i.e. not a whole crown; a figurative expression of less than best or little value (see *OED*, 'half-crown').
29. *brother-in-law*] alluding to the affair between Viner's stepdaughter and Danby's son. 'brothers-in-law' could be a humorous term for the fathers of a married couple: see *OED*, 'brother-in-law', b).
31. *that*] see above, *The Statue in Stocks Market*, l. 17.

35. *twice*] Parliament was in fact prorogued three times since Danby had become treasurer in June 1673: 4 November 1673; 24 February 1674; 9 June 1675. *prorogued*] dismissed (*OED* v. 3).
37. *new ... old*] the statue was of the old king, Charles I; it was an old statue, yet newly erected.
38. *broken*] Viner had been financially damaged by the closure of the Exchequer in 1672: see above, *The Statue in Stocks Market*, l. 4 and n.
39. *copper*] one of the constituents of brass. *Danby of gold*] an allusion to Danby's infamous and extensive practice of bribery.
40. *guineas*] gold coins first struck in 1663, with the original value of twenty shillings. *token*] stamped copper pieces functioning as coinage when precious metals were scarce.
41. *Treasuress*] Danby's wife, originally Lady Bridget Bertie, and regarded as encouraging Danby's venality. *nice*] wanton, lascivious (*OED* a. 2).
43. *go to the price*] i.e. pay the full amount.
44. *crupper*] buttocks, backside (*OED* n. 3).
45. *barties*] i.e. Bertie's (see above, l. 41n.); both of Danby's brothers-in-law received his patronage.
46. *buy*] i.e. from Rivet the brazier (see above, *Headnote, Context*).
48. *gingerbread*] figurative for that which is showy and unsubstantial (*OED* n. 2).
50. *Parliament-list*] Danby's famous lists of his supporters in Parliament and those whom he could bribe.
52. *As ... use*] i.e. the Danbys were financially secure and would indeed make money because they would benefit from the next tax bill, which was bound to become law, because Danby has bought sufficient votes.

69
Scaevola Scoto-Brittannus

Date. ?February–March 1676. On 24 January 1676, James Mitchell (or Mitchel) was tortured in the Parliament House at Edinburgh (*The Register of the Privy Council of Scotland*, 3rd ser., 16 vols, ed. P. Hume Brown (Edinburgh, 1908), IV, 152–3; Paul Mathole, private communication).

Publication. The text was first published in print by Thompson in his preface (xlviii), who used the manuscript copy in *Bod. 1* (264), omitting ll. 23–4 and ll. 33–6.

Text. Yale University, Osborn Collection, MS b 54 (*Y3*), 'A Collection of Witt and Learning . . . from the year 1600, to this present year: 1677' contains a copy of the poem on p. 1225. This copy is thus closer to the point of composition than that in *Bod. 1* and has one significant variant: see below, l. 21n. In addition to *Bod. 1*, a copy of the poem is in BL, Add. MS 34362, fol. 43r-v (*BL 6*) where a different hand to the scribe of the poem attributes it to M.

Authenticity. Thompson was not entirely convinced of M.'s authorship, but, along with several other poems, he placed it in his preface because he thought 'M.'s hand was in it'. We can afford to be more confident of M.'s authorship. It was ascribed to M. in *BL 6*. The poem is playful in its choice of Latin vocabulary in a way that is consistent with M.'s inventiveness. Moreover, it elaborates a principle of doubleness that amounts to reversal: in several places, Mitchell is seen to surpass those who punish him in the very terms that they should apply to him. The willingness with which Mitchell participates in his own torture is also akin to the complicity of Charles I in his own execution (in *An Horatian Ode*) and Archibald Douglas in his own fiery martyrdom (in *The Last Instructions* and *The Loyal Scot*).

Context. Although a member of the Presbyterian kirk before the English invasion of 1650, James Sharp (1613–79), had always had episcopal sympathies. He schemed for the Restoration, and produced some effective propaganda for Monck during his march

south in 1659. He was sent to Charles II at Breda in early May 1660, and induced the King to publish a letter supportive of Presbyterianism. But it was written in a manner that would lay open the way for episcopacy in Scotland again. He had effectively betrayed the Presbyterian cause in Scotland while supposedly speaking in its name. He was consecrated as Bishop of St Andrews on 15 December 1661 at Westminster, and returned to Scotland from another visit to London in 1664 with the title of primate of Scotland. During the 1660s he worked actively to annihilate Presbyterianism and covenanting principles.

Sharp's extremism roused violent passions. On 9 July 1668, he was shot at while sitting in his coach in Blackfriars Wynd, Edinburgh by the Covenanter James Mitchell (d. 1678). Mitchell's pistol missed the archbishop, but the bullet hit the hand of his companion, Andrew Honeyman, Bishop of Orkney. Mitchell escaped and fled the country. He spent five years in Holland, England and Ireland, but, after his return in 1673 (according to his enemies, he returned to fulfil his resolve to assassinate Sharp), was recognized, apprehended, interrogated periodically over the next four years, and threatened with the loss of his right hand and perpetual imprisonment. The torture session that is the subject of the poem was interrupted when the prisoner fainted. Robert Wodrow sets the scene:

> The Executioner was called, and Mr *Mitchel* was tied in a two-armed Chair, and the Boot brought. The Executioner asked which of the Legs he should take. The Lords bade him take any of them. The Executioner laid the left Leg in the Boot, which Mr *Mitchell* lifted out again, and said, Since the Judges have not determined, take the best of the Two, for I freely bestow it in the Cause, and laid his right Leg into the Engine. (R. Wodrow, *The History of the Sufferings of the Church of Scotland*, 2 vols (Edinburgh, 1721), I, 512)

For the 'boot', see below, l. 8 n. Mitchell was tried for the attempted assassination of Sharp and finally executed in January 1678. Sharp's demand that Mitchell's head and hand be set on the city gates was denied on the grounds that legal sentence had already been passed. Sharp was assassinated on Magus Muir by a group of covenanting Fife lairds and farmers on 3 May 1679.

Mitchell's extended trial was sensational in that it involved the perjury of several prominent Scottish noblemen, including Lauderdale (see above, *The Loyal Scot, Headnote, Context*). The case against him was also based on a confession that had been extracted from him on the promise that he would be spared his life if he confessed, and he was not allowed to present some evidence in his favour. Further details are given in Wodrow, op. cit., and George Hickes, *Ravaillac Redivivus* (1682).

Genre and Sources. In English terms, the poem (and indeed its context) resembles many of the poems that made a hero of John Felton, the first Duke of Buckingham's assassin: see Holstun, *ELH*, 59 (1992), 513–52, and (2000), ch. 5. Like the Buckingham assassination, Mitchell's attempt generated some poetry in Latin and English 'which flew abroad like hornets in great swarmes, which were caressed and pleasantly received, speaking much acrimony and ane almost universall discontent' (Fountainhall quoted by James Kirkton, *The Secret and True History of the Church of Scotland* (1817), 387), to which group, *Scaevola Scoto-Brittannus* belongs (see George Hickes, *Ravaillac Redivivus* ('second' edn, 1682 [Wing R 1862]), 33–6). Several were pinned or pasted in public places, such as the Great Cross in Edinburgh. For examples, see 'Deploratio Mortis Jacobi Mitchel', in Hickes, *Ravaillac Redivivus*, 33–6, and an English example in James Kirkton, *The Secret and True History of the Church of Scotland* (1817), 388–9. The location of the poem among M.'s writings against the bishops, as well as the careful moral position adopted by the poet, is discussed by Mathole, in Scott (forthcoming).

Scaevola Scoto-Brittannus

Sharpius exercet dum saevas perfidus iras,
    Et proprii Pastor fit Lupus ipse gregis,
Lenta videbatur coeli vindicta Michello,
    Et fas in talem credidit omne Nefas.
5   Peccat in insonti sed Praesule missile Plumbum
    (Insons si Praesul quilibet esse potest)
Culpa par, at dispar sequitur fortuna Jacobos:
    Ocrea torquet idem, mitra beatque scelus.
Quanta ast Percussor crimen virtute piavit,
10   Judicibusque ipsis quam Reverendus erat!
Quid de se fieret melius Praetore docebat;
    Non poenas illum sed dare jura putes.
Carnificem tremulum jubet abstinuisse sinistra.
    Errorem Dextrae dextera sura luat.
15   Nec mora, feralem Tortore apante Cothurnum,
    Tanquam Sutori commodat usque pedem:
Intima contuso et dum ringitur osse medulla
    Calceus urit ubi cernere nemo queat,
Ut vacat! ut proprii sedet ad spectacula cruris
20   Immotus, populo commiserante, reus:
Non vultu aut ulla confessus voce dolorem,
    Sub cuneo quanquam tibia pressa gemit.
At, ceu mitis herus famulo subridet inepto,
    Infractus Lanium frangere membra videt.
25   Inter lictoris nisus feriatur anheli,
    Nec vult supplicii conscius esse sui
Lassus at interea patitur tormenta minister.
    (Qui sentit solus dicitur ille pati).
Scaevola si Thuscum potuit terrere Tyrannum,
30   Fortius hoc specimen Scotia nostra dedit.
Numina quum temnas, homines ne spernito Sharpi,
    Hic è tercentum Mutius unus erat.

Title. Scaevola] Gaius Mucius Scaevola plotted unsuccessfully to kill the Etruscan king Lars Porsena, who was besieging Rome. Like Mitchell, Scaevola hit the wrong man, killing Porsena's secretary. Porsena threatened to burn Scaevola unless he revealed details of the plot; Scaevola responded by plunging his right hand into the flame. He gained his life and his freedom, but had lost his right hand. The action led Porsena to propose terms of peace with the Romans. See Livy, *Ab Urbe Condita*, II.xii.
1. *dum saevas*] *Bod. 1*; saevus dum *Υ3*.
2. *Et . . . gregis*] for Sharp's betrayal of Presbyterianism, see above, *Headnote, Context*.
5. *insonti . . . Praesule*] Andrew Honeyman, Bishop of Orkney (see above, *Headnote, Context*). *Praesule* means 'president', 'director' or 'patron' (Lewis and Short II), but it can also mean 'public dancer' (Lewis and Short, I). Thus, the word mocks episcopacy.
7. *Culpa . . . at*] *Bod. 1*; par culpa, et *Υ3*.

8. *Ocrea*] the 'boot', a method of torture peculiar to Scotland, used to extract confessions (*OED* n.[3] 3). The prisoner's leg or legs were put into an iron casing, shaped like a boot; wedges were then driven by mallet blows between the leg and the casing.
14. *Errorem*] a) the attempted assassination b) the poor aim (attributed to Kelliher by Legouis).
15. *apante*] *Bod. 1*; aptante *BL 6, Υ3*.
19. *Ut . . . cruris*] Cp. Livy, *Ab Urbe Condita*, II.xii.13: 'Quam cum velut alienato ab sensu torreret animo, prope attontibus miraculo rex cum' (When he allowed his hand to burn as if his spirit were unconscious of sensation, the king was almost beside himself with wonder).
22. *confessus*] *Bod. 1*; testatus *Υ3*.
24. *Lanium*] Lane the executioner.
29. *Scaevola . . . Tyrannum*] see above, l. 1 n.
32. *tercentum*] Scaevola told Porsena that he was one of three hundred Roman youths who had sworn to kill him (Livy, *Ab Urbe Condita*, II.xii.15). *Mutius*] Mucius.

Explosa nequiit quem sternere glande Michellus,
   Explodet saevum Scotia Pontificem.
35 Inter Pontificem quid distat Carnificemque?
   Inter Luciferum Furciferumque quod est.

Scaevola Scoto-Brittannus

While perfidious Sharp practises his cruel anger, and the very shepherd becomes the wolf of his own flock, heaven's vengeance seemed slow to Mitchell, and he believed that against such a man every wrongdoing was right. But his lead missile miscarried upon an innocent bishop (if any bishop can be innocent); equal is the blame but unequal the fortune that attends the Jameses: the boot tortures, the mitre blesses the same crime. But with what courage did the assassin atone for his crime, how venerable he was to the judges themselves! He gave better instructions than the chief magistrate as to what should become of him: you would think he was imposing laws, not paying a penalty. He orders the trembling executioner to keep away from his left side: his right calf should atone for the error of his right hand. And without delay as the torturer applies the deadly boot, he constantly makes available his foot as though to a shoe-maker: and while the innermost marrow is chafed in the crushed bone, the boot stings where no one can see. How unconcerned he is! How unmoved yet pitied by the people does the accused sit to behold the spectacle of his own torture: not by his countenance nor by any utterance did he admit his pain, although the shin bone groans under the wedge's pressure. But, as a gentle master smiles upon his inept servant, unbroken, he sees Lane breaking his limbs. Between the exertions of the panting attendant he is at rest, and does not wish to be aware of his own punishment. But meanwhile the weary official suffers torture (only he who is aware is said to suffer). If Scaevola was able to terrify the Etruscan tyrant, our Scotland has given in this man a braver example. Sharp, although you spurn the divine powers, do not despise men; this one was Mucius out of three hundred. The cruel bishop whom Mitchell was unable to lay low with his exploded bullet, Scotland will explode. What is the difference between a bishop and an executioner? That which is between a Lucifer and a gallows-rogue!

33–6. Explosa . . . est] Margoliouth felt that these four lines, omitted in Thompson, formed a separate epigram.
33. nequiit] *Bod. I+*; nequit *Υ3*.
34. Explodet] a) drive away (originally by clapping or hissing; 'explodo', Lewis and Short, II A) b) reject ('explodo', Lewis and Short, II B) c) punning on the English 'explode': blow up, assassinate. *Pontificem*] originally, a Roman high-priest, then, in the Christian period, a bishop.
36. Luciferum Furciferumque] two opposing senses: a) a light-bearer and a yoke-bearer b) the Devil and a gallows-rogue.

APPENDICES

Appendix 1
On the Victory obtained by Blake over the Spaniards, in the Bay of Santa Cruz, in the Island of Tenerife, 1657

Date. Late May–9 July 1657. The composition date may coincide with Cromwell's congratulatory speech of 9–10 June, referring to the victory: see below, *Headnote, Context.* The Petworth House MS (*P*) is dated 9 July 1657.

Authorship. Lord excluded the poem because it did not appear in *Bod. 1.* Duncan-Jones, *EMS,* 5 (1995), 107–26, argues that M. did not write the poem. She prefers as author the 'R.F.' who signed *P,* and suspects that M., on account of his proximity to Cromwell, received a copy of this inexpert poem in the hope that he would present it to the Lord Protector. She provides detailed evidence that the poem bears little resemblance to M.'s other poems (the second and third of M.'s Cromwell poems refer by intricate textual echoes to M.'s first one, *An Horatian Ode*). In the few cases where resemblance does occur, the coincidence can usually be explained by the presence of common phrases. Further supporting factors against M.'s authorship are the absence of echoes from contemporary published writing, a feature of all of M.'s longer Commonwealth poems, although this was a time when comparatively little literature referring to public events circulated.

Manuscript Circulation. Two MS copies survive:

P Petworth House, West Sussex (old HMC, No. 173; recorded in HMC, 6th report, Part I (1877), Appendix, p. 318); owned by Lord Egremont/Leconfield. Signed or ascribed to 'R.F.'; dated 9 July 1657; written on five 2° pages among papers of Roger Boyle (1621–79), Lord Broghill, later Earl of Orrery. 130 lines long

S University of Sheffield, Hartlib Papers, H50/55/15. Docketed 'A Poem to the Protector'; written on two conjugate 2° leaves among the papers of Samuel Hartlib (*c.* 1601/2–62). 132 lines long

Along with the copy we suppose M. received were copies presented to Samuel Hartlib and Roger Boyle, Lord Broghill, later Earl of Orrery. As with the copy that was the copy text for *1681, H* and *P* were presentation copies, designed to find their way to the Protector by way of the recipients. Duncan-Jones thus disagrees with Stocker and Raylor, *ELR,* 20 (1990), 106–62, who argue that *H* precedes *1681.* Instead, she places the version in *1681* as the earliest, followed by *H,* and then *P.* The latter two are closely related both in terms of various local readings, and have a similar long passage missing. Duncan-Jones believes that *H* and *P* were attempts to improve the earlier version.

Printed Publication. This poem circulated first in manuscript (see above, *Date*). The first printed publication was in John Bulteel's collection *A New Collection of Poems and Songs* (1674), omitting ll. 39–52, where explicit reference to Cromwell is made. Numerous other local alterations were made in order to erase Cromwell's presence from the poem. However, the poem was printed in full in *1681* and not cancelled from most copies, although it does not appear in *Bod. 1.* Duncan-Jones, *EMS,* 5 (1995), 121–4, conjectures that Mary Marvell, or whoever else compiled and printed *1681,* may have substituted, perhaps at a late stage in the publication process, this poem, and *A Dialogue between Thyrsis and Dorinda* (whose authorship by M. is also contested), possibly for a poem by M. that, like the Cromwell poems, was offensive when the volume first appeared.

Context. The movement of the fleet to the Canary Islands, with the intention either of taking them, or of waiting for the Spanish silver fleet, was reported in the English press as early as December, 1656 (see *The Publick Intelligencer,* 62 (8–15 December 1656), 1039). The news of the sinking of the Spanish silver fleet at Santa Cruz, Tenerife on 20 April 1657, first reached London on 28 May. Thurloe read a narrative account from Blake, which was then published in *Mercurius Politicus*, 364 (28 May–4 June 1657), 7814–17, 7822–26, in *The Publick Intelligencer*, 84 (25 May–1 June 1657), 1388–92, and in a pamphlet ordering a day of public thanksgiving (British Library, Thomason Tracts E1065 (14)). The Spanish fleet, consisting of 5–6 galleons and another 10–11 smaller ships had been anchored at Santa Cruz since early February. Having found no enemy ships off Cadiz in late March, Blake's fleet made for the Canary Islands and very shortly after its arrival engaged the Spanish fleet, which was arranged defensively in the harbour. This meant that the English ships had to come in close to land, and took fire from the shore defences. Nonetheless, after four hours the smaller Spanish boats were beaten back, and later, the Vice-Admiral caught fire, and the Admiral exploded (see below, 418). The English losses were comparatively slight: no ships were lost; most of the slain (no more than fifty) or wounded (one hundred and twenty) had succumbed to musket fire from the shore. That the wind had blown directly into the bay during the action, and then changed to enable the English fleet to sail away with ease, was regarded as an act of Providence. The victory concluded Blake's highly successful naval career. He was recalled to England, handsomely rewarded and loudly praised by Cromwell. But being by this time of frail health, he died of scurvy just off Plymouth on 7 August.

Blake's action should be seen within the context of England's war with Spain, and the relationship between foreign events and the survival of the Protectorate regime. The 'Western Design' of 1655 was an expedition against Spanish possessions in the Americas. It was fuelled by ideological hostility towards a Catholic power, as well as being driven by financial and military agendas. Milton's nephew John Phillips resurrected Elizabethan patriotism in his propaganda:

> you are not now to fight against your Country-men, but against your Old and Constant Enemies, the SPANIARDS, a Proud, Deceitful, Cruel, and Treacherous Nation, whose Chiefest Aim hath been the Conquest of this land, and to enslave the People of this Nation; witness those Invasions in the days of Queen ELIZABETH.
>
> Neither need we fear the Vaunts of the Spanish Monarch, whose Government stands not on those strong Foundations that some imagine; Blood and Tyrannie being the chief Pillars of his Greatness, or rather, his Arcana Imperii; and his Empire being onely

strong in this, That the Weaknesses thereof have not yet been well look'd into. Should we chase him from his Indian Treasures, he would soon retire to his Shell, like a Snail tapt upon the horns.

> John Philips, 'To all true English-men', in Philips, trans., Bartholomé de las Casas, *The Tears of the Indians* (1656), sigs. b3^v–b4^r, sig. b5^{r-v}

The campaign failed, but England remained at war with Spain (see Armitage (2000), 136–7). For their part, the Spanish funded the former Leveller Edward Sexby in the hope of inducing an anti-Cromwellian rebellion that would be a prelude to a Spanish invasion of England. Royalist conspirators were also active, and the notorious call for the assassination of Cromwell, *Killing no Murder*, jointly written by Sexby and Silius Titus, was circulating in large numbers (see Holstun (2000), 327–58). Cromwell's refusal to take the crown in May 1657 frustrated Sexby since it avoided certain dissent from the Army, but the enhancement of the Protector's constitutional powers led to further discontent within the Council of State, particularly from Major General Lambert.

Blake's success was useful in that it bolstered patriotic morale, and enhanced English naval prestige, while avoiding a full-scale naval battle, in which a Dutch escort fleet might have augmented the Spanish forces. But if Philip IV was denied a much-needed source of revenue, the English failed to capture the money on board the galleons. 'Most of them had a greate parte of their loading aboarde them, which perished all with the shipes', wrote Thomas Maynard, Consul at Lisbon, to Thurloe on 6 June 1657 (Thurloe State Papers, VI.312), but in fact some of the plate had already been taken ashore before the action began. This loss (reported by *Mercurius Politicus*, 360 (14–21 May 1657), to be worth 15 million ducats) continued to hamper the Protectorate government: its quest for Parliamentary subsidies was a source of discontent, not least because a good deal of the government's expenses were the household costs of the Cromwells. Furthermore, Blake's ill-health meant that the opportunity to capture the Canaries, and hence have a very great stronghold against the Spanish in that region, was not realized. England's disadvantageous position in this respect was underlined by a Spanish invasion of her ally Portugal in late May.

Spain was England's old enemy, and Blake's victory was celebrated at the time and since as of equal stature with the victory over the Spanish Armada in 1588. The poem repeats this sense (see below, l. 125), just as it echoes the frequent reference in contemporary literature to any reference to a Spanish setback as an act of Providence (see, e.g., W. Medley, *A Standard Set Up* ([17 May] 1657), 8).

Sources. The poem is indebted, and in some places, very closely so, to Edmund Waller's *Of a War with Spain, and a Fight at Sea*, which celebrated Stayner's victory of September 1656, without mentioning him by name. But whoever wrote '*Blake's Victory*' must have seen a MS copy of Waller's poem, since it was not printed until 1658 (Thomason acquired his copy on 13 April). Other poems by Waller with a maritime theme are also echoed.

On the Victory obtained by Blake over the Spaniards, in the Bay of Santa Cruz, in the Island of Tenerife, 1657

Now does Spain's fleet her spacious wings unfold,
Leaves the New World and hastens for the old:
But though the wind was fair, they slowly swum
Freighted with acted guilt, and guilt to come:
For this rich load, of which so proud they are,
Was raised by tyranny, and raised for war;
Every capacious gallion's womb was filled,
With what the womb of wealthy kingdoms yield,
The New World's wounded entrails they had tore,
For wealth wherewith to wound the old once more.
Wealth which all others' avarice might cloy,
But yet in them caused as much fear, as joy.
For now upon the main, themselves they saw,

15 That boundless empire, where you give the law,
Of winds' and waters' rage, they fearful be,
But much more fearful are your flags to see.
Day, that to those who sail upon the deep,
More wished for, and more welcome is than sleep,
20 They dreaded to behold, lest the sun's light,
With English streamers, should salute their sight:
In thickest darkness they would choose to steer,
So that such darkness might suppress their fear;
At length their's vanishes, and fortune smiles;
25 For they behold the sweet Canary Isles;
One of which doubtless is by nature blessed
Above both worlds, since 'tis above the rest.
For lest some gloominess might stain her sky,
Trees there the duty of the clouds supply;
30 O noble trust which heav'n on this isle pours,
Fertile to be, yet never need her show'rs.
A happy people, which at once do gain
The benefits without the ills of rain.
Both health and profit, fate cannot deny;
35 Where still the earth is moist, the air still dry;
The jarring elements no discord know,
Fuel and rain together kindly grow;
And coolness there, with heat doth never fight,
This only rules by day, and that by night.
40 Your worth to all these isles, a just right brings,
The best of lands should have the best of kings.
And these want nothing heaven can afford,
Unless it be, the having you their Lord;
But this great want, will not a long one prove,
Your conq'ring sword will soon that want remove.
45 For Spain had better, she'll ere long confess,
Have broken all her swords, than this one peace,
Casting that league off, which she held so long,
She cast off that which only made her strong.

1–2. Now does . . . old] Cp. Waller, *Of a War with Spain*, l. 1: 'Now, for some ages, had the pride of Spain.'
1. spacious] a) covering a large area; expansive (*OED* a. 3) b) bulky (*OED* a. 3b).
2. New World] the American continent. *the old*] Europe.
4. Freighted] loaded (*OED* ppl. a.) *acted*] performed (*OED* ppl. a.) *guilt*] with a pun on 'gilt' (i.e. gold and silver gilt); see also below l. 64.
7. capacious] spacious (*OED* a. 2); cp. Waller, *Of a War with Spain*, l. 35: 'Their huge capacious galleons stuffed with plate.' *womb*] i.e., hold.
10. For wealth . . . once] the introduction of silver bullion by the Spanish into the European economy during the course of the sixteenth century caused great monetary inflation, and was understood to be a cause of war.
11. cloy] a) block up (*OED* v.¹ 5) b) satiate (*OED* v.¹ 8).
12. fear] i.e., of being robbed of the bullion.
13. main] open sea (*OED* n.¹ 5).
14. you] i.e., the Lord Protector.
16. are your] see above, l. 14 n.
20. streamers] long, narrow, pointed flags, flown from mastheads.

24. Canary Isles] archipelago sixty-seven miles at the closest point to the north-west African mainland; a Spanish possession since the 15ᵗʰ-century, and an indispensable replenishment point for Spanish voyages to the New World. Known to the ancients through the account (*c.* 40 B.C.) of Juba II, King of Mauritania, which was preserved by both Pliny and Plutarch.
25. One of which] Tenerife, most prominent of the western group of islands, that rise in mountain peaks directly from the ocean floor.
26. both worlds] earth and Heaven (see below, l. 78).
38. This] i.e., heat. *that*] coolness.
39. Your] see above, l. 14 n. *just right*] i.e., a just right of possession.
40. kings] Cromwell had finally refused the crown on 8 May, 1657. In *The First Anniversary*, M. states that it is right for Cromwell to refuse the crown. M. may have changed his mind, but otherwise the line is further evidence that M. did not write the poem.
41. want] lack.
47. league] alliance (*OED* n.² 1 a); a treaty of 1630 had established peace between England and Spain.

Forces and art, she soon will feel, are vain,
50   Peace, against you, was the sole strength of Spain.
By that alone those islands she secures,
Peace made them hers, but war will make them yours;
There the indulgent soil that rich grape breeds,
Which of the gods the fancied drink exceeds;
55   They still do yield, such is their precious mould,
All that is good, and are not cursed with gold.
With fatal gold, for still where that does grow,
Neither the soil, nor people quiet know.
Which troubles men to raise it when 'tis ore,
60   And when 'tis raised, does trouble them much more.
Ah, why was thither brought that cause of war,
Kind Nature had from thence removed so far?
In vain doth she those islands free from ill,
If Fortune can make guilty what she will.
65   But whilst I draw that scene, where you ere long,
Shall conquests act, your present are unsung.
       For Santa Cruz the glad fleet takes her way,
And safely there casts anchor in the bay.
Never so many with one joyful cry,
70   That place saluted, where they all must die.
Deluded men! Fate with you did but sport,
You 'scaped the sea, to perish in your port.
'Twas more for England's fame you should die there,
Where you had most of strength, and least of fear.
75   The peak's proud height, the Spaniards all admire,
Yet in their breasts, carry a pride much higher.
Only to this vast hill a power is given,
At once both to inhabit earth and heaven.
But this stupendious prospect did not near,
80   Make them admire, so much as they did fear.
       For here they met with news, which did produce,
A grief, above the cure of grapes' best juice.

They learned the terror, that nor summer's heat,
Nor winter's storms, had made your fleet retreat.
85   To fight against such foes was vain, they knew,
Which did the rage of elements subdue.
Who on the ocean that does horror give,
To all besides, triumphantly do live.
       With haste they therefore all their gallions moor,
90   And flank with cannon from the neighb'ring shore.
Forts, lines, and sconces all the bay along,
They build and act all that can make them strong.
       Fond men who know not whilst such works they rais
They only labour to exalt your praise.
95   Yet they by restless toil, became at length,
So proud and confident of their made strength,
That they with joy their boasting general heard,
Wish then for that assault he lately feared.
His wish he has, for now undaunted Blake,
100 With wingèd speed, for Santa Cruz does make.
For your renown, his conqu'ring fleet does ride,
O'er seas as vast as is the Spaniards' pride.
Whose fleets and trenches viewed, he soon did say,
'We to their strength are more obliged than they.
105 Were't not for that, they from their fate would run,
And a third world seek out our arms to shun.
Those forts, which there, so high and strong appear,
Do not so much suppress, as shew their fear.
Of speedy victory let no man doubt,
110 Our worst work's past, now we have found them out.
Behold their Navy does at anchor lie,
And they are ours, for now they cannot fly.'
       This said, the whole fleet gave it their applause,
And all assumes your courage, in your cause.
115 That bay they enter, which unto them owes,
The noblest wreaths, that victory bestows.

---

53. indulgent] a) nurturing b) gratifying.
54. fancied drink] nectar.
55. precious mould] i.e., soft grape skin.
61. cause of war] following in the most general terms the dictum that money is the sinew of war: see Libanius, *Orat.*, xlvi.
64. guilty] see above, l. 4.
67. Santa Cruz] chief port of Tenerife, within a deep and narrow-mouthed bay.
78. earth and heaven] see above, l. 26.
79. stupendious] accepted form of 'stupendous' until the late seventeenth century (*OED*): amazing.
81. news] suggesting a newsbook, and hence a paradox, since news communicated in print was very much an urban phenomenon.
82. Duncan-Jones, *EMS*, 5 (1995), 114, reports that *P* has a cross above the 'w' and conjectures that 'R.F.' intended to write 'Vines.'
87. horror] aversion mixed with dread (OED n 3a).

90–2. And flank . . . strong] 'the Castle, and surrounded besides with six or seven Forts, with almost a continued line for Musqueteers and great shot . . . the whole bay being rounded with 3 brest works one within the other, and that next the water side had stone forts for great Guns, very near adjacent one to the other, and at one part a strong Castle, all which made the Spaniard think himself impregnable', *Mercurius Politicus*, 364 (28 May–4 June, 1657), 7815, 7824.
90. flank] protect by placing artillery along the flank or side (*OED* v. 2).
91. sconces] small forts or earthworks (*OED* n.³).
97. boasting general] 'a Flemming desiring leave of their General to go to Sea, he laughed at him, and told him he might go if he would, but the English fleet might come if he dared, for he would serve them', *Mercurius Politicus*, 364 (21–28 May, 1657), 7822.
99. undaunted] not discouraged (OED ppl. a. 3).
104. obliged] indebted (OED v. III 6a).
106. third world] i.e., neither Europe nor America, but elsewhere.

Bold Stayner leads, this fleet's designed by fate,
To give him laurel, as the last did plate.
　The thund'ring cannon now begins the fight,
And though it be at noon, creates a night.
The air was soon after the fight begun,
Far more enflamed by it, than by the sun.
Never so burning was that climate known,
War turn'd the temperate, to the torrid zone.
　Fate these two fleets, between both worlds had brought.
Who fight, as if for both those worlds they fought.
Thousands of ways, thousands of men there die,
Some ships are sunk, some blown up in the sky.
Nature ne'er made cedars so high aspire,
As oaks did then, urged by the active fire.
Which by quick powder's force, so high was sent,
That it returned to its own element.
Torn limbs some leagues into the island fly,
Whilst others lower, in the sea do lie.
Scarce souls from bodies severed are so far,
By death, as bodies there were by the war.
Th'all-seeing sun, ne'er gazed on such a sight,
Two dreadful navies there at anchor fight.
And neither have, or power, or will to fly
There must one conquer, or there both must die.
Far different motives yet, engaged them thus,
Necessity did them, but Choice did us.

A choice which did the highest worth express,
And was attended by as high success.
145　For your resistless genius there did reign,
By which we laurels reaped ev'n on the main.
So prosperous stars, though absent to the sense,
Bless those they shine for, by their influence.
　Our cannon now tears every ship and sconce,
150　And o'er two elements triumphs at once.
Their gallions sunk, their wealth the sea does fill,
The only place where it can cause no ill.
　Ah would those treasures which both Indies have,
Were buried in as large, and deep a grave,
155　War's chief support with them would buried be,
And the land owe her peace unto the sea.
Ages to come, your conquering arms will bless,
There they destroy, what had destroyed their peace.
And in one war the present age may boast,
160　The certain seeds of many wars are lost.
　All the foe's ships destroyed, by sea or fire,
Victorious Blake, does from the bay retire,
His siege of Spain he then again pursues,
And there first brings of his success the news;
165　The saddest news that e'er to Spain was brought,
Their rich fleet sunk, and ours with laurel fraught.
Whilst Fame in every place, her trumpet blows,
And tells the world, how much to you it owes.

---

117. Stayner] Captain Richard Stayner (a Rear-Admiral) led the attack on the Spanish ships, while Blake directed fire at the shore batteries. Stayner was knighted by Cromwell on 11 June.
117–18. this fleet's . . . plate] Stayner captured some Spanish ships in September, 1656, and hence had a prize, while this victory provides not wealth but fame. M. offers here an honourable picture of events since the silver carried by the Spanish fleet was offloaded and sent ashore before the battle; afterwards both English government and navy considered sending a further fleet to Santa Cruz to capture the silver.
120. And . . . night] Cp. Waller, *Of a War with Spain*, ll. *43–6*: 'Arrived, they soon began that tragic play,/And with their smoky cannons banish day;/Night, horror, slaughter, with confusion meets,/And in their sable arms embrace the fleets.'
124. torrid] scorched (*OED* a. 1).
125. both worlds] see above, l. 78.
127. Thousands . . . die] Cp. Waller, *Of a War with Spain*, l. 48: 'of one wound, hundreds together die.'
128. Some . . . sky] 'their Admiral and Vice-Admiral soon blew up . . . of ships burnt were 14, sunck two besides a smal vessell of about 40 tonnes sunk in all . . . 17 sayle', *Mercurius Politicus*, 364 (21–28 May, 1657), 7824–5.
133–4. Torn limbs . . . lie] Cp. *The Second Advice to a Painter*, ll. 163–70.
135. Scarce] seldom, rarely (*OED* adv. 3).
145. resistless] irresistible.
146. laurels] i.e., laurel wreaths won by Cromwell's panegyrists: see Nevo (1963), 114–15, Smith (1994), 277–94, Norbrook (1999), chs. 7, 8.

147–8. So . . . influence] Cp. Waller, 'Of the Queen', ll. 36–8: 'the rich spangles that adorn the sky/Which, though they shine for ever fixed there,/With light and influence relieve us here.'
149. sconce] see above, l. 91.
150. two elements] earth and water.
151–2. Their . . . ill] Cp. Waller, *Of a War with Spain*, ll. 65–6: 'Some, we made prize; while others, burned and rent,/With their rich lading to the bottom went.' But see above, 424.
153–60. Ah . . . lost] Cp. Waller, *Of a War with Spain*, ll. 67–74: 'Down sinks at once (so Fortune with us sports!)/The pay of armies, and the pride of courts./Vain man! Whose rage buries as low that store,/As avarice had digged for it before;/What earth, in her dark bowels, could not keep/From greedy hands, lies safer in the deep,/Where Thetis kindly does from mortals hide/Those seeds of luxury, debate, and pride.'
163. he . . . pursues] 'General Blake in his returne form thence stopt in Cascais roade, with 18 of the shipes under his command, and 6 he sente directly for the bay of Cadix. Three dayes after his beeinge here, he sente away the vice admiral with eight shipes more; and after eight dayes stay here, havinge refreshed himselfe, and fitted his shipes, he departed for the bay of Cadix with the rest of his fleete, where he now is.' (Thomas Maynard, Consul at Lisbon, to Thurloe, 6 June, 1657 (Thurloe State Papers, VI.312)).
166. fraught] laden.

Appendix 2
Manuscripts and Printed Books

List of seventeenth- and early eighteenth-century manuscripts in which Marvell's poetry appears, together with abbreviated titles

United Kingdom

Aberystwyth

National Library of Wales
NLW 1   Ottley, unnumbered papers
NLW 2   MS Chirk F 12633

Alnwick Castle

AC   Vol. XIX

Arbury Hall

AH 1   MS 185
AH 2   A 414

Bedford

Bedfordshire Record Office
Be.   L 31/340/2

Birmingham

University of Birmingham
Bi.   MS 13/i/22

Bradford

Bradford District Archives
Hopkinson MSS, Vol. XVII

Cambridge

Cambridge University Library
CUL 1   Add. MS 79
CUL 2   Add. MS 42

Fitzwilliam Museum

CF   MU, MS 120

King's College

CK   Hayward Collection, H. 11. 13

Cardiff

Cardiff Central Library
Ca.   MS 1.462

Carlisle

Cumbria Record Office
Cm.   D/Lons/L Miscellaneous 11/6/33

Chelmsford

Essex Record Office
Es.   D/DW Z3 (iii)

Edinburgh

Edinburgh University Library
EUL   MS Dc. 1. 3/1
National Library of Scotland
NLS   Adv. MS 19. 1. 12

Leeds

Brotherton Library, University of Leeds
L 1   Brotherton Collection, MS Lt. 67
L 2   Brotherton Collection, MS Lt. q. 52
L 3   Brotherton Collection, MS Lt. 61
L 4   Brotherton Collection, MS Lt. 55
L 5   Brotherton Collection, MS Lt. 38
L 6   Brotherton Collection, MS Lt. 54

Lincoln

Lincolnshire Archives Office
Li.   Anc 15/B/4

London

British Library
BL 1   Add. MS 29921
BL 2   Add. MS 29396

BL 3	Add. MS 29397
BL 4	Add. MS 31432
BL 5	Burney MS 390
BL 6	Add. MS 34362
BL 7	Add. MS 32096
BL 8	Add. MS 36270
BL 9	Add. MS 4843
BL 10	Add. MS 5831
BL 11	Harley MS 3614
BL 12	Harley MS 7034
BL 13	Lansdowne MS 1233
BL 14	Harley MS 7315
BL 15	Harley MS 7316
BL 16	Harley MS 7319
BL 17	Harley MS 6947
BL 18	Sloane MS 1941
BL 19	Sloane MS 3413
BL 20	Add. MS 23722
BL 21	Add. MS 61903
BL 22	Add. MS 18220
BL 23	Add. MS 21094
BL 24	Lansdowne MS 852
BL 25	Add. MS 72479
BL 26	Sloane MS 655
BL 27	Add. MS 73540
BL 28	Add. MS 47128
BL 29	Add. MS 69823
BL 30	Add. MS 72899; formerly Bowood House, Petty Papers, Vol. 2

Royal Society

RS	MS 32

Society of Antiquaries

SA	MS 330

University College London

UCO	Special Collections, MS Ogden 42

Victoria and Albert Museum

VA 1	Dyce Collection, No. 43 (Pressmark D. 25. F. 38)
VA 2	Dyce Collection, No. 38 (Pressmark D. 25. F. 37)

Longleat House

Lo. 1	Whitelocke Papers, Parcel 5, unbound single folded sheet.
Lo. 2	Whitelocke Papers, MS 124a.
LP	Portland Papers, Vol. XVII

Manchester

Chetham's Library

MCh. 1	Halliwell-Phillipps 2220
MCh. 2	Mun. A 4. 14

Nottingham

University of Nottingham

N 1	Portland MS Pw V 42
N 2	Portland MS Pw V 603
N 3	Portland MS Pw V 46
N 4	Portland MS Pw V 1203
N 5	Portland MS Pw V 40
N 6	Portland MS Pw V 1144
N 7	Portland MS Pw2 V 5 (i)
N 8	Portland MS Pw2 V 5 (ii)
N 9	Portland MS Pw2 V 5 (iii)
N 10	Portland MS Pw2 V 5 (iv)
N 11	Portland MS Pw2 V 6
N 12	Portland MS Pw V 299

Oxford

All Souls College

OA 1	MS 116
OA 2	MS 174

Bodleian Library

Bod. 1	MS Eng. poet d. 49
Bod. 2	MS Rawl. A. 176
Bod. 3	MS Mus. Sch. C. 96
Bod. 4	MS Rawl. poet. 81
Bod. 5	MS Rawl. poet. 90
Bod. 6	MS Rawl. poet. 199
Bod. 7	MS Tanner 306/2
Bod. 8	MS Eng. poet. e. 4
Bod. 9	MS Ashmole 1137
Bod. 10	MS Wood B. 12
Bod. 11	MS Rawl. poet 196
Bod. 12	MS Don. b. 8
Bod. 13	MS Douce 357
Bod. 14	MS Rawl. poet. 181
Bod. 15	MS Broxbourn R 359
Bod. 16	MS Rawl. poet. 171
Bod. 17	MS Top. Oxon. E. 202
Bod. 18	MS Don. e. 23
Bod. 19	MS Ashmole 36/37
Bod. 20	MS Ashmole 1463
Bod. 21	MS Gough London 14
Bod. 22	MS Rawl. poet. 26
Bod. 23	MS Rawl. D. 924
Bod. 24	MS Eng. misc. e. 536
Bod. 25	MS Locke e. 17

Bod. 26   MS Rawl. poet. 123
Bod. 27   MS Rawl. poet. 172
Bod. 28   MS Rawl. poet. 159
Bod. 29   MS Eng. poet. c. 18
Bod. 30   MS Add. A. 48

Worcester College
OW 1   MS 6. 13
OW 2   MS TC. 20. 11

Petworth House
P   formerly HMC 173

Sheffield
University of Sheffield
SH   Hartlib Papers, H50/5515

Stratford-upon-Avon
Shakespeare Birthplace Trust Record Office
SBT 1   DR 18/26/6
SBT 2   ER 93/2

Taunton
Somerset Record Office
T   DD/TB, Box 11, F.L. 14 [no item no.]

Waller Family Papers
WTC   Copy of 'Little T.C.'

Warwick
Warwickshire Record Office
Wa.   CR 341/277

United States of America

Austin, Texas
University of Texas
AT   MS (Killigrew T)/Misc./B

Boston
Boston Public Library
BPL   MS Am. 1502 v. 1

Cambridge, Massachusetts
Harvard University
H 1   MS Eng. 1035
H 2   MS Eng. 624

Chicago
University of Chicago
Ch. 1   MS 554
Ch. 2   MS f553

Columbus, Ohio
Ohio State University
OSU   Spec. MS Eng. 15

Los Angeles, California
Clark Library
LAC 1   P7455M1 [?1712], Bound
LAC 2   M3915M3 S445 [16–], Bound
LAC 3   fC6978M3 [19–], Bound
University of California, Los Angeles
LAUC   170/68

Minneapolis
University of Minnesota
Mn.   MS 690235f

New Brunswick, New Jersey
Rutgers University
R   MS CC (Eng. Misc.)

New Haven, Connecticut
Yale University
Y 1   Osborn Collection, fb 142
Y 2   Osborn Collection, b 52/2
Y 3   Osborn Collection, b 54
Y 4   MS Vault, Section 10, Drawer 3,
           Commonplace Book
Y 5   MS Vault, Section 15, Drawer 3
Y 6   Osborn Collection, b 136
Y 7   Osborn Collection, fb 106
Y 8   Osborn Collection, fb 108
Y 9   Osborn Collection, b 52/1
Y 10   Osborn Collection, fb 140
Y 11   Osborn Collection, c 160
Y 12   Osborn Collection, fc 61
Y 13   Osborn Collection, PB VII/15
Y 14   Osborn Collection, b 150

Princeton, New Jersey
Princeton University
P 1   Robert H. Taylor Collection, Restoration
           MS 3
P 2   Robert H. Taylor Collection, Restoration
           MS 2
P 3   Gen. MS Misc. No. AM 14401
P 4   Robert H. Taylor Collection, Restoration
           MS 1

Washington DC

Folger Shakespeare Library

F 1	MS W. b. 515
F 2	MS M. b. 12
F 3	MS W. a. 135
F 4	MS V. a. 103 (also MS 1.28)
F 5	MS V. a. 220

Georgetown University

G	[no ref. or page nos.]

Wellesley, Massachusetts

WC	MS leaf in exemplum of 1681

Austria

Vienna

Österreichische Nationalbibliothek

V	Cod. 14090

Denmark

Copenhagen

Royal Library

Co.	Gl. Kgl. Saml. 3579, 8°

Printed Books in which Marvell's poetry, and poetry thought to be by Marvell, excluding prefatory poems, appeared in the seventeenth century

1648   *An elegy upon my Lord Francis Villiers.* 1648. Wing M870

1655   *The first Anniversary of the Government under His Highness the Lord Protector.* 1655, W871.

1665   *The Character of Holland.* 1665. Wing M867

1665Y   Another edition. See John Barnard, *PBSA*, 81 (1987), 459–464. No Wing number

1667   *The Second Advice to a Painter, for Drawing the History of our Naval Business; In Imitation of Mr Waller. Being the last work of Sir John Denham. Printed in the Year, 1667.* Wing M868A

1667²   *The Second, and Third Advice to a Painter, for Drawing the History of our Navall Actions, The two last years, 1665. And 1666. In Answer to Mr Waller. A. Breda, 1667.* Wing M887A

1667³   *Directions to a Painter, For Describing our Naval Business: In Imitation of Mr Waller. Being the Last Works of Sir John Denham. Whereunto is annexed, Clarindon's House-Warming. By an unknown Author. Printed in the Year 1667.* Wing M869A

1667³b   Another edition. Wing M869B

1672   *The Character of Holland.* 1672. Wing M868

1681   *Miscellaneous Poems. By Andrew Marvell, Esq; Late Member of the House of Commons. London, Printed for Robert Boulter. 1681.* Wing M872

1689   *The Third Part of the Collection of Poems on Affairs of State. Containing, Esquire Marvel's Further Instructions to a Painter. And the late Lord Rochester's Farewel. London: Printed in the Year 1689.* Wing T913

1694   *Chorus Poetarum: Or, Poems on Several Occasions. By the Duke of Buckingham, the late Lord Rochester, Sir John Denham, or Geo. Etheridge, Andrew Marvel, Esq; the famous Spencer, Madam Behn, And several other Eminent Poets of this Age. Never before Printed. 1694.* Wing B5309

1697   *Poems on Affairs of State: From the Time of Oliver Cromwell, to the Abdication of K. James the Second. Written by the greatest Wits of the Age. Viz. Duke of Buckingham, Earl of Rochester, Lord Bu–st, Sir John Denham, Andrew Marvell, Esq; Mr Milton, Mr Dryden, Mr Sprat, Mr Waller. Mr Ayloffe, &c. With some Miscellany Poems by the same: Most whereof never before printed – Now carefully examined with the originals, and published without any Castration. 1697.* Wing P2719

1697²   *State Poems; Continued From the time of O. Cromwel, to this present Year 1697. Written By the Greatest Wits of the Age, viz.* Wing S5325A

LCP   8° edition containing *The Last Instructions* and *The Loyal Scot*, with a missing title page, in a tract collection originally purchased by Benjamin Franklin and now owned by the Library Company of Philadelphia. Dated by Wing 1667; now thought to be a 1690s printing. Wing M871A

Appendix 3
Textual Variants

Textual variants are listed below for poems where there are several witnesses with many different readings. Variant punctuation and paragraph divisons are not recorded. With the Restoration verse satires, the number of witnesses and variants is enormous. This is especially so in the case of *The Second Advice to a Painter* and *The Third Advice to a Painter*. In these cases, and for the sake of economy, most instances of variant spellings of the same words, including names, and minor variants, where, for instance, a singular/plural difference, or a difference of article or tense, is of no consequence, are not recorded.

A Dialogue between Thyrsis and Dorinda

Title. *BL 1b+*; A Pastorall Dialogue sett by our Mathew Lock her majestes organist *CK*; A Dialogue Dorinda and Thirsis *M. Ch. 1. Dialogue*] *BL 1b+*; Pastorall *P 1*; A Sonnet Sett by Matt. Lock. *Y 1*; Dialogue. Thirsis. Dorinda. *1672*.

1. *part*] *BL 1b+*; snatch *AT, Bod. 5, UCO. 1, 1672, 1681. these*] *BL 1b+*; pour *AT*.

2. *BL 1b+*; Our sports denie; our Love forbids *AT UCO. 1*.

3. *Tell me Thirsis*] *BL 1b+*; Thirsis tell me *AT, Bod. 6 UCO. 1, prithee*] *BL 1b+*; pray thee *1663*.

4. *whither*] *1681*; whether *F 1. thou*] *1681*; thee *Bod. 5. must*] *BL 1b+*; shall *AT, Bod. 4, Bod. 5, Bod. 6, F 1, UCO. 1, M. Ch. 1, UCO. Y 1, 1659, 1663, 1672, 1675*.

5. *To the Elysium*] *BL 1b+*; To Elysium *AT, Bod. 4, Bod. 5, Bod. 6, CK, UCO. 1, 1672. Oh*] *BL 1b+*; But *AT, UCO. 1, Bod. 4*.

7. *way . . . home*] *BL 1b+*; other way but one *M. Ch. 1. to*] *BL 1b+*; one *Bod. 4, Bod. 5, CF, CK, F 1, Y 1, 1659, 1672, 1675, 1681. our*] *BL 1b+*; my *AT UCO. 1*.

8. *Is . . . cell*] *BL 1b+*; Our home is our *M. Ch. 1. Is*] *BL 1b*; Is by *Y 1. our cell*] *BL 1b+*; our *1681*.

9. *Turn thine eye*] *BL 1b+*; Cast thine eye *1681*; Cast thine eyes *Bod. 6*; Turn y[ou]r eyes *P 1*; Cast thy face *AT UCO, eye*] *1681*; eyes *Bod. 6, CUL 1, Y 1, 1663. sky*] *BL 1b*; skies *Y 1*.

10. *There . . . way*] *BL 1b+*; There there the path *P 1. way*] *BL 1b+*; path *AT, Lo. 1. doth*] *BL 1b+*; does *Bod. 5, CK, Y 1*.

11. *'Tis a sure but*] *BL 1b+*; It is a sure the *P 1. but*] *BL 1b+*; though *Bod. 3, CK, 1663. sure . . . rugged*] *BL 1b*; steep but starry *AT*; steepe, though starry *UCO*, straight and easy *Bod. 6*.

13. *nest*] *BL 1b+*; rest *AT, 1663. but*] Not in *CF. can*] *BL 1b+*; shall *CF, CK, F 1, Lo. 1, 1659, 1675*.

14. *That*] *BL 1b+*; Who *Y 1*.

15. *Do not sigh*] *BL 1b*; Dont sight *P 1. sigh*] *BL 1b+*; sight [with the 't' crossed through] *AT*.

16. *Hath*] *BL 1+*; Has *Bod. 5, CK, F 1, L 1, Y 1, 1672, 1675. yet*] *CUL 1, CF*; but *BL 1b+. doth*] does *Bod. 5, CK, Y 1, 1672*.

17. *Till it hit*] *BL 1b+*; and tell itt knock *AT, Bod. 6. hit*] *BL 1b+*; hits *P 1, Y 1*.

18. Assigned to Dorinda in *M. Ch. 1. Heaven's*] *BL 1b+*; Heaven is *AT, Bod. 6, UCO*.

19. *But in*] *BL 1b+*; In *AT, Bod. 6, UCO*.

21. *BL 1b+*; They know not what it is to feare *Bod. 6, UCO. Oh*] *BL 1b+*; Ho *1681. there's*] *BL 1b+*; there is *CF, CK, F 1, P 1, 1659, 1663, 1675. hope*] *BL 1b+*; hopes *Y 1. fear*] *BL 1b+*; fears *Y 1*.

22. *There's . . . bear*] *BL 1b+*; Free from the wolfe and horrid beare *Bod. 6, UCO*; There is no Wolfe nor Fox, nor Bear *Bod. 5, CF, CK, F 1, Y 1, 1659, 1672, 1675. no fox no bear*] *BL 1b+*; nor fox nor bear *M. Ch. 1. no bear*] *BL 1b+*; or bear *Bod. 3*.

23. *dog*] *BL 4*; Dogs *Bod. 5, Y 1. our*] *BL 1b+*; the *CUL 1, 1663*.

24. *Lightfoot*] *BL 1b+*; Whitefoot *P 1*; *CUL 1, 1663*.

25–6. No . . . spheres] BL 1b+; And there most
sweetly thine Ear/May feast with Musick of
the Sphear 1681.

25. oat-pipes] BL 1b+; oat-pipe CK, F 1, 1675;
oatpipe Bod. 3, L 1, Υ 1. there] 1681; sound
P 1. thine] BL 1b+; thy F 1, CF, CK, M.
Ch. 1, 1659; 1675; our Bod. 4.

26. May] 1681; shall CK, P 1, 1663. sleep]
BL 1b+; feast 1681. music] 1681; Musick,
with Musick, Musick 1659.

27. Oh sweet! Oh sweet!] BL 1b+; Sweet sweet
CUL 1, P 1, 1663; O sweet! CK, 1672; Ah
sweet! Bod. 4; Ah Sweet: Ah Sweet Bod. 5;
not in 1681.

28. thinking] BL 1b+; thinking, silent thinking
1659.

29. prithee let us] BL 1b+; prithee P 1, Lo. 1;
Prethee let's 1672; I pray thee 1663. our]
BL 1b+; the M. Ch. 1. to] not in 1681.

31. Then] BL 1b+; Well CUL 1.

32. sweetest grass] BL 1b+; softest grass 1681.

33. consorts] BL 1b+; consort Bod. 3, Bod. 5,
CK, CULF, F 1, CF, 1659, 1663, 1675;
comfort P 1.

34. Cool . . . springs] BL 1b+; Cool . . . streams
Bod. 4.

37. Shepherds there] 1681; There Shepherds all
BL 1b. bear] BL 1b+; bear an Υ 1.

38. Nymph's a] 1681; Nymph is CUL 1, P 1,
1663; Nymph a CF; Nymph 1659.

39. Ah me, ah me!] BL 1b+; Ah! me CK, 1659;
Ah! CUL 1, P 1, Lo. 1, 1663; Aye Mee, Aye
Mee Bod. 5. cry] BL 1b; weep 1672.

40. I'm sick, I'm sick] BL 1b+; I am sick CUL 1,
P 1, 1663.

41. Convince me now, that this] BL 1b+; Shew me
what thou saies CUL 1 [with 'sayst'], 1663.
now, that this] BL 1b+; all thou say'st P 1.

42. all adieu] 1681+; adieu Bod. 5.

43–4. I . . . die] misassigned to Dorinda in 1681;
missing in Υ 1.

43. I . . . I] BL 1b+; Il for thee, much more
with thee die CF, CUL 1.

44–5. 'Chorus together' inserted between these
lines in 1675.

44. Will] BL 1b+; Would P 1, 1672; I'll Bod. 3,
Bod. 5, CK, M. Ch. 1, Lo. 1, 1659, 1663,
1675.

45–8. Then . . . sleep] misassigned to Dorinda in
1681, and [?] 'Cho' in M. Ch. 1. 'Chorus'
inserted after l. 45 in F 1, Donno.

45. Dorinda] BL 1b+; let us] BL 1b+; let's Υ 1.
Carillo] BL 1b+; Corellia 1681; Corella
Bod. 4; Clorido F 1; Corillo Bod. 3, Lo. 1,
1663; Corilla 1659, 1672; Corrilla Bod. 5;
Clorilla CF; Clorillo CK, M. Ch. 1.

46. And thou] BL 1b+; Thou Υ 1. and them]
BL 1b+; which wee'l CUL 1, 1663.

47. on't] BL 1b+; it Υ 1. weep] 1681; weep, 'till
we weep [Dorinda] weep, we weep [Thirsis]
1675. weep, weep [Thirsis] Bod. 3.

48. smoothly pass away in] BL 1b+; pass away in
1659; Passeaway within a Lo. 1; dye away
within a CUL 1, 1663. away] away away
away Bod. 3; Bod. 4; F 1, 1675.

A Letter to Doctor Ingelo, then with my Lord Whitelocke, Ambassador from the Protector to the Queen of Sweden

2. Ingele] 1681; Angele Lo. 2, Arckenholtz.

5. Quae gentes hominum] 1681; Quis
hominum genius Lo. 2, Arckenholtz.

7. obruit] 1681; obterit Lo. 2, Arckenholtz.

8. Jungitur] 1681+; Fungitur Arckenholtz.

10. agricolis] 1681+; agniolis Arckenholtz.

11. saevam] 1681+; Suevam Arckenholtz.

12. Pace vigil] 1681+; Pace viget Arckenholtz.
juste] 1681+; iusta Arckenholtz.

13. Quin] 1681+; Cumque Arckenholtz.

15. Nam] 1681+; Num Arckenholtz.

20. sonetve] 1681+; sonetque Arckenholtz.

21. At] 1681+; Ac Arckenholtz.

33. quoties] 1681+; quotiens Arckenholtz.
demisit] 1681+; dimisit Arckenholtz.

35. falsa] 1681; falsâ Lo. 2; falsos Arckenholtz.

36. tam] 1681; tum Arckenholtz.

38. distribuantur] 1681+; distribuentur
Arckenholtz.

40. sine] 1681+; sin Lo. 2.

41. utrique] 1681; utriq Lo. 2; utrique est
Arckenholtz.

44. Cynthi] 1681; Cynthii Arckenholtz.

45. pariles] 1681+; Paridas Arckenholtz.

47. straverit] 1681+; straverat Lo. 2.

48. Quae] 1681; Qua Arckenholtz.
fovet] Lo. 2. Arckenholtz, Grosart; foret
1681.

49. coopertus] 1681; substratus Lo. 2,
Arckenholtz.

50. Haud ita labentis] 1681; Dignior haud lapsi
Lo. 2, Arckenholtz.

55. *succurrent*] 1681, Arckenholtz; *succerrerit* Lo. 2. *auso*] 1681+; auro Arckenholtz.
57. *Sive*] 1681+; Seu Arckenholtz.
58. *spoliata*] 1681; spoliatae Arckenholtz.
60. *nam*] 1681+; num Arckenholtz.
62. *seris*] 1681+; seriis Arckenholtz.
67. *Aerior*] 1681; Acrior Lo. 2; *curasque*] 1681; curâq Lo. 2.
71–2. *Sic quod in ingenuas* Gothus *peccaverit Artes/Vindicat, & studiis expiat Una suis*] 1681; In literas Gothus sic quod peccaverit olim,/Vindicat, et studijs expiat Illa suis Lo. 2.
81. *sperasse*] 1681; sperare Lo. 2.
85. *Upsalides Musae nunc & majora canemus*] 1681; Upsalides Musae paulo majora canemus Lo. 2.
87. *suorum*] 1681; suarum Lo. 2.
92. *licito pergit*] 1681; pergit licito Lo. 2.
97. *tantos*] 1681; tantis Lo. 2.
99. *ille*] 1681; illa Lo. 2.
103. *Oliverus*] 1681; Olivarus Lo. 2.
116. *petit*] 1681; petet Lo. 2.
127. *Salomon*] 1681; Solomon Lo. 2.
129. *Ingele*] 1681; Angele Lo. 2.
136. *qualiacumque*] 1681+; qualiacunque Lo. 2.

The First Anniversary of the Government under his Highness the Lord Protector

Title. The . . . *Protector*] 1655, Bod. 1; The First Anniversary of the Government under O.C. 1681; Anniversary on the Government of the Ld Protector An: D: 1655 BL 5; An Anniversary on the Government of the Lord Protector 1655 Bod. 8; Copy of Verses upon ye Government under the Protectour Cromwel H 1.
1. *curlings*] 1655+; curling Bod. 8.
2. *does*] 1655+; doth H 1.
4. *circles*] 1655+; circle BL 5.
6. *does*] 1655+; doth H 1.
7–10. *Cromwell . . . before*] missing in Bod. 1.
14. *work*] 1655+; works H 1.
15. *While*] 1655+ whilst BL 5. *a*] 1655+; as H 1.
19. *earthy*] 1655+; early BL 5; earthly H 1. *under*] 1655+; in ye H 1.
21. *to*] 1655+; on Bod. 1. *their son*] 1655, 1681, Bod. 1; your Sun Bod. 8.
24. *Took in*] 1655+; Taken BL 5, Bod. 8. *begs*] 1655+; beg Bod. 8.

26. *have*] 1655+; has Bod. 8.
26. *if he no*] 1655+; because he BL 5.
32. *wreak*] 1655+; turn BL 5.
37. *bear*] 1655+; have BL 5.
38. *with*] 1655+; what Bod. 8. *Jove*] 1655+; love BL 5.
43. *Nor*] 1655+; No BL 5.
45. *hies*] 1655+ flys BL 5.
48. *that higher*] 1655+; the upper BL 5.
50. *god*] 1655+; Gods H 1.
51. *measures*] 1655+; measure H 1.
53. *lower*] 1655+; higher BL 5. *higher*] 1655+; lower BL 5.
55. *story*] 1655, 1681, Bod. 1; stone was BL 5, Bod. 8; stone he H 1.
58. *new*] 1655+; ne're BL 5.
57. *structures*] 1655+; structure BL 5.
61. *strokes*] 1655+; struck H 1.
62. *marbles*] 1655+; marble H 1.
63. *for*] 1655+; yet Bod. 8. *he most the*] 1655+; ye most he H 1.
64. *for*] 1655+; yet BL 5.
70. *that*] 1655+; which H 1.
73. *Amphion*] 1655+; Aphion BL 5.
75. *first*] 1655+; set BL 5.
77. *that*] 1655+; the Bod. 8.
78. *minds of stubborn*] 1655+; stubborn minds of BL 5.
80. *labour*] 1655+; labours Bod. 8. *its*] 1655+; the Bod. 8.
82. *the highest*] 1655+; for highest BL 5.
84. *And*] 1655+; But BL 5, Bod. 8.
85. *his*] 1655+; an H 1.
87. *does*] 1655+; doth Bod. 8.
90. *Fast'ning*] 1655+; Hastn'ing BL 5.
91. *whose*] 1655+; when BL 5.
92. *this*] 1655+; at Bod. 8. *that*] 1655+; this Bod. 8.
100. *world*] 1655+; sun BL 5.
102. *in war*] Bod. 8; a war 1655+.
105. *pattern*] 1655+; pattron BL 5.
106. *nor yet*] 1655+; not yet BL 5, H 1; not the Bod. 8.
107. *their*] 1655+; the BL 5.
112. *not, hate*] 1655+; they hate BL 5.
116. *Not*] Bod. 1, Bod. 8; Nor 1655, 1681, BL 5. *but*] 1655+; or Bod. 8. *or*] 1655+; but Bod. 8.
118. *malice*] 1655+; error BL 5. *error more*] 1655+; malice most BL 5.
119. *to*] 1655+; doth to H 1.
121. *shall*] 1655+; should Bod. 8.

122. *Your*] *1655+*; The *BL 5. your*] *1655+*;
the *BL 5*; *Bod. 8.*
125. *hollow far*] *1655+*; follow (follow) for [sic]
BL 5.
127. *days*] *1655+*; shades *Bod. 8.*
130. *gory*] *1655+*; very *Bod. 8.*
132. *with*] *1655+*; in *H 1.*
136. *conjuncture*] *1655+*; conjunction *H 1.*
138. *a*] *1655+*; an *Bod. 8.*
141. *that*] *1655+*; the *BL 5*; *Bod. 8.*
143. *'tis*] *1655+*; is *BL 5. which*] *1655+*; if *BL 5*,
Bod. 8.
145. *has*] *1655+*; hath *H 1.*
154. *does*] *1655+*; doth *Bod. 8, H 1.*
155. *that*] *1655+*; the *H 1.*
156. *th'elected*] *1655+*; the elected *BL 5.*
158. *authors*] *1655+*; other *BL 5.*
159. *happy*] *1655+*; happ *BL 5.*
165. *does*] *1655+*; doth *BL 5, Bod. 8.*
more] *1655+*; such *BL 5.*
166. *Yet*] *Bod. 8*; But *1655+.*
167. *thine*] *1655+*; thy *BL 5, Bod. 8, H 1.*
unstained] *1655+*; restrain'd *BL 5.*
168. *refrained*] *1655+*; restrain'd *BL 5, Bod. 8, H 1.*
171. *breast*] *1655+*; rest *BL 5.*
173. *Thee*] *1655+*; The *BL 5. or skill*] *1655+*;
and still *H 1.*
174. *one day*] *1655+*; onely *BL 5.*
176. *At once assayed*] *1655+*; Assay'd at once
H 1. assayed] *1655+*; essay'd *BL 5.*
overturn] *1655+*; overthrow *BL 5.*
178. *while*] *1655+*; whilst *BL 5.*
181. *interweave*] *1655+*; intervene *BL 5.*
183. *through the*] *1655+*; though they *H 1.*
185. *past grief*] *1655+*; griefs past *Bod. 8.*
189. *While*] *1655+*; Whilst *BL 5.*
190. *On their own hopes shall find*] *1655+*;
Shall find on their own hopes *BL 5.*
fall] *1655+*; full *H 1.*
191. *their*] *1655+*; the *BL 5.*
192. *guiltily*] *1655+*; quietly *Bod. 8.*
194. *And*] *1655+*; Then *BL 5.*
then their] *1655+*; streight your *BL 5.*
198. *or*] *1655+*; nor *H 1.*
199. *ears*] *1655+*; bits *H 1.*
202. *Or*] *1655+*; Nor *H 1.*
204. *were*] *1655+*; was *BL 5, Bod. 8, H 1.*
212. *ruthless*] *1655+*; restless *Bod. 8.*
215. *Thee*] *1655+*; the *BL 5.*
216. *fiery*] *1655+*; furious *BL 5, Bod. 8.*
had] *1655+*; have *H 1.*

221. *delight*] *1655+*; the light *H 1.*
lose] *1655+*; loose *BL 5.*
224. *headstrong*] *1655+*; mad strong *Bod. 8.*
226. *below*] *1655+*; beneath *H 1. yet*] *1655*;
there *BL 5, Bod. 8*; even *H 1.*
228. *rule*] *1655+*; rate *Bod. 8.*
230. *too*] *1655+*; so *BL 5, Bod. 8.*
231. *field*] *1655+*; fields *Bod. 8.*
232. *An*] *1655+*; A *H 1.*
236. *the*] *1655+*; thy *H 1.*
239. *he*] *1655+*; it *H 1.*
240. *it*] *1655+*; yet *BL 5, Bod. 8.*
241. *Though*] *1655+*; Thou *H 1.*
244. *walk*] *1655+*; walk't *BL 5.*
249. *war*] *1655+*; wars *BL 5.*
253. *Succoth's*] *1655+*; Succoth *Bod. 8.*
suppress] *1655+*; repress *H 1.*
257. *Thou*] *1655+*; Then *H 1.*
and an] *1655+*; and *H 1.*
259. *labour*] *1655+*; labours *Bod. 8.*
260. *thine*] *1655+*; thy *BL 5, H 1.*
261. *flame*] *1655+*; fame *Bod. 8.*
268. *threat'ning*] *1655+*; threating *BL 5.*
269. *shipwrack*] *1655+*; shipwracks *H 1.*
270. *tacklings*] *1655+*; tackling *BL 5, H 1.*
276. *unto*] *1655+*; into *BL 5.*
278. *does*] *1655+*; doth *H 1.*
279. *that*] *1655+*; there *BL 5.*
281. *bounders*] *1655+*; boundrys *BL 5.*
284. *eight*] *1655+*; Arke *BL 5.*
286. *as*] *1655+*; like *Bod. 8. an*] *1655+*; a *BL 5.*
wouldst] *1655+*; didst *Bod. 8.*
287. *didst*] *1655+*; wouldst *BL 5, Bod. 8.*
others] *1655+*; other *H 1.*
288. *its*] *1655+*; the *BL 5.*
291. *parent's*] *1655+*; father's *BL 5, Bod. 8.*
292. *see*] *1655+*; not in *BL 5.*
293. *does*] *1655+*; doth *Bod. 8, H 1.*
295. *deride*] *1655+*; decide *BL 5.*
301. *thy*] *1655+*; they *BL 5*; we *Bod. 8.*
307. *their rant*] *1655+*; the rout *BL 5.*
their] *1655+*; the *H 1.*
308. *thine*] *1655+*; their *H 1.*
309. *band*] *1655+*; land *Bod. 8.*
311. *does*] *1655+*; doth *BL 5, Bod. 8, H 1.*
your] *1655+*; their *Bod. 8*; the *H 1.*
313. *Munser's*] *1655+*; monsters *BL 5*;
Munster's *Bod. 8.*
315. *laws*] *1655+*; law *H 1.*
317. *race*] *1655+*; rare *Bod. 8.*
320. *Aye*] *1655+*; Ah *BL 5, Bod. 8.*

323. *your*] 1655+; their *BL 5.*
327. *unwearied*] 1655+; unweary *H 1.*
328. *moving*] 1655+; morning *H 1.*
339. *mine*] 1655+; my *BL 5.*
333. *their*] 1655+; a *H 1.* *screeching*] 1655+; shrieking *Bod. 8.*
336. *yet*] 1655+; that *H 1.*
338. *as*] 1655+; he *Bod. 8.*
340. *Or*] 1655+; Oh *BL 5.* *last*] 1655+; lasts *BL 5.*
345. *flame*] 1655+; fame *BL 5.* *he darts*] 1655+; doth dart *BL 5, Bod. 8.*
346. *starts*] 1655+; start *BL 5, Bod. 8.*
349. *saith*] 1655+; says *BL 5, Bod. 8.* *saith one, 'the nation*] 1655+; the nation says one *BL 5.*
352. *our*] 1655+; a *BL 5, H 1*; their *Bod. 8.*
357. *Their's*] 1655+; These *Bod. 8.*
359. *islands*] 1655+; island *BL 5.*
362. *Armed*] 1655+; And *Bod. 8.* *three*] 1655+; the *H 1.* *tire*] 1655+; tires *Bod. 8.*
363. *their*] 1655+; your *BL 5.*
364. *does*] 1655+; doth *Bod. 8.*
367. *Needs must we*] 1655+; Needs must we *Bod. 8.*
368. *hold*] 1655+; holds *BL 5.*
370. *took*] 1655+; lock't *BL 5.*
371. *those*] 1655+; they *H 1.*
373. *fears could*] 1655+; fear should *H 1.*
376. *and*] 1655+; or *H 1.*
377. *all*] *Bod. 8*; in 1655+. *night*] *Bod. 8*; nights 1655+.
378. *hanging*] 1655+; to hang *BL 5.*
379. *his*] 1655+; 'tis *H 1.* *one*] 1655+; own *BL 5, H 1.*
380. *bulk*] 1655+; bulks *BL 5.*
381. *hath*] 1655+; has *BL 5.* *secrecy*] 1655+; strong *BL 5.*
384. *our*] 1655+; your *BL 5.*
385. *that*] 1655+; which *Bod. 8.*
388. *does*] 1655+; doth *H 1.*
391. *O*] 1655+; or *Bod. 1.*
392. *yet*] 1655+; that *BL 5.*
395. *or*] 1655+; and *H 1.*
400. *my*] 1655+; our *BL 5, H 1.*

The Second Advice to a Painter

Epigraph. Not in *BL 14, BL 20, BL 30, Bod. 12, Br., Cm., G, LAC 2, NLW 2, OA 1, T, SA.*
Date. Not in *LAC 2.*
1. *Nay*] *Bod. 1+*; Now *BL 14, L 5.*
4. *ev'n*] *Bod. 1+*; made *BL 20, N 10.*

5. *thy*] *Bod. 1+*; the *1667.* *colours*] *Bod. 1+*; colour *AH 1.*
6. *all their*] *Bod. 1+*; make thy *Bod. 8, L 5.*
7. *fit*] *Bod. 1+*; full *Ca. of*] *Bod. 1+*; on *Co., L 5, L6, SA.* *prospect*] not in *Ca.* *vain*] *Bod. 1, BL 30, Bod. 21, N 7, N 8*; main *Bi., BL 14, Bod. 12, Bod. 18, Bod. 24, Bod. 25, CUL 2, Ca., Cm., Es., F 5, G, L 6, NLW 2, Wa., Υ 5, Υ 6, 1667, 1667³*; feigne *AH 1, Be., BL 20, BL 29, Bod. 8, F 4, L 5, OW 2* [written over an illegible word, and with 'main' added in the margin].
8. *Paint*] *Bod. 1, BL 29*; Brave *Be., BL 20, Bod. 8, L 5, OW 2*; Draw *Wa.* *coast*] *Bod. 1+*; court *BL 14.*
9. *heard*] *Bod. 1+*; known *L 5.*
10. *Stemming*] *Bod. 1+*; Sterning *T*; Streaming *Υ 11.* *his*] *Bod. 1+*; her *T*; the *AH 1, G, NLW 2, Υ 5, 1667³b*; yʳ *Es.*
11–12. Not in *Be., BL 20, BL 29, Co., F 4.*
11. *how*] Not in *BL 30, OA 1*; the *LAC 2.* *waft*] *Bod. 1+*; pass *1667³b.*
12. *new*] *Bod. 1+*; not in *N 7.* *marks*] *Bod. 1+*; maske *N 8.*
13–53. Not in *L 5.*
15. *lesser*] *Bod. 1+* fitter *BL 20, BL 29, Co., OW 2.*
16. *the*] *Bod. 1+*; our *Br., Ca.*
18. *cities*] *Bod. 1+*; Cittizens *BL 29, Bod. 8, Bod. 12, Bod. 21, Br., F 4, SA, OW 2, 1667.*
19–24. Not in *Ca.*
19. *insure*] *Yale POAS+*; assure *LAUC, N 7*; ensure *Bod. 1, BL 14, BL 20, AH 1, Bi., BL 30, BL 29, Cm., SA, T*; secure *Be*; assure *OA 1.* *name*] *Bod. 1+*; fame *Υ 11.*
20. *share*] *Bod. 1+*; have *N 9.*
22. *And*] *Bod. 1+*; then *Br.* *are*] *Bod. 1+*; prove *Bi. BL 29, Co., SA.*
23–4. Not in *N 7.*
23. *feigned*] *Bod. 1+*; gained *BL 20, BL 29, BL 30, Bod. 8, SA, OW 2* ['feigned' crossed out]; fram'd *AH 1.*
27–8. Not in *AC, Bod. 1, Bod 12, Bod. 18, Bod. 25, Br., CUL 2, Ca., Cm., L 6, LAC 2, N 7, N 8, N 9, N 10, OA 1, T, F 5, G, NLW 2, Υ 5, Υ 6, Υ 11, 1667, 1667³b,* placed after l. 30 in *BL 30.*
28–34. Not in *Be.*

29. *exactly*] *Bod. 1+*; expressly *Bod. 8, OW 2,
     SA. express*] *Bod. 1+*; depaint *Bod. 8,
     BL 29, Co., OW 2, SA. his hue*] *Bod. 1+*;
     him trew *LAC 2.*

30. *Use . . . blue*] *Bod. 1* [with the spelling
     'oltramarinish'], *Bod. 12, Bod. 18,
     Bod. 25, G, F 5, L 6, LAUC* [with the
     spelling 'alhamarinish'] *N 7, N 8, N 9,
     N 10, NLW 2, Wa., 1667.* Ultramarine
     must do't, the richest blue. *BL 20,
     Bod. 8, BL 14, BL 29, SA.*

31–2. Not in *Ca.*

31. *his*] *Bod. 1+*; him *BL 20*; the *Υ 5.*
     fees one's] *Bod. 1+*; fees the *BL 14,
     BL 30, Br., Cm., LAC 2, LAUC,
     NWL, OA 1*; fees thy *AC*; Fine the *T.*

33. *the*] *Bod. 1+*; their *T, G, NLW 2, Υ 5.*

34. *Until*] *Bod. 1+*; Unless *Bod. 8. that . . .
     point*] *Bod. 1+*; this . . . trick *Ca.*

35. *constant . . . does*] *Bod. 1+*; estant . . .
     doth *G.*

36. *magnet*] *Bod. 1+*; Loadstone *Ca.*;
     Touchstone *Cm.*

37. *hemp . . . tar*] *Bod. 1+*, pitch, and hemp,
     and tar *NLW 2, Υ 5.*

37–8. *pitch . . . Sweden*] *Bod. 1+*; Denmark
     Tar/Pitch, Cordage, Sweden Copper
     BL 20, Bod. 8, BL 29, Co., F 4, OW 2;
     Denmark Pitch & Tar *Bod. 24, SA.*

39–40. *Prize*] *Bod. 1+*; Prizes *Cm., OA 1.
     Warwick . . . away*] *BL 29+*; {Gawden
     victualls/Warwick customes} Carteret/
     Sells pay, but Coventry does seel the
     Fleet. *Bod. 1, AC, N 8, N 9, Bod. 25,
     OA 1*; Carteret/sels pay bᵗ Cᵗʳʸ dos sel yᵉ
     fleet away. *AH 1, BL 30*; Cartaret pay;/
     But Counrntrye does sell the fleet away
     Br., NLW 2; Cartwright/Sells pay, but
     does sell the fleet *LAC 2. Cart'ret pay*]
     Bod. 1+; Cartwright sells pay *Ca.*

39. *Cart'ret*] *Bod. 1+*; Cartwright
     *Bod. 12, BL 20, F 5, LAC 2, LAUC.
     pay*] *Bod. 1+*; sells pay *BL 20.*

40. *sells the whole*] *Bod. 1+*; doth sell yᵉ *G,
     1667, Υ 5*; doth seel his *LAUC*; Sells
     pay *T. sells*] not in *Ca.*

41. *its*] *Bod. 1+* his *BL 20*; her *Ca., SA.*

42. *its*] *BL 20, Bod. 1+*; his *Be., Ca., Es., G,
     LAC 2, NLW 2, T, 1667³b.*

43. *By*] *Bod. 1+*; With *Ca. slow*] *Bod. 1+*;
     ye *BL 30.*

44. *sale . . . sail*] *Bod. 1+*; sail . . . sale *Be.,
     BL 29, BL 30, Bod. 8, Bod. 18, Co., Es.,
     F 4, F 5, G, L 6, NLW 2, SA, Υ 6, Υ 11,
     1667.2, 1667³b*; sail . . . saile *Υ 5.*
     under] *Bod. 1+*; putt to *BL 20.*

45. *kind . . . unto*] *Bod. 1+*; respect of foggy
     BL 29, F 4; respect to foggy *BL 20, Co.,
     OA 1, OW 2* [with 'Obdam' before
     'foggy']; win respect to foggy *Bod. 8,
     SA.*

46. *them*] *Bod. 1+*; [?]thee *Ca.*

48. *them, and*] *Bod. 1*; em, and *BL 14*; the
     game *BL 20, BL 29, BL 30, Bod. 8, Co.,
     SA, OA 1, OW 2*; yᵐ game *Be.*; her, and
     Br. and] not in *BL 20, BL 30, OA 1.*

49. *they*] *Bod. 1+*; you *OA 1.*

50. *at*] *Bod. 1+*; with *G, N 9, NLW 2, SA.*

52. *fisher*] *Bod. 1+*; Angler *Bod. 18, Bod. 24,
     Es., G, L 6, NLW 2, Υ 5, Υ 6, Υ 11,
     1667², 1667³b. river*] *Bod. 1+*; water *SA,
     OW 2.*

53. *thy*] *Bod. 1+*; the *LAC 2.*

55. *the*] *Bod. 1+*; Yorks *LAC 2.*
     tail] *Bod. 1+*; trail *Bod. 21, Co.*
     [corrected to 'tayle'], *Es., G, NLW 2.*

59–68. Not in *Ca.*

59. *then*] *Bod. 1+*; when *G.*

60. *caracole*] *Bod. 1, Be., BL 20, BL 30, Co.,
     LAC 2*; Carocole *BL 30*; Care. cole *N 7*;
     carry coal *BL 14, Bod. 8, Bod. 12, Bod. 18,
     Bod. 24, Br., CUL 2, Es., F 5, G, L 5, L 6,
     NLW 2, SA, Wa., Υ 5, Υ 6, Υ 11, 1667,
     1667³b*; caroll *LAUC*; crawle *OW 2.*

61–2. *So . . . wing*] Not in *BL 29, F 4, SA, Be.,
     Co.*; placed after l. 56 in *N 8, T.*

62. *on*] *BL 29+*; in *Bod. 1, AC, AH 1,
     BL 30, Br., CUL 2, G, N 7, N 8,
     N 9, NLW 2, OA 1, OW 2, T, Wa..
     their*] *Bod. 1+*; the *AC.*

63–82. Missing in *L 5* (fol. 42ʳ).

65. *properties*] *Bod. 1+*; fopperies *L 6, Υ 6,
     1667², 1667³b*; proper toyes *BL 30,
     BL 29* [corrected], *Bod. 8, Co., OW 2,
     Wa.*; proper boys *SA.*

66. *small*] *Bod. 1+*; naval *Υ 11. and*]
     Bod. 1+; are *Br.*; is *BL 14, LAUC. to . . .
     you*] *Bod. 1*; for you my *Be., N 10*; but
     for his *BL 29, Co., OW 2*; but for my
     BL 20, Bod. 8, SA. you] *Bod. 1+*; your
     *AH 1, BL 30, G, LAC 2, NLW 2, OA 1,
     Υ 6, Υ 11, 1667³b*; his *Wa.*

68.   *Venus*] represented by an astrological symbol in *BL 30*. *sport, and*] *Bod. 1+*; pleasure *Bod. 8*; in Pleasure *SA*. *and*] *Bod. 1+*; but *Es., G, NLW 2*. *your*] *Bod. 1+*; her *AH 1, BL 20*; thy *OA 1*.

69.   *nuptial*] *Bod. 1+*; marriage *Be., Co., SA*.

70.   *this*] *Bod. 1+*; thy *NLW 2*.

71.   *Roman . . . Nile*] *Bod. 1+*; Mark Anthony in Pharo's Isle *BL 20, BL 29, Bod. 8, SA*; Anthony . . . Nile *Ca*. we *Ca*. (with 'Isle' as 'Nile'), *F 4, Co., OW 2*. *Nile*] *Bod. 1+*; Pile *Bod. 12*; corrected to 'Isle' *Υ 6*.

72.   *feast*] *Bod. 1+*; treat *BL 29, OW 2, SA*. *the*] *Bod. 1+*; their *G*. *such a*] *Bod. 1+*; so much *N 10*.

73.   *with such a*] *Bod. 1+*; in all his *Bod. 8, Bod. 25* (corrected), *Ca., SA*; in's greatest *BL 20*; with greater *BL 29*; in his great *Co*.; in greater *OW 2*.

74.   *marry*] placed before 'Adriatic' in *SA*.

76.   *draw*] *Bod. 1+*; expresse *OA 1*. *parting*] *Bod. 1+*; panting *Bod. 12, 1667*.

78.   *winds*] *Bod. 1+*; wind *LAC 2, SA*; seas *Bod. 18, G, L 6, NLW 2, Υ 5, Υ 6, 1667², 1667³b*.

79–112. Not in *Ca*.

79.   *as*] *Bod. 1+*; her *Bod. 18*.

80.   *as*] *Bod. 1+*; her *L 6, Bod. 18, G, NLW 2, Υ 5, Υ 6, Υ 11*.

81.   *most*] *Bod. 1+*; next *AH 1, N 9*.

82.   *all more 'fraid*] *Bod. 1+*; more afraid *BL 20, Bod. 8, Bod. 12, Bod. 21, N 8, N 10, OA 1, OW 2*. *'fraid*] *Bod. 1+*; afrayd *Br*.; friends *N 7*; fraile *G*. *she*] *Bod. 1+*; he *BL 30, Bod. 18, Bod. 24, L 6, LAC 2, NLW 2, Υ 5, Υ 6, Υ 11, 1667³b*.

83–8. Not in *BL 20, BL 29, Co*.

84.   *spin*] *Bod. 1+*; swim *OW 2*.

85.   *his*] *Bod. 1+*; the *NLW 2, Υ 5*.

86.   *In*] *Bod. 1+*; By *Υ 5*. *the diving*] *Bod. 1+*; revised to 'a dying' in *N 10*; a diving *SA*.

88.   *Coiled*] *Bod. 1+*; Toyld *Bod. 8, SA*; Wrapt *Be*.

89–90. Missing in *L 5* (fol. 42ᵛ).

89.   *these*] not in *Υ 5*.

90.   *and*] *Bod. 1*; let *Bod. 18, NLW 2, Υ 5, 1667³b*; while *N 7, Bod. 8, SA* ('other'); whilst *Be., BL 30, N 10, 1667²*.

91–100. Not in *Be., BL 20, BL 29, Co*.

91.   *that*] *Bod. 1+*; who *OA 1, SA, T*.

92.   *in a*] not in *OA 1*. *a*] not in *AC*. *chaise-volante*] *Bod. 1+*; la Chalise volant *BL 29*; Chayr volant *LAUC, T, Υ 5*. *chaise*] *Bod. 1+*; chaire *Br., LAC 2, NLW 2*.

93.   *save*] *Bod. 1+*; [?]sawe *OA 1*; butt *T*. *shut*] *Bod. 1+*; kept *BL 30*.

95.   *cap-a-chin*] *Bod. 1+*; Capuchin *LAC 2, LAUC, Wa.*, 1667.

97.   *Dear*] *Bod. 1+*; Neare *OW 2*. *shall*] *Bod. 1+*; how 1667. *twinging*] *Bod. 1+*; winging *OA 1*. *anguish*] *Bod. 1+*; Anger *Br., T*.

98.   *feel*] *Bod. 1+*; see *L 5, Bod. 18, Υ 5, Υ 11*. *whet*] corrected from 'armed' in *NLW 2*.

99.   *trait'ress*] *Bod. 1*; treach'rous *BL 30, Bod. 8, Bod. 18, Bod. 24, F 5, L 5, L 6, LAC 2, Υ 5, 1667², 1667³b*; traiterous *Br., Bod. 12, Bod. 25, N 8, N 10, SA* ('that'); cursed *Wa., LAUC*, 1667. *Jael*] *Bod. 1+*; Jarll *Br*.

100. *That*] *Bod. 1+*; Who *SA*.

101–12. Not in *L 5*.

102. *But*] *Bod. 1+*; Whilst *Be., BL 20, OA 1, OW 2*; And *NLW 2, Υ 5*.

103. *He . . . the*] *Bod. 1+*; Who . . . this *SA*.

104. *pirates*] *Bod. 1+*; pirate *SA*; Puppets 1667; puppett turnd *Wa.. tuned*] *Bod. 1+*; turn'd *Υ 5*.

105. *judicious*] *Bod. 1+*; officious *N 10*.

107–8. Not in *Bod. 1, AC, AH 1, BL 20, BL 30, Br., Co., CUL 2, Bod. 12, Bod. 18, F 4, F 5, L 6, N 8, N 9, NLW 2, OA 1, Υ 5, Υ 6, Υ 11*, 1667, 1667.3. Interlineated in another hand in *N 10, SA* (and written vertically in the left-hand margin).

108. *As . . . Hinchingbrooke*] *Bod. 1+*; at Finchingbrook *N 10, SA*.

110. *but*] *Bod. 1+*; been *AC*. *now*] *Bod. 1+*; to *Be., BL 20, OW 2, SA*.

111. *draw . . . terribler*] *Bod. 1+*; battell drawe, more terrible to showe *Br*.; draw battle more terrible *LAUC*.

112. *Than*] *Bod. 1+*; As *Υ 5*. *Last . . . of*] *Bod. 1+*; Dooms day of Michael *N 10*. *of Angelo*] *Bod. 1+*; of Ameslow *G, NLW 1*; of Anneslow *Υ 5*.

113–20. Follows l. 176 in *F 4*.

115. *very*] *Bod. 1+*; pairy *N 8*.

116. *Hyde*] *Bod. 1+*; H_de *L 6*; H___ *Υ 11*.

117. *Hyde*] *Bod. 1+*; H___ *NLW 2, Υ 5*. *paunch*] *Bod. 1*; 'passion' thinly crossed out and replaced by 'panch' *Υ 5*.

118.   *That . . . seems*] Bod. 1+; [It] He seems the Tympany *L 5*, *BL 29*, *BL 20*, *Bod. 8*, *Bod. 21*, *Co.*, *F 4*, *L 5*, *N 7*, *OW 2* [but with word order of *Bod. 1+*], *SA*. 'Tympany' in margin *AH 1*, *BL 30*; 'rupture' in margin in *OW 2*. *and*] *Bod. 1+*; of and [with 'of' deleted] *Ca*.

119–26.   Not in *Ca*.

119–20.   Not in *G*.

119.   *Paston*] 'Earl of Yarmouth' in margin of *Y 11*.

121–6.   Not in *Be.*, *BL 20*, *BL 29*, *Co.*, *L 5*.

123.   *at gaze*] *Bod. 1+*; our gaze *Br.*; all gaze *NLW 2*, *Y 5*.

125–6.   Not in *Br*, *G*. *But . . . the*] *Bod. 1+*; Still keeping within distance of the fight/ Hoping to gorg with *CUL 2*.

125.   Written vertically up the page and clearly marked for insertion in *F 5*. *gorge yet*] *Bod. 1+*; George keepe *F 5*; George they *Bod. 18*, *L 6*; George yet *BL 30*, *Es.*, *OW 2*, *NLW 2*, *Y 5*, *1667²* (corrected to 'gorge yet'); gorge still *LAUC*; gore still *Bod. 25*. *gorge*] Not in *N 8*, *1667*.

126.   *follow*] *Bod. 1+*; hollow *BL 30*.

127–54.   Follows ll. 113–20, after l. 176, in *F 4*.

127.   *Then*] *Bod. 1+*; Now *SA*, *Co.*, *OW 2*. *With well-*] *Bod. 1+*; to bold *Wa*.

128.   *despair*] *Bod. 1+*; dispute *Wa.. more . . . wish*] *Bod. 1+* as we wishd to *Bod. 25*, *Ca.*; when we withdraw *AH 1*.

129.   Not in *L 6*. *to*] *Bod. 1+*; t'endure *LAC 2*. *the sea but*] *Bod. 1+*; yᵉ fight more *L 5*.

130.   *More to the*] *BL 29*; And more to *Bod. 1*, *AC*, *AH 1*, *Be.*, *BL 20*, *BL 30*, *Br.*, *Ca.*, *Co.*, *LAC 2*, *LAUC*, *N 8*, *N 9*, *N 10*, *NLW 2*, *OA 1*, *OW 2*, *T*, *Wa.*, *Y 5*, *Y 6*, *Y 11*, *1667*, *1667³*. *fight*] *Bod. 1+*; sea *L 5*. *queasy*] *Bod. 1+*; yarely *F 5*; easie *AC*, *AH 1*, *Be.*, *BL 29*, *BL 30*, *Bod. 18*, *L 5*, *L 6*, *LAC 2*, *N 7*, *N 8*, *N 9*, *N 10*, *NLW 2*, *OA 1*, *T*, *Y 5*, *Y 6*, *Y 11*, *OW 2*, *1667³*; squezy *Bod. 8*, *Ca.*, *CUL 2*, *Bod. 8*, *LAUC*, *Wa.*, *1667*.

132.   *beat*] *Bod. 1+*; break *L 5*. *the*] not in *BL 30*.

133.   *most*] not in *Y 5*.

134.   *cast*] *Bod. 1+*; vent *AH 1*, *Be.*, *BL 29*, *Bod. 8*, *Bod. 24*, *Ca.*, *Co.*, *L 6*, *N 9*, *NLW 2*, *Y 5*, *Y 6*, *Y 11*, *1667³b*; ease *N 8*, *1667*; 'vent' corrected to 'cast' *BL 30*.

136.   *That . . . did*] *Bod. 1+*; Who taught in Brine to *Bod. 24*. *sea-*] *Bod. 1+*; salt *OW 2*.

137.   *What*] *Bod. 1+*; Who *Br.*, *LAUC*, *OA 1*. *pines*] *Bod. 1+*; yet *Br.*, *LAUC*; *did* Oakes *BL 20*, *BL 29*, *Bod. 8*, *F 4*, *L 5*, *N 7*, *OW 2*, *SA*.

138.   *drown*] *Bod. 1+*; drone *Y 5*.

139.   *wall*] *Bod. 1+*; Gaole *Bod. 8*, *L 5*, *SA*; Goale *Co.*, *OW 2*; Jayle *BL 29*; hall *1667*; ball *Wa*.

141.   *necromantic*] *Bod. 1+*; Negromanticke *AC*. *be*] not in *AC*, *Bod. 1*, *Bod. 25*, *N 8*, *N 9*.

142.   *And in*] *Bod. 1+*; Into *Ca*. *in*] Not in *N 8*. *own first*] *Bod. 1+*; first one *Ca*.

144.   *brimstone*] *Bod. 1+*; sulphur *BL 29*, *Bod. 8*, *SA*, *Co.*, *OW 2*. *fetched*] *Bod. 1+*; fetch *Br.*, *Y 5*; fought'st *N 10*; took'st *BL 20*, *Bod. 8*, *SA*.

145.   *treble*] *Bod. 1+*; double *AH 1*, *L 5*, *BL 29*, *Bod. 8*, *Co.*, *OW 2*.

145–54.   Not in *G*, although in this MS, l. 15 is written vertically down the leaf, but not marked for insertion.

145.   *house*] *Bod. 1+*; Race *F 5*.

147.   *divert*] *Bod. 1+*; avoid *Wa.. the*] *Bod. 1+*; his *Br.. danger*] *Bod. 1+*; anger *Y 5*.

148.   *hounds us*] *Bod. 1*; throws it *F 5*; bounds us *Bod. 18*, *L 6*, *NLW 2*; hurles us *Br.*; hurles it *Wa.*, *1667*.

149–52.   Not in *Ca*.

149.   *Fool*] *Bod. 1+*; Foul *Bod. 24*, *Y 5*.

155.   *in wrath dispute*] *BL 29*; in reach debut[?e] *Bod. 1*. *wrath*] *BL 29*; reach *Bod. 1*, *AC*, *AH 1*, *Bod. 25*, *Ca.*, *G*, *L 6*, *LAC 2*, *LAUC*, *N 7*, *N 8*, *N 9*, *N 10*, *NLW 2*, *Y 11*, *1667²*.

156–72.   Not in *BL 20*, *L 5*.

156.   *mortally*] *Bod. 1+*; in wrath *Y 5*. *salute*] *Bod. 1+*; confute *LAC 2*.

157–72.   Not in *Be.*, *BL 29*, *Co.*

158.   *whos'e'er o'ercomes*] *Bod. 1+*; who e're o'ercomes *AC*, *Br.*, *Ca.*, *SA*, *LAUC*, *Y 5*; where 'ere he comes *OA 1*.

163.   *in . . . his*] *Bod. 1+*; up mounted on's *LAC 2*, *LAUC*. *in*] *Bod. 1+*; up *Br.*, *OA 1*; not in *NLW 2*, *Y 5*. *placed in*] *Bod. 1+*; placed on *Es.*, *NLW 2*, *Y 5*; mounted on *BL 30*, *Wa.*, *1667*; mounted on's *Br.*, *CUL 2*, *OA 1*, *OW 2*.

168.   *ship*] *Bod. 1+*; chair *LAC 2*.

169.   *Monsieurs*] *Bod. 1*+; Min Heers *Bod. 24*,
            inserted in *L 6*, without deleting the
            original reading. *mount*] *Bod. 1*+; fly *Wa.*
169–70.   Not in *G.*
170.   *dancingly*] *Bod. 1*+; prancingly *BL 30*,
            LAC 2, *LAUC*; dartingly *AH 1*, *Bod. 8*;
            dangerously *OW 2.*
173.   *bullet*] *Bod. 1*+; Blow *L 5*; Ball *BL 29.*
            bullet . . . side] *Bod. 1*+; Opdam's ship
            did *L 5*; Ball from Opdam's ship *BL 20*,
            Co., OW 2.
174.   *battered*] *Bod. 1*+; kill'd brave *BL 29*,
            Co., F 4, L 5, OW 2; kill brave *BL 20.*
            dear] *Bod. 1*+; brave *BL 29.*
175–6.   Comes after ll. 177–8 in *F 4*; not in *Be.*,
            BL 20, BL 29, Co.
176.   *Glory's*] *Bod. 1*+; glorious *Ca.*;
            honnour's *BL 30, Bod. 12, Bod. 24, Br.*,
            CUL 2, F 5, Wa., 1667.
177.   *fate*] *Bod. 1*+; Life *T.*
178.   *through the*] *Bod. 1*+; in the *AC, Be.*,
            *BL 20, Br., CUL 2, Ca., LAC 2, NLW
            2, Wa., Υ 5, Υ 6, Υ 11, Co., 1667³b.*
            lakes] *Bod. 1*+; lake *NLW 2, T, Υ 5*,
            Υ 6, Υ 11, 1667³b; shades *AC, Be., Br.*,
            BL 20, BL 29, BL 30, Bod. 8, Bod. 12,
            Bod. 24, Bod. 25, CUL 2, Ca., CO.,
            F 4, F 5, L 5, L 6, LAC 2, N 10, SA
            ('in the'), *Wa.., 1667*; in the shade *OW 2.*
179–96.   Placed after l. 226 in *AH 1, Bod. 25*,
            Ca., N 9.
179–82.   Not in *G.*
180.   *Yet . . . not*] *Bod. 1*+; Was not quite
            T [also corrected from 'the reach of
            danger's sett']. *not*] *Bod. 1*+; 'quite'
            corrected to 'still' *Bod. 25*. *set*] *Bod. 1*+;
            yet *Bod. 24.*
182.   *Some say 'twas*] *Bod. 1*+; Unless it were
            BL 20, SA, Co., OW 2; Unlesse twere *Br.*;
            Unless twas to *CUL 2, Wa.. say*] *Bod. 1*+;
            thinke *Be. too*] *Bod. 1*+ not in *BL 20*,
            LAC 2. contact] *Bod. 1*+; contract *AC*,
            AH 1, Be., Bod. 24, CUL 2, Ca., F 5,
            L 6, N 7, N 8, NLW 2, SA, Wa., Υ 5,
            Υ 6, Υ 11, 1667, 1667³b cont[r]act
            [with 'r' crossed out] *Co., OW 2.*
183.   *An untaught*] *Bod. 1*+; An unthought
            Ca.; When a round *F 4*; When a rude
            BL 29, BL 20, Co., L 5, SA. its] *Bod. 1*+
            his *Br., Co., N 7, N 8, T. its wanton*]
            Bod. 1+; his mounted *Bod. 25, Ca., N 9.*

184.   *Quashes*] *Bod. 1*+; Dashes *Es., F 4, G*,
            NLW 2, Υ 5, Υ 11, 1667³b; squashes
            BL 29, OW 2; Both squashes *Co.*;
            Justled *N 10.*
185–6.   Not in *Wa.*
186.   Two alternative lines offered in *Bod. 24*:
            '[By a Mischance he both was ruined,
            & rais'd]/[By Chance he fell, by a
            Mischance was rais'd.]' *A*] *Bod. 1*+;
            One *N 7. took*] *Bod. 1*+; felld *T.*
187.   *shattered head*] *Bod. 1*+; scatter'd skull
            BL 29. head] *Bod. 1*+; scull *BL 30*,
            Bod. 8, L 5, SA. fearlesse] *Bod. 1*+;
            peerlesse *BL 29, Bod. 8, Co., OW 2.*
            distains] *Bod. 1*+; disdains *Bod. 18*,
            CUL 2, L 6, 1667; distraines ['r' crossed
            out] *Be.*; bestains *Bod. 24, Ca., N 10*;
            ransome yett *F 4, L 5, Wa.*
188.   *And . . . proof*] *Bod. 1*+; This last-first
            proof to gave *AH 1. last-first*] *Bod. 1*+;
            first last *SA, T. he*] *Bod. 1*+; it *Co., SA.*
189–200.   Not in *G.*
190–4.   Not in *L 6.*
190.   *royal Harding's*] *Bod. 1*+; the Fitz
            Hardings *Br. royal*] *Bod. 1*+; loyal
            LAC 2.
191–4.   Not in *Be., BL 20, BL 29, Bod. 8, Co. SA.*
191.   *was*] *Bod. 1*+; was yet *AC.*
192.   *now the*] *Bod. 1*+; more yⁿ *Ca.*
193.   *it*] Not in *Ca. cost what cost*] not in
            AH 1.
196.   *like*] *Bod. 1*+; yᵉ *Ca. promised*] *Bod. 1*+;
            vow'd *L 6*; vow'd never *Co., OW 2.*
197.   *Urania fairly on*] *BL 20*+; Urania
            carelesse at *OA 1*; Aurania fairly on
            LAC 2; Aurania carelesse at *Bod. 1, AC*,
            AH 1, Be., BL 30, Bod. 12, Bod. 25, Br.,
            CUL 2, Es., L 6, N 7, N 8, N 9, N 10
            (but with 'Aurania' corrected to 'Urania'),
            NLW 2, T, Υ 5, Wa., Υ 6, 1667, 1667³;
            Orania carelesse at us *Ca.*; Aurance fairly
            on *Υ 11. fairly*] *Bod. 1*+; feircely *L 5*;
            fearlesse *F 4, OW 2*; carelesse *F 5.*
198.   *Opdam*] *Bod. 1*+; others *L 5.*
199–200.   Not in *BL 29.*
199.   *intercept*] *Bod. 1*+; interrupt *Bod. 8.*
            her] *Bod. 1*+; his *LAC 2.*
200.   *cleaves*] *Bod. 1*+; stickes *LAC 2. t'her . . .
            the*] *Bod. 1*+; to him . . . the *OA 1*; there
            . . . the *AC, LAC 2*; there . . . a *NLW 2*,
            Υ 5; more closely yⁿ a *Ca.*

201–2.	Not in *Be.*, *BL 20*, *Bod. 8*, *Co.*, *L 5*, *SA.*
204.	*They . . . another's*] *Bod. 1+*; Each others Ship then stabb each others Guns. *T. They stab*] *Bod. 1+*; Stabbing *LAC 2.*
206.	*And ev'n the*] *Bod. 1+*; And bullets even *Ca.*; And flying *Be.*, *BL 29*, *BL 30*, *L 5*; Whilst flying *SA*, *Wa.*; While flying *OW 2*; Whilst fighting *Co.*
207.	*smoke . . . sweat*] *Bod. 1+*; sweat . . . smoke *Br.. sweat . . . fire*] *Bod. 1+*; fire . . . sweat *Ca.*, *LAC 2*, *NLW 2*, *Υ 5.*
208.	*nor*] *Bod. 1+*; scarce *BL 29*, *F 4*, *L 5*, *SA*, *OW 2*; or *N 8*, *T*, *Υ 5.*
209–10.	Not in *Be.*, *BL 20*, *Bod. 8*, *Co.*, *L 5*, *SA*, *Bod. 8*; comes after l. 212 in *Ca.*
211–12.	Comes before l. 209 in *Bod. 25*, *N 9.*
211.	*men*] *Bod. 1+*; brave men *1667.*
213.	*whosoever*] *Bod. 1+*; whereso'ere two *Ca.*
214.	*took*] *Bod. 1+*; takes *AH 1*, *Ca.*, *NLW 2*, *Υ 5*; beats *Co.*, *F 4*, *L 5*; beat *SA*, *Wa.* *and*] *Bod. 1+*; not in *BL 30.*
215.	*dared too*] *Bod. 1+*; durst do *BL 30*, *Bod. 8*, *Bod. 24*, *Co.*, *Es.*, *L 5*, *L 6*, *NLW 2*, *SA*, *Υ 6*, *Υ 11*; durst to *OW 2*, *1667*[2]; durst no *Υ 5. too*] *Bod. 1+*; do *Bod. 12*, *Ca.*, *N 9*, *N 10*, *OA 1*, *1667.*
217–24.	Not in *Be.*, *BL 29*, *BL 20*, *Co.*, *L 5.*
217.	*Dear*] *Bod. 1+*; Brave *Bod. 25.*
218.	*so . . . gloomy*] *Bod. 1+*; more clear, and none more gloomy *T* [corrected to 'clear . . . gloomy']; more gallant, no more gloomy fate *Ca. clear*] *Bod. 1+*; dear *N 8*; brave *Bod. 25.*
219.	*war's*] *Bod. 1+*; Mars *N 10.*
220.	*Death*] *Bod. 1+*; It *N 10.* *the*] Not in *NLW 2.*
221–31.	Not in *G.*
221–2.	Not in *Ca.*
221.	*do vaunt*] *Bod. 1+*; we graunt *F 5.*
223.	*Hence*] *Bod. 1+*; He *Υ 5. life he*] *Bod. 1+*; life time *Υ 5*, *1667.*
226.	*was, or*] *Bod. 1+*: yet none *Ca. or . . . fit*] *Bod. 1+*; none . . . fit *BL 30*, *LAC 2*; none less fit *OA 1*; none less prypard *Co.. or*] *Bod. 1+*; nor *AC*, *Br.*; none *BL 29. less*] not in *1667.*
228.	*Myngs*] *Bod. 1+*; Minus *Υ 5. bravely Sansum*] *Bod. 1+*; Sansum bravely *AH 1. bravely*] *Bod. 1+* Sampson *Be*; Lawson *Ca.. Sansum fell*] *Bod. 1+*; very well *Be.*, *N 10. Sansum*] *Bod. 1+*; Sampson *Br.*;

	AC, *SA*; Sanson *NLW 2*, *Υ 5*; Lawson *CUL 2*, *Bod. 24*; Samson *T*; in battle *Ca. none*] *Bod. 1+*; one *Bod. 18.*
229.	
230.	*shall*] not in *OA 1. brings*] *Bod. 1+*; breaks *1667.*
231.	*unless . . . stories*] *Bod. 1+*; lest yᵗ after ages *Ca. stories*] *Bod. 1+*; ages *Bod. 25.*
233–4.	Not in *Be.*, *BL 20*, *BL 29*, *Co.*
235.	*sleep*] *Bod. 1+*; slumber *BL 29*, *Co.*, *L 5*, *SA.*
238.	*foe*] *Bod. 1+*; Dutch *L 5.*
239.	*But*] *Bod. 1+*; But loe *Υ 5. Brouncker*] *Bod. 1+*; Drunkard *BL 29.*
240.	*Slept not*] *Bod. 1+*; Nor sleeps *Ca. it*] Not in *Ca. needs it*] *Bod. 1+*; need he *Br.*, *LAC 2*, *OA 1*; needed *NLW 2*, *Υ 5. all day*] *Bod. 1+*; all yᵉ time *L 5*, *SA.*
241–2.	Not in *Be.*, *BL 20*, *BL 20*, *Co.*, *L 5*, *SA.*
241–58.	Not in *G.*
241.	*in bed*] *Bod. 1+* wakes *OW 2. first draws*] *Bod. 1+*; drawes out *Br.*
242.	Not in *F 4. makes . . . wheel*] *Bod. 1+*; made . . . reel *LAC 2.*
245–6.	Follows l. 250 in *F 4.*
245.	*dear*] *Bod. 1+*; kind *LAC 2. pains*] not in *OA 1.*
246–50.	Not in *F 4.*
246.	*time*] *Bod. 1+*; fit *Ca.*, *N 10.*
247–51.	Not in *L 5.*
247–50.	Not in *Be.*, *BL 20*, *BL 29*, *Co.*
247.	*all our navy*] *Bod. 1+*; oʳ whole Fleet *Bod. 24.*
248.	*small*] *Bod. 1+*; short *NLW 2*, *Υ 5.* *served*] *Bod. 1+*; reserv'd *Υ 5. space*] *Bod. 1+*; tyme *Bod. 12*; piece *Ca. refresh its*] *Bod. 1+*; recruite itt *Br.*; refresh & *NLW 2*, *Υ 5.*
249.	*tame*] *Bod. 1+*; lame *Ca.*, small *F 5.*
251.	*more*] *Bod. 1* + now *Wa.*
253.	*now*] *Bod. 1+*; we *Υ 5. with . . . maw*] *Bod. 1+*; being better mann'd *N 10.* *better maw*] *Bod. 1+*; confidence *Bod. 18*, *Es.*, *L 6*, *NLW 2*, *Υ 5*, *Υ 6*, *Υ 11*, *1667*[3]*b*; better men *L 5. we*] *Bod. 1+*; made *Υ 6*, *Υ 11*, *1667*[3]*b*; make *NLW 2*, *Υ 5.*
254.	Written vertically up the page in *G*, and marked for insertion between l. 188 and l. 189. *sweet*] *Bod. 1+*; secret *L 6*, *NLW 2*, *Υ 5*, *Υ 6*, *Υ 11. spoils*] *Bod. 1+*; prey *L 5*, *SA*; fruit *F 4. taste*] *Bod. 1+*; vast *BL 29*; waste *OW 2.*

255.	*Though*] *Bod. 1+*; Tom *BL 29, Bod. 8, Co., F 4, L 5, N 9, SA, Wa.*

256.	*supercargo*] *Bod. 1+*; sopracargo *AC, AH 1, T*; sopragarga *Bod. 12*; supracargo *Br., LAC 2, NLW 2, OA 1, SA, Υ 5. theirs*] *Bod. 1+*; their *NLW 2, Υ 5*; [?]steers *OA 1.*

257–8.	Interlineated as one line in another hand in *N 9*; not in *Bod. 25, Ca.*

258.	*And seize*] *Bod. 1+*; T'ensure *N 9.*

259–70.	Not in *BL 29, Be., Co., L 5.*

259–60.	Placed after l. 270 in *G.*

260.	*wasted*] *Bod. 1+*; waited *N 10*; waites at *Wa.* waits till *1667*; wafted o'er [crossed out] in *AH 1.*

261.	*upon*] *Bod. 1+*; just in *LAC 2.*

262.	*disperse*] *Bod. 1+*; dispatch yᵐ *Ca.*

264.	*'scape*] *Bod. 1+*; passe *OW 2. fight*] *Bod. 1+*; flight *N 7, Υ 5.*

265–6.	*And . . . Montagu*] Not in *BL 20, BL 30.*

265.	Not in *OA 1. state and sureness*] *Bod. 1+*; state sureness *Υ 5. Cuttance true*] *Bod. 1*; Cuttings *AC*; Cuttins *T*; curtaines drew *CUL 2* [amended in margin to '[illegible]ting true'] *Bod. 12, Bod. 24, Ca., F 5, LAC 2, OW 2, Wa., Υ 5, 1667*; curtens true Bod. 18; curtanes dren *Br.*; cutting true *NLW 2, SA, 1667²* corrected.

266.	*closes*] *Bod. 1+*; closer *Ca. the right*] *Bod. 1+*; the right eye *Br.*; good night *OW 2.*

267.	*even*] *Bod. 1+*; yⁿ kind *Bod. 24*; when *OA 1*; now Tom *Br.*; truly *Wa., 1667*; now *OW 2.*

268.	*his seal*] *Bod. 1+*; yᶜ zeal [with the 'z' corrected to an 'S' hanging below the line]. *Ca.*

269.	*he . . . Sirens*] *Bod. 1+*; Sirens he had *NLW 2, T, Υ 5*; syrens voice h'had *Bod. 25*; Siren voice was *Ca.*

271–94.	Not in *G.*

271–2.	Not in *Ca.*

272.	*fortune*] *Bod. 1+*; luck on't *Be., BL 29, Bod. 8, Co., L 5, N 9* [replacing 'Fortune'], *F 4, OW 2, SA*; ill luck on't *LAC 2.*

273.	*not yet*] *Bod. 1+*; much lesse *Co., SA.*

274.	*Fools . . . fight*] *Bod. 1+*; Raith fooles doe fight *F 4*; Rash fools do *BL 29, BL 30, Co., OW 2, SA. use to*] *Bod. 1+*; only *SA, OW 2.*

275.	*His*] *Bod. 1+*; Our *Co., OW 2, SA.*

276.	In *SA*, the following two lines come after l. 276: 'Standing on deck, and doesnt looke any Bride,/By an unlucky plot was reach'd and dye'd.'

279–82.	Follow here in *F 4.*

277–90.	Not in *Ca.*

277–84.	Not in *BL 20, L 5.*

277–8.	Comes after l. 286 in *BL 29, Co., L 5.*

277.	*peace*] *Bod. 1+*; brass *N 8. seemed*] *Bod. 1+*; been *Co.*

278.	*ought*] *BL 29+*; nought *Bod. 1.*

279–82.	Not in *Be., BL 29, Bod. 8, Co., SA.*

283.	*that*] Not in *NLW 2, Υ 5.*

283–4.	Comes after ll. 279–82 in *BL 29*, after ll. 277–8 in *L 6*; before l. 287 in *Co.*

285–6.	Follows l. 276 in *F 4.*

286.	*Though . . . too*] *Bod. 1+*; Although . . . too *Br.*; And . . . too *NLW 2, Υ 5*; By an unhappy shot *BL 29, Co., L 5*; Aboard yᶜ Admirall *Be. yet . . . reached*] *Bod. 1+*; not yet was kil'd *1667. yet*] not in *Br. reached*] *Bod. 1+*; kild/kald *Br.*; kill'd shot *Bod. 12, CUL 2*; rash *Bod. 24.*

287–310.	Not in *Be., BL 29, Co.*

287–94.	Not in *BL 20, L 5.*

287–8.	Not in *F 4.*

288.	*Wrinkles our*] *Bod. 1+*; Wrinkled his *NLW 2, Υ 5. fair*] *Bod. 1+*; hair *Br.*

290.	*waft*] *Bod. 1+*; waste *N 9*; wait *1667³b.*

291.	*For*] *Bod. 1+*; The Dutch *Ca. as*] Not in *OA 1. all*] Not in *Ca.*

293–4.	Not in *Ca.*

295.	Two lines inserted before this line appear in *N 10*: 'But a good Pilot & a favouring wind/Brings Sandwich back & once again did blind.'

295–310.	Comes after l. 344 in *L 5*, after l. 368 in *BL 20.*

297.	*reproach*] *Bod. 1+*; approach *N 8, OA 1, T* [corrected to 'Reproach'].

299.	*hatches*] *Bod. 1+*; clutches *Bod. 25, Ca.*

301.	*coast*] *Bod. 1+*; shore *Bod. 18, G, NLW 2, Υ 5, Υ 6, Υ 11.*

305.	*eastern*] *Bod. 1+*; orient *F 4, N 10.*

306.	*sate*] *Bod. 1+*; got *BL 30*; glutt *Br.*; gott *OA 1*; erect *N 7*; serve *F 4*; [?] saves *Wa.*; safe *OW 2. the*] Not in *Ca.*

307.	*warning*] *Bod. 1+*; weary *F 4. it divides*] *Bod. 1+*; did divide *Br.*

307–36. Not in *G*, except for l. 314, 'Embassies bear no arms', which is written in a larger and different hand.

311. *fittest*] *Bod. 1+*; finest *N 9*; better *Co.*

314. *Slips to the*] *Bod. 1+*; Steps into'th *SA*; Shifts to the *Υ 6. Groin*] *Bod. 1+*; grain *L 5*. *Embassies . . . not*] *Bod. 1+*; Embassies . . . no *NLW 2, Υ 5*; Ambassadors.. no *LAC 2*; Embassadours . . . nor [?] *Ca.*

317–44. Occurs after l. 368 in *Bod. 12, F 5*, but a marginal note in the latter signals that it should be read after l. 316.

317–40. Not in *Be., BL 20, BL 29, Co.*; comes after l. 344 in *AC, Bod. 8*; after l. 368 in *Br., OW 2, Wa., 1667*.

321–2. Interlineated as one line in another hand in *N 9*; not in *Ca.*

321. *discharge*] *Bod. 1+*; destroy *Bod. 12, Br., OW 2, 1667. makes*] *Bod. 1+*; breeds *Bod. 24*.

322. *fanatic*] *Bod. 1+*; fanatics *Br., LAC 2, NLW 2, SA, Υ 5. turn . . . or*] *Bod. 1+*; are . . . or *AH 1, LAC 2, SA*; are when they are *Es., N 8, N 9, NLW 2, T, Υ 5, 1667². sick*] *Bod. 1+*; rich *BL 30*.

324. *commissions*] *Bod. 1+*; Comission Officers *Υ 5*.

325. *But*] *Bod. 1+*; If *Br.*; Off *Ca. checkstones*] *Bod. 1+*; cheakstones *SA, Ca.* [blank space], *OW 2. if, and*] *Bod. 1+*; if, a *Br.*; and fine *Ca.*; and rare *N 10*; and for *T.*

326. *For*] *Bod. 1+*; In *Br.. 't has*] *Bod. 1+*; y^t has *Ca.*; 'twas *N 7*; that *Υ 5*.

327. *pass*] Bod. 1+; paste *N 8*.

328. *reserve*] *Bod. 1+*; resert *N 7. alas*] *Bod. 1+*; at last *AC*.

329. *as just*] *Bod 1+*; ye young *Ca. Orange*] *Bod. 1+*, Aura'ge *AH 1*; Orange for *Br.*

330. *giv'n, as*] *Bod. 1*; giv'n & *T*; gone & *Ca. regenerate*] *Bod. 1+*; degenerate *OA 1*.

331. *four*] *Bod. 1+*; five *1667*.

333. *yet*] Not in *OA 1*.

334. *pimp*] *Bod. 1+*; Lord *Ca.*; Prince *1667*.

335. A break is inserted before this line in *N 8*. Missing in *Bod. 12*.

336. *always*] not in *N 8*; hee say *T*.

337. *sheet*] *Bod. 1+*; sute *AC. staff*] *Bod. 1+*; state *G*.

339–40. Not in *G*.

339. *be*] *Bod. 1+*; face *N 9*.

341–4. Repeated as a refrain at the end of *Bod. 12*; placed after l. 316 in *LAC 2, SA*.

341. *O . . . two*] *Bod. 1+*; let our two noble *BL 29, BL 30, Bod. 8, Co., L 5, SA*.

342. *Aumarle*] *Bod. 1+*; Aumarle and *AC, LAC 2, SA, T, Υ 5*; Albermarle *Br.*; Monck & ['&' interlineated] *Ca.*

343–4. Not in *G* (1666).

343. *Since . . . been*] *Bod. 1+*; And since . . . til *SA. Since . . . ship*] repeated once and then deleted in *Ca.*

345–68. Not in *Be., BL 29, Co., L 6*.

345. *King*] *Bod. 1+*; Soveraign *N 10, F 4*.

346. *joys*] *Bod. 1+*; joy *Υ 5*; love *BL 30*; wishes *N 10*; love *BL 30*; Hopes *T*.

347. *it*] *Bod. 1+*; thee *Ca. gild*] *Bod. 1+*; guide *AH 1, Wa.*

348. *basking*] *Bod. 1+*; cherisht *L 5*.

349. 'breath' interlineated and then deleted before 'warmth' in *Ca.*

350. *devour*] *Bod. 1+*; t'endanger *Ca.*; placed before 'Our' in *SA. our*] *Bod. 1+*; the *Br., LAC 2*.

351. *rul'st*] *Bod. 1+*; unlesse *AC*.

352. *And*] *Bod. 1+* Canst *T. hundred . . . fleet*] *Bod. 1+*; absent in *OW 2*.

354. *Who . . . cow*] *Bod. 1+*; Who builds thee but a Labirinth *T* [corrected to 'T'build thee a Labirinth wth out a Clew']. *thee but a lab'rinth and a*] *Bod. 1+*; thee but a labyrinth and *AC*; ye Bull, a Labyrinth, & *Bod. 26* (corrected), *G, NLW 2, Υ 11, 1667². three N 8. cow*] *Bod. 1+*; clue *N 10*.

355. *art Minos*] *Bod. 1+*; a Minos *BL 30, Ca., OW 2, 1667*; aminos *N 7*; O Minos be *N 9*; our Minos *T*; a Man *AC*.

356. *own*] *Bod. 1+*; not in *N 8. confine*] *Bod. 1+*; canst sinck *N 7*; written twice in *Ca.*, the first one crossed out.

357. *Or . . . sun,*] *Bod. 1+*; Art thou o^r sun *BL 30*; O! may our sun *Bod. 26, Es., NLW 2, Υ 5, Υ 11. if*] crossed out and replaced with 't'our' in *LAC 2. he*] *Bod. 1+*; Hide *N 9*.

359. *let him*] *Bod. 1+*; may he *Bod. 26, NLW, Υ 5, Υ 6, Υ 11, 1667³b*; let his *Br.*

362. *sight*] *Bod. 1+*; light *N 8. within*] *Bod. 1+*; through *AC*; into *Ca., N 10*.

363. *calm*] *Bod. 1+*; all *BL 30, N 10*; full *Bod. 24. of joy*] *Bod. 1+*; with joy *Υ 5*; with peace *Bod. 26, Υ 6*.

364.   *universal triump*] *Bod. 1+*; generall
       Triumphs are *Bod. 12. triumph ... fight*]
       Bod. 1+; triumphs have no night *Ca.*
365.   *race*] *Bod. 1+*; care *OW 2, 1667.*
367.   *draw*] *Bod. 1+*; awe *Es.*, *Bod. 26*, *NLW*
       2, *Υ 5*, *Υ 6*, *1667²*.

The Third Advice to a Painter

Title. Epigraph.   *Bod. 1+*; Humano Capiti cervicem
       Pictor equino Iungere si vebit/Pictoribus
       atq Poetis/Quidlibet audendi semper
       fuit aequa Potestas./Horat. De Arte
       Poet./London/Written for the Company
       of Drunken Poets. 1666. *F 5*; not in
       OA 1, *Wa.*
Date.   Placed after l. 456 in *OA 1*; not in *LAC 2.*
3.   *danger*] *Bod. 1+*; dangers *BL 29*, *LAC 2*,
       N 10, *N 11*, *SA*; dangerous *BL 14*,
       BL 20, *Cm.*, *H 2*, *Υ 10.*
6.   *marshalled*] *Bod. 1+*; muscle- *Es.*, *Bod. 8*,
       Bod. 24, *H 2*, *SA*, *Υ 5*, *Υ 6*, *Υ 11*, *1667³.*
7.   *slender*] *Bod. 1+*; little *N 10.*
12.   *Within*] *Bod. 1+*; Both in *Bod. 8*, *SA*, *Υ 11.*
13.   *name*] *Bod. 1+*; flame *Cm.*
14.   *Fame*] *Bod. 1+*; Flame *BL 20.*
15.   *ever*] *Bod. 1+*; so great *BL 20.*
16.   *fierce*] *Bod. 1+*; faire *OA 1.*
21.   *And ... next*] *Bod. 1+*; Go to my boyes
       BL 29.
22.   *loo*] *Bod. 1+*; loose *N 11*, *Υ 10*; lowe
       BL 20, *H 2*, *LAC 2.*
25.   *airy*] *Bod. 1+*; earthy *BL 20*; *Cm.*, *Wa.*,
       Υ 10, *1667².*
26.   *by*] *Bod. 1+*; in *Cm.*, *H 2*; through
       N 10, *Υ 10*; yᵉ *N 11*; per *LAC 2. witchy*]
       Bod. 1+; witched *Bod. 8*; witty *Υ 5.*
27-8. Not in *Bod. 24.*
28.   *quit*] *Bod. 1+*; left *SA.*
29.   *seen*] *Bod. 1+*; won *BL 20.*
31.   *Rumour*] *Bod. 1+*; rumours *BL 14*, *Cm.*,
       Υ 10; meteors *BL 20.*
36.   *And ... the*] *Bod. 1+*; The ... the *SA*;
       In expectation of a *N 11. better*] *Bod. 1*;
       greater *Bod. 24*, *LAC 2*, *OA 1.*
37.   *his*] *Bod. 1+*; the *LAC 2.*
38.   *found*] *Bod. 1+*; felt *Bl 20*, *Cm.*,
       finds *LAC 2*, *OA 1.*
40.   *Thought*] *Bod. 1+*; Though *Υ 10*;
       Thinks *LAC 2.*
41.   *arm*] *Bod. 1+*; fame *Υ 5.*

43.   *conquer ... by*] *Bod. 1+*; subdue ... with *SA.*
55.   *circling*] *Bod. 1+*; encircling *BL 20.*
56.   *Like*] *Bod. 1+*; As *N 10. whirling ... of*]
       Bod. 1; flaming ... like *Bod. 8*, *Wa.* ['like
       a'], *1667²*; flaming ... of *BL 20*, *SA*,
       Υ 10; flaming ... like *Cm.*; whirling ...
       like *BL 14*, *N 10*; whirling ... in *N 11.*
57.   *their*] not in *Υ 11.*
59-60. Not in *Es.*, *Bod. 8*, *Bod. 18*, *Bod. 27*, *SA*,
       Υ 5, *Υ 6*, *Υ 11*, *1667³.*
59.   *trolls*] *Bod. 1*; boul *BL 29*, howles *OA 1.*
60.   *holls*] Howles *Bod. 1*; holds *BL 14*, *BL 29*,
       Bod. 24, *N 10*, *N 11*, *OA 1*; holes *Cm.*,
       LAC 2, *1667².*
64.   *consort*] *Bod. 1+*; courage *BL 20.*
65.   *list'ning*] *Bod. 1+*; lightening *Υ 6.*
68.   *deaf*] *Bod. 1*; dead *Es.*, *Bod. 8*, *Bod. 18*,
       Bod. 24, *Bod. 27*, *LAC 2*, *Υ 11.*
       pulse] *Bod. 1+*; pill *Cm.*, *Wa.*, *1667².*
       Fate] *Bod. 1+*; State *Es.*, *Bod. 18*, *H 2*,
       Υ 5, *Υ 6*, *1667³*, *1667³b.*
72.   *Skill is*] *Bod. 1+*; conduct's *Bod. 21*;
       Conduct *N 10*; conduits' *Υ 10.*
73.   *virtuous envy*] *Bod. 1+*; envious glory *N 10.*
75.   *she*] *Bod. 1+*; he *BL 14*, *BL 20*, *Bod. 24*,
       N 11, *SA.*
76.   *Bricoled*] *Bod. 1*, *Bod. 21*; Recoyl'd *BL 14*,
       Es., *BL 29*, *Bod. 8*, *Bod. 18*, *Bod. 24*, *SA*,
       Υ 5, *Υ 6*, *Υ 11*, *1667³*, *1667³b*; Brusled
       BL 20, *Wa.*, *Υ 10*, *1667².*
79.   *she*] *Bod. 1+*; he *BL 14*, *BL 20*, *Bod. 8*,
       Bod. 18, *Bod. 24*, *Cm.*, *H 2*, *N 11*, *SA*,
       Υ 5, *Υ 6*, *Υ 10.*
80.   *their foible*] *Bod. 1*; their feeble *BL 14*,
       LAC 2, *SA*, *Υ 6*; they're feeble *Es.*, *BL*
       14, *Bod. 8*, *Bod. 18*, *Bod. 24*, *Υ 11*, *1667³*;
       th'are feeble *N 11*; them feeble *Cm.*,
       H 2, *Υ 10*, *1667²*; 'um feeble *BL 20*; nor
       feeble *BL 29* [nor feeble that nor ...].
       Achilles' heel] *Bod. 1+*; Chittereale *1667²*;
       to Chittereale *Cm.*
81.   *crowds*] *Bod. 1+*; clouds *BL 14*, *BL 20*,
       BL 29, *Bod. 24*, *Cm.*, *H 2*, *N 10*, *N 11*,
       OA 1, *SA*, *Wa.*, *Υ 5*, *Υ 6*, *Υ 10*, *Υ 11*,
       1667², *1667³.*
86.   *as*] *Bod. 1+*; at *BL 14.*
87.   *powder's*] *Bod. 1+*; powder *BL 20*;
       fowlers *Wa.*
94.   *imps ... can*] *Bod. 1+*; as he may, doth
       impe his wings *H 2. plumes*] *Bod. 1*;
       sails *LAC 2.*

101.	*losing rooks*] *Bod. 1+*; leering rooks *BL 20*; Parents mockt *Es., Bod. 18, Υ 6, Υ 11, 1667³. losing*] *Bod. 1+*; cheated *Bod. 8, SA.*
103.	Interpolated in *Bod. 8.*
105.	*our scorn*] *Bod. 1*; th'story; *Bod. 8, SA, Υ 6*; yᵉ story *Υ 11*; yᵉ History *Υ 5, 1667³.*
106.	*artist*] *Bod. 1+*; painter *Υ 6.*
107.	*Cashier*] *Bod. 1+*; Where *BL 29.*
108.	*taste*] *Bod. 1+*; take *BL 20.*
109.	*paint*] *Bod. 1+*; tell *BL 14.*
111.	*surveyed . . . so*] *Bod. 1+*; survived the corpse to *Bod. 24. so clear*] *Bod. 1+*; too clear *BL 20*; and neer *Wa., 1667².*
112.	*petrified*] *Bod. 1+*; putrifyd *BL 14.*
113.	*gum*] *Bod. 1+*; a gun *H 2.*
114.	*balm*] *Bod. 1+*; blame *N 10.*
123.	*story*] *Bod. 1+*; sorrow *Υ 5.*
129.	*Rump*] *Bod. 1+*; Dutch *LAC 2*; men *OA 1.*
130.	*Aumerle's*] *Bod. 1+*; Georges *BL 29.*
131.	*The long*] *Bod. 1+*; This great *LAC 2.*
132–6.	Comes after l. 138 in *Bod. 24.*
133–6.	Comes after l. 138 in *SA, Υ 5, Υ 11, 1667³.*
133.	*youthful*] *Bod. 1*; winged *BL 29*; useful *Wa.*
134.	*From . . . chaste*] *Bod. 1+*; To meet the fury of a sea born beast *BL 29.*
137–8.	Comes after l. 132 in *BL 29, Bod. 8, Bod. 24, Υ 6*; not in *Bod. 18.*
137.	*Ruyter*] *Bod. 1+*; not in *Υ 6. chaw*] *Bod. 1+*; chew *BL 20*; 'chaw' corrected to 'claw' *N 10.*
138.	*jaw*] corrected from 'maw' *SA.*
139–40.	Not in *BL 29.*
141.	*late*] *Bod. 1+*; safe *BL 20, Υ 10.*
143–4.	Reverse order in *BL 20.*
144.	*half-eternal*] *Bod. 1+*; half-years *Bod. 8, H 2, Υ 10, 1667²*; a half years *SA.*
146.	*spy*] *Bod. 1+*; meet *H 2. year's*] Not in *LAC 2, OA 1.*
149.	*As our*] Not in *Bod. 18. glad*] *Bod. 1+*; whole *Wa., 1667².*
150.	*wish*] *Bod. 1+*; wᵗʰ *N 10. second*] *Bod. 1+*; other *BL 20, Bod. 24, Υ 10.*
152.	*eagerly assault*] crossed out in *SA.*
154.	*hungry*] *Bod. 1+*; angry *BL 14.*
156.	*wrist*] *Bod. 1+*; wrest *1667².*
164.	*empty*] not in *BL 14.*
170.	*nice*] *Bod. 1+*; my *Bod. 8, SA,* 'any' crossed out and replaced with 'my' *Υ 11. survey*] *Bod. 1+*; with 'delay' crossed out *N 11.*
173.	*tale*] *Bod. 1+*; fate *N 10. outer*] *Bod. 1+*; outward *BL 14, BL 20, Bod. 24, Es., LAC 2, OA 1, SA, Υ 5, Υ 6, Υ 10, Υ 11.*
175.	*roam*] *Bod. 1+*; combe *BL 29.*
178.	*porter*] *Bod. 1+*; coachman *Es., Bod. 18, Bod. 24, SA, Υ 6, Υ 11.*
180.	*Hony-pensy . . . she*] *Bod. 1*; Honi Soit qui mal she bravely *Wa., 1667²*; Honi Pense full honestly *Bod. 18, Bod. 24, Es., LAC 2, SA, Υ 5, Υ 6, Υ 11, 1667³*; Hony pense honestly *BL 20, N 10*; Hony soit qui male pense she *BL 29. she*] *Bod. 1+*; they *OA 1.*
181–2.	Not in *Es., Υ 5, Υ 11, 1667³.*
181.	*She-gen'ral's*] *Bod. 1*; she Gen'rals *1667²*; the Gen'rals *Bod. 29+. britch*] *Bod. 1+*; breech *LAC 2. 1667².*
182.	*piece*] *Bod. 1+*; price *BL 20.*
186.	*just of a*] *Bod. 1+*; of a foul *Bod. 24, N 10*; just of an old *LAC 2. just*] not in *BL 14, Bod. 21, Υ 10.*
189.	*an*] *Bod. 1+*; to *BL 14*; not in *OA 1.*
190.	*neck*] *Bod. 1+*; nose *BL 20.*
191.	*dried*] *Bod. 1+*; shed *Bod. 18, Υ 5, Υ 11.*
192.	*only snuffing*] *Bod. 1+*; only snuffling *BL 20, Bod. 24*; snuffl'd onely *LAC 2.*
194.	*be had in*] *Bod. 1+*; think on as *BL 20. in me(mento)mory*] *Bod. 1+*; in memento mori *LAC 2, Υ 6, Υ 11*; as momento mori *BL 20*; think on momento mori *SA*; think as, as memento mori *Υ 10.*
196.	*spirit*] *Bod. 1+*; fiendly *Es., Bod. 8, Bod. 18, SA, Υ 6, Υ 11, 1667³*; friendly *Υ 5.*
198.	*startle*] *Bod. 1+*; sparkle *Es., Bod. 8, Bod. 18, SA, Υ 5, Υ 11.*
200.	*out did*] *Bod. 1+*; 'gan to *Es., Bod. 18, Bod. 24, SA, Υ 6, Υ 11, 1667.*
201.	*the*] *Bod. 1+*; my *OA 1.*
202.	*grows*] *Bod. 1+*; is *Υ 6, Υ 11.*
203.	*man . . . land*] *Bod. 1+*; alone *LAC 2.*
205–6.	Not in *Wa., 1667².*
212.	*snap*] *Bod. 1+*; fall *BL 20, BL 29, Bod. 8, Bod. 24, SA, Υ 5, Υ 6, 1667², 1667³. gen'ralship*] *Bod. 1+*; Gen'rals ship *BL 29.*
214.	*not . . . me*] *Bod. 1+*; but no man, Mee *LAC 2.*
215.	*ay*] *Bod. 1+*; I *LAC 2. do*] *Bod. 1+*; too *BL 20*; soe *BL 14.*
216.	*shall*] *Bod. 1+*; must *N 10. did*] *Bod. 1+*; told *SA.*

217. *I told*] *Bod. 1+*; Hold *Bod. 8*. *did*] *Bod. 1+*;
      told *BL 20, Bod. 24, Υ 6, Υ 10, Υ 11*.

219–22. Come after l. 224 in *1667³*.

219. *there*] *Bod. 1+*; have *BL 20, Υ 10*; dare *Υ 6*.

220. *intelligence or*] *Bod. 1+*; his secrets or
      to *LAC 2. or*] *Bod. 1+*; not in *Υ 6*.
      buy] *Bod. 1+*; beg *Wa.*

221. *care*] *Bod. 1+*; dare *LAC 2*.

223–4. Placed after l. 218 in *1667²*. Not in *Wa.*

223. *to cheat*] *Bod. 1+*; it is to eat *LAC 2*.

226. *Roy'lists*] *Bod. 1+*; Loyalists *BL 14, BL 20,
      OA 1, Υ 5, 1667²*. *load*] *Bod. 1+*; board
      LAC 2.

225. No plurals in names in *BL 20*.

231. *revel-rout*] *Bod. 1+*; rebel rout *Υ 11*.

232. *same measures*] *Bod. 1+*; small measures
      Υ 11; small measure *SA*; small manners
      Es., Bod. 8, 1667³.

234. *Renew*] *Bod. 1+*; Revue *LAC 2*.

235. *fools*] *Bod. 1+*; fool *1667³*; foule *Υ 5*.

239. *Then*] *Bod. 1+*; When *OA 1*; Next *BL 20,
      Υ 10*.

240. *to content*] *Bod. 1+*; to contents *Υ 10*;
      for contents *BL 14, BL 20, N 10, SA*;
      in spite of *BL 29*; to pleasure *Wa.*

242. *Word*] *Bod. 1+*; wood *Bod. 8*.

243. *their*] *Bod. 1+*; your *LAC 2*.

244. *'jection*] *Bod. 1+*; 'Ejection' *Bod. 21,
      LAC 2, Υ 10, Υ 11*; election *Wa.*

245. *ere*] *Bod. 1+*; 'ere' underlined with 'and'
      interlineated in *N 10*; and *SA, Υ 6, Υ 11*.

246. *interrupts*] *Bod. 1+*; intercepts *BL 29*.

247. *show*] *Bod. 1+*; then *Υ 6*.

249. *scriv'ner*] *Bod. 1+*; pen-man *LAC 2*.

251. *that . . . she*] *Bod. 1+*; that . . . she *SA*;
      who more as oft as he *BL 20*; who . . .
      she *N 10*; who . . . he *BL 20*; that . . .
      he *Υ 5, Υ 11, 1667³*.

252. *she*] *Bod. 1*; he *Bod. 8, Bod. 24*.

253–4. Not in *Wa., 1667²*.

253. *first*] *Bod. 1+*; great *BL 29*.

256. *three*] *Bod. 1+*; four *BL 20*.

258. *taratantar*] *Bod. 1+*; a taratantar *BL 20*;
      tararantar *N 10*.

266. *humours*] *Bod. 1+*; Fancies *1667²*.
      spill] *Bod. 1+*; fill *BL 14, SA, Υ 6, Υ 11*.

267. *one . . . they*] *Bod. 1*; four daies fight,
      they clearly *Es., Bod. 8, Bod. 18, Bod. 27,
      SA, Υ 6, 1667³*; four day's fight they saw
      Υ 11; one day's fight, the clearly saw *Υ 5,
      Υ 11*.

269. *with*] *Bod. 1+*; for *SA, Υ 6, Υ 11*.
      six] not in *BL 14*.

270. *with*] corrected from 'if' *OA 1*.

271. *agree*] corrected from 'appear' in
      BL 20.

272. *less*] *Bod. 1+*; worse *BL 29*.

274. *both*] Not in *1667²*.

275–80. Not in *N 10*.

277. *dazzling*] *Bod. 1+*; darling *BL 20*.

282. *not*] *Bod. 1+*; now *N 10*.

284. *his own*] *Bod. 1+*; the Court *H 2*.

286. *it*] not in *BL 14*.

287. *Hixy*] *Bod. 1+*; hicce *BL 29*.

300. *chink*] *Bod. 1+*; chinks *Υ 10*; thinks
      BL 20, Wa., 1667². *may start*] *Bod. 1+*;
      impart *Bod. 18, Es., SA, Υ 6, Υ 11, 1667³*;
      may part *BL 20, BL 29*.

301–2. Not in *Wa., 1667²*.

303–4. Comes after l. 306 in *Wa., 1667²*.

303. *certain*] *Bod. 1+*; outward *Υ 5*.

304. *write*] *Bod. 1+*; send *BL 29, Bod. 8, Es.,
      SA, Υ 5, Υ 6, 1667³*.

308. *write*] *Bod. 1+*; white *Υ 5*. *it*] Not in
      OA 1. foul] *Es.+*; fair *Bod. 1, BL 20,
      BL 29, LAC 2, N 10, OA 1*; out *Wa.,
      1667² . . out*] not in *SA*.

319–20. Not in *Wa., 1667²*.

321–2. Comes after l. 324 in *Wa., 1667²*.

321. *true*] *Bod. 1+*; time *1667²*.

322. *make*] *Bod. 1+*; still *BL 20*.

332–4. Comes after l. 318 in *1667²*.

327. *See . . . beer*] Written vertically in the left-
      hand margin in *BL 20*, and presumably
      meant to be inserted between l. 325 and
      l. 326, both of which are marked at the
      beginning with a cross. *and*] *Bod. 1+*;
      good *Υ 5*.

329–30. Comes after l. 338 in *Wa., 1667²*; lines
      printed in reversed order in *LAC 2*.

329. *steal*] *Bod. 1+*; sell *Es., BL 29, Bod. 8, SA,
      Υ 5, Υ 6, Υ 11, 1667³*.

330. *out*] not in *SA. from powdered*] Not in
      OA 1.

331–2. Comes after l. 334 in *Wa., 1667²*.

331. *the tub*] *Bod. 1+*; the but *OA 1*; th'beef-
      tub *LAC 2*.

333–4. Comes after l. 328 in *1667²*.

335–6. Not in *Wa.*

336. *Mar'ners*] *Bod. 1+*; Seamen *N 10*.

337–8. Comes after l. 330 in *1667²*.

339–40. Not in *Es., Bod. 18, Υ 5, Υ 11, 1667³*.

339.	Written vertically in left-hand margin in *SA.* countermine] *Bod. 1+;* undermine *LAC 2.*
341–2.	Not in *Wa., 1667².*
342.	*Nor the . . . be]* *Bod. 1;* That sea Dinus be'nt *BL 20;* Nor . . . to be *Υ 10;* Let 'nt . . . be *BL 29.*
351–2.	Comes after l. 354 in *Wa., 1667².*
351.	*arrayed]* *Bod. 1+;* afraid *Bod. 24, Wa., Υ 5, Υ 11.*
352.	*out]* *Bod. 1+;* not in *Υ 6.*
354.	*the]* *Bod. 1+;* at *Υ 6.*
359.	*gores . . . near]* *Bod. 1+;* goes – *Bod. 8. shaft gores]* *Bod. 1+;* swift goes *Es., Bod. 18, Bod. 24, Υ 6, Υ 11, 1667³;* shift goes *SA. their . . . near]* Not in *SA.*
362.	*how]* not in *1667³. lighten, thunder]* *Bod. 1+;* thunder, lighten *Υ 11.* 'lightening' corrected to 'lighten' *BL 20.*
369–70.	In reverse order in *Bod. 8, Bod. 18, 1667³.*
370.	*cut]* *Bod. 1+;* change *LAC 2;* hem *Bod. 18, SA, Υ 5, Υ 6, Υ 11.*
371.	*the . . . ones]* *Bod. 1+;* thy torne Sailes *LAC 2.*
375–6.	*posterior . . . jury]* *Bod. 1+;* back parts George, left/Tho maist have store of masts, of *LAC 2.*
375.	*left]* *Bod. 1+;* George *Bod. 24, Υ 5, Υ 11, 1667³;* not in *Υ 6, 1667². lest]* *Bod. 1+;* ere *Bod. 24, Bod. 21, SA, Υ 5, Υ 6, Υ 11.*
377.	*whet]* *Bod. 1+;* where *Υ 11.*
384.	*out]* not in *Υ 11.*
385.	*steer]* *Bod. 1+;* stir *OA 1.*
386.	*Gold]* *Bod. 1+;* cold *LAC 2.*
387.	*their ships all]* *Bod. 1+;* your ships all *BL 20;* all their ships *Υ 11. their]* *Bod. 1+;* all *LAC 2;* all your *SA, Υ 10. they]* *Bod. 1;* you *Es., Bod. 18, Bod. 24, SA, Υ 5, Υ 11, 1667³b;* they'le *Υ 6.*
388.	*their]* *Bod. 1+;* the *Υ 11;* your *1667³b.*
390.	*richer]* *Bod. 1+;* interlineated in *N 10* above a crossed out 'bigger'.
392.	*we]* *Bod. 1+;* he *BL 14.*
400.	*projects]* *Bod. 1+;* Quarrels *1667². winds]* *Bod. 1+;* wind *BL 20, Lac 2, N 10, OA 1, SA, Υ 10, Υ 11;* men *Υ 6.*
402.	*sends them both]* *Bod. 1+;* sent both fleets *LAC 2.*
403.	*Virginian]* *Bod. 1;* Virginia *LAC 2;* New England *Es., Bod. 8, Bod. 26, SA, Υ 5, Υ 6, Υ 11, 1667³.*
404.	*your]* *Bod. 1+;* our *Bod. 26.*
405.	*get]* *Bod. 1+;* set *Bod. 26.*
406.	*longing]* *Bod. 1;* lingring *Wa., 1667².*
407.	*marchpanes]* *Bod. 1+;* merchants *Υ 10. light]* *BL 29+;* tight *Bod. 1;* rare *BL 20,* not in *Υ 10.*
408.	*ruin]* *Bod. 1+;* hinder *Υ 6.*
409–10.	Not in *1667².*
410.	*down his warder]* *Bod. 1;* down his ward *Υ 11;* down his award *Υ 6;* down's award *Es., Bod. 8, Bod. 18, Bod. 24, Es., SA, 1667³b;* a word *Bod. 26. they've]* *Bod. 1+;* they have *SA.*
411–12.	Comes after l. 420 in *Wa., 1667².*
414.	*utmost date]* *Bod. 1+;* outmost *BL 14.*
415.	*theirs]* *Bod. 1+;* yours *Bod. 26.*
416.	*pile]* *Bod. 1+;* fire *Υ 6.*
417–18.	Comes before l. 421 in *Wa.*
418.	*God]* *Bod. 1+;* Heaven *Bod. 26.* 'but' before 'who' crossed out in *Bod. 26.*
419–20.	Comes after l. 416 in *1667².*
421–2.	Not in *Bod. 26, Es., SA, Υ 5, Υ 6, Υ 11.*
421.	*didst please]* *Bod. 2;* displease *LAC 2.*
422.	*thine]* *Bod. 1+;* mine *BL 29.*
423.	*begot]* *Bod. 1+;* begat *SA,* begun *BL 20, Bod. 26.*
424.	*house]* *Bod. 1+;* houre *BL 20, Bod. 8, Bod. 18, Bod. 26, Υ 6, Υ 10, Υ 11.*
426.	*dies]* *Bod. 1+;* lies *BL 14.*
429.	*though late]* *Bod. 1+;* at last *N 10. here]* *Bod. 1+;* where *OA 1.*
431–2.	Not in *Wa., 1667².*
431.	*help . . . out]* help them out *OA 1;* bear them up *LAC 2.*
433.	*see]* not in *BL 20, Υ 10. Beaufort dares]* *Bod. 1+;* Rup[ert] does *Bod. 26.*
436.	*Faith]* *Bod. 1;* Truth is *Bod. 8, Bod. 18, SA, Υ 5, Υ 11.*
439.	*couns'llors]* *Bod. 1+;* councells *Es., Bod. 26, SA, Υ 6, Υ 11, 1667³.*
440.	*painter . . . poet]* *Bod. 1+;* poet . . . painter *BL 14, N 10.*
443.	*foreign]* *Bod. 1+;* sovreign *Bod. 8.*
450.	*gales]* *Bod. 1+;* calms *Bod. 8, Bod. 18, Bod. 26, Υ 11. oars, will]* *Bod. 1+;* boats oars *Bod. 26.*
451.	*strung]* *Bod. 1+;* 'sung' corrected to 'strung' *BL 20.*
452.	*Needle's]* *Bod. 1+;* Vocall *Bod. 24, Υ 10.*
455.	*increased]* *Bod. 1+;* inclosed *Bod. 26, OA 1, Υ 5, 1667³;* enclos'd *SA, Υ 10;* he clos'd *LAC 2.*

456. *she painted*] *Bod. 1*+; the painter *Es.,*
      Bod. 8, Bod. 26, SA, Υ *5,* Υ *6,* Υ *11, 1667³*;
      the painted *BL 15*.

Clarendon's Housewarming

Title. *1667³*+; The Housewarming to the
          Chancellor *P 4*; A House Warming to
          Chancellor Hyde *V, VA 1*.
2.   *effect*] *1667³*+; effects *Bod. 13*.
4.   *the season*] *1667³*+; th'season *LAC 2*.
6.   *flander*] *1667³*; flanders *Bod. 21, Bod. 13,*
      BL 20, P 4, VA 1.
7.   *kingfisher*] Kings fisher *Bod. 13*; kings-fisher
      Υ *5*. *brume*] *1667³*+; spume *Bod. 13*.
8.   *salamander*] *1667³*+; salamanders *P 4,*
      VA 1.
9.   *that*] *1667³*+; how *Bod. 13*.
10.   *So unreasonable*] *1667³*+; S'unreasonable
      LAC 2. *that they buy*] *1667³*+; they buy
      Bod. 18, SA, V, VA 1; they build *Bod. 13*.
13.   *Rhodopis*] *Bod. 1*; Rhodope *1667³*+;
      Rhodophe *BL 14, LAC 2, VA 1*.
15.   *that his ... as*] *1667³*+; his . . . so *Bod. 13*.
17.   *how*] *Bod. 13*; how the *1667³*+. *the harper*]
      1667³+; th'harper *LAC 2*.
18.   *he*] not in *Bod. 18*.
20.   *with the*] *1667³*+; on a *Bod. 13*.
21.   *fitter*] *1667³*+; after *Bod. 13, P 4, VA 1*.
22.   *Dide*] *Bod. 1, Bod. 13, BL 20*; Dido *1667³*;
      Did' *Bod. 21*.
23.   *he begged*] *1667³*+; she had *Bod. 13*.
24.   *an*] *1667³*+; a *SA, VA 1*.
26.   *expenses*] *1667³*+; expense *LAC 2, P 4*. *of*]
      1667³+ of a *P 4, V*.
27.   *which*] *1667³*+; y^t *V, VA 1*. *brained*] *1667³*+;
      Drained *VA 1*.
30.   *solid*] *1667³*+; strong *LAC 2*. *thong*] *1667³*+;
      strong *Bod. 18, LAC 2, SA*.
32.   *he . . . one*] *1667³*+; many a one hee had
      built *Bod. 13*.
33.   *cattle*] *1667³*+; chattell *BL 14, P 4, V,*
      VA 1.
34.   *and*] *1667³*+; and to *P 4, V, VA 1*.
35.   *by*] *1667³*+; from *V, VA 1*.
36.   *portion*] *1667³*+; portions *P 4*.
37.   *henceforth*] *1667³*+; *hence LAC 2, SA*. *that*]
      1667³+; he *P 4, V, VA 1*.
38.   *make*] *1667³*+; not in *P 4, VA 1*. *allowed*]
      1667³+; low'd *LAC 2*. *them*] *1667³*+ 'em
      P 4, VA 1.

39.   *cared*] *1667³*+; cares *P 4, V, VA 1*.
      distressed] *1667³*+ infest *Bod. 1, Bod. 13,*
      V, VA 1; infect *BL 14, P 4*.
40.   *So*] *1667³*+; Since *LAC 2. to . . . but*] *1667³*+;
      but to build *P 4, VA 1. but*] *1667³*+;
      not in *V. that*] *1667³*+; not in *Bod. 18,*
      LAC 2, SA.
43.   *mould*] *1667³*+; mole *LAC 2, SA, V, VA 1*.
45.   *easier*] *1667³*+; easiest *Bod. 1, Bod. 13, P 4,*
      VA 1.
46.   *So*] *1667³*+; As *P 4, VA 1*.
47.   *friends*] *Bod. 13, Bod. 21*; friend *BL 20,*
      Bod. 18, 1667³.
48.   *framed*] *1667³*+; raised *Bod. 13. them*] *Bod.*
      13, Bod. 21; him *BL 20, Bod. 8, SA, 1667³*.
49.   *the*] *1667³*+; his *V, VA 1*.
50.   *who*] *1667³*+; y^t *V, VA 1*.
51.   *The two*] *1667³*+; Th'two *LAC 2. who*]
      1667³+; y^t *V, VA 1. served*] *1667³*+; serve
      Bod. 18, LAC 2, VA 1. blind justice for]
      1667³+; injustice w^{th} *V, VA 1*.
52.   *who*] *1667³*+; y^t *V. served*] *1667³*+; serve
      Bod. 18, SA. for] *1667³*+; w^{th} *V, VA 1*.
      talons] *1667*+; stallons *BL 20*.
55.   *the*] *1667³*+; his *BL 14, VA 1*.
56.   *For*] *1667³*+; And *P 4, V, VA 1. like*]
      1667³+; as *V, VA 1*.
57.   *would . . . arrear*] *1667³*+; in arrear would
      no more *V*.
58.   *noble*] *1667³*+; nobly *P 4, V, VA 1. cheaper*]
      1667³+; cheap *Bod. 18, SA. too*] *1667³*+ not
      in *P 4, V, VA 1*.
60.   *atom*] *1667³*+; atoms *V, VA 1*.
61.   *then*] *1667³*+; they *Bod. 13. assayed*] *1667³*+;
      essayed *V, VA 1*.
62.   *give*] *1667³*+; shew *BL 14, P 4, V, VA 1*.
66.   *Sumners . . . farmers*] *1667³*+; Governors,
      farmers, sinners *LAC 2. Sumners*] *1667³*+;
      Sinners *Bod. 1, BL 20, Bod. 18, Bod. 21*.
67.   *milk*] *1667³*+; might *BL 20*; mite *Bod. 18,*
      Bod. 21, LAC 2, SA.
68.   *Cheddar . . . cheese*] *Bod. 21*; As Cheddar
      Clubs Dairy to the incorporate Cheese
      Bod. 18, LAC 2, 1667³; as Cheddar Clubbs
      Daries t'incorporate a Cheese *Bod. 13*;
      As Cheddar dairy's clun to ye incorporate
      cheese *V*.
69.   *Beaken's*] *Bod. 21*; Beelings *Bod. 13*; Brake
      BL 20; Beale, Bellins *BL 14, V*; Bulteen's *V*;
      Bulteens, Bellins *VA 1. Morley's*] *Bod. 13*;
      Morley *1667³*; Mortey's *P 4*.

70.   *Clutterbuck's . . . Kipp's*] *1667³*+;
   Clutterbuggs Eyes & Lipps *BL 14, P 4,*
   VA 1. Eager's] *1667³*+; Ayers *Bod. 13;* Eyes
   V. Kipp's] *1667³*+; Pepys *BL 20;* Lipps *V.*

71.   *the*] *1667³*+; th' *LAC 2;* that *P 4, VA 1.*
   selling] *1667³*+; telling *Bod. 13.*

72.   *this*] *1667³*+; the *V. snips*] *1667³*+; ships
   Bod. 18.

73.   *he*] *1667³*+; were *P 4, V, VA 1.*

74.   *he*] *1667³*+; not in *V, VA 1.*

76.   *No, would*] *1667³*+; Not tho' *P 4, VA 1;*
   No, tho' *V. kiss*] *1667³*+ would *P 4.*

78.   *he*] *Bod. 13;* the *1667³*+. *in the*] *1667³*+; i'th'
   LAC 2. bowel] *1667³*+; bowels *P 4.*

79.   *St. John . . . the leads*] *1667³*+; [blank] . . . his
   head *Bod. 13;* St. John . . . lead *P 4, V,*
   VA 1.

80.   *shall*] *1667³*+; shall else *Bod. 18, P 4, VA 1.*
   cut off] *1667³*+; hackt *Bod. 13, V;* hackt off
   BL 14, P 4, VA 1. the] *1667³*+; a *V, VA 1.*

81.   *Pratt*] *1667³*+; Bratt *P 4, V, VA 1.*

82.   *the expense*] *1667³*+; th'expense *LAC 2.*
   Worstenholm] *1667³*+; Woosltenholme *P 4;*
   wors'n ome *LAC 2.*

83.   *sat heretofore*] *1667³*+; was late *P 4, VA 1;*
   was late heretofore *V.*

84.   *received*] *1667³*+; receives *P 4;* not in *V.*
   now] *1667³*+; now takes *V. paid*] *1667³*+;
   pays *P 4, V, VA 1.*

85.   *subsidies*] *1667³*+; subsidy *P 4, V, VA 1.*

86.   *with*] *1667³*+; of *P 4, V, VA 1.*

88.   *excellent*] *1667³*+; famous *Bod. 13.*

89.   *And*] *1667³*+; Then *P 4, VA 1.*

90.   *burnt*] *1667³*+; build *Bod. 13;* whole *LAC 2.*

91.   *And*] *1667³*+; Which *LAC 2. on*] *1667³*+;
   'em *P 4;* them *VA 1. by*] *1667³*+; like *LAC
   2. the*] *1667³*+; a *P 4, VA 1. gilt ball*]
   1667³+; Gold Bull *P 4;* gold ball *V, VA 1.*

92.   *you are*] *1667³*+; y'are *LAC 2.*

93.   *Fond*] *1667³*+; From *Bod. 13. ruins*] *1667*+;
   ruin *P 4, VA 1.*

94.   *its*] *1667³*+; it *LAC 2.*

96.   *you*] *1667³*+; it *P 4. leave*] *1667³*+; want
   Bod. 13, P 4, VA 1.

98.   *this*] *1667³*+; our *P 4, V, VA 1;* thy *SA.*
   adorned] *1667³*+; adored *Bod. 18, P 4, SA,*
   VA 1.

100.   *Buckingham's*] *1667³*+; Buckings *Bod. 13.*

101.   *buildings*] *1667³*+; builders *BL 20.*

102.   *blame*] *1667³*+; blames its *P 4, V.*

103.   *his*] *1667³*+; its *V.*

104.   *expatiation*] *1667³*+; Expectation *V, VA 1.*

105.   *But*] *1667³*+; Such *V. how . . . time*] *1667³*+;
   that . . . times *P 4, V, VA 1.*

106.   *That for*] *1667³*+; For *V. it*] *1667³*+; not in
   P 4, V, VA 1.

107.   *soon*] *1667³*+; hence *P 4;* may hence *V, VA 1.*

108.   *may land*] *1667³*+; arrive *V, VA 1. spare*]
   1667³+; save *BL 20, P 4, V, VA 1.*

110.   *Lest with . . . far*] *1667³*+; Least . . . far
   should *LAC 2.*

111.   *good . . . for*] *1667³*+; whole . . . with *P 4,*
   VA 1; good . . . w^th *V.*

112.   *next St. James'*] *1667³*+; St James' next *P 4,*
   VA 1.

The Last Instructions to a Painter

Title.   *The Last Instructions to a Painter*] *Bod.
   1*+; The Last Instructions to a Painter,
   1667. LCP, Advice to a Painter, 3^d part
   ['A scandalous poem' then written in the
   right-hand margin] *LAUC.*

Date.   *Bod. 1*+; September ye 4th 1667 *BL 27;*
   September: 1667 *Y 13;* not in *LAUC.*

3.   *fall'st*] *Bod. 1*+; fall *LAUC.*

4.   *or*] *Bod. 1*+; & *BL 27.*

11.   *Sketching*] *Bod. 1*+; Stretching *LAUC,
   Y 13.*

13.   *if*] *Bod. 1*+; still *BL 27, LAUC, Y 13.*

15.   *out*] *Bod. 1*+; up *Y 13.*

16.   *the*] *Bod. 1*+; your *LCP, 1697.*

17.   *like*] *Bod. 1*+; ye like *LAUC.*
   Comptroller] *Bod. 1*+; Controller *N 12.*

18.   *the*] *Bod. 1*+; a *Y 13, LCP.*

19.   *guiltless*] *Bod. 1*+; guilty *LAUC, Y 13.*

21.   *so . . . having*] *Bod. 1*+; having so long
   LAUC.

25.   *could*] *Bod. 1*+; did *Y 13.*

28.   *cannot*] *Bod. 1*+; could not *LAUC.*

29.   *then*] *Bod. 1*+; me *BL 22. soup*] *Bod. 1*+;
   sauce *Y 13.*

31.   *courage*] *Bod. 1*+; valour *BL 22.*

34.   *Membered like*] *Bod. 1*+; member of *BL 22.*

35.   *Alban's*] *Bod. 1*+; Alban *LAUC.*

36.   *Bacon never*] *Bod. 1*+; never Bacon
   LAUC, Y 13.

37.   *allaying now*] *Bod. 1*+; having now allayed
   BL 22.

38.   *in*] *Bod. 1*+; from *BL 22;* for *LAUC.*
   treat] *Bod. 1*+; cheat *LCP, 1697.*

39.   *commission*] *Bod. 1*+; commissions *LAUC.*

40. *That*] *Bod. 1+*; And *LCP, 1697. treaty asks*] *Bod. 1+*; treaty want *LAUC*; Treaties ask *BL 22*; Treaty ask *LCP, 1689, 1697.*

42. *were*] *Bod. 1*; wear *BL 22.*

44. *a*] *Bod. 1+*; in *Υ 13*, where the word is scarcely visible, and a word or words before it have been erased.

53. *assayed*] *Bod. 1+*; essay'd *LCP.*

60. *her*] corrected to 'oher' (*sic*) in *BL 27. dukes*] *Bod. 1, BL 27, N 12*; Duke *Υ 13, LAUC, LCP, 1697*; D----s *1689. once*] *Bod. 1+*; but *LAUC, Υ 13.*

61. *lip and*] *Bod. 1+*; lips with *LAUC, Υ 13.*

64. *the*] *Bod. 1+*; her *Υ 13.*

69. *thou*] *Bod. 1+*; yᶜ *LAUC.*

75. *revolves*] *Bod. 1+*; resolves *Υ 13.*

78. *to*] *Bod. 1+*; for *LAUC.*

89. *scorn*] *Bod. 1+*; scorn'd *LCP.*

90. *wished*] *Bod. 1+*; wishes *LAUC.*

93. *her*] *Bod. 1+*; the *Υ 13.*

94. *those*] *Bod. 1+*; her *BL 27, LAUC, Υ 13.*

98. *in's*] *Bod. 1+*; in *LAUC, Υ 13.*

100. *fortune*] *Bod. 1+*; fortunes *LAUC.*

104. *Campaspe thee*] *Bod. 1+*; [blank] she *Υ 13.*

106. *clatt'ring*] *Bod. 1+*; chattring *LAUC.*

107. *both*] *Bod. 1+*; now *LAUC, Υ 13.*

108. *On*] *Bod. 1+*; In *LAUC, Υ 13.*

109. *Those*] *Bod. 1+*; These *LAUC. tric-trac*] *Bod. 1+*; Tick-Tack *BL 27, Υ 13, LAUC, LCP, 1697.*

112. *doth*] does *LCP.*

114. *cheat*] *Bod. 1+*; great *LAUC.*

115. *he so*] *Bod. 1+*; so he *LAUC, Υ 13.*

116. *goes*] *Bod. 1+*; goe *LAUC, LCP, Υ 13.*

120. *oft*] *Bod. 1+*; of *LAUC.*

123. *So*] *Bod. 1+*; Sad *LAUC, Υ 13.*

124. *should*] *Bod. 1+*; would *LAUC, LCP, Υ 13.*

125. *revenue*] *Bod. 1+*; revenues *LAUC.*

130. *they*] *Bod. 1+*; these *LCP, Υ 13.*

133. *and*] *Bod. 1+* a *LAUC, Υ 13.*

136. *trade*] *Bod. 1+*; trades *LAUC, Υ 13*; *cassowar*] *Bod. 1+*; as a Warr *LAUC, Υ 13.*

137. *wheres'e'er*] *Bod. 1+*; where er'e *LAUC. the*] *Bod. 1+*; her *LAUC.*

138. *intended*] *Bod. 1+*; extended *LAUC.*

140. *leathern*] *Bod. 1+*; leather *Υ 13. by*] *Bod. 1+*; at *LAUC.*

141. *cities*] *Bod. 1+*; city *LAUC.*

143. *Birch*] corrected from 'Bitch' in *BL 27.*

146. *Buggered in*] added in *BL 27. Buggered*] *Bod. 1+*; Proceeds *LAUC, Υ 13.*

154. *by*] *Bod. 1+*; with *LCP.*

158. *know*] *Bod. 1+*; knew *Υ 13, LCP. well could*] *Bod. 1+*; how to *LAUC, Υ 13.*

164. *armpit*] *Bod. 1+*; armpits *LAUC.*

166. *Hid*] *Bod. 1+*; And *LAUC.*

175. *arrayed*] *Bod. 1+*; allayed *Υ 13*; are layd *LAUC.*

176. *better . . . so well*] *Bod. 1+*; so well . . . better *Υ 13.*

178. *teal*] *Bod. 1+*; seal *LAUC.*

179. *grossest*] *Bod. 1+*; grosser *1697.*

181. *coif*] *Bod. 1+* ; Wife *LAUC, LCP, Υ 13, 1697*; corrected from 'Noise' in *BL 27.*

182. *Mitre*] *Bod. 1+*; mitred *LAUC, LCP.*

183. *marched*] *Bod. 1+*; marches *LCP. Of*] *Bod. 1+*; wᵗʰ *LAUC.*

185. *band*] *Bod. 1+*; bawds *LAUC.*

190. *further*] *Bod. 1+*; farther *Υ 13.*

192. *still to*] *Bod. 1+*; to do *LCP.*

193. *Pole*] *Bod. 1+*; Poole *LCP, Υ 13.*

195. *come*] *Bod. 1+*; come *LCP.*

196. *other*] *Bod. 1+*; others *LCP, Υ 13.*

200. *or sots*] *1689+*; or Scots *LCP* and Scots *LAUC, 1697.*

201. *quarrel*] *Bod. 1+*; quarrels *LAUC, LCP, Υ 13.*

204. *Cart'ret*] *Bod. 1+*; Cartwright *LAUC.*

205. *these*] *Bod. 1+*; those *LCP.*

209. *drinkers*] *Bod. 1+*; drunkards *LCP, 1697.*

212. *marching*] *Bod. 1+*; leading *LAUC.*

214. *stride*] *Bod. 1+*; pride *LAUC.*

221. *were*] *Bod. 1+*; was *LAUC, LCP.*

226. *one . . . the other*] *Bod. 1+*; th'one . . . t'other *LAUC.*

227. In *N 12*, a square bracket is placed against this line.

228. *by*] *Bod. 1+*; yᶜ *LAUC.*

231. *numbers*] *Bod. 1+*; number *LAUC*

239. *th'other*] *Bod. 1+*; t'other *LAUC. loose*] *Bod. 1+*; close *1697.*

242. *oft'ner*] *Bod. 1+*; often *LAUC, LCP.*

243. *o'er*] *Bod. 1+*; out *LAUC. while*] *Bod. 1+*; whilst *LAUC.*

244. *ere*] *Bod. 1+*; fore *LCP*; for *LAUC.*

249. *Such*] *Bod. 1+*; So *LAUC. strode*] *Bod. 1*; stood *LAUC*; strid *N 12, 1689*; stoo[d] *LCP, 1689, 1697.*

251. *ran*] *Bod. 1+*; man *LAUC.*

266. *in*] *Bod. 1+*; on *LAUC*.
     Montezumes] *Bod. 1+*; Mo-------*LAUC*.
267. *and*] *Bod. 1+*; with *LAUC*, *LCP*.
270. *that*] *Bod. 1+*; his *LAUC*.
271. *theirs*] *Bod. 1+*; them *LAUC*.
272. *conquered*] *Bod. 1+*; conquerour *LAUC*.
277. *bows*] *Bod. 1+*; bent *LAUC*.
285. *these*] *Bod. 1+*; those *LAUC*.
     the . . . long] have still the field *LAUC*.
286. *unknown*] *Bod. 1+*; known *LAUC*.
287. *A . . . gentry*] *Bod. 1+*; Of English gentry
     a gross ['1' and '2' placed respectively
     above the last two words] *LAUC*.
290. *that*] *Bod. 1+*; think *LAUC*.
     think] *Bod. 1+*; thing *LAUC*, *LCP*.
292. *counsel*] *Bod. 1+*; council *LCP*.
298. *Garway . . . great*] *Bod. 1+*; Garroway
     and *LAUC*.
300. *was still*] *Bod. 1+*; still was *LAUC*.
302. *Dunstan*] *Bod. 1+*; Dunstan's *LAUC*.
306. *total*] *Bod. 1+*; fatall *LAUC*.
309. *had*] *Bod. 1+*; t'had *LAUC*.
313. *clamour*] *Bod. 1+*; clamours *LCP*.
314. *want, the*] *Bod. 1+*; want and the *LCP*.
315. *the*] *Bod. 1+*; their *LAUC*.
318. *keels*] *Bod. 1+*; keel *LAUC*.
322. *mine and thine*] *Bod. 1+*; thine and mind
     BL 27, *LAUC*.
324. *lack, nor*] *Bod. 1+*; lacks nor *LCP*; lacks or
     LAUC.
326. *tire*] *Bod. 1+*; fire *BL 27*.
329. *enow*] *Bod. 1+*; enough *LCP*.
334. *But*] *Bod. 1+*; And *LAUC*.
338. *magic*] *Bod. 13+*; replaces a deleted word
     in *N 12*; bitter *Bod. 1*.
340. *fruit*] *Bod. 1+*; fruits *LCP*.
343. *Carteret*] *Bod. 1+*; Cartwright *LAUC*.
345. *morning's*] *Bod. 1+*; morning *LAUC*.
346. *blooms*] *Bod. 1+*; blowes *LAUC*.
     its] *Bod. 1+*; his *LAUC*.
349–50. *Now . . . deflower*] in *N 12*, these lines
     are enclosed within square brackets and
     '(Out' written next to l. 350 in the right-
     hand margin, probably in a hand different
     to that of the text.
354. *holiday*] *Bod. 1+*; Holy-day *LCP*.
355. *palace*] corrected from 'Castle' in *BL 27*.
356. *And*] *Bod. 1+*; He *LAUC*.
357. *durst to him*] *Bod. 1+*; 'gainst *LAUC*,
     LCP, *1697*.
360. *Sisyphus's*] *Bod. 1+*; Sisyphus his *LAUC*.

361. *while*] *Bod. 1+*; whilst *LCP*.
362. *secured . . . be saved*] *Bod. 1+*; might be
     secured . . . saved *LAUC*. *and*] *Bod. 1+*;
     whilst *1697*.
364. *else*] *Bod. 1+*; then *LCP*.
371. *among*] *Bod. 1+*; Amongst *LAUC*.
381. *concerned*] corrected from 'conserv'd'
     in *BL 27*. *for him damage*] *Bod. 1+*;
     dammage for him *LCP*.
383. *just*] *Bod. 1+*; first *LAUC*.
385. *the grains . . . kettle*] *Bod. 1+*; grannyes . . .
     kettles *LAUC*.
388. *crimes*] *Bod. 1+*; Brawls *LCP*.
392. *to*] *Bod. 1+*; would *LAUC*.
393. *chose*] *Bod. 1+*; thought *BL 27*.
398. *Of*] *Donno*; Off *1697+*.
402–5. Not in *LAUC*.
417. *well*] *Bod. 1+*; more *LAUC*; men *LCP*,
     1697.
418. *had . . . before*] *Bod. 1+*; before had lodg'd
     LAUC.
420. *mure*] *Bod. 1+*; barr *BL 27*.
422. *But*] *1689+*; That *Bod. 1*, *LCP*.
424. *flame*] *Bod. 1+*; flames *LAUC*, *LCP*.
     so] *Bod. 1+*; to *BL 27*, *LCP*, *1697*.
427. *to*] *Bod. 1+*; too *LCP*.
428. *Master*] *Bod. 1+*; Mr *LCP*; Monsieur *1697*.
431. *Dolman's*] *Bod. 1+*; Dutchman's *LAUC*.
433. *him*] not in *LAUC*.
442. Not in *LAUC*.
443. *the*] *Bod. 1+*; this *LCP*.
447. *heart*] *Bod. 1+*; hearts *LAUC*.
449. *unto . . . are*] *Bod. 1+*; are unto Breda *LAUC*.
450. *one . . . Harry*] *Bod. 1+*; Harvey one to
     Harvey *LAUC*.
451. *the*] *Bod. 1+*; this *LCP*.
454. *the*] *Bod. 1+*; a *LAUC*.
461. *ordered*] *N 12+*; order *Bod. 1*, *1689*.
462. *grant*] *Bod. 1*; give *N 12*, *LAUC*, *LCP*,
     1689.
463–4. Not in *Bod. 1*.
468. *a*] *Bod. 1*; & *BL 27*.
469. *came*] *Bod. 1+*; comes *LAUC*.
471. *a time*] *Bod. 1+*; times *LAUC*, *LCP*.
475. *in . . . he*] *Bod. 1+*; this . . . him *LAUC*.
479. *most*] *Bod. 1+*; more *LCP*.
481. *our*] *Bod. 1+*; one *LAUC*.
484. *army's*] *Bod. 1+*; armies *LCP*.
485. *loved*] *Bod. 1+*; thought *LAUC*.
486. *thinks . . . but*] *Bod. 1+*; think it is *LAUC*.
492. *was*] *Bod. 1+*; is *LAUC*; are *LCP*.

494. *banquiers*] *Bod. 1*; Bankers *LAUC, LCP, 1697*.

497. *at*] *Bod. 1*+; all *LAUC*.

499. *bid*] *Bod. 1*+; bids *LCP*.

500. *that's*] *Bod. 1*+; cheats *LCP, 1697*.
     at] *Bod. 1*+; yᵉ *LAUC*.

502. *he*] Bod. 1+; yᵃ (i.e., 'they') *BL 27*.

503. *with a scrip*] *Bod. 1*+; in a ship *LAUC*.
     scrip] *Bod. 1*+; skipp *BL 27*.

505. *when*] *Bod. 1*+; and *LAUC, LCP*.

512. *be'n*] *Bod. 1*+; b'on *LCP*.

513. *If*] *Bod. 1*+; Do *LCP*.

517. *call in*] *Bod. 1*+; all *LAUC*.

520. *may*] *Bod. 1*+; must *LAUC*.

522. *would*] *Bod. 1*+; of *LAUC, LCP*.

523. *ocean*] *Bod. 1*+; nation *LAUC*.

524. *among*] *Bod. 1*+; amongst *LCP*; along *LAUC*.

526. *ere*] *Bod. 1*+; o're *LAUC*.

529. *skies*] *Bod. 1*+; sky *LCP*.

535. *His*] *Bod. 1*+; The *LAUC*.

539. *on*] *Bod. 1*+; in *LAUC*.

545. *the*] *Bod. 1*+; not in *BL 27*.

549. A mark and a square bracket are placed before this line in *N 12*. *and*] *Bod. 1*+; the *N 12, LCP, LAUC, 1689*.

556. *calm*] *Bod. 1*+; cold *LAUC*.

565. *pours*] *Bod. 1*+; pour *LAUC*.

566. *thorough*] *Bod. 1*+; through *LCP*.
     bullet showers] *Bod. 1*+; bullets shower *LAUC*; bullets showers *1697*.

568. *So*] *Bod. 1*+; Sad *LAUC*.

569. *dwell*] *Bod. 1*+; live *BL 27*.

570. *Until*] *Bod. 1*+; Unless *BL 27*.

571. *his*] *Bod. 1*+; the *LAUC*.

572. *March*] *Bod. 1*+; March'd *LAUC*.
     the] Bod. 1+; their *LAUC*.

575. *bulk*] *Bod. 1*+; bulks *LAUC*.

576. *or*] *Bod. 1*+; and *LAUC*.

577. *Those*] *Bod. 1*+; These *LAUC*.

579. *The*] *Bod. 1*+; like *LAUC*.
     so] *Bod. 1*+; thô *LCP, 1697*; who *LAUC*.

582. *securely through*] *Bod. 1*+; securely up *LAUC*. *track*] *Bod. 1*; back *LAUC*.

584. *of pay*] *Bod. 1*+; of's pay *LCP*.

586. *And*] *Bod. 1*+; Now *LAUC*.
     now] *Bod. 1*+; do *LAUC*.

588. *so*] *Bod. 1*+; too *BL 27*.

590. *his*] *Bod. 1*+; her *LAUC*.

596. *the dismal*] *Bod. 1*+; that dismal *LCP*.

597. *gallants*] *Bod. 1*+; gallant *LAUC*.

604. *Which*] *Bod. 1*+; Who *LAUC, LCP*.

607. *ill-deserted*] *1689*+; ill-defended *Bod. 1, LAUC*.

609. *succour might*] *Bod. 1*+; doth *LAUC*.

613. *which*] *Bod. 1*+; that *LCP*.

614. *His*] *Bod. 1*+; It's *LAUC, LCP, 1697*.

616. *that*] *Bod. 1*+; it's *LAUC*. *their*] *Bod. 1*+; its *BL 27, LAUC*; his *LCP, 1697*.

618. *this*] *Bod. 1*+; his *LAUC*.

623. *Such*] *Bod. 1*+; So *LAUC*.

624. *the*] *Bod. 1*+; her *LCP*. *robbers for*] *Bod. 1*+; robber of *LAUC*.

628. *since*] *Bod. 1*+; 'cause *LCP*.

629. *chain's . . . fleet's*] *Bod. 1*+; fleet's . . . chain's *LAUC*.

633. *person*] *Bod. 1*+; stature *LAUC*.

635–6. *iv'ry . . . so*] *Bod. 1*; Joy . . too *BL 27*.

636. *and*] *Bod 1*+; or *LAUC*.

640. *nearer*] *Bod. 1*+; loudly *LAUC*.

643. *And*] *Bod. 1*+; But *BL 27, LCP, 1689*.
     he] *Bod. 1*+; next he *LAUC*.

644. *to . . . nearer*] *Bod. 1*+; nearer to him *LAUC, LCP*.

644–96. Not in *1697, LCP. LCP* indicates the lines that repeat in *The Loyal Scot*; *1697* does not.

652. *While*] *Bod. 1*+; Whilst *LAUC*.

654. *but*] *Bod. 1*+; yⁿ *LAUC*.

656. *and*] *Bod. 1*+; or *LAUC*.

660. *That*] *Bod. 1*+; Thou *LAUC*.

661. *Fixed*] *Bod. 1*+; First *LCP*.

662. *run*] *Bod. 1*+; ran *LAUC*.

663. *No*] *Bod. 1*+; Nor *LAUC, LCP*.

664. *Then*] *Bod. 1*+; Than *LCP*.

665. *But*] *Bod. 1*+; That *LCP*.

668. *its*] *Bod. 1*+; his *LAUC*.

673. *honours*] *Bod. 1*+; honour *LCP*.

674. *Inspire*] *Bod. 1*+; Inspir'd *LCP*.

675. *And*] *Bod. 1*+; A *LAUC*.

680. *of*] *Bod. 1*+; on *LAUC*.

681. *the*] *Bod. 1*+; that *LCP*.

685. *mind he*] *Bod. 1*+; soul had *BL 27*.

686. *soldered*] sodred; *BL 27* soder'd *Bod. 1, LAUC, N 12, 1689*.

687. *himself*] *Bod. 1*+; him down *LAUC*.

690. *that's warmed . . . gone*] *Bod. 1*+; yᵗ warmes . . . goes *LAUC*.

694. *if*] *Bod. 1*+; yet *LAUC*.

695. *and*] *Bod. 1*+; or *LAUC*.

696. *youth*] *Bod. 1*+; youths *LAUC*.

704. *tides*] *Bod. 1*+; sides *LCP*.

706.   shook] *Bod. 1*; strook *BL 27, 1689, 1697.*

708.   *had.. then*] *Bod. 1+*; then had been *LAUC.*

712.   *be burned*] *Bod. 1+*; should burn *LAUC, LCP, 1689, 1697.*

715.   *howl*] *1689+*; hole *LAUC, LCP, 1697*; 'howle' corrected to 'hole' in *BL 27.*

718.   *Wines . . . and*] *Bod. 1*; From the South Perfumes *N 12, BL 27, LAUC, LCP, 1689, 1697. and*] crossed out in *N 12.*

722.   *lest*] *Bod. 1+*; least *LAUC, LCP*; less *1697.*

728.   *Her*] *Bod. 1+*; Yᵉ *LAUC. timber*] *Bod. 1+*; timbers *LCP.*

729.   *shapes*] *Bod. 1+*; shape *LAUC, LCP.*

730.   *all*] *Bod. 1+*; much *LAUC. his*] *Bod. 1+*; her *BL 27*; yᵉ *LAUC.*

735-6. 'Sampson' written in left-had margin in *LAUC.*

739.   *in*] *Bod. 1+*; on *LAUC.*

741.   *to . . . right*] *Bod. 1+*; to course yet ever right *BL 27.*

742.   *space*] *Bod. 1+*; course *BL 27.*

747.   *change*] *Bod. 1+*; chance *LCP.*

748.   *When*] *Bod. 1+*; And *LAUC.*

752.   *the*] *Bod. 1+*; their *LAUC.*

753.   *moan*] *Bod. 1+*; mourn *LCP, 1697.*

755.   *Charles*] *Bod. 1+*; Charle *LAUC.*

759.   *swooning*] *Bod. 1+*; sounding *LAUC.*

761.   *farthing*] *Bod. 1+*; farthings *LAUC.*

764.   *her*] *Bod. 1, N 12, LCP*; here *1689.*

771.   *Who . . . follow . . . were beat*] *Bod. 1+*; Who'd . . . pursue . . . fleet was *LAUC.*

775-8. Come after l. 780 in *LAUC.*

777.   *all . . . cheated*] *Bod. 1*; cheated all our seamen *LAUC.*

778.   *And . . . swallow*] *Bod. 1+*; Who was't yᵗ swallowed all our prizes *LAUC.*

780.   *unrepairèd*] *Bod. 1+*; unprepared *LAUC, LCP, 1697.*

783-4. Come after l. 785 in *LAUC.*

785-7. '3,2,1' respectively against these three lines in left-hand margin in *LAUC.*

785.   *in*] *Bod. 1*; of *LAUC.*

788.   *If*] *Bod. 1+*; Of *LAUC.*

800.   *money*] *Bod. 1+*; treasure *LAUC.*

802.   *And*] *Bod. 1+*; He's *LAUC.*

803.   *less*] *Bod. 1+*; least *LAUC.*

804.   *counsellor*] *Bod. 1+*; Chanc'lour *LCP.*

807.   *But*] *Bod. 1+*; And *LCP, 1697.*

808.   *begin again*] *Bod. 1+*; again begin *LAUC.*

810.   *how to*] *Bod. 1+*; that may *LAUC.*

817.   *De*] *Bod. 1+*; not in *N 12, BL 27, 1689.*

819.   *said*] *Bod. 1+*; saith *LCP.*

829.   *are in stagecoach*] corrected to 'in stagecoach are' in *Bod. 1.*

834.   *And all . . . come*] *Bod. 1+*; With sun . . . all come up *LAUC.*

837.   *does*] *Bod. 1+*; doth *LCP.*

838.   *smoothened*] *Bod. 1+*; smoothed *LAUC, LCP.*

840.   *for . . . thence*] *Bod. 1+*; from thence three days *LAUC.*

845.   *While*] *Bod. 1+*; Whilst *LCP.*

848.   *thee*] not in *LAUC.*

853.   *day raised early*] *Bod. 1+*; early raised was *1697.*

854.   *Turnor's*] *Bod. 1+*; Turnor *LAUC.*

855.   *come*] *Bod. 1+*; came *LAUC, LCP.*

858.   *gave*] *Bod. 1+*; gives *LAUC.*
       leave] *Bod. 1+*; time *LAUC.*

861.   *with*] *Bod. 1+*; twixt *LAUC.*

864.   *cannot*] not in *LAUC.*

866.   *in*] *Bod. 1+*; with *LAUC. brain*] *Bod. 1+*; train *LCP, 1697.*

868.   *edge*] *Bod. 1+*; blade *LAUC.*

876.   *mushrumps*] *Bod. 1+*; mushroms *LAUC, LCP. in in*] *Bod. 1+*; in to *LAUC, 1697.*

877.   *grievance*] *Bod. 1+*; grievances *1697.*

885.   *dead*] *Bod. 1+*; dread *LAUC.*

892.   *her*] *Bod. 1+*; yᵉ *LAUC. or*] *Bod. 1+*; & *LAUC.*

896.   *Yet*] *Bod. 1+*; & *LAUC. the*] *Bod. 1+*; her *LCP.*

898.   *would*] *Bod. 1+*; could *LAUC.*

901.   *hand*] *Bod. 1+*; Heart *BL 27.*

903.   *her*] *Bod. 1+*; a *LCP, 1697.*

904.   *the'airy*] *Bod. 1+*; the angry *LAUC.*

907.   *startling*] *1689+*; startled *Bod. 1.*

908.   *that*] *Bod. 1+*; who *LAUC.*

909.   *cannon*] *Bod. 1+*; cannons *LAUC.*

911.   *did he*] *Bod. 1+*; he did *LCP.*
       fled] *Bod. 1+*; led *1689.*

912.   *But*] *Bod. 1+*; And *LAUC. he lies*] *Bod. 1+*; he's laid *LAUC.*

913.   *known*] *Bod. 1+*; vain *LCP.*

915.   *room*] *Bod. 1+*; rooms *LAUC.*

919.   *in*] *Bod. 1+*; on *LAUC.*

921.   *ghastly*] *Bod. 1+*; Ghostly *LCP, 1697.*

929.   *the*] *Bod. 1+*; did *LAUC.*

930.   *its*] *Bod. 1+*; his *LCP, 1697. enclose*] *Bod. 1+*; disclose *BL 27, LAUC.*

931.   *hearts*] *Bod. 1+*; thoughts *LAUC.*

936.   *to such*] *Bod. 1+*; so much *LAUC.*

938. *will*] *Bod. 1+*; would *LAUC.*
943. *arts*] *Bod. 1+*; acts *BL 27.*
948. *the . . . painter*] *Bod. 1+*; the painter and the poet *LAUC.*
951. *obscure*] *Bod. 1+*; obscured *LAUC. please*] *1689+*; prease *Bod. 1*; press *LAUC, 1697.*
956. *Sun*] *Bod. 1+*; Seen *LCP.*
960. *of*] *Bod. 1+*; from *LAUC.*
968. *our*] *Bod. 1*; yᵉ *BL 27*; this *LAUC, LCP, 1697. his*] *Bod. 1+*; this *1697.*
969. *on*] *Bod. 1*; by *BL 27, LAUC, LCP, 1697.*
977. *earthquake*] *Bod. 1+*; earthquakes *LCP.*
980. *hoard their*] *Bod. 1+*; hide yᵉ *LAUC.*
982. *razed*] *Bod. 1*; ras'd *LAUC*; rac't *1697.*
983. *whom*] *Bod. 1+*; who're *LAUC.*
984. *Nor guilt*] *Bod. 1+*; Whom neither *1689, 1697. nor*] *Bod. 1+*; not *BL 27.*
985. *gen'rous*] not in *1689.*
989. *there*] *Bod. 1+*; yᵉ *LAUC.*

The Loyal Scot

Sub-title. *Bod. 13+*; *By* Cleaveland's *Ghost upon the Death of Captain* Douglas *burnt on his Ship at* Chatham. *LCP, 1697*; By Cleveland's Ghost, upon occasion of the death of Capt. Douglas burnt on his ship at Chatham *Bod. 1*; by Cleveland's Ghost. Being a Recantation of his former Satyr; intituled, *The Rebel Scot*, *By Cleveland's Ghost*] not in *Bod. 13. Upon the*] *Bod. 13+*; Upon *NLS.*
1. *Of . . . when*] *Bod. 13*; When . . . of *BL 26, NLS.*
2. *marching*] *Bod. 13*; walking *BL 26, NLS. on*] *Bod. 13+*; thro' *1694.*
3. *straight*] *Bod. 13+*; all *BL 27, 1697. consulting gathered*] *Bod. 13+*; consulted gathering *Mg.*
8. *the warlike*] *Bod. 13+*; the noble *BL 25, BL 27*; their noble *Bod. 1*; their welcome *1694*; that Noble *LCP, 1697.*
9. *tumour*] *Bod. 1+*; humour *BL 26, Bod. 13, NLS.*
11–14. *For . . . art*] not in *BL 27.*
15–62. Not in *LCP.*
19–62. Not in *BL 27.*
19. *shady*] *Bod. 13+*; yellow *1697.*
22. *and cooled*] *Bod. 13+*; with cold *1694.*
24. *rustle*] *Bod. 13+*; rush and *BL 26, NLS*; rush *RS.*

27. *Fixed*] *Bod. 13+*; First *1694, 1697. faced*] *Bod. 13+*; fought *NLS.*
29. *comprehend*] *Bod. 13+*; apprehend *RS.*
31–2. Transposed in *Bod. 1, BL 25, 1694.*
32. *life*] *Bod. 13+*; time *BL 25, Bod. 1, RS, 1697.*
33. *them*] *Bod. 13+*; then *RS.*
34. *its*] *Bod. 13+*; his *BL 25, BL 26.*
36. *safely*] *Bod. 13+*; softly *RS.*
39. *glories*] *Bod. 13+*; Honours *1694.*
41. *soul doth*] *Bod. 13+*; breast doth *BL 26*; brest does *RS.*
43. *glad*] *Bod. 1+*; fierce *Bod. 13.*
45. *shape . . . which*] *Bod. 13+*; ship . . . with *BL 26*; ship . . . in *NLS.*
52. *altered*] *Bod. 13+*; altering *NLS, RS. soldered*] sold'red *1694*; sodered *Bod. 1, BL 25*; sodred *Bod. 13, NLS, 1697.*
53. *him down*] *Bod. 13+*; himself *Bod. 1, NLS, 1694.*
56. *hugs*] *Bod. 13+*; warm'd *1697. in a warm*] *Bod. 13+*; and went to *1697.*
57. *The*] 'His' in *1697* and *The Last Instructions*, l. 691.
60. *fame*] *Bod. 13+*; name *BL 25.*
63–4. Not in *1694, Lord.*
63. *Skip-saddles*] *Bod. 13*; Skip-sadled *Mg*; Skip Saddle *BL 26.*
66. *the . . . the*] *Bod. 13+*; our . . . our *LCP*; our . . . the *Υ 7, 1694.*
69. *or*] *Bod. 13+*; and *LCP, RS, 1697.*
72. *Our*] *Bod. 13+*; Two *BL 26, BL 27, NLS, RS. Nations*] *Bod. 13+*; factions *1694.*
73–4. *Shall . . . before*] not in *BL 25, Bod. 13, LCP, Υ 7, 1694, 1697.*
77. *Anatomists*] *Bod. 13+*; Anathomissos *NLS.*
78. *or*] *Bod. 13+*; and *LCP, 1697.*
79. *exceed their*] *Bod. 13+*; exceeds our *BL 25, Bod. 1, LCP, 1694.*
80. *kill*] *Bod. 13+*; ill *1694, 1697.*
87. *ethic*] *Bod. 13+*; Ethnick *BL 26, Mg. this*] *Bod. 13+*; that *NLS.*
88. *bank*] *Bod. 13+*; side *1694. th'other*] *Bod. 13+*; t'other *RS.*
90. *her*] *Bod. 13+*; the *BL 25. stream*] *Bod. 13+*; Streams *BL 25, NLS, LCP.*
93–5. These three lines are bracketed together in the right-hand margin in *BL 27.*
93. *right*] *Bod. 13+*; well *NLS.*
95–103. Not in *1694, Lord.*

96.   *Scotch*] *Bod. 13+*; Scots *BL 26, NLS, RS.*

99.   *deliver us*] *Bod. 13+*; deliver's *NLS.*
      the] *Bod. 1+*; a *BL 26, BL 27, Bod. 13, NLS, Υ 7, LCP.*

103.   *joint-stools*] *Bod. 13+*; joyn'd stools *BL 25, BL 26, Bod. 1.*

106.   *whisper*] *Bod. 13+*; whip us *1694.*

108–251.   Not in *1694.*

108–250.   Not in *Lord.*

112.   *not*] *Bod. 13+*; but *NLS. bogs*] *Bod. 13+*; boys *BL 25. sands*] *Bod. 13+*; Lands *BL 25, BL 26, Mg., NLS.*

114.   *your*] *Bod. 13+*; the *BL 25, LCP.*

115.   *inhabitable*] *Bod. 13*; unhabitable *BL 25, Bod. 1, LCP, RS, Υ 7, LCP, 1697*; uninhabitable *BL 27.*

116.   *hath*] *Bod. 13+*; had *BL 26.*

118–255.   Not in *1697.*

118.   *tear*] *Bod. 13+*; seize *BL 26, Mg, NLS.*

123.   *sent*] Not in *NLS.*

125.   *A*] *Bod. 13*; The *BL 26, BL 25, BL 27, NLS. an*] *Bod. 13+*; not in *NLS.*

126.   *their earths*] *Bod. 13+*; the earth *BL 26.*

127.   *musk ev'n*] *Bod. 1+*; dung the *Bod. 13, Υ 7*; dung even *BL 26, BL 27, NLS, RS.*

128.   *heat*] *Bod. 13*; hate *BL 25, BL 27, Bod. 1, RS, NLS, LCP.*

130.   *What*] *Bod. 13*; How *BL 25, BL 26.* (*Lord*) *are*] *Bod. 13+*; are Lord *BL 26, Mg.*

132.   *so forsook*] *Bod. 1+*; so mistook *Bod. 13, NLS, RS, Υ 7*; we mistook *BL 25, BL 26.*

137.   *faith*] *BL 26*; Souls *BL 25, Bod. 1, Bod. 13, LCP, Mg.*

139.   *Ah!*] *Bod. 13+*; As *BL 26, Mg.*

144.   *call*] *Bod. 13*; cowl *BL 25, Υ 7*; court *BL 26*; cawl *Bod. 1.*

145.   *The nation*] *Bod. 13*; Their nations *BL 26, NLS*; The nations *Bod. 1. curates*] *Bod. 1+*; court *Bod. 13.*

148.   *moulded*] *Bod. 13+*; modell'd *LCP.*

150–3.   Not in *LCP.*

152.   *That*] *Bod. 13+*; What *BL 27. alone . . . ties*] *Bod. 13+*; can loose this spell that mankind ties *BL 27.*

153.   *For only*] *Bod. 13+*; And none but *Bod. 1. For*] *Bod. 13+*; And *BL 26, Mg., NLS, RS*; 'Tis *BL 27. alone*] *Bod. 13+*; at once *BL 26.*

154.   *treated*] *Bod. 13+*; heated *BL 26, RS*; heald^d *NLS. here*] 'shall' interpolated after 'here' in *NLS.*

155.   *your*] *Bod. 1+*; the *Bod. 13, Υ 7.*

157.   *commendam*] *Bod. 13+*; commendum *BL 25, BL 27.*

158.   *vice*] *Bod. 13+*; [blank space] *BL 26. tempt*] *BL 26, Mg.*; whet *BL 27, Bod. 1, Bod. 13, Υ 7.*

160.   *the*] *Bod. 1*; a *BL 26, BL 27, Bod. 13, NLS, Υ 7. baron*] *BL 26, Mg.*; barren *Bod. 13. bishop*] *Bod. 13+*; prelate *Bod. 1.*

163.   *ordure*] *Bod. 13+*; ordures *BL 27*; orders *BL 26, NLS, Mg.*

164.   *now*] *Bod. 13+*; priest *BL 26*; priests *NLS.*

165.   *fits . . . heads*] *Bod. 13+*; fills . . . head *NLS. heads*] *Bod. 13+*; head *BL 25. four*] *Bod. 13+*; full four *BL 26, BL 27, NLS, Υ 7.*

167.   *Arius*] *Bod. 13+*; [blank space] *BL 26. Athanasian*] *Bod. 13+*; Athanasius *NLS.*

171.   *faith*] *Bod. 13+*; silk *BL 26, BL 27, Mg, NLS, RS*; silks *BL 25, Bod. 1.*

174.   *toils*] *Bod. 13+*; smiles *BL 26, BL 27, BL 26, Mg*; tyles *Bod. 1.*

177.   *armpits*] *NLS+*; armpipes *Bod. 13.*

178.   *one . . . a*] *Bod. 13+*; mist bucks, but Sheldon n'ere mist *Bod. 1. but*] *Bod. 13+*; be *Υ 7.*

179.   *Sheldon*] *Bod. 13+*; Patriarch *Bod. 1.*

182.   *prelate*] *Bod. 13+*; Bishop *RS.*

184.   *adapt*] *Bod. 13+*; adopt *BL 25, RS.*

185.   *smutty*] *Bod. 13+*; smoot *RS. clean*] *Bod. 13+*; pure *Υ 7.*

186.   *uncase*] *Bod. 13+*; uncease *NLS.*

187.   *copes*] *NLS+*; Lopes *Bod. 13.*

188.   *and*] *Bod. 13*; like *NLS, RS.*

189.   *their . . . cat*] *Bod. 13+*; his neighbour bishop grows or eate *NLS. their*] *Bod. 13+*; his *RS. bishop turn*] *Bod. 13+*; Bishops are *LCP*; does Bishop turn *RS. turn*] *Bod. 13+*; grew *BL 25*; grow *BL 27, Bod. 1. and*] *Bod. 13+*; or *RS.*

190–9.   Not in *BL 25, LCP.*

190.   *Archbishop Bel*] *Bod. 13+*; Archbishop's Belly *BL 26, BL 27, Mg, NLS, RS.*

191.   *snake. . . . swell*] *Bod. 13+*; Snakes that Toads do eate to Dragoons Swellye *NLS*; snakes y^t eat toads will to dragons swelly *BL 27. swell*] *Bod. 13+*; swell yee *BL 26*; swell yea *Mg.*

192–9.   Not in *Bod. 1, NLS.*

193.   *distrained*] *Bod. 1+*; restrayn'd *Bod. 13.*

199.   *A*] *Bod. 13+*; The *RS.*

200.   *the . . . that*] *Bod. 13+*; that . . . the *LCP.*

202. *And*] *Bod. 13+*; What *LCP.*
205. *What*] *Bod. 13+*; When *NLS.*
206–7. *But . . . jowl*] not in *Bod. 13, Υ 7.*
207. *bishop's*] *Bod. 13+*; bishop *Mg.*
    perks] *Bod. 13+*; creeps *BL 26.*
    jowl] *Bod. 13+*; joyl *RS.*
213. *It*] *Bod. 13+*; He *BL 26, Mg, NLS,*
    Rs. dwelt] *Bod. 13+* liv'd *LCP.*
216. *moot*] *Bod. 13+*; meet *BL 27, NLS.*
217. *foot*] *Bod. 13+*; feet *BL 27, NLS.*
218. *bishops even*] *Bod. 13+*; even bishops
    BL 26, Mg.
220. *more clam'rous yet*] *Bod. 13+*;
    are Clamourous and *LCP.*
    yet] not in *BL 25, BL 27.*
221. *ceremonies*] *Bod. 13*; ceremonies do *RS.*
222. *with*] *Bod. 13+*; to *BL 25, BL 27, NLS,*
    RS, LCP.
224–36. Written with indented left-hand margin
    in *BL 27.*
224–5. *To . . . indifferent*] not in *BL 27, RS.*
226–7. inserted in *BL 27, Bod. 1, LCP.*
228. *conform's*] *Bod. 13+*; conform *LCP.*
229. *is*] *NLS+*; [?]us *Bod. 13.*
230–1. Placed after l. 225 in *Bod. 1.*
231. *cheat . . . plague-*] *Bod. 13+*; steal . . .
    poors *NLS. indifferent*] is indifferent *LCP.*
232. *rebabel*] *Bod. 13+*; rebuild St. *BL 27,*
    Mg, RS; rebuilt *NLS*; build Babel *LCP.*
236. *with . . . their*] *Bod. 13+*; without a *NLS.*
240. *cool*] *Bod. 13+*; jool *NLS.*
242. *though so*] *Bod. 13+*; so much *NLS.*
243. *his postern*] *Bod. 13+*; this postren *NLS.*
250. *bias*] *Bod. 13+*; barr *BL 27.*
253. *those*] *Bod. 13+*; these *LCP.*
256. *climes*] *Bod. 13+*; times *BL 25* 'times'
    corrected from 'climes' in *Bod. 1.*
257. *For*] *Bod. 13+*; Her *BL 27.*
261. *heart*] *Bod. 13+*; hears *Bod. 1.*
262. *as*] *Bod. 13+*; a *1694.*
263. *accent*] *Bod. 1+*; Action *Bod. 13.*
266. *men*] *Bod. 13+*; man *RS.*
269. *Does*] *Bod. 13+*; Do *BL 25, NLS, LCP,*
    1697.
270. *we*] *Bod. 13+*; they *1694.*
272. *men's*] *Bod. 13+*; Man *BL 27, Bod. 1,*
    RS, LCP. all] *Bod. 1*; are *BL 27,*
    Bod. 13, NLS, Υ 7, LCP.
274. *For*] *Bod. 13+*; From *BL 27.*
    each loyal breast] *Bod. 13+*; loyal
    breast ['all breasts' crossed out] *Υ 7.*
275. *interest*] *Bod. 13+*; innocence *Υ 7.*

277. *and Scotch*] *Bod. 13+*; or Scotch *Bod. 1.*
279. *will*] *Bod. 13+*; wills *LCP.*
280. *twin*] *Bod. 13+*; two *NLS.*
    atone] *Bod. 1+*; Alone *Bod. 13.*
281. *them*] *Bod. 13+*; us *Bod. 1, NLS, RS,*
    LCP, 1694, 1697; as *BL 27.*
282. *who*] that *LCP, 1697.*
285. *comb-case*] *Bod. 13+*; combat *BL 26,*
    BL 27, Mg, NLS, RS, 1694.
286. *discern*] *Bod. 13+*; discerns *LCP.*
    their] *Bod. 13+*; his *BL 25, Bod. 1.*
287. *close*] *Bod. 13*; loose *BL 27, NLS, RS*;
    lose *Bod. 1, Mg, LCP, 1694, 1697.*
291. *noble*] *Bod. 13+*; nobly *BL 27, 1694. exhort*]
    Bod. 1+; extort *Bod. 13, BL 25, 1697.*
293. *The . . . set*] *Bod. 13+*; My fault against my
    Recantation set *1694, Lord*; not in *1697.*
295. *singly*] *Bod. 1+*; single *Bod. 1, LCP,*
    1694, 1697.
296. *crime*] *Bod. 13+*; crimes *1697.*
301. *Metempsychosed*] *Bod. 13+*; Metamorphos'd
    NLS. to] *Bod. 13+*; in *BL 25, Bod. 1.*

The Statue in Stocks-Market

Title. *Bod. 1*; Vpon Sʳ Robert Viners setting up
    yᵉ Kings Statue on Horsebacke. &c. *Bod.*
    12; Upon Sʳ Vyners setting up the Statue,
    &c. *LAC 3*; Vpon Sʳ Robert's setting up ye
    statue *Bod. 14*; On Sir Robt Vyner setting
    up the Kings Statue in Stocks Markett
    1673 P 1; On Sʳ. Robert Viners erecting
    the Kings Statue *P 5*; On the Statue in the
    Stock Markett *Li.*
1. *cities, that to the fierce*] *Bod. 1*; Cittizens,
    that to the *N 5*; Citizens, that to their
    1689. to the] *Bod. 1*; unto *BL 14. the fierce*]
    their first *Li.*; the first *N 5.*
2. *their . . . citadells*] their owne Cittadell *Li.,*
    N 5.
3. *the King's*] *Bod. 1*; this *Bod. 14, BL 14,*
    LAC 3, N 6, VA 1.
4. *banker*] *Bod. 1, LAC 3*; Bankers *BL 14*;
    a Broker *1689.*
5. *knightly . . . generous*] *Bod. 1*;
    mighty . . . gracious Li., N 5.
7. *word*] *Bod. 1*; honour *P 5.*
8. *vows*] *Li., N 6, 1689*; waits *Bod. 1*; prays
    VA 1. for] *Bod. 1*; not in *BL 14. for a*
    calm] *Bod. 1*; in a storm *BL 20. absolved*]
    Bod. 1; dissolv'd *P 1. wreck*] *Bod. 1*; wrack
    LAC 3; rack *Bod. 14.*

10.   *a revenge and a malice*] *Bod. 1*; a plot and malice *P 5*.

12.   *monster*] *Bod. 1*; Monkey *Li.*, *N 5*; *1689*.

14.   *Yet*] *Bod. 1+*; But *LAC 3*, *VA 1*. *affirm*] *Bod. 1*; assure *Li.*, *N 5*.

15–16.   Not in *N 6*.

17.   *disfigured*] *Bod. 1*; disguised *Li.*, *N 5*, *1671*; corrected from 'disguised' in *Bod. 14*.

19.   *in his seat*] in the saddle *P 3*; are his feet *Li.*

20.   *Even*] Not in *Li. firmer*] *Bod. 1*; faster *Li.*; finer *VA 1*.

21–4.   Not in *N 6*.

21.   *suit*] *Bod. 1*; fitt *Li.*

22.   *the*] *Bod. 1*; oft *Li.*

24.   *bought too*] Bod. 1; oft bought *Li.*

25–8.   Not in *P 5*.

25.   *This . . . surely*] *Bod. 1*; That . . . sure *BL 14*; The . . . sure *BL 20*. *scandalous*] *Bod. 1*; dangerous *Li.*, *1689*.

26.   *pictures*] *Bod. 1*; peices *BL 20*.

28.   *reasons more*] *Bod. 1+*; treason most *N 5*.

31.   *workmanship . . . not*] *Bod. 1+*; the thing is none of *Li.*, *N 5*.

34.   *liege*] *Bod. 1*; King *P 1*.

35.   *deals*] *Bod. 1*; Deale *BL 14*, *LAC 3*. *do*] *Bod. 1+*; did *LAC 3*.

36.   *meant it*] *Bod. 1+*; it meant *LAC 3*.

39.   *in*] *Bod. 1*; with the *Li.*, *N 5*.

40.   *Compter removed*] *Bod. 1*; Counter removed *LAC 3*, *N 6*; Counter, convey'd *BL 14*, *VA 1*.

41–4 and 45–8 transposed in *P 1*.

41.   *Methinks*] *Bod. 1*; Men *P 5*.

45.   *beams*] *Bod. 1*; errors *Li.*

46.   express] *Bod. 1+*; expose *Li. shattered*] *Bod. 1+*; scatterd *P 5*; shallow *BL 20*. *rags*] *Bod. 1+*; ragg *LAC 3*, *N 6*.

47.   *shattered*] *Bod. 1+*; scattered *P 5*; tattered *BL 20*, *LAC 3*, *N 6*, *VA 1*.

49.   *Sure*] *Bod. 1*; Surely ___ [set a line above] in *BL 14*. *repaying*] *Bod. 1*; repairing *BL 14*, *N 6*, *P 5*; restoring *Bod. 14*. *king . . . his*] *Bod. 1+*; Knight . . . the *Li.*, *N 5*.

50.   *now*] not in *BL 14*, *Li.*, *VA 1*.

51.   *If*] *Bod. 1*; Now *BL 14*, *VA 1*. *Indies . . . Smryna*] *Bod. 1*; Judges . . . Parliament *Li.*, *N 5*. *not*] not in *BL 20*.

53.   *we*] *Bod. 1+*; y^t we; they Li.

54.   *reform*] *Bod. 1*; refine *Bod. 12*; deform *P 5*.

55.   *never*] *Bod. 1+*; nere *LAC 3*.

56.   *'tis*] *Bod. 1+*; it is *LAC 3*; he's *BL 20*.

57.   *restore*] *Bod. 1*; pray restore *LAC 3*, *VA 1*; pray give *Li.*, *N 5*; return *P 5*.

58.   *in . . . for*] *Bod. 1+*; for . . . in *BL 20*. *December*] *Bod. 1*; Summer *BL 20*; September *VA 1*.

60.   *better*] *Bod. 1*; rather *P 1*. *brother*] *Bod. 1*; P_fyd Brother *Li.*, *N 5*.

The Statue at Charing Cross

Title.]   *Bod. 13+*; Upon the old Kings Statue seet up in Brass at Chareing Cross *P 1*; no title in *LAC 3*; Upon the Statue at Charing Cross/Charles the first *N 5*; On the Statue at Charing Crosse *VA 1*.

1.   Not in *BL 6*.

2.   *continues*] *Bod. 13+*; continue *BL 14*. *blinded*] *Bod. 13+*; buffld *BL 6*. *board*] *Bod. 13+*; boards *LAC 3*.

4.   *Punchinello . . . be*] *Bod. 13+*; we must have Punchinello *BL 6*. *be*] *Bod. 13+*; is *BL 14*, *N 5*, *VA 1*.

6.   *theatre*] *Bod. 13+*; feather *N 5*.

5.   *great disrespect*] *Bod. 13+*; much Respect *BL 14*.

8.   *legally*] *Bod. 13+*; lately *VA 1*. *of*] *Bod. 18+*; at *LAC 3*; not in *N 5*.

10.   *the . . . it*] *Bod. 13+*; a Guard & a Garden could not me [?one] *Bod. 17*, *Bod. 28*, *LAC 3*, *N 5*, *P 1*, *VA 1*; a Guard and a Garden, would not one *BL 14*.

11.   *And . . . never*] *Bod. 13+*; For . . . not *LAC 3*.

12.   *Any*] not in *LAC 3*. *mispend*] *Bod. 13+*; may spend *LAC 3*.

13.   *Were . . . kept . . . sheathing*] *Bod. 13+*; Now . . . yet . . . sheaving *LAC 3*; Were . . . *VA 1*.

14.   *armado*] *Bod. 13+*; Armada *BL 6*.

17.   *No*] *Bod. 13+*; Nor *LAC 3*. *poor*] *Bod. 12*, *P 1*; old *Bod. 13+*.

18.   *here*] *Bod. 13+*; now *LAC 3*.

19.   *the . . . and the*] *Bod. 13+*; your . . . and yor *BL 6*; the . . . and *LAC 3*.

21.   *the . . . men*] *Bod. 13+*; this . . . us *LAC 3*.

22.   *their*] *Bod. 13+*; the *LAC 3*. *stopped*] *Bod. 13+*; lost *Bod. 28*, *VA 1*. *fooled*] *Bod. 13+*; fed *VA 1*.

23.   *And . . . the old*] *Bod. 13+*; Now . . . on him *LAC 3*; No . . . on his *N 5*. *forty*] *Bod. 13+*; twenty *VA 1*.

24. *He'll*] *Bod. 13+*; But he'll *LAC 3*. 'ere long' after 'us' in *BL 6*.

25. *but of*] *Bod. 13+*; nor *LAC 3*.

26. *up*] *Bod. 13+*; down *LAC 3, P 1*.

29. *had gained*] *Bod. 13+*; gaine *LAC 3*.

30. *though prudent*] *Bod. 13+*; thought fitt *LAC 3*; Trick thought *VA 1*.

31. *herbs . . . of fruit*] *Bod. 13+*; yᵉ herbs . . . yᵉ fruit *LAC 3*.

33. *then*] *Bod. 13+*; pray *LAC 3*.

35. *twice*] *Bod. 13+*; heire *LAC 3*.

36. *far*] *Bod. 13*; long *LAC 3*.

37. *then . . . new be*] *Bod. 13+*; Sʳ . . . never so *LAC 3*.

38. *was*] *Bod. 13+*; were *BL 6*.

40. *guineas . . . of*] *Bod. 13+*; guinea grudge us prince of a *LAC 3*.

41. *nice*] *Bod. 13+*; wise *BL 6*.

42. *That*] *Bod. 13+*; And *BL 6*.

44. *we've lost*] *Bod. 13+*; we lose *P 1, BL 14, Bod. 12*.

45. *barties*] *Bod. 13+*; Bartu's *BL 6*; bartues *Bod. 28, N 5, VA 1*; partys we *P 1*.

48. *That a*] *Bod. 13+*; A *LAC 3*.

50. *list*] *Bod. 13+*; Roll *Bod. 12, LAC 3, P 1*.

51. *that so many voters*] *Bod. 13+*; her so many notes *P 1*.

52. *As would . . . with*] *Bod. 13+*; Would . . . at *LAC 3*. *tax*] *Bod. 13+*; session *P 1*. *them*] *Bod. 13+*; him *P 1, VA 1*.

On the Victory obtained by Blake over the Spaniards, in the Bay of Santa Cruz, in the Island of Tenerife, 1657

Title. *1681*; To His Highness On His late Victory in the Bay of Santa Cruz, in the Island of Tenerife *H* To his Highnesse on his late victory in the Bay of Sancta Cruze in the Island of Tenneriff *57'* *P*; On the Victory over the Spaniards in the Bay of Santa Cruz, in the island of Tenerife *1674*.

1–2. *Now does . . . old*] *1681*; The Spaniards Fleet from the Havanna now,/With sails extended doth the Ocean plow *H, P*.

1.   *for*] *1681*; to *1674*.

3.   *swum*] *1681*; swoome *P*.

9.   *entrails*] *P, H*; intrails *1674*; intails *1681*.

12. *caused*] *1681*; bred *H*.

14. *you*] *1681*; we *1674*.

16. *are your*] *1681*; th'English *1674*.

17. *who*] *1681*; that *P*.

19. *lest*] *1681*; least *P*.

20. *English*] *1681*; our dread *1674*.

21. *choose*] *1681*; 'chose' or 'chase' *P*.

22. *suppress*] *1681*; dispell *P*; subdue it.

23. *their's*] their fear. *vanishes*] *1681*; vanisheth *H*.

24. *sweet Canary*] *1681*; blest Canarian *P*.

25–52. Not in *H, P*.

53. *There the*] *1681*; Isles whose *H, P* (25).

55. *They*] *1681*; Who *H, P* (27).

57. *With . . . grow*] *1681*; Gold which so guilty is, that where it grows *H, P* (29). *still where that*] *1681*; where e're it *1674*.

58. *know*] *1681*; knows *H, P* (30).

59–60. Not in *P*.

59. *when*] *1681*; while *1674*.

60. *does*] *1681*; it *1674*.

62. *from thence removed*] *1681*; removed from them *H* (34).

64. *If*] *1681*; Since *H, P* (36).

65–6. Not in *H, P*.

65. *you*] *1681*; we *1674*.

66. *1681*; Again may conquer, this is left unsung *1674*.

68. *there*] *1681*; doth *H* (38); does *P*.

70. *That place . . . die*] *1681*; That place did greet, where they are doomed to die *H, P* (40).

71. *did*] *1681*; doth *H* (41); does *P*.

72. *your*] *1681*; the *H, P* (42), *1674*.

73–4. Not in *H, P*.

75. *all*] *1681*; do *1674*.

76. *much*] *1681*; that's *H* (44).

79–80. Not in *H, P*.

81. *For*] *1681* But *H, P* (47).

82. *grief*] *1681*; fear *H, P* (48). *grape's*] *1681*; wine's *H* (48), wynes *P*.

83. *learned*] *1681*; learn *H, P* (49). *terror*] *1681*; wonder *H, P* (49)g. *nor*] *1681*; no *H* (49).

85. *was*] *1681*; 'twas *H* (51).

86. *Which*] *1681*; Who *H, P* (52).

87. *on*] *1681*; in *P*. *that*] *1681*; which *H, P* (53).

93. *Fond*] stupid. *who*] *1681*; that *P*. *works*] *1681*; work *H* (59).

94. *your*] *1681*; our *H, P* (60).

95. *toil*] *1681*; toils *P, 1674*. *became*] *1681*; become *H* (61).

98. *Wish*] *1681*; wished *1674*. *he*] *1681*; they *1681*.

99.	*Has*] *1681*; Hath *H* (65), *1674*.		135.	*severed are so far*] *1681*; so far severed are *1674*.
100.	*does*] *1681*; doth *H* (66).			
101.	*your renown*] *1681*; England's fame *P*, *H* (67). *your*] *1681*; our *1674*. *does*] *1681*; doth *H* (67).		136.	*the*] *1681*; fierce *1674*.
			138.	*there*] *1681*; do *P*.
			139.	*or . . . or*] either . . . or. *or*] *1681*; a *P*.
103.	*Who . . . say*] *1681*; Whose trenches viewed, he to his men did say *H*, *P* (69).		140.	*must one*] *1681*; one must *P*. *there*] *1681*; here *H*, *P* (106).
104.	*their strength*] *1681*; those works *H* (70); those Forts *P*.		141.	*engaged*] *1681*; engage *H* (107).
			144.	*with*] *1681*; by H (110).
105.	*that*] *1681*; them *H*, *P* (71).		145.	*For your*] *1681*; England's *1674*. *there*] *1681*; Here *H* (111).
107–8.	Placed after 110 in *H*, *P*.			
107.	*there*] *1681*; do *P*. *so . . . strong*] *1681*; in every place *H*, *P*.		146.	*ev'n*] *1681*; upon *H* (112). *on*] *1681*; in *P*.
108.	*Do not*] *1681*; Cannot *P*.		148.	*those*] *1681*; them *P*.
111.	*does*] *1681*; doth *H* (77).		151.	*their . . . sea*] *1681*; the sea theire Wealth *P*. *does*] *1681*; doth *H* (117).
112.	*for now*] *1681*; because *H* (78).			
114.	*And all . . . cause*] *1681*; And all assum'd his courage for the Cause *1674*. *assume*] *1681*; assumes *P*.		152.	*cause*] *1681*; do *H* (118).
			153.	*those treasures*] *1681*; that Treasure *P*.
			154.	*large, and deep*] *1681*; bottomless *H*, *P* (120).
115.	*unto them*] *1681*; our nation *H*, *P* (81).		155.	*them*] *1681*; it *P*.
118.	*laurel*] *1681*; laurels *H* (84).		156.	*place unto*] *1681*; quiet to *H*, *P* (122) [corrected from 'quitt' in *P*].
119.	*now begins*] *1681*; doth begin *H* (85). *begins the*] *1681*; begin a *P*.			
			157.	*your*] *1681*; our *1674*.
125.	*Fate . . . brought*] *1681*; Fate had these fleets, betwixt the two worlds brought *H*, *P* (91); Fate had those fleets just between both worlds brought *1674*.		158.	*There they*] *1681*; They here *H*, *P* (124). *destroy*] *1681*; destroyed *1674*.
			159.	*the*] *1681*; this *P*.
			162.	*does*] *1681*; doth *H* (128).
127.	*Thousands of ways*] *1681*; By thousand ways *H*, *P* (93).		163.	*then*] *1681*; soon *H*, *P* (129).
			164.	*brings*] *1681*; bringst *H* (130).
129.	*aspire*] *1674*; a spire *1681*.		165–6.	Not in *H*, *P*.
130.	*then*] *1681*; there *1674*.		165.	*that*] *1681*; which *1674*.
131.	*was*] *1681*; is *P*.		167.	*in every place*] *1681*; for you, aloud *P*.
133.	*leagues*] *1681*; miles *P*.		168.	*you*] *1681*; us *1674*.

Appendix 4
List of Poems of Uncertain Attribution

Advice to a Painter to draw the Duke by
  In *Bod. 1*; first print publication in 1679; attrib.
  John Ayloffe, Henry Savile and Rochester.
A Ballad call'd the Chequer Inn
  In *Bod. 1*; first print publication in 1726; rejected
  by Lord; attrib. in some MSS to Henry Savile.
A Ballad called the Haymarket Hectors (Upon the
Cutting of Sir John Coventry's Nose)
  In *Bod. 1*; first print publication in 1704; anonymous in most MSS and print witnesses.
Britannia and Rawleigh
  In *Bod. 1*; first print publication in 1689;
  attributed to John Ayloffe.
A Country Clowne call'd Hodge Went to view the
Pyramid, pray mark what did ensue
  In *Bod. 12*; first print publication in 1726 (*Cooke*);
  anonymous in most MS witnesses.
A Dialogue between the Two Horses
  In *Bod. 13*; first print publication in 1689; rejected
  by Lord.
The Doctor turn'd Justice
  In *Bod. 1*; appears anonymously.
The Dream of the Cabal: A Prophetical Satire Anno
1672
The Fifth Advice to a Painter
  In *BL 20*; first print publication in *1667³*; regarded
  as anonymous by all editors.
The Fourth Advice to a Painter
  In *Bod. 12*; first print publication in *1667³*;
  regarded as anonymous by all editors.

Further Advice to a Painter
  In *Bod. 12*, *Bod. 13*; first print publication in 1697;
  rejected by Lord, doubted by Chernaik.
An Historical Poem
  In *Bod. 12*; first print publication in 1689; rejected
  by Lord.
The Kings Vowes
  In *Bod. 1*; first print publication in 1689.
  Attributed to Lord Buckhurst in *Υ 3*, and to the
  Duke of Buckingham.
Nostradamus' Prophecy
  In *Bod. 12*; first print publication in 1689; rejected
  by Lord; associated with John Ayloffe.
Oceana and Britannia
  In *Bod. 12*, *Bod. 13*; first print publication in 1726
  (*Cooke*); anonymous in all MSS witnesses.
On the Monument
  In *Bod. 1*; first print publication in 1703–4;
  anonymous in all MSS witnesses.
Upon his Grand-Children
  First print publication in *1667³*; rejected by Lord
  and Chernaik.
Upon his House
  First print publication in *1667³*; rejected by Lord
  and Chernaik.
Upon his Majesties being made free of the City
  In *Bod. 1*, *Bod. 12*; first print publication 1689.

BIBLIOGRAPHY OF REFERENCES CITED

Unless otherwise stated, the place of publication is London.

ABBOTT, WILBUR CORTEZ (1937–47). *The Writings and Speeches of Oliver Cromwell*. 4 vols. Cambridge, MA.

ABRAHAM, LYNDY (1990). *Marvell and Alchemy*. Aldershot and Brookfield, VT.

ÅKERMAN, SUSANNA (1991). *Queen Christina of Sweden and her Circle: the Transformation of a Seventeenth-century Philosophical Libertine*. Leiden and New York.

ALLEN, DON CAMERON (1960). *Image and Meaning; Metaphoric Traditions in Renaissance Poetry*. Baltimore, MD.

ALPERS, PAUL (1996). *What is Pastoral?* Chicago.

AMUSSEN, SUSAN and KISHLANSKY, MARK A., eds (1995). *Political Culture and Cultural Politics in Early Modern England: Essays Presented to David Underdown*. Manchester.

ARCKENHOLTZ, JOHANN (1751–60). *Mémoires concernant Christine reine de Suède: pour servir d'éclaircissement à l'histoire de son regne et principalement de sa vie privée, et aux événemens de l'histoire de son tems civile et littéraire: suivis de deux ouvrages de cette savante princesse, qui n'ont jamais été imprimés*. Amsterdam and Leipzig.

ARMITAGE, DAVID, HIMY, ARMAND and SKINNER, QUENTIN, eds (1995). *Milton and Republicanism*. Cambridge and New York.

—— (2000). *The Ideological Origins of the British Empire*. Cambridge and New York.

ASHTON, ROBERT (1994). *Counter-Revolution: the Second Civil War and its Origins, 1646–8*. New Haven, CT and London.

ATTWATER, Donald (1965). *A Dictionary of Saints*. Harmondsworth.

AUBIN, ROBERT ARNOLD, ed. (1943). *London in Flames, London in Glory; Poems on the Fire and Rebuilding of London, 1666–1709*. New Brunswick, NJ.

AUBREY, JOHN (1898). *'Brief Lives', Chiefly of Contemporaries, Set Down by John Aubrey, Between the Years 1669 and 1696*. ed. Andrew Clark, 2 vols. Oxford.

BADLEY, WILLIAM JOHN (1994). 'A New Reading of Andrew Marvell's Mower Poems' (unpublished PhD dissertation, Middle Tennessee State University).

BAKER, DAVID J. (1997). *Between Nations: Shakespeare, Spenſer, Marvell and the Question of Britain*. Stanford, CA.

BEALES, DEREK and BEST, GEOFFREY, eds (1985). *History, Society and the Churches: Essays in Honour of Owen Chadwick*. Cambridge.

BELL, MAUREEN, *et al.*, eds (2001). *Re-constructing the Book. Literary Texts in Transmission*. Aldershot, Burlington, VT, Singapore and Sydney.

BERGERON, DAVID M. (1971). *English Civic Pageantry, 1558–1642*. Columbia, SC.

BERTHOFF, ANNE E. (1970). *The Resolved Soul: a Study of Marvell's Major Poems*. Princeton, NJ.

BLACK, JEREMY, ed. (1997). *Culture and Society in Britain 1660–1800*. Manchester and New York.

BOLD, JOHN (1989). *John Webb: Architectural Theory and Practice in the Seventeenth Century*. Oxford and New York.

BRADBROOK, M.C. and LLOYD-THOMAS, M.G. (1940). *Andrew Marvell*. Cambridge.

BRETT, R.L., ed. (1979). *Andrew Marvell: Essays on the Tercentenary of his Death*. Oxford.

BROOKS, CLEANTH (1991). *Historical Evidence and the Reading of Seventeenth-Century Poetry*. Columbia, MO.

BROWER, REUBEN, VENDLER, HELEN and HOLLANDER, JOHN, eds (1973). *I. A. Richards: Essays in His Honor*. New York and London.

BURNS, J.H., ed., assisted by Mark Goldie (1991). *The Cambridge History of Political Thought, 1450–1700*. Cambridge and New York.

BURT, RICHARD and ARCHER, JOHN MICHAEL, eds (1994). *Enclosure Acts: Sexuality, Property, and Culture in Early Modern England*. Ithaca, NY.

CAMPBELL, THOMAS, ed. (1819). *Specimens of the British Poets*.

CAPP, B.S. (1972). *The Fifth Monarchy Men. A Study in Seventeenth-Century English Millenarianism*.

—— (1989). *Cromwell's Navy: The Fleet and the English Revolution, 1648–1660*. Oxford and New York.

CAREY, JOHN, ed. (1969). *Andrew Marvell. A Critical Anthology*. Harmondsworth.

CARR-GOMM, PHILIP (1991). *The Elements of the Druid tradition*. Shaftesbury.

CHAMBERS, A.B. (1991). *Andrew Marvell and Edmund Waller: Seventeenth-Century Praise and Restoration Satire*. University Park, PA.

CHANEY, EDWARD (1985). *The Grand Tour and the Great Rebellion: Richard Lassels and 'The Voyage of Italy' in the Seventeenth Century*. Geneva.

CHAUDHURI, SUKANTA (1989). *Renaissance Pastoral and its English Developments*. Oxford and New York.

CHERNAIK, WARREN (1983). *The Poet's Time: Politics and Religion in the Work of Andrew Marvell*. Cambridge.

CHERNAIK, WARREN and DZELZAINIS, MARTIN, eds (1999). *Marvell and Liberty*. Basingstoke and New York.

CHESTER, ALLAN GRIFFITH (1932). *Thomas May: Man of Letters, 1595–1650*. Philadelphia, PA.

CHEVALIER, JEAN, *et al.* (1996). *The Penguin Dictionary of Symbols*. Harmondsworth.

CLARENDON, EDWARD HYDE, EARL OF (1992). *The History of the Rebellion and Civil Wars in England Begun in the Year 1641*, ed. W. Dunn Macray, 6 vols. Oxford and New York.

CLEVELAND, JOHN (1967). *Poems*, eds Brian Morris and Eleanor Withington. Oxford.

COLENBRANDER, H.T. (1919). *Bescheiden uit Vreemde Archieven Omtrent de Groote Nederlandsche Zeeoorlogen 1652–1676*, 2 vols. The Hague.

COLIE, ROSALIE L. (1966). *Paradoxia Epidemica. The Renaissance Tradition of Paradox*. Princeton, NJ.

—— (1970). *'My Ecchoing Song': Andrew Marvell's Poetry of Criticism*. Princeton, NJ.

CONDREN, CONAL and COUSINS, A.D., eds (1990). *The Political Identity of Andrew Marvell*. Aldershot and Brookfield, VT.

COOK, ELIZABETH (1986). *Seeing through Words: The Scope of Late Renaissance Poetry*. New Haven, CT.

CORNS, THOMAS N. (1990). *Milton's Language*. Oxford and Cambridge, MA.

—— (1992). *Uncloistered Virtue: English Political Literature, 1640–1660*. Oxford and New York.

COUGHLAN, PATRICIA (1980). 'Classical Theory and Influences in the Non-Satiric Poetry of Andrew Marvell' (unpublished PhD thesis, University of London).

COX, VIRGINIA (1992). *The Renaissance Dialogue: Literary Dialogue in its Social and Political Contexts, Castiglione to Galileo*. Cambridge and New York.

CRAZE, MICHAEL (1979). *The Life and Lyrics of Andrew Marvell*.

CRESSY, DAVID (2000). *Travesties and Transgressions in Tudor and Stuart England: Tales of Discord and Dissession*. Oxford and New York.

CROMWELL, OLIVER (1846). *Letters and Speeches: with Elucidations*, by Thomas Carlyle. 2nd edn.

—— (1937–47; repr. 1988). ed. W.A. Abbott. *The Writings and Speeches of Oliver Cromwell*. 4 vols. Cambridge, MA.

CROSS, CLAIRE and VICKERS, NOREEN (1995). *Monks, Friars and Nuns in Sixteenth-Century Yorkshire*. Yorkshire Archaeological Society, vol. 150. Leeds.

CULLEN, PATRICK (1970). *Spenser, Marvell, and Renaissance Pastoral*. Cambridge, MA.

CUTHBERT, DENISE (1987). 'A Re-Examination of Andrew Marvell: A Study of the Poems of the Cromwell Era' (unpublished PhD thesis, University of Sydney, 1987).

DASH, MIKE (2000). *Tulipomania: The Story of the World's Most Coveted Flower and the Extraordinary Passions it aroused*. New York.

DAVIES, LADY ELEANOR (1995). *Prophetic writings of Lady Eleanor Davies*, ed. Esther S. Cope. New York.

DAVIES, GODFREY (1959, 1991). *The Early Stuarts, 1603–1660*. Oxford and New York.

DENHAM, SIR JOHN (1969). *The Poetical Works of Sir John Denham*, ed. Theodore Howard Banks, 2nd edn. Archon Books.

DENNIS, JOHN (1883). *Heroes of English Literature: English Poets. A Book for Young Readers*.

DOLLIMORE, JONATHAN (1998). *Death, Desire, and Loss in Western Culture*. London and New York.

DONNE, JOHN (1953–62). *Sermons*, ed. with introductions and critical apparatus by George R. Potter and Evelyn M. Simpson, 10 vols. Berkeley, CA.

DRAPER, J.W. (1929). *The Funeral Elegy and the Rise of English Romanticism*. New York.

DUNCAN-JONES, E.E. (1976). *A Great Master of Words: Some Aspects of Marvell's Poems of Praise and Blame*. British Academy Warton lecture on English poetry, 1975.

DYSON, A.E. and LOVELOCK, JULIAN (1976). *Masterful Images: English Poetry from Metaphysicals to Romantics*. London and New York.

EMPSON, WILLIAM (1930, 3rd edn rev. 1953). *Seven Types of Ambiguity*.

—— (1935). *Some Versions of Pastoral*.

ERDMAN, DAVID V. and FOGEL, EPHIM G., eds (1966). *Evidence for Authorship. Essays on Problems of Attribution, with an Annotated Bibliography of Selected Readings*. Ithaca, NY.

ERSKINE-HILL, HOWARD (1983). *The Augustan Idea in English Literature*.

—— (1996). *Poetry and the Realm of Politics: Shakespeare to Dryden*. Oxford and New York.

EVANS, J. MARTIN (1996). *Milton's Imperial Epic: Paradise Lost and the Discourse of Colonialism*. Ithaca, NY.

FABER, BENNE KLAAS (1992). 'The Poetics of Subversion and Conservatism: Popular Satire, *c.* 1640–*c.* 1649' (unpublished DPhil thesis, University of Oxford).

FAIRHOLT, F.W., ed. (1850). *Poems and Songs relating to George Villiers, Duke of Buckingham; and his Assassination by John Felton 23 August 1628*. Percy Society, Vol. 29.

FARLEY-HILLS, DAVID (1974). *The Benevolence of Laughter: Comic Poetry of the Commonwealth and Restoration*. London and Totowa, NJ.

FITTER, CHRIS (1995). *Poetry, Space, Landscape: Toward a New Theory*. Cambridge.

FLECKNOE, RICHARD (1987). *The Prose Characters of Richard Flecknoe: a Critical Edition*, ed. Fred Mayer. New York.

FOWLER, ALASTAIR (1970). *Triumphal Forms: Structural Patterns in Elizabethan Poetry*. Cambridge.

——, ed. (1994). *The Country House Poem. An Anthology of Seventeenth-Century Estate Poems and Related Items*. Edinburgh.

FOX, ADAM, GRIFFITHS, PAUL and HINDLE, STEVE, eds (1996). *The Experience of Authority in Early Modern England*. London and New York.

FOX, FRANK L. (1996). *A Distant Storm. The Four Days' Battle of 1666*. Rotherfield, East Sussex.

FOX, GEORGE (1998). *The Journal*, ed. Nigel Smith. Harmondsworth.

FRASER, ANTONIA (1973, 1989). *Cromwell, Our Chief of Men*.

FRIEDENREICH, KENNETH, ed. (1977). *Tercentenary Essays in Honor of Andrew Marvell*. Hamden, CT.

FRIEDMAN, D.M. (1970). *Marvell's Pastoral Art*.

GARDINER, S.R. (1897). *History of the Commonwealth and Protectorate*.

GARRARD, MARY (1989). *Artemisia Gentileschi: The Image of the Female Hero in Italian Baroque Art*. Princeton, NJ.

GARSTEIN, OSKAR (1992). *Rome and the Counter-Reformation in Scandinavia: the Age of Gustavus Adolphus and Queen Christina of Sweden, 1622–1656*. Leiden.

GLOBE, ALEXANDER (1985). *Peter Stent, London Printseller, circa 1642–1665: Being a Catalogue Raisonné of his Engraved Prints and Books with an Historical and Bibliographical Introduction*. Vancouver.

GOLDBERG, JONATHAN (1986). *Voice Terminal Echo: Postmodernism and English Renaissance Texts.* London and New York.

GOLDSWORTHY, CEPHAS (2001). *The Satyr: An Account of the Life and Work, Death and Salvation of John Wilmot, Second Earl of Rochester.* London.

GREENGRASS, MARK, LESLIE, MICHAEL and RAYLOR, TIMOTHY, eds (1994). *Samuel Hartlib and Universal Reformation: Studies in Intellectual Communication.* Cambridge and New York.

GREY, ANCHITELL (1769). *Debates of the House of Commons: from the Year 1667 to the Year 1694.* 10 vols.

GRIFFIN, PATSY (1995). *The Modest Ambition of Andrew Marvell.* Newark, DA.

GROVE, RICHARD (1995). *Green Imperialism: Colonial Expansion, Tropical Island Edens, and the Origins of Environmentalism, 1600–1860.* Cambridge and New York.

HAAN, ESTELLE (2003). *Andrew Marvell's Latin Poetry: From Text to Context.* Brussels.

HABER, JUDITH (1992). *Pastoral and the Poetics of Self-Contradiction: Theocritus to Marvell.* Cambridge.

HAGSTRUM, JEAN H. (1958). *The Sister Arts: The Tradition of Literary Pictorialism and English Poetry from Dryden to Gray.* Chicage, IL.

HARDIN, RICHARD F. (2000). *Love in a Green Shade. Idyllic Romance Ancient to Modern.* Lincoln, NE and London.

HARRIS, TIM, SEAWARD, PAUL and GOLDIE, MARK, eds (1990). *The Politics of Religion in Restoration England.* Oxford and Cambridge, MA.

HARTMANN, C.H. (1924). *La Belle Stuart.*

HARVEY, ELIZABETH and MAUS, KATHARINE EISAMAN, eds (1990). *Soliciting Interpretation: Literary Theory and Seventeenth-Century English Poetry.* Chicago, IL.

HEALY, THOMAS and SAWDAY, JONATHAN, eds (1990). *Literature and the English Civil War.* Cambridge and New York.

HEFELE, KARL JOSEPH VON (1871). *A History of the Christian Councils: from the Original Documents, to the Close of the Council of Nicæa, AD 325,* trans. William R. Clark. Edinburgh.

HENINGER, S.K., JR (1977). *The Cosmographical Glass.* San Marino, CA.

HENKEL, ARTHUR and SCHONE, ALBRECHT, eds (1967). *Emblemata; Handbuch zur Sinnbildkunst des XVI. und XVII. Jahrhunderts.* Stuttgart.

HESSAYSON, ARIEL (1997). ' "Gold tried in the Fire": The Prophet Theaurau John Tany and the Puritan revolution' (unpublished PhD thesis, University of Cambridge).

HESSE, WERNER (1981). *Hier Wittelsbach hier Pfalz. Die Geschichte der pfälzischen Wittelsbacher von 1214–1803.* Landau.

HILL, CHRISTOPHER (1974). *Change and Continuity in Seventeenth-Century England.*

HODGE, R.I.V. (1978). *Foreshortened Time. Andrew Marvell and Seventeenth-Century Revolutions.* Cambridge, Ipswich and Totowa, NJ.

HOLLANDER, JOHN (1961). *The Untuning of the Sky: Ideas of Music in English poetry, 1500–1700.* Princeton, NJ.

HOLSTUN, JAMES, ed. (1992). *Pamphlet Wars: Prose in the English Revolution.* London and Portland, OR.

—— (2000). *Ehud's Dagger: Class Struggle in the English Revolution.* London and New York.

HOULBROOKE, RALPH (1998). *Death, Religion and the Family in England, 1480–1750.* Oxford.

HOXBY, BLAIR (2002). *Mammon's Music: Literature and Economics in the Age of Milton.* New Haven, CT and London.

HUNT, JOHN DIXON (1978). *Andrew Marvell: his Life and Writings.*

HUTTON, RONALD (1989). *Charles the Second King of England, Scotland, and Ireland.* Oxford.

JOHNS, ADRIAN (1998). *The Nature of the Book: Print and Knowledge in the Making.* Chicago, IL.

KAJANTO, IIRO (1993). *Christina Heroina: Mythological and Historical Exemplification in the Latin Panegyrics on Christina Queen of Sweden.* Helsinki.

KATZ, DAVID S. (1982). *Philo-Semitism and the Readmission of the Jews to England, 1603–1655.* Oxford.

KAUFMANN, U. MILO (1978). *Paradise in the Age of Milton.* Victoria, BC.

KEEBLE, N.H. (1987). *The Literary Culture of Nonconformity in Later Seventeenth-Century England.* Leicester and Athens, GA.

KEGEL-BRINKGREVE, ELIZABETH (1991). *The Echoing Woods: Bucolic and Pastoral from Theocritus to Wordsworth.* Amsterdam.

KELLIHER, HILTON (1978). *Andrew Marvell. Poet & Politician, 1621–78. An Exhibition to Commemorate the Tercentenary of his Death.*

KELSEY, SEAN (1997). *Inventing a Republic: The Political Culture of the English Commonwealth, 1649–1653.* Manchester and New York.

KERMODE, FRANK, ed. (1952). *English Pastoral Poetry: From the Beginnings to Marvell.*

—— (1971). *Shakespeare, Spenser, Donne: Renaissance Essays.*

KERRIGAN, JOHN, ed. (1991). *Motives of Woe. Shakespeare and 'Female Complaint': A Critical Anthology.* Oxford and New York.

KING, BRUCE (1977). *Marvell's Allegorical Poetry.* New York.

KLAUSE, JOHN (1983). *The Unfortunate Fall: Theodicy and the Moral Imagination of Andrew Marvell.* Hamden, CT.

KNOPPERS, LAURA LUNGER (1994). *Historicizing Milton: Spectacle, Power, and Poetry in Restoration England.* Athens, GA.

—— (2000). *Constructing Cromwell: Ceremony, Portrait, and Print, 1645–1661.* Cambridge and New York.

KNOTT, JOHN R. (1993). *Discourses of Martyrdom in English Literature, 1563–1694.* Cambridge and New York.

KORSHIN, PAUL J. (1973). *From Concord to Dissent: Major Themes in English Poetic Theory, 1640–1700.* Menston, Yorkshire, 1973.

LAING, ROSEMARY (1982). 'The Disintegration of Pastoral' (unpublished DPhil thesis, University of Oxford).

LAKE, PETER and SHARPE, KEVIN, eds (1994). *Culture and Politics in early Stuart England.* Basingstoke and London.

LEGOUIS, PIERRE (1928). *André Marvell, Poète, Puritain, Patriote, 1621–1678.* Paris.

—— (1965). *Andrew Marvell. Poet, Puritan, Patriot.* Oxford.

LEISHMAN, J.B. (1966, 2nd edn, 1968). *The Art of Marvell's Poetry*.

LENNARD, JOHN (1991). *'But I digress': the Exploitation of Parentheses in English Printed Verse*. Oxford and New York.

LESLIE, MICHAEL and RAYLOR, TIMOTHY, eds (1992). *Culture and Cultivation in Early Modern England: Writing and the Land*. Leicester and New York.

LOEWENSTEIN, DAVID (2001). *Representing Revolution in Milton and his Contemporaries: Religion, Politics, and Polemics in Radical Puritanism*. Cambridge.

LORD, GEORGE de F., ed. (1968). *Andrew Marvell. A Collection of Critical Essays*. Englewood Cliffs, NJ.

—— (1987). *Classical Presences in Seventeenth-Century English Poetry*. New Haven.

LOW, ANTHONY (1978). *Love's Architecture: Devotional Modes in Seventeenth-Century English Poetry*. New York.

—— (1985). *The Georgic Revolution*. Princeton, NJ.

LUDLOW, EDMUND (1894). *The Memoirs of Edmund Ludlow, Lieutenant-General of the Horse in the Army of the Commonwealth of England, 1625–1672*, ed. C.H. Firth, 2 vols. Oxford.

MACKELLAR, WALTER, ed. (1930). *The Latin Poems of John Milton*. New Haven, CT.

MCLACHLAN, H. JOHN (1952). *Socinianism in Seventeenth-Century England*.

MACLEAN, GERALD M., ed. (1995). *Culture and Society in the Stuart Restoration: Literature, Drama, History*. Cambridge.

MACHIN, RICHARD and NORRIS, CHISTOPHER, eds (1987). *Post-Structuralist Readings of English Poetry*. Cambridge and New York.

MAGUIRE, NANCY KLEIN (1992). *Regicide and Restoration: English Tragicomedy, 1660–1671*. Cambridge and New York.

MARCUS, LEAH (1986). *Childhood and Cultural Despair: a Theme and Variations in Seventeenth-Century Literature*. Pittsburgh, PA.

—— (1986). *The Politics of Mirth: Jonson, Herrick, Milton, Marvell, and the Defense of Old Holiday Pastimes*. Chicago, IL.

MARKHAM, CLEMENTS R. (1870). *A Life of the Great Lord Fairfax, Commander-in-Chief of the Army of the Parliament of England*.

MAROTTI, ARTHUR (1995). *Manuscript, Print, and the English Renaissance Lyric*. Ithaca, NY.

MATHOLE, PAUL J. (2004). 'Marvell and Violence' (unpublished Ph. D. thesis, University of London).

MILTON, JOHN (1968, rev. 2nd edn 1997). *Complete Shorter Poems*, ed. John Carey. Harlow and New York.

—— (1968, rev. 2nd edn 1998). *Paradise Lost*, ed. Alastair Fowler. Harlow and New York.

MILWARD, JOHN (1938). *The Diary of John Milward, Esq., Member of Parliament for Derbyshire, September 1666 to May 1668*, ed. with some notes and an introduction on his life, by Caroline Robbins. Cambridge.

MINER, EARL, ed. (1971). *Seventeenth-Century Imagery. Essays on Uses of Figurative Language from Donne to Farquhar*. Berkeley, CA.

MIROLLO, JAMES V. (1963). *The Poet of the Marvelous: Giambattista Marino*. New York.

MURRAY, NICHOLAS (1999). *World Enough and Time: The Life of Andrew Marvell*.

MURRIN, MICHAEL (1994). *History and Warfare in Renaissance Epic*. Chicago, IL and London.

NARDO, ANNA K. (1991). *The Ludic Self in Seventeenth-Century English Literature*. Albany, NY.

NEVO, RUTH (1963). *The Dial of Virtue: A Study of Poems on Affairs of State in the Seventeenth Century*. Princeton, NJ.

NISPEN, WIM VAN (1991). *De Teems in Brant: een Verzameling Teksten en Afbeeldingen Rond de Tweede Engelse Zeeoorlog (1665–1667)*. Hilversum.

NORBROOK, DAVID (1999). *Writing the English Republic. Poetry, Rhetoric and Politics 1627–1660*. Cambridge and New York.

NORTH, ROGER (1742). *The Life of the Right Hon. Francis North, Baron Guilford*.

NORTON, GLYN P. (2000). *The Cambridge History of Literary Criticism. Vol. 3. The Renaissance*. Cambridge.

NUTTALL, GEOFFREY F. (1946). *The Holy Spirit in Puritan Faith and Experience*. Oxford.

—— (1957). *Visible Saints: The Congregational Way, 1640–1660*. Oxford.

OGG, DAVID (1934). *England in the Reign of Charles II*. 2 vols. Oxford.

O HEHIR, BRENDAN (1968). *Harmony from Discords; a Life of Sir John Denham*. Berkeley, CA.

OLLARD, RICHARD (1994). *Cromwell's Earl: A Life of Edward Mountagu, 1st Earl of Sandwich*.

ONIANS, JOHN (1988). *Bearers of Meaning: The Classical Orders in Antiquity, the Middle Ages, and the Renaissance*. Princeton, NJ.

ORESKO, ROBERT, GIBBS, G.C. and SCOTT, H.M. eds (1997). *Royal and Republican Sovereignty in Early Modern Europe: Essays in Memory of Ragnhild Hatton*. Cambridge and New York.

OSBORNE, MARY TOM (1949). *Advice-to-a-Painter Poems, 1633–1856: An Annotated Finding List*. Austin, TX.

PAGDEN, ANTHONY, ed. (1987). *The Languages of Political Theory in Early-Modern Europe*. Cambridge.

PARKES, M.B. (1992). *Pause and Effect. An Introduction to the History of Punctuation in the West*. Aldershot.

PATRIDES, C.A., ed. (1978). *Approaches to Marvell: The York Tercentenary Lectures*. London and Boston, MA.

PATTERSON, ANNABEL M. (1978). *Marvell and the Civic Crown*. Princeton, NJ.

—— (2000). *Marvell: The Writer in Public Life*. Harlow and New York.

PEPYS, SAMUEL (1926). *Samuel Pepys's Naval Minutes*. Navy Records Society.

PETRUCCI, ARMANDO (1993). *Public lettering: Script, Power, and Culture*, trans. Linda Lappin. Chicago, IL.

PEVSNER, SIR NIKOLAUS and LLOYD, DAVID (1967). *Hampshire and the Isle of Wight* (The Buildings of England. no. 32.) Harmondsworth.

PHILIPS, JACQUELINE LOUISE (1998). 'Transformation by Allegory in John Bunyan's *The Pilgrim's Progress*' (unpublished DPhil thesis, University of Oxford).

PHIPPS, CHRISTINE (1985). *Buckingham, Public and Private Man: the Prose, Poems, and Commonplace Book of George Villiers, second Duke of Buckingham (1628–1687)*. New York.

PICCIOTTO, JOANNA (forthcoming). *The Work that Remains: Experimentalism in Seventeenth- and Eighteenth-Century England.*

PINCUS, STEVEN C.A. (1996). *Protestantism and Patriotism: Ideologies and the Making of English Foreign Policy, 1650–1668.* Cambridge and New York.

PIPER, WILLIAM BOWMAN (1969). *The Heroic Couplet.* Cleveland, OH.

POTTER, LOIS (1989). *Secret Rites and Secret Writing: Royalist Literature, 1641–1660.* Cambridge and New York.

PURKISS, DIANE (2000). *Troublesome Things: A History of Fairies and Fairy Stories.*

RANDALL, DALE J.B. (1995). *Winter Fruit: English Drama, 1642–1660.* Lexington, KY.

RANKIN, DEANA M. (1999). 'The Art of War: Military Writing in Ireland in the Mid-Seventeenth Century' (unpublished DPhil thesis University of Oxford, 1999).

RAY, ROBERT H. (1998). *An Andrew Marvell Companion.* New York.

RAYLOR, TIMOTHY (1994). *Cavaliers, Clubs, and Literary Culture: Sir John Mennes, James Smith, and the Order of the Fancy.* Newark, DE.

REED, EDWARD BLISS (1912). *English Lyrical Poetry from its Origins to the Present Time.* New Haven, CT.

REES, CHRISTINE (1989). *The Judgement of Marvell.* London and New York.

RERESBY, SIR JOHN (1991). *Memoirs of Sir John Reresby: the Complete Text and a Selection from his Letters,* ed., with introduction and notes by Andrew Browning, 2nd edn with new preface and notes by Mary K. Geiter and W.A. Speck. London and Woodbridge.

RICHARDS, JENNIFER and THORNE, ALISON, eds. *Renaissance Rhetoric: Gender and Politics.* (Routledge, forthcoming).

RIVERS, ISABEL (1991). *Reason, Grace, and Sentiment: a Study of the Language of Religion and Ethics in England, 1660–1780.* Cambridge and New York.

ROGERS, JOHN (1996). *The Matter of Revolution: Science, Poetry, and Politics in the Age of Milton.* Ithaca, NY.

RØSTVIG, MAREN-SOPHIE (1954). *The Happy Man: Studies in the Metamorphoses of a Classical Ideal, 1600–1700,* Oslo.

ROWLAND, INGRID D. (1998). *The Culture of the High Renaissance. Ancients and Moderns in Sixteenth-Century Rome.* Cambridge.

RUSHWORTH, JOHN (1659–1701). *Historical Collections,* 4 parts, 7 vols.

SAWDAY, JONATHAN (1995). *The Body Emblazoned: Dissection and the Human Body in Renaissance Culture.* London and New York.

SCHAMA, SIMON (1987). *The Embarrassment of Riches. An Interpretation of Dutch Culture in the Golden Age.* New York.

SCHOLES, PERCY A. (1934, 2nd edn 1969). *The Puritans and Music in England and New England: a Contribution to the Cultural History of Two Nations.* Oxford.

SCODEL, JOSHUA (1991). *The English Poetic Epitaph: Commemoration and Conflict from Jonson to Wordsworth.* Ithaca, NY.

SCOTT, PAUL, ed. (forthcoming). *Early Modern Perspectives on Martyrs and Martyrdom.* Leiden.

SCOULAR, KITTY W. (1965). *Natural Magic: Studies in the Presentation of Nature in English Poetry from Spenser to Marvell.* Oxford.

SEAWARD, PAUL (1989). *The Cavalier Parliament and the Reconstruction of the Old Regime, 1661–1667.* Cambridge.

SELDEN, RAMAN (1978). *English Verse Satire 1590–1765.* London, Boston, MA and Sydney.

SENECA, LUCIUS ANNAEUS (1985). *Thyestes,* ed. with introduction and commentary by R.J. Tarrant. Atlanta, GA.

SEYMOUR, CHARLES, JR (1966). *Sculpture in Italy 1400–1500.* The Pelican History of Art.

SEZNEC, JEAN (1953). *The Survival of the Pagan Gods: the Mythological Tradition and its Place in Renaissance Humanism and Art,* trans. Barbara F. Sessions. New York.

SHELL, ALISON (1999). *Catholicism, Controversy and the English Literary Imagination, 1558–1660.* Cambridge and New York.

SHERWOOD, ROY (1977). *The Court of Oliver Cromwell.* London and Totowa, NJ.

SHIFFLETT, ANDREW (1998). *Stoicism, Politics and Literature in the Age of Milton. War and Peace Reconciled.* Cambridge, New York and Melbourne.

SMET, INGRID DE (1996). *Menippean Satire and the Republic of Letters 1581–1655.* Geneva.

SMITH, NIGEL (1989). *Perfection Proclaimed: Language and Literature in English Radical Religion, 1640–1660.* Oxford and New York.

——, ed. (1993). *Literature and Censorship.* Woodbridge.

—— (1994). *Literature and Revolution in England, 1640–1660.* New Haven, CT and London.

SMUTS, MALCOLM, ed. (1996). *The Stuart Court and Europe: Essays in Politics and Political Culture.* Cambridge and New York.

SPENSER, EDMUND (1977). *The Faerie Queene,* ed. A.C. Hamilton. London and New York.

STANIVUKOVIC, GORAN V., ed. (2001). *Ovid and the Renaissance Body.* Toronto and Buffalo.

STEVENSON, JANE and DAVIDSON, PETER, eds (2001). *Early Modern Women Poets: An Anthology.* Oxford and New York.

STEWART, STANLEY (1966). *The Enclosed Garden.* Madison and Milwaukee, WI.

STOCKER, MARGARITA (1986). *Apocalyptic Marvell: The Second Coming in Seventeenth-Century Poetry.* Brighton.

SUMMERS, CLAUDE J. and PEBWORTH, TED-LARRY eds (1988). *'The Muses Common-weale': Poetry and Politics in the Earlier Seventeenth Century.* Columbia, MO.

—— eds (1992). *On the Celebrated and Neglected Poems of Andrew Marvell.* Columbia, MO.

SUMMERS, JOSEPH H. (1970). *The Heirs of Donne and Jonson.*

SWARDSON, H.R. (1962). *Poetry and the Fountain of Light: Observations on the Conflict between Christian and Classical Traditions in Seventeenth-Century Poetry.*

THURLOE, JOHN (1742). *A Collection of the State Papers of John Thurloe,* 7 vols.

TOLAND, JOHN (1699). *Amyntor, or, A Defence of Milton's Life.*

TOLIVER, HAROLD (1965). *Marvell's Ironic Vision.* New Haven, CT.

TUCK, RICHARD (1993). *Philosophy and Government, 1572–1651.* Cambridge and New York.

TURNER, JAMES (1979). *The Politics of Landscape: Rural Scenery and Society in English Poetry 1630–1660.* Oxford.

—— (2002). *Libertines and Radicals in Early Modern London: Sexuality, Politics and Literary Culture, 1650–1685.* Cambridge and New York.

UNDERDOWN, DAVID (1985). *Revel, Riot, and Rebellion: Popular Politics and Culture in England, 1603–1660.* Oxford and New York.

VAN WANING, C.J.W., and VAN DER MOER, A. (1981). *Dese Aengenaeme Tocht. Chatham 1667 Herbezien door Zeemansogen.* Zutphen.

VEEVERS, ERICA (1989). *Images of Love and Religion: Queen Henrietta Maria and Court Entertainments.* Cambridge and New York.

VERTUE, GEORGE (1930–35). *Note Books,* 6 vols. Oxford.

VON MALTZAHN (2005). NICHOLAS, *An Andrew Marvell Chronology.* Basingstoke and New York.

WALLACE, JOHN M. (1968). *Destiny His Choice: The Loyalism of Andrew Marvell.* Cambridge.

——, ed. (1985). *The Golden and the Brazen World: Papers in Literature and History, 1650–1800.* Berkeley, CA.

WALLERSTEIN, RUTH (1950). *Studies in Seventeenth-Century Poetic.* Madison, WI.

WALTON, GEOFFREY (1955). *Metaphysical to Augustan. Studies in Tone and Sensibility in the Seventeenth Century.*

WANAMAKER, MELISSA C. (1975). *Discordia Concors: the Wit of Metaphysical Poetry.* Port Washington, NY.

WHEATLEY, HENRY BENJAMIN (1891). *London Past and Present: Its History, Associations and Traditions.*

WHITELOCKE, BULSTRODE (1772). *A Journal of the Swedish Ambassy, in the years 1653 and 1654, from the Commonwealth of England, Scotland, and Ireland,* 2 vols.

—— (1990). *The Diary of Bulstrode Whitelocke, 1605–1675,* ed. Ruth Spalding. Oxford and New York.

WILCHER, ROBERT (1985). *Andrew Marvell.* Cambridge and New York.

—— (2001). *The Writing of Royalism, 1628–1660.* Cambridge and New York.

WILDING, MICHAEL (1985). *Dragons Teeth: Literature in the English Revolution.* Oxford and New York.

WILLIAMSON, GEORGE (1967). *Six Metaphysical Poets: a Reader's Guide.* New York.

WILSON, JOHN (1985). *Fairfax: a Life of Thomas, Lord Fairfax, Captain-General of all the Parliament's Forces in the English Civil War, Creator & Commander of the New Model Army.*

WILSON, TIM (1986). *Flags at Sea.*

WINN, JAMES A. (1987). *John Dryden and his World.* New Haven, CT.

WIND, EDGAR (1958). *Pagan Mysteries in the Renaissance.*

WISEMAN, SUSAN (1998). *Drama and Politics in the English Civil War.* Cambridge and New York.

WOOD, ANTHONY Á (1691–92). *Athenae Oxonienses,* 2 vols.

WORDEN, BLAIR, LLOYD-JONES, HUGH and PEARL, VALERIE, eds (1981). *History and Imagination: Essays in Honour of H.R. Trevor-Roper.*

YATES, FRANCES (1975). *Astraea: the Imperial Theme in the Sixteenth Century.* London and Boston.

YOUNG, ALAN R. (1995). *Emblematic Flag Devices of the English Civil Wars 1642–1660.* The English Emblem Tradition, 3. Toronto, Buffalo, NY and London.

ZWICKER, STEVEN N. (1993). *Lines of Authority: Politics and English Literary Culture, 1649–1689.* Ithaca, NY.

INDEX OF TITLES AND FIRST LINES